Philosophic Classics, Third Edition
Volume III

MODERN PHILOSOPHY

FORREST E. BAIRD, EDITOR
Whitworth College

WALTER KAUFMANN
Late, of Princeton University

Prentice Hall, Upper Saddle River, New Jersey 07458

Library of Congress Cataloging-in-Publication Data

Philosophic classics / Forrest E. Baird, editor.—3rd ed.
    p. cm.
    "Walter Kaufmann, late, of Princeton University."
    Includes bibliographical references.
    Contents: v. 1. Ancient philosophy—v. 2. Medieval philosophy—
v. 3. Modern philosophy—v. 4. Nineteenth-century philosophy. 2nd
ed.—v. 5. Twentiety-century philosophy. 2nd ed.
    ISBN 0–13–021314–4 (v. 1).—ISBN 0–13–021315–2 (v. 2).—ISBN
0–13–021316–0 (v. 3).—ISBN 0–13–021533–3 (v. 4).—ISBN
0–13–021534–1 (v. 5)
    1. Philosophy. I. Baird, Forrest E. II. Kaufmann, Walter
Arnold.
  B21.P39   2000
  100—dc21   98–32332
                                          CIP

Editor-in-chief: Charlyce Jones-Owen
Acquisitions editor: Karita France
Editorial assistant: Jennifer Ackerman
Production liaison: Fran Russello
Editorial/production supervision:
  Bruce Hobart (Pine Tree Composition)
Prepress and manufacturing buyer:
  Tricia Kenny
Cover director: Jayne Conte
Cover photo: *Experiment with an Air Pump* by Joseph
  Wright of Derby. National Gallery, London,
  UK/Bridgeman Art Library, London/New York.
Marketing manager: Ilse Wolfe

This volume is dedicated to:

James R. Edwards
J. Michele Graham
Stephen C. Meyer
Terence P. McGonigal
Roger L. Mohrlang
Gerald L. Sittser, Jr.
and Keith Wyma
Whitworth College

This book was set in 10/12 Times Roman by Pine Tree Composition, Inc.,
and was printed and bound by R.R. Donnelley & Sons Company.
The cover was printed by Phoenix Color Corp.

©2000, 1997, 1994 by Prentice-Hall, Inc.
Upper Saddle River, New Jersey 07458

ISBN 0-13-021316-0

Prentice-Hall International (UK) Limited, *London*
Prentice-Hall of Australia Pty. Limited, *Sydney*
Prentice-Hall Canada, Inc., *Toronto*
Prentice-Hall Hispanoamericana, S.A., *Mexico*
Prentice-Hall of India Private Limited, *New Dehli*
Prentice-Hall of Japan, Ltd., *Tokyo*
Pearson Education Asia Pte. Ltd., *Singapore*
Editora Prentice-Hall do Brasil, Ltda., *Rio de Janeiro*

Contents

Preface

To a large extent, modern philosphy begins with a rejection of tradition. While medieval philosophers such as Thomas Aquinas took great pains to incorporate and reconcile ancient writings, smoothing over any apparent contradictions, early modern philosophers such as Francis Bason and René Descartes encouraged their readers to simply make a clean sweep of the past and start over. Previous thinkers had been deluded by "idols" or mistakes in thinking or had relied too heavily on authority. In the modern age, the wisdom of the past was to be discarded as error-prone. As Descartes observed,

> Some years ago I was struck by the large number of falsehoods that I had accepted as true in my childhood, and by the highly doubtful nature of the whole edifice that I had subsequently based on them. I realized that it was necessary, once in the course of my life, to demolish everything completely and start again right from the foundations if I wanted to establish anything at all in the sciences that was stable and likely to last.*

This quest to establish a stable intellectual foundation on which to build something "likely to last" characterized seventeenth- and eighteenth-century European philosophy. British Empiricists, such as Bacon, Thomas Hobbes, John Locke, David Hume, and Thomas Reid, found such a foundation in sensory experience and developed their thought on that basis. On the other hand, the Continental Rationalists, philosophers such as Descartes, Baruch Spinoza, and Gottfried Leibniz, thought the senses inade-

*Descartes, *Meditations* (see p. 15 of this volume).

quate for such a task. They considered reason superior to experience and sought to establish their philosophies on the basis of more certain principles. Immanuel Kant, the greatest of the modern philosophers, sought to combine these two approaches and in so doing developed a uniquely influential system of philosophy.

This volume in the *Philosophic Classics* series includes the key writings of the British Empiricists and Continental Rationalists, along with the work of Kant. In choosing texts for this volume, I have tried wherever possible to follow three principles: (1) to use complete works or, where more appropriate, complete sections of works (2) in clear translations (3) of texts central to the thinker's philosophy or widely accepted as part of the "canon." To make the works more accessible to students, most footnotes treating textual matters (variant readings, etc.) have been omitted and all Greek words have been transliterated and put in angle brackets. In addition, each thinker is introduced by a brief essay composed of three sections: (1) biographical (a glimpse of the life), (2) philosophical (a résumé of the philosopher's thought), and (3) bibliographical (suggestions for further reading).

This third edition now includes a brief selection from Blaise Pascal, and a longer selection using a different translation from Immanuel Kant's *Critique of Pure Reason*. To make room for these additions I have changed the selection from Francis Bacon and dropped the epilogue on Mary Wollstonecraft.

Those who use this volume in a one-term course in modern philosophy will notice more material here than can easily fit a normal semester. But this embarrassment of riches gives teachers some choice and, for those who offer the same course year after year, an opportunity to change the menu.

*   *   *

I would like to thank the many people who assisted me in this volume, including the library staff of Whitworth College, especially Hans Bynagle, Gail Fielding, and Jeanette Langston; my colleagues, F. Dale Bruner, who made helpful suggestions on all the introductions, Barbara Filo, who helped make selections for the artwork, and Bryan Yorton, who made suggestions for the Pascal and Kant selections; Wayne Pomerleau, Gonzaga University, and Arthur F. Holmes, Wheaton College, who read the introductions and made helpful suggestions; Nicholas Wolterstorff, Yale University, who made suggestions for the Locke and Reid selections; John Justice, Randolph-Macon Woman's College, who made several helpful suggestions; my secretary, Michelle Seefried; and my production editor, Bruce Hobart, my acquisitions editor, Karita France of Prentice Hall; and my former acquisitions editors, Angela Stone and Ted Bolen. I would also like to acknowledge the following reviewers: James W. Allard, Montana State University; Robert C. Bennett, El Centro College; Herbert L. Carson, Ferris State University; Steven M. Emmanuel, Virginia Wesleyan College; Wolfgang Fuchs, Towsen State University; Helen S. Lang, Trinity College; Scott MacDonald, University of Iowa; Eric Palmer, Allegheny College; Stephen Scott, Eastern Washington University; Jeffrey T. Tlumak, Vanderbilt University; Donald Phillip Verene, Emory University; and Richard T. Zee, Trinity College.

I am especially thankful to my wife, Joy Lynn Fulton Baird, and to our children, Whitney Jaye, Sydney Tev, and Soren David, who have supported me in this process.

Finally, this volume is dedicated to my departmental colleagues, James R. Edwards, J. Michele Graham, Terence P. McGonigal, Stephen C. Meyer, Roger L. Mohrlang, Gerald L. Sittser, Jr., and Keith Wyma, who have helped make working at Whitworth College such a rewarding experience.

Forrest E. Baird
Professor of Philosophy
Whitworth College
Spokane, WA 99251
email: fbaird@whitworth.edu

Philosophers In This Volume

Francis Bacon

Thomas Hobbes
René Descartes

Blaise Pascal

Baruch Spinoza
John Locke
Gottfried Leibniz

Other Important Figures

Akbar the Great
Giordano Bruno
William Shakespeare
Galileo Galilei
Johann Kepler

Rembrandt

Christopher Wren
Louis XIV of France
Nicolas Malebranche
Isaac Newton
Fenelon
Giovanni
Battista Vico

A Sampling of Major Events

French religious wars
Portuguese settle in Rio de Janeiro
English defeat Spanish Armada
English settle In Virginia

Manchu Dynasty in China
Charles I of England
executed

| 1550 | 1575 | 1600 | 1625 | 1650 | 1675 |

George Berkeley
Thomas Reid
David Hume
Immanuel Kant

J.S. Bach
Voltaire
Benjamin Franklin
Jean-Jacque Rousseau

Johan Wolfgang Goethe
Wolfgang Amadeus Mozart
Napolean I
Ludwig van Beethoven
Simón Bolívar

"Glorious Revolution" in England
Salem witchcraft trials

Great Lisbon Earthquake
British Rule in India
Declaration of
Independence
French
Revolution
begins

| 1700 | 1725 | 1750 | 1775 | 1800 |

FRANCIS BACON
1561–1626

Francis Bacon's life can be characterized as a mercurial search for power. As the youngest son of Sir Nicholas Bacon, Lord Keeper of the Great Seal for Queen Elizabeth I, Francis's early life was one of prestige and privilege. His uncle, Lord Burghley, was one of the most powerful men in the kingdom. His mother, Lady Bacon, was a woman of uncommon learning (and a committed Puritan). As a young man, Francis displayed remarkable intellect. He entered Trinity College, Cambridge, when he was only twelve years old. There he came to the conviction that the prevailing Aristotelian philosophy was hopelessly sterile. As a result, much of Bacon's later work has a strong antischolastic cast. Upon graduating three years later, his intellectual gifts attracted the interest of the queen herself, and he was sent to France (at age sixteen) as part of the English ambassador's staff.

Bacon's shooting star came hurtling down two years later at the death of his father. Under the inheritance laws of the time, he found himself, as the youngest son, penniless at age eighteen. He took up law—a promising career for a man with connections and little money. In 1584 (at age twenty-three), he won a seat in Parliament. For the next twenty-three years, he was prominent in public affairs—and, notoriously, in controversies. Once, he publicly opposed the queen and lost his high position. Subsequently, however, he supported the queen's decision to hang his best friend. His motivations and his reasonings in this case have frequently been debated.

After the death of Queen Elizabeth I and the ascension of James I, Bacon's star rose once more. He was made Solicitor-General in 1607 and six years later Attorney-General; in 1617, he was given his father's former position, Lord

Keeper of the Great Seal; the following year he was named Lord Chancellor and the Baron Verulam. During the reign of James I, Bacon also wrote his two most important philosophical works. The first, *The Advancement of Learning* (1605), argued that scholars should be freed from the past and encouraged to seek new discoveries in science. The second, his *Novum Organum* (1620), explained the various ways scholars had been held in intellectual bondage and proposed an inductive method to escape such bondage.

Bacon's career reached a peak in 1621 when he was named the Viscount St. Albans. But exactly one week after this last, and highest, investiture, Bacon was accused of bribery, to which he later pleaded guilty. He received a heavy fine (£40,000) and was imprisoned in the Tower of London. Even though the king forgave the fine, and Bacon spent only four days in the Tower, he was disqualified from public office for life. As he later cryptically wrote: "I was the justes judge that was in England these fifty years; but it was the justes censure in Parliament that was these two hundred years." Although he followed his time's practice of accepting gifts from litigants, he insisted that his judgment had never been swayed by a bribe. Again, his conduct has been the subject of much discussion. The last years of Bacon's life were spent in research and writing.

*   *   *

Bacon's drive for power extended beyond politics. He saw knowledge, especially scientific knowledge, as a means to power. He was not interested in abstract "Truth," but in "that knowledge whose dignity is maintained by works of utility and power." He sought to make humans masters of the natural world. The goal of science is "the glory of the Creator and the relief of man's estate." To this end, he sought a "total reconstruction of the sciences, arts, and all human knowledge"—what he called "The Great Instauration."

Bacon's total reconstruction begins with dismantling all past errors. He argues that medieval philosophers, the Scholastics, were consumed with disputing questions but never approached knowledge of the real world. Renaissance humanists were not much better. They were obsessed with the eloquence of ancient Greeks and Romans but inclined to "hunt after words more than matter." According to Bacon, all previous thinkers, and most thinkers of his own day as well, had developed bad mental habits or what he called "Idols of the Mind." In the passage that follows, *Aphorisms Concerning the Interpretation of Nature and the Kingdom of Man* from his *Novum Organum,* Bacon explains how these idols have impeded real knowledge.

Having removed past errors and the "Idols of the Mind," Bacon presents his positive program. Instead of the deductive methods of the Scholastics, Bacon claims "Our only hope . . . lies in a true induction." Bacon argues for a careful return to the empirical data in order to develop axioms and then derive experiments from those axioms. In a later passage (not included here), Bacon says that if one would know the cause of a phenomenon, one must begin by tirelessly collecting data and constructing three tables: (1) instances exhibiting the phenomenon, (2) instances not exhibiting the phenomenon, and (3) instances in which the phenomenon is present in different degrees. Using heat, for example, one would construct tables of "What's Hot," "What's Not," and "What's Sort of Hot and Sort of Not." From such tables, one could discover the "form" of heat. Contemporary philosophers of science point out that Bacon's "scientific method" of "true induction" leaves out both working hypotheses and mathematics. Moreover, simply listing phenomena does not necessarily yield knowledge—after all, every phenomenon in the universe could be on at least one "What's Hot" list! But Bacon is still appreciated for encouraging the systematic empirical study of science.

Besides *The Advancement of Learning* and *Novum Oreganum,* Bacon's major works include *Essays* (1597—expanded by him in 1612 and 1625) and *New Atlantis* (1624). In addition, he planned, but never completed, a much larger work, *The Great Instauration,* of which the *Novum Organum* was to be but one small part. (At various times, Bacon has been credited with writing Shakespeare's plays by those who found it inconceivable that Shakespeare himself, a mere actor, could have written them.)

*   *   *

For a complete biography with a sympathetic discussion of Bacon's political controversies, see Fulton H. Anderson, *Francis Bacon: His Career and His Thought* (Los Angeles: University of Southern California Press, 1962). For overviews of Bacon's thought, see the short classic, C.D. Broad, *The Philosophy of Francis Bacon* (Cambridge: Cambridge University Press, 1926); Fulton H. Anderson, *The Philosophy of Francis Bacon* (Chicago: University of Chicago Press, 1948); Paolo Rossi, *Francis Bacon: From Magic to Science* (London: Routledge & Kegan Paul, 1968); Loren Eiseley, *The Man Who Saw Through Time* (New York: Scribner's, 1973); Lisa Jardine, *Francis Bacon: Discovery and the Art of Discourse* (Cambridge: Cambridge University Press, 1974); and Perez Zagorin, *Francis Bacon* (Princeton: Princeton University Press, 1998). Markku Peltonen, ed., *The Cambridge Companion to Bacon* (Cambridge: Cambridge University Press, 1974) provides critical essays.

NOVUM ORGANUM (in part)

Aphorisms Concerning the Interpretation of Nature and the Kingdom of Man

PREFACE

. . . Now my method, though hard to practice, is easy to explain; and it is this. I propose to establish progressive stages of certainty. The evidence of the sense, helped and guarded by a certain process of correction, I retain. But the mental operation which follows the act of sense I for the most part reject; and instead of it I open and lay out a new and certain path for the mind to proceed in, starting directly from the simple sensuous perception. The necessity of this was felt, no doubt, by those who attributed so much importance to logic, showing thereby that they were in search of helps for the understanding, and had no confidence in the native and spontaneous process of the mind. But this remedy comes too late to do any good, when the mind is already, through the daily intercourse and conversation of life, occupied with unsound doctrines and beset on all sides by vain imaginations. And therefore that art of logic, coming (as I said) too late to the rescue, and no way able to set matters right again, has had the effect of fixing errors rather than disclosing truth. There remains but one course for the recovery of a sound and healthy condition—namely, that the entire work of the understanding be commenced afresh, and the mind itself be from the very outset not left to take its own course, but guided at every step; and the business be done as if by machinery. Certainly if in things mechanical men had set to work with their naked hands, without help or force of instruments, just as in things intellectual they have set to work with little else than the naked forces of the understanding, very small would the matters have been which, even with their best efforts applied in conjunction, they could have attempted or accomplished.

APHORISMS, BOOK ONE

III

Human knowledge and human power meet in one; for where the cause is not known the effect cannot be produced. Nature to be commanded must be obeyed; and that which in contemplation is as the cause is in operation as the rule.

IV

Toward the effecting of works, all that man can do is to put together or put asunder natural bodies. The rest is done by nature working within.

VII

The productions of the mind and hand seem very numerous in books and manufactures. But all this variety lies in an exquisite subtlety and derivations from a few things already known, not in the number of axioms.

VIII

Moreover, the works already known are due to chance and experiment rather than to sciences; for the sciences we now possess are merely systems for the nice ordering and setting forth of things already invented, not methods of invention or directions for new works.

XI

As the sciences which we now have do not help us in finding out new works, so neither does the logic which we now have help us in finding out new sciences.

XII

The logic now in use serves rather to fix and give stability to the errors which have their foundation in commonly received notions than to help the search after truth. So it does more harm than good.

The title page of Bacon's *Novum Organum* (1620). (*The Bettmann Archive*)

XIV

The syllogism consists of propositions, propositions consist of words, words are symbols of notions. Therefore if the notions themselves (which is the root of the matter) are confused and overhastily abstracted from the facts, there can be no firmness in the superstructure. Our only hope therefore lies in a true induction.

XIX

There are and can be only two ways of searching into and discovering truth. The one flies from the senses and particulars to the most general axioms, and from these principles, the truth of which it takes for settled and immovable, proceeds to judgment and to the discovery of middle axioms. And this way is now in fashion. The other derives axioms from the senses and particulars, rising by a gradual and unbroken ascent, so that it arrives at the most general axioms last of all. This is the true way, but as yet untried.

XXII

Both ways set out from the senses and particulars, and rest in the highest generalities; but the difference between them is infinite. For the one just glances at experiment and particulars in passing, the other dwells duly and orderly among them. The one, again, begins at once by establishing certain abstract and useless generalities, the other rises by gradual steps to that which is prior and better known in the order of nature.

XXIV

It cannot be that axioms established by argumentation should avail for the discovery of new works, since the subtlety of nature is greater many times over than the subtlety of argument. But axioms duly and orderly formed from particulars easily discover the way to new particulars, and thus render sciences active.

XXV

The axioms now in use, having been suggested by a scanty and manipular experience and a few particulars of most general occurrence, are made for the most part just large enough to fit and take these in; and therefore it is no wonder if they do not lead to new particulars. And if some opposite instance, not observed or not known before, chance to come in the way, the axiom is rescued and preserved by some frivolous distinction; whereas the truer course would be to correct the axiom itself.

XXXI

It is idle to expect any great advancement in science from the superinducing and engrafting of new things upon old. We must begin anew from the very foundations, unless we would revolve forever in a circle with mean and contemptible progress.

XXXVI

One method of delivery alone remains to us which is simply this: we must lead men to the particulars themselves, and their series and order; while men on their side must force themselves for a while to lay their notions by and begin to familiarize themselves with facts.

XXXVIII

The idols and false notions which are now in possession of the human understanding, and have taken deep root therein, not only so beset men's minds that truth can hardly find entrance, but even after entrance is obtained, they will again in the very instauration of the sciences meet and trouble us, unless men being forewarned of the danger fortify themselves as far as may be against their assaults.

XXXIX

There are four classes of idols which beset men's minds. To these for distinction's sake I have assigned names,—calling the first class *Idols of the Tribe*; the second, *Idols of the Cave*; the third, *Idols of the Market-place*; the fourth, *Idols of the Theater*.

XL

The formation of ideas and axioms by true induction is no doubt the proper remedy to be applied for the keeping off and clearing away of idols. To point them out, however, is of great use, for the doctrine of idols is to the interpretation of nature what the doctrine of the refutation of sophisms is to common logic.

XLI

The Idols of the Tribe have their foundation in human nature itself, and in the tribe or race of men. For it is a false assertion that the sense of man is the measure of things. On the contrary, all perceptions, as well of the sense as of the mind, are according to the measure of the individual and not according to the measure of the universe. And the human understanding is like a false mirror, which, receiving rays irregularly, distorts and discolors the nature of things by mingling its own nature with it.

XLII

The Idols of the Cave are the idols of the individual man. For everyone (besides the errors common to human nature in general) has a cave or den of his own, which refracts and discolors the light of nature; owing either to his own proper and peculiar nature or to his education and conversation with others; or to the reading of books, and the authority of those whom he esteems and admires; or to the differences of impressions, accordingly as they take place in a mind preoccupied and predisposed or in a mind indifferent and settled; or the like. So that the spirit of man (according as it is meted out to different individuals) is in fact a thing variable and full of perturbation, and governed as it were by chance. Whence it was well observed by Heraclitus that men look for sciences in their own lesser worlds, and not in the greater or common world.

XLIII

There are also idols formed by the intercourse and association of men with each other, which I call Idols of the Market-place, on account of the commerce and consort of men there. For it is by discourse that men associate; and words are imposed according to the apprehension of the vulgar. And therefore the ill and unfit choice of words wonderfully obstructs the understanding. Nor do the definitions or explanations wherewith in some things learned men are wont to guard and defend themselves, by any means set the matter right. But words plainly force and overrule the understanding, and throw all into confusion, and lead men away into numberless empty controversies and idle fancies.

XLIV

Lastly, there are idols which have immigrated into men's minds from the various dogmas of philosophies, and also from wrong laws of demonstration. These I call Idols of the Theater; because in my judgment all the received systems are but so many stage-plays, representing worlds of their own creation after an unreal and scenic fashion. Nor is it only of the systems now in vogue, or only of the ancient sects and philosophies, that I speak: for many more plays of the same kind may yet be composed and in like artificial manner set forth; seeing that errors the most widely different have nevertheless causes for the most part alike. Neither again do I mean this only of entire systems, but also of many principles and axioms in science, which by tradition, credulity, and negligence have come to be received. . . .

XLV

The human understanding is of its own nature prone to suppose the existence of more order and regularity in the world than it finds. And though there be many things in nature which are singular and unmatched, yet it devises for them parallels and conjugates and relatives which do not exist. Hence the fiction that all celestial bodies move in perfect circles; spirals and dragons being (except in name) utterly rejected. Hence too the element of fire with its orb is brought in, to make up the square with the other three which the sense perceives. Hence also the ratio of density of the so-called elements is arbitrarily fixed at ten to one. And so on of other dreams. And these fancies affect not dogmas only, but simple notions also.

XLVI

The human understanding when it has once adopted an opinion (either as being the received opinion or as being agreeable to itself) draws all things else to support and agree with it. And though there be a greater number and weight of instances to be found on the other side, yet these it either neglects and despises, or else by some distinction sets aside and rejects; in order that by this great and pernicious predetermination the authority of its former conclusions may remain inviolate. And therefore it was a good answer that was made by one who when they showed him hanging in a temple a picture of those who had paid their vows as having escaped shipwreck, and would have him say whether he did not now acknowledge the power of the gods,—"Aye," asked he again, "but where are they painted that were drowned after their vows?" And such is the way of all superstition, whether in astrology, dreams, omens, divine judgments, or the like; wherein men, having a delight in such vanities, mark the events where they are fulfilled, but where they fail, though this happen much oftener, neglect and pass them by. But with far more subtlety does this mischief insinuate itself into philosophy and the sciences; in which the first conclusion colors and brings into conformity with itself all that come after, though far sounder and better. Besides, independently of that delight and vanity which I have described, it is the peculiar and perpetual error of the human intellect to be more moved and excited by affirmatives than by negatives; whereas it ought properly to hold itself indifferently disposed towards both alike. Indeed in the establishment of any true axiom, the negative instance is the more forcible of the two.

C

But not only is a greater abundance of experiments to be sought for and procured, and that too of a different kind from those hitherto tried; an entirely different method, order, and process for carrying on and advancing experience must also be introduced. For experience, when it wanders in its own track, is, as I have already remarked, mere groping in the dark, and confounds men rather than instructs them. But when it shall proceed in accordance with a fixed law, in regular order, and without interruption, then may better things be hoped of knowledge.

CIV

The understanding must not, however, be allowed to jump and fly from particulars to axioms remote and of almost the highest generality (such as the first principles, as they are called, of arts and things), and taking stand upon them as truths that cannot be shaken, proceed to prove and frame the middle axioms by reference to them; which has been the practice hitherto, the understanding being not only carried that way by a natural impulse, but also by the use of syllogistic demonstration trained and inured to it. But then, and then only, may we hope well of the sciences when in a just scale of ascent, and by successive steps not interrupted or broken, we rise from particulars to lesser axioms; and then to middle axioms, one above the other; and last of all to the most general. For the lowest axioms differ but slightly from bare experience, while the highest and most general (which we now have) are notional and abstract and without solidity. But the middle are the true and solid and living axioms, on which depend the affairs and fortunes of men; and above them again, last of all, those which are indeed the most general; such, I mean, as are not abstract, but of which those intermediate axioms are really limitations.

The understanding must not therefore be supplied with wings, but rather hung with weights, to keep it from leaping and flying. Now this has never yet been done; when it is done, we may entertain better hopes of the sciences.

CV

In establishing axioms, another form of induction must be devised than has hitherto been employed, and it must be used for proving and discovering not first principles (as they are called) only, but also the lesser axioms, and the middle, and indeed all. For the induction which proceeds by simple enumeration is childish; its conclusions are precarious and exposed to peril from a contradictory instance; and it generally decides on too small a number of facts, and on those only which are at hand. But the induction which is to be available for the discovery and demonstration of sciences and arts, must analyze nature by proper rejections and exclusions; and then, after a sufficient number of negatives, come to a conclusion on the affirmative instances—which has not yet been done or even attempted, save only by Plato, who does indeed employ this form of induction to a certain extent for the purpose of discussing definitions and ideas. But in order to furnish this induction or demonstration well and duly for its work, very many things are to be provided which no mortal has yet thought of; insomuch that greater labor will have to be spent in it than has hitherto been spent on the syllogism. And this induction must be used not only to discover axioms, but also in the formation of notions. And it is in this induction that our chief hope lies.

CVI

But in establishing axioms by this kind of induction, we must also examine and try whether the axiom so established be framed to the measure of those particulars only from which it is derived, or whether it be larger and wider. And if it be larger and wider, we must observe whether by indicating to us new particulars it confirm that wideness and largeness as by a collateral security, that we may not either stick fast in things already known, or loosely grasp at shadows and abstract forms, not at things solid and realized in matter. And when this process shall have come into use, then at last shall we see the dawn of a solid hope.

APHORISMS, BOOK 2

X

. . . Now my directions for the interpretation of nature embrace two generic divisions: the one how to educe and form axioms from experience; the other how to deduce and derive new experiments from axioms. The former again is divided into three ministrations: a ministration to the sense, a ministration to the memory, and a ministration to the mind or reason.

For first of all we must prepare a natural and experimental history, sufficient and good; and this is the foundation of all, for we are not to imagine or suppose, but to discover, what nature does or may be made to do.

But natural and experimental history is so various and diffuse that it confounds and distracts the understanding, unless it be ranged and presented to view in a suitable order. We must therefore form tables and arrangements of instances, in such a method and order that the understanding may be able to deal with them.

And even when this is done, still the understanding, if left to itself and its own spontaneous movements, is incompetent and unfit to form axioms, unless it be directed and guarded. Therefore in the third place we must use induction, true and legitimate induction, which is the very key of interpretation. But of this, which is the last, I must speak first, and then go back to the other ministrations.

RENÉ DESCARTES
1596–1650

René Descartes was born into the family of a minor noble in the town of La Haye in Touraine, France. At ten, René began a nine-year course of studies at the Royal Jesuit College of La Flèche. There he studied the humanities, theology, and philosophy (which included morals, logic, mathematics, metaphysics, and science). Though he did well in school, he was disillusioned by the uncertainty of his studies and their contradictory conclusions. Like many modern students, he felt overwhelmed by the multitude of opinions he encountered. He later wrote in his *Discourse on Method* that upon completing his course of study, "I found myself embarrassed with so many doubts and errors that it seemed to me that the effort to instruct myself had no effect other than the increasing discovery of my own ignorance."

However, there was one discipline in which he found the certainty he was seeking: mathematics. The truths of mathematics were assured regardless of one's metaphysical or epistemological assumptions: $2 + 2 = 4$ whether one is a Platonist or an Aristotelian; $3 \times 3 = 9$ whether one is a Roman Catholic or a Protestant. Given mathematical certainty, Descartes found it odd that on such a firm basis "no loftier edifice had been reared."

Left a modest inheritance by his father, Descartes spent the rest of his life seeking the certainty not found in college. After receiving a law degree at Poitiers in 1616, he served as a gentleman volunteer in the army of Maurice of Nassau. While soldiering, he began to develop the idea of connecting mathematical certainty with philosophy. In 1619, he had a series of dreams convincing him that the "spirit of truth" was leading him and that he had divine approval for his studies. For the next ten years, while traveling and serving in the army, he developed his ideas. In 1628, he had a debate with Chandoux, a scientist who claimed that science could only be founded on probability. Descartes argued eloquently that knowledge must be based on certainty and that he had a system that provided that basis. Encouraged by others to develop his system, he retired to Holland, where he found a greater degree of intellectual freedom and spent the next twenty years writing and publishing his ideas. His major philosophical works include *Rules for the Direction of the Mind* (written 1628, but not published until 1701), *Discourse on Method* (published in 1637 as a preface to the essays *Geometry*, *Dioptric*, and *Meteors*), and *Meditations on First Philosophy* (1641). Descartes also published seven sets of Objections to the Meditations of such thinkers as Hobbes, Arnauld, and Gassendi, accompanied by his Reply to Objections. In addition to his work in philosophy, Descartes made major contributions to the fields of optics, anatomy, physiology, and mathematics (especially analytic geometry in which "Cartesian coordinates" are still used).

Descartes chose to write his works in French as well as Latin in order to reach beyond the academics to a wider audience. His writings did, indeed, reach learned people throughout Europe and that fact, unfortunately, led indirectly to his death. In 1649, Queen Christina of Sweden invited Descartes to join a circle of leading thinkers to instruct her in philosophy. Although he initially resisted the invitation, he finally felt compelled to accept. Upon arriving in Sweden, Descartes discovered that Queen Christina had time to see him only at five each morning. Descartes had been used to lying in bed until late in the morning, reflecting and philosophizing. Within a year the rigorous new schedule, together with Sweden's harsh weather, led to his death.

*   *   *

Like Bacon before him, Descartes began his philosophy by sweeping away all the "errors of the past." Whereas Bacon turned to empirical observation to escape the "tyranny" of the past, Descartes turned to mathematics, specifically geometry. He began by establishing twenty-one *Rules for the Direction of the Mind*. He would begin by finding knowledge that he could "clearly and evidently intuit, or deduce with certainty." Then he would build from this knowledge deductively, one step at a time. This procedure would parallel the geometrical method of moving with deductive certainty from postulates to axioms. His *Meditations on First Philosophy*, reprinted here (complete) in the latest John Cottingham translation, chronicles this process.

The key was to find the knowledge that he could "clearly and evidently intuit" that could serve as his starting point. Although uncertainty and doubt were the enemies, Descartes hit upon the idea of using doubt as a tool or a weapon. Instead of fighting doubt, he would use it to find certainty. He would use doubt as an acid to pour over every "truth" to see if there was anything that would not be dissolved, any "truth" that could not be doubted. Some of his doubts may seem extreme (such as that the earth may not exist or that I may be dreaming all this), but in order to find 100-percent certainty he had to find a starting point with zero-percent doubt.

After subjecting all his knowledge to the acid of doubt, he concluded that there was one thing he could not doubt: that he was doubting. The one fact the acid of doubt could not dissolve was doubt itself. This meant there had to be an "I" who was doing the doubting. Even if he were deceived about everything else, he had to exist in order to be deceived. This led Descartes to his famous statement, *Cogito ergo sum,* meaning "I think, therefore I am" (although these exact words do not appear in the *Meditations*). Here was the "clearly and evidently intuited" knowledge, the starting point, that Descartes had been seeking.

Having established that there is an "I," a self, a starting point, Descartes began to explore the nature of this "I":

> But what then am I? A thing that thinks. What is that? A thing that doubts, understands, affirms, denies, is willing, is unwilling, and also imagines and has sensory perceptions.

Among the ideas of this "thinking thing" called the "I" is the idea of a perfect God. Descartes went on to argue that nothing less than God could have caused the idea of God. He therefore concluded with a second certainty: that God exists.

From here Descartes moved to his third certainty: We have a strong tendency to believe in the existence of a reality beyond our consciousness. If there is no such external world, then we are terribly deceived. But a perfect God would not allow us to be unavoidably deceived, since deceit implies imperfection. Accordingly, we can conclude that we are not misled about those natural beliefs, such as the existence of an external world, so long as they can withstand the scrutiny of reason and are not willfully disregarded.

The Anatomy Lesson, 1632, by Rembrandt (1606–1669). Members of the Surgeons and Physicians Guild personify the Age of Observation with their intense scientific inquiry into human anatomy. Descartes was also interested in anatomy, making such important discoveries as that muscles work in opposition to each other. (*Mauritshuis, The Hague*)

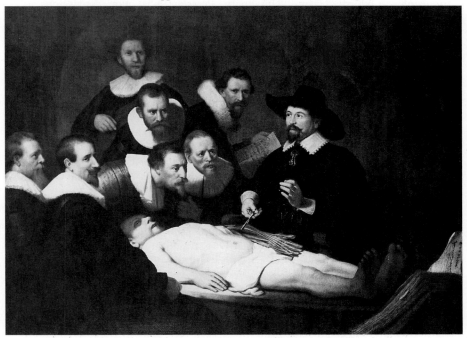

Descartes had now established a basis for accepting the "obvious" truths he had thrown out earlier by his method of doubt. He had at the same time identified the criterion needed to distinguish the foundational truths upon which his knowledge rested, namely, the criterion that a truth must be "clearly and distinctly perceived." An example of his rationalistic dependence upon such intuitions is his claim that the essential nature of a material object can only be known intuitively, not through sense perceptions.

One final point needs to be noted. The "I" that Descartes found at the end of his methodological doubting was "entirely distinct from the body." This "I" was an immaterial mind, a "spiritual" thing. The body is an "extended, non-thinking thing." As such, it is part of the material world, subject to the same laws of motion as a billiard ball. The "I," or the mind, on the other hand, is not bound by physical laws. This Cartesian distinction leads to a problem about the relationship between body and mind. One of the first to raise the issue was Princess Elisabeth of Bohemia (1618–1680). Her correspondence with Descartes, given here in the Anscombe and Geach translation, addresses questions with which we still struggle today.

*   *   *

For a concise treatment of Descartes' thought in its historical context, see Alexandre Koyré, "Introduction," in E. Anscombe and P.T. Geach, eds., *René Descartes' Philosophical Writings* (Edinburgh: Nelson, 1954). Among the best of several excellent general studies of Descartes are Anthony Kenny, *Descartes: A Study of His Philosophy* (New York: Random House, 1968); Margaret Dauler Wilson, *Descartes* (Oxford: Routledge, 1983); John Cottingham, *Descartes* (Oxford: Basil Blackwell, 1986); and Stephen Gauktoger, *Descartes: An Intellectual Biography* (Oxford: Oxford University Press, 1995). For discussions of Descartes' *Meditations*, see L.J. Beck, *The Metaphysics of Descartes: A Study of the Meditations* (Oxford: Clarendon Press, 1965); E.M. Curley, *Descartes Against the Skeptics* (Cambridge, MA: Harvard University Press, 1978); Stanley Tweyman, ed., *Rene Descartes' Meditations on First Philosophy in Focus* (Oxford: Routledge, 1993); Georges Dicker, *Descartes* (Oxford: Oxford University Press, 1993); and Vere Chappel, ed., *Descartes's Meditations: Critical Essays* (Lanham, MD: Rowan & Littlefield, 1997). Roger Ariew and Marjorie Grene, eds., *Descartes and his Contemporaries: Meditations, Objections, and Replies* (Chicago: University of Chicago Press, 1995) includes the responses of Descartes' contemporaries to the *Meditations*. S. Woolhouse, *Descartes, Spinoza, Leibniz: The Concept of Substance in Seventeenth-Century Metaphysics* (London: Routledge, 1993) provides a comparative study, whereas John Cottingham, *A Descartes Dictionary* (Oxford: Basil Blackwell, 1993) provides a helpful reference work. For collections of essays on Descartes, see Willis Doney, ed., *Descartes: A Collection of Critical Essays* (Garden City, NY: Doubleday, 1967); Michael Hooker, ed., *Descartes: Critical and Interpretive Essays* (Baltimore, MD: Johns Hopkins University Press, 1978); Amelie O. Rorty, ed., *Essays on Descartes' Meditations* (Berkeley: University of California Press, 1986); Georges J.D. Moyal, ed., *René Descartes: Critical Assessments* (London: Routledge, 1991); Vere Chappell, ed., *Essays on Early Modern Philosophers: René Descartes* (Hamden, CT: Garland, 1992); John Cottingham, ed., *The Cambridge Companion to Descartes* (Cambridge: Cambridge University Press, 1992); the multi-volume George J.D. Moyal, *Rene Descartes: Critical Assessments* (Oxford: Routledge, 1992); and Stephen Voss, *Essays on the Philosophy and Science of René Descartes* (Oxford: Oxford University Press, 1993). Gilbert Ryle, *The Concept of Mind* (London: Hutchinson's University Library, 1949) is the classic critique of Descartes' views on body and mind.

MEDITATIONS ON THE FIRST PHILOSOPHY

[Dedicatory letter to the Sorbonne]

To those most learned and distinguished men, the Dean and Doctors of the sacred Faculty of Theology at Paris, from René Descartes.   1

I have a very good reason for offering this book to you, and I am confident that you will have an equally good reason for giving it your protection once you understand the principle behind my undertaking; so much so, that my best way of commending it to you will be to tell you briefly of the goal which I shall be aiming at in the book.

I have always thought that two topics—namely God and the soul—are prime examples of subjects where demonstrative proofs ought to be given with the aid of philosophy rather than theology. For us who are believers, it is enough to accept on faith that the human soul does not die with the body, and that God exists; but in the case of   2 unbelievers, it seems that there is no religion, and practically no moral virtue, that they can be persuaded to adopt until these two truths are proved to them by natural reason. And since in this life the rewards offered to vice are often greater than the rewards of virtue, few people would prefer what is right to what is expedient if they did not fear God or have the expectation of an after-life. It is of course quite true that we must believe in the existence of God because it is a doctrine of Holy Scripture, and conversely, that we must believe Holy Scripture because it comes from God; for since faith is the gift of God, he who gives us grace to believe other things can also give us grace to believe that he exists. But this argument cannot be put to unbelievers because they would judge it to be circular. Moreover, I have noticed both that you and all other theologians assert that the existence of God is capable of proof by natural reason, and also that the inference from Holy Scripture is that the knowledge of God is easier to acquire than the knowledge we have of many created things—so easy, indeed, that those who do not acquire it are at fault. This is clear from a passage in the Book of Wisdom, Chapter 13: "Howbeit they are not to be excused; for if their knowledge was so great that they could value this world, why did they not rather find out the Lord thereof?" And in Romans, Chapter I it is said that they are "without excuse." And in the same place, in the passage "that which is known of God is manifest in them," we seem to be told that

René Descartes, *Meditations on the First Philosophy with Selections from the Objections and Replies,* translated by John Cottingham (Cambridge: Cambridge University Press, 1986). Copyright © 1986 by Cambridge University Press. Reprinted with the permission of Cambridge University Press.

everything that may be known of God can be demonstrated by reasoning which has no other source but our own mind. Hence I thought it was quite proper for me to inquire how this may be, and how God may be more easily and more certainly known than the things of this world.

3   As regards the soul, many people have considered that it is not easy to discover its nature, and some have even had the audacity to assert that, as far as human reasoning goes, there are persuasive grounds for holding that the soul dies along with the body and that the opposite view is based on faith alone. But in its eighth session the Lateran Council held under Leo X condemned those who take this position,* and expressly enjoined Christian philosophers to refute their arguments and use all their powers to establish the truth; so I have not hesitated to attempt this task as well.

In addition, I know that the only reason why many irreligious people are unwilling to believe that God exists and that the human mind is distinct from the body is the alleged fact that no one has hitherto been able to demonstrate these points. Now I completely disagree with this: I think that when properly understood almost all the arguments that have been put forward on these issues by the great men have the force of demonstrations, and I am convinced that it is scarcely possible to provide any arguments which have not already been produced by someone else. Nevertheless, I think there can be no more useful service to be rendered in philosophy than to conduct a careful search, once and for all, for the best of these arguments, and to set them out so precisely and clearly as to produce for the future a general agreement that they amount to demonstrative proofs. And finally, I was strongly pressed to undertake this task by several people who knew that I had developed a method for resolving certain difficulties in the sciences—not a new method (for nothing is older than the truth), but one which they had seen me use with some success in other areas; and I therefore thought it my duty to make some attempt to apply it to the matter in hand.

4   The present treatise contains everything that I have been able to accomplish in this area. Not that I have attempted to collect here all the different arguments that could be put forward to establish the same results, for this does not seem worthwhile except in cases where no single argument is regarded as sufficiently reliable. What I have done is to take merely the principal and most important arguments and develop them in such a way that I would now venture to put them forward as very certain and evident demonstrations. I will add that these proofs are of such a kind that I reckon they leave no room for the possibility that the human mind will ever discover better ones. The vital importance of the cause and the glory of God, to which the entire undertaking is directed, here compel me to speak somewhat more freely about my own achievements than is my custom. But although I regard the proofs as quite certain and evident, I cannot therefore persuade myself that they are suitable to be grasped by everyone. In geometry there are many writings left by Archimedes, Apollonius, Pappus, and others which are accepted by everyone as evident and certain because they contain absolutely nothing that is not very easy to understand when considered on its own, and each step fits in precisely with what has gone before; yet because they are somewhat long, and demand a very attentive reader, it is only comparatively few people who understand them. In the same way, although the proofs I employ here are in my view as certain and evident as the proofs of geometry, if not more so, it will, I fear, be impossible for many people to achieve an adequate perception of them, both because they are rather

*The Lateran Council of 1513 condemned the Averroist heresy that denied personal immortality.

long and some depend on others, and also, above all, because they require a mind which is completely free from preconceived opinions and which can easily detach itself from involvement with the senses. Moreover, people who have an aptitude for metaphysical studies are certainly not to be found in the world in any greater numbers than those who have an aptitude for geometry. What is more, there is the difference that in geometry everyone has been taught to accept that as a rule no proposition is put forward in a book without there being a conclusive demonstration available; so inexperienced students make the mistake of accepting what is false, in their desire to appear to understand it, more often than they make the mistake of rejecting what is true. In philosophy, by contrast, the belief is that everything can be argued either way; so few people pursue the truth, while the great majority build up their reputation for ingenuity by boldly attacking whatever is most sound.

Hence, whatever the quality of my arguments may be, because they have to do with philosophy I do not expect they will enable me to achieve any very worthwhile results unless you come to my aid by granting me your patronage.* The reputation of your Faculty is so firmly fixed in the minds of all, and the name of the Sorbonne has such authority that, with the exception of the Sacred Councils, no institution carries more weight than yours in matters of faith; while as regards human philosophy, you are thought of as second to none, both for insight and soundness and also for the integrity and wisdom of your pronouncements. Because of this, the results of your careful attention to this book, if you deigned to give it, would be threefold. First, the errors in it would be corrected—for when I remember not only that I am a human being, but above all that I am an ignorant one, I cannot claim it is free of mistakes. Secondly, any passages which are defective, or insufficiently developed or requiring further explanation, would be supplemented, completed and clarified, either by yourselves or by me after you have given me your advice. And lastly, once the arguments in the book proving that God exists and that the mind is distinct from the body have been brought, as I am sure they can be, to such a pitch of clarity that they are fit to be regarded as very exact demonstrations, you may be willing to declare as much, and make a public statement to that effect. If all this were to happen, I do not doubt that all the errors which have ever existed on these subjects would soon be eradicated from the minds of men. In the case of all those who share your intelligence and learning, the truth itself will readily ensure that they subscribe to your opinion. As for the atheists, who are generally posers rather than people of real intelligence or learning, your authority will induce them to lay aside the spirit of contradiction; and, since they know that the arguments are regarded as demonstrations by all who are intellectually gifted, they may even go so far as to defend them, rather than appear not to understand them. And finally, everyone else will confidently go along with so many declarations of assent, and there will be no one left in the world who will dare to call into doubt either the existence of God or the real distinction between the human soul and body. The great advantage that this would bring is something which you, in your singular wisdom, are in a better position to evaluate than anyone; and it would ill become me to spend any more time commending the cause of God and religion to you, who have always been the greatest tower of strength to the Catholic Church.

---

*Although the title page of the first edition of the *Meditations* carries the words "with the approval of the learned doctors," Descartes never, in fact, obtained the endorsement from the Sorbonne which he sought.

7 PREFACE TO READER

I briefly touched on the topics of God and the human mind in my *Discourse on the method of rightly conducting reason and seeking the truth in the sciences*, which was published in French in 1637. My purpose there was not to provide a full treatment, but merely to offer a sample, and learn from the views of my readers how I should handle these topics at a later date. The issues seemed to me of such great importance that I considered they ought to be dealt with more than once; and the route which I follow in explaining them is so untrodden and so remote from the normal way, that I thought it would not be helpful to give a full account of it in a book written in French and designed to be read by all and sundry, in case weaker intellects might believe that they ought to set out on the same path.

In the *Discourse* I asked anyone who found anything worth criticizing in what I had written to be kind enough to point it out to me. In the case of my remarks concerning God and the soul, only two objections worth mentioning were put to me, which I shall now briefly answer before embarking on a more precise elucidation of these topics.

8   The first objection is this. From the fact that the human mind, when directed towards itself, does not perceive itself to be anything other than a thinking thing, it does not follow that its nature or essence consists only in its being a thinking thing, where the word "only" excludes everything else that could be said to belong to the nature of the soul. My answer to this objection is that in that passage it was not my intention to make those exclusions in an order corresponding to the actual truth of the matter (which I was not dealing with at that stage) but merely in an order corresponding to my own perception. So the sense of the passage was that I was aware of nothing at all that I knew belonged to my essence, except that I was a thinking thing, or a thing possessing within itself the faculty of thinking. I shall, however, show below how it follows from the fact that I am aware of nothing else belonging to my essence, that nothing else does in fact belong to it.

The second objection is this. From the fact that I have within me an idea of a thing more perfect than myself, it does not follow that the idea itself is more perfect than me, still less that what is represented by the idea exists. My reply is that there is an ambiguity here in the word "idea." "Idea" can be taken materially, as an operation of the intellect, in which case it cannot be said to be more perfect than me. Alternatively, it can be taken objectively, as the thing represented by that operation; and this thing, even if it is not regarded as existing outside the intellect, can still, in virtue of its essence, be more perfect than myself. As to how, from the mere fact that there is within me an idea of something more perfect than me, it follows that this thing really exists, this is something which will be fully explained below.

Apart from these objections, there are two fairly lengthy essays which I have looked at, but these did not attack my reasoning on these matters so much as my conclusions, and employed arguments lifted from the standard sources of the atheists. But

9   arguments of this sort can carry no weight with those who understand my reasoning. Moreover, the judgement of many people is so silly and weak that, once they have accepted a view, they continue to believe it, however false and irrational it may be, in preference to a true and well-grounded refutation which they hear subsequently. So I do not wish to reply to such arguments here, if only to avoid having to state them. I will only make the general point that all the objections commonly tossed around by atheists to attack the existence of God invariably depend either on attributing human

feelings to God or on arrogantly supposing our own minds to be so powerful and wise that we can attempt to grasp and set limits to what God can or should perform. So, provided only that we remember that our minds must be regarded as finite, while God is infinite and beyond our comprehension, such objections will not cause us any difficulty.

But now that I have, after a fashion, taken an initial sample of people's opinions, I am again tackling the same questions concerning God and the human mind; and this time I am also going to deal with the foundations of First Philosophy in its entirety. But I do not expect any popular approval, or indeed any wide audience. On the contrary I would not urge anyone to read this book except those who are able and willing to meditate seriously with me, and to withdraw their minds from the senses and from all preconceived opinions. Such readers, as I well know, are few and far between. Those who do not bother to grasp the proper order of my arguments and the connection between them, but merely try to carp at individual sentences, as is the fashion, will not   10 get much benefit from reading this book. They may well find an opportunity to quibble in many places, but it will not be easy for them to produce objections which are telling or worth replying to.

But I certainly do not promise to satisfy my other readers straightaway on all points, and I am not so presumptuous as to believe that I am capable of foreseeing all the difficulties which anyone may find. So first of all, in the *Meditations*, I will set out the very thoughts which have enabled me, in my view, to arrive at a certain and evident knowledge of the truth, so that I can find out whether the same arguments which have convinced me will enable me to convince others. Next, I will reply to the objections of various men of outstanding intellect and scholarship who had these *Meditations* sent to them for scrutiny before they went to press. For the objections they raised were so many and so varied that I would venture to hope that it will be hard for anyone else to think of any point—at least of any importance—which these critics have not touched on. I therefore ask my readers not to pass judgement on the *Meditations* until they have been kind enough to read through all these objections and my replies to them.

SYNOPSIS OF FOLLOWING SIX MEDITATIONS   12

In the First Meditation reasons are provided which give us possible grounds for doubt about all things, especially material things, so long as we have no foundations for the sciences other than those which we have had up till now. Although the usefulness of such extensive doubt is not apparent at first sight, its greatest benefit lies in freeing us from all our preconceived opinions, and providing the easiest route by which the mind may be led away from the senses. The eventual result of this doubt is to make it impossible for us to have any further doubts about what we subsequently discover to be true.

In the Second Meditation, the mind uses its own freedom and supposes the non-existence of all the things about whose existence it can have even the slightest doubt; and in so doing the mind notices that it is impossible that it should not itself exist during this time. This exercise is also of the greatest benefit, since it enables the mind to distinguish without difficulty what belongs to itself, i.e. to an intellectual nature, from what belongs to the body. But since some people may perhaps expect arguments for the immortality of the soul in this section, I think they should be warned here and now that I have tried not to put down anything which I could not precisely demon-   13 strate. Hence the only order which I could follow was that normally employed by geometers, namely to set out all the premises on which a desired proposition depends, before drawing any conclusions about it. Now the first and most important prerequisite for knowledge of the immortality of the soul is for us to form a concept of the soul which is as clear as possible and is also quite distinct from every concept of body; and that is just what has been done in this section. A further requirement is that we should know that everything that we clearly and distinctly understand is true in a way which corresponds exactly to our understanding of it; but it was not possible to prove this before the Fourth Meditation. In addition we need to have a distinct concept of corporeal nature, and this is developed partly in the Second Meditation itself, and partly in the Fifth and Sixth Meditations. The inference to be drawn from these results is that all the things that we clearly and distinctly conceive of as different substances (as we do in the case of mind and body) are in fact substances which are really distinct one from the other; and this conclusion is drawn in the Sixth Meditation. This conclusion is confirmed in the same Meditation by the fact that we cannot understand a body except as being divisible, while by contrast we cannot understand a mind except as being indivisible. For we cannot conceive of half of a mind, while we can always conceive of half of a body, however small; and this leads us to recognize that the natures of mind and body are not only different, but in some way opposite. But I have not pursued this topic any further in this book, first because these arguments are enough to show that the decay of the body does not imply the destruction of the mind, and are hence enough to give mortals the hope of an after-life, and secondly because the premises which lead to the conclusion that the soul is immortal depend on an account of the whole of physics. This is required for two reasons. First, we need to know that absolutely all substances, or things which must be created by God in order to exist, are by their nature incorruptible and cannot ever cease to exist unless they are reduced to nothingness by God's denying his concurrence* to them. Secondly, we need to recognize that body, taken in the general sense, is a substance, so that it too never perishes. But the human body, in so far as it differs from other bodies, is simply made up of a certain configuration of limbs and other accidents** of this sort; whereas the human mind is not made up of any accidents in this way, but is a pure substance. For even if all the accidents of the mind change, so that it has different objects of the understanding and different desires and sensations, it does not on that account become a different mind; whereas a human body loses its identity merely as a result of a change in the shape of some of its parts. And it follows from this that while the body can very easily perish, the mind*** is immortal by its very nature.

In the Third Meditation I have explained quite fully enough, I think, my principal argument for proving the existence of God. But in order to draw my readers' minds away from the senses as far as possible, I was not willing to use any comparison taken from bodily things. So it may be that many obscurities remain; but I hope they will be completely removed later, in my Replies to the Objections. One such problem, among others, is how the idea of a supremely perfect being, which is in us, possesses so much objective reality that it can come only from a cause which is supremely perfect. In the Replies this is illustrated by the comparison of a very perfect machine, the idea of

---

*The continuous divine action necessary to maintain things in existence.

**Descartes here uses this scholastic term to refer to those features of a thing which may alter, e.g. the particular size, shape, etc. of a body, or the particular thoughts, desires, etc. of a mind.

***". . . or the soul of man, for I make no distinction between them" (added in French version).

which is in the mind of some engineer. Just as the objective intricacy belonging to the idea must have some cause, namely the scientific knowledge of the engineer, or of someone else who passed the idea on to him, so the idea of God which is in us must   15
have God himself as its cause.

In the Fourth Meditation it is proved that everything that we clearly and distinctly perceive is true, and I also explain what the nature of falsity consists in. These results need to be known both in order to confirm what has gone before and also to make intelligible what is to come later. (But here it should be noted in passing that I do not deal at all with sin, i.e. the error which is committed in pursuing good and evil, but only with the error that occurs in distinguishing truth from falsehood. And there is no discussion of matters pertaining to faith or the conduct of life, but simply of speculative truths which are known solely by means of the natural light.)

In the Fifth Meditation, besides an account of corporeal nature taken in general, there is a new argument demonstrating the existence of God. Again, several difficulties may arise here, but these are resolved later in the Replies to the Objections. Finally I explain the sense in which it is true that the certainty even of geometrical demonstrations depends on the knowledge of God.

Lastly, in the Sixth Meditation, the intellect is distinguished from the imagination; the criteria for this distinction are explained; the mind is proved to be really distinct from the body, but is shown, notwithstanding, to be so closely joined to it that the mind and the body make up a kind of unit; there is a survey of all the errors which commonly come from the senses, and an explanation of how they may be avoided; and, lastly, there is a presentation of all the arguments which enable the existence of material things to be inferred. The great benefit of these arguments is not, in my view, that they prove what they establish—namely that there really is a world, and that   16
human beings have bodies and so on—since no sane person has ever seriously doubted these things. The point is that in considering these arguments we come to realize that they are not as solid or as transparent as the arguments which lead us to knowledge of our own minds and of God, so that the latter are the most certain and evident of all possible objects of knowledge for the human intellect. Indeed, this is the one thing that I set myself to prove in these Meditations. And for that reason I will not now go over the various other issues in the book which are dealt with as they come up.

17 # MEDITATIONS ON FIRST PHILOSOPHY
IN WHICH ARE DEMONSTRATED
THE EXISTENCE OF GOD
AND THE DISTINCTION BETWEEN
THE HUMAN SOUL AND THE BODY

FIRST MEDITATION

What can be called into doubt

Some years ago I was struck by the large number of falsehoods that I had accepted as true in my childhood, and by the highly doubtful nature of the whole edifice that I had subsequently based on them. I realized that it was necessary, once in the course of my life, to demolish everything completely and start again right from the foundations if I wanted to establish anything at all in the sciences that was stable and likely to last. But the task looked an enormous one, and I began to wait until I should reach a mature enough age to ensure that no subsequent time of life would be more suitable for tackling such inquiries. This led me to put the project off for so long that I would now be to blame if by pondering over it any further I wasted the time still left

18 for carrying it out. So today I have expressly rid my mind of all worries and arranged for myself a clear stretch of free time. I am here quite alone, and at last I will devote myself sincerely and without reservation to the general demolition of my opinions.

But to accomplish this, it will not be necessary for me to show that all my opinions are false, which is something I could perhaps never manage. Reason now leads me to think that I should hold back my assent from opinions which are not completely certain and indubitable just as carefully as I do from those which are patently false. So, for the purpose of rejecting all my opinions, it will be enough if I find in each of them at least some reason for doubt. And to do this I will not need to run through them all individually, which would be an endless task. Once the foundations of a building are undermined, anything built on them collapses of its own accord; so I will go straight for the basic principles on which all my former beliefs rested.

Whatever I have up till now accepted as most true I have acquired either from the senses or through the senses. But from time to time I have found that the senses deceive, and it is prudent never to trust completely those who have deceived us even once.

Yet although the senses occasionally deceive us with respect to objects which are very small or in the distance, there are many other beliefs about which doubt is quite impossible, even though they are derived from the senses—for example, that I am here, sitting by the fire, wearing a winter dressing-gown, holding this piece of paper in my hands, and so on Again, how could it be denied that these hands or this whole body

19 are mine? Unless perhaps I were to liken myself to madmen, whose brains are so damaged by the persistent vapours of melancholia that they firmly maintain they are kings when they are paupers, or say they are dressed in purple when they are naked, or that their heads are made of earthenware or that they are pumpkins, or made of glass. But such people are insane and I would be thought equally mad if I took anything from them as: model for myself.

A brilliant piece of reasoning! As if I were not a man who sleeps a night, and regularly has all the same experiences while asleep a madmen do when awake—indeed sometimes even more improbable ones. How often, asleep at night, am I convinced of just such familiar events—that I am here in my dressing-gown, sitting by the fire—when in fact I am lying undressed in bed! Yet at the moment my eyes are certainly wide awake when I look at this piece of paper; I shake my head and it is not asleep; as I stretch out and feel my hand I do so deliberately, and I know what I am doing. All this would not happen with such distinctness to someone asleep. Indeed! As if I did not remember other occasions when I have been tricked by exactly similar thoughts while asleep! As I think about this more carefully, I see plainly that there are never any sure signs by means of which being awake can be distinguished from being asleep. The result is that I begin to feel dazed, and this very feeling only reinforces the notion that I may be asleep.

Suppose then that I am dreaming, and that these particulars—that my eyes are open, that I am moving my head and stretching out my hands—are not true. Perhaps, indeed, I do not even have such hands or such a body at all. Nonetheless, it must surely be admitted that the visions which come in sleep are like paintings, which must have been fashioned in the likeness of things that are real, and hence that at least these general kinds of things—eyes, head, hands and the body as a whole—are things which are not imaginary but are real and exist. For even when painters try to create sirens and satyrs with the most extraordinary bodies, they cannot give them natures which are new in all respects; they simply jumble up the limbs of different animals. Or if perhaps they manage to think up something so new that nothing remotely similar has ever been seen before—something which is therefore completely fictitious and unreal—at least the colours used in the composition must be real. By similar reasoning, although these general kinds of things—eyes, head, hands and so on—could be imaginary, it must at least be admitted that certain other even simpler and more universal things are real. These are as it were the real colours from which we form all the images of things, whether true or false, that occur in our thought. 20

This class appears to include corporeal nature in general, and its extension; the shape of extended things; the quantity, or size and number of these things; the place in which they may exist, the time through which they may endure, and so on.

So a reasonable conclusion from this might be that physics, astronomy, medicine, and all other disciplines which depend on the study of composite things, are doubtful; while arithmetic, geometry and other subjects of this kind, which deal only with the simplest and most general things, regardless of whether they really exist in nature or not, contain something certain and indubitable. For whether I am awake or asleep, two and three added together are five, and a square has no more than four sides. It seems impossible that such transparent truths should incur any suspicion of being false.

And yet firmly rooted in my mind is the long-standing opinion that there is an omnipotent God who made me the kind of creature that I am. How do I know that he has not brought it about that there is no earth, no sky, no extended thing, no shape, no size, no place, while at the same time ensuring that all these things appear to me to exist just as they do now? What is more, since I sometimes believe that others go astray in cases where they think they have the most perfect knowledge, may I not similarly go wrong every time I add two and three or count the sides of a square, or in some even simpler matter, if that is imaginable? But perhaps God would not have allowed me to be deceived in this way, since he is said to be supremely good. But if it were inconsistent with his goodness to have created me such that I am deceived all the time, it would seem equally foreign to his goodness to allow me to be deceived even occasionally; yet this last assertion cannot be made. 21

Perhaps there may be some who would prefer to deny the existence of so powerful a God rather than believe that everything else is uncertain. Let us not argue with them, but grant them that everything said about God is a fiction. According to their supposition, then, I have arrived at my present state by fate or chance or a continuous chain of events, or by some other means; yet since deception and error seem to be imperfections, the less powerful they make my original cause, the more likely it is that I am so imperfect as to be deceived all the time. I have no answer to these arguments, but am finally compelled to admit that there is not one of my former beliefs about which a doubt may not properly be raised; and this is not a flippant or ill-considered conclusion, but is based on powerful and well thought-out reasons. So in future I must withhold my assent from these former beliefs just as carefully as I would from obvious falsehoods, if I want to discover any certainty.

22

But it is not enough merely to have noticed this; I must make an effort to remember it. My habitual opinions keep coming back, and, despite my wishes, they capture my belief, which is as it were bound over to them as a result of long occupation and the law of custom. I shall never get out of the habit of confidently assenting to these opinions, so long as I suppose them to be what in fact they are, namely highly probable opinions—opinions which, despite the fact that they are in a sense doubtful, as has just been shown, it is still much more reasonable to believe than to deny. In view of this, I think it will be a good plan to turn my will in completely the opposite direction and deceive myself, by pretending for a time that these former opinions are utterly false and imaginary. I shall do this until the weight of preconceived opinion is counter-balanced and the distorting influence of habit no longer prevents my judgement from perceiving things correctly. In the meantime, I know that no danger or error will result from my plan, and that I cannot possibly go too far in my distrustful attitude. This is because the task now in hand does not involve action but merely the acquisition of knowledge.

I will suppose therefore that not God, who is supremely good and the source of truth, but rather some malicious demon of the utmost power and cunning has employed all his energies in order to deceive me. I shall think that the sky, the air, the earth, colours, shapes, sounds and all external things are merely the delusions of dreams which he has devised to ensnare my judgement. I shall consider myself as not having hands or eyes, or flesh, or blood or senses, but as falsely believing that I have all these things. I shall stubbornly and firmly persist in this meditation; and, even if it is not in my power to know any truth, I shall at least do what is in my power, that is, resolutely guard against assenting to any falsehoods, so that the deceiver, however powerful and cunning he may be, will be unable to impose on me in the slightest degree. But this is an arduous undertaking, and a kind of laziness brings me back to normal life. I am like a prisoner who is enjoying an imaginary freedom while asleep; as he begins to suspect that he is asleep, he dreads being woken up, and goes along with the pleasant illusion as long as he can. In the same way, I happily slide back into my old opinions and dread being shaken out of them, for fear that my peaceful sleep may be followed by hard labour when I wake, and that I shall have to toil not in the light, but amid the inextricable darkness of the problems I have now raised.

23

SECOND MEDITATION

The nature of the human mind, and how it is better known than the body

So serious are the doubts into which I have been thrown as a result of yesterday's meditation that I can neither put them out of my mind nor see any way of resolving

them. It feels as if I have fallen unexpectedly into a deep whirlpool which tumbles me   24
around so that I can neither stand on the bottom nor swim up to the top. Nevertheless I
will make an effort and once more attempt the same path which I started on yesterday.
Anything which admits of the slightest doubt I will set aside just as if I had found it to
be wholly false; and I will proceed in this way until I recognize something certain, or,
if nothing else, until I at least recognize for certain that there is no certainty.
Archimedes used to demand just one firm and immovable point in order to shift the entire earth; so I too can hope for great things if I manage to find just one thing, however
slight, that is certain and unshakeable.

I will suppose then, that everything I see is spurious. I will believe that my memory tells me lies, and that none of the things that it reports ever happened. I have no
senses. Body, shape, extension, movement and place are chimeras. So what remains
true? Perhaps just the one fact that nothing is certain.

Yet apart from everything I have just listed, how do I know that there is not
something else which does not allow even the slightest occasion for doubt? Is there not
a God, or whatever I may call him, who puts into me the thoughts I am now having?
But why do I think this, since I myself may perhaps be the author of these thoughts? In
that case am not I, at least, something? But I have just said that I have no senses and no
body. This is the sticking point: what follows from this? Am I not so bound up with a   25
body and with senses that I cannot exist without them? But I have convinced myself
that there is absolutely nothing in the world, no sky, no earth, no minds, no bodies.
Does it now follow that I too do not exist? No: if I convinced myself of something then
I certainly existed. But there is a deceiver of supreme power and cunning who is deliberately and constantly deceiving me. In that case I too undoubtedly exist, if he is deceiving me; and let him deceive me as much as he can, he will never bring it about that
I am nothing so long as I think that I am something. So after considering everything
very thoroughly, I must finally conclude that this proposition, *I am, I exist*, is necessarily true whenever it is put forward by me or conceived in my mind.

But I do not yet have a sufficient understanding of what this "I" is, that now necessarily exists. So I must be on my guard against carelessly taking something else to be
this "I," and so making a mistake in the very item of knowledge that I maintain is the
most certain and evident of all. I will therefore go back and meditate on what I originally believed myself to be, before I embarked on this present train of thought. I will
then subtract anything capable of being weakened, even minimally, by the arguments
now introduced, so that what is left at the end may be exactly and only what is certain
and unshakeable.

What then did I formerly think I was? A man. But what is a man? Shall I say "a
rational animal"? No; for then I should have to inquire what an animal is, what rationality is, and in this way one question would lead me down the slope to other harder
ones, and I do not now have the time to waste on subtleties of this kind. Instead I propose to concentrate on what came into my thoughts spontaneously and quite naturally   26
whenever I used to consider what I was. Well, the first thought to come to mind was
that I had a face, hands, arms and the whole mechanical structure of limbs which can
be seen in a corpse, and which I called the body. The next thought was that I was nourished, that I moved about, and that I engaged in sense-perception and thinking; and
these actions I attributed to the soul. But as to the nature of this soul, either I did not
think about this or else I imagined it to be something tenuous, like a wind or fire or
ether, which permeated my more solid parts. As to the body, however, I had no doubts
about it, but thought I knew its nature distinctly. If I had tried to describe the mental
conception I had of it, I would have expressed it as follows: by a body I understand

whatever has a determinable shape and a definable location and can occupy a space in such a way as to exclude any other body; it can be perceived by touch, sight, hearing, taste or smell, and can be moved in various ways, not by itself but by whatever else comes into contact with it. For, according to my judgement, the power of self-movement, like the power of sensation or of thought, was quite foreign to the nature of a body; indeed, it was a source of wonder to me that certain bodies were found to contain faculties of this kind.

But what shall I now say that I am, when I am supposing that there is some supremely powerful and, if it is permissible to say so, malicious deceiver, who is deliberately trying to trick me in every way he can? Can I now assert that I possess even the most insignificant of all the attributes which I have just said belong to the nature of a

27   body? I scrutinize them, think about them, go over them again, but nothing suggests itself; it is tiresome and pointless to go through the list once more. But what about the attributes I assigned to the soul? Nutrition or movement? Since now I do not have a body, these are mere fabrications. Sense-perception? This surely does not occur without a body, and besides, when asleep I have appeared to perceive through the senses many things which I afterwards realized I did not perceive through the senses at all. Thinking? At last I have discovered it—thought; this alone is inseparable from me. I am, I exist—that is certain. But for how long? For as long as I am thinking. For it could be that were I totally to cease from thinking, I should totally cease to exist. At present I am not admitting anything except what is necessarily true. I am, then, in the strict sense only a thing that thinks; that is, I am a mind, or intelligence, or intellect, or reason—words whose meaning I have been ignorant of until now. But for all that I am a thing which is real and which truly exists. But what kind of a thing? As I have just said—a thinking thing.

What else am I? I will use my imagination. I am not that structure of limbs which is called a human body. I am not even some thin vapour which permeates the limbs—a wind, fire, air, breath, or whatever I depict in my imagination; for these are things which I have supposed to be nothing. Let this supposition stand; for all that I am still something. And yet may it not perhaps be the case that these very things which I am supposing to be nothing, because they are unknown to me, are in reality identical with the "I" of which I am aware? I do not know, and for the moment I shall not argue the point, since I can make judgements only about things which are known to me. I know that I exist; the question is, what is this "I" that I know? If the "I" is understood strictly as we have been taking it, then it is quite certain that knowledge of it does not depend

28   on things of whose existence I am as yet unaware; so it cannot depend on any of the things which I invent in my imagination. And this very word "invent" shows me my mistake. It would indeed be a case of fictitious invention if I used my imagination to establish that I was something or other; for imagining is simply contemplating the shape or image of a corporeal thing. Yet now I know for certain both that I exist and at the same time that all such images and, in general, everything relating to the nature of body, could be mere dreams [and chimeras]. Once this point has been grasped, to say "I will use my imagination to get to know more distinctly what I am" would seem to be as silly as saying "I am now awake, and see some truth; but since my vision is not yet clear enough, I will deliberately fall asleep so that my dreams may provide a truer and clearer representation." I thus realize that none of the things that the imagination enables me to grasp is at all relevant to this knowledge of myself which I possess, and that the mind must therefore be most carefully diverted from such things if it is to perceive its own nature as distinctly as possible.

But what then am I? A thing that thinks. What is that? A thing that doubts, understands, affirms, denies, is willing, is unwilling, and also imagines and has sensory perceptions.

This is a considerable list, if everything on it belongs to me. But does it? Is it not one and the same "I" who is now doubting almost everything, who nonetheless understands some things, who affirms that this one thing is true, denies everything else, desires to know more, is unwilling to be deceived, imagines many things even involuntarily, and is aware of many things which apparently come from the senses? Are not all these things just as true as the fact that I exist, even if I am asleep all the time, and even if he who created me is doing all he can to deceive me? Which of all these activities is distinct from my thinking? Which of them can be said to be separate from myself? The fact that it is I who am doubting and understanding and willing is so evident that I see no way of making it any clearer. But it is also the case that the "I" who imagines is the same "I." For even if, as I have supposed, none of the objects of imagination are real, the power of imagination is something which really exists and is part of my thinking. Lastly, it is also the same "I" who has sensory perceptions, or is aware of bodily things as it were through the senses. For example, I am now seeing light, hearing a noise, feeling heat. But I am asleep, so all this is false. Yet I certainly *seem* to see, to hear, and to be warmed. This cannot be false; what is called "having a sensory perception" is strictly just this, and in this restricted sense of the term it is simply thinking.

From all this I am beginning to have a rather better understanding of what I am. But it still appears—and I cannot stop thinking this—that the corporeal things of which images are formed in my thought, and which the senses investigate, are known with much more distinctness than this puzzling "I" which cannot be pictured in the imagination. And yet it is surely surprising that I should have a more distinct grasp of things which I realize are doubtful, unknown and foreign to me, than I have of that which is true and known—my own self. But I see what it is: my mind enjoys wandering off and will not yet submit to being restrained within the bounds of truth. Very well then; just this once let us give it a completely free rein, so that after a while, when it is time to tighten the reins, it may more readily submit to being curbed.

Let us consider the things which people commonly think they understand most distinctly of all; that is, the bodies which we touch and see. I do not mean bodies in general—for general perceptions are apt to be somewhat more confused—but one particular body. Let us take, for example, this piece of wax. It has just been taken from the honeycomb; it has not yet quite lost the taste of the honey; it retains some of the scent of the flowers from which it was gathered; its colour, shape and size are plain to see; it is hard, cold and can be handled without difficulty; if you rap it with your knuckle it makes a sound. In short, it has everything which appears necessary to enable a body to be known as distinctly as possible. But even as I speak, I put the wax by the fire, and look: the residual taste is eliminated, the smell goes away, the colour changes, the shape is lost, the size increases; it becomes liquid and hot; you can hardly touch it, and if you strike it, it no longer makes a sound. But does the same wax remain? It must be admitted that it does; no one denies it, no one thinks otherwise. So what was it in the wax that I understood with such distinctness? Evidently none of the features which I arrived at by means of the senses; for whatever came under taste, smell, sight, touch or hearing has now altered—yet the wax remains.

Perhaps the answer lies in the thought which now comes to my mind; namely, the wax was not after all the sweetness of the honey, or the fragrance of the flowers, or the whiteness, or the shape, or the sound, but was rather a body which presented itself

29

30

to me in these various forms a little while ago, but which now exhibits different ones.
31   But what exactly is it that I am now imagining? Let us concentrate, take away everything which does not belong to the wax, and see what is left: merely something extended, flexible and changeable. But what is meant here by "flexible" and "changeable"? Is it what I picture in my imagination: that this piece of wax is capable of
changing from a round shape to a square shape, or from a square shape to a triangular
shape? Not at all; for I can grasp that the wax is capable of countless changes of this
kind, yet I am unable to run through this immeasurable number of changes in my
imagination, from which it follows that it is not the faculty of imagination that gives
me my grasp of the wax as flexible and changeable. And what is meant by "extended"?
Is the extension of the wax also unknown? For it increases if the wax melts, increases
again if it boils, and is greater still if the heat is increased. I would not be making a correct judgement about the nature of wax unless I believed it capable of being extended
in many more different ways than I will ever encompass in my imagination. I must
therefore admit that the nature of this piece of wax is in no way revealed by my imagination, but is perceived by the mind alone. (I am speaking of this particular piece of
wax; the point is even clearer with regard to wax in general.) But what is this wax
which is perceived by the mind alone? It is of course the same wax which I see, which
I touch, which I picture in my imagination, in short the same wax which I thought it to
be from the start. And yet, and here is the point, the perception I have of it is a case not
of vision or touch or imagination—nor has it ever been, despite previous appearances—but of purely mental scrutiny; and this can be imperfect and confused, as it was
before, or clear and distinct as it is now, depending on how carefully I concentrate on
what the wax consists in.

But as I reach this conclusion I am amazed at how [weak and] prone to error my
mind is. For although I am thinking about these matters within myself, silently and
32   without speaking, nonetheless the actual words bring me up short, and I am almost
tricked by ordinary ways of talking. We say that we see the wax itself, if it is there before us, not that we judge it to be there from its colour or shape; and this might lead me
to conclude without more ado that knowledge of the wax comes from what the eye
sees, and not from the scrutiny of the mind alone. But then if I look out of the window
and see men crossing the square, as I just happen to have done, I normally say that I
see the men themselves, just as I say that I see the wax. Yet do I see any more than hats
and coats which could conceal automatons? I *judge* that they are men. And so something which I thought I was seeing with my eyes is in fact grasped solely by the faculty
of judgement which is in my mind.

However, one who wants to achieve knowledge above the ordinary level should
feel ashamed at having taken ordinary ways of talking as a basis for doubt. So let us
proceed, and consider on which occasion my perception of the nature of the wax was
more perfect and evident. Was it when I first looked at it, and believed I knew it by my
external senses, or at least by what they call the "common" sense—that is, the power
of imagination? Or is my knowledge more perfect now, after a more careful investigation of the nature of the wax and of the means by which it is known? Any doubt on this
issue would clearly be foolish; for what distinctness was there in my earlier perception? Was there anything in it which an animal could not possess? But when I distinguish the wax from its outward forms—take the clothes off, as it were, and consider it
naked—then although my judgement may still contain errors, at least my perception
now requires a human mind.

33   But what am I to say about this mind, or about myself? (So far, remember, I am
not admitting that there is anything else in me except a mind.) What, I ask, is this "I"

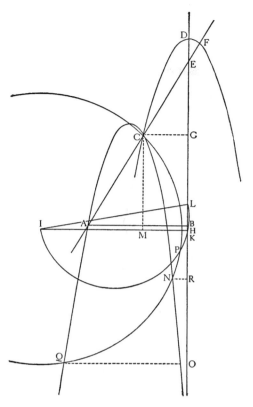

Geometry formula from Descartes' *Geometry* (1637). The X–Y axes in analytic geometry, which Descartes invented, are still called "Cartesian coordinates." (*Library of Congress*)

which seems to perceive the wax so distinctly? Surely my awareness of my own self is not merely much truer and more certain than my awareness of the wax, but also much more distinct and evident. For if I judge that the wax exists from the fact that I see it, clearly this same fact entails much more evidently that I myself also exist. It is possible that what I see is not really the wax; it is possible that I do not even have eyes with which to see anything. But when I see, or think I see (I am not here distinguishing the two), it is simply not possible that I who am now thinking am not something. By the same token, if I judge that the wax exists from the fact that I touch it, the same result follows, namely that I exist. If I judge that it exists from the fact that I imagine it, or for any other reason, exactly the same thing follows. And the result that I have grasped in the case of the wax may be applied to everything else located outside me. Moreover, if my perception of the wax seemed more distinct after it was established not just by sight or touch but by many other considerations, it must be admitted that I now know myself even more distinctly. This is because every consideration whatsoever which contributes to my perception of the wax, or of any other body, cannot but establish even more effectively the nature of my own mind. But besides this, there is so much else in the mind itself which can serve to make my knowledge of it more distinct, that it scarcely seems worth going through the contributions made by considering bodily things.

I see that without any effort I have now finally got back to where I wanted. I now   34
know that even bodies are not strictly perceived by the senses or the faculty of imagi-

nation but by the intellect alone, and that this perception derives not from their being touched or seen but from their being understood; and in view of this I know plainly that I can achieve an easier and more evident perception of my own mind than of anything else. But since the habit of holding on to old opinions cannot be set aside so quickly, I should like to stop here and meditate for some time on this new knowledge I have gained, so as to fix it more deeply in my memory.

THIRD MEDITATION

The existence of God
    I will now shut my eyes, stop my ears, and withdraw all my senses. I will eliminate from my thoughts all images of bodily things, or rather, since this is hardly possible, I will regard all such images as vacuous, false and worthless. I will converse with myself and scrutinize myself more deeply; and in this way I will attempt to achieve, little by little, a more intimate knowledge of myself. I am a thing that thinks: that is, a thing that doubts, affirms, denies, understands a few things, is ignorant of many things, is willing, is unwilling, and also which imagines and has sensory perceptions; for as I have noted before, even though the objects of my sensory experience and imagination may have no existence outside me, nonetheless the modes of thinking which I refer to
35   as cases of sensory perception and imagination, in so far as they are simply modes of thinking, do exist within me—of that I am certain.

    In this brief list I have gone through everything I truly know, or at least everything I have so far discovered that I know. Now I will cast around more carefully to see whether there may be other things within me which I have not yet noticed. I am certain that I am a thinking thing. Do I not therefore also know what is required for my being certain about anything? In this first item of knowledge there is simply a clear and distinct perception of what I am asserting; this would not be enough to make me certain of the truth of the matter if it could ever turn out that something which I perceived with such clarity and distinctness was false. So I now seem to be able to lay it down as a general rule that whatever I perceive very clearly and distinctly is true.

    Yet I previously accepted as wholly certain and evident many things which I afterwards realized were doubtful. What were these? The earth, sky, stars, and everything else that I apprehended with the senses. But what was it about them that I perceived clearly? Just that the ideas, or thoughts, of such things appeared before my mind. Yet even now I am not denying that these ideas occur within me. But there was something else which I used to assert, and which through habitual belief I thought I perceived clearly, although I did not in fact do so. This was that there were things outside me which were the sources of my ideas and which resembled them in all respects. Here was my mistake; or at any rate, if my judgement was true, it was not thanks to the strength of my perception.

    But what about when I was considering something very simple and straightfor-
36   ward in arithmetic or geometry, for example that two and three added together make five, and so on? Did I not see at least these things clearly enough to affirm their truth? Indeed, the only reason for my later judgement that they were open to doubt was that it occurred to me that perhaps some God could have given me a nature such that I was deceived even in matters which seemed most evident. And whenever my preconceived belief in the supreme power of God comes to mind, I cannot but admit that it would be

easy for him, if he so desired, to bring it about that I go wrong even in those matters which I think I see utterly clearly with my mind's eye. Yet when I turn to the things themselves which I think I perceive very clearly, I am so convinced by them that I spontaneously declare: let whoever can do so deceive me, he will never bring it about that I am nothing, so long as I continue to think I am something; or make it true at some future time that I have never existed, since it is now true that I exist; or bring it about that two and three added together are more or less than five, or anything of this kind in which I see a manifest contradiction. And since I have no cause to think that there is a deceiving God, and I do not yet even know for sure whether there is a God at all, any reason for doubt which depends simply on this supposition is a very slight and, so to speak, metaphysical one. But in order to remove even this slight reason for doubt, as soon as the opportunity arises I must examine whether there is a God, and, if there is, whether he can be a deceiver. For if I do not know this, it seems that I can never be quite certain about anything else.

First, however, considerations of order appear to dictate that I now classify my thoughts into definite kinds, and ask which of them can properly be said to be the bearers of truth and falsity. Some of my thoughts are as it were the images of things, and it is only in these cases that the term "idea" is strictly appropriate—for example, when I think of a man, or a chimera, or the sky, or an angel, or God. Other thoughts have various additional forms: thus when I will, or am afraid, or affirm, or deny, there is always a particular thing which I take as the object of my thought, but my thought includes something more than the likeness of that thing. Some thoughts in this category are called volitions or emotions, while others are called judgements. 37

Now as far as ideas are concerned, provided they are considered solely in themselves and I do not refer them to anything else, they cannot strictly speaking be false; for whether it is a goat or a chimera that I am imagining, it is just as true that I imagine the former as the latter. As for the will and the emotions, here too one need not worry about falsity; for even if the things which I may desire are wicked or even non-existent, that does not make it any less true that I desire them. Thus the only remaining thoughts where I must be on my guard against making a mistake are judgements. And the chief and most common mistake which is to be found here consists in my judging that the ideas which are in me resemble, or conform to, things located outside me. Of course, if I considered just the ideas themselves simply as modes of my thought, without referring them to anything else, they could scarcely give me any material for error.

Among my ideas, some appear to be innate, some to be adventitious,* and others to have been invented by me. My understanding of what a thing is, what truth is, and what thought is, seems to derive simply from my own nature. But my hearing a noise, as I do now, or seeing the sun, or feeling the fire, comes from things which are located outside me, or so I have hitherto judged. Lastly, sirens, hippogriffs and the like are my own invention. But perhaps all my ideas may be thought of as adventitious, or they may all be innate, or all made up; for as yet I have not clearly perceived their true origin. 38

But the chief question at this point concerns the ideas which I take to be derived from things existing outside me: what is my reason for thinking that they resemble these things? Nature has apparently taught me to think this. But in addition I know by experience that these ideas do not depend on my will, and hence that they do not depend simply on me. Frequently I notice them even when I do not want to: now, for example, I feel the heat whether I want to or not, and this is why I think that this sensa-

---

*". . . foreign to me and coming from outside" (French version).

tion or idea of heat comes to me from something other than myself, namely the heat of the fire by which I am sitting. And the most obvious judgement for me to make is that the thing in question transmits to me its own likeness rather than something else.

I will now see if these arguments are strong enough. When I say "Nature taught me to think this," all I mean is that a spontaneous impulse leads me to believe it, not that its truth has been revealed to me by some natural light. There is a big difference here. Whatever is revealed to me by the natural light—for example that from the fact that I am doubting it follows that I exist, and so on—cannot in any way be open to doubt. This is because there cannot be another faculty both as trustworthy as the natural light and also capable of showing me that such things are not true. But as for my natural impulses, I have often judged in the past that they were pushing me in the wrong direction when it was a question of choosing the good, and I do not see why I should place any greater confidence in them in other matters.

Then again, although these ideas do not depend on my will, it does not follow that they must come from things located outside me. Just as the impulses which I was speaking of a moment ago seem opposed to my will even though they are within me, so there may be some other faculty not yet fully known to me, which produces these ideas without any assistance from external things; this is, after all, just how I have always thought ideas are produced in me when I am dreaming.

And finally, even if these ideas did come from things other than myself, it would not follow that they must resemble those things. Indeed, I think I have often discovered a great disparity [between an object and its idea] in many cases. For example, there are two different ideas of the sun which I find within me. One of them, which is acquired as it were from the senses and which is a prime example of an idea which I reckon to come from an external source, makes the sun appear very small. The other idea is based on astronomical reasoning, that is, it is derived from certain notions which are innate in me (or else it is constructed by me in some other way), and this idea shows the sun to be several times larger than the earth. Obviously both these ideas cannot resemble the sun which exists outside me; and reason persuades me that the idea which seems to have emanated most directly from the sun itself has in fact no resemblance to it at all.

All these considerations are enough to establish that it is not reliable judgement but merely some blind impulse that has made me believe up till now that there exist things distinct from myself which transmit to me ideas or images of themselves through the sense organs or in some other way.

But it now occurs to me that there is another way of investigating whether some of the things of which I possess ideas exist outside me. In so far as the ideas are [considered] simply [as] modes of thought, there is no recognizable inequality among them: they all appear to come from within me in the same fashion. But in so far as different ideas [are considered as images which] represent different things, it is clear that they differ widely. Undoubtedly, the ideas which represent substances to me amount to something more and, so to speak, contain within themselves more objective reality than the ideas which merely represent modes or accidents. Again, the idea that gives me my understanding of a supreme God, eternal, infinite, [immutable,] omniscient, omnipotent and the creator of all things that exist apart from him, certainly has in it more objective reality than the ideas that represent finite substances.

Now it is manifest by the natural light that there must be at least as much [reality] in the efficient and total cause as in the effect of that cause. For where, I ask, could the effect get its reality from, if not from the cause? And how could the cause give it to the effect unless it possessed it? It follows from this both that something cannot arise from nothing, and also that what is more perfect—that is, contains in itself more real-

ity—cannot arise from what is less perfect. And this is transparently true not only in   41
the case of effects which possess [what the philosophers call] actual or formal reality,
but also in the case of ideas, where one is considering only [what they call] objective
reality. A stone, for example, which previously did not exist, cannot begin to exist unless it is produced by something which contains, either formally or eminently everything to be found in the stone; similarly, heat cannot be produced in an object which
was not previously hot, except by something of at least the same order [degree or kind]
of perfection as heat, and so on. But it is also true that the idea of heat, or of a stone,
cannot exist in me unless it is put there by some cause which contains at least as much
reality as I conceive to be in the heat or in the stone. For although this cause does not
transfer any of its actual or formal reality to my idea, it should not on that account be
supposed that it must be less real. The nature of an idea is such that of itself it requires
no formal reality except what it derives from my thought, of which it is a mode. But in
order for a given idea to contain such and such objective reality, it must surely derive it
from some cause which contains at least as much formal reality as there is objective reality in the idea. For if we suppose that an idea contains something which was not in its
cause, it must have got this from nothing; yet the mode of being by which a thing exists objectively [or representatively] in the intellect by way of an idea, imperfect
though it may be, is certainly not nothing, and so it cannot come from nothing.

And although the reality which I am considering in my ideas is merely objective
reality, I must not on that account suppose that the same reality need not exist formally   42
in the causes of my ideas, but that it is enough for it to be present in them objectively.
For just as the objective mode of being belongs to ideas by their very nature, so the formal mode of being belongs to the causes of ideas—or at least the first and most important ones—by *their* very nature. And although one idea may perhaps originate from another, there cannot be an infinite regress here; eventually one must reach a primary
idea, the cause of which will be like an archetype which contains formally [and in fact]
all the reality [or perfection] which is present only objectively [or representatively] in
the idea. So it is clear to me, by the natural light, that the ideas in me are like [pictures,
or] images which can easily fall short of the perfection of the things from which they
are taken, but which cannot contain anything greater or more perfect.

The longer and more carefully I examine all these points, the more clearly and
distinctly I recognize their truth. But what is my conclusion to be? If the objective reality of any of my ideas turns out to be so great that I am sure the same reality does not
reside in me, either formally or eminently, and hence that I myself cannot be its cause,
it will necessarily follow that I am not alone in the world, but that some other thing
which is the cause of this idea also exists. But if no such idea is to be found in me, I
shall have no arguments to convince me of the existence of anything apart from myself. For despite a most careful and comprehensive survey, this is the only argument I
have so far been able to find.

Among my ideas, apart from the idea which gives me a representation of myself,
which cannot present any difficulty in this context, there are ideas which variously rep-   43
resent God, corporeal and inanimate things, angels, animals and finally other men like
myself.

As far as concerns the ideas which represent other men, or animals, or angels, I
have no difficulty in understanding that they could be put together from the ideas I
have of myself, of corporeal things and of God, even if the world contained no men besides me, no animals and no angels.

As to my ideas of corporeal things, I can see nothing in them which is so great
[or excellent] as to make it seem impossible that it originated in myself. For if I scruti-

nize them thoroughly and examine them one by one, In the way in which I examined the idea of the wax yesterday, I notice that the things which I perceive clearly and distinctly in them are very few in number. The list comprises size, or extension in length, breadth and depth; shape, which is a function of the boundaries of this extension; position, which is a relation between various items possessing shape; and motion, or change in position; to these may be added substance, duration and number. But as for all the rest, including light and colours, sounds, smells, tastes, heat and cold and the other tactile qualities, I think of these only in a very confused and obscure way, to the extent that I do not even know whether they are true or false, that is, whether the ideas I have of them are ideas of real things or of non-things. For although, as I have noted before, falsity in the strict sense, or formal falsity, can occur only in judgements, there is another kind of falsity, material falsity, which occurs in ideas, when they represent non-things as things. For example, the ideas which I have of heat and cold contain so little clarity and distinctness that they do not enable me to tell whether cold is merely the absence of heat or vice versa, or whether both of them are real qualities, or neither is. And since there can be no ideas which are not as it were of things, if it is true that cold is nothing but the absence of heat, the idea which represents it to me as something real and positive deserves to be called false; and the same goes for other ideas of this kind.

44

Such ideas obviously do not require me to posit a source distinct from myself. For on the one hand, if they are false, that is, represent non-things, I know by the natural light that they arise from nothing—that is, they are in me only because of a deficiency and lack of perfection in my nature. If on the other hand they are true, then since the reality which they represent is so extremely slight that I cannot even distinguish it from a non-thing, I do not see why they cannot originate from myself.

With regard to the clear and distinct elements in my ideas of corporeal things, it appears that I could have borrowed some of these from my idea of myself, namely substance, duration, number and anything else of this kind. For example, I think that a stone is a substance, or is a thing capable of existing independently, and I also think that I am a substance. Admittedly I conceive of myself as a thing that thinks and is not extended, whereas I conceive of the stone as a thing that is extended and does not think, so that the two conceptions differ enormously; but they seem to agree with respect to the classification "substance." Again, I perceive that I now exist, and remember that I have existed for some time; moreover, I have various thoughts which I can count; it is in these ways that I acquire the ideas of duration and number which I can then transfer to other things. As for all the other elements which make up the ideas of corporeal things, namely extension, shape, position and movement, these are not formally contained in me, since I am nothing but a thinking thing; but since they are merely modes of a substance, and I am a substance, it seems possible that they are contained in me eminently.

45

So there remains only the idea of God; and I must consider whether there is anything in the idea which could not have originated in myself. By the word "God" I understand a substance that is infinite, [eternal, immutable,] independent, supremely intelligent, supremely powerful, and which created both myself and everything else (if anything else there be) that exists. All these attributes are such that, the more carefully I concentrate on them, the less possible it seems that they could have originated from me alone. So from what has been said it must be concluded that God necessarily exists.

It is true that I have the idea of substance in me in virtue of the fact that I am a substance; but this would not account for my having the idea of an infinite substance, when I am finite, unless this idea proceeded from some substance which really was infinite.

And I must not think that, just as my conceptions of rest and darkness are arrived at by negating movement and light, so my perception of the infinite is arrived at not by means of a true idea but merely by negating the finite. On the contrary, I clearly understand that there is more reality in an infinite substance than in a finite one, and hence that my perception of the infinite, that is God, is in some way prior to my perception of the finite, that is myself. For how could I understand that I doubted or desired—that is, lacked something—and that I was not wholly perfect, unless there were in me some idea of a more perfect being which enabled me to recognize my own defects by comparison?   46

Nor can it be said that this idea of God is perhaps materially false and so could have come from nothing, which is what I observed just a moment ago in the case of the ideas of heat and cold, and so on. On the contrary, it is utterly clear and distinct, and contains in itself more objective reality than any other idea; hence there is no idea which is in itself truer or less liable to be suspected of falsehood. This idea of a supremely perfect and infinite being is, I say, true in the highest degree; for although perhaps one may imagine that such a being does not exist, it cannot be supposed that the idea of such a being represents something unreal, as I said with regard to the idea of cold. The idea is, moreover, utterly clear and distinct; for whatever I clearly and distinctly perceive as being real and true, and implying any perfection, is wholly contained in it. It does not matter that I do not grasp the infinite, or that there are countless additional attributes of God which I cannot in any way grasp, and perhaps cannot even reach in my thought; for it is in the nature of the infinite not to be grasped by a finite being like myself. It is enough that I understand the infinite,* and that I judge that all the attributes which I clearly perceive and know to imply some perfection—and perhaps countless others of which I am ignorant—are present in God either formally or eminently. This is enough to make the idea that I have of God the truest and most clear and distinct of all my ideas.

But perhaps I am something greater than I myself understand, and all the perfections which I attribute to God are somehow in me potentially, though not yet emerging or actualized. For I am now experiencing a gradual increase in my knowledge, and I   47 see nothing to prevent its increasing more and more to infinity. Further, I see no reason why I should not be able to use this increased knowledge to acquire all the other perfections of God. And finally, if the potentiality for these perfections is already within me, why should not this be enough to generate the idea of such perfections?

But all this is impossible. First, though it is true that there is a gradual increase in my knowledge, and that I have many potentialities which are not yet actual, this is all quite irrelevant to the idea of God, which contains absolutely nothing that is potential; indeed, this gradual increase in knowledge is itself the surest sign of imperfection. What is more, even if my knowledge always increases more and more, I recognize that it will never actually be infinite, since it will never reach the point where it is not capable of a further increase; God, on the other hand, I take to be actually infinite, so that nothing can be added to his perfection. And finally, I perceive that the objective being of an idea cannot be produced merely by potential being, which strictly speaking is nothing, but only by actual or formal being.

If one concentrates carefully, all this is quite evident by the natural light. But when I relax my concentration, and my mental vision is blinded by the images of

---

*According to Descartes one can know or understand something without fully grasping it "just as we can touch a mountain but not put our arms around it. To grasp something is to embrace it in one's thought; to know something, it suffices to touch it with one's thought" (letter to Mersenne, 26 May 1630).

things perceived by the senses, it is not so easy for me to remember why the idea of a being more perfect than myself must necessarily proceed from some being which is in reality more perfect. I should therefore like to go further and inquire whether I myself, who have this idea, could exist if no such being existed.

From whom, in that case, would I derive my existence? From myself presumably, or from my parents, or from some other beings less perfect than God; for nothing more perfect than God, or even as perfect, can be thought of or imagined.

Yet if I derived my existence from myself, then I should neither doubt nor want, nor lack anything at all; for I should have given myself all the perfections of which I have any idea, and thus I should myself be God. I must not suppose that the items I lack would be more difficult to acquire than those I now have. On the contrary, it is clear that, since I am a thinking thing or substance, it would have been far more difficult for me to emerge out of nothing than merely to acquire knowledge of the many things of which I am ignorant—such knowledge being merely an accident of that substance. And if I had derived my existence from myself, which is a greater achievement, I should certainly not have denied myself the knowledge in question, which is something much easier to acquire, or indeed any of the attributes which I perceive to be contained in the idea of God; for none of them seem any harder to achieve. And if any of them were harder to achieve, they would certainly appear so to me, if I had indeed got all my other attributes from myself, since I should experience a limitation of my power in this respect.

I do not escape the force of these arguments by supposing that I have always existed as I do now, as if it followed from this that there was no need to look for any author of my existence. For a life-span can be divided into countless parts, each completely independent of the others, so that it does not follow from the fact that I existed a little while ago that I must exist now, unless there is some cause which as it were creates me afresh at this moment—that is, which preserves me. For it is quite clear to anyone who attentively considers the nature of time that the same power and action are needed to preserve anything at each individual moment of its duration as would be required to create that thing anew if it were not yet in existence. Hence the distinction between preservation and creation is only a conceptual one, and this is one of the things that are evident by the natural light.

I must therefore now ask myself whether I possess some power enabling me to bring it about that I who now exist will still exist a little while from now. For since I am nothing but a thinking thing—or at least since I am now concerned only and precisely with that part of me which is a thinking thing—if there were such a power in me, I should undoubtedly be aware of it. But I experience no such power, and this very fact makes me recognize most clearly that I depend on some being distinct from myself.

But perhaps this being is not God, and perhaps I was produced either by my parents or by other causes less perfect than God. No; for as I have said before, it is quite clear that there must be at least as much in the cause as in the effect. And therefore whatever kind of cause is eventually proposed, since I am a thinking thing and have within me some idea of God, it must be admitted that what caused me is itself a thinking thing and possesses the idea of all the perfections which I attribute to God. In respect of this cause one may again inquire whether it derives its existence from itself or from another cause. If from itself, then it is clear from what has been said that it is itself God, since if it has the power of existing through its own might, then undoubtedly it also has the power of actually possessing all the perfections of which it has an idea—that is, all the perfections which I conceive to be in God. If, on the other hand, it derives its existence from another cause, then the same question may be repeated concerning this further cause, namely whether it derives its existence from itself or from another cause, until eventually the ultimate cause is reached, and this will be God.

It is clear enough that an infinite regress is impossible here, especially since I am dealing not just with the cause that produced me in the past, but also and most importantly with the cause that preserves me at the present moment.

Nor can it be supposed that several partial causes contributed to my creation, or that I received the idea of one of the perfections which I attribute to God from one cause and the idea of another from another—the supposition here being that all the perfections are to be found somewhere in the universe but not joined together in a single being, God. On the contrary, the unity, the simplicity, or the inseparability of all the attributes of God is one of the most important of the perfections which I understand him to have. And surely the idea of the unity of all his perfections could not have been placed in me by any cause which did not also provide me with the ideas of the other perfections; for no cause could have made me understand the interconnection and inseparability of the perfections without at the same time making me recognize what they were.

Lastly, as regards my parents, even if everything I have ever believed about them is true, it is certainly not they who preserve me; and in so far as I am a thinking thing, they did not even make me; they merely placed certain dispositions in the matter which I have always regarded as containing me, or rather my mind, for that is all I now take   51 myself to be. So there can be no difficulty regarding my parents in this context. Altogether then, it must be concluded that the mere fact that I exist and have within me an idea of a most perfect being, that is, God, provides a very clear proof that God indeed exists.

It only remains for me to examine how I received this idea from God. For I did not acquire it from the senses; it has never come to me unexpectedly, as usually happens with the ideas of things that are perceivable by the senses, when these things present themselves to the external sense organs—or seem to do so. And it was not invented by me either; for I am plainly unable either to take away anything from it or to add anything to it. The only remaining alternative is that it is innate in me, just as the idea of myself is innate in me.

And indeed it is no surprise that God, in creating me, should have placed this idea in me to be, as it were, the mark of the craftsman stamped on his work—not that the mark need be anything distinct from the work itself. But the mere fact that God created me is a very strong basis for believing that I am somehow made in his image and likeness, and that I perceive that likeness, which includes the idea of God, by the same faculty which enables me to perceive myself. That is, when I turn my mind's eye upon myself, I understand that I am a thing which is incomplete and dependent on another and which aspires without limit to ever greater and better things; but I also understand at the same time that he on whom I depend has within him all those greater things, not just indefinitely and potentially but actually and infinitely, and hence that he is God. The whole force of the argument lies in this: I recognize that it would be impossible for me to exist with the kind of nature I have—that is, having within me the idea of God—   52 were it not the case that God really existed. By "God" I mean the very being the idea of whom is within me, that is, the possessor of all the perfections which I cannot grasp, but can somehow reach in my thought, who is subject to no defects whatsoever. It is clear enough from this that he cannot be a deceiver, since it is manifest by the natural light that all fraud and deception depend on some defect.

But before examining this point more carefully and investigating other truths which may be derived from it, I should like to pause here and spend some time in the contemplation of God; to reflect on his attributes, and to gaze with wonder and adoration on the beauty of this immense light, so far as the eye of my darkened intellect can bear it. For just as we believe through faith that the supreme happiness of the next life consists solely in the contemplation of the divine majesty, so experience tells us that this same contemplation, albeit much less perfect, enables us to know the greatest joy of which we are capable in this life.

FOURTH MEDITATION

Truth and falsity

During these past few days I have accustomed myself to leading my mind away from the senses; and I have taken careful note of the fact that there is very little about corporeal things that is truly perceived, whereas much more is known about the human mind, and still more about God. The result is that I now have no difficulty in turning my mind away from imaginable things and towards things which are objects of the intellect alone and are totally separate from matter. And indeed the idea I have of the human mind, in so far as it is a thinking thing, which is not extended in length, breadth or height and has no other bodily characteristics, is much more distinct than the idea of any corporeal thing. And when I consider the fact that I have doubts, or that I am a thing that is incomplete and dependent, then there arises in me a clear and distinct idea of a being who is independent and complete, that is, an idea of God. And from the mere fact that there is such an idea within me, or that I who possess this idea exist, I clearly infer that God also exists, and that every single moment of my entire existence depends on him. So clear is this conclusion that I am confident that the human intellect cannot know anything that is more evident or more certain. And now, from this contemplation of the true God, in whom all the treasures of wisdom and the sciences lie hidden, I think I can see a way forward to the knowledge of other things.

To begin with, I recognize that it is impossible that God should ever deceive me. For in every case of trickery or deception some imperfection is to be found; and although the ability to deceive appears to be an indication of cleverness or power, the will to deceive is undoubtedly evidence of malice or weakness, and so cannot apply to God.

Next, I know by experience that there is in me a faculty of judgement which, like everything else which is in me, I certainly received from God. And since God does not wish to deceive me, he surely did not give me the kind of faculty which would ever enable me to go wrong while using it correctly.

There would be no further doubt on this issue were it not that what I have just said appears to imply that I am incapable of ever going wrong. For if everything that is in me comes from God, and he did not endow me with a faculty for making mistakes, it appears that I can never go wrong. And certainly, so long as I think only of God, and turn my whole attention to him, I can find no cause of error or falsity. But when I turn back to myself, I know by experience that I am prone to countless errors. On looking for the cause of these errors, I find that I possess not only a real and positive idea of God, or a being who is supremely perfect, but also what may be described as a negative idea of nothingness, or of that which is farthest removed from all perfection. I realize that I am, as it were, something intermediate between God and nothingness, or between supreme being and non-being: my nature is such that in so far as I was created by the supreme being, there is nothing in me to enable me to go wrong or lead me astray; but in so far as I participate in nothingness or non-being, that is, in so far as I am not myself the supreme being and am lacking in countless respects, it is no wonder that I make mistakes. I understand, then, that error as such is not something real which depends on God, but merely a defect. Hence my going wrong does not require me to have a faculty specially bestowed on me by God; it simply happens as a result of the fact that the faculty of true judgement which I have from God is in my case not infinite.

But this is still not entirely satisfactory. For error is not a pure negation, but   55 rather a privation or lack of some knowledge which somehow should be in me. And when I concentrate on the nature of God, it seems impossible that he should have placed in me a faculty which is not perfect of its kind, or which lacks some perfection which it ought to have. The more skilled the craftsman the more perfect the work produced by him; if this is so, how can anything produced by the supreme creator of all things not be complete and perfect in all respects? There is, moreover, no doubt that God could have given me a nature such that I was never mistaken; again, there is no doubt that he always wills what is best. Is it then better that I should make mistakes than that I should not do so?

As I reflect on these matters more attentively, it occurs to me first of all that it is no cause for surprise if I do not understand the reasons for some of God's actions; and there is no call to doubt his existence if I happen to find that there are other instances where I do not grasp why or how certain things were made by him. For since I now know that my own nature is very weak and limited, whereas the nature of God is immense, incomprehensible and infinite, I also know without more ado that he is capable of countless things whose causes are beyond my knowledge. And for this reason alone I consider the customary search for final causes to be totally useless in physics; there is considerable rashness in thinking myself capable of investigating the [impenetrable] purposes of God.

It also occurs to me that whenever we are inquiring whether the works of God are perfect, we ought to look at the whole universe, not just at one created thing on its own. For what would perhaps rightly appear very imperfect if it existed on its own is quite perfect when its function as a part of the universe is considered. It is true that,   56 since my decision to doubt everything, it is so far only myself and God whose existence I have been able to know with certainty; but after considering the immense power of God, I cannot deny that many other things have been made by him, or at least could have been made, and hence that I may have a place in the universal scheme of things.

Next, when I look more closely at myself and inquire into the nature of my errors (for these are the only evidence of some imperfection in me), I notice that they depend on two concurrent causes, namely on the faculty of knowledge which is in me, and on the faculty of choice or freedom of the will; that is, they depend on both the intellect and the will simultaneously. Now all that the intellect does is to enable me to perceive the ideas which are subjects for possible judgements; and when regarded strictly in this light, it turns out to contain no error in the proper sense of that term. For although countless things may exist without there being any corresponding ideas in me, it should not, strictly speaking, be said that I am deprived of these ideas, but merely that I lack them, in a negative sense. This is because I cannot produce any reason to prove that God ought to have given me a greater faculty of knowledge than he did; and no matter how skilled I understand a craftsman to be, this does not make me think he ought to have put into every one of his works all the perfections which he is able to put into some of them. Besides, I cannot complain that the will or freedom of choice which

I received from God is not sufficiently extensive or perfect, since I know by experience
57   that it is not restricted in any way. Indeed, I think it is very noteworthy that there is
nothing else in me which is so perfect and so great that the possibility of a further increase in its perfection or greatness is beyond my understanding. If, for example, I consider the faculty of understanding, I immediately recognize that in my case it is extremely slight and very finite, and I at once form the idea of an understanding which is
much greater—indeed supremely great and infinite; and from the very fact that I can
form an idea of it, I perceive that it belongs to the nature of God. Similarly, if I examine the faculties of memory or imagination, or any others, I discover that in my case
each one of these faculties is weak and limited, while in the case of God it is immeasurable. It is only the will, or freedom of choice, which I experience within me to be so
great that the idea of any greater faculty is beyond my grasp; so much so that it is
above all in virtue of the will that I understand myself to bear in some way the image
and likeness of God. For although God's will is incomparably greater than mine, both
in virtue of the knowledge and power that accompany it and make it more firm and efficacious, and also in virtue of its object, in that it ranges over a greater number of
items, nevertheless it does not seem any greater than mine when considered as will in
the essential and strict sense. This is because the will simply consists in our ability to
do or not do something (that is, to affirm or deny, to pursue or avoid); or rather, it consists simply in the fact that when the intellect puts something forward for affirmation
or denial or for pursuit or avoidance, our inclinations are such that we do not feel we
are determined by any external force. In order to be free, there is no need for me to be
inclined both ways; on the contrary, the more I incline in one direction—either because
58   I clearly understand that reasons of truth and goodness point that way, or because of a
divinely produced disposition of my inmost thoughts—the freer is my choice. Neither
divine grace nor natural knowledge ever diminishes freedom; on the contrary, they increase and strengthen it. But the indifference I feel when there is no reason pushing me
in one direction rather than another is the lowest grade of freedom; it is evidence not of
any perfection of freedom, but rather of a defect in knowledge or a kind of negation.
For if I always saw clearly what was true and good, I should never have to deliberate
about the right judgement or choice; in that case, although I should be wholly free, it
would be impossible for me ever to be in a state of indifference.

From these considerations I perceive that the power of willing which I received
from God is not, when considered in itself, the cause of my mistakes; for it is both extremely ample and also perfect of its kind. Nor is my power of understanding to blame;
for since my understanding comes from God, everything that I understand I undoubtedly understand correctly, and any error here is impossible. So what then is the source
of my mistakes? It must be simply this: the scope of the will is wider than that of the
intellect; but instead of restricting it within the same limits, I extend its use to matters
which I do not understand. Since the will is indifferent in such cases, it easily turns
aside from what is true and good, and this is the source of my error and sin.

For example, during these past few days I have been asking whether anything in
the world exists, and I have realized that from the very fact of my raising this question
it follows quite evidently that I exist. I could not but judge that something which I un-
59   derstood so clearly was true; but this was not because I was compelled so to judge by
any external force, but because a great light in the intellect was followed by a great inclination in the will, and thus the spontaneity and freedom of my belief was all the
greater in proportion to my lack of indifference. But now, besides the knowledge that I
exist, in so far as I am a thinking thing, an idea of corporeal nature comes into my
mind; and I happen to be in doubt as to whether the thinking nature which is in me, or

rather which I am, is distinct from this corporeal nature or identical with it. I am making the further supposition that my intellect has not yet come upon any persuasive reason in favour of one alternative rather than the other. This obviously implies that I am indifferent as to whether I should assert or deny either alternative, or indeed refrain from making any judgement on the matter.

What is more, this indifference does not merely apply to cases where the intellect is wholly ignorant, but extends in general to every case where the intellect does not have sufficiently clear knowledge at the time when the will deliberates. For although probable conjectures may pull me in one direction, the mere knowledge that they are simply conjectures, and not certain and indubitable reasons, is itself quite enough to push my assent the other way. My experience in the last few days confirms this: the mere fact that I found that all my previous beliefs were in some sense open to doubt was enough to turn my absolutely confident belief in their truth into the supposition that they were wholly false.

If, however, I simply refrain from making a judgement in cases where I do not perceive the truth with sufficient clarity and distinctness, then it is clear that I am behaving correctly and avoiding error. But if in such cases I either affirm or deny, then I am not using my free will correctly. If I go for the alternative which is false, then obvi-   60 ously I shall be in error; if I take the other side, then it is by pure chance that I arrive at the truth, and I shall still be at fault since it is clear by the natural light that the perception of the intellect should always precede the determination of the will. In this incorrect use of free will may be found the privation which constitutes the essence of error. The privation, I say, lies in the operation of the will in so far as it proceeds from me, but not in the faculty of will which I received from God, nor even in its operation, in so far as it depends on him.

And I have no cause for complaint on the grounds that the power of understanding or the natural light which God gave me is no greater than it is; for it is in the nature of a finite intellect to lack understanding of many things, and it is in the nature of a created intellect to be finite. Indeed, I have reason to give thanks to him who has never owed me anything for the great bounty that he has shown me, rather than thinking myself deprived or robbed of any gifts he did not bestow.

Nor do I have any cause for complaint on the grounds that God gave me a will which extends more widely than my intellect. For since the will consists simply of one thing which is, as it were, indivisible, it seems that its nature rules out the possibility of anything being taken away from it. And surely, the more widely my will extends, then the greater thanks I owe to him who gave it to me.

Finally, I must not complain that the forming of those acts of will or judgements in which I go wrong happens with God's concurrence. For in so far as these acts depend on God, they are wholly true and good; and my ability to perform them means that there is in a sense more perfection in me than would be the case if I lacked this ability. As for the privation involved—which is all that the essential definition of fal-   61 sity and wrong consists in—this does not in any way require the concurrence of God, since it is not a thing; indeed, when it is referred to God as its cause, it should be called not a privation but simply a negation. For it is surely no imperfection in God that he has given me the freedom to assent or not to assent in those cases where he did not endow my intellect with a clear and distinct perception; but it is undoubtedly an imperfection in me to misuse that freedom and make judgements about matters which I do not fully understand. I can see, however, that God could easily have brought it about that without losing my freedom, and despite the limitations in my knowledge, I should nonetheless never make a mistake. He could, for example, have endowed my intellect with a clear and distinct perception of everything about which I was ever likely to deliberate; or he could simply have impressed it unforgettably on my memory that I should never make a judgement about anything which I did not clearly and distinctly understand. Had God made me this way, then I can easily understand that, considered as a totality, I would have been more perfect than I am now. But I cannot therefore deny that there may in some way be more perfection in the universe as a whole because some of its parts are not immune from error, while others are immune, than there would be if all the parts were exactly alike. And I have no right to complain that the role God wished me to undertake in the world is not the principal one or the most perfect of all.

62   What is more, even if I have no power to avoid error in the first way just mentioned, which requires a clear perception of everything I have to deliberate on, I can avoid error in the second way, which depends merely on my remembering to withhold judgement on any occasion when the truth of the matter is not clear. Admittedly, I am aware of a certain weakness in me, in that I am unable to keep my attention fixed on one and the same item of knowledge at all times; but by attentive and repeated meditation I am nevertheless able to make myself remember it as often as the need arises, and thus get into the habit of avoiding error.

It is here that man's greatest and most important perfection is to be found, and I therefore think that today's meditation, involving an investigation into the cause of error and falsity, has been very profitable. The cause of error must surely be the one I have explained; for if, whenever I have to make a judgement, I restrain my will so that it extends to what the intellect clearly and distinctly reveals, and no further, then it is quite impossible for me to go wrong. This is because every clear and distinct perception is undoubtedly something, and hence cannot come from nothing, but must necessarily have God for its author. Its author, I say, is God, who is supremely perfect, and who cannot be a deceiver on pain of contradiction; hence the perception is undoubtedly true. So today I have learned not only what precautions to take to avoid ever going wrong, but also what to do to arrive at the truth. For I shall unquestionably reach the truth, if only I give sufficient attention to all the things which I perfectly understand, and separate these from all the other cases where my apprehension is more confused and obscure. And this is just what I shall take good care to do from now on.

63   # FIFTH MEDITATION

The essence of material things, and the existence of God considered a second time

There are many matters which remain to be investigated concerning the attributes of God and the nature of myself, or my mind; and perhaps I shall take these up at another time. But now that I have seen what to do and what to avoid in order to reach the truth, the most pressing task seems to be to try to escape from the doubts into which I fell a few days ago, and see whether any certainty can be achieved regarding material objects.

But before I inquire whether any such things exist outside me, I must consider the ideas of these things, in so far as they exist in my thought, and see which of them are distinct, and which confused.

Quantity, for example, or "continuous" quantity as the philosophers commonly call it, is something I distinctly imagine. That is, I distinctly imagine the extension of the quantity (or rather of the thing which is quantified) in length, breadth and depth. I also enumerate various parts of the thing, and to these parts I assign various sizes, shapes, positions and local motions; and to the motions I assign various durations.

Not only are all these things very well known and transparent to me when regarded in this general way, but in addition there are countless particular features regarding shape, number, motion, and so on, which I perceive when I give them my attention. And the truth of these matters is so open and so much in harmony with my 64 nature, that on first discovering them it seems that I am not so much learning something new as remembering what I knew before; or it seems like noticing for the first time things which were long present within me although I had never turned my mental gaze on them before.

But I think the most important consideration at this point is that I find within me countless ideas of things which even though they may not exist anywhere outside me still cannot be called nothing; for although in a sense they can be thought of at will, they are not my invention but have their own true and immutable natures. When, for example, I imagine a triangle, even if perhaps no such figure exists, or has ever existed, anywhere outside my thought, there is still a determinate nature, or essence, or form of the triangle which is immutable and eternal, and not invented by me or dependent on my mind. This is clear from the fact that various properties can be demonstrated of the triangle, for example that its three angles equal two right angles, that its greatest side subtends its greatest angle, and the like; and since these properties are ones which I now clearly recognize whether I want to or not, even if I never thought of them at all when I previously imagined the triangle, it follows that they cannot have been invented by me.

It would be beside the point for me to say that since I have from time to time seen bodies of triangular shape, the idea of the triangle may have come to me from external things by means of the sense organs. For I can think up countless other shapes which there can be no suspicion of my ever having encountered through the senses, and yet I can demonstrate various properties of these shapes, just as I can with the tri- 65 angle. All these properties are certainly true, since I am clearly aware of them, and therefore they are something, and not merely nothing; for it is obvious that whatever is true is something; and I have already amply demonstrated that everything of which I am clearly aware is true. And even if I had not demonstrated this, the nature of my mind is such that I cannot but assent to these things, at least so long as I clearly perceive them. I also remember that even before, when I was completely preoccupied with the objects of the senses, I always held that the most certain truths of all were the kind which I recognized clearly in connection with shapes, or numbers or other items relating to arithmetic or geometry, or in general to pure and abstract mathematics.

But if the mere fact that I can produce from my thought the idea of something entails that everything which I clearly and distinctly perceive to belong to that thing really does belong to it, is not this a possible basis for another argument to prove the existence of God? Certainly, the idea of God, or a supremely perfect being, is one which I find within me just as surely as the idea of any shape or number. And my understanding that it belongs to his nature that he always exists is no less clear and distinct than is the case when I prove of any shape or number that some property belongs to its nature. Hence, even if it turned out that not everything on which I have meditated in these past days is true, I ought still to regard the existence of God as having at least the same 66 level of certainty as I have hitherto attributed to the truths of mathematics.

At first sight, however, this is not transparently clear, but has some appearance of being a sophism. Since I have been accustomed to distinguish between existence and essence in everything else, I find it easy to persuade myself that existence can also be separated from the essence of God, and hence that God can be thought of as not existing. But when I concentrate more carefully, it is quite evident that existence can no more be separated from the essence of God than the fact that its three angles equal two right angles can be separated from the essence of a triangle, or than the idea of a mountain can be separated from the idea of a valley. Hence it is just as much of a contradiction to think of God (that is, a supremely perfect being) lacking existence (that is, lacking a perfection), as it is to think of a mountain without a valley.

However, even granted that I cannot think of God except as existing, just as I cannot think of a mountain without a valley, it certainly does not follow from the fact that I think of a mountain with a valley that there is any mountain in the world; and similarly, it does not seem to follow from the fact that I think of God as existing that he does exist. For my thought does not impose any necessity on things; and just as I may imagine a winged horse even though no horse has wings, so I may be able to attach existence to God even though no God exists.

But there is a sophism concealed here. From the fact that I cannot think of a mountain without a valley, it does not follow that a mountain and valley exist anywhere, but simply that a mountain and a valley, whether they exist or not, are mutually inseparable. But from the fact that I cannot think of God except as existing, it follows that existence is inseparable from God, and hence that he really exists. It is not that my thought makes it so, or imposes any necessity on any thing; on the contrary, it is the necessity of the thing itself, namely the existence of God, which determines my thinking in this respect. For I am not free to think of God without existence (that is, a supremely perfect being without a supreme perfection) as I am free to imagine a horse with or without wings.

And it must not be objected at this point that while it is indeed necessary for me to suppose God exists, once I have made the supposition that he has all perfections (since existence is one of the perfections), nevertheless the original supposition was not necessary. Similarly, the objection would run, it is not necessary for me to think that all quadrilaterals can be inscribed in a circle; but given this supposition, it will be necessary for me to admit that a rhombus can be inscribed in a circle—which is patently false. Now admittedly, it is not necessary that I ever light upon any thought of God; but whenever I do choose to think of the first and supreme being, and bring forth the idea of God from the treasure house of my mind as it were, it is necessary that I attribute all perfections to him, even if I do not at that time enumerate them or attend to them individually. And this necessity plainly guarantees that, when I later realize that existence is a perfection, I am correct in inferring that the first and supreme being exists. In the same way, it is not necessary for me ever to imagine a triangle; but whenever I do wish to consider a rectilinear figure having just three angles, it is necessary that I attribute to it the properties which license the inference that its three angles equal no more than two right angles, even if I do not notice this at the time. By contrast, when I examine what figures can be inscribed in a circle, it is in no way necessary for me to think that this class includes all quadrilaterals. Indeed, I cannot even imagine this, so long as I am willing to admit only what I clearly and distinctly understand. So there is a great difference between this kind of false supposition and the true ideas which are innate in me, of which the first and most important is the idea of God. There are many ways in which I understand that this idea is not something fictitious which is dependent on my thought, but is an image of a true and immutable nature. First of all, there is the fact that, apart from God, there is nothing else of which I am capable of thinking such that existence belongs to its essence. Second, I cannot understand how there could be two or more Gods of this kind; and after supposing that one God exists, I plainly see that it is necessary that he has existed from eternity and will abide for eternity. And finally, I perceive many other attributes of God, none of which I can remove or alter.

But whatever method of proof I use, I am always brought back to the fact that it is only what I clearly and distinctly perceive that completely convinces me. Some of the things I clearly and distinctly perceive are obvious to everyone, while others are discovered only by those who look more closely and investigate more carefully; but once they have been discovered, the latter are judged to be just as certain as the former. In the case of a right-angled triangle, for example, the fact that the square on the hypotenuse is equal to the square on the other two sides is not so readily apparent as the fact that the hypotenuse subtends the largest angle; but once one has seen it, one believes it just as strongly. But as regards God, if I were not overwhelmed by preconceived opinions, and if the images of things perceived by the senses did not besiege my thought on every side, I would certainly acknowledge him sooner and more easily than anything else. For what is more self-evident than the fact that the supreme being exists, or that God, to whose essence alone existence belongs, exists? 69

Although it needed close attention for me to perceive this, I am now just as certain of it as I am of everything else which appears most certain. And what is more, I see that the certainty of all other things depends on this, so that without it nothing can ever be perfectly known.

Admittedly my nature is such that so long as I perceive something very clearly and distinctly I cannot but believe it to be true. But my nature is also such that I cannot fix my mental vision continually on the same thing, so as to keep perceiving it clearly; and often the memory of a previously made judgement may come back, when I am no longer attending to the arguments which led me to make it. And so other arguments can now occur to me which might easily undermine my opinion, if I did not possess knowledge of God; and I should thus never have true and certain knowledge about anything, but only shifting and changeable opinions. For example, when I consider the nature of a triangle, it appears most evident to me, steeped as I am in the principles of geometry, that its three angles are equal to two right angles; and so long as I attend to the proof, I cannot but believe this to be true. But as soon as I turn my mind's eye away from the proof, then in spite of still remembering that I perceived it very clearly, I can easily fall into doubt about its truth, if I am without knowledge of God. For I can convince myself that I have a natural disposition to go wrong from time to time in matters which I think I perceive as evidently as can be. This will seem even more likely when I remember that there have been frequent cases where I have regarded things as true and certain, but have later been led by other arguments to judge them to be false. 70

Now, however, I have perceived that God exists, and at the same time I have understood that everything else depends on him, and that he is no deceiver; and I have drawn the conclusion that everything which I clearly and distinctly perceive is of necessity true. Accordingly, even if I am no longer attending to the arguments which led me to judge that this is true, as long as I remember that I clearly and distinctly perceived it, there are no counter-arguments which can be adduced to make me doubt it, but on the contrary I have true and certain knowledge of it. And I have knowledge not just of this matter, but of all matters which I remember ever having demonstrated, in geometry and so on. For what objections can now be raised? That the way I am made makes me prone to frequent error? But I now know that I am incapable of error in those cases where my understanding is transparently clear. Or can it be objected that I have in the past regarded as true and certain many things which I afterwards recognized to be false? But none of these were things which I clearly and distinctly perceived: I was ignorant of this rule for establishing the truth, and believed these things for other reasons which I later discovered to be less reliable. So what is left to say? Can one raise the objection I put to myself a while ago, that I may be dreaming, or that everything which I am now thinking has as little truth as what comes to the mind of one who is asleep? Yet even this does not change anything. For even though I might be dreaming, if there is anything which is evident to my intellect, then it is wholly true.

Thus I see plainly that the certainty and truth of all knowledge depends uniquely on my knowledge of the true God, to such an extent that I was incapable of perfect knowledge about anything else until I knew him. And now it is possible for me to achieve full and certain knowledge of countless matters, both concerning God himself and other things whose nature is intellectual, and also concerning the whole of that corporeal nature which is the subject-matter of pure mathematics.

SIXTH MEDITATION

The existence of material things, and the real distinction between mind and body

It remains for me to examine whether material things exist. And at least I now know they are capable of existing, in so far as they are the subject-matter of pure mathematics, since I perceive them clearly and distinctly. For there is no doubt that God is capable of creating everything that I am capable of perceiving in this manner; and I have never judged that something could not be made by him except on the grounds that there would be a contradiction in my perceiving it distinctly. The conclusion that material things exist is also suggested by the faculty of imagination, which I am aware of using when I turn my mind to material things. For when I give more attentive consideration to what imagination is, it seems to be nothing else but an application of the cognitive faculty to a body which is intimately present to it, and which therefore exists.

To make this clear, I will first examine the difference between imagination and pure understanding. When I imagine a triangle, for example, I do not merely understand that it is a figure bounded by three lines, but at the same time I also see the three lines with my mind's eye as if they were present before me; and this is what I call imagining. But if I want to think of a chiliagon, although I understand that it is a figure consisting of a thousand sides just as well as I understand the triangle to be a three-sided figure, I do not in the same way imagine the thousand sides or see them as if they were present before me. It is true that since I am in the habit of imagining something whenever I think of a corporeal thing, I may construct in my mind a confused representation of some figure; but it is clear that this is not a chiliagon. For it differs in no way from the representation I should form if I were thinking of a myriagon, or any figure with very many sides. Moreover, such a representation is useless for recognizing the properties which distinguish a chiliagon from other polygons. But suppose I am dealing with a pentagon: I can of course understand the figure of a pentagon, just as I can the figure of a chiliagon, without the help of the imagination; but I can also imagine a pentagon, by applying my mind's eye to its five sides and the area contained within them. And in doing this I notice quite clearly that imagination requires a peculiar effort of mind which is not required for understanding; this additional effort of mind clearly shows the difference between imagination and pure understanding.

Besides this, I consider that this power of imagining which is in me, differing as it does from the power of understanding, is not a necessary constituent of my own essence, that is, of the essence of my mind. For if I lacked it, I should undoubtedly remain the same individual as I now am; from which it seems to follow that it depends on something distinct from myself. And I can easily understand that, if there does exist some body to which the mind is so joined that it can apply itself to contemplate it, as it were, whenever it pleases, then it may possibly be this very body that enables me to imagine corporeal things. So the difference between this mode of thinking and pure understanding may simply be this: when the mind understands, it in some way turns towards itself and inspects one of the ideas which are within it; but when it imagines, it turns towards the body and looks at something in the body which conforms to an idea understood by the mind or perceived by the senses. I can, as I say, easily understand that this is how imagination comes about, if the body exists; and since there is no other equally suitable way of explaining imagination that comes to mind, I can make a probable conjecture that the body exists. But this is only a probability; and despite a careful and comprehensive investigation, I do not yet see how the distinct idea of corporeal nature which I find in my imagination can provide any basis for a necessary inference that some body exists.

But besides that corporeal nature which is the subject-matter of pure mathematics, there is much else that I habitually imagine, such as colours, sounds, tastes, pain and so on—though not so distinctly. Now I perceive these things much better by means of the senses, which is how, with the assistance of memory, they appear to have reached the imagination. So in order to deal with them more fully, I must pay equal attention to the senses, and see whether the things which are perceived by means of that mode of thinking which I call "sensory perception" provide me with any sure argument for the existence of corporeal things. 74

To begin with, I will go back over all the things which I previously took to be perceived by the senses, and reckoned to be true; and I will go over my reasons for thinking this. Next, I will set out my reasons for subsequently calling these things into doubt. And finally I will consider what I should now believe about them.

First of all then, I perceived by my senses that I had a head, hands, feet and other limbs making up the body which I regarded as part of myself, or perhaps even as my whole self. I also perceived by my senses that this body was situated among many other bodies which could affect it in various favourable or unfavourable ways; and I gauged the favourable effects by a sensation of pleasure, and the unfavourable ones by a sensation of pain. In addition to pain and pleasure, I also had sensations within me of hunger, thirst, and other such appetites, and also of physical propensities towards cheerfulness, sadness, anger and similar emotions. And outside me, besides the exten- 75 sion, shapes and movements of bodies, I also had sensations of their hardness and heat, and of the other tactile qualities. In addition, I had sensations of light, colours, smells, tastes and sounds, the variety of which enabled me to distinguish the sky, the earth, the seas, and all other bodies, one from another. Considering the ideas of all these qualities which presented themselves to my thought, although the ideas were, strictly speaking, the only immediate objects of my sensory awareness, it was not unreasonable for me to think that the items which I was perceiving through the senses were things quite distinct from my thought, namely bodies which produced the ideas. For my experience was that these ideas came to me quite without my consent, so that I could not have sensory awareness of any object, even if I wanted to, unless it was present to my sense organs; and I could not avoid having sensory awareness of it when it was present. And since the ideas perceived by the senses were much more lively and vivid and even, in their own way, more distinct than any of those which I deliberately formed through meditating or which I found impressed on my memory, it seemed impossible that they should have come from within me; so the only alternative was that they came from other things. Since the sole source of my knowledge of these things was the ideas themselves, the supposition that the things resembled the ideas was bound to occur to me. In addition, I remembered that the use of my senses had come first, while the use of my reason came only later; and I saw that the ideas which I formed myself were less vivid than those which I perceived with the senses and were, for the most part, made up of elements of sensory ideas. In this way I easily convinced myself that I had noth-

76   ing at all in the intellect which I had not previously had in sensation. As for the body which by some special right I called "mine," my belief that this body, more than any other, belonged to me had some justification. For I could never be separated from it, as I could from other bodies; and I felt all my appetites and emotions in, and on account of, this body; and finally, I was aware of pain and pleasurable ticklings in parts of this body, but not in other bodies external to it. But why should that curious sensation of pain give rise to a particular distress of mind; or why should a certain kind of delight follow on a tickling sensation? Again, why should that curious tugging in the stomach which I call hunger tell me that I should eat, or a dryness of the throat tell me to drink, and so on? I was not able to give any explanation of all this, except that nature taught me so. For there is absolutely no connection (at least that I can understand) between the tugging sensation and the decision to take food, or between the sensation of something causing pain and the mental apprehension of distress that arises from that sensation. These and other judgements that I made concerning sensory objects, I was apparently taught to make by nature; for I had already made up my mind that this was how things were, before working out any arguments to prove it.

Later on, however, I had many experiences which gradually undermined all the faith I had had in the senses. Sometimes towers which had looked round from a distance appeared square from close up; and enormous statues standing on their pediments did not seem large when observed from the ground. In these and countless other such cases, I found that the judgements of the external senses were mistaken. And this applied not just to the external senses but to the internal senses as well. For what can

77   be more internal than pain? And yet I had heard that those who had had a leg or an arm amputated sometimes still seemed to feel pain intermittently in the missing part of the body. So even in my own case it was apparently not quite certain that a particular limb was hurting, even if I felt pain in it. To these reasons for doubting, I recently added two very general ones. The first was that every sensory experience I have ever thought I was having while awake I can also think of myself as sometimes having while asleep; and since I do not believe that what I seem to perceive in sleep comes from things located outside me, I did not see why I should be any more inclined to believe this of what I think I perceive while awake. The second reason for doubt was that since I did not know the author of my being (or at least was pretending not to), I saw nothing to rule out the possibility that my natural constitution made me prone to error even in matters which seemed to me most true. As for the reasons for my previous confident belief in the truth of the things perceived by the senses, I had no trouble in refuting them. For since I apparently had natural impulses towards many things which reason told me to avoid, I reckoned that a great deal of confidence should not be placed in what I was taught by nature. And despite the fact that the perceptions of the senses were not dependent on my will, I did not think that I should on that account infer that they proceeded from things distinct from myself, since I might perhaps have a faculty not yet known to me which produced them.

But now, when I am beginning to achieve a better knowledge of myself and the author of my being, although I do not think I should heedlessly accept everything I seem to have acquired from the senses, neither do I think that everything should be called into doubt.

First, I know that everything which I clearly and distinctly understand is capable of being created by God so as to correspond exactly with my understanding of it. Hence the fact that I can clearly and distinctly understand one thing apart from another is enough to make me certain that the two things are distinct, since they are capable of being separated, at least by God. The question of what kind of power is required to bring about such a separation does not affect the judgement that the two things are distinct. Thus, simply by knowing that I exist and seeing at the same time that absolutely nothing else belongs to my nature or essence except that I am a thinking thing, I can infer correctly that my essence consists solely in the fact that I am a thinking thing. It is true that I may have (or, to anticipate, that I certainly have) a body that is very closely joined to me. But nevertheless, on the one hand I have a clear and distinct idea of myself, in so far as I am simply a thinking, non-extended thing; and on the other hand I have a distinct idea of body,* in so far as this is simply an extended, non-thinking thing. And accordingly, it is certain that I am really distinct from my body, and can exist without it.

Besides this, I find in myself faculties for certain special modes of thinking, namely imagination and sensory perception. Now I can clearly and distinctly understand myself as a whole without these faculties; but I cannot, conversely, understand these faculties without me, that is, without an intellectual substance to inhere in. This is because there is an intellectual act included in their essential definition; and hence I perceive that the distinction between them and myself corresponds to the distinction between the modes of a thing and the thing itself. Of course I also recognize that there are other faculties (like those of changing position, of taking on various shapes, and so on) which, like sensory perception and imagination, cannot be understood apart from some substance for them to inhere in, and hence cannot exist without it. But it is clear that these other faculties, if they exist, must be in a corporeal or extended substance and not an intellectual one; for the clear and distinct conception of them includes extension, but does not include any intellectual act whatsoever. Now there is in me a passive faculty of sensory perception, that is, a faculty for receiving and recognizing the ideas of sensible objects; but I could not make use of it unless there was also an active faculty, either in me or in something else, which produced or brought about these ideas. But this faculty cannot be in me, since clearly it presupposes no intellectual act on my part, and the ideas in question are produced without my cooperation and often even against my will. So the only alternative is that it is in another substance distinct from me—a substance which contains either formally or eminently all the reality which exists objectively in the ideas produced by this faculty (as I have just noted). This substance is either a body, that is, a corporeal nature, in which case it will contain formally [and in fact] everything which is to be found objectively [or representatively] in the ideas; or else it is God, or some creature more noble than a body, in which case it will contain eminently whatever is to be found in the ideas. But since God is not a deceiver, it is quite clear that he does not transmit the ideas to me either directly from himself, or indirectly, via some creature which contains the objective reality of the ideas not formally but only eminently. For God has given me no faculty at all for

78

79

---

*The Latin term corpus as used here by Descartes is ambiguous between "body" (i.e. corporeal matter in general) and "the body" (i.e. this particular body of mine). The French version preserves the ambiguity.

recognizing any such source for these ideas; on the contrary, he has given me a great propensity to believe that they are produced by corporeal things. So I do not see how God could be understood to be anything but a deceiver if the ideas were transmitted from a source other than corporeal things. It follows that corporeal things exist. They may not all exist in a way that exactly corresponds with my sensory grasp of them, for in many cases the grasp of the senses is very obscure and confused. But at least they possess all the properties which I clearly and distinctly understand, that is, all those which, viewed in general terms, are comprised within the subject-matter of pure mathematics.

What of the other aspects of corporeal things which are either particular (for example that the sun is of such and such a size or shape), or less clearly understood, such as light or sound or pain, and so on? Despite the high degree of doubt and uncertainty involved here, the very fact that God is not a deceiver, and the consequent impossibility of there being any falsity in my opinions which cannot be corrected by some other faculty supplied by God, offers me a sure hope that I can attain the truth even in these matters. Indeed, there is no doubt that everything that I am taught by nature contains some truth. For if nature is considered in its general aspect, then I understand by the term nothing other than God himself, or the ordered system of created things established by God. And by my own nature in particular I understand nothing other than the totality of things bestowed on me by God.

There is nothing that my own nature teaches me more vividly than that I have a body, and that when I feel pain there is something wrong with the body, and that when I am hungry or thirsty the body needs food and drink, and so on. So I should not doubt that there is some truth in this.

Nature also teaches me, by these sensations of pain, hunger, thirst and so on, that I am not merely present in my body as a sailor is present in a ship, but that I am very closely joined and, as it were, intermingled with it, so that I and the body form a unit. If this were not so, I, who am nothing but a thinking thing, would not feel pain when the body was hurt, but would perceive the damage purely by the intellect, just as a sailor perceives by sight if anything in his ship is broken. Similarly, when the body needed food or drink, I should have an explicit understanding of the fact, instead of having confused sensations of hunger and thirst. For these sensations of hunger, thirst, pain and so on are nothing but confused modes of thinking which arise from the union and, as it were, intermingling of the mind with the body.

I am also taught by nature that various other bodies exist in the vicinity of my body, and that some of these are to be sought out and others avoided. And from the fact that I perceive by my senses a great variety of colours, sounds, smells and tastes, as well as differences in heat, hardness and the like, I am correct in inferring that the bodies which are the source of these various sensory perceptions possess differences corresponding to them, though perhaps not resembling them. Also, the fact that some of the perceptions are agreeable to me while others are disagreeable makes it quite certain that my body, or rather my whole self, in so far as I am a combination of body and mind, can be affected by the various beneficial or harmful bodies which surround it.

There are, however, many other things which I may appear to have been taught by nature, but which in reality I acquired not from nature but from a habit of making ill-considered judgements; and it is therefore quite possible that these are false. Cases in point are the belief that any space in which nothing is occurring to stimulate my senses must be empty; or that the heat in a body is something exactly resembling the idea of heat which is in me; or that when a body is white or green, the selfsame whiteness or greenness which I perceive through my senses is present in the body; or that in a body which is bitter or sweet there is the selfsame taste which I experience, and so on; or, finally, that stars and towers and other distant bodies have the same size and shape which they present to my senses, and other examples of this kind. But to make sure that my perceptions in this matter are sufficiently distinct, I must more accurately define exactly what I mean when I say that I am taught something by nature. In this context I am taking nature to be something more limited than the totality of things bestowed on me by God. For this includes many things that belong to the mind alone—for example my perception that what is done cannot be undone, and all other things that are known by the natural light; but at this stage I am not speaking of these matters. It also includes much that relates to the body alone, like the tendency to move in a downward direction, and so on; but I am not speaking of these matters either. My sole concern here is with what God has bestowed on me as a combination of mind and body. My nature, then, in this limited sense, does indeed teach me to avoid what induces a feeling of pain and to seek out what induces feelings of pleasure, and so on. But it does not appear to teach us to draw any conclusions from these sensory perceptions about things located outside us without waiting until the intellect has examined the matter. For knowledge of the truth about such things seems to belong to the mind alone, not to the combination of mind and body. Hence, although a star has no greater effect on my eye than the flame of a small light, that does not mean that there is any real or positive inclination in me to believe that the star is no bigger than the light; I have simply made this judgement from childhood onwards without any rational basis. Similarly, although I feel heat when I go near a fire and feel pain when I go too near, there is no convincing argument for supposing that there is something in the fire which resembles the heat, any more than for supposing that there is something which resembles the pain. There is simply reason to suppose that there is something in the fire, whatever it may eventually turn out to be, which produces in us the feelings of heat or pain. And likewise, even though there is nothing in any given space that stimulates the senses, it does not follow that there is no body there. In these cases and many others I see that I have been in the habit of misusing the order of nature. For the proper purpose of the sensory perceptions given me by nature is simply to inform the mind of what is beneficial or harmful for the composite of which the mind is a part; and to this extent they are sufficiently clear and distinct. But I misuse them by treating them as reliable touchstones for immediate judgements about the essential nature of the bodies located outside us; yet this is an area where they provide only very obscure information.

83

I have already looked in sufficient detail at how, notwithstanding the goodness of God, it may happen that my judgements are false. But a further problem now comes to mind regarding those very things which nature presents to me as objects which I should seek out or avoid, and also regarding the internal sensations, where I seem to have detected errors—e.g. when someone is tricked by the pleasant taste of some food into eating the poison concealed inside it. Yet in this case, what the man's nature urges him to go for is simply what is responsible for the pleasant taste, and not the poison, which his nature knows nothing about. The only inference that can be drawn from this is that his nature is not omniscient. And this is not surprising, since man is a limited thing, and so it is only fitting that his perfection should be limited.

84

And yet it is not unusual for us to go wrong even in cases where nature does urge us towards something. Those who are ill, for example, may desire food or drink that will shortly afterwards turn out to be bad for them. Perhaps it may be said that they go wrong because their nature is disordered, but this does not remove the difficulty. A sick man is no less one of God's creatures than a healthy one, and it seems no less a contradiction to suppose that he has received from God a nature which deceives him.

Yet a clock constructed with wheels and weights observes all the laws of its nature just as closely when it is badly made and tells the wrong time as when it completely fulfils the wishes of the clockmaker. In the same way, I might consider the body of a man as a kind of machine equipped with and made up of bones, nerves, muscles, veins, blood and skin in such a way that, even if there were no mind in it, it would still perform all the same movements as it now does in those cases where movement is not under the control of the will or, consequently, of the mind. I can easily see that if such a body suffers from dropsy, for example, and is affected by the dryness of the throat which normally produces in the mind the sensation of thirst, the resulting condition of the nerves and other parts will dispose the body to take a drink, with the result that the disease will be aggravated. Yet this is just as natural as the body's being stimulated by a similar dryness of the throat to take a drink when there is no such illness and the drink is beneficial. Admittedly, when I consider the purpose of the clock, I may say that it is departing from its nature when it does not tell the right time; and similarly when I consider the mechanism of the human body, I may think that, in relation to the movements which normally occur in it, it too is deviating from its nature if the throat is dry at a time when drinking is not beneficial to its continued health. But I am well aware that "nature" as I have just used it has a very different significance from "nature" in the other sense. As I have just used it, "nature" is simply a label which depends on my thought; it is quite extraneous to the things to which it is applied, and depends simply on my comparison between the idea of a sick man and a badly-made clock, and the idea of a healthy man and a well-made clock. But by "nature" in the other sense I understand something which is really to be found in the things themselves; in this sense, therefore, the term contains something of the truth.

85

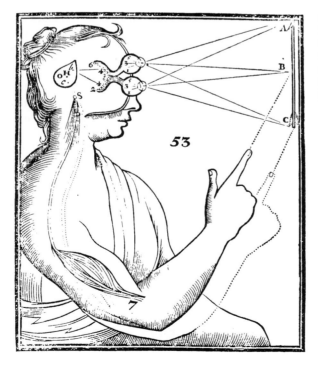

A diagram from Descartes' *Tractatus de Homine* (1677) showing how the pineal gland (shown here at the back of the head) connects sensory images from the eyes to the muscles of the arm. (*Library of Congress*)

When we say, then, with respect to the body suffering from dropsy, that it has a disordered nature because it has a dry throat and yet does not need drink, the term "nature" is here used merely as an extraneous label. However, with respect to the composite, that is, the mind united with this body, what is involved is not a mere label, but a true error of nature, namely that it is thirsty at a time when drink is going to cause it harm. It thus remains to inquire how it is that the goodness of God does not prevent nature, in this sense, from deceiving us.

The first observation I make at this point is that there is a great difference between the mind and the body, inasmuch as the body is by its very nature always divisible, while the mind is utterly indivisible. For when I consider the mind, or myself in so   86
far as I am merely a thinking thing, I am unable to distinguish any parts within myself; I understand myself to be something quite single and complete. Although the whole mind seems to be united to the whole body, I recognize that if a foot or arm or any other part of the body is cut off, nothing has thereby been taken away from the mind. As for the faculties of willing, of understanding, of sensory perception and so on, these cannot be termed parts of the mind, since it is one and the same mind that wills, and understands and has sensory perceptions. By contrast, there is no corporeal or extended thing that I can think of which in my thought I cannot easily divide into parts; and this very fact makes me understand that it is divisible. This one argument would be enough to show me that the mind is completely different from the body, even if I did not already know as much from other considerations.

My next observation is that the mind is not immediately affected by all parts of the body, but only by the brain, or perhaps just by one small part of the brain, namely the part which is said to contain the "common" sense. Every time this part of the brain is in a given state, it presents the same signals to the mind, even though the other parts of the body may be in a different condition at the time. This is established by countless observations, which there is no need to review here.

I observe, in addition, that the nature of the body is such that whenever any part of it is moved by another part which is some distance away, it can always be moved in the same fashion by any of the parts which lie in between, even if the more distant part does nothing. For example, in a cord ABCD, if one end D is pulled so that the other   87
end A moves, the exact same movement could have been brought about if one of the intermediate points B or C had been pulled, and D had not moved at all. In similar fashion, when I feel a pain in my foot, physiology tells me that this happens by means of nerves distributed throughout the foot, and that these nerves are like cords which go from the foot right up to the brain. When the nerves are pulled in the foot, they in turn pull on inner parts of the brain to which they are attached, and produce a certain motion in them; and nature has laid it down that this motion should produce in the mind a sensation of pain, as occurring in the foot. But since these nerves, in passing from the foot to the brain, must pass through the calf, the thigh, the lumbar region, the back and the neck, it can happen that, even if it is not the part in the foot but one of the intermediate parts which is being pulled, the same motion will occur in the brain as occurs when the foot is hurt, and so it will necessarily come about that the mind feels the same sensation of pain. And we must suppose the same thing happens with regard to any other sensation.

My final observation is that any given movement occurring in the part of the brain that immediately affects the mind produces just one corresponding sensation; and hence the best system that could be devised is that it should produce the one sensation which, of all possible sensations, is most especially and most frequently conducive to the preservation of the healthy man. And experience shows that the sensations which

nature has given us are all of this kind; and so there is absolutely nothing to be found in
88   them that does not bear witness to the power and goodness of God. For example, when
the nerves in the foot are set in motion in a violent and unusual manner, this motion, by
way of the spinal cord, reaches the inner parts of the brain, and there gives the mind its
signal for having a certain sensation, namely the sensation of a pain as occurring in the
foot. This stimulates the mind to do its best to get rid of the cause of the pain, which it
takes to be harmful to the foot. It is true that God could have made the nature of man
such that this particular motion in the brain indicated something else to the mind; it
might, for example, have made the mind aware of the actual motion occurring in the
brain, or in the foot, or in any of the intermediate regions; or it might have indicated
something else entirely. But there is nothing else which would have been so conducive
to the continued well-being of the body. In the same way, when we need drink, there
arises a certain dryness in the throat; this sets in motion the nerves of the throat, which
in turn move the inner parts of the brain. This motion produces in the mind a sensation
of thirst, because the most useful thing for us to know about the whole business is that
we need drink in order to stay healthy. And so it is in the other cases.

It is quite clear from all this that, notwithstanding the immense goodness of God,
the nature of man as a combination of mind and body is such that it is bound to mislead
him from time to time. For there may be some occurrence, not in the foot but in one of
the other areas through which the nerves travel in their route from the foot to the brain,
or even in the brain itself; and if this cause produces the same motion which is generally produced by injury to the foot, then pain will be felt as if it were in the foot. This
deception of the senses is natural, because a given motion in the brain must always
produce the same sensation in the mind; and the origin of the motion in question is
much more often going to be something which is hurting the foot, rather than some-
89   thing existing elsewhere. So it is reasonable that this motion should always indicate to
the mind a pain in the foot rather than in any other part of the body. Again, dryness of
the throat may sometimes arise not, as it normally does, from the fact that a drink is
necessary to the health of the body, but from some quite opposite cause, as happens in
the case of the man with dropsy. Yet it is much better that it should mislead on this occasion than that it should always mislead when the body is in good health. And the
same goes for the other cases.

This consideration is the greatest help to me, not only for noticing all the errors
to which my nature is liable, but also for enabling me to correct or avoid them without
difficulty. For I know that in matters regarding the well-being of the body, all my
senses report the truth much more frequently than not. Also, I can almost always make
use of more than one sense to investigate the same thing; and in addition, I can use
both my memory, which connects present experiences with preceding ones, and my intellect, which has by now examined all the causes of error. Accordingly, I should not
have any further fears about the falsity of what my senses tell me every day; on the
contrary, the exaggerated doubts of the last few days should be dismissed as laughable.
This applies especially to the principal reason for doubt, namely my inability to distinguish between being asleep and being awake. For I now notice that there is a vast difference between the two, in that dreams are never linked by memory with all the other
actions of life as waking experiences are. If, while I am awake, anyone were suddenly
to appear to me and then disappear immediately, as happens in sleep, so that I could
90   not see where he had come from or where he had gone to, it would not be unreasonable
for me to judge that he was a ghost, or a vision created in my brain, rather than a real
man. But when I distinctly see where things come from and where and when they
come to me, and when I can connect my perceptions of them with the whole of the rest

of my life without a break, then I am quite certain that when I encounter these things I am not asleep but awake. And I ought not to have even the slightest doubt of their reality if, after calling upon all the senses as well as my memory and my intellect in order to check them, I receive no conflicting reports from any of these sources. For from the fact that God is not a deceiver it follows that in cases like these I am completely free from error. But since the pressure of things to be done does not always allow us to stop and make such a meticulous check, it must be admitted that in this human life we are often liable to make mistakes about particular things, and we must acknowledge the weakness of our nature.

CORRESPONDENCE WITH PRINCESS ELIZABETH (selections)

1.a. Princess Elizabeth to Descartes [On the Relation of Soul and Body]

The Hague, 6–16 May 1643.

. . . I beg of you to tell me how the human soul can determine the movement of the animal spirits in the body so as to perform voluntary acts—being as it is merely a conscious (*pensante*) substance. For the determination of movement seems always to come about from the moving body's being propelled—to depend on the kind of impulse it gets from what sets it in motion, or again, on the nature and shape of this latter thing's surface. Now the first two conditions involve contact, and the third involves that the impelling thing has extension; but you utterly exclude extension from your notion of soul, and contact seems to me incompatible with a thing's being immaterial.

I therefore ask you for a more specific definition of the soul than you give in your metaphysics: a definition of its substance, as distinct from its activity, consciousness (*pensée*). Even if we supposed these to be in fact inseparable—a matter hard to prove in regard to children in their mother's womb and severe fainting-fits—to be inseparable as the divine attributes are: nevertheless we may get a more perfect idea of them by considering them apart.

1.b. Descartes to Princess Elizabeth

Egmond, 21 May 1643.

. . . I may truly say that what your Highness is propounding seems to me to be the question people have most right to ask me in view of my published works. For there are two facts about the human soul on which there depends any knowledge we may have as to its nature: first, that it is conscious; secondly, that, being united to a body, it is able to act and suffer along with it. Of the second fact I said almost nothing;

René Descartes, "Correspondence with Princess Elizabeth," from Descartes, *Philosophical Writings*, translated by Elizabeth Anscombe and Peter Thomas Geach (New York: Macmillan/Library of the Liberal Arts, 1971).

my aim was simply to make the first properly understood; for my main object was to prove the distinction of soul and body; and to this end only the first was serviceable, the second might have been prejudicial. But since your Highness sees too clearly for dissimulation to be possible, I will here try to explain how I conceive the union of soul and body and how the soul has the power of moving the body.

My first observation is that there are in us certain primitive notions—the originals, so to say, on the pattern of which we form all other knowledge. These notions are very few in number. First, there are the most general ones, existence, number, duration, etc., which apply to everything we can conceive. As regards body in particular, we have merely the notion of extension and the consequent notions of shape and movement. As regards the soul taken by itself, we have merely the notion of consciousness, which comprises the conceptions (*perceptions*) of the intellect and the inclinations of the will. Finally, as regards the soul and body together, we have merely the notion of their union; and on this there depend our notions of the soul's power to move the body, and of the body's power to act on the soul and cause sensations and emotions.

I would also observe that all human knowledge consists just in properly distinguishing these notions and attaching each of them only to the objects that it applies to. If we try to explain some problem by means of a notion that does not apply, we cannot help making mistakes; we are just as wrong if we try to explain one of these notions in terms of another, since, being primitive, each such notion has to be understood in itself. The use of our senses has made us much more familiar with notions of extension, shape, and movement than with others; thus the chief cause of our errors is that ordinarily we try to use these notions to explain matters to which they do not apply; e.g. we try to use our imagination in conceiving the nature of the soul, or to conceive the way the soul moves the body in terms of the way that one body is moved by another body.

In the Meditations that your Highness condescended to read, I tried to bring before the mind the notions that apply to the soul taken by itself, and to distinguish them from those that apply to the body taken by itself. Accordingly, the next thing I have to explain is how we are to form the notions that apply to the union of the soul with the body, as opposed to those that apply to the body taken by itself or the mind taken by itself. . . . These simple notions are to be sought only within the soul, which is naturally endowed with all of them, but does not always adequately distinguish between them, or again, does not always attach them to the right objects.

So I think people have hitherto confused the notions of the soul's power to act within the body and the power one body has to act within another; and they have ascribed both powers not to soul, whose nature was so far unknown, but to various qualities of bodies—gravity, heat, etc. These qualities were imagined to be real, i.e. to have an existence distinct from the existence of bodies; consequently, they were imagined to be substances, although they were called qualities. In order to conceive of them, people have used sometimes notions that we have for the purpose of knowing body, and sometimes those that we have for the purpose of knowing the soul, according as they were ascribing to them a material or an immaterial nature. For example, on the supposition that gravity is a real quality, about which we know no more than its power of moving the body in which it occurs towards the centre of the Earth, we find no difficulty in conceiving how it moves the body or how it is united to it; and we do not think of this as taking place by means of real mutual contact between two surfaces; our inner experience shows (*nous expérimentons*) that that notion is a specific one. Now I hold that we misuse this notion by applying it to gravity (which, as I hope to show in my Physics, is nothing really distinct from body), but that it has been given to us in order that we may conceive of the way that the soul moves the body.

2.a. Princess Elizabeth to Descartes [On the Relation of Soul and Body]

The Hague, 10–20 June 1643.

. . . [I cannot] understand the idea by means of which we are to judge of the way that the soul, unextended and immaterial, moves the body, in terms of the idea you used to have about gravity. You used falsely to ascribe to gravity, under the style of a "quality," the power of carrying bodies towards the centre of the Earth. But I cannot see why this should convince us that a body may be impelled by something immaterial; why we should not rather be confirmed in the view that this is impossible, by the demonstration of a true [view of gravity], opposed [to this], which you promise us in your *Physics;* especially as the idea [that a body may be so impelled] cannot claim the same degree of perfection and representative reality (*réalité objective*) as the idea of God, and may be a figment resulting from ignorance of what really moves bodies towards the centre. Since no material cause was apparent to the senses, people may well have ascribed this to the opposite cause, the immaterial, but I have never been able to conceive *that,* except as a negation of matter, which can have no communication with matter.

And I must confess that I could more readily allow that the soul has matter and extension than that an immaterial being has the capacity of moving a body and being affected by it. If the first, [the soul's moving the body], took place by [the soul's giving] information [to the body], then the [animal] spirits, which carry out the movement, would have to be intelligent; but you do not allow intelligence to anything corporeal. You do indeed show the possibility of the second thing [the body's affecting the soul], in your Metaphysical Meditations; but it is very hard to see how a soul such as you describe, after possessing the power and the habit of correct reasoning, may lose all that because of some vapours [in the brain]; or why the soul is so much governed by the body, when it can subsist separately, and has nothing in common with it. . . .

2.b. Descartes to Princess Elizabeth

Egmond, 28 June 1643.

I am most deeply obliged to your Highness for condescending, after experience of my previous ill success in explaining the problem you were pleased to propound to me, to be patient enough to listen to me once more on the same subject, and to give me an opportunity of making remarks on matters I had passed over. My chief omissions seem to be the following. I began by distinguishing three kinds of primitive ideas or notions, each of which is known in a specific way and not by comparison to another kind; viz. the notion of soul, the notion of body, and the notion of the union between soul and body. I still had to explain the difference between the operations of the soul by means of which we get them, and to show the means of becoming readily familiar with each kind. Further, I had to explain why I used the comparison of gravity. Next, I had to show that even if we try to conceive of the soul as material (which means, properly speaking, to conceive of its union with the body), we cannot help going on to recognise that it is separable from the body. This, I think, is the sum of the task your Highness has set me.

In the first place, then, I discern this great difference between the three kinds of notions: the soul is conceived only by pure intellect; body (i.e. extension, shape, and movement) can likewise be known by pure intellect, but is known much better when intellect is aided by imagination; finally, what belongs to the union of soul and body can be understood only in an obscure way either by pure intellect or even when the intellect is aided by imagination, but is understood very clearly by means of the senses. Consequently, those who never do philosophise and make use only of their senses have no doubt that the soul moves the body and the body acts on the soul; indeed, they consider the two as a single thing, i.e. they conceive of their union; for to conceive of the union between two things is to conceive of them as a single thing. Metaphysical reflections, which exercise the pure intellect, are what make us familiar with the notion of soul; the study of mathematics, which chiefly exercises the imagination in considering figures and movements, accustoms us to form very distinct notions of body; finally, it is just by means of ordinary life and conversation, by abstaining from meditating and from studying things that exercise the imagination, that one learns to conceive the union of soul and body.

I am half afraid that your Highness may think I am not speaking seriously here; but that would be contrary to the respect that I owe to your Highness and will never fail to pay. I can truly say that the chief rule I have always observed in my studies, and the one I think has been most serviceable to me in acquiring some measure of knowledge, has been never to spend more than a few hours a day in thoughts that demand imagination, or more than a few hours a year in thoughts that demand pure intellect; I have given all the rest of my time to the relaxation of my senses and the repose of my mind. I here count among exercises of imagination all serious conversations, and everything that demands attention. This is what made me retire to the country; it is true that in the busiest city in the world I might have as many hours to myself as I now spend in study, but I could not employ them so usefully when my mind was wearied by the attention that the troubles of life demand.

I take the liberty of writing thus to your Highness, to express my sincere admiration of your Highness's ability, among all the business and cares that are never lacking to persons who combine high intelligence and high birth, to find leisure for the meditations that are necessary for proper understanding of the distinction between soul and body. I formed the opinion that it was these meditations, rather than thoughts demanding less attention, that made your Highness find some obscurity in our notion of their union. It seems to me that the human mind is incapable of distinctly conceiving both the distinction between body and soul and their union, at one and the same time; for that requires our conceiving them as a single thing and simultaneously conceiving them as two things, which is self-contradictory. I supposed that your Highness still had very much in mind the arguments proving the distinction of soul and body; and I did not wish to ask you to lay them aside, in order to represent to yourself that notion of their union which everybody always has in himself without doing philosophy—viz. that there is one single person who has at once body and consciousness, so that this consciousness can move the body and be aware of the events that happen to it. Accordingly, I used in my previous letter the simile of gravity and other qualities, which we imagine to be united to bodies as consciousness is united to ours. I did not worry over the fact that this simile is lame, because these qualities are not, as one imagines, realities; for I thought your Highness was already fully convinced that the soul is a substance distinct from the body.

Your Highness, however, makes the remark that it is easier to ascribe matter and extension to the soul than to ascribe to it the power of moving a body and being moved by it without having any matter. Now I would ask your Highness to hold yourself free to ascribe "matter and extension" to the soul; for this is nothing else than to conceive the soul as united to the body. After forming a proper conception of this, and experiencing it in your own case, your Highness will find it easy to reflect that the matter you thus ascribe to your consciousness (*pensée*) is not the consciousness itself; again, the extension of the matter is essentially different from the extension of the consciousness, for the first extension is determined to a certain place, and excludes any other corporeal extension from that place, whereas the second does not. In this way your Highness will assuredly find it easy to come back to a realisation of the distinction between soul and body, in spite of having conceived of them as united.

Finally, I think it is very necessary to have got a good understanding, for once in one's life, of the principles of metaphysics, because it is from these that we have knowledge of God and of our soul. But I also think it would be very harmful to occupy one's intellect often with meditating on them, for it would be the less able to find leisure for the functioning of the imagination and the senses; the best thing is to be content with retaining in memory and in belief the conclusions one has drawn once for all, and to spend the rest of one's time for study in reflections in which the intellect co-operates with the imagination and the senses. . . .

THOMAS HOBBES
1588–1679

Born prematurely when his mother heard of the approach of the Spanish Armada, Thomas Hobbes often quipped that he was born "a twin with fear." Hobbes saw much to fear in his long life. He observed a civil war, the execution of Charles I, and periods of great political and social upheaval. On more than one occasion, he was forced to flee England; and he often feared for his life. It is not surprising, then, that he developed a political philosophy emphasizing fear of death and the need for security.

Hobbes was born in Malmesbury, Whiltshire, England, the son of a disreputable vicar. His father was forced to leave the Whiltshire area after brawling outside his church. Young Thomas was sent to live with a rich uncle. At the age of fourteen, he went to Oxford University. Like Descartes, he found most of his schooling to be a waste of time. He particularly disliked the Aristotelianism of his college, Magdalen Hall. In 1608, he became the tutor to the son of William Cavendish, Earl of Devonshire. For the rest of his life, Hobbes remained a friend of the Cavendish family and a royalist sympathizer.

Hobbes made several extended visits to the Continent—some voluntary, some a result of running for his life. At home and on the Continent, Hobbes met and conversed with such leading thinkers as Descartes, Galileo, and Bacon. Although he, of course, had differences with them, he nevertheless used each thinker's ideas to refine his own philosophy. From Descartes, he learned to value the geometric method. Descartes used geometry to establish epistemological certainty. Hobbes used geometry to develop a political theory. In opposition to the dominant Aristotelian thesis that rest is the natural state of objects, Galileo had proposed that all bodies are naturally in motion. Hobbes took Galileo's postulate and proceeded to argue that all things in the world, including human beings, are bodies in motion. With Bacon, Hobbes agreed that scientific knowledge was primarily useful for improving the human condition.

In 1628, Hobbes published his first literary work: a translation of *Thucydides*, by which he hoped to use history to enlighten the English people. In Thucydides' *Peloponnesian War,* democratic Athens had been defeated by monarchical Sparta. Hobbes wanted to warn his fellow citizens of the creeping democracy threatening England. Hobbes was convinced that democracy led to chaos and that a strong central government was essential for national stability. In 1640, Hobbes was forced to flee England for Paris when the Long Parliament supplanted the king. In Paris, Hobbes wrote the book for which he is famous, *Leviathan, or the Matter, Form, and Power of a Commonwealth, Ecclesiastical and Civil.* The book was published between the execution of Charles I (1649) and the Protectorate of Cromwell (1653), a time ripe for political philosophy.

Cromwell permitted Hobbes to return to England in 1652. Although Hobbes had always been a royalist, his argument for the absolute power of the sovereign was not restricted to kings. Thus Cromwell had no reason to consider Hobbes's doctrine seditious—nor did Charles II, whom Hobbes had tutored in Paris, and who was later restored to the monarchy.

Hobbes's later years were spent writing and arguing for his ideas. Although he continued to have enemies, with the king's friendship he managed to stay out of serious trouble. In his early-eighties, Hobbes wrote a history of the period 1640 to 1660, which he called *Behemoth*. When he was eighty-four, Hobbes published his autobiography in Latin verse; at eighty-six, he produced a verse translation of both the *Iliad* and the *Odyssey* (for lack of anything better to do, he commented). He died in 1679 at the age of 91.

*   *   *

The *Leviathan* is known primarily for its political philosophy, but it touches on a number of other issues including epistemology, metaphysics, ethics, and religion. Hobbes begins with a thoroughgoing version of materialism. Everything in the world, including humans, consists of bodies in motion. Knowledge of the world begins in sensation. Bodies in motion outside of a person cause motion within the person. Memories, imagination, and other "mental" phenomena are the aftershocks of sensations—what Hobbes calls "decaying sense." *Willing* is that "beginning of motion" that leads to action when individuals move and so move other bodies.

Using a mechanistic explanation of "voluntary motions," which he calls "endeavors," Hobbes believes that in human life self-interest and the desire for power are the basic motive powers. According to Hobbes, each person constantly seeks an advantage over everyone else. Yet since all are born equal, there is no inherent reason why one person should give way to another. The result is what Hobbes calls "a war of every man against every man . . . [in which] the notions of right and wrong, justice and injustice, have no place." In such an environment, life is "solitary, poor, nasty, brutish, and short."

To avoid this natural state of anarchy, individuals must enter into a social contract or covenant with all other individuals to give up their power irrevocably to a sovereign: "This is the generation of that great LEVIATHAN, or rather, to speak more reverently, of that 'mortal god,' to which we owe under the 'immortal God,' our peace and defence." This contract is not binding on the sovereign, as the sovereign is not a party to it. Hence there is no legal limitation on the sovereign's power. The sovereign is the essence of the commonwealth, which can be defined as

> one person, of whose acts a great multitude, by mutual covenants one with another, have made themselves every one the author, to the end he may use the strength and means of them all, as he shall think expedient, for their peace and common defence. . . . And he that carries this person, is called SOVEREIGN, and said to have sovereign power; and every one besides, his SUBJECT.

Hobbes believes this sovereign did not have to be a single person—sovereignty could reside in an individual (a monarchy), a small group (an aristocracy), or in the entire population (a democracy)—though he shows a marked preference for monarchy because of its greater stability and efficiency. What matters to Hobbes above all else is that the sovereign has absolute power in order to keep the peace and to guarantee security. To be sure, an absolute sovereign might abuse power, but the only alternative to this possible abuse, Hobbes claims, is an unthinkable anarchy.

$$*\quad*\quad*$$

Hobbes wrote many books over the course of his long life—the standard Oxford edition of his English works includes eleven volumes with another five volumes of his Latin works—but *Leviathan* (1651) is the basis of his fame. The key sections of this work, from Chapters 1–3, 6, 9, 12, 15, 17–18, and 21, are reprinted here. The spelling has been updated and standardized.

For a general introduction to Hobbes's life and thought, see John Laird, Hobbes (London: Ernest Benn, 1934); Richard Peters, *Hobbes* (Baltimore, MD: Penguin Books, 1956); G.C. Robertson, *Hobbes* (New York: AMS Press, 1968); and Tom Sorell, *Hobbes* (London: Routledge, 1986). For discussions of Hobbes's ethical and political thought as developed in *Leviathan*, see Leo Strauss, *The Political Philosophy of Hobbes* (Chicago: University of Chicago Press, 1952); Howard Warrender, *The Political Philosophy of Hobbes: His Theory of Obligation* (Oxford: Clarendon Press, 1957); David P. Gauthier, *The Logic of Leviathan: The Moral and Political Theory of Thomas Hobbes* (Oxford: Clarendon Press, 1969); and Michael Oakeshott, *Hobbes on Civil Association* (Berkeley: University of California Press, 1975). G.A.J. Rogers, ed., *Leviathan: Contemporary Responses to the Political Theory of Thomas Hobbes* (Bristol, UK: Thoemmes Press, 1995) includes the responses of Hobbes's contemporaries to the *Leviathan*. A.P. Martinish, *A Hobbes Dictionary* (Oxford: Basil Blackwell, 1995) provides a helpful reference work. For collections of essays on Hobbes, see Keith Brown, ed., *Hobbes Studies* (Cambridge, MA: Harvard University Press, 1965); G.A.J. Rogers and Alan Ryan, eds., *Perspectives on Thomas Hobbes* (Oxford: Oxford University Press, 1989); Vere Chappell, ed., *Essays on Early Modern Philosophers: Thomas Hobbes* (Hamden, CT: Garland, 1992); Tom Sorell, ed., *The Cambridge Companion to Hobbes* (Cambridge: Cambridge University Press, 1996); and the multi-volume G.A.J. Rogers, ed., *Critical Responses to Hobbes* (Oxford: Routledge, 1997).

LEVIATHAN OR THE MATTER, FORM, AND POWER OF A COMMONWEALTH, ECCLESIASTICAL AND CIVIL (in part)

PART I—OF MAN

CHAPTER 1. OF SENSE

Concerning the thoughts of man, I will consider them first singly, and afterwards in train, or dependence upon one another. Singly, they are every one a "representation" or "appearance" of some quality, or other accident of a body without us, which is commonly called an "object." Which object works on the eyes, ears, and other parts of a man's body, and, by diversity of working, produces diversity of appearances.

The title page of Hobbes's *Leviathan* (1651). The sovereign in the background, whose body is composed of the people, is supreme. He is shown here holding the symbols of both church and state. (*Library of Congress*)

The original of them all is that which we call "sense," for there is no conception in a man's mind which hath not at first, totally or by parts, been begotten upon the organs of sense. The rest are derived from that original.

To know the natural cause of sense is not very necessary to the business now in hand; and I have elsewhere written of the same at large. Nevertheless, to fill each part of my present method I will briefly deliver the same in this place.

The cause of sense is the external body, or object, which presses the organ proper to each sense, either immediately, as in the taste and touch, or mediately, as in seeing, hearing, and smelling; which pressure, by the mediation of the nerves and other strings and membranes of the body continued inwards to the brain and heart, causes there a resistance, or counter-pressure, or endeavor of the heart to deliver itself, which endeavor, because "outward," seems to be some matter without. And this "seeming" or "fancy" is that which men call "sense" and consists, as to the eye, in a "light" or "color figured"; to the ear, in a "sound"; to the nostril, in an "odor"; to the tongue and palate, in a "savor"; and to the rest of the body, in "heat," "cold," "hardness," "softness," and such other qualities as we discern by "feeling." All which qualities, called "sensible" are in the object that causes them but so many several motions of the matter, by which it presses our organs diversely. Neither in us that are pressed are they anything else but divers motions; for motion produces nothing but motion. But their appearance to us is fancy, the same waking that dreaming. And as pressing, rubbing, or striking the eye, makes us fancy a light, and pressing the ear produces a din, so do the bodies also we see or hear produce the same by their strong, though unobserved, action. For if those colors and sounds were in the bodies, or objects that cause them, they could not be severed from them, as by glasses, and in echoes by reflection, we see they are, where we know the thing we see is in one place, the appearance in another. And though at some certain distance the real and very object seem invested with the fancy it begets in us, yet still the object is one thing, the image or fancy is another. So that sense in all cases is nothing else but original fancy, caused, as I have said, by the pressure, that is by the motion, of external things upon our eyes, ears, and other organs thereunto ordained.

But the philosophy schools through all the universities of Christendom, grounded upon certain texts of Aristotle, teach another doctrine, and say, for the cause of "vision," that the thing seen sends forth on every side a "visible species," in English, a "visible show," "apparition," or "aspect," or "a being seen"; the receiving whereof into the eye is "seeing." And for the cause of "hearing," that the thing heard sends forth an "audible species," that is an "audible aspect," or "audible being seen," which entering at the ear makes "hearing." Nay, for the cause of "understanding" also, they say the thing understood sends forth an "intelligible species," that is, an "intelligible being seen," which, coming into the understanding, makes us understand. I say not this as disproving the use of universities; but, because I am to speak hereafter of their office in a commonwealth. I must let you see on all occasions by the way what things would be amended in them, amongst which the frequency of insignificant speech is one.

Chapter 2. Of Imagination

That when a thing lies still, unless somewhat else stir it, it will lie still for ever, is a truth that no man doubts of. But that when a thing is in motion, it will eternally be in motion, unless somewhat else stay it, though the reason be the same, namely that nothing can change itself, is not so easily assented to. For men measure not only other men but all other things, by themselves; and, because they find themselves subject after motion to pain and lassitude, think everything else grows weary of motion, and seeks repose of its own accord; little considering whether it be not some other motion wherein that desire of rest they find in themselves consists. From hence it is that the schools say heavy bodies fall downwards out of an appetite to rest, and to conserve their nature in that place which is most proper for them; ascribing appetite and knowledge of what is good for their conservation, which is more than man has, to things inanimate, absurdly.

When a body is once in motion, it moves, unless something else hinder it, eternally; and whatsoever hinders it cannot in an instant, but in time and by degrees, quite extinguish it; and, as we see in the water though the wind cease the waves give not over rolling for a long time after: so also it happens in that motion which is made in the internal parts of a man, then, when he sees, dreams, etc. For, after the object is removed, or the eye shut, we still retain an image of the thing seen, though more obscure than when we see it. And this is it the Latins call "imagination," from the image made in seeing; and apply the same, though improperly, to all the other senses. But the Greeks call it "fancy," which signifies "appearance," and is as proper to one sense as to another. "Imagination," therefore, is nothing but "decaying sense," and is found in men, and many other living creatures, as well sleeping as waking.

The decay of sense in men waking is not the decay of the motion made in sense, but an obscuring of it in such manner as the light of the sun obscures the light of the stars, which stars do no less exercise their virtue, by which they are visible, in the day than in the night. But because amongst many strokes which our eyes, ears, and other organs, receive from external bodies, the predominant only is sensible; therefore, the light of the sun being predominant, we are not affected with the action of the stars. And any object being removed from our eyes, though the impression it made in us remain, yet other objects more present succeeding and working on us, the imagination of the past is obscured and made weak, as the voice of a man is in the noise of the day. From whence it follows that the longer the time is, after the sight or sense of any object, the weaker is the imagination. For the continual change of man's body destroys in time the parts which in sense were moved; so that distance of time, and of place, hath one and the same effect in us. For as at a great distance of place that which we look at appears dim and without distinction of the smaller parts, and as voices grow weak and inarticulate, so also after great distance of time our imagination of the past is weak; and we lose, for example, of cities we have seen many particular streets, and of actions many particular circumstances. This "decaying sense," when we would express the thing itself, I mean "fancy" itself, we call "imagination," as I said before; but when we would express the decay, and signify that the sense is fading, old, and past, it is called "memory." So that imagination and memory are but one thing, which for divers considerations hath divers names.

Much memory, or memory of many things, is called "experience." Again, imagination being only of those things which have been formerly perceived by sense, either all at once or by parts at several times the former, which is the imagining the whole object as it was presented to the sense, is "simple" imagination, as when one imagines a man, or horse, which he hath seen before. The other is "compounded," as when, from the sight of a man at one time, and of a horse at another, we conceive in our mind a Centaur. So when a man compounds the image of his own person with the image of the actions of another man, as when a man images himself a Hercules or an Alexander, which happens often to them that are much taken with reading of romances, it is a compound imagination, and properly but a fiction of the mind. There be also other imaginations that rise in men, though waking, from the great impression made in sense; as, from gazing upon the sun, the impression leaves an image of the sun before our eyes a long time after; and, from being long and vehemently intent upon geometrical figures, a man shall in the dark, though awake, have the images of lines and angles before his eyes; which kind of fancy hath no particular name, as being a thing that doth not commonly fall into men's discourse.

The imaginations of them that sleep are those we call "dreams." And these also, as also all other imaginations, have been before, either totally or by parcels, in the sense. And, because in sense, the brain and nerves, which are the necessary organs of sense, are so benumbed in sleep as not easily to be moved by the action of external objects, there can happen in sleep no imagination, and therefore no dream, but what proceeds from the agitation of the inward parts of man's body; which inward parts, for the connection they have with the brain and other organs, when they be distempered, do keep the same in motion; whereby the imaginations there formerly made, appear as if a man were waking; saving that the organs of sense being now benumbed, so as there is no new object which can master and obscure them with a more vigorous impression, a dream must needs be more clear in this silence of sense than our waking thoughts. And hence it comes to pass that it is a hard matter, and by many thought impossible, to distinguish exactly between sense and dreaming. For my part, when I consider that in dreams I do not often nor constantly think of the same persons, places, objects, and actions, that I do waking, nor remember so long a train of coherent thoughts, dreaming, as at other times, and because waking I often observe the absurdity of dreams, but never dream of the absurdities of my waking thoughts, I am well satisfied, that, being awake, I know I dream not, though when I dream I think myself awake.

And, seeing dreams are caused by the distemper of some of the inward parts of the body, divers distempers must needs cause different dreams. And hence it is that lying cold breeds dreams of fear, and raises the thought and image of some fearful object, the motion from the brain to the inner parts and from the inner parts to the brain being reciprocal; and that, as anger causes heat in some parts of the body when we are awake, so when we sleep the overheating of the same parts causes anger, and raises up in the brain the imagination of an enemy. In the same manner, as natural kindness, when we are awake, causes desire, and desire makes heat in certain other parts of the body; so also too much heat in those parts, while we sleep, raises in the brain an imagination of some kindness shown. In sum, our dreams are the reverse of our waking imaginations, the motion when we are awake beginning at one end, and when we dream at another.

The most difficult discerning of a man's dream from his waking thoughts is, then, when by some accident we observe not that we have slept: which is easy to happen to a man full of fearful thoughts, and whose conscience is much troubled, and that sleeps without the circumstances of going to bed or putting off his clothes, as one that nods in a chair. For he that takes pains, and industriously lays himself to sleep, in case any uncouth and exorbitant fancy come unto him, cannot easily think it other than a dream. We read of Marcus Brutus (one that had his life given him by Julius Cæsar, and was also his favorite, and notwithstanding murdered him) how at Philippi, the night before he gave battle to Augustus Cæsar, he saw a fearful apparition, which is commonly related by historians as a vision; but, considering the circumstances, one may easily judge to have been but a short dream. For, sitting in his tent, pensive and troubled with the horror of his rash act, it was not hard for him, slumbering in the cold, to dream of that which most frightened him; which fear, as by degrees it made him wake, so also it must needs make the apparition by degrees to vanish; and, having no assurance that he slept, he could have no cause to think it a dream or anything but a vision. And this is no very rare accident; for even they that be perfectly awake, if they be timorous and superstitious, possessed with fearful tales, and alone in the dark, are subject to the like fancies, and believe they see spirits and dead men's ghosts walking in churchyards; whereas it is either their fancy only, or else the knavery of such persons as make use of such superstitious fear to pass disguised in the night to places they would not be known to haunt.

From this ignorance of how to distinguish dreams and other strong fancies from vision and sense, did arise the greatest part of the religion of the Gentiles in time past, that worshipped satyrs, fawns, nymphs, and the like; and now-a-days the opinion that rude people have of fairies, ghosts, and goblins, and of the power of witches. For as for witches, I think not that their witchcraft is any real power; but yet that they are justly punished for the false belief they have that they can do such mischief, joined with their purpose to do it if they can; their trade being nearer to a new religion than to a craft or science. And for fairies and walking ghosts, the opinion of them has, I think, been on purpose either taught, or not confuted, to keep in credit the use of exorcism, of crosses, of holy water, and other such inventions of ghostly men. Nevertheless there is no doubt but God can make unnatural apparitions; but that He does it so often as men need to fear such things more than they fear the stay or change of the course of nature, which He also can stay and change, is no point of Christian faith. But evil men, under pretext that God can do anything, are so bold as to say anything when it serves their turn, though they think it untrue; it is the part of a wise man to believe them no farther than right reason makes that which they say appear credible. If this superstitious fear of spirits were taken away, and with it prognostics from dreams, false prophecies, and many other things depending thereon, by which crafty ambitious persons abuse the simple people, men would be much more fitted than they are for civil obedience.

And this ought to be the work of the schools; but they rather nourish such doctrine. For, not knowing what imagination or the senses are, what they receive they teach; some saying that imaginations rise of themselves and have no cause; others that they rise most commonly from the will, and that good thoughts are blown (inspired) into a man by God, and evil thoughts by the devil; or that good thoughts are poured (infused) into a man by God, and evil ones by the devil. Some say the senses receive the species of things, and deliver them to the common sense, and the common sense delivers them over to the fancy, and the fancy to the memory, and the memory to the judgment, like handling of things from one to another, with many words making nothing understood.

The imagination that is raised in man, or any other creature endowed with the faculty of imagining, by words or other voluntary signs, is that we generally call "understanding," and is common to man and beast. For a dog by custom will understand the call or the rating of his master; and so will many other beasts. That understanding which is peculiar to man, is the understanding not only his will, but his conceptions and thoughts, by the sequel and contexture of the names of things into affirmations, negations, and other forms of speech; and of this kind of understanding I shall speak hereafter.

CHAPTER 3. OF THE CONSEQUENCE OR TRAIN OF IMAGINATIONS

By "consequence," or "train," of thoughts I understand that succession of one thought to another which is called, to distinguish it from discourse in words, "mental discourse."

When a man thinks on anything whatever, his next thought after is not altogether so casual as it seems to be. Not every thought to every thought succeeds indifferently.

But as we have no imagination whereof we have not formerly had sense, in whole or in parts, so we have no transition from one imagination to another whereof we never had the like before in our senses. The reason whereof is this. All fancies are motions within us, relics of those made in the sense, and those motions that immediately succeeded one another in the sense continue also together after sense: in so much as the former coming again to take place, and be predominant, the latter followeth, by coherence of the matter moved, in such manner as water upon a plane table is drawn which way any one part of it is guided by the finger. But because in sense to one and the same thing perceived, sometimes one thing sometimes another, succeeds, it comes to pass in time that in the imagining of anything there is no certainty what we shall imagine next: only this is certain, it shall be something that succeeded the same before, at one time or another.

This train of thoughts, or mental discourse, is of two sorts. The first is "unguided," "without design," and inconstant; wherein there is no passionate thought, to govern and direct those that follow, to itself, as the end and scope of some desire or other passion: in which case the thoughts are said to wander, and seem impertinent one to another as in a dream. Such are commonly the thoughts of men that are not only without company but also without care of anything; though even then their thoughts are as busy as at other times, but without harmony; as the sound which a lute out of tune would yield to any man, or in tune to one that could not play. And yet in this wild ranging of the mind a man may oft-times perceive the way of it, and the dependence of one thought upon another. For in a discourse of our present civil war, what could seem more impertinent than to ask, as one did, what was the value of a Roman penny. Yet the coherence to me was manifest enough. For the thought of the war introduced the thought of the delivering up the king to his enemies, the thought of that brought in the thought of the delivering up of Christ; and that again the thought of the thirty pence, which was the price of that treason; and thence easily followed that malicious question; and all this in a moment of time—for thought is quick.

The second is more constant; as being "regulated" by some desire and design. For the impression made by such things as we desire, or fear, is strong and permanent, or, if it cease for a time, of quick return: so strong it is sometimes as to hinder and break our sleep. From desire arises the thought of some means we have seen produce the like of that which we aim at; and from the thought of that, the thought of means to that mean, and so continually till we come to some beginning within our own power. And because the end, by the greatness of the impression, comes often to mind, in case our thoughts begin to wander, they are quickly again reduced into the way: which observed by one of the Seven Wise Men, made him give men this precept, which is now worn out, *Respice finem;* that is to say, in all your actions look often upon what you would have as the thing that directs all your thoughts in the way to attain it.

The train of regulated thoughts is of two kinds; one, when of an effect imagined we seek the causes or means that produce it; and this is common to man and beast. The other is when imagining anything whatsoever we seek all the possible effects that can by it be produced, that is to say, we imagine what we can do with it when we have it. Of which I have not at any time seen any sign but in man only; for this is a curiosity hardly incident to the nature of any living creature that has no other passion but sensual, such as are hunger, thirst, lust, and anger. In sum, the discourse of the mind, when it is governed by design, is nothing but "seeking," or the faculty of invention, which the Latins called sagacitas, and solertia; a hunting out of the causes, of some effect, present or past; or of the effects, of some present or past cause. Sometimes a man seeks what he hath lost; and from that place and time wherein he misses it his mind runs back, from place to place, and time to time, to find where and when he had it, that is to say, to find some certain and limited time and place in which to begin a method of seeking. Again, from thence his thoughts run over the same places and times to find what action or other occasion might make him lose it. This we call "remembrance," or calling to mind: the Latins call it *reminiscentia*, as it were a "re-conning" of our former actions.

Sometimes a man knows a place determinate, within the compass whereof he is to seek; and then his thoughts run over all the parts thereof, in the same manner as one would sweep a room to find a jewel, or as a spaniel ranges the field till he find a scent, or as a man should run over the alphabet to start a rhyme.

Sometimes a man desires to know the event of an action; and then he thinks of some like action past, and the events thereof one after another, supposing like events will follow like actions. As he that foresees what will become of a criminal recons what he has seen follow on the like crime before, having this order of thoughts, the crime, the officer, the prison, the judge, and the gallows. Which kind of thoughts is called "foresight," and "prudence," or "providence," and sometimes "wisdom," though such conjecture, through the difficulty of observing all circumstances, be very fallacious. But this is certain: by how much one man has more experience of things past than another, by so much also he is more prudent, and his expectations the seldomer fail him. The "present" only has a being in nature; things "past" have a being in the memory only, but things "to come" have no being at all, the "future" being but a fiction of the mind, applying the sequels of actions past to the actions that are present; which with most certainty is done by him that has most experience, but not with certainty enough. And though it be called prudence, when the event answers our expectation, yet, in its own nature, it is but presumption. For the foresight of things to come, which is providence, belongs only to him by whose will they are to come. From him only, and supernaturally, proceeds prophecy. The best prophet naturally is the best guesser; and the best guesser he that is most versed and studied in the matters he guesses at, for he hath most "signs" to guess by.

A "sign" is the event antecedent of the consequent; and, contrarily, the consequent of the antecedent, when the like consequences have been observed before; and the oftener they have been observed, the less uncertain is the sign. And therefore he that has most experience in any kind of business has most signs whereby to guess at the future time, and consequently is the most prudent; and so much more prudent than he that is new in that kind of business as not to be equalled by any advantage of natural and extemporary wit; though perhaps many young men think the contrary.

Nevertheless it is not prudence that distinguishes man from beast. There be beasts that at a year old observe more, and pursue that which is for their good more prudently than a child can do at ten.

As prudence is a "presumption" of the "future" contracted from the "experience" of time "past," so there is a presumption of things past taken from other things, not future, but past also. For he that hath seen by what courses and degrees a flourishing state hath first come into civil war, and then to ruin, upon the sight of the ruins of any other state will guess the like war and the like courses have been there also. But this conjecture has the same uncertainty almost with the conjecture of the future, both being grounded only upon experience.

There is no other act of man's mind that I can remember naturally planted in him, so as to need no other thing to the exercise of it but to be born a man, and live with the use of his five senses. Those other faculties of which I shall speak by and by, and which seem proper to man only, are acquired and increased by study and industry, and of most men learned by instruction and discipline; and proceed all from the invention of words and speech. For besides sense, and thoughts, and the train of thoughts, the mind of man has no other motion, though by the help of speech and method the same faculties may be improved to such a height as to distinguish men from all other living creatures.

Whatsoever we imagine is "finite." Therefore there is no idea or conception of any thing we call "infinite." No man can have in his mind an image of infinite magnitude, nor conceive infinite swiftness, infinite time, or infinite force, or infinite power. When we say anything is infinite, we signify only that we are not able to conceive the ends and bounds of the things named; having no conception of the thing, but of our own inability. And therefore the name of God is used, not to make us conceive Him, for He is incomprehensible, and His greatness and power are inconceivable, but that we may honor Him. Also because, whatsoever, as I said before, we conceive, has been perceived first by sense, either all at once or by parts; a man can have no thought representing anything not subject to sense. No man therefore can conceive anything but he must conceive it in some place, and endowed with some determinate magnitude, and which may be divided into parts; nor that anything is all in this place and all in another place at the same time; nor that two or more things can be in one and the same place at once: for none of these things ever have or can be incident to sense, but are absurd speeches, taken upon credit, without any signification at all, from deceived philosophers, and deceived or deceiving schoolmen.

*   *   *

CHAPTER 6. OF THE INTERIOR BEGINNINGS OF VOLUNTARY MOTIONS; COMMONLY CALLED THE PASSIONS; AND THE SPEECHES BY WHICH THEY ARE EXPRESSED

There be in animals two sorts of "motions" peculiar to them: one called "vital," begun in generation, and continued without interruption through their whole life, such as are the "course" of the "blood," the "pulse," the "breathing," the "concoction, nutrition, excretion," etc., to which motions there needs no help of imagination: the other is "animal motion," otherwise called "voluntary motion," as to "go," to "speak," to "move" any of our limbs in such manner as is first fancied in our minds. That sense is motion in the organs and interior parts of man's body, caused by the action of the things we see, hear, etc.; and that fancy is but the relics of the same motion, remaining after sense, has been already said in the first and second chapters. And, because "going," "speaking," and the like voluntary motions, depend always upon a precedent thought of "whither," "which way," and "what," it is evident that the imagination is the first internal beginning of all voluntary motion. And, although unstudied men do not conceive any motion at all to be there where the thing moved is invisible, or the space it is moved in is, for the shortness of it, insensible, yet that doth not hinder but that such motions are. For, let a space be never so little, that which is moved over a greater space, whereof that little one is part, must first be moved over that. These small beginnings of motion within the body of man before they appear in walking, speaking, striking, and other visible actions, are commonly called "endeavor."

This endeavor, when it is toward something which causes it, is called "appetite," or "desire," the latter being the general name, and the other oftentimes restrained to signify the desire of food, namely "hunger" and "thirst." And, when the endeavor is fromward something, it is generally called "aversion." These words, "appetite" and "aversion," we have from the Latins—and they both of them signify the motions, one of approaching, the other of retiring. So also do the Greek words for the same, which are ⟨horma⟩ and ⟨aphorma⟩. For Nature itself does often press upon men those truths which afterwards, when they look for somewhat beyond Nature, they stumble at. For the schools find in mere appetite to go, or move, no actual motion at all; but, because some motion they must acknowledge, they call it metaphorical motion, which is but an absurd speech; for though words may be called metaphorical, bodies and motions cannot.

That which men desire they are also said to "love"; and to "hate" those things for which they have aversion. So that desire and love are the same thing, save that by desire we always signify the absence of the object, by love most commonly the presence of the same. So also by aversion we signify the absence, and by hate, the presence of the object.

Of appetites and aversions, some are born with men, as appetite of food, appetite of excretion, and exoneration, which may also and more properly be called aversions from somewhat they feel in their bodies; and some other appetites, not many. The rest, which are appetites of particular things, proceed from experience and trial of their effects upon themselves or other men. For of things we know not at all, or believe not to be, we can have no further desire than to taste and try. But aversion we have for things not only which we know have hurt us, but also that we do not know whether they will hurt us or not.

Those things which we neither desire nor hate we are said to "contemn," "contempt" being nothing else but an immobility or contumacy of the heart in resisting the action of certain things, and proceeding from that the heart is already moved otherwise by other more potent objects, or from want of experience of them.

And, because the constitution of a man's body is in continual mutation, it is impossible that all the same things should always cause in him the same appetites and aversions: much less can all men consent in the desire of almost any one and the same object.

But whatsoever is the object of any man's appetite or desire, that is it which he for his part calls "good"; and the object of his hate and aversion, "evil"; and of his contempt "vile" and "inconsiderable." For these words of good, evil, and contemptible, are ever used with relation to the person that uses them, there being nothing simply and absolutely so; nor any common rule of good and evil, to be taken from the nature of the objects themselves; but from the person of the man, where there is no commonwealth, or, in a commonwealth, from the person that represents it; or from an arbitrator or judge, whom men disagreeing shall by consent set up, and make his sentence the rule thereof.

The Latin tongue has two words whose significations approach to those of good and evil, but are not precisely the same; and those are *pulchrum* and *turpe*. Whereof the former signifies that which by some apparent signs promises good; and the latter that which promises evil. But in our tongue we have not so general names to express them by. But for pulchrum we say in some things "fair," in others, "beautiful," or "handsome," or "gallant," or "honorable," or "comely," or "amiable"; and for *turpe*, "foul," "deformed," "ugly," "base," "nauseous," and the like, as the subject shall require; all which words, in their proper places, signify nothing else but the "mien," or countenance, that promises good and evil. So that of good there be three kinds: good in the promise, that is *pulchrum*; good in effect, as the end desired, which is called *jucundum,* "delightful"; and good as the means which is called *utile,* "profitable"; and as many of evil: for "evil" in promise is that they call *turpe;* evil in effect, and end is *molestum,* "unpleasant," "troublesome"; and evil in the means, *inutile,* "unprofitable," "hurtful."

As, in sense, that which is really within us is, as I have said before, only motion caused by the action of external objects but in appearance—to the sight, light and color; to the ear, sound; to the nostril, odor, etc.; so, when the action of the same object is continued from the eyes, ears, and other organs to the heart, the real effect there is nothing but motion or endeavor which consists in appetite, or aversion, to or from the object moving. But the appearance, or sense of that motion, is that we either call "delight" or "trouble of mind."

This motion, which is called appetite, and for the appearance of it "delight" and "pleasure," seems to be a corroboration of vital motion, and a help thereunto; and therefore such things as caused delight were not improperly called *jucunda—juvando,* from helping or fortifying; and the contrary *molesta,* "offensive," from hindering and troubling the motion vital.

"Pleasure," therefore, or "delight," is the appearance or sense of good; and "molestation," or "displeasure," the appearance or sense of evil. And consequently all appetite, desire, and love, is accompanied with some delight more or less; and all hatred and aversion with more or less displeasure and offence.

Of pleasures or delights some arise from the sense of an object present; and those may be called "pleasures of sense," the word "sensual," as it is used by those only that condemn them, having no place till there be laws. Of this kind are all onerations and exonerations of the body, as also all that is pleasant in the "sight," "hearing," "smell," "taste," or "touch." Others arise from the expectation that proceeds from foresight of the end or consequence of things, whether those things in the sense please or displease. And these are "pleasures of the mind" of him that draws those consequences, and are generally called "joy." In the like manner, displeasures are some in the sense, and called "pain"; others in the expectation of consequences, and are called "grief."

These simple passions called "appetite," "desire," "love," "aversion," "hate," "joy," and "grief," have their names for divers considerations diversified. As first, when they one succeed another, they are diversely called from the opinion men have of the likelihood of attaining what they desire. Secondly, from the object loved or hated. Thirdly, from the consideration of many of them together. Fourthly, from the alteration or succession itself.

For "appetite" with an opinion of attaining is called "hope."

The same without such opinion, "despair."

"Aversion" with opinion of "hurt" from the object "fear."

The same with hope of avoiding that hurt by resistance, "courage."

Sudden "courage," "anger."

Constant "hope," "confidence" of ourselves.

Constant "despair," "diffidence" of ourselves.

"Anger" for great hurt done to another, when we conceive the same to be done by injury, "indignation."

"Desire" of good to another, ''benevolence,'' "good will," "charity." If to man generally, "good-nature."

"Desire" of riches, "covetousness," a name used always in signification of blame, because men contending for them are displeased with one another attaining them, though the desire in itself be to be blamed, or allowed, according to the means by which those riches are sought.

"Desire" of office, or precedence, "ambition," a name used also in the worse sense, for the reason before mentioned.

"Desire" of things that conduce but a little to our ends, and fear of things that are but of little hindrance, "pusillanimity."

"Contempt" of little helps and hindrances, "magnanimity."

"Magnanimity" in danger of death or wounds, "valor," "fortitude."

"Magnanimity" in the use of riches, "liberality."

"Pusillanimity" in the same, "wretchedness," "miserableness," or "parsimony," as it is liked or disliked.

"Love" of persons for society, "kindness."

"Love" of persons for pleasing the sense only, "natural lust."

"Love" of the same, acquired from rumination, that is imagination of pleasure past, "luxury."

"Love" of one singularly, with desire to be singularly beloved, "the passion of love." The same, with fear that the love is not mutual, "jealousy."

"Desire," by doing hurt to another, to make him condemn some fact of his own, "revengefulness."

"Desire" to know why and how, "curiosity," such as is in no living creature but "man," so that man is distinguished not only by his reason but also by this singular passion from other "animals," in whom the appetite of food, and other pleasures of sense, by predominance take away the care of knowing causes, which is a lust of the mind, that by a perseverance of delight in the continual and indefatigable generation of knowledge exceeds the short vehemence of any carnal pleasure.

"Fear" of power invisible, feigned by the mind or imagined from tales publicly allowed, "religion," not allowed, "superstition." And when the power imagined is truly such as we imagine, "true religion."

"Fear," without the apprehension of why or what, "panic terror," called so from the fables that make Pan the author of them, whereas in truth there is always in him that so fears, first some apprehension of the cause, though the rest run away by example, every one supposing his fellow to know why. And therefore this passion happens to none but in a throng or multitude of people.

"Joy," from apprehension of novelty "admiration," proper to man, because it excites the appetite of knowing the cause.

"Joy," arising from imagination of a man's own power and ability is that exultation of the mind which is called "glorying," which, if grounded upon the experience of his own former actions, is the same as "confidence," but if grounded on the flattery of others or only supposed by himself for delight in the consequences of it, is called "vain-glory," which name is properly given, because a well-grounded "confidence" begets attempt, whereas the supposing of power does not, and is therefore rightly called "vain."

"Grief" from opinion of want of power is called "dejection of mind."

The "vain-glory" which consists in the feigning or supposing of abilities in ourselves which we know are not is most incident to young men, and nourished by the histories or fictions of gallant persons, and is corrected oftentimes by age and employment.

"Sudden glory" is the passion which makes those "grimaces" called "laughter"; and is caused either by some sudden act of their own that pleases them, or by the apprehension of some deformed thing in another by comparison whereof they suddenly applaud themselves. And it is incident most to them that are conscious of the fewest abilities in themselves; who are forced to keep themselves in their own favor by observing the imperfections of other men. And therefore much laughter at the defects of others is a sign of pusillanimity. For of great minds one of the proper works is to help and free others from scorn and compare themselves only with the most able.

On the contrary, "sudden dejection" is the passion that causes "weeping," and is caused by such accidents as suddenly take away some vehement hope or some prop of their power; and they are most subject to it that rely principally on helps external, such as are women and children. Therefore some weep for the loss of friends, others for their unkindness, others for the sudden stop made to their thoughts of revenge by reconciliation. But in all cases, both laughter and weeping, are sudden motions, custom taking them both away. For no man laughs at old jests, or weeps for an old calamity.

"Grief" for the discovery of some defect of ability is "shame," or the passion that discovers itself in "blushing," and consists in the apprehension of something dishonorable; and in young men is a sign of the love of good reputation, and commendable: in old men it is a sign of the same; but, because it comes too late, not commendable.

The "contempt" of good reputation is called "impudence."

"Grief" for the calamity of another is "pity," and arises from the imagination that the like calamity may befall himself; and therefore is called also "compassion," and in the phrase of this present time a "fellow-feeling"; and therefore for calamity arriving from great wickedness the best men have the least pity; and for the same calamity those have least pity that think themselves least obnoxious to the same.

"Contempt," or little sense of the calamity of others, is that which men call "cruelty," proceeding from security of their own fortune. For, that any man should take pleasure in other men's great harms without other end of his own, I do not conceive it possible.

"Grief" for the success of a competitor in wealth, honor, or other good, if it be joined with endeavor to enforce our own abilities to equal or exceed him, is called "emulation"; but joined with endeavor to supplant or hinder a competitor, "envy."

When in the mind of man, appetites and aversions, hopes and fears, concerning one and the same thing, arise alternately, and divers good and evil consequences of the doing or omitting the thing propounded, come successively into our thoughts, so that sometimes we have an appetite to it, sometimes an aversion from it, sometimes hope to be able to do it, sometimes despair or fear to attempt it, the whole sum of desires, aversions, hopes, and fears, continued till the thing be either done or thought impossible, is that we call "deliberation."

Therefore of things past there is no "deliberation," because manifestly impossible to be changed; nor of things known to be impossible, or thought so, because men know, or think, such deliberation vain. But of things impossible which we think possible we may deliberate, not knowing it is in vain. And it is called "deliberation," because it is a putting an end to the "liberty" we had of doing or omitting according to our own appetite or aversion.

This alternate succession of appetites, aversions, hopes, and fears, is no less in other living creatures than in man; and therefore beasts also deliberate.

Every "deliberation" is then said to "end" when that whereof they deliberate is either done or thought impossible because till then we retain the liberty of doing or omitting according to our appetite or aversion.

In "deliberation," the last appetite, or aversion, immediately adhering to the action, or to the omission thereof, is that we call the "will," the act, not the faculty, of "willing." And beasts that have "deliberation" must necessarily also have "will." The definition of the "will" given commonly by the schools, that it is a "rational appetite," is not good. For if it were, then could there be no voluntary act against reason. For a "voluntary act" is that which proceeds from the "will" and no other. But if instead of a rational appetite we shall say an appetite resulting from a precedent deliberation, then the definition is the same that I have given here. Will, therefore, is the last appetite in deliberating. And, though we say in common discourse a man had a will once to do a thing, that nevertheless he forbore to do, yet that is properly but an inclination, which makes no action voluntary; because the action depends not of it, but of the last inclination or appetite. For if the intervenient appetites make any action voluntary, then by the same reason all intervenient aversions should make the same action involuntary; and so one and the same action should be both voluntary and involuntary.

By this it is manifest that not only actions that have their beginning from covetousness, ambition, lust, or other appetites to the thing propounded, but also those that have their beginning from aversion, or fear of those consequences that follow the omission, are "voluntary actions."

The forms of speech by which the passions are expressed are partly the same, and partly different from those by which we express our thoughts. And, first, generally all passions may be expressed "indicatively," as "I love," "I fear," "I joy," "I deliberate," "I will," "I command," but some of them have particular expressions by themselves, which nevertheless are not affirmations, unless it be when they serve to make other inferences besides that of the passion they proceed from. Deliberation is expressed "subjunctively," which is a speech proper to signify suppositions, with their consequences: as, "if this be done, then this will follow," and differs not from the language of reasoning, save that reasoning is in general words—but deliberation for the most part is of particulars. The language of desire, and aversion, is "imperative," as "do this," "forbear that," which when the party is obliged to do, or forbear, is "command"; otherwise "prayer," or else "counsel." The language of vain-glory, of indignation, pity and revengefulness, "optative," but of the desire to know there is a peculiar expression, called "interrogative," as "what is it"? "when shall it"? "how is it done"? and "why so"? Other language of the passions I find none; for cursing, swearing, reviling, and the like, do not signify as speech, but as the actions of a tongue accustomed.

These forms of speech, I say, are expressions, or voluntary significations of our passions—but certain signs they be not, because they may be used arbitrarily, whether they that use them have such passions or not. The best signs of passions present are either in the countenance, motions of the body, actions, and ends, or aims, which we otherwise know the man to have.

And because in deliberation the appetites and aversions are raised by foresight of the good and evil consequences, and sequels of the action whereof we deliberate, the good or evil effect thereof depends on the foresight of a long chain of consequences of which very seldom any man is able to see to the end. But for so far as a man sees, if the good in those consequences be greater than the evil, the whole chain is that which writers call "apparent" or "seeming good." And, contrarily, when the evil exceeds the good, the whole is "apparent" or "seeming evil," so that he who hath by experience, or reason, the greatest and surest prospect of consequences, deliberates best himself, and is able, when he will, to give the best counsel unto others.

"Continual success" in obtaining those things which a man from time to time desires, that is to say continual prospering, is that men call "felicity"; I mean the felicity of this life. For there is no such thing as perpetual tranquility of mind while we live here, because life itself is but motion, and can never be without desire, nor without fear, no more than without sense. What kind of felicity God hath ordained to them that devoutly honor Him a man shall no sooner know than enjoy, being joys that now are as incomprehensible as the word of schoolmen "beatifical vision" is unintelligible.

The form of speech whereby men signify their opinion of the goodness of anything is "praise." That whereby they signify the power and greatness of anything is "magnifying." And that whereby they signify the opinion they have of a man's felicity is by the Greeks called ⟨*makarismos*⟩ for which we have no name in our tongue. And thus much is sufficient for the present purpose, to have been said of the "passions."

*   *   *

CHAPTER 9. OF THE SEVERAL SUBJECTS OF KNOWLEDGE

There are of "knowledge" two kinds, whereof one is "knowledge of fact," the other "knowledge of the consequence of one affirmation to another." The former is nothing else but sense and memory, and is "absolute knowledge," as when we see a fact doing or remember it done; and this is the knowledge required in a witness. The latter is called "science," and is "conditional," as when we know that "if the figure shown be a circle, then any straight line through the center shall divide it into two equal parts." And this is the knowledge required in a philosopher, that is to say of him that pretends to reasoning.

The register of "knowledge of fact" is called "history," whereof there be two sorts: one called "natural history," which is the history of such facts or effects of Nature as have no dependence on man's "will," such as are the histories of "metals," "plants," "animals," "regions," and the like. The other is "civil history," which is the history of the voluntary actions of men in commonwealths.

The registers of science are such "books," as contain the "demonstrations" of consequences of one affirmation to another, and are commonly called "books of philosophy," whereof the sorts are many, according to the diversity of the matter, and may be divided in such manner as I have divided them in the . . . table [see following page].

*   *   *

CHAPTER 12. OF RELIGION

Seeing there are no signs nor fruit of "religion" but in man only, there is no cause to doubt but that the seed of "religion" is also only in man—and consists in some peculiar quality or at least in some eminent degree thereof not to be found in other living creatures.

And, first, it is peculiar to the nature of man to be inquisitive into the causes of the events they see, some more, some less; but all men so much as to be curious in the search of the causes of their own good and evil fortune.

Secondly, upon the sight of anything that hath a beginning to think also it had a cause which determined the same to begin, then when it did, rather than sooner or later.

Thirdly, whereas there is no other felicity of beasts but the enjoying of their quotidian food, ease, and lusts, as having little or no foresight of the time to come, for want of observation and memory of the order, consequence, and dependence of the things they see, man observes how one event hath been produced by another, and remembers in them antecedence and consequence; and, when he cannot assure himself

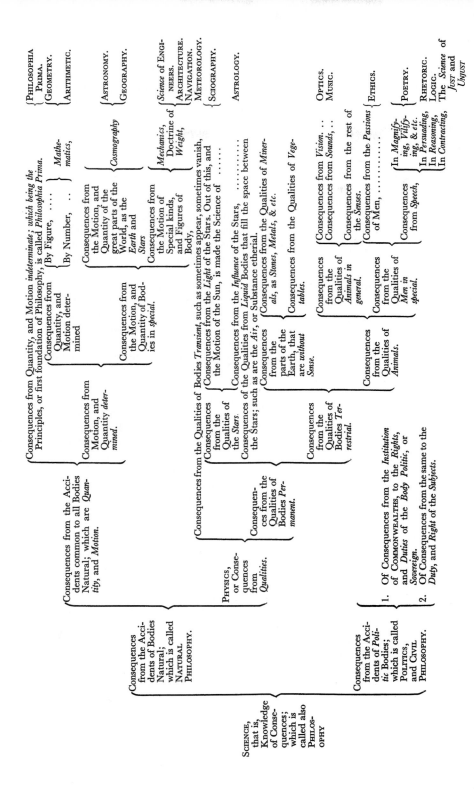

of the true causes of things (for the causes of good and evil fortune for the most part are invisible), he supposes causes of them, either such as his own fancy suggests, or trusts the authority of other men, such as he thinks to be his friends and wiser than himself.

The two first make anxiety. For, being assured that there be causes of all things that have arrived hitherto or shall arrive hereafter, it is impossible for a man, who continually endeavors to secure himself against the evil he fears and procure the good he desires, not to be in a perpetual solicitude of the time to come; so that every man, especially those that are over-provident, are in a state like to that of Prometheus. For as Prometheus, which interpreted is "the prudent man," was bound to the hill Caucasus, a place of large prospect, where an eagle feeding on his liver devoured in the day as much as was repaired in the night, so that man, which looks too far before him in the care of future time, hath his heart all the day long gnawed on by fear of death, poverty, or other calamity, and has no repose nor pause of his anxiety but in sleep.

This perpetual fear, always accompanying mankind in the ignorance of causes, as it were in the dark, must needs have for object something. And therefore, when there is nothing to be seen, there is nothing to accuse, either of their good or evil fortune, but some ''power'' or agent "invisible" in which sense perhaps it was that some of the old poets said that the gods were at first created by human fear; which spoken of the gods, that is to say of the many gods of the Gentiles, is very true. But the acknowledging of one God, eternal, infinite, and omnipotent, may more easily be derived, from the desire men have to know the causes of natural bodies and their several virtues and operations, than from the fear of what was to befall them in time to come. For he that from any effect he sees come to pass should reason to the next and immediate cause thereof, and from thence to the cause of that cause, and plunge himself profoundly in the pursuit of causes, shall at last come to this, that there must be, as even the heathen philosophers confessed, one first mover, that is, a first and an eternal cause of all things, which is that which men mean by the name of God, and all this without thought of their fortune; the solicitude whereof both inclines to fear and hinders them from the search of the causes of other things, and thereby gives occasion of feigning of as many gods as there be men that feign them.

And, for the matter or substance of the invisible agents so fancied, they could not by natural cogitation fall upon any other conceit, but that it was the same with that of the soul of man; and that the soul of man was of the same substance with that which appears in a dream to one that sleeps or in a looking-glass to one that is awake, which, men not knowing that such apparitions are nothing else but creatures of the fancy, think to be real and external substances, and therefore call them ghosts; as the Latins called them *imagines* and *umbræ*, and thought them spirits, that is thin aerial bodies, and those invisible agents which they feared, to be like them, save that they appear and vanish when they please. But the opinion that such spirits were incorporeal, or immaterial, could never enter into the mind of any man by nature, because, though men may put together words of contradictory signification, as "spirit" and "incorporeal," yet they can never have the imagination of anything answering to them; and therefore men that by their own meditation arrive to the acknowledgment of one infinite, omnipotent, and eternal God chose rather to confess He is incomprehensible and above their understanding than to define His nature by "spirit incorporeal," and then confess their definition to be unintelligible; or, if they give Him such a title, it is not "dogmatically" with intention to make the divine nature understood, but "piously," to honor Him with attributes of significations as remote as they can from the grossness of bodies visible.

Then for the way by which they think these invisible agents wrought their effects, that is to say, what immediate causes they used in bringing things to pass, men that know not what it is that we call "causing," that is almost all men, have no other rule to guess by but by observing and remembering what they have seen to precede the like effect at some other time or times before, without seeing between the antecedent and subsequent event any dependence or connection at all; and therefore from the like things past they expect the like things to come, and hope for good or evil luck, superstitiously, from things that have no part at all in the causing of it: as the Athenians did for their war at Lepanto, demand another Phormio; the Pompeian faction for their war in Africa, another Scipio, and others have done in divers other occasions since. In like manner they attribute their fortune to a stander-by, to a lucky or unlucky place, to words spoken, especially if the name God be amongst them, as charming and conjuring, the liturgy of witches; inasmuch as to believe they have power to turn a stone into bread, bread into a man, or anything into anything.

Thirdly, for the worship which naturally men exhibit to powers invisible, it can be no other but such expressions of their reverence, as they would use towards men; gifts, petitions, thanks, submission of body, considerate addresses, sober behavior, premeditated words, swearing, that is assuring one another of their promises by invoking them. Beyond that, reason suggests nothing, but leaves them either to rest there, or, for further ceremonies, to rely on those they believe to be wiser than themselves.

Lastly, concerning how these invisible powers declare to men the things which shall hereafter come to pass, especially concerning their good or evil fortune in general or good or ill success in any particular undertaking, men are naturally at a stand, save that, using to conjecture of the time to come by the time past, they are very apt not only to take casual things, after one or two encounters, for prognostics of the like encounter ever after, but also to believe the like prognostics from other men of whom they have once conceived a good opinion.

And, in these four things, opinion of ghosts, ignorance of second causes, devotion towards what men fear, and taking of things casual for prognostics, consists the natural seed of "religion," which, by reason of the different fancies, judgments, and passions of several men, hath grown up into ceremonies so different that those which are used by one man are for the most part ridiculous to another.

For these seeds have received culture from two sorts of men. One sort have been they that have nourished and ordered them according to their own invention. The other have done it by God's commandment and direction; but both sorts have done it with a purpose to make those men that relied on them the more apt to obedience, laws, peace, charity and civil society. So that the religion of the former sort is a part of human politics, and teaches part of the duty which earthly kings require of their subjects. And the religion of the latter sort is divine politics, and contains precepts to those that have yielded themselves subjects in the kingdom of God. Of the former sort were all the founders of commonwealths and the lawgivers of the Gentiles; of the latter sort, were Abraham, Moses, and our blessed Savior, by whom have been derived unto us the laws of the kingdom of God.

* * *

CHAPTER 13. OF THE NATURAL CONDITION OF MANKIND AS CONCERNING THEIR FELICITY AND MISERY

Nature hath made men so equal in the faculties of the body and mind, as that, though there be found one man sometimes manifestly stronger in body or of quicker mind than another, yet when all is reckoned together the difference between man and man is not so considerable as that one man can thereupon claim to himself any benefit to which another may not pretend as well as he. For, as to the strength of body, the weakest has strength enough to kill the strongest, either by secret machination or by confederacy with others that are in the same danger with himself.

And, as to the faculties of the mind, setting aside the arts grounded upon words and especially that skill of proceeding upon general and infallible rules called science, which very few have and but in few things, as being not a native faculty born with us, nor attained, as prudence, while we look after somewhat else, I find yet a greater equality amongst men than that of strength. For prudence is but experience, which equal time equally bestows on all men in those things they equally apply themselves unto. That which may perhaps make such equality incredible is but a vain conceit of one's own wisdom, which almost all men think they have in a greater degree than the vulgar, that is, than all men but themselves, and a few others whom by fame or for concurring with themselves they approve. For such is the nature of men that, howsoever they may acknowledge many others to be more witty or more eloquent or more learned, yet they will hardly believe there be many so wise as themselves, for they see their own wit at hand and other men's at a distance. But this proves rather that men are in that point equal than unequal. For there is not ordinarily a greater sign of the equal distribution of anything than that every man is contented with his share.

From this equality of ability arises equality of hope in the attaining of our ends. And therefore, if any two men desire the same thing which nevertheless they cannot both enjoy, they become enemies—and, in the way to their end, which is principally their own conservation and sometimes their delectation only, endeavor to destroy or subdue one another. And from hence it comes to pass that, where an invader hath no more to fear than another man's single power, if one plant, sow, build, or possess, a convenient seat others may probably be expected to come prepared with forces united to dispossess and deprive him not only of the fruit of his labor but also of his life or liberty. And the invader again is in the like danger of another.

And from this diffidence of one another there is no way for any man to secure himself so reasonable as anticipation, that is, by force or wiles to master the persons of all men he can so long till he see no other power great enough to endanger him; and this is no more than his own conservation requires and is generally allowed. Also, because there be some that, taking pleasure in contemplating their own power in the acts of conquest, which they pursue farther than their security requires, if others, that otherwise would be glad to be at ease within the modest bounds, should not by invasion increase their power, they would not be able for a long time, by standing only on their defence, to subsist. And by consequence, such augmentation of dominion over men being necessary to a man's conservation, it ought to be allowed him.

Again, men have no pleasure, but on the contrary a great deal of grief, in keeping company where there is no power able to overawe them all. For every man looks that his companion should value him at the same rate he sets upon himself, and, upon all signs of contempt or undervaluing, naturally endeavors as far as he dares (which amongst them that have no common power to keep them in quiet, is far enough to make them destroy each other) to extort a greater value from his condemners by damage, and from others by the example.

So that in the nature of man we find three principal causes of quarrel. First, competition; secondly, diffidence; thirdly, glory.

The first makes man invade for gain; the second, for safety; and the third, for reputation. The first use violence, to make themselves masters of other men's persons, wives, children, and cattle; the second, to defend them; the third, for trifles, as a word, a smile, a different opinion, and any other sign of undervalue, either direct in their persons or by reflection in their kindred, their friends, their nation, their profession, or their name.

Hereby it is manifest that, during the time men live without a common power to keep them all in awe, they are in that condition which is called war, and such a war as is of every man against every man. For "war" consists not in battle only or the act of fighting, but in a tract of time wherein the will to contend by battle is sufficiently known, and therefore the notion of "time" is to be considered in the nature of war, as it is in the nature of weather. For as the nature of foul weather lies not in a shower or two of rain but in an inclination thereto of many days together, so the nature of war consists not in actual fighting but in the known disposition thereto during all the time there is no assurance to the contrary. All other time is "peace."

Whatsoever therefore is consequent to a time of war where every man is enemy to every man, the same is consequent to the time wherein men live without other security than what their own strength and their own invention shall furnish them withal. In such condition there is no place for industry, because the fruit thereof is uncertain, and consequently no culture of the earth, no navigation nor use of the commodities that may be imported by sea, no commodious building, no instruments of moving and removing such things as require much force, no knowledge of the face of the earth; no account of time, no arts, no letters, no society, and, which is worst of all, continual fear and danger of violent death, and the life of man solitary, poor, nasty, brutish, and short.

It may seem strange to some man that has not well weighed these things that Nature should thus dissociate and render men apt to invade and destroy one another; and he may therefore, not trusting to this inference made from the passions, desire perhaps to have the same confirmed by experience. Let him therefore consider with himself, when taking a journey, he arms himself and seeks to go well accompanied; when going to sleep, he locks his doors; when even in his house, he locks his chests; and this when he knows there be laws and public officers armed to revenge all injuries shall be done him; what opinion he has of his fellow-subjects, when he rides armed—of his fellow-citizens, when he locks his doors; and of his children and servants, when he locks his chests. Does he not there as much accuse mankind by his actions as I do by my words? But neither of us accuse man's nature in it. The desires and other passions of man are in themselves no sin. No more are the actions that proceed from those passions, till they know a law that forbids them; which, till laws be made, they cannot know, nor can any law be made till they have agreed upon the person that shall make it.

It may peradventure be thought there was never such a time nor condition of war as this; and I believe it was never generally so over all the world, but there are many places where they live so now. For the savage people in many places of America, except the government of small families the concord whereof depends on natural lust, have no government at all, and live at this day in that brutish manner as I said before. Howsoever, it may be perceived what manner of life there would be where there were no common power to fear, by the manner of life which men that have formerly lived under a peaceful government use to degenerate into, in a civil war. But, though there had never been any time wherein particular men were in a condition of war one against another, yet in all times kings and persons of sovereign authority, because of their independence, are in continual jealousies and in the state and posture of gladiators, having their weapons pointing, and their eyes fixed on one another, that is, their forts, garrisons, and guns, upon the frontiers of their kingdoms, and continual spies upon their neighbors: which is a posture of war. But because they uphold thereby the industry of their subjects, there does not follow from it that misery which accompanies the liberty of particular men.

To this war of every man against every man this also is consequent, that nothing can be unjust. The notions of right and wrong, justice and injustice, have there no place. Where there is no common power, there is no law; where no law, no injustice. Force and fraud are in war the two cardinal virtues. Justice and injustice are none of the faculties neither of the body nor mind. If they were, they might be in a man that were alone in the world, as well as his senses and passions. They are qualities that relate to men in society, not in solitude. It is consequent also to the same condition that there be no propriety, no dominion, no "mine" and "thine" distinct, but only that to be every man's that he can get, and for so long as he can keep it. And thus much for the ill condition which man by mere nature is actually placed in, though with a possibility to come out of it, consisting partly in the passions, partly in his reason.

The passions that incline men to peace are fear of death, desire of such things as are necessary to commodious living, and a hope by their industry to obtain them. And reason suggests convenient articles of peace, upon which men may be drawn to agreement. These articles are they which otherwise are called the Laws of Nature, whereof I shall speak more particularly in the two following chapters.

CHAPTER 14. OF THE FIRST AND SECOND NATURAL LAWS, AND OF CONTRACTS

"The right of Nature," which writers commonly call *jus naturale*, is the liberty each man hath to use his own power as he will himself for the preservation of his own nature, that is to say, of his own life; and consequently of doing anything which in his own judgment and reason he shall conceive to be the aptest means thereunto.

By "liberty" is understood, according to the proper signification of the word, the absence of external impediments which impediments may oft take away part of a man's power to do what he would, but cannot hinder him from using the power left him according as his judgment and reason shall dictate to him.

A "law of Nature," *lex naturalis*, is a precept or general rule found out by reason by which a man is forbidden to do that which is destructive of his life or takes away the means of preserving the same, and to omit that by which he thinks it may be best preserved. For, though they that speak of this subject use to confound *jus* and *lex*, "right" and "law," yet they ought to be distinguished; because "right" consists in liberty to do or to forbear, whereas "law" determines and binds to one of them: so that law and right differ as much as obligation and liberty; which in one and the same matter are inconsistent.

And because the condition of man, as hath been declared in the precedent chapter, is a condition of war of every one against every one, in which case every one is governed by his own reason, and there is nothing he can make use of that may not be a help unto him in preserving his life against his enemies, it follows that in such a condition every man has a right to everything, even to one another's body. And therefore, as long as this natural right of every man to everything endures, there can be no security to any man, how strong or wise soever he be, of living out the time which Nature ordinarily allows men to live. And consequently it is a precept or general rule of reason "that every man ought to endeavor peace as far as he has hope of obtaining it, and, when he cannot obtain it, that he may seek and use all helps and advantages of war." The first branch of which rule contains the first and fundamental law of Nature, which is, "to seek peace, and follow it." The second, the sum of the right of Nature, which is, "by all means we can, to defend ourselves."

From this fundamental law of Nature, by which men are commanded to endeavor peace, is derived this second law, "that a man be willing, when others are so too, as far-forth as for peace and defence of himself he shall think it necessary, to lay down this right to all things, and be contented with so much liberty against other men as he would allow other men against himself." For as long as every man holds this right of doing anything he likes, so long are all men in the condition of war. But if other men will not lay down their right as well as he, then there is no reason for any one to divest himself of his: for that were to expose himself to prey, which no man is bound to, rather than to dispose himself to peace. This is that law of the Gospel: "whatsoever you require that others should do to you, that do ye to them." And that law of all men, *quod tibi fieri non vis, alteri ne feceris.*

To "lay down" a man's "right" to anything is to "divest" himself of the "liberty," of hindering another of the benefit of his own right to the same. For he that renounces or passes away his right gives not to any other man a right which he had not before, because there is nothing to which every man had not right by Nature; but only stands out of his way that he may enjoy his own original right without hindrance from him, not without hindrance from another. So that the effect which redounds to one man, by another man's defect of right, is but so much diminution of impediments to the use of his own right original.

Right is laid aside either by simply renouncing it, or by transferring it to another. By "simply renouncing" when he cares not to whom the benefit thereof redounds. By "transferring," when he intends the benefit thereof to some certain person or persons. And, when a man hath in either manner abandoned or granted away his right, then is he said to be "obliged" or "bound" not to hinder those to whom such right is granted or abandoned from the benefit of it; and that he "ought," and it is his "duty," not to make void that voluntary act of his own; and that such hindrance is "injustice" and "injury" as being sine jure, the right being before renounced or transferred. So that "injury" or "injustice," in the controversies of the world, is somewhat like to that which in the disputations of scholars is called "absurdity." For, as it is there called an absurdity to contradict what one maintained in the beginning, so in the world it is called injustice and injury voluntarily to undo that from the beginning he had voluntarily done. The way by which a man either simply renounces or transfers his right is a declaration or signification, by some voluntary and sufficient sign or signs, that he doth so renounce or transfer, or hath so renounced or transferred, the same, to him that accepts it. And these signs are either words only or actions only, or, as it happens most often, both words and actions. And the same are the "bonds" by which men are bound and obliged: bonds that have their strength not from their own nature, for nothing is more easily broken than a man's word, but from fear of some evil consequence upon the rupture.

Whensoever a man transfers his right or renounces it, it is either in consideration of some right reciprocally transferred to himself, or for some other good he hopes for thereby. For it is a voluntary act: and of the voluntary acts of every man the object is some good "to himself." And therefore there be some rights which no man can be understood by any words or other signs to have abandoned or transferred. As first a man cannot lay down the right of resisting them that assault him by force to take away his life, because he cannot be understood to aim thereby at any good to himself. The same may be said of wounds, and chains, and imprisonment, both because there is no benefit consequent to such patience, as there is to the patience of suffering another to be wounded or imprisoned, as also because a man cannot tell when he sees men proceed against him by violence whether they intend his death or not. And lastly the motive and end for which this renouncing and transferring of right is introduced is nothing else but the security of a man's person in his life and in the means of so preserving life as not to be weary of it. And therefore if a man by words or other signs seem to despoil himself of the end for which those signs were intended, he is not to be understood as if he meant it or that it was his will, but that he was ignorant of how such words and actions were to be interpreted.

The mutual transferring of right is that which men call "contract."

*　　*　　*

CHAPTER 15. OTHER LAWS OF NATURE

From that law of Nature by which we are obliged to transfer to another such rights as, being retained, hinder the peace of mankind, there follows a third, which is this, "that men perform their covenants made"; without which covenants are in vain, and but empty words: and the right of all men to all things remaining, we are still in the condition of war.

And in this law of Nature consists the fountain and original of "justice." For, where no covenant hath preceded, there hath no right been transferred, and every man has right to everything; and consequently, no action can be unjust. But when a covenant is made, then to break it is "unjust"; and the definition of "injustice" is no other than "the not performance of covenant." And whatsoever is not unjust is "just."

But because covenants of mutual trust, where there is a fear of not performance on either part, as hath been said in the former chapter, are invalid, though the original of justice be the making of covenants, yet injustice actually there can be none, till the cause of such fear be taken away, which, while men are in the natural condition of war, cannot be done. Therefore, before the names of just and unjust can have place, there must be some coercive power to compel men equally to the performance of their covenants, by the terror of some punishment greater than the benefit they expect by the breach of their covenant; and to make good that propriety which by mutual contract men acquire in recompense of the universal right they abandon; and such power there is none before the erection of a commonwealth. And this is also to be gathered out of the ordinary definition of justice in the schools; for they say that "justice is the constant will of giving to every man his own." And therefore where there is no "own" there is no propriety, there is no injustice; and where there is no coercive power erected, that is, where there is no commonwealth, there is no propriety, all men having right to all things: therefore, where there is no commonwealth, there nothing is unjust. So that the nature of justice consists in keeping of valid covenants; but the validity of covenants begins not but with the constitution of a civil power sufficient to compel men to keep them; and then it is also that propriety begins.

The fool hath said in his heart there is no such thing as justice, and sometimes also with his tongue, seriously alleging that every man's conservation and contentment, being committed to his own care, there could be no reason why every man might not do what he thought conduced thereunto; and therefore also to make or not make, keep or not keep, covenants was not against reason when it conduced to one's benefit. He does not therein deny that there be covenants, and that they are sometimes broken, sometimes kept, and that such breach of them may be called injustice, and the observance of them justice; but he questions whether injustice taking away the fear of God, for the same fool hath said in his heart there is no God, may not sometimes stand with that reason which dictates to every man his own good; and particularly then when it conduces to such a benefit as shall put a man in a condition to neglect not only the dispraise and revilings, but also the power, of other men. The kingdom of God is gotten by violence; but what if it could be gotten by unjust violence? Were it against reason so to get it, when it is impossible to receive hurt by it? And, if it be not against reason, it is not against justice, or else justice is not to be approved for good. From such reasoning as this, successful wickedness hath obtained the name of virtue, and some that in all other things have disallowed the violation of faith, yet have allowed it when it is for the getting of a kingdom. And the heathen that believed that Saturn was deposed by his son Jupiter believed nevertheless the same Jupiter to be the avenger of injustice somewhat like to a piece of law in Coke's *Commentaries on Littleton*, where he says, if the right heir of the crown be attainted of treason, yet the crown shall descend to him, and *eo instante* the attainder be void; from which instances a man will be very prone to infer that, when the heir apparent of a kingdom shall kill him that is in possession, though his father, you may call it injustice or by what other name you will, yet it can never be against reason seeing all the voluntary actions of men tend to the benefit of themselves; and those actions are most reasonable that conduce most to their ends. This specious reasoning is nevertheless false.

For the question is not of promises mutual, where there is no security of performance on either side, as when there is no civil power erected over the parties promising, for such promises are no covenants, but either where one of the parties has performed already, or where there is a power to make him perform, there is the question whether it be against reason, that is against the benefit of the other to perform or not. And I say it is not against reason. For the manifestation whereof we are to consider, first that when a man doth a thing which notwithstanding anything can be foreseen and reckoned on tends to his own destruction, howsoever some accident which he could not expect, arriving may turn it to his benefit, yet such events do not make it reasonably or wisely done. Secondly, that, in a condition of war, wherein every man to every man, for want of a common power to keep them all in awe, is an enemy, there is no man who can hope by his own strength or wit to defend himself from destruction without the help of confederates; where every one expects the same defence by the confederation that any one else does; and therefore he which declares he thinks it reason to deceive those that help him can in reason expect no other means of safety than what can be had from his own single power. He therefore that breaks his covenant, and consequently declares that he thinks he may with reason do so, cannot be received into any society that unite themselves for peace and defence but by the error of them that receive him; nor, when he is received, be retained in it without seeing the danger of their error; which errors a man cannot reasonably reckon upon as the means of his security; and therefore, if he be left or cast out of society, he perishes; and if he live in society, it is by the errors of other men which he could not foresee nor reckon upon, and consequently against the reason of his preservation; and so, as all men that contribute not to his destruction, forbear him only out of ignorance of what is good for themselves.

As for the instance of gaining the secure and perpetual felicity of heaven by any way, it is frivolous; there being but one way imaginable; and that is not breaking, but keeping of covenant.

And, for the other instance of attaining sovereignty by rebellion, it is manifest that, though the event follow, yet, because it cannot reasonably be expected, but rather the contrary, and because by gaining it so, others are taught to gain the same in like manner, the attempt thereof is against reason. Justice therefore, that is to say keeping of covenant, is a rule of reason by which we are forbidden to do anything destructive to our life; and consequently a law of Nature.

There be some that proceed further, and will not have the law of Nature to be those rules which conduce to the preservation of man's life on earth, but to the attaining of an eternal felicity after death; to which they think the breach of covenant may conduce; and consequently be just and reasonable; such are they that think it a work of merit to kill or depose or rebel against the sovereign power constituted over them by their own consent. But, because there is no natural knowledge of man's estate after death, much less of the reward that is then to be given to breach of faith, but only a belief grounded upon other men's saying that they know it supernaturally, or that they know those that knew them, that knew others, that knew it supernaturally; breach of faith cannot be called a precept of reason or nature.

Others that allow for a law of Nature the keeping of faith do nevertheless make exception of certain persons as heretics and such as use not to perform their covenant to others; and this also is against reason. For if any fault of a man be sufficient to discharge our covenant made, the same ought in reason to have been sufficient to have hindered the making of it.

The names of just and unjust, when they are attributed to men, signify one thing; and when they are attributed to actions, another. When they are attributed to men they signify conformity or inconformity of manners to reason. But, when they are attributed to actions, they signify the conformity or inconformity to reason, not of manners or manner of life but of particular actions. A just man, therefore, is he that takes all the care he can that his actions may be all just, and an unjust man is he that neglects it. And such men are more often in our language styled by the names of righteous and unrighteous than just and unjust, though the meaning be the same. Therefore a righteous man does not lose that title by one or a few unjust actions that proceed from sudden passion or mistake of things or persons; nor does an unrighteous man lose his character for such actions as he does, or forbears to do, for fear, because his will is not framed by the justice but by the apparent benefit of what he is to do. That which gives to human actions the relish of justice is a certain nobleness or gallantness of courage, rarely found, by which a man scorns to be beholden for the contentment of his life to fraud or breach of promise. This justice of the manners is that which is meant where justice is called a virtue, and injustice a vice.

But the justice of actions denominates men not just, "guiltless"; and the injustice of the same, which is also called injury, gives them but the name of "guilty."

Again, the injustice of manners is the disposition or aptitude to do injury, and is injustice before it proceeds to act, and without supposing any individual person injured. But the injustice of an action, that is to say injury, supposes an individual person injured, namely him to whom the covenant was made; and therefore many times the injury is received by one man when the damage redounds to another. As when the master commands his servant to give money to a stranger: if it be not done, the injury is done to the master, whom he had before covenanted to obey; but the damage redounds to the stranger, to whom he had no obligation, and therefore could not injure him. And so also in commonwealths. Private men may remit to one another their debts, but not robberies or other violences whereby they are endamaged, because the detaining of debt is an injury to themselves, but robbery and violence are injuries to the person of the commonwealth.

Whatsoever is done to a man conformable to his own will signified to the doer is no injury to him. For, if he that does it hath not passed away his original right to do what he please by some antecedent covenant, there is no breach of covenant, and therefore no injury done him. And if he have, then his will to have it done being signified is a release of that covenant, and so again there is no injury done him.

Justice of action is by writers divided into "commutative" and "distributive"; and the former they say consists in proportion arithmetical, the latter in proportion geometrical. Commutative, therefore, they place in the equality of value of the things contracted for—and distributive, in the distribution of equal benefit to men of equal merit. As if it were injustice to sell dearer than we buy, or to give more to a man than he merits. The value of all things contracted for is measured by the appetite of the contractors; and therefore the just value is that which they be contented to give. And merit, besides that which is by covenant, where the performance on one part merits the performance of the other part, and falls under justice commutative not distributive, is not due by justice, but is rewarded of grace only. And therefore this distinction, in the sense wherein it uses to be expounded, is not right. To speak properly, commutative justice is the justice of a contractor; that is, a performance of covenant in buying and selling, hiring and letting to hire, lending and borrowing, exchanging, bartering, and other acts of contract.

And distributive justice, the justice of an arbitrator; that is to say, the act of defining what is just. Wherein, being trusted by them that make him arbitrator, if he perform his trust he is said to distribute to every man his own; and this is indeed just distribution, and may be called, though improperly, distributive justice, but more properly equity, which also is a law of Nature, as shall be shown in due place.

As justice depends on antecedent covenant, so does "gratitude" depend on antecedent grace, that is to say, antecedent free gift; and is the fourth law of Nature; which may be conceived in this form, "that a man, which receives benefit from another of mere grace, endeavor that he which gives it have no reasonable cause to repent him of his good will." For no man gives but with intention of good to himself; because gift is voluntary; and of all voluntary acts the object is to every man his own good, of which, if men see they shall be frustrated, there will be no beginning of benevolence, or trust, nor consequently of mutual help, nor of reconciliation of one man to another; and therefore they are to remain still in the condition of "war," which is contrary to the first and fundamental law of Nature, which commands men to "seek peace." The breach of this law is called "ingratitude," and hath the same relation to grace that injustice hath to obligation by covenant.

A fifth law of Nature, is "complaisance," that is to say, "that every man strive to accommodate himself to the rest." For the understanding whereof, we may consider that there is in men's aptness to society, a diversity of nature, rising from their diversity of affections, not unlike to that we see in stones brought together for building of an edifice. For as that stone which by the asperity and irregularity of figure takes more room from others than itself fills, and for the hardness cannot be easily made plain, and thereby hinders the building, is by the builders cast away as unprofitable and troublesome, so also a man that by asperity of nature will strive to retain those things which to himself are superfluous and to others necessary, and for the stubbornness of his passions cannot be corrected, is to be left or cast out of society as cumbersome thereunto.

For seeing every man, not only by right but also by necessity of nature, is supposed to endeavor all he can to obtain that which is necessary for his conversation, he that shall oppose himself against it for things superfluous is guilty of the war that thereupon is to follow; and therefore doth that which is contrary to the fundamental law of Nature, which commands "to seek peace." The observers of this law may be called "sociable"— the Latins call them *commodi;* the contrary, "stubborn," "insociable," "froward," "intractable."

A sixth law of Nature is this, "that, upon caution of the future time, a man ought to pardon the offenses past of them that, repenting, desire it." For "pardon" is nothing but granting of peace, which, though granted to them that persevere in their hostility, be not peace but fear; yet not granted to them that give caution of the future time is sign of an aversion to peace, and therefore contrary to the law of Nature.

A seventh is, "that in revenges," that is, retribution of evil for evil, "men look not at the greatness of the evil past but the greatness of the good to follow." Whereby we are forbidden to inflict punishment with any other design than for correction of the offender or direction of others. For this law is consequent to the next before it, that commands pardon, upon security of the future time. Besides, revenge, without respect to the example and profit to come, is a triumph or glorying in the hurt of another tending to no end; for the end is always somewhat to come; and glorying to no end is vainglory and contrary to reason, and to hurt without reason tends to the introduction of war, which is against the law of Nature, and is commonly by the name of "cruelty."

*   *   *

PART II—OF COMMONWEALTH

CHAPTER 17. OF THE CAUSES, GENERATION, AND DEFINITION OF A COMMONWEALTH

The final cause, end, or design of men, who naturally love liberty, and dominion over others, in the introduction of that restraint upon themselves, in which we see them live in commonwealths, is the foresight of their own preservation, and of a more contented life thereby; that is to say, of getting themselves out from that miserable condition of war, which is necessarily consequent, as hath been shown in Chapter XIII, to the natural passions of men, when there is no visible power to keep them in awe, and tie them by fear of punishment to the performance of their covenants, and observation of those laws of nature set down in the fourteenth and fifteenth chapters.

For the laws of nature, as "justice," "equity," "modesty," "mercy," and, in sum, "doing to others, as we would be done to," of themselves, without the terror of some power, to cause them to be observed, are contrary to our natural passions, that carry us to partiality, pride, revenge, and the like. And covenants, without the sword, are but words, and of no strength to secure a man at all. Therefore notwithstanding the laws of nature (which every one hath then kept, when he has the will to keep them, when he can do it safely) if there be no power erected, or not great enough for our security; every man will, and may lawfully rely on his own strength and art, for caution against all other men. And in all places, where men have lived by small families, to rob and spoil one another, has been a trade, and so far from being reputed against the law of nature, that the greater spoils they gained, the greater was their honor; and men observed no other laws therein, but the laws of honor; that is, to abstain from cruelty, leaving to men their lives, and instruments of husbandry. And as small families did then; so now do cities and kingdoms which are but greater families, for their own security, enlarge their dominions, upon all pretenses of danger, and fear of invasion, or assistance that may be given to invaders, and endeavor as much as they can, to subdue, or weaken their neighbors, by open force, and secret arts, for want of other caution, justly; and are remembered for it in after ages with honor.

Nor is it the joining together of a small number of men, that gives them this security; because in small numbers, small additions on the one side or the other, make the advantage of strength so great, as is sufficient to carry the victory; and therefore gives encouragement to an invasion. The multitude sufficient to confide in for our security, is not determined by any certain number, but by comparison with the enemy we fear; and is then sufficient, when the odds of the enemy is not of so visible and conspicuous moment, to determine the event of war, as to move him to attempt.

And be there never so great a multitude; yet if their actions be directed according to their particular judgments, and particular appetites, they can expect thereby no defence, nor protection, neither against a common enemy, nor against the injuries of one another. For being distracted in opinions concerning the best use and application of their strength, they do not help but hinder one another; and reduce their strength by

The execution of King Charles I of England, 1649, engraving by Wenceslaus Holler (1607–1677). Hobbes considered this event a horrible example of what happens when the sovereign does not have absolute power. (*Library of Congress*)

mutual opposition to nothing: whereby they are easily, not only subdued by a very few that agree together; but also when there is no common enemy, they make war upon each other, for their particular interests. For if we could suppose a great multitude of men to consent in the observation of justice, and other laws of nature, without a common power to keep them all in awe; we might as well suppose all mankind to do the same; and then there neither would be, nor need to be any civil government, or commonwealth at all; because there would be peace without subjection.

Nor is it enough for the security, which men desire should last all the time of their life, that they be governed, and directed by one judgment, for a limited time; as in one battle, or one war. For though they obtain a victory by their unanimous endeavor against a foreign enemy; yet afterwards, when either they have no common enemy, or he that by one part is held for an enemy, is by another part held for a friend, they must needs by the difference of their interests dissolve, and fall again into a war amongst themselves.

It is true that certain living creatures, as bees, and ants, live sociably one with another, which are therefore by Aristotle numbered amongst political creatures; and yet have no other direction, than their particular judgments and appetites; nor speech, whereby one of them can signify to another, what he thinks expedient for the common benefit: and therefore some man may perhaps desire to know, why mankind cannot do the same. To which I answer,

First, that men are continually in competition for honor and dignity, which these creatures are not; and consequently amongst men there arises on that ground, envy and hatred, and finally war; but amongst these not so.

Secondly, that amongst these creatures, the common good differs not from the private; and being by nature inclined to their private, they procure thereby the common benefit. But man, whose joy consists in comparing himself with other men, can relish nothing but what is eminent.

Thirdly, that these creatures, having not, as man, the use of reason, do not see, nor think they see any fault, in the administration of their common business; whereas amongst men, there are very many, that think themselves wiser, and abler to govern the public, better than the rest; and these strive to reform and innovate, one this way, another that way; and thereby bring it into distraction and civil war.

Fourthly, that these creatures, though they have some use of voice, in making known to one another their desires, and other affections; yet they want that art of words, by which some men can represent to others, that which is good, in the likeness of evil; and evil, in the likeness of good; and augment, or diminish the apparent greatness of good and evil; discontenting men, and troubling their peace at their pleasure.

Fifthly, irrational creatures cannot distinguish between "injury," and "damage"; and therefore as long as they be at ease, they are not offended with their fellows: whereas man is then most troublesome, when he is most at ease: for then it is that he loves to shew his wisdom, and control the actions of them that govern the commonwealth.

Lastly, the agreement of these creatures is natural; that of men, is by covenant only, which is artificial: and therefore it is no wonder if there be somewhat else required, besides covenant, to make their agreement constant and lasting; which is a common power, to keep them in awe, and to direct their actions to the common benefit.

The only way to erect such a common power, as may be able to defend them from the invasion of foreigners, and the injuries of one another, and thereby to secure them in such sort, as that by their own industry, and by the fruits of the earth, they may nourish themselves and live contentedly; is, to confer all their power and strength upon one man, or upon one assembly of men, that may reduce all their wills, by plurality of voices, unto one will: which is as much as to say, to appoint one man, or assembly of men, to bear their person; and every one to own, and acknowledge himself to be author of whatsoever he that so bears their person, shall act, or cause to be acted, in those things which concern the common Peace and safety; and therein to submit their wills, every one to his will, and their judgments, to his judgment. This is more than consent, or concord; it is a real unity of them all, in one and the same person, made by covenant of every man with every man, in such manner, as if every man should say to every man, "I authorize and give up my right of governing myself to this man, or to this assembly of men, on this condition, that thou give up thy right to him, and authorize all his actions in like manner." This done, the multitude so united in one person, is called a COMMONWEALTH, in Latin *CIVITAS*. This is the generation of that great LEVIATHAN, or rather, to speak more reverently, of that "mortal god," to which we owe under the "immortal God," our peace and defence. For by this authority, given him by every particular man in the commonwealth, he hath the use of so much power and strength conferred on him, that by terror thereof, he is enabled to form the wills of them all, to peace at home, and mutual aid against their enemies abroad. And in him consists the essence of the commonwealth; which, to define it, "is one person, of whose acts a great multitude, by mutual covenants one with another, have made themselves every one the author, to the end he may use the strength and means of them all, as he shall think expedient, for their peace and common defence."

And he that carries this person, is called SOVEREIGN, and said to have sovereign power; and every one besides, his SUBJECT.

The attaining to this sovereign power, is by two ways. One, by natural force; as when a man makes his children, to submit themselves, and their children to his government, as being able to destroy them if they refuse; or by war subdues his enemies to his will, giving them their lives on that condition. The other, is when men agree amongst themselves, to submit to some man, or assembly of men, voluntarily, on confidence to be protected by him against all others. This latter, may be called a political commonwealth, or commonwealth by "institution"; and the former, a commonwealth by "acquisition." And first, I shall speak of a commonwealth by institution.

Chapter 18. Of the Rights of Sovereigns by Institution

A "commonwealth" is said to be "instituted," when a "multitude" of men do agree, and "covenant, every one, with every one," that to whatsoever "man," or "assembly of men," shall be given by the major part, the "right" to "present" the person of them all, that is to say, to be their "representative"; every one, as well he that "voted for it," as he that "voted against it," shall "authorize" all the actions and judgments, of that man, or assembly of men, in the same manner, as if they were his own, to the end, to live peaceably amongst themselves, and be protected against other men.

From this institution of a commonwealth are derived all the "rights," and faculties of him, or them, on whom the sovereign power is conferred by the consent of the people assembled.

First, because they covenant, it is to be understood, they are not obliged by former covenant to any thing repugnant hereunto. And consequently they that have already instituted a commonwealth, being thereby bound by covenant, to own the actions, and judgments of one, cannot lawfully make a new covenant, amongst themselves, to be obedient to any other, in any thing whatsoever, without his permission.

And therefore, they that are subjects to a monarch, cannot without his leave cast off monarchy, and return to the confusion of a disunited multitude; nor transfer their person from him that bears it, to another man, or other assembly of men: for they are bound, every man to every man, to own, and be reputed author of all, that he that already is their sovereign, shall do, and judge fit to be done: so that any one man dissenting, all the rest should break their covenant made to that man, which is injustice: and they have also every man given the sovereignty to him that bears their person; and therefore if they depose him, they take from him that which is his own, and so again it is injustice. Besides, if he that attempts to depose his sovereign, be killed, or punished by him for such attempt, he is author of his own punishment, as being by the institution, author of all his sovereign shall do: and because it is injustice for a man to do any thing, for which he may be punished by his own authority, he is also upon that title, unjust. And whereas some men have pretended for their disobedience to their sovereign, a new covenant, made, not with men, but with God; this also is unjust: for there is no covenant with God, but by mediation of somebody that represents God's person which none doth but God's lieutenant, who hath the sovereignty under God. But this pretence of covenant with God, is so evident a lie, even in the pretenders' own consciences, that it is not only an act of an unjust, but also of a vile, and unmanly disposition.

Secondly, because the right of bearing the person of them all, is given to him they make sovereign, by covenant only of one to another, and not of him to any of them; there can happen no breach of covenant on the part of the sovereign; and consequently none of his subjects, by any pretence of forfeiture, can be freed from his subjection. That he which is made sovereign makes no covenant with his subjects beforehand, is manifest; because either he must make it with the whole multitude, as one party to the covenant; or he must make a several covenant with every man. With the whole, as one party, it is impossible; because as yet they are not one person: and if he make so many several covenants as there be men, those covenants after he hath the sovereignty are void; because what act soever can be pretended by any one of them for breach thereof, is the act both of himself, and of all the rest, because done in the person, and by the right of every one of them in particular. Besides, if any one, or more of them, pretend a breach of the covenant made by the sovereign at his institution; and others, or one other of his subjects, or himself alone, pretend there was no such breach, there is in this case, no judge to decide the controversy; it returns therefore to the sword again; and every man recovers the right of protecting himself by his own strength, contrary to the design they had in the institution. It is therefore in vain to grant sovereignty by way of precedent covenant. The opinion that any monarch receives his power by covenant, that is to say, on condition, proceeds from want of understanding this easy truth, that covenants being but words and breath, have no force to oblige, contain, constrain, or protect any man, but what it has from the public sword; that is, from the untied hands of that man, or assembly of men that hath the sovereignty, and whose actions are avouched by them all, and performed by the strength of them all, in him united. But when an assembly of men is made sovereign; then no man imagines any such covenant to have passed in the institution; for no man is so dull as to say, for example, the people of Rome made a covenant with the Romans, to hold the sovereignty on such or such conditions; which not performed, the Romans might lawfully depose the Roman people. That men see not the reason to be alike in a monarchy, and in a popular government, proceeds from the ambition of some, that are kinder to the government of an assembly, whereof they may hope to participate, than of monarchy, which they despair to enjoy.

Thirdly, because the major part hath by consenting voices declared a sovereign; he that dissented must now consent with the rest—that is, be contented to avow all the actions he shall do, or else justly be destroyed by the rest. For if he voluntarily entered into the congregation of them that were assembled, he sufficiently declared thereby his will, and therefore tacitly covenanted, to stand to what the major part should ordain: and therefore if he refuse to stand thereto, or make protestation against any of their decrees, he does contrary to his covenant, and therefore unjustly. And whether he be of the congregation, or not; and whether his consent be asked, or not, he must either submit to their decrees, or be left in the condition of war he was in before; wherein he might without injustice be destroyed by any man whatsoever.

Fourthly, because every subject is by this institution author of all the actions, and judgments of the sovereign instituted; it follows, that whatsoever he doth, it can be no injury to any of his subjects; nor ought he to be by any of them accused of injustice. For he that doth anything by authority from another, doth therein no injury to him by whose authority he acts: but by this institution of a commonwealth, every particular man is author of all the sovereign doth: and consequently he that complains of injury from his sovereign, complains of that whereof he himself is author, and therefore ought not to accuse any man but himself; no nor himself of injury; because to do injury to one's self, is impossible. It is true that they that have sovereign power may commit iniquity; but not injustice, or injury in the proper signification.

Fifthly, and consequently to that which was said last, no man that hath sovereign power can justly be put to death, or otherwise in any manner by his subject punished. For seeing every subject is author of the actions of his sovereign; he punishes another for the actions committed by himself.

And because the end of this institution, is the peace and defence of them all; and whosoever has right to the end, has right to the means; it belongs of right, to whatsoever man, or assembly that hath the sovereignty, to be judge both of the means of peace and defence, and also of the hindrances, and disturbances of the same; and to do whatsoever he shall think necessary to be done, both beforehand, for the preserving of peace and security, by prevention of discord at home, and hostility from abroad; and, when peace and security are lost, for the recovery of the same. And therefore,

Sixthly, it is annexed to the sovereignty, to be judge of what opinions and doctrines are averse, and what conducing to peace; and consequently, on what occasions, how far, and what men are to be trusted withal, in speaking to multitudes of people; and who shall examine the doctrines of all books before they be published. For the actions of men proceed from their opinions; and in the well-governing of opinions, consists the well-governing of men's actions, in order to their peace, and concord. And though in matter of doctrine, nothing ought to be regarded but the truth; yet this is not repugnant to regulating the same by peace. For doctrine repugnant to peace, can no more be true, than peace and concord can be against the law of nature. It is true, that in a commonwealth, where by the negligence, or unskillfulness of governors, and teachers, false doctrines are by time generally received; the contrary truths may be generally offensive. Yet the most sudden, and rough bustling in of a new truth, that can be, does never break the peace, but only sometimes awake the war. For those men that are so remissly governed, that they dare take up arms to defend, or introduce an opinion, are still in war; and their condition not peace, but only a cessation of arms for fear of one another; and they live, as it were, in the precincts of battle continually. It belongs therefore to him that hath the sovereign power, to be judge, or constitute all judges of opinions and doctrines, as a thing necessary to peace; thereby to prevent discord and civil war.

Seventhly, is annexed to the sovereignty, the whole power of prescribing the rules, whereby every man may know, what goods he may enjoy, and what actions he may do, without being molested by any of his fellow-subjects; and this is it men call "propriety." For before constitution of sovereign power, as hath already been shown, all men had right to all things; which necessarily causes war: and therefore this propriety, being necessary to peace, and depending on sovereign power, is the act of that power, in order to the public peace. These rules of propriety, or *meum* and *tuum*, and of "good," "evil," "lawful," and "unlawful" in the actions of subjects, are the civil laws; that is to say, the laws of each commonwealth in particular; though the name of civil law be now restrained to the ancient civil laws of the city of Rome—which being the head of a great part of the world, her laws at that time were in these parts the civil law.

Eighthly, is annexed to the sovereignty, the right judicature; that is to say, of hearing and deciding all controversies, which may arise concerning law, either civil, or natural; or concerning fact. For without the decision of controversies, there is no protection of one subject, against the injuries of another; the laws concerning *meum* and *tuum* are in vain; and to every man remains, from the natural and necessary appetite of his own conservation, the right of protecting himself by his private strength, which is the condition of war, and contrary to the end for which every commonwealth is instituted.

Ninthly, is annexed to the sovereignty, the right of making war and peace with other nations, and commonwealths; that is to say, of judging when it is for the public good, and how great forces are to be assembled, armed, and paid for that end; and to levy money upon the subjects, to defray the expenses thereof. For the power by which the people are to be defended, consists in their armies; and the strength of an army, in the union of their strength under one command, which command the sovereign instituted, therefore hath; because the command of the "militia," without other institution, makes him that hath it sovereign. And therefore whosoever is made general of an army, he that hath the sovereign power is always generalissimo.

Tenthly, is annexed to the sovereignty, the choosing of all counsellors, ministers, magistrates, and officers, both in peace, and war. For seeing the sovereign is charged with the end, which is the common peace and defence, he is understood to have power to use such means, as he shall think most fit for his discharge.

Eleventhly, to the sovereign is committed the power of rewarding with riches, or honor, and of punishing with corporal or pecuniary punishment, or with ignominy, every subject according to the law he hath formerly made; or if there be no law made, according as he shall judge most to conduce to the encouraging of men to serve the commonwealth, or deterring of them from doing disservice to the same.

Lastly, considering what value men are naturally apt to set upon themselves; what respect they look for from others; and how little they value other men; from whence continually arise amongst them, emulation, quarrels, factions, and at last war, to the destroying of one another, and diminution of their strength against a common enemy; it is necessary that there be laws of honor, and a public rate of the worth of such men as have deserved, or are able to deserve well of the commonwealth; and that there be force in the hands of some or other, to put those laws in execution. But it hath already been shown, that not only the whole "militia," or forces of the commonwealth; but also the judicature of all controversies, is annexed to the sovereignty. To the sovereign therefore it belongs also to give titles of honor; and to appoint what order of place, and dignity, each man shall hold; and what signs of respect, in public or private meetings, they shall give to one another.

These are the rights, which make the essence of sovereignty, and which are the marks, whereby a man may discern in what man, or assembly of men, the sovereign power is placed, and resides. For these are incommunicable, and inseparable. The power to coin money; to dispose of the estate and persons of infant heirs; to have preemption in markets; and all other statute prerogatives, may be transferred by the sovereign; and yet the power to protect his subjects be retained. But if he transfer the "militia," he retains the judicature in vain, for want of execution of the laws: or if he grant away the power of raising money; the "militia" is in vain; or if he give away the government of doctrines, men will be frighted into rebellion with the fear of spirits. And so if we consider any one of the said rights, we shall presently see, that the holding of all the rest will produce no effect, in the conservation of peace and justice, the end for which all commonwealths are instituted. And this division is it, whereof it is said, "a kingdom divided in itself cannot stand": for unless this division precede, division into opposite armies can never happen. If there had not first been an opinion received of the greatest part of England, that these powers were divided between the King, and the Lords, and the House of Commons, the people had never been divided and fallen into this civil war; first between those that disagreed in politics; and after between the dissenters about the liberty of religion; which have so instructed men in this point of sovereign right, that there be few now in England that do not see, that these rights are inseparable, and will be so generally acknowledged at the next return of peace; and so continue, till their miseries are forgotten; and no longer, except the vulgar be better taught than they have hitherto been.

And because they are essential and inseparable rights, it follows necessarily, that in whatsoever words any of them seem to be granted away, yet if the sovereign power itself be not in direct terms renounced, and the name of sovereign no more given by the grantees to him that grants them, the grant is void: for when he has granted all he can, if we grant back the sovereignty, all is restored, as inseparably annexed thereunto.

This great authority being indivisible and inseparably annexed to the sovereignty, there is little ground for the opinion of them, that say of sovereign kings, though they be *singulis majores*, of greater power than every one of their subjects, yet they be *universis minores*, of less power than them all together. For if by "all together," they mean not the collective body as one person, then "all together," and "every one," signify the same; and the speech is absurd. But if by "all together," they understand them as one person, which person the sovereign bears, then the power of all together, is the same with the sovereign's power; and so again the speech is absurd: which absurdity they see well enough, when the sovereignty is in an assembly of the people; but in a monarch they see it not; and yet the power of sovereignty is the same in whomsoever it be placed.

And as the power, so also the honor of the sovereign, ought to be greater, than that of any, or all the subjects. For in the sovereignty is the fountain of honor. The dignities of lord, earl, duke, and prince are his creatures. As in the presence of the master, the servants are equal, and without any honor at all; so are the subjects, in the presence of the sovereign. And though they shine some more, some less, when they are out of his sight; yet in his presence, they shine no more than the stars in the presence of the sun.

But a man may here object, that the condition of subjects is very miserable; as being obnoxious to the lusts, and other irregular passions of him, or them that have so unlimited a power in their hands. And commonly they that live under a monarch, think it the fault of monarchy; and they that live under the government of democracy, or other sovereign assembly, attribute all the inconvenience to that form of commonwealth; whereas the power in all forms, if they be perfect enough to protect them, is the same: not considering that the state of man can never be without some incommodity or other; and that the greatest, that in any form of government can possibly happen to the people in general, is scarce sensible in respect of the miseries, and horrible calamities, that accompany a civil war, or that dissolute condition of masterless men, without subjection to laws, and a coercive power to tie their hands from rapine and revenge: nor considering that the greatest pressure of sovereign governors, proceeds not from any delight, or profit they can expect in the damage or weakening of their subjects, in whose vigor, consists their own strength and glory; but in the restiveness of themselves, that unwillingly contributing to their own defence, make it necessary for their governors to draw from them what they can in time of peace, that they may have means on any emergent occasion, or sudden need, to resist, or take advantage on their enemies. For all men are by nature provided of notable multiplying glasses, that is their passions and self-love, through which, every little payment appears a great grievance; but are destitute of those prospective glasses, namely moral and civil science, to see afar off the miseries that hang over them, and cannot without such payments be avoided.

*   *   *

CHAPTER 21. OF THE LIBERTY OF SUBJECTS

LIBERTY, or FREEDOM, signifies, properly, the absence of opposition; by opposition, I mean external impediments of motion; and may be applied no less to irrational, and inanimate creatures, than to rational. For whatsoever is so tied, or environed, as it cannot move but within a certain space, which space is determined by the opposition of some external body, we say it hath not liberty to go further. And so of all living creatures, whilst they are imprisoned, or restrained, with walls, or chains; and of the water whilst it is kept in by banks, or vessels, that otherwise would spread itself into a larger space, we use to say, they are not at liberty, to move in such manner, as without those external impediments they would. But when the impediment of motion, is in the constitution of the thing itself, we use not to say; it wants the liberty; but the power to move; as when a stone lies still, or a man is fastened to his bed by sickness.

And according to this proper, and generally received meaning of the word, a FREEMAN, is he, that in those things, which by his strength and wit he is able to do, is not hindered to do what he has a will to. But when the words "free," and "liberty," are applied to any thing but "bodies," they are abused; for that which is not subject to motion, is not subject to impediment: and therefore, when it is said, for example, the way is free, no liberty of the way is signified, but of those that walk in it without stop. And when we say a gift is free, there is not meant any liberty of the gift but of the giver, that was not bound by any law or covenant to give it. So when we "speak freely," it is not the liberty of voice, or pronunciation, but of the man, whom no law hath obliged to speak otherwise than he did. Lastly, from the use of the word "free-will," no liberty can be inferred of the will, desire, or inclination, but the liberty of the man; which consists in this, that he finds no stop, in doing what he has the will, desire, or inclination to do.

Fear and liberty are consistent; as when a man throws his goods into the sea for "fear" the ship should sink, he doth it nevertheless very willingly, and may refuse to do it if he will: it is therefore the action of one that was "free"; so a man sometimes pays his debt, only for "fear" of imprisonment, which because nobody hindered him from detaining, was the action of a man at "liberty." And generally all actions which men do in commonwealths, for fear of the law, are actions, which the doers had liberty to omit.

"Liberty," and "necessity" are consistent: as in the water, that hath not only "liberty," but a "necessity" of descending by the channel; so likewise in the actions which men voluntarily do: which, because they proceed from their will, proceed from liberty; and yet, because every act of man's will, and every desire, and inclination proceeds from some cause, and that from another cause, in a continual chain, whose first link is in the hand of God the first of all causes, proceed from "necessity." So that to him that could see the connection of those causes, the necessity of all men's voluntary actions, would appear manifest. And therefore God, that sees, and disposes all things, sees also that the "liberty" of man in doing what he will, is accompanied with the "necessity" of doing that which God will, and no more, nor less. For though men may do many things, which God does not command, nor is therefore author of them; yet they can have no passion, nor appetite to any thing, of which appetite God's will is not the cause. And did not his will assure the "necessity" of man's will, and consequently of all that on man's will depends, the "liberty" of men would be a contradiction, and impediment to the omnipotence and "liberty" of God. And this shall suffice, as to the matter in hand, of that natural "liberty," which only is properly called "liberty."

But as men, for the attaining of peace, and conservation of themselves thereby, have made an artificial man, which we call a commonwealth; so also have they made artificial chains, called "civil laws," which they themselves, by mutual covenants, have fastened at one end, to the lips of that man, or assembly, to whom they have given the sovereign power; and at the other end to their own ears. These bonds, in their own nature but weak, may nevertheless be made to hold, by the danger, though not by the difficulty of breaking them.

In relation to these bonds only it is, that I am to speak now, of the "liberty" of "subjects." For seeing there is no commonwealth in the world, wherein there be rules enough set down, for the regulating of all the actions, and words of men; as being a thing impossible: it follows necessarily, that in all kinds of actions by the laws pretermitted, men have the liberty, of doing what their own reasons shall suggest, for the most profitable to themselves. For if we take liberty in the proper sense, for corporal liberty; that is to say, freedom from chains and prison; it were very absurd for men to clamor as they do, for the liberty they so manifestly enjoy. Again, if we take liberty, for an exemption from laws, it is no less absurd, for men to demand as they do, that liberty, by which all other men may be masters of their lives. And yet, as absurd as it is, this is it they demand; not knowing that the laws are of no power to protect them, without a sword in the hands of a man, or men, to cause those laws to be put in execution. The liberty of a subject, lies therefore only in those things, which in regulating their actions, the sovereign hath pretermitted: such as is the liberty to buy, and sell, and otherwise contract with one another; to choose their own abode, their own diet, their own trade of life, and institute their children as they themselves think fit; and the like.

Nevertheless we are not to understand, that by such liberty, the sovereign power of life and death, is either abolished, or limited. For it has been already shown, that nothing the sovereign representative can do to a subject, on what pretence soever, can properly be called injustice, or injury; because every subject is author of every act the sovereign doth; so that he never wants right to any thing, otherwise, than as he himself is the subject of God, and bound thereby to observe the laws of nature. And therefore it may, and doth often happen in commonwealths, that a subject may be put to death, by the command of the sovereign power; and yet neither do the other wrong: as when Jephtha caused his daughter to be sacrificed: in which, and the like cases, he that so dies, had liberty to do the action, for which he is nevertheless, without injury put to death. And the same holds also in a sovereign prince, that puts to death an innocent subject. For though the action be against the law of nature, as being contrary to equity, as was the killing of Uriah, by David; yet it was not an injury to Uriah, but to God. Not to Uriah, because the right to do what he pleased was given him by Uriah himself: and yet to God, because David was God's subject, and prohibited all iniquity by the law of nature: which distinction, David himself, when he repented the fact, evidently confirmed, saying, "To thee only have I sinned." In the same manner, the people of Athens, when they banished the most potent of their commonwealth for ten years, thought they committed no injustice; and yet they never questioned what crime he had done; but what hurt he would do: nay they commanded the banishment of they knew not whom; and every citizen bringing his oystershell into the market place, written with the name of him he desired should be banished, without actually accusing him, sometimes banished an Aristides, for his reputation of justice; and sometimes a scurrilous jester, as Hyperbolus, to make a jest of it. And yet a man cannot say, the sovereign people of Athens wanted right to banish them; or an Athenian the liberty to jest, or to be just.

The liberty, whereof there is so frequent and honorable mention, in the histories, and philosophy of the ancient Greeks, and Romans, and in the writings, and discourse of those that from them have received all their learning in the politics, is not the liberty of particular men; but the liberty of the commonwealth: which is the same with that which every man then should have, if there were no civil laws, nor commonwealth at all. And the effects of it also be the same. For as amongst masterless men, there is perpetual war, of every man against his neighbor; no inheritance, to transmit to the son, nor to expect from the father; no propriety of goods, or lands; no security; but a full and absolute liberty in every particular man: so in states, and commonwealths not dependent on one another, every commonwealth, not every man, has an absolute liberty, to do what it shall judge, that is to say, what that man, or assembly that represents it, shall judge most conducing to their benefit. But withal, they live in the condition of a perpetual war, and upon the confines of battle, with their frontiers armed, and cannons planted against their neighbors round about. The Athenians, and Romans were free; that is, free commonwealths: not that any particular men had the liberty to resist their own representative; but that their representative had the liberty to resist, or invade other people. There is written on the turrets of the city of Lucca in great characters at this day, the word LIBERTAS; yet no man can thence infer, that a particular man has more liberty, or immunity from the service of the commonwealth there, than in Constantinople. Whether a commonwealth be monarchical, or popular, the freedom is still the same.

But it is an easy thing, for men to be deceived, by the specious name of liberty; and for want of judgment to distinguish, mistake that for their private inheritance, and birth-right, which is the right of the public only. And when the same error is confirmed by the authority of men in reputation for their writings on this subject, it is no wonder if it produce sedition, and change of government. In these western parts of the world, we are made to receive our opinions concerning the institution, and rights of commonwealths, from Aristotle, Cicero, and other men, Greeks and Romans, that living under popular states, derived those rights, not from the principles of nature, but transcribed them into their books, out of the practice of their own commonwealths, which were popular; as the grammarians describe the rules of language, out of the practice of the time; or the rules of poetry, out of the poems of Homer and Virgil. And because the Athenians were taught, to keep them from desire of changing their government, that they were freemen, and all that lived under monarchy were slaves; therefore Aristotle puts it down in his Politics (lib. 6. cap. ii.): "In democracy, LIBERTY is to be supposed: for it is commonly held, that no man is FREE in any other government." And as Aristotle; so Cicero, and other writers have grounded their civil doctrine, on the opinions of the Romans, who were taught to hate monarchy, at first, by them that having deposed their sovereign, shared amongst them the sovereignty of Rome; and afterwards by their successors. And by reading of these Greek, and Latin authors, men from their childhood have gotten a habit, under a false show of liberty, of favoring tumults, and of licentious controlling the actions of their sovereigns, and again of controlling those controllers; with the effusion of so much blood, as I think I may truly say, there was never any thing so dearly bought, as these western parts have bought the learning of the Greek and Latin tongues.

To come now to the particulars of the true liberty of a subject; that is to say, what are the things, which though commanded by the sovereign, he may nevertheless, without injustice, refuse to do; we are to consider, what rights we pass away, when we make a commonwealth; or, which is all one, what liberty we deny ourselves, by owning all the actions, without exception, of the man, or assembly we make our sovereign. For in the act of our "submission," consists both our "obligation," and our "liberty"; which must therefore be inferred by arguments taken from thence; there being no obligation on any man, which arises not from some act of his own; for all men equally, are by nature free. And because such arguments, must either be drawn from the express words, I "authorize all his actions," or from the intention of him that submits himself to his power, which intention is to be understood by the end for which he so submits; the obligation, and liberty of the subject, is to be derived, either from those words, or others equivalent; or else from the end of the institution of sovereignty, namely, the peace of the subjects within themselves, and their defence against a common enemy.

First therefore, seeing sovereignty by institution, is by covenant of every one to every one; and sovereignty by acquisition, by covenants of the vanquished to the victor, or child to the parent; it is manifest, that every subject has liberty in all those things, the right whereof cannot by covenant be transferred. I have shown before in the 14th chapter, that covenants, not to defend a man's own body, are void. Therefore,

If the sovereign command a man, though justly condemned, to kill, wound, or maim himself; or not to resist those that assault him; or to abstain from the use of food, air, medicine, or any other thing, without which he cannot live; yet hath that man the liberty to disobey.

If a man be interrogated by the sovereign, or his authority, concerning a crime done by himself, he is not bound, without assurance of pardon, to confess it; because no man, as I have shown in the same chapter, can be obliged by covenant to accuse himself.

Again, the consent of a subject to sovereign power, is contained in these words, "I authorize, or take upon me, all his actions"; in which there is no restriction at all, of his own former natural liberty: for by allowing him to "kill me," I am not bound to kill myself when he commands me. It is one thing to say, "kill me, or my fellow, if you please"; another thing to say, "I will kill myself, or my fellow." It follows therefore, that

No man is bound by the words themselves, either to kill himself, or any other man; and consequently, that the obligation a man may sometimes have, upon the command of the sovereign to execute any dangerous, or dishonorable office, depends not on the words of our submission; but on the intention, which is to be understood by the end thereof. When therefore our refusal to obey, frustrates the end for which the sovereignty was ordained; then there is no liberty to refuse: otherwise there is.

Upon this ground, a man that is commanded as a soldier to fight against the enemy, though his sovereign have right enough to punish his refusal with death, may nevertheless in many cases refuse, without injustice; as when he substitutes a sufficient soldier in his place: for in this case he deserts not the service of the commonwealth. And there is allowance to be made for natural timorousness; not only to women, of whom no such dangerous duty is expected, but also to men of feminine courage. When armies fight, there is on one side, or both, a running away; yet when they do it not out of treachery, but fear, they are not esteemed to do it unjustly, but dishonorably. For the same reason, to avoid battle, is not injustice, but cowardice. But he that enrolls himself a soldier, or takes imprest money, takes away the excuse of a timorous nature; and is obliged, not only to go to the battle, but also not to run from it, without his captain's leave. And when the defence of the commonwealth, requires at once the help of all that are able to bear arms, every one is obliged; because otherwise the institution of the commonwealth, which they have not the purpose, or courage to preserve, was in vain.

To resist the sword of the commonwealth, in defence of another man, guilty, or innocent, no man hath liberty; because such liberty, takes away from the sovereign, the means of protecting us; and is therefore destructive of the very essence of government. But in case a great many men together, have already resisted the sovereign power unjustly, or committed some capital crime, for which every one of them expects death, whether have they not the liberty then to join together, and assist, and defend one another? Certainly they have: for they but defend their lives, which the guilty man may as well do, as the innocent. There was indeed injustice in the first breach of their duty; their bearing of arms subsequent to it, though it be to maintain what they have done, is no new unjust act. And if it be only to defend their persons, it is not unjust at all. But the offer of pardon takes from them, to whom it is offered, the plea of self-defence, and makes their perseverance in assisting, or defending the rest, unlawful.

As for other liberties, they depend on the silence of the law. In cases where the sovereign has prescribed no rule, there the subject hath the liberty to do, or forbear, according to his own discretion. And therefore such liberty is in some places more, and in some less; and in some times more, in other times less, according as they that have the sovereignty shall think most convenient. As for example, there was a time, when in England a man might enter into his own land, and dispossess such as wrongfully possessed it, by force. But in aftertimes, that liberty of forcible entry, was taken away by a statute made, by the king, in parliament. And in some places of the world, men have the liberty of many wives: in other places, such liberty is not allowed.

If a subject have a controversy with his sovereign, of debt, or of right of possession of lands or goods, or concerning any service required at his hands, or concerning any penalty, corporal, or pecuniary, grounded on a precedent law; he hath the same liberty to sue for his right, as if it were against a subject; and before such judges, as are appointed by the sovereign. For seeing the sovereign demands by force of a former law, and not by virtue of his power; he declares thereby, that he requires no more, than shall appear to be due by that law. The suit therefore is not contrary to the will of the sovereign; and consequently the subject hath the liberty to demand the hearing of his cause; and sentence, according to that law. But if he demand, or take any thing by pretence of his power; there lies, in that case, no action of law; for all that is done by him in virtue of his power, is done by the authority of every subject, and consequently he that brings an action against the sovereign, brings it against himself.

If a monarch, or sovereign assembly, grant a liberty to all, or any of his subjects, which grant standing, he is disabled to provide for their safety, the grant is void; unless he directly renounce, or transfer the sovereignty to another. For in that he might openly, if it had been his will, and in plain terms, have renounced, or transferred it, and did not; it is to be understood it was not his will, but that the grant proceeded from ignorance of the repugnancy between such a liberty and the sovereign power; and therefore the sovereignty is still retained; and consequently all those powers, which are necessary to the exercising thereof; such as are the power of war, and peace, of judicature, of appointing officers, and councilors, of levying money, and the rest named in the eighteenth chapter.

The obligation of subjects to the sovereign, is understood to last as long, and no longer, than the power lasts, by which he is able to protect them. For the right men have by nature to protect themselves, when none else can protect them, can by no covenant be relinquished. The sovereignty is the soul of the commonwealth which once departed from the body, the members do no more receive their motion from it. The end of obedience is protection; which, wheresoever a man sees it, either in his own, or in another's sword, nature applies his obedience to it, and his endeavor to maintain it. And though sovereignty, in the intention of them that make it, be immortal; yet is it in its own nature, not only subject to violent death, by foreign war; but also through the ignorance, and passions of men, it hath in it, from the very institution, many seeds of a natural mortality, by intestine discord.

If a subject be taken prisoner in war; or his person, or his means of life be within the guards of the enemy, and hath his life and corporal liberty given him, on condition to be subject to the victor, he hath liberty to accept the condition; and having accepted it, is the subject of him that took him; because he had no other way to preserve himself. The case is the same, if he be detained on the same terms, in a foreign country. But if a man be held in prison, or bonds, or is not trusted with the liberty of his body; he cannot be understood to be bound by covenant to subjection; and therefore may, if he can, make his escape by any means whatsoever.

If a monarch shall relinquish the sovereignty, both for himself, and his heirs; his subjects return to the absolute liberty of nature; because, though nature may declare who are his sons, and who are the nearest of his kin; yet it depends on his own will, as hath been said in the precedent chapter, who shall be his heir. If therefore he will have no heir, there is no sovereignty, nor subjection. The case is the same, if he die without known kindred, and without declaration of his heir. For then there can no heir be known, and consequently no subjection be due.

If the sovereign banish his subject; during the banishment, he is not subject. But he that is sent on a message, or hath leave to travel, is still subject; but it is, by contract between sovereigns, not by virtue of the covenant of subjection. For whosoever enters into another's dominion, is subject to all the laws thereof; unless he have a privilege by the amity of the sovereigns, or by special license.

If a monarch subdued by war, render himself subject to the victor; his subjects are delivered from their former obligation, and become obliged to the victor. But if he be held prisoner, or have not the liberty of his own body; he is not understood to have given away the right of sovereignty; and therefore his subjects are obliged to yield obedience to the magistrates formerly placed, governing not in their own name, but in his. For, his right remaining, the question is only of the administration; that is to say, of the magistrates and officers; which, if he have not means to name, he is supposed to approve those, which he himself had formerly appointed.

BLAISE PASCAL
1623–1662

Blaise Pascal was the middle child of an upper-class magistrate in Clermont-Ferrand, France. His mother died when he was three years old, and five years later Pascal's father moved the family to Paris. His father, Etienne, an excellent amateur mathematician, educated young Blaise at home. Etienne first taught young Blaise Latin and Greek, deciding to wait on his own love, mathematics, until his son was older. By the age of twelve, however, Blaise had figured out many of the principles of Euclidian geometry on his own. His father finally relented and bought Blaise a copy of Euclid, which he devoured. Over the next several years, father and son attended weekly mathematical lectures and were regular guests at important intellectual salons in Paris. In 1638, the family underwent another trauma when Etienne Pascal was forced by a conflict with the powerful Cardinal Richelieu to flee Paris. However, Blaise Pascal's younger sister, Jacqueline, performed so well in a children's play for the Cardinal that their father was given a pardon and installed as tax commissioner for Rouen.

At Rouen Blaise Pascal began to concentrate on mathematics. While still a teenager, he wrote his first book (on conic sections in geometry) and developed a plan for a calculating machine to help his father with his tax work. In 1644, he built the first of the machine's several working models—no small feat given the state of metalworking at the time. Pascal's contributions to mathematics and computing machines were so important that a major contemporary programming language is named in his honor. Pascal also experimented on the nature of a vacuum showing that, contrary to Artistotle's belief, "Nature has no abhorrence of a vacuum."

In 1647 Pascal became seriously ill and returned to Paris with his younger sister to recover. Following his father's death in 1651, his sister entered a convent, leaving Pascal alone. Over the next several years Pascal seemed to drift: he out-wardly enjoying the social life of Paris as a successful mathematician and eligi-ble bachelor, but he was inwardly dissatisfied. Although he had undergone a conversion in 1646 under the influence of the Jansenists, a group of devout Catholics, Pascal still found himself without direction. On the night of Novem-ber 23, 1654, Pascal had a remarkable second conversion experience, the de-scription of which he sewed inside his coat:

> . . . From about half past ten in the evening until about half past midnight.
> Fire.
> God of Abraham, God of Isaac, God of Jacob, not of philosophers and scholars.
> Certainty, joy, certainty, emotion, sight, joy
> God of Jesus Christ. . . .
> Oblivious to the world and to everything except GOD. . . .
> This is life eternal, that they might know you,
> the only true God, and him whom you sent,
> Jesus Christ
> Jesus Christ
> I have cut myself off from him for ever. I have fled from him, denied
> him, crucified him.
> Let me never be cut off from him.
> He can only be kept by the ways taught in the Gospel.
> Sweet and total renunciation.
> Total submission to Jesus Christ and my director.
> Everlasting joy for one day's tribulation on earth.
> *I will not forget thy word.* Amen.*

Pascal committed himself to living out his faith by doing good works. He wrote a remarkable series of *Provincial Letters* defending the Jansenists against the Je-suits. Pascal also worked on one of the first regularly-scheduled public transit services, with profits for the poor; the line became operational shortly before Pascal's death in 1662. But Pascal's most important mature work was his *Apol-ogy for the Christian Religion,* the completed portion of which is now known as the *Pensées (Thoughts).*

*   *   *

Collected and published after Pascal's death at age thirty-nine, the *Pensées* is considered French classic—despite its fragmentary character. Touching on nu-merous areas of religious and philosophical thought, the *Pensées* portray human-ity "engulfed in the infinite immensity" of the universe. Unlike Descartes, Pascal claims that reason is insufficient to find certainty. While the *cogito* ("I think") is indeed one of God's greatest gift to humanity and "all our dignity consists . . . in thought," there is nevertheless something more important than thought and rea-son: the heart. As Pascal put it, "The heart has its reasons, which reason does not know."

As for knowledge of God, Pascal claims that reason is utterly insufficient for the enterprise. Against Descartes, St. Thomas Aquinas, and others, proofs for God's existence and the Christian truth "are not of such a nature that they can be

---

*"The Memorial," Blaise Pascal, *Pensées and Other Writings,* translated by Honor Levi (Oxford: Oxford University Press, 1995), p. 178.

said to be absolutely convincing." There is always "both evidence and obscurity [enough] to enlighten some and [to] confuse others." Given that one can never *know* if there is a God, how can one *live* one's life? According to Pascal, one can never have true knowledge of *anything* until one has submitted to it—and so there can be no true knowledge of God until one has submitted to God as revealed in Jesus Christ. Is there, then, no rational basis for making the Christian commitment? In the selection given here, Pascal appeals to the *bon vivants* of Paris by asking them to consider faith as a wager. If you bet your life on God and you turn out to be right, you have gained eternity. If you are wrong and there is no God, what have you lost—except the possibility of "those poisonous pleasures, glory and luxury?" But, if you bet your life against the reality of God, you gain little if correct, but lose eternally if wrong.

Some critics have argued that Pascal's Wager hardly seems like faith at all—that it is a "calculating and self-regarding attitude" and is "profoundly irreligious."* Others have claimed that the wager leads not to Christianity, but to any religion with a great reward for belief and a great penalty for disbelief. Still others argue that the most reasonable choice is to avoid wagering at all until the evidence is clear. (See the suggested readings below.) However, to be fair, Pascal never claimed the wager was the *way* to faith or that it provided the *means* for proving Christian truth. His two goals were to show that while being *supra*rational, belief is not *ir*rational and one *must* decide. As Pascal put it,

> Do not then reprove for error those who have made a choice; for you know nothing about it. "No, but I blame them for having made, not this choice, but a choice . . . The true course is not to wager at all."
>
> Yes; but you must wager. It is not optional. You are embarked. Which will you choose then?

*   *   *

There is little consistency in the numbering of different editions of the *Pensées.* The system used here is from W.F. Trotter's translation.

The best general introduction to Pascal remains J.H. Broome, *Pascal* (London: E. Arnold, 1972). Other general studies include Émile Cailliet, *Pascal: The Emergence of Genius,* 2nd edition (New York: Harper, 1961); Morris Bishop, *Pascal: The Life of a Genius* (1936; reprint Westport, CO: Greenwood Press, 1968); Jean Mesnard, *Pascal,* translated by Claude and Marcia Abraham (University, AL: University of Alabama Press, 1969); Alban Krailsheimer, *Pascal,* Past Masters Series (Oxford: Oxford University Press, 1980); and Hugh M. Davidson, *Blaise Pascal* (Boston: Twayne, 1983). More specialized studies include F.T.H. Fletcher, *Pascal and the Mystical Tradition* (Oxford: Basil Blackwell, 1954); Jan Miel, *Pascal and Theology* (Baltimore, MD: Johns Hopkins University Press, 1969); Robert James Nelson, *Pascal: Adversary and Advocate* (Cambridge, MA: Harvard University Press, 1981); Sara E. Melzer, *Discourses of the Fall: A Study of Pascal's Pensées* (Berkeley, CA: University of California Press, 1986); and Nicholas Hammond, *Playing with Truth: Language and the Human Condition in Pascal's 'Pensées'* (Oxford: Oxford University Press, 1994).

---

*John Hick, *Philosophy of Religion,* 4th edition (Englewood Cliffs, NJ: Prentice Hall, 1990), p. 59.

For discussions of Pascal's wager, see Nicholas Rescher, *Pascal's Wager: A Study of Practical Reasoning in Philosophical Theology* (Notre Dame, IN: University of Notre Dame Press, 1985) and Jeff Jordan, ed., *Gambling on God: Essays on Pascal's Wager* (Lanham, MD: Rowman & Littlefield, 1994).

PENSÉES (in part)

1. The difference between the mathematical and the intuitive minds.—In the [mathematical mind] the principles are evident, but removed from ordinary use; so that for want of habit it is difficult to turn one's mind in that direction: but if one turns it there ever so little, one sees the principles fully, and one must have a quite inaccurate mind who reasons wrongly from principles so plain that it is almost impossible they should escape notice.

But in the intuitive mind the principles are found in common use, and are before the eyes of everybody. One has only to look, and no effort is necessary; it is only a question of good eyesight, but it must be good, for the principles are so subtle and so numerous, that it is almost impossible but that some escape notice. Now the omission of one principle leads to error; thus one must have very clear sight to see all the principles, and an accurate mind not to draw false deductions from known principles. . . .

Mathematicians who are only mathematicians have exact minds, provided all things are explained to them by means of definitions and axioms; otherwise they are inaccurate and insufferable, for they are only right when the principles are quite clear.

And men of intuition who are only intuitive cannot have the patience to reach to first principles of things speculative and conceptual, which they have never seen in the world, and which are altogether out of the common.

72. The whole visible world is only an imperceptible atom in the ample bosom of nature. No idea approaches it. We may enlarge our conceptions beyond all imaginable space; we only produce atoms in comparison with the reality of things. It is an infinite sphere, the center of which is everywhere, the circumference nowhere. In short it is the greatest sensible mark of the almighty power of God, that imagination loses itself in that thought.

Returning to himself, let man consider what he is in comparison with all existence; let him regard himself as lost in this remote corner of nature and from the little cell in which he finds himself lodged. I mean the universe, let him estimate at their true value the earth, kingdoms, cities, and himself. What is a man in the Infinite?

But to show him another prodigy equally astonishing, let him examine the most delicate things he knows. Let a mite be given him, with its minute body parts incomparably more minute, limbs with their joints, veins in the limbs, blood in the veins, humors in the blood, drops in the humors, vapors in the drops. Dividing these last things again, let him exhaust his powers of conception, and let the last object at which he can arrive be now that of our discourse. Perhaps he will think that here is the smallest point in nature. I will let him see therein a new abyss. I will paint for him not only the visible universe, but all that he can conceive of nature's immensity in the womb of this abridged atom. Let him see therein an infinity of universes, each of which has its firmament, its planet, its earth, in the same proportion as in the visible world; in each earth animals, and in the last mites, in which he will find again all that the first had, finding still in these others the same thing without end and without cessation. Let him lose himself in wonders as amazing in their littleness as the others in their vastness. For who will not be astounded at the fact that our body, which a little while ago was imperceptible in the universe, itself imperceptible in the bosom of the whole, is now colossus, a world, or rather a whole, in respect of the nothingness which we cannot reach? He who regards himself in this light will be afraid of himself, and observing himself sustained in the body given him by nature between those two abysses of the Infinite and Nothing, will tremble at the sight of these marvels; and I think that, as his curiosity changes into admiration, he will be more disposed to contemplate then in silence than to examine them with presumption.

For in fact what is man in nature? A Nothing in comparison with the Infinite, and All in comparison with the Nothing, a mean between nothing and everything. Since he is infinitely removed from comprehending the extremes, the end of things and their beginning are hopelessly hidden from him in an impenetrable secret; he is equally incapable of seeing the Nothing from which he was made, and the Infinite in which he is swallowed up.

What will he do then, but perceive the appearance of the middle of things, in an eternal despair of knowing either their beginning or their end. All things proceed from the Nothing, and are borne towards the Infinite. Who will follow these marvelous processes? The Author of these wonders understands them. None other can do so.

Through failure to contemplate these Infinites, men have rashly rushed into the examination of nature, as though they bore some proportion to her. . . .

Who would not think, seeing us compose all things of mind and body, but that this mixture would be quite intelligible to us? Yet it is the very thing we least understand. Man is to himself the most wonderful object in nature; for he cannot conceive what the body is, still less what the mind is, and least of all how a body should be united to a mind. This is the consummation of his difficulties, and yet it is his very being.

77. I cannot forgive Descartes. In all his philosophy he would have been quite willing to dispense with God. But he had to make Him give a [finger snap] to set the world in motion; beyond this, he has no further need of God.

78. Descartes useless and uncertain.

82. Imagination.—It is that deceitful part in man, that mistress of error and falsity, the more deceptive because she is not always so; for she would be an infallible rule of truth, if she were an infallible rule of falsehood. But being most generally false, she gives no sign of her nature, impressing the same character on the true and the false.

I do not speak of fools, I speak of the wisest men; and it is among them that the imagination has the great gift of persuasion. Reason protests in vain; it cannot set a true value on things.

This arrogant power, the enemy of reason, who likes to rule and dominate it, has established in man a second nature to show how all-powerful she is. She makes men happy and sad, healthy and sick, rich and poor; she compels reason to believe, doubt, and deny; she blunts the senses, or quickens them; she has her fools and sages; and nothing vexes us more than to see that she fills her devotees with a satisfaction far more full and entire than does reason. Those who have a lively imagination are a great deal more pleased with themselves than the wise can reasonably be.

If the greatest philosopher in the world finds himself upon a plank wider than actually necessary, but hanging over a precipice, his imagination will prevail, though his reason convince him of his safety. Many cannot bear the thought without a cold sweat.

83. We must thus begin the chapter on the deceptive powers. Man is only a subject full of error, natural and indelible, without grace. Nothing shows him the truth. Everything deceives him. These two sources of truth, reason and the senses, besides being both wanting in sincerity, deceive each other in turn. The senses mislead the reason with false appearances, and receive from reason in their turn the same trickery which they apply to her; reason has her revenge. The passions of the soul trouble the senses, and make false impressions upon them. They rival each other in falsehood and deception.

139. When I have occasionally set myself to consider the different distractions of men, the pains and perils to which they expose themselves at court or in war, whence arise so many quarrels, passions, bold and often bad ventures, etc., I have discovered that all the unhappiness of men arises from one single fact, that they cannot stay quietly in their own chamber. A man who has enough to live on, if he knew how to stay with pleasure at home, would not leave it to go to sea or to besiege a town. A commission in the army would not be bought so dearly, but that it is found insufferable not to budge from the town; and men only seek conversation and entering games, because they cannot remain with pleasure at home.

But on further consideration, when, after finding the cause of all our ills, I have sought to discover the reason of it, I have found that there is one very real reason, namely, the natural poverty of our feeble and mortal condition, so miserable that nothing can comfort us when we think of it closely.

144. I spent a long time in the study of the abstract sciences, and was disheartened by the small number of fellow-students in them. When I commenced the study of man, I saw that these abstract sciences are not suited to man, and that I was wandering farther from my own state in examining them, than others in not knowing them. I pardoned their little knowledge; but I thought at least to find many companions in the study of man, and that it was the true study which is suited to him. I have been deceived; still fewer study it than geometry. It is only from the want of knowing how to study this that we seek the other studies. But is it not that even here is not the knowledge which man should have, and that for the purpose of happiness it is better for him not to know himself?

146. Man is obviously made to think. It is his whole dignity and his whole merit; and his whole duty is to think as he ought. Now, the order of thought is to begin with self, and with its Author and its end.

Now, of what does the world think? Never of this, but of dancing, playing the lute, singing, making verses, running at the ring etc., fighting, making oneself king, without thinking what it is to be a king and what to be a man.

148. We are so presumptuous that we would wish to be known by all the world, even by people who shall come after, when we shall be no more; and we are so vain that the esteem of five or six neighbors delights and contents us.

150. Vanity is so anchored in the heart of man that a soldier, a soldier's servant, a cook, a porter brags, and wishes to have his admirers. Even philosophers wish for them. Those who write against it want to have the glory of having written well; and those who read it desire the glory of having read it. I who write this have perhaps this desire, and perhaps those who will read it. . . .

168. Diversion.—As men are not able to fight against death, misery, ignorance, they have taken it into their heads, in order to be happy, not to think of them at all.

172. Let each one examine his thoughts, and he will find them all occupied with the past and the future. We scarcely ever think of the present; and if we think of it, it is only to take light from it to arrange the future. The present is never our end. The past and the present are our means; the future alone is our end. So we never live, but we hope to live; and, as we are always preparing to be happy, it is inevitable we should never be so.

185. The conduct of God, who disposes all things kindly, is to put religion into the mind by reason, and into the heart by grace. But to will to put it into the mind and heart by force and threats is not to put religion there, but terror. . . .

187. Order.—Men despise religion; they hate it, and fear it is true. To remedy this, we must begin by showing that religion is not contrary to reason; that it is venerable, to inspire respect for it; then we must make it lovable, to make good men hope it is true; finally, we must prove it is true.

194. . . . Let them at least learn what is the religion they attack, before attacking it. If this religion boasted of having a clear view of God, and of possessing it open and unveiled, it would be attacking it to say that we see nothing in the world which shows it with this clearness. But since, on the contrary, it says that men are in darkness and estranged from God, that He has hidden Himself from their knowledge, that this is in fact the name which He gives Himself in the Scriptures, *Deus absconditus* [hidden God]; and finally, if it endeavors equally to establish these two things: that God has set up in the Church visible signs to make Himself known to those who should seek Him sincerely, and that He has nevertheless so disguised them that He will only be perceived by those who seek Him with all their heart; . . .

We do not require great education of the mind to understand that here is no real and lasting satisfaction; that our pleasures are only vanity; that our evils are infinite; and, lastly, that death, which threatens us every moment, must infallibly place us within a few years under the dreadful necessity of being for ever either annihilated or unhappy.

There is nothing more real than this, nothing more terrible. Be we as heroic as we like, that is the end which awaits the noblest life in the world. Let us reflect on this, and then say whether it is not beyond doubt that there is no good in this life but in the hope of another; that we are happy only in proportion as we draw near it; and that, as there are no more woes for those who have complete assurance of eternity, so there is no more happiness for those who have no insight into it.

199. Let us imagine a number of men in chains, and all condemned to death, where some are killed each day in the sight of the others, and those who remain see their own

fate in that of their fellows, and wait their turn, looking at each other sorrowfully and without hope. It is an image of the condition of men.

205. When I consider the short duration of my life, swallowed up in the eternity before and after, the little space which I fill, and even can see, engulfed in the infinite immensity of spaces of which I am ignorant, and which know me not, I am frightened, and am astonished at being here rather than there; for there is no reason why here rather than there, why now rather than then. Who has put me here? By whose order and direction have this place and time been allotted to me? . . .

206. The eternal silence of these infinite spaces frightens me.

210. The last act is tragic, however happy all the rest of the play is; at the last a little earth is thrown upon our head, and that is the end for ever.

229. . . . If I saw nothing there which revealed a Divinity, I would come to a negative conclusion; if I saw everywhere the signs of a Creator, I would remain peacefully in faith. But, seeing too much to deny and too little to be sure, I am in a state to be pitied; wherefore I have a hundred times wished that if a God maintains nature, she should testify to Him unequivocally, and that, if the signs she gives are deceptive, she should suppress them altogether; that she should say everything or nothing, that I might see which cause I ought to follow. Whereas in my present state, ignorant of what I am or of what I ought to do, I know neither my condition nor my duty. My heart inclines wholly to know where is the true good, in order to follow it; nothing would be too dear to me for eternity.

I envy those whom I see living in the faith with such carelessness, and who make such a bad use of a gift of which it seems to me I would make such a different use.

230. It is incomprehensible that God should exist, and it is incomprehensible that He should not exist; that the soul should be joined to the body, and that we should have no soul; that the world should be created, and that it should not be created, etc., that original sin should be, and that it should not be.

233. [*The Wager*] . . . Let us then examine this point, and say, "God is, or He is not."

But to which side shall we incline? Reason can decide nothing here. There is an infinite chaos which separated us. A game is being played at the extremity of this infinite distance where heads or tails will turn up. What will you wager? According to reason, you can do neither the one thing nor the other; according to reason, you can defend neither of the propositions.

Do not then reprove for error those who have made a choice; for you know nothing about it. "No, but I blame them for having made, not this choice, but a choice; for again both he who chooses heads and he who chooses tails are equally at fault, they are both in the wrong. The true course is not to wager at all."

Yes; but you must wager. It is not optional. You are embarked. Which will you choose then? Let us see. Since you must choose, let us see which interests you least. You have two things to lose, the true and the good; and two things to stake, your reason and your will, your knowledge and your happiness; and your nature has two things to shun, error and misery. Your reason is no more shocked in choosing one rather than the other, since you must of necessity choose. This is one point settled. But your happiness? Let us weight the gain and the loss in wagering that God is. Let us estimate these two chances. If you gain, you gain all; if you lose, you lose nothing. Wager, then, without hesitation that He is.— "That is very fine. Yes, I must wager; but I may perhaps wager too much."—Let us see. Since there is an equal risk of gain and of loss, but if you had only to gain two lives, instead of one, you might still wager. But if there were three lives to gain, you would have to play (since you are under the necessity of playing), and you would be imprudent, when you are forced to play, not chance your life to gain three at a game where there is an equal risk of loss and gain. But there is an eternity of life and happiness. And this being so, if there were an infinity of chances, of which one only would be for you, you would still be right in wagering one to win two, and you would act stupidly, being obliged to play, by refusing to stake one life against three at a game in which out of an infinity of chances there is one for you, if there were an infinity of an infinitely happy life to gain. But there is here an infinity of an infinitely happy life to gain, a chance to gain against a finite number of chances to lose, and what you stake is finite. . . .

And so our proposition is of infinite force, when there is the finite to stake in a game where there are equal risks of gain and of loss, and the infinite to gain. This is demonstrable: and if men are capable of any truths, this is one.

"I confess it, I admit it. But, still, is there no means of seeing the faces of the cards?"—Yes, Scripture and the rest, etc. "Yes, but I have my hands tied and my mouth closed; I am forced to wager, and am not free. I am not released, and am so made that I cannot believe. What, then, would you have me do?"

True. But at least learn your inability to believe, since reason brings you to this, and yet you cannot believe. Endeavour then to convince yourself, not by increase of proofs of God, but by the abatement of your passions. You would like to attain faith, and do not know the way; you would like to cure yourself of unbelief, and ask the remedy for it. Learn of those who have been bound like you, and who now stake all their possessions. These are people who know the way which you would follow, and who are cured of an ill of which you would be cured. Follow the way by which they began; by acting as if they believed, taking the holy water, having masses said, etc. Even this will naturally make you believe, and deaden your acuteness.—"But this is what I am afraid of."—And why? What have you to lose? . . .

The end of this discourse.—Now, what harm will befall you in taking this side? You will be faithful, honest, humble, grateful, generous, a sincere friend, truthful. Certainly you will not have those poisonous pleasures, glory and luxury; but will you not have other? I will tell you that you will thereby gain in this life, and that, at each step you take on this road, you will see so great certainty of gain, so much nothingness in what you risk, that you will at last recognize that you have wagered for something certain and infinite, for which you have given nothing.

"Ah! This discourse transports me, charms me," etc.

If this discourse pleases you and seems impressive, know that it is made by a man who has knelt, both before and after it, in prayer to that Being, infinite and without parts, before whom he lays all he has, for you also to lay before Him all you have for your own good and for His glory, so that strength may be given to lowliness.

240. "I would soon have renounced pleasure," say they, "had I faith."

For my part I tell you, "You would soon have faith, if you renounced pleasure." Now, it is for you to begin. . . .

242. I admire the boldness with which these persons undertake to speak of God. In addressing their argument to infidels, their first chapter is to prove Divinity from the

works of nature. I should not be astonished at their enterprise, if they were addressing their argument to the faithful; for it is certain that those who have the living faith in their heart see at once that all existence is none other than the work of the God whom they adore. But for those in whom this light is extinguished, and in whom we purpose to rekindle it, persons destitute of faith and grace, who, seeking with all their light, whatever they see in nature that can bring them to this knowledge, find only obscurity and darkness; to tell them that they have only to look at the smallest things which surround them, and they will see God openly, to give them, as a complete proof of this great and important matter, the course of the moon and planets, and to claim to have concluded the proof with such an argument, is to give them ground for believing that the proofs of our religion are very weak. And I see by reason and experience that nothing is more calculated to arouse their contempt.

It is not after this manner that Scripture speaks, which has a better knowledge of the things that are of God. It says, on the contrary, that God is a hidden God, and that, since the corruption of nature, He has left men in a darkness from which they can escape only through Jesus Christ, without whom all communion with God is cut off. . . .

253. Two extremes: to exclude reason, to admit reason only.

277. The heart has its reasons, which reason does not know. We feel it in a thousand things. I say that the heart naturally loves the Universal Being, and also itself naturally, according as it gives itself to them; and it hardens itself against one or the other at its will. You have rejected the one, and kept the other at its will. You have rejected the one, and kept the other. Is it by reason that you love yourself?

278. It is the heart which experiences God, and not the reason. This, then, is faith: God felt by the heart, not by the reason.

Faith is a gift of God; do not believe that we said it was a gift of reasoning. Other religions do not say this of their faith. They only give reasoning in order to arrive at it, and yet it does not bring them to it.

280. The knowledge of God is very far from the love of Him.

282. We know truth, not only by the reason, but also by the heart, and it is in this last way that we know first principles; and reason, which has no part in it, tries in vain to impugn them. The skeptics, who have only this for their object, labor to no purpose. We know that we do not dream, and however impossible it is for us to prove it by reason, this inability demonstrates only the weakness of our reason, but not, as they affirm, the uncertainty of all our knowledge. For the knowledge of first principles, as space, time, motion, number, is as sure as any of those which we get from reasoning. And reason must trust these intuitions of the heart, and must base on them every argument. (We have intuitive knowledge of the tri-dimensional nature of space, and of the infinity of number, and reason then shows that there are no two square numbers one of which is double of the other. Principles are intuited, propositions are inferred, all with certainty, though in different ways.) And it is as useless and absurd for reason to demand from the heart proofs of her first principles, before admitting them, as it would be for the heart to demand from reason an intuition of all demonstrated propositions before accepting them.

This inability ought, then, to serve only to humble reason, which would judge all, but not to impugn our certainty, as if only reason were capable of instructing us.

Would to God, on the contrary, that we had never need of it, and that we knew everything by instinct and intuition! But nature has refused us this boon. On the contrary, she has given us but very little knowledge of this kind; and all the rest can be acquired only by reasoning.

Therefore, those to whom God has imparted religion by intuition are very fortunate, and justly convinced. But to those who do not have it, we can give it only by reasoning, waiting for God to give them spiritual insight, without which faith is only human, and useless for salvation.

347. Man is but a reed, the most feeble thing in nature; but he is a thinking reed. The entire universe need not arm itself to crush him. A vapor, a drop of water suffices to kill him. But, if the universe were to crush him, man would still be more noble than that which killed him, because he knows that he dies and the advantage which the universe has over him; the universe knows nothing of this.

All our dignity consists, then, in thought. By it we must elevate ourselves, and not by space and time which we cannot fill. Let us endeavour, then, to think well; this is the principle of morality.

365. Thought.—All the dignity of man consists in thought. Thought is therefore by its nature a wonderful and incomparable thing. It must have strange defects to be contemptible. But it has such, so that nothing is more ridiculous. How great it is in its nature! How vile it is in its defects!

But what is this thought? How foolish it is!

409. The greatness of man.—The greatness of man is so evident, that it is even proved by his wretchedness. For what in animals is nature we call in man wretchedness; by which we recognize that, his nature being now like that of animals, he has fallen from a better nature which once was his.

For who is unhappy at not being a king, except a deposed king? Was Paulus Aemilius unhappy at being no longer consul? On the contrary, everybody thought him happy in having been consul, because the office could only be held for a time. But men thought Perseus so unhappy in being no longer king, because the condition of kingship implied his being always king, that they thought it strange that he endured life. Who is unhappy at having only one eye? Probably no man ever ventured to mourn at not having three eyes. But any one is inconsolable at having none.

430. The greatness and the wretchedness of man are so evident that the true religion must necessarily teach us both that there is in man some great source of greatness, and a great source of wretchedness. It must then give us a reason for these astonishing contradictions. . . .

434. . . . Again, no person is certain, apart from faith, whether he is awake or sleeps, seeing that during sleep we believe that we are awake as firmly as we do when we are awake; we believe that we see space, figure, and motion; we are aware of the passage of time, we measure it; and in fact we act as if we were awake. So that half of our life being passed in sleep, we have on our own admission no idea of truth, whatever we may imagine. As all our intuitions are then illusions, who knows whether the other half of our life, in which we think we are awake, is not another sleep a little different from the former, from which we awake when we suppose ourselves asleep? . . .

What then shall man do in this state? Shall he doubt everything? Shall he doubt whether he is awake, whether he is being pinched, or whether he is being burned? Shall he doubt whether he doubts? Shall he doubt whether he exists? We cannot go so far as that; and I lay it down as a fact that there never has been a real complete skeptic. Nature sustains our feeble reason, and prevents it raving to this extent.

Shall he then say, on the contrary, that he certainly possesses truth—he who, when pressed ever so little, can show no title to it, and is forced to let go his hold?

What a chimera then is man! What a novelty! What a monster, what a chaos, what a contradiction, what a prodigy! Judge of all things, imbecile worm of the earth; depositary of truth, a sink of uncertainty and error; the pride and refuse of the universe!

Who will unravel this tangle? Nature confutes the skeptics, and reason confutes the dogmatists. What then will you become, O men! who try to find out by your natural reason what is your true condition? You cannot avoid one of these sects, nor adhere to one of them.

Know then, proud man, what a paradox you are to yourself. Humble yourself, weak reason; be silent, foolish nature; learn that man infinitely transcends man, and learn from your Master your true condition, of which you are ignorant. Hear God. . . .

555. . . . The Christian religion, then, teaches men these two truths; that there is a God whom men can know, and that there is a corruption in their nature which renders them unworthy of Him. It is equally important to men to know both these points; and it is equally dangerous for man to know God without knowing his own wretchedness, and to know his own wretchedness without knowing the Redeemer who can free him from it. The knowledge of only one of these points gives rise either to the pride of philosophers, who have known God, and not their own wretchedness, or to the despair of atheists, who know their own wretchedness, but not the Redeemer.

And, as it is alike necessary to man to know these two points, so is it alike merciful to God to have made us know them. The Christian religion does this; it is in this that it consists.

Let us herein examine the order of the world, and see if all things do not tend to establish these two chief points of this religion: Jesus Christ is the end of all, and the center to which all tends. Whoever knows Him knows the reason of everything.

Those who fall into error err only through failure to see one of these two things. We can then have an excellent knowledge of God without that of our own wretchedness, and of our own wretchedness without that of God. But we cannot know Jesus Christ without knowing at the same time both God and our own wretchedness. . . .

The God of Christians is not a God who is simply the author of mathematical truths, or of the order of the elements; that is the view of heathens and Epicureans. He is not merely a God who exercises His providence over the life and fortunes of men, to bestow on those who worship Him a long and happy life. That was the portion of the Jews. But the God of Abraham, the God of Isaac, and God of Jacob, and God of Christians, is a God of love and of comfort, a God who fills the soul and heart of those whom He possesses, a God who makes them conscious of their inward wretchedness, and His infinite mercy, who unites Himself to their inmost soul, who fills it with humility and joy, with confidence and love, who renders them incapable of any other end than Himself.

All who seek God without Jesus Christ, and who rest in nature, either find no light to satisfy them, or come to form for themselves a means of knowing God and serving Him without a mediator. Thereby they fall either into atheism, or into deism, two things which the Christian religion abhors almost equally. . . .

563. The prophecies, the very miracles and proofs of our religion, are not of such a nature that they can be said to be absolutely convincing. But they are also of such a kind that it cannot be said that it is unreasonable to believe them. Thus there is both evidence and obscurity to enlighten some and confuse others. But the evidence is such that it surpasses, or at least equals, the evidence to the contrary; so that it is not reason which can determine men not to follow it, and thus it can only be lust or malice of heart. And by this means there is sufficient evidence to condemn, and insufficient to convince; so that it appears in those who follow it, that it is grace, and not reason, which makes them follow it; and in those who shun it, that it is lust, not reason, which makes them shun it.

BARUCH SPINOZA
1632–1677

Except for Socrates himself, it would be difficult to find a philosopher who was a more highly regarded person than Benedict (Baruch) Spinoza. Like Socrates, he was not interested in power or wealth. Like Socrates, he was accused of atheism and was hounded for his unorthodox beliefs. Like Socrates, he was interested in philosophy as a way of life, not as a professional discipline.

Spinoza was born in Amsterdam the son of Jewish refugees who had fled from Portugal to escape persecution. As a young man, he was trained in Jewish tradition under a celebrated Talmudist, Saul Levi Morteira. He later studied with Manasseh ben Israel, the man who persuaded Cromwell to allow Jews to return to England, and with a Dutch physician, Franz van der Ende.

As a Jew, Spinoza was an outsider in Holland—not even entitled to citizenship because of his faith. As an original thinker, Spinoza soon became an outsider within the Jewish community as well. He was accused of heresy by the synagogue of Amsterdam and required to disavow his teachings. Spinoza refused and was officially excommunicated in 1656, when he was twenty-three years old. (In the twentieth century, the new state of Israel formally revoked the ban.)

With no wish to join any other religious community, Spinoza left Amsterdam and eventually settled in The Hague. He lived very simply, supporting himself by grinding and polishing lenses, a craft he had adopted out of respect for the Jewish tradition, which required scholars to learn a trade.

Spinoza published only two works during his lifetime. His first work was *Principles of Descartes' Philosophy* (1663), which critically examined the presuppositions and structure of Descartes' system. Using what later came to be called "higher criticism," his second book, *Theological-Political Treatise* (1670), subjected Scripture to rational analysis. He concluded that the Bible does not aim at truth but at pious and obedient behavior. Writing soon after the Thirty Years War (1618–1648), he proposed that religion and truth be separated altogether. This separation, he believed, would be the best safeguard against fanaticism. And pious conduct flourishes best in an atmosphere of free speech.

His *Theological-Political Treatise* attracted a great deal of criticism. It also brought an invitation to the chair of philosophy at the University of Heidelberg, Germany. Although the invitation included a guarantee of academic freedom, Spinoza rejected it out of his passion for freedom to speak and write as he saw fit.

The rigor of his simple life, with the glass dust of his trade, hastened his death from consumption at the age of forty-four, two years before Hobbes died at ninety-one. Immediately following his death, Spinoza's other works, including *Political Treatise* (which supports individual liberty, religious tolerance, and democracy), *On the Improvement of the Intellect*, and his masterpiece, *Ethics*, were published.

*   *   *

Whereas Descartes and Hobbes used the geometrical *method*, Spinoza used geometrical *form* as well. The *Ethics* is presented as a geometrical system, developing propositions from axioms and definitions.

In Books I and II of his *Ethics,* reprinted here in the E. Curley translation, Spinoza explores God and the nature and origin of mind. He begins by accepting Descartes' idea that "infinite substance" is completely independent and necessary. But he claims that Descartes had contradicted himself by allowing for "finite substances" as well. Instead, Spinoza claims that there could only be one substance: God. God exists necessarily and as God is the only substance, what we call "Nature" is also God. This also means that whatever happens is necessary (though individuals are often confused and do not understand the connections).

Although God is the only substance, God has infinite attributes. The only two divine attributes we can know are thought (of which minds are modifications) and extension (of which bodies are modifications). To Spinoza, Descartes was wrong to present mind and body as two separate substances (with all the concomitant problems of interaction). Instead, says Spinoza, body and mind are both attributes of the One substance. Thinking substance and extended substance are really the same substance.

In Books III to V of the *Ethics*, Spinoza argues that we must free ourselves from the tyranny of the passions. The key to this freedom is an understanding of God that allows us to see the necessary, rational structure of reality: "The more this knowledge, that things are necessary, is applied to particular things . . . the greater is the power of the mind over the emotions." The final goal of this knowledge is "blessedness," which consists of intellectual love towards God. This program of overcoming the passions by reason may be difficult, but Spinoza concludes that "all things excellent are as difficult as they are rare" (an apt description of Spinoza's classic).

*   *   *

For a general introduction to Spinoza's life and thought, see Stuart Hampshire, *Spinoza* (Baltimore, MD: Penguin Books, 1952); Henry E. Allison, *Benedict De Spinoza*, rev. ed. (New Haven, CT: Yale University Press, 1987); Alan Donagan, *Spinoza* (Chicago: University of Chicago Press, 1988); and Herman De Dijn, *Spinoza:*

The Way to Wisdom (West Lafayette, IN: Purdue University Press, 1996). For an interesting study of Spinoza's thought in relation to the other Continental rationalists, see John Cottingham, *The Rationalists* (Oxford: Oxford University Press, 1988). The generally accepted "classic" commentary on the *Ethics* remains Harry Austryn Wolfson, *The Philosophy of Spinoza: Unfolding the Latent Processes of His Reasoning* (1934; reprint New York: Schocken, 1969). For more recent discussions of Spinoza's *Ethics,* see Jonathan Bennett, *A Study of Spinoza's Ethics* (Indianapolis, IN: Hackett, 1984); Edwin Curley, *Behind the Geometrical Method: A Reading of Spinoza's Ethics* (Princeton, NJ: Princeton University Press, 1988); and Genevieve Lloyd, *Spinoza and the Ethics* (Oxford: Routledge, 1996). For collections of essays on Spinoza, see S. Paul Kashap, ed., *Studies in Spinoza* (Berkeley: University of California Press, 1972); Robert W. Shahan and J.I. Biro, eds., *Spinoza: New Perspectives* (Norman, OK: University of Oklahoma Press, 1978); Richard Kennington, ed., *The Philosophy of Baruch Spinoza* (Washington, DC: Catholic University of America Press, 1980); Vere Chappell, ed., *Essays on Early Modern Philosophers: Baruch De Spinoza* (Hamden, CT: Garland, 1992); Graeme Hunter, ed., *Spinoza: The Enduring Questions* (Toronto: University of Toronto Press, 1994); and Don Garrett, ed., *The Cambridge Companion to Spinoza* (Cambridge: Cambridge University Press, 1995); and Warren Montag and Ted Stolze, eds., *The New Spinoza* (Minneapolis, MN: University of Minnesota Press, 1998). Richard Mason, *The God of Spinoza: A Philosophical Study* (Cambridge: Cambridge University Press, 1997) is a study of Spinoza's philosophy of religion while the Jewish character of Spinoza's thought is discussed in Yirmiyahu Yovel's pair of books, *The Marrano of Reason* and *The Adventures of Immanence* (both Princeton, NJ: Princeton University Press, 1991) and Steven Smith, *Spinoza, Liberalism, and the Question of Jewish Identity* (New Haven, CT: Yale University Press, 1997).

ETHICS (in part)

FIRST PART OF THE ETHICS

ON GOD

Definitions

D1: By cause of itself I understand that whose essence involves existence, or that whose nature cannot be conceived except as existing.

D2: That thing is said to be finite in its own kind that can be limited by another of the same nature.

Baruch Spinoza, *Ethics* from *Collected Works of Spinoza,* Vol. 1, edited and translated by Edwin Curley (Princeton, NJ: Princeton University Press, 1985). © 1985 by Princeton University Press. Reprinted by permission of Princeton University Press. [Material within square brackets is from *De Nagelate Schriften van B.D.S.,* a later edition of the *Ethics,* and is included by Curley in the primary text.]

For example, a body is called finite because we always conceive another that is greater. Thus a thought is limited by another thought. But a body is not limited by a thought nor a thought by a body.

D3: By substance I understand what is in itself and is conceived through itself, i.e., that whose concept does not require the concept of another thing, from which it must be formed.

D4: By attribute I understand what the intellect perceives of a substance, as constituting its essence.

D5: By mode I understand the affections of a substance, or that which is in another through which it is also conceived.

D6: By God I understand a being absolutely infinite, i.e., a substance consisting of an infinity of attributes, of which each one expresses an eternal and infinite essence.
    Exp.: I say absolutely infinite, not infinite in its own kind; for if something is only infinite in its own kind, we can deny infinite attributes of it [(i.e., we can conceive infinite attributes which do not pertain to its nature)]; but if something is absolutely infinite, whatever expresses essence and involves no negation pertains to its essence.

D7: That thing is called free which exists from the necessity of its nature alone, and is determined to act by itself alone. But a thing is called necessary, or rather compelled, which is determined by another to exist and to produce an effect in a certain and determinate manner.

D8: By eternity I understand existence itself, insofar as it is conceived to follow necessarily from the definition alone of the eternal thing.
    Exp.: For such existence, like the essence of a thing, is conceived as an eternal truth, and on that account cannot be explained by duration or time, even if the duration is conceived to be without beginning or end.

Axioms

A1: Whatever is, is either in itself or in another.

A2: What cannot be conceived through another, must be conceived through itself.

A3: From a given determinate cause the effect follows necessarily; and conversely, if there is no determinate cause, it is impossible for an effect to follow.

A4: The knowledge of an effect depends on, and involves, the knowledge of its cause.

A5: Things that have nothing in common with one another also cannot be understood through one another, or the concept of the one does not involve the concept of the other.

A6: A true idea must agree with its object.

A7: If a thing can be conceived as not existing, its essence does not involve existence.

P1: *A substance is prior in nature to its affections.*
    Dem.: This is evident from D3 and D5.

P2: *Two substances having different attributes have nothing in common with one another.*
    Dem.: This is also evident from D3. For each must be in itself and be conceived through itself, *or* the concept of the one does not involve the concept of the other.

P3: *If things have nothing in common with one another, one of them cannot be the cause of the other.*
    Dem.: If they have nothing in common with one another, then (by A5) they cannot be understood through one another, and so (by A4) one cannot be the cause of the other, q.e.d.*

P4: *Two or more distinct things are distinguished from one another, either by a difference in the attributes of the substances or by a difference in their affections.*
    Dem.: Whatever is, is either in itself or in another (by A1), i.e. (by D3 and D5), outside the intellect there is nothing except substances and their affections. Therefore, there is nothing outside the intellect through which a number of things can be distinguished from one another except substances, or what is the same (by D4), their attributes, and their affections, q.e.d.

P5: *In nature there cannot be two or more substances of the same nature or attribute.*
    Dem.: If there were two or more distinct substances, they would have to be distinguished from one another either by a difference in their attributes, or by a difference in their affections (by P4). If only by a difference in their attributes, then it will be conceded that there is only one of the same attribute. But if by a difference in their affections, then since a substance is prior in nature to its affections (by P1), if the affections are put to one side and [the substance] is considered in itself, i.e. (by D3 and A6), considered truly, one cannot be conceived to be distinguished from another, i.e. (by P4), there cannot be many, but only one [of the same nature or attribute], q.e.d.

P6: *One substance cannot be produced by another substance.*
    Dem.: In nature there cannot be two substances of the same attribute (by P5), i.e. (by P2), which have something in common with each other. Therefore (by P3) one cannot be the cause of the other, or cannot be produced by the other, q.e.d.
    Cor.: From this it follows that a substance cannot be produced by anything else. For in nature there is nothing except substances and their affections, as is evident from A1, D3, and D5. But it cannot be produced by a substance (by P6). Therefore, substance absolutely cannot be produced by anything else, q.e.d.
    Alternatively: This is demonstrated even more easily from the absurdity of its contradictory. For if a substance could be produced by something else, the knowledge of it would have to depend on the knowledge of its cause (by A4). And so (by D3) it would not be a substance.

---

*[*quod erat demonstandum*—"which was to be demonstrated"]

P7: *It pertains to the nature of a substance to exist.*

Dem.: A substance cannot be produced by anything else (by P6C); therefore it will be the cause of itself, i.e. (by D1), its essence necessarily involves existence, or it pertains to its nature to exist, q.e.d.

P8: *Every substance is necessarily infinite.*

Dem.: A substance of one attribute does not exist unless it is unique (P5), and it pertains to its nature to exist (P7). Of its nature, therefore, it will exist either as finite or as infinite. But not as finite. For then (by D2) it would have to be limited by something else of the same nature, which would also have to exist necessarily (by P7), and so there would be two substances of the same attribute, which is absurd (by P5). There-fore, it exists as infinite, q.e.d.

Schol. 1: Since being finite is really, in part, a negation, and being infinite is an absolute affirmation of the existence of some nature, it follows from P7 alone that every substance must be infinite. [For if we assumed a finite substance, we would, in part, deny existence to its nature, which (by P7) is absurd.]

Schol. 2: I do not doubt that the demonstration of P7 will be difficult to conceive for all who judge things confusedly, and have not been accustomed to know things through their first causes—because they do not distinguish between the modifications of substances and the substances themselves, nor do they know how things are pro-duced. So it happens that they fictitiously ascribe to substances the beginning which they see that natural things have; for those who do not know the true causes of things confuse everything and without any conflict of mind feign that both trees and men speak, imagine that men are formed both from stones and from seed, and that any form whatever is changed into any other. So also, those who confuse the divine nature with the human easily ascribe human affects to God, particularly so long as they are also ig-norant of how those affects are produced in the mind.

But if men would attend to the nature of substance, they would have no doubt at all of the truth of P7. Indeed, this proposition would be an axiom for everyone, and would be numbered among the common notions. For by substance they would under-stand what is in itself and is conceived through itself, i.e., that the knowledge of which does not require the knowledge of any other thing. But by modifications they would understand what is in another, those things whose concept is formed from the concept of the thing in which they are.

This is how we can have true ideas of modifications which do not exist; for though they do not actually exist outside the intellect, nevertheless their essences are comprehended in another in such a way that they can be conceived through it. But the truth of substances is not outside the intellect unless it is in them themselves, because they are conceived through themselves.

Hence, if someone were to say that he had a clear and distinct, i.e., true, idea of a substance, and nevertheless doubted whether such a substance existed, that would in-deed be the same as if he were to say that he had a true idea, and nevertheless doubted whether it was false (as is evident to anyone who is sufficiently attentive). Or if some-one maintains that a substance is created, he maintains at the same time that a false idea has become true. Of course nothing more absurd can be conceived. So it must be confessed that the existence of a substance, like its essence, is an eternal truth.

And from this we can infer in another way that there is only one [substance] of the same nature, which I have considered it worth the trouble of showing here. But to do this in order, it must be noted,

    I. that the true definition of each thing neither involves nor expresses anything except the nature of the thing defined.

From which it follows,

    II. that no definition involves or expresses any certain number of individuals,

since it expresses nothing other than the nature of the thing defined. E.g., the definition of the triangle expresses nothing but the simple nature of the triangle, but not any certain number of triangles. It is to be noted,

    III. that there must be, for each existing thing, a certain cause on account of which it exists.

Finally, it is to be noted,

    IV. that this cause, on account of which a thing exists, either must be contained in the very nature and definition of the existing thing (viz. that it pertains to its nature to exist) or must be outside it.

From these propositions it follows that if, in nature, a certain number of individuals exists, there must be a cause why those individuals, and why neither more nor fewer, exist.

    For example, if 20 men exist in nature (to make the matter clearer, I assume that they exist at the same time, and that no others previously existed in nature), it will not be enough (i.e., to give a reason why 20 men exist) to show the cause of human nature in general; but it will be necessary in addition to show the cause why not more and not fewer than 20 exist. For (by III) there must necessarily be a cause why each [particular man] exists. But this cause (by II and III) cannot be contained in human nature itself, since the true definition of man does not involve the number 20. So (by IV) the cause why these 20 men exist, and consequently, why each of them exists, must necessarily be outside each of them.

    For that reason it is to be inferred absolutely that whatever is of such a nature that there can be many individuals [of that nature] must, to exist, have an external cause to exist. Now since it pertains to the nature of a substance to exist (by what we have already shown in this Scholium), its definition must involve necessary existence, and consequently its existence must be inferred from its definition alone. But from its definition (as we have shown from II and III) the existence of a number of substances cannot follow. Therefore it follows necessarily from this, that there exists only one of the same nature, as was proposed.

P9: *The more reality or being each thing has, the more attributes belong to it.*
    Dem.: This is evident from D4.

P10: *Each attribute of a substance must be conceived through itself.*
    Dem.: For an attribute is what the intellect perceives concerning a substance, as constituting its essence (by D4); so (by D3) it must be conceived through itself, q.e.d.
    Schol.: From these propositions it is evident that although two attributes may be conceived to be really distinct (i.e., one may be conceived without the aid of the other),

we still cannot infer from that that they constitute two beings, *or* two different substances. For it is of the nature of a substance that each of its attributes is conceived through itself, since all the attributes it has have always been in it together, and one could not be produced by another, but each expresses the reality, *or* being of substance.

So it is far from absurd to attribute many attributes to one substance. Indeed, nothing in nature is clearer than that each being must be conceived under some attribute, and the more reality, or being it has, the more it has attributes which express necessity, *or* eternity, and infinity. And consequently there is also nothing clearer than that a being absolutely infinite must be defined (as we taught in D6) as a being that consists of infinite attributes, each of which expresses a certain eternal and infinite essence.

But if someone now asks by what sign we shall be able to distinguish the diversity of substances, let him read the following propositions, which show that in Nature there exists only one substance, and that it is absolutely infinite. So that sign would be sought in vain.

P11: *God, or a substance consisting of infinite attributes, each of which expresses eternal and infinite essence, necessarily exists.*

Dem.: If you deny this, conceive, if you can, that God does not exist. Therefore (by A7) his essence does not involve existence. But this (by P7) is absurd. Therefore God necessarily exists, q.e.d.

Alternatively: For each thing there must be assigned a cause, or reason, as much for its existence as for its nonexistence. For example, if a triangle exists, there must be a reason *or* cause why it exists; but if it does not exist, there must also be a reason or cause which prevents it from existing, *or* which takes its existence away.

But this reason, *or* cause, must either be contained in the nature of the thing, or be outside it. E.g., the very nature of a square circle indicates the reason why it does not exist, viz. because it involves a contradiction. On the other hand, the reason why a substance exists also follows from its nature alone, because it involves existence (see P7). But the reason why a circle or triangle exists, or why it does not exist, does not follow from the nature of these things, but from the order of the whole of corporeal Nature. For from this [order] it must follow either that the triangle necessarily exists now or that it is impossible for it to exist now.

These things are evident through themselves, but from them it follows that a thing necessarily exists if there is no reason or cause which prevents it from existing. Therefore, if there is no reason or cause which prevents God from existing, or which takes his existence away, it must certainly be inferred that he necessarily exists.

But if there were such a reason, *or* cause, it would have to be either in God's very nature or outside it, i.e., in another substance of another nature. For if it were of the same nature, that very supposition would concede that God exists. But a substance which was of another nature [than the divine] would have nothing in common with God (by P2), and therefore could neither give him existence nor take it away.

Since, then, there can be, outside the divine nature, no reason, *or* cause, which takes away the divine existence, the reason will necessarily have to be in his nature itself, if indeed he does not exist. That is, his nature would involve a contradiction [as in our second Example]. But it is absurd to affirm this of a Being absolutely infinite and supremely perfect. Therefore, there is no cause, *or* reason, either in God or outside God, which takes his existence away. And therefore, God necessarily exists, q.e.d.

Alternatively: To be able not to exist is to lack power, and conversely, to be able to exist is to have power (as is known through itself). So, if what now necessarily exists are only finite beings, then finite beings are more powerful than an absolutely infinite Being. But this, as is known through itself, is absurd. So, either nothing exists or an absolutely infinite Being also exists. But we exist, either in ourselves, or in something else, which necessarily exists (see A1 and P7). Therefore an absolutely infinite Being—i.e. (by D6), God—necessarily exists, q.e.d.

Schol.: In this last demonstration I wanted to show God's existence a posteriori, so that the demonstration would be perceived more easily—but not because God's existence does not follow a priori from the same foundation. For since being able to exist is power, it follows that the more reality belongs to the nature of a thing, the more powers it has, of itself, to exist. Therefore, an absolutely infinite Being, *or* God, has, of himself, an absolutely infinite power of existing. For that reason, he exists absolutely.

Still, there may be many who will not easily be able to see how evident this demonstration is, because they have been accustomed to contemplate only those things that flow from external causes. And of these, they see that those which quickly come to be, i.e., which easily exist, also easily perish. And conversely, they judge that those things to which they conceive more things to pertain are more difficult to do, i.e., that they do not exist so easily. But to free them from these prejudices, I have no need to show here in what manner this proposition—*what quickly comes to be, quickly perishes*—is true, nor whether or not all things are equally easy in respect to the whole of Nature. It is sufficient to note only this, that I am not here speaking of things that come to be from external causes, but only of substances that (by P6) can be produced by no external cause.

For things that come to be from external causes—whether they consist of many parts or of few—owe all the perfection or reality they have to the power of the external cause; and therefore their existence arises only from the perfection of their external cause, and not from their own perfection. On the other hand, whatever perfection substance has is not owed to any external cause. So its existence must follow from its nature alone; hence its existence is nothing but its essence.

Perfection, therefore, does not take away the existence of a thing, but on the contrary asserts it. But imperfection takes it away. So there is nothing of whose existence we can be more certain than we are of the existence of an absolutely infinite, or perfect, Being—i.e., God. For since his essence excludes all imperfection, and involves absolute perfection, by that very fact it takes away every cause of doubting his existence, and gives the greatest certainty concerning it. I believe this will be clear even to those who are only moderately attentive.

P12: *No attribute of a substance can be truly conceived from which it follows that the substance can be divided.*

Dem.: For the parts into which a substance so conceived would be divided either will retain the nature of the substance or will not. If the first [viz. they retain the nature of the substance], then (by P8) each part will have to be infinite, and (by P7) its own cause, and (by P5) each part will have to consist of a different attribute. And so many substances will be able to be formed from one, which is absurd (by P6). Furthermore, the parts (by P2) would have nothing in common with their whole, and the whole (by D4 and P10) could both be and be conceived without its parts, which is absurd, as no one will be able to doubt.

But if the second is asserted, viz. that the parts will not retain the nature of substance, then since the whole substance would be divided into equal parts, it would lose the nature of substance, and would cease to be, which (by P7) is absurd.

P13: *A substance which is absolutely infinite is indivisible.*

Dem.: For if it were divisible, the parts into which it would be divided will either retain the nature of an absolutely infinite substance or they will not. If the first, then there will be a number of substances of the same nature, which (by P5) is absurd. But if the second is asserted, then (as above [P12]), an absolutely infinite substance will be able to cease to be, which (by P11) is also absurd.

Cor.: From these [propositions] it follows that no substance, and consequently no corporeal substance, insofar as it is a substance, is divisible.

Schol.: That substance is indivisible, is understood more simply merely from this, that the nature of substance cannot be conceived unless as infinite, and that by a part of substance nothing can be understood except a finite substance, which (by P8) implies a plain contradiction.

P14: *Except God, no substance can be or be conceived.*

Dem.: Since God is an absolutely infinite being, of whom no attribute which expresses an essence of substance can be denied (by D6), and he necessarily exists (by P11), if there were any substance except God, it would have to be explained through some attribute of God, and so two substances of the same attribute would exist, which (by P5) is absurd. And so except God, no substance can be or, consequently, be conceived. For if it could be conceived, it would have to be conceived as existing. But this (by the first part of this demonstration) is absurd. Therefore, except for God no substance can be or be conceived, q.e.d.

Cor. 1: From this it follows most clearly, first, that God is unique, i.e. (by D6), that in Nature there is only one substance, and that it is absolutely infinite (as we indicated in P10S).

Cor. 2: It follows, second, that an extended thing and a thinking thing are either attributes of God, or (by A1) affections of God's attributes.

P15: *Whatever is, is in God, and nothing can be or be conceived without God.*

Dem.: Except for God, there neither is, nor can be conceived, any substance (by P14), i.e. (by D3), thing that is in itself and is conceived through itself. But modes (by D5) can neither be nor be conceived without substance. So they can be in the divine nature alone, and can be conceived through it alone. But except for substances and modes there is nothing (by A1). Therefore, [everything is in God and] nothing can be or be conceived without God, q.e.d.

Schol.: [I.] There are those who feign a God, like man, consisting of a body and a mind, and subject to passions. But how far they wander from the true knowledge of God, is sufficiently established by what has already been demonstrated. Them I dismiss. For everyone who has to any extent contemplated the divine nature denies that God is corporeal. They prove this best from the fact that by body we understand any quantity, with length, breadth, and depth, limited by some certain figure. Nothing more absurd than this can be said of God, viz. of a being absolutely infinite.

But meanwhile, by the other arguments by which they strive to demonstrate this same conclusion they clearly show that they entirely remove corporeal, *or* extended, substance itself from the divine nature. And they maintain that it has been created by God. But by what divine power could it be created? They are completely ignorant of that. And this shows clearly that they do not understand what they themselves say.

At any rate, I have demonstrated clearly enough—in my judgment, at least—that no substance can be produced or created by any other (see P6C and P8S2). Next, we have shown (P14) that except for God, no substance can either be or be conceived, and hence [in P14C2] we have concluded that extended substance is one of God's infinite attributes. But to provide a fuller explanation, I shall refute my opponents' arguments, which all reduce to these.

[II.] *First*, they think that corporeal substance, insofar as it is substance, consists of parts. And therefore they deny that it can be infinite, and consequently, that it can pertain to God. They explain this by many examples, of which I shall mention one or two.

[i] If corporeal substance is infinite, they say, let us conceive it to be divided in two parts. Each part will be either finite or infinite. If the former, then an infinite is composed of two finite parts, which is absurd. If the latter [i.e., if each part is infinite], then there is one infinite twice as large as another, which is also absurd. [ii] Again, if an infinite quantity is measured by parts [each] equal to a foot, it will consist of infinitely many such parts, as it will also, if it is measured by parts [each] equal to an inch. And therefore, one infinite number will be twelve times greater than another [which is no less absurd]. [iii] Finally, if we conceive that from one point of a certain infinite quantity two lines, say AB and AC, are extended to infinity, it is certain that, although in the beginning they are a certain, determinate distance apart, the distance between B and C is continuously increased, and at last, from being determinate, it will become indeterminable.

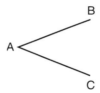

Since these absurdities follow—so they think—from the fact that an infinite quantity is supposed, they infer that corporeal substance must be finite, and consequently cannot pertain to God's essence.

[III.] Their *second* argument is also drawn from God's supreme perfection. For God, they say, since he is a supremely perfect being, cannot be acted on. But corporeal substance, since it is divisible, can be acted on. It follows, therefore, that it does not pertain to God's essence.

[IV.] These are the arguments which I find authors using, to try to show that corporeal substance is unworthy of the divine nature, and cannot pertain to it. But anyone who is properly attentive will find that I have already replied to them, since these arguments are founded only on their supposition that corporeal substance is composed of parts, which I have already (P12 and P13C) shown to be absurd. And then anyone who wishes to consider the matter rightly will see that all those absurdities (*if indeed they are all absurd, which I am not now disputing*), from which they wish to infer that extended substance is finite, do not follow at all from the fact that an infinite quantity is supposed, but from the fact that they suppose an infinite quantity to be measurable and composed of finite parts. So from the absurdities which follow from that they can infer only that infinite quantity is not measurable, and that it is not composed of finite parts. This is the same thing we have already demonstrated above (P12, etc.). So the weapon they aim at us, they really turn against themselves.

If, therefore, they still wish to infer from this absurdity of theirs that extended substance must be finite, they are indeed doing nothing more than if someone feigned that a circle has the properties of a square, and inferred from that the circle has no center, from which all lines drawn to the circumference are equal. For corporeal substance, which cannot be conceived except as infinite, unique, and indivisible (see P8, 5 and 12), they conceive to be composed of finite parts, to be many, and to be divisible, in order to infer that it is finite.

So also others, after they feign that a line is composed of points, know how to invent many arguments, by which they show that a line cannot be divided to infinity. And indeed it is no less absurd to assert that corporeal substance is composed of bodies, or parts, than that a body is composed of surfaces, the surfaces of lines, and the lines, finally, of points.

All those who know that clear reason is infallible must confess this—particularly those who deny that there is a vacuum. For if corporeal substance could be so divided that its parts were really distinct, why, then, could one part not be annihilated, the rest remaining connected with one another as before? And why must they all be so fitted together that there is no vacuum? Truly, of things which are really distinct from one another, one can be, and remain in its condition, without the other. Since, therefore, there is no vacuum in nature (a subject I discuss elsewhere), but all its parts must so concur that there is no vacuum, it follows also that they cannot be really distinguished, i.e., that corporeal substance, insofar as it is a substance, cannot be divided.

[V.] If someone should now ask why we are, by nature, so inclined to divide quantity, I shall answer that we conceive quantity in two ways: abstractly, or superficially, as we [commonly] imagine it, *or* as substance, which is done by the intellect alone [without the help of the imagination]. So if we attend to quantity as it is in the imagination, which we do often and more easily, it will be found to be finite, divisible, and composed of parts; but if we attend to it as it is in the intellect, and conceive it insofar as it is a substance, which happens [seldom and] with great difficulty, then (as we have already sufficiently demonstrated) it will be found to be infinite, unique, and indivisible.

This will be sufficiently plain to everyone who knows how to distinguish between the intellect and the imagination—particularly if it is also noted that matter is everywhere the same, and that parts are distinguished in it only insofar as we conceive matter to be affected in different ways, so that its parts are distinguished only modally, but not really.

For example, we conceive that water is divided and its parts separated from one another—insofar as it is water, but not insofar as it is corporeal substance. For insofar as it is substance, it is neither separated nor divided. Again, water, insofar as it is water, is generated and corrupted, but insofar as it is substance, it is neither generated nor corrupted.

[VI.] And with this I think I have replied to the second argument also, since it is based on the supposition that matter, insofar as it is substance, is divisible, and composed of parts. Even if this [reply] were not [sufficient], I do not know why [divisibility] would be unworthy of the divine nature. For (by P14) apart from God there can be no substance by which [the divine nature] would be acted on. All things, I say, are in God, and all things that happen, happen only through the laws of God's infinite nature and follow (as I shall show) from the necessity of his essence. So it cannot be said in any way that God is acted on by another, or that extended substance is unworthy of the divine nature, even if it is supposed to be divisible, so long as it is granted to be eternal and infinite. But enough of this for the present.

P16: *From the necessity of the divine nature there must follow infinitely many things in infinitely many modes (i.e., everything which can fall under an infinite intellect).*

Dem.: This Proposition must be plain to anyone, provided he attends to the fact that the intellect infers from the given definition of any thing a number of properties that really do follow necessarily from it (i.e., from the very essence of the thing); and that it infers more properties the more the definition of the thing expresses reality, i.e., the more reality the essence of the defined thing involves. But since the divine nature has absolutely infinite attributes (by D6), each of which also expresses an essence infinite in its own kind, from its necessity there must follow infinitely many things in infinite modes (i.e., everything which can fall under an infinite intellect), q.e.d.

Cor. 1: From this it follows that God is the efficient cause of all things which can fall under an infinite intellect.

Cor. 2: It follows, secondly, that God is a cause through himself and not an accidental cause.

Cor. 3: It follows, thirdly, that God is absolutely the first cause.

P17: *God acts from the laws of his nature alone, and is compelled by no one.*

Dem.: We have just shown (P16) that from the necessity of the divine nature alone, or (what is the same thing) from the laws of his nature alone, absolutely infinite things follow, and in P15 we have demonstrated that nothing can be or be conceived without God, but that all things are in God. So there can be nothing outside him by which he is determined or compelled to act. Therefore, God acts from the laws of his nature alone, and is compelled by no one, q.e.d.

Cor. 1: From this it follows, first, that there is no cause, either extrinsically or intrinsically, which prompts God to action, except the perfection of his nature.

Cor. 2: It follows, secondly, that God alone is a free cause. For God alone exists only from the necessity of his nature (by P11 and P14C1), and acts from the necessity of his nature (by P17). Therefore (by D7) God alone is a free cause, q.e.d.

Schol.: [I.] Others think that God is a free cause because he can (so they think) bring it about that the things which we have said follow from his nature (i.e., which are in his power) do not happen or are not produced by him. But this is the same as if they were to say that God can bring it about that it would not follow from the nature of a triangle that its three angles are equal to two right angles; or that from a given cause the effect would not follow—which is absurd.

Further, I shall show later, without the aid of this Proposition, that neither intellect nor will pertain to God's nature. Of course I know there are many who think they can demonstrate that a supreme intellect and a free will pertain to God's nature. For they say they know nothing they can ascribe to God more perfect than what is the highest perfection in us.

Moreover, even if they conceive God to actually understand in the highest degree, they still do not believe that he can bring it about that all the things he actually understands exist. For they think that in that way they would destroy God's power. If he had created all the things in his intellect (they say), then he would have been able to create nothing more, which they believe to be incompatible with God's omnipotence. So they preferred to maintain that God is indifferent to all things, not creating anything except what he has decreed to create by some absolute will.

But I think I have shown clearly enough (see P16) that from God's supreme power, *or* infinite nature, infinitely many things in infinitely many modes, i.e., all things, have necessarily flowed, or always follow, by the same necessity and in the same way as from the nature of a triangle it follows, from eternity and to eternity, that its three angles are equal to two right angles. So God's omnipotence has been actual from eternity and will remain in the same actuality to eternity. And in this way, at least in my opinion, God's omnipotence is maintained far more perfectly.

Indeed—to speak openly—my opponents seem to deny God's omnipotence. For they are forced to confess that God understands infinitely many creatable things, which nevertheless he will never be able to create. For otherwise, if he created everything he understood [to be creatable] he would (according to them) exhaust his omnipotence and render himself imperfect. Therefore to maintain that God is perfect, they are driven to maintain at the same time that he cannot bring about everything to which his power extends. I do not see what could be feigned which would be more absurd than this or more contrary to God's omnipotence.

[II.] Further—to say something here also about the intellect and will which we commonly attribute to God—if will and intellect do pertain to the eternal essence of God, we must of course understand by each of these attributes something different from what men commonly understand. For the intellect and will which would constitute God's essence would have to differ entirely from our intellect and will, and could not agree with them in anything except the name. They would not agree with one another any more than do the dog that is a heavenly constellation and the dog that is a barking animal. I shall demonstrate this.

If intellect pertains to the divine nature, it will not be able to be (like our intellect) by nature either posterior to (as most would have it), or simultaneous with, the things understood, since God is prior in causality to all things (by P16C1). On the contrary, the truth and formal essence of things is what it is because it exists objectively in that way in God's intellect. So God's intellect, insofar as it is conceived to constitute God's essence, is really the cause both of the essence and of the existence of things. This seems also to have been noticed by those who asserted that God's intellect, will and power are one and the same.

Therefore, since God's intellect is the only cause of things (viz. as we have shown, both of their essence and of their existence), he must necessarily differ from them both as to his essence and as to his existence. For what is caused differs from its cause precisely in what it has from the cause [for that reason it is called the effect of such a cause]. E.g., a man is the cause of the existence of another man, but not of his essence, for the latter is an eternal truth. Hence, they can agree entirely according to their essence. But in existing they must differ. And for that reason, if the existence of one perishes, the other's existence will not thereby perish. But if the essence of one could be destroyed, and become false, the other's essence would also be destroyed [and become false].

So the thing that is the cause both of the essence and of the existence of some effect, must differ from such an effect, both as to its essence and as to its existence. But God's intellect is the cause both of the essence and of the existence of our intellect. Therefore, God's intellect, insofar as it is conceived to constitute the divine essence, differs from our intellect both as to its essence and as to its existence, and cannot agree with it in anything except in name, as we supposed. The proof proceeds in the same way concerning the will, as anyone can easily see.

P18: *God is the immanent, not the transitive, cause of all things.*

Dem.: Everything that is, is in God, and must be conceived through God (by P15), and so (by P16C1) God is the cause of [all] things, which are in him. That is the first [thing to be proven]. And then outside God there can be no substance (by P14), i.e. (by D3), thing which is in itself outside God. That was the second. God, therefore, is the immanent, not the transitive cause of all things, q.e.d.

P19: *God is eternal, or all God's attributes are eternal.*

Dem.: For God (by D6) is substance, which (by P11) necessarily exists, i.e. (by P7), to whose nature it pertains to exist, or (what is the same) from whose definition it follows that he exists; and therefore (by D8), he is eternal.

Next, by God's attributes are to be understood what (by D4) expresses an essence of the Divine substance, i.e., what pertains to substance. The attributes themselves, I say, must involve it itself. But eternity pertains to the nature of substance (as I have already demonstrated from P7). Therefore each of the attributes must involve eternity, and so, they are all eternal, q.e.d.

Schol.: This Proposition is also as clear as possible from the way I have demonstrated God's existence (P11). For from that demonstration, I say, it is established that God's existence, like his essence, is an eternal truth. And then I have also demonstrated God's eternity in another way (Descartes' *Principles* IP19), and there is no need to repeat it here.

P20: *God's existence and his essence are one and the same.*

Dem.: God (by P19) and all of his attributes are eternal, i.e. (by D8), each of his attributes expresses existence. Therefore, the same attributes of God which (by D4) explain God's eternal essence at the same time explain his eternal existence, i.e., that itself which constitutes God's essence at the same time constitutes his existence. So his existence and his essence are one and the same, q.e.d.

Cor. 1: From this it follows, first, that God's existence, like his essence, is an eternal truth.

Cor. 2: It follows, secondly, that God, or all of God's attributes, are immutable. For if they changed as to their existence, they would also (by P20) change as to their essence, i.e. (as is known through itself), from being true become false, which is absurd.

P21: *All the things which follow from the absolute nature of any of God's attributes have always had to exist and be infinite, or are, through the same attribute, eternal and infinite.*

Dem.: If you deny this, then conceive (if you can) that in some attribute of God there follows from its absolute nature something that is finite and has a determinate existence, or duration, e.g., God's idea in thought. Now since thought is supposed to be an attribute of God, it is necessarily (by P11) infinite by its nature. But insofar as it has God's idea, [thought] is supposed to be finite. But (by D2) [thought] cannot be conceived to be finite unless it is determined through thought itself. But [thought can] not [be determined] through thought itself, insofar as it constitutes God's idea, for to that extent [thought] is supposed to be finite. Therefore, [thought must be determined] through thought insofar as it does not constitute God's idea, which [thought] nevertheless (by P11) must necessarily exist. Therefore, there is thought which does not constitute God's idea, and on that account God's idea does not follow necessarily from the nature [of this thought] insofar as it is absolute thought (for [thought] is conceived both as constituting God's idea and as not constituting it). [That God's idea does not follow from thought, insofar as it is absolute thought] is contrary to the hypothesis. So if God's idea in thought, or anything else in any attribute of God (for it does not matter what example is taken, since the demonstration is universal), follows from the necessity of the absolute nature of the attribute itself, it must necessarily be infinite. This was the first thing to be proven.

Next, what follows in this way from the necessity of the nature of any attribute cannot have a determinate [existence, or] duration. For if you deny this, then suppose

there is, in some attribute of God, a thing which follows from the necessity of the nature of that attribute—e.g., God's idea in thought—and suppose that at some time [this
idea] did not exist or will not exist. But since thought is supposed to be an attribute of
God, it must exist necessarily and be immutable (by P11 and P20C2). So beyond the
limits of the duration of God's idea (for it is supposed that at some time [this idea] did
not exist or will not exist) thought will have to exist without God's idea. But this is
contrary to the hypothesis, for it is supposed that God's idea follows necessarily from
the given thought. Therefore, God's idea in thought, or anything else which follows
necessarily from the absolute nature of some attribute of God, cannot have a determinate duration, but through the same attribute is eternal. This was the second thing [to
be proven]. Note that the same is to be affirmed of any thing which, in some attribute
of God, follows necessarily from God's absolute nature.

P22: *Whatever follows from some attribute of God insofar as it is modified by a modification which, through the same attribute, exists necessarily and is infinite, must also
exist necessarily and be infinite.*

Dem.: The demonstration of this proposition proceeds in the same way as the
demonstration of the preceding one.

P23: *Every mode which exists necessarily and is infinite has necessarily had to follow
either from the absolute nature of some attribute of God, or from some attribute, modified by a modification which exists necessarily and is infinite.*

Dem.: For a mode is in another, through which it must be conceived (by D5), i.e.
(by P15), it is in God alone, and can be conceived through God alone. So if a mode is
conceived to exist necessarily and be infinite, [its necessary existence and infinitude]
must necessarily be inferred, or perceived through some attribute of God, insofar as
that attribute is conceived to express infinity and necessity of existence, or (what is the
same, by D8) eternity, i.e. (by D6 and P19), insofar as it is considered absolutely.
Therefore, the mode, which exists necessarily and is infinite, has had to follow from
the absolute nature of some attribute of God—either immediately (see P21) or by some
mediating modification, which follows from its absolute nature, i.e. (by P22), which
exists necessarily and is infinite, q.e.d.

P24: *The essence of things produced by God does not involve existence.*

Dem.: This is evident from D1. For that whose nature involves existence (considered in itself), is its own cause, and exists only from the necessity of its nature.

Cor.: From this it follows that God is not only the cause of things' beginning to
exist, but also of their persevering in existing, or (to use a Scholastic term) God is the
cause of the being of things. For—whether the things [produced] exist or not—so long
as we attend to their essence, we shall find that it involves neither existence nor duration. So their essence can be the cause neither of their existence nor of their duration,
but only God, to whose nature alone it pertains to exist [can be the cause] (by P14C1).

P25: *God is the efficient cause, not only of the existence of things, but also of their
essence.*

Dem.: If you deny this, then God is not the cause of the essence of things; and so
(by A4) the essence of things can be conceived without God. But (by P15) this is absurd. Therefore God is also the cause of the essence of things, q.e.d.

Schol.: This Proposition follows more clearly from P16. For from that it follows
that from the given divine nature both the essence of things and their existence must

necessarily be inferred; and in a word, God must be called the cause of all things in the same sense in which he is called the cause of himself. This will be established still more clearly from the following corollary.

Cor.: Particular things are nothing but affections of God's attributes, or modes by which God's attributes are expressed in a certain and determinate way. The demonstration is evident from P15 and D5.

P26: *A thing which has been determined to produce an effect has necessarily been determined in this way by God; and one which has not been determined by God cannot determine itself to produce an effect.*

Dem.: That through which things are said to be determined to produce an effect must be something positive (as is known through itself). And so, God, from the necessity of his nature, is the efficient cause both of its essence and of its existence (by P15 and 16); this was the first thing. And from it the second thing asserted also follows very clearly. For if a thing which has not been determined by God could determine itself, the first part of this [proposition] would be false, which is absurd, as we have shown.

P27: *A thing which has been determined by God to produce an effect, cannot render itself undetermined.*

Dem.: This proposition is evident from A3.

The Synagogue, Amsterdam, n.d., by Rembrandt (1606–1669). Spinoza was a member of the Amsterdam Synagogue until he was excommunicated in 1656. (*Musée de la Ville de Paris, Musée du Petit-Palais/Art Resource*)

P28: *Every singular thing, or any thing which is finite and has a determinate existence, can neither exist nor be determined to produce an effect unless it is determined to exist and produce an effect by another cause, which is also finite and has a determinate existence; and again, this cause also can neither exist nor be determined to produce an effect unless it is determined to exist and produce an effect by another, which is also finite and has a determinate existence, and so on, to infinity.*

Dem.: Whatever has been determined to exist and produce an effect has been so determined by God (by P16 and P24C). But what is finite and has a determinate existence could not have been produced by the absolute nature of an attribute of God; for whatever follows from the absolute nature of an attribute of God is eternal and infinite (by P21). It had, therefore, to follow either from God or from an attribute of God insofar as it is considered to be affected by some mode. For there is nothing except substance and its modes (by A1, D3, and D5) and modes (by P25C) are nothing but affections of God's attributes. But it also could not follow from God, or from an attribute of God, insofar as it is affected by a modification which is eternal and infinite (by P22). It had, therefore, to follow from, or be determined to exist and produce an effect by God or an attribute of God insofar as it is modified by a modification which is finite and has a determinate existence. This was the first thing to be proven.

And in turn, this cause, or this mode (by the same reasoning by which we have already demonstrated the first part of this proposition) had also to be determined by another, which is also finite and has a determinate existence; and again, this last (by the same reasoning) by another, and so always (by the same reasoning) to infinity, q.e.d.

Schol.: Since certain things had to be produced by God immediately, viz. those which follow necessarily from his absolute nature, and others (which nevertheless can neither be nor be conceived without God) had to be produced by the mediation of these first things, it follows:

I. That God is absolutely the proximate cause of the things produced immediately by him, and not [a proximate cause] in his own kind, as they say. For God's effects can neither be nor be conceived without their cause (by P15 and P24C).

II. That God cannot properly be called the remote cause of singular things, except perhaps so that we may distinguish them from those things that he has produced immediately, or rather, that follow from his absolute nature. For by a remote cause we understand one which is not conjoined in any way with its effect. But all things that are, are in God, and so depend on God that they can neither be nor be conceived without him.

P29: *In nature there is nothing contingent, but all things have been determined from the necessity of the divine nature to exist and produce an effect in a certain way.*

Dem.: Whatever is, is in God (by P15); but God cannot be called a contingent thing. For (by P11) he exists necessarily, not contingently. Next, the modes of the divine nature have also followed from it necessarily and not contingently (by P16)—either insofar as the divine nature is considered absolutely (by P21) or insofar as it is considered to be determined to act in a certain way (by P18). Further, God is the cause of these modes not only insofar as they simply exist (by P24C), but also (by P16) insofar as they are considered to be determined to produce an effect. For if they have not been determined by God, then (by P16) it is impossible, not contingent, that they should determine themselves. Conversely (by P17) if they have been determined by God, it is not contingent, but impossible, that they should render themselves undetermined. So all things have been determined from the necessity of the divine nature, not only to exist, but to exist in a certain way, and to produce effects in a certain way. There is nothing contingent, q.e.d.

Schol.: Before I proceed further, I wish to explain here—or rather to advise [the reader]—what we must understand by *Natura naturans* and *Natura naturata*. For from the preceding I think it is already established that by *Natura naturans* we must understand what is in itself and is conceived through itself, or such attributes of substance as express an eternal and infinite essence, i.e. (by P14C1 and P17C2), God, insofar as he is considered as a free cause.

But by *Natura naturata* I understand whatever follows from the necessity of God's nature, or from any of God's attributes, i.e., all the modes of God's attributes insofar as they are considered as things which are in God, and can neither be nor be conceived without God.

P30: *An actual intellect, whether finite or infinite, must comprehend God's attributes and God's affections, and nothing else.*

Dem.: A true idea must agree with its object (by A6), i.e. (as is known through itself), what is contained objectively in the intellect must necessarily be in nature. But in nature (by P14C1) there is only one substance, viz. God, and there are no affections other than those which are in God (by P15) and which can neither be nor be conceived without God (by P15). Therefore, an actual intellect, whether finite or infinite, must comprehend God's attributes and God's affections, and nothing else, q.e.d.

P31: *The actual intellect, whether finite or infinite, like will, desire, love, etc., must be referred to* Natura naturata, *not to* Natura naturans.

Dem.: By intellect (as is known through itself) we understand not absolute thought, but only a certain mode of thinking, which mode differs from the others, such as desire, love, etc., and so (by D5) must be conceived through absolute thought, i.e. (by P15 and D6), it must be so conceived through an attribute of God, which expresses the eternal and infinite essence of thought, that can neither be nor be conceived without [that attribute]; and so (by P29S), like the other modes of thinking, it must be referred to *Natura naturata*, not to *Natura naturans*, q.e.d.

Schol.: The reason why I speak here of actual intellect is not because I concede that there is any potential intellect, but because, wishing to avoid all confusion, I wanted to speak only of what we perceive as clearly as possible, i.e., of the intellection itself. We perceive nothing more clearly than that. For we can understand nothing that does not lead to more perfect knowledge of the intellection.

P32: *The will cannot be called a free cause, but only a necessary one.*

Dem.: The will, like the intellect, is only a certain mode of thinking. And so (by P18) each volition can neither exist nor be determined to produce an effect unless it is determined by another cause, and this cause again by another, and so on, to infinity. Even if the will be supposed to be infinite, it must still be determined to exist and produce an effect by God, not insofar as he is an absolutely infinite substance, but insofar as he has an attribute that expresses the infinite and eternal essence of thought (by P13). So in whatever way it is conceived, whether as finite or as infinite, it requires a cause by which it is determined to exist and produce an effect. And so (by D7) it cannot be called a free cause, but only a necessary or compelled one, q.e.d.

Cor. 1: From this it follows, first, that God does not produce any effect by freedom of the will.

Cor. 2: It follows, secondly, that will and intellect are related to God's nature as motion and rest are, and as are absolutely all natural things, which (by P29) must be determined by God to exist and produce an effect in a certain way. For the will, like all other things, requires a cause by which it is determined to exist and produce an effect in a certain way. And although from a given will, *or* intellect infinitely many things may follow, God still cannot be said, on that account, to act from freedom of the will, any more than he can be said to act from freedom of motion and rest on account of those things that follow from motion and rest (for infinitely many things also follow from motion and rest). So will does not pertain to God's nature any more than do the other natural things, but is related to him in the same way as motion and rest, and all the other things which, as we have shown, follow from the necessity of the divine nature and are determined by it to exist and produce an effect in a certain way.

P33: *Things could have been produced by God in no other way, and in no other order than they have been produced.*

Dem.: For all things have necessarily followed from God's given nature (by P16), and have been determined from the necessity of God's nature to exist and produce an effect in a certain way (by P29). Therefore, if things could have been of another nature, or could have been determined to produce an effect in another way, so that the order of Nature was different, then God's nature could also have been other than it is now, and therefore (by P11) that [other nature] would also have had to exist, and consequently, there could have been two or more Gods, which is absurd (by P14C1). So things could have been produced in no other way and no other order, etc., q.e.d.

Schol. 1: Since by these propositions I have shown more clearly than the noon light that there is absolutely nothing in things on account of which they can be called contingent, I wish now to explain briefly what we must understand by contingent—but first, what [we must understand] by necessary and impossible.

A thing is called necessary either by reason of its essence or by reason of its cause. For a thing's existence follows necessarily either from its essence and definition or from a given efficient cause. And a thing is also called impossible from these same causes—viz. either because its essence, or definition, involves a contradiction, or because there is no external cause which has been determined to produce such a thing.

But a thing is called contingent only because of a defect of our knowledge. For if we do not know that the thing's essence involves a contradiction, or if we do know very well that its essence does not involve a contradiction, and nevertheless can affirm nothing certainly about its existence, because the order of causes is hidden from us, it can never seem to us either necessary or impossible. So we call it contingent or possible.

Schol. 2: From the preceding it clearly follows that things have been produced by God with the highest perfection, since they have followed necessarily from a given most perfect nature. Nor does this convict God of any imperfection, for his perfection compels us to affirm this. Indeed, from the opposite, it would clearly follow (as I have just shown), that God is not supremely perfect; because if things had been produced by God in another way, we would have to attribute to God another nature, different from that which we have been compelled to attribute to him from the consideration of the most perfect Being.

Of course, I have no doubt that many will reject this opinion as absurd, without even being willing to examine it—for no other reason than because they have been accustomed to attribute another freedom to God, far different from that we have taught

(D7), viz. an absolute will. But I also have no doubt that, if they are willing to reflect on the matter, and consider properly the chain of our demonstrations, in the end they will utterly reject the freedom they now attribute to God, not only as futile, but as a great obstacle to science. Nor is it necessary for me to repeat here what I said in P17S.

Nevertheless, to please them, I shall show that even if it is conceded that will pertains to God's essence, it still follows from his perfection that things could have been created by God in no other way or order. It will be easy to show this if we consider, first, what they themselves concede, viz. that it depends on God's decree and will alone that each thing is what it is. For otherwise God would not be the cause of all things. Next, that all God's decrees have been established by God himself from eternity. For otherwise he would be convicted of imperfection and inconstancy. But since, in eternity, there is neither when, nor *before*, nor *after*, it follows, from God's perfection alone, that he can never decree anything different, and never could have, or that God was not before his decrees, and cannot be without them.

But they will say that even if it were supposed that God had made another nature of things, or that from eternity he had decreed something else concerning nature and its order, no imperfection in God would follow from that.

Still, if they say this, they will concede at the same time that God can change his decrees. For if God had decreed, concerning nature and its order, something other than what he did decree, i.e., had willed and conceived something else concerning nature, he would necessarily have had an intellect other than he now has, and a will other than he now has. And if it is permitted to attribute to God another intellect and another will, without any change of his essence and of his perfection, why can he not now change his decrees concerning created things, and nevertheless remain equally perfect? For his intellect and will concerning created things and their order are the same in respect to his essence and his perfection, however his will and intellect may be conceived.

Further, all the Philosophers I have seen concede that in God there is no potential intellect, but only an actual one. But since his intellect and his will are not distinguished from his essence, as they all also concede, it follows that if God had had another actual intellect, and another will, his essence would also necessarily be other. And therefore (as I inferred at the beginning) if things had been produced by God otherwise than they now are, God's intellect and his will, i.e. (as is conceded), his essence, would have to be different [from what it now is]. And this is absurd.

Therefore, since things could have been produced by God in no other way, and no other order, and since it follows from God's supreme perfection that this is true, no truly sound reason can persuade us to believe that God did not will to create all the things that are in his intellect, with that same perfection with which he understands them.

But they will say that there is no perfection or imperfection in things; what is in them, on account of which they are perfect or imperfect, and are called good or bad, depends only on God's will. And so, if God had willed, he could have brought it about that what is now perfection would have been the greatest imperfection, and conversely [that what is now an imperfection in things would have been the most perfect]. How would this be different from saying openly that God, who necessarily understands what he wills, can bring it about by his will that he understands things in another way than he does understand them? As I have just shown, this is a great absurdity.

So I can turn the argument against them in the following way. All things depend on God's power. So in order for things to be able to be different, God's will would necessarily also have to be different. But God's will cannot be different (as we have just shown most evidently from God's perfection). So things also cannot be different.

I confess that this opinion, which subjects all things to a certain indifferent will of God, and makes all things depend on his good pleasure, is nearer the truth than that of those who maintain that God does all things for the sake of the good. For they seem to place something outside God, which does not depend on God, to which God attends, as a model, in what he does, and at which he aims, as at a certain goal. This is simply to subject God to fate. Nothing more absurd can be maintained about God, whom we have shown to be the first and only free cause, both of the essence of all things, and of their existence. So I shall waste no time in refuting this absurdity.

P34: *God's power is his essence itself.*

Dem.: For from the necessity alone of God's essence it follows that God is the cause of himself (by P11) and (by P16 and P16C) of all things. Therefore, God's power, by which he and all things are and act, is his essence itself, q.e.d.

P35: *Whatever we conceive to be in God's power, necessarily exists.*

Dem.: For whatever is in God's power must (by P34) be so comprehended by his essence that it necessarily follows from it, and therefore necessarily exists, q.e.d.

P36: *Nothing exists from whose nature some effect does not follow.*

Dem.: Whatever exists expresses the nature, or essence of God in a certain and determinate way (by P25C), i.e. (by P34), whatever exists expresses in a certain and determinate way the power of God, which is the cause of all things. So (by P16), from [everything that exists] some effect must follow, q.e.d.

Appendix

With these [demonstrations] I have explained God's nature and properties: that he exists necessarily; that he is unique; that he is and acts from the necessity alone of his nature; that (and how) he is the free cause of all things; that all things are in God and so depend on him that without him they can neither be nor be conceived; and finally, that all things have been predetermined by God, not from freedom of the will *or* absolute good pleasure, but from God's absolute nature, or infinite power.

Further, I have taken care, whenever the occasion arose, to remove prejudices that could prevent my demonstrations from being perceived. But because many prejudices remain that could, and can, be a great obstacle to men's understanding the connection of things in the way I have explained it, I considered it worthwhile to submit them here to the scrutiny of reason. All the prejudices I here undertake to expose depend on this one: that men commonly suppose that all natural things act, as men do, on account of an end; indeed, they maintain as certain that God himself directs all things to some certain end, for they say that God has made all things for man, and man that he might worship God.

So I shall begin by considering this one prejudice, asking *first* [I] why most people are satisfied that it is true, and why all are so inclined by nature to embrace it. Then [II] I shall show its falsity, and finally [III] how, from this, prejudices have arisen concerning *good* and *evil*, *merit* and *sin*, *praise* and *blame*, *order* and *confusion*, *beauty* and *ugliness*, and other things of this kind.

[I.] Of course this is not the place to deduce these things from the nature of the human mind. It will be sufficient here if I take as a foundation what everyone must acknowledge: that all men are born ignorant of the causes of things, and that they all want to seek their own advantage, and are conscious of this appetite.

From these [assumptions] it follows, *first*, that men think themselves free, because they are conscious of their volitions and their appetite, and do not think, even in their dreams, of the causes by which they are disposed to wanting and willing, because they are ignorant of [those causes]. It follows, *secondly*, that men act always on account of an end, viz. on account of their advantage, which they want. Hence they seek to know only the final causes of what has been done, and when they have heard them, they are satisfied, because they have no reason to doubt further. But if they cannot hear them from another, nothing remains for them but to turn toward themselves, and reflect on the ends by which they are usually determined to do such things; so they necessarily judge the temperament of other men from their own temperament.

Furthermore, they find—both in themselves and outside themselves—many means that are very helpful in seeking their own advantage, e.g., eyes for seeing, teeth for chewing, plants and animals for food, the sun for light, the sea for supporting fish [and so with almost all other things whose natural causes they have no reason to doubt]. Hence, they consider all natural things as means to their own advantage. And knowing that they had found these means, not provided them for themselves, they had reason to believe that there was someone else who had prepared those means for their use. For after they considered things as means, they could not believe that the things had made themselves; but from the means they were accustomed to prepare for themselves, they had to infer that there was a ruler, or a number of rulers of nature, endowed with human freedom, who had taken care of all things for them, and made all things for their use.

And since they had never heard anything about the temperament of these rulers, they had to judge it from their own. Hence, they maintained that the Gods direct all things for the use of men in order to bind men to them and be held by men in the highest honor. So it has happened that each of them has thought up from his own temperament different ways of worshipping God, so that God might love them above all the rest, and direct the whole of Nature according to the needs of their blind desire and insatiable greed. Thus this prejudice was changed into superstition, and struck deep roots in their minds. This was why each of them strove with great diligence to understand and explain the final causes of all things.

But while they sought to show that nature does nothing in vain (i.e., nothing which is not of use to men), they seem to have shown only that nature and the Gods are as mad as men. See, I ask you, how the matter has turned out in the end! Among so many conveniences in nature they had to find many inconveniences: storms, earthquakes, diseases, etc. These, they maintain, happen because the Gods [(whom they judge to be of the same nature as themselves)] are angry on account of wrongs done to them by men, or on account of sins committed in their worship. And though their daily experience contradicted this, and though infinitely many examples showed that conveniences and inconveniences happen indiscriminately to the pious and the impious alike, they did not on that account give up their longstanding prejudice. It was easier for them to put this among the other unknown things, whose use they were ignorant of, and so remain in the state of ignorance in which they had been born, than to destroy that whole construction, and think up a new one.

So they maintained it as certain that the judgments of the Gods far surpass man's grasp. This alone, of course, would have caused the truth to be hidden from the human race to eternity, if Mathematics, which is concerned not with ends, but only with the essences and properties of figures, had not shown men another standard of truth. And besides Mathematics, we can assign other causes also (which it is unnecessary to enumerate here), which were able to bring it about that men [—but very few, in relation to the whole human race—] would notice these common prejudices and be led to the true knowledge of things.

[II.] With this I have sufficiently explained what I promised in the first place [viz. why men are so inclined to believe that all things act for an end]. Not many words will be required now to show that Nature has no end set before it, and that all final causes are nothing but human fictions. For I believe I have already sufficiently established it, both by the foundations and causes from which I have shown this prejudice to have had its origin, and also by P16, P32C1 and C2, and all those [propositions] by which I have shown that all things proceed by a certain eternal necessity of nature, and with the greatest perfection.

I shall, however, add this: this doctrine concerning the end turns nature completely upside down. For what is really a cause, it considers as an effect, and conversely [what is an effect it considers as a cause]. What is by nature prior, it makes posterior. And finally, what is supreme and most perfect, it makes imperfect.

For—to pass over the first two, since they are manifest through themselves—as has been established in PP21–23, that effect is most perfect which is produced immediately by God, and the more something requires intermediate causes to produce it, the more imperfect it is. But if the things which have been produced immediately by God had been made so that God would achieve his end, then the last things, for the sake of which the first would have been made, would be the most excellent of all.

Again, this doctrine takes away God's perfection. For if God acts for the sake of an end, he necessarily wants something which he lacks. And though the Theologians and Metaphysicians distinguish between an end of need and an end of assimilation, they nevertheless confess that God did all things for his own sake, not for the sake of the things to be created. For before creation they can assign nothing except God for whose sake God would act. And so they are necessarily compelled to confess that God lacked those things for the sake of which he willed to prepare means, and that he desired them. This is clear through itself.

Nor ought we here to pass over the fact that the Followers of this doctrine, who have wanted to show off their cleverness in assigning the ends of things, have introduced—to prove this doctrine of theirs—a new way of arguing: by reducing things, not to the impossible, but to ignorance. This shows that no other way of defending their doctrine was open to them.

For example, if a stone has fallen from a roof onto someone's head and killed him, they will show, in the following way, that the stone fell in order to kill the man. For if it did not fall to that end, God willing it, how could so many circumstances have concurred by chance (for often many circumstances do concur at once)? Perhaps you will answer that it happened because the wind was blowing hard and the man was walking that way. But they will persist: why was the wind blowing hard at that time? why was the man walking that way at that same time? If you answer again that the wind arose then because on the preceding day, while the weather was still calm, the sea began to toss, and that the man had been invited by a friend, they will press on—for there is no end to the questions which can be asked: but why was the sea tossing? why was the man invited at just that time? And so they will not stop asking for the causes of causes until you take refuge in the will of God, i.e., the sanctuary of ignorance.

Similarly, when they see the structure of the human body, they are struck by a foolish wonder, and because they do not know the causes of so great an art, they infer that it is constructed, not by mechanical, but by divine, or supernatural art, and constituted in such a way that one part does not injure another.

Hence it happens that one who seeks the true causes of miracles, and is eager, like an educated man, to understand natural things, not to wonder at them, like a fool, is generally considered and denounced as an impious heretic by those whom the people honor as interpreters of nature and the Gods. For they know that if ignorance is taken away, then foolish wonder, the only means they have of arguing and defending their authority, is also taken away. But I leave these things, and pass on to what I have decided to treat here in the third place.

[III.] After men persuaded themselves that everything that happens, happens on their account, they had to judge that what is most important in each thing is what is most useful to them, and to rate as most excellent all those things by which they were most pleased. Hence, they had to form these notions, by which they explained natural things: *good, evil, order, confusion, warm, cold, beauty, ugliness.* And because they think themselves free, those notions have arisen: *praise* and *blame, sin* and *merit.* The latter I shall explain after I have treated human nature; but the former I shall briefly explain here.

Whatever conduces to health and the worship of God, they have called *good*; but what is contrary to these, *evil.*

And because those who do not understand the nature of things, but only imagine them, affirm nothing concerning things, and take the imagination for the intellect, they firmly believe, in their ignorance of things and of their own nature, that there is an order in things. For when things are so disposed that, when they are presented to us through the senses, we can easily imagine them, and so can easily remember them, we say that they are wellordered; but if the opposite is true, we say that they are badly ordered, or confused.

And since those things we can easily imagine are especially pleasing to us, men prefer order to confusion, as if order were anything in nature more than a relation to our imagination. They also say that God has created all things in order, and so, unknowingly attribute imagination to God—unless, perhaps, they mean that God, to provide for human imagination, has disposed all things so that men can very easily imagine them. Nor will it, perhaps, give them pause that infinitely many things are found which far surpass our imagination, and a great many which confuse it on account of its weakness. But enough of this.

The other notions are also nothing but modes of imagining, by which the imagination is variously affected; and yet the ignorant consider them the chief attributes of things, because, as we have already said, they believe all things have been made for their sake, and call the nature of a thing good or evil, sound or rotten and corrupt, as they are affected by it. For example, if the motion the nerves receive from objects presented through the eyes is conducive to health, the objects by which it is caused are called beautiful; those which cause a contrary motion are called ugly. Those which move the sense through the nose, they call pleasant-smelling or stinking; through the tongue, sweet or bitter, tasty or tasteless; through touch, hard or soft, rough or smooth, etc.; and finally, those which move the ears are said to produce noise, sound or harmony. Men have been so mad as to believe that God is pleased by harmony. Indeed there are Philosophers who have persuaded themselves that the motions of the heavens produce a harmony.

All of these things show sufficiently that each one has judged things according to the disposition of his brain; or rather, has accepted affections of the imagination as things. So it is no wonder (to note this, too, in passing) that we find so many controversies to have arisen among men, and that they have finally given rise to Skepticism. For although human bodies agree in many things, they still differ in very many. And for that reason what seems good to one, seems bad to another; what seems ordered to one, seems confused to another; what seems pleasing to one, seems displeasing to another, and so on.

I pass over the [other notions] here, both because this is not the place to treat them at length, and because everyone has experienced this [variability] sufficiently for himself. That is why we have such sayings as "So many heads, so many attitudes," "everyone finds his own judgment more than enough," and "there are as many differences of brains as of palates." These proverbs show sufficiently that men judge things according to the disposition of their brain, and imagine, rather than understand them. For if men had understood them, the things would at least convince them all, even if they did not attract them all, as the example of mathematics shows.

We see, therefore, that all the notions by which ordinary people are accustomed to explain nature are only modes of imagining, and do not indicate the nature of anything, only the constitution of the imagination. And because they have names, as if they were [notions] of beings existing outside the imagination, I call them beings, not of reason, but of imagination. So all the arguments in which people try to use such notions against us can easily be warded off.

For many are accustomed to arguing in this way: if all things have followed from the necessity of God's most perfect nature, why are there so many imperfections in nature? why are things corrupt to the point where they stink? so ugly that they produce nausea? why is there confusion, evil, and sin?

As I have just said, those who argue in this way are easily answered. For the perfection of things is to be judged solely from their nature and power; things are not more or less perfect because they please or offend men's senses, or because they are of use to, or are incompatible with, human nature.

But to those who ask "why God did not create all men so that they would be governed by the command of reason?" I answer only "because he did not lack material to create all things, from the highest degree of perfection to the lowest"; or, to speak more properly, "because the laws of his nature have been so ample that they sufficed for producing all things which can be conceived by an infinite intellect" (as I have demonstrated in P16).

These are the prejudices I undertook to note here. If any of this kind still remain, they can be corrected by anyone with only a little meditation. [And so I find no reason to devote more time to these matters, etc.]

SECOND PART OF THE ETHICS

ON THE NATURE AND ORIGIN OF THE MIND

I pass now to explaining those things which must necessarily follow from the essence of God, or the infinite and eternal Being—not, indeed, all of them, for we have demonstrated (IP16) that infinitely many things must follow from it in infinitely many modes, but only those that can lead us, by the hand, as it were, to the knowledge of the human Mind and its highest blessedness.

Definitions

D1: By body I understand a mode that in a certain and determinate way expresses God's essence insofar as he is considered as an extended thing (see IP25C).

D2: I say that to the essence of any thing belongs that which, being given, the thing is [also] necessarily posited and which, being taken away, the thing is necessarily [also] taken away; or that without which the thing can neither be nor be conceived, and which can neither be nor be conceived without the thing.

D3: By idea I understand a concept of the Mind that the Mind forms because it is a thinking thing.
    Exp.: *I say concept rather than perception, because the word perception seems to indicate that the Mind is acted on by the object. But concept seems to express an action of the Mind.*

D4: By adequate idea I understand an idea which, insofar as it is considered in itself, without relation to an object, has all the properties, or intrinsic denominations of a true idea.

Exp.: *I say intrinsic to exclude what is extrinsic, viz. the agreement of the idea with its object.*

D5: Duration is an indefinite continuation of existing.

Exp.: *I say indefinite because it cannot be determined at all through the very nature of the existing thing, nor even by the efficient cause, which necessarily posits the existence of the thing, and does not take it away.*

D6: By reality and perfection I understand the same thing.

D7: By singular things I understand things that are finite and have a determinate existence. And if a number of Individuals so concur in one action that together they are all the cause of one effect, I consider them all, to that extent, as one singular thing.

Axioms

A1: The essence of man does not involve necessary existence, i.e., from the order of nature it can happen equally that this or that man does exist, or that he does not exist.

A2: Man thinks.

A3: There are no modes of thinking, such as love, desire, or whatever is designated by the word affects of the mind, unless there is in the same Individual the idea of the thing loved, desired, etc. But there can be an idea, even though there is no other mode of thinking.

A4: We feel that a certain body is affected in many ways.

A5: We neither feel nor perceive any singular things [or anything of *natura naturata*], except bodies and modes of thinking.
   See the postulates after P13.

P1: *Thought is an attribute of God, or God is a thinking thing.*
   Dem.: Singular thoughts, or this or that thought, are modes that express God's nature in a certain and determinate way (by IP25C). Therefore (by ID5) there belongs to God an attribute whose concept all singular thoughts involve, and through which they are also conceived. Therefore, Thought is one of God's infinite attributes, which expresses an eternal and infinite essence of God (see ID6), *or* God is a thinking thing, q.e.d.
   Schol.: This Proposition is also evident from the fact that we can conceive an infinite thinking being. For the more things a thinking being can think, the more reality, or perfection, we conceive it to contain. Therefore, a being that can think infinitely many things in infinitely many ways is necessarily infinite in its power of thinking. So since we can conceive an infinite Being by attending to thought alone, Thought (by ID4 and D6) is necessarily one of God's infinite attributes, as we maintained.

P2: *Extension is an attribute of God, or God is an extended thing.*
   Dem.: The demonstration of this proceeds in the same way as that of the preceding Proposition.

P3: *In God there is necessarily an idea, both of his essence and of everything that necessarily follows from his essence.*
   Dem.: For God (by P1) can think infinitely many things in infinitely many modes, *or* (what is the same, by IP16) can form the idea of his essence and of all the things which necessarily follow from it. But whatever is in God's power necessarily exists (by IP35); therefore, there is necessarily such an idea, and (by IP15) it is only in God, q.e.d.
   Schol.: By God's power ordinary people understand God's free will and his right over all things which are, things which on that account are commonly considered to be contingent. For they say that God has the power of destroying all things and reducing them to nothing. Further, they very often compare God's power with the power of Kings.
   But we have refuted this in IP32C1 and C2, and we have shown in IP16 that God acts with the same necessity by which he understands himself, i.e., just as it follows from the necessity of the divine nature (as everyone maintains unanimously) that God understands himself, with the same necessity it also follows that God does infinitely many things in infinitely many modes. And then we have shown in IP34 that God's power is nothing except God's active essence. And so it is as impossible for us to conceive that God does not act as it is to conceive that he does not exist.
   Again, if it were agreeable to pursue these matters further, I could also show here that that power which ordinary people fictitiously ascribe to God is not only human (which shows that ordinary people conceive God as a man, or as like a man), but also involves lack of power. But I do not wish to speak so often about the same topic. I only ask the reader to reflect repeatedly on what is said concerning this matter in Part I, from P16 to the end. For no one will be able to perceive rightly the things I maintain unless he takes great care not to confuse God's power with the human power or right of Kings.

P4: *God's idea, from which infinitely many things follow in infinitely many modes, must be unique.*

Dem.: An infinite intellect comprehends nothing except God's attributes and his affections (by IP30). But God is unique (by IP14C1). Therefore God's idea, from which infinitely many things follow in infinitely many modes, must be unique, q.e.d.

P5: *The formal being of ideas admits God as a cause only insofar as he is considered as a thinking thing, and not insofar as he is explained by any other attribute. I.e., ideas, both of God's attributes and of singular things, admit not the objects themselves, or the things perceived, as their efficient cause, but God himself, insofar as he is a thinking thing.*

Dem.: This is evident from P3. For there we inferred that God can form the idea of his essence, and of all the things that follow necessarily from it, solely from the fact that God is a thinking thing, and not from the fact that he is the object of his own idea. So the formal being of ideas admits God as its cause insofar as he is a thinking thing.

But another way of demonstrating this is the following. The formal being of ideas is a mode of thinking (as is known through itself), i.e. (by IP25C), a mode that expresses, in a certain way, God's nature insofar as he is a thinking thing. And so (by IP10) it involves the concept of no other attribute of God, and consequently (by IA4) is the effect of no other attribute than thought. And so the formal being of ideas admits God as its cause insofar as he is considered only as a thinking thing, etc., q.e.d.

P6: *The modes of each attribute have God for their cause only insofar as he is considered under the attribute of which they are modes, and not insofar as he is considered under any other attribute.*

Dem.: For each attribute is conceived through itself without any other (by IP10). So the modes of each attribute involve the concept of their own attribute, but not of another one; and so (by IA4) they have God for their cause only insofar as he is considered under the attribute of which they are modes, and not insofar as he is considered under any other, q.e.d.

Cor.: From this it follows that the formal being of things which are not modes of thinking does not follow from the divine nature because [God] has first known the things; rather the objects of ideas follow and are inferred from their attributes in the same way and by the same necessity as that with which we have shown ideas to follow from the attribute of Thought.

P7: *The order and connection of ideas is the same as the order and connection of things.*

Dem.: This is clear from IA4. For the idea of each thing caused depends on the knowledge of the cause of which it is the effect.

Cor.: From this it follows that God's [actual] power of thinking is equal to his actual power of acting. I.e., whatever follows formally from God's infinite nature follows objectively in God from his idea in the same order and with the same connection.

Schol.: Before we proceed further, we must recall here what we showed [in the First Part], viz. that whatever can be perceived by an infinite intellect as constituting an essence of substance pertains to one substance only, and consequently that the thinking substance and the extended substance are one and the same substance, which is now comprehended under this attribute, now under that. So also a mode of extension and the idea of that mode are one and the same thing, but expressed in two ways. Some of the Hebrews seem to have seen this, as if through a cloud, when they maintained that God, God's intellect, and the things understood by him are one and the same.

For example, a circle existing in nature and the idea of the existing circle, which is also in God, are one and the same thing, which is explained through different attributes. Therefore, whether we conceive nature under the attribute of Extension, or under the attribute of Thought, or under any other attribute, we shall find one and the same order, or one and the same connection of causes, i.e., that the same things follow one another.

When I said [before] that God is the cause of the idea, say of a circle, only insofar as he is a thinking thing, and [the cause] of the circle, only insofar as he is an extended thing, this was for no other reason than because the formal being of the idea of the circle can be perceived only through another mode of thinking, as its proximate cause, and that mode again through another, and so on, to infinity. Hence, so long as things are considered as modes of thinking, we must explain the order of the whole of nature, *or* the connection of causes, through the attribute of Thought alone. And insofar as they are considered as modes of Extension, the order of the whole of nature must be explained through the attribute of Extension alone. I understand the same concerning the other attributes.

So of things as they are in themselves, God is really the cause insofar as he consists of infinite attributes. For the present, I cannot explain these matters more clearly.

P8: *The ideas of singular things, or of modes, that do not exist must be comprehended in God's infinite idea in the same way as the formal essences of the singular things, or modes, are contained in God's attributes.*

Dem.: This Proposition is evident from the preceding one, but is understood more clearly from the preceding scholium.

Cor.: From this it follows that so long as singular things do not exist, except insofar as they are comprehended in God's attributes, their objective being, *or* ideas, do not exist except insofar as God's infinite idea exists. And when singular things are said to exist, not only insofar as they are comprehended in God's attributes, but insofar also as they are said to have duration, their ideas also involve the existence through which they are said to have duration.

Schol.: If anyone wishes me to explain this further by an example, I will, of course, not be able to give one which adequately explains what I speak of here, since it is unique. Still I shall try as far as possible to illustrate the matter: the circle is of such a nature that the rectangles formed from the segments of all the straight lines intersecting in it are equal to one another. So in a circle there are contained infinitely many rectangles that are equal to one another. Nevertheless, none of them can be said to exist except insofar as the circle exists, nor also can the idea of any of these rectangles be said to exist except insofar as it is comprehended in the idea of the circle. Now of these infinitely many [rectangles] let two only, viz. [those formed from the segments of lines] D and E, exist.

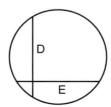

Of course their ideas also exist now, not only insofar as they are only comprehended in the idea of the circle, but also insofar as they involve the existence of those
rectangles. By this they are distinguished from the other ideas of the other rectangles.

P9: *The idea of a singular thing which actually exists has God for a cause not insofar
as he is infinite, but insofar as he is considered to be affected by another idea of a singular thing which actually exists; and of this [idea] God is also the cause, insofar as
he is affected by another third [idea], and so on, to infinity.*

Dem.: The idea of a singular thing which actually exists is a singular mode of
thinking, and distinct from the others (by P8C and S), and so (by P6) has God for a
cause only insofar as he is a thinking thing. But not (by IP28) insofar as he is a thing
thinking absolutely; rather insofar as he is considered to be affected by another [deter-
minate] mode of thinking. And God is also the cause of this mode, insofar as he is affected by another [determinate mode of thinking], and so on, to infinity. But the order
and connection of ideas (by P7) is the same as the order and connection of causes.
Therefore, the cause of one singular idea is another idea, or God, insofar as he is considered to be affected by another idea; and of this also [God is the cause], insofar as he
is affected by another, and so on, to infinity, q.e.d.

Cor.: Whatever happens in the singular object of any idea, there is knowledge of
it in God, only insofar as he has the idea of the same object.

Dem.: Whatever happens in the object of any idea, there is an idea of it in God
(by P3), not insofar as he is infinite, but insofar as he is considered to be affected by
another idea of [an existing] singular thing (by P9); but the order and connection of
ideas (by P7) is the same as the order and connection of things; therefore, knowledge
of what happens in a singular object will be in God only insofar as he has the idea of
the same object, q.e.d.

P10: *The being of substance does not pertain to the essence of man, or substance does
not constitute the form of man.*

Dem.: For the being of substance involves necessary existence (by IP7). Therefore, if the being of substance pertained to the essence of man, then substance being
given, man would necessarily be given (by D2), and consequently man would exist
necessarily, which (by A1) is absurd, q.e.d.

Schol.: This proposition is also demonstrated from IP5, viz. that there are not
two substances of the same nature. Since a number of men can exist, what constitutes
the form of man is not the being of substance. Further, this proposition is evident from
the other properties of substance, viz. that substance is, by its nature, infinite, immutable, indivisible, etc., as anyone can easily see.

Cor.: From this it follows that the essence of man is constituted by certain modifications of God's attributes.

Dem.: For the being of substance does not pertain to the essence of man (by
P10). Therefore, it is something (by IP15) which is in God, and which can neither be
nor be conceived without God, *or* (by IP25C) an affection, *or* mode, which expresses
God's nature in a certain and determinate way.

Schol.: Everyone, of course, must concede that nothing can either be or be conceived without God. For all confess that God is the only cause of all things, both of
their essence and of their existence. I.e., God is not only the cause of the coming to be
of things, as they say, but also of their being.

But in the meantime many say that anything without which a thing can neither be
nor be conceived pertains to the nature of the thing. And so they believe either that the

nature of God pertains to the essence of created things, or that created things can be or be conceived without God—or what is more certain, they are not sufficiently consistent.

The cause of this, I believe, was that they did not observe the [proper] order of Philosophizing. For they believed that the divine nature, which they should have contemplated before all else (because it is prior both in knowledge and in nature) is last in the order of knowledge, and that the things that are called objects of the senses are prior to all. That is why, when they contemplated natural things, they thought of nothing less than they did of the divine nature; and when afterwards they directed their minds to contemplating the divine nature, they could think of nothing less than of their first fictions, on which they had built the knowledge of natural things, because these could not assist knowledge of the divine nature. So it is no wonder that they have generally contradicted themselves.

But I pass over this. For my intent here was only to give a reason why I did not say that anything without which a thing can neither be nor be conceived pertains to its nature—viz. because singular things can neither be nor be conceived without God, and nevertheless, God does not pertain to their essence. But I have said that what necessarily constitutes the essence of a thing is that which, if it is given, the thing is posited, and if it is taken away, the thing is taken away, i.e., the essence is what the thing can neither be nor be conceived without, and vice versa, what can neither be nor be conceived without the thing.

P11: *The first thing that constitutes the actual being of a human Mind is nothing but the idea of a singular thing which actually exists.*

Dem.: The essence of man (by P10C) is constituted by certain modes of God's attributes, viz. (by A2) by modes of thinking, of all of which (by A3) the idea is prior in nature, and when it is given, the other modes (to which the idea is prior in nature) must be in the same individual (by A3). And therefore an idea is the first thing that constitutes the being of a human Mind. But not the idea of a thing which does not exist. For then (by P8C) the idea itself could not be said to exist. Therefore, it will be the idea of a thing which actually exists. But not of an infinite thing. For an infinite thing (by IP21 and 22) must always exist necessarily. But (by A1) it is absurd [that this idea should be of a necessarily existing object]. Therefore, the first thing that constitutes the actual being of a human Mind is the idea of a singular thing which actually exists, q.e.d.

Cor.: From this it follows that the human Mind is a part of the infinite intellect of God. Therefore, when we say that the human Mind perceives this or that, we are saying nothing but that God, not insofar as he is infinite, but insofar as he is explained through the nature of the human Mind, *or* insofar as he constitutes the essence of the human Mind, has this or that idea; and when we say that God has this or that idea, not only insofar as he constitutes the nature of the human Mind, but insofar as he also has the idea of another thing together with the human Mind, then we say that the human Mind perceives the thing only partially, *or* inadequately.

Schol.: Here, no doubt, my readers will come to a halt, and think of many things which will give them pause. For this reason I ask them to continue on with me slowly, step by step, and to make no judgment on these matters until they have read through them all.

P12: *Whatever happens in the object of the idea constituting the human Mind must be perceived by the human Mind, or there will necessarily be an idea of that thing in the*

Mind; i.e., if the object of the idea constituting a human Mind is a body, nothing can happen in that body which is not perceived by the Mind.

Dem.: For whatever happens in the object of any idea, the knowledge of that thing is necessarily in God (by P9C), insofar as he is considered to be affected by the idea of the same object, i.e. (by P11), insofar as he constitutes the mind of some thing. Therefore, whatever happens in the object of the idea constituting the human Mind, the knowledge of it is necessarily in God insofar as he constitutes the nature of the human Mind, i.e. (by P11C), knowledge of this thing will necessarily be in the Mind, or the Mind will perceive it, q.e.d.

Schol.: This Proposition is also evident, and more clearly understood from P7S, which you should consult.

P13: *The object of the idea constituting the human Mind is the Body, or a certain mode of Extension which actually exists, and nothing else.*

Dem.: For if the object of the human Mind were not the Body, the ideas of the affections of the Body would not be in God (by P9C) insofar as he constituted our Mind, but insofar as he constituted the mind of another thing, i.e. (by P11C), the ideas of the affections of the Body would not be in our Mind; but (by A4) we have ideas of the affections of the body. Therefore, the object of the idea that constitutes the human Mind is the Body, and it (by P11) actually exists.

Next, if the object of the Mind were something else also, in addition to the Body, then since (by IP36) nothing exists from which there does not follow some effect, there would necessarily (by P12) be an idea in our Mind of some effect of it. But (by A5) there is no idea of it. Therefore, the object of our Mind is the existing Body and nothing else, q.e.d.

Cor.: From this it follows that man consists of a Mind and a Body, and that the human Body exists, as we are aware of it.

Schol.: From these [propositions] we understand not only that the human Mind is united to the Body, but also what should be understood by the union of Mind and Body. But no one will be able to understand it adequately, or distinctly, unless he first knows adequately the nature of our Body. For the things we have shown so far are completely general and do not pertain more to man than to other Individuals, all of which, though in different degrees, are nevertheless animate. For of each thing there is necessarily an idea in God, of which God is the cause in the same way as he is of the idea of the human Body. And so, whatever we have said of the idea of the human Body must also be said of the idea of any thing.

However, we also cannot deny that ideas differ among themselves, as the objects themselves do, and that one is more excellent than the other, and contains more reality, just as the object of the one is more excellent than the object of the other and contains more reality. And so to determine what is the difference between the human Mind and the others, and how it surpasses them, it is necessary for us, as we have said, to know the nature of its object, i.e., of the human Body. I cannot explain this here, nor is that necessary for the things I wish to demonstrate. Nevertheless, I say this in general, that in proportion as a Body is more capable than others of doing many things at once, or being acted on in many ways at once, so its Mind is more capable than others of perceiving many things at once. And in proportion as the actions of a body depend more on itself alone, and as other bodies concur with it less in acting, so its mind is more capable of understanding distinctly. And from these [truths] we can know the excellence of one mind over the others, and also see the cause why we have only a completely confused knowledge of our Body, and many other things which I shall deduce from them in the following [propositions]. For this reason I have thought it worthwhile to explain and demonstrate these things more accurately. To do this it is necessary to premise a few things concerning the nature of bodies.

A1′: All bodies either move or are at rest.

A2′: Each body moves now more slowly, now more quickly.

L1: *Bodies are distinguished from one another by reason of motion and rest, speed and slowness, and not by reason of substance.*
    Dem.: I suppose that the first part of this is known through itself. But that bodies are not distinguished by reason of substance is evident both from IP5 and from IP8. But it is more clearly evident from those things which are said in IP15S.

L2: *All bodies agree in certain things.*
    Dem.: For all bodies agree in that they involve the concept of one and the same attribute (by D1), and in that they can move now more slowly, now more quickly, and absolutely, that now they move, now they are at rest.

L3: *A body which moves or is at rest must be determined to motion or rest by another body, which has also been determined to motion or rest by another, and that again by another, and so on, to infinity.*
    Dem.: Bodies (by D1) are singular things which (by L1) are distinguished from one another by reason of motion and rest; and so (by IP28), each must be determined necessarily to motion or rest by another singular thing, viz. (by P6) by another body, which (by A19) either moves or is at rest. But this body also (by the same reasoning) could not move or be at rest if it had not been determined by another to motion or rest, and this again (by the same reasoning) by another, and so on, to infinity, q.e.d.
    Cor.: From this it follows that a body in motion moves until it is determined by another body to rest; and that a body at rest also remains at rest until it is determined to motion by another.
    This is also known through itself. For when I suppose that body A, say, is at rest, and do not attend to any other body in motion, I can say nothing about body A except that it is at rest. If afterwards it happens that body A moves, that of course could not have come about from the fact that it was at rest. For from that nothing else could follow but that body A would be at rest.
    If, on the other hand, A is supposed to move, then as often as we attend only to A, we shall be able to affirm nothing concerning it except that it moves. If afterwards it happens that A is at rest, that of course also could not have come about from the motion it had. For from the motion nothing else could follow but that A would move. Therefore, it happens by a thing which was not in A, viz. by an external cause, by which [the Body in motion, A] has been determined to rest.

A1″: All modes by which a body is affected by another body follow both from the nature of the body affected and at the same time from the nature of the affecting body, so that one and the same body may be moved differently according to differences in the nature of the bodies moving it. And conversely, different bodies may be moved differently by one and the same body.

A2″: When a body in motion strikes against another which is at rest and cannot give way, then it is reflected, so that it continues to move, and the angle of the line of the reflected motion with the surface of the body at rest which it struck against will be equal to the angle which the line of the incident motion makes with the same surface.

This will be sufficient concerning the simplest bodies, which are distinguished from one another only by motion and rest, speed and slowness. Now let us move up to composite bodies.

Definition: *When a number of bodies, whether of the same or of different size, are so constrained by other bodies that they lie upon one another, or if they so move, whether with the same degree or different degrees of speed, that they communicate their motions to each other in a certain fixed manner, we shall say that those bodies are united with one another and that they all together compose one body or Individual, which is distinguished from the others by this union of bodies.*

A3″: As the parts of an Individual, or composite body, lie upon one another over a larger or smaller surface, so they can be forced to change their position with more or less difficulty; and consequently the more or less will be the difficulty of bringing it about that the Individual changes its shape. And therefore the bodies whose parts lie upon one another over a large surface, I shall call *hard;* those whose parts lie upon one another over a small surface, I shall call *soft;* and finally those whose parts are in motion, I shall call *fluid.*

L4: *If, of a body, or of an Individual, which is composed of a number of bodies, some are removed, and at the same time as many others of the same nature take their place, the [body, or the] Individual will retain its nature, as before, without any change of its form.*
    Dem.: For (by L1) bodies are not distinguished in respect to substance; what constitutes the form of the Individual consists [only] in the union of the bodies (by the preceding definition). But this [union] (by hypothesis) is retained even if a continual change of bodies occurs. Therefore, the Individual will retain its nature, as before, both in respect to substance, and in respect to mode, q.e.d.

L5: *If the parts composing an Individual become greater or less, but in such a proportion that they all keep the same ratio of motion and rest to each other as before, then the Individual will likewise retain its nature, as before, without any change of form.*
    Dem.: The demonstration of this is the same as that of the preceding Lemma.

L6: *If certain bodies composing an Individual are compelled to alter the motion they have from one direction to another, but so that they can continue their motions and communicate them to each other in the same ratio as before, the Individual will likewise retain its nature, without any change of form.*

Dem.: This is evident through itself. For it is supposed that it retains everything which, in its definition, we said constitutes its form. [See the Definition before L4.]

L7: *Furthermore, the Individual so composed retains its nature, whether it, as a whole, moves or is at rest, or whether it moves in this or that direction, so long as each part retains its motion, and communicates it, as before, to the others.*

Dem.: This [also] is evident from the definition preceding L4.

Schol.: By this, then, we see how a composite Individual can be affected in many ways, and still preserve its nature. So far we have conceived an Individual which is composed only of bodies which are distinguished from one another only by motion and rest, speed and slowness, i.e., which is composed of the simplest bodies. But if we should now conceive of another, composed of a number of Individuals of a different nature, we shall find that it can be affected in a great many other ways, and still preserve its nature. For since each part of it is composed of a number of bodies, each part will therefore (by L7) be able, without any change of its nature, to move now more slowly, now more quickly, and consequently communicate its motion more quickly or more slowly to the others.

But if we should further conceive a third kind of Individual, composed [of many individuals] of this second kind, we shall find that it can be affected in many other ways, without any change of its form. And if we proceed in this way to infinity, we shall easily conceive that the whole of nature is one Individual, whose parts, i.e., all bodies, vary in infinite ways, without any change of the whole Individual.

If it had been my intention to deal expressly with body, I ought to have explained and demonstrated these things more fully. But I have already said that I intended something else, and brought these things forward only because I can easily deduce from them the things I have decided to demonstrate.

Postulates

I. The human Body is composed of a great many individuals of different natures, each of which is highly composite.

II. Some of the individuals of which the human Body is composed are fluid, some soft, and others, finally are hard.

III. The individuals composing the human Body, and consequently, the human Body itself, are affected by external bodies in very many ways.

IV. The human Body, to be preserved, requires a great many other bodies, by which it is, as it were, continually regenerated.

V. When a fluid part of the human Body is determined by an external body so that it frequently thrusts against a soft part [of the Body], it changes its surface and, as it were, impresses on [the soft part] certain traces of the external body striking against [the fluid part].

VI. The human Body can move and dispose external bodies in a great many ways.

P14: *The human Mind is capable of perceiving a great many things, and is the more capable, the more its body can be disposed in a great many ways.*

Dem.: For the human Body (by Post. 3 and 6) is affected in a great many ways by external bodies, and is disposed to affect external bodies in a great many ways. But the human Mind must perceive everything which happens in the human body (by P12). Therefore, the human Mind is capable of perceiving a great many things, and is the more capable [as the human Body is more capable], q.e.d.

P15: *The idea that constitutes the formal being [esse] of the human Mind is not simple, but composed of a great many ideas.*

Dem.: The idea that constitutes the formal being of the human Mind is the idea of a body (by P13), which (by Post. 1) is composed of a great many highly composite Individuals. But of each Individual composing the body, there is necessarily (by P8C) an idea in God. Therefore (by P7), the idea of the human Body is composed of these many ideas of the parts composing the Body, q.e.d.

P16: *The idea of any mode in which the human Body is affected by external bodies must involve the nature of the human Body and at the same time the nature of the external body.*

Dem.: For all the modes in which a body is affected follow from the nature of the affected body, and at the same time from the nature of the affecting body (by A10 [II/99]). So the idea of them (by IA4) will necessarily involve the nature of each body. And so the idea of each mode in which the human Body is affected by an external body involves the nature of the human body and of the external body, q.e.d.

Cor. 1: From this it follows, first, that the human Mind perceives the nature of a great many bodies together with the nature of its own body.

Cor. 2: It follows, second, that the ideas which we have of external bodies indicate the condition of our own body more than the nature of the external bodies. I have explained this by many examples in the Appendix of Part I.

P17: *If the human Body is affected with a mode that involves the nature of an external body, the human Mind will regard the same external body as actually existing, or as present to it, until the Body is affected by an affect that excludes the existence or presence of that body.*

Dem.: This is evident. For so long as the human Body is so affected, the human Mind (by P12) will regard this affection of the body, i.e. (by P16), it will have the idea of a mode that actually exists, an idea that involves the nature of the external body, i.e., an idea that does not exclude, but posits, the existence or presence of the nature of the external body. And so the Mind (by P16C1) will regard the external body as actually existing, or as present, until it is affected, etc., q.e.d.

Cor.: Although the external bodies by which the human body has once been affected neither exist nor are present, the mind will still be able to regard them as if they were present.

Dem.: While external bodies so determine the fluid parts of the human body that they often thrust against the softer parts, they change (by Post. 5) their surfaces with the result (see A20 after L3) that they are reflected from it in another way than they used to be before, and still later, when the fluid parts, by their spontaneous motion, encounter those new surfaces, they are reflected in the same way as when they were driven against those surfaces by the external bodies. Consequently, while, thus reflected, they continue to move, they will affect the human Body with the same mode, concerning which the Mind (by P12) will think again, i.e. (by P17), the Mind will again regard the external body as present; this will happen as often as the fluid parts of the human body encounter the same surfaces by their spontaneous motion. So although the external bodies by which the human Body has once been affected do not exist, the

Mind will still regard them as present, as often as this action of the body is repeated, q.e.d.

Schol.: We see, therefore, how it can happen (as it often does) that we regard as present things that do not exist. This can happen from other causes also, but it is sufficient for me here to have shown one through which I can explain it as if I had shown it through its true cause; still, I do not believe that I wander far from the true [cause] since all those postulates which I have assumed contain hardly anything that is not established by experience which we cannot doubt, after we have shown that the human Body exists as we are aware of it (see P13C).

Furthermore (from P17C and P16C2), we clearly understand what is the difference between the idea of, say, Peter, which constitutes the essence of Peter's mind, and the idea of Peter which is in another man, say in Paul. For the former directly explains the essence of Peter's body, and does not involve existence, except so long as Peter exists; but the latter indicates the condition of Paul's body more than Peter's nature [see P16C2], and therefore, while that condition of Paul's body lasts, Paul's Mind will still regard Peter as present to itself, even though Peter does not exist.

Next, to retain the customary words, the affections of the human Body whose ideas present external bodies as present to us, we shall call images of things, even if they do not reproduce the [external] figures of things. And when the Mind regards bodies in this way, we shall say that it imagines.

And here, in order to begin to indicate what error is, I should like you to note that the imaginations of the Mind, considered in themselves contain no error, or that the Mind does not err from the fact that it imagines, but only insofar as it is considered to lack an idea that excludes the existence of those things that it imagines to be present to it. For if the Mind, while it imagined nonexistent things as present to it, at the same time knew that those things did not exist, it would, of course, attribute this power of imagining to a virtue of its nature, not to a vice—especially if this faculty of imagining depended only on its own nature, i.e. (by ID7), if the Mind's faculty of imagining were free.

P18: *If the human Body has once been affected by two or more bodies at the same time, then when the Mind subsequently imagines one of them, it will immediately recollect the others also.*

Dem.: The Mind (by P17C) imagines a body because the human Body is affected and disposed as it was affected when certain of its parts were struck by the external body itself. But (by hypothesis) the Body was then so disposed that the Mind imagined two [or more] bodies at once; therefore it will now also imagine two [or more] at once, and when the Mind imagines one, it will immediately recollect the other also, q.e.d.

Schol.: From this we clearly understand what Memory is. For it is nothing other than a certain connection of ideas involving the nature of things which are outside the human Body—a connection that is in the Mind according to the order and connection of the affections of the human Body.

I say, *first*, that the connection is only of those ideas that involve the nature of things which are outside the human Body, but not of the ideas that explain the nature of the same things. For they are really (by P16) ideas of affections of the human Body which involve both its nature and that of external bodies.

I say, *second*, that this connection happens according to the order and connection of the affections of the human Body in order to distinguish it from the connection of ideas which happens according to the order of the intellect, by which the Mind perceives things through their first causes, and which is the same in all men.

And from this we clearly understand why the Mind, from the thought of one thing, immediately passes to the thought of another, which has no likeness to the first: as, for example, from the thought of the word *pomum* a Roman will immediately pass to the thought of the fruit [viz. an apple], which has no similarity to that articulate sound and nothing in common with it except that the Body of the same man has often been affected by these two [at the same time], i.e., that the man often heard the word pomum while he saw the fruit.

And in this way each of us will pass from one thought to another, as each one's association has ordered the images of things in the body. For example, a soldier, having seen traces of a horse in the sand, will immediately pass from the thought of a horse to the thought of a horseman, and from that to the thought of war, etc. But a Farmer will pass from the thought of a horse to the thought of a plow, and then to that of a field, etc. And so each one, according as he has been accustomed to join and connect the images of things in this or that way, will pass from one thought to another.

P19: *The human Mind does not know the human Body itself, nor does it know that it exists, except through ideas of affections by which the Body is affected.*

Dem.: For the human Mind is the idea itself, or knowledge of the human Body (by P13), which (by P9) is indeed in God insofar as he is considered to be affected by another idea of a singular thing, or because (by Post. 4) the human Body requires a great many bodies by which it is, as it were, continually regenerated; and [because] the order and connection of ideas is (by P7) the same as the order and connection of causes, this idea will be in God insofar as he is considered to be affected by the ideas of a great many singular things. Therefore, God has the idea of the human Body, or knows the human Body, insofar as he is affected by a great many other ideas, and not insofar as he constitutes the nature of the human Mind, i.e. (by P11C), the human Mind does not know the human Body.

But the ideas of affections of the Body are in God insofar as he constitutes the nature of the human Mind, or the human Mind perceives the same affections (by P12), and consequently (by P16) the human Body itself, as actually existing (by P17).

Therefore to that extent only, the human Mind perceives the human Body itself, q.e.d.

P20: *There is also in God an idea, or knowledge, of the human Mind, which follows in God in the same way and is related to God in the same way as the idea, or knowledge, of the human Body.*

Dem.: Thought is an attribute of God (by P1), and so (by P3) there must necessarily be in God an idea both of [thought] and of all of its affections, and consequently (by P11), of the human Mind also. Next, this idea, or knowledge, of the Mind does not follow in God insofar as he is infinite, but insofar as he is affected by another idea of a singular thing (by P9). But the order and connection of ideas is the same as the order and connection of causes (by P7). Therefore, this idea, *or* knowledge, of the Mind follows in God and is related to God in the same way as the idea, *or* knowledge, of the Body, q.e.d.

P21: *This idea of the Mind is united to the Mind in the same way as the Mind is united to the Body.*

Dem.: We have shown that the Mind is united to the Body from the fact that the Body is the object of the Mind (see P12 and 13); and so by the same reasoning the idea of the Mind must be united with its own object, i.e., with the Mind itself, in the same way as the Mind is united with the Body, q.e.d.

Schol.: This proposition is understood far more clearly from what is said in P7S; for there we have shown that the idea of the Body and the Body, i.e. (by P13), the Mind and the Body, are one and the same Individual, which is conceived now under the attribute of Thought, now under the attribute of Extension. So the idea of the Mind and the Mind itself are one and the same thing, which is conceived under one and the same attribute, viz. Thought. The idea of the Mind, I say, and the Mind itself follow in God from the same power of thinking and by the same necessity. For the idea of the Mind, i.e., the idea of the idea, is nothing but the form of the idea insofar as this is considered as a mode of thinking without relation to the object. For as soon as someone knows something, he thereby knows that he knows it, and at the same time knows that he knows that he knows, and so on, to infinity. But more on these matters later.

P22: *The human Mind perceives not only the affections of the Body, but also the ideas of these affections.*

Dem.: The ideas of the ideas of the affections follow in God in the same way and are related to God in the same way as the ideas themselves of the affections (this is demonstrated in the same way as P20). But the ideas of the affections of the Body are in the human Mind (by P12), i.e. (by P11C), in God, insofar as he constitutes the essence of the human Mind. Therefore, the ideas of these ideas will be in God insofar as he has the knowledge, *or* idea, of the human Mind, i.e. (by P21), they will be in the human Mind itself, which for that reason perceives not only the affections of the Body, but also their ideas, q.e.d.

P23: *The Mind does not know itself, except insofar as it perceives the ideas of the affections of the Body.*

Dem.: The idea, *or* knowledge, of the Mind (by P20) follows in God in the same way, and is related to God in the same way as the idea, *or* knowledge, of the body. But since (by P19) the human Mind does not know the human Body itself, i.e. (by P11C), since the knowledge of the human Body is not related to God insofar as he constitutes the nature of the human Mind, the knowledge of the Mind is also not related to God insofar as he constitutes the essence of the human Mind. And so (again by P11C) to that extent the human Mind does not know itself.

Next, the ideas of the affections by which the Body is affected involve the nature of the human Body itself (by P16), i.e. (by P13), agree with the nature of the Mind. So knowledge of these ideas will necessarily involve knowledge of the Mind. But (by P22) knowledge of these ideas is in the human Mind itself. Therefore, the human Mind, to that extent only, knows itself, q.e.d.

P24: *The human Mind does not involve adequate knowledge of the parts composing the human Body.*

Dem.: The parts composing the human Body pertain to the essence of the Body itself only insofar as they communicate their motions to one another in a certain fixed manner (see the Definition after L3C), and not insofar as they can be considered as Individuals, without relation to the human Body. For (by Post. 1) the parts of the human Body are highly composite Individuals, whose parts (by L4) can be separated from the human Body and communicate their motions (see A10 after L3) to other bodies in another manner, while the human Body completely preserves its nature and form. And so the idea, *or* knowledge, of each part will be in God (by P3), insofar as he is considered to be affected by another idea of a singular thing (by P9), a singular thing which is prior, in the order of nature, to the part itself (by P7). The same must also be said of each part of the Individual composing the human Body. And so, the knowledge of each part composing the human Body is in God insofar as he is affected with a great many ideas of things, and not insofar as he has only the idea of the human Body, i.e. (by P13), the idea that constitutes the nature of the human Mind. And so, (by P11C) the human Mind does not involve adequate knowledge of the parts composing the human Body, q.e.d.

P25: *The idea of any affection of the human Body does not involve adequate knowledge of an external body.*

Dem.: We have shown (P16) that the idea of an affection of the human Body involves the nature of an external body insofar as the external body determines the human Body in a certain fixed way. But insofar as the external body is an Individual that is not related to the human Body, the idea, *or* knowledge, of it is in God (by P9) insofar as God is considered to be affected with the idea of another thing which (by P7) is prior in nature to the external body itself. So adequate knowledge of the external body is not in God insofar as he has the idea of an affection of the human Body, *or* the idea of an affection of the human Body does not involve adequate knowledge of the external body, q.e.d.

P26: *The human Mind does not perceive any external body as actually existing, except through the ideas of the affections of its own Body.*

Dem.: If the human Body is not affected by an external body in any way, then (by P7) the idea of the human Body, i.e. (by P13), the human Mind, is also not affected in any way by the idea of the existence of that body, *or* it does not perceive the existence of that external body in any way. But insofar as the human Body is affected by an external body in some way, to that extent [the human Mind] (by P16 and P16C1) perceives the external body, q.e.d.

Cor.: Insofar as the human Mind imagines an external body, it does not have adequate knowledge of it.

Dem.: When the human Mind regards external bodies through ideas of the affections of its own Body, then we say that it imagines (see P17S); and the Mind cannot in any other way (by P16) imagine external bodies as actually existing. And so (by P15), insofar as the Mind imagines external bodies, it does not have adequate knowledge of them, q.e.d.

P27: *The idea of any affection of the human Body does not involve adequate knowledge of the human body itself.*

Dem.: Any idea of any affection of the human Body involves the nature of the human Body insofar as the human Body itself is considered to be affected with a certain definite mode (see P16). But insofar as the human Body is an Individual, which can be affected with many other modes, the idea of this [affection] etc. (See P25D.)

P28: *The ideas of the affections of the human Body, insofar as they are related only to the human Mind, are not clear and distinct, but confused.*

Dem.: For the ideas of the affections of the human Body involve the nature of external bodies as much as that of the human Body (by P16), and must involve the nature not only of the human Body [as a whole], but also of its parts; for the affections are modes (by Post. 3), with which the parts of the human Body, and consequently the whole Body, are affected. But (by P14 and P15) adequate knowledge of external bodies and of the parts composing the human Body is in God, not insofar as he is considered to be affected with the human Mind, but insofar as he is considered to be affected with other ideas. Therefore, these ideas of the affections, insofar as they are related only to the human Mind, are like conclusions without premises, i.e. (as is known through itself), they are confused ideas, q.e.d.

Schol.: In the same way we can demonstrate that the idea that constitutes the nature of the human Mind is not, considered in itself alone, clear and distinct; we can also demonstrate the same of the idea of the human Mind and the ideas of the ideas of the human Body's affections [viz. that are confused], insofar as they are referred to the Mind alone. Anyone can easily see this.

P29: *The idea of the idea of any affection of the human Body does not involve adequate knowledge of the human Mind.*

Dem.: For the idea of an affection of the human Body (by P17) does not involve adequate knowledge of the Body itself, *or* does not express its nature adequately, i.e. (by P13), does not agree adequately with the nature of the Mind; and so (by IA6) the idea of this idea does not express the nature of the human mind adequately, or does not involve adequate knowledge of it, q.e.d.

Cor.: From this it follows that so long as the human Mind perceives things from the common order of nature, it does not have an adequate, but only a confused and mutilated knowledge of itself, of its own Body, and of external bodies. For the Mind does not know itself except insofar as it perceives ideas of the affections of the body (by P13). But it does not perceive its own Body (by P19) except through the very ideas themselves of the affections [of the body], and it is also through them alone that it perceives external bodies (by P16). And so, insofar as it has these [ideas], then neither of itself (by P29), nor of its own Body (by P17), nor of external bodies (by P15) does it have an adequate knowledge, but only (by P18 and P28S) a mutilated and confused knowledge, q.e.d.

Schol.: I say expressly that the Mind has, not an adequate, but only a confused [and mutilated] knowledge, of itself, of its own Body, and of external bodies, so long as it perceives things from the common order of nature, i.e., so long as it is determined externally, from fortuitous encounters with things, to regard this or that, and not so long as it is determined internally, from the fact that it regards a number of things at once, to understand their agreements, differences, and oppositions. For so often as it is disposed internally, in this or another way, then it regards things clearly and distinctly, as I shall show below.

P30: *We can have only an entirely inadequate knowledge of the duration of our Body.*

Dem.: Our body's duration depends neither on its essence (by A1), nor even on God's absolute nature (by IP21). But (by IP28) it is determined to exist and produce an effect from such [other] causes as are also determined by others to exist and produce an effect in a certain and determinate manner, and these again by others, and so to infinity. Therefore, the duration of our Body depends on the common order of nature and the constitution of things. But adequate knowledge of how things are constituted is in God, insofar as he has the ideas of all of them, and not insofar as he has only the idea of the human Body (by P9C). So the knowledge of the duration of our Body is quite inadequate in God, insofar as he is considered to constitute only the nature of the human Mind, i.e. (by P11C), this knowledge is quite inadequate in our Mind, q.e.d.

P31: *We can have only an entirely inadequate knowledge of the duration of the singular things which are outside us.*

Dem.: For each singular thing, like the human Body, must be determined by another singular thing to exist and produce effects in a certain and determinate way, and this again by another, and so to infinity (by IP28). But since (in P30) we have demonstrated from this common property of singular things that we have only a very inadequate knowledge of the duration of our Body, we shall have to draw the same conclusion concerning the duration of singular things [outside us], viz. that we can have only a very inadequate knowledge of their duration, q.e.d.

Cor.: From this it follows that all particular things are contingent and corruptible. For we can have no adequate knowledge of their duration (by P31), and that is what we must understand by the contingency of things and the possibility of their corruption (see IP33S1). For (by IP29) beyond that there is no contingency.

P32: *All ideas, insofar as they are related to God, are true.*

Dem.: For all ideas which are in God agree entirely with their objects (by P7C), and so (by IA6) they are all true, q.e.d.

P33: *There is nothing positive in ideas on account of which they are called false.*

Dem.: If you deny this, conceive (if possible) a positive mode of thinking which constitutes the form of error, or falsity. This mode of thinking cannot be in God (by P32). But it also can neither be nor be conceived outside God (by IP15). And so there can be nothing positive in ideas on account of which they are called false, q.e.d.

P34: *Every idea that in us is absolute, or adequate and perfect, is true.*

Dem.: When we say that there is in us an adequate and perfect idea, we are saying nothing but that (by P11C) there is an adequate and perfect idea in God insofar as he constitutes the essence of our Mind, and consequently (by P32) we are saying nothing but that such an idea is true, q.e.d.

P35: *Falsity consists in the privation of knowledge which inadequate, or mutilated and confused, ideas involve.*

Dem.: There is nothing positive in ideas that constitutes the form of falsity (by P33); but falsity cannot consist in an absolute privation (for it is Minds, not Bodies, which are said to err, or be deceived), nor also in absolute ignorance. For to be ignorant and to err are different. So it consists in the privation of knowledge that inadequate knowledge of things, *or* inadequate and confused ideas, involve, q.e.d.

Schol.: In P17S I explained how error consists in the privation of knowledge. But to explain the matter more fully, I shall give [one or two examples]: men are deceived in that they think themselves free [i.e., they think that, of their own free will, they can either do a thing or forbear doing it], an opinion which consists only in this, that they are conscious of their actions and ignorant of the causes by which they are determined. This, then, is their idea of freedom—that they do not know any cause of their actions. They say, of course, that human actions depend on the will, but these are only words for which they have no idea. For all are ignorant of what the will is, and how it moves the Body; those who boast of something else, who feign seats and dwelling places of the soul, usually provoke either ridicule or disgust.

Similarly, when we look at the sun, we imagine it as about 200 feet away from us, an error that does not consist simply in this imagining, but in the fact that while we imagine it in this way, we are ignorant of its true distance and of the cause of this imagining. For even if we later come to know that it is more than 600 diameters of the earth away from us, we nevertheless imagine it as near. For we imagine the sun so near not because we do not know its true distance, but because an affection of our body involves the essence of the sun insofar as our body is affected by the sun.

P36: *Inadequate and confused ideas follow with the same necessity as adequate, or clear and distinct ideas.*

Dem.: All ideas are in God (by IP15); and, insofar as they are related to God, are true (by P32), and (by P7C) adequate. And so there are no inadequate or confused ideas except insofar as they are related to the singular Mind of someone (see P14 and P18). And so all ideas—both the adequate and the inadequate—follow with the same necessity (by P6C), q.e.d.

P37: *What is common to all things (on this see L2, above) and is equally in the part and in the whole, does not constitute the essence of any singular thing.*

Dem.: If you deny this, conceive (if possible) that it does constitute the essence of some singular thing, say the essence of B. Then (by D2) it can neither be nor be conceived without B. But this is contrary to the hypothesis. Therefore, it does not pertain to the essence of B, nor does it constitute the essence of any other singular thing, q.e.d.

P38: *Those things which are common to all, and which are equally in the part and in the whole, can only be conceived adequately.*

Dem.: Let A be something which is common to all bodies, and which is equally in the part of each body and in the whole. I say that A can only be conceived adequately. For its idea (by P7C) will necessarily be adequate in God, both insofar as he has the idea of the human Body and insofar as he has ideas of its affections, which (by P16, P15, and P17) involve in part both the nature of the human Body and that of external bodies. That is (by P12 and P13), this idea will necessarily be adequate in God insofar as he constitutes the human Mind, *or* insofar as he has ideas that are in the human Mind. The Mind therefore (by P11C) necessarily perceives A adequately, and does so both insofar as it perceives itself and insofar as it perceives its own or any external body. Nor can A be conceived in another way, q.e.d.

Cor.: From this it follows that there are certain ideas, or notions, common to all men. For (by L2) all bodies agree in certain things, which (by P38) must be perceived adequately, or clearly and distinctly, by all.

P39: *If something is common to, and peculiar to, the human Body and certain external bodies by which the human Body is usually affected, and is equally in the part and in the whole of each of them, its idea will also be adequate in the Mind.*

Dem.: Let A be that which is common to, and peculiar to, the human Body and certain external bodies, which is equally in the human Body and in the same external bodies, and finally, which is equally in the part of each external body and in the whole. There will be an adequate idea of A in God (by P7C), both insofar as he has the idea of the human Body, and insofar as he has ideas of the posited external bodies. Let it be posited now that the human Body is affected by an external body through what it has in common with it, i.e., by A; the idea of this affection will involve property A (by P16), and so (by P7C) the idea of this affection, insofar as it involves property A, will be adequate in God insofar as he is affected with the idea of the human Body, i.e. (by P13), insofar as he constitutes the nature of the human Mind. And so (by P11C), this idea is also adequate in the human Mind, q.e.d.

Cor.: From this it follows that the Mind is the more capable of perceiving many things adequately as its Body has many things in common with other bodies.

P40: *Whatever ideas follow in the Mind from ideas that are adequate in the mind are also adequate.*

Dem.: This is evident. For when we say that an idea in the human Mind follows from ideas that are adequate in it, we are saying nothing but that (by P11C) in the Divine intellect there is an idea of which God is the cause, not insofar as he is infinite, nor insofar as he is affected with the ideas of a great many singular things, but insofar as he constitutes only the essence of the human Mind [and therefore, it must be adequate].

Schol. 1: With this I have explained the cause of those notions which are called *common*, and which are the foundations of our reasoning.

But some axioms, or notions, result from other causes which it would be helpful to explain by this method of ours. For from these [explanations] it would be established which notions are more useful than the others, and which are of hardly any use; and then, which are common, which are clear and distinct only to those who have no prejudices, and finally, which are ill-founded. Moreover, we would establish what is the origin of those notions they call *Second*, and consequently of the axioms founded on them, and other things I have thought about, from time to time, concerning these matters. But since I have set these aside for another Treatise, and do not wish to give rise to disgust by too long a discussion, I have decided to pass over them here.

But not to omit anything it is necessary to know, I shall briefly add something about the causes from which the terms called *Transcendental* have had their origin—I

Interior of a House, ca. 1660, by Pieter De Hooch (1629–1684). This Dutch Baroque painting provides a visual metaphor for the precise geometry of Spinoza's *Ethics.* (*Wallace Collection, London,* © *Archivi Alinari, 1990/Art Resource*)

mean terms like Being, Thing and something. These terms arise from the fact that the human Body, being limited, is capable of forming distinctly only a certain number of images at the same time (I have explained what an image is in P17S). If that number is exceeded, the images will begin to be confused, and if the number of images the Body is capable of forming distinctly in itself at once is greatly exceeded, they will all be completely confused with one another.

Since this is so, it is evident from P17C and P18, that the human Mind will be able to imagine distinctly, at the same time, as many bodies as there can be images formed at the same time in its body. But when the images in the body are completely confused, the Mind also will imagine all the bodies confusedly, without any distinction, and comprehend them as if under one attribute, viz. under the attribute of Being, Thing, etc. This can also be deduced from the fact that images are not always equally vigorous and from other causes like these, which it is not necessary to explain here. For our purpose it is sufficient to consider only one. For they all reduce to this: these terms signify ideas that are confused in the highest degree.

Those notions they call *Universal*, like Man, Horse, Dog, etc., have arisen from similar causes, viz. because so many images (e.g., of men) are formed at one time in the human Body that they surpass the power of imagining—not entirely, of course, but still to the point where the Mind can imagine neither slight differences of the singular [men] (such as the color and size of each one, etc.) nor their determinate number, and imagines distinctly only what they all agree in, insofar as they affect the body. For the body has been affected most [forcefully] by [what is common], since each singular has affected it [by this property]. And [the mind] expresses this by the word *man*, and predicates it of infinitely many singulars. For as we have said, it cannot imagine a determinate number of singulars.

But it should be noted that these notions are not formed by all [men] in the same way, but vary from one to another, in accordance with what the body has more often been affected by, and what the Mind imagines or recollects more easily. For example, those who have more often regarded men's stature with wonder will understand by the word *man* an animal of erect stature. But those who have been accustomed to consider something else, will form another common image of men—e.g., that man is an animal capable of laughter, or a featherless biped, or a rational animal.

And similarly concerning the others—each will form universal images of things according to the disposition of his body. Hence it is not surprising that so many controversies have arisen among the philosophers, who have wished to explain natural things by mere images of things.

Schol. 2: From what has been said above, it is clear that we perceive many things and form universal notions:

I. from singular things which have been represented to us through the senses in a way that is mutilated, confused, and without order for the intellect (see P29C); for that reason I have been accustomed to call such perceptions knowledge from random experience;

II. from signs, e.g., from the fact that, having heard or read certain words, we recollect things, and form certain ideas of them, which are like them, and through which we imagine the things (P18S). These two ways of regarding things I shall henceforth call knowledge of the first kind, opinion or imagination.

III. Finally, from the fact that we have common notions and adequate ideas of the properties of things (see P38C, P39, P39C, and P40). This I shall call reason and the second kind of knowledge.

[IV]. In addition to these two kinds of knowledge, there is (as I shall show in what follows) another, third kind, which we shall call intuitive knowledge. And this kind of knowing proceeds from an adequate idea of the formal essence of certain attributes of God to the adequate knowledge of the [formal] essence of things.

I shall explain all these with one example. Suppose there are three numbers, and the problem is to find a fourth which is to the third as the second is to the first. Merchants do not hesitate to multiply the second by the third, and divide the product by the first, because they have not yet forgotten what they heard from their teacher without any demonstration, or because they have often found this in the simplest numbers, or from the force of the Demonstration of P7 in Bk. VII of Euclid, viz. from the common property of proportionals. But in the simplest numbers none of this is necessary. Given the numbers 1, 2, and 3, no one fails to see that the fourth proportional number is 6— and we see this much more clearly because we infer the fourth number from the ratio which, in one glance, we see the first number to have the second.

P41: *Knowledge of the first kind is the only cause of falsity, whereas knowledge of the second and of the third kind is necessarily true.*
    Dem.: We have said in the preceding scholium that to knowledge of the first kind pertain all those ideas which are inadequate and confused; and so (by P35) this knowledge is the only cause of falsity. Next, we have said that to knowledge of the second and third kinds pertain those which are adequate; and so (by P34) this knowledge is necessarily true.

P42: *Knowledge of the second and third kinds, and not of the first kind, teaches us to distinguish the true from the false.*
    Dem.: This Proposition is evident through itself. For he who knows how to distinguish between the true and the false must have an adequate idea of the true and of the false, i.e. (P40S2), must know the true and the false by the second or third kind of knowledge.

P43: *He who has a true idea at the same time knows that he has a true idea, and cannot doubt the truth of the thing.*
    Dem.: An idea true in us is that which is adequate in God insofar as he is explained through the nature of the human Mind (by P11C). Let us posit, therefore, that there is in God, insofar as he is explained through the nature of the human Mind, an adequate idea, A. Of this idea there must necessarily also be in God an idea which is related to God in the same way as idea A (by P20, whose demonstration is universal [and can be applied to all ideas]). But idea A is supposed to be related to God insofar as he is explained through the nature of the human Mind; therefore the idea of idea A must also be related to God in the same way, i.e. (by the same P11C), this adequate idea of idea A will be in the Mind itself which has the adequate idea A. And so he who has an adequate idea, *or* (by P34) who knows a thing truly, must at the same time have an adequate idea, *or* true knowledge, of his own knowledge. I.e. (as is manifest through itself), he must at the same time be certain, q.e.d.
    Schol.: In P21S I have explained what an idea of an idea is. But it should be noted that the preceding proposition is sufficiently manifest through itself. For no one who has a true idea is unaware that a true idea involves the highest certainty. For to have a true idea means nothing other than knowing a thing perfectly, *or* in the best way. And of course no one can doubt this unless he thinks that an idea is something

mute, like a picture on a tablet, and not a mode of thinking, viz. the very [act of] understanding. And I ask, who can know that he understands some thing unless he first understands it? I.e., who can know that he is certain about some thing unless he is first certain about it? What can there be which is clearer and more certain than a true idea, to serve as a standard of truth? As the light makes both itself and the darkness plain, so truth is the standard both of itself and of the false.

By this I think we have replied to these questions: if a true idea is distinguished from a false one, [not insofar as it is said to be a mode of thinking, but] only insofar as it is said to agree with its object, then a true idea has no more reality or perfection than a false one (since they are distinguished only through the extrinsic denomination [and not through the intrinsic denomination])—and so, does the man who has true ideas [have any more reality or perfection] than him who has only false ideas? Again, why do men have false ideas? And finally, how can someone know certainly that he has ideas which agree with their objects?

To these questions, I say, I think I have already replied. For as far as the difference between a true and a false idea is concerned, it is established from P35 that the true is related to the false as being is to nonbeing. And the causes of falsity I have shown most clearly from P19 to P35S. From this it is also clear what is the difference between the man who has true ideas and the man who has only false ideas. Finally, as to the last, viz. how a man can know that he has an idea that agrees with its object? I have just shown, more than sufficiently, that this arises solely from his having an idea that does agree with its object—or that truth is its own standard. Add to this that our Mind, insofar as it perceives things truly, is part of the infinite intellect of God (by P11C); hence, it is as necessary that the mind's clear and distinct ideas are true as that God's ideas are.

P44: *It is of the nature of Reason to regard things as necessary, not as contingent.*

Dem.: It is of the nature of reason to perceive things truly (by P41), viz. (by IA6) as they are in themselves, i.e. (by IP29), not as contingent but as necessary, q.e.d.

Cor. 1: From this it follows that it depends only on the imagination that we regard things as contingent, both in respect to the past and in respect to the future.

Schol.: I shall explain briefly how this happens. We have shown above (by P17 and P17C) that even though things do not exist, the Mind still imagines them always as present to itself, unless causes occur which exclude their present existence. Next, we have shown (P18) that if the human Body has once been affected by two external bodies at the same time, then afterwards, when the Mind imagines one of them, it will immediately recollect the other also, i.e., it will regard both as present to itself unless causes occur which exclude their present existence. Moreover, no one doubts but what we also imagine time, viz. from the fact that we imagine some bodies to move more slowly, or more quickly, or with the same speed.

Let us suppose, then, a child, who saw Peter for the first time yesterday, in the morning, but saw Paul at noon, and Simon in the evening, and today again saw Peter in the morning. It is clear from P18 that as soon as he sees the morning light, he will immediately imagine the sun taking the same course through the sky as he saw on the preceding day, or he will imagine the whole day, and Peter together with the morning, Paul with noon, and Simon with the evening. That is, he will imagine the existence of Paul and of Simon with a relation to future time. On the other hand, if he sees Simon in the evening, he will relate Paul and Peter to the time past, by imagining them together with past time. And he will do this more uniformly, the more often he has seen them in this same order.

But if it should happen at some time that on some other evening he sees James instead of Simon, then on the following morning he will imagine now Simon, now James, together with the evening time, but not both at once. For it is supposed that he has seen one or the other of them in the evening, but not both at once. His imagination, therefore, will vacillate and he will imagine now this one, now that one, with the future evening time, i.e., he will regard neither of them as certainly future, but both of them as contingently future.

And this vacillation of the imagination will be the same if the imagination is of things we regard in the same way with relation to past time or to present time. Consequently we shall imagine things as contingent in relation to present time as well as to past and future time.

Cor. 2: It is of the nature of Reason to perceive things under a certain species of eternity.

Dem.: It is of the nature of Reason to regard things as necessary and not as contingent (by P44). And it perceives this necessity of things truly (by P41), i.e. (by IA6), as it is in itself. But (by IP16) this necessity of things is the very necessity of God's eternal nature. Therefore, it is of the nature of Reason to regard things under this species of eternity.

Add to this that the foundations of Reason are notions (by P38) which explain those things that are common to all, and which (by P37) do not explain the essence of any singular thing. On that account, they must be conceived without any relation to time, but under a certain species of eternity, q.e.d.

P45: *Each idea of each body, or of each singular thing which actually exists, necessarily involves an eternal and infinite essence of God.*

Dem.: The idea of a singular thing which actually exists necessarily involves both the essence of the thing and its existence (by P8C). But singular things (by IP15) cannot be conceived without God—on the contrary, because (by P6) they have God for a cause insofar as he is considered under the attribute of which the things are modes, their ideas must involve the concept of their attribute (by IA4), i.e. (by ID6), must involve an eternal and infinite essence of God, q.e.d.

Schol.: By existence here I do not understand duration, i.e., existence insofar as it is conceived abstractly, and as a certain species of quantity. For I am speaking of the very nature of existence, which is attributed to singular things because infinitely many things follow from the eternal necessity of God's nature in infinitely many modes (see IP16). I am speaking, I say, of the very existence of singular things insofar as they are in God. For even if each one is determined by another singular thing to exist in a certain way, still the force by which each one perseveres in existing follows from the eternal necessity of God's nature. Concerning this, see IP24C.

P46: *The knowledge of God's eternal and infinite essence which each idea involves is adequate and perfect.*

Dem.: The demonstration of the preceding Proposition is Universal, and whether the thing is considered as a part or as a whole, its idea, whether of the whole or a part (by P45), will involve God's eternal and infinite essence. So what gives knowledge of an eternal and infinite essence of God is common to all, and is equally in the part and in the whole. And so (by P38) this knowledge will be adequate, q.e.d.

P47: *The human Mind has an adequate knowledge of God's eternal and infinite essence.*

Dem.: The human Mind has ideas (by P22) from which it perceives (by P13) itself, (by P19) its own Body, and (by P16C1 and P17) external bodies as actually existing. And so (by P45 and P46) it has an adequate knowledge of God's eternal and infinite essence, q.e.d.

Schol.: From this we see that God's infinite essence and his eternity are known to all. And since all things are in God and are conceived through God, it follows that we can deduce from this knowledge a great many things which we know adequately, and so can form that third kind of knowledge of which we spoke in P40S2 and of whose excellence and utility we shall speak in Part V.

But that men do not have so clear a knowledge of God as they do of the common notions comes from the fact that they cannot imagine God, as they can bodies, and that they have joined the name *God* to the images of things which they are used to seeing. Men can hardly avoid this, because they are continually affected by bodies.

And indeed, most errors consist only in our not rightly applying names to things. For when someone says that the lines which are drawn from the center of a circle to its circumference are unequal, he surely understands (then at least) by a circle something different from what Mathematicians understand. Similarly, when men err in calculating, they have certain numbers in their mind and different ones on the paper. So if you consider what they have in Mind, they really do not err, though they seem to err because we think they have in their mind the numbers which are on the paper. If this were not so, we would not believe that they were erring, just as I did not believe that he was erring whom I recently heard cry out that his courtyard had flown into his neighbor's hen [although his words were absurd], because what he had in mind seemed sufficiently clear to me [viz. that his hen had flown into his neighbor's courtyard].

And most controversies have arisen from this, that men do not rightly explain their own mind, or interpret the mind of the other man badly. For really, when they contradict one another most vehemently, they either have the same thoughts, or they are thinking of different things, so that what they think are errors and absurdities in the other are not.

P48: *In the Mind there is no absolute, or free, will, but the Mind is determined to will this or that by a cause which is also determined by another, and this again by another, and so to infinity.*

Dem.: The Mind is a certain and determinate mode of thinking (by P11), and so (by IP17C2) cannot be a free cause of its own actions, or cannot have an absolute faculty of willing and not willing. Rather, it must be determined to willing this or that (by IP28) by a cause which is also determined by another, and this cause again by another, etc., q.e.d.

Schol.: In this same way it is also demonstrated that there is in the Mind no absolute faculty of understanding, desiring, loving, etc. From this it follows that these and similar faculties are either complete fictions *or* nothing but Metaphysical beings, or universals, which we are used to forming from particulars. So intellect and will are to this or that idea, or to this or that volition as "stone-ness" is to this or that stone, or man to Peter or Paul.

We have explained the cause of men's thinking themselves free in the Appendix of Part I. But before I proceed further, it should be noted here that by will I understand a faculty of affirming and denying, and not desire. I say that I understand the faculty by which the Mind affirms or denies something true or something false, and not the desire by which the Mind wants a thing or avoids it.

But after we have demonstrated that these faculties are universal notions which are not distinguished from the singulars from which we form them, we must now investigate whether the volitions themselves are anything beyond the very ideas of things. We must investigate, I say, whether there is any other affirmation or negation in the Mind except that which the idea involves, insofar as it is an idea—on this see the following Proposition and also D3—so that our thought does not fall into pictures. For by ideas I understand, not the images that are formed at the back of the eye (and, if you like, in the middle of the brain), but concepts of Thought [or the objective Being of a thing insofar as it consists only in Thought].

P49: *In the Mind there is no volition, or affirmation and negation, except that which the idea involves insofar as it is an idea.*

Dem.: In the Mind (by P48) there is no absolute faculty of willing and not willing, but only singular volitions, viz. this and that affirmation, and this and that negation. Let us conceive, therefore, some singular volition, say a mode of thinking by which the Mind affirms that the three angles of a triangle are equal to two right angles.

This affirmation involves the concept, *or* idea, of the triangle, i.e., it cannot be conceived without the idea of the triangle. For to say that A must involve the concept of B is the same as to say that A cannot be conceived without B. Further, this affirmation (by A3) also cannot be without the idea of the triangle. Therefore, this affirmation can neither be nor be conceived without the idea of the triangle.

Next, this idea of the triangle must involve this same affirmation, viz. that its three angles equal two right angles. So conversely, this idea of the triangle also can neither be nor be conceived without this affirmation.

So (by D2) this affirmation pertains to the essence of the idea of the triangle, and is nothing beyond it. And what we have said concerning this volition (since we have selected it at random), must also be said concerning any volition, viz. that it is nothing apart from the idea, q.e.d.

Cor.: The will and the intellect are one and the same.

Dem.: The will and the intellect are nothing apart from the singular volitions and ideas themselves (by P48 and P48S). But the singular volitions and ideas are one and the same (by P49). Therefore the will and the intellect are one and the same, q.e.d.

Schol.: [I.] By this we have removed what is commonly maintained to be the cause of error. Moreover, we have shown above that falsity consists only in the privation that mutilated and confused ideas involve. So a false idea, insofar as it is false, does not involve certainty. When we say that a man rests in false ideas, and does not doubt them, we do not, on that account, say that he is certain, but only that he does not doubt, or that he rests in false ideas because there are no causes to bring it about that his imagination wavers [or to cause him to doubt them]. On this, see P44S.

Therefore, however stubbornly a man may cling to something false [so that we cannot in any way make him doubt it], we shall still never say that he is certain of it. For by certainty we understand something positive (see P43 and P43S), not the privation of doubt. But by the privation of certainty, we understand falsity.

However, to explain the preceding Proposition more fully, there remain certain things I must warn you of. And then I must reply to the objections that can be made against this doctrine of ours. And finally, to remove every uneasiness, I thought it worthwhile to indicate some of the advantages of this doctrine. Some, I say—for the most important ones will be better understood from what we shall say in Part V.

[II.] I begin, therefore, by warning my Readers, first, to distinguish accurately between an idea, *or* concept, of the Mind, and the images of things that we imagine. And then it is necessary to distinguish between ideas and the words by which we signify things. For because many people either completely confuse these three—ideas, images, and words—or do not distinguish them accurately enough, or carefully enough, they have been completely ignorant of this doctrine concerning the will. But it is quite necessary to know it, both for the sake of speculation and in order to arrange one's life wisely.

Indeed, those who think that ideas consist in images which are formed in us from encounters with [external] bodies, are convinced that those ideas of things [which can make no trace in our brains, or] of which we can form no similar image [in our brain] are not ideas, but only fictions which we feign from a free choice of the will. They look on ideas, therefore, as mute pictures on a panel and preoccupied with this prejudice, do not see that an idea, insofar as it is an idea, involves an affirmation or negation.

And then, those who confuse words with the idea, or with the very affirmation that the idea involves, think that they can will something contrary to what they are aware of, when they only affirm or deny with words something contrary to what they are aware of. But these prejudices can easily be put aside by anyone who attends to the nature of thought, which does not at all involve the concept of extension. He will then understand clearly that an idea (since it is a mode of thinking) consists neither in the image of anything, nor in words. For the essence of words and of images is constituted only by corporeal motions, which do not at all involve the concept of thought.

It should suffice to have issued these few words of warning on this matter, so I pass to objections mentioned above.

[III.A.(i)] The first of these is that they think it clear that the will extends more widely than the intellect, and so is different from the intellect. The reason why they think the will extends more widely than the intellect is that they say they know by experience that they do not require a greater faculty of assenting, or affirming, and denying, than we already have, in order to assent to infinitely many other things which we do not perceive—but they do require a greater faculty of understanding. The will, therefore, is distinguished from the intellect because the intellect is finite and the will is infinite.

[III.A.(ii)] Secondly, it can be objected to us that experience seems to teach nothing more clearly than that we can suspend our judgment so as not to assent to things we perceive. This also seems to be confirmed from the fact that no one is said to be deceived insofar as he perceives something, but only insofar as he assents or dissents. E.g., someone who feigns a winged horse does not on that account grant that there is a winged horse, i.e., he is not on that account deceived unless at the same time he grants that there is a winged horse. Therefore, experience seems to teach nothing more clearly than that the will, or faculty of assenting, is free, and different from the faculty of understanding.

[III.A.(iii)] Thirdly, it can be objected that one affirmation does not seem to contain more reality than another, i.e., we do not seem to require a greater power to affirm that what is true, is true, than to affirm that something false is true. But [with ideas it is different, for] we perceive that one idea has more reality, or perfection, than another. As some objects are more excellent than others, so also some ideas of objects are more perfect than others. This also seems to establish a difference between the will and the intellect.

[III.A.(iv)] Fourth, it can be objected that if man does not act from freedom of the will, what will happen if he is in a state of equilibrium, like Buridan's ass? Will he perish of hunger and of thirst? If I concede that he will, I would seem to conceive an ass, or a statue of a man, not a man. But if I deny that he will, then he will determine himself, and consequently have the faculty of going where he wills and doing what he wills.

Perhaps other things in addition to these can be objected. But because I am not bound to force on you what anyone can dream, I shall only take the trouble to reply to these objections—and that as briefly as I can.

[III.B.(i)] To the first I say that I grant that the will extends more widely than the intellect, if by intellect they understand only clear and distinct ideas. But I deny that the will extends more widely than perceptions, *or* the faculty of conceiving. And indeed, I do not see why the faculty of willing should be called infinite, when the faculty of sensing is not. For just as we can affirm infinitely many things by the same faculty of willing (but one after another, for we cannot affirm infinitely many things at once), so also we can sense, *or* perceive, infinitely many bodies by the same faculty of sensing (viz. one after another [and not at once]).

If they say that there are infinitely many things which we cannot perceive, I reply that we cannot reach them by any thought, and consequently, not by any faculty of willing. But, they say, if God willed to bring it about that we should perceive them also, he would have to give us a greater faculty of perceiving, but not a greater faculty of willing than he has given us. This is the same as if they said that, if God should will to bring it about that we understood infinitely many other beings, it would indeed be necessary for him to give us a greater intellect, but not a more universal idea of being, in order for us to embrace the same infinity of beings. For we have shown that the will is a universal being, *or* idea, by which we explain all the singular volitions, i.e., it is what is common to them all.

Therefore, since they believe that this common or universal idea of all volitions is a faculty, it is not at all surprising if they say that this faculty extends beyond the limits of the intellect to infinity. For the universal is said equally of one, a great many, or infinitely many individuals.

[III.B.(ii)] To the second objection I reply by denying that we have a free power of suspending judgment. For when we say that someone suspends judgment, we are saying nothing but that he sees that he does not perceive the thing adequately. Suspension of judgment, therefore, is really a perception, not [an act of] free will.

To understand this clearly, let us conceive a child imagining a winged horse, and not perceiving anything else. Since this imagination involves the existence of the horse (by P17C), and the child does not perceive anything else that excludes the existence of the horse, he will necessarily regard the horse as present. Nor will he be able to doubt its existence, though he will not be certain of it.

We find this daily in our dreams, and I do not believe there is anyone who thinks that while he is dreaming he has a free power of suspending judgment concerning the things he dreams, and of bringing it about that he does not dream the things he dreams he sees. Nevertheless, it happens that even in dreams we suspend judgment, viz. when we dream that we dream.

Next, I grant that no one is deceived insofar as he perceives, i.e., I grant that the imaginations of the Mind, considered in themselves, involve no error. But I deny that a man affirms nothing insofar as he perceives. For what is perceiving a winged horse other than affirming wings of the horse? For if the Mind perceived nothing else except the winged horse, it would regard it as present to itself, and would not have any cause of doubting its existence, or any faculty of dissenting, unless either the imagination of the winged horse were joined to an idea which excluded the existence of the same horse, or the Mind perceived that its idea of a winged horse was inadequate. And then either it will necessarily deny the horse's existence, or it will necessarily doubt it.

[III.B.(iii)] As for the third objection, I think what has been said will be an answer to it too: viz. that the will is something universal, which is predicated of all ideas, and which signifies only what is common to all ideas, viz. the affirmation, whose adequate essence, therefore, insofar as it is thus conceived abstractly, must be in each idea, and in this way only must be the same in all, but not insofar as it is considered to constitute the idea's essence; for in that regard the singular affirmations differ from one another as much as the ideas themselves do. For example, the affirmation that the idea of a circle involves differs from that which the idea of a triangle involves as much as the idea of the circle differs from the idea of the triangle.

Next, I deny absolutely that we require an equal power of thinking, to affirm that what is true is true, as to affirm that what is false is true. For if you consider the mind, they are related to one another as being to not-being. For there is nothing positive in ideas which constitutes the form of falsity (see P35, P35S, and P47S). So the thing to note here, above all, is how easily we are deceived when we confuse universals with singulars, and beings of reason and abstractions with real beings.

[III.B.(iv)] Finally, as far as the fourth objection is concerned, I say that I grant entirely that a man placed in such an equilibrium (viz. who perceives nothing but thirst and hunger, and such food and drink as are equally distant from him) will perish of hunger and thirst. If they ask me whether such a man should not be thought an ass, rather than a man, I say that I do not know—just as I also do not know how highly we should esteem one who hangs himself, or children, fools, and madmen, etc.

[IV.] It remains now to indicate how much knowledge of this doctrine is to our advantage in life. We shall see this easily from the following considerations:

[A.] Insofar as it teaches that we act only from God's command, that we share in the divine nature, and that we do this the more, the more perfect our actions are, and the more and more we understand God. This doctrine, then, in addition to giving us complete peace of mind, also teaches us wherein our greatest happiness, *or* blessedness, consists: viz. in the knowledge of God alone, by which we are led to do only those things which love and morality advise. From this we clearly understand how far they stray from the true valuation of virtue, who expect to be honored by God with the greatest rewards for their virtue and best actions, as for the greatest bondage—as if virtue itself, and the service of God, were not happiness itself, and the greatest freedom.

[B.] Insofar as it teaches us how we must bear ourselves concerning matters of fortune, or things which are not in our power, i.e., concerning things which do not follow from our nature—that we must expect and bear calmly both good fortune and bad. For all things follow from God's eternal decree with the same necessity as from the essence of a triangle it follows that its three angles are equal to two right angles.

[C.] This doctrine contributes to social life, insofar as it teaches us to hate no one, to disesteem no one, to mock no one, to be angry at no one, to envy no one; and also insofar as it teaches that each of us should be content with his own things, and should be helpful to his neighbor, not from unmanly compassion, partiality, or superstition, but from the guidance of reason, as the time and occasion demand. I shall show this in the Fourth Part.

[D.] Finally, this doctrine also contributes, to no small extent, to the common society insofar as it teaches how citizens are to be governed and led, not so that they may be slaves, but that they may do freely the things that are best.

And with this I have finished what I had decided to treat in this scholium, and put an end to this our Second Part. In it I think that I have explained the nature and properties of the human Mind in sufficient detail, and as clearly as the difficulty of the subject allows, and that I have set out doctrines from which we can infer many excellent things, which are highly useful and necessary to know.

JOHN LOCKE
1632–1704

John Locke was born in Wrington, Somerset, the son of a Puritan lawyer. His father fought on the side of the Parliament against Charles I, and Locke himself was a lifelong defender of the parliamentary system.

As a teenager, Locke attended Westminster School, studying classics under the harsh discipline of the time. He later condemned the English educational system for its brutality and one-sided emphasis on the past. In 1652, he entered Christ Church, Oxford, where he received his B.A. in 1656 and an M.A. in 1658. Again, he found his Oxford education obsessed with the past—in particular the Scholasticism of the late Middle Ages. Hence, he sought knowledge in the emerging sciences. In 1659, he was named a Senior Student at Oxford—a position he held until he lost it for political reasons in 1684.

In 1662, Locke met Lord Ashley, the Earl of Shaftesbury. Locke and Shaftesbury became close friends and in 1667 Locke went to live with Shaftesbury as his personal physician, securing his medical degree and license in 1674. Locke also helped Shaftesbury with several projects, including writing a constitution for the colony of Carolina. As a member of Shaftesbury's entourage, Locke traveled extensively and met many of the leading thinkers of his day.

When Shaftesbury became the leader of the parliamentary opposition to the king, Locke's friendship became a liability. Shaftesbury was tried for treason in 1681; and although he was acquitted, he fled to Holland where he died in 1683. Without the backing of his powerful patron, Locke also fled to Holland where he became an advisor to William and Mary of Orange. Following the Glorious Revolution of 1688, which removed Locke's enemy, James II, from the throne,

Locke returned home in the company of William and Mary—now king and queen of England.

Following his return to England, Locke published his two most important works, *Essay Concerning Human Understanding* (1690) and *Two Treatises of Government* (1690). Locke spent the rest of his life writing and serving the new government as Commissioner of Appeals and, later, as Commissioner of Trade and Plantations. He died quietly at the home of a friend in 1704.

*   *   *

Locke begins his first major work, *Essays Concerning Human Understanding*, with several arguments against the Cartesian notion of innate ideas. He claims that the mind is a *tabula rasa*, a blank tablet or "white paper, void of all characters, without any ideas." All ideas come from one source: experience. Experience, in turn, is of two types: sensation or reflection. Sensations are derived from our sensory perceptions of the external world. Reflection, on the other hand, provides ideas by the mind "reflecting on its own operations within itself."

Having explained the *origin* of ideas, Locke then explains the *nature* of ideas. All ideas are either simple or complex. Simple ideas are uncompounded; that is, they cannot be broken down further, such as the ideas of "sweetness" or "redness." Complex ideas are composed of two or more simple ideas, such as the idea of a red, sweet apple. Locke then classifies simple and complex ideas by sources (sensation, reflection, or both).

Having explained the sources of ideas, Locke next asks if the ideas that come from sensation actually resemble the qualities of the external objects that gave rise to them. He answers first by dividing qualities into primary and secondary. Primary qualities are "utterly inseparable" from external objects regardless of their state—such qualities include solidity, extension, figure, motion, rest, and number. On the other hand, secondary qualities are "nothing in the objects themselves, but powers to produce various sensations in us by their primary qualities." These secondary qualities would include such things as colors, sounds, tastes, and the like. So, for example, the primary qualities of an apple (a solid, being extended in space, etc.) have the power to produce the secondary quality of a sweet taste and a red color. This analysis means that the world *as we experience it* is only a representation of the way the world actually is. The blooming, buzzing, colorful world of our experience is not the real world.

Finally, Locke asks what these primary and secondary qualities are qualities *of*. He argues that there must be "some *substratum* wherein [ideas] do subsist, and from which they do result, which therefore we call *substance*." Although we cannot have any idea of substance, nor can we explain the concept, we must posit substance as a "supporter" of qualities—a "something I know not what," Locke said.

Locke's other major work, *Two Treatises Concerning Civil Government*, treats political theory. The *First Treatise* attacks the patriarchal absolutism of Sir Robert Filmer, a contemporary royalist, and the *Second Treatise* presents Locke's own ideas. Using much of Hobbes's terminology, Locke agrees with Hobbes that in a state of nature all persons are free and equal. While such a state is clearly inconvenient, it is not "a war of every man against every man," requiring all to surrender their rights to a sovereign. Instead, Locke argues for a social contract where people do not relinquish their rights to a sovereign but enter into an agreement with mutual rights and responsibilities. Locke insists that the rights of "life, liberty, and property" remain with the people. If the government does not abide by the terms of the contract, the people have the right to dissolve the contract and establish a new government. Locke's views greatly influenced Thomas Jefferson and the structure of American government.

*   *   *

Locke spent twenty years preparing his *Essay Concerning Human Understanding* for publication in 1690. The *Essay* went through several editions while Locke was still living, including an abridgment with his consent. The following selection is an abridgment by Walter Kaufmann, which I have modified. This abridgment owes much to John Wynne's (1695) editing and to the modern work of A.S. Pringle-Pattison.

The selection from the *Second Treatise* of Locke's *Two Treatises of Government* gives Locke's view of the state of nature and his argument against absolute monarchy.

In addition to these two works, Locke wrote *The Reasonableness of Christianity as Delivered in the Scriptures* (1695), *Vindications of the Reasonableness of Christianity* (1695 and 1697), and several "Letters" concerning toleration.

The best commentary on Locke's thought in general and on the *Essay* in particular is Richard I. Aaron, *John Locke* (Oxford: Clarendon Press, 1971). Also useful as a general overview are D.J. O'Connor, *John Locke* (Harmondsworth, Middlesex: Penguin Books, 1952); John W. Yolton, *Locke and the Way of Ideas* (Oxford: Clarendon Press, 1968); R.S. Woolhouse, *Locke* (Minneapolis: University of Minnesota Press, 1983); John Dunn, *Locke* (New York: Oxford University Press, 1984)—part of the "Past Masters" series, now reprinted in the combined volume of John Dunn et al., eds., *The British Empiricists* (Oxford: Oxford University Press, 1992); and Michael Ayers, *Locke* (Oxford: Routledge, 1994). For help with Locke's *Essay*, see John W. Yolton, *Locke and the Compass of Human Understanding: A Selective Commentary on the "Essay"* (London: Cambridge University Press, 1970), and John L. Mackie, *Problems from Locke* (Oxford: Oxford University Press, 1976). Nicholas Wolterstorff, *John Locke and the Ethics of Belief* (Cambridge: Cambridge University Press, 1996) provides guidance to the last section of the *Essay*. For guides to Locke's political thought, see John Dunn, *The Political Thought of John Locke* (Cambridge: Cambridge University Press, 1969), and J.W. Gough, *John Locke's Political Philosophy* (Oxford: Clarendon Press, 1973). John Yolton, *A Locke Dictionary* (Oxford: Basil Blackwell, 1993) provides a useful reference work. For collections of essays on Locke's thought, see C.B. Martin and D.M. Armstrong, eds., *Locke and Berkeley: A Collection of Critical Essays* (Notre Dame, IN: Notre Dame University Press, 1968); John W. Yolton, ed., *John Locke: Problems and Perspectives: A Collection of New Essays* (Cambridge: Cambridge University Press, 1969); and Vere Chappell's trio of books, *Essays on Early Modern Philosophers: John Locke—Theory of Knowledge, John Locke—Political Philosophy* (both Hamden, CT: Garland Press, 1992), and *The Cambridge Companion to Locke* (Cambridge: Cambridge University Press, 1994). For an interesting, if unusual, analysis of Locke's political thought, see Leo Strauss, *Natural Right and History* (Chicago: University of Chicago Press, 1952).

AN ESSAY CONCERNING HUMAN UNDERSTANDING (in part)

INTRODUCTION

1. *An enquiry into the understanding, pleasant and useful.*—Since it is the *understanding* that sets man above the rest of sensible beings, and gives him all the advantage and dominion which he has over them, it is certainly a subject, even for its nobleness, worth our labour to enquire into. The understanding, like the eye, whilst it makes us see and perceive all other things, takes no notice of itself; and it requires art and pains to set it at a distance, and make it its own object. But whatever be the difficulties that lie in the way of this enquiry; whatever it be that keeps us so much in the dark to ourselves; sure I am that all the light we can let in upon our own minds, all the acquaintance we can make with our own understandings, will not only be very pleasant, but bring us great advantage in directing our thoughts in the search of other things.

2. *Design.*—This, therefore, being my purpose, to enquire into the original, certainty, and extent of *human knowledge*, together with the grounds and degrees of *belief, opinion*, and *assent*, I shall not at present meddle with the physical consideration of the mind, or trouble myself to examine wherein its essence consists, or by what motions of our spirits, or alterations of our bodies, we come to have any *sensation* by our organs, or any *ideas* in our understandings; and whether those ideas do, in their formation, any or all of them, depend on matter or no. These are speculations which, however curious and entertaining, I shall decline, as lying out of my way in the design I am now upon. It shall suffice to my present purpose, to consider the discerning faculties of a man as they are employed about the objects which they have to do with: and I shall imagine I have not wholly misemployed myself in the thoughts I shall have on this occasion, if, in this historical, plain method, I can give any account of the ways whereby our understandings come to attain those notions of things we have, and can set down any measures of the certainty of our knowledge, or the grounds of those persuasions which are to be found amongst men, so various, different, and wholly contradictory; and yet asserted somewhere or other with such assurance, and confidence, that he that shall take a view of the opinions of mankind, observe their opposition, and at the same time consider the fondness and devotion wherewith they are embraced, the resolution and eagerness wherewith they are maintained, may perhaps have reason to suspect that either there is no such thing as truth at all, or that mankind hath no sufficient means to attain a certain knowledge of it.

3. *Method.*—It is therefore worth while to search out the bounds between opinion and knowledge, and examine by what measures, in things whereof we have no certain knowledge, we ought to regulate our assent, and moderate our persuasions. In order whereunto, I shall pursue this following method:—

First, I shall enquire into the original of those *ideas*, notions, or whatever else you please to call them, which a man observes, and is conscious to himself he has in his mind; and the ways whereby the understanding comes to be furnished with them.

Secondly, I shall endeavour to show what *knowledge* the understanding hath by those ideas, and the certainty, evidence, and extent of it.

Thirdly, I shall make some enquiry into the nature and grounds of *faith* or *opinion*: whereby I mean that assent which we give to any proposition as true, of whose truth yet we have no certain knowledge. And here we shall have occasion to examine the reasons and degrees of assent.

4. *Useful to know the extent of our comprehension.*—If by this enquiry into the nature of the understanding, I can discover the powers thereof, how far they reach, to what things they are in any degree proportionate, and where they fail us, I suppose it may be of use, to prevail with the busy mind of man to be more cautious in meddling with things exceeding its comprehension, to stop when it is at the utmost extent of its tether, and to sit down in a quiet ignorance of those things which, upon examination, are found to be beyond the reach of our capacities. We should not then perhaps be so forward, out of an affection of an universal knowledge, to raise questions, and perplex ourselves and others with disputes about things to which our understandings are not suited, and of which we cannot frame in our minds any clear or distinct perceptions, or whereof (as it has, perhaps, too often happened) we have not any notions at all. If we can find out how far the understanding can extend its view, how far it has faculties to attain certainty, and in what cases it can only judge and guess, we may learn to content ourselves with what is attainable by us in this state.

*   *   *

8. *What "idea" stands for.*—Thus much I thought necessary to say concerning the occasion of this enquiry into human understanding. But, before I proceed on to what I have thought on this subject, I must here, in the entrance, beg pardon of my reader for the frequent use of the word *idea* which he will find in the following treatise. It being that term which, I think, serves best to stand for whatsoever is the object of the understanding when a man thinks, I have used it to express whatever is meant by *phantasm, notion, species, or whatever it is which the mind can be employed about in thinking*; and I could not avoid frequently using it.

I presume it will be easily granted me, that there are such *ideas* in men's minds; every one is conscious of them in himself, and men's words and actions will satisfy him that they are in others.

Our first enquiry then shall be,—how they come into the mind.

BOOK I. NEITHER PRINCIPLES NOR IDEAS ARE INNATE

CHAPTER 1. NO INNATE PRINCIPLES IN THE MIND

1. *The way shown how we come by any knowledge, sufficient to prove it not innate.*—It is an established opinion amongst some men, that there are in the understanding certain innate principles; some primary notions, ⟨*koinai ennoiai*⟩, characters, as it were stamped upon the mind of man, which the soul receives in its very first being, and brings into the world with it. It would be sufficient to convince unprejudiced readers of the falseness of this supposition, if I should only show (as I hope I shall in the following parts of this discourse) how men, barely by the use of their natural faculties, may attain to all the knowledge they have, without the help of any innate impressions; and may arrive at certainty, without any such original notions or principles. For I imagine any one will easily grant, that it would be impertinent to suppose the ideas of colours innate in a creature to whom God hath given sight, and a power to receive them by the

eyes from external objects: and no less unreasonable would it be to attribute several truths to the impressions of nature and innate characters, when we may observe in ourselves faculties fit to attain as easy and certain knowledge of them as if they were originally imprinted on the mind.

But because a man is not permitted without censure to follow his own thoughts in the search of truth, when they lead him ever so little out of the common road, I shall set down the reasons that made me doubt of the truth of that opinion, as an excuse for my mistake, if I be in one; which I leave to be considered by those who, with me, dispose themselves to embrace truth wherever they find it.

2. *General assent the great argument.*—There is nothing more commonly taken for granted, than that there are certain principles, both *speculative* and *practical* (for they speak of both), universally agreed upon by all mankind; which therefore, they argue, must needs be the constant impressions which the souls of men receive in their first beings and which they bring into the world with them, as necessarily and really as they do any of their inherent faculties.

3. *Universal consent proves nothing innate.*—This argument, drawn from universal consent, has this misfortune in it, that if it were true in matter of fact, that there were certain truths wherein all mankind agreed, it would not prove them innate, if there can be any other way shown, how men may come to that universal agreement in the things they do consent in; which I presume may be done.

4. *"What is, is,"* and *"It is impossible for the same Thing to be and not to be," not universally assented to.*—But, which is worse, this argument of universal consent which is made use of to prove innate principles, seems to me a demonstration that there are none such: because there are none to which all mankind give an universal assent. I shall begin with the speculative, and instance in those magnified principles of demonstration, "Whatsoever is, is," and "It is impossible for the same thing to be and not to be"; which, of all others, I think have the most allowed title to innate. These have so settled a reputation of maxims universally received, that it will no doubt be thought strange if any one should seem to question it. But yet I take liberty to say, that these propositions are so far from having an universal assent, that there are a great part of mankind to whom they are not so much as known.

5. *Not on the mind naturally imprinted, because not known to children, idiots, etc.*—For, first, it is evident, that all children and idiots have not the least apprehension or thought of them. And the want of that is enough to destroy that universal assent, which must needs be the necessary concomitant of all innate truths: it seeming to me near a contradiction to say, that there are truths imprinted on the soul which it perceives or understands not; imprinting, if it signify anything, being nothing else but the making certain truths to be perceived. . . . No proposition can be said to be in the mind which it never yet knew, which it was never yet conscious of. For if any one may, then, by the same reason, all propositions that are true, and the mind is *capable* ever of assenting to, may be said to be in the mind, and to be imprinted; since if any one can be said to be in the mind, which it never yet knew, it must be only because it is capable of knowing it; and so the mind is of all truths it ever shall know. Nay, thus truths may be imprinted on the mind which it never did, nor ever shall know: for a man may live long, and die at last in ignorance of many truths which his mind was capable of knowing, and that with certainty. So that if the capacity of knowing be the natural impression contended for, all the truths a man ever comes to know will, by this account, be every one of them innate: and this great point will amount to no more, but only to a very high improper way of speaking. But then, to what end such contest for certain in-

nate maxims? If truths can be imprinted on the understanding without being perceived, I can see no difference there can be between any truths the mind is capable of knowing in respect of their original: they must all be innate, or all adventitious; in vain shall a man go about to distinguish them. He therefore that talks of innate notions in the understanding, cannot (if he intend thereby any distinct sort of truths) mean such truths to be in the understanding as it never perceived, and is yet wholly ignorant of. For if these words "to be in the understanding" have any propriety, they signify to be understood. If therefore these two propositions: "Whatsoever is, is," and, "It is impossible for the same thing to be, and not to be," are by nature imprinted, children cannot be ignorant of them; infants, and all that have souls, must necessarily have them in their understandings, know the truth of them, and assent to it.

*   *   *

Chapter 2. No Innate Practical Principles

1. *No moral principles so clear and so generally received as the forementioned speculative maxims.*—If those speculative maxims whereof we discoursed in the foregoing chapter have not an actual universal assent from all mankind, as we there proved, it is much more visible concerning practical principles, that they come short of an universal reception. . . .

2. *Faith and justice not owned as principles by all men.*—Whether there be any such moral principles wherein all men do agree, I appeal to any who have been but moderately conversant in the history of mankind, and looked abroad beyond the smoke of their own chimneys. Where is that practical truth that is universally received without doubt or question, as it must be if innate? *Justice*, and keeping of contracts, is that which most men seem to agree in. This is a principle which is thought to extend itself to the dens of thieves, and the confederacies of the greatest villains; and they who have gone farthest towards the putting off of humanity itself, keep faith and rules of justice one with another. I grant that outlaws themselves do this one amongst another; but it is without receiving these as the innate laws of nature. They practice them as rules of convenience within their own communities: but it is impossible to conceive that he embraces justice as a practical principle who acts fairly with his fellow-highwayman, and at the same plunders or kills the next honest man he meets with.

*   *   *

Chapter 3. Considerations on Innate Principles

8. *Idea of God not innate.*—If any idea can be imagined innate, the idea of God may, of all others, for many reasons, be thought so; since it is hard to conceive how there should be innate moral principles without an innate idea of a Deity: without a notion of a lawmaker, it is impossible to have a notion of a law, and an obligation to observe it. Besides the atheists taken notice of amongst the ancients, and left branded upon the records of history, hath not navigation discovered, in these latter ages, whole

St. Paul's Cathedral, London, facade, built 1675–1710. Like Locke,
Sir Christopher Wren (1632–1723) was interested in science and
combining reason and religion. The left turret of the facade he
designed for St. Paul's conceals an observatory (opposite the clock in
the right turret). (*The British Tourist Authority*)

nations, at the Bay of Soldania, in Brazil, in Boranday, and the Caribbee Islands, etc.,
amongst whom there was to be found no notion of a God, no religion? . . . Perhaps, if
we should with attention mind the lives and discourses of people not so far off, we
should have too much reason to fear that many, in more civilized countries, have no
very strong and clear impressions of a Deity upon their minds; and that the complaints
of atheism made from the pulpit are not without reason. . . .

9. *The name of God not universal or obscure in meaning.*—But had all mankind
everywhere a notion of a God (whereof yet history tells us the contrary), it would not
from thence follow that the idea of him was innate, . . . especially if it be such an idea
as is agreeable to the common light of reason, and naturally deducible from every part
of our knowledge, as that of a God is. For the visible marks of extraordinary wisdom
and power appear so plainly in all the work of the creation, that a rational creature who
will but seriously reflect on them, cannot miss the discovery of a Deity; and the influence that the discovery of such a Being must necessarily have on the minds of all that
have but once heard of it, is so great, and carries such a weight of thought and communication with it, that it seems stranger to me that a whole nation of men should be anywhere found so brutish as to want the notion of a God, than that they should be without
any notion of numbers, or fire.

*   *   *

Book II. Of Ideas

Chapter 1. Of Ideas in General and Their Original

1. *Idea is the object of thinking.*—Every man being conscious to himself that he thinks, and that which his mind is applied about whilst thinking being the ideas that are there, it is past doubt that men have in their minds several ideas, such as are those expressed by the words *whiteness, hardness, sweetness, thinking, motion, man, elephant, army, drunkenness,* and others. It is in the first place then to be enquired, How he comes by them?

I know it is a received doctrine, that men have native ideas and original characters stamped upon their minds in their very first being. This opinion I have at large examined already; and, I suppose, what I have said in the foregoing Book will be much more easily admitted, when I have shown whence the understanding may get all the ideas it has, and by what ways and degrees they may come into the mind; for which I shall appeal to every one's own observation and experience.

2. *All ideas come from sensation or reflection.*—Let us then suppose the mind to be, as we say, white paper, void of all characters, without any ideas; how comes it to be furnished? Whence comes it by that vast store, which the busy and boundless fancy of man has painted on it with an almost endless variety? Whence has it all the *materials* of reason and knowledge? To this I answer, in one word, from EXPERIENCE; in that all our knowledge is founded, and from that it ultimately derives itself. Our observation, employed either about external sensible objects, or about the internal operations of our minds, perceived and reflected on by ourselves, is that which supplies our understandings with all the materials of thinking. These two are the fountains of knowledge, from whence all the ideas we have or can naturally have, do spring.

3. *The objects of sensation one source of ideas.*—First, our senses, conversant about particular sensible objects, do convey into the mind several distinct perceptions of things, according to those various ways wherein those objects do affect them; and thus we come by those *ideas* we have of *yellow, white, heat, cold, soft, hard, bitter, sweet,* and all those which we call sensible qualities; which when I say the senses convey into the mind, I mean, they from external objects convey into the mind what produces there those perceptions. This great source of most of the ideas we have, depending wholly upon our senses, and derived by them to the understanding, I call, SENSATION.

4. *The operations of our minds the other source of them.*—Secondly, the other fountain, from which experience furnishes the understanding with ideas, is the perception of the operations of our mind within us, as it is employed about the ideas it has got; which operations, when the soul comes to reflect on and consider, do furnish the understanding with another set of ideas which could not be had from things without: and such are *perception, thinking, doubting, believing, reasoning, knowing, willing,* and all the different actings of our own minds; which we being conscious of, and observing in ourselves, do from these receive into our understanding as distinct ideas, as

we do from bodies affecting our senses. This source of ideas every man has wholly in himself: and though it be not sense, as having nothing to do with external objects, yet it is very like it, and might properly enough be called *internal sense*. But as I call the other SENSATION, so I call this REFLECTION, the ideas it affords being such only as the mind gets by reflecting on its own operations within itself. By Reflection, then, in the following part of this discourse, I would be understood to mean that notice which the mind takes of its own operations, and the manner of them, by reason whereof there come to be ideas of these operations in the understanding. These two, I say, viz., external material things as the objects of SENSATION, and the operations of our own minds within as the objects of REFLECTION are, to me, the only originals from whence all our ideas take their beginnings. The term *operations* here, I use in a large sense, as comprehending not barely the actions of the mind about its ideas, but some sort of passions arising sometimes from them, such as is the satisfaction or uneasiness arising from any thought.

5. *All our ideas are of the one or the other of these.*—The understanding seems to me not to have the least glimmering of any ideas which it doth not receive from one of these two. *External objects* furnish the mind with the ideas of sensible qualities, which are all those different perceptions they produce in us; and *the mind* furnishes the understanding with ideas of its own operations. These, when we have taken a full survey of them, and their several modes, combinations, and relations, we shall find to contain all our whole stock of ideas; and that we have nothing in our minds which did not come in one of these two ways. Let any one examine his own thoughts, and thoroughly search into his understanding, and then let him tell me, whether all the original ideas he has there, are any other than of the objects of his senses, or of the operations of his mind considered as objects of his reflection; and how great a mass of knowledge soever he imagines to be lodged there, he will, upon taking a strict view, see that he has not any idea in his mind but what one of these two have imprinted, though perhaps with infinite variety compounded and enlarged by the understanding, as we shall see hereafter.

6. *Observable in children.*—He that attentively considers the state of a child at his first coming into the world, will have little reason to think him stored with plenty of ideas that are to be the matter of his future knowledge. It is *by degrees* he comes to be furnished with them: and though the ideas of obvious and familiar qualities themselves before the memory begins to keep a register of time and order, yet it is often so late before some unusual qualities come in the way, that there are few men that cannot recollect the beginning of their acquaintance with them: and if it were worth while, no doubt a child might be so ordered as to have but a very few even of the ordinary ideas till he were grown up to a man. But all that are born into the world being surrounded with bodies that perpetually and diversely affect them, variety of ideas, whether care be taken about it or no, are imprinted on the minds of children. Light and colours are busy and at hand everywhere when the eye is but open; sounds and some tangible qualities fail not to solicit their proper senses, and force an entrance to the mind; but yet I think it will be granted easily, that if a child were kept in a place where he never saw any other but black and white till he were a man, he would have no more ideas of scarlet or green, than he that from his childhood never tasted an oyster or a pineapple has of those particular relishes.

7. *Men are differently furnished with these according to the different objects they converse with.*—Men then come to be furnished with fewer or more simple ideas from without, according as the objects they converse with afford greater or less variety; and from the operations of their minds within, according as they more or less reflect on

them. For, though he that contemplates the operations of his mind cannot but have plain and clear ideas of them; yet, unless he turn his thoughts that way, and considers them *attentively*, he will no more have clear and distinct ideas of all the operations of his mind, and all that may be observed therein, than he will have all the particular ideas of any landscape, or of the parts and motions of a clock, who will not turn his eyes to it, and with attention heed all the parts of it. The picture or clock may be so placed, that they may come in his way every day; but yet he will have but a confused idea of all the parts they are made up of, till he applies himself with attention to consider them each in particular.

8. *Ideas of reflection later, because they need attention.*—And hence we see the reason why it is pretty late before most children get ideas of the operations of their own minds; and some have not any very clear or perfect ideas of the greatest part of them all their lives. Because, though they pass there continually, yet, like floating visions, they make not deep impressions enough to leave in the mind clear, distinct, lasting ideas, till the understanding turns inward upon itself, reflects on its own operations, and makes them the object of its own contemplation. Children, when they come first into it, are surrounded with a world of new things, which, by a constant solicitation of their senses, draw the mind constantly to them, forward to take notice of new, and apt to be delighted with the variety of changing objects. Thus the first years are usually employed and diverted in looking abroad. Men's business in them is to acquaint themselves with what is to be found without; and so, growing up in a constant attention to outward sensations, seldom make any considerable reflection on what passes within them till they come to be of riper years; and some scarce ever at all.

9. *The soul begins to have ideas when it begins to perceive.*—To ask, at what time a man has first any ideas, is to ask when he begins to perceive; having ideas, and perception, being the same thing. I know it is an opinion, that the soul always thinks; and that it has the actual perception of ideas in itself constantly, as long as it exists; and that actual thinking is as inseparable from the soul, as actual extension is from the body: which if true, to enquire after the beginning of a man's ideas is the same as to enquire after the beginning of his soul. For by this account, soul and its ideas, as body and its extension, will begin to exist both at the same time.

*   *   *

CHAPTER 2. OF SIMPLE IDEAS

1. *Uncompounded appearances.*—The better to understand the nature, manner, and extent of our knowledge, one thing is carefully to be observed concerning the ideas we have; and that is, that some of them are *simple*, and some *complex*.

Though the qualities that affect our senses are, in the things themselves, so united and blended that there is no separation, no distance between them; yet it is plain the ideas they produce in the mind enter by the senses simple and unmixed. For though the sight and touch often take in from the same object at the same time different ideas; as a man sees at once motion and colour, the hand feels softness and warmth in the same piece of wax; yet the simple ideas thus united in the same subject are as perfectly distinct as those that come in by different senses. The coldness and hardness which a man feels in a piece of ice being as distinct ideas in the mind as the smell and whiteness of a lily, or as the taste of sugar and smell of a rose: and there is nothing can be plainer to a man than the clear and distinct perception he has of those simple ideas; which, being each in itself uncompounded, contains in it nothing but *one uniform appearance or conception in the mind*, and is not distinguishable into different ideas.

2. *The mind can neither make nor destroy them.*—These simple ideas, the materials of all our knowledge, are suggested and furnished to the mind only by those two ways above mentioned, viz., sensation and reflection. When the understanding is once stored with these simple ideas, it has the power to repeat, compare, and unite them, even to an almost infinite variety, and so can make at pleasure new complex ideas. But it is not in the power of the most exalted wit or enlarged understanding, by any quickness or variety of thought, to *invent* or *frame* one new simple idea in the mind, not taken in by the ways before mentioned; nor can any force of the understanding *destroy* those that are there. The dominion of man in this little world of his own understanding, being much-what the same as it is in the great world of visible things, wherein his power, however managed by art and skill, reaches no farther than to compound and divide the materials that are made to his hand, but can do nothing towards the making the least particle of new matter, or destroying one atom of what is already in being. The same inability will every one find in himself, who shall go about to fashion in his understanding any simple idea not received in by his senses from external objects, or by reflection from the operations of his own mind about them. I would have any one try to fancy any taste which had never affected his palate, or frame the idea of a scent he had never smelt; and when he can do this, I will also conclude, that a blind man hath ideas of colours, and a deaf man true distinct notions of sounds.

3. *Only the qualities that affect the sense are imaginable.*—This is the reason why, though we cannot believe it impossible to God to make a creature with other organs, and more ways to convey into the understanding the notice of corporeal things than those five, as they are usually counted, which he has given to man—yet I think it is *not possible* for any one to imagine any other qualities in bodies, howsoever constituted, whereby they can be taken notice of, besides sounds, tastes, smells, visible and tangible qualities. And had mankind been made with but four senses, the qualities then which are the object of the fifth sense, had been as far from our notice, imagination, and conception, as now any belonging to a sixth, seventh, or eighth sense, can possibly be: which, whether yet some other creatures, in some other parts of this vast and stupendous universe, may not have, will be a great presumption to deny. He that will not set himself proudly at the top of all things, but will consider the immensity of this fabric, and the great variety that is to be found in this little and inconsiderable part of it which he has to do with, may be apt to think, that in other mansions of it there may be other and different intelligible beings, of whose faculties he has as little knowledge or apprehension, as a worm shut up in one drawer of a cabinet hath of the senses or understanding of a man; such variety and excellency being suitable to the wisdom and power of the Maker. I have here followed the common opinion of man's having but five senses, though perhaps there may be justly counted more, but either supposition serves equally to my present purpose.

CHAPTER 3. OF IDEAS OF ONE SENSE

1. *Division of simple ideas.*—The better to conceive the ideas we receive from sensation, it may not be amiss for us to consider them in reference to the different ways whereby they make their approaches to our minds, and make themselves perceivable by us.

First, then, There are some which come into our minds *by one sense only*.

Secondly. There are others that convey themselves into the mind *by more senses than one*.

Thirdly. Others that are from *reflection only*.

Fourthly. There are some that make themselves way, and are suggested to the mind *by all the ways of sensation and reflection*.

We shall consider them apart under these several heads.

Ideas of one sense. There are some ideas which have admittance only through one sense, which is peculiarly adapted to receive them. Thus light and colours, as white, red, yellow, blue, with their several degrees or shades and mixtures, as green, scarlet, purple, sea-green, and the rest come in only by the eyes; all kinds of noises, sounds, and tones, only by the ears; the several tastes and smells, by the nose and palate. And if these organs, or the nerves which are the conduits to convey them from without to their audience in the brain, the mind's presence-room (as I may so call it), are, any of them, so disordered as not to perform their functions, they have no postern to be admitted by, no other way to bring themselves into view, and be perceived by the understanding.

The most considerable of those belonging to the touch are heat, and cold, and solidity; all the rest, consisting almost wholly in the sensible configuration, as smooth and rough; or else, more or less firm adhesion of the parts, as hard and soft, tough and brittle, are obvious enough.

2. *Few simple ideas have names.*—I think it will be needless to enumerate all the particular simple ideas belonging to each sense. Nor indeed is it possible if we would, there being a great many more of them belonging to most of the senses than we have names for. The variety of smells, which are as many almost, if not more than species of bodies in the world, do most of them want names. Sweet and stinking commonly serve our turn for these ideas, which in effect is little more than to call them pleasing or displeasing; though the smell of a rose and violet, both sweet, are certainly very distinct ideas. Nor are the different tastes that by our palates we receive ideas of, much better provided with names. Sweet, bitter, sour, harsh, and salt, are almost all the epithets we have to denominate that numberless variety of relishes which are to be found distinct, not only in almost every sort of creatures, but in the different parts of the same plant, fruit, or animal. The same may be said of colours and sounds. I shall therefore, in the account of simple ideas I am here giving, content myself to set down only such as are most material to our present purpose, or are in themselves less apt to be taken notice of, though they are very frequently the ingredients of our complex ideas; amongst which, I think, I may well account solidity, which therefore I shall treat of in the next chapter.

CHAPTER 4. OF SOLIDITY

1. *We receive this idea from touch.*—The idea of solidity we receive by our touch; and it arises from the resistance which we find in body to the entrance of any other body into the place it possesses, till it has left it. There is no idea which we receive more constantly from sensation than solidity. Whether we move or rest, in what posture soever we are, we always feel something under us that supports us, and hinders our farther sinking downwards; and the bodies which we daily handle make us perceive that whilst they remain between them, they do, by an insurmountable force, hinder the approach of the parts of our hands that press them. *That which thus hinders the*

approach of two bodies, when they are moving one towards another, I call solidity. I will not dispute whether this acceptation of the word solid be nearer to its original signification than that which mathematicians use it in: it suffices that, I think, the common notion of solidity will allow, if not justify, this use of it; but if any one think it better to call it *impenetrability*, he has my consent. Only I have thought the term solidity the more proper to express this idea, not only because of its vulgar use in that sense, but also because it carries something more of positive in it than impenetrability, which is negative, and is, perhaps, more a consequence of solidity than solidity itself. This, of all other, seems the idea most intimately connected with and essential to body, so as nowhere else to be found or imagined, but only in matter; and though our senses take no notice of it, but in masses of matter, of a bulk sufficient to cause a sensation in us; yet the mind, having once got this idea from such grosser sensible bodies, traces it farther, and considers it, as well as figure, in the minutest particle of matter that can exist, and finds it inseparably inherent in body, wherever or however modified.

2. *Solidity fills space.*—This is the idea which belongs to body, whereby we conceive it to fill space. The idea of which filling of space is,—that where we imagine any space taken up by a solid substance, we conceive it so to possess it, that it excludes all other solid substances; and will for ever hinder any other two bodies, that move towards one another in a straight line, from coming to touch one another, unless it removes from between them in a line not parallel to that which they move in. This idea of it, the bodies which we ordinarily handle sufficiently furnish us with.

3. *Distinct from space.*—This resistance, whereby it keeps other bodies out of the space which it possesses, is so great, that no force, how great soever, can surmount it. All the bodies in the world, pressing a drop of water on all sides, will never be able to overcome the resistance which it will make, as soft as it is, to their approaching one another, till it be removed out of their way: whereby our idea of solidity is distinguished both from pure space, which is capable neither of resistance nor motion, and from the ordinary idea of hardness. For a man may conceive two bodies at a distance so as they may approach one another without touching or displacing any solid thing till their superficies come to meet; whereby, I think, we have the clear idea of space without solidity. For (not to go so far as annihilation of any particular body) I ask, whether a man cannot have the idea of the motion of one single body alone, without any other succeeding immediately into its place? I think it is evident he can: the idea of motion in one body no more including the idea of motion in another, than the idea of a square figure in one body includes the idea of a square figure in another. I do not ask, whether bodies do so exist, that the motion of one body cannot really be without the motion of another? To determine this either way is to beg the question for or against a *vacuum*. But my question is, whether one cannot have the *idea* of one body moved, whilst others are at rest? And I think this no one will deny: if so, then the place it deserted gives us the idea of pure space without solidity, whereinto another body may enter without either resistance or protrusion of anything. When the sucker in a pump is drawn, the space it filled in the tube is certainly the same, whether any other body follows the motion of the sucker or no; nor does it imply a contradiction that upon the motion of one body, another that is only contiguous to it should not follow it. The necessity of such a motion is built only on the supposition, that the world is full, but not on the distinct *ideas* of space and solidity; which are as different as resistance and not resistance, protrusion and not protrusion. And that men have ideas of space without body, their very disputes a vacuum plainly demonstrate as is showed in another place.

4. *From hardness.*—Solidity is hereby also differenced from hardness, in that solidity consists in repletion, and so an utter exclusion of other bodies out of the space it

possesses; but hardness, in a firm cohesion of the parts of matter, making up masses of a sensible bulk, so that the whole does not easily change its figure. And, indeed, hard and soft are names that we give to things only in relation to the constitutions of our own bodies; that being generally called hard by us which will put us to pain sooner than change figure by the pressure of any part of our bodies; and that, on the contrary, soft which changes the situation of its parts upon an easy and unpainful touch.

But this difficulty of changing the situation of the sensible parts amongst themselves, or of the figure of the whole, gives no more solidity to the hardest body in the world than to the softest; nor is an adamant one jot more solid than water. For though the two flat sides of two pieces of marble will more easily approach each other, between there is nothing but water or air, than if there be a diamond between them; yet it is not that the parts of the diamond are more solid than those of water, or resist more, but because the parts of water being more easily separable from each other, they will by a side-motion be more easily removed and give way to the approach of the two pieces of marble: but if they could be kept from making place by that side-motion, they would eternally hinder the approach of these two pieces of marble as much as the diamond. The softest body in the world will as invincibly resist the coming together of any two other bodies, if it be not put out of the way, but remain between them, as the hardest that can be found or imagined. He that shall fill a yielding soft body well with air or water will quickly find its resistance: and he that thinks that nothing but bodies that are hard can keep his hands from approaching one another, may be pleased to make a trial with the air enclosed in a football. The experiment I have been told was made at Florence, with a hollow globe of gold filled with water, and exactly closed, farther shows the solidity of so soft a body as water. For the golden globe thus filled being put into a press which was driven by the extreme force of screws, the water made its way through the pores of that very close metal, and finding no room for a nearer approach of its particles within, got to the outside, where it rose like a dew, and so fell in drops before the sides of the globe could be made to yield to the violent compression of the engine that squeezed it.

5. *On solidity depend impulse, resistance, and protrusion.*—By this idea of solidity is the extension of body distinguished from the extension of space. The extension of body being nothing but the cohesion or continuity of solid, separable parts; and the extension of space, the continuity of unsolid, inseparable, and immovable parts. Upon the solidity of bodies also depend their mutual impulse, resistance, and protrusion. Of pure space then, and solidity, there are several (amongst which I confess myself one) who persuade themselves they have clear and distinct ideas; and that they can think on space without anything in it that resists or is protruded by body. This is the idea of pure space, which they think they have as clear as any idea they can have of the extension of body. . . .

6. *What solidity is.*—If any one asks me, *what this solidity is*, I send him to his senses to inform him: let him put a flint or a football between his hands, and then endeavour to join them, and he will know. If he thinks this is not a sufficient explanation of solidity, what it is, and wherein it consists, I promise to tell him what it is, and wherein it consists, when he tells me what thinking is, or wherein it consists; or explains to me what extension or motion is, which perhaps seems much easier. The simple ideas we have are such as experience teaches them to us; but if, beyond that, we endeavour by words to make them clearer in the mind, we shall succeed no better than if we went about to clear up the darkness of a blind man's mind by talking, and to discourse into him the ideas of light and colours. The reason of this I shall show in another place.

CHAPTER 5. OF SIMPLE IDEAS OF DIVERS SENSES

Ideas received both by seeing and touching.—The ideas we get by more than one sense are of space or extension, figure, rest and motion: for these make perceivable impressions both on the eyes and touch; and we can receive and convey into our minds the ideas of the extension, figure, motion, and rest of bodies, both by seeing and feeling. But having occasion to speak more at large of these in another place, I here only enumerate them.

CHAPTER 6. OF SIMPLE IDEAS OF REFLECTION

1. *Simple ideas are the operations of the mind about its other ideas.*—The mind, receiving the ideas mentioned in the foregoing chapters from without, when it turns its view inward upon itself, and observes its own actions about those ideas it has, takes from thence other ideas, which are as capable to be the objects of its contemplation as any of those it received from foreign things.

2. *The idea of perception, and idea of willing, we have from reflection.*—The two great and principal actions of the mind, which are most frequently considered, and which are so frequent that every one that pleases may take notice of them in himself, are these two:—*Perception* or *Thinking*, and *Volition* or *Willing*. The power of thinking is called the *Understanding* and the power of volition is called the *Will*; and these two powers of abilities in the mind are denominated *faculties*. Of some of the *modes* of these simple ideas of reflection, such as are *remembrance, discerning, reasoning, judging, knowledge, faith, etc.*, I shall have occasion to speak hereafter.

CHAPTER 7. OF SIMPLE IDEAS OF BOTH SENSATION AND REFLECTION

1. *Ideas of pleasure and pain.*—There be other simple ideas which convey themselves into the mind by all the ways of sensation and reflection; viz., *pleasure* or *delight*, and its opposite, *pain* or *uneasiness*; *power*; *existence*; *unity*.

2. *Mix with almost all our other ideas.*—Delight or uneasiness, one or other of them, join themselves to almost all our ideas both of sensation and reflection; and there is scarce any affection of our senses from without, any retired thought of our mind within, which is not able to produce in us pleasure or pain. By pleasure and pain, I would be understood to signify whatsoever delights or molests us; whether it arises from the thoughts of our minds, or anything operating on our bodies. For whether we call it satisfaction, delight, pleasure, happiness, etc., on the one side, or uneasiness, trouble, pain, torment, anguish, misery, etc., on the other, they are still but different degrees of the same thing, and belong to the ideas of pleasure and pain, delight or uneasiness; which are the names I shall most commonly use for those two sorts of ideas.

3. *As motives of our actions.*—The infinite wise Author of our being, . . . to excite us to these actions of thinking and motion that we are capable of, has been pleased to join to several thoughts and several sensations a perception of delight. If this were wholly separated from all our outward sensations and inward thoughts, we should have no reason to prefer one thought or action to another, negligence to attention, or motion to rest. And so we should neither stir our bodies, nor employ our minds, but let our thoughts (if I may so call it) run adrift, without any direction or design; and suffer the

ideas of our minds, like unregarded shadows, to make their appearances there as it happened, without attending to them. In which state man, however furnished with the faculties of understanding and will, would be a very idle, unactive creature, and pass his time only in a lazy, lethargic dream. . . .

4. *An end and use of pain.*—Pain has the same efficacy and use to set us on work that pleasure has, we being as ready to employ our faculties to avoid that, as to pursue this: only this is worth our consideration, that pain is often produced by the same objects and ideas that produce pleasure in us. . . . Thus heat, that is very agreeable to us in one degree, by a little greater increase of it proves no ordinary torment; and the most pleasant of all sensible objects, light itself, if there be too much of it, if increased beyond a due proportion to our eyes, causes a very painful sensation. Which is wisely and favourably so ordered by nature, that when any object does by the vehemency of its operation disorder the instruments of sensation, whose structures cannot but be very nice and delicate, we might by the pain be warned to withdraw before the organ be quite put out of order, and so be unfitted for its proper functions for the future.

*   *   *

7. *Ideas of existence and unity.*—Existence and unity are two other ideas that are suggested to the understanding by every object without, and every idea within. When ideas are in our minds, we consider them as being actually there, as well as we consider things to be actually without us: which is, that they exist, or have existence. And whatever we can consider as one thing, whether a real being or idea, suggests to the understanding the idea of unity.

8. *Idea of power.*—Power also is another of those ideas which we receive from sensation and reflection. For, observing in ourselves that we do and can think, and that we can at pleasure move several parts of our bodies which were at rest, the effects also that natural bodies are able to produce in one another occurring every moment to our senses, we both these ways get the idea of power.

9. *Idea of succession.*—Besides these there is another idea, which though suggested by our senses yet is more constantly offered us by what passes in our own minds; and that is the idea of succession. For if we look immediately into ourselves, and reflect on what is observable there, we shall find our ideas always, whilst we are awake or have any thought, passing in train, one going and another coming without intermission.

10. *Simple ideas the materials of all our knowledge.*—These, if they are not all, are at least (as I think) the most considerable of those simple ideas which the mind has, and out of which is made all its other knowledge: all of which it receives only by the two forementioned ways of sensation and reflection.

Nor let any one think these too narrow bounds for the capacious mind of man to expatiate in, which takes its flight farther than the stars, and cannot be confined by the limits of the world. I grant all this, but desire any one to assign any *simple idea* which is not received from one of those inlets before mentioned, or any *complex idea* not made out of those simple ones.

Nor will it be so strange to think these few simple ideas sufficient to employ the quickest thought or largest capacity, and to furnish the materials of all that various knowledge and more various fancies and opinions of all mankind, if we consider how many words may be made out of the various composition of twenty-four letters; or if, going one step farther, we will but reflect on the variety of combinations may be made with barely one of the above-mentioned ideas, viz., number, whose stock is inexhaustible and truly infinite: and what a large and immense field doth extension alone afford the mathematicians?

CHAPTER 8. SOME FURTHER CONSIDERATIONS CONCERNING OUR SIMPLE IDEAS OF SENSATION

1. *Positive ideas from privative causes.*—Concerning the simple ideas of sensation it is to be considered, that whatsoever is so constituted in nature as to be able by affecting our senses to cause any perception in the mind, doth thereby produce in the understanding a simple idea; which, whatever be the external cause of it, when it comes to be taken notice of by our discerning faculty, it is by the mind looked on and considered there to be a real positive idea in the understanding, as much as any other whatsoever; though perhaps the cause of it be but a privation in the subject.

2. *Ideas in the mind distinguished from that in things which gives rise to them.*— Thus the ideas of heat and cold, light and darkness, white and black, motion and rest, are equally clear and positive ideas in the mind; though perhaps some of the causes which produce them are barely privations in those subjects from whence our senses derive those ideas. These the understanding, in its view of them, considers all as distinct positive ideas without taking notice of the causes that produce them: which is an enquiry not belonging to the idea as it is in the understanding, but to the nature of the things existing without us. These are two very different things, and carefully to be distinguished; it being one thing to perceive and know the idea of white or black, and quite another to examine what kind of particles they must be, and how ranged in the superficies, to make any object appear white or black.

3. *We may have ideas when we are ignorant of their physical causes.*—A painter or dyer who never enquired into their causes, hath the ideas of white and black and other colours as clearly, perfectly, and distinctly in his understanding, and perhaps more distinctly than the philosopher who hath busied himself in considering their natures, and thinks he knows how far either of them is in its cause positive or privative; and the idea of black is no less positive in his mind than that of white, however the cause of that colour in the external object may be only a privation.

4. *Why a privative cause in nature may occasion a positive idea.*—If it were the design of my present undertaking to enquire into the natural causes and manner of perception, I should offer this as a reason why a privative cause might, in some cases at least, produce a positive idea, viz., that all sensation being produced in us only by different degrees and modes of motion in our animal spirits, variously agitated by external objects, the abatement of any former motion must as necessarily produce a new sensation as the variation or increase of it; and so introduce a new idea, which depends only on a different motion of the animal spirits in that organ.

5. *Negative names need not be meaningless.*—But whether this be so or no I will not here determine, but appeal to every one's own experience, whether the shadow of a man, though it consists of nothing but the absence of light (and the more the absence of light is, the more discernible is the shadow), does not, when a man looks on it, cause as clear and positive an idea in his mind as a man himself, though covered over with clear sunshine. And the picture of a shadow is a positive thing. Indeed, we have negative names, which stand not directly for positive ideas, but for their absence, such as *insipid, silence, nihil,* etc., which words denote positive ideas, v.g., *taste, sound, being,* with a signification of their absence.

6. *Whether any ideas are due to causes really privative.*—And thus one may truly be said to see darkness. . . . The privative causes I have here assigned of positive ideas are according to the common opinion; but in truth it will be hard to determine whether there be really any ideas from a privative cause, till it be determined whether rest be any more a privation than motion.

7. *Ideas in the mind, qualities in bodies.*—To discover the nature of our ideas the better, and to discourse of them intelligibly, it will be convenient to distinguish them *as they are ideas or perceptions in our minds, and as they are modifications of matter in the bodies that cause such perceptions in us:* that so we may not think (as perhaps usually is done) that they are exactly the images and resemblances of something inherent in the subject; most of those of sensation being in the mind no more the likeness of something existing without us than the names that stand for them are the likeness of our ideas, which yet upon hearing they are apt to excite in us.

8. *Our ideas and the qualities of bodies.*—Whatsoever the mind perceives *in itself*, or is the immediate object of perception, thought, or understanding, that I call *idea*; and the power to produce any idea in our mind, I call *quality* of the subject wherein that power is. Thus a snowball having the power to produce in us the ideas of white, cold, and round, the powers to produce those ideas in us as they are in the snowball, I call qualities; and as they are sensations or perceptions in our understandings, I call them ideas; which *ideas*, if I speak of them sometimes as in the things themselves, I would be understood to mean those qualities in the objects which produce them in us.

9. *Primary qualities of bodies.*—Qualities thus considered in bodies are, *First*, such as are utterly inseparable from the body, in what estate soever it be; such as, in all the alterations and changes it suffers, all the force can be used upon it, it constantly keeps; and such as sense constantly finds in every particle of matter which has bulk enough to be perceived, and the mind finds inseparable from every particle of matter, though less than to make itself singly be perceived by our senses: v.g., take a grain of wheat, divide it into two parts, each part has still solidity, extension, figure, and mobility; divide it again, and it retains still the same qualities: and so divide it on, till the parts become insensible; they must retain still each of them all those qualities. . . . These I call *original* or *primary qualities* of body, which I think we may observe to produce simple ideas in us, viz., solidity, extension, figure, motion or rest, and number.

10. *Secondary qualities of bodies.*—Secondly, such qualities, which in truth are nothing in the objects themselves, but powers to produce various sensations in us by their primary qualities, i.e., by the bulk, figure, texture, and motion of their insensible parts, as colours, sounds, tastes, etc., these I call *secondary qualities*. To these might be added a third sort, which are allowed to be barely powers, though they are as much real qualities in the subject as those which I, to comply with the common way of speaking, call qualities, but, for distinction, secondary qualities. For the power in fire to produce a new colour or consistence in *wax* or *clay* by its primary qualities, is as much a quality in fire as the power it has to produce in me a new idea or sensation of warmth or burning, which I felt not before, by the same primary qualities, viz., the bulk, texture, and motion of its insensible parts.

11. *How bodies produce ideas in us.*—The next thing to be considered is, how bodies produce ideas in us; and that is manifestly by impulse, the only way which we can conceive bodies operate in.

12. *By motions, external, and in our organism.*—If, then, external objects be not united to our minds when they produce ideas in it, and yet we perceive these original qualities in such of them as singly fall under senses, it is evident that some motion must be thence continued by our nerves or animal spirits, by some parts of our bodies,

to the brains or the seat of sensation, there to produce in our minds the particular ideas we have of them. And since the extension, figure, number, and motion of bodies of an observable bigness, may be perceived at a distance by the sight, it is evident some singly imperceptible bodies must come from them to the eyes, and thereby convey to the brain some motion which produces these ideas which we have of them in us.

13. *How secondary qualities produce their ideas.*—After the same manner that the ideas of these original qualities are produced in us, we may conceive that the ideas of *secondary* qualities are also produced, viz., by the operation of insensible particles on our senses. . . . The different motions and figures, bulk and number of such particles, affecting the several organs of our senses, produce in us those different sensations which we have from the colours and smells of bodies; v.g., that a violet, by the impulse of such insensible particle, of matter of peculiar figures and bulks, and in different degrees and modifications of their motions, causes the ideas of the blue colour and sweet scent of that flower to be produced in our minds. It being no more impossible to conceive that God should annex such ideas to such motions with which they have no similitude, than that he should annex the idea of pain to the motion of a piece of steel dividing our flesh, with which that idea hath no resemblance.

14. *They depend on the primary qualities.*—What I have said concerning colours and smells may be understood also of tastes and sounds, and other the like sensible qualities; which, whatever reality we by mistake attribute to them, are in truth nothing in the objects themselves, but powers to produce various sensations in us, and depend on those primary qualities, viz., bulk, figure, texture, and motion of parts, as I have said.

15. *Ideas of primary qualities are resemblances; of secondary, not.*—From whence I think it is easy to draw this observation, that the ideas of primary qualities of bodies are resemblances of them, and their patterns do really exist in the bodies themselves; but the ideas produced in us by these secondary qualities have no resemblance of them at all. There is nothing like our ideas existing in the bodies themselves. They are, in the bodies we denominate from them, only a power to produce those sensations in us: and what is sweet, blue, or warm in idea, is but the certain bulk, figure, and motion of the insensible parts in the bodies themselves, which we call so.

16. *Examples.*—Flame is denominated hot and light; snow, white and cold; and manna, white and sweet, from the ideas they produce in us. Which qualities are commonly thought to be the same in those bodies that those ideas are in us, the one the perfect resemblance of the other, as they are in a mirror; and it would by most men be judged very extravagant, if one should say otherwise. And yet he that will consider that the same fire that at one distance produces in us the sensation of warmth, does at a nearer approach produce in us the far different sensation of pain, ought to bethink himself what reason he has to say, that his idea of warmth which was produced in him by the fire, is *actually in the fire*; and his idea of pain which the same fire produced in him the same way is not in the fire. Why is whiteness and coldness in snow, and pain not, when it produces the one and the other idea in us, and can do neither, but by the bulk, figure, number, and motion of its solid parts?

17. *The ideas of the primary alone really exist.*—The particular bulk, number, figure, and motion of the parts of fire or snow are really in them, whether any one's senses perceive them or no; and therefore they may be called *real* qualities, because they really exist in those bodies. But light, heat, whiteness, or coldness, are no more really in them than sickness or pain is in manna. Take away the sensation of them; let not the eyes see light or colours, nor the ears hear sounds; let the palate not taste, nor the nose smell; and all colours, tastes, odours, and sounds, *as they are such particular ideas*, vanish and cease, and are reduced to their causes, i.e., bulk, figure, and motion of parts.

18. *Secondary exist only as modes of the primary.*—A piece of manna of a sensible bulk is able to produce in us the idea of a round or square figure; and, by being removed from one place to another, the idea of motion. This idea of motion represents it as it really is in the manna moving; a circle or square are the same, whether in idea or existence, in the mind or in the manna; and this, both motion and figure are really in the manna, whether we take notice of them or no: this everybody is ready to agree to. Besides, manna, by the bulk, figure, texture, and motion of its parts, has a power to produce the sensations of sickness, and sometimes of acute pains or gripings, in us. That these ideas of sickness and pain are not in the manna, but effects of its operations on us, and are nowhere when we feel them not: this also every one readily agrees to. And yet men are hardly to be brought to think that sweetness and whiteness are not really in manna, which are but the effects of the operations of manna by the motion, size, and figure of its particles on the eyes and palate: as the pain and sickness caused by manna are confessedly nothing but the effects of its operations on the stomach. . . . Why the pain and sickness, ideas that are the effects of manna, should be thought to be nowhere when they are not felt; and yet the sweetness and whiteness, effects of the same manna on other parts of the body, by ways equally as unknown, should be thought to exist in the manna, when they are not seen nor tasted, would need some reason to explain.

19. *Examples.*—Let us consider the red and white colours in porphyry: hinder light but from striking on it, and its colours vanish; it no longer produces any such ideas in us. Upon the return of light, it produces these appearances on us again. Can any one think any real alterations are made in the porphyry by the presence or absence of light, and that those ideas of whiteness and redness are really in porphyry in the light, when it is plain *it has no colour in the dark?* It has indeed such a configuration of particles, both night and day, as are apt, by the rays of light rebounding from some parts of that hard stone, to produce in us the idea of redness, and from others the idea of whiteness: but whiteness or redness are not in it at any time, but such a texture that hath the power to produce such a sensation in us.

*   *   *

22. *Excursion into natural philosophy.*—I have, in what just goes before, been engaged in physical enquiries a little farther than perhaps I intended. But it being necessary to make the nature of sensation a little understood, and to make the difference between the *qualities* in bodies and the *ideas* produced by them in the mind to be distinctly conceived, without which it were impossible to discourse intelligibly of them, I hope I shall be pardoned this little excursion into natural philosophy, it being necessary in our present enquiry to distinguish the *primary* and *real* qualities of bodies, which are always in them (viz., solidity, extension, figure, number, and motion or rest, and are sometimes perceived by us, viz., when the bodies they are in are big enough singly to be discerned), from those *secondary* and *imputed* qualities, which are but the powers of several combinations of those primary ones, when they operate without being distinctly discerned: whereby we also may come to know what ideas are, and what are not, resemblances of something really existing in the bodies we denominate from them.

23. *Three sorts of qualities in bodies.*—The qualities then that are in bodies, rightly considered, are of three sorts:

First, the bulk, figure, number, situation, and motion or rest of their solid parts. Those are in them, whether we perceive them or no; and when they are of that size that we can discover them, we have by these an idea of the thing as it is in itself, as is plain in artificial things. These I call *primary qualities.*

Secondly, the power that is in any body, by reason of its insensible primary qualities, to operate after a peculiar manner on any of our senses, and thereby produce in us the different ideas of several colours, sounds, smells, tastes, etc. These are usually called *sensible qualities.*

Thirdly, the power that is in any body, by reason of the particular constitution of its primary qualities, to make such a change in the bulk, figure, texture, and motion of *another body,* as to make it operate on our senses differently from what it did before. Thus the sun has a power to make wax white, and fire, to make lead fluid. These are usually called *powers.*

The first of these, as has been said, I think may be properly called real, original, or primary qualities, because they are in the things themselves, whether they are perceived or no: and upon their different modifications it is that the secondary qualities depend.

The other two are only powers to act differently upon other things, which powers result from the different modifications of those primary qualities.

24. *The first are resemblances; the second thought to be resemblances, but are not; the third neither are, nor are thought so.*—But though these two latter sorts of qualities are powers barely, and nothing but powers, relating to several other bodies, and resulting from the different modifications of the original qualities, yet they are generally otherwise thought of. . . . V.g., the idea of heat or light which we receive by our eyes or touch from the sun, are commonly thought real qualities existing in the sun, and something more than mere powers in it. But when we consider the sun in reference to wax, which it melts or blanches, we look upon the whiteness and softness produced in the wax, not as qualities in the sun, but effects produced by powers in it: whereas, if rightly considered, these qualities of light and warmth, which are perceptions in me when I am warmed or enlightened by the sun, are no otherwise in the sun than the changes made in the wax, when it is blanched or melted, are in the sun. They are all of them equally powers in the sun, depending on its primary qualities. . . .

25. *Why the secondary are ordinarily taken for real qualities, and not for bare powers.*—The reason why the one are ordinarily taken for real qualities, and the other only for bare powers, seems to be because the ideas we have of distinct colours, sounds, etc., containing nothing at all in them of bulk, figure, or motion, we are not apt to think them the effects of these primary qualities which appear not to our senses to operate in their production, and with which they have not any apparent congruity, or conceivable connexion. Hence it is that we are so forward to imagine that those ideas are the resemblances of something really existing in the objects themselves. . . . But, in the other case, in the operations of bodies changing the qualities one of another, we plainly discover that the quality produced hath commonly no resemblance with anything in the thing producing it; wherefore we look on it as a bare effect of power. . . .

*   *   *

CHAPTER 9. OF PERCEPTION

1. *Perception the first simple idea of reflection.*—PERCEPTION, as it is the first faculty of the mind exercised about our ideas; so it is the first and simplest idea we

have from reflection, and is by some called thinking in general. Though thinking, in the propriety of the English tongue, signifies that sort of operation in the mind about its ideas, wherein the mind is active; where it, with some degree of voluntary attention, considers anything. For in bare naked perception, the mind is, for the most part, only passive; and what it perceives, it cannot avoid perceiving.

2. *Reflection alone can give us the idea of what, perception is.*—What perception is, every one will know better by reflecting on what he does himself, when he sees, hears, feels, etc., or thinks, than by any discourse of mine. Whoever reflects on what passes in his own mind cannot miss it. And if he does not reflect, all the words in the world cannot make him have any notion of it.

3. *Arises in sensation only when the mind notices the organic impression.*—This is certain, that whatever alterations are made in the body, if they reach not the mind; whatever impressions are made on the outward parts, if they are not taken notice of within, there is no perception. Fire may burn our bodies with no other effect than it does a billet, unless the motion be continued to the brain, and there the sense of heat, or idea of pain, produced in the mind; wherein consists actual perception.

4. *Impulse on the organ insufficient.*—How often may a man observe in himself, that whilst his mind is intently employed in the contemplation of some objects, and curiously surveying some ideas that are there, it takes no notice of impressions of sounding bodies made upon the organ of hearing, with the same alteration that uses to be for the producing the idea of sound? A sufficient impulse there may be on the organ; but it not reaching the observation of the mind, there follows no perception: and though the motion that uses to produce the idea of sound be made in the ear, yet no sound is heard. Want of sensation, in this case, is not through any defect in the organ, or that the man's ears are less affected than at other times when he does hear: but that which uses to produce the idea, though conveyed in by the usual organ, not being taken notice of in the understanding, and so imprinting no idea in the mind, there follows no sensation. So that wherever there is sense or perception, there some idea is actually produced, and present in the understanding.

*   *   *

8. *Sensations often changed by the judgment.*—We are further to consider concerning perception, that the ideas we receive by sensation are often, in grown people, altered by the judgment, without our taking notice of it. When we set before our eyes a round globe of any uniform colour, v.g., gold, alabaster, or jet, it is certain that the idea thereby imprinted on our mind is of a flat circle, variously shadowed, with several degrees of light and brightness coming to our eyes. But we having, by use, been accustomed to perceive what kind of appearance convex bodies are wont to make in us; what alterations are made in the reflections of light by the difference of the sensible figures of bodies;—the judgment presently, by an habitual custom, alters the appearances into their causes. So that from that which is truly variety of shadow or colour, collecting the figure, it makes it pass for a mark of figure, and frames to itself the perception of a convex figure and an uniform colour; when the idea we receive from thence is only a plane variously coloured, as is evident in painting. To which purpose I shall here insert a problem of that very ingenious and studious promoter of real knowledge, the learned and worthy Mr. Molyneux, which he was pleased to send me in a letter some months since; and it is this:—"Suppose a man born blind, and now adult, and taught by his touch to distinguish between a cube and a sphere of the same metal, and nighly of the same bigness, so as to tell, when he felt one and the other, which is the

cube, which the sphere. Suppose then the cube and sphere placed on a table, and the blind man be made to see: *quære* whether *by his sight, before he touched them*, he could now distinguish and tell which is the globe, which the cube?" To which the acute and judicious proposer answers, "Not. For, though he has obtained the experience of how a globe, how a cube affects his touch, yet he has not yet obtained the experience, that what affects his touch so or so, must affect his sight so or so; or that a protuberant angle in the cube, that pressed his hand unequally, shall appear to his eye as it does in the cube."—I agree with this thinking gentleman, whom I am proud to call my friend, in his answer to this problem; and am of opinion that the blind man, at first sight, would not be able with certainty to say which was the globe, which the cube, whilst he only saw them; though he could unerringly name them by his touch, and certainly distinguish them by the difference of their figures felt. This I have set down, and leave with my reader, as an occasion for him to consider how much he may be beholden to experience, improvement, and acquired notions, where he thinks he had not the least use of, or help from them. And the rather, because this observing gentleman further adds, that "having, upon the occasion of my book, proposed this to divers very ingenious men, he hardly ever met with one that at first gave the answer to it which he thinks true, till by hearing his reasons they were convinced."

*   *   *

CHAPTER 11. OF DISCERNING, AND OTHER OPERATIONS OF THE MIND

*   *   *

8. *Naming.*—When children have, by repeated sensations, got ideas fixed in their memories, they begin by degrees to learn the use of signs; and when they have got the skill to apply the organs of speech to the framing of articulate sounds, they begin to make use of words to signify their ideas to others. These verbal signs they sometimes borrow from others, and sometimes make themselves, as one may observe among the new and unusual names children often give to things in the first use of language.

9. *Abstraction.*—The use of words, then, being to stand as outward marks of our internal ideas, and those ideas being taken from particular things, if every particular idea that we take in should have a distinct name, names must be endless. To prevent this, the mind makes the particular ideas received from particular objects to become general; which is done by considering them as they are in the mind, such appearances, separate from all other existences, and the circumstances of real existence, as time, place, or any other concomitant ideas. This is called abstraction, whereby ideas taken from particular beings become general representatives of all of the same kind, and their names general names, applicable to whatever exists conformable to such abstract ideas. Such precise, naked appearances in the mind, without considering how, whence, or with what others they came there, the understanding lays up (with names commonly annexed to them) as the standard to rank real existences into sorts, as they agree with these patterns, and to denominate them accordingly. Thus the same colour being observed today in chalk or snow, which the mind yesterday received from milk, it considers that appearance alone makes it a representative of all of that kind; and having given it the name whiteness, it by that sound signifies the same quality, where-

soever to be imagined or met with, and thus universals, whether ideas or terms, are made.

10. *Brutes abstract not.*—If it may be doubted whether beasts compound and enlarge their ideas that way to any degree; this, I think, I may be positive in, that the power of abstracting is not at all in them; and that the having of general ideas is that which puts a perfect distinction betwixt man and brutes, and is an excellency which the faculties of brutes do by no means attain to; for it is evident we observe no footsteps in them of making use of general signs for universal ideas; from which we have reason to imagine that they have not the faculty of abstracting, or making general ideas, since they have no use of words, or any other general signs.

*   *   *

CHAPTER 12. OF COMPLEX IDEAS

1. *Made by the mind out of simple ones.*—We have hitherto considered those ideas, in the reception whereof the mind is only passive, which are those simple ones received from sensation and reflection before mentioned, whereof the mind cannot make one to itself, nor have any idea which does not wholly consist of them. [But as the mind is wholly passive in the reception of all its simple ideas, so it exerts several acts of its own, whereby out of its simple ideas, as the materials and foundations of the rest, the other are framed. The acts of the mind wherein it exerts its power over its simple ideas are chiefly these three: (1) Combining several simple ideas into one compound one; and thus all *complex ideas* are made. (2) The second is bringing two ideas, whether simple or complex, together, and setting them by one another, so as to take a view of them at once, without uniting them into one; by which it gets all its *ideas of relations*. (3) The third is separating them from all other ideas that accompany them in their real existence; this is called abstraction: and thus all its *general ideas* are made. This shows man's power and its way of operation to be much the same in the material and intellectual world. For, the materials in both being such as he has no power over, either to make or destroy, all that man can do is either to unite them together, or to set them by one another, or wholly separate them. I shall here begin with the first of these in the consideration of complex ideas, and come to the other two in their due places.] As simple ideas are observed to exist in several combinations united together, so the mind has a power to consider several of them united together as one idea; and that not only as they are united in external objects, but as itself has joined them. Ideas thus made up of several simple ones put together I call *complex*; such as are beauty, gratitude, a man, an army, the universe; which, though complicated of various simple ideas or complex ideas made up of simple ones, yet are, when the mind pleases, considered each by itself as one entire thing, and signified by one name.

2. *Made voluntarily.*—In this faculty of repeating and joining together its ideas, the mind has great power in varying and multiplying the objects of its thoughts infinitely beyond what sensation or reflection furnished it with: but all this still confined to those simple ideas which it received from those two sources, and which are the ultimate materials of all its compositions. For simple ideas are all from things themselves; and of these the mind can have no more nor other than what are suggested to it. It can have no other ideas of sensible qualities than what come from without by the senses,

nor any ideas of other kind of operations of a thinking substance than what it finds in itself: but when it has once got these simple ideas, it is not confined barely to observation, and what offers itself from without; it can, by its own power, put together those ideas it has, and make new complex ones which it never received so united.

3. *Complex ideas are either modes, substances, or relations.*—COMPLEX IDEAS, however compounded and decompounded, though their number be infinite, and the variety endless wherewith they fill and entertain the thoughts of men, yet I think they may be all reduced under these three heads: 1. *Modes.* 2. *Substances.* 3. *Relations.*

4. *Ideas of modes.*—First, *Modes* I call such complex ideas which, however compounded, contain not in them the supposition of subsisting by themselves, but are considered as dependences on, or affections of substances; such as are the ideas signified by the words triangle, gratitude, murder, etc. And if in this I use the word mode in somewhat a different sense from its ordinary signification, I beg pardon; it being unavoidable in discourses differing from the ordinary received notions, either to make new words, or to use old words in somewhat a new signification: the latter whereof, in our present case, is perhaps the more tolerable of the two.

5. *Simple and mixed modes of simple ideas.*—Of these modes there are two sorts which deserve distinct consideration. First, there are some which are only variations or different combinations of the same simple idea, without the mixture of any other, as a dozen, or score; which are nothing but the ideas of so many distinct units added together: and these I call *simple modes*, as being contained within the bounds of one simple idea. Secondly, there are others compounded of simple ideas of several kinds, put together to make one complex one; v.g., beauty, consisting of a certain composition of colour and figure, causing delight in the beholder; theft, which, being the concealed change of the possession of anything, without the consent of the proprietor, contains, as is visible, a combination of several ideas of several kinds: and these I call *mixed modes.*

6. *Ideas of substances, single or collective.*—Secondly, the ideas of *Substances* are such combinations of simple ideas as are taken to represent distinct particular things subsisting by themselves, in which the supposed or confused idea of substance, such as it is, is always the first and chief. Thus, if to substance be joined the simple idea of a certain dull whitish colour, with certain degrees of weight, hardness, ductility, and fusibility, we have the idea of lead; and a combination of the ideas of a certain sort of figure, with the powers of motion, thought, and reasoning, joined to substance, make the ordinary idea of a man. Now of substances also there are two sorts of ideas, one of single substances, as they exist separately, as of a man or a sheep; the other of several of those put together, as an army of men, or flock of sheep; which *collective* ideas of several substances thus put together, are as much each of them one single idea as that of a man or an unit.

7. *Ideas of relation.*—Thirdly, the last sort of complex ideas is that we call Relation, which consists in the consideration and comparing one idea with another. Of these several kinds we shall treat in their order.

8. *The abstrusest ideas we can have are all from two sources.*—If we will trace the progress of our minds, and with attention observe how it repeats, adds together, and unites its simple ideas received from sensation or reflection, it will lead us farther than at first perhaps we should have imagined. And I believe we shall find, if we warily observe the originals of our notions, that *even the most abstruse ideas*, how remote soever they may seem from sense, or from any operation of our own minds, are yet only such as the understanding frames to itself, by repeating and joining together ideas that

it had either from objects of sense, or from its own operations about them: so that those even large and abstract ideas are *derived from sensation or reflection*, being no other than what the mind, by the ordinary use of its own faculties, employed about ideas received from objects of sense, or from the operations it observes in itself about them, may and does attain unto. This I shall endeavour to show in the ideas we have of space, time, and infinity, and some few other, that seem the most remote from those originals.

*   *   *

CHAPTER 21. OF POWER

1. *This idea how got.*—The mind being every day informed, by the senses, of the alteration of those simple ideas it observes in things without; and taking notice how one comes to an end and ceases to be, and another begins to exist which was not before; reflecting also, on what passes within itself, and observing a constant change of its ideas, sometimes by the impression of outward objects on the senses, and sometimes by the determination of its own choice; and concluding from what it has so constantly observed to have been, that the like changes will for the future be made in the same things by like agents, and by the like ways; considers in one thing the possibility of having any of its simple ideas changed, and in another the possibility of making that change; and so comes by that idea which we call *power*. Thus we say, fire has a power to melt gold, i.e., to destroy the consistency of its insensible parts, and consequently its hardness, and make it fluid; and gold has a power to be melted: that the sun has a power to blanch wax; and wax a power to be blanched by the sun, whereby the yellowness is destroyed, and whiteness made to exist in its room. In which and the like cases, the power we consider is in reference to the change of perceivable ideas. For we cannot observe any alteration to be made in, or operation upon, anything, but by the observable change of its sensible ideas: nor conceive any alteration to be made, but by conceiving a change of some of its ideas.

2. *Power, active and passive.*—Power thus considered is twofold, viz., as able to make, or able to receive, any change: the one may be called *active*, and the other passive, power. Whether matter be not wholly destitute of active power, as its author, God, is truly above all passive power; and whether the intermediate state of created spirits be not that alone which is capable of both active and passive power, may be worth consideration. I shall not now enter into that enquiry: my present business being not to search into the original of power, but how we come by the *idea* of it. But since active powers make so great a part of our complex ideas of natural substances (as we shall see hereafter), yet they being not, perhaps, so truly active powers as our hasty thoughts are apt to represent them, I judge it not amiss, by this intimation, to direct our minds to the consideration of God and spirits, for the clearest idea of *active* power.

3. *Power includes relation.*—I confess power includes in it some kind of relation (a relation to action or change), as indeed, which of our ideas, of what kind soever, when attentively considered, does not? For our ideas of extension, duration, and number, do they not all contain in them a secret relation of the parts? Figure and motion have something relative in them much more visibly: and sensible qualities, as colours and smells, etc., what are they but the powers of different bodies in relation to our perception? And if considered in the things themselves, do they not depend on the bulk, figure, texture, and motion of the parts? All which include some kind of relation in

them. Our idea therefore of power, I think, may well have a place amongst other *simple ideas*, and be considered as one of them, being one of those that make a principal ingredient in our complex ideas of substances, as we shall hereafter have occasion to observe.

4. *The clearest idea of active power had from spirit.*—We are abundantly furnished with the idea of passive power, by almost all sorts of sensible things. In most of them we cannot avoid observing their sensible qualities, nay, their very substances, to be in a continual flux: and therefore with reason we look on them as liable still to the same change. Nor have we of *active* power (which is the more proper signification of the word power) fewer instances. Since whatever change is observed, the mind must collect a power somewhere, able to make that change, as well as a possibility in the thing itself to receive it. But yet, if we will consider it attentively, bodies by our senses do not afford us so clear and distinct an idea of active power as we have from reflection on the operations of our minds. For all power relating to action, and there being but two sorts of action whereof we have any idea, viz., thinking and motion, let us consider whence we have the clearest ideas of the powers which produce these actions. (1) Of thinking, body affords us no idea at all: it is only from reflection that we have that. (2) Neither have we from body any idea of the beginning of motion. A body at rest affords us no idea of any active power to move; and when it is set in motion itself, that motion is rather a passion than an action in it. For when the ball obeys the stroke of a billiard-stick, it is not any action of the ball, but bare passion. Also when by impulse it sets another ball in motion that lay in its way, it only communicates the motion it had received from another, and loses in itself so much as the other received: which gives us but a very obscure idea of an *active* power of moving in body, whilst we observe it only to *transfer*, but not *produce* any motion. . . . The idea of the *beginning* of motion we have only from reflection on what passes in ourselves, where we find by experience, that, barely by willing it, barely by a thought of the mind, we can move the parts of our bodies which were before at rest. So that it seems to me, we have, from the observation of the operation of bodies by our senses, but a very imperfect, obscure idea of *active* power, since they afford us not any idea in themselves of the power to begin any action, either motion or thought. But if, from the impulse bodies are observed to make one upon another, any one thinks he has a clear idea of power, it serves as well to my purpose, sensation being one of those ways whereby the mind comes by its ideas: only I thought it worth while to consider here by the way, whether the mind doth not receive its idea of active power clearer from reflection on its own operations, than it doth from any external sensation.

5. *Will and understanding two powers in mind or spirit.*—This, at least, I think evident,—That we find in ourselves a power to begin or forbear, continue or end several actions of our minds, and motions of our bodies, barely by a thought or preference of the mind ordering, or as it were commanding, the doing or not doing such or such a particular action. This power which the mind has thus to order the consideration of any idea, or the forbearing to consider it; or to prefer the motion of any part of the body to its rest, and *vice versa*, in any particular instance, is that which we call the *Will*. The actual exercise of that power, by directing any particular action, or its forbearance, is that which we call *volition* or *willing*. The forbearance of that action, consequent to such order or command of the mind, is called *voluntary*. And whatsoever action is performed without such a thought of the mind, is called *involuntary*. The power of perception is that which we call the *Understanding*. Perception, which we make the act of the understanding, is of three sorts:—1. The perception of ideas in our minds. 2. The perception of the signification of signs. 3. The perception of the connexion or repugnancy,

agreement or disagreement, that there is between any of our ideas. All these are attributed to the understanding, or perceptive power, though it be the two latter only that use allows us to say we understand.

*   *   *

7. *Whence the idea of liberty and necessity.*—Everyone, I think, finds in himself a power to begin or forbear, continue or put an end to several actions in himself. From the consideration of the extent of this power of the mind over the actions of the man, which everyone finds in himself, arise the ideas of liberty and necessity.

8. *Liberty, what.*—All the actions that we have any idea of reducing themselves, as has been said, to these two, viz., thinking and motion; so far as a man has power to think or not to think, to move or not to move, according to the preference or direction of his own mind, so far is a man *free*. Wherever any performance or forbearance are not equally in a man's power; wherever doing or not doing will not equally *follow* upon the preference of his mind directing it, there he is not free, though perhaps the action may be voluntary. So, that the idea of *liberty* is, the idea of a power in any agent to do or forbear any particular action, according to the determination or thought of the mind, whereby either of them is preferred to the other: where either of them is not in the power of the agent to be produced by him according to his volition, there he is not at liberty; that agent is under *necessity*. So that liberty cannot be where there is no thought, no volition, no will; but there may be thought, there may be will, there may be volition, where there is no liberty. A little consideration of an obvious instance or two may make this clear.

9. *Supposes understanding and will.*—A tennis-ball, whether in motion by the stroke of a racket, or lying still at rest, is not by any one taken to be a free agent.—If we inquire into the reason, we shall find it is because we conceive not a tennis-ball to think, and consequently not to have any volition, or *preference* of motion to rest, or *vice versa*; and therefore has not liberty, is not a free agent; but all its both motion and rest come under our idea of necessary, and are so called. Likewise a man falling into the water, (a bridge breaking under him,) has not herein liberty, is not a free agent. For though he has volition, though he prefers his not falling to falling; yet the forbearance of that motion not being in his power, the stop or cessation of that motion follows not upon his volition; and therefore therein he is not free. So a man striking himself, or his friend, by a convulsive motion of his arm, which it is not in his power, by volition or the direction of his mind, to stop or forbear, nobody thinks he has in this liberty; every one pities him, as acting by necessity and constraint.

10. *Belongs not to volition.*—Again: suppose a man be carried, whilst fast asleep, into a room where is a person he longs to see and speak with; and be there locked fast in, beyond his power to get out: he awakes, and is glad to find himself in so desirable company, which he stays willingly in, i.e., prefers his stay to going away. I ask, is not this stay voluntary? I think nobody will doubt it: and yet, being locked fast in, it is evident he is not at liberty not to stay, he has not freedom to be gone. So that liberty is not an idea belonging to volition, or preferring; but to the person having the power of doing, or forbearing to do, according as the mind shall choose or direct. Our idea of liberty reaches as far as that power, and no farther. For wherever restraint comes to check that power, or compulsion takes away that indifferency of ability to act, or to forbear acting, there liberty, and our notion of it, presently ceases.

11. *Voluntary opposed to involuntary, not to necessary.*—We have instances enough, and often more than enough, in our own bodies. A man's heart beats, and the

blood circulates, which it is not in his power by any thought or volition to stop; and therefore in respect of these motions, where rest depends not on his choice, nor would follow the determination of his mind, if it should prefer it, he is not a free agent. Convulsive motions agitate his legs, so that though he wills it ever so much, he cannot by any power of his mind stop their motion, (as in that odd disease called *chorea sancti viti*), but he is perpetually dancing; he is not at liberty in this action, but under as much necessity of moving, as a stone that falls, or a tennis-ball struck with a racket. On the other side, a palsy or the stocks hinder his legs from obeying the determination of his mind, if it would thereby transfer his body to another place. In all these there is want of freedom; though the sitting still, even of a paralytic, whilst he prefers it to a removal, is truly voluntary. Voluntary, then, is not opposed to necessary, but to involuntary. For a man may prefer what he can do, to what he cannot do; the state he is in, to its absence or change; though necessity has made it in itself unalterable.

12. *Liberty, what.*—As it is in the motions of the body, so it is in the thoughts of our minds: where any one is such, that we have power to take it up, or lay it by, according to the preference of the mind, there we are at liberty. A waking man, being under the necessity of having some ideas constantly in his mind, is not at liberty to think or not to think; no more than he is at liberty, whether his body shall touch any other or no: but whether he will remove his contemplation from one idea to another is many times in his choice; and then he is, in respect of his ideas, as much at liberty as he is in respect of bodies he rests on; he can at pleasure remove himself from one to another. But yet some ideas to the mind, like some motions to the body, are such as in certain circumstances it cannot avoid, nor obtain their absence by the utmost effort it can use. A man on the rack is not at liberty to lay by the idea of pain, and divert himself with other contemplations: and sometimes a boisterous passion hurries our thoughts, as a hurricane does our bodies, without leaving us the liberty of thinking on other things, which we would rather choose. But as soon as the mind regains the power to stop or continue, begin or forbear, any of these motions of the body without, or thoughts within, according as it thinks fit to prefer either to the other, we then consider the man as a *free agent* again.

13. *Necessity, what.*—Wherever thought is wholly wanting, or the power to act or forbear according to the direction of thought, there necessity takes place. This, in an agent capable of volition, when the beginning or continuation of any action is contrary to that preference of his mind, is called compulsion; when the hindering or stopping any action is contrary to his volition, it is called restraint. Agents that have no thought, no volition at all, are in everything *necessary agents*.

14. *Liberty belongs not to the will.*—If this be so, (as I imagine it is,) I leave it to be considered, whether it may not help to put an end to that long agitated, and, I think, unreasonable, because unintelligible question, viz., *Whether man's will be free or no?* For if I mistake not, it follows from what I have said, that the question itself is altogether improper; and it is as insignificant to ask whether man's will be free, as to ask whether his sleep be swift, or his virtue square: liberty being as little applicable to the will, as swiftness of motion is to sleep, or squareness to virtue. Every one would laugh at the absurdity of such a question as either of these: because it is obvious that the modifications of motion belong not to sleep, nor the difference of figure to virtue; and when any one well considers it, I think he will as plainly perceive that liberty, which is but a power, belongs only to *agents*, and cannot be an attribute or modification of the will, which is also but a power.

15. *Volition.*—Such is the difficulty of explaining and giving clear notions of internal actions by sounds, that I must here warn my reader, that *ordering, directing,*

choosing, preferring, etc., which I have made use of, will not distinctly enough express volition, unless he will reflect on what he himself does when he wills. For example, preferring, which seems perhaps best to express the act of volition, does it not precisely. For though a man would prefer flying to walking, yet who can say he ever wills it? Volition, it is plain, is an act of the mind knowingly exerting that dominion it takes itself to have over any part of the man, by employing it in, or withholding it from, any particular action. And what is the will, but the faculty to do this? And is that faculty anything more in effect than a power; the power of the mind to determine its thought, to the producing, continuing, or stopping any action, as far as it depends on us? For can it be denied that whatever agent has a power to think on its own actions, and to prefer their doing or omission either to other, has that faculty called will? *Will*, then, is nothing but such a power. *Liberty*, on the other side, is the power a *man* has to do or forbear doing any particular action according as its doing or forbearance has the actual preference in the mind; which is the same thing as to say, according as he himself wills it.

16. *Powers, belonging to agents.*—It is plain then that the will is nothing but one power or ability, and *freedom* another power or ability so that, to ask, whether the will has freedom, is to ask whether one power has another power, one ability another ability; a question at first sight too grossly absurd to make a dispute, or need an answer. For, who is it that sees not that powers belong only to agents, and are attributes only of substances, and not of powers themselves? So that this way of putting the question (viz., whether the will be free) is in effect to ask, whether the will be a substance, an agent, or at least to suppose it, since freedom can properly be attributed to nothing else. If freedom can with any propriety of speech be applied to power, it may be attributed to the power that is in a man to produce, or forbear producing, motion in parts of his body, by choice or preference; which is that which denominates him free, and is freedom itself. But if any one should ask, whether freedom were free, he would be suspected not to understand well what he said; and he would be thought to deserve Midas's ears, who, knowing that rich was a denomination for the possession of riches, should demand whether riches themselves were rich.

*   *   *

21. *But to the agent or man.*—To return, then, to the inquiry about liberty, I think the question is not proper, *whether the will be free*, but *whether a man be free*. Thus, I think.

First, That so far as any one can, by the direction or choice of his mind, preferring the existence of any action to the non-existence of that action, and *vice versa*, make it to exist or not exist, so far he is free. For if I can, by a thought directing the motion of my finger, make it move when it was at rest, or *vice versa*, it is evident, that in respect of that I am free: and if I can, by a like thought of my mind, preferring one to the other, produce either words or silence, I am at liberty to speak or hold my peace: and as far as this power reaches, of acting or not acting, by the determination of his own thought preferring either, so far is a man free. For how can we think any one freer, than to have the power to do what he will? And so far as any one can, by preferring any action to its not being, or rest to any action, produce that action or rest, so far can he do what he will. For such a preferring of action to its absence, is the willing of it: and we can scarce tell how to imagine any being freer, than to be able to do what he wills. So that in respect of actions within the reach of such a power in him, a man seems as free as it is possible for freedom to make him.

22. *In respect of willing, a man is not free.*—But the inquisitive mind of man, willing to shift off from himself, as far as he can, all thoughts of guilt, though it be by putting himself into a worse state than that of fatal necessity, is not content with this: freedom, unless it reaches further than this, will not serve the turn: and it passes for a good plea, that a man is not free at all, if he be not as *free to will* as he is to *act what he wills.* Concerning a man's liberty, there yet, therefore, is raised this further question, *Whether a man be free to will?* which I think is what is meant, when it is disputed whether the will be free. And as to that I imagine.

23. *How a man cannot be free to will.*—Secondly, That willing, or volition, being an action, and freedom consisting in a power of acting or not acting, a man in respect of willing or the act of volition, when any action in his power is once proposed to his thoughts, as presently to be done, cannot be free. The reason whereof is very manifest. For, it being unavoidable that the action depending on his will should exist or not exist, and its existence or not existence following perfectly the determination and preference of his will, he cannot avoid willing the existence or non-existence of that action; it is absolutely necessary that he will the one or the other; i.e., prefer the one to the other: since one of them must necessarily follow; and that which does follow follows by the choice and determination of his mind; that is, by his willing it: for if he did not will it, it would not be. So that, in respect of the act of willing, a man in such a case is not free: liberty consisting in a power to act or not to act; which, in regard of volition, a man, upon such a proposal, has not. For it is unavoidably necessary to prefer the doing or forbearance of an action in a man's power, which is once so proposed to his thoughts; a man must necessarily will the one or the other of them; upon which preference or volition, the action or its forbearance certainly follows, and is truly voluntary. But the act of volition, or preferring one of the two, being that which he cannot avoid, a man, in respect of that act of willing, is under a necessity, and so cannot be free; unless necessity and freedom can consist together, and a man can be free and bound at once. Besides to make a man free after this manner, by making the action of willing to depend on his will, there must be another antecedent will, to determine the acts of this will, and another to determine that, and so *in infinitum*: for wherever one stops, the actions of the last will cannot be free. Nor is any being, as far I can comprehend beings above me, capable of such a freedom of will, that it can forbear to will, i.e., to prefer the being or not being of anything in its power, which it has once considered as such.

24. *Liberty is freedom to execute what is willed.*—This, then, is evident, That *a man is not at liberty to will, or not to will, anything in his power that he once considers of*: liberty consisting in a power to act or to forbear acting, and in that only. For a man that sits still is said yet to be at liberty; because he can walk if he wills it. A man that walks is at liberty also, not because he walks or moves; but because he can stand still if he wills it. But if a man sitting still has not a power to remove himself, he is not at liberty; so likewise a man falling down a precipice, though in motion, is not at liberty, because he cannot stop that motion if he would. This being so, it is plain that a man that is walking, to whom it is proposed to give off walking, is not at liberty, whether he will determine himself to walk, or give off walking or not: he must necessarily prefer one or the other of them; walking or not walking. And so it is in regard of all other actions in our power so proposed, which are the far greater number. For, considering the vast number of voluntary actions that succeed one another every moment that we are awake in the course of our lives, there are but few of them that are thought on or proposed to the will, till the time they are to be done; and in all such actions, as I have shown, the mind, in respect of willing, has not a power to act or not to act, wherein consists liberty. The mind, in that case, has not a power to forbear *willing*; it cannot avoid some

determination concerning them, let the consideration be as short, the thought as quick as it will, it either leaves the man in the state he was before thinking, or changes it; continues the action, or puts an end to it. Whereby it is manifest, that it orders and directs one, in preference to, or with neglect of the other, and thereby either the continuation or change becomes unavoidably voluntary.

25. *The will determined by something without it.*— Since then it is plain that, in most cases, a man is not at liberty, whether he will or no, (for, when an action in his power is proposed to his thoughts, he *cannot* forbear volition; he *must* determine one way or the other); the next thing demanded is,—*Whether a man be at liberty to will which of the two he pleases, motion or rest?* This question carries the absurdity of it so manifestly in itself, that one might thereby sufficiently be convinced that liberty concerns not the will. For, to ask whether a man be at liberty to will either motion or rest, speaking or silence, which he pleases, is to ask whether a man can will what he wills, or be pleased with what he is pleased with? A question which, I think, needs no answer: and they who can make a question of it must suppose one will to determine the acts of another, and another to determine that, and so on *in infinitum.*

26. *The ideas of* liberty *and* volition *must be defined.*—To avoid these and the like absurdities, nothing can be of greater use than to establish in our minds determined ideas of the things under consideration. If the ideas of liberty and volition were well fixed in our understandings, and carried along with us in our minds, as they ought, through all the questions that are raised about them, I suppose a great part of the difficulties that perplex men's thoughts, and entangle their understandings, would be much easier resolved; and we should perceive where the confused signification of terms, or where the nature of the thing caused the obscurity.

27. *Freedom.*—First, then, it is carefully to be remembered, That freedom consists in the dependence of the existence, or not existence of any *action*, upon our *volition* of it; and not in the dependence of any action, or its contrary, on our *preference.* A man standing on a cliff, is at liberty to leap twenty yards downwards into the sea, not because he has a power to do the contrary action, which is to leap twenty yards upwards, for that he cannot do; but he is therefore free, because he has a power to leap or not to leap. But if a greater force than his, either holds him fast, or tumbles him down, he is no longer free in that case; because the doing or forbearance of that particular action is no longer in his power. He that is a close prisoner in a room twenty feet square, being at the north side of his chamber, is at liberty to walk twenty feet southward, because he can walk or not walk it; but is not, at the same time, at liberty to do the contrary, i.e., to walk twenty feet northward.

In this, then, consists freedom*, viz., in our being able to act or not to act, according as we shall choose or will.*

28. *What volition and action mean.*—Secondly, we must remember, that *volition* or willing is an act of the mind directing its thought to the production of any action, and thereby exerting its power to produce it. To avoid multiplying of words, I would crave leave here, under the word action, to comprehend the forbearance too of any action proposed: sitting still, or holding one's peace, when walking or speaking are proposed, though mere forbearances, requiring as much the determination of the will, and being as often weighty in their consequences, as the contrary actions, may, on that consideration, well enough pass for actions too: but this I say, that I may not be mistaken, if (for brevity's sake) I speak thus.

29. *What determines the will.*—Thirdly, the will being nothing but a power in the mind to direct the operative faculties of a man to motion or rest, as far as they depend on such direction; to the question, What is it determines the will? the true and proper

answer is, The mind. For that which determines the general power of directing, to this or that particular direction, is nothing but the agent itself exercising the power it has that particular way. If this answer satisfies not, it is plain the meaning of the question, What determines the will? is this,—What moves the mind, in every particular instance, to determine its general power of directing, to this or that particular motion or rest? And to this I answer,—The motive for continuing in the same state or action, is only the present satisfaction in it; the motive to change is always some uneasiness: nothing setting us upon the change of state, or upon any new action, but some uneasiness. This is the great motive that works on the mind to put it upon action, which for shortness' sake we will call determining of the will, which I shall more at large explain.

*   *   *

73. *Recapitulation—liberty of indifferency.*—To conclude this inquiry into *human liberty*, which, as it stood before, I myself from the beginning fearing, and a very judicious friend of mine, since the publication, suspecting to have some mistake in it, though he could not particularly show it me, I was put upon a stricter review of this chapter. Wherein lighting upon a very easy and scarce observable slip I had made, in putting one seemingly indifferent word for another that discovery opened to me this present view, which here, in this second edition, I submit to the learned world, and which, in short, is this: *Liberty* is a power to act or not to act, according as the mind directs. A power to direct the operative faculties to motion or rest in particular instances is that which we call the *will*. That which in the train of our voluntary actions determines the will to any change of operation is *some present uneasiness*, which is, or at least is always accompanied with that of *desire*. Desire is always moved by evil, to fly it: because a total freedom from pain always makes a necessary part of our happiness: but every good, nay, every greater good, does not constantly move desire, because it may not make, or may not be taken to make, any necessary part of our happiness. For all that we desire, is only to be happy. But, though this general desire of happiness operates constantly and invariably, yet the satisfaction of any particular desire *can be suspended* from determining the will to any subservient action, till we have maturely examined whether the particular apparent good which we then desire makes a part of our real happiness, or be consistent or inconsistent with it. The result of our judgment upon that examination is what ultimately determines the man; who could not be *free* if his will were determined by some, is placed in an indifferency of the man; antecedent to the determination of his will. I wish they who lay so much stress on such an antecedent indifferency, as they call it, had told us plainly, whether this supposed indifferency be antecedent to the thought and judgment of the understanding, as well as to the decree of the will. For it is pretty hard to state it between them, i.e., immediately *after* the judgment of the understanding, and *before* the determination of the will: because the determination of the will immediately follows the judgment of the understanding: and to place liberty in an indifferency, antecedent to the thought and judgment of the understanding, seems to me to place liberty in a state of darkness, wherein we can neither see nor say anything of it; at least it places it in a subject incapable of it, no agent being allowed capable of liberty, but in consequence of thought and judgment. I am not nice about phrases, and therefore consent to say with those that love to speak so, that liberty is placed in indifferency; but it is an indifferency which remains after the judgment of the understanding, yea, even after the determination of the will: and that is an indifferency not of the *man*, (for after he has once judged which is best, viz., to do or forbear, he is no longer indifferent,) but an indifferency of *the operative powers of the man,*

which remaining equally able to operate or to forbear operating after as before the decree of the will, are in a state, which, if one pleases, may be called indifferency; and as far as this indifferency reaches, a man is free, and no further: v.g., I have the ability to move my hand, or to let it rest; that operative power is indifferent to move or not to move my hand. I am then, in that respect perfectly free; my will determines that operative power to rest: I am yet free, because the indifferency of that my operative power to act, or not to act, still remains; the power of moving my hand is not at all impaired by the determination of my will, which at present orders rest; the indifferency of that power to act, or not to act, is just as it was before, as will appear, if the will puts it to the trial, by ordering the contrary. But if, during the rest of my hand, it be seized with a sudden palsy, the indifferency of that operative power is gone, and with it my liberty; I have no longer freedom in that respect, but am under a necessity of letting my hand rest. On the other side, if my hand be put into motion by a convulsion, the indifferency of that operative faculty is taken away by that motion; and my liberty in that case is lost, for I am under a necessity of having my hand move. I have added this, to show in what sort of indifferency liberty seems to me to consist, and not in any other, real or imaginary.

74. *Active and passive power, in motions and in thinking.*— ... Before I close this chapter, it may perhaps be to our purpose, and help to give us clearer conceptions about power, if we make our thoughts take a little more exact survey of *action*. I have said above, that we have ideas but of two sorts of action, viz., motion and thinking. These, in truth, though called and counted actions, yet, if nearly considered, will not be found to be always perfectly so. For, if I mistake not, there are instances of both kinds, which, upon due consideration, will be found rather passions than actions; and consequently so far the effects barely of *passive powers* in those subjects, which yet on their accounts are thought agents. For, in these instances, the substance that hath motion or thought receives the impression, whereby it is put into that action, purely from without, and so acts merely by the capacity it has to receive such an impression from some external agent; and such a power is not properly an *active power*, but a mere passive capacity in the subject. Sometimes the substance or agent puts itself into action by its own power, and this is properly active power. Whatsoever modification a substance has, whereby it produces any effect, that is called action: v.g., a solid substance, by motion, operates on or alters the sensible ideas of another substance, and therefore this modification of motion we call action. But yet this motion in that solid substance is, when rightly considered, but a passion, if it received it only from some external agent. So that the active power of motion is in no substance which cannot begin motion in itself or in another substance when at rest. So likewise in thinking, a power to receive ideas or thoughts from the operation of any external substance is called a power of thinking: but this is but a passive power, or capacity. But to be able to bring into view ideas out of sight at one's own choice, and to compare which of them one thinks fit, this is an active power. This reflection may be of some use to preserve us from mistakes about powers and actions, which grammar, and the common frame of languages, may be apt to lead us into. Since what is signified by verbs that grammarians call active, does not always signify action: v.g., this proposition: I see the moon, or a star, or I *feel* the heat of the sun, though expressed by a verb active, does not signify any action in me, whereby I operate on those substances, but only the reception of the ideas of light, roundness, and heat; wherein I am not active, but barely passive, and cannot, in that position of my eyes or body, avoid receiving them. But when I turn my eyes another way, or remove my body out of the sunbeams, I am properly active; because of my own choice, by a power within myself, I put myself into that motion. Such an action is the product of active power.

The Funeral of Phocion, 1648, by Nicholas Poussin (1594–1665). In this classical-style painting, nature is depicted in geometrical terms that imply a sense of permanence. Locke believed that the complex ideas we have about such scenes are built up out of "a great number of the simple ideas conveyed in by the senses." (*Louvre/Paris*)

*   *   *

CHAPTER 23. OF OUR COMPLEX IDEAS OF SUBSTANCES

1. *Ideas of particular substances, how made.*—The mind being, as I have declared, furnished with a great number of the simple ideas conveyed in by the senses, as they are found in exterior things, or by reflection on its own operations, takes notice also, that a certain number of these simple ideas go constantly together; which being presumed to belong to one thing, and words being suited to common apprehensions, and made use of for quick dispatch, are called, so united in one subject, by one name; which, by inadvertency, we are apt afterward to talk of and consider as one simple idea, which indeed is a complication of many ideas together: because, as I have said, not imagining how these simple ideas can subsist by themselves, we accustom ourselves to suppose some *substratum* wherein they do subsist, and from which they do result, which therefore we call *substance.*

2. *Our obscure idea of substance in general.*—So that if any one will examine himself concerning his notion of pure substance in general, he will find he has no other idea of it at all, but only a supposition of he knows not what of such qualities which are

capable of producing simple ideas in us; which qualities are commonly called accidents. If any one should be asked, what is the subject wherein colour or weight inheres, he would have nothing to say, but the solid extended parts: and if he were demanded, what is it that that solidity and extension inhere in, he would not be in a much better case than the Indian before mentioned, who saying that the world was supported by a great elephant, was asked, what the elephant rested on; to which his answer was, a great tortoise: but being again pressed to know what gave support to the broad-backed tortoise, replied, *something, he knew not what*. And thus here, as in all other cases where we use words without having clear and distinct ideas, we talk like children; who being questioned what such a thing is which they know not, readily give this satisfactory answer, that it is *something*; which in truth signifies no more, when so used, either by children or men, but that they know not what; and that the thing they pretend to know, and talk of, is what they have no distinct idea of at all, and so are perfectly ignorant of it, and in the dark. The idea, then, we have, to which we give the general name substance, being nothing but the supposed, but unknown, support of those qualities we find existing, which we imagine cannot subsist *sine re substante*, without something to support them, we call that support *substantia*; which, according to the true import of the word, is, in plain English, standing under, or upholding.

3. *Of the sorts of substances.*—An obscure and relative idea of *substance in general* being thus made, we come to have the ideas of *particular sorts of substances*, by collecting *such* combinations of simple ideas as are, by experience and observation of men's senses, taken notice of to exist together, and are therefore supposed to flow from the particular internal constitution or unknown essence of that substance. Thus we come to have the ideas of a man, horse, gold, water, etc., of which substances, whether any one has any other *clear* idea, farther than of certain simple ideas coexisting together, I appeal to every one's own experience. It is the ordinary qualities observable in iron or a diamond, put together, that make the true complex idea of those substances, which a smith or a jeweller commonly knows better than a philosopher; who, whatever *substantial forms* he may talk of, has no other idea of those substances than what is framed by a collection of those simple ideas which are to be found in them. Only we must take notice, that our complex ideas of substances, besides all these simple ideas they are made up of, have always the confused idea of something to which they belong and in which they subsist. And therefore, when we speak of any sort of substance, we say it is a thing having such or such qualities; as body is a thing that is extended, figured, and capable of motion; a spirit, a thing capable of thinking; and so hardness, friability, and power to draw iron, we say, are qualities to be found in a loadstone. These and the like fashions of speaking intimate that the substance is supposed always *something besides* the extension, figure, solidity, motion, thinking, or other observable ideas, though we know not what it is.

4. *No clear or distinct idea of substance in general.*—Hence, when we talk or think of any particular sort of corporeal substances, as horse, stone, etc., though the idea we have of either of them be but the complication or collection of those several simple ideas of sensible qualities which we use to find united in the thing called horse or stone; yet *because we cannot conceive how they should subsist alone, nor one in another*, we suppose them existing in, and supported by, some common subject; which support we denote by the name substance, though it be certain we have no clear or distinct idea of that thing we suppose a support.

5. *As clear an idea of spiritual substance as of corporeal substance.*—The same happens concerning the operations of the mind, viz., thinking, reasoning, fearing, etc., which we concluding not to subsist of themselves, nor apprehending how they can be-

long to body, or be produced by it, we are apt to think these the actions of some other *substance*, which we call *spirit*; whereby yet it is evident, that having no other idea or notion of matter, but something wherein those many sensible qualities which affect our senses do subsist; by supposing a substance wherein thinking, knowing, doubting, and a power of moving, etc., do subsist; we have as clear a notion of the substance of spirit as we have of body; the one being supposed to be (without knowing what it is) the *substratum* to those simple ideas we have from without; and the other supposed (with a like ignorance of what it is) to be the *substratum* to those operations which we experiment in ourselves within. It is plain, then, that the idea of *corporeal substance* in matter is as remote from our conceptions and apprehensions as that of *spiritual substance* or spirit; and therefore, from our not having any notion of the substance of spirit, we can no more conclude its nonexistence than we can, for the same reason, deny the existence of body: it being as rational to affirm there is no body, because we have no clear and distinct idea of the substance of matter, as to say there is no spirit, because we have no clear and distinct idea of the substance of a spirit.

6. *Our ideas of particular sorts of substances.*—Whatever therefore be the secret and abstract nature of substance in general, all the ideas we have of particular distinct sorts of substances are nothing but several combinations of simple ideas coexisting in such, though unknown, cause of their union, as makes the whole subsist of itself. It is by such combinations of simple ideas, and nothing else, that we represent particular sorts of substances to ourselves. Such are the ideas we have of their several species in our minds; and such only do we, by their specific names, signify to others, v.g., man, horse, sun, water, iron; upon hearing which words, every one who understands the language frames in his mind a combination of those several simple ideas which he has usually observed or fancied to exist together under that denomination; all which he supposes to rest in, and be, as it were, adherent to, that unknown common subject, which inheres not in anything else. Though in the meantime it be manifest, and every one upon enquiry into his own thoughts will find, that he has no other idea of any substance but what he has barely of those sensible qualities, which he supposes to inhere, with a supposition of such a *substratum*, as gives, as it were, a support to those qualities or simple ideas, which he has observed to exist united together. Thus the idea of the sun, what is it but an aggregate of those several simple ideas, bright, hot, roundish, having a constant regular motion, at a certain distance from us, and perhaps some other? As he who thinks and discourses of the sun, has been more or less accurate in observing those sensible qualities, ideas, or properties, which are in that thing which he calls the sun.

7. *Their active and passive powers a great part of our complex ideas of substances.*—For he has the perfectest idea of any of the particular sorts of substances who has gathered and put together most of those simple ideas which do exist in it, among which are to be reckoned its active powers and passive capacities; which, though not simple ideas, yet in this respect, for brevity's sake, may conveniently enough be reckoned amongst them; . . . We immediately by our senses perceive in fire its heat and colour; which are, if rightly considered, nothing but powers in it to produce those ideas in us: we also by our senses perceive the colour and brittleness of charcoal, whereby we come by the knowledge of another power in fire, which it has to change the colour and consistency of *wood*. By the former, fire immediately, by the latter, it mediately discovers to us these several powers; which therefore we look upon to be a part of the qualities of fire, and so make them a part of the complex idea of it. For all those powers that we take cognizance of, terminating only in the alteration of some sensible qualities in those subjects on which they operate, and so making them exhibit

to us new sensible ideas; therefore it is that I have reckoned these powers amongst the simple ideas which make the complex ones of the sorts of substances; though these powers, considered in themselves, are truly complex ideas. . . .

8. *And why.*—Nor are we to wonder that powers make a great part of our complex ideas of substances, since their secondary qualities are those which, in most of them, serve principally to distinguish substances one from another and commonly make a considerable part of the complex idea of the several sorts of them. For our senses failing us in the discovery of the bulk, texture, and figure of the minute parts of bodies, on which their real constitutions and differences depend, we are fain to make use of their secondary qualities as the characteristical notes and marks whereby to frame ideas of them in our minds, and distinguish them one from another. All which secondary qualities, as has been shown, are nothing but bare powers. For the colour and taste of opium are, as well as its soporific or anodyne virtues, mere powers depending on its primary qualities, whereby it is fitted to produce different operations on different parts of our bodies.

9. *Three sorts of ideas make our complex ones of corporeal substances.*—The ideas that make our complex ones of corporeal substances are of these three sorts. First, the ideas of the primary qualities of things which are discovered by our senses, and are in them even when we perceive them not: such are the bulk, figure, number, situation, and motion of the parts of bodies, which are really in them, whether we take notice of them or no. Secondly, the sensible secondary qualities which, depending on these, are nothing but the powers those substances have to produce several ideas in us by our senses; which ideas are not in the things themselves otherwise than as anything is in its cause. Thirdly, the aptness we consider in any substance to give or receive such alterations of primary qualities as that the substance so altered should produce in us different ideas from what it did before; these are called active and passive powers: all which powers, as far as we have any notice or notion of them, terminate only in sensible simple ideas. For whatever alteration a loadstone has the power to make in the minute particles of iron, we should have no notion of any power it had at all to operate on iron, did not its sensible motion discover it; and I doubt not but there are a thousand changes that bodies we daily handle have a power to cause in one another, which we never suspect, because they never appear in sensible effects.

10. *Powers thus make a great part of our complex ideas of particular substances.*—Powers therefore justly make a great part of our complex ideas of substances. He that will examine his complex idea of gold, will find several of its ideas that make it up to be only powers: as the power of being melted, but of not spending itself in the fire, of being dissolved in *aqua regia*, are ideas as necessary to make up our complex idea of gold, as its colour and weight: which, if duly considered, are also nothing but different powers. For to speak truly, yellowness is not actually in gold, but is a power in gold to produce that idea in us by our eyes when placed in a due light: and the heat which we cannot leave out of our idea of the sun, is no more really in the sun than the white colour it introduces into wax. . . .

11. *The now secondary qualities of bodies would disappear, if we could discover the primary ones of their minute parts.*—Had we senses acute enough to discern the minute particles of bodies, and the real constitution on which their sensible qualities depend, I doubt not but they would produce quite different ideas in us, and that which is now the yellow colour of gold would then disappear, and instead of it we should see an admirable texture of parts of a certain size and figure. This microscopes plainly discover to us; for what to our naked eyes produces a certain colour is, by thus augmenting the acuteness of our senses, discovered to be quite a different thing; and the thus al-

tering, as it were, the proportion of the bulk of the minute parts of a coloured object to our usual sight, produces different ideas from what it did before. Thus sand, or pounded glass, which is opaque and white to the naked eye, is pellucid in a microscope: ... blood to the naked eye appears all red; but by a good microscope, wherein its lesser parts appear, shows only some few globules of red, swimming in a pellucid liquor; and how these red globules would appear, if glasses could be found that yet could magnify them one thousand or ten thousand times more, is uncertain.

* * *

30. *Our idea of spirit and our idea of body compared.*—So that, in short, the idea we have of spirit, compared with the idea we have of body, stands thus: The substance of spirit is unknown to us; and so is the substance of body equally unknown to us. Two primary qualities or properties of body, viz., solid coherent parts and impulse, we have distinct clear ideas of: so likewise we know and have distinct clear ideas of two primary qualities or properties of spirit, viz., thinking, and a power of action; i.e., a power of beginning or stopping several thoughts or motions. We have also the ideas of several qualities inherent in bodies, and have the clear distinct ideas of them: which qualities are but the various modifications of the extension of cohering solid parts and their motion. We have likewise the ideas of the several modes of thinking, viz., believing, doubting, intending, fearing, hoping; all which are but the several modes of thinking. We have also the ideas of willing, and moving the body consequent to it, and with the body itself too; for, as has been showed, spirit is capable of motion.

* * *

33. *Our complex idea of God.*—For if we examine the idea we have of the incomprehensible Supreme Being, we shall find, that we come by it the same way; and that the complex ideas we have both of God and separate spirits are made up of the simple ideas we receive from reflection: v.g., having, from what we experiment in ourselves, got the ideas of existence and duration, of knowledge and power, of pleasure and happiness, and of several other qualities and powers which it is better to have than to be without; when we would frame an idea the most suitable we can to the Supreme Being, we enlarge every one of these with our idea of infinity; and so, putting them together, make our complex idea of God. For that the mind has such a power of enlarging some of its ideas, received from sensation and reflection, has been already showed.

* * *

35. *God in his own essence incognisable.*—It is infinity which, joined to our ideas of existence, power, knowledge, etc., makes that complex idea whereby we represent to ourselves, the best we can, the Supreme Being. For though in his own essence (which certainly we do not know, not knowing the real essence of a pebble, or a fly, or of our own selves) God be simple and uncompounded; yet, I think, I may say we have no other idea of him but a complex one of existence, knowledge, power, happiness, etc., infinite and eternal: which are all distinct ideas, and some of them being relative are again compounded of others; all which being, as has been shown, originally got from sensation and reflection, go to make up the idea or notion we have of God.

*   *   *

37. *Recapitulation.*—And thus we have seen what kind of ideas we have of *substances of all kinds*, wherein they consist, and how we come by them. From whence, I think, it is very evident,

First, That all our ideas of the several *sorts* of substances are nothing but collections of simple ideas, with a supposition of *something* to which they belong, and in which they subsist; though of this supposed something we have no clear distinct idea at all.

Secondly, That all the simple ideas that, thus united in one common *substratum*, make up our complex ideas of several *sorts* of substances, are no other but such as we have received from sensation or reflection. . . .

Thirdly, That most of the simple ideas that make up our complex ideas of substances, when truly considered, are only *powers*, however we are apt to take them for positive qualities: v.g., the greatest part of the ideas that make our complex idea of *gold* are yellowness, great weight, ductility, fusibility, and solubility in *aqua regia*, etc., all united together in an unknown *substratum*; all which ideas are nothing else but so many relations to other substances, and are not really in the gold considered barely in itself, though they depend on those real and primary qualities of its internal constitution, whereby it has a fitness differently to operate and be operated on by several other substances.

*   *   *

Chapter 27. Of Identity and Diversity

1. *Wherein identity consists.*—Another occasion the mind often takes of comparing, is the very being of things, when, considering *anything as existing at any determined time and place*, we compare it with *itself existing at another time*, and thereon form the ideas of *identity* and *diversity*. When we see anything to be in any place in any instant of time, we are sure (be it what it will) that it is that very thing, and not another which at that same time exists in another place, how like and undistinguishable soever it may be in all other respects: and in this consists *identity*, when the ideas it is attributed to vary not at all from what they were that moment wherein we consider their former existence, and to which we compare the present. For we never finding, nor conceiving it possible, that two things of the same kind should exist in the same place at the same time, we rightly conclude, that, whatever exists anywhere at any time, excludes all of the same kind, and is there itself alone. When therefore we demand whether anything be the *same* or no, it refers always to something that existed such a time in such a place, which it was certain, at that instant, was the same with itself, and no other. From whence it follows, that one thing cannot have two beginnings of existence, nor two things one beginning; it being impossible for two things of the same kind to be or exist in the same instant, in the very same place; or one and the same thing in different places. That, therefore, that had one beginning, is the same thing; and that which had a different beginning in time and place from that, is not the same, but diverse. That which has made the difficulty about this relation has been the little care and attention used in having precise notions of the things to which it is attributed.

2. *Identity of substances.*—We have the ideas but of three sorts of substances: 1. *God.* 2. *Finite intelligences.* 3. *Bodies.*

First, *God* is without beginning, eternal, unalterable, and everywhere, and therefore concerning his identity there can be no doubt.

Secondly, *finite spirits* having had each its determinate time and place of beginning to exist, the relation to that time and place will always determine to each of them its identity, as long as it exists.

Thirdly, The same will hold of every *particle of matter*, to which no addition or subtraction of matter being made, it is the same. For, though these three sorts of substances, as we term them, do not exclude one another out of the same place, yet we cannot conceive but that they must necessarily each of them exclude any of the same kind out of the same place: or else the notions and names of identity and diversity would be in vain, and there could be no such distinctions of substances, or anything else one from another. For example: could two bodies be in the same place at the same time; then those two parcels of matter must be one and the same, take them great or little; nay, all bodies must be one and the same. For, by the same reason that two particles of matter may be in one place, all bodies may be in one place: which, when it can be supposed, takes away the distinction of identity and diversity of one and more, and renders it ridiculous. But it being a contradiction that two or more should be one, identity and diversity are relations and ways of comparing well founded, and of use to the understanding.

Identity of modes and relations.—All other things being but modes or relations ultimately terminated in substances, the identity and diversity of each particular existence of them too will be by the same way determined: only as to things whose existence is in succession, such as are the actions of finite beings, v.g., *motion* and *thought*, both which consist in a continued train of succession, concerning *their* diversity there can be no question: because each perishing the moment it begins, they cannot exist in different times, or in different places, as permanent beings can at different times exist in distant places; and therefore no motion or thought, considered as at different times, can be the same, each part thereof having a different beginning of existence.

3. *Principium individuationis.*—From what has been said, it is easy to discover what is so much inquired after, the *principium individuationis*; and that, it is plain, is existence itself; which determines a being of any sort to a particular time and place, incommunicable to two beings of the same kind. This, though it seems easier to conceive in simple substances or modes; yet, when reflected on, is not more difficult in compound ones, if care be taken to what it is applied: v.g., let us suppose an atom, i.e., a continued body under one immutable superficies, existing in a determined time and place; it is evident, that, considered in any instant of its existence, it is in that instant the same with itself. For, being at that instant what it is, and nothing else, it is the same, and so must continue as long as its existence is continued; for so long it will be the same, and no other. In like manner, if two or more atoms be joined together into the same mass, every one of those atoms will be the same, by the foregoing rule: and whilst they exist united together, the mass, consisting of the same atoms, must be the same mass, or the same body, let the parts be ever so differently jumbled. But if one of these atoms be taken away, or one new one added, it is no longer the same mass or the same body. In the state of living creatures, their identity depends not on a mass of the same particles, but on something else. For in them the variation of great parcels of matter alters not the identity: an oak growing from a plant to a great tree, and then lopped, is still the same oak; and a colt grown up to a horse, sometimes fat, sometimes lean, is all the while the same horse: though, in both these cases, there may be a manifest

change of the parts; so that truly they are not either of them the same masses of matter, though they be truly one of them the same oak, and the other the same horse. The reason whereof is, that, in these two cases—a *mass of matter* and a *living body*—identity is not applied to the same thing.

4. *Identity of vegetables.*—We must therefore consider wherein an oak differs from a mass of matter, and that seems to me to be in this, that the one is only the cohesion of particles of matter any how united, the other such a disposition of them as constitutes the parts of an oak; and such an organization of those parts as is fit to receive and distribute nourishment, so as to continue and frame the wood, bark, and leaves, etc., of an oak, in which consists the vegetable life. That being then one plant which has such an organization of parts in one coherent body, partaking of one common life, it continues to be the same plant as long as it partakes of the same life, though that life be communicated to new particles of matter vitally united to the living plant, in a like continued organization conformable to that sort of plants. For this organization, being at any one instant in any one collection of matter, is in that particular concrete distinguished from all other, and is that individual life, which existing constantly from that moment both forwards and backwards, in the same continuity of insensibly succeeding parts united to the living body of the plant, it has that identity which makes the same plant, and all the parts of it, parts of the same plant, during all the time that they exist united in that continued organization, which is fit to convey that common life to all the parts so united.

5. *Identity of animals.*—The case is not so much different in brutes but that any one may hence see what makes an animal and continues it the same. Something we have like this in machines, and may serve to illustrate it. For example, what is a watch? It is plain it is nothing but a fit organization or construction of parts to a certain end, which, when a sufficient force is added to it, it is capable to attain. If we would suppose this machine one continued body, all whose organized parts were repaired, increased, or diminished by a constant addition or separation of insensible parts, with one common life, we should have something very much like the body of an animal; with this difference, That, in an animal the fitness of the organization, and the motion wherein life consists, begin together, the motion coming from within; but in machines the force coming sensibly from without, is often away when the organ is in order, and well fitted to receive it.

6. *The identity of man.*—This also shows wherein the identity of the same *man* consists; viz., in nothing but a participation of the same continued life, by constantly fleeting particles of matter, in succession vitally united to the same organized body. He that shall place the identity of man in anything else, but, like that of other animals, in one fitly organized body, taken in any one instant, and from thence continued, under one organization of life, in several successively fleeting particles of matter united to it, will find it hard to make an embryo, one of years, mad and sober, the *same* man, by any supposition, that will not make it possible for Seth, Ismael, Socrates, Pilate, St. Austin, and Caesar Borgia, to be the same man. For if the identity of *soul alone* makes the same *man*; and there be nothing in the nature of matter why the same individual spirit may not be united to different bodies, it will be possible that those men, living in distant ages, and of different tempers, may have been the same man: which way of speaking must be from a very strange use of the word man, applied to an idea out of which body and shape are excluded. And that way of speaking would agree yet worse with the notions of those philosophers who allow of transmigration, and are of opinion that the souls of men may, for their miscarriages, be detruded into the bodies of beasts, as fit habitations, with organs suited to the satisfaction of their brutal inclinations. But

yet I think nobody, could he be sure that the *soul* of Heliogabalus were in one of his hogs, would yet say that hog were a *man* or Heliogabalus.

*   *   *

9. *Personal identity.*—This being premised, to find wherein personal identity consists, we must consider what *person* stands for;—which, I think, is a thinking intelligent being, that has reason and reflection, and can consider itself as itself, the same thinking thing, in different times and places; which it does only by that consciousness which is inseparable from thinking, and, as it seems to me, essential to it: it being impossible for any one to perceive without *perceiving* that he does perceive. When we see, hear, smell, taste, feel, meditate, or will anything, we know that we do so. Thus it is always as to our present sensations and perceptions: and by this every one is to himself that which he calls *self*:—it not being considered, in this case, whether the same self be continued in the same or divers substances. For, since consciousness always accompanies thinking, and it is that which makes every one to be what he calls self, and thereby distinguishes himself from all other thinking things, in this alone consists personal identity, i.e., the sameness of a rational being: and as far as this consciousness can be extended backwards to any past action or thought, so far reaches the identity of that person; it is the same self now it was then; and it is by the same self with this present one that now reflects on it, that that action was done.

10. *Consciousness makes personal identity.*—But it is further inquired, whether it be the same identical substance. This few would think they had reason to doubt of, if these perceptions, with their consciousness, always remained present in the mind, whereby the same thinking thing would be always consciously present, and, as would be thought, evidently the same to itself. But that which seems to make the difficulty is this, that this consciousness being interrupted always by forgetfulness, there being no moment of our lives wherein we have the whole train of all our past actions before our eyes in one view, but even the best memories losing the sight of one part whilst they are viewing another; and we sometimes, and that the greatest part of our lives, not reflecting on our past selves, being intent on our present thoughts, and in sound sleep having no thoughts at all, or at least none with that consciousness which remarks our waking thoughts,—I say, in all these cases, our consciousness being interrupted, and we losing the sight of our past selves, doubts are raised whether we are the same thinking thing, i.e., the same *substance* or no. Which, however reasonable or unreasonable, concerns not *personal* identity at all. The question being what makes the same person, and not whether it be the same identical substance, which always thinks in the same person, which, in this case, matters not at all: different substances, by the same consciousness (where they do partake in it) being united into one person, as well as different bodies by the same life are united into one animal, whose identity is preserved in that change of substances by the unity of one continued life. For, it being the same consciousness that makes a man be himself to himself, personal identity depends on that only, whether it be annexed solely to one individual substance, or can be continued in a succession of several substances. For as far as any intelligent being *can* repeat the idea of any past action with the same consciousness it had of it at first, and with the same consciousness it has of any present action; so far it is the same personal self. For it is by the consciousness it has of its present thoughts and actions, that it is *self* to *itself* now, and so will be the same self, as far as the same consciousness can extend to actions past or to come; and would be by distance of time, or change of substance, no more two persons, than a man be two men by wearing other clothes

today than he did yesterday, with a long or a short sleep between: the same consciousness uniting those distant actions into the same person, whatever substances contributed to their production.

*   *   *

16. *Consciousness alone unites actions into the same person.*—But though the same immaterial substance or soul does not alone, wherever it be, and in whatsoever state, make the same *man*; yet it is plain, consciousness, as far as ever it can be extended—should it be to ages past—unites existences and actions very remote in time into the same *person*, as well as it does the existences and actions of the immediately preceding moment: so that whatever has the consciousness of present and past actions, is the same person to whom they both belong. Had I the same consciousness that I saw the ark and Noah's flood, as that I saw an overflowing of the Thames last winter, or as that I write now, I could no more doubt that I who write this now, that saw the Thames overflowed last winter, and that viewed the flood at the general deluge, was the same *self*,—place that self in what *substance* you please—than that I who write this am the same myself now whilst I write (whether I consist of all the same substance, material or immaterial, or no) that I was yesterday. For as to this point of being the same self, it matters not whether this present self be made up of the same or other substances—I being as much concerned, and as justly accountable for any action that was done a thousand years since, appropriated to me now by this self consciousness, as I am for what I did the last moment.

17. *Self depends on consciousness, not on substance.*—Self is that conscious thinking thing,—whatever substance made up of, (whether spiritual or material, simple or compounded, it matters not)—which is sensible or conscious of pleasure and pain, capable of happiness or misery, and so is concerned for itself, as far as that consciousness extends. Thus every one finds that, whilst comprehended under that consciousness, the little finger is as much a part of himself as what is most so. Upon separation of this little finger, should this consciousness go along with the little finger, and leave the rest of the body, it is evident the little finger would be the person, the same person; and self then would have nothing to do with the rest of the body. As in this case it is the consciousness that goes along with the substance, when one part is separate from another, which makes the same person, and constitutes this inseparable self: so it is in reference to substances remote in time. That with which the consciousness of this present thinking thing *can* join itself, makes the same person, and is one self with it, and with nothing else; and so attributes to itself, and owns all the actions of that thing, as its own, as far as that consciousness reaches, and no further; as every one who reflects will perceive.

18. *Persons, not substances, the objects of reward and punishment.*—In this personal identity is founded all the right and justice of reward and punishment; happiness and misery being that for which every one is concerned for *himself*, and not mattering what becomes of any *substance*, not joined to, or affected with that consciousness. For, as it is evident in the instance I gave but now, if the consciousness went along with the little finger when it was cut off, that would be the same self which was concerned for the whole body yesterday, as making part of itself, whose actions then it cannot but admit as its own now. Though, if the same body should still live, and immediately from the separation of the little finger have its own peculiar consciousness, whereof the little finger knew nothing, it would not at all be concerned for it, as a part of itself, or could own any of its actions, or have any of them imputed to him.

19. *Which shows wherein personal identity consists.*—This may show us wherein personal identity consists: not in the identity of substance, but, as I have said, in the identity of consciousness, wherein if Socrates and the present mayor of Queinborough agree, they are the same person: if the same Socrates waking and sleeping do not partake of the same consciousness, Socrates waking and sleeping are not the same person. And to punish Socrates waking for what Socrates sleeping thought, and waking Socrates was never conscious of, would be no more of right, than to punish one twin for what his brother-twin did, whereof he knew nothing, because their outsides were so alike, that they could not be distinguished; for such twins have been seen.

20. *Absolute oblivion separates what is thus forgotten from the person, but not from the man.*—But yet possibly it will still be objected,—Suppose I wholly lose the memory of some parts of my life, beyond a possibility of retrieving them, so that perhaps I shall never be conscious of them again; yet am I not the same person that did those actions, had those thoughts that I once was conscious of, though I have now forgot them? To which I answer, that we must here take notice what the word *I* is applied to; which, in this case, is the *man* only. And the same man being presumed to be the same person, I is easily here supposed to stand also for the same person. But if it be possible for the same man to have distinct incommunicable consciousness at different times, it is past doubt the same man would at different times make different persons; which, we see, is the sense of mankind in the solemnest declaration of their opinions, human laws not punishing the mad man for the sober man's actions, nor the sober man for what the mad man did,—thereby making them two persons: which is somewhat explained by our way of speaking in English when we say such an one is "not himself," or is "beside himself"; in which phrases it is insinuated, as if those who now, or at least first used them, thought that self was changed; the self-same person was no longer in that man.

*   *   *

22. *Is not a man drunk and sober the same person?*—Why else is he punished for the fact he commits when drunk, though he be never afterwards conscious of it? Just as much the same person as a man that walks, and does other things in his sleep, is the same person, and is answerable for any mischief he shall do in it. Human laws punish both, with a justice suitable to *their* way of knowledge;—because, in these cases, they cannot distinguish certainly what is real, what counterfeit: and so the ignorance in drunkenness or sleep is not admitted as a plea. For, though punishment be annexed to personality, and personality to consciousness, and the drunkard perhaps be not conscious of what he did, yet human judicatures justly punish him; because the fact is proved against him, but want of consciousness cannot be proved for him. But in the Great Day, wherein the secrets of all hearts shall be laid open, it may be reasonable to think, no one shall be made to answer for what he knows nothing of; but shall receive his doom, his conscience accusing or excusing him.

*   *   *

25. *Consciousness unites substances, material or spiritual, with the same personality.*—I agree, that more probable opinion is, that this consciousness is annexed to, and the affection of, one individual immaterial substance.

But let men, according to their diverse hypotheses, resolve of that as they please. This every intelligent being, sensible of happiness or misery, must grant—that there is something that is *himself*, that he is concerned for, and would have happy; that this self has existed in a continued duration more than one instant, and therefore it is possible may exist, as it has done, months and years to come, without any certain bounds to be set to its duration; and may be the same self, by the same consciousness continued on for the future. And thus, by this consciousness he finds himself to be the same self which did such and such an action some years since, by which he comes to be happy or miserable now. In all which account of self, the same numerical substance is not considered as making the same self; but the same continued *consciousness*, in which several substances may have been united, and again separated from it, which, whilst they continued in a vital union with that wherein this consciousness then resided, made a part of that same self. Thus any part of our bodies, vitally united to that which is conscious in us, makes a part of ourselves: but upon separation from the vital union by which that consciousness is communicated, that which a moment since was part of ourselves, is now no more so than a part of another man's self is a part of me: and it is not impossible but in a little time may become a real part of another person. And so we have the same numerical substance become a part of two different persons; and the same person preserved under the change of various substances. Could we suppose any spirit wholly stripped of all its memory or consciousness of past actions, as we find our minds always are of a great part of ours, and sometimes of them all; the union or separation of such a spiritual substance would make no variation of personal identity, any more than that of any particle of matter does. Any substance vitally united to the present thinking being is a part of that very same self which now is; anything united to it by a consciousness of former actions, makes also a part of the same self, which is the same both then and now.

*   *   *

Book III. Of Words

Chapter 2. Of the Signification of Words

1. *Words are sensible signs, necessary for communication of ideas.*—Man, though he have great variety of thoughts, and such from which others as well as himself might receive profit and delight; yet they are all within his own breast, invisible and hidden from others, nor can of themselves be made to appear. The comfort and advantage of society not being to be had without communication of thoughts, it was necessary that man should find out some external sensible signs, whereof those invisible ideas, which his thoughts are made up of, might be made known to others. For this purpose nothing was so fit, either for plenty or quickness, as those articulate sounds, which with so much ease and variety he found himself able to make. Thus we may conceive how words, which were by nature so well adapted to that purpose, came to be made use of by men as the signs of their ideas; not by any natural connexion that there is between particular articulate sounds and certain ideas, for then there would be but one language amongst all men; but by a voluntary imposition, whereby such a word is made arbitrarily the mark of such an idea. The use, then, of words, is to be sensible marks of ideas; and the ideas they stand for are their proper and immediate signification.

*   *   *

3. *Examples of this.*—This is so necessary in the use of language, that in this respect the knowing and the ignorant, the learned and the unlearned, use the words they speak (with any meaning) all alike. They, in every man's mouth, stand for the ideas he has, and which he would express by them. A child having taken notice of nothing in the metal he hears called *gold*, but the bright shining yellow colour, he applies the word gold only to his own idea of that colour, and nothing else; and therefore calls the same colour in a peacock's tail gold. Another that hath better observed, adds to shining yellow great weight: and then the sound gold, when he uses it, stands for a complex idea of a shining yellow and a very weighty substance. Another adds to those qualities fusibility: and then the word gold signifies to him a body, bright, yellow, fusible, and very heavy. Another adds malleability. Each of these uses equally the word gold, when they have occasion to express the idea which they have applied it to: but it is evident that each can apply it only to his own idea; nor can he make it stand as a sign of such a complex idea as he has not.

*   *   *

CHAPTER 3. OF GENERAL TERMS

1. *The greatest part of words are general terms.*—All things that exist being particulars, it may perhaps be thought reasonable that words, which ought to be conformed to things, should be so too,—I mean in their signification: but yet we find quite the contrary. The far greatest part of words that make all languages are general terms: which has not been the effect of neglect or chance, but of reason and necessity.

2. *That every particular thing should have a name for itself is impossible.*—First, It is impossible that every particular thing should have a distinct peculiar name. For, the signification and use of words depending on that connexion which the mind makes between its ideas and the sounds it uses as signs of them, it is necessary, in the application of names to things, that the mind should have distinct ideas of the things, and retain also the particular name that belongs to every one, with its peculiar appropriation to that idea. But it is beyond the power of human capacity to frame and retain distinct ideas of all the particular things we meet with: every bird and beast men saw; every tree and plant that affected the senses, could not find a place in the most capacious understanding. If it be looked on as an instance of a prodigious memory, that some generals have been able to call every soldier in their army by his proper name, we may easily find a reason why men have never attempted to give names to each sheep in their flock, or crow that flies over their heads; much less to call every leaf of plants, or grain of sand that came in their way, by a peculiar name.

3. *And would be useless, if it were possible.*—Secondly, If it were possible, it would yet be useless; because it would not serve to the chief end of language. Men would in vain heap up names of particular things, that would not serve them to communicate their thoughts. Men learn names, and use them in talk with others, only that they may be understood: which is then only done when, by use or consent, the sound I make by the organs of speech, excites in another man's mind who hears it, the idea I apply it to in mine, when I speak it. This cannot be done by names applied to particular things; whereof I alone having the ideas in my mind, the names of them could not be

significant or intelligible to another, who was not acquainted with all those very particular things which had fallen under my notice.

4. *A distinct name for every particular thing, not fitted for enlargement of knowledge.*—Thirdly, But yet, granting this also feasible, (which I think is not), yet a distinct name for every particular thing would not be of any great use for the improvement of knowledge: which, though founded in particular things, enlarges itself by general views; to which things reduced into sorts, under general names, are properly subservient. These, with the names belonging to them, come within some compass, and do not multiply every moment, beyond what either the mind can contain, or use requires. And therefore, in these, men have for the most part stopped: but yet not so as to hinder themselves from distinguishing particular things by appropriated names, where convenience demands it. And therefore in their own species, which they have most to do with, and wherein they have often occasion to mention particular persons, they make use of proper names; and there distinct individuals have distinct denominations.

5. *What things have proper names, and why.*—Besides persons, countries also, cities, rivers, mountains, and other the like distinctions of place have usually found peculiar names, and that for the same reason; they being such as men have often an occasion to mark particularly, and, as it were, set before others in their discourses with them. And I doubt not but, if we had reason to mention particular horses as often as we have to mention particular men, we should have proper names for the one, as familiar as for the other, and Bucephalus would be a word as much in use as Alexander. And therefore we see that, amongst jockeys, horses have their proper names to be known and distinguished by, as commonly as their servants: because, amongst them, there is often occasion to mention this or that particular horse when he is out of sight.

6. *How general words are made.*—The next thing to be considered is,—How general words come to be made. For, since all things that exist are only particulars, how come we by general terms; or where find we those general natures they are supposed to stand for? Words become general by being made the signs of general ideas: and ideas become general, by separating from them the circumstances of time and place, and any other ideas that may determine them to this or that particular existence. By this way of abstraction they are made capable of representing more individuals than one; each of which having in it a conformity to that abstract idea, is (as we call it) of that sort.

7. *Shown by the way we enlarge our complex ideas from infancy.*—But, to deduce this a little more distinctly, it will not perhaps be amiss to trace our notions and names from their beginning, and observe by what degrees we proceed, and by what steps we enlarge our ideas from our first infancy. There is nothing more evident, than that the ideas of the persons children converse with (to instance in them alone) are like the persons themselves, only particular. The ideas of the nurse and the mother are well framed in their minds; and, like pictures of them there, represent only those individuals. The names they first gave to them are confined to these individuals; and the names of *nurse* and *mamma*, the child uses, determine themselves to those persons. Afterwards, when time and a larger acquaintance have made them observe that there are a great many other things in the world, that in some common agreements of shape, and several other qualities, resemble their father and mother, and those persons they have been used to, they frame an idea, which they find those many particulars do partake in; and to that they give, with others, the name *man*, for example. And thus they come to have a general name, and a general idea. Wherein they make nothing new; but only leave out of the complex idea they had of Peter and James, Mary and Jane, that which is peculiar to each, and retain only what is common to them all.

8. *And further enlarge our complex ideas, by still leaving out properties contained in them.*—By the same way that they come by the general name and idea of man, they easily advance to more general names and notions. For, observing that several things that differ from their idea of man, and cannot therefore be comprehended under that name, have yet certain qualities wherein they agree with man, by retaining only those qualities, and uniting them into one idea, they have again another and more general idea; to which having given a name they make a term of a more comprehensive extension: which new idea is made, not by any new addition, but only as before, by leaving out the shape, and some other properties signified by the name man, and retaining only a body, with life, sense, and spontaneous motion, comprehended under the name animal.

9. *General natures are nothing but abstract end partial ideas of more complex ones.*—That this is the way whereby men first formed general ideas, and general names to them, I think is so evident, that there needs no other proof of it but the considering of a man's self, or others, and the ordinary proceedings of their minds in knowledge. And he that thinks *general natures* or *notions* are anything else but such abstract and partial ideas of more complex ones, taken at first from particular existences, will, I fear, be at a loss where to find them. For let any one effect, and then tell me, wherein does his idea of *man* differ from that of *Peter* and *Paul*, or his idea of horse from that of *Bucephalus*, but in the leaving out something that is peculiar to each individual, and retaining so much of those particular complex ideas of several particular existences as they are found to agree in? Of the complex ideas signified by the names *man* and *horse*, leaving out but those particulars wherein they differ, and retaining only those wherein they agree, and of those making a new distinct complex idea, and giving the name *animal* to it, one has a more general term, that comprehends with man several other creatures. Leave out of the idea of *animal*, sense and spontaneous motion, and the remaining complex idea, made up of the remaining simple ones of body, life, and nourishment, becomes a more general one, under the more comprehensive term, *vivens*. And, not to dwell longer upon this particular, so evident in itself; by the same way the mind proceeds to *body, substance,* and at last to *being, thing,* and such universal terms, which stand for any of our ideas whatsoever. To conclude: this whole mystery of genera and species, which make such a noise in the schools, and are with justice so little regarded out of them, is nothing else but *abstract ideas*, more or less comprehensive, with names annexed to them. In all which this is constant and unvariable, that every more general term stands for such an idea, and is but a part of any of those contained under it.

10. *Why the genus is ordinarily made use of in definitions.*—This may show us the reason why, in the defining of words, which is nothing but declaring their signification, we make use of the *genus*, or next general word that comprehends it. Which is not out of necessity, but only to save the labour of enumerating the several simple ideas which the next general word or genus stands for; or, perhaps, sometimes the shame of not being able to do it. But though defining by *genus* and *differentia* (I crave leave to use these terms of art, though originally Latin, since they most properly suit those notions they are applied to), I say, though defining by the *genus* be the shortest way, yet I think it may be doubted whether it be the best. This I am sure, it is not the only, and so not absolutely necessary. For, definition being nothing but making another understand by words what idea the term defined stands for, a definition is best made by enumerating those simple ideas that are combined in the signification of the term defined: and, if, instead of such an enumeration, men have accustomed themselves to use the next general term, it has not been out of necessity, or for greater clearness, but for quickness

and dispatch sake. For I think that, to one who desired to know what idea the word man stood for; if it should be said, that man was a solid extended substance, having life, sense, spontaneous motion, and the faculty of reasoning, I doubt not but the meaning of the term man would be as well understood, and the idea it stands for be at least as clearly made known, as when it is defined to be a rational animal: which, by the several definitions of *animal, vivens,* and *corpus,* resolves itself into those enumerated ideas. I have, in explaining the term man, followed here the ordinary definition of the schools; which, though perhaps not the most exact, yet serves well enough to my present purpose. And one may, in this instance, see what gave occasion to the rule, that a definition must consist of *genus* and *differentia;* and it suffices to show us the little necessity there is of such a rule, or advantage in the strict observing of it. For, definitions, as has been said, being only the explaining of one word by several others, so that the meaning or idea it stands for may be certainly known; languages are not always so made according to the rules of logic, that every term can have its signification exactly and clearly expressed by two others. Experience sufficiently satisfies us to the contrary; or else those who have made this rule have done ill, that they have given us so few definitions conformable to it. But of definitions more in the next chapter.

11. *General and universal are creatures of the understanding, and belong not to the real existence of things.*—To return to general words: it is plain, by what has been said, that *general* and *universal* belong not to the real existence of things; but are the inventions and creatures of the understanding, made by it for its own use, and concern only signs, whether words or ideas. Words are general, as has been said, when used for signs of general ideas, and so are applicable indifferently to many particular things; and ideas are general when they are set up as the representatives of many particular things: but universality belongs not to things themselves, which are all of them particular in their existence, even those words and ideas which in their signification are general. When therefore we quit particulars, the generals that rest are only creatures of our own making; their general nature being nothing but the capacity they are put into, by the understanding, of signifying or representing many particulars. For the signification they have is nothing but a relation that, by the mind of man, is added to them.

12. *Abstract ideas are the essences of genera and species.*—The next thing therefore to be considered is, What kind of signification it is that general words have. For, as it is evident that they do not signify barely one particular thing; for then they would not be general terms, but proper names, so, on the other side, it is as evident they do not signify a plurality; for *man* and *men* would then signify the same; and the distinction of numbers (as the grammarians call them) would be superfluous and useless. That then which general words signify is a *sort* of things; and each of them does that, by being a sign of an abstract idea in the mind; to which idea, as things existing are found to agree, so they come to be ranked under that name, or, which is all one, be of that sort. Whereby it is evident that the *essences* of the sorts, or, if the Latin word pleases better, *species* of things, are nothing else but these abstract ideas. For the having the essence of any species, being that which makes anything to be of that species; and the conformity to the idea to which the name is annexed being that which gives a right to that name; the having the essence, and the having that conformity, must needs be the same thing: since to be of any species, and to have a right to the name of that species, is all one. As, for example, to be a *man,* or of the *species* man, and to have right to the *name* man, is the same thing. Again, to be a man, or of the species man, and have the *essence* of a man, is the same thing. Now, since nothing can be a man, or have a right to the name man, but what has a conformity to the abstract idea the name man stands for, nor anything be a man, or have a right to the species man, but what has

the essence of that species; it follows, that the abstract idea for which the name stands, and the essence of the species, is one and the same. From whence it is easy to observe, that the essences of the sorts of things, and, consequently, the sorting of things, is the workmanship of the understanding that abstracts and makes those general ideas.

13. *They are the workmanship of the understanding, but have their foundation in the similitude of things.*—I would not here be thought to forget, much less to deny, that Nature, in the production of things, makes several of them alike: there is nothing more obvious, especially in the races of animals, and all things propagated by seed. But yet I think we may say, *the sorting of them under names is the workmanship of the understanding, taking occasion, from the similitude it observes amongst them, to make abstract general ideas*, and set them up in the mind, with names annexed to them, as patterns or forms (for, in that sense, the word *form* has a very proper signification) to which as particular things existing are found to agree, so they come to be of that species, have that denomination, or are put into that *classis*. For when we say this is a man, that a horse; this justice, that cruelty; this a watch, that a jack; what do we else but rank things under different specific names, as agreeing to those abstract ideas, of which we have made those names the signs? And what are the essences of those species set out and marked by names, but those abstract ideas in the mind; which are, as it were, the bonds between particular things that exist, and the names they are to be ranked under? And when general names have any connexion with particular beings, these abstract ideas are the medium that unites them: so that the essences of species, as distinguished and denominated by us, neither are nor can be anything but those precise abstract ideas we have in our minds. And therefore the supposed real essences of substances, if different from our abstract ideas, cannot be the essences of the species we rank things into. For two species may be one, as rationally as two different essences be the essence of one species: and I demand what are the alterations [which] may, or may not be made in a *horse* or *lead*, without making either of them to be of another species? In determining the species of things by *our* abstract ideas, this is easy to resolve, but if any one will regulate himself herein by supposed *real* essences, he will, I suppose, be at a loss: and he will never be able to know when anything precisely ceases to be of the species of a *horse* or *lead*.

14. *Each distinct abstract idea is a distinct essence.*—Nor will any one wonder that I say these essences, or abstract ideas (which are the measures of name, and the boundaries of species) are the workmanship of the understanding, who considers that at least the complex ones are often, in several men, different collections of simple ideas; and therefore that is *covetousness* to one man, which is not so to another. Nay, even in substances, where their abstract ideas seem to be taken from the things themselves, they are not constantly the same; no, not in that species which is most familiar to us, and with which we have the most intimate acquaintance: it having been more than once doubted, whether the *fetus* born of a woman were a *man*, even so far as that it hath been debated, whether it were or were not to be nourished and baptized: which could not be, if the abstract idea or essence to which the name man belonged were of nature's making; and were not the uncertain and various collection of simple ideas, which the understanding put together, and then, abstracting it, affixed a name to it. So that, in truth, every distinct abstract idea is a distinct essence; and the names that stand for such distinct ideas are the names of things essentially different. Thus a circle is as essentially different from an oval as a sheep from a goat; and rain is as essentially different from snow as water from earth: that abstract idea which is the essence of one being impossible to be communicated to the other. And thus any two abstract ideas, that in any part vary one from another, with two distinct names annexed to them, con-

stitute two distinct sorts, or, if you please, species, as essentially different as any two of the most remote or opposite in the world.

15. *Several significations of the word "essence."*—But since the essences of things are thought by some (and not without reason) to be wholly unknown, it may not be amiss to consider the several significations of the word essence.

Real essence.—First, Essence may be taken for the very being of anything, whereby it is what it is. And thus the real internal, but generally (in substances) unknown constitution of things, whereon their discoverable qualities depend, may be called their essence. This is the proper original signification of the word, as is evident from the formation of it; *essentia*, in its primary notation, signifying properly, being. And in this sense it is still used, when we speak of the essence of *particular* things, without giving them any name.

Nominal essences.—Secondly, The learning and disputes of the schools having been much busied about *genus* and *species*, the word *essence* has almost lost its primary signification: and, instead of the real constitution of things, has been almost wholly applied to the artificial constitution of *genus* and *species*. It is true, there is ordinarily supposed a real constitution of the sorts of things; and it is past doubt there must be some real constitution, on which any collection of simple ideas co-existing must depend. But, it being evident that things are ranked under names into sorts or species, only as they agree to certain abstract ideas, to which we have annexed those names, the essence of each *genus*, or sort, comes to be nothing but that abstract idea which the general, or sortal (if I may have leave so to call it from sort, as I do general from genus) name stands for. And this we shall find to be that which the word essence imports in its most familiar use.

These two sorts of essences, I suppose, may not unfitly be termed, the one the *real*, the other *nominal essence*.

*   *   *

Book IV. Of Knowledge and Probability

Chapter 1. Of Knowledge in General

1. *Our knowledge conversant about our ideas only.*—Since the mind, in all its thoughts and reasonings, hath no other immediate object but its own ideas, which it alone does or can contemplate, it is evident that our knowledge is only conversant about them.

2. *Knowledge is the perception of the agreement or disagreement of two ideas.*—*Knowledge* then seems to me to be nothing but the *perception of the connexion and agreement, or disagreement and repugnancy, of any of our ideas*. In this alone it consists. Where this perception is, there is knowledge; and where it is not, there, though we may fancy, guess, or believe, yet we always come short of knowledge. For when we know that white is not black, what do we else but perceive that these two ideas do not agree? When we possess ourselves with the utmost security of the demonstration that the three angles of a triangle are equal to two right ones, what do we more but perceive, that equality to two right ones does necessarily agree to, and is inseparable from, the three angles of a triangle?

3. *This agreement or disagreement may be any of four sorts.*—But to understand a little more distinctly wherein this agreement or disagreement consists, I think we may reduce it all to these four sorts: (1) *Identity,* or *diversity.* (2) *Relation.* (3) *Coexistence,* or *necessary connexion.* (4) *Real existence.*

4. *Of identity, or diversity in ideas.*—*First,* As to the first sort of agreement or disagreement, viz., *identity,* or *diversity.* It is the first act of the mind, when it has any sentiments or ideas at all, to perceive its ideas, and, so far as it perceives them, to know each what it is, and thereby also to perceive their difference, and that one is not another. This is so absolutely necessary, that without it there could be no knowledge, no reasoning, no imagination, no distinct thoughts at all. By this the mind clearly and infallibly perceives each idea to agree with itself, and to be what it is; and all distinct ideas to disagree, i.e., the one not to be the other: and this it does without pains, labour, or deduction; but at first view, by its natural power of perception and distinction. And though men of art have reduced this into those general rules, *What is, is*; and, *It is impossible for the same thing to be and not to be,* for ready application in all cases wherein there may be occasion to reflect on it; yet it is certain that the first exercise of this faculty is about particular ideas. A man infallibly knows, as soon as ever he has them in his mind, that the ideas he calls *white* and *round* are the very ideas they are, and that they are not other ideas which he calls *red* or *square.* Nor can any maxim or proposition in the world make him know it clearer or surer than he did before, and without any such general rule. This then is the first agreement or disagreement which the mind perceives in its ideas; which it always perceives at first sight; and if there ever happen any doubt about it, it will always be found to be about the names, and not the ideas themselves, whose identity and diversity will always be perceived as soon and as clearly as the ideas themselves are, nor can it possibly be otherwise.

5. *Of abstract relations between ideas.*—*Secondly,* The next sort of agreement or disagreement the mind perceives in any of its ideas may, I think, be called *relative,* and is nothing but the perception of the *relation* between any two ideas, of what kind soever, whether substances, modes, or any other. For, since all distinct ideas must eternally be known not to be the same, and so be universally and constantly denied one of another, there could be no room for any positive knowledge at all, if we could not perceive any relation between our ideas, and find out the agreement or disagreement they have one with another, in several ways the mind takes of comparing them.

6. *Of their necessary coexistence in substances.*—*Thirdly,* The third sort of agreement or disagreement to be found in our ideas, which the perception of the mind is employed about, is *coexistence,* or *non-coexistence* in the *same subject*; and this belongs particularly to substances. Thus when we pronounce concerning gold that it is fixed, our knowledge of this truth amounts to no more but this, that fixedness, or a power to remain in the fire unconsumed, is an idea that always accompanies and is joined with that particular sort of yellowness, weight, fusibility, malleableness, and solubility in aqua regia, which make our complex idea, signified by the word gold.

7. *Of real existence agreeing to any idea.*—*Fourthly,* The fourth and last sort is that of *actual real existence* agreeing to any idea. Within these four sorts of agreement or disagreement is, I suppose, contained all the knowledge we have or are capable of; for all the enquiries that we can make concerning any of our ideas, all that we know or can affirm concerning any of them, is, that it is or is not the same with some other; that it does or does not always coexist with some other idea in the same subject; that it has this or that relation to some other idea; or that it has a real existence without the mind. Thus, "Blue is not yellow," is of identity. "Two triangles upon equal bases between two parallels are equal," is of relation. "Iron is susceptible of magnetical impressions,"

is of coexistence. "God is," is of real existence. Though identity and coexistence are truly nothing but relations, yet they are so peculiar ways of agreement or disagreement of our ideas, that they deserve well to be considered as distinct heads, and not under relation in general: since they are so different grounds of affirmation and negation, as will easily appear to any one who will but reflect on what is said in several places of this Essay. I should now proceed to examine the several degrees of our knowledge, but that it is necessary first to consider the different acceptations of the word knowledge.

8. *Knowledge is either actual or habitual.*—There are several ways wherein the mind is possessed of truth, each of which is called knowledge.

(1) There is *actual knowledge*, which is the present view the mind has of the agreement or disagreement of any of its ideas, or of the relation they have one to another.

(2) A man is said to know any proposition which having been once laid before his thoughts, he evidently perceived the agreement or disagreement of the ideas whereof it consists; and so lodged it in his memory, that whenever that proposition comes again to be reflected on, he, without doubt or hesitation, embraces the right side, assents to and is certain of the truth of it. This, I think, one may call *habitual knowledge.* . . . For our finite understandings being able to think clearly and distinctly but on one thing at once, if men had no knowledge of any more than what they actually thought on, they would all be very ignorant; and he that knew most would know but one truth, that being all he was able to think on at one time.

9. *Habitual knowledge is of two degrees.*—Of habitual knowledge there are also, vulgarly speaking, two degrees:—

First, The one of such truths laid up in the memory as, whenever they occur to the mind, it *actually perceives the relation is between those ideas*. And this is in all those truths whereof we have an intuitive knowledge, where the ideas themselves, by an immediate view, discover their agreement or disagreement one with another.

Secondly, The other is of such truths, whereof the mind having been convinced, it retains *the memory of the conviction without the proofs*. Thus a man that remembers certainly that he once perceived the demonstration that the three angles of a triangle are equal to two right ones, is certain that he knows it, because he cannot doubt of the truth of it. In his adherence to a truth where the demonstration by which it was at first known is forgot, though a man may be thought rather to believe his memory than really to know, and this way of entertaining a truth seemed formerly to me like something between opinion and knowledge, a sort of assurance which exceeds bare belief, for that relies on the testimony of another; yet, upon a due examination, I find it comes not short of perfect certainty, and is, in effect, true knowledge. That which is apt to mislead our first thoughts into a mistake in this matter is, that the agreement or disagreement of the ideas in this case is not perceived, as it was at first, by an actual view of all the intermediate ideas whereby the agreement or disagreement of those in the proposition was at first perceived; but by other intermediate ideas, that show the agreement or disagreement of the ideas contained in the proposition whose certainty we remember. For example: in this proposition, that "the three angles of a triangle are equal to two right ones," one who has seen and clearly perceived the demonstration of this truth knows it to be true, when that demonstration is gone out of his mind, so that at present it is not actually in view, and possibly cannot be recollected; but he knows it in a different way from what he did before. The agreement of the two ideas joined in that proposition is perceived; but it is by the intervention of other ideas than those which at first produced that perception. He remembers, i.e., he knows (for remembrance is but the reviving of some past knowledge) that he was once certain of the truth of this proposition, that "the three angles of a triangle are equal to two right ones." The immutability of the same relations between the same immutable things is now the idea that shows him, that if the three angles of a triangle were once equal to two right ones, they will always be equal to two right ones. And hence he comes to be certain, that what was once true in the case is always true; what ideas once agreed will always agree: and consequently, what he once knew to be true he will always know to be true, as long as he can remember that he once knew it. Upon this ground it is that particular demonstrations in mathematics afford general knowledge. If then the perception that the same ideas will eternally have the same habitudes and relations be not a sufficient ground of knowledge, there could be no knowledge of general propositions in mathematics; for no mathematical demonstration would be any other than particular and when a man had demonstrated any proposition concerning one triangle or circle, his knowledge would not reach beyond that particular diagram. If he would extend it farther, he must renew his demonstration in another instance, before he could know it to be true in another like triangle, and so on by which means one could never come to the knowledge of any general propositions. Nobody, I think, can deny that Mr. Newton certainly knows any proposition that he now at any time reads in his book to be true, though he has not in actual view that admirable chain of intermediate ideas whereby he at first discovered it to be true. Such a memory as that, able to retain such a train of particulars, may be well thought beyond the reach of human faculties, when the very discovery, perception, and laying together that wonderful connexion of ideas is found to surpass most readers' comprehension. But yet it is evident the author himself knows the proposition to be true, remembering he once saw the connexion of those ideas, as certainly as he knows such a man wounded another, remembering that he saw him run him through. But because the memory is not always so clear as actual perception, and does in all men more or less decay in length of time, this amongst other differences, is one which shows that *demonstrative* knowledge is much more imperfect than *intuitive*, as we shall see in the following chapter.

CHAPTER 2. OF THE DEGREES OF OUR KNOWLEDGE

1. *Of the degree, or differences in clearness, of our knowledge*: I. *Intuitive*—All our knowledge consisting, as I have said, in the view the mind has of its own ideas, which is the utmost light and greatest certainty we, with our faculties and in our way of knowledge, are capable of, it may not be amiss to consider a little the degrees of its evidence. The different clearness of our knowledge seems to me to lie in the different way of perception the mind has of the agreement or disagreement of any of its ideas. For if we will reflect on our own ways of thinking, we shall find that sometimes the mind perceives the agreement or disagreement of two ideas *immediately by themselves*, without the intervention of any other and this, I think, we may call *intuitive knowledge*. For in this the mind is at no pains of proving or examining, but perceives the truth, as the eye doth light, only by being directed towards it. Thus the mind perceives that *white* is not black, that a *circle* is not a *triangle*, that *three* are more than *two*, and equal to *one and two*. Such kind of truths the mind perceives at the first sight of the ideas together, by bare intuition, without the intervention of any other idea; and this kind of knowledge is the clearest and most certain that human frailty is capable of. This part of knowledge is irresistible, and like bright sunshine, forces itself immediately to be perceived as soon as ever the mind turns its view that way; and leaves no room for hesitation, doubt, or examination, but the mind is presently filled with the clear light of it. *It*

is on this intuition that depends all the certainty and evidence of all our knowledge;
which certainty every one finds to be so great, that he cannot imagine, and therefore
not require, a greater for a man cannot conceive himself capable of a greater certainty,
than to know that any idea in his mind is such as he perceives it to be; and that two
ideas wherein he perceives a difference, are different, and not precisely the same. He
that demands a greater certainty that this demands he knows not what, and shows only
that he has a mind to be a skeptic without being able to be so. Certainty depends so
wholly on this intuition, that in the next degree of knowledge, which I call demonstrative, this intuition is necessary in all the connexions of the intermediate ideas, without
which we cannot attain knowledge and certainty.

2. II. *Demonstrative.*—The next degree of knowledge is, where the mind perceives the agreement or disagreement of any ideas, but not immediately. . . . In this
case, when the mind cannot so bring its ideas together as, by their immediate comparison and, as it were, juxtaposition or application one to another, to perceive their agreement or disagreement, it is fain, by the intervention of other ideas (one or more, as it
happens), to discover the agreement or disagreement which it searches; and this is that
which we call *reasoning*. Thus the mind, being willing to know the agreement or disagreement in bigness between the three angles of a triangle and two right ones, cannot,
by an immediate view and comparing them, do it: because the three angles of a triangle
cannot be brought at once, and be compared with any other one or two angles; and so
of this the mind has no immediate, no intuitive knowledge. In this case the mind is fain
to find out some other angles, to which the three angles of a triangle have an equality;
and finding those equal to two right ones, comes to know their equality to two right
ones.

3. *Demonstration depends on clearly perceived proofs.*—Those intervening
ideas which serve to show the agreement of any two others, are called *proofs*; and
where the agreement or disagreement is by this means plainly and clearly perceived, it
is called *demonstration*, it being *shown* to the understanding, and the mind made to see
that it is so. A quickness in the mind to find out these intermediate ideas (that shall discover the agreement or disagreement of any other), and to apply them right, is, I suppose, that which is called *sagacity*.

4. *As certain, but not so easy and ready as intuitive knowledge.*—This knowledge by intervening proofs, though it be certain, yet the evidence of it is not altogether
so clear and bright, nor the assent so ready, as in intuitive knowledge. For though in
demonstration the mind does at last perceive the agreement or disagreement of the
ideas it considers, yet it is not without pains and attention: there must be more than one
transient view to find it. A steady application and pursuit is required to this discovery:
and there must be a progression by steps and degrees before the mind can in this way
arrive at certainty. . . .

5. *The demonstrated conclusion not without doubt, precedent to the demonstration.*—Another difference between intuitive and demonstrative knowledge is, that
though in the latter all doubt be removed, when by the intervention of the intermediate
ideas the agreement or disagreement is perceived; yet before the demonstration there
was a doubt; which in intuitive knowledge cannot happen to the mind that has its faculty of perception left to a degree capable of distinct ideas, no more than it can be a
doubt to the eye (that can distinctly see white and black), whether this ink and this
paper be all of a colour. . . .

6. *Not so clear as intuitive knowledge.*—It is true, the perception produced by
demonstration is also very clear; yet it is often with a great abatement of that evident
lustre and full assurance that always accompany that which I call intuitive; like a face

reflected by several mirrors one to another, where, as long as it retains the similitude and agreement with the object, it produces a knowledge; but it is still, in every successive reflection, with a lessening of that perfect clearness and distinctness which is in the first, till at last, after many removes, it has a great mixture of dimness, and is not at first sight so knowable, especially to weak eyes. Thus it is with knowledge made out by a long train of proofs.

7. *Each step in demonstrated knowledge must have intuitive evidence.*—Now, in every step reason makes in demonstrative knowledge, there is an intuitive knowledge of that agreement or disagreement it seeks with the next intermediate idea, which it uses as a proof: for it were not so, that yet would need a proof; since without the perception of such agreement or disagreement there is no knowledge produced. . . . This intuitive perception of the agreement or disagreement of the intermediate ideas, in each step and progression of the demonstration, must also be carried exactly in the mind, and a man must be sure that no part is left out: which, because in long deductions, and the use of many proofs, the memory does not always so readily and exactly retain; therefore it comes to pass, that this is more imperfect than intuitive knowledge, and men embrace often falsehood for demonstrations.

8. *Hence the mistake, ex præcognitis et præconcessis.*—The necessity of this intuitive knowledge, in each step of scientifical or demonstrative reasoning, gave occasion, I imagine, to that mistaken axiom, that all reasoning was *ex præcognitis et præconcessis*; which how far it is mistaken, I shall have occasion to show more at large where I come to consider propositions, and particularly those propositions which are called "maxims"; and to show that it is by a mistake that they are supposed to be the foundations of all our knowledge and reasonings.

9. *Demonstration not limited to ideas of mathematical quantity.*—It has been generally taken for granted, that mathematics alone are capable of demonstrative certainty: but to have such an agreement or disagreement as may intuitively be perceived being, as I imagine, not the privilege of the ideas of number, extension, and figure alone, it may possibly be the want of due method and application in us, and not of sufficient evidence in things, that demonstration has been thought to have so little to do in other parts of knowledge, and been scarce so much as aimed at by any but mathematicians. . . .

10. *Why it has been thought to be so limited.*—The reason why it has been generally sought for and supposed to be only in those, I imagine, has been not only the general usefulness of those sciences, but because, in comparing their equality or excess, the modes of numbers have every the least difference very clear and perceivable: and though in extension every the least excess is not so perceptible, yet the mind has found out ways to examine and discover demonstratively the just equality of two angles, or extensions, or figures. . . .

11. *Modes of qualities not demonstrable like modes of quantity.*—But in other simple ideas, whose modes and differences are made and counted by degrees, and not quantity, we have not so nice and accurate a distinction of their differences as to perceive or find ways to measure their just equality or the least differences. For those other simple ideas, being appearances or sensations produced in us by the size, figure, number, and motion of minute corpuscles singly insensible, their different degrees also depend upon the variation of some or all of those causes; which since it cannot be observed by us in particles of matter whereof each is too subtle to be perceived, it is impossible for us to have any exact measures of the different degrees of these simple ideas. . . .

*   *   *

13. *The secondary qualities of things not discovered by demonstration.*—Not knowing what number of particles, nor what motion of them, is fit to produce any precise degree of whiteness, we cannot demonstrate the certain equality of any two degrees of whiteness; because we have no certain standard to measure them by, nor means to distinguish every the least real difference; the only help we have being from our senses, which in this point fail us. But where the difference is so great as to produce in the mind clearly distinct ideas, whose differences can be perfectly retained, there these ideas of colours, as we see in different kinds, as blue and red, are as capable of demonstration as ideas of number and extension. What I have here said of whiteness and colours, I think, holds true in all secondary qualities, and their modes.

14. *Sensitive knowledge of the particular existence of finite beings without us.*—These two, viz., intuition and demonstration, are the degrees of our *knowledge*; whatever comes short of one of these, with what assurance soever embraced, is but *faith* or *opinion*, but not knowledge, at least in all general truths. There is, indeed, another perception of the mind employed about *the particular existence of finite beings without us*, which, going beyond bare probability, and yet not reaching perfectly to either of the foregoing degrees of certainty, passes under the name of *knowledge*. There can be nothing more certain, than that the idea we receive from an external object is in our minds; this is intuitive knowledge. But whether there be anything more than barely that idea in our minds, whether we can thence certainly infer the existence of anything without us which corresponds to that idea, is that whereof some men think there may be a question made; because men may have such ideas in their minds when no such thing exists, no such object affects their senses. But yet here, I think, we are provided with an evidence that puts us past doubting; for I ask any one, whether he be not invincibly conscious to himself of a different perception when he looks on the sun by day, and thinks on it by night; when he actually tastes wormwood, or smells a rose, or only thinks on that savour or odour? We as plainly find the difference there is between any idea revived in our minds by our own memory, and actually coming into our minds by our senses, as we do between any two distinct ideas. If any one say, a dream may do the same thing, and all these ideas may be produced in us without any external objects; he may please to dream that I make him this answer: (1) That it is no great matter whether I remove his scruple or no: where all is but dream, reasoning and arguments are of no use, truth and knowledge nothing. (2) That I believe he will allow a very manifest difference between dreaming of being in the fire, and being actually in it. But yet if he be resolved to appear so skeptical as to maintain, that what I call being actually in the fire is nothing but a dream; and that we cannot thereby certainly know that any such thing as fire actually exists without us; I answer, that we certainly finding that pleasure or pain follows upon the application of certain objects to us, whose existence we perceive, or dream that we perceive, by our senses; this certainly is as great as our happiness or misery, beyond which we have no concernment to know or to be. So that, I think, we may add to the two former sorts of knowledge this also, of the existence of particular external objects by that perception and consciousness we have of the actual entrance of ideas from them, and allow these three degrees of knowledge, viz., *intuitive*, *demonstrative*, and *sensitive*: in each of which there are different degrees and ways of evidence and certainty.

*   *   *

CHAPTER 3. OF THE EXTENT OF HUMAN KNOWLEDGE

1. *Extent of our knowledge.*—KNOWLEDGE, as has been said, lying in the perception of the agreement or disagreement of any of our ideas, it follows from hence that,

It extends no farther than we have ideas.—First, We can have knowledge no farther than we have ideas.

2. *It extends no farther than we can perceive their agreement or disagreement.*—Secondly, That we can have no knowledge farther than we can have perception of that agreement or disagreement: which perception being, (1) Either by *intuition*, or the immediate comparing any two ideas; or, (2) By *reason*, examining the agreement or disagreement of two ideas by the intervention of some others; or (3) By *sensation*, perceiving the existence of particular things; hence it also follows,

3. *Intuitive knowledge extends itself not to all the relations of all our ideas.*—Thirdly, that we cannot have an *intuitive knowledge* that shall extend itself to all our ideas, and all that we would know about them; because we cannot examine and perceive all the relations they have one to another by juxtaposition, or an immediate comparison one with another. Thus having the ideas of an obtuse and an acute angled triangle, both drawn from equal bases, and between parallels, I can by intuitive knowledge perceive the one not to be the other; but cannot that way know whether they be equal or no: because their agreement or disagreement in equality can never be perceived by an immediate comparing them; the difference of figure makes their parts incapable of an exact immediate application; and therefore there is need of some intervening quantities to measure them by, which is demonstration or rational knowledge.

4. *Nor does demonstrative knowledge.*—Fourthly, It follows also, from what is above observed, that our *rational knowledge* cannot reach to the whole extent of our ideas. Because between two different ideas we would examine, we cannot always find such mediums as we can connect one to another with an intuitive knowledge, in all the parts of the deduction; and wherever that fails, we come short of knowledge and demonstration.

5. *Sensitive knowledge narrower than either.*—Fifthly, *Sensitive knowledge*, reaching no farther than the existence of things actually present to our senses, is yet much narrower than either of the former.

*   *   *

CHAPTER 9. OF OUR THREEFOLD KNOWLEDGE OF EXISTENCE

1. *General propositions that are certain concern not existence.*—Hitherto we have only considered the essences of things; which being only abstract ideas, and thereby removed in our thoughts from particular existence, (that being the proper operation of the mind, in abstraction, to consider an idea under no other existence but what it has in the understanding,) gives us no knowledge of real existence at all. Where, by the way, we may take notice, that universal propositions of whose truth or falsehood

we can have certain knowledge concern not existence: and further, that all particular affirmations or negations that would not be certain if they were made general, are only concerning existence; they declaring only the accidental union or separation of ideas in things existing, which, in their abstract natures, have no known necessary union or repugnancy.

2. *A threefold knowledge of existence.*—But, leaving the nature of propositions, and different ways of predication to be considered more at large in another place, let us proceed now to inquire concerning our knowledge of the *existence of things*, and how we come by it. I say, then, that we have the knowledge of *our own* existence by intuition; of the existence of *God* by demonstration; and of *other things* by sensation.

3. *Our knowledge of our own existence is intuitive.*—As for our own existence, we perceive it so plainly and so certainly, that it neither needs nor is capable of any proof. For nothing can be more evident to us than our own existence. I think, I reason, I feel pleasure and pain: can any of these be more evident to me than my own existence? If I doubt of all other things, that very doubt makes me perceive my own existence, and will not suffer me to doubt of that. For if I know I feel pain, it is evident I have as certain perception of my own existence, as of the existence of the pain I feel: or if I know I doubt, I have as certain perception of the existence of the thing doubting, as of that thought which I *call doubt*. Experience then convinces us, that we have an *intuitive knowledge* of our own existence, and an internal infallible perception that we are. In every act of sensation, reasoning, or thinking, we are conscious to ourselves of our own being; and, in this matter, come not short of the highest degree of certainty.

CHAPTER 10. OF OUR KNOWLEDGE OF THE EXISTENCE OF A GOD

1. *We are capable of knowing certainly that there is a God.*—Though God has given us no innate ideas of himself; though he has stamped no original characters on our minds, wherein we may read his being; yet having furnished us with those faculties our minds are endowed with, he hath not left himself without witness: since we have sense, perception, and reason, and cannot want a clear proof of him, as long as we carry *ourselves* about us. Nor can we justly complain of our ignorance in this great point; since he has so plentifully provided us with the means to discover and know him; so far as is necessary to the end of our being, and the great concernment of our happiness. But, though this be the most obvious truth that reason discovers, and though its evidence be (if I mistake not) equal to mathematical certainty: yet it requires thought and attention; and the mind must apply itself to a regular deduction of it from some part of our intuitive knowledge, or else we shall be as uncertain and ignorant of this as of other propositions, which are in themselves capable of clear demonstration. To show, therefore, that we are capable of *knowing*, i.e., *being certain* that there is a God, and *how we may come by* this certainty, I think we need go no further than *ourselves*, and that undoubted knowledge we have of our own existence.

2. *For man knows that he himself exists.*—I think it is beyond question, that man has a clear idea of his own being; he knows certainly he exists, and that he is something. He that can doubt—whether he be anything or no, I speak not to; no more than I would argue with pure nothing, or endeavour to convince nonentity that it were something. If any one pretends to be so sceptical as to deny his own existence, (for really to doubt of it is manifestly impossible,) let him for me enjoy his beloved happiness of being nothing, until hunger or some other pain convince him of the contrary. This,

then, I think I may take for a truth, which every one's certain knowledge assures him of, beyond the liberty of doubting, viz., that he is something that actually exists.

3. *He knows also that nothing cannot produce a being; therefore something must have existed from eternity.*—In the next place, man knows, by an intuitive certainty, that bare *nothing can no more produce any real being, than it can be equal to two right angles.* If a man knows not that nonentity, or the absence of all being, cannot be equal to two right angles, it is impossible he should know any demonstration in Euclid. If, therefore, we know there is some real being, and that nonentity cannot produce any real being, it is an evident demonstration, that *from eternity there has been something*; since what was not from eternity had a beginning; and what had a beginning must be produced by something else.

4. *And that eternal Being must be most powerful.*—Next, it is evident, that what had its being and beginning from another, must also have all that which is in and belongs to its being from another too. All the powers it has must be owing to and received from the same source. This eternal source, then, of all being must also be the source and original of all power; and so *this eternal Being must be also the most powerful.*

5. *And most knowing.*—Again, a man finds in *himself* perception and knowledge. We have then got one step further; and we are certain now that there is not only some being, but some knowing, intelligent being in the world. There was a time, then, when there was no knowing being and when knowledge began to be; or else there has been also a *knowing being from eternity.* If it be said, there was a time when no being had any knowledge, when that eternal being was void of all understanding; I reply, that then it was impossible there should ever have been any knowledge: it being as impossible that things wholly void of knowledge, and operating blindly, and without any perception, should produce a knowing being, as it is impossible that a triangle should make itself three angles bigger than two right ones. For it is as repugnant to the idea of senseless matter, that it should put into itself sense, perception, and knowledge, as it is repugnant to the idea of a triangle, that it should put into itself greater angles than two right ones.

6. *And therefore God.*—Thus, from the consideration of ourselves, and what we infallibly find in our own constitutions, our reason leads us to the knowledge of this certain and evident truth,—*That there is an eternal, most powerful, and most knowing Being*; which whether any one will please to call God, it matters not. The thing is evident, and from this idea duly considered, will easily be deduced all those other attributes, which we ought to ascribe to this eternal Being. If, nevertheless, any one should be found so senselessly arrogant, as to suppose man alone knowing and wise, but yet the product of mere ignorance and chance; and that all the rest of the universe acted only by that blind haphazard; I shall leave with him that very rational and emphatical rebuke of Tully, to be considered at his leisure: "What can be more sillily arrogant and misbecoming, than for a man to think that he has a mind and understanding in him, but yet in all the universe beside there is no such thing? Or that those things, which with the utmost stretch of his reason he can scarce comprehend, should be moved and managed without any reason at all?" . . .

From what has been said, it is plain to me we have a more certain knowledge of the existence of a God, than of anything our senses have not immediately discovered to us. Nay, I presume I may say, that we more certainly know that there is a God, than that there is anything else without us. When I say we *know*, I mean there is such a knowledge within our reach which we cannot miss, if we will but apply our minds to that, as we do to several other inquiries.

*   *   *

Chapter 11. Of our Knowledge of the Existence of Other Things

1. *Knowledge of the existence of other finite beings is to be had only by actual sensation.*—The knowledge of our own being we have by intuition. The existence of a God, reason clearly makes known to us, as has been shown.

The knowledge of the existence of *any other thing* we can have only by sensation: for there being no necessary connexion of real existence with any idea a man hath in his memory; nor of any other existence but that of God with the existence of any particular man: no particular man can know the existence of any other being, but only when, by actual operating upon him, it makes itself perceived by him. For, the having the idea of anything in our mind, no more proves the existence of that thing, than the picture of a man evidences his being in the world, or the visions of a dream make thereby a true history.

2. *Instance: whiteness of this paper.*—It is therefore the *actual receiving* of ideas from without that gives us notice of the existence of other things, and makes us know, that something doth exist at that time without us, which causes that idea in us; though perhaps we neither know nor consider how it does it. For it takes not from the certainty of our senses, and the ideas we receive by them, that we know not the manner wherein they are produced: v.g., whilst I write this, I have, by the paper affecting my eyes, that idea produced in my mind, which, whatever object causes, I call *white*; by which I know that that quality or accident (i.e., whose appearance before my eyes always causes that idea) doth really exist, and hath a being without me. And of this, the greatest assurance I can possibly have, and to which my faculties can attain, is the testimony of my eyes, which are the proper and sole judges of this thing; whose testimony I have reason to rely on as so certain, that I can no more doubt, whilst I write this, that I see white and black, and that something really exists that causes that sensation in me, than that I write or move my hand; which is a certainty as great as human nature is capable of, concerning the existence of anything, but a man's self alone, and of God.

3. *This notice by our senses, though not so certain as demonstration, yet may be called knowledge, and proves the existence of things without us.*—The notice we have by our senses of the existing of things without us, though it be not altogether so certain as our intuitive knowledge, or the deductions of our reason employed about the clear abstract ideas of our own minds; yet it is an assurance that deserves the name of *knowledge*. If we persuade ourselves that our faculties act and inform us right concerning the existence of those objects that affect them, it cannot pass for an ill-grounded confidence: for I think nobody can, in earnest, be so sceptical as to be uncertain of the existence of those things which he sees and feels. At least, he that can doubt so far, (whatever he may have with his own thoughts,) will never have any controversy with me; since he can never be sure I say anything contrary to his own opinion. As to myself, I think God has given me assurance enough of the existence of things without me: since, by their different application, I can produce in myself both pleasure and pain, which is one great concernment of my present state. This is certain: the confidence that our faculties do not herein deceive us, is the greatest assurance we are capable of concerning the existence of material beings. For we cannot act anything but by our faculties; nor talk of knowledge itself, but by the help of those faculties which are fitted to apprehend even what knowledge is.

But besides the assurance we have from our senses themselves, that they do not err in the information they give us of the existence of things without us, when they are affected by them, we are further confirmed in this assurance by other concurrent reasons:—

4. I. *Confirmed by concurrent reasons:—First, because we cannot have ideas of sensation but by the inlet of the senses.*—It is plain those perceptions are produced in us by exterior causes affecting our senses: because those that want the organs of any sense, never can have the ideas belonging to that sense produced in their minds. This is too evident to be doubted: and therefore we cannot but be assured that they come in by the organs of that sense, and no other way. The organs themselves, it is plain, do not produce them: for then the eyes of a man in the dark would produce colours, and his nose smell roses in the winter: but we see nobody gets the relish of a pineapple, till he goes to the Indies, where it is, and tastes it.

5. II. *Secondly, Because we find that an idea from actual sensation, and another from memory, are very distinct perceptions.*—Because sometimes I find that *I cannot avoid the having those ideas produced in my mind.* For though, when my eyes are shut, or windows fast, I can at pleasure recall to my mind the ideas of light, or the sun, which former sensations had lodged in my memory; so I can at pleasure lay by *that* idea, and take into my view that of the smell of a rose, or taste of sugar. But, if I turn my eyes at noon towards the sun, I cannot avoid the ideas which the light or sun then produces in me. So that there is a manifest difference between the ideas laid up in my memory, (over which, if they were there only, I should have constantly the same power to dispose of them, and lay them by at pleasure,) and those which force themselves upon me, and I cannot avoid having. And therefore it must needs be some exterior cause, and the brisk acting of some objects without me, whose efficacy I cannot resist, that produces those ideas in my mind, whether I will or no. Besides, there is nobody who doth not perceive the difference in himself between contemplating the sun, as he hath the idea of it in his memory, and actually looking upon it: of which two, his perception is so distinct, that few of his ideas are more distinguishable one from another. And therefore he hath certain knowledge that they are not *both* memory, or the actions of his mind, and fancies only within him; but that actual seeing hath a cause without.

6. III. *Thirdly, because pleasure or pain, which accompanies actual sensation, accompanies not the returning of those ideas without the external objects.*—Add to this, that many of those ideas are *produced in us with pain*, which afterwards we remember without the least offence. Thus, the pain of heat or cold, when the idea of it is revived in our minds, gives us no disturbance; which, when felt, was very troublesome; and is again, when actually repeated: which is occasioned by the disorder the external object causes in our bodies when applied to them: and we remember the pains of hunger, thirst, or the headache, without any pain at all; which would either never disturb us, or else constantly do it, as often as we thought of it, were there nothing more but ideas floating in our minds, and appearances entertaining our fancies, without the real existence of things affecting us from abroad. The same may be said of *pleasure*, accompanying several actual sensations. And though mathematical demonstration depends not upon sense, yet the examining them by diagrams gives great credit to the evidence of our sight, and seems to give it a certainty approaching to that of demonstration itself. For, it would be very strange, that a man should allow it for an undeniable truth, that two angles of a figure, which he measures by lines and angles of a diagram, should be bigger one than the other, and yet doubt of the existence of those lines and angles, which by looking on he makes use of to measure that by.

7. IV. *Fourthly, because our senses assist one Another's testimony of the existence of outward things, and enable us to predict.*—Our senses in many cases *bear witness to the truth of each other's report*, concerning the existence of sensible things without us. He that sees a fire, may, if he doubt whether it be anything more than a bare fancy, *feel* it too; and be convinced, by putting his hand in it. Which certainly could never be put into such exquisite pain by a bare idea or phantom, unless that the pain be a fancy too: which yet he cannot, when the burn is well, by raising the idea of it, bring upon himself again.

Thus I see, whilst I write this, I can change the appearance of the paper; and by designing the letters, tell *beforehand* what new idea it shall exhibit the very next moment, by barely drawing my pen over it: which will neither appear (let me fancy as much as I will) if my hands stand still; or though I move my pen, if my eyes be shut: nor, when those characters are once made on the paper, can I choose afterwards but see them as they are; that is, have the ideas of such letters as I have made. Whence it is manifest, that they are not barely the sport and play of my own imagination, when I find that the characters that were made at the pleasure of my own thoughts, do not obey them; nor yet cease to be, whenever I shall fancy it, but continue to affect my senses constantly and regularly, according to the figures I made them. To which if we will add, that the sight of those shall, from another man, draw such sounds as I beforehand design they shall stand for, there will be little reason left to doubt that those words I write do really exist without me, when they cause a long series of regular sounds to affect my ears, which could not be the effect of my imagination, nor could my memory retain them in that order.

8. *This certainty is as great as our condition needs.*—But yet, if after all this any one will be so sceptical as to distrust his senses, and to affirm that all we see and hear, feel and taste, think and do, during our whole being, is but the series and deluding appearances of a long dream, whereof there is no reality; and therefore will question the existence of all things, or our knowledge of anything: I must desire him to consider, that, if all be a dream, then he doth but dream that he makes the question, and so it is not much matter that a waking man should answer him. But yet, if he pleases, he may dream that I make him this answer, That the certainty of things existing in *rerum natura* when we have the testimony of our senses for it is not only as great as our frame can attain to, but as our condition needs. For, our faculties being suited not to the full extent of being, nor to a perfect, clear, comprehensive knowledge of things free from all doubt and scruple; but to the preservation of us, in whom they are; and accommodated to the use of life: they serve to our purpose well enough, if they will but give us certain notice of those things, which are convenient or inconvenient to us. For he that sees a candle burning, and hath experimented the force of its flame by putting his finger in it, will little doubt that this is something existing without him, which does him harm, and puts him to great pain: which is assurance enough, when no man requires greater certainty to govern his actions by than what is as certain as his actions themselves. And if our dreamer pleases to try whether the glowing heat of a glass furnace be barely a wandering imagination in a drowsy man's fancy, by putting his hand into it, he may perhaps be wakened into a certainty greater than he could wish, that it is something more than bare imagination. So that this evidence is as great as we can desire, being as certain to us as our pleasure or pain, i.e., happiness or misery; beyond which we have no concernment, either of knowing or being. Such an assurance of the existence of things without us is sufficient to direct us in the attaining the good and avoiding the evil which is caused by them, which is the important concernment we have of being made acquainted with them.

9. *But reaches no further than actual sensation.*—In fine, then, when our senses do actually convey into our understandings any idea, we cannot but be satisfied that there doth something *at that time* really exist without us, which doth affect our senses, and by them give notice of itself to our apprehensive faculties, and actually produce that idea which we then perceive: and we cannot so far distrust their testimony, as to doubt that such *collections* of simple ideas as we have observed by our senses to be united together, do really exist together. But this knowledge extends as far as the present testimony of our senses, employed about particular objects that do then affect them, and no further. For if I saw such a collection of simple ideas as is wont to be called *man*, existing together one minute since, and am now alone, I cannot be certain that the same man exists now, since there is no *necessary connexion* of his existence a minute since with his existence now: by a thousand ways he may cease to be, since I had the testimony of my senses for his existence. And if I cannot be certain that the man I saw last today is now in being, I can less be certain that he is so who hath been longer removed from my senses, and I have not seen since yesterday, or since the last year: and much less can I be certain of the existence of men that I never saw. And, therefore, though it be highly probable that millions of men do now exist, yet, whilst I am alone, writing this, I have not that certainty of it which we strictly call knowledge; though the great likelihood of it puts me past doubt, and it be reasonable for me to do several things upon the confidence that there are men (and men also of my acquaintance, with whom I have to do) now in the world: but this is but probability, not knowledge.

10. *Folly to expect demonstration in everything.*—Whereby yet we may observe how foolish and vain a thing it is for a man of a narrow knowledge, who having reason given him to judge of the different evidence and probability of things, and to be swayed accordingly; how vain, I say, it is to expect demonstration and certainty in things not capable of it—and refuse assent to very rational propositions, and act contrary to very plain and clear truths, because they cannot be made out so evident, as to surmount every the least (I will not say reason, but) pretence of doubting. He that, in the ordinary affairs of life, would admit of nothing but direct plain demonstration would be sure of nothing in this world but of perishing quickly. The wholesomeness of his meat or drink would not give him reason to venture on it: and I would fain know what it is he could do upon such grounds as are capable of no doubt, no objection.

11. *Past existence of other things is known by memory.*—As *when our senses are actually employed about any object*, we do know that it does exist; so *by our memory we may be assured*, that heretofore things that affected our senses have existed. And thus we have knowledge of the past existence of several things, whereof our senses having informed us, our memories still retain the ideas; and of this we are past all doubt, so long as we remember well. But this knowledge also reaches no further than our senses have formerly assured us. Thus, seeing water at this instant, it is an unquestionable truth to me that water doth exist: and remembering that I saw it yesterday, it will also be always true, and as long as my memory retains it always an undoubted proposition to me, that water did exist the 10th of July, 1688; as it will also be equally true that a certain number of very fine colours did exist, which at the same time I saw upon a bubble of that water: but, being now quite out of sight both of the water and bubbles too, it is no more certainly known to me that the water doth now exist, than that the bubbles or colours therein do so: it being no more necessary that water should exist today, because it existed yesterday, than that the colours or bubbles exist today, because they existed yesterday, though it be exceedingly much more probable; because water hath been observed to continue long in existence, but bubbles, and the colours on them, quickly cease to be.

12. *The existence of other finite spirits not knowable, and rests on faith.*—What ideas we have of spirits, and how we come by them, I have already shown. But though we have those ideas in our minds, and know we have them there, the having the ideas of spirits does not make us know that any such things do exist without us, or that there are any finite spirits, or any other spiritual beings, but the Eternal God. We have ground from revelation, and several other reasons, to believe with assurance that there are such creatures: but our senses not being able to discover them, we want the means of knowing their particular existences. For we can no more know that there are finite spirits really existing, by the idea we have of such beings in our minds, than by the ideas any one has of fairies or centaurs, he can come to know that things answering those ideas do really exist.

And therefore concerning the existence of finite spirits, as well as several other things, we must content ourselves with the evidence of faith; but universal, certain propositions concerning this matter are beyond our reach. For however true it may be, v.g., that all the intelligent spirits that God ever created do still exist, yet it can never make a part of our certain knowledge. These and the like propositions we may assent to, as highly probable, but are not, I fear, in this state capable of knowing. We are not, then, to put others upon demonstrating, nor ourselves upon search of universal certainty in all those matters; wherein we are not capable of any other knowledge, but what our senses give us in this or that particular.

13. *Only particular propositions concerning concrete existences are knowable.*—By which it appears that there are two sorts of propositions:—(1) There is one sort of propositions concerning the *existence* of anything answerable to such an idea: as having the idea of an elephant, phoenix, motion, or an angel, in my mind, the first and natural inquiry is, Whether such a thing does anywhere exist? And this knowledge is only of particulars. No existence of anything without us, but only of God, can certainly be known further than our senses inform us. (2) There is another sort of propositions, wherein is expressed the agreement or disagreement of *our abstract ideas*, and their dependence on one another. Such propositions may be universal and certain. So, having the idea of God and myself, of fear and obedience, I cannot but be sure that God is to be feared and obeyed by me: and this proposition will be certain, concerning man in general, if I have made an abstract idea of such a species, whereof I am one particular. But yet this proposition, how certain soever, that "men ought to fear and obey God" proves not to me the *existence* of *men* in the world but will be true of all such creatures, whenever they do exist: which certainty of such general propositions depends on the agreement or disagreement to be discovered in those abstract ideas.

14. *And all general propositions that are known to be true concern abstract ideas.*—In the former case, our knowledge is the consequence of the existence of things, producing ideas in our minds by our senses: in the latter, knowledge is the consequence of the ideas (be they what they will) that are in our minds, producing there general certain propositions. Many of these are called *aeternae veritates*, and all of them indeed are so; not from being written, all or any of them, in the minds of all men; or that they were any of them propositions in any one's mind, till he, having got the abstract ideas, joined or separated them by affirmation or negation. But wheresoever we can suppose such a creature as man is, endowed with such faculties, and thereby furnished with such ideas as we have, we must conclude, he must needs, when he applies his thoughts to the consideration of his ideas, know the truth of certain propositions that will arise from the agreement or disagreement which he will perceive in his own ideas. Such propositions are therefore called *eternal truths*, not because they are eternal propositions actually formed, and antecedent to the understanding that at any time

makes them; nor because they are imprinted on the mind from any patterns that are anywhere out of the mind, and existed before: but because, being once made about abstract ideas, so as to be true, they will, whenever they can be supposed to be made again at any time, past or to come, by a mind having those ideas, always actually be true. For names being supposed to stand perpetually for the same ideas, and the same ideas having immutably the same habitudes one to another, propositions concerning any abstract ideas that are once true must needs be *eternal verities*.

AN ESSAY CONCERNING THE TRUE ORIGINAL EXTENT AND END OF CIVIL GOVERNMENT (SECOND ESSAY) (in part)

*   *   *

CHAPTER 2. OF THE STATE OF NATURE

4. To understand political power aright, and derive it from its original, we must consider what estate all men are naturally in, and that is, a state of perfect freedom to order their actions, and dispose of their possessions and persons as they think fit, within the bounds of the law of Nature, without asking leave or depending upon the will of any other man.

A state also of equality, wherein all the power and jurisdiction is reciprocal, no one having more than another, there being nothing more evident than that creatures of the same species and rank, promiscuously born to all the same advantages of Nature, and the use of the same faculties, should also be equal one amongst another, without subordination or subjection, unless the lord and master of them all should, by any manifest declaration of his will, set one above another, and confer on him, by an evident and clear appointment, an undoubted right to dominion and sovereignty.

*   *   *

6. But though this be a state of liberty, yet it is not a state of licence; though man in that state have an uncontrollable liberty to dispose of his person or possessions, yet he has not liberty to destroy himself, or so much as any creature in his possession, but where some nobler use than its bare preservation calls for it. The state of Nature has a law of Nature to govern it, which obliges every one, and reason, which is that law, teaches all mankind who will but consult it, that being all equal and independent, no one ought to harm another in his life, health, liberty or possessions; for men being all the workmanship of one omnipotent and infinitely wise Maker; all the servants of one sovereign Master, sent into the world by His order and about His business; they are His property, whose workmanship they are made to last during His, not one another's pleasure. And, being furnished with like faculties, sharing all in one community of Nature,

there cannot be supposed any such subordination among us that may authorise us to destroy one another, as if we were made for one another's uses, as the inferior ranks of creatures are for ours. Every one as he is bound to preserve himself, and not to quit his station wilfully, so by the like reason, when his own preservation comes not in competition, ought he as much as he can to preserve the rest of mankind, and not unless it be to do justice on an offender, take away or impair the life, or what tends to the preservation of the life, the liberty, health, limb, or goods of another.

7. And that all men may be restrained from invading others' rights, and from doing hurt to one another, and the law of Nature be observed, which willeth the peace and preservation of all mankind, the execution of the law of Nature is in that state put into every man's hands, whereby every one has a right to punish the transgressors of that law to such a degree as may hinder its violation. For the law of Nature would, as all other laws that concern men in this world, be in vain if there were nobody that in the state of Nature had a power to execute that law, and thereby preserve the innocent and restrain offenders; and if any one in the state of Nature may punish another for any evil he has done, every one may do so. For in that state of perfect equality, where naturally there is no superiority or jurisdiction of one over another, what any may do in prosecution of that law, every one must needs have a right to do.

8. And thus, in the state of Nature, one man comes by a power over another, but yet no absolute or arbitrary power to use a criminal, when he has got him in his hands, according to the passionate heats or boundless extravagancy of his own will, but only to retribute to him so far as calm reason and conscience dictate, what is proportionate to his transgression, which is so much as may serve for reparation and restraint. For these two are the only reasons why one man may lawfully do harm to another, which is that we call punishment. In transgressing the law of Nature, the offender declares himself to live by another rule than that of reason and common equity, which is that measure God has set to the actions of men for their mutual security, and so he becomes dangerous to mankind; the tie which is to secure them from injury and violence being slighted and broken by him, which being a trespass against the whole species, and the peace and safety of it, provided for by the law of Nature, every man upon this score, by the right he hath to preserve mankind in general, may restrain, or where it is necessary, destroy things noxious to them, and so may bring such evil on any one who hath transgressed that law, as may make him repent the doing of it, and thereby deter him, and, by his example, others from doing the like mischief. And in this case, and upon this ground every man hath a right to punish the offender, and be executioner of the law of Nature.

*   *   *

13. To this strange doctrine—viz., That in the state of Nature every one has the executive power of the law of Nature—I doubt not but it will be objected that it is unreasonable for men to be judges in their own cases, that self-love will make men partial to themselves and their friends; and, on the other side, ill-nature, passion, and revenge will carry them too far in punishing others, and hence nothing but confusion and disorder will follow, and that therefore God hath certainly appointed government to restrain the partiality and violence of men. I easily grant that civil government is the proper remedy for the inconveniences of the state of Nature, which must certainly be great where men may be judges in their own case, since it is easy to be imagined that he who was so unjust as to do his brother an injury will scarce be so just as to condemn himself for it. But I shall desire those who make this objection to remember that absolute

monarchs are but men; and if government is to be the remedy of those evils which necessarily follow from men being judges in their own cases, and the state of Nature is therefore not to be endured, I desire to know what kind of government that is, and how much better it is than the state of Nature, where one man commanding a multitude has the liberty to be judge in his own case, and may do to all his subjects whatever he pleases without the least question or control of those who execute his pleasure? and in whatsoever he doth, whether led by reason, mistake, or passion, must be submitted to? which men in the state of Nature are not bound to do one to another. And if he that judges, judges amiss in his own or any other case, he is answerable for it to the rest of mankind.

14. It is often asked as a mighty objection, where are, or ever were, there any men in such a state of Nature? To which it may suffice as an answer at present, that since all princes and rulers of "independent" governments all through the world are in a state of Nature, it is plain the world never was, nor never will be, without numbers of men in that state. I have named all governors of "independent" communities, whether they are, or are not, in league with others; for it is not every compact that puts an end to the state of Nature between men, but only this one of agreeing together mutually to enter into one community, and make one body politic; other promises and compacts men may make one with another, and yet still be in the state of Nature. The promises and bargains for truck, etc., between the two men in Soldania, in or between a Swiss and an Indian, in the woods of America, are binding to them, though they are perfectly in a state of Nature in reference to one another for truth, and keeping of faith belongs to men as men, and not as members of society.

*   *   *

CHAPTER 7. OF POLITICAL OR CIVIL SOCIETY

87. Man being born, as has been proved, with a title to perfect freedom and an uncontrolled enjoyment of all the rights and privileges of the law of Nature, equally with any other man, or number of men in the world hath by nature a power not only to preserve his property—that is, his life, liberty, and estate, against the injuries and attempts of other men, but to judge of and punish the breaches of that law in others, as he is persuaded the offence deserves, even with death itself, in crimes where the heinousness of the fact, in his opinion, requires it. But because no political society can be, nor subsist, without having in itself the power to preserve the property, and in order thereunto punish the offences of all those of that society, there, and there only, is political society where every one of the members hath quitted this natural power, resigned it up into the hands of the community in all cases that exclude him not from appealing for protection to the law established by it. And thus all private judgment of every particular member being excluded, the community comes to be umpire, and by understanding indifferent rules and men authorised by the community for their execution, decides all the differences that may happen between any members of that society concerning any matter of right, and punishes those offences which any member hath committed against the society with such penalties as the law has established; whereby it is easy to discern who are, and are not, in political society together. Those who are united into one body, and have a common established law and judicature to appeal to, with authority to decide controversies between them and punish offenders, are in civil society one

with another; but those who have no such common appeal, I mean on earth, are still in the state of Nature, each being where there is no other, judge for himself and executioner, which is, as I have before showed it, the perfect state of Nature.

88. And thus the commonwealth comes by a power to set down what punishment shall belong to the several transgressions they think worthy of it, committed amongst the members of that society (which is the power of making laws), as well as it has the power to punish any injury done unto any of its members by any one that is not of it (which is the power of war and peace); and all this for the preservation of the property of all the members of that society, as far as is possible. But though every man entered into society has quitted his power to punish offences against the law of Nature in prosecution of his own private judgment, yet with the judgment of offences which he has given up to the legislative, in all cases where he can appeal to the magistrate, he has given up a right to the commonwealth to employ his force for the execution of the judgments of the commonwealth whenever he shall be called to it, which, indeed, are his own judgments, they being made by himself or his representative. And herein we have the original of the legislative and executive power of civil society, which is to judge by standing laws how far offences are to be punished when committed within the commonwealth; and also by occasional judgments founded on the present circumstances of the fact, how far injuries from without are to be vindicated, and in both these to employ all the force of all the members when there shall be need.

89. Wherever, therefore, any number of men so unite into one society as to quit every one his executive power of the law of Nature, and to resign it to the public, there and there only is a political or civil society. And this is done wherever any number of men, in the state of Nature, enter into society to make one people one body politic under one supreme government or else when any one joins himself to, and incorporates with any government already made. For hereby he authorises the society, or which is all one, the legislative thereof, to make laws for him as the public good of the society shall require, to the execution whereof his own assistance (as to his own decrees) is due. And this puts men out of a state of Nature into that of a commonwealth, by setting up a judge on earth with authority to determine all the controversies and redress the injuries that may happen to any member of the commonwealth, which judge is the legislative or magistrates appointed by it. And wherever there are any number of men, however associated, that have no such decisive power to appeal to, there they are still in the state of Nature.

90. And hence it is evident that absolute monarchy, which by some men is counted for the only government in the world, is indeed inconsistent with civil society, and so can be no form of civil government at all. For the end of civil society being to avoid and remedy those inconveniencies of the state of Nature which necessarily follow from every man's being judge in his own case, by setting up a known authority to which every one of that society may appeal upon any injury received, or controversy that may arise, and which every one of the society ought to obey. Wherever any persons are who have not such an authority to appeal to, and decide any difference between them there, those persons are still in the state of Nature. And so is every absolute prince in respect of those who are under his dominion.

91. For he being supposed to have all, both legislative and executive, power in himself alone, there is no judge to be found, no appeal lies open to any one, who may fairly and indifferently, and with authority decide, and from whence relief and redress may be expected of any injury or inconveniency that may be suffered from him, or by his order. So that such a man, however entitled, Czar, or Grand Signior, or how you please, is as much in the state of Nature, with all under his dominion, as he is with the

rest of mankind. For wherever any two men are, who have no standing rule and common judge to appeal to on earth, for the determination of controversies of right betwixt them, there they are still in the state of Nature, and under all the inconveniencies of it, with only this woeful difference to the subject, or rather slave of an absolute prince. That whereas, in the ordinary state of Nature, he has a liberty to judge of his right, according to the best of his power to maintain it; but whenever his property is invaded by the will and order of his monarch, he has not only no appeal, as those in society ought to have, but, as if he were degraded from the common state of rational creatures, is denied a liberty to judge of, or defend his right, and so is exposed to all the misery and inconveniencies that a man can fear from one, who being in the unrestrained state of Nature, is yet corrupted with flattery and armed with power.

92. For he that thinks absolute power purifies men's blood, and corrects the baseness of human nature, need read but the history of this, or any other age, to be convinced to the contrary. He that would have been insolent and injurious in the woods of America would not probably be much better on a throne, where perhaps learning and religion shall be found out to justify all that he shall do to his subjects, and the sword presently silence all those that dare question it. For what the protection of absolute monarchy is, what kind of fathers of their countries it makes princes to be, and to what a degree of happiness and security it carries civil society, where this sort of government is grown to perfection, he that will look into the late relation of Ceylon may easily see.

93. In absolute monarchies, indeed, as well as other governments of the world, the subjects have an appeal to the law, and judges to decide any controversies, and restrain any violence that may happen betwixt the subjects themselves, one amongst another. This every one thinks necessary, and believes; he deserves to be thought a declared enemy to society and mankind who should go about to take it away. But whether this be from a true love of mankind and society, and such a charity as we owe all one to another there is reason to doubt. For this is no more than what every man, who loves his own power, profit, or greatness, may, and naturally must do, keep those animals from hurting or destroying one another who labour and drudge only for his pleasure and advantage; and so are taken care of, not out of any love the master has for them, but love of himself, and the profit they bring him. For if it be asked what security, what fence is there in such a state against the violence and oppression of this absolute ruler, the very question can scarce be borne. They are ready to tell you that it deserves death only to ask after safety. Betwixt subject and subject, they will grant, there must be measures, laws, and judges for their mutual peace and security. But as for the ruler, he ought to be absolute, and is above all such circumstances; because he has a power to do more hurt and wrong, it is right when he does it. To ask how you may be guarded from or injury on that side, where the strongest hand is to do it, is presently the voice of faction and rebellion. As if when men, quitting the state of Nature, entered into society, they agreed that all of them but one should be under the restraint of laws; but that he should still retain all the liberty of the state of Nature, increased with power, and made licentious by impunity. This is to think that men are so foolish that they take care to avoid what mischiefs may be done them by polecats or foxes, but are content, nay, think it safety, to be devoured by lions.

94. But, whatever flatterers may talk to amuse people's understandings, it never hinders men from feeling; and when they perceive that any man, in what station soever, is out of the bounds of the civil society they are of, and that they have no appeal, on earth, against any harm they may receive from him, they are apt to think themselves in the state of Nature, in respect of him whom they find to be so; and to take care, as

Coronation of William and Mary, 1688. Locke was an advisor to William and Mary of Orange while they were still in Holland and continued to serve them after they came to the English throne. Their peaceful accession to the crown under contract with Parliament reinforced Locke's belief in limited monarchy. (*Library of Congress*)

soon as they can, to have that safety and security, in civil society, for which it was first instituted, and for which only they entered into it. And therefore, though perhaps at first, as shall be showed more at large hereafter, in the following part of this discourse, some one good and excellent man having got a preeminency amongst the rest, had this deference paid to his goodness and virtue, as to a kind of natural authority, that the chief rule, with arbitration of their differences, by a tacit consent devolved into his hands, without any other caution but the assurance they had of his uprightness and wisdom; yet when time giving authority, and, as some men would persuade us, sacredness to customs, which the negligent and unforeseeing innocence of the first ages began, had brought in successors of another stamp, the people finding their properties not secure under the government as then it was (whereas government has no other end but the preservation of property), could never be safe, nor at rest, nor think themselves in civil society, till the legislative was so placed in collective bodies of men, call them senate, parliament, or what you please, by which means every single person became subject equally, with other the meanest men, to those laws, which he himself, as part of the legislative, had established; nor could any one, by his own authority, avoid the force of the law, when once made, nor by any pretence of superiority plead exemption, thereby to license his own, or the miscarriages of any of his dependents. No man in civil society can be exempted from the laws of it. For if any man may do what he thinks fit and there be no appeal on earth for redress or security against any harm he shall do, I ask whether he be not perfectly still in the state of Nature, and so can be no part or member of that civil society, unless any one will say the state of Nature and civil society are one and the same thing, which I have never yet found any one so great a patron of anarchy as to affirm.

GOTTFRIED LEIBNIZ
1646–1716

Gottfried Wilhelm Von Leibniz was born and raised in academe. His father was a professor of moral philosophy at the University of Leipzig and his mother was the daughter of a law professor at the same institution. His advance was prodigious: At fifteen, he began his study of the history of philosophy at the university; at seventeen, after defending his thesis, he proceeded to the University of Jena where he studied mathematics and law; at eighteen, he published his treatise on law; and at twenty, he was ready to present himself as a candidate for the doctor of law degree, but he was declared too young. So he moved to the University of Altdorf, where he not only received his doctoral degree but was offered a professorship. He declined this invitation and settled into a position with Johann Philipp von Schönborn, elector of Mainz.

While in the service of the Mainz court, he lived for a time in Paris, where he made the acquaintance of leading thinkers of his day, such as the physicist Christian Huygens and the philosophers Antoine Arnauld and Nicolas Malebranche. As part of his mission in Paris, Leibniz prepared a plan for invading Egypt for Louis XIV (hoping to deflect Louis from military action in Europe). Though Louis never acted on the plan, many scholars believe that Napoleon used the scheme 120 years later.

In addition to diplomatic initiatives, Leibniz worked extensively on mathematics while he was in Paris. He invented a calculating machine that could add, subtract, multiply, divide, and extract square roots. When he demonstrated his machine in London, he was made a member of the Royal Society (1673). He also discovered differential and integral calculus—though years later there was an unpleasant dispute over whether Leibniz or Newton should get the credit for it.

Did one of these great men steal the idea from the other? The Royal Society officially belittled Leibniz's achievement (quite unjustly according to the verdict of subsequent scholarship). It has been said that the dispute "redounded to the discredit of all concerned." It may be best to credit both men with the discovery. Interestingly, Leibniz's notation proved the more convenient and is the system currently used.

In 1676, Leibniz went into the service of the Duke of Brunswick in Hanover, where he remained the rest of his life. He traveled extensively and met such notable people as Spinoza and the chemist Robert Boyle. In 1700, he was elected a foreign member of the French Academy. In the same year, by his inspiration, the *Akademie der Wissenschaften* was founded in Berlin and he was elected its first president. He was a close friend of Sophie Charlotte, the wife of the Elector of Brandenburg (subsequently the first king of Prussia). The only large systematic philosophic work he published, *Theodicy* (1710), grew out of his discussions with Sophie Charlotte.

Despite his accomplishments, Leibniz was not well liked. As Bertrand Russell later commented, "Leibniz was one of the supreme intellects of all time, but he was not admirable." Leibniz's death in 1716 was ignored not only by the Royal Society in London but also by the *Akademie* in Berlin and by the court at Hanover. His secretary is said to have been his only mourner, and an eyewitness reports in his memoirs that Leibniz "was buried more like a robber than what he really was, the ornament of his country."

At his death, he left an enormous number of unpublished letters and manuscripts. One major work was published in 1765: his detailed critique of Locke's *Essay,* entitled *Nouveaux essais sur L'entendement humain.* Leibniz had completed the book in 1704 but withheld it from publication when Locke died the same year. The book greatly stimulated Immanuel Kant, particularly his *Critique of Pure Reason.* In this century, thinkers such as Bertrand Russell and Ernst Cassirer have focused attention on Leibniz's work in logic. The neglect of Leibniz in his lifetime has given way in this century to great admiration for the scope and originality of his thought.

*   *   *

Leibniz's philosophy begins by rejecting the notion that extension is a substance (as Descartes claimed) or an attribute of substance (as Spinoza thought). Instead of understanding nature as a collection of discrete extended entities, such as atoms, Leibniz says that the basic substance is a "Monad," or a unit of psychic force. Such Monads are without parts (i.e., simple) and have no interaction with one another. As Leibniz puts it, they have "no windows through which anything may come in or go out." Each Monad has within itself an internal principle of "appetition" that causes it to change. Although there is no causal interaction between Monads, they may *appear* to influence one another. This connection is merely a reflection of the "pre-established harmony" by which God created each of the Monads to "mirror" the others. A Monad's entire past and present are contained within it so that whatever it does, it does so by necessity. If we could know the entire past of a given Monad, we could predict its entire future.

Monads all differ qualitatively and occupy different points of view. This means that each Monad "mirrors" the world in a slightly different way and with different levels of clarity. Rocks and dirt are made of colonies of "low level"

Monads that have only dull and confused perceptions as they mirror the world. It might seem odd to talk about rocks as having perceptions at all, but according to Leibniz, every Monad has some sort of psychic life: Each Monad has an "internal state [by which it] represent[s] external things." Those Monads whose perceptions are "more distinct and are accompanied by memory" are on a higher level. The dominant Monad of an animal, for example, has distinct perceptions and memory of those perceptions: "If you show a stick to a dog, for instance, it remembers the pain caused by it and howls or runs away." This dominant Monad Leibniz calls a "soul" to distinguish it from lower level or "naked" Monads. Human beings are Monad aggregates of yet a higher degree. Whereas human bodies are colonies of lower Monads, the dominant Monad in a person is a "spirit," because it is capable of performing "reflective acts." Spirits are also capable of knowing the universe and of entering into a relationship with the chief Monad, God.

Leibniz's metaphysics seems to exclude the possibility of freedom. If each Monad has its entire future within it, and if it thus unfolds that future by necessity, how can we, as colonies of a dominant "spirit" Monad and lower "body" Monads, be free? Leibniz's answer to this question turns on his definition of "freedom." To be "free," claims Leibniz, does not mean "liberty of indifference." Instead we are "free" in that our actions flow from our wills and there is no logical contradiction in our willing other than we do. As Leibniz put it, "there is always a prevailing reason which prompts the will to its choice, and for the maintenance of freedom for the will it suffices that this reason should incline without necessitating." Of course, he also claims that our wills are created by God and that God foreknows what we will will ourselves to do. But the action of our wills is not necessary in the sense that willing something else involves a logical contradiction; hence, our wills can be said to be "free."

In creating the world, God considered all possibilities and actualized only those ensuring the greatest perfection. As Leibniz explained in his *Theodicy,* God creates only those substances that will harmonize with other entities to the fullest possible extent. Whereas we may not understand it fully, the world as it actually exists is "the best of all possible worlds." It is this point that is satirized so ruthlessly in Voltaire's *Candide* (1759).

*   *   *

Leibniz never wrote a *magnum opus* that clearly defined his position on philosophical issues. *The Discourse on Metaphysics* (1686), reprinted here (complete) in the Martin and Brown translation, gives his early ideas on metaphysics. The *Monadology* (1714), also reprinted here (complete) in the Paul Schrecker and Anne Martin Schrecker translation, presents his mature position on metaphysics.

After the publication of *Theodicy* in 1710, Leibniz wrote a brief summary of his argument. This summary is presented (complete) in the George M. Duncan translation.

For general introductions to Leibniz's philosophy, see Herbert Wildon Carr, *Leibniz* (Boston: Little, Brown, 1929); Ruth Lydia Saw, *Leibniz* (Baltimore, MD: Penguin Books, 1954); Nicholas Rescher, *The Philosophy of Leibniz* (Englewood Cliffs, NJ: Prentice Hall, 1967); C.D. Broad, *Leibniz: An Introduction,* edited by C. Lewy (Cambridge: Cambridge University Press, 1975); Stuart

Brown, *Leibniz* (Minneapolis: University of Minnesota Press, 1984); and Robert Merrihew Adams, *Leibniz: Determinist, Theist, Idealist* (Oxford: Oxford University Press, 1994). For a discussion of the logic and metaphysics of Leibniz, Bertrand Russell, *A Critical Exposition of the Philosophy of Leibniz* (London: George Allen & Unwin, 1900), is still a valuable source. For more recent treatments of these issues, see Hidé Ishiguro, *Leibniz's Philosophy of Logic and Language* (Ithaca, NY: Cornell University Press, 1972); Robert McRae, *Leibniz: Perception, Apperception, and Thought* (Toronto: University of Toronto Press, 1976); Benson Mates, *The Philosophy of Leibniz: Metaphysics and Language* (Oxford: Oxford University Press, 1986); and Reginald Osburn Savage, *Real Alternatives: Leibniz's Metaphysics of Choice* (Norwell, MA: Kluwer, 1998). For a commentary on *The Monadology*, see Herbert Wildon Carr, *The Monadology of Leibniz* (Los Angeles: University of Southern California Press, 1930). For an interesting discussion of the *Theodicy*, see John Hick, *Evil and the God of Love* (New York: Harper & Row, 1966). For collections of essays, see Harry G. Frankfurt, ed., *Leibniz: A Collection of Critical Essays* (Garden City, NY: Doubleday, 1972); R.S. Woolhouse, ed., *Leibniz: Metaphysics and Philosophy of Science* (Oxford: Oxford University Press, 1981); Michael Hooker, *Leibniz: Critical and Interpretive Essays* (Minneapolis: University of Minnesota Press, 1984); Vere Chappell, ed., *Essays on Early Modern Philosophers: Gottfried Wilhelm Leibniz* (Hamden, CT: Garland Press, 1992); and Nicholas Jolley, ed., *The Cambridge Companion to Leibniz* (Cambridge: Cambridge University Press, 1995).

DISCOURSE ON METAPHYSICS

1. On the Divine Perfection: God Does Everything in the Most Desirable Way.

The most commonly accepted notion of God we have, and the one most full of meaning, is well enough expressed in these terms: God is an absolutely perfect being. Not enough thought, however, is given to its consequences. If we are to make progress, it is relevant to note that in nature there are several entirely different perfections, that God possesses them all together, and that each belongs to Him to the highest degree.

We also need to understand what a perfection is. A sure enough mark of one is that forms or natures not admitting of an ultimate degree are not perfections, as for example the nature of numbers or of shape. For the greatest of all numbers (or rather the number of all numbers), and the greatest of all shapes imply contradictions while omniscience and omnipotence involve no impossibility. Consequently, power and knowledge are perfections, and to the extent that they belong to God, they have no limits.

Gottfried Liebniz, *Discourse on Metaphysics and Related Writings*, edited and translated by R.N.D. Martin and Stuart Brown (Manchester and New York: Manchester University Press, 1988). Reprinted by permission of Manchester University Press.

[Liebniz made minor additions, deletions, and/or changes to virtually every paragraph of this work. I have chosen to reproduce Liebniz's text minus all material deleted by Leibniz.]

Hence it follows that since God possesses supreme and infinite wisdom, He acts in the most perfect manner, not only in the metaphysical sense, but also morally speaking. From our point of view we can express ourselves thus: the more we are enlightened and informed about the works of God, the more we shall be disposed to find that they are excellent and satisfactory in every way we could hope.

2. AGAINST THOSE WHO MAINTAIN THAT THERE IS NO GOODNESS IN THE WORKS OF GOD, OR THAT THE RULES OF GOODNESS AND BEAUTY ARE ARBITRARY.

Thus I am far removed from the opinion of those who maintain that there are no rules of goodness or perfection in the nature of things or in the ideas God has of them, and that the works of God are good only for the formal reason that God made them. For if that were so, since God knew He was their author, He had only to look at them after making them to find them good, in accordance with the testimony of Holy Scripture. But Scripture seems to have made use of this anthropomorphic way of speaking only to make us realise that we recognise the excellence of God's works by considering them by themselves, even when we disregard the purely extrinsic denomination that refers them to their cause. This is all the more true in that it is by considering the works that we can discover the Worker, so that the works must carry His marks in themselves. I confess that the contrary opinion seems to me extremely dangerous, and very close to the way the Spinozists think of goodness and harmony. Their opinion is that the beauty of the universe and the goodness we attribute to the works of God are no more than the chimeras of men who conceive God according to their own way of thinking. Also, if we say that things are good by no rule of goodness beyond the will of God alone, we thoughtlessly destroy, I feel, all the love and glory of God. For why praise Him for what He had done if He would be equally praiseworthy for doing the opposite? Where will His justice and His wisdom be, if all that remains of Him is some kind of a despotic power, if His will takes the place of reason, and if, by the very definition of tyranny, what pleases the Almighty is *ipso facto* just? Besides, it seems that every act of willing presupposes some reason for willing, and that reason is naturally prior to will. That is why I still find altogether strange the expression of Descartes who says that even the eternal truths of metaphysics and geometry, and consequently also the rules of goodness, justice and perfection are no more than the effects of God's will. It seems to me, rather, that they are no more than the consequences of His understanding, which certainly does not depend on His will, any more His essence does.

3. AGAINST THOSE WHO THINK GOD COULD HAVE DONE BETTER.

Neither can I approve the opinion of some scholastics who maintain boldly that what God has done is not absolutely perfect, and that He could have done much better. For it seems to me that the consequences of this opinion are altogether contrary to the glory of God. "Just as the lesser evil contains a proportion of good, so the lesser good contains a proportion of evil." To act with less perfection than one could have done is to act imperfectly. To show that an architect could have done better is to find fault with his work. It also runs counter to the assurance of the goodness of God's works in Holy Scripture. For, since perfections decrease to infinity, however God did his work, it would always be good in comparison with the less perfect, if that were enough. But a thing is not very praiseworthy if it is only so in that way. I also think that a very large number of passages favouring my opinion could be found in the divine Scriptures and the holy Fathers, with scarcely any favouring that of those new scholastics a view unknown, in my opinion, to the whole of antiquity. It is based on our insufficient knowledge of the general harmony of the universe and of the hidden reasons for God's conduct which lead us to the rash judgement that many things could have been done better. Besides, these moderns insist on some subtleties that are not very sound, for they imagine that nothing is so perfect but that there is something that is more perfect, which is a mistake. There is an infinity of regular figures, but one is the most perfect, namely the circle. If a triangle had to be made and there was no further specification of the kind of triangle, God would assuredly make an equilateral triangle because, absolutely speaking, that is the most perfect.

They also think that in this way they are providing for the liberty of God, as if it were not the highest liberty to act in accordance with sovereign reason. For, apart from its apparent impossibility, the belief that God acts in some matter without any reason for His act of will is hardly consistent with His glory. Suppose, for example, that God chooses between A and B, and that He takes A without any reason for preferring it to B; I say that that action of God would at the least not be praiseworthy. For every praise must be based on some reason and here *ex hypothesi* there is none. On the contrary, I hold that God does nothing for which He does not merit being glorified.

4. Loving God Demands Complete Satisfaction with and Acquiescence in what He Does, but We Do Not, on that Account, Have to be Quietists.

The general recognition of this great truth—that God always acts in the most perfect and desirable manner possible—is to my mind the basis of the love we owe to God concerning all things. For he who loves seeks his satisfaction in the happiness or perfection of the loved one and his actions. "True friendship is to want the same and to reject the same." And I think that it is difficult to love God well when not disposed to will what He wills, if changing that were in our power. Indeed those who are not satisfied with what He does seem to me like discontented subjects of a king or of a republic whose intentions are little different from those of rebels.

Hence, in accordance with these principles, I hold that to act in conformity with the love of God it is not enough to be patient under duress. We must be truly satisfied with all that happens to us in consequence of His will. I mean this acquiescence to apply to the past. As far as the future is concerned, we must not be quietists nor wait ridiculously with arms folded for what God will do, in accordance with the sophism the Ancients called ⟨*logon aegon*⟩ lazy reason. On the contrary, we must act in accordance with the presumptive will of God, as far as we can judge it, trying with all our ability to contribute to the general good, especially to the adornment and perfection of what concerns us or is near us, or, so to speak, within our range. For when the outcome shows that God may perhaps not want our good will to have its effect for the present, it does not follow that He does not want us to do what we have done. On the contrary, since He is the best of all masters, He never asks for more than the right intentions, and it is for Him to know the hour and the place for bringing good plans to fruition.

5. WHAT ARE THE RULES OF PERFECTION OF GOD'S CONDUCT; AND THAT THE SIMPLICITY OF MEANS IS BALANCED BY THE RICHNESS OF EFFECTS.

Hence it is enough to have this confidence in God, that He does everything for the best and that nothing can harm those who love him. But to know in detail the reasons that could have moved Him to choose this order of the universe, to allow sins, or to dispense His saving grace in a particular way, is beyond the power of a finite mind, particularly of a finite mind that has not yet attained enjoyment of the sight of God.

Nevertheless, some general remarks can be made on the conduct of Providence in the government of things. Thus it can be said that whatever encloses more reality in less volume is more perfect, that he who acts perfectly is like an excellent geometer who knows how to find the best constructions for a problem; like a good architect who arranges his site and the funds intended for the building in the most advantageous manner, so as to leave nothing that jars or lacks the beauty of which it is capable; like a good householder who uses his property so that nothing is left uncultivated or barren; like a skilled engineer who achieves his result by the least complicated way that could be chosen; like an experienced author who includes as much reality as he is able in the least space. Now the most perfect of all beings, occupying the least volume, in other words, those which hinder the least, are minds, and their perfections are the virtues. That is why we must not doubt that the happiness of minds is the principal objective of God and that He pursues it as much as the general harmony allows. More will be said of this presently.

As for the simplicity of God's ways, that applies properly in respect of means whereas the variety, richness or abundance applies to aims or effects. The one has to be in balance with the other, like the expenses of a building with the size and beauty expected of it. It is true that nothing costs God anything, much less than it costs a philosopher to make hypotheses for the construction of his imaginary world, since God has only to make decrees to bring a real world to birth; but in relation to wisdom, in so far as they are mutually independent, decrees or hypotheses take the place of expenditure, for reason demands that we avoid a multiplicity of hypotheses or principles; in almost the same way the simplest system is always preferred in astronomy.

6. GOD DOES NOTHING OUT OF ORDER AND IT IS NOT EVEN POSSIBLE TO IMAGINE EVENTS THAT ARE NOT REGULAR.

The decisions or actions of God are commonly divided into ordinary and extraordinary. But it is well to bear in mind that God does nothing out of order. So, whatever passes for extraordinary is only so in relation to some particular order established among creatures. For, in relation to the universal order, everything conforms to it. So true is this, that not only does nothing happen in the world that is absolutely irregular, but such a thing cannot even be imagined. Suppose, for example, that someone puts a number of points on paper completely at random like those who practise the ridiculous art of geomancy, then I say that it is possible to find a geometric line whose notion is constant and uniform according to some rule, so that this line passes through all these points and does so in the same order as they were made by the hand.

And if someone were to draw in one movement a line that was sometimes straight, sometimes circular, and sometimes of some other kind, it is possible to find a notion, a rule, or an equation common to all the points in that line and in virtue of which these same changes had to occur. For example there is no face whose contour is not part of a geometric line and cannot be drawn all in one movement by some rule-governed motion. But when a rule is very complicated, what conforms to it is taken to be irregular.

Thus it can be said that however God might have created the world, it would always have been regular and within some general order. But God chose that world that is the most perfect, i.e. the one that is simultaneously the simplest in hypotheses and richest in phenomena, just as a geometric line might be if its construction was easy but its properties most admirable and extensive. I make use of these comparisons to sketch some kind of imperfect resemblance to the divine wisdom and to say something that could at least raise our minds to conceive in some way what cannot be adequately expressed. But by this I do not claim to explain the great mystery on which the whole universe depends.

7. MIRACLES CONFORM TO THE GENERAL ORDER ALTHOUGH THEY ARE CONTRARY TO SUBALTERN NORMS. WHAT GOD WISHES OR PERMITS BY A GENERAL OR PARTICULAR WILL.

Now, since nothing can take place that is not within the order, it can be said that miracles are just as much within the order as natural operations, are so called because they conform to certain subaltern norms we call the nature of things. For it can be said that this "nature" is no more than a custom of God from which He can exempt Himself in virtue of a stronger reason than the one that moved Him to make use of these norms.

As for the general and particular wills, depending on how we take the matter, it can be said that God does everything in accordance with His most general will, the one in conformity with the most perfect order He chose. But it can also be said that He has particular wills, which are exceptions to the subaltern norms mentioned above; for the most general of the laws of God, by means of which He regulates the whole universe, are without exception.

It can also be said that God wills everything that is an object of His particular will. But as for the objects of His general will, such as the actions of other creatures, particularly of those that are rational, and with which, (i.e. the *actions*) God wishes to concur, we must draw a distinction: if the action is good in itself, it can be said that God wills it and sometimes commands it, even when it does not happen; but if it is evil in itself, and only becomes good by accident, it has to be said that God permits it and not that He wills it, though He concurs in it through the laws of nature established by Him, and because he is able to draw from it greater good. This comes about because the sequence of things, particularly punishment and recompense, corrects its evil nature, and compensates for the evil with interest, so that in the end there is more perfection in all that follows than if none of the evil had happened.

8. IN ORDER TO DISTINGUISH THE ACTIONS OF GOD FROM THOSE OF CREATURES, AN EXPLANATION IS GIVEN OF THE NOTION OF AN INDIVIDUAL SUBSTANCE.

It is rather difficult to distinguish the actions of God from those of creatures as well as the actions and passions of these same creatures. For there are those who think that God does everything, while others imagine that He does no more than conserve the force He has given to creatures. What follows will show how far either of these can be said. Now since, properly speaking, actions belong to individual substances ("actions belong to supposita"), it will be necessary to explain just what such a substance is.

It seems to me that when several predications are attributed to the same subject and this subject is not attributed to any other, this subject is called an individual substance. But that is not enough and such an explanation is merely nominal, so we need to consider what it is to be truly attributed to a particular subject.

Now it is acknowledged that all true predication has some basis in the nature of things, and when a proposition is not an identity, that is, when the predicate is not expressly included in the subject, it must be so included virtually. That is what the Philosophers call *inesse*, when they say that the predicate is in the subject. Thus the subject term must always include that of the predicate, so that whoever understood the notion of the subject perfectly would also judge that the predicate belongs to it.

That being so, we can say that the nature of an individual substance or complete being is to have such a complete notion as to include and entail all the predicates of the subject that notion is attributed to. In contrast, an accident is a being whose notion does not include all that can be attributed to the subject it is attributed to. Thus* the quality of being king that belongs to Alexander the Great, taken in abstraction from the subject, is not sufficiently determinate for one individual, and does not include the other qualities of the same subject, nor everything that the notion of this prince includes, whereas God who sees the individual notion or *haecceity*** of Alexander sees in it at the same time the foundation and reason for all the predicates that can truly be ascribed to him, such as that he would defeat Darius and Porus even to the point of knowing *a priori* (and not by experience) whether he died naturally or by poison, something we can only know historically. Also, when we consider well the connection of things, we can say that there is in the soul of Alexander for all time traces of everything that happened to him, and marks of everything that will happen to him, and even traces of everything happening in the universe, though to recognise them all belongs to God alone.

9. Each Unique Substance Expresses the Whole Universe in Its Own Way, and Included in Its Notion Are All the Events that Happen to It With all their Circumstances, and the Whole Sequence of External Things.

Among several paradoxical conclusions following from this, is that it is not true that two substances are completely alike, differing only numerically, and what St Thomas has to say on this point about angels and intelligences ("in these cases every individual is a lowest species") is true of all substances provided that the specific difference is taken in the way geometers take it in relation to their figures. Likewise, if bodies are substances, their natures cannot possibly consist solely in size, figure and motion:

---

*The first edition of the text used the following example: "Thus the circular figure of the ring of Gyges, does not contain everything that makes up the individual notion of this ring. Whereas God sees in it at the same time the foundation and cause for all the predicates that can truly be applied to it, such as that it would be swallowed by a fish and nevertheless returned to its master. I speak here as if this ring were a substance."

**Literally "thisness," an allusion to the theory of what makes something an individual substance produced by Duns Scotus and in which Leibniz had taken an interest when writing a student dissertation. Every individual has its own *haecceity*, according to Duns Scotus, though (like Leibniz) he believed it was only known to God.

something else is needed. Likewise, a substance can begin only by creation and perish only by annihilation; a substance cannot be divided into two, nor can two substances become one, and so the number of substances does not naturally increase or diminish, though they are frequently transformed.

Moreover every substance is as it were an entire world and a mirror of God, or rather of the whole universe, expressing it in its own way, somewhat as the same town is variously represented according to the different positions of an observer. It can even be said that every substance bears in some way the mark of the infinite wisdom and omnipotence of God, imitating Him as far as it is capable. For it expresses, if only confusedly, all that happens in the universe, past, present and future, and this has some resemblance to an infinite perception or knowledge. And since all other substances in turn express it and are accommodated to it, it can be said to extend its power over all the others in imitation of the omnipotence of the Creator.

10. There is Some Soundness to the Belief in Substantial Forms, but These Make no Difference to the Phenomena, and Should Not Be Used to Explain Particular Effects.

It seems that the ancients in distinguishing an *ens per se* from an *ens per accidens* and in introducing substantial forms, as well as the many able people who were accustomed to profound meditations and who taught theology and philosophy centuries ago, many of them praiseworthy for their sanctity, had some knowledge of what we have just said. This is what led them to introduce and uphold the substantial forms so much in disfavour today. But they are neither so far from the truth nor as ridiculous as the common run of our modern philosophers imagine.

I agree that the knowledge of forms is of no use in the details of physics and should not be used for explaining the particulars of phenomena. That is where our scholastics went wrong, and with them the physicians of the past who followed their example, in thinking to account for the properties of bodies by mentioning forms and qualities without taking the trouble to examine their manner of operation. It is as if we were to content ourselves with saying that a clock has the horodictic [time-telling] quality deriving from its form without considering what that consists in. That indeed might be enough for whoever buys the clock, provided he left its maintenance to someone else.

But this shortcoming and misuse of forms should not make us reject something whose knowledge is so necessary in metaphysics that without it, I hold, the first principles cannot be well understood, nor the mind sufficiently raised to the knowledge of incorporeal natures and the wonders of God.

Nevertheless, a geometer has no need to trouble his mind with the famous labyrinth of the composition of the continuum, and neither has any moral philosopher, and still less any legal expert or politician, any need to trouble himself with the great difficulties involved in reconciling the freedom of the will with the providence of God. For the geometer can complete all his demonstrations and the politician conclude all his deliberations without entering into these discussions, important as they are in philosophy and theology. In the same way, a physicist can account for experiments, sometimes by means of simpler experiments carried out before, and sometimes by means of geometrical and mechanical demonstrations, without the need of forms and other general considerations belonging to another sphere. If he employs the extraordinary concurrence of God, or some soul, *arché* or other thing of that nature, he is wandering as far off course as he who tries to introduce the nature of destiny and our liberty into a deliberation about an important practical matter. Men often make this mistake without thinking when they trouble their minds by considering fate, and sometimes they are even diverted from some good resolution or necessary care as a result.

11. THE MEDITATIONS OF THE THEOLOGIANS AND PHILOSOPHERS CALLED "SCHOLASTICS" ARE NOT TO BE DESPISED ENTIRELY.

I know that in claiming in some way to rehabilitate the old philosophy and restore the all but banished substantial forms to which not enough justice has been done to life, I am proposing a big paradox. But I only do this on the supposition that it is possible to speak of bodies as substances. But perhaps I shall not be lightly condemned if it is known that I have long meditated on modern philosophy, and spent much time on physical experiments and geometrical demonstrations, and that I was long persuaded of the vanity of such beings. But I was eventually obliged to take them up again against my will and as if by force. It was as a result of carrying out my own researches that I was made to recognise that our moderns do not do full justice to St. Thomas and other great men of those times, and that the opinions of scholastic philosophers and theologians are much more sound than is imagined, as long as they are used appropriately and in their place. I am even convinced that if some exact and reflecting mind took the trouble to clarify and digest their thoughts in the manner of analytical geometry, he would find a treasure store of very important truths which could be demonstrated completely.

12. NOTIONS DEFINED BY EXTENSION INVOLVE SOMETHING IMAGINARY AND CANNOT CONSTITUTE THE ESSENCE OF BODIES.

But, to take up again the thread of our considerations, I believe that any one who meditates on the nature of substance as I have explained it above will find that either bodies are not substances in strict metaphysical rigour (the view indeed of the Platonists), or that the whole nature of body does not consist solely in extension, i.e. in size, shape and motion. On the contrary, something related to souls which is commonly called a "substantial form" has necessarily to be recognised in them, though that makes no more difference to the phenomena than the souls of animals, if they have any. It can even be demonstrated that the notions of size, shape and motion are not so distinct as is imagined and that they involve something imaginary and relative to our perceptions, just as colour, heat and other similar qualities also do, (to an even greater extent)—we may doubt that these are truly in the nature of external things. That is why qualities of these kinds could not constitute any substance. And if there were no other principle of identity in body than the one just considered, no body would ever last more than a moment.

Nevertheless, souls and substantial forms of other bodies are very different from intelligent souls, who alone know what they do, and which not only do not naturally perish but even for ever retain the basis of the knowledge of what they are. This makes them liable to punishment and reward, and makes them citizens of the republic of the universe whose monarch is God. It also follows that all other creatures ought to serve them, something we shall discuss more fully presently.

13. SINCE THE INDIVIDUAL NOTION OF EVERY PERSON INCLUDES
ONCE FOR ALL EVERYTHING THAT WILL EVER HAPPEN TO HIM,
IN IT ARE TO BE SEEN THE *A PRIORI* PROOFS OF EACH EVENT,
OR RATHER WHY ONE HAPPENED RATHER THAN THE OTHER.
BUT ALTHOUGH THESE TRUTHS ARE ASSURED, THEY DO NOT
CEASE TO BE CONTINGENT, SINCE THEY ARE BASED ON THE FREE
WILL OF GOD OR OF CREATURES. THERE ARE ALWAYS REASONS
FOR THEIR CHOICES BUT THESE INCLINE WITHOUT NECESSITATING.

But a great difficulty can arise from the foundations laid above, and before proceeding further, we must try to deal with it. We said that the notion of an individual substance includes once for all everything that can ever happen to it, and that by considering this notion, we can see in it everything that can truly be stated about it, just as we can see in the nature of the circle all the properties that can be derived from it. But from that it seems that all events will become fatally necessary that the difference between necessary and contingent truths will be destroyed, that all the fate of the Stoics will take the place of liberty, there will no longer be any room for human liberty, and absolute fate will reign over all our actions as well as over all other events in the world. My reply is: we must distinguish between what is certain and what is necessary. Everyone agrees that future contingents are assured since God foresees them, but it is not for all that admitted that they are necessary. But (it will be said) if some conclusion can be infallibly deduced from a definition or notion, it will be necessary. Now in fact we do maintain that everything that is to happen to a person is already included virtually in his nature or notion, just as the properties of a circle are included in its definition. So the difficulty remains. In order to give a sound answer, I claim that connection or derivation is of two kinds: one is absolutely necessary (its contrary implies a contradiction) and occurs with eternal truths like those of geometry; the other is necessary only *ex hypothesi*, by accident, so to speak, but in itself it is contingent, since its contrary does not imply a contradiction. This connection is based, not on the absolutely pure ideas and God's bare understanding alone, but also on His free decrees and the connection of the universe.

Let us take an example. Since Peter will deny our Lord, that action is included in his notion, for we are supposing it to be in the nature of such a perfect notion to include everything, so that the predicate should be included in it, *ut possit inesse subjecto*. We could say that it is not in virtue of this notion or idea or nature that he must sin, since that only applies to him because God knows everything. But, it will be insisted, his nature or form corresponds to his notion. I reply that it is indeed true and since God imposed this personality on him he must henceforth conform to it. I could reply with the objection of future contingents, for these have as yet no reality outside the understanding and the will, and since God gave them this form in advance, they will have to conform to it all the same.

But I prefer to deal with difficulties than make excuses for them with examples of some other similar difficulties, and what I am going to say will help clarify both. Thus it is here that we must apply the distinction between the kinds of connection. I say that what happens in accordance with these prior conditions is assured, but that it is not necessary; and if he did the opposite, he would be doing nothing impossible in itself though it would be *ex hypothesi* impossible that this should happen. For if someone were capable of completing the whole of the demonstration by virtue of which he proved the connection between the subject Peter and the predicate (namely, his denial), he would show that this fact had its basis in his notion or nature, and that it was reasonable and consequently assured that it should come about; but he would not show that it was necessary in itself, nor that its contrary implied a contradiction. In almost the same way, it is reasonable and assured that God will always do the best, although what is less perfect involves no contradiction in itself.

For it would be found that this demonstration of this predicate of Peter is not as absolute as those of numbers and geometry, but that it supposes the sequence of things freely chosen by God and founded on the first free decree of God, which always leads him to do what is most perfect, as well as on the decree God made (in consequence of the first) concerning human nature, which is that man will always (although freely) do what seems best. Now every truth founded on decrees of this kind is contingent, although certain, since those decrees make no difference to the possibility of things and, as I have already said, although God assuredly always chooses the best, that does not prevent what is less perfect remaining possible in itself, though it does not happen. It is not its impossibility but its imperfection that causes it to be rejected. Nothing is necessary if its contrary is possible.

Hence, we are in a position to meet such difficulties, great as they may appear to be (and indeed they are no less pressing for all others who have ever dealt with this matter,) provided it is fully realised that contingent propositions have reasons for being that way rather than otherwise, or (what comes to the same thing) that there are *a priori* proofs of their truth which make them certain and show that the subject-predicate connection in these propositions has its basis in the nature of each. But these are not necessary demonstrations, since these reasons are only based on the principle of the contingency or of the existence of things, i.e. on what is or seems to be the best of several equally possible things; whereas necessary truths are founded on the principle of contradiction and on the possibility or impossibility of the essences themselves, without regard to the free will of God or of creatures.

14. GOD PRODUCES DIFFERENT SUBSTANCES ACCORDING TO THE DIFFERENT VIEWS HE HAS OF THE UNIVERSE. THE DISTINCTIVE NATURE OF EACH SUBSTANCE ENSURES, BY THE (MEDIATION) OF GOD, THAT WHAT HAPPENS TO EACH CORRESPONDS TO WHAT HAPPENS TO ALL THE OTHERS, WITHOUT THEM ACTING DIRECTLY ON EACH OTHER.

Having after a fashion come to know what the nature of created substances consists in, we must try to explain their mutual dependence and their actions and passions. Now, in the first place, it is altogether obvious that created substances depend on God who conserves them—and even continually produces them by a kind of emanation, as we do our thoughts. For as God, so to speak, turns on all its sides and in all ways the general system of phenomena which He finds it good to produce to manifest His glory, and as He looks at all the faces of the world in all possible ways—because there is no relation that escapes His omniscience—the result of each view of the universe as if seen from a particular place is a substance expressing the universe in conformity with that view, if God finds it good to make His thought effective and produce this substance. And since the view of God is always true, our perceptions are so too; it is those of our judgements that derive from us that deceive us.

Now we have said above, and it follows from what we have just said, that each substance is like a world on its own, independent of everything else apart from God.

Hence all our phenomena, that is, all that can ever happen to us, are consequences of our natures and, since we are free substances, of our wills. Since these phenomena preserve a particular order conforming to our nature or, so to speak, the world within us, so that we are able (to make observations useful for regulating our conduct which are justified by the favourable outcome of future phenomena) and to judge the future by the past without error, this enables us to say that these phenomena are true, without worrying whether they are outside us or whether others perceive them as well. Nevertheless, it is very true that the perceptions or qualities of all substances correspond with each other, so that each, carefully following the particular reasons or laws it has observed, fits in with the other in doing the same, just as when several people agree with each other to be at a particular place at a prearranged day, they can in fact do so if they wish. Now although all express the same phenomena, it does not follow from this that their expressions should be perfectly similar: it is enough that they are proportionate to each other. In the same way several spectators think they have seen the same thing and indeed agree with each other, although each sees and speaks according to his point of view.

Now it is God from whom all substances emanate continually and He sees the universe, not only as they see it, but quite differently from them all as well. He is the only cause of this correspondence between their phenomena, and He alone makes what is peculiar to one public to all, otherwise there would be no connection between them. Hence it can be said in a manner of speaking and in a sense that is good, though remote from ordinary usage that a particular substance never acts on another particular substance and is not acted upon by another either. This follows if we remember that what happens to each is only a consequence of its idea or complete notion alone, since that idea already includes all the predicates or events, and expresses the whole universe. Indeed, nothing can happen to us but thoughts and perceptions, and all our thoughts and our future perceptions are no more than consequences, albeit contingent, of our previous thoughts and perceptions. Hence, if I were capable of considering distinctly everything happening or appearing to me at the present time, I would be able to see therein everything that would ever happen or appear to me. This would not fail, but would happen in any case, if everything outside me were destroyed and only God and myself remained. But as we attribute to other things, as if to causes acting on us, what we perceive in some way in other things, we have to consider the basis of this judgement, and what truth there is in it.

It is above all agreed that if we desire some phenomenon to happen at a certain time and it occurs in the ordinary course of things, we say that we acted and that we were the cause of it, as when I want to, as we say, "move my hand." Also, when it seems to me that by my will something happens to what I call another substance (and that this is the way it would happen as I judge from frequent observation) although it was not willed by it, I judge that this substance is acted upon. I admit this of myself when something happens to me in accordance with the will of another substance. Also, when we will something to happen, and something else follows from it that we did not want, we still say that we did it, provided that we understood how it followed. There are also some phenomena of extension that we attribute to ourselves more particularly and which have their basis *a parte rei* in what is called our body. As everything of importance happening to it (i.e. all the notable changes appearing to us in it) make themselves strongly felt in it, ordinarily at least, we attribute all the passions to this body to ourselves. We do so with very good reason, for even if we did not perceive them at the time, we do not fail to become well aware of the consequences, just as if we had been transported from one place to another while asleep. We also attribute to ourselves the actions of this body, as when we run, hit or fall, and when our body, continuing the motion once begun, has some effect. But I do not attribute to myself what happens to other bodies, because I realise that great changes can happen that I cannot perceive, unless my body is exposed to them in a way I conceive appropriate to that assumption.

So it is quite clear that although all the bodies of the universe belong to us in some way and harmonise with ours, we do not attribute to ourselves what happens to them. For when my body is pushed, I say that I myself have been pushed, but if someone else is pushed, I do not say that I have been pushed, even though I may perceive it and some passion in me may arise from it, since I measure where I am by the place my body is in. And this language is highly reasonable because it is appropriate for clear expression in everyday practice. As for the mind, it can be said briefly that our acts of will and judgements or reasonings are actions while our perceptions or sensations are passions. As for the body, we say that a change that happens to it is an action when it follows from a previous change, but otherwise it is a passion.

In general, to give our terms a meaning that reconciles metaphysics with practice, it can be said that when several powers are affected by the same change the one that passes to a higher degree of perfection or continues in the same acts, while the one that immediately becomes more limited thereby, so that its expressions become more confused, is acted upon.

15. THE ACTION OF ONE FINITE SUBSTANCE ON ANOTHER CONSISTS SOLELY IN THE INCREASE IN THE DEGREE OF ITS EXPRESSION TOGETHER WITH THE DIMINUTION OF THAT OF THE OTHER, IN SO FAR AS GOD HAS MADE THEM CONFORM TO EACH OTHER.

But without getting involved in a long discussion, it is enough for the present to reconcile the language of metaphysics with that of practice by noting that we attribute to ourselves our more clear and distinct perceptions and that we can in general attribute to a substance its more clear and distinct expression and, with reason, the phenomena we express more perfectly, while we attribute to other substances what each best expresses. Thus a substance of infinite extension, in so far as it expresses everything, becomes limited by its more or less perfect manner of expression. Thus in this way it is possible to conceive that substances mutually hinder or limit each other and, consequently, in this sense, to say that they act on each other and, so to speak, are obliged to conform to each other. For it can happen that a change which increases the expression of the one diminishes that of the other. Now, the virtue of a particular substance is to express well the glory of God, and it is there that it is least limited, and everything that exerts its virtue or power, that is when it acts, changes for the better and is extended in so far as it acts. Thus when a change affects several substances (since indeed every change touches all of them), I think that it can be said that the one that thereby passes to a higher degree of perfection or to a more perfect expression exerts its power and acts, while the other one that passes to a lesser degree shows its weakness and is acted upon. So I hold that every action of a substance possessing perception implies some pleasure and every passion some pain, and vice versa. This notwithstanding that it can easily happen that a present advantage is destroyed in what follows. Hence it follows that it is possible to sin by acting or exerting one's power and finding pleasure therein.

16. THE EXTRAORDINARY CONCURRENCE OF GOD IS INCLUDED
IN THE EXPRESSION OF OUR ESSENCE BECAUSE IT APPLIES TO
EVERYTHING, BUT IT TRANSCENDS THE POWERS OF OUR NATURE
OF DISTINCT EXPRESSION (WHICH IS FINITE AND FOLLOWS
PARTICULAR SUBALTERN NORMS).

All that remains for the present is to explain how it is sometimes possible for God to
have influence on men or other substances through an extraordinary or miraculous concurrence, since it seems that everything that has to happen to them is natural in so far
as it is a consequence of their substance. But what we said above about miracles in the
universe must be remembered: they always conform to the universal laws of the general order, even though these transcend the subordinate norms. And, to the extent that
every person or substance is like a little world expressing the great one, it can even be
said that this extraordinary concurrence of God is included in the general order of the
universe in so far as that is expressed by the nature of this person, but it does not cease
to be miraculous and to be beyond the norms. That is why, if everything it expresses is
included in our nature, nothing is supernatural with respect to it, for it extends to
everything, since an effect always expresses its cause and God is the true cause of substances. But since what our nature expresses more perfectly particularly belongs to it,
that is what its power consists in—and since, as I have just explained, it is limited,
there are many things that surpass the powers of our natures, and even those of every
limited nature. Consequently, to speak more clearly, I say that miracles and the extraordinary acts of God's concurrence have the particular character that they could not be
foreseen by the reasoning of any created mind, however enlightened it might be, since
the comprehension of the general order surpasses them all, while everything called natural depends on the less general norms creatures can understand. Hence, in order to say
nothing of these norms or laws of nature that might cause offence, it would be good to
link particular ways of speaking with particular thoughts: whatever includes everything we express could then be called our essence or idea, and since it expresses our
union with God, it has no limits and nothing exceeds it. But what is limited in us could
be called our nature or power, and in this respect what exceeds the natures of all created substances is supernatural.

17. EXAMPLE OF A SUBALTERN NORM OR LAW OF NATURE;
IN WHICH IT IS SHOWN THAT GOD ALWAYS PRESERVES
THE SAME FORCE, BUT NOT THE SAME QUANTITY OF MOTION . . .
AGAINST THE CARTESIANS AND SOME OTHERS.

I have often mentioned subaltern maxims or laws of nature already, and it would be
good to give an example. Our new philosophers commonly make use of that famous
rule advanced by Descartes that God always preserves the same quantity of motion in
the world. It seems highly plausible indeed, and in the past I held it to be indubitable.
But I have since come to recognise wherein lay its error. It is that Descartes and many
other able mathematicians thought that the quantity of motion (i.e. the speed times the
size of the mobile) was the same thing as the force, or at least expressed it perfectly, or
geometrically speaking, that the forces are in compound proportion of the speeds and
the bodies. Now it is obvious indeed that the same force should always be preserved in
the universe. So, when we attend to the phenomena with care, we see clearly that mechanical perpetual motion does not occur, because then the force of a machine, which

is continually being slightly diminished by friction, and must consequently soon cease, would be replaced and so would increase of itself without any new impulsion from outside. We also note that the force of a body is diminished solely to the extent that it gives some of it to neighbouring bodies or to its own parts in so far as these have independent motions.

Thus they thought that what can be said of force could also be said of quantity of motion. But, to show the difference, I suppose that a body falling from a particular height acquires the force needed to climb up again, if its direction of travel should take it that way, unless there are hindrances. For example, a pendulum would rise right back again to the height it had fallen from if the resistance of the air and other small obstacles did not somehow diminish the force acquired.

I *suppose* also that as much force is needed to raise a body A of one pound a height CD of four fathoms as to raise a body B of four pounds a height EF of one fathom. All this is accepted by our new philosophers.

Hence, it is manifest that body (A), after falling from the height CD has acquired as much force precisely as body (B) after falling from the height EF. For when body (B) has arrived at F and has the force to climb back to E (by the first supposition), it has in consequence the force to carry a body of four pounds, that is its own body, to the height EF of one fathom, and similarly, when body (A) has reached D and has the force to climb back to C, it has the force to carry a body of one pound, that is its own body, to the height CD of four fathoms. Hence (by the second supposition), the forces of the two bodies are equal.

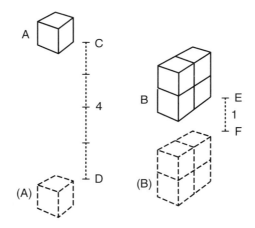

Now let us see whether the quantity of motion is also the same in both cases: but it is here that there will be surprise at finding a very great difference. For it has been demonstrated by Galileo that the speed acquired in the fall CD is twice that acquired in the fall EF, though the height is quadruple. If then, we multiply the body (A), in the proportion 1, by the speed, in the proportion 2, the product or quantity of motion will be as 2, and if on the other hand, we multiply the body (B), which is as 4, by its speed, which is as 1, then the product or quantity of motion will be as 4. Hence the quantity of motion of body (A) at point D is half the quantity of motion of body (B) at point F, though their forces are equal. Hence there is a great difference between the quantity of motion and the force, as was to be proved.

From this it is seen that the force must be measured by the quantity of the effect it can produce, e.g. by the height to which a heavy body of a particular size and kind can be raised, something very different from the speed that can be given it, and that to give it twice the speed more than twice the force is needed.

Nothing is simpler than this proof. Descartes only fell into error here because he trusted too much in his thoughts before they had matured enough with a confidence based on the happy success of some of his thoughts and on his experience of the penetration of his mind, which rendered him rather too rash in the end. But I am astonished that his followers have not recognised this error since, and I fear that little by little they begin to imitate the Peripatetics they so make fun of, and that like them they grow accustomed to consulting the books of their master rather than reason and nature.

18. IMPORTANCE OF THE DISTINCTION BETWEEN FORCE AND QUANTITY OF MOTION INTER ALIA IN DECIDING THAT WE MUST HAVE RECOURSE TO METAPHYSICAL CONSIDERATIONS DISTINCT FROM EXTENSION TO EXPLAIN THE NATURE OF BODIES.

This consideration of the distinction of force from quantity of motion is important enough, not only in physics and mechanics in the discovery of the true laws of nature and rules of motions, and even in the correction of several practical errors that have slipped into the writings of some able mathematicians, but also in metaphysics, in the better understanding of the principles of things. For motion, if its precise formal content only—i.e. change of place—is considered, is not a completely real thing, and when several bodies mutually exchange their places, it is impossible to determine from these changes alone which of them ought to have motion or rest attributed to it, as I could show geometrically if I wanted to dwell on this point now.

But the force or direct cause of these changes is something more real, and there is some basis for attributing it to one body rather than to another, and it is only thereby that we can know which one the motion is best attributed to. Now, this force is something different from size and motion, and it can be concluded from this that what is conceived in bodies does not consist solely in extension and its modifications, contrary to the conviction of our moderns. Hence, too, we are obliged to re-establish some of the beings or forms banished by them. And although all the particular phenomena of corporeal nature can be explained mathematically or mechanically by those who understand them, it nevertheless appears more and more that the general principles of corporeal mechanical nature itself are metaphysical rather than geometrical, belonging to forms or indivisible natures functioning as causes of the matter or extension rather than to corporeal or extended mass—a reflection capable of reconciling the mechanical philosophy of the moderns with the circumspection of some intelligent well-intentioned people who fear quite reasonably that we are moving too far from immaterial beings to the disadvantage of piety.

19. USEFULNESS OF FINAL CAUSES IN PHYSICS.

As I do not like to judge people's intentions, or only do so favourably if I can, I am not accusing our new philosophers of impiety when they claim to banish final causes in physics. Nevertheless I am obliged to admit that I do not recognise their usual intelligence and prudence therein and that the consequences of this opinion seem dangerous to me, particularly when it is connected with that refuted by me at the beginning of this discourse, which seems to lead to their removal altogether, as if God never had any aim, whether good or active, or as if the good were not the object of His will. . . . For my part, I hold on the contrary that it is just there that we have to seek the principle of all existences and even of the laws of nature, since God always intends what is best and most perfect.

I am happy to admit that we are liable to error when we want to determine the aims and counsels of God, but that is only when we try to restrict them to a particular plan, in the belief that He has only one single thing in view, whereas in fact He considers everything at once. Thus, when we think that God made the world for us alone, we are greatly mistaken, although it is true that He made it in its totality for us and that there is nothing in the world that does not affect us and does not also conform to His concerns for us, in accordance with the above principles. Thus, when we see some good effect or perfection happening or resulting from the works of God, we can certainly say that God intended it, for He does nothing by chance and unlike us does not sometimes fail to do well. That is why, far from being in an error here, akin to that of the overly political who attribute excessive refinement to the designs of princes, or to that of commentators who search for too much erudition in their authors, we cannot attribute too many reflections to this infinite Wisdom, and there is no matter in which there is less danger of error as long as we only affirm and avoid negative propositions here that limit the plans of God.

Everyone who sees the admirable structure of animals is led to recognise the wisdom of the Author of things, and I advise those with any feeling of piety or even of true Philosophy to avoid the expression of some would-be tough minds who say that we see because we happen to have eyes, without noting that the eyes were made to see. If we are seriously involved in these opinions that assign everything to the necessity of matter or to a particular chance (although both must seem ridiculous to those who understand what we have explained above), we will inevitably fail to recognise an intelligent Author of nature. For it is ridiculous to introduce a Sovereign Intelligence as the Ordainer of things and not use His wisdom to account for phenomena. As if, in accounting for the conquest of a great prince in capturing an important position, a historian tried to say that it was because the particles of the gunpowder liberated by lighting the fuse escaped at a speed capable of pushing a hard heavy body against the walls of the position, while the branches of the particles composing the copper of the cannon were sufficiently intertwined not to be separated by this speed, instead of showing how the foresight of the victor caused him to choose the appropriate time and means, and how his power overcame all the obstacles.

20. REMARKABLE PASSAGE OF SOCRATES IN PLATO AGAINST EXCESSIVELY MATERIALISTIC PHILOSOPHERS.

This point reminds me of a fine passage of Socrates in Plato's *Phaedo*. In marvellous agreement with my thoughts on this point, it seems to be written expressly against our excessively materialistic philosophers. So this account made me want to translate it, and though it is rather long, perhaps this sample will give one of us the occasion to share many other fine sound thoughts from the writings of the great man.

"One day," he said, "I heard someone read a book of Anaxagoras, where there were these words 'that an Intelligent Being was the cause of all things, and that He arranged and adorned them.' I was extremely pleased with that, for I thought that if the world was the result of an Intelligence, everything would have been made in the most perfect way possible. That is why I thought that he who wanted to explain why things came to be, perished or subsisted had to search for what suited the perfection of each. Thus man would only have to consider in himself or in some other thing, what was best or most perfect, alone. For he who knew the most perfect would easily decide thereby what was imperfect, since there is only one true knowledge of both.

"In view of all this, I rejoiced to have found a master able to teach the reason of things: whether, for example, the earth was round or flat, and why it was best that way rather than otherwise. . . . Moreover, I expected that when he said that the earth was or was not at the centre of the universe, he would explain to me why that was the most suitable. And when he said the same of the sun, the moon, the stars and their motions. . . . And finally, after showing what was suitable to each thing individually, he would show me what was best in general.

"Full of this hope, I took and skimmed through the books of Anaxagoras with great eagerness, but I was far from my expectation, for I was surprised to see that he made no use of this governing Intelligence, set out in advance, that he spoke no more of the adornment and the perfection of things, and introduced some rather implausible ethereal matters.

"In this he was rather like the man who said that Socrates did things intelligently, but when he came to explaining in particular the causes of his actions, thereupon said that he was sitting here because he had a body composed of bone, flesh and nerves, that the bones were solid, but had gaps and joints, that the nerves could be tensed or re-laxed, and that was why the body was flexible and I was sitting. Or if he wanted to ex-plain the present speech, he had recourse to the air, to vocal and aural organs and like things, while forgetting the true causes, that is that the Athenians thought it better to condemn than to acquit me, and I for my part thought it better to sit here than to take flight. For, by my faith, these nerves and these bones would long since be with the Boeotians and the Megarans, if I had not found it more just and more honest for me to suffer the penalty the fatherland wants to impose on me than live elsewhere a wanderer in exile. That is why it is unreasonable to call these bones and nerves and their motions causes.

"It is true that whoever said that I could not do all this without bones and nerves would be right, but the true cause is something else . . . and that is no more than a con-dition without which the cause could not be the cause. . . .

"People who say no more than, for example, that the motions of the bodies sur-rounding the earth support the earth where it is, forget that the divine power arranges everything in the finest way, and do not understand that it is the good and the beautiful that join, form and preserve the world. . . ." Thus far Socrates, for the things about ideas or forms that follow in Plato are not less excellent but a bit more difficult.

21. IF THE RULES OF MECHANICS DEPENDED ON GEOMETRY ALONE WITHOUT METAPHYSICS, THE PHENOMENA WOULD BE QUITE DIFFERENT.

Now, since the wisdom of God has always been recognised in the details of the me-chanical structures of particular bodies, it is very necessary that it should also be shown in the general set-up of the world and the constitution of the laws of nature. This is so true that the counsels of this Wisdom are observed in the laws of motion in general. For if there were nothing else to bodies but an extended mass and nothing to motion but change of place, and if everything had to and could be deduced from these definitions alone by geometrical necessity, it would follow, as I have shown elsewhere, that the least body would give the same speed as its own to the largest resting body it met without losing any of its own, and many other rules of this sort would have to be accepted, such as are altogether contrary to the construction of a system. But the decree of the divine wisdom to preserve always the same total force and direction has provided for this.

I even find that many natural effects can be demonstrated doubly, i.e. through the efficient cause and separately through the final cause as well, by using for example the decree of God to produce His effect by the simplest and most determinate ways, as I have shown elsewhere in my account of the rules of catoptrics and dioptrics, and I shall say more of it below.

22. RECONCILIATION OF THE TWO WAYS BY FINAL AND EFFICIENT CAUSES IN DEFENCE OF BOTH THOSE WHO EXPLAIN NATURE MECHANICALLY AND THOSE WHO HAVE RECOURSE TO INCORPOREAL NATURES.

It is good to note this point to reconcile those who hope to explain mechanically the formation of the first tissues of an animal and the complete machine of its parts with those who account for the same structure by final causes. Both are good and both can be useful, not only for admiring the artifice of the great Workman, but also in discovering something useful in physics and medicine. Authors who follow these different routes should not be hard on each other.

For I see that those who concentrate on explaining the beauty of divine Anatomy laugh at others who imagine that an apparently fortuitous motion of particular fluids can make such a beautiful variety of members, and call such people rash and profane, while on the other hand the latter call the former simple and superstitious like the ancients who took it that the physicists were impious when they held that it was not Jupiter that thundered but some matter in the clouds. The best thing would be to unite both considerations, for, to use a vulgar comparison, the skill of a workman is recognised and praised not only by showing what designs he had when he made the parts of his machine, but also by explaining the tools he used to make each part, particularly when these tools are simple and ingeniously contrived. *God is skilful enough an artisan* to produce a machine a thousand times still more ingenious than that of our body if that were possible, using only a few simple enough fluids expressly formed so that only the ordinary laws of nature are needed to sort them out as necessary to produce such an admirable effect, but it is also true that this would not happen if God were not the Author of nature.

I find, nevertheless, that the way of efficient causes is while indeed more profound and in one way more direct and *a priori*, on the other hand rather difficult when we get down to details and I think that our Philosophers are most often still rather far from that. In contrast, the way of final causes is easier and is moreover often helpful in guessing important and useful truths that would have been a long time in the searching by the former more physical route, and of this Anatomy can furnish important examples. I also hold that Snell, the first discoverer of the rules of refraction, would have taken a long time to find them if he had tried to find out first how light was formed. But he seems to have followed the method the ancients used in catoptrics, that of final causes in fact. For, in the search for the easiest way of conducting a ray from one given point to another by reflection at a given plane (supposing that this is nature's design), they discovered the equality of the angles of incidence and reflection, as can be seen in a little treatise of Heliodorus of Larissa and elsewhere. That is what in my opinion Snell, and after him (though without knowing anything about him) Fermat, applied more ingeniously to refraction. For when in the same media the rays observe the same proportion of sines which is also that of the resistances of the media, it turns out to be the easiest, or at least the most determinate way of passing from a given point in one medium to a given point in the other. The demonstration Descartes tried to give of this same theorem by the way of efficient causes is far from being as good. At least there are grounds for suspecting that he would never have found it that way if he had not heard something of Snell's discovery in Holland.

23. RETURNING TO IMMATERIAL SUBSTANCES; THE EXPLANATION OF HOW GOD ACTS ON THE UNDERSTANDING OF MINDS AND OF WHETHER WE ALWAYS HAVE AN IDEA OF WHAT WE THINK.

I have found it relevant to insist somewhat on these considerations concerning final causes, incorporeal natures and an Intelligent Cause in relation to bodies, to make known their use even in physics and mathematics. On the one hand, this is to purge the mechanical philosophy of the profanity imputed to it. On the other hand it is to raise the minds of our philosophers from mere material considerations to more noble meditations. It is now time to return from bodies to immaterial natures, to minds in particular, and to say something of the ways God uses to illumine them and act on them, for we must not doubt that here too there are laws of nature, a point I could discuss more fully elsewhere. For now, it is enough to touch a little on ideas, on whether we see all things in God, and on how God is our light.

Now, it is relevant to note that several errors are occasioned by the misuse of ideas. For when we reason on something we imagine we have an idea of it, and on that foundation some recent authors have built a demonstration of God that is, rigorously speaking, very imperfect. For, they say, I must have an idea of God or of a perfect being, since I am thinking of Him, and it is impossible to think without an idea. Now the idea of this Being includes all the perfections and existence is one of these, so that consequently He exists. But as we often think of impossible chimerae, such as the ultimate degree of speed or the greatest number or the meeting of the conchoid [a plane curve in geometry] with its base or rule, this reasoning is not enough. Hence in this sense a person can say he has true or false ideas according as the thing in question is possible or not, and it is only when we are assured of its possibility that we can boast of having an idea of the thing. Thus the above argument proves at least that God necessarily exists if He is possible. This is indeed an excellent privilege of the divine nature: to need only its possibility or essence to exist in fact, just what is called an *Ens a se*.

24. JUST WHAT IS CLEAR OR OBSCURE, DISTINCT OR CONFUSED, ADEQUATE AND INTUITIVE OR SUPPOSITIVE KNOWLEDGE, AND WHAT ARE NOMINAL, REAL, CAUSAL AND ESSENTIAL DEFINITIONS.

The better to understand the nature of ideas, we have to touch a little on the varieties of knowledge. When I know only through experience that something is possible, because everything that exists is possible, my knowledge is confused. It is in this way that we know bodies and their qualities. But when I can prove *a priori* that something is possible, this knowledge is distinct. When I can recognise one thing among others without being able to say in what its *differentiae* or properties consist, my knowledge is confused. Thus it is that we sometimes know *clearly* without being in any doubt at all whether a poem or picture is well or badly made, because there is an I don't know what that satisfies or shocks us. But only when I can explain the marks available to me is my knowledge called *distinct*. Such is the knowledge of the assayer who discerns the true and the false by particular tests or marks comprising the definition of gold.

But there are degrees of distinct knowledge, for the notions that enter the definition would ordinarily themselves need definition and are only confusedly known. But when every thing that enters a definition or distinct item of knowledge is distinctly known right back to the primitive notions, I call this knowledge *adequate*, and when my mind understands all the primitive ingredients of a notion all at once and distinctly, then it has an intuitive knowledge of it, something very rare since most human knowledge is confused or even *suppositive*.

It is also good to distinguish nominal definitions from real ones. I refer to a nominal definition when it is still possible to doubt that the notion defined is possible. Thus, for example, when I say that an endless screw is a solid line whose parts are congruent or can coincide with each other, whoever did not otherwise know what an endless screw was could doubt the possibility of such a line, though indeed it was a reciprocal property of an endless screw, since the other lines whose parts are congruent are planar (the circumference of the circle and the straight line only), that is they can be drawn *in a plane*. This shows that every reciprocal property can be used in a nominal definition, whereas when the property makes known the possibility of the thing, it makes the definition real. As long as we have a mere nominal definition, we could never be sure of the consequences drawn from it, for if it concealed some contradiction or impossibility, contrary conclusions could be drawn from it. That is why truths do not depend on names and are not arbitrary as held by some new philosophers.

25. IN WHAT CASE OUR KNOWLEDGE IS JOINED TO THE CONTEMPLATION OF THE IDEA.

Now it is obvious that we have no idea of a notion when it is impossible. And when our knowledge is merely *suppositive*, when we have the idea we do not contemplate it, for such a notion is known only in the same way as those that are occultly impossible, and if it is possible it is not learned by that method of knowing. For example, when I think of a thousand, or of chiliagon [a group of one thousand things], I often do so without contemplating the idea, as when I say that a thousand is ten times a hundred without putting myself to the trouble of thinking what ten and a hundred are. That is because I *suppose* I know it and see no need for the present to pause to conceive it. Thus it can easily happen, as indeed it does often enough, that I am in error with respect to a notion I suppose or believe I understand, although in truth it is impossible, or at least incompatible with the others I join it to. Whether or not I am in error, this suppositive way of conceiving remains the same. Hence, it is only when our knowledge of confused things is *clear* or our knowledge of distinct things intuitive, that we contemplate the complete idea of them.

26. WE HAVE ALL IDEAS IN US; PLATO'S NOTION OF REMINISCENCE.

If we are to conceive properly what an idea is, we must avoid an ambiguity. For there are some who take the idea to be the form or way of distinguishing our thoughts. On this view we have the idea in our minds only to the extent that we think of it, and whenever we think of it again, we have ideas of the same thing different from though similar to the previous ones. But it seems that others take the idea to be an immediate object of thought, or some permanent form remaining when we do not contemplate it. Indeed, there is always in our souls the capacity to conceive any nature or form whatever, when the opportunity of thinking of it presents itself. I think that this capacity of our souls, to the extent that it expresses some nature, form or essence, is properly speaking the idea of the thing, in us and always in us, whether we think of it or not. For our soul expresses God and the universe, and all essences as well as all existences.

This follows from my principles, for nothing enters our minds naturally from outside, and it is a bad habit of ours to think as if our souls received some messenger—species or had gates and windows. We have all the forms in our minds, for all time even, because the mind always expresses all its future thoughts, and already thinks confusedly everything it will ever think distinctly. Nothing could be taught us whose idea was not already present in our minds as the matter from which this thought was formed.

That is what Plato understood so well when he put forward his doctrine of reminiscence, which is very sound provided we take it the right way and purge it of the error of pre-existence, and do not imagine that the soul has to have once known and distinctly thought what it is now learning and thinking. He also confirmed his opinion by a beautiful experiment. He introduced a little boy in his dialogue called *Meno* whom he led insensibly into the most difficult geometrical truths concerning incommensurables, without teaching him anything, merely putting relevant questions in order. This shows that our souls have virtual knowledge of everything. They need only attention to know the truths, and consequently have at least the truths on which these truths depend. It can even be said, if the latter are taken for the relations of ideas, that they already possess these truths.

27. IN WHAT SENSE OUR SOULS MAY BE COMPARED TO EMPTY TABLETS, AND HOW OUR NOTIONS COME FROM THE SENSES.

Aristotle preferred to compare our souls to tablets that were still bare with space for writing on, and he claimed that nothing was in our understanding that did not come from the senses. As is the way with Aristotle, this is more in conformity with popular notions, whereas Plato goes deeper. Nevertheless, such everyday expressions or practical sayings are liable to pass into common usage, almost as with the followers of Copernicus who continue to say that the sun rises and sets. I often find, even, that a good sense can be given to them in accordance with which there is nothing wrong with them. Just as I have already remarked on the way it is possible to say truly that particular substances act on each other, in this same sense it can be said that we receive some knowledge from outside by the ministry of the senses, because some external things contain, or more particularly express, the reasons determining our souls to particular thoughts. But when we are concerned with the accuracy of metaphysical truths, it is important to recognise the extent and independence of our souls. This goes infinitely further than is vulgarly supposed, although in the ordinary course of life only what is more certainly perceived and belongs to us in a particular way is attributed to it, since there is no purpose in going further.

Nevertheless, it would be good to choose special terms for both senses to avoid ambiguity. Hence, expressions in our souls, whether conceived or not, can be called ideas, while those we conceive or form can be called *notions* or *concepts*. But however we take it, it is always false to say that all our notions come from the senses called external, since the one I have of myself, and of my thoughts, and consequently of being, substance, action, identity and many others, comes from internal experience.

28. GOD ALONE IS THE IMMEDIATE OBJECT OF OUR PERCEPTIONS EXISTING OUTSIDE US, FOR HE ALONE IS OUR LIGHT.

Now, in the rigour of metaphysical truth, there is no external cause acting on us but God alone, and He alone communicates himself to us directly in virtue of our continual dependence. It follows from this that there is no other external object touching our souls and exciting our perceptions directly. So it is only in virtue of the continual action of God on us that we have in our souls the ideas of everything, i.e. because every effect expresses its cause and hence the essence of our souls is a particular expression, imitation, or image of the essence, thought and will of God and of all the ideas included in Him. Hence, it can be said that God alone is our immediate object outside us, and that it is in Him that we see all things. For example, when we see the sun and the stars, it is God who gave us them and preserves their ideas in us, and in fact determines us to think of them at the time at which our senses are disposed in a particular way, through His ordinary concurrence and in accordance with the laws established by Him. God is the sun and light of souls, "the light enlightening every man born into the world." It is not just today that people are of this opinion. After Holy Scripture and the Fathers—always more for Plato than for Aristotle—I recall noticing once that in the time of the Scholastics some believed that God was the light of the soul and, in their way of speaking, "the active intellect of the rational soul." The Averroists gave this a bad meaning, but others such as, I think, William of St. Amour, doctor of the Sorbonne, and several mystical theologians, took it in a manner worthy of God and capable of raising the soul to the knowledge of its good.

29. NEVERTHELESS WE THINK DIRECTLY BY OUR OWN IDEAS AND NOT BY THOSE OF GOD.

Nevertheless I am not of the opinion of some able philosophers who seem to maintain that our very ideas are in God, and not at all in us. In my opinion, this comes about because they have still not pondered enough what we have just explained concerning substances, nor the entire extent and independence of our souls (which means that they include everything happening to them and express the essence of God, and with Him all possible and actual beings, like an effect its cause). Also, it is inconceivable that I should think by means of the thoughts of someone else. It is very necessary that an effect should express its cause and it is also very necessary that the soul should be actually affected in a particular way when it thinks of something and that it should have in advance, not only the passive power of being affected in this way, something already determined, but also an active power, in virtue of which there has always been in its nature the marks of the future production of that thought and dispositions to produce it when the time came. All this already includes the idea contained in that thought.

30. How God Inclines Without Necessitating; We Have No Right to Complain, and We Must Not Ask Why Judas Sins Since this Free Action Is Included in His Notion, Only Why Judas the Sinner Is Admitted to Existence in Preference to Other Possible Persons. The Origin of Evil Comes From this, the Original Imperfection Before Sin, and the Degrees of Grace.

Concerning the action of God on the human will, there are many rather difficult questions that would take time to pursue here. Nevertheless, in outline, this is what can be said. When God concurs in our actions, He ordinarily does no more than follow the laws of nature He has established, i.e. He preserves and continually produces our nature, so that the thoughts spontaneously and naturally or freely happen to us in the order carried by the notion of our individual substance, within which they could have been foreseen from all eternity. Moreover, in virtue of the decree that the will should always tend towards the apparent good, and so express or imitate God's will in certain particular respects in respect of which this apparent good always has something of the true, He determines our will to choose what seems the best without nonetheless necessitating it. For, absolutely speaking, in so far as it may be opposed to necessity, our will is indifferent and has the power to do otherwise or to suspend its action altogether, since both are and remain possible.

Hence it falls to the soul to take precautions against the appearances taking it by surprise by means of a firm resolve to reflect and to refuse to act or judge on particular occasions without thorough deliberation. Nevertheless it is true and even certain from all eternity that a particular soul will not use this power on one such occasion. But who could do anything about it or do other than complain about himself? For all complaints after the fact are unjust when they would have been unjust before. Now would this soul, shortly before sinning, be in the right to complain of God, who has not determined him to flee from the sin as if He had determined him to sin? Since God's determinations in these matters are unforeseeable, how does he know himself to be determined to sin, unless in fact he is already actually sinning? It is only a matter of not willing, and God could propose no easier or juster condition. Moreover, any judge stops only to consider how far a man's will is bad without searching for the reasons disposing him to have a bad will. But perhaps it is certain from all eternity that I will sin? Answer yourself: perhaps not. Do not think about what you cannot know and cannot enlighten you, but act in accordance with the duty you know.

But, someone else will ask, whence comes it that that man will certainly do this sin? The answer is easy: otherwise he would not be that man. For God sees for all time that there will be a certain Judas whose notion, or idea God has of him, contains this future free action. Hence the only question that remains is why such a Judas, the traitor, who is merely a possible in the idea of God actually exists. But to that question there is no answer to be expected here below, unless that in general we must say that since God thought it good for him to exist, despite the sin he foresaw this evil must be repaid with interest in the universe, that God will obtain a greater good from it; and that in all He will find this sequence of things including the existence of this sinner the most perfect of all the other possible ones. But to explain in all cases the admirable economy of this choice is not possible while we are travellers in this vale of tears in this world. It is enough to know without understanding it. It is time here to recognise "the height of the riches," the width and depth of the divine wisdom, without seeking a detail involving these infinite considerations.

Nevertheless, it is clear that God is not the cause of evil. For not only did original sin take hold of the soul after the loss of innocence but before then there was a limitation or original imperfection common to the natures of all creatures making them capable of sin or liable to fail. Thus there is no more difficulty with regard to the supralapsarians* than with the others. In my opinion, it is to this that the opinion of St. Augustine and other authors that the root of evil is in nothingness should be reduced, i.e. in the privation or the limitation of creatures that God graciously remedies by giving them the degree of perfection it pleases Him to give. Whether ordinary or extraordinary, this grace of God has its degrees and measures, always in itself efficacious in producing a proportionate effect. Moreover it is always sufficient, not only to guarantee us against sin, but to produce salvation, if the man joins himself to it with his will, though it is not always sufficient to surmount human inclinations, otherwise it would depend on nothing more, and that is reserved to the absolutely efficacious grace alone that is always victorious whether by itself or by the congruity of circumstances.

31. THE FOREKNOWLEDGE OF MERIT, THE DISPENSING OF GRACE,
THE MOTIVES OF ELECTION, THE MIDDLE KNOWLEDGE,
THE ABSOLUTE DECREE; THAT EVERYTHING REDUCES
TO THE REASON WHY GOD CHOSE A PARTICULAR POSSIBLE PERSON
FOR EXISTENCE, WHOSE NOTION INCLUDES THAT PARTICULAR
SEQUENCE OF GRACES AND FREE ACTIONS, SO THAT ALL
THE DIFFICULTIES ARE REMOVED AT ONCE.

In the end, the graces of God are graces pure and simple over which creatures have no claim. However, just as when we are giving an account of the action of God in dispensing these graces it is not enough to have recourse to His fore-sight, whether absolute or conditional, of the future actions of men, so we must not imagine absolute decrees with no reasonable motive. As regards God's fore-sight of faith and good works, it is very true that God has elected only those whose faith and charity He foresaw, "those He foreknew He would give faith to," but the same question returns: why God will give the grace of faith and good works to some rather than to others. As for this middle knowledge of God's, the fore-sight, not of good works, but of their matter and predisposition, or of what the man would contribute from his side (since it is true that there is diversity on the human side wherever there is on the side of grace, and since indeed, although man needs to be excited towards the good and converted, it is very necessary that he should also play his part here after the fact) some people think that it could be said that since God sees what man would do without grace or extraordinary assistance, or at least what he will have on his side apart from grace, He could resolve to give grace to those whose natural disposition was the best or at any rate the least imperfect or least evil. But if that was the case, it could be said that these natural dispositions, in so far as they are good, are still the effect of an act of grace, even if an ordinary one, since God has advantaged some more than others. And since He well knows that these

*[Calvinists who believe that election to heaven or hell was a part of God's original plan.]

natural advantages He gives will provide the motive for grace or extraordinary assistance, does it not follow from the doctrine that truly everything in the end reduces to His mercy?

Hence, I believe (since we do not know how much or how God takes account of natural dispositions in dispensing grace) that the most accurate and certain thing to say is, as already noted and in conformity with our principles, that among the possible beings there should be the person of Peter or John whose notion or idea contains the whole sequence of ordinary and extraordinary graces and all the other events along with their circumstances, and that it pleased God to choose him from among an infinity of other equally possible persons for actual existence. After that it seems that there is no more to ask and that all the difficulties disappear.

For, considering this single great question, why it pleased God to choose one from so many other possible persons, we would have to be unreasonable indeed not to be satisfied with the general reasons given, for which the detail is beyond our reach. So, we should not have recourse to an absolute decree, which is unreasonable since there is no reason for it, or to reasons that do not succeed in resolving the difficulty. Instead the best will be to say with St. Paul that there are certain grand reasons for this unknown to mortals and founded in the general order whose aim is the greatest perfection of the universe, and that God has observed these. It is to this that the motives of the glory of God and the manifestation of His justice reduce, as well as His mercy and His perfections generally, and finally that immense depth of His riches Paul's soul was enchanted with.

32. Usefulness of These Principles in Matters of Piety and Religion.

For the rest, it seems that the thoughts we have just explained, particularly the grand principle of the perfection of the operations of God and the notion of the substance including all the events with all their circumstances, far from harming religion, serve to confirm it, removing very great difficulties, inflaming souls with a divine love and raising minds to the knowledge of incorporeal substances to a much greater extent than the hypotheses we have seen up to now. For it is clear that just as thoughts depend on our substance, all other substances depend on God, that God is all in all, and that He is intimately united with all creatures (though to the extent of their perfection), and that He alone determines them externally by His influence. And if to act is to determine directly, it can be said in this sense, in the language of metaphysics, that God operates on me and is alone able to do me good or ill, while other substances are nothing but occasional causes, for the reason that as God considers all of them, He distributes His acts of goodness and obliges them to conform to each other. Also, God alone makes the connection and communication of substances, and it is by Him that phenomena of any given substance meet and fit with those of the others, and consequently that there is reality in our perceptions. But in practice action is attributed to particular occasional causes in the sense explained above, because it is not always necessary to mention the universal cause in particular cases.

It is seen also that every substance has a perfect spontaneity (which in intelligent substances becomes liberty): that everything that happens to it is a consequence of its ideas or being, and that it is determined by nothing but God alone. That is why a person of noble mind whose sanctity is greatly revered used to say that the soul must often think as if there were only God and it in the world.

Now nothing makes immortality more completely comprehensible than this independence and extent of the soul. It protects it absolutely from all external things, since it alone constitutes the whole world and, with God, suffices to itself. It is also impossible for it to perish other than by annihilation, and impossible for the world (of which it is a living and perpetual expression) to destroy itself. Hence, it is not possible for the changes in that extended mass called our body to do anything to our soul, or for the disappearance of that body to destroy what is indivisible.

33. Explanation of the Union of Soul and Body Something Once Thought Inexplicable or Miraculous, and the Origin of Confused Perceptions.

Also clear is the unexpected solution of that great mystery of the union of soul and body, i.e. how it happens that the actions and passions of the one are accompanied by the actions and passions, or rather appropriate phenomena, of the other. For there is no way of conceiving any influence of the one on the other, and it is unreasonable simply to have recourse to the extraordinary operation of the universal cause in something ordinary and particular. But here is the true reason. We have said that everything happening to the soul and to every substance is a consequence of its notion. Hence the very idea or essence of the soul makes all its appearances or perceptions arise spontaneously out of its own nature, and just so, that they answer of themselves to what happens in the whole universe, though particularly in the body assigned to it, because in a way and for a time, it is in accordance with the relation of other bodies to its own that the soul expresses the state of the universe. This shows yet again how our bodies belong to us without nevertheless being attached to our essences. I believe that persons able to meditate will see advantage in our principles in just this, that it is easy to see in what exactly the connection between soul and body—apparently inexplicable by any other means—consists.

It can also be seen that the perceptions of our senses, even when they are clear, must necessarily contain some confused sensations. For as all the bodies in the universe are in sympathy, ours receive the impressions of all the others. Although our senses relate to everything, it is not possible for our souls to attend to all individually, and that is why our confused sensations are the result of a variety, altogether infinite, of perceptions. It is almost like the confused murmur heard by those approaching the shores of the sea that arises from the accumulation of the reverberations of innumerable waves. Now if of several perceptions (not coming together to become a single one) none stands out above the others, and if they make almost equally strong impressions, or are equally capable of determining the attention of the soul, it can only register them confusedly.

34. The Excellence of Minds Compared with Other Substances or Substantial Forms. The Immortality Called for Implies Memory.

One thing I do not propose to decide is whether in metaphysical rigour bodies are substances or are no more than *true* phenomena like the rainbow, nor consequently whether there are substances, souls or substantial forms that are not intelligent. But if we suppose that bodies like man that constitute unities in themselves are substances and have substantial forms, we are obliged to admit that these souls and substantial forms could no more entirely perish than atoms if there are any or ultimate particles of matter can, in the opinion of other philosophers. For though it may become quite different, no substance perishes. Although more imperfectly than minds, they too express the whole universe. But the principal difference is that they do not know what they are nor what they are doing. Consequently, since they have no power of reflection, they are unable to discover necessary and universal truths. It is also for want of reflection on themselves that they have no moral qualities, so that, when we consider how a caterpillar changes into a butterfly through almost a thousand transformations, it comes to the same for morals and practice as saying that they perish, as can indeed be said physically (as we say of bodies that they perish by corruption). But the intelligent soul that knows what it is, and is capable of pronouncing this me which says so much, not only remains the same metaphysically to a greater extent than the others, but it also remains morally the same and constitutes the same personality. For it is the memory and knowledge of this me that makes it liable to punishment and reward. Also, the immortality called for both in morality and religion does not consist merely in that perpetual subsistence proper to all substances. For without the memory of what has been, there would be nothing desirable about it. Let us suppose that some poor wretch suddenly became King of China, but only on condition that he forgot what he had been, as if he had just been reborn: does that not come to the same in practice, or in the effects that could be registered, as if he had to be annihilated and a King of China created at the same instant and at the same place? Something this individual has no reason to desire.

35. THE EXCELLENCE OF MINDS. GOD CONSIDERS THEM IN PREFERENCE TO OTHER CREATURES. MINDS EXPRESS GOD RATHER THAN THE WORLD, BUT OTHER SUBSTANCES EXPRESS THE WORLD RATHER THAN GOD.

But to show by natural reasons that God always will preserve not only our substance but also our personality, that is memory and knowledge of what we are although distinct knowledge of that may sometimes be suspended when asleep or unconscious, morality must be joined to Metaphysics. That is, God has not only to be considered as the principle and cause of all substances and all beings, but also as the chief of all persons or intelligent substances and the absolute monarch of the most perfect city or republic, like that of the universe composed of all minds together, since God himself is the most accomplished of all Minds as well as the greatest of all Beings. For assuredly, minds are either the only substances existing in the world if bodies are no more than true phenomena, or else they are at least the most perfect ones. And since the whole nature, end, virtue and function of substances is merely to express God and the universe, as has been sufficiently explained, there are no grounds for doubting that substances expressing Him in the knowledge of what they are doing, and capable of knowing great truths regarding God and the universe, express Him incomparably better than those natures that are either animal and incapable of knowing truths, or altogether destitute of sense and knowledge; and the difference between intelligent substances and those that are not is as great as that between the mirror and he who sees.

And since God Himself is the greatest and wisest of minds, it is easy to conclude that beings with whom He can so to speak enter into conversation or even into fellowship, communicating His thoughts and intentions individually, so that they can know and love their Benefactor, must concern Him infinitely more than all other beings, able only to pass for the tools of minds, just as we can see wise persons taking infinitely more account of a man than of some other thing, however precious that may be. It seems that the greatest satisfaction an otherwise contented soul can have is to see himself loved by others although in respect of God there is this difference that His glory and our worship can add nothing to His satisfaction, since the knowledge of creatures is no more than a consequence of His sovereign and perfect happiness and very far from contributing to the latter or being part of the cause thereof. Nevertheless, what is good and reasonable in finite minds is supremely so in Him and just as we would praise a king who preferred to preserve the life of a man before the most precious and rare of animals, we should not doubt that the most enlightened and just of all Monarchs is of the same opinion.

36. GOD IS THE MONARCH OF THAT MOST PERFECT REPUBLIC THAT CONSISTS OF ALL MINDS, AND THE HAPPINESS OF THIS CITY OF GOD IS HIS PRINCIPAL DESIGN.

In fact, minds are the most perfectible of all substances and their perfections have this characteristic that they hinder each other the least, or rather that they assist each other, for only the most virtuous can be the most perfect friends. Hence it manifestly follows that God who always looks to the greatest perfection in general, will have the most care of minds, and will give them, not only generally but to each individually, the greatest perfection the universal harmony can permit.

It can even be said that God, in so far as He is a mind, is the origin of existent things—if there were no will to choose best there would be no reason for one possible thing to exist in preference to others. Hence God's quality of being Himself a mind precedes all other considerations He may have with respect to creatures. Minds only are made in His image, and it is as if they are of His race and children of His house, since they alone can serve Him freely and act consciously in imitation of the divine nature. One mind is worth an entire world, since it does not only express it, but knows it, and governs itself there in the manner of God. So much so that it seems that while every substance expresses the whole universe, other substances express the world rather than God while minds express God rather than the world. And this natural nobility of minds, which brings them as near to the divine as is possible for mere creatures, means that God receives from them infinitely more glory than from other beings, or rather other beings merely give minds matter for glorifying Him.

That is why this moral quality of God that makes Him the Lord and Monarch of Minds, affects Him so to speak personally in a quite special manner. It is in this that He becomes human and is willing to allow human ways of speaking about Him, and enters into fellowship with us like a Prince with his subjects. This consideration is so dear to Him that the happy and flourishing state of His empire, that consists in the greatest possible happiness of the inhabitants, becomes the supreme subaltern law of His conduct. For happiness is to persons what perfection is to beings, and if the first principle of existence of the physical world is the decree giving it the greatest possible perfection, the first principle of existence of the moral world or City of God, the most noble part of the universe, must be to spread as much happiness as possible in it.

Hence it must not be doubted that God so ordained (not only that minds could live forever, which is inevitable, but also that they should conserve forever their moral nature) so that this city should lose no person just as the world loses no substance. And consequently, they will always know what they are, otherwise they would not be liable to reward or punishment, which however is the essence of any republic, above all of one that is the most perfect, in which nothing can be neglected.

Finally, since God is at once the most just and the most good-natured of monarchs, and asks only for good will, provided that it is sincere and serious, His subjects could not hope for better conditions: to make them perfectly happy, He wants only that they love Him.

37. Jesus Christ Has Revealed to Men the Mystery and Admirable Laws of the Kingdom of Heaven and the Greatness of the Supreme Happiness God Prepares for Those Who Love Him.

The ancient philosophers had very little knowledge of these important truths. Jesus Christ alone expressed them divinely well and in such a clear and familiar way, that the most crude minds came to understand them. So His gospel changed the entire face of human affairs. He brought us knowledge of the Kingdom of Heaven or this perfect republic of minds that merits the title "City of God" whose admirable laws he revealed to us, and he alone shows us how much God loves us; the exactness with which He has provided for all that concerns us; that since He cares for sparrows, He will not neglect the reasonable creatures who are infinitely more dear to Him; that all the hairs in our heads are counted; that heaven and earth will pass away before the Word of God and everything belonging to the pattern of our salvation is changed; God has more concern with the least of intelligent souls than with the whole machine of the world; that we must not fear those who can destroy the body but are unable to harm souls, since God alone can make them happy or unhappy; that the just are in His hand protected from all the revolutions of the universe, since nothing can act on them but God alone; that none of our actions is forgotten; that everything is taken into account, right down to unguarded words, and a spoonful of water well used; and finally that all things must result in the greatest good for those that are good; that the just are like suns and that neither our senses nor our minds have ever tasted anything approaching the happiness God prepares for those who love Him.

THEODICY (Leibniz's abridgement)

Abridgement of the Argument Reduced to Syllogistic Form

Some intelligent persons have desired that this supplement be made [to the Theodicy], and I have the more readily yielded to their wishes as in this way I have an opportunity again to remove certain difficulties and to make some observations which were not sufficiently emphasized in the work itself.

I. *Objection.* Whoever does not choose the best is lacking in power, or in knowledge, or in goodness.

God did not choose the best in creating this world.

Therefore, God has been lacking in power, or in knowledge, or in goodness.

Answer. I deny the minor, that is, the second premise of this syllogism; and our opponent proves it by this.

Prosyllogism. Whoever makes things in which there is evil, which could have been made without any evil, or the making of which could have been omitted, does not choose the best.

God has made a world in which there is evil, a world, I say, which could have been made without any evil, or the making of which could have been omitted altogether.

Therefore, God has not chosen the best.

Answer. I grant the minor of this prosyllogism; for it must be confessed that there is evil in this world which God has made, and that it was possible to make a world without evil, or even not to create a world at all, for its creation has depended on the free will of God; but I deny the major, that is, the first of the two premises of the prosyllogism, and I might content myself with simply demanding its proof; but in order to make the matter clearer, I have wished to justify this denial by showing that the best plan is not always that which seeks to avoid evil, since it may happen that *the evil is accompanied by a greater good*. For example, a general of an army will prefer a great victory with a slight wound to a condition without wound and without victory. We have proved this more fully in the large work by making it clear, by instances taken from mathematics and elsewhere, that an imperfection in the part may be required for a greater perfection in the whole. In this I have followed the opinion of St. Augustine, who has said a hundred times, that God has permitted evil in order to bring about good, that is, a greater good; and that of Thomas Aquinas (in libr. II. sent. dist. 32, qu. I, art. 1), that the permitting of evil tends to the good of the universe. I have shown that the ancients called Adam's fall *felix culpa*, a happy sin, because it had been retrieved with immense advantage by the incarnation of the Son of God, who has given to the universe something nobler than anything that ever would have been among creatures except for it. For the sake of a clearer understanding, I have added, following many good authors, that it was in accordance with order and the general good that God allowed to certain creatures the opportunity of exercising their liberty, even when he foresaw that they would turn to evil, but which he could so well rectify; because it was not fitting that, in order to hinder sin, God should always act in an extraordinary manner. To overthrow this objection, therefore, it is sufficient to show that a world with evil might be better than a world without evil; but I have gone even farther, in the work, and have even proved that this universe must be in reality better than every other possible universe.

II. *Objection.* If there is more evil than good in intelligent creatures, then there is more evil than good in the whole work of God.

Now, there is more evil than good in intelligent creatures.

Therefore, there is more evil than good in the whole work of God.

Answer. I deny the major and the minor of this conditional syllogism. As to the major, I do not admit it at all, because this pretended deduction from a part to the whole, from intelligent creatures to all creatures, supposes tacitly and without proof that creatures destitute of reason cannot enter into comparison nor into account with those which possess it. But why may it not be that the surplus of good in the non-intelligent creatures which fill the world, compensates for, and even incomparably surpasses, the surplus of evil in the rational creatures? It is true that the value of the latter is greater; but, in compensation, the others are beyond comparison the more numerous, and it may be that the proportion of number and quantity surpasses that of value and of quality.

As to the minor, that is no more to be admitted; that is, it is not at all to be admitted that there is more evil than good in the intelligent creatures. There is no need even of granting that there is more evil than good in the human race, because it is possible, and in fact very probable, that the glory and the perfection of the blessed are incomparably greater than the misery and the imperfection of the damned, and that here the excellence of the total good in the smaller number exceeds the total evil in the greater number. The blessed approach the Divinity, by means of a Divine Mediator, as near as may suit these creatures, and make such progress in good as is impossible for the damned to make in evil, approach as nearly as they may to the nature of demons. God is infinite, and the devil is limited; the good may and does go to infinity, while evil has its bounds. It is therefore possible, and is credible, that in the comparison of the blessed and the damned, the contrary of that which I have said might happen in the comparison of intelligent and nonintelligent creatures, takes place; namely, it is possible that in the comparison of the happy and the unhappy, the proportion of degree exceeds that of number, and that in the comparison of intelligent and nonintelligent creatures, the proportion of number is greater than that of value. I have the right to suppose that a thing is possible so long as its impossibility is not proved; and indeed that which I have here advanced is more than a supposition.

But in the second place, if I should admit that there is more evil than good in the human race, I have still good grounds for not admitting that there is more evil than good in all intelligent creatures. For there is an inconceivable number of genii, and perhaps of other rational creatures. And an opponent could not prove that in all the City of God, composed as well of genii as of rational animals without number and of an infinity of kinds, evil exceeds good. And although in order to answer an objection, there is no need of proving that a thing is, when its mere possibility suffices; yet, in this work, I have not omitted to show that it is a consequence of the supreme perfection of the Sovereign of the universe, that the kingdom of God is the most perfect of all possible states or governments, and that consequently the little evil there is, is required for the consummation of the immense good which is found there.

III. *Objection.* If it is always impossible not to sin, it is always unjust to punish.

Now, it is always impossible not to sin; or, in other words, every sin is necessary.

Therefore, it is always unjust to punish.

The minor of this is proved thus:

1. *Prosyllogism.* All that is predetermined is necessary.

Every event is predetermined.

Therefore, every event (and consequently sin also) is necessary.

Again this second minor is proved thus:

2. *Prosyllogism.* That which is future, that which is foreseen, that which is involved in the causes, is predetermined.

Every event is such.

Therefore, every event is predetermined.

Answer. I admit in a certain sense the conclusion of the second prosyllogism, which is the minor of the first; but I shall deny the major of the first prosyllogism, namely, that every thing predetermined is necessary; understanding by the necessity of sinning, for example, or by the impossibility of not sinning, or of not performing any action, the necessity with which we are here concerned, that is, that which is essential and absolute, and which destroys the morality of an action and the justice of punishments. For if anyone understood another necessity or impossibility, namely, a necessity which should be only moral, or which was only hypothetical (as will be explained shortly); it is clear that I should deny the major of the objection itself. I might content myself with this answer and demand the proof of the proposition denied; but I have again desired to explain my procedure in this work, in order to better elucidate the matter and to throw more light on the whole subject, by explaining the necessity which ought to be rejected and the determination which must take place. That *necessity* which is contrary to morality and which ought to be rejected, and which would render punishment unjust, is an insurmountable necessity which would make all opposition useless, even if we should wish with all our heart to avoid the necessary action, and should make all possible efforts to that end. Now, it is manifest that this is not applicable to voluntary actions, because we would not perform them if we did not choose to. Also their prevision and predetermination are not absolute, but presuppose the will: if it is certain that we shall perform them, it is not less certain that we shall choose to perform them. These voluntary actions and their consequences will not take place no matter what we do or whether we wish them or not; but, *through* that which we shall do and through that which we shall wish to do, which leads to them. And this is involved in prevision and in predetermination, and even constitutes their ground. And the necessity of such an event is called conditional or hypothetical, or the necessity of consequence, because it supposes the will, and the other *requisites*; whereas the necessity which destroys morality and renders punishment unjust and reward useless, exists in things which will be whatever we may do or whatever we may wish to do, and, in a word, is in that which is essential; and this is what is called an absolute necessity. Thus it is to no purpose, as regards what is absolutely necessary, to make prohibitions or commands, to propose penalties or prizes, to praise or to blame; it will be none the less. On the other hand, in voluntary actions and in that which depends upon them, precepts armed with power to punish and to recompense are very often of use and are included in the order of causes which make an action exist. And it is for this reason that not only cares and labors but also prayers are useful; God having had these prayers in view before he regulated things and having had that consideration for them which was proper. This is why the precept which says *ora et labora* (pray and work), holds altogether good; and not only those who (under the vain pretext of the necessity of events) pretend that the care which business demands may be neglected, but also those who reason against prayer, fall into what the ancients even then called the *lazy sophism*. Thus the predetermination of events by causes is just what contributes to morality instead of destroying it, and causes incline the will, without compelling it. This is why the *determination* in question is not a necessitation—it is certain (to him who knows all) that the effect will follow this inclination; but this effect does not follow by a necessary consequence, that is, one the contrary of which implies contradiction. It is also by an internal inclination such as this that the will is determined, without there being any necessity. Suppose that one has the greatest passion in the world (a great thirst, for example), you will admit to me that the soul can find some reason for resisting it, if it were only that of showing its power. Thus, although one may never be in a perfect indifference of equilibrium and there may be always a preponderance of inclination for the side taken, it, nevertheless, never renders the resolution taken absolutely necessary.

IV. *Objection.* Whoever can prevent the sin of another and does not do so but rather contributes to it although he is well informed of it, is accessory to it.

God can prevent the sin of intelligent creatures; but he does not do so, and rather contributes to it by his concurrence and by the opportunities which he brings about, although he has a perfect knowledge of it.

Hence, etc.

Answer. I deny the major of this syllogism. For it is possible that one could prevent sin, but ought not, because he could not do it without himself committing a sin, or (when God is in question) without performing an unreasonable action. Examples have been given and the application to God himself has been made. It is possible also that we contribute to evil and that sometimes we even open the road to it, in doing things which we are obliged to do; and, when we do our duty or (in speaking of God) when, after thorough consideration, we do that which reason demands, we are not responsible for the results, even when we foresee them. We do not desire these evils; but we are willing to permit them for the sake of a greater good which we cannot reasonably help preferring to other considerations. And this is a *consequent* will, which results from *antecedent* wills by which we will the good. I know that some persons, in speaking of the *antecedent* and consequent will of God, have understood by the antecedent that which wills that all men should be saved; and by the *consequent*, that which wills, in consequence of persistent sin, that some should be damned. But these are merely illustrations of a more general idea, and it may be said for the same reason that God, by his antecedent will, wills that men should not sin; and by his consequent or final and decreeing will (that which is always followed by its effect), he wills to permit them to sin, this permission being the result of superior reasons. And we have the right to say in general that the antecedent will of God tends to the production of good and the prevention of evil, each taken in itself and as if alone (*particulariter et secundum quid,* Thom. I, qu. 19, art. 6), according to the measure of the degree of each good and of each evil; but that the divine consequent or final or total will tends toward the production of as many goods as may be put together, the combination of which becomes in this way determined, and includes also the permission of some evils and the exclusion of some goods, as the best possible plan for the universe demands. Arminius, in his Anti-perkinsus, has very well explained that the will of God may be called consequent, not only in relation to the action of the creature considered beforehand in the divine understanding, but also in relation to other anterior divine acts of will. But this consideration of the passage cited from Thomas Aquinas, and that from Scotus (I. dist. 46, qu. XI), is enough to show that they make this distinction as I have done here. Nevertheless, if anyone objects to this use of terms let him substitute *deliberating* will, in place of antecedent, and final or decreeing will, in place of consequent. For I do not wish to dispute over words.

V. *Objection.* Whoever produces all that is real in a thing, is its cause.

God produces all that is real in sin.

Hence, God is the cause of sin.

Answer. I might content myself with denying the major or the minor, since the term real admits of interpretations which would render these propositions false. But in order to explain more clearly, I will make a distinction. *Real* signifies either that which is positive only, or, it includes also privative beings: in the first case, I deny the major and admit the minor; in the second case, I do the contrary. I might have limited myself to this, but I have chosen to proceed still farther and give the reason for this distinction. I have been very glad therefore to draw attention to the fact that every reality purely positive or absolute is a perfection; and that imperfection comes from limitation, that is, from the privative: for to limit is to refuse progress, or the greatest possible progress. Now God is the cause of all perfections and consequently of all realities considered as purely positive. But limitations or privations result from the original imperfection of creatures, which limits their receptivity. And it is with them as with a loaded vessel, which the river causes to move more or less slowly according to the weight which it carries: thus its speed depends upon the river, but the retardation which limits this speed comes from the load. Thus in the *Theodicy*, we have shown how the creature, in causing sin, is a defective cause; how errors and evil inclinations are born of privation; and how privation is accidentally efficient; and I have justified the opinion of St. Augustine (lib. I. ad Simpl. qu. 2) who explains, for example, how God makes the soul obdurate, not by giving it something evil, but because the effect of his good impression is limited by the soul's resistance and by the circumstances which contribute to this resistance, so that he does not give it all the good which would overcome its evil. *Nec* (inquit) *ab illo erogatur aliquid quo homo fit deterior, sed tantum quo fit melior non erogatur.* But if God had wished to do more, he would have had to make either other natures for creatures or other miracles to change their natures, things which the best plan could not admit. It is as if the current of the river must be more rapid than its fall admitted or that the boats should be loaded more lightly, if it were necessary to make them move more quickly. And the original limitation or imperfection of creatures requires that even the best plan of the universe could not receive more good, and could not be exempt from certain evils, which, however, are to result in a greater good. There are certain disorders in the parts which marvelously enhance the beauty of the whole; just as certain dissonances, when properly used, render harmony more beautiful. But this depends on what has already been said in answer to the first objection.

VI. *Objection.* Whoever punishes those who have done as well as it was in their power to do, is unjust.

God does so.

Hence, etc.

Answer. I deny the minor of this argument. And I believe that God always gives sufficient aid and grace to those who have a good will, that is, to those who do not reject this grace by new sin. Thus I do not admit the damnation of infants who have died without baptism or outside of the church; nor the damnation of adults who have acted according to the light which God has given them. And I believe that *if any one has followed the light which has been given him*, he will undoubtedly receive greater light when he has need of it, as the late M. Hulseman, a profound and celebrated theologian at Leipzig, has somewhere remarked; and if such a man has failed to receive it during his lifetime he will at least receive it when at the point of death.

VII. *Objection.* Whoever gives only to some, and not to all, the means which produces in them effectively a good will and salutary final faith, has not sufficient goodness.

God does this.

Hence, etc.

Answer. I deny the major of this. It is true that God could overcome the greatest resistance of the human heart; and does it, too, sometimes, either by internal grace, or by external circumstances which have a great effect on souls; but he does not always do this. Whence comes this distinction? it may be asked, and why does his goodness seem limited? It is because, as I have already said in answering the first objection, it would not have been in order always to act in an extraordinary manner, and to reverse the connection of things. The reasons of this connection, by means of which one is placed in more favorable circumstances than another, are hidden in the depths of the wisdom of God: they depend upon the universal harmony. The best plan of the universe, which God could not fail to choose, made it so. We judge from the event itself; since God has made it, it was not possible to do better. Far from being true that this conduct is contrary to goodness, it is supreme goodness which led him to it. This objection with its solution might have been drawn from what was said in regard to the first objection; but it seemed useful to touch upon it separately.

VIII. *Objection.* Whoever cannot fail to choose the best, is not free.

God cannot fail to choose the best.

Hence, God is not free.

Answer. I deny the major of this argument; it is rather true liberty, and the most perfect, to be able to use one's free will for the best, and to always exercise this power, without ever being turned aside either by external force or by internal passions, the first of which causes slavery of the body, the second, slavery of the soul. There is nothing less servile, and nothing more in accordance with the highest degree of freedom, than to be always led toward the good, and always by one's own inclination, without any constraint and without any displeasure. And to object therefore that God had need of external things, is only a sophism. He created them freely; but having proposed to himself an end, which is to exercise his goodness, wisdom has determined him to choose the means best fitted to attain this end. To call this a need, is to take that term in an unusual sense which frees it from all imperfection, just as when we speak of the wrath of God.

Seneca has somewhere said that God commanded but once but that he obeys always, because he obeys laws which he willed to prescribe to himself: *semel jussit, semper paret.* But he might better have said that God always commands and that he is always obeyed; for in willing, he always follows the inclination of his own nature, and all other things always follow his will. And as this will is always the same, it cannot be said that he obeys only that will which he formerly had. Nevertheless, although his will is always infallible and always tends toward the best, the evil, or the lesser good, which he rejects, does not cease to be possible in itself; otherwise the necessity of the good would be geometrical (so to speak), or metaphysical, and altogether absolute; the contingency of things would be destroyed, and there would be no choice. But this sort of necessity, which does not destroy the possibility of the contrary, has this name only by analogy; it becomes effective, not by the pure essence of things, but by that which is outside of them, above them, namely, by the will of God. This necessity is called moral, because, to the sage, *necessity* and *what ought to be* are equivalent things; and when it always has its effect, as it really has in the perfect sage, that is, in God, it may be said that it is a happy necessity. The nearer creatures approach to it, the nearer they approach to perfect happiness. Also this kind of necessity is not that which we try to avoid and which destroys morality, rewards and praise. For that which it brings, does not happen whatever we may do or will, but because we will it so. And a will to which it is natural to choose well, merits praise so much the more; also it carries its reward with it, which is sovereign happiness. And as this constitution of the divine nature gives entire satisfaction to him who possesses it, it is also the best and the most desirable for the creatures who are all dependent on God. If the will of God did not have for a rule the principle of the best, it would either tend toward evil, which would be the worst; or it would be in some way indifferent to good and to evil, and would be guided by chance: but a will which would allow itself always to act by chance, would not be worth more for the government of the universe than the fortuitous concourse of atoms, without there being any divinity therein. And even if God should abandon himself to chance only in some cases and in a certain way (as he would do, if he did not always work entirely for the best and if he were capable of preferring a lesser work to a greater, that is, an evil to a good, since that which prevents a greater good is an evil), he would be imperfect, as well as the object of his choice; he would not merit entire confidence; he would act without reason in such a case, and the government of the universe would be like certain games, equally divided between reason and chance. All this proves that this objection which is made against the choice of the best, perverts the notions of the free and of the necessary, and represents to us the best even as evil: which is either malicious or ridiculous.

THE MONADOLOGY

1. The object of this discourse, the *monad*, is nothing else than a simple substance, which enters into the composites; *simple* meaning, which has no parts.

2. And there must be simple substances, since there are composites; for the composite is nothing else than an accumulation or aggregate of the simples.

3. But where there are no parts, neither extension, nor figure, nor divisibility is possible. Thus, these monads are the veritable atoms of nature, and, in one word, the elements of all things.

4. Hence no dissolution is to be feared for them, and a simple substance cannot perish naturally in any conceivable manner.

5. For the same reason, no simple substance can come into being naturally, since it cannot be formed by composition.

6. Thus it may be maintained that monads cannot begin or end otherwise than instantaneously, that is, they can begin only by creation, and end only by annihilation; while what is complete begins and ends through and in its parts.

7. It is impossible also to explain how a monad can be altered, that is, internally changed, by any other creature. For there is nothing in it which might be transposed, nor can there be conceived in it any internal movement which could be excited, directed, or diminished. In composites this is possible, since the parts can interchange place. The monads have no windows through which anything could come in or go out.

8. Nevertheless, the monads must have some qualities, otherwise they would not even be beings. And if the simple substances did not differ through their qualities, there would be no means at all of perceiving any change in things. For what is in the composites can come only from the ingredient simples. So the monads, if they were without qualities, would be indistinguishable the one from the other, since they do not differ in quantity either. The plenum being presupposed, no space, consequently, could ever receive through movement anything but the equivalent of what has been in it, and one state of things would be indiscernible from another.

9. Each monad must even be different from every other. For in nature there are never two beings which are perfectly like one another, and between which it would not be possible to find an internal difference, that is, a difference founded on an intrinsic denomination.

10. I take it also for granted that all created beings, consequently the created monads as well, are subject to change, and that this change is even continual in each one.

11. In consequence of what has been said, the natural changes of the monads must result from an *internal principle*, since no external cause could influence their interior.

12. But besides the principle of change, there must be a *particular trait of what is changing*, which produces, so to speak, the specification and variety of the simple substances.

13. This particular must comprehend a multiplicity in the unity, that is, in the simple. For since all natural change proceeds by degrees, something changes and something remains. Consequently, there must be in the simple substance a plurality of affections and relations, though it has no parts.

Gottfried Wilhelm Von Leibniz, *Monadology and Other Philosophical Essays*, translated by Paul Schrecker and Anne Martin Schrecker (New York: Macmillan/Library of the Liberal Arts, 1965).

14. The passing state which comprehends and represents a multiplicity in the unity or simple substance is nothing but what is called *perception*; it must be clearly distinguished from apperception or consciousness, as will become clear later on. On this point the Cartesian doctrine has been very defective, since it has entirely neglected those perceptions which are not apperceived; the same failure to distinguish has made the Cartesians believe that only spirits are monads, and that there are neither animal souls nor other entelechies. Therefore, they, like the unlearned, have confused a long swoon with death, strictly speaking, and yielded to the scholastic prejudice that there are entirely separated souls. The same error has even confirmed unsound minds in the opinion that souls are mortal.

15. The action of the internal principle which produces change, that is, the passage from one perception to another, may be called *appetition*. It is true that appetition may not always entirely attain the whole perception toward which it tends, but it always obtains something and arrives at new perceptions.

16. We ourselves experience a multiplicity in the simple substance, when we observe that the least thought which we apperceive in ourselves comprehends a variety in its object. Thus, all those who recognize that the soul is a simple substance must recognize this multiplicity in the monad. Pierre Bayle should not have found a difficulty in this theory, as he indeed did in the article "Rorarius" of his *Dictionary*.

17. Moreover, it must be avowed that *perception* and what depends upon it *cannot possibly be explained by mechanical reasons*, that is, by figure and movement. Suppose that there be a machine, the structure of which produces thinking, feeling, and perceiving; imagine this machine enlarged but preserving the same proportions, so that you could enter it as if it were a mill. This being supposed, you might visit its inside; but what would you observe there? Nothing but parts which push and move each other, and never anything that could explain perception. This explanation must therefore be sought in the simple substance, not in the composite, that is, in the machine. However, there is nothing else to be found in the simple substance but perceptions and their changes. In this alone can consist all the *internal actions* of simple substances.

18. The name *entelechies* would fit all the simple substances or created monads. For they have in themselves a certain perfection *[echousi to enteles]*, and they are endowed with a selfsufficiency *[autarkeia]* which makes them the sources of their own actions and, so to speak, incorporeal automata.

19. If we want to call *soul* all that has perception and appetition, in the general sense explained above, we might give the name soul to all simple substances or created monads. But since sensation is something more than a simple perception, I agree that the general name monad or entelechy may suffice for those simple substances which have nothing but perception and appetition; the name souls may then be reserved for those having perception that is more distinct and is accompanied by memory.

20. Indeed, we experience in ourselves a state in which we remember nothing and have no distinct perception at all, e.g., when we faint or are overcome by a deep and dreamless sleep. In this state the soul is not noticeably different from a simple monad. However, since this state does not last, the soul being able to pull itself out of it, the soul is more than a simple monad.

21. Besides, it does not follow at all that in such a state the simple substance entirely lacks perception. For the reasons propounded a while ago, this lack is not possible; for the monad cannot perish, nor can it subsist without some affection, which is nothing but its perception. But when there is a great multitude of minute perceptions lacking distinctness, one becomes dizzy: for example, when you turn around several

consecutive times, you get a vertigo which may make you faint and leave you without any distinct perception. Death may throw animals into such a state for a time.

22. The present state of a simple substance is the natural result of its precedent state, so much so that the present is pregnant with the future.

23. Therefore, since on awakening from such a swoon, you apperceive your perceptions, it follows that you must have had some perceptions immediately before, though you did not apperceive them. For a perception cannot come naturally except from another perception, just as movement cannot come naturally except from another movement.

24. Hence it is evident that if in our perceptions there were nothing distinct nor anything, so to speak, in relief and of a more marked taste, we would always be in a swoon. And that is the state of the mere naked monads.

25. We see indeed that nature has given distinct perceptions to the animals, for care has been taken to provide them with organs which collect several light rays or several air waves, to unite them and thereby give them greater effect. Something similar occurs in scent, taste, and touch, and perhaps in many other senses unknown to us. I shall explain soon how what occurs in the soul represents what occurs in the sense organs.

26. Memory provides the souls with a sort of *consistency* which imitates reason but has to be distinguished from it. For we see that animals, perceiving something which impresses them and of which they have previously had a resembling perception, are brought by the representation of their memory to expect what has been associated with this perception in the past and are moved to feelings similar to those they had then. If you show a stick to a dog, for instance, it remembers the pain caused by it and howls or runs away.

27. The vividness of the imagination which strikes and moves animals comes from either the strength or the frequency of preceding perceptions. For often one strong impression produces at once the effect of a long *habit* or of many reiterated impressions of minor strength.

28. Men act like animals in so far as the succession of their perceptions is brought about by the principle of memory. In this they resemble medical empiricists whose practice is not backed by theory. In fact, we are mere empiricists in three quarters of all our actions. If you expect, for instance, that the sun will rise tomorrow because up to now it has always happened, you act as an empiricist. The astronomer alone judges by reason.

29. Knowledge of necessary and eternal truths, however, distinguishes us from mere animals and grants us *reason* and the sciences, elevating us to the knowledge of ourselves and of God. This possession is what is called our reasonable soul or *spirit*.

30. By this knowledge of necessary truths and by the abstractions made possible through them, we also are raised to *acts of reflection* which enable us to think of the so-called *self* and to consider this or that to be in us. Thinking thus about ourselves, we think of being, substance, the simple and the composite, the immaterial, and even of God, conceiving what is limited in us as without limit in him. These acts of reflection furnish the principal objects of our reasoning.

31. Our reasoning is founded on two great principles: The first is the principle of *contradiction*, by virtue of which we consider as false what implies a contradiction and as true what is the opposite of the contradictory or false.

32. The second is the principle of *sufficient reason*, by virtue of which we hold that no fact can be true or existing and no statement truthful without a sufficient reason for its being so and not different; albeit these reasons most frequently must remain unknown to us.

33. There are also two kinds of *truths*: those of *reason*, which are necessary and of which the opposite is impossible, and those of *fact*, which are contingent and of which the opposite is possible. When a truth is necessary, the reasons for it can be found through analysis, that is, by resolving it into simpler ideas and truths until one comes to primitives.

34. Thus the mathematicians, using the analytical method, reduce the speculative theorems and the practical canons to *definitions*, *axioms*, and *postulates*.

35. In the end, there are simple ideas of which no definition can be given. Moreover, there are axioms and postulates, in short, *primitive principles*, which cannot be demonstrated and do not need demonstration. They are *identical propositions*, the opposite of which contains an express contradiction.

36. A *sufficient reason*, however, must also exist for *contingent truths* or *truths of fact*, that is, for the series of things comprehended in the universe of creatures. Here the resolution into particular reasons could be continued without limit; for the variety of natural things is immense, and bodies are infinitely divided. There is an infinity of figures and movements, past and present, which contribute to the efficient cause of my presently writing this. And there is an infinity of minute inclinations and dispositions of my soul, which contribute to the final cause of my writing.

37. Now, all of this detail implies previous or more particular contingents, each of which again stands in need of a similar analysis to be accounted for, so that nothing is gained by such an analysis. The sufficient or ultimate reason must therefore exist outside the succession or series of contingent particulars, infinite though this series may be.

38. Consequently, the ultimate reason of all things must subsist in a necessary substance, in which all particular changes may exist only virtually as in its source: this substance is what we call *God*.

39. Now, this substance is the sufficient reason for all this particular existence which is, moreover, interconnected throughout. Hence, there is but one God, and this God suffices.

40. This Supreme Substance is unique, universal, and necessary. There is nothing existing apart from it which would be independent of it, and the existence of this being is a simple consequence of its possibility. It follows that this substance does not admit of any limitation and must contain as much reality as is possible.

41. God, therefore, is absolutely perfect, *perfection* meaning the quantity of positive reality. In things which have limits, that is, in finite things, this perfection has to be strictly interpreted, namely as the quantity of positive reality within their given limits. But where there are no limits, namely in God, perfection is absolutely infinite.

42. It follows that creatures owe their perfections to the divine influence, but their imperfections to their proper nature, which is incapable of being without limits. For it is in this that they are distinguished from God. The created things' *original imperfection* manifests itself through the *natural inertia* of all bodies.

43. Moreover, it is true that in God is the source not only of all existence, but also of all essence endowed with reality, that is, the source of what is real in the possibles. For the divine understanding is the region of the eternal truths and of the ideas on which they depend, and without him there would not be anything real in the possibles; that is, without him there would not only be nothing existing, but even nothing possible.

44. Indeed, if there is to be any reality in the essences or possibles, that is, in the necessary truths, this reality must be founded on the existence of the necessary being whose essence implies its existence, that is, to which it suffices to be possible in order to be actual.

45. Thus God alone (or the necessary being) has the privilege of existing necessarily, provided only he be possible. Now, since nothing can hinder the possibility of the substance which contains no limits, no negation, and hence no contradiction, this provides a sufficient reason for the knowledge *a priori* of God's existence. Besides, we have proved it by the reality of the eternal truths. In addition, we also have proved this existence *a posteriori* by the existence of contingent beings. For the sufficient and ultimate reason of these can lie only in the necessary being which has in itself the reason of its existence.

46. It must not be imagined, however, as certain authors have imagined, that since the eternal truths depend upon God, they are arbitrary and depend upon his will. Descartes seems to have thought so, and after him Poiret. This is true only of the contingent truths which are based on the principle of fitness, that is, the choice of the best possible; while the necessary truths depend only on his understanding, of which they are the internal object.

47. Thus God is the only primitive unit or the only original simple substance, of which all the created or derivative monads are the products, born, so to speak, every moment by continual fulgurations from the divinity, and limited by the capacities of creatures, to which limitation is essential.

48. In God there are his *power* which is the source of everything, his *knowledge* which contains the particulars of the ideas, and finally his *will* which is the source of change or production and acts according to the principle of the best possible. Corresponding to these divine attributes, there is in the created monads the subject or basis, namely, the faculty of perception and the faculty of appetition. In God, however, these attributes are absolutely infinite and perfect, whereas in the created monads or *entelechies* (Hermolaus Barbarus translated this word into Latin by *perfectihabies*) these attributes are only likenesses, possessed by the monads in proportion to their perfections.

49. Creatures are said to act outwardly in so far as they have perfection, and to *suffer* from other creatures in so far as they are imperfect. Thus *activity* has to be attributed to the monad in so far as it has distinct perceptions, and passivity in so far as it has confused perceptions.

50. One creature is more perfect than another, in so far as there is found in the former a reason to account *a priori* for what is happening in the latter; this is why one says that the former acts upon the latter.

51. But in the simple substances this influence of one monad upon the other is but *ideal* and can take effect only through the intervention of God; in the ideas of God, indeed, any monad reasonably requires that in his ruling of all others, God, from the beginning, take that monad into consideration. For since no created monad can exercise a physical influence upon the interior of any other, this is the only means by which the one can depend upon the other.

52. By this means actions and passions among creatures are mutual. For when God compares two simple substances, he finds in either one reasons which oblige him to adjust the other to it. What appears as active in certain respects, consequently appears as passive from another point of view: it appears as *active* in so far as what is distinctly known in one monad serves to account for what happens in another; it appears as passive in so far as the reason for what happens in it is to be found in what is distinctly known in another.

53. Now, since in the divine ideas there is an infinity of possible universes of which only one can exist, the choice made by God must have a sufficient reason which determines him to the one rather than to another.

54. This reason can be found only in fitness, that is, in the degree of perfection contained in these worlds. For each possible has a right to claim existence in proportion to the perfection it involves. Thus nothing is entirely arbitrary.

55. This is the cause for the existence of the best, which is disclosed to him by his wisdom, determines his choice by his goodness, and is produced by his power.

56. This *connection* of all created things with every single one of them and their adaptation to every single one, as well as the connection and adaptation of every single thing to all others, has the result that every single substance stands in relations which express all the others. Whence every single substance is a perpetual living mirror of the universe.

57. Just as the same city regarded from different sides offers quite different aspects, and thus appears multiplied *by the perspective*, so it also happens that the infinite multitude of simple substances creates the appearance of as many different universes. Yet they are but perspectives of a single universe, varied according to the *points of view*, which differ in each monad.

58. This is the means of obtaining the greatest possible variety, together with the greatest possible order; in other words, it is the means of obtaining as much perfection as possible.

59. Only by this hypothesis (which I dare to call demonstrated) can the greatness of God be exalted as it ought to be. Pierre Bayle has recognized this when he objected to the hypothesis in the article "Rorarius" of his *Dictionary*. In that passage he was inclined to believe that I attributed to God too much, and even more than is possible. But he was unable to adduce any reason why this universal harmony, due to which every substance exactly expresses all the others through the relations it has with them, should be impossible.

60. In what I have just stated, there can also be discerned reasons *a priori* why things could not be different. For God, legislating the whole, has considered every part and particularly every monad. And since the nature of every monad is representative, there is nothing which could limit it to representing only a part of all things. It is true, however, that this representation is but confused concerning the particulars of the whole universe and can be distinct concerning only a small part of all things, namely those which are either the nearest or the largest in respect to each of the monads. For otherwise every monad would be a deity. It is not in the objects of their knowledge, but in the modes of this knowledge that the monads are limited. All of them have a confused knowledge of the infinite, that is, of the whole; but they are limited and distinguished by the degrees of distinct perception.

61. The composite substances are in this respect symbols of the simples. For since all is a plenum, all matter is connected and all movement in the plenum produces some effect on the distant bodies, in proportion to the distance. Hence every body is affected not only by those with which it is in contact, and thus feels in some way everything that happens to them; but through them it also feels those that touch the ones with which it is in immediate contact. Hence it follows that this communication extends over any distance whatever. Consequently, every body experiences everything that goes on in the universe, so much so that he who sees everything might read in any body what is happening anywhere, and even what has happened or will happen. He would be able to observe in the present what is remote in both time and space: [*sumpnoia panta*], as Hippocrates stated. A soul, however, can read in itself only what is distinctly represented in it; it is unable to unfold all at once all its folds; for these go on into infinity.

62. Thus, every created monad represents the whole universe; nevertheless, it represents more distinctly the body which is particularly attached to it and of which it

is the entelechy. And since this body expresses the whole universe through the interconnection of all the matter in the plenum, the soul, too, represents the whole universe by representing this body which in a particular manner belongs to it.

63. The body belonging to a monad which is its entelechy or its soul constitutes, together with this entelechy, what may be called a *living unit*, and together with this soul what may be called an *animal*. This body of a living being or of an animal is always an organism. For since every monad is, in its way, a mirror of the universe, and since the universe is ruled in a perfect order, there must also be an order in the representing, that is, in the perceptions of the soul, and consequently in the body. The representation of the universe in the body evinces this order.

64. Thus every body of a living being is a sort of divine machine or natural automaton, which infinitely surpasses all artificial automata. For a machine made by human art is not a machine in all its parts. The cog on a brass wheel, for instance, has parts or fragments which for us are no longer artificial things, and are no longer proper to the machine with respect to the purpose for which the wheel was designed. The machines of nature (namely, the living bodies) are, on the contrary, machines even in their smallest parts without any limit. Herein lies the difference between nature and art, that is, between divine and human art.

65. The author of nature, indeed, has been able to practice this divine and infinitely marvellous art because any portion of matter is not only infinitely divisible, as the ancients recognized, but also actually subdivided *ad infinitum*: every part having parts each of which has its own particular movement. For otherwise it would be impossible for every portion of matter to express the whole universe.

66. Hence it can be seen that in the smallest portion of matter there is a world of creatures, living beings, animals, entelechies, and souls.

67. Thus every portion of matter can be conceived as a garden full of plants or as a pond full of fish. But every branch of the plant, every limb of the animal, every drop of its humors, is again such a garden or such a pond.

68. And though the soil and the air in the intervals between the plants of the garden is not a plant, nor the water between the fishes a fish, yet these intervals contain again plants or fishes. But these living beings most frequently are so minute that they remain imperceptible to us.

69. Thus there is nothing uncultured, sterile or dead in the universe, no chaos, no disorder, though this may be what appears. It would be about the same with a pond seen from a distance: you would perceive a confused movement, a squirming of fishes, if I may say so, without discerning the single fish.

70. Hence it becomes clear that every living body has a dominant entelechy which in an animal is its soul. But the limbs of this living body are full of other living beings, plants or animals, each of which again has its entelechy or its dominant soul.

71. But you must not imagine—like some authors who have misinterpreted my thought—that each soul has a mass or portion of matter forever belonging or attached to it and that, consequently, it owns other living, though inferior, beings forever destined to serve it. For all bodies are, like rivers, in a perpetual flux; small parts enter and leave them continually.

72. Thus the soul changes its body bit by bit, and by degrees, so that it never is deprived all at once of all its organs; in animals there is frequently metamorphosis. Never, however, is there metempsychosis nor transmigration of souls. Nor are there any totally separate *souls*, nor *genii* without body. God alone is entirely bodiless.

73. This also proves that, strictly speaking, there never is either complete generation or perfect death, which would consist in the separation of the soul. What we call

generation consists in developments and growths, just as what we call *death* consists in involutions and diminutions.

74. Philosophers formerly have been very perplexed concerning the origin of forms, entelechies, or souls. Today, however, it has been discovered through precise observations made on plants, insects, and animals that the organized bodies of nature are never produced out of a chaos or putrefaction, but always out of seeds, in which doubtless there has been some *preformation*. Hence it has been concluded, not only that the organized body was already in the seed before conception, but also that there was a soul in this body, and, in short, the animal itself. Through the conception, furthermore, the animal has only been disposed to a great transformation, namely to become an animal of a different species. Something similar can even be observed outside generation, as, for instance, when worms become flies, or caterpillars butterflies.

75. Those animals among which some are elevated by means of the conception to the grade of larger animals, may be called *spermatic*; while those among them which remain within their species, that is, the majority, are born, multiply, and are destroyed like the large animals. Only a small number of elect pass on to a greater stage.

76. This, so far, has been but half the truth. Therefore I have concluded that if it be true that the animal never begins naturally, it will not end naturally either, and that consequently there will be, strictly speaking, neither generation nor entire destruction, that is, death. These arguments made a posteriori and drawn from experience agree perfectly with my principles deduced *a priori* a while ago.

77. Thus it may be said that not only the soul (mirror of an indestructible universe) is indestructible, but also that the animal itself is indestructible, albeit its machine often partly perishes, and casts off or takes on organic accretions.

78. These principles have enabled me to propose a natural explanation for the union or conformity of the soul and the organized body. The soul follows its own laws, and so does the body. They meet by virtue of the *pre-established harmony* prevailing among all substances, since they all are representations of one and the same universe.

79. The souls act according to the laws of final causes, through appetitions, ends, and means. The bodies act according to the laws of efficient causes, that is, of motion. And the two realms, that of efficient causes and that of final causes, are in mutual harmony.

80. Descartes has recognized that souls cannot impart force to bodies, because there is always the same quantity of force in matter. He believed, however, that the soul was able to change the directions of bodies. For at his time it was unknown yet that there is a law of nature according to which the total direction of matter is equally conserved. If he had been aware of this, he would have hit upon my system of pre-established harmony.

81. This system maintains that bodies act as though there were no souls (assuming the impossible); and that souls act as though there were no bodies; and that both act as though the one influenced the other.

82. As to *spirits* or reasonable souls, I find that essentially all the living beings and animals have the same nature, as I have said before, namely that the animal and the soul begin with the world and end no more than the world. Nevertheless, the reasonable souls have this in particular, that their little spermatic animals have only ordinary or sensitive souls, as long as they remain undeveloped. As soon, however, as those who, so to speak, are elected attain human nature through an actual conception, their sensitive souls are promoted to the rank of human nature and to the prerogative of spirits.

83. Among other differences existing between ordinary souls and spirits, some of which I have already pointed out, there is also this one, that souls in general are living

mirrors or images of the created universe, while the spirits are in addition the images of the Deity itself or of the author of nature himself. They are capable of knowing the system of the universe and of imitating some of it by architectonic specimens, each spirit being like a small deity in his field.

84. This is the reason why the spirits are capable of entering a kind of society with God, and why with respect to them he is not only as an inventor is to his machine (this being the relation of God to the other creatures), but also as a prince to his subjects and even as a father to his children.

85. Hence it may easily be concluded that the assemblage of all the spirits must compose the City of God, that is, the most perfect city possible, under the most perfect monarch possible.

86. This City of God, this truly universal monarchy, is a moral world within the natural world; it is among the works of God the most exalted and the most divine. In it consists veritably the glory of God: for he would be without glory unless his greatness and goodness were recognized and admired by the spirits. Properly speaking, his goodness is directed toward this divine City, while his wisdom and power manifest themselves everywhere.

87. We have established above the perfect harmony between two natural realms, that of efficient causes and the other of final causes. To this we must add here still another harmony, namely, between the physical realm of nature and the moral realm of grace, that is, between God considered as the architect of the machine of the universe, and God considered as the monarch of the divine city of the spirits.

88. This harmony has the result that events lead to grace through the very processes of nature, and that our globe, for instance, must be destroyed and repaired through natural processes at the moments when the government of the spirits so demands, to chastise some and to reward others.

89. One may add that God as the architect satisfies in all respects God as the legislator. Thus sin must entail punishment according to the order of nature and as the very result of the mechanical structure of the universe; and, analogously, good actions will attract their rewards through machinelike corporeal processes. Of course, these results cannot be and ought not always to be obtained as an immediate consequence.

90. Finally, under this perfect government, no good action will remain without its reward, no evil action without its punishment. All events in this city conspire to the advantage of the good people, that is, of those who are not discontented in this great State; who, once they have fulfilled their duties, trust in providence and duly love and imitate the author of all good; who enjoy the contemplation of his perfections as required by the nature of the true *pure love*, which consists in taking pleasure in the felicity of the beloved. This pure love makes the wise and virtuous people work at everything that seems conformable to the divine will, presumed or antecedent, and yet renders them contented with any event that God actually brings about through his secret, consequent, and decisive will. They realize that, could we only understand sufficiently the order of the universe, we should find that this order surpasses all the wishes of the wisest and that it is impossible to improve it; that it is the best not only for the whole in general, but also for ourselves in particular. For ourselves, that is, provided we are duly attached to the author of all things, not only as to the architect and efficient cause of our being, but also as to the master and to the final cause who ought to provide the sole goal of our will and who alone can give us happiness.

GEORGE BERKELEY
1685–1753

George Berkeley was born near Kilkenny, Ireland, and, although an Anglican of English descent, he emphatically considered himself to be Irish. He studied at Kilkenny College and in 1700 went on to Trinity College, Dublin. There he read Descartes, Newton, and Locke. In 1707, he became a Fellow of the College and was ordained in the Anglican church. The next six years were to be the most philosophically productive in his life. In 1709, he published his *New Theory of Vision,* and in the following year his most important philosophic work, *A Treatise Concerning the Principles of Human Knowledge.* In 1711, he wrote *Discourse on Passive Obedience.* Two years later, he published a more popular exposition of the doctrine of his *Principles* in the form of *Three Dialogues Between Hylas and Philonous.*

For the next eleven years, Berkeley traveled widely, visiting with many of the great thinkers of his day. He became Dean of Derry in 1724, though most of his energy at this time seems to have been given to the founding of a college in the Bermudas. With promises of financial support, he sailed for Rhode Island in 1728 to establish farms for supplying his future college with food. Berkeley spent two and a half years in Rhode Island with his new wife and friends, waiting for the twenty-thousand pounds the government had promised. When the funds never arrived, he finally gave up and returned to London.

In 1733, he published *Alciphron, or The Minute Philosopher,* against the free-thinkers (agnostics), and in the following year *The Analyst,* a criticism of Newton. That same year, he was made Bishop of Cloyne. For the next eighteen years, he energetically served his remote, poor diocese. Among the works he wrote during this period are *The Querist* (1737), which used questions to propose public works and education as remedies to the crushing poverty he observed, and *Siris* (1744), an unusual work dealing with the medicinal value of tar water. In 1751, he lost his eldest son, and the next year he moved to Oxford, where another son was beginning his studies. On January 14, 1753, Berkeley died suddenly; he was buried at Christ Church, Oxford.

*   *   *

Like Locke before him, Berkeley accepted the empiricist doctrine that all we can know are ideas and that ideas come from perception or reflection. But Berkeley saw a problem in Locke's assertion of an external world of material "substances" giving rise to perceptions. If all we can know are ideas, how can we know there is a world "out there" giving rise to our ideas? Locke had said that the primary qualities of an "external object" (such as extension and solidity) are "utterly inseparable" from the objects themselves, whereas this is not the case with secondary qualities (such as color, taste, etc.). But again, asked Berkeley, how can Locke know this? He cannot get "outside himself" to see which of his perceptions are actually a part of objects "out there." Berkeley concluded that Locke's philosophy will lead to skepticism, whereby we must admit that we cannot really know anything about the world "out there."

To avoid this skepticism, Berkeley made the radical claim that there is no "out there," or, more precisely, there is no *matter*. Berkeley's position, which is called "idealism," can be summed up in his famous phrase "*esse* is *percipi*": to be is to be perceived. What we call "bodies," or physical objects, are simply stable collections of perceptions to which we give names such as "apples," "trees," and so on. These collections of perceptions have no existence apart from a perceiving mind. The answer to the famous conundrum "If a tree falls in the forest and no one hears it, does it make a sound?" is that if no one is perceiving it, it not only does not make a sound, the tree does not even exist!

Does this mean that trees go out of existence when no one is left in the forest to perceive them and that they come back into existence when someone enters the forest to perceive them again? It would seem that Berkeley must accept this odd conclusion were it not for one important point: God never leaves the forest, and God is *always* perceiving the trees. By always holding all collections of perceptions in the divine mind, God ensures their continued existence and the perceived regularity in what we call "nature." This point has been classically formulated in the following limericks:

> There was a young man who said, "God,
> Must think it exceedingly odd
> If he finds that this tree
> Continues to be
> When there's no one about in the Quad."

> REPLY:
> "Dear Sir: Your astonishment's odd:
> I am always about in the Quad.
> And that's why the tree
> Continues to be,
> Since observed by, Yours faithfully, God."

Berkeley saw his philosophy as a common-sense attack on the metaphysical excesses of medieval Scholastics, Continental Rationalists, and even fellow empiricists such as Hobbes and Locke. Although Berkeley understood his philosophy to be common sense, his readers drew different conclusions. One prominent physician of his day claimed Berkeley was insane. The great Dr. Samuel Johnson dismissed Berkeley's ideas with his famous "I refute Berkeley *thus*" and then he kicked a rock. Of course, this did not refute Berkeley at all. It only proved Johnson had not understood Berkeley's point. Berkeley did not claim the non-existence of stones or that kicking a stone will not produce sensation. He claimed the rock did not exist apart from the perception of its solidity or the perception of pain when struck, and so on. An oft-repeated epitaph summarizes the general reaction to Berkeley: "His arguments produce no conviction, though they cannot be refuted."

*　　*　　*

Berkeley's major work, *A Treatise Concerning the Principles of Human Knowledge*, is reprinted here (complete) using the revised text of 1734.

For general introductions to Berkeley, see G.J. Warnock, *Berkeley* (Harmondsworth, Middlesex: Penguin Books, 1953); Harry M. Bracken, *Berkeley* (New York: St. Martin's Press, 1974); J.O. Urmson, *Berkeley* (Oxford: Oxford University Press, 1982)—part of the Past Masters series, now reprinted in the combined volume John Dunn et al., eds., *The British Empiricists* (Oxford: Oxford University Press, 1992); and David Berman, *George Berkeley: Idealism and the Man* (Oxford: Oxford University Press, 1994). For interesting but difficult discussions of Berkeley's arguments, see George Pitcher, *Berkeley* (London: Routledge, 1977) or Kenneth Winkler, *Berkeley: An Interpretation* (Oxford: Oxford University Press, 1989). For collections of essays, see Gale W. Engle and Gabriele Taylor, eds., *Berkeley's Principles of Human Knowledge* (Belmont, CA: Wadsworth, 1968); Colin M. Turbayne, ed., *Berkeley: Critical and Interpretive Essays* (Minneapolis: University of Minnesota Press, 1982); John Foster and Howard Robinson, eds., *Essays on Berkeley: A Tercentennial Celebration* (Oxford: Oxford University Press, 1985); and D.M. Armstrong and C.B. Martin, *Berkeley: A Collection of Critical Essays* (Hamden, CT: Garland, 1992)—a reprint of the second half of *Locke and Berkeley: A Collection of Critical Essays* (Garden City, NY: Doubleday, 1968).

A TREATISE CONCERNING
THE PRINCIPLES OF HUMAN KNOWLEDGE

Preface

What I here make public has, after a long and scrupulous inquiry, seemed to me evidently true and not unuseful to be known—particularly to those who are tainted with Scepticism, or want a demonstration of the existence and immateriality of God, or the natural immortality of the soul. Whether it be so or no I am content the reader should impartially examine; since I do not think myself any farther concerned for the success of what I have written than as it is agreeable to truth. But, to the end this may not suffer, I make it my request that the reader suspend his judgment till he has once at least read the whole through with that degree of attention and thought which the subject-matter shall seem to deserve. For, as there are some passages that, taken by themselves, are very liable (nor could it be remedied) to gross misinterpretation, and to be charged with most absurd consequences, which, nevertheless, upon an entire perusal will appear not to follow from them; so likewise, though the whole should be read over, yet, if this be done transiently, it is very probable my sense may be mistaken; but to a thinking reader, I flatter myself it will be throughout clear and obvious. As for the characters of novelty and singularity which some of the following notions may seem to bear, it is, I hope, needless to make any apology on that account. He must surely be either very weak, or very little acquainted with the sciences, who shall reject a truth that is capable of demonstration, for no other reason but because it is newly known, and contrary to the prejudices of mankind. Thus much I thought fit to premise, in order to prevent, if possible, the hasty censures of a sort of men who are too apt to condemn an opinion before they rightly comprehend it.

INTRODUCTION

1. Philosophy being nothing else but the study of wisdom and truth, it may with reason be expected that those who have spent most time and pains in it should enjoy a greater calm and serenity of mind, a greater clearness and evidence of knowledge, and be less disturbed with doubts and difficulties than other men. Yet so it is, we see the illiterate bulk of mankind that walk the high-road of plain common sense, and are governed by the dictates of nature, for the most part easy and undisturbed. To them nothing that is familiar appears unaccountable or difficult to comprehend. They complain not of any want of evidence in their senses, and are out of all danger of becoming Sceptics. But no sooner do we depart from sense and instinct to follow the light of a superior principle, to reason, meditate, and reflect on the nature of things, but a thousand scruples spring up in our minds concerning those things which before we seemed fully to comprehend. Prejudices and errors of sense do from all parts discover themselves to our view; and, endeavouring to correct these by reason, we are insensibly drawn into uncouth paradoxes, difficulties, and inconsistencies, which multiply and grow upon us as we advance in speculation, till at length, having wandered through many intricate mazes, we find ourselves just where we were, or, which is worse, sit down in a forlorn Scepticism.

2. The cause of this is thought to be the obscurity of things, or the natural weakness and imperfection of our understandings. It is said, the faculties we have are few, and those designed by nature for the support and comfort of life, and not to penetrate into the inward essence and constitution of things. Besides, the mind of man being finite, when it treats of things which partake of infinity, it is not to be wondered at if it run into absurdities and contradictions, out of which it is impossible it should ever extricate itself, it being of the nature of infinite not to be comprehended by that which is finite.

3. But, perhaps, we may be too partial to ourselves in placing the fault originally in our faculties, and not rather in the wrong use we make of them. It is a hard thing to

suppose that right deductions from true principles should ever end in consequences which cannot be maintained or made consistent. We should believe that God has dealt more bountifully with the sons of men than to give them a strong desire for that knowledge which he had placed quite out of their reach. This were not agreeable to the wonted indulgent methods of Providence, which, whatever appetites it may have implanted in the creatures, doth usually furnish them with such means as, if rightly made use of, will not fail to satisfy them. Upon the whole, I am inclined to think that the far greater part, if not all, of those difficulties which have hitherto amused philosophers, and blocked up the way to knowledge, are entirely owing to ourselves—that we have first raised a dust and then complain we cannot see.

4. My purpose therefore is, to try if I can discover what those Principles are which have introduced all that doubtfulness and uncertainty, those absurdities and contradictions, into the several sects of philosophy; insomuch that the wisest men have thought our ignorance incurable, conceiving it to arise from the natural dulness and limitation of our faculties. And surely it is a work well deserving our pains to make a strict inquiry concerning the First Principles of Human Knowledge, to sift and examine them on all sides, especially since there may be some grounds to suspect that those lets and difficulties, which stay and embarrass the mind in its search after truth, do not spring from any darkness and intricacy in the objects, or natural defect in the understanding, so much as from false Principles which have been insisted on, and might have been avoided.

5. How difficult and discouraging soever this attempt may seem, when I consider how many great and extraordinary men have gone before me in the like designs, yet I am not without some hopes—upon the consideration that the largest views are not always the clearest, and that he who is short-sighted will be obliged to draw the object nearer, and may, perhaps, by a close and narrow survey, discern that which had escaped far better eyes.

6. In order to prepare the mind of the reader for the easier conceiving what follows, it is proper to premise somewhat, by way of Introduction, concerning the nature and abuse of Language. But the unravelling this matter leads me in some measure to anticipate my design, by taking notice of what seems to have had a chief part in rendering speculation intricate and perplexed, and to have occasioned innumerable errors and difficulties in almost all parts of knowledge. And that is the opinion that the mind hath a power of framing *abstract ideas* or notions of things. He who is not a perfect stranger to the writings and disputes of philosophers must needs acknowledge that no small part of them are spent about abstract ideas. These are in a more especial manner thought to be the object of those sciences which go by the name of Logic and Metaphysics, and of all that which passes under the notion of the most abstracted and sublime learning, in all which one shall scarce find any question handled in such a manner as does not suppose their existence in the mind, and that it is well acquainted with them.

7. It is agreed on all hands that the qualities or modes of things do never really exist each of them apart by itself, and separated from all others, but are mixed, as it were, and blended together, several in the same object. But, we are told, the mind being able to consider each quality singly, or abstracted from those other qualities with which it is united, does by that means frame to itself abstract ideas. For example, there is perceived by sight an object extended, coloured, and moved: this mixed or compound idea the mind resolving into its simple, constituent parts, and viewing each by itself, exclusive of the rest, does frame the abstract ideas of extension, colour, and motion. Not that it is possible for colour or motion to exist without extension; but only that the mind can frame to itself by *abstraction* the idea of colour exclusive of extension, and of motion exclusive of both colour and extension.

8. Again, the mind having observed that in the particular extensions perceived by sense there is something common and alike in all, and some other things peculiar, as this or that figure or magnitude, which distinguish them one from another; it considers apart or singles out by itself that which is common, making thereof a most abstract idea of extension, which is neither line surface, nor solid, nor has any figure or magnitude, but is an idea entirely prescinded from all these. So likewise the mind, by leaving out of the particular colours perceived by sense that which distinguishes them one from another, and retaining that only which is common to all, makes an idea of colour in abstract which is neither red nor blue, nor white, nor any other determinate colour. And, in like manner, by considering motion abstractedly not only from the body moved, but likewise from the figure it describes, and all particular directions and velocities, the abstract idea of motion is framed; which equally corresponds to all particular motions whatsoever that may be perceived by sense.

9. And as the mind frames to itself abstract ideas of qualities or modes, so does it, by the same precision or mental separation, attain abstract ideas of the more compounded beings which include several coexistent qualities. For example, the mind having observed that Peter, James, and John resemble each other in certain common agreements of shape and other qualities, leaves out of the complex or compounded idea it has of Peter, James, and any other particular man, that which is peculiar to each, retaining only what is common to all, and so makes an abstract idea wherein all the particulars equally partake—abstracting entirely from and cutting off all those circumstances and differences which might determine it to any particular existence. And after this manner it is said we come by the abstract idea of man, or, if you please, humanity, or human nature; wherein it is true there is included colour, because there is no man but has some colour, but then it can be neither white, nor black, nor any particular colour, because there is no one particular colour wherein all men partake. So likewise there is included stature, but then it is neither tall stature, nor low stature, nor yet middle stature, but something abstracted from all these. And so of the rest. Moreover, there being a great variety of other creatures that partake in some parts, but not all, of the complex idea of man, the mind, leaving out those parts which are peculiar to men, and retaining those only which are common to all the living creatures, frames the idea of *animal*, which abstracts not only from all particular men, but also all: birds, beasts, fishes, and insects. The constituent parts of the abstract idea of animal are body, life, sense, and spontaneous motion. By *body* is meant body without any particular shape or figure, there being no one shape or figure common to all animals, without covering, either of hair, or feathers, or scales, etc., nor yet naked: hair, feathers, scales, and nakedness being the distinguishing properties of particular animals, and for that reason left out of the *abstract idea*. Upon the same account the spontaneous motion must be neither walking, nor flying, nor creeping; it is nevertheless a motion, but what that motion is it is not easy to conceive.

10. Whether others have this wonderful faculty of abstracting their ideas, they best can tell: for myself, I find indeed I have a faculty of imagining, or representing to myself, the ideas of those particular things I have perceived, and of variously compounding and dividing them. I can imagine a man with two heads, or the upper parts of a man joined to the body of a horse. I can consider the hand, the eye, the nose, each by itself abstracted or separated from the rest of the body. But then whatever hand or eye I imagine, it must have some particular shape and colour. Likewise the idea of man that I frame to myself must be either of a white, or a black, or a tawny, a straight, or a crooked, a tall, or a low, or a middle-sized man. I cannot by any effort of thought conceive the abstract idea above described. And it is equally impossible for me to form the

abstract idea of motion distinct from the body moving, and which is neither swift nor slow, curvilinear nor rectilinear; and the like may be said of all other abstract general ideas whatsoever. To be plain, I own myself able to abstract in one sense, as when I consider some particular parts or qualities separated from others, with which, though they are united in some object, yet it is possible they may really exist without them. But I deny that I can abstract from one another, or conceive separately, those qualities which it is impossible should exist so separated; or that I can frame a general notion, by abstracting from particulars in the manner aforesaid—which last are the two proper acceptations of *abstraction*. And there are grounds to think most men will acknowledge themselves to be in my case. The generality of men which are simple and illiterate never pretend to *abstract notions*. It is said they are difficult and not to be attained without pains and study; we may therefore reasonably conclude that, if such there be, they are confined only to the learned.

11. I proceed to examine what can be alleged in defence of the doctrine of abstraction, and try if I can discover what it is that inclines the men of speculation to embrace an opinion so remote from common sense as that seems to be. There has been a late deservedly esteemed philosopher who, no doubt, has given it very much countenance, by seeming to think the having of abstract general ideas is what puts the widest difference in point of understanding betwixt man and beast. "The having of general ideas," saith he, "is that which puts a perfect distinction betwixt man and brutes, and is an excellency which the faculties of brutes do by no means attain unto. For, it is evident we observe no foot-steps in them of making use of general signs for universal ideas; from which we have reason to imagine that they have not the faculty of abstracting, or making general ideas, since they have no use of words or any other general signs." And a little after: "Therefore, I think, we may suppose that it is in this that the species of brutes are discriminated from men, and it is that proper difference wherein they are wholly separated, and which at last widens to so wide a distance. For, if they have any ideas at all, and are not bare machines (as some would have them), we cannot deny them to have some reason. It seems as evident to me that they do, some of them, in certain instances reason as that they have sense; but it is only in particular ideas, just as they receive them from their senses. They are the best of them tied up within those narrow bounds, and have not (as I think) the faculty to enlarge them by any kind of abstraction."—*Essay on Human Understanding*, Bk. II, Chap. xi, §§ 10 and 11. I readily agree with this learned author, that the faculties of brutes can by no means attain to abstraction. But then if this be made the distinguishing property of that sort of animals, I fear a great many of those that pass for men must be reckoned into their number. The reason that is here assigned why we have no grounds to think brutes have abstract general ideas is, that we observe in them no use of words or any other general signs; which is built on this supposition—that the making use of words implies the having general ideas. From which it follows that men who use language are able to abstract or generalize their ideas. That this is the sense and arguing of the author will further appear by his answering the question he in another place puts: "Since all things that exist are only particulars, how come we by general terms?" His answer is: "Words become general by being made the signs of general ideas."—*Essay on Human Understanding*, Bk. III, Chap. iii, § 6. But it seems that a word becomes general by being made the sign, not of an *abstract* general idea, but of several particular ideas, any one of which it indifferently suggests to the mind. For example, when it is said "the change of motion is proportional to the impressed force," or that "whatever has extension is divisible," these propositions are to be understood of motion and extension in general; and nevertheless it will not follow that they suggest to my thoughts an idea of motion without a body

moved, or any determinate direction and velocity, or that I must conceive an abstract general idea of extension, which is neither line, surface, nor solid, neither great nor small, black, white, nor red, nor of any other determinate colour. It is only implied that whatever particular motion I consider, whether it be swift or slow, perpendicular, horizontal, or oblique, or in whatever object, the axiom concerning it holds equally true. As does the other of every particular extension, it matters not whether line, surface, or solid, whether of this or that magnitude or figure.

12. By observing how ideas become general we may the better judge how words are made so. And here it is to be noted that I do not deny absolutely there are general ideas, but only that there are any abstract general ideas; for, in the passages we have quoted wherein there is mention of general ideas, it is always supposed that they are formed by abstraction, after the manner set forth in sections 8 and 9. Now, if we will annex a meaning to our words, and speak only of what we can conceive, I believe we shall acknowledge that an idea which, considered in itself, is particular, becomes general by being made to represent or stand for all other particular ideas of the same sort. To make this plain by an example, suppose a geometrician is demonstrating the method of cutting a line in two equal parts. He draws, for instance a black line of an inch in length: this, which in itself is a particular line, is nevertheless with regard to its signification general, since, as it is there used, it represents all particular lines whatsoever; so that what is demonstrated of it is demonstrated of all lines, or, in other words, of a line in general. And, as that *particular* line becomes general by being made a sign, so the *name* "line," which taken absolutely is particular, by being a sign is made general. And as the former owes its generality not to its being the sign of an abstract or general line, but of all particular right lines that may possibly exist, so the latter must be thought to derive its generality from the same cause, namely, the various particular lines which it indifferently denotes.

13. To give the reader a yet clearer view of the nature of abstract ideas, and the uses they are thought necessary to, I shall add one more passage out of the *Essay on Human Understanding*, (Bk. IV, Chap. vii. § 9) which is as follows:

> *Abstract ideas* are not so obvious or easy to children or the yet unexercised mind as particular ones. If they seem so to grown men it is only because by constant and familiar use they are made so. For, when we nicely reflect upon them, we shall find that general ideas are fictions and contrivances of the mind, that carry difficulty with them, and do not so easily offer themselves as we are apt to imagine. For example, does it not require some pains and skill to form the general idea of a triangle (which is yet none of the most abstract, comprehensive, and difficult); for it must be neither oblique nor rectangle, neither equilateral, equicrural, nor scalenon, but *all and none* of these at once? In effect, it is something imperfect that cannot exist, an idea wherein some parts of several different and *inconsistent* ideas are put together. It is true the mind in this imperfect state has need of such ideas, and makes all the haste to them it can, for the conveniency of communication and enlargement of knowledge, to both which it is naturally very much inclined. But yet one has reason to suspect such ideas are marks of our imperfection. At least this is enough to show that the most abstract and general ideas are not those that the mind is first and most easily acquainted with, nor such as its earliest knowledge is conversant about.

If any man has the faculty of framing in his mind such an idea of a triangle as is here described, it is in vain to pretend to dispute him out of it, nor would I go about it. All I desire is that the reader would fully and certainly inform himself whether he has such an idea or no. And this, methinks, can be no hard task for anyone to perform. What more easy than for anyone to look a little into his own thoughts, and there try whether he has, or can attain to have, an idea that shall correspond with the description that is here given of the general idea of a triangle, which is "neither oblique nor rectangle, equilateral, equicrural nor scalenon, but all and none of these at once?"

14. Much is here said of the difficulty that abstract ideas carry with them, and the pains and skill requisite to the forming them. And it is on all hands agreed that there is need of great toil and labour of the mind, to emancipate our thoughts from particular objects, and raise them to those sublime speculations that are conversant about abstract ideas. From all which the natural consequence should seem to be, that so difficult a thing as the forming abstract ideas was not necessary for *communication*, which is so easy and familiar to all sorts of men. But, we are told, if they seem obvious and easy to grown men, it is only because by constant and familiar use they are made so. Now, I would fain know at what time it is men are employed in surmounting that difficulty, and furnishing themselves with those necessary helps for discourse. It cannot be when they are grown up, for then it seems they are not conscious of any such painstaking; it remains therefore to be the business of their childhood. And surely the great and multiplied labour of framing abstract notions will be found a hard task for that tender age. Is it not a hard thing to imagine that a couple of children cannot prate together of their sugar-plums and rattles and the rest of their little trinkets, till they have first tacked together numberless inconsistencies, and so framed in their minds abstract general ideas, and annexed them to every common name they make use of?

15. Nor do I think them a whit more needful for the *enlargement of knowledge* than for *communication*. It is, I know, a point much insisted on, that all knowledge and demonstration are about universal notions, to which I fully agree: but then it doth not appear to me that those notions are formed by abstraction in the manner premised— *universality*, so far as I can comprehend, not consisting in the absolute, positive nature or conception of anything, but in the relation it bears to the particulars signified or represented by it; by virtue whereof it is that things, names, or notions, being in their own nature *particular*, are rendered *universal*. Thus, when I demonstrate any proposition concerning triangles, it is to be supposed that I have in view the universal idea of a triangle; which ought not to be understood as if I could frame an idea of a triangle which was neither equilateral, nor scalenon, nor equicrural; but only that the particular triangle I consider, whether of this or that sort it matters not, doth equally stand for and represent all rectilinear triangles whatsoever, and is in that sense universal. All which seems very plain and not to include any difficulty in it.

16. But here it will be demanded, how we can know any proposition to be true of all particular triangles, except we have first seen it demonstrated of the abstract idea of a triangle which equally agrees to all? For, because a property may be demonstrated to agree to some one particular triangle, it will not thence follow that it equally belongs to any other triangle, which in all respects is not the same with it. For example, having demonstrated that the three angles of an isoceles rectangular triangle are equal to two right ones, I cannot therefore conclude this affection agrees to all other triangles which have neither a right angle nor two equal sides. It seems therefore that, to be certain this proposition is universally true, we must either make a particular demonstration for every particular triangle, which is impossible, or once for all demonstrate it of the abstract idea of a triangle, in which all the particulars do indifferently partake and by which they are all equally represented. To which I answer, that, though the idea I have in view whilst I make the demonstration be, for instance, that of an isosceles rectangular triangle whose sides are of a determinate length, I may nevertheless be certain it extends to all other rectilinear triangles, of what sort or bigness soever. And that because neither the right angle, nor the equality, nor determinate length of the sides are at all

concerned in the demonstration. It is true the diagram I have in view includes all these particulars, but then there is not the least mention made of them in the proof of the proposition. It is not said the three angles are equal to two right ones, because one of them is a right angle, or because the sides comprehending it are of the same length. Which sufficiently shows that the right angle might have been oblique, and the sides unequal, and for all that the demonstration have held good. And for this reason it is that I conclude that to be true of any obliquangular or scalenon which I had demonstrated of a particular right-angled equicrural triangle, and not because I demonstrated the proposition of the abstract idea of a triangle. And here it must be acknowledged that a man may consider a figure merely as triangular, without attending to the particular qualities of the angles, or relations of the sides. So far he may abstract; but this will never prove that he can frame an abstract, general, inconsistent idea of a triangle. In like manner we may consider Peter so far forth as man, or so far forth as animal, without framing the fore-mentioned abstract idea, either of man or of animal, inasmuch as all that is perceived is not considered.

17. It were an endless as well as an useless thing to trace the Schoolmen, those great masters of abstraction, through all the manifold inextricable labyrinths of error and dispute which their doctrine of abstract natures and notions seems to have led them into. What bickerings and controversies, and what a learned dust have been raised about those matters, and what mighty advantage has been from thence derived to mankind, are things at this day too clearly known to need being insisted on. And it had been well if the ill effects of that doctrine were confined to those only who make the most avowed profession of it. When men consider the great pains, industry, and parts that have for so many ages been laid out on the cultivation and advancement of the sciences, and that notwithstanding all this the far greater part of them remains full of darkness and uncertainty, and disputes that are like never to have an end, and even those that are thought to be supported by the most clear and cogent demonstrations contain in them paradoxes which are perfectly irreconcilable to the understandings of men, and that, taking all together, a very small portion of them does supply any real benefit to mankind, otherwise than by being an innocent diversion and amusement—I say the consideration of all this is apt to throw them into a despondency and perfect contempt of all study. But this may perhaps cease upon a view of the false principles that have obtained in the world, amongst all which there is none, methinks, hath a more wide and extended sway over the thoughts of speculative men than this of *abstract* general ideas.

18. I come now to consider the *source* of this prevailing notion, and that seems to me to be language. And surely nothing of less extent than reason itself could have been the source of an opinion so universally received. The truth of this appears as from other reasons so also from the plain confession of the ablest patrons of abstract ideas, who acknowledge that they are made in order to naming; from which it is a clear consequence that if there had been no such things as speech or universal signs there never had been any thought of abstraction. See Bk. III, Chap. vi, § 39, and elsewhere of the *Essay on Human Understanding*. Let us examine the manner wherein words have contributed to the origin of that mistake.—First then, it is thought that every name has, or ought to have, one only precise and settled signification, which inclines men to think there are certain abstract, determinate ideas that constitute the true and only immediate signification of each general name; and that it is by the mediation of these abstract ideas that a general name comes to signify any particular thing. Whereas, in truth, there is no such thing as one precise and definite signification annexed to any general name, they all signifying indifferently a great number of particular ideas. All which doth evi-

dently follow from what has been already said, and will clearly appear to anyone by a little reflexion. To this it will be objected that every name that has a definition is thereby restrained to one certain signification. For example, a triangle is defined to be "a plain surface comprehended by three right lines," by which that name is limited to denote one certain idea and no other. To which I answer, that in the definition it is not said whether the surface be great or small, black or white, nor whether the sides are long or short, equal or unequal, nor with what angles they are inclined to each other, in all which there may be great variety, and consequently there is no one settled idea which limits the signification of the word triangle. It is one thing for to keep a name constantly to the same definition, and another to make it stand everywhere for the same idea; the one is necessary, the other useless and impracticable.

19. But, to give a farther account how words came to produce the doctrine of abstract ideas, it must be observed that it is a received opinion that language has no other end but the communicating our ideas, and that every significant name stands for an idea. This being so, and it being withal certain that names which yet are not thought altogether insignificant do not always mark out particular conceivable ideas, it is straightway concluded that they stand for abstract notions. That there are many names in use amongst speculative men which do not always suggest to others determinate, particular ideas, or in truth anything at all, is what nobody will deny. And a little attention will discover that it is not necessary (even in the strictest reasonings) significant names which stand for ideas should, every time they are used, excite in the understanding the ideas they are made to stand for—in reading and discoursing, names being for the most part used as letters are in Algebra, in which, though a particular quantity be marked by each letter, yet to proceed right it is not requisite that in every step each letter suggest to your thoughts that particular quantity it was appointed to stand for.

20. Besides, the communicating of ideas marked by words is not the chief and only end of language, as is commonly supposed. There are other ends, as the raising of some passion, the exciting to or deterring from an action, the putting the mind in some particular disposition—to which the former is in many cases barely subservient, and sometimes entirely omitted, when these can be obtained without it, as I think does not unfrequently happen in the familiar use of language. I entreat the reader to reflect with himself, and see if it doth not often happen, either in hearing or reading a discourse, that the passions of fear, love, hatred, admiration, disdain, and the like, arise immediately in his mind upon the perception of certain words, without any ideas coming between. At first, indeed, the words might have occasioned ideas that were fitting to produce those emotions; but, if I mistake not, it will be found that, when language is once grown familiar, the hearing of the sounds or sight of the characters is oft immediately attended with those passions which at first were wont to be produced by the intervention of ideas that are now quite omitted. May we not, for example, be affected with the promise of a *good thing*, though we have not an idea of what it is? Or is not the being threatened with danger sufficient to excite a dread, though we think not of any particular evil likely to befall us, nor yet frame to ourselves an idea of danger in abstract? If any one shall join ever so little reflexion of his own to what has been said, I believe that it will evidently appear to him that general names are often used in the propriety of language without the speaker's designing them for marks of ideas in his own, which he would have them raise in the mind of the hearer. Even proper names themselves do not seem always spoken with a design to bring into our view the ideas of those individuals that are supposed to be marked by them. For example, when a schoolman tells me "Aristotle hath said it," all I conceive he means by it is to dispose me to embrace his opinion with the deference and submission which custom has annexed to that name.

And this effect is often so instantly produced in the minds of those who are accustomed to resign their judgment to authority of that philosopher, as it is impossible any idea either of his person, writings, or reputation should go before. Innumerable examples of this kind may be given, but why should I insist on those things which every one's experience will, I doubt not, plentifully suggest unto him?

21. We have, I think, shewn the impossibility of Abstract Ideas. We have considered what has been said for them by their ablest patrons, and endeavored to show they are of no use for those ends to which they are thought necessary. And lastly, we have traced them to the source from whence they flow, which appears evidently to be language.—It cannot be denied that words are of excellent use, in that by their means all that stock of knowledge which has been purchased by the joint labours of inquisitive men in all ages and nations may be drawn into the view and made the possession of one single person. But at the same time it must be owned that most parts of knowledge have been strangely perplexed and darkened by the abuse of words, and general ways of speech wherein they are delivered. Since therefore words are so apt to impose on the understanding, whatever ideas I consider, I shall endeavour to take them bare and naked into my view, keeping out of my thoughts so far as I am able, those names which long and constant use hath so strictly united with them; from which I may expect to derive the following advantages:

22. *First*, I shall be sure to get clear of all controversies purely verbal—the springing up of which weeds in almost all the sciences has been a main hindrance to the growth of true and sound knowledge. *Secondly*, this seems to be a sure way to extricate myself out of that fine and subtle net of *abstract ideas* which has so miserably perplexed and entangled the minds of men; and that with this peculiar circumstance, that by how much the finer and more curious was the wit of any man, by so much the deeper was he likely to be ensnared and faster held therein. *Thirdly*, so long as I confine my thoughts to my own ideas divested of words, I do not see how I can easily be mistaken. The objects I consider, I clearly and adequately know. I cannot be deceived in thinking I have an idea which I have not. It is not possible for me to imagine that any of my own ideas are alike or unlike that are not truly so. To discern the agreements or disagreements there are between my ideas, to see what ideas are included in any compound idea and what not there is nothing more requisite than an attentive perception of what passes in my own understanding.

23. But the attainment of all these advantages doth presuppose an entire deliverance from the deception of words, which I dare hardly promise myself; so difficult a thing it is to dissolve an union so early begun, and confirmed by so long a habit as that betwixt words and ideas. Which difficulty seems to have been very much increased by the doctrine of *abstraction*. For, so long as men thought abstract ideas were annexed to their words, it doth not seem strange that they should use words for ideas—it being found an impracticable thing to lay aside the word, and retain the *abstract* idea in the mind, which in itself was perfectly inconceivable. This seems to me the principal cause why those men who have so emphatically recommended to others the laying aside all use of words in their meditations, and contemplating their bare ideas, have yet failed to perform it themselves. Of late many have been very sensible of the absurd opinions and insignificant disputes which grow out of the abuse of words. And, in order to remedy these evils, they advise well, that we attend to the ideas signified and draw off our attention from the words which signify them. But, how good soever this advice may be they have given others, it is plain they could not have a due regard to it themselves, so long as they thought the only immediate use of words was to signify ideas, and that the immediate signification of every general name was a determinate abstract idea.

24. But, these being known to be mistakes, a man may with greater ease prevent his being imposed on by words. He that knows he has no other than *particular* ideas, will not puzzle himself in vain to find out and conceive the *abstract* idea annexed to any name. And he that knows names do not always stand for ideas will spare himself the labour of looking for ideas where there are none to be had. It were, therefore, to be wished that everyone would use his utmost endeavours to obtain a clear view of the ideas he would consider, separating from them all that dress and incumbrance of words which so much contribute to blind the judgment and divide the attention. In vain do we extend our view into the heavens and pry into the entrails of the earth, in vain do we consult the writings of learned men and trace the dark footsteps of antiquity—we need only draw the curtain of words, to hold the fairest tree of knowledge, whose fruit is excellent, and within the reach of our hand.

25. Unless we take care to clear the First Principles of Knowledge from the embarrassment and delusion of words, we may make infinite reasonings upon them to no purpose; we may draw consequences from consequences, and be never the wiser. The farther we go, we shall only lose ourselves the more irrecoverably, and be the deeper entangled in difficulties and mistakes. Whoever therefore designs to read the following sheets, I entreat him to make my words the occasion of his own thinking, and endeavour to attain the same train of thoughts in reading that I had in writing them. By this means it will be easy for him to discover the truth or falsity of what I say. He will be out of all danger of being deceived by my words, and I do not see how he can be led into an error by considering his own naked, undisguised ideas.

A Treatise Concerning the Principles of Human Knowledge

1. It is evident to any one who takes a survey of the *objects* of human knowledge, that they are either ideas actually imprinted on the senses; or else such as are perceived by attending to the passions and operations of the mind; or lastly, ideas formed by help of memory and imagination—either compounding, dividing, or barely representing those originally perceived in the aforesaid ways. By sight I have the ideas of light and colours, with their several degrees and variations. By touch I perceive hard and soft, heat and cold, motion and resistance, and of all these more and less either as to quantity or degree. Smelling furnishes me with odours; the palate with tastes; and hearing conveys sounds to the mind in all their variety of tone and composition. And as several of these are observed to accompany each other, they come to be marked by one name, and so to be reputed as one thing. Thus, for example a certain colour, taste, smell, figure and consistence having been observed to go together, are accounted one distinct thing, signified by the name *apple*; other collections of ideas constitute a stone, a tree, a book, and the like sensible things—which as they are pleasing or disagreeable excite the passions of love, hatred, joy, grief, and so forth.

2. But, besides all that endless variety of ideas or objects of knowledge, there is likewise something which knows or perceives them, and exercises divers operations, as willing, imagining, remembering, about them. This perceiving, active being is what I call *mind, spirit, soul*, or *myself*. By which words I do not denote any one of my ideas, but a thing entirely distinct from them, wherein, they exist, or, which is the same thing, whereby they are perceived—for the existence of an idea consists in being perceived.

3. That neither our thoughts, nor passions, nor ideas formed by the imagination, exist without the mind, is what everybody will allow. And it seems no less evident that the various sensations or ideas imprinted on the sense, however blended or combined together (that is, whatever objects they compose), cannot exist otherwise than in a mind perceiving them.—I think an intuitive knowledge may be obtained of this by any one that shall attend to what is meant by the term *exists*, when applied to sensible things. The table I write on I say exists, that is, I see and feel it; and if I were out of my study I should say it existed—meaning thereby that if I was in my study I might perceive it, or that some other spirit actually does perceive it. There was an odour, that is, it was smelt; there was a sound, that is, it was heard; a colour or figure, and it was perceived by sight or touch. This is all that I can understand by these and the like expressions. For as to what is said of the absolute existence of unthinking things without any relation to their being perceived, that seems perfectly unintelligible. Their *esse* is *percepi*, nor is it possible they should have any existence out of the minds or thinking things which perceive them.

4. It is indeed an opinion strangely prevailing amongst men, that houses, mountains, rivers, and in a word all sensible objects, have an existence, natural or real, distinct from their being perceived by the understanding. But, with how great an assurance and acquiescence soever this principle may be entertained in the world, yet whoever shall find in his heart to call it in question may, if I mistake not, perceive it to involve a manifest contradiction. For, what are the forementioned objects but the things we perceive by sense? and what do we perceive besides our own ideas or sensations? and is it not plainly repugnant that any one of these, or any combination of them, should exist unperceived?

5. If we thoroughly examine this tenet it will, perhaps, be found at bottom to depend on the doctrine of *abstract ideas*. For can there be a nicer strain of abstraction than to distinguish the existence of sensible objects from their being perceived, so as to conceive them existing unperceived? Light and colours, heat and cold, extension and figures—in a word the things we see and feel—what are they but so many sensations, notions, ideas, or impressions on the sense? and is it possible to separate, even in thought, any of these from perception? For my part, I might as easily divide a thing from itself. I may, indeed, divide in my thoughts, or conceive apart from each other, those things which, perhaps I never perceived by sense so divided. Thus, I imagine the trunk of a human body without the limbs, or conceive the smell of a rose without thinking on the rose itself. So far, I will not deny, I can abstract—if that may properly be called *abstraction* which extends only to the conceiving separately such objects as it is possible may really exist or be actually perceived asunder. But my conceiving or imagining power does not extend beyond the possibility of real existence or perception. Hence, as it is impossible for me to see or feel anything without an actual sensation of that thing, so is it impossible for me to conceive in my thoughts any sensible thing or object distinct from the sensation or perception of it.

6. Some truths there are so near and obvious to the mind that a man need only open his eyes to see them. Such I take this important one to be, viz., that all the choir of heaven and furniture of the earth, in a word all those bodies which compose the mighty frame of the world, have not any subsistence without a mind, that their *being* is to be perceived or known; that consequently so long as they are not actually perceived by me, or do not exist in my mind or that of any other created spirit, they must either have no existence at all, or else subsist in the mind of some Eternal Spirit—it being perfectly unintelligible, and involving all the absurdity of abstraction, to attribute to any single part of them an existence independent of a spirit. To be convinced of which, the reader need only reflect, and try to separate in his own thoughts the *being* of a sensible thing from its *being perceived*.

7. From what has been said it follows there is not any other Substance than Spirit, or that which perceives. But, for the fuller proof of this point, let it be considered the sensible qualities are colour, figure, motion, smell, taste, etc., i.e. the ideas perceived by sense. Now, for an idea to exist in an unperceiving thing is a manifest contradiction, for to have an idea is all one as to perceive; that therefore wherein colour, figure, and the like qualities exist must perceive them; hence it is clear there can be no unthinking substance or *substratum* of those ideas.

8. But, say you, though the ideas themselves do not exist without the mind, yet there may be things like them, whereof they are copies or resemblances, which things exist without the mind in an unthinking substance. I answer, an idea can be like nothing but an idea; a colour or figure can be like nothing but another colour or figure. If we look but never so little into our thoughts, we shall find it impossible for us to conceive a likeness except only between our ideas. Again, I ask whether those supposed originals or external things, of which our ideas are the pictures or representations, be themselves perceivable or no? If they are, then they are ideas and we have gained our point; but if you say they are not, I appeal to any one whether it be sense to assert a colour is like something which is invisible; hard or soft, like something which is intangible; and so of the rest.

9. Some there are who make a distinction between *primary* and *secondary* qualities. By the former they mean extension, figure, motion, rest, solidity or impenetrability, and number; by the latter they denote all other sensible qualities, as colours, sounds, tastes, and so forth. The ideas we have of these they acknowledge not to be the resemblances of anything existing without the mind, or unperceived, but they will have our ideas of the primary qualities to be patterns or images of things which exist without the mind, in an unthinking substance which they call Matter. By Matter, therefore, we are to understand an inert, senseless substance, in which extension, figure, and motion do actually subsist. But it is evident from what we have already shown, that extension, figure, and motion are only ideas existing in the mind, and that an idea can be like nothing but another idea, and that consequently neither they nor their archetypes can exist in an unperceiving substance. Hence, it is plain that the very notion of what is called *Matter* or *corporeal substance* involves a contradiction in it.

10. They who assert that figure, motion, and the rest of the primary or original qualities do exist without the mind in unthinking substances, do at the same time acknowledge that colours, sounds, heat, cold, and suchlike secondary qualities, do not— which they tell us are sensations existing in the mind alone, that depend on and are occasioned by the different size, texture, and motion of the minute particles of matter. This they take for an undoubted truth, which they can demonstrate beyond all exception. Now, if it be certain that those original qualities are inseparably united with the other sensible qualities, and not, even in thought, capable of being abstracted from them, it plainly follows that they exist only in the mind. But I desire any one to reflect and try whether he can, by any abstraction of thought, conceive the extension and motion of a body without all other sensible qualities. For my own part, I see evidently that it is not in my power to frame an idea of a body extended and moving, but I must withal give it some colour or other sensible quality which is acknowledged to exist only in the mind. In short, extension, figure, and motion, abstracted from all other qualities, are inconceivable. Where therefore the other sensible qualities are, there must these be also, to wit, in the mind and nowhere else.

11. Again, *great* and *small*, *swift* and *slow*, are allowed to exist nowhere without the mind, being entirely relative, and changing as the frame or position of the organs of sense varies. The extension therefore which exists without the mind is neither great nor small, the motion neither swift nor slow, that is, they are nothing at all. But, say you,

Fruits and Dishes on the Table, by Jan Davids de Heem (1606–1683). The underlying theme of *Vanitas* in Dutch still life presents a dual message in the arrangement of fine and rare objects. On the one hand, the objects represent the joy of possessions and the good life, yet the half-eaten pie and the peeled fruit cause reflection on the brevity of human existence and the fleeting nature of material objects. Berkeley takes this a step further by denying material substance and claiming that such objects do not exist apart from a perceiving mind. (*Lauros-Giraudon/Art Resource*)

they are extension in general, and motion in general: thus we see how much the tenet of extended movable substances existing without the mind depends on the strange doctrine of *abstract ideas*. And here I cannot but remark how nearly the vague and indeterminate description of Matter or corporeal substance, which the modern philosophers are run into by their own principles, resembles that antiquated and so much ridiculed notion of *materia prima*, to be met with in Aristotle and his followers. Without extension solidity cannot be conceived; since therefore it has been shewn that extension exists not in an unthinking substance, the same must also be true of solidity.

12. That number is entirely the creature of the mind, even though the other qualities be allowed to exist without, will be evident to whoever considers that the same thing bears a different denomination of number as the mind views it with different respects. Thus, the same extension is one, or three, or thirty-six, according as the mind considers it with reference to a yard, a foot or an inch. Number is so visibly relative, and dependent on men's understanding, that it is strange to think how any one should give it an absolute existence without the mind. We say one book, one page, one line, etc.; all these are equally units, though some contain several of the others. And in each instance, it is plain, the unit relates to some particular combination of ideas arbitrarily put together by the mind.

13. Unity I know some will have to be a simple or uncompounded idea, accompanying all other ideas into the mind. That I have any such idea answering the word unity I do not find; and if I had, methinks I could not miss finding it: on the contrary, it should be the most familiar to my understanding, since it is said to accompany all other ideas, and to be perceived by all the ways of sensation and reflexion. To say no more, it is an *abstract* idea.

14. I shall farther add, that, after the same manner as modern philosophers prove certain sensible qualities to have no existence in Matter, or without the mind, the same thing may be likewise proved of all other sensible qualities whatsoever. Thus, for instance, it is said that heat and cold are affections only of the mind, and not at all patterns of real beings, existing in the corporeal substances which excite them, for that the same body which appears cold to one hand seems warm to another. Now, why may we not as well argue that figure and extension are not patterns or resemblances of qualities existing in Matter, because to the same eye at different stations or eyes of a different texture at the same station, they appear various, and cannot therefore be the images of anything settled and determinate without the mind? Again, it is proved that sweetness is not really in the sapid thing, because the thing remaining unaltered the sweetness is changed into bitter, as in case of a fever or otherwise vitiated palate. Is it not as reasonable to say that motion is not without the mind, since if the succession of ideas in the mind become swifter, the motion, it is acknowledged, shall appear slower without any alteration in any external object?

15. In short, let any one consider those arguments which are thought manifestly to prove that colours and taste exist only in the mind, and he shall find they may with equal force be brought to prove the same thing of extension, figure, and motion. Though it must be confessed this method of arguing does not so much prove that there is no extension or colour in an outward object, as that we do not know by sense which is the true extension or colour of the object. But the arguments foregoing plainly shew it to be impossible that any colour or extension at all, or other sensible quality whatsoever, should exist in an unthinking subject without the mind, or in truth, that there should be any such thing as an outward object.

16. But let us examine a little the received opinion.—It is said extension is a mode or accident of Matter, and that Matter is the substratum that supports it. Now I desire that you would explain to me what is meant by Matter's supporting extension. Say you, I have no idea of Matter and therefore cannot explain it. I answer, though you have no positive, yet, if you have any meaning at all, you must at least have a relative idea of Matter; though you know not what it is, yet you must be supposed to know what relation it bears to accidents, and what is meant by its supporting them. It is evident "support" cannot here be taken in its usual or literal sense—as when we say that pillars support a building; in what sense therefore must it be taken?

17. If we inquire into what the most accurate philosophers declare themselves to mean by material substance, we shall find them acknowledging they have no other meaning annexed to those sounds but the idea of Being in general, together with the relative notion of its supporting accidents. The general idea of Being appeareth to me the most abstract and incomprehensible of all other; and as for its supporting accidents, this, as we have just now observed, cannot be understood in the common sense of those words; it must therefore be taken in some other sense, but what that is they do not explain. So that when I consider the two parts or branches which make the signification of the words material substance, I am convinced there is no distinct meaning annexed to them. But why should we trouble ourselves any farther, in discussing this material substratum or support of figure and motion, and other sensible qualities? Does it

not suppose they have an existence without the mind? And is not this a direct repugnancy, and altogether inconceivable?

18. But, though it were possible that solid, figured, movable substances may exist without the mind, corresponding to the ideas we have of bodies, yet how is it possible for us to know this? Either we must know it by sense or by reason. As for our senses, by them we have the knowledge only of our sensations, ideas, or those things that are immediately perceived by sense, call them what you will: but they do not inform us that things exist without the mind, or unperceived, like to those which are perceived. This the materialists themselves acknowledge. It remains therefore that if we have any knowledge at all of external things, it must be by reason, inferring their existence from what is immediately perceived by sense. But what reason can induce us to believe the existence of bodies without the mind, from what we perceive, since the very patrons of Matter themselves do not pretend there is any necessary connexion betwixt them and our ideas? I say it is granted on all hands (and what happens in dreams, phrensies, and the like, puts it beyond dispute) that it is possible we might be affected with all the ideas we have now, though there were no bodies existing without resembling them. Hence, it is evident the supposition of external bodies is not necessary for the producing our ideas; since it is granted they are produced sometimes, and might possibly be produced always in the same order, we see them in at present, without their concurrence.

19. But, though we might possibly have all our sensations without them, yet perhaps it may be thought easier to conceive and explain the manner of their production, by supposing external bodies in their likeness rather than otherwise; and so it might be at least probable there are such things as bodies that excite their ideas in our minds. But neither can this be said; for, though we give the materialists their external bodies, they by their own confession are never the nearer knowing how our ideas are produced; since they own themselves unable to comprehend in what manner body can act upon spirit, or how it is possible it should imprint any idea in the mind. Hence it is evident the production of ideas or sensations in our minds can be no reason why we should suppose Matter or corporeal substances, since that is acknowledged to remain equally inexplicable with or without this supposition. If therefore it were possible for bodies to exist without the mind, yet to hold they do so, must needs be a very precarious opinion; since it is to suppose, without any reason at all, that God has created innumerable beings that are entirely useless, and serve to no manner of purpose.

20. In short, if there were external bodies, it is impossible we should ever come to know it; and if there were not, we might have the very same reasons to think there were that we have now. Suppose—what no one can deny possible—an intelligence without the help of external bodies, to be affected with the same train of sensations or ideas that you are, imprinted in the same order and with like vividness in his mind. I ask whether that intelligence hath not all the reason to believe the existence of corporeal substances, represented by his ideas, and exciting them in his mind, that you can possibly have for believing the same thing? Of this there can be no question—which one consideration were enough to make any reasonable person suspect the strength of whatever arguments he may think himself to have, for the existence of bodies without the mind.

21. Were it necessary to add any farther proof against the existence of Matter after what has been said, I could instance several of those errors and difficulties (not to mention impieties) which have sprung from that tenet. It has occasioned numberless controversies and disputes in philosophy, and not a few of far greater moment in religion. But I shall not enter into the detail of them in this place, as well because I think

arguments *a posteriori* are unnecessary for confirming what has been, if I mistake not, sufficiently demonstrated *a priori*, as because I shall hereafter find occasion to speak somewhat of them.

22. I am afraid I have given cause to think I am needlessly prolix in handling this subject. For, to what purpose is it to dilate on that which may be demonstrated with the utmost evidence in a line or two, to any one that is capable of the least reflexion? It is but looking in to your own thoughts, and so trying whether you can conceive it possible for a sound, or figure, or motion, or colour to exist without the mind or unperceived. This easy trial may perhaps make you see that what you contend for is a downright contradiction. Insomuch that I am content to put the whole upon this issue:—If you can but conceive it possible for one extended movable substance, or, in general, for any one idea, or anything like an idea, to exist otherwise than in a mind perceiving it, I shall readily give up the cause. And, as for all that compages [complex system] of external bodies you contend for, I shall grant you its existence, though you cannot either give me any reason why you believe it exists, or assign any use to it when it is supposed to exist. I say, the bare possibility of your opinions being true shall pass for an argument that it is so.

23. But, say you, surely there is nothing easier than for me to imagine trees, for instance, in a park, or books existing in a closet, and nobody by to perceive them. I answer, you may so, there is no difficulty in it; but what is all this, I beseech you, more than framing in your mind certain ideas which you call books and trees, and the same time omitting to frame the idea of any one that may perceive them? But do not you yourself perceive or think of them all the while? This therefore is nothing to the purpose; it only shews you have the power of imagining or forming ideas in your mind: but it does not shew that you can conceive it possible the objects of your thought may exist without the mind. To make out this, it is necessary that you conceive them existing unconceived or unthought of, which is a manifest repugnancy. When we do our utmost to conceive the existence of external bodies, we are all the while only contemplating our own ideas. But the mind taking no notice of itself, is deluded to think it can and does conceive bodies existing unthought of or without the mind, though at the same time they are apprehended by or exist in itself. A little attention will discover to any one the truth and evidence of what is here said, and make it unnecessary to insist on any other proofs against the existence of *material substance*.

24. It is very obvious, upon the least inquiry into our thoughts, to know whether it is possible for us to understand what is meant by the *absolute existence of sensible objects in themselves, or without the mind*. To me it is evident those words mark out either a direct contradiction, or else nothing at all. And to convince others of this, I know no readier or fairer way than to entreat they would calmly attend to their own thoughts; and if by this attention the emptiness or repugnancy of those expressions does appear, surely nothing more is requisite for the conviction. It is on this therefore that I insist, to wit, that the absolute existence of unthinking things are words without a meaning, or which include a contradiction. This is what I repeat and inculcate, and earnestly recommend to the attentive thoughts of the reader.

25. All our ideas, sensations, notions, or the things which we perceive, by whatsoever names they may be distinguished, are visibly inactive—there is nothing of power or agency included in them. So that one idea or object of thought cannot produce or make any alteration in another. To be satisfied of the truth of this, there is nothing else requisite but a bare observation of our ideas. For, since they and every part of them exist only in the mind, it follows that there is nothing in them but what is perceived: but whoever shall attend to his ideas, whether of sense or reflexion, will not

perceive in them any power or activity; there is, therefore, no such thing contained in them. A little attention will discover to us that the very being of an idea implies passiveness and inertness in it, insomuch that it is impossible for an idea to do anything, or, strictly speaking, to be the cause of anything: neither can it be the resemblance or pattern of any active being, as is evident from sect. 8. Whence it plainly follows that extension, figure, and motion cannot be the cause of our sensations. To say, therefore, that these are the effects of powers resulting from the configuration, number, motion, and size of corpuscles, must certainly be false.

26. We perceive a continual succession of ideas, some are anew excited, others are changed or totally disappear. There is therefore some cause of these ideas, whereon they depend, and which produces and changes them. That this cause cannot be any quality or idea or combination of ideas, is clear from the preceding section. It must therefore be a substance; but it has been shewn that there is no corporeal or material substance: it remains therefore that the cause of ideas is an incorporeal active substance or Spirit.

27. A spirit is one simple, undivided, active being—as it perceives ideas it is called the *understanding*, and as it produces or otherwise operates about them it is called the *will*. Hence there can be no *idea* formed of a soul or spirit, for all ideas whatever, being passive and inert (*vide* sect. 25), they cannot represent unto us, by way of image or likeness, that which acts. A little attention will make it plain to any one, that to have an idea which shall be like that active principle of motion and change of ideas is absolutely impossible. Such is the nature of *spirit*, or that which acts, that it cannot be of itself perceived, but only by the effects which it produceth. If any man shall doubt of the truth of what is here delivered, let him but reflect and try if he can frame the idea of any power or active being, and whether he has ideas of two principal powers, marked by the names *will* and *understanding*, distinct from each other as well as from a third idea of Substance or Being in general, with a relative notion of its supporting or being the subject of the aforesaid powers—which is signified by the name *soul* or *spirit*. This is what some hold; but, so far as I can see, the words *will*, *soul*, *spirit*, do not stand for different ideas, or, in truth, for any idea at all, but for something which is very different from ideas, and which, being an agent, cannot be like unto, or represented by, any idea whatsoever. Though it must be owned at the same time that we have some *notion* of soul, spirit, and the operations of the mind: such as willing, loving, hating—inasmuch as we know or understand the meaning of these words.

28. I find I can excite ideas in my mind at pleasure, and vary and shift the scene as oft as I think fit. It is no more than willing, and straightway this or that idea arises in my fancy; and by the same power it is obliterated and makes way for another. This making and unmaking of ideas doth very properly denominate the mind active. Thus much is certain and grounded on experience; but when we think of unthinking agents or of exciting ideas exclusive of volition, we only amuse ourselves with words.

29. But, whatever power I may have over my own thoughts, I find the ideas actually perceived by Sense have not a like dependence on my will. When in broad daylight I open my eyes, it is not in my power to choose whether I shall see or no, or to determine what particular objects shall present themselves to my view; and so likewise as to the hearing and other senses; the ideas imprinted on them are not creatures of my will. There is therefore some *other* Will or Spirit that produces them.

30. The ideas of Sense are more strong, lively, and distinct than those of the imagination; they have likewise a steadiness, order, and coherence, and are not excited at random, as those which are the effects of human wills often are, but in a regular train or series, the admirable connexion whereof sufficiently testifies the wisdom and benev-

olence of its Author. Now the set rules or established methods wherein the Mind we depend on excites in us the ideas of sense, are called the *laws of nature*; and these we learn by experience, which teaches us that such and such ideas are attended with such and such other ideas, in the ordinary course of things.

31. This gives us a sort of foresight which enables us to regulate our actions for the benefit of life. And without this we should be eternally at a loss; we could not know how to act anything that might procure us the least pleasure, or remove the least pain of sense. That food nourishes, sleep refreshes, and fire warms us; that to sow in the seed-time is the way to reap in the harvest; and in general that to obtain such or such ends, such or such means are conducive—all this we know, not by discovering any necessary connexion between our ideas, but only by the observation of the settled laws of nature, without which we should be all in uncertainty and confusion, and a grown man no more know how to manage himself in the affairs of life than an infant just born.

32. And yet this consistent uniform working, which so evidently displays the goodness and wisdom of that Governing Spirit whose Will constitutes the laws of nature, is so far from leading our thoughts to Him, that it rather sends them wandering after second causes. For, when we perceive certain ideas of Sense constantly followed by other ideas and we know this is not of our own doing, we forthwith attribute power and agency to the ideas themselves, and make one the cause of another, than which nothing can be more absurd and unintelligible. Thus, for example, having observed that when we perceive by sight a certain round luminous figure we at the same time perceive by touch the idea or sensation called heat, we do from thence conclude the sun to be the cause of heat. And in like manner perceiving the motion and collision of bodies to be attended with sound, we are inclined to think the latter the effect of the former.

33. The ideas imprinted on the Senses by the Author of nature are called *real things*; and those excited in the imagination being less regular, vivid, and constant, are more properly termed *ideas*, or *images of things*, which they copy and represent. But then our sensations, be they never so vivid and distinct, are nevertheless ideas, that is, they exist in the mind, or are perceived by it, as truly as the ideas of its own framing. The ideas of Sense are allowed to have more reality in them, that is, to be more strong, orderly, and coherent than the creatures of the mind; but this is no argument that they exist without the mind. They are also less dependent on the spirit, or thinking substance which perceives them, in that they are excited by the will of another and more powerful spirit; yet still they are *ideas*, and certainly no idea, whether faint or strong, can exist otherwise than in a mind perceiving it.

34. Before we proceed any farther it is necessary we spend some time in answering objections which may probably be made against the principles we have hitherto laid down. In doing of which, if I seem too prolix to those of quick apprehensions, I hope it may be pardoned, since all men do not equally apprehend things of this nature, and I am willing to be understood by every one.

First, then, it will be objected that by the foregoing principles all that is real and substantial in nature is banished out of the world, and instead thereof a chimerical scheme of *ideas* takes place. All things that exist, exist only in the mind, that is, they are purely notional. What therefore becomes of the sun, moon and stars? What must we think of houses, rivers, mountains, trees, stones; nay, even of our own bodies? Are all these but so many chimeras and illusions on the fancy? To all which, and whatever else of the same sort may be objected, I answer, that by the principles premised we are not deprived of any one thing in nature. Whatever we see, feel, hear, or anywise conceive or understand remains as secure as ever and is as real as ever. There is a *rerum natura*, and the distinction between realities and chimeras retains its full force. This is evident from sect. 29, 30, and 33, where we have shewn what is meant by *real things* in opposition to *chimeras* or ideas of our own framing; but then they both equally exist in the mind, and in that sense they are alike ideas.

35. I do not argue against the existence of any one thing that we can apprehend either by sense or reflexion. That the things I see with my eyes and touch with my hands do exist, really exist, I make not the least question. The only thing whose existence we deny is that which *philosophers* call Matter or corporeal substance. And in doing of this there is no damage done to the rest of mankind, who, I dare say, will never miss it. The Atheist indeed will want the colour of an empty name to support his impiety; and the Philosophers may possibly find they have lost a great handle for trifling and disputation.

36. If any man thinks this detracts from the existence or reality of things, he is very far from understanding what hath been premised in the plainest terms I could think of. Take here an abstract of what has been said:—There are spiritual substances, minds, or human souls, which will or excite ideas in themselves at pleasure; but these are faint, weak, and unsteady in respect of others they perceive by sense—which, being impressed upon them according to certain rules or laws of nature, speak themselves the effects of a mind more powerful and wise than human spirits. These latter are said to have more *reality* in them than the former:—by which is meant that they are more affecting, orderly, and distinct, and that they are not fictions of the mind perceiving them. And in this sense the sun that I see by day is the real sun, and that which I imagine by night is the idea of the former. In the sense here given of *reality* it is evident that every vegetable, star, mineral, and in general each part of the mundane system, is as much a *real being* by our principles as by any other. Whether others mean anything by the term reality different from what I do, I entreat them to look into their own thoughts and see.

37. It will be urged that thus much at least is true, to wit, that we take away all corporeal substances. To this my answer is, that if the word *substance* be taken in the vulgar sense—for a combination of sensible qualities, such as extension, solidity, weight, and the like—this we cannot be accused of taking away: but if it be taken in a philosophic sense—for the support of accidents or qualities without the mind—then indeed I acknowledge that we take it away, if one may be said to take away that which never had any existence, not even in the imagination.

38. But after all, say you, it sounds very harsh to say we eat and drink ideas, and are clothed with ideas. I acknowledge it does so—the word *idea* not being used in common discourse to signify the several combinations of sensible qualities which are called *things*; and it is certain that any expression which varies from the familiar use of language will seem harsh and ridiculous. But this doth not concern the truth of the proposition, which in other words is no more than to say, we are fed and clothed with those things which we perceive immediately by our senses. The hardness or softness, the colour, taste, warmth, figure, or suchlike qualities, which combined together constitute the several sorts of victuals and apparel, have been shewn to exist only in the mind that perceives them; and this is all that is meant by calling them *ideas*; which word if it was as ordinarily used as *thing*, would sound no harsher nor more ridiculous than it. I am not for disputing about the propriety, but the truth of the expression. If therefore you agree with me that we eat and drink and are clad with the immediate objects of sense, which cannot exist unperceived or without the mind, I shall readily grant it is more proper or conformable to custom that they should be called things rather than ideas.

39. If it be demanded why I make use of the word *idea*, and do not rather in compliance with custom call them *things*; I answer, I do it for two reasons:—first, because the term *thing* in contradistinction to *idea*, is generally supposed to denote somewhat existing without the mind; secondly, because *thing* hath a more comprehensive signification than *idea*, including spirit or thinking things as well as ideas. Since therefore the objects of sense exist only in the mind, and are withal thoughtless and inactive, I chose to mark them by the word *idea*, which implies those properties.

40. But, say what we can, some one perhaps may be apt to reply, he will still believe his senses, and never suffer any arguments, how plausible soever, to prevail over the certainty of them. Be it so; assert the evidence of sense as high as you please, we are willing to do the same. That what I see, hear, and feel doth exist, that is to say, is perceived by me, I no more doubt than I do of my own being. But I do not see how the testimony of sense can be alleged as a proof for the existence of anything which is not perceived by sense. We are not for having any man turn sceptic and disbelieve his senses; on the contrary, we give them all the stress and assurance imaginable; nor are there any principles more opposite to Scepticism than those we have laid down, as shall be hereafter clearly shewn.

41. *Secondly*, it will be objected that there is a great difference betwixt real fire for instance, and the idea of fire, betwixt dreaming or imagining oneself burnt, and actually being so: if you suspect it to be only the idea of fire which you see, do but put your hand into it and you will be convinced with a witness. This and the like may be urged in opposition to our tenets. To all which the answer is evident from what hath been already said; and I shall only add in this place, that if real fire be very different from the idea of fire, so also is the real pain that it occasions very different from the idea of the same pain, and yet nobody will pretend that real pain either is, or can possibly be, in an unperceiving thing, or without the mind, any more than its idea.

42. *Thirdly*, it will be objected that we see things actually without or at distance from us, and which consequently do not exist in the mind; it being absurd that those things which are seen at the distance of several miles should be as near to us as our own thoughts. In answer to this, I desire it may be considered that in a dream we do oft perceive things as existing at a great distance off; and yet for all that, those things are acknowledged to have their existence only in the mind.

43. But, for the fuller clearing of this point, it may be worth while to consider how it is that we perceive distance and things placed at a distance by sight. For, that we should in truth see external space, and bodies actually existing in it, some nearer, others farther off, seems to carry with it some opposition to what hath been said of their existing nowhere without the mind. The consideration of this difficulty it was that gave birth to my "Essay towards a New Theory of Vision," which was published not long since wherein it is shewn that distance or outness is neither immediately of itself perceived by sight, nor yet apprehended or judged of by lines and angles, or any thing that hath a necessary connexion with it; but that it is only suggested to our thoughts by certain visible ideas and sensations attending vision, which in their own nature have no manner of similitude or relation either with distance or things placed at a distance; but, by a connexion taught us by experience, they come to signify and suggest them to us, after the same manner that words of any language suggest the ideas they are made to stand for; insomuch that a man born blind and afterwards made to see, would not, at first sight, think the things he saw to be without his mind, or at any distance from him. See sect. 41 of the forementioned treatise.

44. The ideas of sight and touch make two species entirely distinct and heterogeneous. The former are marks and prognostics of the latter. That the proper objects of

sight neither exist without mind, nor are the images of external things, was shewn even in that treatise. Though throughout the same the contrary be supposed true of tangible objects—not that to suppose that vulgar error was necessary for establishing the notion therein laid down, but because it was beside my purpose to examine and refute it in a discourse concerning *Vision*. So that in strict truth the ideas of sight, when we apprehend by them distance and things placed at a distance, do not suggest or mark out to us things actually existing at a distance, but only admonish us what ideas of touch will be imprinted in our minds at such and such distances of time, and in consequence of such or such actions. It is, I say, evident from what has been said in the foregoing parts of this Treatise, and in sect. 147 and elsewhere of the Essay concerning Vision, that visible ideas are the Language whereby the Governing Spirit on whom we depend informs us what tangible ideas he is about to imprint upon us, in case we excite this or that motion in our own bodies. But for a fuller information in this point I refer to the Essay itself.

45. *Fourthly*, it will be objected that from the foregoing principles it follows things are every moment annihilated and created anew. The objects of sense exist only when they are perceived; the trees therefore are in the garden, or the chairs in the parlour, no longer than while there is somebody by to perceive them. Upon shutting my eyes all the furniture in the room is reduced to nothing, and barely upon opening them it is again created. In answer to all which, I refer the reader to what has been said in sect. 3, 4, etc., and desire he will consider whether he means anything by the actual existence of an idea distinct from its being perceived. For my part, after the nicest inquiry I could make, I am not able to discover that anything else is meant by those words; and I once more entreat the reader to sound his own thoughts, and not suffer himself to be imposed on by words. If he can conceive it possible either for his ideas or their archetypes to exist without being perceived, then I give up the cause; but if he cannot, he will acknowledge it is unreasonable for him to stand up in defence of he knows not what, and pretend to charge on me as an absurdity the not assenting to those propositions which at bottom have no meaning in them.

46. It will not be amiss to observe how far the received principles of philosophy are themselves chargeable with those pretended absurdities. It is thought strangely absurd that upon closing my eyelids all the visible objects around me should be reduced to nothing; and yet is not this what philosophers commonly acknowledge, when they agree on all hands that light and colours, which alone are the proper and immediate objects of sight, are mere sensations that exist no longer than they are perceived? Again, it may to some perhaps seem very incredible that things should be every moment creating, yet this very notion is commonly taught in the schools. For the Schoolmen, though they acknowledge the existence of Matter, and that the whole mundane fabric is framed out of it, are nevertheless of opinion that it cannot subsist without the divine conservation, which by them is expounded to be a continual creation.

47. Farther, a little thought will discover to us that though we allow the existence of Matter or corporeal substance, yet it will unavoidably follow, from the principles which are now generally admitted, that the particular bodies, of what kind soever, do none of them exist whilst they are not perceived. For, it is evident from sect. 11 and the following sections, that the Matter philosophers contend for is an incomprehensible somewhat, which hath none of those particular qualities whereby the bodies falling under our senses are distinguished one from another. But, to make this more plain, it must be remarked that the infinite divisibility of Matter is now universally allowed, at least by the most approved and considerable philosophers, who on the received principles demonstrate it beyond all exception. Hence, it follows there is an infinite number

of parts in each particle of Matter which are not perceived by sense. The reason therefore that any particular body seems to be of a finite magnitude, or exhibits only a finite number of parts to sense, is, not because it contains no more, since in itself it contains an infinite number of parts, but because the sense is not acute enough to discern them. In proportion therefore as the sense is rendered more acute, it perceives a greater number of parts in the object, that is, the object appears greater, and its figure varies, those parts in its extremities which were before unperceivable appearing now to bound it in very different lines and angles from those perceived by an obtuser sense. And at length, after various changes of size and shape, when the sense becomes infinitely acute the body shall seem infinite. During all which there is no alteration in the body, but only in the sense. Each body therefore, considered in itself, is infinitely extended, and consequently void of all shape or figure. From which it follows that, though we should grant the existence of Matter to be never so certain, yet it is withal as certain, the materialists themselves are by their own principles forced to acknowledge, that neither the particular bodies perceived by sense, nor anything like them, exists without the mind. Matter, I say, and each particle thereof, is according to them infinite and shapeless, and it is the mind that frames all that variety of bodies which compose the visible world, any one whereof does not exist longer than it is perceived.

48. If we consider it, the objection proposed in sect. 45 will not be found reasonably charged on the principles we have premised, so as in truth to make any objection at all against our notions. For, though we hold indeed the objects of sense to be nothing else but ideas which cannot exist unperceived; yet we may not hence conclude they have no existence except only while they are perceived by us, since there may be some other spirit that perceives them though we do not. Wherever bodies are said to have no existence without the mind, I would not be understood to mean this or that particular mind, but all minds whatsoever. It does not therefore follow from the foregoing principles that bodies are annihilated and created every moment, or exist not at all during the intervals between our perception of them.

49. *Fifthly*, it may perhaps be objected that if extension and figure exist only in the mind, it follows that the mind is extended and figured; since extension is a mode or attribute which (to speak with the schools) is predicated of the subject in which it exists. I answer, those qualities are in the mind only as they are perceived by it—that is, not by way of *mode* or *attribute*, but only by way of *idea*; and it no more follows the soul or mind is extended, because extension exists in it alone, than it does that it is red or blue, because those colours are on all hands acknowledged to exist in it, and nowhere else. As to what philosophers say of subject and mode, that seems very groundless and unintelligible. For instance, in this proposition "a die is hard, extended, and square," they will have it that the word *die* denotes a subject or substance, distinct from the hardness, extension, and figure which are predicated of it, and in which they exist. This I cannot comprehend: to me a die seems to be nothing distinct from those things which are termed its modes or accidents. And, to say a die is hard, extended, and square is not to attribute those qualities to a subject distinct from and supporting them, but only an explication of the meaning of the word *die*.

50. *Sixthly*, you will say there have been a great many things explained by matter and motion; take away these and you destroy the whole corpuscular philosophy, and undermine those mechanical principles which have been applied with so much success to account for the phenomena. In short, whatever advances have been made, either by ancient or modern philosophers, in the study of nature do all proceed on the supposition that corporeal substance or Matter doth really exist. To this I answer that there is not any one phenomenon explained on that supposition which may not as well be ex-

plained without it as might easily be made to appear by an induction of particulars. To explain the phenomena, is all one as to shew why, upon such and such occasions, we are affected with such and such ideas. But how Matter should operate on a Spirit, or produce any idea in it, is what no philosopher will pretend to explain; it is therefore evident there can be no use of Matter in natural philosophy. Besides, they who attempt to account for things do it not by corporeal substance, but by figure, motion, and other qualities, which are in truth no more than mere ideas, and, therefore, cannot be the cause of anything, as hath been already shewn. See sect. 25.

51. *Seventhly*, it will upon this be demanded whether it does not seem absurd to take away natural causes, and ascribe everything to the immediate operation of Spirits? We must no longer say upon these principles that fire heats, or water cools, but that a Spirit heats, and so forth. Would not a man be deservedly laughed at, who should talk after this manner? I answer, he would so; in such things we ought to "think with the learned, and speak with the vulgar." They who to demonstration are convinced of the truth of the Copernican system do nevertheless say "the sun rises," "the sun sets," or "comes to the meridian"; and if they affected a contrary style in common talk it would without doubt appear very ridiculous. A little reflexion on what is here said will make it manifest that the common use of language would receive no manner of alteration or disturbance from the admission of our tenets.

52. In the ordinary affairs of life, any phrases may be retained, so long as they excite in us proper sentiments, or dispositions to act in such a manner as is necessary for our well-being, how false soever they may be if taken in a strict and speculative sense. Nay, this is unavoidable, since, propriety being regulated by custom, language is suited to the received opinions, which are not always the truest. Hence it is impossible, even in the most rigid, philosophic reasonings, so far to alter the bent and genius of the tongue we speak as never to give a handle for cavillers to pretend difficulties and inconsistencies. But, a fair and ingenuous reader will collect the sense from the scope and tenor and connexion of a discourse, making allowances for those inaccurate modes of speech which use has made inevitable.

53. As to the opinion that there are no Corporeal Causes, this has been heretofore maintained by some of the Schoolmen, as it is of late by others among the modern philosophers, who though they allow Matter to exist, yet will have God alone to be the immediate efficient cause of all things. These men saw that amongst all the objects of sense there was none which had any power or activity included in it; and that by consequence this was likewise true of whatever bodies they supposed to exist without the mind, like unto the immediate objects of sense. But then, that they should suppose an innumerable multitude of created beings, which they acknowledge are not capable of producing any one effect in nature, and which therefore are made to no manner of purpose, since God might have done everything as well without them: this I say, though we should allow it possible, must yet be a very unaccountable and extravagant supposition.

54. In the *eighth* place, the universal concurrent assent of mankind may be thought by some an invincible argument in behalf of Matter, or the existence of external things. Must we suppose the whole world to be mistaken? And if so, what cause can be assigned of so widespread and predominant an error? I answer, first, that, upon a narrow inquiry, it will not perhaps be found so many as is imagined do really believe the existence of Matter or things without the mind. Strictly speaking, to believe that which involves a contradiction, or has no meaning in it, is impossible; and whether the foregoing expressions are not of that sort, I refer it to the impartial examination of the reader. In one sense, indeed, men may be said to believe that Matter exists, that is, they

act as if the immediate cause of their sensations, which affects them every moment, and is so nearly present to them, were some senseless unthinking being. But, that they should clearly apprehend any meaning marked by those words, and form thereof a settled speculative opinion, is what I am not able to conceive. This is not the only instance wherein men impose upon themselves, by imagining they believe those propositions which they have often heard, though at bottom they have no meaning in them.

55. But secondly, though we should grant a notion to be never so universally and steadfastly adhered to, yet this is weak argument of its truth to whoever considers what a vast number of prejudices and false opinions are everywhere embraced with the utmost tenaciousness, by the unreflecting (which are the far greater) part of mankind. There was a time when the antipodes and motion of the earth were looked upon as monstrous absurdities even by men of learning: and if it be considered what a small proportion they bear to the rest of mankind, we shall find that at this day those notions have gained but a very inconsiderable footing in the world.

56. But it is demanded that we assign a cause of this prejudice, and account for its obtaining in the world. To this I answer, that men knowing they perceived several ideas, whereof they themselves were not the authors—as not being excited from within nor depending on the operation of their wills—this made them maintain those ideas, or objects of perception had an existence independent of and without the mind, without ever dreaming that a contradiction was involved in those words. But, philosophers having plainly seen that the immediate objects of perception do not exist without the mind, they in some degree corrected the mistake of the vulgar, but at the same time run into another which seems no less absurd, to wit, that there are certain objects really existing without the mind, or having a subsistence distinct from being perceived, of which our ideas are only images or resemblances imprinted by those objects on the mind. And this notion of the philosophers owes its origin to the same cause with the former, namely, their being conscious that they were not the authors of their own sensations, which they evidently knew were imprinted from without, and which therefore must have some cause distinct from the minds on which they are imprinted.

57. But why they should suppose the ideas of sense to be excited in us by things in their likeness, and not rather have recourse to *Spirit* which alone can act, may be accounted for, first, because they were not aware of the repugnancy there is, as well in supposing things like unto our ideas existing without, as in attributing to them power or activity. Secondly, because the Supreme Spirit which excites those ideas in our minds, is not marked out and limited to our view by any particular finite collection of sensible ideas, as human agents are by their size, complexion, limbs, and motions. And thirdly, because His operations are regular and uniform. Whenever the course of nature is interrupted by a miracle, men are ready to own the presence of a superior agent. But, when we see things go on in the ordinary course they do not excite in us any reflexion; their order and concatenation, though it be an argument of the greatest wisdom, power, and goodness in their creator, is yet so constant and familiar to us that we do not think them the immediate effects of a *Free Spirit*; especially since inconsistency and mutability in acting, though it be an imperfection, is looked on as a mark of *freedom*.

58. *Tenthly*, it will be objected that the notions we advance are inconsistent with several sound truths in philosophy and mathematics. For example, the motion of the earth is now universally admitted by astronomers as a truth grounded on the clearest and most convincing reasons. But, on the foregoing principles, there can be no such thing. For, motion being only an idea, it follows that if it be not perceived it exists not; but the motion of the earth is not perceived by sense. I answer, that tenet, if rightly understood, will be found to agree with the principles we have premised; for, the question

whether the earth moves or no amounts in reality to no more than this, to wit, whether we have reason to conclude, from what has been observed by astronomers, that if we were placed in such and such circumstances, and such or such a position and distance both from the earth and sun, we should perceive the former to move among the choir of the planets, and appearing in all respects like one of them; and this, by the established rules of nature which we have no reason to mistrust, is reasonably collected from the phenomena.

59. We may, from the experience we have had of the train and succession of ideas in our minds, often make, I will not say uncertain conjectures, but sure and well-grounded predictions concerning the ideas we shall be affected with pursuant to a great train of actions, and be enabled to pass a right judgment of what would have appeared to us, in case we were placed in circumstances very different from those we are in at present. Herein consists the knowledge of nature, which may preserve its use and certainty very consistently with what hath been said. It will be easy to apply this to whatever objections of the like sort may be drawn from the magnitude of the stars, or any other discoveries in astronomy or nature.

60. In the *eleventh* place, it will be demanded to what purpose serves that curious organization of plants, and the animal mechanism in the parts of animals; might not vegetables grow, and shoot forth leaves of blossoms, and animals perform all their motions as well without as with all that variety of internal parts so elegantly contrived and put together; which, being ideas, have nothing powerful or operative in them, nor have any necessary connexion with the effects ascribed to them? If it be a Spirit that immediately produces every effect by a *fiat* or act of his will, we must think all that is fine and artificial in the works, whether of man or nature, to be made in vain. By this doctrine, though an artist hath made the spring and wheels, and every movement of a watch, and adjusted them in such a manner as he knew would produce the motions he designed, yet he must think all this done to no purpose, and that it is an Intelligence which directs the index, and points to the hour of the day. If so, why may not the Intelligence do it, without his being at the pains of making the movements and putting them together? Why does not an empty case serve as well as another? And how comes it to pass that whenever there is any fault in the going of a watch, there is some corresponding disorder to be found in the movements, which being mended by a skilful hand all is right again? The like may be said of all the clockwork of nature, great part whereof is so wonderfully fine and subtle as scarce to be discerned by the best microscope. In short, it will be asked, how, upon our principles, any tolerable account can be given, or any final cause assigned of an innumerable multitude of bodies and machines, framed with the most exquisite art, which in the common philosophy have very apposite uses assigned them, and serve to explain abundance of phenomena?

61. To all which I answer, first, that though there were some difficulties relating to the administration of Providence, and the uses by it assigned to the several parts of nature, which I could not solve by the foregoing principles, yet this objection could be of small weight against the truth and certainty of those things which may be proved *a priori*, with the utmost evidence and rigor of demonstration. Secondly, but neither are the received principles free from the like difficulties; for, it may still be demanded to what end God should take those roundabout methods of effecting things by instruments and machines, which no one can deny might have been effected by the mere command of His will without all that apparatus; nay, if we narrowly consider it, we shall find the objection may be retorted with greater force on those who hold the existence of those machines without of mind; for it has been made evident that solidity, bulk, figure, motion, and the like have no *activity* or *efficacy* in them, so as to be capa-

ble of producing any one effect in nature. See sect. 25. Whoever therefore supposes them to exist (allowing the supposition possible) when they are not perceived does it manifestly to no purpose; since the only use that is assigned to them, as they exist unperceived, is that they produce those perceivable effects which in truth cannot be ascribed to anything but Spirit.

62. But, to come nigher the difficulty, it must be observed that though the fabrication of all those parts and organs be not absolutely necessary to the producing any effect, yet it is necessary to the producing of things in a constant regular way according to the laws of nature. There are certain general laws that run through the whole chain of natural effects; these are learned by the observation and study of nature, and are by men applied as well to the framing artificial things for the use and ornament of life as to the explaining various phenomena—which explication consists only in shewing the conformity any particular phenomenon hath to the general laws of nature, or, which is the same thing, in discovering the *uniformity* there is in the production of natural effects; as will be evident to whoever shall attend to the several instances wherein philosophers pretend to account for appearances. That there is a great and conspicuous use in these regular constant methods of working observed by the Supreme Agent hath been shewn in sect. 31. And it is no less visible that a particular size, figure, motion, and disposition of parts are necessary, though not absolutely to the producing any effect, yet to the producing it according to the standing mechanical laws of nature. Thus, for instance, it cannot be denied that God, or the Intelligence that sustains and rules the ordinary course of things, might if He were minded to produce a miracle, cause all the motions on the dialplate of a watch, though nobody had ever made the movements and put them in it: but yet, if He will act agreeably to the rules of mechanism, by Him for wise ends established and maintained in the creation, it is necessary that those actions of the watchmaker, whereby he makes the movements and rightly adjusts them, precede the production of the aforesaid motions; as also that any disorder in them be attended with the perception of some corresponding disorder in the movements, which being once corrected all is right again.

63. It may indeed on some occasions be necessary that the Author of nature display His overruling power in producing some appearance out of the ordinary series of things. Such exceptions from the general rules of nature are proper to surprise and awe men into an acknowledgement of the Divine Being; but then they are to be used but seldom, otherwise there is a plain reason why they should fail of that effect. Besides, God seems to choose the convincing our reason of His attributes by the works of nature, which discover so much harmony and contrivance in their make and are such plain indications of wisdom and beneficence in their Author, rather than to astonish us into a belief of His Being by anomalous and surprising events.

64. To set this matter in a yet clearer light, I shall observe that what has been objected in sect. 60 amounts in reality to no more than this:—ideas are not anyhow and at random produced, there being a certain order and connexion between them, like to that of cause and effect; there are also several combinations of them made in a very regular and artificial manner, which seem like so many instruments in the hand of nature that, being hid as it were behind the scenes, have a secret operation in producing those appearances which are seen on the theatre of the world, being themselves discernible only to the curious eye of the philosopher. But, since one idea cannot be the cause of another, to what purpose is that connexion? And, since those instruments, being barely *inefficacious perceptions* in the mind, are not subservient to the production of natural effects, it is demanded why they are made; or, in other words, what reason can be assigned why God should make us, upon a close inspection into His works, behold so

great variety of ideas so artfully laid together, and so much according to rule; it not being credible that He would be at the expense (if one may so speak) of all that art and regularity to no purpose.

65. To all which my answer is, first, that the connexion of ideas does not imply the relation of *cause* and *effect*, but only of a mark or sign with the thing *signified*. The fire which I see is not the cause of the pain I suffer upon my approaching it, but the mark that forewarns me of it. In like manner the noise that I hear is not the effect of this or that motion or collision of the ambient bodies, but the sign thereof. Secondly, the reason why ideas are formed into machines, that is, artificial and regular combinations, is the same with that for combining letters into words. That a few original ideas may be made to signify a great number of effects and actions, it is necessary they be variously combined together. And, to the end their use be permanent and universal, these combinations must be made by *rule, and with* wise contrivance. By this means abundance of information is conveyed unto us, concerning what we are to expect from such and such actions and what methods are proper to be taken for the exciting such and such ideas; which in effect is all that I conceive to be distinctly meant when it is said that, by discerning a figure, texture, and mechanism of the inward parts of bodies, whether natural or artificial, we may attain to know the several uses and properties depending thereon, or the nature of the thing.

66. Hence, it is evident that those things which, under the notion of a cause co-operating or concurring to the production of effects, are altogether inexplicable, and run us into great absurdities, may be very naturally explained, and have a proper and obvious use assigned to them, when they are considered only as marks or signs for our information. And it is the searching after and endeavouring to understand those signs instituted by the Author of Nature, that ought to be the employment of the natural philosopher; and not the pretending to explain things by corporeal causes, which doctrine seems to have too much estranged the minds of men from that active principle, that supreme and wise Spirit "in whom we live, move, and have our being."

67. In the *twelfth* place, it may perhaps be objected that—though it be clear from what has been said that there can be no such thing as an inert, senseless, extended, solid, figured, movable substance existing without the mind, such as philosophers describe Matter—yet, if any man shall leave out of his idea of matter the positive ideas of extension, figure, solidity and motion, and say that he means only by that word an inert, senseless substance, that exists without the mind or unperceived, which is the occasion of our ideas, or at the presence whereof God is pleased to excite ideas in us: it doth not appear but that Matter taken in this sense may possibly exist. In answer to which I say, first, that it seems no less absurd to suppose a substance without accidents, than it is to suppose accidents without a substance. But secondly, though we should grant this unknown substance may possibly exist, yet where can it be supposed to be? That it exists not in the mind is agreed; and that it exists not in place is no less certain—since all place or extension exists only in the mind, as hath been already proved. It remains therefore that it exists nowhere at all.

68. Let us examine a little the description that is here given us of *matter*. It neither acts, nor perceives, nor is perceived; for this is all that is meant by saying it is an inert, senseless, unknown substance; which is a definition entirely made up of negatives, excepting only the relative notion of its standing under or supporting. But then it must be observed that it supports nothing at all, and how nearly this comes to the description of a *nonentity* I desire may be considered. But, say you, it is the *unknown occasion*, at the presence of which ideas are excited in us by the will of God. Now, I would fain know how anything can be present to us, which is neither perceivable by

sense nor reflexion, nor capable of producing any idea in our minds, nor is at all extended, nor hath any form, nor exists in any place. The words "to be present," when thus applied, must needs be taken in some abstract and strange meaning, and which I am not able to comprehend.

69. Again, let us examine what is meant by occasion. So far as I can gather from the common use of language, that word signifies either the agent which produces any effect, or else something that is observed to accompany or go before it in the ordinary course of things. But when it is applied to Matter as above described, it can be taken in neither of those senses; for Matter is said to be passive and inert, and so cannot be an agent or efficient cause. It is also unperceivable, as being devoid of all sensible qualities, and so cannot be the occasion of our perceptions in the latter sense: as when the burning my finger is said to be the occasion of the pain that attends it. What therefore can be meant by calling matter an *occasion*? The term is either used in no sense at all, or else in some very distant from its received signification.

70. You will perhaps say that Matter, though it be not perceived by us, is nevertheless perceived by God, to whom it is the occasion of exciting ideas in our minds. For, say you, since we observe our sensations to be imprinted in an orderly and constant manner, it is but reasonable to suppose there are certain constant and regular occasions of their being produced. That is to say, that there are certain permanent and distinct parcels of Matter, corresponding to our ideas, which, though they do not excite them in our minds, or anywise immediately affect us, as being altogether passive and unperceivable to us, they are nevertheless to God, by whom they are perceived, as it were so many occasions to remind Him when and what ideas to imprint on our minds; that so things may go on in a constant uniform manner.

71. In answer to this, I observe that, as the notion of Matter is here stated, the question is no longer concerning the existence of a thing distinct from *Spirit* and *idea*, from perceiving and being perceived; but whether there are not certain ideas of I know not what sort, in the mind of God which are so many marks or notes that direct Him how to produce sensations in our minds in a constant and regular method—much after the same manner as a musician is directed by the notes of music to produce that harmonious train and composition of sound which is called a tune, though they who hear the music do not perceive the notes, and may be entirely ignorant of them. But, this notion of Matter seems too extravagant to deserve a confutation. Besides, it is in effect no objection against what we have advanced, viz. that there is no senseless unperceived substance.

72. If we follow the light of reason, we shall, from the constant uniform method of our sensations, collect the goodness and wisdom of the Spirit who excites them in our minds; but this is all that I can see reasonably concluded from thence. To me, I say, it is evident that the being of a spirit infinitely wise, good, and powerful is abundantly sufficient to explain all the appearances of nature. But, as for *inert, senseless Matter*, nothing that I perceive has any the least connexion with it, or leads to the thoughts of it. And I would fain see any one explain any the meanest phenomenon in nature by it, or shew any manner of reason, though in the lowest rank of probability, that he can have for its existence, or even make any tolerable sense or meaning of that supposition. For, as to its being an occasion, we have, I think, evidently shewn that with regard to us it is no occasion. It remains therefore that it must be, if at all, the occasion to God of exciting ideas in us; and what this amounts to we have just now seen.

73. It is worth while to reflect a little on the motives which induced men to suppose the existence of *material substance*; that so having observed the gradual ceasing and expiration of those motives or reasons, we may proportionably withdraw the assent

that was grounded on them. First, therefore, it was thought that colour, figure, motion, and the rest of the sensible qualities or accidents, did really exist without the mind; and for this reason it seemed needful to suppose some unthinking *substratum* or substance wherein they did exist, since they could not be conceived to exist by themselves. Afterwards, in process of time, men being convinced that colours, sounds, and the rest of the sensible, secondary qualities had no existence without the mind, they stripped this *substratum* or material substance of those qualities, leaving only the primary ones, figure, motion, and suchlike, which they still conceived to exist without the mind, and consequently to stand in need of a material support. But, it having been shewn that none even of these can possibly exist otherwise than in a Spirit or Mind which perceives them it follows that we have no longer any reason to suppose the being of Matter; nay, that it is utterly impossible there should be any such thing, so long as that word is taken to denote an *unthinking substratum* of qualities or accidents wherein they exist without the mind.

74. But though it be allowed by the materialists themselves that Matter was thought of only for the sake of supporting accidents, and, the reason entirely ceasing, one might expect the mind should naturally, and without any reluctance at all, quit the belief of what was solely grounded thereon; yet the prejudice is riveted so deeply in our thoughts, that we can scarce tell how to part with it, and are therefore inclined, since the *thing* itself is indefensible, at least to retain the *name*, which we apply to I know not what abstracted and indefinite notions of being, or occasion, though without any show of reason, at least so far as I can see. For, what is there on our part, or what do we perceive, amongst all the ideas, sensations, notions which are imprinted on our minds, either by sense or reflexion, from whence may be inferred the existence of an inert, thoughtless, unperceived occasion? and, on the other hand, on the part of an All-sufficient Spirit, what can there be that should make us believe or even suspect He is directed by an inert occasion to excite ideas in our minds?

75. It is a very extraordinary instance of the force of prejudice, and much to be lamented, that the mind of man retains so great a fondness, against all the evidence of reason, for a stupid thoughtless *somewhat*, by the interposition whereof it would as it were screen hat itself from the Providence of God, and remove it farther off from the affairs of the world. But, though we do the utmost we can to secure the belief of Matter, though, when reason forsakes us, we endeavour to support our opinion on the bare possibility of the thing, and though we indulge ourselves in the full scope of an imagination not regulated by reason to make out that poor possibility, yet the upshot of all is, that there are certain *unknown Ideas* in the mind of God; for this, if anything, is all that I conceive to be meant by *occasion* with regard to God. And this at the bottom is no longer contending for the thing, but for the name.

76. Whether therefore there are such Ideas in the mind of God, and whether they may be called by the name *Matter*, I shall not dispute. But, if you stick to the notion of an unthinking substance or support of extension, motion, and other sensible qualities, then to me it is most evidently impossible there should be any such thing: since it is a plain repugnancy that those qualities should exist in or be supported by an unperceiving substance.

77. But, say you, though it be granted that there is no thoughtless support of extension and the other qualities or accidents which we perceive, yet there may perhaps be some inert, unperceiving substance or *substratum* of some other qualities, as incomprehensible to us as colours are to a man born blind, because we have not a sense adapted to them. But, if we had a new sense, we should possibly no more doubt of their existence than a blind man made to see does of the existence of light and colours. I an-

swer, first, if what you mean by the word Matter be only the unknown support of un-known qualities, it is no matter whether there is such a thing or no, since it no way con-cerns us; and I do not see the advantage there is in disputing about what we know not *what*, and we know not *why*.

78. But, secondly, if we had a new sense it could only furnish us with new ideas or sensations; and then we should have the same reason against their existing in an unperceiving substance that has been already offered with relation to figure, motion, colour and the like. Qualities, as hath been shewn, are nothing else but *sen-sations* or *ideas*, which exist only in a *mind* perceiving them; and this is true not only of the ideas we are acquainted with at present, but likewise of all possible ideas whatsoever.

79. But, you will insist, what if I have no reason to believe the existence of Mat-ter? what if I cannot assign any use to it or explain anything by it, or even conceive what is meant by that word? yet still it is no contradiction to say that Matter exists, and that this Matter is in general a *substance*, or *occasion of ideas*; though indeed to go about to unfold the meaning or adhere to any particular explication of those words may be attended with great difficulties. I answer, when words are used without a meaning, you may put them together as you please without danger of running into a contradic-tion. You may say, for example, that twice two is equal to seven, so long as you de-clare you do not take the words of that proposition in their usual acceptation but for marks of you know not what. And, by the same reason, you may say there is an inert thoughtless substance without accidents which is the occasion of our ideas. And we shall understand just as much by one proposition as the other.

80. In the *last* place, you will say, what if we give up the cause of material Sub-stance, and stand to it that Matter is an unknown *somewhat*—neither substance nor ac-cident, spirit nor idea, inert, thoughtless, indivisible, immovable, unextended, existing in no place. For, say you, whatever may be urged against *substance* or *occasion*, or any other positive or relative notion of Matter, hath no place at all, so long as this *negative* definition of Matter is adhered to. I answer, you may, if so it shall seem good, use the word "Matter" in the same sense as other men use "nothing," and so make those terms convertible in your style. For, after all, this is what appears to me to be the result of that definition, the parts whereof when I consider with attention, either collectively or separate from each other, I do not find that there is any kind of effect or impression made on my mind different from what is excited by the term *nothing*.

81. You will reply, perhaps, that in the foresaid definition is included what doth sufficiently distinguish it from nothing—the positive abstract idea of *quiddity*, *entity*, or *existence*. I own, indeed, that those who pretend to the faculty of framing abstract general ideas do talk as if they had such an idea, which is, say they, the most abstract and general notion of all; that is, to me, the most incomprehensible of all others. That there are a great variety of spirits of different orders and capacities, whose faculties both in number and extent are far exceeding those the Author of my being has be-stowed on me, I see no reason to deny. And for me to pretend to determine by my own few, stinted narrow inlets of perception, what ideas the inexhaustible power of the Supreme Spirit may imprint upon them were certainly the utmost folly and presump-tion—since there may be, for aught that I know, innumerable sorts of ideas or sensa-tions, as different from one another, and from all that I have perceived, as colours are from sounds. But, how ready soever I may be to acknowledge the scantiness of my comprehension with regard to the endless variety of spirits and ideas that may possibly exist, yet for any one to pretend to a notion of Entity or Existence, *abstracted* from *spirit* and *idea*, from perceived and being perceived, is, I suspect, a downright repug-

nancy and trifling with words.—It remains that we consider the objections which may possibly be made on the part of Religion.

82. Some there are who think that, though the arguments for the real existence of bodies which are drawn from Reason be allowed not to amount to demonstration, yet the Holy Scriptures are so clear in the point as will sufficiently convince every good Christian that bodies do really exist, and are something more than mere ideas; there being in Holy Writ innumerable facts related which evidently suppose the reality of timber and stone, mountains and rivers, and cities, and human bodies. To which I answer that no sort of writings whatever, sacred or profane, which use those and the like words in the vulgar acceptation, or so as to have a meaning in them, are in danger of having their truth called in question by our doctrine. That all those things do really exist, that there are bodies, even corporeal substances, when taken in the vulgar sense, has been shewn to be agreeable to our principles; and the difference betwixt *things* and *ideas*, *realities* and *chimeras*, has been distinctly explained. See sect. 29, 30, 33, 36, etc. And I do not think that either what philosophers call *Matter*, or the existence of objects without the mind, is anywhere mentioned in Scripture.

83. Again, whether there can be or be not external things, it is agreed on all hands that the proper use of words is the marking our conceptions, or things only as they are known and perceived by us; whence it plainly follows that in the tenets we have laid down there is nothing inconsistent with the right use and significancy of language, and that discourse, of what kind soever, so far as it is intelligible, remains undisturbed. But all this seems so manifest, from what has been largely set forth in the premises, that it is needless to insist any farther on it.

84. But, it will be urged that miracles do, at least, lose much of their stress and import by our principles. What must we think of Moses' rod? was it not *really* turned into a serpent, or was there only a change of *ideas* in the minds of the spectators? And, can it be supposed that our Saviour did no more at the marriage-feast in Cana than impose on the sight, and smell, and taste of the guests, so as to create in them the appearance or idea only of wine? The same may be said of all other miracles; which, in consequence of the foregoing principles, must be looked upon only as so many cheats, or illusions of fancy. To this I reply, that the rod was changed into a real serpent, and the water into real wine. That this does not in the least contradict what I have elsewhere said will be evident from sect. 34 and 35. But this business of *real* and *imaginary* has been already so plainly and fully explained, and so often referred to, and the difficulties about it are so easily answered from what has gone before, that it were an affront to the reader's understanding to resume the explication of it in its place. I shall only observe that if at table all who were present should see, and smell, and taste, and drink wine, and find the effects of it, with me there could be no doubt of its reality; so that at bottom the scruple concerning real miracles has no place at all on ours, but only on the received principles, and consequently makes rather for than against what has been said.

85. Having done with the Objections, which I endeavoured to propose in the clearest light, and gave them all the force and weight I could, we proceed in the next place to take a view of our tenets in their Consequences. Some of these appear at first sight—as that several difficult and obscure questions, on which abundance of speculation has been thrown away, are entirely banished from philosophy. "Whether corporeal substance can think," "whether Matter be infinitely divisible," and "how it operates on spirit"—these and like inquiries have given infinite amusement to philosophers in all ages; but depending on the existence of Matter, they have no longer any place on our principles. Many other advantages there are, as well with regard to religion as the sci-

ences, which it is easy for any one to deduce from what has been premised; but this will appear more plainly in the sequel.

86. From the principles we have laid down it follows human knowledge may naturally be reduced to two heads—that of *ideas* and that of *spirits*. Of each of these I shall treat in order.

And first as to ideas or unthinking things. Our knowledge of these hath been very much obscured and confounded, and we have been led into very dangerous errors, by supposing a twofold existence of the objects of sense—the one *intelligible or in the mind, the other* real and without the mind; whereby unthinking things are thought to have a natural subsistence of their own distinct from being perceived by spirits. This, which, if I mistake not, hath been shewn to be a most groundless and absurd notion, is the very root of Scepticism; for, so long as men thought that real things subsisted without the mind, and that their knowledge was only so far forth *real* as it was conformable to *real things*, it follows they could not be certain they had any real knowledge at all. For how can it be known that the things which are perceived are conformable to those which are not perceived, or exist without the mind?

87. Colour, figure, motion, extension, and the like, considered only as so many *sensations* in the mind, are perfectly known, there being nothing in them which is not perceived. But, if they are looked on as notes or images, referred to *things* or *archetypes* existing without the mind, then are we involved all in scepticism. We see only the appearances, and not the real qualities of things. What may be the extension, figure, or motion of anything really and absolutely, or in itself, it is impossible for us to know, but only the proportion or relation they bear to our senses. Things remaining the same, our ideas vary, and which of them, or even whether any of them at all, represent the true quality really existing in the thing, it is out of our reach to determine. So that, for aught we know, all we see, hear, and feel may be only phantom and vain chimera, and not at all agree with the real things existing in *rerum natura*. All this scepticism follows from our supposing a difference between *things* and *ideas*, and that the former have a subsistence without the mind or unperceived. It were easy to dilate on this subject, and show how the arguments urged by sceptics in all ages depend on the supposition of external objects.

88. So long as we attribute a real existence to unthinking things, distinct from their being perceived, it is not only impossible for us to know with evidence the nature of any real unthinking being, but even that it exists. Hence it is that we see philosophers distrust their senses, and doubt of the existence of heaven and earth, of everything they see or feel, even of their own bodies. And, after all their labour and struggle of thought, they are forced to own we cannot attain to any self-evident or demonstrative knowledge of the existence of sensible things. But, all this doubtfulness, which so bewilders and confounds the mind and makes philosophy ridiculous in the eyes of the world, vanishes if we annex a meaning to our words, and not amuse ourselves with the terms "absolute," "external," "exist," and suchlike, signifying we know not what. I can as well doubt of my own being as of the being of those things which I actually perceive by *sense*; it being a manifest contradiction that any sensible object should be immediately perceived by sight or touch, and at the same time have no *existence* in nature, since the very existence of an unthinking being consists in *being perceived*.

89. Nothing seems of more importance towards erecting a firm system of sound and real knowledge, which may be proof against the assaults of Scepticism, than to lay the beginning in a distinct explication of what is meant by *thing, reality, existence*; for in vain shall we dispute concerning the real existence of things, or pretend to any knowledge thereof, so long as we have not fixed the meaning of those words. *Thing* or

Being is the most general name of all; it comprehends under it two kinds entirely distinct and heterogeneous, and which have nothing common but the name, viz. spirits and ideas. The former are active indivisible substances: the latter are inert, fleeting, dependent beings, which subsist not by themselves, but are supported by, or exist in minds or spiritual substances. We comprehend our own existence by inward feeling or reflexion, and that of other spirits by reason. We may be said to have some knowledge or notion of our own minds, of spirits and active beings, whereof in a strict sense we have not ideas. In like manner, we know and have a notion of relations between things or ideas—which relations are distinct from the ideas or things related, inasmuch as the latter may be perceived by us without our perceiving the former. To me it seems that *ideas*, *spirits*, and *relations* are all in their respective kinds the object of human knowledge and subject of discourse; and that the term *idea* would be improperly extended to signify everything we know or have any notion of.

90. Ideas imprinted on the senses are real things, or do really exist; this we do not deny, but we deny they can subsist without the minds which perceive them, or that they are resemblances of any archetypes existing without the mind; since the very being of a sensation or idea consists in being perceived, and an idea can be like nothing but an idea. Again, the things perceived by sense may be termed *external*, with regard to their origin—in that they are not generated from within by the mind itself, but imprinted by a Spirit distinct from that which perceives them. Sensible objects may likewise be said to be "without the mind" in another sense, namely when they exist in some other mind; thus, when I shut my eyes, the things I saw may still exist, but it must be in another mind.

91. It were a mistake to think that what is here said derogates in the least from the reality of things. It is acknowledged, on the received principles, that extension, motion, and in a word all sensible qualities have need of a support as not being able to subsist by themselves. But the objects perceived by sense are allowed to be nothing but combinations of those qualities, and consequently cannot subsist by themselves. Thus far it is agreed on all hand. So that in denying the things perceived by sense an existence independent of a substance of support wherein they may exist, we detract nothing from the received opinion of their *reality*, and are guilty of no innovation in that respect. All the difference is that, according to us, the unthinking beings perceived by sense have no existence distinct from being perceived, and cannot therefore exist in any other substance than those unextended indivisible substances or *spirits* which act and think and perceive them; whereas philosophers vulgarly hold that the sensible qualities do exist in an inert, extended, unperceiving substance which they call *Matter*, to which they attribute a natural subsistence, exterior to all thinking beings, or distinct from being perceived by any mind whatsoever, even the eternal mind of the Creator, wherein they suppose only ideas of the corporeal substances created by him; if indeed they allow them to be at all created.

92. For, as we have shewn the doctrine of Matter or corporeal substance to have been the main pillar and support of Scepticism, so likewise upon the same foundation have been raised all the impious schemes of Atheism and Irreligion. Nay, so great a difficulty has it been thought to conceive Matter produced out of nothing, that the most celebrated among the ancient philosophers, even of those who maintained the being of a God, have thought Matter to be uncreated and coeternal with Him. How great a friend *material substance* has been to Atheists in all ages were needless to relate. All their monstrous systems have so visible and necessary a dependence on it that, when this cornerstone is once removed, the whole fabric cannot choose but fall to the

ground, insomuch that it is no longer worth while to bestow a particular consideration on the absurdities of every wretched sect of Atheists.

93. That impious and profane persons should readily fall in with those systems which favour their inclinations, by deriding immaterial substance, and supposing the soul to be divisible and subject to corruption as the body; which exclude all freedom, intelligence, and design from the formation of things, and instead thereof make a self-existent, stupid, unthinking substance the root and origin of all beings; that they should hearken to those who deny a Providence, or inspection of a Superior Mind over the affairs of the world, attributing the whole series of events either to blind chance or fatal necessity arising from the impulse of one body or another—all this is very natural. And, on the other hand, when men of better principles observe the enemies of religion lay so great a stress on *unthinking Matter*, and all of them use so much industry and artifice to reduce everything to it, methinks they should rejoice to see them deprived of their grand support, and driven from that only fortress, without which your Epicureans, Hobbists, and the like, have not even the shadow of a pretence, but become the most cheap and easy triumph in the world.

94. The existence of Matter, or bodies unperceived, has not only been the main support of Atheists and Fatalists, but on the same principle doth Idolatry likewise in all its various forms depend. Did men but consider that the sun, moon, and stars, and every other object of the senses are only so many sensations in their minds, which have no other existence but barely being perceived, doubtless they would never fall down and worship their own *ideas*, but rather address their homage to that ETERNAL INVISIBLE MIND which produces and sustains all things.

95. The same absurd principle, by mingling itself with the articles of our faith, has occasioned no small difficulties to Christians. For example, about the Resurrection, how many scruples and objections have been raised by Socinians and others? But do not the most plausible of them depend on the supposition that a body is denominated the *same*, with regard not to the form or that which is perceived by sense, but the material substance, which remains the same under several forms? Take away this *material substance*, about the identity whereof all the dispute is, and mean by *body* what every plain ordinary person means by that word, to wit, that which is immediately seen and felt which is only a combination of sensible qualities or ideas, and then their most unanswerable objections come to nothing.

96. Matter being once expelled out of nature drags with it so many sceptical and impious notions, such an incredible number of disputes and puzzling questions, which have been thorns in the sides of divines as well as philosophers, and made so much fruitless work for mankind, that if the arguments we have produced against it are not found equal to demonstration (as to me they evidently seem), yet I am sure all friends to knowledge, peace, and religion have reason to wish they were.

97. Beside the external existence of the objects of perception, another great source of errors and difficulties with regard to ideal knowledge is the doctrine of *abstract ideas*, such as it hath been set forth in the Introduction. The plainest things in the world, those we are most intimately acquainted with and perfectly know, when they are considered in an abstract way, appear strangely difficult and incomprehensible. Time, place, and motion, taken in particular or concrete, are what everybody knows, but, having passed through the hands of a metaphysician, they become too abstract and fine to be apprehended by men of ordinary sense. Bid your servant meet you at such a *time* in such a *place*, and he shall never stay to deliberate on the meaning of those words; in conceiving that particular time and place, or the motion by which he is to get

thither, he finds not the least difficulty. But if *time* be taken exclusive of all those particular actions and ideas that diversify the day, merely for the continuation of existence or duration in abstract, then it will perhaps gravel even a philosopher to comprehend it.

98. For my own part, whenever I attempt to frame a simple idea of *time*, abstracted from the succession of ideas in my mind, which flows uniformly and is participated by all beings, I am lost and embrangled in inextricable difficulties. I have no notion of it at all, only I hear others say it is infinitely divisible, and speak of it in such a manner as leads me to entertain odd thoughts of my existence; since that doctrine lays one under an absolute necessity of thinking, either that he passes away innumerable ages without a thought, or else that he is annihilated every moment of his life, both which seem equally absurd. Time therefore being nothing, abstracted from the succession of ideas in our minds, it follows that the duration of any finite spirit must be estimated by the number of ideas or actions succeeding each other in that same spirit or mind. Hence, it is a plain consequence that the soul always thinks; and in truth whoever shall go about to divide in his thoughts, or abstract the *existence* of a spirit from its *cogitation*, will, I believe, find it no easy task.

99. So likewise when we attempt to abstract extension and motion from all other qualities, and consider them by themselves, we presently lose sight of them, and run into great extravagances. All which depend on a twofold abstraction; first, it is supposed that extension, for example, may be abstracted from all other sensible qualities; and secondly, that the entity of extension may be abstracted from its being perceived. But, whoever shall reflect, and take care to understand what he says, will, if I mistake not, acknowledge that all sensible qualities are alike *sensations* and alike *real*; that where the extension is, there is the colour, too, i.e., in his mind, and that their archetypes can exist only in some other *mind*; and that the objects of sense are nothing but those sensations combined, blended, or (if one may so speak) concreted together; none of all which can be supposed to exist unperceived.

100. What it is for a man to be happy, or an object good, every one may think he knows. But to frame an abstract idea of happiness, prescinded from all particular pleasure, or of goodness from everything that is good, this is what few can pretend to. So likewise a man may be just and virtuous without having precise ideas of justice and virtue. The opinion that those and the like words stand for general notions, abstracted from all particular persons and actions, seems to have rendered morality very difficult, and the study thereof of small use to mankind. And in effect the doctrine of *abstraction* has not a little contributed towards spoiling the most useful parts of knowledge.

101. The two great provinces of speculative science conversant about ideas received from sense, are Natural Philosophy and Mathematics; with regard to each of these I shall make some observations. And first I shall say somewhat of Natural Philosophy. On this subject it is that the sceptics triumph. All that stock of arguments they produce to depreciate our faculties and make mankind appear ignorant and low, are drawn principally from this head, namely, that we are under an invincible blindness as to the *true* and *real* nature of things. This they exaggerate, and love to enlarge on. We are miserably bantered, say they, by our senses, and amused only with the outside and show of things. The real essence, the internal qualities and constitution of even the meanest object, is hid from our view; something there is in every drop of water, every grain of sand, which it is beyond the power of human understanding to fathom or comprehend. But, it is evident from what has been shewn that all this complaint is groundless, and that we are influenced by false principles to that degree as to mistrust our senses, and think we know nothing of those things which we perfectly comprehend.

102. One great inducement to our pronouncing ourselves ignorant of the nature of things is the current opinion that everything includes within itself the cause of its properties; or that there is in each object an inward essence which is the source whence its discernible qualities flow, and whereon they depend. Some have pretended to account for appearances by occult qualities, but of late they are mostly resolved into mechanical causes, to wit, the figure, motion, weight, and suchlike qualities, of insensible particles; whereas, in truth, there is no other agent or efficient cause than *spirit*, it being evident that motion, as well as all other *ideas*, is perfectly inert. See sect. 25. Hence, to endeavour to explain the production of colours or sounds, by figure, motion, magnitude, and the like, must needs be labour in vain. And accordingly we see the attempts of that kind are not at all satisfactory. Which may be said in general of those instances wherein one idea or quality is assigned for the cause of another. I need not say how many hypotheses and speculations are left out, and how much the study of nature is abridged by this doctrine.

103. The great mechanical principle now in vogue is *attraction*. That a stone falls to the earth, or the sea swells towards the moon, may to some appear sufficiently explained thereby. But how are we enlightened by being told this is done by attraction? Is it that that word signifies the manner of the tendency, and that it is by the mutual drawing of bodies instead of their being impelled or protruded towards each other? But, nothing is determined of the manner or action, and it may as truly (for aught we know) be termed "impulse," or "protrusion," as "attraction." Again, the parts of steel we see cohere firmly together, and this also is accounted for by attraction; but, in this as in the other instances, I do not perceive that anything is signified besides the effect itself for as to the manner of the action whereby it is produced, or the cause which produces it, these are not so much as aimed at.

104. Indeed, if we take a view of the several phenomena, and compare them together, we may observe some likeness and conformity between them. For example, in the falling of a stone to the ground, in the rising of the sea towards the moon, in cohesion, crystallization, etc., there is something alike, namely, an union or mutual approach of bodies. So that any one of these or the like phenomena may not seem strange or surprising to a man who has nicely observed and compared the effects of nature. For that only is thought so which is uncommon, or a thing by itself, and out of the ordinary course of our observation. That bodies should tend towards the centre of the earth is not thought strange, because it is what we perceive every moment of our lives. But, that they should have a like gravitation towards the centre of the moon may seem odd and unaccountable to most men, because it is discerned only in the tides. But a philosopher, whose thoughts take in a larger compass of nature, having observed a certain similitude of appearances, as well in the heavens as the earth, that argue innumerable bodies to have a mutual tendency towards each other, which he denotes by the general name "attraction," whatever can be reduced to that he thinks justly accounted for. Thus he explains the tides by the attraction of the terraqueous globe towards the moon, which to him does not appear odd or anomalous, but only a particular example of a general rule or law of nature.

105. If therefore we consider the difference there is betwixt natural philosophers and other men, with regard to their knowledge of the phenomena, we shall find it consists not in an exacter knowledge of the efficient cause that produces them—for that can be no other than the will of a *spirit*—but only in a greater largeness of comprehension, whereby analogies, harmonies, and agreements are discovered in the works of nature, and the particular effects explained, that is, reduced to general rules, see sect. 62, which rules, grounded on the analogy and uniformness observed in the production of

natural effects, are most agreeable and sought after by the mind; for that they extend our prospect beyond what is present and near to us, and enable us to make very probable conjectures touching things that may have happened at very great distances of time and place, as well as to predict things to come; which sort of endeavour towards omniscience is much affected by the mind.

106. But we should proceed warily in such things, for we are apt to lay too great stress on analogies, and, to the prejudice of truth, humour that eagerness of the mind whereby it is carried to extend its knowledge into general theorems. For example, in the business of gravitation or mutual attraction, because it appears in many instances, some are straightway for pronouncing it *universal*; and that to attract and be attracted by every other body is an essential quality inherent in all bodies whatsoever. Whereas it is evident the fixed stars have no such tendency towards each other; and, so far is that gravitation from being *essential* to bodies that in some instances a quite contrary principle seems to shew itself; as in the perpendicular growth of plants, and the elasticity of the air. There is nothing necessary or essential in the case, but it depends entirely on the will of the Governing Spirit, who causes certain bodies to cleave together or tend towards each other according to various laws, whilst He keeps others at a fixed distance; and to some He gives a quite contrary tendency to fly asunder just as He sees convenient.

107. After what has been premised, I think we may lay down the following conclusions. First, it is plain philosophers amuse themselves in vain, when they inquire for any natural efficient cause, distinct from a *mind* or *spirit*. Secondly, considering the whole creation is the workmanship of a *wise and good Agent*, it should seem to become philosophers to employ their thoughts (contrary to what some hold) about the final causes of things; and I confess I see no reason why pointing out the various ends to which natural things are adapted, and for which they were originally with unspeakable wisdom contrived, should not be thought one good way of accounting for them, and altogether worthy a philosopher. Thirdly, from what has been premised no reason can be drawn why the history of nature should not still be studied, and observations and experiments made, which, that they are of use to mankind, and enable us to draw any general conclusions, is not the result of any immutable habitudes or relations between things themselves, but only of God's goodness and kindness to men in the administration of the world. See sect. 30 and 31. Fourthly, by a diligent observation of the phenomena within our view, we may discover the general laws of nature, and from them deduce the other phenomena; I do not say *demonstrate*, for all deductions of that kind depend on a supposition that the Author of nature always operates uniformly, and in a constant observance of those rules we take for principles: which we cannot evidently know.

108. Those men who frame general rules from the phenomena and afterwards derive the phenomena from those rules, seem to consider signs rather than causes. A man may well understand natural signs without knowing their analogy, or being able to say by what rule a thing is so or so. And, as it is very possible to write improperly, through too strict an observance of general grammar rules; so, in arguing from general laws of nature, it is not impossible we may extend the analogy too far, and by that means run into mistakes.

109. As in reading other books a wise man will choose to fix his thoughts on the sense and apply it to use, rather than lay them out in grammatical remarks on the language; so, in perusing the volume of nature, it seems beneath the dignity of the mind to affect an exactness in reducing each particular phenomenon to general rules, or shewing how it follows from them. We should propose to ourselves nobler views, namely,

to recreate and exalt the mind with a prospect of the beauty, order, extent, and variety of natural things: hence, by proper inferences, to enlarge our notions of the grandeur, wisdom, and beneficence of the Creator; and lastly, to make the several parts of the creation, so far as in us lies, subservient to the ends they were designed for, God's glory, and the sustentation and comfort of ourselves and fellow-creatures.

110. The best key for the aforesaid analogy or natural Science will be easily acknowledged to be a certain celebrated Treatise of *Mechanics*. In the entrance of which justly admired treatise, Time, Space, and Motion are distinguished into *absolute* and *relative, true* and *apparent, mathematical* and *vulgar*; which distinction, as it is at large explained by the author, does suppose these quantities to have an existence without the mind; and that they are ordinarily conceived with relation to sensible things, to which nevertheless in their own nature they bear no relation at all.

111. As for *Time*, as it is there taken in an absolute or abstracted sense, for the duration or perseverance of the existence of things, I have nothing more to add concerning it after what has been already said on that subject. Sect. 97 and 98. For the rest, this celebrated author holds there is an *absolute Space*, which, being unperceivable to sense, remains in itself similar and immovable; and relative space to be the measure thereof, which, being movable and defined by its situation in respect of sensible bodies, is vulgarly taken for immovable space. *Place* he defines to be that part of space which is occupied by any body; and according as the space is absolute or relative so also is the place. *Absolute Motion* is said to be the translation of a body from absolute place to absolute place, as relative motion is from one relative place to another. And, because the parts of absolute space do not fall under our senses, instead of them we are obliged to use their sensible measures, and so define both place and motion with respect to bodies which we regard as immovable. But, it is said in philosophical matters we must abstract from our senses, since it may be that none of those bodies which seem to be quiescent are truly so, and the same thing which is moved relatively may be really at rest; as likewise one and the same body may be in relative rest and motion, or even moved with contrary relative motions at the same time, according as its place is variously defined. All which ambiguity is to be found in the apparent motions but not at all in the true or absolute, which should therefore be alone regarded in philosophy. And the true as we are told are distinguished from apparent or relative motions by the following properties.—First, in true or absolute motion all parts which preserve the same position with respect of the whole, partake of the motions of the whole. Secondly, the place being moved, that which is placed therein is also moved; so that a body moving in a place which is in motion doth participate the motion of its place. Thirdly, true motion is never generated or changed otherwise than by force impressed on the body itself. Fourthly, true motion is always changed by force impressed on the body moved. Fifthly, in circular motion barely relative there is no centrifugal force, which, nevertheless, in that which is true or absolute, is proportional to the quantity of motion.

112. But, notwithstanding what has been said, I must confess it does not appear to me that there can be any motion other than *relative*; so that to conceive motion there must be at least conceived two bodies, whereof the distance or position in regard to each other is varied. Hence, if there was one only body in being it could not possibly be moved. This seems evident, in that the idea I have of motion doth necessarily include relation.

113. But, though in every motion it be necessary to conceive more bodies than one, yet it may be that one only is moved, namely, that on which the force causing the change in the distance or situation of the bodies, is impressed. For, however some may

define relative motion, so as to term that body *moved* which changes its distance from some other body, whether the force or action causing that change were impressed on it or no, yet as relative motion is that which is perceived by sense, and regarded in the ordinary affairs of life, it should seem that every man of common sense knows what it is as well as the best philosopher. Now, I ask any one whether, in his sense of motion as he walks along the streets, the stones he passes over may be said to *move*, because they change distance with his feet? To me it appears that though motion includes a relation of one thing to another, yet it is not necessary that each term of the relation be denominated from it. As a man may think of somewhat which does not think, so a body may be moved to or from another body which is not therefore itself in motion.

114. As the place happens to be variously defined, the motion which is related to it varies. A man in a ship may be said to be quiescent with relation to the sides of the vessel, and yet move with relation to the land. Or he may move eastward in respect of the one, and westward in respect of the other. In the common affairs of life men never go beyond the earth to define the place of any body; and what is quiescent in respect of that is accounted *absolutely* to be so. But philosophers, who have a greater extent of thought, and juster notions of the system of things, discover even the earth itself to be moved. In order therefore to fix their notions they seem to conceive the corporeal world as finite, and the utmost unmoved walls or shell thereof to be the place whereby they estimate true motions. If we sound our own conceptions, I believe we may find all the absolute motion we can frame an idea of to be at bottom no other than relative motion thus defined. For, as hath been already observed, absolute motion, exclusive of all external relation, is incomprehensible; and to this kind of relative motion all the above-mentioned properties, causes, and effects ascribed to absolute motion will, if I mistake not, be found to agree. As to what is said of the centrifugal force, that it does not at all belong to circular relative motion, I do not see how this follows from the experiment which is brought to prove it. See *Philosophiae Naturalis Principia Mathematica, in Schol. Def. VIII.* For the water in the vessel at that time wherein it is said to have the greatest relative circular motion, hath, I think, no motion at all; as is plain from the foregoing section.

115. For, to denominate a body *moved* it is requisite, first, that it change its distance or situation with regard to some other body; and secondly, that the force occasioning that change be applied to it. If either of these be wanting, I do not think that, agreeably to the sense of mankind, or the propriety of language, a body can be said to be in motion. I grant indeed that it is possible for us to think a body which we see change its distance from some other to be moved, though it have no force applied to it (in which sense there may be apparent motion), but then it is because the force causing the change of distance is imagined by us to be applied or impressed on that body thought to move; which indeed shews we are capable of mistaking a thing to be in motion which is not, and that is all.

116. From what has been said it follows that the philosophic consideration of motion does not imply the being of an absolute *Space*, distinct from that which is perceived by sense and related bodies; which that it cannot exist without the mind is clear upon the same principles that demonstrate the like of all other objects of sense. And perhaps, if we inquire narrowly, we shall find we cannot even frame an idea of *pure Space* exclusive of all body. This I must confess seems impossible, as being a most abstract idea. When I excite a motion in some part of my body if it be free or without resistance, I say there is *Space*; but if I find a resistance, then I say there is *Body*; and in proportion as the resistance to motion is lesser or greater, I say the space is more or less pure. So that when I speak of pure or empty space, it is not to be supposed that the

word "space" stands for an idea distinct from or conceivable without body and mo-tion—though indeed we are apt to think every noun substantive stands for a distinct idea that may be separated from all others; which has occasioned infinite mistakes. When, therefore, supposing all the world to be annihilated besides my own body, I say there still remains *pure Space*, thereby nothing else is meant but only that I conceive it possible for the limbs of my body to be moved on all sides without the least resistance, but if that, too, were annihilated then there could be no motion, and consequently no Space. Some, perhaps, may think the sense of seeing doth furnish them with the idea of pure space; but it is plain from what we have elsewhere shewn, that the ideas of space and distance are not obtained by that sense. See the Essay concerning Vision.

117. What is here laid down seems to put an end to all those disputes and diffi-culties that have sprung up amongst the learned concerning the nature of *pure Space*. But the chief advantage arising from it is that we are freed from that dangerous dilemma, to which several who have employed their thoughts on that subject imagine themselves reduced, to wit, of thinking either that Real Space is God, or else that there is something beside God which is eternal, uncreated, infinite, indivisible, immutable. Both which may justly be thought pernicious and absurd notions. It is certain that not a few divines, as well as philosophers of great note, have, from the difficulty they found in conceiving either limits or annihilation of space, concluded it must be divine. And some of late have set themselves particularly to shew the incommunicable attributes of God agree to it. Which doctrine, how unworthy soever it may seem of the Divine Na-ture, yet I do not see how we can get clear of it, so long as we adhere to the received opinions.

118. Hitherto of Natural Philosophy: we come now to make some inquiry con-cerning that other great branch of speculative knowledge, to wit, Mathematics. These, how celebrated soever they may be for their clearness and certainty of demonstration, which is hardly anywhere else to be found, cannot nevertheless be supposed altogether free from mistakes, if in their principles there lurks some secret error which is common to the professors of those sciences with the rest of mankind. Mathematicians, though they deduce their theorems from a great height of evidence, yet their first principles are limited by the consideration of quantity: and they do not ascend into any inquiry con-cerning those transcendental maxims which influence all the particular sciences, each part whereof, Mathematics not excepted, does consequently participate of the errors in-volved in them. That the principles laid down by mathematicians are true, and their way of deduction from those principles clear and incontestible, we do not deny; but, we hold there may be certain erroneous maxims of greater extent than the object of Mathematics, and for that reason not expressly mentioned, though tacitly supposed throughout the whole progress of that science; and that the ill effects of those secret unexamined errors are diffused through all the branches thereof. To be plain, we sus-pect the mathematicians are as well as other men concerned in the errors arising from the doctrine of abstract general ideas, and the existence of objects without the mind.

119. Arithmetic has been thought to have for its object abstract ideas of *Number*; of which to understand the properties and mutual habitudes, is supposed no mean part of speculative knowledge. The opinion of the pure and intellectual nature of numbers in abstract has made them in esteem with those philosophers who seem to have af-fected an uncommon fineness and elevation of thought. It hath set a price on the most trifling numerical speculations which in practice are of no use, but serve only for amusement; and hath therefore so far infected the minds of some, that they have dreamed of mighty mysteries involved in numbers, and attempted the explication of natural things by them. But, if we inquire into our own thoughts, and consider what has

been premised, we may perhaps entertain a low opinion of those high flights and abstractions, and look on all inquiries, about numbers only as so many *difficiles nugae* [troublesome trifles], so far as they are not subservient to practice, and promote the benefit of life.

120. Unity in abstract we have before considered in sect. 13, from which and what has been said in the Introduction, it plainly follows there is not any such idea. But, number being defined a "collection of units," we may conclude that, if there be no such thing as unity or unit in abstract, there are no ideas of number in abstract denoted by the numeral names and figures. The theories therefore in Arithmetic, if they are abstracted from the names and figures, as likewise from all use and practice as well as from the particular things numbered, can be supposed to have nothing at all for their object; hence we may see how entirely the science of numbers is subordinate to practice, and how jejune and trifling it becomes when considered as a matter of mere speculation.

121. However, since there may be some who, deluded by the specious show of discovering abstracted verities, waste their time in arithmetical theorems and problems which have not any use, it will not be amiss if we more fully consider and expose the vanity of that pretence; and this will plainly appear by taking a view of Arithmetic in its infancy, and observing what it was that originally put men on the study of that science, and to what scope they directed it. It is natural to think that at first, men, for ease of memory and help of computation, made use of counters, or in writing of single strokes, points, or the like, each whereof was made to signify an unit, *i.e.*, some one thing of whatever kind they had occasion to reckon. Afterwards they found out the more compendious ways of making one character stand in place of several strokes or points. And, lastly, the notation of the Arabians or Indians came into use, wherein, by the repetition of a few characters or figures, and varying the signification of each figure according to the place it obtains, all numbers may be most aptly expressed; which seems to have been done in imitation of language, so that an exact analogy is observed betwixt the notation by figures and names, the nine simple figures answering the nine first numeral names and places in the former, corresponding to denominations in the latter. And agreeably to those conditions of the simple and local value of figures, were contrived methods of finding, from the given figures or marks of the parts, what figures and how placed are proper to denote the whole, or *vice versa*. And having found the sought figures, the same rule or analogy being observed throughout, it is easy to read them into words; and so the number becomes perfectly known. For then the number of any particular things is said to be known, when we know the name of figures (with their due arrangement) that according to the standing analogy belong to them. For, these signs being known, we can by the operations of arithmetic know the signs of any part of the particular sums signified by them; and, thus computing in signs (because of the connexion established betwixt them and the distinct multitudes of things whereof one is taken for an unit), we may be able rightly to sum up, divide, and proportion the things themselves that we intend to number.

122. In Arithmetic, therefore, we regard not the *things*, but the *signs*, which nevertheless are not regarded for their own sake, but because they direct us how to act with relation to things, and dispose rightly of them. Now, agreeably to what we have before observed of words in general (sect. 19, Introd.) it happens here likewise that abstract ideas are thought to be signified by numeral names or characters, while they do not suggest ideas of particular things to our minds. I shall not at present enter into a more particular dissertation on this subject, but only observe that it is evident from what has been said, those things which pass for abstract truths and theorems concern-

ing numbers, are in reality conversant about no object distinct from particular numeral things, except only names and characters, which originally came to be considered on no other account but their being signs, or capable to represent aptly whatever particular things men had need to compute. Whence it follows that to study them for their own sake would be just as wise, and to as good purpose as if a man, neglecting the true use or original intention and subserviency of language, should spend his time in impertinent criticisms upon words, or seasonings and controversies purely verbal.

123. From numbers we proceed to speak of *Extension*, which, considered as relative, is the object of Geometry. The *infinite* divisibility of *finite* extension, though it is not expressly laid down either as an axiom or theorem in the elements of that science, yet is throughout the same everywhere supposed and thought to have so inseparable and essential a connexion with the principles and demonstrations in Geometry, that mathematicians never admit it into doubt, or make the least question of it. And, as this notion is the source from whence do spring all those amusing geometrical paradoxes which have such a direct repugnancy to the plain common sense of mankind, and are admitted with so much reluctance into a mind not yet debauched by learning; so it is the principal occasion of all that nice and extreme subtilty which renders the study of Mathematics so difficult and tedious. Hence, if we can make it appear that no finite extension contains innumerable parts, or is infinitely divisible, it follows that we shall at once clear the science of Geometry from a great number of difficulties and contradictions which have ever been esteemed a reproach to human reason, and withal make the attainment thereof a business of much less time and pains than it hitherto has been.

124. Every particular finite extension which may possibly be the object of our thought is an *idea* existing only in the mind, and consequently each part thereof must be perceived. If, therefore, I cannot perceive innumerable parts in any finite extension that I consider, it is certain they are not contained in it; but, it is evident that I cannot distinguish innumerable parts in any particular line, surface, or solid, which I either perceive by sense, or figure to myself in my mind: wherefore I conclude they are not contained in it. Nothing can be plainer to me than that the extensions I have in view are no other than my own ideas; and it is no less plain that I cannot resolve any one of my ideas into an infinite number of other ideas, that is, that they are not infinitely divisible. If by finite extension be meant something distinct from a finite idea, I declare I do not know what that is, and so cannot affirm or deny anything of it. But if the terms "extension," "parts," etc., are taken in any sense conceivable, that is, for ideas, then to say a finite quantity or extension consists of parts infinite in number is so manifest a contradiction, that every one at first sight acknowledges it to be so; and it is impossible it should ever gain the assent of any reasonable creature who is not brought to it by gentle and slow degrees, as a converted Gentile to the belief of transubstantiation. Ancient and rooted prejudices do often pass into principles; and those propositions which once obtain the force and credit of a *principle*, are not only themselves, but likewise whatever is deducible from them, thought privileged from all examination. And there is no absurdity so gross, which, by this means, the mind of man may not be prepared to swallow.

125. He whose understanding is possessed with the doctrine of abstract general ideas may be persuaded that (whatever be thought of the ideas of sense) extension in *abstract* is infinitely divisible. And one who thinks the objects of sense exist without the mind will perhaps in virtue thereof be brought to admit that a line but an inch long may contain innumerable parts—really existing, though too small to be discerned. These errors are grafted as well in the minds of geometricians as of other men, and have a like influence on their reasonings; and it were no difficult thing to show how the

arguments from Geometry made use of to support the infinite divisibility of extension are bottomed on them. At present we shall only observe in general whence it is the mathematicians are all so fond and tenacious of that doctrine.

126. It has been observed in another place that the theorems and demonstrations in Geometry are conversant about universal ideas (sect. 15, Introd.); where it is explained in what sense this ought to be understood, to wit, the particular lines and figures included in the diagram are supposed to stand for innumerable others of different sizes; or, in other words, the geometer considers them abstracting from their magnitude—which does not imply that he forms an abstract idea, but only that he cares not what the particular magnitude is, whether great or small, but looks on that as a thing different to the demonstration. Hence it follows that a line in the scheme but an inch long must be spoken of as though it contained ten thousand parts, since it is regarded not in itself, but as it is universal; and it is universal only in its signification, whereby it represents innumerable lines greater than itself, in which may be distinguished ten thousand parts or more, though there may not be above an inch in it. After this manner, the properties of the lines signified are (by a very usual figure) transferred to the sign, and thence, through mistake, though to appertain to it considered in its own nature.

127. Because there is no number of parts so great but it is possible there may be a line containing more, the inch-line is said to contain parts more than any assignable number; which is true, not of the inch taken absolutely, but only for the things signified by it. But men, not retaining that distinction in their thoughts, slide into a belief that the small particular line described on paper contains in itself parts innumerable. There is no such thing as the ten-thousandth part of an inch; but there is of a mile or diameter of the earth, which may be signified by that inch. When therefore I delineate a triangle on paper, and take one side not above an inch, for example, in length to be the radius this I consider as divided into 10,000 or 100,000 parts or more; for, though the ten-thousandth part of that line considered in itself is nothing at all, and consequently may be neglected without an error or inconvenience, yet these described lines, being only marks standing for greater quantities, whereof it may be the ten-thousandth part is very considerable, it follows that, to prevent notable errors in practice, the radius must be taken of 10,000 parts or more.

128. From what has been said the reason is plain why, to the end any theorem become universal in its use, it is necessary we speak of the lines described on paper as though they contained parts which really they do not. In doing of which, if we examine the matter thoroughly, we shall perhaps discover that we cannot conceive an inch itself as consisting of, or being divisible into, a thousand parts, but only some other line which is far greater than an inch, and represented by it; and that when we say a line is infinitely divisible, we must mean a line which is infinitely great. What we have here observed seems to be the chief cause why, to suppose the infinite divisibility of finite extension has been thought necessary in geometry.

129. The several absurdities and contradictions which flowed from this false principle might, one would think, have been esteemed so many demonstrations against it. But, by I know not what logic, it is held that proofs *a posteriori* are not to be admitted against propositions relating to infinity, as though it were not impossible even for an infinite mind to reconcile contradictions; or as if anything absurd and repugnant could have a necessary connexion with truth or flow from it. But, whoever considers the weakness of this pretence will think it was contrived on purpose to humour the laziness of the mind which had rather acquiesce in an indolent scepticism than be at the pains to go through with a severe examination of those principles it has ever embraced for true.

130. Of late the speculations about Infinities have run so high, and grown to such strange notions, as have occasioned no small scruples and disputes among the geometers of the present age. Some there are of great note who, not content with holding that finite lines may be divided into an infinite number of parts, do yet farther maintain that each of those infinitesimals is itself subdivisible into an infinity of other parts or infinitesimals of a second order, and so on *ad infinitum*. These, I say, assert there are infinitesimals of infinitesimals of infinitesimals, etc., without ever coming to an end; so that according to them an inch does not barely contain an infinite number of parts, but an infinity of an infinity of an infinity *ad infinitum* of parts. Others there be who hold all orders of infinitesimals below the first to be nothing at all; thinking it with good reason absurd to imagine there is any positive quantity or part of extension which, though multiplied infinitely, can never equal the smallest given extension. And yet on the other hand it seems no less absurd to think the square, cube or other power of a positive real root, should itself be nothing at all; which they who hold infinitesimals of the first order, denying all of the subsequent orders, are obliged to maintain.

131. Have we not therefore reason to conclude they are *both* in the wrong, and that there is in effect no such thing as parts infinitely small, or an infinite number of parts contained in any finite quantity? But you will say that if this doctrine obtains it will follow the very foundations of Geometry are destroyed, and those great men who have raised that science to so astonishing a height, have been all the while building a castle in the air. To this it may be replied that whatever is useful in geometry, and promotes the benefit of human life, does still remain firm and unshaken on our principles; that science considered as practical will rather receive advantage than any prejudice from what has been said. But to set this in a due light may be the proper business of another place. For the rest, though it should follow that some of the more intricate and subtle parts of Speculative Mathematics may be pared off without any prejudice to truth, yet I do not see what damage will be thence derived to mankind. On the contrary, I think it were highly to be wished that men of great abilities and obstinate application would draw off their thoughts from those amusements, and employ them in the study of such things as lie nearer the concerns of life, or have a more direct influence on the manners.

132. If it be said that several theorems undoubtedly true are discovered by methods in which infinitesimals are made use of, which could never have been if their existence included a contradiction in it; I answer that upon a thorough examination it will not be found that in any instance it is necessary to make use of or conceive infinitesimal parts of finite lines, or even quantities less than the *minimum sensible*; nay, it will be evident this is never done, it being impossible.

133. By what we have premised, it is plain that very numerous and important errors have taken their rise from those false Principles which were impugned in the foregoing parts of this treatise; and the opposites of those erroneous tenets at the same time appear to be most fruitful Principles, from whence do flow innumerable consequences highly advantageous to true philosophy as well as to religion. Particularly *Matter*, or *the absolute existence of corporeal objects*, hath been shewn to be that wherein the most avowed and pernicious enemies of all knowledge, whether human or divine, have ever placed their chief strength and confidence. And surely, if by distinguishing the real existence of unthinking things from their being perceived, and allowing them a subsistance of their own out of the minds of spirits, no one thing is explained in nature, but on the contrary a great many inexplicable difficulties arise; if the supposition of *Matter* is barely precarious, as not being grounded on so much as one single reason; if its consequences cannot endure the light of examination and free inquiry, but screen

themselves under the dark and general pretence of "infinites being incomprehensible"; if withal the removal of this Matter be not attended with the least evil consequence; if it be not even missed in the world but everything as well, nay much easier conceived without it; if, lastly, both Sceptics and Atheists are for ever silenced upon supposing only spirits and ideas, and this scheme of things is perfectly agreeable both to Reason and Religion: methinks we may expect it should be admitted and firmly embraced, though it were proposed only as an *hypothesis*, and the existence of Matter had been allowed possible, which yet I think we have evidently demonstrated that it is not.

134. True it is that, in consequence of the foregoing principles, several disputes and speculations which are esteemed no mean parts of learning, are rejected as useless. But, how great a prejudice soever against our notions this may give to those who have already been deeply engaged, and make large advances in studies of that nature, yet by others we hope it will not be thought any just ground of dislike to the principles and tenets herein laid down, that they abridge the labour of study, and make human sciences far more clear, compendious and attainable than they were before.

135. Having despatched what we intended to say concerning the knowledge of IDEAS, the method we proposed leads us in the next place to treat of SPIRITS—with regard to which, perhaps, human knowledge is not so deficient as is vulgarly imagined. The great reason that is assigned for our being thought ignorant of the nature of spirits is our not having an *idea* of it. But, surely it ought not to be looked on as a defect in a human understanding that it does not perceive the idea of spirit, if it is manifestly impossible there should be any such idea. And this if I mistake not has been demonstrated in sect. 27; to which I shall here add that a spirit has been shewn to be the only substance or support wherein unthinking beings or ideas can exist; but that this *substance* which supports or perceives ideas should itself be an idea or like an idea is evidently absurd.

136. It will perhaps be said that we want a sense (as some have imagined) proper to know substances withal, which, if we had, we might know our own soul as we do a triangle. To this I answer, that, in case we had a new sense bestowed upon us, we could only receive thereby some new sensations or ideas of sense. But I believe nobody will say that what he means by the terms *soul* and *substance* is only some particular sort of idea or sensation. We may therefore infer that, all things duly considered, it is not more reasonable to think our faculties defective, in that they do not furnish us with an idea of spirit or active thinking substance, than it would be if we should blame them for not being able to comprehend a *round square*.

137. From the opinion that spirits are to be known after the manner of an idea or sensation have risen many absurd and heterodox tenets, and much scepticism about the nature of the soul. It is even probable that this opinion may have produced a doubt in some whether they had any soul at all distinct from their body since upon inquiry they could not find they had an idea of it. That an *idea* which is inactive, and the existence whereof consists in being perceived, should be the image or likeness of an agent subsisting by itself, seems to need no other refutation than barely attending to what is meant by those words. But, perhaps you will say that though an idea cannot resemble a spirit in its thinking, acting, or subsisting by itself, yet it may in some other respects; and it is not necessary that an idea or image be in all respects like the original.

138. I answer, if it does not in those mentioned, it is impossible it should represent it in any other thing. Do but leave out the power of willing, thinking, and perceiving ideas, and there remains nothing else wherein the idea can be like a spirit. For, by the word *spirit* we mean only that which thinks, wills, and perceives; this, and this alone, constitutes the signification of the term. If therefore it is impossible that any de-

gree of those powers should be represented in an idea, it is evident there can be no idea of a spirit.

139. But it will be objected that, if there is no idea signified by the terms *soul*, *spirit*, and *substance*, they are wholly insignificant, or have no meaning in them. I answer, those words do mean or signify a real thing, which is neither an idea nor like an idea, but that which perceives ideas, and wills, and reasons about them. What I am myself, that which I denote by the term I, is the same with what is meant by *soul* or *spiritual substance*. If it be said that this is only quarreling at a word, and that, since the immediate significations of other names are by common consent called ideas, no reason can be assigned why that which is signified by the name *spirit* or *soul* may not partake in the same appellation. I answer, all the unthinking objects of the mind agree in that they are entirely passive, and their existence consists only in being perceived; where as a soul or spirit is an active being, whose existence consists not in being perceived, but in perceiving ideas and thinking. It is therefore necessary, in order to prevent equivocation and confounding natures perfectly disagreeing and unlike, that we distinguish between *spirit* and *idea*. See sect. 27.

140. In a large sense, indeed, we may be said to have an idea or rather a notion of *spirit*; that is, we understand the meaning of the word, otherwise we could not affirm or deny anything of it. Moreover, as we conceive the ideas that are in the minds of other spirits by means of our own, which we suppose to be resemblances of them; so we know other spirits by means of our own soul—which in that sense is the image or idea of them; it having a like respect to other spirits that blueness or heat by me perceived has to those ideas perceived by another.

141. It must not be supposed that they who assert the natural immortality of the soul are of opinion that it is absolutely incapable of annihilation even by the infinite power of the Creator who first gave it being, but only that it is not liable to be broken or dissolved by the ordinary laws of nature or motion. They indeed who hold the soul of man to be only a thin vital flame, or system of animal spirits, make it perishing and corruptible as the body; since there is nothing more easily dissipated than such a being, which it is naturally impossible should survive the ruin of the tabernacle wherein it is enclosed. And this notion has been greedily embraced and cherished by the worst part of mankind, as the most effectual antidote against all impressions of virtue and religion. But it has been made evident that bodies, of what frame or texture soever, are barely passive ideas in the mind, which is more distant and heterogeneous from them than light is from darkness. We have shewn that the soul is indivisible, incorporeal, unextended, and it is consequently incorruptible. Nothing can be plainer than that the motions, changes, decays, and dissolutions which we hourly see befall natural bodies (and which is what we mean by the *course of nature*) cannot possibly affect an active, simple, uncompounded substance; such a being therefore is indissoluble by the force of nature; that is to say, "the soul of man is naturally immortal."

142. After what has been said, it is, I suppose, plain that our souls are not to be known in the same manner as senseless, inactive objects, or by way of *idea*. *Spirits* and *ideas* are things so wholly different, that when we say "they exist," "they are known," or the like, these words must not be thought to signify anything common to both natures. There is nothing alike or common in them: and to expect that by any multiplication or enlargement of our faculties we may be enabled to know a spirit as we do a triangle, seems as absurd as if we should hope to see a sound. This is inculcated because I imagine it may be of moment towards clearing several important questions, and preventing some very dangerous errors concerning the nature of the soul. We may not, I think, strictly be said to have an *idea* of an active being, or of an action, although we

may be said to have a *notion* of them. I have some knowledge or notion of my mind, and its acts about ideas, inasmuch as I know or understand what is meant by these words. What I know, that I have some notion of. I will not say that the terms *idea* and *notion* may not be used convertibly, if the world will have it so; but yet it conduceth to clearness and propriety that we distinguish things very different by different names. It is also to be remarked that, all relations including an act of the mind, we cannot so properly be said to have an idea, but rather a notion of the relations and habitudes between things. But if, in the modern way, the word *idea* is extended to spirits, and relations, and acts, this is, after all, an affair of verbal concern.

143. It will not be amiss to add, that the doctrine of *abstract ideas* has had no small share in rendering those sciences intricate and obscure which are particularly conversant about spiritual things. Men have imagined they could frame abstract notions of the powers and acts of the mind, and consider them prescinded as well from the mind or spirit itself, as from their respective objects and effects. Hence a great number of dark and ambiguous terms, presumed to stand for abstract notions, have been introduced into metaphysics and morality, and from these have grown infinite distractions and disputes amongst the learned.

144. But, nothing seems more to have contributed towards engaging men in controversies and mistakes with regard to the nature and operations of the mind, than the being used to speak of those things in terms borrowed from sensible ideas. For example, the will is termed the *motion* of the soul; this infuses a belief that the mind of man is as a ball in motion, impelled and determined by the objects of sense, as necessarily as that is by the stroke of a racket. Hence arise endless scruples and errors of dangerous consequence in morality. All which, I doubt not, may be cleared, and truth appear plain, uniform, and consistent, could but philosophers be prevailed on to retire into themselves, and attentively consider their own meaning.

145. From what has been said, it is plain that we cannot know the existence of other spirits otherwise than by their operations, or the ideas by them excited in us. I perceive several motions, changes, and combinations of ideas, that inform me there are certain particular agents, like myself, which accompany them and concur in their production. Hence, the knowledge I have of other spirits is not immediate, as is the knowledge of my ideas; but depending on the intervention of ideas, by me referred to agents or spirits distinct from myself, as effects or concomitant signs.

146. But, though there be some things which convince us human agents are concerned in producing them; yet it is evident to every one that those things which are called the Works of Nature, that is, the far greater part of the ideas or sensations perceived by us, are not produced by, or dependent on, the wills of men. There is therefore some other Spirit that causes them; since it is repugnant that they should subsist by themselves. See sect. 29. But, if we attentively consider the constant regularity, order, and concatenation of natural things, the surprising magnificence, beauty, and perfection of the larger, and the exquisite contrivance of the smaller parts of creation, together with the exact harmony and correspondence of the whole, but above all the never-enough-admired laws of pain and pleasure, and the instincts or natural inclinations, appetites, and passions of animals; I say if we consider all these things, and at the same time attend to the meaning and import of the attributes One, Eternal, Infinitely Wise, Good, and Perfect, we shall clearly perceive that they belong to the aforesaid Spirit, "who works all in all," and "by whom all things consist."

147. Hence, it is evident that God is known as certainly and immediately as any other mind or spirit whatsoever distinct from ourselves. We may even assert that the existence of God is far more evidently perceived than the existence of men; because the

effects of nature are infinitely more numerous and considerable than those ascribed to human agents. There is not any one mark that denotes a man, or effect produced by him, which does not more strongly evince the being of that Spirit who is the Author of Nature. For, it is evident that in affecting other persons the will of man has no other object than barely the motion of the limbs of his body; but that such a motion should be attended by, or excite any idea in the mind of another, depends wholly on the will of the Creator. He alone it is who "upholding all things by the word of His power," maintains that intercourse between spirits whereby they are able to perceive the existence of each other. And yet this pure and clear light which enlightens every one is itself invisible.

148. It seems to be a general pretence of the unthinking herd that they cannot see God. Could we but see Him, say they, as we see a man, we should believe that He is, and believing obey His commands. But alas, we need only open our eyes to see the Sovereign Lord of all things, with a more full and clear view than we do any one of our fellow-creatures. Not that I imagine we see God (as some will have it) by a direct and immediate view; or see corporeal things, not by themselves, but by seeing that which represents them in the essence of God, which doctrine is, I must confess, to me incomprehensible. But I shall explain my meaning;—A human spirit or person is not perceived by sense, as not being an idea; when therefore we see the colour, size, figure, and motions of a man, we perceive only certain sensations or ideas excited in our own minds; and these being exhibited to our view in sundry distinct collections, serve to mark out unto us the existence of finite and created spirits like ourselves. Hence it is plain we do not see a man—if by *man* is meant that which lives, moves, perceives, and thinks as we do—but only such a certain collection of ideas as directs us to think there is a distinct principle of thought and motion, like to ourselves, accompanying and represented by it. And after the same manner we see God; all the difference is that, whereas some one finite and narrow assemblage of ideas denotes a particular human mind, whithersoever we direct our view, we do at all times and in all places perceive manifest tokens of the Divinity: everything we see, hear, feel, or anywise perceive by sense, being a sign or effect of the power of God; as is our perception of those very motions which are produced by men.

149. It is therefore plain that nothing can be more evident to any one that is capable of the least reflexion than the existence of God, or a Spirit who is intimately present to our minds, producing in them all that variety of ideas or sensations which continually affect us, on whom we have an absolute and entire dependence, in short "in whom we live, and move, and have our being." That the discovery of this great truth, which lies so near and obvious to the mind, should be attained to by the reason of so very few, is a sad instance of the stupidity and inattention of men, who, though they are surrounded with such clear manifestations of the Deity, are yet so little affected by them that they seem, as it were, blinded with excess of light.

150. But you will say, Hath Nature no share in the production of natural things, and must they be all ascribed to the immediate and sole operation of God? I answer, if by *Nature* is meant only the visible *series* of effects or sensations imprinted on our minds, according to certain fixed and general laws, then it is plain that Nature, taken in this sense, cannot produce anything at all. But, if by *Nature* is meant some being distinct from God, as well as from the laws of nature, and things perceived by sense, I must confess that word is to me an empty sound without any intelligible meaning annexed to it. Nature, in this acceptation, is a vain chimera, introduced by those heathens who had not just notions of the omnipresence and infinite perfection of God. But, it is more unaccountable that it should be received among Christians, professing belief in the Holy Scriptures, which constantly ascribe those effects to the immediate hand of

God that heathen philosophers are wont to impute to Nature. "The Lord He causeth the vapours to ascend; He maketh lightnings with rain; He bringeth forth the wind out of his treasures." Jerem., 10. 13. "He turneth the shadow of death into the morning, and maketh the day dark with night." Amos, 5. 8. "He visiteth the earth, and maketh it soft with showers: He blesseth the springing thereof, and crowneth the year with His goodness; so that the pastures are clothed with flocks, and the valleys are covered over with corn." See Psalm 65. But, notwithstanding that this is the constant language of Scripture, yet we have I know not what aversion from believing that God concerns Himself so nearly in our affairs. Fain would we suppose Him at a great distance off, and substitute some blind unthinking deputy in His stead, though (if we may believe Saint Paul) "He be not far from every one of us."

151. It will, I doubt not, be objected that the slow and gradual methods observed in the production of natural things do not seem to have for their cause the immediate hand of an Almighty Agent. Besides, monsters, untimely births, fruits blasted in the blossom, rains falling in desert places, miseries incident to human life, and the like, are so many arguments that the whole frame of nature is not immediately actuated and superintended by a Spirit of infinite wisdom and goodness. But the answer to this objection is in a good measure plain from sect. 62; it being visible that the aforesaid methods of nature are absolutely necessary, in order to working by the most simple and general rules, and after a steady and consistent manner; which argues both the wisdom and goodness of God. Such is the artificial contrivance of this mighty machine of nature that, whilst its motions and various phenomena strike on our senses, the hand which actuates the whole is itself unperceivable to men of flesh and blood. "Verily" (saith the prophet) "thou art a God that hidest thyself." Isaiah, 45. 15. But, though the Lord conceal Himself from the eyes of the sensual and lazy, who will not be at the least expense of thought, yet to an unbiased and attentive mind nothing can be more plainly legible than the intimate presence of an All-wise Spirit, who fashions, regulates and sustains the whole system of beings. It is clear, from what we have elsewhere observed, that the operating according to general and stated laws is so necessary for our guidance in the affairs of life, and letting us into the secret of nature, that without it all reach and compass of thought, all human sagacity and design, could serve to no manner of purpose; it were even impossible there should be any such faculties or powers in the mind. See sect. 31. Which one consideration abundantly outbalances whatever particular inconveniences may thence arise.

152. We should further consider that the very blemishes and defects of nature are not without their use, in that they make an agreeable sort of variety, and augment the beauty of the rest of the creation, as shades in a picture serve to set off the brighter and more enlightened parts. We would likewise do well to examine whether our taxing the waste of seeds and embryos, and accidental destruction of plants and animals, before they come to full maturity, as an imprudence in the Author of nature, be not the effect of prejudice contracted by our familiarity with impotent and saving mortals. In man indeed a thrifty management of those things which he cannot procure without much pains and industry may be esteemed wisdom. But, we must not imagine that the inexplicably fine machine of an animal or vegetable costs the great Creator any more pains or trouble in its production than a pebble does; nothing being more evident than that an Omnipotent Spirit can indifferently produce everything by a mere *fiat* or act of His will. Hence, it is plain that the splendid profusion of natural things should not be interpreted weakness or prodigality in the agent who produces them, but rather be looked on as an argument of the riches of His power.

153. As for the mixture of pain or uneasiness which is in the world, pursuant to the general laws of nature, and the actions of finite, imperfect spirits, this, in the state we are in at present, is indispensably necessary to our well-being. But our prospects are too narrow. We take, for instance, the idea of some one particular pain into our thoughts, and account it *evil*; whereas, if we enlarge our view, so as to comprehend the various ends, connexions, and dependencies of things, on what occasions and in what proportions we are affected with pain and pleasure, the nature of human freedom, and the design with which we are put into the world; we shall be forced to acknowledge that those particular things which, considered in themselves, appear to be evil, have the nature of good, when considered as linked with the whole system of beings.

154. From what has been said, it will be manifest to any considering person, that it is merely for want of attention and comprehensiveness of mind that there are any favourers of Atheism or the Manichean Heresy to be found. Little and unreflecting souls may indeed burlesque the works of Providence, the beauty and order whereof they have not capacity, or will not be at the pains, to comprehend; but those who are masters of any justness and extent of thought, and are withal used to reflect, can never sufficiently admire the divine traces of Wisdom and Goodness that shine throughout the Economy of Nature. But what truth is there which shineth so strongly on the mind that by an aversion of thought, a wilful shutting of the eyes, we may not escape seeing it? Is it therefore to be wondered at, if the generality of men, who are ever intent on business or pleasure, and little used to fix or open the eye of their mind, should not have all that conviction and evidence of the Being of God which might be expected in reasonable creatures?

155. We should rather wonder that men can be found so stupid as to neglect, than that neglecting they should be unconvinced of such an evident and momentous truth. And yet it is to be feared that too many of parts and leisure, who live in Christian countries, are, merely through a supine and dreadful negligence, sunk into Atheism. Since it is downright impossible that a soul pierced and enlightened with a thorough sense of the omnipresence, holiness, and justice of that Almighty Spirit should persist in a remorseless violation of His laws. We ought, therefore, earnestly to meditate and dwell on those important points; that so we may attain conviction without all scruple "that the eyes of the Lord are in every place beholding the evil and the good; that He is with us and keepeth us in all places whither we go, and giveth us bread to eat and raiment to put on"; that He is present and conscious to our innermost thoughts; and that we have a most absolute and immediate dependence on Him. A clear view of which great truths cannot choose but fill our hearts with an awful circumspection and holy fear, which is the strongest incentive to *Virtue*, and the best guard against *Vice*.

156. For, after all, what deserves the first place in our studies is the consideration of GOD and our DUTY; which to promote, as it was the main drift and design of my labours, so shall I esteem them altogether useless and ineffectual if, by what I have said, I cannot inspire my readers with a pious sense of the Presence of God; and, having shewn the falseness or vanity of those barren speculations which make the chief employment of learned men, the better dispose them to reverence and embrace the salutary truths of the Gospel, which to know and to practice is the highest perfection of human nature.

DAVID HUME
1711–1776

David Hume was born in Edinburgh, Scotland, in 1711. His father, a lawyer, died before David was two years old. He was raised by his mother, a deeply religious woman, on a pleasant, but modest, family estate at Ninewells, near Berwick in southern Scotland. Young David was very religious as a boy, often making lists of his sins so that he could seek forgiveness. But shortly after beginning his studies at the University of Edinburgh, at age twelve, he seems to have lost his faith.

Although the family was not poor, there was not enough wealth to provide a comfortable life of study for David, the youngest child. His family decided, therefore, that Hume should follow his father into law. This was not to be, however, for as Hume later wrote, "I found an unsurmountable aversion to everything but the pursuit of philosophy and general learning."

In 1729, when he was only eighteen, Hume had a breakthrough, discovering what he called "a new Science of Thought." He gave up all pretense of becoming a lawyer and applied his energies to his new insight. To conserve his limited finances, he moved to a small town in France, La Flèche, where Descartes had studied. There he completed his first work, *A Treatise of Human Nature, Being an Attempt to Introduce the Experimental Method of Reasoning into Moral Subjects*, published in 1739 and 1740. Hume hoped this work would give him his "love of literary fame"—while putting him in a more comfortable financial situation. But, as he later said, the work "fell dead-born from the press, without reaching such distinction as even to excite a murmur among the zealots."

For the next thirteen years, Hume held a variety of positions, including tutor to a mad marquess and secretary to a general. During this time, Hume wrote and published his *Essays, Moral and Political* (1741–1742). The success of this work led him to rewrite Book I of his earlier *Treatise*, this time titled as *An Enquiry Concerning Human Understanding* (1748). He added chapters on miracles, free will, and the argument from design, which he had left out of the earlier work, and he omitted many of his psychological speculations. This book enjoyed some success, though its antireligious nature may have contributed to Hume's rejected applications for two different chairs of philosophy. In 1751, he also recast Book III of the earlier *Treatise*, under the title *Enquiry Concerning the Principles of Morals.*

Hume was appointed Librarian to the Faculty of Advocates in Edinburgh in 1752. In this post, he wrote a multivolume history of England. He also managed to infuriate the library curators with his selections, and in 1757 he was forced to resign when he refused to remove books the curators considered obscene. In the same year, he published *Four Dissertations*, including "The Natural History of Religion," "Of the Passions" (a truncated version of Book II of the *Treatise*), "Of Tragedy," and "Of the Standard of Taste." By now Hume's works had become well known on the Continent, and when he returned to France in 1763 as part of the British ambassador's staff, he was lionized by French intellectual society. Hume was a favorite at French soirées: Sociable and witty, he was called "le bon David" by his French friends.

When Hume returned to England in 1766, he found that his works had finally brought him the literary fame at home that he had so long desired. In 1767, he took another government post, but two years later he resigned and retired to Edinburgh. There he spent his last years quietly, until his death, probably from cancer, in 1776. His *Dialogues Concerning Natural Religion*, written in the 1750s, was published posthumously in 1779.

$$* \quad * \quad *$$

Hume's philosophy, as developed in the *Enquiry*, begins with a rejection of the "abstruse speculations" and "superstitions" of contemporary thought. With Locke, Hume agrees that there are no such things as innate ideas; all knowledge comes through sensory experience. Yet as he worked out the implications of these convictions, he came to conclusions quite different from those of his predecessor.

According to Hume, all the perceptions of the mind may be divided into "impressions" and "ideas." Using an empirical distinction, Hume believes impressions to be "more lively" than ideas. These impressions and ideas are then divided into simple and complex, impressions of sensation and impressions of reflection, and so on. The source of impressions cannot be known empirically, so Hume does not address this question. Simple ideas, on the other hand, must come from impressions. In fact, for an idea to have any meaning whatever, it must be derived from an impression or from a combination of impressions. If I have the idea of a gold mountain, for instance, it is because I have previously had impressions that gave rise to the ideas of "gold" and "mountain" that I am now associating. Using this empirical criterion of meaning, it becomes clear that ideas such as "substance," "God," or even "the self" are without a clear meaning. So according to Hume, Locke's idea of an eternal world of "substances" and Berkeley's idea of an all-perceiving God are without meaning.

Hume then considers the association between ideas and argues that there are "only three principles of connexion among ideas, namely, *Resemblance, Contiguity* in time or place, and *Cause* or *Effect.*" These associations of ideas are really nothing more than habit or "custom" and so do not necessarily reflect the "real world." Take causality, for example. One could imagine Pavlov's dogs hearing the bell, getting the food, hearing the bell, getting the food, hearing the bell . . . and after a period of time concluding, "bells cause food." But there is obviously no necessary relation between cause and effect in this case. There is no logical reason why the bell might not sound and yet no food appear. Hume argues that all supposed instances of cause and effect are of this kind. We get so used to seeing two events joined that we conclude that one caused the other. Thus, according to Hume, Locke's claim that the "external world" causes sensations and the Thomistic First-Cause argument for God's existence are without empirical foundation. It also means that the "laws of nature" are founded only on past experience and that we have no *a priori* evidence that tomorrow will be the same as today.

The remainder of the *Enquiry* develops the implications of Hume's radical empiricism and deals with the skepticism arising from it. He acknowledges that his own practice does not always reflect his philosophical position. Hume recognizes that despite his causal skepticism, it would not be wise to "throw himself out at the window." As he wrote early on in this work, we must "be modest in our pretensions; and even to discover the difficulty ourselves before it is objected to us. By this means, we may make a kind of merit of our very ignorance."

Hume's *Dialogues Concerning Natural Religion* applies the insights of the *Enquiry* to the question of God. Since there is no necessary relationship between cause and effect, we cannot argue with certainty from an effect, such as apparent design in nature, back to a cause, such as God the Designer. Further, deductions we might make about God from design would make God finite and imperfect because that is how the world is. Finally, Hume argues that even if we allow an analogy between the world and God, it would not necessarily mean a monotheistic God who wills, thinks, and so on. The world might be the result of a cosmic spider or even of divine "animal birth and copulation." Hume's point is that such discussions are ultimately meaningless, given our inability to know anything beyond impressions and ideas.

Philosophers differ in their appraisals of Hume's two greatest works, the *Treatise* and its reworking, the *Enquiry*. Many consider the *Enquiry* more mature; others think the *Treatise* more brilliant. Hume himself said that the *Enquiry*, not the *Treatise*, contained his "philosophical sentiments and principles." The *Enquiry* is reprinted here complete, as is Hume's *Dialogues Concerning Natural Religion*.

*   *   *

For a comprehensive biography of Hume, including interesting material from his letters, see Ernest Campbell Mossner, *The Life of David Hume* (Oxford: Clarendon Press, 1954, 1980). The classic studies of Hume's thought are Charles William Hendel, *Studies in the Philosophy of David Hume* (Princeton, NJ: Princeton University Press, 1925); and, especially, Norman Kemp Smith, *The Philosophy of David Hume* (London: Macmillan, 1941). A short, clear overview of his thought is A.J. Ayer, *Hume* (New York: Oxford University Press, 1981)— part of the "Past Masters" series, now reprinted in a combined volume, John Dunn et al., eds., *The British Empiricists* (Oxford: Oxford University Press, 1992). Barry Stroud, *Hume* (Oxford: Routledge, 1981) and Terence Penelhum, *David Hume: An Introduction to His Philosophical System* (West Lafayette, IN: Purdue University Press, 1995) are also useful. For studies in specific areas of

Hume's thought, see Tom L. Beauchamp, *Hume and the Problem of Causation* (New York: Oxford University Press, 1981); Robert J. Fogelin, *Hume's Skepticism in the Treatise of Human Nature* (London: Routledge, 1985); and David Pears, *Hume's System* (Oxford: Oxford University Press, 1991), George Dicker, *Hume's Epistemology and Metaphysics* (London: Routledge, 1998); H.O. Mounce, *Hume's Naturalism* (London: Routledge, 1999), for epistemology and philosophy of mind; Jonathan Harrison, *Hume's Moral Epistemology* (Oxford: Clarendon Press, 1976), and J.L. Mackie, *Hume's Moral Theory* (London: Routledge & Kegan Paul, 1980), for ethics; and Antony Flew, *Hume's Philosophy of Belief* (London: Routledge & Kegan Paul; New York: Humanities Press, 1961); J.C.A. Gaskin, *Hume's Philosophy of Religion* (New York: Barnes & Noble, 1978); and Keith E. Yandell, *Hume's "Inexplicable Mystery": His Views on Religion* (Philadelphia: Temple University Press, 1990); Stanley Tweyman, ed., *David Hume—Dialogues Concerning Natural Religion in Focus* (Oxford: Routledge, 1991), for philosophy of religion. For collections of essays, see David Pears, ed., *David Hume: A Symposium* (London: St. Martin's Press, 1963); A. Sesonke and N. Fleming, eds., *Human Understanding: Studies in the Philosophy of David Hume* (Belmont, CA: Wadsworth, 1965); and the excellent V.C. Chappell, ed., *Hume: A Collection of Critical Essays* (Notre Dame, IN: Notre Dame University Press, 1968); and Stanley Tweyman, ed., *David Hume: Critical Assessments,* six volumes (London: Routledge, 1996).

AN ENQUIRY CONCERNING HUMAN UNDERSTANDING

Section I. Of the Different Species of Philosophy

Moral philosophy, or the science of human nature, may be treated after two different manners; each of which has its peculiar merit, and may contribute to the entertainment, instruction, and reformation of mankind. The one considers man chiefly as born for action; and as influenced in his measures by taste and sentiment; pursuing one object, and avoiding another, according to the value which these objects seem to possess, and according to the light in which they present themselves. As virtue, of all objects, is allowed to be the most valuable, this species of philosophers paint her in the most amiable colours; borrowing all helps from poetry and eloquence, and treating their subject in an easy and obvious manner, and such as is best fitted to please the imagination, and engage the affections. They select the most striking observations and instances from common life; place opposite characters in a proper contrast; and alluring us into the paths of virtue by the views of glory and happiness, direct our steps in these paths by the soundest precepts and most illustrious examples. They make us *feel* the difference between vice and virtue; they excite and regulate our sentiments; and so they can but bend our hearts to the love of probity and true honour, they think, that they have fully attained the end of all their labours.

The other species of philosophers consider man in the light of a reasonable rather than an active being, and endeavour to form his understanding more than cultivate his manners. They regard human nature as a subject of speculation; and with a narrow scrutiny examine it, in order to find those principles, which regulate our understanding, excite our sentiments, and make us to approve or blame any particular object, action, or behaviour. They think it a reproach to all literature, that philosophy should not yet have fixed, beyond controversy, the foundation of morals, reasoning, and criticism; and should for ever talk of truth and falsehood, vice and virtue, beauty and deformity, without being able to determine the source of these distinctions. While they attempt this arduous task, they are deterred by no difficulties; but proceeding from particular instances to general principles, they still push on their enquiries to principles more general, and rest not satisfied till they arrive at those original principles, by which, in every science, all human curiosity must be bounded. Though their speculations seem abstract, and even unintelligible to common readers, they aim at the approbation of the learned and the wise; and think themselves sufficiently compensated for the labour of their whole lives, if they can discover some hidden truths, which may contribute to the instruction of posterity.

It is certain that the easy and obvious philosophy will always, with the generality of mankind, have the preference above the accurate and abstruse; and by many will be recommended, not only as more agreeable, but more useful than the other. It enters more into common life; moulds the heart and affections; and, by touching those principles which actuate men, reforms their conduct, and brings them nearer to that model of perfection which it describes. On the contrary, the abstruse philosophy, being founded on a turn of mind, which cannot enter into business and action, vanishes when the philosopher leaves the shade, and comes into open day; nor can its principles easily retain any influence over our conduct and behaviour. The feelings of our heart, the agitation of our passions, the vehemence of our affections, dissipate all its conclusions, and reduce the profound philosopher to a mere plebeian.

This also must be confessed, that the most durable, as well as justest fame, has been acquired by the easy philosophy, and that abstract reasoners seem hitherto to have enjoyed only a momentary reputation, from the caprice or ignorance of their own age, but have not been able to support their renown with more equitable posterity. It is easy for a profound philosopher to commit a mistake in his subtile reasonings; and one mistake is the necessary parent of another, while he pushes on his consequences, and is not deterred from embracing any conclusion, by its unusual appearance, or its contradiction to popular opinion. But a philosopher, who purposes only to represent the common sense of mankind in more beautiful and more engaging colours, if by accident he falls into error, goes not farther; but renewing his appeal to common sense, and the natural sentiments of the mind, returns into the right path, and secures himself from any dangerous illusions. The fame of Cicero flourishes at present; but that of Aristotle is utterly decayed. La Bruyere passes the seas, and still maintains his reputation: But the glory of Malebranche is confined to his own nation, and to his own age. And Addison, perhaps, will be read with pleasure, when Locke shall be entirely forgotten.

The mere philosopher is a character, which is commonly but little acceptable in the world, as being supposed to contribute nothing either to the advantage or pleasure of society; while he lives remote from communication with mankind, and is wrapped up in principles and notions equally remote from their comprehension. On the other hand, the mere ignorant is still more despised; nor is any thing deemed a surer sign of an illiberal genius in an age and nation where the sciences flourish, than to be entirely destitute of all relish for those noble entertainments. The most perfect character is supposed to lie between those extremes; retaining an equal ability and taste for books, company, and business; preserving in conversation that discernment and delicacy which arise from polite letters; and in business, that probity and accuracy which are the natural result of a just philosophy. In order to diffuse and cultivate so accomplished a character, nothing can be more useful than compositions of the easy style and manner, which draw not too much from life, require no deep application or retreat to be comprehended, and send back the student among mankind full of noble sentiments and wise precepts, applicable to every exigence of human life. By means of such compositions, virtue becomes amiable, science agreeable, company instructive, and retirement entertaining.

Man is a reasonable being; and as such, receives from science his proper food and nourishment: But so narrow are the bounds of human understanding, that little satisfaction can be hoped for in this particular, either from the extent or security of his acquisitions. Man is a sociable, no less than a reasonable being: But neither can he always enjoy company agreeable and amusing, or preserve the proper relish for them. Man is also an active being; and from that disposition, as well as from the various necessities of human life, must submit to business and occupation: But the mind requires some relaxation, and cannot always support its bent to care and industry. It seems, then, that nature has pointed out a mixed kind of life as most suitable to the human race, and secretly admonished them to allow none of these biases to draw too much, so as to incapacitate them for other occupations and entertainments. Indulge your passion for science, says she, but let your science be human, and such as may have a direct reference to action and society. Abstruse thought and profound researches I prohibit, and will severely punish, by the pensive melancholy which they introduce, by the endless uncertainty in which they involve you, and by the cold reception which your pretended discoveries shall meet with, when communicated. Be a philosopher; but, amidst all your philosophy, be still a man.

Were the generality of mankind contented to prefer the easy philosophy to the abstract and profound, without throwing any blame or contempt on the latter, it might not be improper, perhaps, to comply with this general opinion, and allow every man to enjoy, without opposition, his own taste and sentiment. But as the matter is often carried farther, even to the absolute rejecting of all profound reasonings, or what is commonly called *metaphysics*, we shall now proceed to consider what can reasonably be pleaded in their behalf.

We may begin with observing, that one considerable advantage, which results from the accurate and abstract philosophy, is, its subserviency to the easy and humane, which, without the former, can never attain a sufficient degree of exactness in its sentiments, precepts, or reasonings. All polite letters are nothing but pictures of human life in various attitudes and situations; and inspire us with different sentiments, of praise or blame, admiration or ridicule, according to the qualities of the object, which they set before us. An artist must be better qualified to succeed in this undertaking, who, besides a delicate taste and a quick apprehension, possesses an accurate knowledge of the internal fabric, the operations of the understanding, the workings of the passions, and the various species of sentiment which discriminate vice and virtue. How painful soever this inward search or enquiry may appear, it becomes, in some measure, requisite to those, who would describe with success the obvious and outward appearances of life and manners. The anatomist presents to the eye the most hideous and disagreeable objects; but his science is useful to the painter in delineating even a Venus or an Helen. While the latter employs all the richest colours of his art, and gives his figures the most graceful and engaging airs; he must still carry his attention to the inward structure of

An Experiment on a Bird in the Air Pump, ca. 1767–1768, by Joseph Wright of Derby
(1734–1797). The artist is showing the interplay between rational analysis and human
emotion, between reason and feeling. The scientist in the center is demonstrating that a
bird cannot fly in a vacuum. In doing so he is also killing the bird—a fact not lost on the
little girls to the right. (*Tate Gallery, London*)

the human body, the position of the muscles, the fabric of the bones, and the use and
figure of every part or organ. Accuracy is, in every case, advantageous to beauty and
just reasoning to delicate sentiment. In vain would we exalt the one by depreciating the
other.

Besides, we may observe, in every art or profession, even those which most concern life or action, that a spirit of accuracy, however acquired, carries all of them
nearer their perfection, and renders them more subservient to the interests of society.
And though a philosopher may live remote from business, the genius of philosophy, if
carefully cultivated by several, must gradually diffuse itself throughout the whole society, and bestow a similar correctness on every art and calling. The politician will acquire greater foresight and subtlety, in the subdividing and balancing of power; the
lawyer more method and finer principles in his reasonings; and the general more regularity in his discipline, and more caution in his plans and operations. The stability of
modern governments above the ancient, and the accuracy of modern philosophy, have
improved, and probably will still improve, by similar gradations.

Were there no advantage to be reaped from these studies, beyond the gratification of an innocent curiosity, yet ought not even this to be despised; as being one accession to those few safe and harmless pleasures, which are bestowed on the human
race. The sweetest and most inoffensive path of life leads through the avenues of sci-

ence and learning; and whoever can either remove any obstructions in this way, or open up any new prospect, ought so far to be esteemed a benefactor to mankind. And though these researches may appear painful and fatiguing, it is with some minds as with some bodies, which being endowed with vigorous and florid health, require severe exercise, and reap a pleasure from what, to the generality of mankind, may seem burdensome and laborious. Obscurity, indeed, is painful to the mind as well as to the eye; but to bring light from obscurity, by whatever labour, must needs be delightful and rejoicing.

But this obscurity in the profound and abstract philosophy, is objected to, not only as painful and fatiguing, but as the inevitable source of uncertainty and error. Here indeed lies the justest and most plausible objection against a considerable part of metaphysics, that they are not properly a science; but arise either from the fruitless efforts of human vanity, which would penetrate into subjects utterly inaccessible to the understanding, or from the craft of popular superstitions, which, being unable to defend themselves on fair ground, raise these entangling brambles to cover and protect their weakness. Chased from the open country, these robbers fly into the forest, and lie in wait to break in upon every unguarded avenue of the mind, and overwhelm it with religious fears and prejudices. The stoutest antagonist, if he remit his watch a moment, is oppressed. And many, through cowardice and folly, open the gates to the enemies, and willingly receive them with reverence and submission, as their legal sovereigns.

But is this a sufficient reason, why philosophers should desist from such researches, and leave superstition still in possession of her retreat? Is it not proper to draw an opposite conclusion, and perceive the necessity of carrying the war into the most secret recesses of the enemy? In vain do we hope, that men, from frequent disappointment, will at last abandon such airy sciences, and discover the proper province of human reason. For, besides, that many persons find too sensible an interest in perpetually recalling such topics; besides this, I say, the motive of blind despair can never reasonably have place in the sciences; since, however unsuccessful former attempts may have proved, there is still room to hope, that the industry, good fortune, or improved sagacity of succeeding generations may reach discoveries unknown to former ages. Each adventurous genius will leap at the arduous prize, and find himself stimulated, rather than discouraged, by the failures of his predecessors; while he hopes that the glory of achieving so hard an adventure is reserved for him alone. The only method of freeing learning, at once, from these abstruse questions, is to enquire seriously into the nature of human understanding, and show, from an exact analysis of its powers and capacity, that it is by no means fitted for such remote and abstruse subjects. We must submit to this fatigue, in order to live at ease ever after: And must cultivate true metaphysics with some care, in order to destroy the false and adulterate. Indolence, which, to some persons, affords a safeguard against this deceitful philosophy, is, with others, overbalanced by curiosity; and despair, which, at some moments, prevails, may give place afterwards to sanguine hopes and expectations. Accurate and just reasoning is the only catholic remedy, fitted for all persons and all dispositions; and is alone able to subvert that abstruse philosophy and metaphysical jargon, which, being mixed up with popular superstition, renders it in a manner impenetrable to careless reasoners, and gives it the air of science and wisdom.

Besides this advantage of rejecting, after deliberate enquiry, the most uncertain and disagreeable part of learning, there are many positive advantages, which result from an accurate scrutiny into the powers and faculties of human nature. It is remarkable concerning the operations of the mind, that, though most intimately present to us, yet, whenever they become the object of reflection, they seem involved in obscurity;

nor can the eye readily find those lines and boundaries, which discriminate and distinguish them. The objects are too fine to remain long in the same aspect or situation; and must be apprehended in an instant, by a superior penetration, derived from nature, and improved by habit and reflection. It becomes, therefore, no inconsiderable part of science barely to know the different operations of the mind, to separate them from each other, to class them under their proper heads, and to correct all that seeming disorder, in which they lie involved, when made the object of reflection and enquiry. This talk of ordering and distinguishing, which has no merit, when performed with regard to external bodies, the objects of our senses, rises in its value, when directed towards the operations of the mind, in proportion to the difficulty and labour, which we meet with in performing it. And if we can go no farther than this mental geography, or delineation of the distinct parts and powers of the mind, it is at least a satisfaction to go so far; and the more obvious this science may appear (and it is by no means obvious) the more contemptible still must the ignorance of it be esteemed, in all pretenders to learning and philosophy.

Nor can there remain any suspicion, that this science is uncertain and chimerical; unless we should entertain such a scepticism as is entirely subversive of all speculation, and even action. It cannot be doubted, that the mind is endowed with several powers and faculties, that these powers are distinct from each other, that what is really distinct to the immediate perception may be distinguished by reflection; and consequently, that there is a truth and falsehood in all propositions on this subject, and a truth and falsehood, which lie not beyond the compass of human understanding. There are many obvious distinctions of this kind, such as those between the will and understanding, the imagination and passions, which fall within the comprehension of every human creature; and the finer and more philosophical distinctions are no less real and certain, though more difficult to be comprehended. Some instances, especially late ones, of success in these enquiries, may give us a juster notion of the certainty and solidity of this branch of learning. And shall we esteem it worthy the labour of a philosopher to give us a true system of the planets, and adjust the position and order of those remote bodies; while we affect to overlook those, who, with so much success, delineate the parts of the mind, in which we are so intimately concerned?

But may we not hope, that philosophy, if cultivated with care, and encouraged by the attention of the public, may carry its researches still farther, and discover, at least in some degree, the secret springs and principles, by which the human mind is actuated in its operations? Astronomers had long contented themselves with proving, from the phenomena, the true motions, order, and magnitude of the heavenly bodies: Till a philosopher, at last, arose, who seems, from the happiest reasoning, to have also determined the laws and forces, by which the revolutions of the planets are governed and directed. The like has been performed with regard to other parts of nature. And there is no reason to despair of equal success in our enquiries concerning the mental powers and economy, if prosecuted with equal capacity and caution. It is probable, that one operation and principle of the mind depends on another; which, again, may be resolved into one more general and universal: And how far these researches may possibly be carried, it will be difficult for us, before, or even after, a careful trial, exactly to determine. This is certain, that attempts of this kind are every day made even by those who philosophize the most negligently: And nothing can be more requisite than to enter upon the enterprize with thorough care and attention; that, if it lie within the compass of human understanding, it may at last be happily achieved; if not, it may, however, be rejected with some confidence and security. This last conclusion, surely, is not desirable; nor ought it to be embraced too rashly. For how much must we diminish from the beauty and value of this species of philosophy, upon such a supposition? Moralists have hitherto been accustomed, when they considered the vast multitude and diversity of those actions that excite our approbation or dislike, to search for some common principle, on which this variety of sentiments might depend. And though they have sometimes carried the matter too far, by their passion for some one general principle; it must, however, be confessed, that they are excusable in expecting to find some general principles, into which all the vices and virtues were justly to be resolved. The like has been the endeavour of critics, logicians, and even politicians: Nor have their attempts been wholly unsuccessful; though perhaps longer time, greater accuracy, and more ardent application may bring these sciences still nearer their perfection. To throw up at once all pretensions of this kind may justly be deemed more rash, precipitate, and dogmatical, than even the boldest and most affirmative philosophy, that has ever attempted to impose its crude dictates and principles on mankind.

What though these reasonings concerning human nature seem abstract, and of difficult comprehension? This affords no presumption of their falsehood. On the contrary, it seems impossible, that what has hitherto escaped so many wise and profound philosophers can be very obvious and easy. And whatever pains these researches may cost us, we may think ourselves sufficiently rewarded, not only in point of profit but of pleasure, if, by that means, we can make any addition to our stock of knowledge, in subjects of such unspeakable importance.

But as, after all, the abstractedness of these speculations is no recommendation, but rather a disadvantage to them, and as this difficulty may perhaps be surmounted by care and art, and the avoiding of all unnecessary detail, we have, in the following enquiry, attempted to throw some light upon subjects, from which uncertainty has hitherto deterred the wise, and obscurity the ignorant. Happy, if we can unite the boundaries of the different species of philosophy, by reconciling profound enquiry with clearness, and truth with novelty! And still more happy, if reasoning in this easy manner, we can undermine the foundations of an abstruse philosophy, which seems to have hitherto served only as a shelter to superstition, and a cover to absurdity and error!

Section II. Of the Origin of Ideas

Every one will readily allow, that there is a considerable difference between the perceptions of the mind, when a man feels the pain of excessive heat, or the pleasure of moderate warmth, and when he afterwards recalls to his memory this sensation, or anticipates it by his imagination. These faculties may mimic or copy the perceptions of the senses; but they never can entirely reach the force and vivacity of the original sentiment. The utmost we say of them, even when they operate with greatest vigour, is, that they represent their object in so lively a manner, that we could almost say we feel or see it: But, except the mind be disordered by disease or madness, they never can arrive at such a pitch of vivacity, as to render these perceptions altogether undistinguishable. All the colours of poetry, however splendid, can never paint natural objects in such a manner as to make the description be taken for a real landscape. The most lively thought is still inferior to the dullest sensation.

We may observe a like distinction to run through all the other perceptions of the mind. A man in a fit of anger, is actuated in a very different manner from one who only thinks of that emotion. If you tell me, that any person is in love, I easily understand your meaning, and form a just conception of his situation; but never can mistake that conception for the real disorders and agitations of the passion. When we reflect on our past sentiments and affections, our thought is a faithful mirror, and copies its objects truly; but the colours which it employs are faint and dull, in comparison of those in which our original perceptions were clothed. It requires no nice discernment or metaphysical head to mark the distinction between them.

Here therefore we may divide all the perceptions of the mind into two classes or species, which are distinguished by their different degrees of force and vivacity. The less forcible and lively are commonly denominated *Thoughts* or *Ideas*. The other species want a name in our language, and in most others; I suppose, because it was not requisite for any, but philosophical purposes, to rank them under a general term or appellation. Let us, therefore, use a little freedom, and call them *Impressions*; employing that word in a sense somewhat different from the usual. By the term impression, then, I mean all our more lively perceptions, when we hear, or see, or feel, or love, or hate, or desire, or will. And *impressions* are distinguished from ideas which are the less lively perceptions, of which we are conscious, when we reflect on any of those sensations or movements above mentioned.

Nothing, at first view, may seem more unbounded than the thought of man, which not only escapes all human power and authority, but is not even restrained within the limits of nature and reality. To form monsters, and join incongruous shapes and appearances, costs the imagination no more trouble than to conceive the most natural and familiar objects. And while the body is confined to one planet, along which it creeps with pain and difficulty; the thought can in an instant transport us into the most distant regions of the universe; or even beyond the universe, into the unbounded chaos, where nature is supposed to lie in total confusion. What never was seen, or heard of, may yet be conceived; nor is any thing beyond the power of thought, except what implies an absolute contradiction.

But though our thought seems to possess this unbounded liberty, we shall find, upon a nearer examination, that it is really confined within very narrow limits, and that all this creative power of the mind amounts to no more than the faculty of compounding, transposing, augmenting, or diminishing the materials afforded us by the senses and experience. When we think of a golden mountain, we only join two consistent ideas, *gold* and *mountain*, with which we were formerly acquainted. A virtuous horse we can conceive; because, from our own feeling, we can conceive virtue; and this we may unite to the figure and shape of a horse, which is an animal familiar to us. In short, all the materials of thinking are derived either from our outward or inward sentiment: the mixture and composition of these belongs alone to the mind and will. Or, to express myself in philosophical language, all our ideas or more feeble perceptions are copies of our impressions or more lively ones.

To prove this, the two following arguments will, I hope, be sufficient. First, when we analyze our thoughts or ideas, however compounded or sublime, we always find that they resolve themselves into such simple ideas as were copied from a precedent feeling or sentiment. Even those ideas, which, at first view, seem the most wide of this origin, are found, upon a nearer scrutiny, to be derived from it. The idea of God, as meaning an infinitely intelligent, wise, and good Being, arises from reflecting on the operations of our own mind, and augmenting, without limit, those qualities of goodness and wisdom. We may prosecute this enquiry to what length we please; where we shall always find, that every idea which we examine is copied from a similar impression. Those who would assert that this position is not universally true nor without exception, have only one, and that an easy method of refuting it; by producing that idea, which, in their opinion, is not derived from this source. It will then be incumbent on us, if we would maintain our doctrine, to produce the impression, or lively perception, which corresponds to it.

Secondly. If it happens, from a defect of the organ, that a man is not susceptible of any species of sensation, we always find that he is as little susceptible of the correspondent ideas. A blind man can form no notion of colours; a deaf man of sounds. Restore either of them that sense in which he is deficient; by opening this new inlet for his sensations, you also open an inlet for the ideas; and he finds no difficulty in conceiving these objects. The case is the same, if the object, proper for exciting any sensation, has never been applied to the organ. A Laplander or Negro has no notion of the relish of wine. And though there are few or no instances of a like deficiency in the mind, where a person has never felt or is wholly incapable of a sentiment or passion that belongs to his species; yet we find the same observation to take place in a less degree. A man of mild manners can form no idea of inveterate revenge or cruelty; nor can a selfish heart easily conceive the heights of friendship and generosity. It is readily allowed, that other beings may possess many senses of which we can have no conception, because the ideas of them have never been introduced to us in the only manner by which an idea can have access to the mind, to wit, by the actual feeling and sensation.

There is, however, one contradictory phenomenon, which may prove that it is not absolutely impossible for ideas to arise, independent of their correspondent impressions. I believe it will readily be allowed, that the several distinct ideas of colour, which enter by the eye, or those of sound, which are conveyed by the ear, are really different from each other; though, at the same time, resembling. Now if this be true of different colours, it must be no less so of the different shades of the same colour; and each shade produces a distinct idea, independent of the rest. For if this should be denied, it is possible, by the continual gradation of shades, to run a colour insensibly into what is most remote from it; and if you will not allow any of the means to be different, you cannot, without absurdity, deny the extremes to be the same. Suppose, therefore, a person to have enjoyed his sight for thirty years, and to have become perfectly acquainted with colours of all kinds except one particular shade of blue, for instance, which it never has been his fortune to meet with. Let all the different shades of that colour, except that single one, be placed before him, descending gradually from the deepest to lightest; it is plain that he will perceive a blank, where that shade is wanting, and will be sensible that there is a greater distance in that place between the contiguous colours than in any other. Now I ask, whether it be possible for him, from his own imagination, to supply this deficiency, and raise up to himself the idea of that particular shade, though it had never been conveyed to him by his senses? I believe there are few but will be of opinion that he can: and this may serve as a proof that the simple ideas are not always, in every instance, derived from the correspondent impressions; though this instance is so singular, that it is scarcely worth our observing, and does not merit that for it alone we should alter our general maxim.

Here, therefore, is a proposition, which not only seems, in itself, simple and intelligible; but, if a proper use were made of it, might render every dispute equally intelligible, and banish all that jargon, which has so long taken possession of metaphysical reasonings, and drawn disgrace upon them. All ideas, especially abstract ones, are naturally faint and obscure: the mind has but a slender hold of them: they are apt to be confounded with other resembling ideas; and when we have often employed any term, though without a distinct meaning, we are apt to imagine it has a determinate idea annexed to it. On the contrary, all impressions, that is, all sensations, either outward or inward, are strong and vivid: the limits between them are more exactly determined: nor is it easy to fall into any error or mistake with regard to them. When we entertain, therefore, any suspicion that a philosophical term is employed without any meaning or idea (as is but too frequent), we need but enquire, *from what impressions is that supposed idea derived*? And if it be impossible to assign any, this will serve to confirm our suspicion.* By bringing ideas into so clear a light we may reasonably hope to remove all dispute, which may arise, concerning their nature and reality.

SECTION III. OF THE ASSOCIATION OF IDEAS

It is evident that there is a principle of connexion between the different thoughts or ideas of the mind, and that, in their appearance to the memory or imagination, they introduce each other with a certain degree of method and regularity. In our more serious thinking or discourse this is so observable that any particular thought, which breaks in upon the regular tract or chain of ideas, is immediately remarked and rejected. And even in our wildest and most wandering reveries, nay in our very dreams, we shall find, if we reflect, that the imagination ran not altogether at adventures, but that there was still a connexion upheld among the different ideas, which succeeded each other. Were the loosest and freest conversation to be transcribed, there would immediately be observed something which connected it in all its transitions. Or where this is wanting, the person who broke the thread of discourse might still inform you, that there had secretly revolved in his mind a succession of thought, which had gradually led him from the subject of conversation. Among different languages, even where we cannot suspect the least connexion or communication, it is found, that the words, expressive of ideas, the most compounded, do yet nearly correspond to each other: a certain proof that the simple ideas, comprehended in the compound ones, were bound together by some universal principle, which had an equal influence on all mankind.

Though it be too obvious to escape observation, that different ideas are connected together; I do not find that any philosopher has attempted to enumerate or class all the principles of association; a subject, however, that seems worthy of curiosity. To

---

*It is probable that no more was meant by those, who denied innate ideas, than that all ideas were copies of our impressions; though it must be confessed, that the terms, which they employed, were not chosen with such caution, nor so exactly defined, as to prevent all mistakes about their doctrine. For what is meant by *innate*? If innate be equivalent to natural, then all the perceptions and ideas of the mind must be allowed to be innate or natural, in whatever sense we take the latter word, whether in opposition to what is uncommon, artificial, or miraculous. If by innate be meant, contemporary to our birth, the dispute seems to be frivolous; nor is it worth while to enquire at what time thinking begins, whether before, at, or after our birth. Again, the word idea, seems to be commonly taken in a very loose sense, by LOCKE and others; as standing for any of our perceptions, our sensations and passions, as well as thoughts. Now in this sense, I should desire to know, what can be meant by asserting, that self-love, or resentment of injuries, or the passion between the sexes is not innate?

But admitting these terms, *impressions* and *ideas*, in the sense above explained, and understanding by *innate*, what is original or copied from no precedent perception, then may we assert that all our impressions are innate and our ideas not innate.

To be ingenuous, I must own it to be my opinion, that LOCKE was betrayed into this question by the schoolmen, who, making use of undefined terms, draw out their disputes to a tedious length, without ever touching the point in question. A like ambiguity and circumlocution seem to run through that philosopher's reasonings on this as well as most other subjects.

me, there appear to be only three principles of connexion among ideas, namely, *Resemblance*, *Contiguity* in time or place, and *Cause* or *Effect*.

That these principles serve to connect ideas will not, I believe, be much doubted. A picture naturally leads our thoughts to the original:* the mention of one apartment in a building naturally introduces an enquiry or discourse concerning the others:** and if we think of a wound, we can scarcely forbear reflecting on the pain which follows it.*** But that this enumeration is complete, and that there are no other principles of association except these, may be difficult to prove to the satisfaction of the reader, or even to a man's own satisfaction. All we can do, in such cases, is to run over several instances, and examine carefully the principle which binds the different thoughts to each other, never stopping till we render the principle as general as possible.† The more instances we examine, and the more care we employ, the more assurance shall we acquire, that the enumeration, which we form from the whole, is complete and entire.

Section IV. Sceptical Doubts Concerning the Operations of the Understanding

Part I

All the objects of human reason or enquiry may naturally be divided into two kinds, to wit, *Relations of Ideas*, and *Matters of Fact*. Of the first kind are the sciences of Geometry, Algebra, and Arithmetic; and in short, every affirmation which is either intuitively or demonstratively certain. *That the square of the hypothenuse is equal to the squares of the two sides*, is a proposition which expresses a relation between these figures. *That three times five is equal to the half of thirty*, expresses a relation between these numbers. Propositions of this kind are discoverable by the mere operation of thought, without dependence on what is anywhere existent in the universe. Though there never were a circle or triangle in nature, the truths demonstrated by Euclid would for ever retain their certainty and evidence.

Matters of fact, which are the second objects of human reason, are not ascertained in the same manner; nor is our evidence of their truth however great, of a like nature with the foregoing. The contrary of every matter of fact is still possible; because it can never imply a contradiction, and is conceived by the mind with the same facility and distinctness, as if ever so conformable to reality. *That the sun will not rise tomorrow* is no less intelligible a proposition, and implies no more contradiction than the affirmation, *that it will rise*. We should in vain, therefore, attempt to demonstrate its falsehood. Were it demonstratively false, it would imply a contradiction, and could never be distinctly conceived by the mind.

---

*Resemblance.
**Continguity.
***Cause and effect.
†For instance, Contrast or Contrariety is also a connexion among Ideas but it may, perhaps, be considered as a mixture of *Causation* and *Resemblance*. Where two objects are contrary, the one destroys the other; that is, the cause of its annihilation, and the idea of the annihilation of an object implies the idea of its former existence.

It may, therefore, be a subject worthy of curiosity, to enquire what is the nature of that evidence which assures us of any real existence and matter of fact, beyond the present testimony of our senses, or the records of our memory. This part of philosophy, it is observable, has been little cultivated, either by the ancients or moderns; and therefore our doubts and errors, in the prosecution of so important an enquiry, may be the more excusable; while we march through such difficult paths without any guide or direction. They may even prove useful, by exciting curiosity, and destroying that implicit faith and security, which is the bane of all reasoning and free enquiry. The discovery of defects in the common philosophy, if any such there be, will not, I presume, be a discouragement, but rather an incitement, as is usual, to attempt something more full and satisfactory than has yet been proposed to the public.

All reasonings concerning matter of fact seem to be founded on the relation of *Cause* and *Effect*. By means of that relation alone we can go beyond the evidence of our memory and senses. If you were to ask a man, why he believes any matter of fact, which is absent; for instance, that his friend is in the country, or in France; he would give you a reason; and this reason would be some other fact; as a letter received from him, or the knowledge of his former resolutions and promises. A man finding a watch or any other machine in a desert island, would conclude that there had once been men in that island. All our reasonings concerning fact are of the same nature. And here it is constantly supposed that there is a connexion between the present fact and that which is inferred from it. Were there nothing to bind them together, the inference would be entirely precarious. The hearing of an articulate voice and rational discourse in the dark assures us of the presence of some person: Why? because these are the effects of the human make and fabric, and closely connected with it. If we anatomize all the other reasonings of this nature, we shall find that they are founded on the relation of cause and effect, and that this relation is either near or remote, direct or collateral. Heat and light are collateral effects of fire, and the one effect may justly be inferred from the other.

If we would satisfy ourselves, therefore, concerning the nature of that evidence, which assures us of matters of fact, we must enquire how we arrive at the knowledge of cause and effect.

I shall venture to affirm, as a general proposition, which admits of no exception, that the knowledge of this relation is not, in any instance, attained by reasonings a priori; but arises entirely from experience, when we find that any particular objects are constantly conjoined with each other. Let an object be presented to a man of ever so strong natural reason and abilities; if that object be entirely new to him, he will not be able, by the most accurate examination of its sensible qualities, to discover any of its causes or effects. Adam, though his rational faculties be supposed, at the very first, entirely perfect, could not have inferred from the fluidity and transparency of water that it would suffocate him, or from the light and warmth of fire that it would consume him. No object ever discovers, by the qualities which appear to the senses, either the causes which produced it, or the effects which will arise from it; nor can our reason, unassisted by experience, ever draw any inference concerning real existence and matter of fact.

This proposition, *that causes and effects are discoverable, not by reason but by experience*, will readily be admitted with regard to such objects, as we remember to have once been altogether unknown to us; since we must be conscious of the utter inability, which we then lay under, of foretelling what would arise from them. Present two smooth pieces of marble to a man who has no tincture of natural philosophy; he will never discover that they will adhere together in such a manner as to require great force to separate them in a direct line, while they make so small a resistance to a lateral pressure. Such events, as bear little analogy to the common course of nature, are also readily confessed to be known only by experience; nor does any man imagine that the explosion of gunpowder, or the attraction of a loadstone, could ever be discovered by arguments *a priori*. In like manner, when an effect is supposed to depend upon an intricate machinery or secret structure of parts, we make no difficulty in attributing all our knowledge of it to experience. Who will assert that he can give the ultimate reason, why milk or bread is proper nourishment for a man, not for a lion or a tiger?

But the same truth may not appear, at first sight, to have the same evidence with regard to events, which have become familiar to us from our first appearance in the world, which bear a close analogy to the whole course of nature, and which are supposed to depend on the simple qualities of objects, without any secret structure of parts. We are apt to imagine that we could discover these effects by the mere operation of our reason, without experience. We fancy, that were we brought on a sudden into this world, we could at first have inferred that one Billiard-ball would communicate motion to another upon impulse; and that we needed not to have waited for the event, in order to pronounce with certainty concerning it. Such is the influence of custom, that, where it is strongest, it not only covers our natural ignorance, but even conceals itself, and seems not to take place, merely because it is found in the highest degree.

But to convince us that all the laws of nature, and all the operations of bodies without exception, are known only by experience, the following reflections may, perhaps, suffice. Were any object presented to us, and were we required to pronounce concerning the effect, which will result from it, without consulting past observation; after what manner, I beseech you, must the mind proceed in this operation? It must invent or imagine some event, which it ascribes to the object as its effect; and it is plain that this invention must be entirely arbitrary. The mind can never possibly find the effect in the supposed cause, by the most accurate scrutiny and examination. For the effect is totally different from the cause, and consequently can never be discovered in it. Motion in the second Billiard-ball is a quite distinct event from motion in the first: nor is there anything in the one to suggest the smallest hint of the other. A stone or piece of metal raised into the air, and left without any support, immediately falls: but to consider the matter *a priori*, is there anything we discover in this situation which can beget the idea of a downward, rather than an upward, or any other motion, in the stone or metal?

And as the first imagination or invention of a particular effect, in all natural operations, is arbitrary, where we consult not experience; so must we also esteem the supposed tie or connexion between the cause and effect, which binds them together, and renders it impossible that any other effect could result from the operation of that cause. When I see, for instance, a Billiard-ball moving in a straight line towards another; even suppose motion in the second ball should by accident be suggested to me, as the result of their contact or impulse; may I not conceive, that a hundred different events might as well follow from that cause? May not both these balls remain at absolute rest? May not the first ball return in a straight line, or leap off from the second in any line or direction? All these suppositions are consistent and conceivable. Why then should we give the preference to one, which is no more consistent or conceivable than the rest? All our reasonings *a priori* will never be able to show us any foundation for this preference.

In a word, then, every effect is a distinct event from its cause. It could not, therefore, be discovered in the cause, and the first invention or conception of it, *a priori*, must be entirely arbitrary. And even after it is suggested, the conjunction of it with the cause must appear equally arbitrary; since there are always many other effects, which, to reason, must seem fully as consistent and natural. In vain, therefore, should we pretend to determine any single event, or infer any cause or effect, without the assistance of observation and experience.

Hence we may discover the reason why no philosopher, who is rational and modest, has ever pretended to assign the ultimate cause of any natural operation, or to show distinctly the action of that power, which produces any single effect in the universe. It is confessed, that the utmost effort of human reason is to reduce the principles, productive of natural phenomena, to a greater simplicity, and to resolve the many particular effects into a few general causes, by means of reasonings from analogy, experience, and observation. But as to the causes of these general causes, we should in vain attempt their discovery; nor shall we ever be able to satisfy ourselves, by any particular explication of them. These ultimate springs and principles are totally shut up from human curiosity and enquiry. Elasticity, gravity, cohesion of parts, communication of motion by impulse; these are probably the ultimate causes and principles which we ever discover in nature; and we may esteem ourselves sufficiently happy, if, by accurate inquiry and reasoning, we can trace up the particular phenomena to, or near to, these general principles. The most perfect philosophy of the natural kind only staves off our ignorance a little longer: as perhaps the most perfect philosophy of the moral or metaphysical kind serves only to discover larger portions of it. Thus the observation of human blindness and weakness is the result of all philosophy, and meets us at every turn, in spite of our endeavours to elude or avoid it.

Nor is geometry, when taken into the assistance of natural philosophy, ever able to remedy this defect, or lead us into the knowledge of ultimate causes, by all that accuracy of reasoning for which it is so justly celebrated. Every part of mixed mathematics proceeds upon the supposition that certain laws are established by nature in her operations; and abstract reasonings are employed, either to assist experience in the discovery of these laws, or to determine their influence in particular instances, where it depends upon any precise degree of distance and quantity. Thus, it is a law of motion, discovered by experience, that the movement or force of any body in motion is in the compound ratio or proportion of its solid contents and its velocity; and consequently, that a small force may remove the greatest obstacle or raise the greatest weight, if, by any contrivance or machinery, we can increase the velocity of that force, so as to make it an overmatch for its antagonist. Geometry assists us in the application of this law, by giving us the just dimensions of all the parts and figures which can enter into any species of machines; but still the discovery of the law itself is owing merely to experience, and all the abstract reasonings in the world could never lead us one step towards the knowledge of it. When we reason *a priori*, and consider merely any object or cause, as it appears to the mind, independent of all observation, it never could suggest to us the notion of any distinct object, such as its effect; much less, show us the inseparable and inviolable connexion between them. A man must be very sagacious who could discover by reasoning that crystal is the effect of heat, and ice of cold, without being previously acquainted with the operation of these qualities.

PART II

But we have not yet attained any tolerable satisfaction with regard to the question first proposed. Each solution still gives rise to a new question as difficult as the foregoing, and leads us on to farther enquiries. When it is asked, *What is the nature of all our rea-*

sonings concerning matter of fact? the proper answer seems to be, that they are founded on the relation of cause and effect. When again it is asked, *What is the foundation of all our reasonings and conclusions concerning that relation?* it may be replied in one word, Experience. But if we still carry on our sifting humour, and ask, *What is the foundation of all conclusions from experience?* this implies a new question, which may be of more difficult solution and explication. Philosophers, that give themselves airs of superior wisdom and sufficiency, have a hard task when they encounter persons of inquisitive dispositions, who push them from every corner to which they retreat, and who are sure at last to bring them to some dangerous dilemma. The best expedient to prevent this confusion, is to be modest in our pretensions; and even to discover the difficulty ourselves before it is objected to us. By this means, we may make a kind of merit of our very ignorance.

I shall content myself, in this section, with an easy task, and shall pretend only to give a negative answer to the question here proposed. I say then, that, even after we have experience of the operations of cause and effect, our conclusions from that experience are not founded on reasoning, or any process of the understanding. This answer we must endeavour both to explain and to defend.

It must certainly be allowed, that nature has kept us at a great distance from all her secrets, and has afforded us only the knowledge of a few superficial qualities of objects; while she conceals from us those powers and principles on which the influence of those objects entirely depends. Our senses inform us of the colour, weight, and consistence of bread; but neither sense nor reason can ever inform us of those qualities which fit it for the nourishment and support of a human body. Sight or feeling conveys an idea of the actual motion of bodies; but as to that wonderful force or power, which would carry on a moving body for ever in a continued change of place, and which bodies never lose but by communicating it to others; of this we cannot form the most distant conception. But notwithstanding this ignorance of natural powers* and principles, we always presume, when we see like sensible qualities, that they have like secret powers, and expect that effects, similar to those which we have experienced, will follow from them. If a body of like colour and consistence with that bread, which we have formerly eat, be presented to us, we make no scruple of repeating the experiment, and foresee, with certainty, like nourishment and support. Now this is a process of the mind or thought, of which I would willingly know the foundation. It is allowed on all hands that there is no known connexion between the sensible qualities and the secret powers; and consequently, that the mind is not led to form such a conclusion concerning their constant and regular conjunction, by anything which it knows of their nature. As to past Experience, it can be allowed to give direct and certain information of those precise objects only, and that precise period of time, which fell under its cognizance: but why this experience should be extended to future times, and to other objects, which, for aught we know, may be only in appearance similar; this is the main question on which I would insist. The bread, which I formerly eat, nourished me; that is, a body of such sensible qualities was, at that time, endued with such secret powers: but does it follow, that other bread must also nourish me at another time, and that like sensible qualities must always be attended with like secret powers? The consequence seems nowise necessary. At least, it must be acknowledged that there is here a consequence drawn by the mind; that there is a certain step taken; a process of thought, and an inference, which wants to be explained. These two propositions are far from being the

---

*The word, Power, is here used in a loose and popular sense. The most accurate explication of it would give additional evidence to this argument. See Sec. 7.

same, *I have found that such an object has always been attended with such an effect, and I foresee, that other objects, which are, in appearance, similar, will be attended with similar effects.* I shall allow, if you please, that the one proposition may justly be inferred from the other; I know, in fact, that it always is inferred. But if you insist that the inference is made by a chain of reasoning, I desire you to produce that reasoning. The connexion between these propositions is not intuitive. There is required a medium, which may enable the mind to draw such an inference, if indeed it be drawn by reasoning and argument. What that medium is, I must confess, passes my comprehension; and it is incumbent on those to produce it, who assert that it really exists, and is the origin of all our conclusions concerning matter of fact.

This negative argument must certainly, in process of time, become altogether convincing, if many penetrating and able philosophers shall turn their enquiries this way and no one be ever able to discover any connecting proposition or intermediate step, which supports the understanding in this conclusion. But as the question is yet new, every reader may not trust so far to his own penetration, as to conclude, because an argument escapes his enquiry, that therefore it does not really exist. For this reason it may be requisite to venture upon a more difficult task; and enumerating all the branches of human knowledge, endeavour to show that none of them can afford such an argument.

All reasonings may be divided into two kinds, namely, demonstrative reasoning, or that concerning relations of ideas, and moral reasoning, or that concerning matter of fact and existence. That there are no demonstrative arguments in the case seems evident; since it implies no contradiction that the course of nature may change, and that an object, seemingly like those which we have experienced, may be attended with different or contrary effects. May I not clearly and distinctly conceive that a body, falling from the clouds, and which, in all other respects, resembles snow, has yet the taste of salt or feeling of fire? Is there any more intelligible proposition than to affirm, that all the trees will flourish in December and January, and decay in May and June? Now whatever is intelligible, and can be distinctly conceived, implies no contradiction, and can never be proved false by any demonstrative argument or abstract reasoning *a priori*.

If we be, therefore, engaged by arguments to put trust in past experience, and make it the standard of our future judgement, these arguments must be probable only, or such as regard matter of fact and real existence, according to the division above mentioned. But that there is no argument of this kind, must appear, if our explication of that species of reasoning be admitted as solid and satisfactory. We have said that all arguments concerning existence are founded on the relation of cause and effect; that our knowledge of that relation is derived entirely from experience; and that all our experimental conclusions proceed upon the supposition that the future will be conformable to the past. To endeavour, therefore, the proof of this last supposition by probable arguments, or arguments regarding existence, must be evidently going in a circle, and taking that for granted, which is the very point in question.

In reality, all arguments from experience are founded on the similarity which we discover among natural objects, and by which we are induced to expect effects similar to those which we have found to follow from such objects. And though none but a fool or madman will ever pretend to dispute the authority of experience, or to reject that great guide of human life, it may surely be allowed a philosopher to have so much curiosity at least as to examine the principle of human nature, which gives this mighty authority to experience, and makes us draw advantage from that similarity which nature has placed among different objects. From causes which appear similar we expect similar effects. This is the sum of all our experimental conclusions. Now it seems evident that, if this conclusion were formed by reason, it would be as perfect at first, and upon one instance, as after ever so long a course of experience. But the case is far otherwise. Nothing so like as eggs; yet no one, on account of this appearing similarity, expects the same taste and relish in all of them. It is only after a long course of uniform experiments in any kind, that we attain a firm reliance and security with regard to a particular event. Now where is that process of reasoning which, from one instance, draws a conclusion, so different from that which it infers from a hundred instances that are nowise different from that single one? This question I propose as much for the sake of information, as with an intention of raising difficulties. I cannot find, I cannot imagine any such reasoning. But I keep my mind still open to instruction, if any one will vouchsafe to bestow it on me.

Should it be said that, from a number of uniform experiments, we *infer* a connexion between the sensible qualities and the secret powers; this, I must confess, seems the same difficulty, couched in different terms. The question still recurs, on what process of argument this *inference* is founded? Where is the medium, the interposing ideas, which join propositions so very wide of each other? It is confessed that the colour, consistence, and other sensible qualities of bread appear not, of themselves, to have any connexion with the secret powers of nourishment and support. For otherwise we could infer these secret powers from the first appearance of these sensible qualities, without the aid of experience; contrary to the sentiment of all philosophers, and contrary to plain matter of fact. Here, then, is our natural state of ignorance with regard to the powers and influence of all objects. How is this remedied by experience? It only shows us a number of uniform effects, resulting from certain objects, and teaches us that those particular objects, at that particular time, were endowed with such powers and forces. When a new object, endowed with similar sensible qualities, is produced, we expect similar powers and forces, and look for a like effect. From a body of like colour and consistence with bread we expect like nourishment and support. But this surely is a step or progress of the mind, which wants to be explained. When a man says, *I have found, in all past instances, such sensible qualities conjoined with such secret powers*: And when he says, *Similar sensible qualities will always be conjoined with similar secret powers*, he is not guilty of a tautology, nor are these propositions in any respect the same. You say that the one proposition is an inference from the other. But you must confess that the inference is not intuitive; neither is it demonstrative: Of what nature is it, then? To say it is experimental, is begging the question. For all inferences from experience suppose, as their foundation, that the future will resemble the past, and that similar powers will be conjoined with similar sensible qualities. If there be any suspicion that the course of nature may change, and that the past may be no rule for the future, all experience becomes useless, and can give rise to no inference or conclusion. It is impossible, therefore, that any arguments from experience can prove this resemblance of the past to the future: since all these arguments are founded on the supposition of that resemblance. Let the course of things be allowed hitherto ever so regular; that alone, without some new argument or inference, proves not that, for the future, it will continue so. In vain do you pretend to have learned the nature of bodies from your past experience. Their secret nature, and consequently all their effects and influence, may change, without any change in their sensible qualities. This happens sometimes, and with regard to some objects: Why may it not happen always, and with regard to all objects? What logic, what process of argument secures you against this supposition? My practice, you say, refutes my doubts. But you mistake the purport of my question. As an agent, I am quite satisfied in the point; but as a philosopher, who has some share of curiosity, I will not say scepticism, I want to learn the foundation of this inference. No reading, no enquiry has yet been able to remove my difficulty, or give me satisfaction in a matter of such importance. Can I do better than propose the difficulty to the public, even though, perhaps, I have small hopes of obtaining a solution? We shall, at least, by this means, be sensible of our ignorance, if we do not augment our knowledge.

I must confess that a man is guilty of unpardonable arrogance who concludes, because an argument has escaped his own investigation, that therefore it does not really exist. I must also confess that, though all the learned, for several ages, should have employed themselves in fruitless search upon any subject, it may still, perhaps, be rash to conclude positively that the subject must, therefore, pass all human comprehension. Even though we examine all the sources of our knowledge, and conclude them unfit for such a subject, there may still remain a suspicion, that the enumeration is not complete, or the examination not accurate. But with regard to the present subject, there are some considerations which seem to remove all this accusation of arrogance or suspicion of mistake.

It is certain that the most ignorant and stupid peasants—nay infants, nay even brute beasts—improve by experience, and learn the qualities of natural objects, by observing the effects which result from them. When a child has felt the sensation of pain from touching the flame of a candle, he will be careful not to put his hand near any candle; but will expect a similar effect from a cause which is similar in its sensible qualities and appearance. If you assert, therefore, that the understanding of the child is led into this conclusion by any process of argument or ratiocination, I may justly require you to produce that argument; nor have you any pretense to refuse so equitable a demand. You cannot say that the argument is abstruse, and may possibly escape your enquiry; since you confess that it is obvious to the capacity of a mere infant. If you hesitate, therefore, a moment, or if, after reflection, you produce any intricate or profound argument, you, in a manner, give up the question, and confess that it is not reasoning which engages us to suppose the past resembling the future, and to expect similar effects from causes which are, to appearance, similar. This is the proposition which I intended to enforce in the present section. If I be right, I pretend not to have made any mighty discovery. And if I be wrong, I must acknowledge myself to be indeed a very backward scholar; since I cannot now discover an argument which, it seems, was perfectly familiar to me long before I was out of my cradle.

SECTION V. SCEPTICAL SOLUTION OF THESE DOUBTS

PART I

The passion for philosophy, like that for religion, seems liable to this inconvenience, that, though it aims at the correction of our manners, and extirpation of our vices, it may only serve, by imprudent management, to foster a predominant inclination, and push the mind, with more determined resolution, towards that side which already *draws* too much, by the bias and propensity of the natural temper. It is certain that, while we aspire to the magnanimous firmness of the philosophic sage, and endeavour to confine our pleasures altogether within our own minds, we may, at last, render our philosophy like that of Epictetus, and other *Stoics*, only a more refined system of self-ishness, and reason ourselves out of all virtue as well as social enjoyment. While we study with attention the vanity of human life, and turn all our thoughts towards the empty and transitory nature of riches and honours, we are, perhaps, all the while flattering our natural indolence, which, hating the bustle of the world, and drudgery of business, seeks a pretence of reason to give itself a full and uncontrolled indulgence. There is, however, one species of philosophy which seems little liable to this inconvenience, and that because it strikes in with no disorderly passion of the human mind, nor can mingle itself with any natural affection or propensity; and that is the Academic or Sceptical philosophy. The academics always talk of doubt and suspense of judgement, of danger in hasty determinations, of confining to very narrow bounds the enquiries of the understanding, and of renouncing all speculations which lie not within the limits of common life and practice. Nothing, therefore, can be more contrary than such a philosophy to the supine indolence of the mind, its rash arrogance, its lofty pretensions, and its superstitious credulity. Every passion is mortified by it, except the love of truth; and that passion never is, nor can be, carried to too high a degree. It is surprising, therefore, that this philosophy, which, in almost every instance, must be harmless and innocent, should be the subject of so much groundless reproach and obloquy. But, perhaps, the very circumstance which renders it so innocent is what chiefly exposes it to the public hatred and resentment. By flattering no irregular passion, it gains few partizans: By opposing so many vices and follies, it raises to itself abundance of enemies, who stigmatize it as libertine, profane, and irreligious.

Nor need we fear that this philosophy, while it endeavours to limit our enquiries to common life, should ever undermine the reasonings of common life, and carry its doubts so far as to destroy all action, as well as speculation. Nature will always maintain her rights, and prevail in the end over any abstract reasoning whatsoever. Though we should conclude, for instance, as in the foregoing section, that, in all reasonings from experience, there is a step taken by the mind which is not supported by any argument or process of the understanding; there is no danger that these reasonings, on which almost all knowledge depends, will ever be affected by such a discovery. If the mind be not engaged by argument to make this step, it must be induced by some other principle of equal weight and authority; and that principle will preserve its influence as long as human nature remains the same. What that principle is may well be worth the pains of enquiry.

Suppose a person, though endowed with the strongest faculties of reason and reflection, to be brought on a sudden into this world; he would, indeed, immediately observe a continual succession of objects, and one event following another; but he would not be able to discover anything farther. He would not, at first, by any reasoning, be able to reach the idea of cause and effect; since the particular powers, by which all natural operations are performed, never appear to the senses; nor is it reasonable to conclude, merely because one event, in one instance, precedes another, that therefore the one is the cause, the other the effect. Their conjunction may be arbitrary and casual. There may be no reason to infer the existence of one from the appearance of the other. And in a word, such a person, without more experience, could never employ his conjecture or reasoning concerning any matter of fact, or be assured of anything beyond what was immediately present to his memory and senses.

Suppose, again, that he has acquired more experience, and has lived so long in the world as to have observed familiar objects or events to be constantly conjoined together; what is the consequence of this experience? He immediately infers the existence of one object from the appearance of the other. Yet he has not, by all his experience, acquired any idea or knowledge of the secret power by which the one object produces the other; nor is it, by any process of reasoning, he is engaged to draw this inference. But still he finds himself determined to draw it: And though he should be convinced that his understanding has no part in the operation, he would nevertheless continue in the same course of thinking. There is some other principle which determines him to form such a conclusion.

This principle is Custom or Habit. For wherever the repetition of any particular act or operation produces a propensity to renew the same act or operation, without being impelled by any reasoning or process of the understanding, we always say, that this propensity is the effect of *Custom*. By employing that word, we pretend not to have given the ultimate reason of such a propensity. We only point out a principle of human nature, which is universally acknowledged, and which is well known by its effects. Perhaps we can push our enquiries no farther, or pretend to give the cause of this cause; but must rest contented with it as the ultimate principle, which we can assign, of all our conclusions from experience. It is sufficient satisfaction, that we can go so far, without repining at the narrowness of our faculties because they will carry us no farther. And it is certain we here advance a very intelligible proposition at least, if not a true one, when we assert that, after the constant conjunction of two objects—heat and flame, for instance, weight and solidity—we are determined by custom alone to expect the one from the appearance of the other. This hypothesis seems even the only one which explains the difficulty, why we draw, from a thousand instances, an inference which we are not able to draw from one instance, that is, in no respect, different from them. Reason is incapable of any such variation. The conclusions which it draws from considering one circle are the same which it would form upon surveying all the circles in the universe. But no man, having seen only one body move after being impelled by another, could infer that every other body will move after a like impulse. All inferences from experience, therefore, are effects of custom, not of reasoning.*

---

*Nothing is more useful than for writers, even, on *moral, political,* or *physical* subjects to distinguish between *reason* and *experience,* and to suppose, that these species of argumentation are entirely different from each other. The former are taken for the mere result of our intellectual faculties, which, by considering *a priori* the nature of things, and examining the effects that must follow from their operation, establish particular principles of science and philosophy. The latter are supposed to be derived entirely from sense and observation, by which we learn what has actually resulted from the operation of particular objects, and are thence able to infer, what will, for the future, result from them. Thus, for instance, the limitations and restraints of civil government, and a legal constitution, may be defended, either from *reason,* which reflecting on the great frailty and corruption of human nature, teaches, that no man can safely be trusted with unlimited authority; or from *experience* and history which inform us of the enormous abuses, that ambition, in every age and country, has been found to make of so imprudent a confidence.

The same distribution between reason and experience is maintained in all our deliberations concerning the conduct of life; while the experienced statesman, general, physician, or merchant is trusted and followed; and the unpractised novice, with whatever natural talents endowed, neglected and despised. Though it be allowed, that reason may form very plausible conjectures with regard to the consequences of such a particular conduct in such the assistance of experience, which is alone able to give stability and certainty to the maxims, derived from study and reflection.

But notwithstanding that this distinction be thus universally received, both in the active speculative scenes of life, I shall not scruple to pronounce, that it is, at bottom, erroneous, at least, superficial.

If we examine those arguments, which, in any of the sciences above mentioned, are supposed to be the mere effects of reasoning and reflection, they will be found to terminate at last, in some general principle or conclusion, for which we can assign no reason but observation and experience. The only difference between them and those maxims, which are vulgarly esteemed the result of pure experience, is, that the former cannot be established without some process of thought, and some reflection on what we have observed, in order to distinguish its circumstances, and trace its consequences: Whereas in the latter, the experienced

Custom, then, is the great guide of human life. It is that principle alone which renders our experience useful to us, and makes us expect, for the future, a similar train of events with those which have appeared in the past. Without the influence of custom, we should be entirely ignorant of every matter of fact beyond what is immediately present to the memory and senses. We should never know to adjust means to ends, or to employ our natural powers in the production of any effect. There would be an end at once of all action, as well as of the chief part of speculation.

But here it may be proper to remark, that though our conclusions from experience carry us beyond our memory and senses, and assure us of matters of fact which happened in the most distant places and most remote ages, yet some fact must always be present to the senses or memory, from which we may first proceed in drawing these conclusions. A man, who should find in a desert country the remains of pompous buildings, would conclude that the country had, in ancient times, been cultivated by civilized inhabitants; but did nothing of this nature occur to him, he could never form such an inference. We learn the events of former ages from history; but then we must peruse the volumes in which this instruction is contained, and thence carry up our inferences from one testimony to another, till we arrive at the eyewitnesses and spectators of these distant events. In a word, if we proceed not upon some fact, present to the memory or senses, our reasonings would be merely hypothetical; and however the particular links might be connected with each other, the whole chain of inferences would have nothing to support it, nor could we ever, by its means, arrive at the knowledge of any real existence. If I ask why you believe any particular matter of fact, which you relate, you must tell me some reason; and this reason will be some other fact, connected with it. But as you cannot proceed after this manner, *in infinitum*, you must at last terminate in some fact, which is present to your memory or senses; or must allow that your belief is entirely without foundation.

What, then, is the conclusion of the whole matter? A simple one; though, it must be confessed, pretty remote from the common theories of philosophy. All belief of matter of fact or real existence is derived merely from some object, present to the memory or senses, and a customary conjunction between that and some other object. Or in other words; having found in many instances, that any two kinds of objects— flame and heat, snow and cold—have always been conjoined together; if flame or snow be presented anew to the senses, the mind is carried by custom to expect heat or cold,

---

event is exactly and fully familiar to that which we infer as the result of any particular situation. The history of a Tiberius or a Nero makes us dread a like tyranny, were our monarchs freed from the restraints of laws and senates. But the observation of any fraud or cruelty in private life is sufficient, with the aid of a little thought, to give us the same apprehension; while it serves as an instance of the general corruption of human nature, and shows us the danger which we must incur by reposing an entire confidence in mankind. In both cases, it is experience which is ultimately the foundation of our inference and conclusion.

There is no man so young and experienced, as not to have formed, from observation, many general and just maxims concerning human affairs and the conduct of life; but it must be confessed, that, when a man comes to put these in practice, he will be extremely liable to error, till time and farther experience both enlarge these maxims, and teach him their proper use and application. In every situation or incident, there are many particular and seemingly minute circumstances, which the man of greatest talent is, at first, apt to overlook, though on them the justness of his conclusions, and consequently the prudence of his conduct, entirely depend. Not to mention, that, to a young beginner, the general observations and maxims occur not always on the proper occasions, nor can be immediately applied with due calmness and distinction. The truth is, an unexperienced reasoner could be no reasoner at all, were he absolutely unexperienced; and when we assign that character to any one, we mean it only in a comparative sense, and suppose him possessed of experience, in a smaller and more imperfect degree.

and to *believe* that such a quality does exist, and will discover itself upon a nearer approach. This belief is the necessary result of placing the mind in such circumstances. It is an operation of the soul, when we are so situated, as unavoidable as to feel the passion of love, when we receive benefits; or hatred, when we meet with injuries. All these operations are a species of natural instincts, which no reasoning or process of the thought and understanding is able either to produce or to prevent.

At this point, it would be very allowable for us to stop our philosophical researches. In most questions we can never make a single step farther; and in all questions we must terminate here at last, after our most restless and curious enquiries. But still our curiosity will be pardonable, perhaps commendable, if it carry us on to still farther researches, and make us examine more accurately the nature of this belief, and of the *customary conjunction*, whence it is derived. By this means we may meet with some explications and analogies that will give satisfaction; at least to such as love the abstract sciences, and can be entertained with speculations, which, however accurate, may still retain a degree of doubt and uncertainty. As to readers of a different taste; the remaining part of this section is not calculated for them, and the following enquiries may well be understood, though it be neglected.

PART II

Nothing is more free than the imagination of man; and though it cannot exceed that original stock of ideas furnished by the internal and external senses, it has unlimited power of mixing, compounding, separating, and dividing these ideas, in all the varieties of fiction and vision. It can feign a train of events, with all the appearance of reality, ascribe to them a particular time and place, conceive them as existent, and paint them out to itself with every circumstance, that belongs to any historical fact, which it believes with the greatest certainty. Wherein, therefore, consists the difference between such a *fiction* and *belief*? It lies not merely in any peculiar idea, which is annexed to such a conception as commands our assent, and which is wanting to every known fiction. For as the mind has authority over all its ideas, it could voluntarily annex this particular idea to any fiction, and consequently be able to believe whatever it pleases; contrary to what we find by daily experience. We can, in our conception, join the head of a man to the body of a horse; but it is not in our power to believe that such an animal has ever really existed.

It follows, therefore, that the difference between fiction and belief lies in some sentiment or feeling, which is annexed to the latter, not to the former, and which depends not on the will, nor can be commanded at pleasure. It must be excited by nature, like all other sentiments; and must arise from the particular situation, in which the mind is placed at any particular juncture. Whenever any object is presented to the memory or senses, it immediately, by the force of custom, carries the imagination to conceive that object, which is usually conjoined to it; and this conception is attended with a feeling or sentiment, different from the loose reveries of the fancy. In this consists the whole nature of belief. For as there is no matter of fact which we believe so firmly that we cannot conceive the contrary, there would be no difference between the conception assented to and that which is rejected, were it not for some sentiment which distinguishes the one from the other. If I see a Billiard-ball moving towards another, on a smooth table, I can easily conceive it to stop upon contact. This conception implies no contradiction; but still it feels very differently from that conception by which I represent to myself the impulse and the communication of motion from one ball to another.

Were we to attempt a *definition* of this sentiment, we should, perhaps, find it a very difficult, if not an impossible task; in the same manner as if we should endeavour to define the feeling of cold or passion of anger, to a creature who never had any experience of these sentiments. Belief is the true and proper name of this feeling; and no one is ever at a loss to know the meaning of that term; because every man is every moment conscious of the sentiment represented by it. It may not, however, be improper to attempt a *description* of this sentiment; in hopes we may, by that means, arrive at some analogies, which may afford a more perfect explication of it. I say, then, that belief is nothing but a more vivid, lively, forcible, firm, steady conception of an object, than what the imagination alone is ever able to attain. This variety of terms, which may seem so unphilosophical, is intended only to express that act of the mind, which renders realities, or what is taken for such, more present to us than fictions, causes them to weigh more in the thought, and gives them a superior influence on the passions and imagination. Provided we agree about the thing, it is needless to dispute about the terms. The imagination has the command over all its ideas, and can join and mix and vary them, in all the ways possible. It may conceive fictitious objects with all the circumstances of place and time. It may set them, in a manner, before our eyes, in their true colours, just as they might have existed. But as it is impossible that this faculty of imagination can ever, of itself, reach belief, it is evident that belief consists not in the peculiar nature or order of ideas, but in the *manner* of their conception, and in their *feeling* to the mind. I confess, that it is impossible perfectly to explain this feeling or manner of conception. We may make use of words which express something near it. But its true and proper name, as we observed before, is *belief;* which is a term that every one sufficiently understands in common life. And in philosophy, we can go no farther than assert, that *belief* is something felt by the mind, which distinguishes the ideas of the judgement from the fictions of the imagination. It gives them more weight and influence; makes them appear of greater importance; enforces them in the mind; and renders them the governing principle of our actions. I hear at present, for instance, a person's voice, with whom I am acquainted; and the sound comes as from the next room. This impression of my senses immediately conveys my thought to the person, together with all the surrounding objects. I paint them out to myself as existing at present, with the same qualities and relations, of which I formerly knew them possessed. These ideas take faster hold of my mind than ideas of an enchanted castle. They are very different to the feeling, and have a much greater influence of every kind, either to give pleasure or pain, joy or sorrow.

Let us, then, take in the whole compass of this doctrine, and allow, that the sentiment of belief is nothing but a conception more intense and steady than what attends the mere fictions of the imagination, and that this manner of conception arises from a customary conjunction of the object with something present to the memory or senses: I believe that it will not be difficult, upon these suppositions, to find other operations of the mind analogous to it, and to trace up these phenomena to principles still more general.

We have already observed that nature has established connexions among particular ideas, and that no sooner one idea occurs to our thoughts than it introduces its correlative, and carries our attention towards it, by a gentle and insensible movement. These principles of connexion or association we have reduced to three, namely, *Resemblance, Contiguity* and *Causation;* which are the only bonds that unite our thoughts together, and beget that regular train of reflection or discourse, which, in a greater or less degree, takes place among mankind. Now here arises a question, on which the solution of the present difficulty will depend. Does it happen, in all these relations, that, when one of the objects is presented to the senses or memory the mind is not only carried to the conception of the correlative, but reaches a steadier and stronger conception of it than what otherwise it would have been able to attain? This seems to be the case with that belief which arises from the relation of cause and effect. And if the case be the same with the other relations or principles of associations, this may be established as a general law, which takes place in all the operations of the mind.

We may, therefore, observe, as the first experiment to our present purpose, that, upon the appearance of the picture of an absent friend, our idea of him is evidently enlivened by the *resemblance*, and that every passion, which that idea occasions, whether of joy or sorrow, acquires new force and vigour. In producing this effect, there concur both a relation and a present impression. Where the picture bears him no resemblance, at least was not intended for him, it never so much as conveys our thought to him: And where it is absent, as well as the person, though the mind may pass from the thought of the one to that of the other, it feels its idea to be rather weakened than enlivened by that transition. We take a pleasure in viewing the picture of a friend, when it is set before us; but when it is removed, rather choose to consider him directly than by reflection in an image, which is equally distant and obscure.

The ceremonies of the Roman Catholic religion may be considered as instances of the same nature. The devotees of that superstition usually plead in excuse for the mummeries, with which they were upbraided, that they feel the good effect of those external motions, and postures, and actions, in enlivening their devotion and quickening their fervour, which otherwise would decay, if directed entirely to distant and immaterial objects. We shadow out the objects of our faith, say they, in sensible types and images, and render them more present to us by the immediate presence of these types, than it is possible for us to do merely by an intellectual view and contemplation. Sensible objects have always a greater influence on the fancy than any other; and this influence they readily convey to those ideas to which they are related, and which they resemble. I shall only infer from these practices, and reasoning, that the effect of resemblance in enlivening the ideas is very common; and as in every case a resemblance and a present impression must concur, we are abundantly supplied with experiments to prove the reality of the foregoing principle.

We may add force to these experiments by others of a different kind, in considering the effects of *contiguity* as well as of *resemblance*. It is certain that distance diminishes the force of every idea, and that, upon our approach to any object; though it does not discover itself to our senses; it operates upon the mind with an influence, which imitates an immediate impression. The thinking on any object readily transports the mind to what is contiguous; but it is only the actual presence of an object, that transports it with a superior vivacity. When I am a few miles from home, whatever relates to it touches me more nearly than when I am two hundred leagues distant; though even at that distance the reflecting on any thing in the neighbourhood of my friends or family naturally produces an idea of them. But as in this latter case, both the objects of the mind are ideas; notwithstanding there is an easy transition between them; that transition alone is not able to give a superior vivacity to any of the ideas, for want of some immediate impression.* No one can doubt but causation has the same influence as the other two relations of resemblance and contiguity. Superstitious people are fond of the relics of saints and holy men, for the same reason, that they seek after types or images,

---

*"Should I call it our nature or some error that leads us to feel more deeply moved upon seeing places where memorable men are said to have spent much time than we feel when hearing of their deeds or reading their writings? Thus I feel deeply moved now. For Plato comes to my mind, who is said to have been the first philosopher to have made a practice of holding discussions here; and his little garden nearby not only stirs memories but makes me all but see him in the flesh. Here is Speusippus, here Xenocrates, here his student Polemo; it was his seat that we see before us. Even looking at our senate building—that of Hostilius,

in order to enliven their devotion, and give them a more intimate and strong conception of those exemplary lives, which they desire to imitate. Now it is evident, that one of the best relics, which a devotee could procure, would be the handywork of a saint; and if his clothes and furniture are ever to be considered in this light, it is because they were once at his disposal, and were moved and affected by him; in which respect they are to be considered as imperfect effects, and as connected with him by a shorter chain of consequences than any of those, by which we learn the reality of his existence.

Suppose, that the son of a friend, who had been long dead or absent, were presented to us; it is evident, that this object would instantly revive its correlative idea, and recall to our thoughts all past intimacies and familiarities, in more lively colours than they would otherwise have appeared to us. This is another phenomenon, which seems to prove the principle above mentioned.

We may observe, that, in these phenomena, the belief of the correlative object is always presupposed; without which the relation could have no effect. The influence of the picture supposes, that we *believe* our friend to have once existed. Contiguity to home can never excite our ideas of home, unless we *believe* that it really exists. Now I assert, that this belief, where it reaches beyond the memory or senses, is of a similar nature, and arises from similar causes, with the transition of thought and vivacity of conception here explained. When I throw a piece of dry wood into a fire, my mind is immediately carried to conceive, that it augments, not extinguishes the flame. This transition of thought from the cause to the effect proceeds not from reason. It derives its origin altogether from custom and experience. And as it first begins from an object, present to the senses, it renders the idea or conception of flame more strong and lively than any loose, floating reverie of the imagination. That idea arises immediately. The thought moves instantly towards it, and conveys to it all that force of conception, which is derived from the impression present to the senses. When a sword is levelled at my breast, does not the idea of wound and pain strike me more strongly, than when a glass of wine is presented to me, even though by accident this idea should occur after the appearance of the latter object? But what is there in this whole matter to cause such a strong conception, except only a present object and a customary transition to the idea of another object, which we have been accustomed to conjoin with the former? This is the whole operation of the mind, in all our conclusions concerning matter of fact and existence; and it is a satisfaction to find some analogies, by which it may be explained. The transition from a present object does in all cases give strength and solidity to the related idea.

Here, then, is a kind of pre-established harmony between the course of nature and the succession of our ideas; and though the powers and forces, by which the former is governed, be wholly unknown to us; yet our thoughts and conceptions have still, we find, gone on in the same train with the other work of nature. Custom is that principle, by which this correspondence has been effected; so necessary to the subsistence of our species, and the regulation of our conduct, in every circumstance and occurrence of human life. Had not the presence of an object, instantly excited the idea of those objects, commonly conjoined with it, all our knowledge must have been limited to the narrow sphere of our memory and senses; and we should never have been able to adjust means to ends, or employ our natural powers, either to the producing of good, or avoiding of evil. Those, who delight in the discovery and contemplation of *final causes*, have here ample subject to employ their wonder and admiration.

---

not the new building which looks smaller to me since it was made larger—made me think of Scipio, Cato, Laelius, and above all my grandfather. Such power of stirring recollection resides in places: no wonder that the training of the memory is based on them." Cicero, *De Finibus*, Book V. [Hume's footnote is in Latin, translation by W.K.]

I shall add, for a further confirmation of the foregoing theory, that, as this operation of the mind, by which we infer like effects from like causes, and *vice versa*, is so essential to the subsistence of all human creatures, it is not probable, that it could be trusted to the fallacious deductions of our reason, which is slow in its operations; appears not, in any degree, during the first years of infancy; and at best is, in every age and period of human life, extremely liable to error and mistake. It is more conformable to the ordinary wisdom of nature to secure so necessary an act of the mind, by some instinct or mechanical tendency, which may be infallible in its operations, may discover itself at the first appearance of life and thought, and may be independent of all the laboured deductions of the understanding. As nature has taught us the use of our limbs, without giving us the knowledge of the muscles and nerves, by which they are actuated; so has she implanted in us an instinct, which carries forward the thought in a correspondent course to that which she has established among external objects; though we are ignorant of those powers and forces, on which this regular course and succession of objects totally depends.

SECTION VI. OF PROBABILITY[*]

Though there be no such thing as *Chance* in the world; our ignorance of the real cause of any event has the same influence on the understanding, and begets a like species of belief or opinion.

There is certainly a probability, which arises from a superiority of chances on any side; and according as this superiority increases, and surpasses the opposite chances, the probability receives a proportionable increase, and begets still a higher degree of belief or assent to that side, in which we discover the superiority. If a dye were marked with one figure or number of spots on four sides, and with another figure or number of spots on the two remaining sides, it would be more probable, that the former would turn up than the latter; though, if it had a thousand sides marked in the same manner, and only one side different, the probability would be much higher, and our belief or expectation of the event more steady and secure. This process of the thought or reasoning may seem trivial and obvious; but to those who consider it more narrowly, it may, perhaps, afford matter for curious speculation.

It seems evident, that, when the mind looks forward to discover the event, which may result from the throw of such a dye, it considers the turning up of each particular side as alike probable; and this is the very nature of chance, to render all the particular events, comprehended in it, entirely equal. But finding a greater number of sides concur in the one event than in the other, the mind is carried more frequently to that event, and meets it oftener, in revolving the various possibilities or chances, on which the ultimate result depends. This concurrence of several views in one particular event begets immediately, by an inexplicable contrivance of nature, the sentiment of belief, and gives that event the advantage over its antagonist, which is supported by a smaller number of views, and recurs less frequently to the mind. If we allow, that belief is nothing but a firmer and stronger conception of an object than what attends the mere fictions of the imagination, this operation may, perhaps, in some measure, be ac-

*Mr. Locke divides all arguments into demonstrative and probable. In this view, we must say, that it is only probable all men must die, or that the sun will rise tomorrow. But to conform our language more to common use, we ought to divide arguments into *demonstrations*, *proofs*, and *probabilities*. By proofs meaning such arguments from experience as leave no room for doubt or opposition.

counted for. The concurrence of these several views or glimpses imprints the idea more strongly on the imagination; gives it superior force and vigour; renders its influence on the passions and affections more sensible; and in a word, begets that reliance or security, which constitutes the nature of belief and opinion.

The case is the same with the probability of causes, as with that of chance. There are some causes, which are entirely uniform and constant in producing a particular effect; and no instance has ever yet been found of any failure or irregularity in their operation. Fire has always burned, and water suffocated every human creature: The production of motion by impulse and gravity is an universal law, which has hitherto admitted of no exception. But there are other causes which have been found more irregular and uncertain; nor has rhubarb always proved a purge, or opium a soporific to every one, who has taken these medicines. It is true, when any cause fails of producing its usual effect, philosophers ascribe not this to any irregularity in nature; but suppose, that some secret causes, in the particular structure of parts, have prevented the operation. Our reasonings, however, and conclusions concerning the event are the same as if this principle had no place. Being determined by custom to transfer the past to the future, in all our inferences; where the past has been entirely regular and uniform, we expect the event with the greatest assurance, and leave no room for any contrary supposition. But where different effects have been found to follow from causes, which are to *appearance* exactly similar, all these various effects must occur to the mind in transferring the past to the future, and enter into our consideration, when we determine the probability of the event. Though we give the preference to that which has been found most usual, and believe that this effect will exist, we must not overlook the other effects, but must assign to each of them a particular weight and authority, in proportion as we have found it to be more or less frequent. It is more probable, in almost every country of Europe, that there will be frost sometime in January, than that the weather will continue open throughout the whole month; though this probability varies according to the different climates, and approaches to a certainty in the more northern kingdoms. Here then it seems evident, that, when we transfer the past to the future, in order to determine the effect, which will result from any cause, we transfer all the different events, in the same proportion as they have appeared in the past, and conceive one to have existed a hundred times, for instance, another ten times, and another once. As a great number of views do here concur in one event, they fortify and confirm it to the imagination, beget that sentiment which we call *belief*, and give its object the preference above the contrary event, which is not supported by an equal number of experiments, and recurs not so frequently to the thought in transferring the past to the future. Let any one try to account for this operation of the mind upon any of the received systems of philosophy, and he will be sensible of the difficulty. For my part, I shall think it sufficient, if the present hints excite the curiosity of philosophers, and make them sensible how defective all common theories are in treating of such curious and such sublime subjects.

Section VII. Of the Idea of Necessary Connexion

Part I

The great advantage of the mathematical sciences above the moral consists in this, that the ideas of the former, being sensible, are always clear and determinate, the smallest distinction between them is immediately perceptible, and the same terms are still expressive of the same ideas, without ambiguity or variation. An oval is never mistaken for a circle, nor an hyperbola for an ellipsis. The isosceles and scalenum are distinguished by boundaries more exact than vice and virtue, right and wrong. If any term be defined in geometry, the mind readily, of itself, substitutes, on all occasions, the definition for the term defined: Or even when no definition is employed, the object itself may be presented to the senses, and by that means be steadily and clearly apprehended. But the finer sentiments of the mind, the operations of the understanding, the various agitations of the passions, though really in themselves distinct, easily escape us, when surveyed by reflection; nor is it in our power to recall the original object, as often as we have occasion to contemplate it. Ambiguity, by this means, is gradually introduced into our reasonings: Similar objects are readily taken to be the same: And the conclusion becomes at last very wide of the premises.

One may safely, however, affirm, that, if we consider these sciences in a proper light, their advantages and disadvantages nearly compensate each other, and reduce both of them to a state of equality. If the mind, with greater facility, retains the ideas of geometry clear and determinate, it must carry on a much longer and more intricate chain of reasoning, and compare ideas much wider of each other, in order to reach the abstruser truths of that science. And if moral ideas are apt, without extreme care, to fall into obscurity and confusion, the inferences are always much shorter in these disquisitions, and the intermediate steps, which lead to the conclusion, much fewer than in the sciences which treat of quantity and number. In reality, there is scarcely a proposition in Euclid so simple, as not to consist of more parts, than are to be found in any moral reasoning which runs not into chimera and conceit. Where we trace the principles of the human mind through a few steps, we may be very well satisfied with our progress; considering how soon nature throws a bar to all our enquiries concerning causes, and reduces us to an acknowledgment of our ignorance. The chief obstacle, therefore, to our improvement in the moral or metaphysical sciences is the obscurity of the ideas, and ambiguity of the terms. The principal difficulty in the mathematics is the length of inferences and compass of thought, requisite to the forming of any conclusion. And, perhaps, our progress in natural philosophy is chiefly retarded by the want of proper experiments and phenomena, which are often discovered by chance, and cannot always be found, when requisite, even by the most diligent and prudent enquiry. As moral philosophy seems hitherto to have received less improvement than either geometry or physics, we may conclude, that, if there be any difference in this respect among these sciences, the difficulties, which obstruct the progress of the former, require superior care and capacity to be surmounted.

There are no ideas, which occur in metaphysics, more obscure and uncertain, than those of *power*, *force*, *energy* or *necessary connexion*, of which it is every moment necessary for us to treat in all our disquisitions. We shall, therefore, endeavour, in this section, to fix, if possible, the precise meaning of these terms, and thereby remove some part of that obscurity, which is so much complained of in this species of philosophy.

It seems a proposition, which will not admit of much dispute, that all our ideas are nothing but copies of our impressions, or, in other words, that it is impossible for us to *think* of any thing, which we have not antecedently *felt*, either by our external or internal senses. I have endeavoured* to explain and prove this proposition, and have expressed my hopes, that, by a proper application of it, men may reach a greater clearness and precision in philosophical reasonings, than what they have hitherto been able

---

*Section II.

to attain. Complex ideas may, perhaps, be well known by definition, which is nothing but an enumeration of those parts or simple ideas, that compose them. But when we have pushed up definitions to the most simple ideas, and find still some ambiguity and obscurity; what resource are we then possessed of? By what invention can we throw light upon these ideas, and render them altogether precise and determinate to our intellectual view? Produce the impressions or original sentiments, from which the ideas are copied. These impressions are all strong and sensible. They admit not of ambiguity. They are not only placed in a full light themselves, but may throw light on their correspondent ideas, which lie in obscurity. And by this means, we may, perhaps, attain a new microscope or species of optics, by which, in the moral sciences, the most minute, and most simple ideas may be so enlarged as to fall readily under our apprehension, and be equally known with the grossest and most sensible ideas, that can be the object of our enquiry.

To be fully acquainted, therefore, with the idea of power or necessary connexion, let us examine its impression; and in order to find the impression with greater certainty, let us search for it in all the sources, from which it may possibly be derived.

When we look about us towards external objects, and consider the operation of causes, we are never able, in a single instance, to discover any power or necessary connexion; and quality, which binds the effect to the cause, and renders the one an infallible consequence of the other. We only find, that the one does actually, in fact, follow the other. The impulse of one Billiard-ball is attended with motion in the second. This is the whole that appears to the *outward senses*. The mind feels no sentiment or *inward* impression from this succession of objects: Consequently there is not, in any single, particular instance of cause and effect, any thing which can suggest the idea of power or necessary connexion.

From the first appearance of an object, we never can conjecture what effect will result from it. But were the power or energy of any cause discoverable by the mind, we could foresee the effect, even without experience; and might, at first, pronounce with certainty concerning it, by mere dint of thought and reasoning.

In reality, there is no part of matter, that does ever, by its sensible qualities, discover any power or energy, or give us ground to imagine, that it could produce any thing, or be followed by any other object, which we could denominate its effect. Solidity, extension, motion; these qualities are all complete in themselves, and never point out any other event which may result from them. The scenes of the universe are continually shifting, and one object follows another in an uninterrupted succession; but the power of force, which actuates the whole machine, is entirely concealed from us, and never discovers itself in any of the sensible qualities of body. We know, that, in fact, heat is a constant attendant of flame; but what is the connexion between them, we have no room so much as to conjecture or imagine. It is impossible, therefore, that the idea of power can be derived from the contemplation of bodies, in single instances of their operation; because no bodies ever discover any power, which can be the original of this idea.*

Since, therefore, external objects as they appear to the senses, give us no idea of power or necessary connexion, by their operation in particular instances, let us see, whether this idea be derived from reflection on the operations of our own minds, and

---

*Mr. Locke, in his chapter of power, says, that, finding from experience, that there are several new productions in matter, and concluding that there must somewhere be a power capable of producing them, we arrive at last by this reasoning at the idea of power. But no reasoning can ever give us a new, original, simple idea; as this philosopher himself confesses. This, therefore, can never be the origin of that idea.

be copied from any internal impression. It may be said, that we are every moment conscious of internal power; while we feel, that, by the simple command of our will, we can move the organs of our body, or direct the faculties of our mind. An act of volition produces motion in our limbs, or raises a new idea in our imagination. This influence of the will we know by consciousness. Hence we acquire the idea of power or energy; and are certain, that we ourselves and all other intelligent beings are possessed of power. This idea, then, is an idea of reflection, since it arises from reflecting on the operations of our own mind, and on the command which is exercised by will, both over the organs of the body and faculties of the soul.

We shall proceed to examine this pretension; and first with regard to the influence of volition over the organs of the body. This influence, we may observe, is a fact, which, like all other natural events, can be known only by experience, and can never be foreseen from any apparent energy or power in the cause, which connects it with the effect, and renders the one an infallible consequence of the other. The motion of our body follows upon the command of our will. Of this we are every moment conscious. But the means, by which this is effected; the energy, by which the will performs so extraordinary an operation; of this we are so far from being immediately conscious, that it must for ever escape our most diligent enquiry.

For *first;* is there any principle in all nature more mysterious than the union of soul with body; by which a supposed spiritual substance acquires such an influence over a material one, that the most refined thought is able to actuate the grossest matter? Were we empowered, by a secret wish, to remove mountains, or control the planets in their orbit; this extensive authority would not be more extraordinary, nor more beyond our comprehension. But if by consciousness we perceived any power or energy in the will, we must know this power; we must know its connexion with the effect; we must know the secret union of soul and body, and the nature of both these substances; by which the one is able to operate, in so many instances, upon the other.

Secondly, We are not able to move all the organs of the body with a like authority; though we cannot assign any reason besides experience, for so remarkable a difference between one and the other. Why has the will an influence over the tongue and fingers, not over the heart and liver? This question would never embarrass us, were we conscious of a power in the former case, not in the latter. We should then perceive, independent of experience, why the authority of will over the organs of the body is circumscribed within such particular limits. Being in that case fully acquainted with the power or force, by which it operates; we should also know, why its influence reaches precisely to such boundaries, and no farther.

A man, suddenly struck with palsy in the leg or arm, or who had newly lost those members, frequently endeavours, at first to move them, and employ them in their usual offices. Here he is as much conscious of power to command such limbs, as a man in perfect health is conscious of power to actuate any member which remains in its natural state and condition. But consciousness never deceives. Consequently, neither in the one case nor in the other, are we ever conscious of any power. We learn the influence of our will from experience alone. And experience only teaches us, how one event constantly follows another; without instructing us in the secret connexion, which binds them together, and renders them inseparable.

Thirdly, We learn from anatomy, that the immediate object of power in voluntary motion, is not the member itself which is moved, but certain muscles, and nerves, and animal spirits, and, perhaps, something still more minute and more unknown, through which the motion is successfully propagated, ere it reach the member itself whose motion is the immediate object of volition. Can there be a more certain proof that the power, by which this whole operation is performed, so far from being directly and fully known by an inward sentiment or consciousness, is, to the last degree, mysterious and unintelligible? Here the mind wills a certain event: Immediately another event, unknown to ourselves, and totally different from the one intended, is produced: This event produces another, equally unknown: Till at last, through a long succession, the desired event is produced. But if the original power were felt, it must be known: Were it known, its effect also must be known; since all power is relative to its effect. And *vice versa,* if the effect be not known, the power cannot be known nor felt. How indeed can we be conscious of a power to move our limbs, when we have no such power; but only that to move certain animal spirits, which, though they produce at last the motion of our limbs, yet operate in such a manner as is wholly beyond our comprehension?

We may, therefore, conclude from the whole, I hope, without any temerity, though with assurance; that our idea of power is not copied from any sentiment or consciousness of power within ourselves, when we give rise to animal motion, or apply our limbs, to their proper use and office. That their motion follows the command of the will is a matter of common experience, like other natural events: But the power or energy by which this is effected, like that in other natural events, is unknown and inconceivable.*

Shall we then assert, that we are conscious of a power or energy in our own minds, when, by an act or command of our will, we raise up a new idea, fix the mind to the contemplation of it, turn it on all sides, and at last dismiss it for some other idea, when we think that we have surveyed it with sufficient accuracy? I believe the same arguments will prove, that even this command of the will gives us no real idea of force or energy.

First, It must be allowed, that, when we know a power, we know that very circumstance is the cause, by which it is enabled to produce the effect: For these are supposed to be synonymous. We must, therefore, know both the cause and effect, and the relation between them. But do we pretend to be acquainted with the nature of the human soul and the nature of an idea, or the aptitude of the one to produce the other? This is a real creation; a production of something out of nothing: Which implies a power so great, that it may seem, at first sight, beyond the reach of any being, less than infinite. At least it must be owned, that such a power is not felt, nor known, nor even conceivable by the mind. We only feel the event, namely, the existence of an idea, consequent to a command of the will: But the manner, in which this operation is performed, the power by which it is produced, is entirely beyond our comprehension.

Secondly, The command of the mind over itself is limited, as well as its command over the body; and these limits are not known by reason, or any acquaintance with the nature of cause and effect, but only by experience and observation, as in all other natural events and in the operation of external objects. Our authority over our

---

*It may be pretended, that the resistance which we meet with in bodies, obliging us frequently to exert our force, and call up all our power, this gives us the idea of force and power. It is this nisus, or strong endeavour, of which we are conscious, that is the original impression from which this idea is copied. But, *first,* we attribute power to a vast number of objects, where we never can suppose this resistance or exertion of force to take place, to the Supreme Being, who never meets with any resistance; to the mind in its command over its ideas and limbs, in common thinking and motion, where the effect follows immediately upon the will, without any exertion or summoning up of force, to inanimate matter, which is not capable of this sentiment. *Secondly,* This sentiment of an endeavour to overcome resistance has no known connexion with any event: What follows it we know by experience; but could not know it *a priori.* It must, however, be confessed that the animal nisus, which we experience though it can afford no accurate precise idea of power, enters very much into that vulgar, inaccurate idea, which is formed of it.

sentiments and passions is much weaker than that over our ideas; and even the latter authority is circumscribed within very narrow boundaries, or show why the power is deficient in one case, not in another.

Thirdly, This self-command is very different at different times. A man in health possesses more of it than one languishing with sickness. We are more master of our thoughts in the morning than in the evening: Fasting, than after a full meal. Can we give any reason for these variations, except experience? Where then is the power, of which we pretend to be conscious? Is there not here, either in a spiritual or material substance, or both, some secret mechanism or structure of parts, upon which the effect depends, and which, being entirely unknown to us, renders the power or energy of the will equally unknown and incomprehensible?

Volition is surely an act of the mind, with which we are sufficiently acquainted. Reflect upon it. Consider it on all sides. Do you find anything in it like this creative power, by which it raises from nothing a new idea, and with a kind of *Fiat*, imitates the omnipotence of its Maker, if I may be allowed so to speak, who called forth into existence all the various scenes of nature? So far from being conscious of this energy in the will, it requires as certain experience as that of which we are possessed, to convince us that such extraordinary effects do ever result from a simple act of volition.

The generality of mankind never find any difficulty in accounting for the more common and familiar operations of nature—such as the descent of heavy bodies, the growth of plants, the generation of animals, or the nourishment of bodies by food: But suppose that, in all these cases, they perceive the very force or energy of the cause, by which it is connected with its effect, and is for ever infallible in its operation. They acquire, by long habit, such a turn of mind, that, upon the appearance of the cause, they immediately expect with assurance its usual attendant, and hardly conceive it possible that any other event could result from it. It is only on the discovery of extraordinary phenomena, such as earthquakes, pestilence, and prodigies of any kind, that they find themselves at a loss to assign a proper cause, and to explain the manner in which the effect is produced by it. It is usual for men, in such difficulties, to have recourse to some invisible intelligent principle as the Immediate cause of that event which surprises them, and which, they think, cannot be accounted for from the common powers of nature. But philosophers, who carry their scrutiny a little farther, immediately perceive that, even in the most familiar events, the energy of the cause is as unintelligible as in the most unusual, and that we only learn by experience the frequent *Conjunction* of objects, without being ever able to comprehend anything like *Connexion* between them. Here, then, many philosophers think themselves obliged by reason to have recourse, on all occasions, to the same principle, which the vulgar never appeal to but in cases that appear miraculous and supernatural. They acknowledge mind and intelligence to be, not only the ultimate and original cause of all things, but the immediate and sole cause of every event which appears in nature. They pretend that those objects which are commonly denominated *causes*, are in reality nothing but *occasions*; and that the true and direct principle of every effect is not any power or force in nature, but a volition of the Supreme Being, who wills that such particular objects should for ever be conjoined with each other. Instead of saying that one Billiard-ball moves another by a force which it has derived from the author of nature, it is the Deity himself, they say, who, by a particular volition, moves the second ball, being determined to this operation by the impulse of the first ball, in consequence of those general laws which he has laid down to himself in the government of the universe. But philosophers advancing still in their inquiries, discover that, as we are totally ignorant of the power on which depends the mutual operation of bodies, we are no less ignorant of that power on which depends the operation of mind on body, or of body on mind; nor are we able, either from our sense or consciousness, to assign the ultimate principle in one case more than in the other. The same ignorance, therefore, reduces them to the same conclusion. They assert that the Deity is the immediate cause of the union between soul and body; and that they are not the organs of sense, which, being agitated by external objects, produce sensations in the mind; but that it is a particular volition of our omnipotent Maker, which excites such a sensation, in consequence of such a motion in the organ. In like manner, it is not any energy in the will that produces local motion in our members: It is God himself, who is pleased to second our will, in itself important, and to command that motion which we erroneously attribute to our own power and efficacy. Nor do philosophers stop at this conclusion. They sometimes extend the same inference to the mind itself, in its internal operations. Our mental vision or conception of ideas is nothing but a revelation made to us by our Maker. When we voluntarily turn our thoughts to any object, and raise up its image in the fancy, it is not the will which creates that idea: It is the universal Creator, who discovers it to the mind, and renders it present to us.

Thus, according to these philosophers, every thing is full of God. Not content with the principle, that nothing exists but by his will, that nothing possesses any power but by his concession: They rob nature, and all created beings, of every power, in order to render their dependence on the Deity still more sensible and immediate. They consider not that, by this theory, they diminish, instead of magnifying, the grandeur of those attributes, which they affect so much to celebrate. It argues surely more power in the Deity to delegate a certain degree of power to inferior creatures, than to produce every thing by his own immediate volition. It argues more wisdom to contrive at first the fabric of the world with such perfect foresight that, of itself, and by its proper operation, it may serve all the purposes of providence, than if the great Creator were obliged every moment to adjust its parts, and animate by his breath all the wheels of that stupendous machine.

But if we would have a more philosophical confutation of this theory, perhaps the two following reflections may suffice.

First, It seems to me that this theory of the universal energy and operation of the Supreme Being is too bold ever to carry conviction with it to a man, sufficiently apprized of the weakness of human reason, and the narrow limits to which it is confined in all its operations. Though the chain of arguments which conduct to it were ever so logical, there must arise a strong suspicion, if not an absolute assurance, that it has carried us quite beyond the reach of our faculties, when it leads to conclusions so extraordinary, and so remote from common life and experience. We are got into fairy land, long ere we have reached the last steps of our theory; and *there* we have no reason to trust our common methods of argument, or to think that our usual analogies and probabilities have any authority. Our line is too short to fathom such immense abysses. And however we may flatter ourselves that we are guided, in every step which we take, by a kind of verisimilitude and experience, we may be assured that this fancied experience has no authority when we thus apply it to subjects that lie entirely out of the sphere of experience. But on this we shall have occasion to touch afterwards.*

Secondly, I cannot perceive any force in the arguments on which this theory is founded. We are ignorant, it is true, of the manner in which bodies operate on each other: Their force or energy is entirely incomprehensible: But are we not equally ignorant of the manner of force by which a mind, even the supreme mind, operates either on itself or on body? Whence, I beseech you, do we acquire any idea of it? We have no sentiment or consciousness of this power in ourselves. We have no idea of the Supreme Being but what we learn from reflection on our own faculties. Were our igno-

*Section XII.

rance, therefore, a good reason for rejecting any thing, we should be led into that principle of denying all energy in the Supreme Being as much as in the grossest matter. We surely comprehend as little the operations of one as of the other. Is it more difficult to conceive that motion may arise from impulse than that it may arise from volition? All we know is our profound ignorance in both cases.*

PART II

But to hasten to a conclusion of this argument, which is already drawn out to too great a length: We have sought in vain for an idea of power or necessary connexion in all the sources from which we could suppose it to be derived. It appears that, in single instances of the operation of bodies, we never can, by our utmost scrutiny, discover any thing but one event following another, without being able to comprehend any force or power by which the cause operates, or any connexion between it and its supposed effect. The same difficulty occurs in contemplating the operations of mind on body— where we observe the motion of the latter to follow upon the volition of the former, but are not able to observe or conceive the tie which binds together the motion and volition, or the energy by which the mind produces this effect. The authority of the will over its own faculties and ideas is not a whit more comprehensible: So that, upon the whole, there appears not, throughout all nature, any one instance of connexion which is conceivable by us. All events seem entirely loose and separate. One event follows another; but we never can observe any tie between them. They seem *conjoined,* but never connected. And as we can have no idea of any thing which never appeared to our outward sense or inward sentiment, the necessary conclusion *seems* to be that we have no idea of connexion or power at all, and that these words are absolutely without any meaning, when employed either in philosophical reasonings or common life.

But there still remains one method of avoiding this conclusion, and one source which we have not yet examined. When any natural object or event is presented, it is impossible for us, by any sagacity or penetration, to discover, or even conjecture, without experience, what event will result from it, or to carry our foresight beyond that object which is immediately present to the memory and senses. Even after one instance or experiment where we have observed a particular event to follow upon another, we are not entitled to form a general rule, or foretell what will happen in like cases; it being justly esteemed an unpardonable temerity to judge of the whole course of nature from one single experiment, however accurate or certain. But when one particular species of event has always, in all instances, been conjoined with another, we make no longer any

---

*I need not examine at length the *vis inertiae* [force of inertia] which is so much talked of in the new philosophy, and which is ascribed to matter. We find by experience, that a body at rest or in motion continues for ever in its present state, till put from it by some new cause; and that a body impelled takes as much motion from the impelling body as it acquires itself. These are facts. When we call this a *vis inertiae,* we only mark these facts, without pretending to have any idea of the inert power; in the same manner as, when we talk of gravity, we mean certain effects without comprehending that active power. It was never the meaning of SIR ISAAC NEWTON to rob second causes of all forces of energy though some of his followers have endeavoured to establish that theory upon his authority. On the contrary, that great philosopher had recourse to an etherial active fluid to explain his universal attraction; though he was so cautious and modest as to allow that it was a mere hypothesis, not to be insisted on, without more experiments. I must confess, that there is something in the fate of opinions a little extraordinary. DESCARTES insinuated that doctrine of the universal and sole efficacy of the Deity, without insisting on it. MALEBRANCHE and other CARTESIANS made it the foundation of all their philosophy. It had, however, no authority in England. LOCKE, CLARKE, and CUDWORTH, never so much as take notice of it, but suppose all along, that matter has a real, though subordinate and derived power. By what means has it become so prevalent among our modern metaphysicians?

scruple of foretelling one upon the appearance of the other, and of employing that reasoning which can alone assure us of any matter of fact or existence. We then call the one object, *Cause*; the other, *Effect.* We suppose that there is some connexion between them; some power in the one, by which it infallibly produces the other, and operates with the greatest certainty and strongest necessity.

It appears, then, that this idea of a necessary connexion among events arises from a number of similar instances which occur of the constant conjunction of these events; nor can that idea ever be suggested by any one of these instances, surveyed in all possible lights and positions. But there is nothing in a number of instances, different from every single instance, which is supposed to be exactly similar; except only, that after a repetition of similar instances, the mind is carried by habit, upon the appearance of one event, to expect its usual attendant, and to believe that it will exist. This connexion, therefore, which we *feel* in the mind, this customary transition of the imagination from one object to its usual attendant, is the sentiment or impression from which we form the idea of power or necessary connexion. Nothing farther is in the case. Contemplate the subject on all sides; you will never find any other origin of that idea. This is the sole difference between one instance, from which we can never receive the idea of connexion, and a number of similar instances, by which it is suggested. The first time a man saw the communication of motion by impulse, as by the shock of two Billiard-balls, he could not pronounce that the one event was *connected*: but only that it was *conjoined* with the other. After he has observed several instances of this nature, he then pronounces them to be *connected.* What alteration has happened to give rise to this new idea of connexion? Nothing but that he now *feels* these events to be *connected* in his imagination, and can readily foretell the existence of one from the appearance of the other. When we say, therefore, that one object is connected with another, we mean only that they have acquired a connexion in our thought, and give rise to this inference, by which they become proofs of each other's existence: A conclusion which is somewhat extraordinary, but which seems founded on sufficient evidence. Nor will its evidence be weakened by any general diffidence of the understanding, or sceptical suspicion concerning every conclusion which is new and extraordinary. No conclusions can be more agreeable to scepticism than such as make discoveries concerning the weakness and narrow limits of human reason and capacity.

And what stronger instance can be produced of the surprising ignorance and weakness of the understanding than the present? For surely, if there be any relation among objects which it imports to us to know perfectly, it is that of cause and effect. On this are founded all our reasonings concerning matter of fact or existence. By means of it alone we attain any assurance concerning objects which are removed from the present testimony of our memory and senses. The only immediate utility of all sciences, is to teach us, how to control and regulate future events by their causes. Our thoughts and enquiries are, therefore, every moment, employed about this relation: Yet so imperfect are the ideas which we form concerning it, that it is impossible to give any just definition of cause, except what is drawn from something extraneous and foreign to it. Similar objects are always conjoined with similar. Of this we have experience. Suitably to this experience, therefore, we may define a cause to be *an object, followed by another, and where all the objects similar to the first are followed by objects similar to the second. Or in other words where, if the first object had not been, the second never had existed.* The appearance of a cause always conveys the mind, by a customary transition, to the idea of the effect. Of this also we have experience. We may, therefore, suitably to this experience, form another definition of cause, and call it, *an object followed by another and whose appearance always conveys the thought to that other.* But though both these definitions be drawn from circumstances foreign to the cause, we cannot remedy this inconvenience, or attain any more perfect definition, which may point out that circumstance in the cause, which gives it a connexion with its effect. We have no idea of this connexion, nor even any distinct notion what it is we desire to know, when we endeavour at a conception of it. We say, for instance, that the vibration of this string is the cause of this particular sound. But what do we mean by that affirmation? We either mean *that this vibration is followed by this sound, and that all similar vibrations have been followed by similar sounds*: Or, that this vibration is followed by this sound, and that upon the appearance of one the mind anticipates the senses, and forms immediately an idea of the other. We may consider the relation of cause and effect in either of these two lights; but beyond these, we have no idea of it.*

To recapitulate, therefore, the reasonings of this section: Every idea is copied from some preceding impression or sentiment; and where we cannot find any impression, we may be certain that there is no idea. In all single instances of the operation of bodies or minds, there is nothing that produces any impression, nor consequently can suggest any idea of power or necessary connexion. But when many uniform instances appear, and the same object is always followed by the same event; we then begin to entertain the notion of cause and connexion. We then *feel* a new sentiment or impression, to wit, a customary connexion in the thought or imagination between one object and its usual attendant; and this sentiment is the original of that idea which we seek for. For as this idea arises from a number of similar instances, and not from any single instance, it must arise from that circumstance, in which the number of instances differ from every individual instance. But this customary connexion or transition of the imagination is the only circumstance in which they differ. In every other particular they are alike. The first instance which we saw of motion communicated by the shock of two Billiard-balls (to return to this obvious illustration) is exactly similar to any instance that may, at present, occur to us; except only, that we could not, at first, *infer* one event from the other; which we are enabled to do at present, after so long a course of uniform experience. I know not whether the reader will readily apprehend this reasoning. I am afraid that, should I multiply words about it, or throw it into a greater variety of lights, it would only become more obscure and intricate. In all abstract reasonings there is one point of view which, if we can happily hit, we shall go farther towards illustrating the subject than by all the eloquence in the world. This point of view we should endeavour to reach, and reserve the flowers of rhetoric for subjects which are more adapted to them.

*According to these explanations and definitions, the idea of *power* is relative as much as that of cause; and both have a reference to an effect, or some other event constantly conjoined with the former. When we consider the *unknown* circumstance of an object, by which the degree of quantity of its effect is fixed and determined, we call that its power: And accordingly, it is allowed by all philosophers, that the effect is the measure of the power. But if they had any idea of power, as it is in itself, why could not they measure it in itself? The dispute whether the force of a body in motion be as its velocity, or the square of its velocity; this dispute, I say, need not be decided by comparing its effects in equal or unequal times; but by a direct mensuration and comparison.

As to the frequent use of the words, Force, Power, Energy, etc., which every where occur in common conversation, as well as in philosophy; that is no proof, that we are acquainted, in any instance, with the connecting principle between cause and effect or can account ultimately for the production of one thing to another. These words, as commonly used, have very loose meanings annexed to them; and their ideas in motion without the sentiment of a *nisus* or endeavour; and every animal has a sentiment or feeling from the stroke or blow of an external object, that is in motion. These sensations, which are merely animal, and from which we can *a priori* draw no inference, we are apt to transfer to inanimate objects, and to suppose, that they have some such feelings, whenever they transfer or receive motion. With regard to energies, which are exerted, without our annexing to them any idea of communicated motion, we consider only the constant experienced conjunction of the events; and as we *feel* a customary connexion between the ideas, we transfer that feeling to the objects; as nothing is more usual than to apply to external bodies every internal sensation which they occasion.

Section VIII. Of Liberty and Necessity

Part I

It might reasonably be expected in questions which have been canvassed and disputed with great eagerness, since the first origin of science and philosophy, that the meaning of all the terms, at least, should have been agreed upon among the disputants; and our enquiries, in the course of two thousand years, been able to pass from words to the true and real subject of the controversy. For how easy may it seem to give exact definitions of the terms employed in reasoning, and make these definitions, not the mere sound of words, the object of future scrutiny and examination? But if we consider the matter more narrowly, we shall be apt to draw a quite opposite conclusion. From this circumstance alone, that a controversy has been long kept on foot, and remains still undecided, we may presume that there is some ambiguity in the expression, and that the disputants affix different ideas to the terms employed in the controversy. For as the faculties of the mind are supposed to be naturally alike in every individual; otherwise nothing could be more fruitless than to reason or dispute together; it were impossible, if men affix the same ideas to their terms, that they could so long form different opinions of the same subject; especially when they communicate their views, and each party turn themselves on all sides, in search of arguments which may give them the victory over their antagonists. It is true, if men attempt the discussion of questions which lie entirely beyond the reach of human capacity, such as those concerning the origin of worlds, or the economy of the intellectual system or region of spirits, they may long beat the air in their fruitless contests, and never arrive at any determinate conclusion. But if the question regard any subject of common life and experience, nothing, one would think, could preserve the dispute so long undecided but some ambiguous expressions, which keep the antagonists still at a distance, and hinder them from grappling with each other.

This has been the case in the long disputed question concerning liberty and necessity; and to so remarkable a degree that, if I be not much mistaken, we shall find, that all mankind, both learned and ignorant, have always been of the same opinion with regard to this subject, and that a few intelligible definitions would immediately have put an end to the whole controversy. I own that this dispute has been so much canvassed on all hands, and has led philosophers into such a labyrinth of obscure sophistry, that it is no wonder, if a sensible reader indulge his ease so far as to turn a deaf ear to the proposal of such a question, from which he can expect neither instruction nor entertainment. But the state of the argument here proposed may, perhaps, serve to renew his attention; as it has more novelty, promises at least some decision of the controversy, and will not much disturb his ease by any intricate or obscure reasoning.

I hope, therefore, to make it appear that all men have ever agreed in the doctrine both of necessity and of liberty, according to any reasonable sense, which can be put on these terms; and that the whole controversy has hitherto turned merely upon words. We shall begin with examining the doctrine of necessity.

It is universally allowed that matter, in all its operations, is actuated by a necessary force, and that every natural effect is so precisely determined by the energy of its cause that no other effect, in such particular circumstances, could possibly have resulted from it. The degree and direction of every motion is, by the laws of nature, prescribed with such exactness that a living creature may as soon arise from the shock of two bodies as motion in any other degree or direction than what is actually produced by it. Would we, therefore, form a just and precise idea of *necessity* we must consider whence that idea arises when we apply it to the operation of bodies.

It seems evident that, if all the scenes of nature were continually shifted in such a manner that no two events bore any resemblance to each other, but every object was entirely new, without any similitude to whatever had been seen before, we should never, in that case, have attained the least idea of necessity, or of a connexion among these objects. We might say, upon such a supposition, that one object or event has followed another; not that one was produced by the other. The relation of cause and effect must be utterly unknown to mankind. Inference and reasoning concerning the operations of nature would, from that moment, be at an end; and the memory and senses remain the only canals, by which the knowledge of any real existence could possibly have access to the mind. Our idea, therefore, of necessity and causation arises entirely from the uniformity observable in the operations of nature, where similar objects are constantly conjoined together, and the mind is determined by custom to infer the one from the appearance of the other. These two circumstances form the whole of that necessity, which we ascribe to matter. Beyond the constant conjunction of similar objects, and the consequent *inference* from one to the other, we have no notion of any necessity or connexion.

If it appear, therefore, that all mankind have ever allowed, without any doubt or hesitation, that these two circumstances take place in the voluntary actions of men, and in the operations of mind; it must follow, that all mankind have ever agreed in the doctrine of necessity, and that they have hitherto disputed, merely for not understanding each other.

As to the first circumstance, the constant and regular conjunction of similar events, we may possibly satisfy ourselves by the following considerations. It is universally acknowledged that there is a great uniformity among the actions of men, in all nations and ages, and that human nature remains still the same, in its principles and operations. The same motives always produce the same actions: The same events follow from the same causes. Ambition, avarice, self-love, vanity, friendship, generosity, public spirit: these passions, mixed in various degrees, and distributed through society, have been, from the beginning of the world, and still are, the source of all the actions and enterprises, which have ever been observed among mankind. Would you know the sentiments, inclinations, and course of life of the Greeks and Romans? Study well the temper and actions of the French and English: You cannot be much mistaken in transferring to the former *most* of the observations which you have made with regard to the latter. Mankind are so much the same, in all times and places, that history informs us of nothing new or strange in this particular. Its chief use is only to discover the constant and universal principles of human nature, by showing men in all varieties of circumstances and situations, and furnishing us with materials from which we may form our observations and become acquainted with the regular springs of human action and behaviour. These records of wars, intrigues, factions, and revolutions, are so many collections of experiments, by which the politician or moral philosopher fixes the principles of his science, in the same manner as the physician or natural philosopher becomes acquainted with the nature of plants, minerals, and other external objects, by the experiments which he forms concerning them. Nor are the earth, water, and other elements, examined by Aristotle, and Hippocrates, more like to those which at present lie under our observation than the men described by Polybius and Tacitus are to those who now govern the world.

Should a traveller, returning from a far country, bring us an account of men, wholly different from any with whom we were ever acquainted; men, who were entirely divested of avarice, ambition, or revenge; who knew no pleasure but friendship, generosity, and public spirit; we should immediately, from these circumstances, detect the falsehood, and prove him a liar, with the same certainty as if he had stuffed his narration with stories of centaurs and dragons, miracles and prodigies. And if we would explode any forgery in history, we cannot make use of a more convincing argument, than to prove, that the actions ascribed to any person are directly contrary to the course of nature, and that no human motives, in such circumstances, could ever induce him to such a conduct. The veracity of Quintus Curtius is as much to be suspected, when he describes the supernatural courage of Alexander, by which he was hurried on singly to attack multitudes, as when he describes his supernatural force and activity, by which he was able to resist them. So readily and universally do we acknowledge a uniformity in human motives and actions as well as in the operations of body.

Hence likewise the benefit of that experience, acquired by long life and a variety of business and company, in order to instruct us in the principles of human nature, and regulate our future conduct, as well as speculation. By means of this guide, we mount up to the knowledge of men's inclinations and motives, from their actions, expressions, and even gestures; and again descend to the interpretation of their actions from our knowledge of their motives and inclinations. The general observations treasured up by a course of experience, give us the clue of human nature, and teach us to unravel all its intricacies. Pretexts and appearances no longer deceive us. Public declarations pass for the specious colouring of a cause. And though virtue and honour be allowed their proper weight and authority, that perfect disinterestedness, so often pretended to, is never expected in multitudes and parties; seldom in their leaders; and scarcely even in individuals of any rank or station. But were there no uniformity in human actions, and were every experiment which we could form of this kind irregular and anomalous, it were impossible to collect any general observations concerning mankind; and no experience, however accurately digested by reflection, would ever serve to any purpose. Why is the aged husbandman more skilful in his calling than the young beginner but because there is a certain uniformity in the operation of the sun, rain, and earth towards the production of vegetables; and experience teaches the old practitioner the rules by which this operation is governed and directed.

We must not, however, expect that this uniformity of human actions should be carried to such a length as that all men, in the same circumstances, will always act precisely in the same manner, without making any allowance for the diversity of characters, prejudices, and opinions. Such a uniformity in every particular, is found in no part of nature. On the contrary, from observing the variety of conduct in different men, we are enabled to form a greater variety of maxims, which still suppose a degree of uniformity and regularity.

Are the manners of men different in different ages and countries? We learn thence the great force of custom and education, which mould the human mind from its infancy and form it into a fixed and established character. Is the behaviour and conduct of the one sex very unlike that of the other? Is it thence we become acquainted with the different characters which nature has impressed upon the sexes, and which she preserves with constancy and regularity? Are the actions of the same person much diversified in the different periods of his life, from infancy to old age? This affords room for many general observations concerning the gradual change of our sentiments and inclinations, and the different maxims which prevail in the different ages of human creatures. Even the characters, which are peculiar to each individual, have a uniformity in their influence; otherwise our acquaintance with the persons and our observation of their conduct could never teach us their dispositions, or serve to direct our behaviour with regard to them.

I grant it possible to find some actions, which seem to have no regular connexion with any known motives, and are exceptions to all the measures of conduct which have ever been established for the government of men. But if we would willingly know what judgement should be formed of such irregular and extraordinary actions, we may consider the sentiments commonly entertained with regard to those irregular events which appear in the course of nature, and the operations of external objects. All causes are not conjoined to their usual effects with like uniformity. An artificer, who handles only dead matter, may be disappointed of his aim, as well as the politician, who directs the conduct of sensible and intelligent agents.

The vulgar, who take things according to their first appearance, attribute the uncertainty of events to such an uncertainty in the causes as makes the latter often fail of their usual influence; though they meet with no impediment in their operation. But philosophers, observing that, almost in every part of nature, there is contained a vast variety of springs and principles, which are hid, by reason of their minuteness or remoteness, find, that it is at least possible the contrariety of events may not proceed from any contingency in the cause, but from the secret operation of contrary causes. This possibility is converted into certainty by farther observation, when they remark that, upon an exact scrutiny, a contrariety of effects always betrays a contrariety of causes, and proceeds from their mutual opposition. A peasant can give no better reason for the stopping of any clock or watch than to say that it does not commonly go right: But an artist easily perceives that the same force in the spring or pendulum has always the same influence on the wheels; but fails of its usual effect, perhaps by reason of a grain of dust, which puts a stop to the whole movement. From the observation of several parallel instances, philosophers form a maxim that the connexion between all causes and effects is equally necessary, and that its seeming uncertainty in some instances proceeds from the secret opposition of contrary causes.

Thus, for instance, in the human body, when the usual symptoms of health or sickness disappoint our expectation; when medicines operate not with their wonted powers; when irregular events follow from any particular cause; the philosopher and physician are not surprised at the matter, nor are ever tempted to deny, in general, the necessity and uniformity of those principles by which the animal economy is conducted. They know that a human body is a mighty complicated machine: That many secret powers lurk in it, which are altogether beyond our comprehension: That to us it must often appear very uncertain in its operations: And that therefore the irregular events, which outwardly discover themselves, can be no proof that the laws of nature are not observed with the greatest regularity in its internal operations and government.

The philosopher, if he be consistent, must apply the same reasoning to the actions and volitions of intelligent agents. The most irregular and unexpected resolutions of men may frequently be accounted for by those who know every particular circumstance of their character and situation. A person of an obliging disposition gives a peevish answer: But he has the toothache, or has not dined. A stupid fellow discovers an uncommon alacrity in his carriage: But he has met with a sudden piece of good fortune. Or even when an action, as sometimes happens, cannot be particularly accounted for, either by the person himself or by others; we know, in general, that the characters of men are, to a certain degree, inconstant and irregular. This is, in a manner, the constant character of human nature; though it be applicable, in a more particular manner, to some persons who have no fixed rule for their conduct, but proceed in a continued course of caprice and inconstancy. The internal principles and motives may operate in a uniform manner, notwithstanding these seeming irregularities; in the same manner as the winds, rain, clouds, and other variations of the weather are supposed to be gov-

erned by steady principles; though not easily discoverable by human sagacity and enquiry.

Thus it appears, not only that the conjunction between motives and voluntary actions is as regular and uniform as that between the cause and effect in any part of nature; but also that this regular conjunction has been universally acknowledged among
mankind, and has never been the subject of dispute, either in philosophy or common
life. Now, as it is from past experience that we draw all inferences concerning the future, and as we conclude that objects will always be conjoined together which we find
to have always been conjoined; it may seem superfluous to prove that this experienced
uniformity in human actions is a source whence we draw *inferences* concerning them.
But in order to throw the argument into a greater variety of lights we shall also insist,
though briefly, on this latter topic.

The mutual dependence of men is so great in all societies that scarce any human
action is entirely complete in itself, or is performed without some reference to the actions of others, which are requisite to make it answer fully the intention of the agent.
The poorest artificer, who labours alone, expects at least the protection of the magistrate, to ensure him the enjoyment of the fruits of his labour. He also expects that,
when he carries his goods to market, and offers them at a reasonable price, he shall find
purchasers, and shall be able, by the money he acquires, to engage others to supply
him with those commodities which are requisite for his subsistence. In proportion as
men extend their dealings, and render their intercourse with others more complicated,
they always comprehend, in their schemes of life, a greater variety of voluntary actions, which they expect, from the proper motives, to co-operate with their own. In all
these conclusions they take their measures from past experience, in the same manner
as in their reasonings concerning external objects; and firmly believe that men, as well
as all the elements, are to continue, in their operations, the same that they have ever
found them. A manufacturer reckons upon the labour of his servants for the execution
of any work as much as upon the tools which he employs, and would be equally surprised were his expectations disappointed. In short, this experimental inference and
reasoning concerning the actions of others enters so much into human life, that no
man, while awake, is ever a moment without employing it. Have we not reason, therefore, to affirm that all mankind have always agreed in the doctrine of necessity according to the foregoing definition and explication of it?

Nor have philosophers ever entertained a different opinion from the people in
this particular. For, not to mention that almost every action of their life supposes that
opinion, there are even few of the speculative parts of learning to which it is not essential. What would become of *history*, had we not a dependence on the veracity of the
historian according to the experience which we have had of mankind? How could *politics* be a science, if laws and forms of government had not a uniform influence upon
society? Where would be the foundation of *morals*, if particular characters had no certain or determinate power to produce particular sentiments, and if these sentiments had
no constant operation on actions? And with what pretence could we employ our *criticism* upon any poet or polite author, if we could not pronounce the conduct and sentiments of his actors either natural or unnatural to such characters, and in such circumstances? It seems almost impossible, therefore, to engage either in science or action of
any kind without acknowledging the doctrine of necessity, and this *inference* from motive to voluntary actions, from characters to conduct.

And indeed, when we consider how aptly *natural* and *moral* evidence link together, and form only one chain of argument, we shall make no scruple to allow that
they are of the same nature, and derived from the same principles. A prisoner who has

neither money nor interest, discovers the impossibility of his escape, as well when he considers the obstinacy of the gaoler, as the walls and bars with which he is surrounded; and, in all attempts for his freedom, chooses rather to work upon the stone and iron of the one, than upon the inflexible nature of the other. The same prisoner, when conducted to the scaffold, foresees his death as certainly from the constancy and fidelity of his guards, as from the operation of the axe or wheel. His mind runs along a certain train of ideas: The refusal of the soldiers to consent to his escape; the action of the executioner; the separation of the head and body; bleeding, convulsive motions, and death. Here is a connected chain of natural causes and voluntary actions; but the mind feels no difference between them in passing from one link to another: Nor is less certain of the future event than if it were connected with the objects present to the memory or senses, by a train of causes, cemented together by what we are pleased to call a *physical* necessity. The same experienced union has the same effect on the mind, whether the united objects be motives, volition, and actions; or figure and motion. We may change the name of things; but their nature and their operation on the understanding never change.

Were a man, whom I know to be honest and opulent, and with whom I live in intimate friendship, to come into my house, where I am surrounded with my servants, I rest assured that he is not to stab me before he leaves it in order to rob me of my silver standish; and I no more suspect this event than the falling of the house itself, which is new, and solidly built and founded.—*But he may have been seized with a sudden and unknown frenzy.*—So may a sudden earthquake arise, and shake and tumble my house about my ears. I shall therefore change the suppositions. I shall say that I know with certainty that he is not to put his hand into the fire and hold it there till it be consumed: And this event I think I can foretell with the same assurance, as that, if he throw himself out at the window, and meet with no obstruction, he will not remain a moment suspended in the air. No suspicion of an unknown frenzy can give the least possibility to the former event, which is so contrary to all the known principles of human nature. A man who at noon leaves his purse full of gold on the pavement at Charing-Cross, may as well expect that it will fly away like a feather, as that he will find it untouched an hour after. Above one half of human reasonings contain inferences of a similar nature, attended with more or less degrees of certainty proportioned to our experience of the usual conduct of mankind in such particular situations.

I have frequently considered, what could possibly be the reason why all mankind, though they have ever, without hesitation, acknowledged the doctrine of necessity in their whole practice and reasoning, have yet not discovered such a reluctance to acknowledge it in words, and have rather shown a propensity, in all ages, to profess the contrary opinion. The matter, I think, may be accounted for after the following manner. If we examine the operations of body, and the production of effects from their causes, we shall find that all our faculties can never carry us farther in our knowledge of this relation than barely to observe that particular objects are *constantly conjoined* together, and that the mind is carried, by a *customary transition*, from the appearance of one to the belief of the other. But though this conclusion concerning human ignorance be the result of the strictest scrutiny of this subject, men still entertain a strong propensity to believe that they penetrate farther into the powers of nature, and perceive something like a necessary connexion between the cause and the effect. When again they turn their reflections towards the operations of their own minds, and *feel* no such connexion of the motive and the action; they are thence apt to suppose, that there is a difference between the effects which result from material force, and those which arise from thought and intelligence. But being once convinced that we know nothing farther of causation of any kind than merely the *constant conjunction* of objects, and the consequent *inference* of the mind from one to another, and finding that these two circumstances are universally allowed to have place in voluntary actions; we may be more easily led to own the same necessity common to all causes. And though this reasoning may contradict the systems of many philosophers, in ascribing necessity to the determinations of the will, we shall find, upon reflection, that they dissent from it in words only, not in their real sentiment. Necessity, according to the sense in which it is here taken, has never yet been rejected, nor can ever, I think, be rejected by any philosopher. It may only, perhaps, be pretended that the mind can perceive, in the operations of matter, some farther connexion between the cause and effect; and connexion that has no place in voluntary actions of intelligent beings. Now whether it be so or not, can only appear upon examination; and it is incumbent on these philosophers to make good their assertion, by defining or describing that necessity, and pointing it out to us in the operations of material causes.

It would seem, indeed, that men begin at the wrong end of this question concerning liberty and necessity, when they enter upon it by examining the faculties of the soul, the influence of the understanding, and the operations of the will. Let them first discuss a more simple question, namely, the operations of body and of brute unintelligent matter; and try whether they can there form any idea of causation and necessity, except that of a constant conjunction of objects, and subsequent inference of the mind from one to another. If these circumstances form, in reality, the whole of that necessity, which we conceive in matter, and if these circumstances be also universally acknowledged to take place in the operations of the mind, the dispute is at an end; at least, must be owned to be thenceforth merely verbal. But as long as we will rashly suppose, that we have some farther idea of necessity and causation in the operations of external objects; at the same time, that we can find nothing farther in the voluntary actions of the mind; there is no possibility of bringing the question to any determinate issue, while we proceed upon so erroneous a supposition. The only method of undeceiving us is to mount up higher; to examine the narrow extent of science when applied to material causes; and to convince ourselves that all we know of them is the constant conjunction and inference above mentioned. We may, perhaps, find that it is with difficulty we are induced to fix such narrow limits to human understanding: But we can afterwards find no difficulty when we come to apply this doctrine to the actions of the will. For as it is evident that these have a regular conjunction with motives and circumstances and characters, and as we always draw inferences from one to the other, we must be obliged to acknowledge in words that necessity, which we have already avowed, in every deliberation of our lives, and in every step of our conduct and behaviour.*

*The prevalence of the doctrine of liberty may be accounted for, from another cause viz. a false sensation or seeming experience which we have, or may have, of liberty or indifference, in many of our actions. The necessity of any action, whether of matter or of mind, is not, properly speaking, a quality in the agent, but in any thinking or intelligent being, who may consider the action; and it consists chiefly in the determination of his thoughts to infer the existence of that action from some preceding objects; as liberty, when opposed to necessity, is nothing but the want of that determination, and a certain looseness or indifference, which we feel, in passing or not passing, from the idea of one object to that of any succeeding one. Now we may observe, that, though, in *reflecting* on human actions, we seldom feel such a looseness, or indifference, but are commonly able to infer them with considerable certainty from their motives, and from the dispositions of the agent; yet it frequently happens, that, in *performing* the actions themselves, we are sensible of something like it: And as all resembling objects are readily taken for each other, this has been employed as a demonstrative and even intuitive proof of human liberty. We feel, that our actions are subject to our will, on most occasions; and imagine we feel, that the will itself is subject to nothing, because, when by a denial of it we are provoked to try, we feel, that it moves easily every way, and produces an image of itself (or a

But to proceed in this reconciling project with regard to the question of liberty and necessity; the most contentious question of metaphysics, the most contentious science; it will not require many words to prove, that all mankind have ever agreed in the doctrine of liberty as well as in that of necessity, and that the whole dispute, in this respect also, has been hitherto merely verbal. For what is meant by liberty, when applied to voluntary actions? We cannot surely mean that actions have so little connexion with motives, inclinations, and circumstances, that one does not follow with a certain degree of uniformity from the other, and that one affords no inference by which we can conclude the existence of the other. For these are plain and acknowledged matters of fact. By liberty, then, we can only mean *a power of acting or not acting, according to the determinations of the will;* that is, if we choose to remain at rest, we may; if we choose to move, we also may. Now this hypothetical liberty is universally allowed to belong to every one who is not a prisoner and in chains. Here, then, is no subject of dispute.

Whatever definition we may give of liberty, we should be careful to observe two requisite circumstances; *first,* that it be consistent with plain matter of fact; *secondly,* that it be consistent with itself. If we observe these circumstances, and render our definition intelligible, I am persuaded that all mankind will be found of one opinion with regard to it.

It is universally allowed that nothing exists without a cause of its existence, and that chance, when strictly examined, is a mere negative word, and means not any real power which has anywhere a being in nature. But it is pretended that some causes are necessary, some not necessary. Here then is the advantage of definitions. Let any one *define* a cause, without comprehending, as a part of the definition, a *necessary connexion* with its effect; and let him show distinctly the origin of the idea, expressed by the definition; and I shall readily give up the whole controversy. But if the foregoing explication of the matter be received, this must be absolutely impracticable. Had not objects a regular conjunction with each other, we should never have entertained any notion of cause and effect; and this regular conjunction produces that inference of the understanding, which is the only connexion, that we can have any comprehension of. Whoever attempts a definition of cause, exclusive of these circumstances, will be obliged either to employ unintelligible terms or such as are synonymous to the term which he endeavours to define.* And if the definition above mentioned be admitted; liberty, when opposed to necessity, not to constraint, is the same thing with chance; which is universally allowed to have no existence.

Velleïty, as it is called in the schools) even on that side, on which it did not settle. This image, or faint motion, we persuade ourselves, could, at that time, have been completed into the thing itself; because, should that be denied, we find, upon a second trial, that, at present it can. We consider not that the fantastical desire of showing liberty, is here the motive of our actions. And it seems certain, that, however, we may imagine we feel a liberty within ourselves, a spectator can commonly infer our actions from our motives and character, and even where he cannot, he concludes in general, that he might, were he perfectly acquainted with every circumstance of our situation and temper, and the most secret springs of our complexion and disposition. Now this is the very essence of necessity, according to the foregoing doctrine.

*Thus, if a cause be defined, *that which produces any thing;* it is easy to observe, that *producing* is synonymous to *causing.* In like manner, if a cause be defined, *that by which any thing exists;* this is liable to the same objection. For what is meant by these words, *by which?* Had it been said, that a cause is *that* after which *any thing constantly exists;* we should have understood the terms. For this is, indeed, all we know of the matter. And this constancy forms the very essence of necessity, nor have we any other idea of it.

PART II

There is no method of reasoning more common, and yet none more blameable, than, in philosophical disputes, to endeavour the refutation of any hypothesis, by a pretence of its dangerous consequences to religion and morality. When any opinion leads to absurdities, it is certainly false; but it is not certain that an opinion is false, because it is of dangerous consequence. Such topics, therefore, ought entirely to be forborne; as serving nothing to the discovery of truth, but only to make the person of an antagonist odious. This I observe in general, without pretending to draw any advantage from it. I frankly submit to an examination of this kind, and shall venture to affirm that the doctrines, both of necessity and of liberty, as above explained, are not only consistent with morality, but are absolutely essential to its support.

Necessity may be defined two ways, conformably to the two definitions of *cause,* of which it makes an essential part. It consists either in the constant conjunction of like objects, or in the inference of the understanding from one object to another. Now necessity, in both these senses, (which, indeed, are at bottom the same) has universally, though tacitly, in the schools, in the pulpit, and in common life, been allowed to belong to the will of man; and no one has ever pretended to deny that we can draw inferences concerning human actions, and that those inferences are founded on the experienced union of like actions, with like motives, inclinations, and circumstances. The only particular in which any one can differ, is, that either, perhaps, he will refuse to give the name of necessity to this property of human actions: But as long as the meaning is understood, I hope the word can do no harm: Or that he will maintain it possible to discover something farther in the operations of matter. But this, it must be acknowledged, can be of no consequence to morality or religion, whatever it may be to natural philosophy or metaphysics. We may here be mistaken in asserting that there is no idea of any other necessity or connexion in the actions of body: But surely we ascribe nothing to the actions of the mind, but what everyone does, and must readily allow of. We change no circumstance in the received orthodox system with regard to the will, but only in that with regard to material objects and causes. Nothing, therefore, can be more innocent, at least, than this doctrine.

All laws being founded on rewards and punishments, it is supposed as a fundamental principle, that these motives have a regular and uniform influence on the mind, and both produce the good and prevent the evil actions. We may give to this influence what name we please; but, as it is usually conjoined with the action, it must be esteemed a *cause,* and be looked upon as an instance of that necessity, which we would here establish.

The only proper object of hatred or vengeance is a person or creature, endowed with thought and consciousness; and when any criminal or injurious actions excite that passion, it is only by their relation to the person, or connexion with him. Actions are, by their very nature, temporary and perishing; and where they proceed not from some cause in the character and disposition of the person who performed them, they can neither redound to his honour, if good; nor infamy, if evil. The actions themselves may be blameable; they may be contrary to all the rules of morality and religion: But the person is not answerable for them; and as they proceeded from nothing in him that is durable and constant, and leave nothing of that nature behind them, it is impossible he can, upon their account, become the object of punishment or vengeance. According to the principle, therefore, which denies necessity, and consequently causes, a man is as pure and untainted, after having committed the most horrid crime, as at the first moment of his birth, nor is his character anywise concerned in his actions, since they are not derived from it, and the wickedness of the one can never be used as a proof of the depravity of the other.

Men are not blamed for such actions as they perform ignorantly and casually, whatever may be the consequences. Why? but because the principles of these actions are only momentary, and terminate in them alone. Men are less blamed for such actions as they perform hastily and unpremeditately than for such as proceed from deliberation. For what reason? but because a hasty temper, though a constant cause or principle in the mind, operates only by intervals, and infects not the whole character. Again, repentance wipes off every crime, if attended with a reformation of life and manners. How is this to be accounted for? but by asserting that actions render a person criminal merely as they are proofs of criminal principles in the mind; and when, by an alteration of these principles, they cease to be just proofs, they likewise cease to be criminal. But, except upon the doctrine of necessity, they never were just proofs, and consequently never were criminal.

It will be equally easy to prove, and from the same arguments, that *liberty*, according to that definition above mentioned, in which all men agree, is also essential to morality, and that no human actions, where it is wanting, are susceptible of any moral qualities, or can be the objects either of approbation or dislike. For as actions are objects of our moral sentiment, so far only as they are indications of the internal character, passions, and affections; it is impossible that they can give rise either to praise or blame, where they proceed not from these principles, but are derived altogether from external violence.

I pretend not to have obviated or removed all objections to this theory, with regard to necessity and liberty. I can foresee other objections, derived from topics which have not here been treated of. It may be said, for instance, that, if voluntary actions be subjected to the same laws of necessity with the operations of matter, there is a continued chain of necessary causes, pre-ordained and pre-determined, reaching from the original cause of all to every single volition of every human creature. No contingency anywhere in the universe; no indifference; no liberty. While we act, we are, at the same time, acted upon. The ultimate Author of all our volitions is the Creator of the world, who first bestowed motion on this immense machine, and placed all beings in that particular position, whence every subsequent event, by an inevitable necessity, must result. Human actions, therefore, either can have no moral turpitude at all, as proceeding from so good a cause; or if they have any turpitude, they must involve our Creator in the same guilt, while he is acknowledged to be their ultimate cause and author. For as a man, who fired a mine, is answerable for all the consequences whether the train he employed be long or short; so wherever a continued chain of necessary causes is fixed, that Being, either finite or infinite, who produces the first, is likewise the author of all the rest, and must both bear the blame and acquire the praise which belong to them. Our clear and unalterable ideas of morality establish this rule, upon unquestionable reasons, when we examine the consequences of any human action; and these reasons must still have greater force when applied to the volitions and intentions of a Being infinitely wise and powerful. Ignorance or impotence may be pleaded for so limited a creature as man; but those imperfections have no place in our Creator. He foresaw, he ordained, he intended all those actions of men, which we so rashly pronounce criminal. And we must therefore conclude, either that they are not criminal, or that the Deity, not man, is accountable for them. But as either of these positions is absurd and impious, it follows, that the doctrine from which they are deduced cannot possibly be true, as being liable to all the same objections. An absurd consequence, if necessary, proves the original doctrine to be absurd in the same manner as criminal actions render criminal the original cause, if the connexion between them be necessary and inevitable.

This objection consists of two parts, which we shall examine separately; *First*, that, if human actions can be traced up, by a necessary chain, to the Deity, they can never be criminal; on account of the infinite perfection of that Being from whom they are derived, and who can intend nothing but what is altogether good and laudable. Or, *Secondly*, if they be criminal, we must retract the attribute of perfection, which we ascribe to the Deity, and must acknowledge him to be the ultimate author of guilt and moral turpitude in all his creatures.

The answer to the first objection seems obvious and convincing. There are many philosophers who, after an exact scrutiny of all the phenomena of nature, conclude, that the WHOLE, considered as one system is, in every period of its existence, ordered with perfect benevolence; and that the utmost possible happiness will, in the end, result to all created beings, without any mixture of positive or absolute ill or misery. Every physical ill, say they, makes an essential part of this benevolent system, and could not possibly be removed, even by the Deity himself, considered as a wise agent, without giving entrance to greater ill, or excluding greater good, which will result from it. From this theory, some philosophers, and the ancient *Stoics* among the rest, derived a topic of consolation under all afflictions, while they taught their pupils that those ills under which they laboured were, in reality, goods to the universe; and that to an enlarged view, which could comprehend the whole system of nature, every event became an object of joy and exultation. But though this topic be specious and sublime, it was soon found in practice weak and ineffectual. You would surely more irritate than appease a man lying under the racking pains of the gout by preaching up to him the rectitude of those general laws, which produced the malignant humours in his body, and led them through the proper canals, to the sinews and nerves, where they now excite such acute torments. These enlarged views may, for a moment, please the imagination of a speculative man, who is placed in ease and security; but neither can they dwell with constancy on his mind, even though undisturbed by the emotions of pain or passion; much less can they maintain their ground when attacked by such powerful antagonists. The affections take a narrower and more natural survey of their object; and by an economy, more suitable to the infirmity of human minds, regard alone the beings around us, and are actuated by such events as appear good or ill to the private system.

The case is the same with *moral* as with *physical* ill. It cannot reasonably be supposed, that those remote considerations, which are found of so little efficacy with regard to one, will have a more powerful influence with regard to the other. The mind of man is so formed by nature that, upon the appearance of certain characters, dispositions, and actions, it immediately feels the sentiment of approbation or blame; nor are there any emotions more essential to its frame and constitution. The characters which engage our approbation are chiefly such as contribute to the peace and security of human society; as the characters which excite blame are chiefly such as tend to public detriment and disturbance: Whence it may reasonably be presumed, that the moral sentiments arise, either mediately or immediately, from a reflection of these opposite interests. What though philosophical meditations establish a different opinion or conjecture; that everything is right with regard to the WHOLE, and that the qualities, which disturb society, are, in the main, as beneficial, and are as suitable to the primary intention of nature as those which more directly promote its happiness and welfare? Are such remote and uncertain speculations able to counterbalance the sentiments which arise from the natural and immediate view of the objects? A man who is robbed of a considerable sum; does

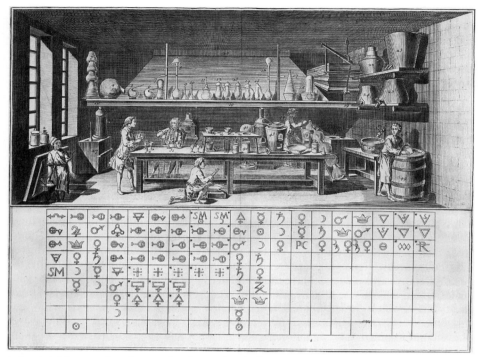

A chemist's laboratory from Denis Diderot's *Encyclopedia* (1751–1772) illustrates the
state of empirical science during Hume's lifetime. The symbols below are an early periodic
table of elements. (*The Bettmann Archive*)

he find his vexation for the loss anywise diminished by these sublime reflections? Why
then should his moral resentment against the crime be supposed incompatible with
them? Or why should not the acknowledgment of a real distinction between vice and
virtue be reconcileable to all speculative systems of philosophy, as well as that of a real
distinction between personal beauty and deformity? Both these distinctions are founded
in the natural sentiments of the human mind: And these sentiments are not to be controlled or altered by any philosophical theory or speculation whatsoever.

The *second* objection admits not of so easy and satisfactory an answer; nor is it
possible to explain distinctly, how the Deity can be the mediate cause of all the actions of men, without being the author of sin and moral turpitude. These are mysteries, which mere natural and unassisted reason is very unfit to handle; and whatever
system she embraces, she must find herself involved in inextricable difficulties, and
even contradictions, at every step which she takes with regard to such subjects. To
reconcile the indifference and contingency of human actions with prescience; or to
defend absolute decrees, and yet free the Deity from being the author of sin, has been
found hitherto to exceed all the power of philosophy. Happy, if she be thence sensible
of her temerity, when she pries into these sublime mysteries; and leaving a scene so
full of obscurities and perplexities, return, with suitable modesty, to her true and
proper province, the examination of common life; where she will find difficulties
enough to employ her enquiries, without launching into so boundless an ocean of
doubt, uncertainty, and contradiction!

Section IX. Of the Reason of Animals

All our reasonings concerning matter of fact are founded on a species of Analogy, which leads us to expect from any cause the same events, which we have observed to result from similar causes. Where the causes are entirely similar, the analogy is perfect, and the inference, drawn from it, is regarded as certain and conclusive: nor does any man ever entertain a doubt, when he sees a piece of iron, that it will have weight and cohesion of parts; as in all other instances, which have ever fallen under his observation. But where the objects have not so exact a similarity, the analogy is less perfect, and the inference is less conclusive; though still it has some force, in proportion to the degree of similarity and resemblance. The anatomical observations, formed upon one animal, are, by this species of reasoning, extended to all animals; and it is certain, that when the circulation of the blood for instance, is clearly proved to have place in one creature, as a frog, or fish, it forms a strong presumption, that the same principle has place in all. These analogical observations may be carried farther, even to this science, of which we are now treating; and any theory, by which we explain the operations of the understanding, or the origin and connexion of the passions in man, will acquire additional authority, if we find, that the same theory is requisite to explain the same phenomena in all other animals. We shall make trial of this, with regard to the hypothesis, by which we have, in the foregoing discourse, endeavoured to account for all experimental reasonings; and it is hoped, that this new point of view will serve to confirm all our former observations.

First, It seems evident, that animals as well as men learn many things from experience, and infer, that the same events will always follow from the same causes. By this principle they become acquainted with the more obvious properties of external objects, and gradually, from their birth, treasure up a knowledge of the nature of fire, water, earth, stones, heights, depths, etc., and of the effects which result from their operation. The ignorance and inexperience of the young are here plainly distinguishable from the cunning and sagacity of the old, who have learned, by long observation, to avoid what hurt them, and to pursue what gave ease or pleasure. A horse, that has been accustomed to the field, becomes acquainted with the proper height which he can leap, and will never attempt what exceeds his force and ability. An old greyhound will trust the more fatiguing part of the chase to the younger, and will place himself so as to meet the hare in her doubles; nor are the conjectures, which he forms on this occasion, founded in any thing but his observation and experience.

This is still more evident from the effects of discipline and education on animals, who, by the proper application of rewards and punishments, may be taught any course of action, and most contrary to their natural instincts and propensities. Is it not experience, which renders a dog apprehensive of pain, when you menace him, or lift up the whip to beat him? Is it not even experience, which makes him answer to his name, and infer, from such an arbitrary sound, that you mean him rather than any of his fellows, and intend to call him, when you pronounce it in a certain manner, and with a certain tone and accent?

In all these cases, we may observe, that the animal infers some fact beyond what immediately strikes his senses; and that this inference is altogether founded on past experience, while the creature expects from the present object the same consequences, which it has always found in its observation to result from similar objects.

Secondly, It is impossible, that this inference of the animal can be founded on any process of argument or reasoning, by which he concludes, that like events must follow like objects, and that the course of nature will always be regular in its operations. For if there be in reality any arguments of this nature, they surely lie too abstruse for the observation of such imperfect understandings; since it may well employ the utmost care and attention of a philosophic genius to discover and observe them. Animals, therefore, are not guided in these inferences by reasoning: Neither are children: Neither are the generality of mankind, in their ordinary actions and conclusions: Neither are philosophers themselves, who, in all the active parts of life, are, in the main, the same with the vulgar, and are governed by the same maxims. Nature must have provided some other principle, of more ready, and more general use and application; nor can an operation of such immense consequence in life, as that of inferring effects from causes, be trusted to the uncertain process of reasoning and argumentation. Were this doubtful with regard to men, it seems to admit of no question with regard to the brute creation; and the conclusion being once firmly established in the one, we have a strong presumption, from all the rules of analogy, that it ought to be universally admitted, without any exception or reserve. It is custom alone, which engages animals, from every object, that strikes their senses, to infer its usual attendant, and carries their imagination, from the appearance of the one, to conceive the other, in that particular manner, which we denominate *belief*. No other explication can be given of this operation, in all the higher, as well as lower classes of sensitive beings, which fall under our notice and observation.*

But though animals learn many parts of their knowledge from observation, there are also many parts of it, which they derive from the original hand of nature; which much exceed the share of capacity they possess on ordinary occasions; and in which they improve, little or nothing, by the longest practice and experience. These we denominate Instincts, and are so apt to admire as something very extraordinary, and inexplicable by all the disquisitions of human understanding. But our wonder will, perhaps, cease or diminish, when we consider, that the experimental reasoning itself, which we possess in common with beasts, and on which the whole conduct of life depends, is nothing but a species of instinct or mechanical power, that acts in us unknown to ourselves; and in its chief operations, is not directed by any such relations or comparisons of ideas, as are the proper objects of our intellectual faculties. Though the instinct be different, yet still it is an instinct, which teaches a man to avoid the fire; as much as that, which teaches a bird, with such exactness, the art of incubation, and the whole economy and order of its nursery.

SECTION X. OF MIRACLES**

PART I

There is, in Dr. Tillotson's writings, an argument against the *real presence*, which is as concise, and elegant, and strong as any argument can possibly be supposed against a doctrine, so little worthy of a serious refutation. It is acknowledged on all hands, says that learned prelate, that the authority, either of the scripture or of tradition, is founded

---

*Since all reasonings concerning facts or causes is derived merely from custom, it may be asked how it happens, that men so much surpass animals in reasoning, and one man so much surpasses another? Has not the same custom the same influence on all?

We shall here endeavour briefly to explain the great difference in human understandings: After which the reason of the difference between men and animals will easily be comprehended.

**1. When we have lived any time, and have been accustomed to the uniformity of nature we acquire a general habit, by which we always transfer the known to the unknown, and conceive the latter to re-

merely in the testimony of the apostles, who were eye-witnesses to those miracles of our Saviour, by which he proved his divine mission. Our evidence, then, for the truth of the *Christian* religion is less than the evidence for the truth of our senses; because, even in the first authors of our religion, it was no greater; and it is evident it must diminish in passing from them to their disciples; nor can any one rest such confidence in their testimony, as in the immediate object of his senses. But a weaker evidence can never destroy a stronger; and therefore, were the doctrine of the real presence ever so clearly revealed in scripture, it were directly contrary to the rules of just reasoning to give our assent to it. It contradicts sense, though both the scripture and tradition, on which it is supposed to be built, carry not such evidence with them as sense, when they are considered merely as external evidences, and are not brought home to every one's breast, by the immediate operation of the Holy Spirit.

Nothing is so convenient as a decisive argument of this kind, which must at least *silence* the most arrogant bigotry and superstition, and free us from their impertinent solicitations. I flatter myself, that I have discovered an argument of a like nature, which, if just, will, with the wise and learned, be an everlasting check to all kinds of superstitious delusion, and consequently, will be useful as long as the world endures; for so long, I presume, will the accounts of miracles and prodigies be found in all history, sacred and profane.

Though experience be our only guide in reasoning concerning matters of fact; it must be acknowledged, that this guide is not altogether infallible, but in some cases is apt to lead us into errors. One, who in our climate, should expect better weather in any week of June than in one of December, would reason justly, and conformably to experience; but it is certain, that he may happen, in the event, to find himself mistaken. However, we may observe, that, in such a case, he would have no cause to complain of experience; because it commonly informs us beforehand of the uncertainty, by that contrariety of events, which we may learn from a diligent observation. All effects follow not with like certainty from their supposed causes. Some events are found, in all countries and all ages, to have been constantly conjoined together: Others are found to have been more variable, and sometimes to disappoint our expectations; so that, in our

---

semble the former. By means of this general habitual principle, we regard even one experiment as the foundation of reasoning, and expect a similar event with some degree of certainty, where the experiment has been made accurately, and free from all foreign circumstances. It is therefore considered as a matter of great importance to observe the consequences of things; and as one man may very much surpass another in attention and memory and observation, this will make a very great difference in their reasoning.

2. Where there is a complication of causes to produce any effect, one mind may be much larger than another, and better able to comprehend the whole system of objects, and to infer justly their consequences.

3. One man is able to carry on a chain of consequences to a greater length than another.

4. Few men can think long without running into a confusion of ideas, and mistaking one for another; and there are various degrees of this infirmity.

5. The circumstance, on which the effect depends, is frequently involved in other circumstances, which are foreign and extrinsic. The separation of it often requires great attention, accuracy, and subtilty.

6. The forming of general maxims from particular observation is a very nice operation; and nothing is more usual, from haste or narrowness of mind which sees not on all sides than to commit mistakes in this particular.

7. When we reason from analogies, the man, who has the greater experience of the greater promptitude of suggesting analogies, will be the better reasoner.

8. Biases from prejudice, education, passion, party, etc., hang more upon one mind than another.

9. After we have acquired a confidence in human testimony, books and conversation enlarge much more the sphere of one man's experience and thought than those of another.

It would be easy to discover many other circumstances that make a difference in the understandings of men.

reasonings concerning matter of fact, there are all imaginable degrees of assurance, from the highest certainty to the lowest species of moral evidence.

A wise man, therefore, proportions his belief to the evidence. In such conclusions as are founded on an infallible experience, he expects the event with the last degree of assurance, and regards his past experience as a full *proof* of the future existence of that event. In other cases, he proceeds with more caution: He weighs the opposite experiments: He considers which side is supported by the greater number of experiments: to that side he inclines, with doubt and hesitation; and when at last he fixes his judgement, the evidence exceeds not what we properly call *probability*. All probability, then, supposes an opposition of experiments and observations, where the one side is found to overbalance the other, and to produce a degree of evidence, proportioned to the superiority. A hundred instances or experiments on one side, and fifty on another, afford a doubtful expectation of any event; though a hundred uniform experiments, with only one that is contradictory, reasonably begets a pretty strong degree of assurance. In all cases, we must balance the opposite experiments, where they are opposite, and deduct the smaller number from the greater, in order to know the exact force of the superior evidence.

To apply these principles to a particular instance; we may observe, that there is no species of reasoning more common, more useful, and even necessary to human life, than that which is derived from the testimony of men, and the reports of eye-witnesses and spectators. This species of reasoning, perhaps, one may deny to be founded on the relation of cause and effect. I shall not dispute about a word. It will be sufficient to observe that our assurance in any argument of this kind is derived from no other principle than our observation of the veracity of human testimony, and of the usual conformity of facts to the reports of witnesses. It being a general maxim, that no objects have any discoverable connexion together, and that all the inferences, which we can draw from one to another, are founded merely on our experience of their constant and regular conjunction; it is evident, that we ought not to make an exception to this maxim in favour of human testimony, whose connexion with any event seems, in itself, as little necessary as any other. Were not the memory tenacious to a certain degree; had not men commonly an inclination to truth and a principle of probity, were they not sensible to shame, when detected in a falsehood: Were not these, I say, discovered by *experience* to be qualities, inherent in human nature, we should never repose the least confidence in human testimony. A man delirious, or noted for falsehood and villainy, has no manner of authority with us.

And as the evidence, derived from witnesses and human testimony, is founded on past experience, so it varies with the experience, and is regarded either as *proof* or a *probability*, according as the conjunction between any particular kind of report and any kind of object has been found to be constant or variable. There are a number of circumstances to be taken into consideration in all judgements of this kind; and the ultimate standard, by which we determine all disputes, that may arise concerning them, is always derived from experience and observation. Where this experience is not entirely uniform on any side, it is attended with an unavoidable contrariety in our judgements, and with the same opposition and mutual destruction of argument as in every other kind of evidence. We frequently hesitate concerning the reports of others. We balance the opposite circumstances, which cause any doubt or uncertainty; and when we discover a superiority on one side, we incline to it; but still with a diminution of assurance, in proportion to the force of its antagonist.

This contrariety of evidence, in the present case, may be derived from several different causes; from the opposition of contrary testimony; from the character or number of the witnesses; from the manner of their delivering their testimony; or from the union of all these circumstances. We entertain a suspicion concerning any matter of fact, when the witnesses contradict each other; when they are but few, or of a doubtful character; when they have an interest in what they affirm; when they deliver their testimony with hesitation, or on the contrary, with too violent asseverations. There are many other particulars of the same kind, which may diminish or destroy the force of any argument, derived from human testimony.

Suppose, for instance, that the fact, which the testimony endeavours to establish, partakes of the extraordinary and the marvellous; in that case, the evidence, resulting from the testimony, admits of a diminution, greater or less, in proportion as the fact is more or less unusual. The reason why we place any credit in witnesses and historians, is not derived from any *connexion*, which we perceive *a priori*, between testimony and reality, but because we are accustomed to find a conformity between them. But when the fact attested is such a one as has seldom fallen under our observation, here is a contest of two opposite experiences; of which the one destroys the other, as far as its force goes, and the superior can only operate on the mind by the force, which remains. The very same principle of experience, which gives us a certain degree of assurance in the testimony of witnesses, gives us also, in this case, another degree of assurance against the fact, which they endeavour to establish; from which contradiction there necessarily arises a counterpoise, and mutual destruction of belief and authority.

I should not believe such a story were it told me by Cato, was a proverbial saying in Rome, even during the lifetime of that philosophical patriot.* The incredibility of a fact, it was allowed, might invalidate so great an authority.

The Indian prince, who refused to believe the first relations concerning the effects of frost, reasoned justly; and it naturally required very strong testimony to engage his assent to facts, that arose from a state of nature, with which he was unacquainted, and which bore so little analogy to those events, of which he had had constant and uniform experience. Though they were not contrary to his experience, they were not conformable to it.**

But in order to increase the probability against the testimony of witnesses, let us suppose, that the fact, which they affirm, instead of being only marvellous, is really miraculous; and suppose also, that the testimony considered apart and in itself, amounts to an entire proof; in that case, there is proof against proof, of which the strongest must prevail, but still with a diminution of its force, in proportion to that of its antagonist.

A miracle is a violation of the laws of nature; and as a firm and unalterable experience has established these laws, the proof against a miracle, from the very nature of

*Plutarch, *Marcus Cato* [*The Life of Cato*].

**No Indian, it is evident, could have experience that water did not freeze in cold climates. This is placing nature in a situation quite unknown to him; and it is impossible for him to tell *a priori* what will result from it. It is making a new experiment, the consequence of which is always uncertain. One may sometimes conjecture from analogy what will follow; but still this is but conjecture. And it must be confessed, that, in the present case of freezing, the event follows contrary to the rules of analogy, and is such as a rational Indian would not look for. The operations of cold upon water are not gradual according to the degrees of cold; but whenever it comes to the freezing point, the water passes in a moment, from the utmost liquidity to perfect hardness. Such an event, therefore, may be denominated *extraordinary*, and requires a pretty strong testimony, to render it credible to people in a warm climate: But still it is not *miraculous*, nor contrary to uniform experience of the course of nature in cases where all the circumstances are the same. The inhabitants of Sumatra have always seen water fluid in their own climate, and the freezing of their rivers ought to be deemed a prodigy: But they never saw water in Muscovy during the winter, and therefore they cannot reasonably be positive what would there be the consequence.

the fact, is as entire as any argument from experience can possibly be imagined. Why is it more than probable, that all men must die; that lead cannot, of itself, remain suspended in the air; that fire consumes wood, and is extinguished by water; unless it be, that these events are found agreeable to the laws of nature, and there is required a violation of these laws, or in other words, a miracle to prevent them? Nothing is esteemed a miracle, if it ever happen in the common course of nature. It is no miracle that a man, seemingly in good health, should die on a sudden: because such a kind of death, though more unusual than any other, has yet been frequently observed to happen. But it is a miracle, that a dead man should come to life; because that has never been observed in any age or country. There must, therefore, be a uniform experience against every miraculous event, otherwise the event would not merit that appellation. And as a uniform experience amounts to a proof, there is here a direct and full *proof*, from the nature of the fact, against the existence of any miracle; nor can such a proof be destroyed, or the miracle rendered credible, but by an opposite proof, which is superior.*

The plain consequence is (and it is a general maxim worthy of our attention), "That no testimony is sufficient to establish a miracle, unless the testimony be of such a kind, that its falsehood would be more miraculous, than the fact, which it endeavours to establish; and even in that case there is a mutual destruction of arguments, and the superior only gives us an assurance suitable to that degree of force, which remains, after deducting the inferior." When anyone tells me, that he saw a dead man restored to life, I immediately consider with myself, whether it be more probable, that this person should either deceive or be deceived, or that the fact, which he relates, should really have happened. I weigh the one miracle against the other; and according to the superiority, which I discover, I pronounce my decision, and always reject the greater miracle. If the falsehood of his testimony would be more miraculous, than the event which he relates; then, and not till then, can he pretend to command my belief or opinion.

PART II

In the foregoing reasoning we have supposed, that the testimony, upon which a miracle is founded, may possibly amount to an entire proof, and that the falsehood of that testimony would be a real prodigy: But it is easy to shew, that we have been a great deal too liberal in our concession, and that there never was a miraculous event established on so full an evidence.

For *first*, there is not to be found, in all history, any miracle attested by a sufficient number of men, of such unquestioned good-sense, education, and learning, as to

---

*Sometimes an event may not, *in itself*, seem to be contrary to the laws of nature, and yet, if it were real, it might, by reason of some circumstances, be denominated a miracle, because, *in fact*, it is contrary to these laws. Thus if a person, claiming a divine authority, should command a sick person to be well, a healthful man to fall down dead, the clouds to pour rain, the winds to blow, in short, should order many natural events, which immediately follow upon his command; these might justly be esteemed miracles, because they are really, in this case, contrary to the laws of nature. For if any suspicion remain, that the event and command concurred by accident, there is no miracle and no transgression of the laws of nature. If this suspicion be removed, there is evidently a miracle, and a transgression of these laws; because nothing can be more contrary to nature than that the voice or command of a man should have such an influence. A miracle may be accurately defined, *a transgression of a law of nature by a particular volition of the Deity, or by the interposition of some invisible agent.* A miracle may either be discovered by men or not. This alters not its nature and essence. The raising of a house or ship into the air is a visible miracle. The raising of a feather, when the wind wants ever so little of a force requisite for that purpose, is as real a miracle, though not so sensible with regard to us.

secure us against all delusion in themselves; of such undoubted integrity, as to place them beyond all suspicion of any design to deceive others; of such credit and reputation in the eyes of mankind, as to have a great deal to lose in case of their being detected in any falsehood; and at the same time, attesting facts performed in such a public manner and in so celebrated a part of the world, as to render the detection unavoidable: All which circumstances are requisite to give us a full assurance in the testimony of men.

Secondly, We may observe in human nature a principle which, if strictly examined, will be found to diminish extremely the assurance, which we might, from human testimony, have, in any kind of prodigy. The maxim, by which we commonly conduct ourselves in our reasonings, is, that the objects, of which we have no experience, resemble those, of which we have; that what we have found to be most usual is always most probable; and that where there is an opposition of arguments, we ought to give the preference to such as are founded on the greatest number of past observations. But though, in proceeding by this rule, we readily reject any fact which is unusual and incredible in an ordinary degree; yet in advancing farther, the mind observes not always the same rule; but when anything is affirmed utterly absurd and miraculous, it rather the more readily admits of such a fact, upon account of that very circumstance, which ought to destroy all its authority. The passion of *surprise* and *wonder*, arising from miracles, being an agreeable emotion, gives a sensible tendency towards the belief of those events, from which it is derived. And this goes so far, that even those who cannot enjoy this pleasure immediately, nor can believe those miraculous events, of which they are informed, yet love to partake of the satisfaction at second-hand or by rebound, and place a pride and delight in exciting the admiration of others.

With what greediness are the miraculous accounts of travellers received, their descriptions of sea and land monsters, their relations of wonderful adventures, strange men, and uncouth manners? But if the spirit of religion join itself to the love of wonder, there is an end of common sense; and human testimony, in these circumstances, loses all pretensions to authority. A religionist may be an enthusiast, and imagine he sees what has no reality: he may know his narrative to be false, and yet persevere in it, with the best intentions in the world, for the sake of promoting so holy a cause: or even where this delusion has no place, vanity, excited by so strong a temptation, operates on him more powerfully than on the rest of mankind in any other circumstances; and self-interest with equal force. His auditors may not have, and commonly have not, sufficient judgement to canvass his evidence: what judgement they have, they renounce by principle, in these sublime and mysterious subjects: or if they were ever so willing to employ it, passion and a heated imagination disturb the regularity of its operations. Their credulity increases his impudence: and his impudence overpowers their credulity.

Eloquence, when at its highest pitch, leaves little room for reason or reflection; but addressing itself entirely to the fancy or the affections, captivates the willing hearers, and subdues their understanding. Happily, this pitch it seldom attains. But what a Tully or a Demosthenes could scarcely effect over a Roman or Athenian audience, every *Capuchin*, every itinerant or stationary teacher can perform over the generality of mankind, and in a higher degree, by touching such gross and vulgar passions.

The many instances of forged miracles, and prophecies, and supernatural events, which, in all ages, have either been detected by contrary evidence, or which detect themselves by their absurdity, prove sufficiently the strong propensity of mankind to the extraordinary and the marvellous, and ought reasonably to beget a suspicion against all relations of this kind. This is our natural way of thinking, even with regard to the most common and most credible events. For instance: There is no kind of report which rises so easily, and spreads so quickly, especially in country places and provincial towns, as those concerning marriages; insomuch that two young persons of equal condition never see each other twice, but the whole neighbourhood immediately join them together. The pleasure of telling a piece of news so interesting, of propagating it, and of being the first reporters of it, spreads the intelligence. And this is so well known, that no man of sense gives attention to these reports, till he find them confirmed by some greater evidence. Do not the same passions, and others still stronger, incline the generality of mankind to believe and report, with the greatest vehemence and assurance, all religious miracles?

Thirdly. It forms a strong presumption against all supernatural and miraculous relations, that they are observed chiefly to abound among ignorant and barbarous nations; or if a civilized people has ever given admission to any of them, that people will be found to have received them from ignorant and barbarous ancestors, who transmitted them with that inviolable sanction and authority, which always attend received opinions. When we peruse the first histories of all nations, we are apt to imagine ourselves transported into some new world; where the whole frame of nature is disjointed, and every element performs its operations in a different manner, from what it does at present. Battles, revolutions, pestilence, famine and death, are never the effect of those natural causes, which we experience. Prodigies, omens, oracles, judgements, quite obscure the few natural events, that are intermingled with them. But as the former grow thinner every page, in proportion as we advance nearer the enlightened ages, we soon learn, that there is nothing mysterious or super-natural in the case, but that all proceeds from the usual propensity of mankind towards the marvellous, and that, though this inclination may at intervals receive a check from sense and learning, it can never be thoroughly extirpated from human nature.

It is strange, a judicious reader is apt to say, upon the perusal of these wonderful historians, *that such prodigious events never happen in our days*. But it is nothing strange, I hope, that men should lie in all ages. You must surely have seen instances enough of that frailty. You have yourself heard many such marvellous relations started, which, being treated with scorn by all the wise and judicious, have at last been abandoned even by the vulgar. Be assured, that those renowned lies, which have spread and flourished to such a monstrous height, arose from like beginnings; but being sown in a more proper soil, shot up at last into prodigies almost equal to those which they relate.

It was a wise policy in that false prophet, Alexander, who though now forgotten, was once so famous, to lay the first scene of his impostures in Paphlagonia, where, as Lucian tells us, the people were extremely ignorant and stupid, and ready to swallow even the grossest delusion. People at a distance, who are weak enough to think the matter at all worth enquiry, have no opportunity of receiving better information. The stories come magnified to them by a hundred circumstances. Fools are industrious in propagating the imposture; while the wise and learned are contented, in general, to deride its absurdity, without informing themselves of the particular facts, by which it may be distinctly refuted. And thus the impostor above mentioned was enabled to proceed, from his ignorant Paphlagonians, to the enlisting of votaries, even among the Grecian philosophers, and men of the most eminent rank and distinction in Rome: nay, could engage the attention of that sage emperor Marcus Aurelius; so far as to make him trust the success of a military expedition to his delusive prophecies.

The advantages are so great, of starting an imposture among an ignorant people, that, even though the delusion should be too gross to impose on the generality of them (*which, though seldom, is sometimes the case*) it has a much better chance for succeeding in remote countries, than if the first scene had been laid in a city renowned for arts and knowledge. The most ignorant and barbarous of these barbarians carry the report abroad. None of their countrymen have a large correspondence, or sufficient credit and authority to contradict and beat down the delusion. Men's inclination to the marvellous has full opportunity to display itself. And thus a story, which is universally exploded in the place where it was first started, shall pass for certain at a thousand miles distance. But had Alexander fixed his residence at Athens, the philosophers of that renowned mart of learning had immediately spread, throughout the whole Roman empire, their sense of the matter; which, being supported by so great authority, and displayed by all the force of reason and eloquence, had entirely opened the eyes of mankind. It is true; Lucian, passing by chance through Paphlagonia, had an opportunity of performing this good office. But, though much to be wished, it does not always happen, that every Alexander meets with a Lucian, ready to expose and detect his impostures.

I may add as a *fourth* reason, which diminishes the authority of prodigies, that there is no testimony for any, even those which have not been expressly detected, that is not opposed by an infinite number of witnesses; so that not only the miracle destroys the credit of testimony, but the testimony destroys itself. To make this the better understood, let us consider, that, in matters of religion, whatever is different is contrary; and that it is impossible the religions of ancient Rome, of Turkey, of Siam, and of China should, all of them, be established on any solid foundation. Every miracle, therefore, pretended to have been wrought in any of these religions (and all of them abound in miracles), as its direct scope is to establish the particular system to which it is attributed; so has it the same force, though more indirectly, to overthrow every other system. In destroying a rival system, it likewise destroys the credit of those miracles, on which that system was established; so that all the prodigies of different religions are to be regarded as contrary facts, and the evidences of these prodigies, whether weak or strong, as opposite to each other. According to this method of reasoning, when we believe any miracle of Mahomet or his successors, we have for our warrant the testimony of a few barbarous Arabians: And on the other hand, we are to regard the authority of Titus Livius, Plutarch, Tacitus, and, in short, of all the authors and witnesses, Grecian, Chinese, and Roman Catholic, who have related any miracle in their particular religion; I say, we are to regard their testimony in the same light as if they had mentioned that Mahometan miracle, and had in express terms contradicted it, with the same certainty as they have for the miracle they relate. This argument may appear over subtile and refined; but is not in reality different from the reasoning of a judge, who supposes, that the credit of two witnesses, maintaining a crime against any one, is destroyed by the testimony of two others, who affirm him to have been two hundred leagues distant, at the same instant when the crime is said to have been committed.

One of the best attested miracles in all profane history, is that which Tacitus reports of Vespasian, who cured a blind man in Alexandria, by means of his spittle, and a lame man by the mere touch of his foot; in obedience to a vision of the god Serapis, who had enjoined them to have recourse to the Emperor, for these miraculous cures. The story may be seen in that fine historian;* where every circumstance seems to add weight to the testimony, and might be displayed at large with all the force of argument and eloquence, if any one were now concerned to enforce the evidence of that exploded and idolatrous superstition. The gravity, solidity, age, and probity of so great an emperor, who, through the whole course of his life, conversed in a familiar manner with his friends and courtiers, and never affected those extraordinary airs of divinity assumed by Alexander and Demetrius. The historian, a contemporary writer, noted for candour and veracity, and withal, the greatest and most penetrating genius, perhaps, of

*Histories, iv. 81. Suetonius gives nearly the same account, *Lives of the Caesars* (Vespasian).

all antiquity; and so free from any tendency to credulity, that he even lies under the contrary imputation, of atheism and profaneness: The persons, from whose authority he related the miracle, of established character for judgement and veracity, as we may well presume; eye-witnesses of the fact, and confirming their testimony, after the Flavian family was despoiled of the empire, and could no longer give any reward, as the price of a lie. *Utrumque, qui interfuere, nunc quoque memorant, postquam nullum mendacio pretium.** To which if we add the public nature of the facts, as related, it will appear, that no evidence can well be supposed stronger for so gross and so palpable a falsehood.

There is also a memorable story related by Cardinal de Retz, which may well deserve our consideration. When that intriguing politician fled into Spain, to avoid the persecution of his enemies, he passed through Saragossa, the capital of Arragon, where he was shown, in the cathedral, a man, who had served seven years as a doorkeeper, and was well known to every body in town, that had ever paid his devotions at that church. He had been seen, for so long a time, wanting a leg; but recovered that limb by the rubbing of holy oil upon the stump; and the cardinal assures us that he saw him with two legs. This miracle was vouched by all the canons of the church; and the whole company in town were appealed to for a confirmation of the fact; whom the cardinal found, by their zealous devotion, to be thorough believers of the miracle. Here the relater was also contemporary to the supposed prodigy, of an incredulous and libertine character, as well as of great genius; the miracle of so *singular* a nature as could scarcely admit of a counterfeit, and the witnesses very numerous, and all of them, in a manner, spectators of the fact, to which they gave their testimony. And what adds mightily to the force of the evidence, and may double our surprise on this occasion, is, that the cardinal himself, who relates the story, seems not to give any credit to it, and consequently cannot be suspected of any concurrence in the holy fraud. He considered justly, that it was not requisite, in order to reject a fact of this nature, to be able accurately to disprove the testimony, and to trace its falsehood, through all the circumstances of knavery and credulity which produced it. He knew, that, as this was commonly altogether impossible at any small distance of time and place; so was it extremely difficult, even where one was immediately present, by reason of the bigotry, ignorance, cunning, and roguery of a great part of mankind. He therefore concluded, like a just reasoner, that such an evidence carried falsehood upon the very face of it, and that a miracle, supported by any human testimony, was more properly a subject of derision than of argument.

There surely never was a greater number of miracles ascribed to one person, than those, which were lately said to have been wrought in France upon the tomb of Abbe Paris, the famous Jansenist, with whose sanctity the people were so long deluded. The curing of the sick, giving hearing to the deaf, and sight to the blind, were every where talked of as the usual effects of that holy sepulchre. But what is more extraordinary; many of the miracles were immediately proved upon the spot, before judges of unquestioned integrity, attested by witnesses of credit and distinction, in a learned age, and on the most eminent theatre that is now in the world. Nor is this all: a relation of them was published and dispersed everywhere; nor were the *Jesuits,* though a learned body, supported by the civil magistrate, and determined enemies to those opinions, in whose favour the miracles were said to have been wrought, ever able distinctly to refute or detect them. Where shall we find such a number of circumstances, agreeing to the corroboration of one fact? And what have we to oppose to

---

*[Those who were present recount both even now that a lie is no longer rewarded.]

such a cloud of witnesses, but the absolute impossibility or miraculous nature of the events, which they relate? And this surely, in the eyes of all reasonable people, will alone be regarded as a sufficient refutation.

Is the consequence just, because some human testimony has the utmost force and authority in some cases, when it relates the battle of Philippi or Pharsalia for instance; that therefore all kinds of testimony must, in all cases, have equal force and authority? Suppose that the Caesarean and Pompeian factions had, each of them, claimed the victory in these battles, and that the historians of each party had uniformly ascribed the advantage to their own side; how could mankind, at this distance, have been able to determine between them? The contrariety is equally strong between the miracles related by Herodotus or Plutarch, and those delivered by Mariana, Bede, or any monkish historian.

The wise lend a very academic faith to every report which favours the passion of the reporter; whether it magnifies his country, his family, or himself, or in any other way strikes in with his natural inclinations and propensities. But what greater temptation than to appear a missionary, a prophet, an ambassador from heaven? Who would not encounter many dangers and difficulties, in order to attain so sublime a character? Or if, by the help of vanity and a heated imagination, a man has first made a convert of himself, and entered seriously into the delusion; who ever scruples to make use of pious frauds, in support of so holy and meritorious a cause?

The smallest spark may here kindle into the greatest flame; because the materials are always prepared for it. The *avidum genus auricularum,** the gazing populace, receive greedily, without examination, whatever soothes superstition, and promotes wonder.

How many stories of this nature have, in all ages, been detected and exploded in their infancy? How many more have been celebrated for a time, and have afterwards sunk into neglect and oblivion? Where such reports, therefore, fly about, the solution of the phenomenon is obvious; and we judge in conformity to regular experience and observation, when we account for it by the known and natural principles of credulity and delusion. And shall we, rather than have a recourse to so natural a solution, allow of a miraculous violation of the most established laws of nature?

I need not mention the difficulty of detecting, a falsehood in any private or even public history, at the place, where it is said to happen; much more when the scene is removed to ever so small a distance. Even a court of judicature, with all the authority, accuracy, and judgement, which they can employ, find themselves often at a loss to distinguish between truth and falsehood in the most recent actions. But the matter never comes to any issue, if trusted to the common method of altercations and debate and flying rumours; especially when men's passions have taken part on either side.

In the infancy of new religions, the wise and learned commonly esteem the matter too inconsiderable to deserve their attention or regard. And when afterwards they would willingly detect the cheat, in order to undeceive the deluded multitude, the season is now past, and the records and witnesses, which might clear up the matter, have perished beyond recovery.

No means of detection remain, but those which must be drawn from the very testimony itself of the reporters: and these, though always sufficient with the judicious and knowing, are commonly too fine to fall under the comprehension of the vulgar.

Upon the whole, then, it appears, that no testimony for any kind of miracle has ever amounted to a probability, much less to a proof; and that, even supposing it amounted to a proof, it would be opposed by another proof; derived from the very na-

*[a genus hungry for gossip] Lucretius, De Rerum Natura, iv.

ture of the fact, which it would endeavour to establish. It is experience only, which gives authority to human testimony; and it is the same experience, which assures us of the laws of nature. When, therefore, these two kinds of experience are contrary, we have nothing to do but subtract the one from the other, and embrace an opinion, either on one side or the other, with that assurance which arises from the remainder. But according to the principle here explained, this substraction, with regard to all popular religions, amounts to an entire annihilation; and therefore we may establish it as a maxim, that no human testimony can have such force as to prove a miracle, and make it a just foundation for any such system of religion.

I beg the limitations here made may be remarked, when I say, that a miracle can never be proved, so as to be the foundation of a system of religion. For I own, that otherwise, there may possibly be miracles, or violations of the usual course of nature, of such a kind as to admit of proof from human testimony; though, perhaps, it will be impossible to find any such in all the records of history. Thus, suppose, all authors, in all languages, agree, that, from the first of January 1600, there was a total darkness over the whole earth for eight days: suppose that the tradition of this extraordinary event is still strong and lively among the people: that all travellers, who return from foreign countries, bring us accounts of the same tradition, without the least variation or contradiction: it is evident, that our present philosophers, instead of doubting the fact, ought to receive it as certain, and ought to search for the causes whence it might be derived. The decay, corruption, and dissolution of nature, is an event rendered probable by so many analogies, that any phenomenon, which seems to have a tendency towards that catastrophe, comes within the reach of human testimony, if that testimony be very extensive and uniform.

But suppose, that all the historians who treat of England, should agree, that, on the first of January 1600, Queen Elizabeth died; that both before and after her death she was seen by her physicians and the whole court, as is usual with persons of her rank; that her successor was acknowledged and proclaimed by the parliament; and that, after being interred a month, she again appeared, resumed the throne, and governed England for three years: I must confess that I should be surprised at the concurrence of so many odd circumstances, but should not have the least inclination to believe so miraculous an event. I should not doubt of her pretended death, and of those other public circumstances that followed it: I should only assert it to have been pretended, and that it neither was, nor possibly could be real. You would in vain object to me the difficulty, and almost impossibility of deceiving the world in an affair of such consequence; the wisdom and solid judgement of that renowned queen; with the little or no advantage which she could reap from so poor an artifice: All this might astonish me; but I would still reply, that the knavery and folly of men are such common phenomena, that I should rather believe the most extraordinary events to arise from their concurrence, then admit of so signal a violation of the laws of nature.

But should this miracle be ascribed to any new system of religion; men, in all ages, have been so much imposed on by ridiculous stories of that kind, that this very circumstance would be a full proof of a cheat, and sufficient, with all men of sense, not only to make them reject the fact, but even reject it without farther examination. Though the Being to whom the miracle is ascribed, be, in this case, Almighty, it does not, upon that account, become a whit more probable; since it is impossible for us to know the attributes or actions of such a Being, otherwise than from the experience which we have of his productions, in the usual course of nature. This still reduces us to past observation, and obliges us to compare the instances of the violation of truth in the testimony of men, with those of the violation of the laws of nature by miracles, in order to judge which of them is most likely and probable. As the violations of truth are more common in the testimony concerning religious miracles, than in that concerning any other matter of fact; this must diminish very much the authority of the former testimony, and make us form a general resolution, never to lend any attention to it, with whatever specious pretence it may be covered.

Lord Bacon seems to have embraced the same principles of reasoning. "We ought," says he, "to make a collection or particular history of all monsters and prodigious births or productions, and in a word of every thing new, rare, and extraordinary in nature. But this must be done with the most severe scrutiny, lest we depart from truth. Above all, every relation must be considered as suspicious, which depends in any degree upon religion, as the prodigies of Livy: And no less so, every thing that is to be found in the writers of natural magic or alchemy, or such authors, who seem, all of them, to have an unconquerable appetite for falsehood and fable.*

I am the better pleased with the method of reasoning here delivered, as I think it may serve to confound those dangerous friends or disguised enemies to the *Christian Religion*, who have undertaken to defend it by the principles of human reason. Our most holy religion is founded on *Faith*, not on reason; and it is a sure method of exposing it to put it to such a trial as it is, by no means, fitted to endure. To make this more evident, let us examine those miracles, related in scripture; and not to lose ourselves in too wide a field, let us confine ourselves to such as we find in the *Pentateuch*, which we shall examine, according to the principles of these pretended Christians, not as the word or testimony of God himself, but as the production of a mere human writer and historian. Here then we are first to consider a book, presented to us by a barbarous and ignorant people, written in an age when they were still more barbarous, and in all probability long after the facts which it relates, corroborated by no concurring testimony, and resembling those fabulous accounts, which every nation gives of its origin. Upon reading this book, we find it full of prodigies and miracles. It gives an account of a state of the world and of human nature entirely different from the present: Of our fall from that state: Of the age of man, extended to near a thousand years: Of the destruction of the world by a deluge: Of the arbitrary choice of one people, as the favourites of heaven; and that people the countrymen of the author: Of their deliverance from bondage by prodigies the most astonishing imaginable: I desire any one to lay his hand upon his heart, and after a serious consideration declare, whether he thinks that the falsehood of such a book, supported by such a testimony, would be more extraordinary and miraculous than all the miracles it relates; which is, however, necessary to make it be received, according to the measures of probability above established.

What we have said of miracles may be applied, without any variation, to prophecies; and indeed, all prophecies are real miracles, and as such only, can be admitted as proofs of any revelation. If it did not exceed the capacity of human nature to foretell future events, it would be absurd to employ any prophecy as an argument for a divine mission or authority from heaven. So that, upon the whole, we may conclude, that the *Christian Religion* not only was at first attended with miracles, but even at this day cannot be believed by any reasonable person without one. Mere reason is insufficient to convince us of its veracity: And whoever is moved by *Faith* to assent to it, is conscious of a continued miracle in his own person, which subverts all the principles of his understanding, and gives him a determination to believe what is most contrary to custom and experience.

Novum Organum, II, aphorism 29.

Section XI. Of a Particular Providence and of a Future State

I was lately engaged in conversation with a friend who loves sceptical paradoxes; where, though he advanced many principles, of which I can by no means approve, yet as they seem to be curious, and to bear some relation to the chain of reasoning carried on throughout this enquiry, I shall here copy them from my memory as accurately as I can, in order to submit them to the judgement of the reader.

Our conversation began with my admiring the singular good fortune of philosophy, which, as it requires entire liberty above all other privileges, and chiefly flourishes from the free opposition of sentiments and argumentation, received its first birth in an age and country of freedom and toleration, and was never cramped, even in its most extravagant principles, by any creeds, concessions, or penal statutes. For, except the banishment of Protagoras, and the death of Socrates, which last event proceeded partly from other motives, there are scarcely any instances to be met with, in ancient history, of this bigoted jealousy, with which the present age is so much infested. Epicurus lived at Athens to an advanced age, in peace and tranquillity: Epicureans were even admitted to receive the sacerdotal character, and to officiate at the altar, in the most sacred rites of the established religion: And the public encouragement of pensions and salaries was afforded equally, by the wisest of all the Roman emperors, to the professors of every sect of philosophy. How requisite such kind of treatment was to philosophy, in her early youth, will easily be conceived, if we reflect, that, even at present, when she may be supposed more hardy and robust, she bears with much difficulty the inclemency of the seasons, and those harsh winds of calumny and persecution, which blow upon her.

You admire, says my friend, as the singular good fortune of philosophy, what seems to result from the natural course of things, and to be unavoidable in every age and nation. This pertinacious bigotry, of which you complain, as so fatal to philosophy, is really her offspring, who, after allying with superstition, separates himself entirely from the interest of his parent, and becomes her most inveterate enemy and persecutor. Speculative dogmas of religion, the present occasions of such furious dispute, could not possibly be conceived or admitted in the early ages of the world; when mankind, being wholly illiterate, formed an idea of religion more suitable to their weak apprehension, and composed their sacred tenets of such tales chiefly as were the objects of traditional belief, more than of argument or disputation. After the first alarm, therefore, was over, which arose from the new paradoxes and principles of the philosophers; these teachers seem ever after, during the ages of antiquity, to have lived in great harmony with the established superstition, and to have made a fair partition of mankind between them; the former claiming all the learned and wise, the latter possessing all the vulgar and illiterate.

It seems then, say I, that you leave politics entirely out of the question, and never suppose, that a wise magistrate can justly be jealous of certain tenets of philosophy, such as those of Epicurus, which, denying a divine existence, and consequently a providence and a future state, seem to loosen, in a great measure, the ties of morality, and may be supposed, for that reason, pernicious to the peace of civil society.

I know, replied he, that in fact these persecutions never, in any age, proceeded from calm reason, or from experience of the pernicious consequences of philosophy; but arose entirely from passion and prejudice. But what if I should advance farther, and assert, that if Epicurus had been accused before the people, by any of the *sycophants* or informers of those days, he could easily have defended his cause, and proved his principles of philosophy to be as salutary as those of his adversaries, who endeavoured, with such zeal, to expose him to the public hatred and jealousy?

I wish, said I, you would try your eloquence upon so extraordinary a topic, and make a speech for Epicurus, which might satisfy, not the mob of Athens, if you will allow that ancient and polite city to have contained any mob, but the more philosophical part of his audience, such as might be supposed capable of comprehending his arguments.

The matter would not be difficult, upon such conditions, replied he: And if you please, I shall suppose myself Epicurus for a moment, and make you stand for the Athenian people, and shall deliver you such an harangue as will fill all the urn with white beans, and leave not a black one to gratify the malice of my adversaries.

Very well: Pray proceed upon these suppositions.

I come hither, O ye Athenians, to justify in your assembly what I maintained in my school, and I find myself impeached by furious antagonists, instead of reasoning with calm and dispassionate enquirers. Your deliberations, which of right should be directed to questions of public good, and the interest of the commonwealth, are diverted to the disquisitions of speculative philosophy; and these magnificent, but perhaps fruitless enquiries, take place of your more familiar but more useful occupations. But so far as in me lies, I will prevent this abuse. We shall not here dispute concerning the origin and government of worlds. We shall only enquire how far such questions concern the public interest. And if I can persuade you, that they are entirely indifferent to the peace of society and security of government, I hope that you will presently send us back to our schools, there to examine, at leisure, the question the most sublime, but at the same time, the most speculative of all philosophy.

The religious philosophers, not satisfied with the tradition of your forefathers, and doctrine of your priests (in which I willingly acquiesce), indulge a rash curiosity, in trying how far they can establish religion upon the principles of reason; and they thereby excite, instead of satisfying, the doubts, which naturally arise from a diligent and scrutinous enquiry. They paint, in the most magnificent colours, the order, beauty, and wise arrangement of the universe; and then ask, if such a glorious display of intelligence could proceed from the fortuitous concourse of atoms, or if chance could produce what the greatest genius can never sufficiently admire. I shall not examine the justness of this argument. I shall allow it to be as solid as my antagonists and accusers can desire. It is sufficient, if I can prove, from this very reasoning, that the question is entirely speculative, and that, when, in my philosophical disquisitions, I deny a providence and a future state, I undermine not the foundations of society, but advance principles, which they themselves, upon their own topics, if they argue consistently, must allow to be solid and satisfactory.

You then, who are my accusers, have acknowledged, that the chief or sole argument for a divine existence (which I never questioned) is derived from the order of nature; where there appear such marks of intelligence and design, that you think it extravagant to assign for its cause, either chance, or the blind and unguided force of matter. You allow, that this is an argument drawn from effects to causes. From the order of the work, you infer, that there must have been project and forethought in the workman. If you cannot make out this point, you allow, that your conclusion fails; and you pretend not to establish the conclusion in a greater latitude than the phenomena of nature will justify. These are your concessions. I desire you to mark the consequences.

When we infer any particular cause from an effect, we must proportion the one to the other, and can never be allowed to ascribe to the cause any qualities, but what are exactly sufficient to produce the effect. A body of ten ounces raised in any scale may serve as a proof, that the counterbalancing weight exceeds ten ounces; but can never afford a reason that it exceeds a hundred. If the cause, assigned for any effect, be not sufficient to produce it, we must either reject that cause, or add to it such qualities as will give it a just proportion to the effect. But if we ascribe to it further qualities, or affirm it capable of producing other effects, we can only indulge the licence of conjecture, and arbitrarily suppose the existence of qualities and energies, without reason or authority.

The same rule holds, whether the cause assigned be brute unconscious matter, or a rational intelligent being. If the cause be known only by the effect, we never ought to ascribe to it any qualities, beyond what are precisely requisite to produce the effect: Nor can we, by any rules of just reasoning, return back from the cause, and infer other effects from it, beyond those by which alone it is known to us. No one, merely from the sight of one of Zeuxis's pictures, could know, that he was also a statuary or architect, and was an artist no less skilful in stone and marble than in colours. The talents and taste, displayed in the particular work before us; these we may safely conclude the workmen to be possessed of. The cause must be proportioned to the effect; and if we exactly and precisely proportion it, we shall never find in it any qualities, that point farther, or afford an inference concerning any other design or performance. Such qualities must be somewhat beyond what is merely requisite for producing the effect, which we examine.

Allowing, therefore, the gods to be the authors of the existence or order of the universe; it follows, that they possess that precise degree of power, intelligence, and benevolence, which appears in their workmanship; but nothing farther can ever be proved, except we call in the assistance of exaggeration and flattery to supply the defects of argument and reasoning. So far as the traces of any attributes, at present, appear, so far may we conclude these attributes to exist. The supposition of farther attributes is mere hypothesis; much more the supposition, that, in distant regions of space or periods of time, there has been, or will be, a more magnificent display of these attributes, and a scheme of administration more suitable to such imaginary virtues. We can never be allowed to mount up from the universe, the effect, to Jupiter, the cause; and then descend downwards, to infer any new effect from that cause; as if the present effects alone were not entirely worthy of the glorious attributes, which we ascribe to that deity. The knowledge of the cause being derived solely from the effect, they must be exactly adjusted to each other; and the one can never refer to anything farther, or be the foundation of any new inference and conclusion.

You find certain phenomena in nature. You seek a cause or author. You imagine that you have found him. You afterwards become so enamoured of this offspring of your brain, that you imagine it impossible, but he must produce something greater and more perfect than the present scene of things, which is so full of ill and disorder. You forget, that this superlative intelligence and benevolence are entirely imaginary, or, at least, without any foundation in reason; and that you have no ground to ascribe to him any qualities, but what you see he has actually exerted and displayed in his productions. Let your gods, therefore, O philosophers, be suited to the present appearances of nature: and presume not to alter these appearances by arbitrary suppositions, in order to suit them to the attributes, which you so fondly ascribe to your deities.

When priests and poets, supported by your authority, O Athenians, talk of a golden or silver age, which preceded the present state of vice and misery, I hear them with attention and with reverence. But when philosophers, who pretend to neglect authority, and to cultivate reason, hold the same discourse, I pay them not, I own, the same obsequious submission and pious deference. I ask, who carried them into the celestial regions, who admitted them into the councils of the gods, who opened to them the book of fate, that they thus rashly affirm, that their deities have executed, or will execute, any purpose beyond what has actually appeared? If they tell me, that they have mounted on the steps or by the gradual ascent of reason, and by drawing inferences from effects to causes, I still insist, that they have aided the ascent of reason by the wings of imagination; otherwise they could not thus change their manner of inference, and argue from causes to effects; presuming, that a more perfect production than the present world would be more suitable to such perfect beings as the gods, and forgetting that they have no reason to ascribe to these celestial beings any perfection or any attribute, but what can be found in the present world.

Hence all the fruitless industry to account for the ill appearance of nature, and save the honour of the gods; while we must acknowledge the reality of that evil and disorder, with which the world so much abounds. The obstinate and intractable qualities of matter, we are told, or the observance of general laws, or some such reason, is the sole cause, which controlled the power and benevolence of Jupiter, and obliged him to create mankind and every sensible creature so imperfect and so unhappy. These attributes then, are, it seems, beforehand, taken for granted, in their greatest latitude. And upon that supposition, I own that such conjectures may, perhaps, be admitted as plausible solutions of the ill phenomena. But still I ask, Why take these attributes for granted, or why ascribe to the cause any qualities but what actually appear in the effect? Why torture your brain to justify the course of nature upon suppositions, which, for aught you know, may be entirely imaginary, and of which there are to be found no traces in the course of nature?

The religious hypothesis, therefore, must be considered only as a particular method of accounting for the visible phenomena of the universe: but no just reasoner will ever presume to infer from it any single fact, and alter or add to the phenomena, in any single particular. If you think, that the appearances of things prove such causes, it is allowable for you to draw an inference concerning the existence of these causes. In such complicated and sublime subjects, every one should be indulged in the liberty of conjecture and argument. But here you ought to rest. If you come backward, and arguing from your inferred causes, conclude, that any other fact has existed, or will exist, in the course of nature, which may serve as a fuller display of particular attributes; I must admonish you, that you have departed from the method of reasoning, attached to the present subject, and have certainly added something to the attributes of the cause, beyond what appears in the effect; otherwise you could never, with tolerable sense or propriety, add anything to the effect, in order to render it more worthy of the cause.

Where, then, is the odiousness of that doctrine, which I teach in my school, or rather, which I examine in my gardens? Or what do you find in this whole question, wherein the security of good morals, or the peace and order of society, is in the least concerned?

I deny a providence, you say, and supreme governor of the world, who guides the course of events, and punishes the vicious with infamy and disappointment, and rewards the virtuous with honour and success, in all their undertakings. But surely, I deny not the course itself of events, which lies open to every one's inquiry and examination. I acknowledge, that, in the present order of things, virtue is attended with more peace of mind than vice, and meets with a more favour able reception from the world. I am sensible, that, according to the past experience of mankind, friendship is the chief joy of human life, and moderation the only source of tranquillity and happiness. I never balance between the virtuous and the vicious course of life; but am sensible, that, to a well-disposed mind, every advantage is on the side of the former. And what can you say more, allowing all your suppositions and reasonings? You tell me, indeed, that this disposition of things proceeds from intelligence and design. But whatever it proceeds from, the disposition itself, on which depends our happiness or misery, and consequently our conduct and deportment in life is still the same. It is still open for me, as well as you, to regulate my behaviour, by my experience of past events. And if you affirm, that, while a divine providence is allowed, and a supreme distributive justice in the universe, I ought to expect some more particular reward of the good, and punishment of the bad, beyond the ordinary course of events; I here find the same fallacy, which I have before endeavoured to detect. You persist in imagining, that, if we grant that divine existence, for which you so earnestly contend, you may safely infer consequences from it, and add something to the experienced order of nature, by arguing from the attributes which you ascribe to your gods. You seem not to remember, that all your reasonings on this subject can only be drawn from effects to causes; and that every argument, deducted from causes to effects, must of necessity be a gross sophism; since it is impossible for you to know anything of the cause, but what you have antecedently, not inferred, but discovered to the full, in the effect.

But what must a philosopher think of those vain reasoners, who, instead of regarding the present scene of things as the sole object of their contemplation, so far reverse the whole course of nature, as to render this life merely a passage to something farther; a porch, which leads to a greater, and vastly different building; a prologue, which serves only to introduce the piece, and give it more grace and propriety? Whence, do you think, can such philosophers derive their idea of the gods? From their own conceit and imagination surely. For if they derived it from the present phenomena, it would never point to anything farther, but must be exactly adjusted to them. That the divinity may *possibly* be endowed with attributes, which we have never seen exerted, may be governed by principles of action, which we cannot discover to be satisfied: all this will freely be allowed. But still this is mere *possibility* and hypothesis. We never can have reason to *infer* any attributes, or any principles of action in him, but so far as we know them to have been exerted and satisfied.

Are there *any marks of a distributive justice in the world?* If you answer in the affirmative, I conclude, that, since justice here exerts itself, it is satisfied. If you reply in the negative, I conclude, that you have then no reason to ascribe justice, in our sense of it, to the gods. If you hold a medium between affirmation and negation, by saying, that the justice of the gods, at present, exerts itself in part, but not in its full extent; I answer, that you have no reason to give it any particular extent, but only so far as you see it, *at present,* exert itself.

Thus I bring the dispute, O Athenians, to a short issue with my antagonists. The course of nature lies open to my contemplation as well as to theirs. The experienced train of events is the great standard, by which we all regulate our conduct. Nothing else can be appealed to in the field, or in the senate. Nothing else ought ever to be heard of in the schools, or in the closet. In vain would our limited understanding break through those boundaries, which are too narrow for our fond imagination. While we argue from the course of nature, and infer a particular intelligent cause, which first bestowed, and still preserves order in the universe, we embrace a principle, which is both uncertain and useless. It is uncertain; because the subject lies entirely beyond the reach of human experience. It is useless; because our knowledge of this cause being derived entirely from the course of nature, we can never, according to the rules of just reasoning, return back from the cause with any new inference, or making additions to the common and experienced course of nature, establish any new principles of conduct and behaviour.

I observe (said I, finding he had finished his harangue) that you neglect not the artifice of the demagogues of old; and as you were pleased to make me stand for the people, you insinuate yourself into my favour by embracing those principles, to which, you know, I have always expressed a particular attachment. But allowing you to make experience (as indeed I think you ought) the only standard of our judgement concerning this, and all other questions of fact; I doubt not but, from the very same experience, to which you appeal, it may be possible to refute this reasoning, which you have put into the mouth of Epicurus. If you saw, for instance, a half-finished building, surrounded with heaps of brick and stone and mortar, and all the instruments of masonry; could you not *infer* from the effect, that it was a work of design and contrivance? And could you not return again, from this inferred cause, to infer new additions to the effect, and conclude, that the building would soon be finished, and receive all the further improvements, which art could bestow upon it? If you saw upon the sea-shore the print of one human foot, you would conclude, that a man had passed that way, and that he had also left the traces of the other foot, though effaced by the rolling of the sands or inundation of the waters. Why then do you refuse to admit the same method of reasoning with regard to the order of nature? Consider the world and the present life only as an imperfect building, from which you can infer a superior intelligence; and arguing from that superior intelligence, which can leave nothing imperfect; why may you not infer a more finished scheme or plan, which will receive its completion in some distant point of space or time? Are not these methods of reasoning exactly similar? And under what pretence can you embrace the one, while you reject the other?

The infinite difference of the subjects, replied he, is a sufficient foundation for this difference in my conclusions. In works of *human* art and contrivance, it is allowable to advance from the effect to the cause, and returning back from the cause, to form new inferences concerning the effect, and examine the alterations, which it has probably undergone, or may still undergo. But what is the foundation of this method of reasoning? Plainly this: that man is a being, whom we know by experience, whose motives and designs we are acquainted with, and whose projects and inclinations have a certain connexion and coherence, according to the laws which nature has established for the government of such a creature. When, therefore, we find, that any work has proceeded from the skill and industry of man; as we are otherwise acquainted with the nature of the animal, we can draw a hundred inferences concerning what may be expected from him; and these inferences will all be founded in experience and observation. But did we know man only from the single work or production which we examine, it were impossible for us to argue in this manner; because our knowledge of all the qualities, which we ascribe to him, being in that case derived from the production, it is impossible they could point to anything further, or be the foundation of any new inference. The print of a foot in the sand can only prove, when considered alone, that there was some figure adapted to it, by which it was produced: but the print of a human foot proves likewise, from our other experience, that there was probably another foot, which also left its impression, though effaced by time or other accidents. Here we mount from the effect to the cause; and descending again from the cause, infer alterations in the effect; but this is not a continuation of the same simple chain of reasoning. We comprehend in this case a hundred other experiences and observations, concerning the *usual* figure and members of that species of animal, without which this method of argument must be considered as fallacious and sophistical.

The case is not the same with our reasonings from the works of nature. The Deity is known to us only by his productions, and is a single being in the universe, not comprehended under any species or genus, from whose experienced attributes or qualities, we can, by analogy, infer any attribute or quality in him. As the universe shows wisdom and goodness, we infer wisdom and goodness. As it shows a particular degree of these perfections, we infer a particular degree of them, precisely adapted to the effect which we examine. But further attributes or further degrees of the same attributes, we can never be authorized to infer or suppose, by any rules of just reasoning. Now, without some such license of supposition, it is impossible for us to argue from the cause, or infer any alteration in the effect, beyond what has immediately fallen under our observation. Greater good produced by this Being must still prove a greater degree of goodness: a more impartial distribution of rewards and punishments must proceed from a greater regard to justice and equity. Every supposed addition to the works of nature makes an addition to the attributes of the Author of nature; and consequently, being entirely unsupported by any reason or argument, can never be admitted but as mere conjecture and hypothesis.*

The great source of our mistake in this subject, and of the unbounded licence of conjecture, which we indulge, is, that we tacitly consider ourselves, as in the place of the Supreme Being, and conclude, that he will, on every occasion, observe the same conduct, which we ourselves, in his situation, would have embraced as reasonable and eligible. But, besides that the ordinary course of nature may convince us, that almost everything is regulated by principles and maxims very different from ours; besides, this, I say, it must evidently appear contrary to all rules of analogy to reason, from the intentions and projects of men, to those of a Being so different, and so much superior. In human nature, there is a certain experienced coherence of designs and inclinations; so that when, from any fact, we have discovered one intention of any man, it may often be reasonable, from experience, to infer another, and draw a long chain of conclusions concerning his past or future conduct. But this method of reasoning can never have place with regard to a Being, so remote and incomprehensible, who bears much less analogy to any other being in the universe than the sun to a waxen taper, and who discovers himself only by some faint traces or outlines, beyond which we have no authority to ascribe to him any attribute or perfection. What we imagine to be a superior perfection, may really be a defect. Or were it ever so much a perfection, the ascribing of it to the Supreme Being, where it appears not to have been really exerted, to the full, in his works, savours more of flattery and panegyric, than of just reasoning and sound philosophy. All the philosophy, therefore, in the world, and all the religion, which is nothing but a species of philosophy, will never be able to carry us beyond the usual course of experience, or give us measures of conduct and behaviour different from those which are furnished by reflections on common life. No new fact can ever be inferred from the religious hypothesis; no event foreseen or foretold: no reward or punishment expected or dreaded, beyond what is already known by practice and observation. So that my apology for Epicurus will still appear solid and satisfactory; nor have the political interests of society any connexion with the philosophical disputes concerning metaphysics and religion.

There is still one circumstance, replied I, which you seem to have overlooked. Though I should allow your premises, I must deny your conclusion. You conclude, that religious doctrines and reasonings *can* have no influence on life, because they *ought* to

---

*In general, it may, I think, be established as a maxim, that where any cause is known only by its particular effects, it must be impossible to infer any new effects from that cause; since the qualities, which are requisite to produce these new effects along with the former, must either be different, or superior, or of more extensive operation, than those which simply produced the effect, whence alone the cause is supposed to be known to us. We can never, therefore, have any reason to suppose the existence of these qualities. To say, that the new effects proceed only from a continuation of the same energy, which is already known from the first effects, will not remove the difficulty. For even granting this to be the case (which can seldom be supposed), the very continuation and exertion of a like energy (for it is impossible it can be absolutely the same), I say, this exertion of a like energy, in a different period of space and time, is a very arbitrary supposition, and what there cannot possibly be any traces of in the effects, from which all our knowledge of the cause is originally derived. Let the *inferred* cause be exactly proportioned (as it should be) to the known effect; and it is impossible that it can possess any qualities, from which new or different effects can be *inferred*.

have no influence; never considering, that men reason not in the same manner you do, but draw many consequences from the belief of a divine Existence, and suppose that the Deity will inflict punishments on vice, and bestow rewards on virtue, beyond what appear in the ordinary course of nature. Whether this reasoning of theirs be just or not, is no matter. Its influence on their life and conduct must still be the same. And, those, who attempt to disabuse them of such prejudices, may, for aught I know, be good reasoners, but I cannot allow them to be good citizens and politicians; since they free men from one restraint upon their passions, and make the infringement of the laws of society, in one respect, more easy and secure.

After all, I may, perhaps, agree to your general conclusion in favour of liberty, though upon different premises from those, on which you endeavour to found it. I think, that the state ought to tolerate every principle of philosophy; nor is there an instance, that any government has suffered in its political interests by such indulgence. There is no enthusiasm among philosophers; their doctrines are not very alluring to the people; and no restraint can be put upon their reasonings, but what must be of dangerous consequences to the sciences, and even to the state, by paving the way for persecution and oppression in points, where the generality of mankind are more deeply interested and concerned.

But there occurs to me (continued I) with regard to your main topic, a difficulty, which I shall just propose to you without insisting on it; lest it lead into reasonings of too nice and delicate a nature. In a word, I much doubt whether it be possible for a cause to be known only by its effect (as you have all along supposed) or to be of so singular and particular a nature as to have no parallel and no similarity with any other cause or object, that has ever fallen under our observation. It is only when two *species* of objects are found to be constantly conjoined, that we can infer the one from the other; and were an effect presented, which was entirely singular, and could not be comprehended under any known species, I do not see, that we could form any conjecture or inference at all concerning its cause. If experience and observation and analogy be, indeed, the only guides which we can reasonably follow in inferences of this nature; both the effect and cause must bear a similarity and resemblance to other effects and causes, which we know, and which we have found, in many instances, to be conjoined with each other. I leave it to your own reflection to pursue the consequences of this principle. I shall just observe, that, as the antagonists of Epicurus always suppose the universe, an effect quite singular and unparalleled, to be the proof of a Deity, a cause no less singular and unparalleled; your reasonings, upon that supposition, seem, at least, to merit our attention. There is, I own, some difficulty, how we can ever return from the cause to the effect, and, reasoning from our ideas of the former, infer any alteration on the latter, or any addition to it.

Section XII. Of the Academical or Sceptical Philosophy

Part I

There is not a greater number of philosophical reasonings, displayed upon any subject, than those, which prove the existence of a Deity, and refute the fallacies of *Atheists;* and yet the most religious philosophers still dispute whether any man can be so blinded as to be a speculative atheist. How shall we reconcile these contradictions? The knightserrant, who wandered about to clear the world of dragons and giants, never entertained the least doubt with regard to the existence of these monsters.

The *Sceptic* is another enemy of religion, who naturally provokes the indignation of all divines and graver philosophers; though it is certain, that no man ever met with any such absurd creature, or conversed with a man, who had no opinion or principle concerning any subject, either of action or speculation. This begets a very natural question; What is meant by a sceptic? And how far is it possible to push these philosophical principles of doubt and uncertainty?

There is a species of scepticism, *antecedent* to all study and philosophy, which is much inculcated by Des Cartes and others, as a sovereign preservative against error and precipitate judgement. It recommends an universal doubt, not only of all our former opinions and principles, but also of our very faculties; of whose veracity, say they, we must assure ourselves, by a chain of reasoning, deduced from some original principle, which cannot possibly be fallacious or deceitful. But neither is there any such original principle, which has a prerogative above others, that are self-evident and convincing: or if there were, could we advance a step beyond it, but by the use of those very faculties, of which we are supposed to be already diffident. The Cartesian doubt, therefore, were it ever possible to be attained by any human creature (as it plainly is not) would be entirely incurable; and no reasoning could ever bring us to a state of assurance and conviction upon any subject.

It must, however, be confessed, that this species of scepticism, when more moderate, may be understood in a very reasonable sense, and is a necessary preparative to the study of philosophy, by preserving a proper impartiality in our judgements, and weaning our mind from all those prejudices, which we may have imbibed from education or rash opinion. To begin with clear and self-evident principles, to advance by timorous and sure steps, to review frequently our conclusions, and examine accurately all their consequences; though by these means we shall make both a slow and a short progress in our systems; are the only methods, by which we can ever hope to reach truth, and attain a proper stability and certainty in our determinations.

There is another species of scepticism, *consequent* to science and enquiry, when men are supposed to have discovered either the absolute fallaciousness of their mental faculties, or their unfitness to reach any fixed determination in all those curious subjects of speculation, about which they are commonly employed. Even our very senses are brought into dispute, by a certain species of philosophers; and the maxims of common life are subjected to the same doubt as the most profound principles or conclusions of metaphysics and theology. As these paradoxical tenets (if they may be called tenets) are to be met with in some philosophers, and the refutation of them in several, they naturally excite our curiosity, and make us enquire into the arguments, on which they may be founded.

I need not insist upon the more trite topics, employed by the sceptics in all ages, against the evidence of *sense*; such as those which are derived from the imperfection and fallaciousness of our organs, on numberless occasions; the crooked appearance of an oar in water; the various aspects of objects, according to their different distances; the double images which arise from the pressing one eye; with many other appearances of a like nature. These sceptical topics, indeed, are only sufficient to prove, that the senses alone are not implicitly to be depended on; but that we must correct their evidence by reason, and by considerations, derived from the nature of the medium, the distance of the object, and the disposition of the organ, in order to render them, without their sphere, the proper *criteria* of truth and falsehood. There are other more profound arguments against the senses, which admit not of so easy a solution.

It seems evident, that men are carried, by a natural instinct or prepossession, to repose faith in their senses; and that, without any reasoning, or even almost before the use of reason, we always suppose an external universe, which depends not on our perception, but would exist, though we and every sensible creature were absent or annihilated. Even the animal creations are governed by a like opinion, and preserve this belief of external objects, in all their thoughts, designs, and actions.

It seems also evident, that, when men follow this blind and powerful instinct of nature, they always suppose the very images, presented by the senses, to be the external objects, and never entertain any suspicion, that the one are nothing but representations of the other. This very table, which we see white, and which we feel hard, is believed to exist, independent of our perception, and to be something external to our mind, which perceives it. Our presence bestows not being on it: our absence does not annihilate it. It preserves its existence uniform and entire, independent of the situation of intelligent beings, who perceive or contemplate it.

But this universal and primary opinion of all men is soon destroyed by the slightest philosophy, which teaches us, that nothing can ever be present to the mind but an image or perception, and that the senses are only the inlets, through which these images are conveyed, without being able to produce any immediate intercourse between the mind and the object. The table, which we see, seems to diminish, as we remove farther from it: but the real table, which exists independent of us, suffers no alteration: it was, therefore, nothing but its image, which was present to the mind. These are the obvious dictates of reason; and no man, who reflects, ever doubted, that the existences, which we consider, when we say, *this house* and *that tree*, are nothing but perceptions in the mind, and fleeting copies or representations of other existences, which remain uniform and independent.

So far, then, are we necessitated by reasoning to contradict or depart from the primary instincts of nature, and to embrace a new system with regard to the evidence of our senses. But here philosophy finds herself extremely embarrassed, when she would justify this new system, and obviate the cavils and objections of the sceptics. She can no longer plead the infallible and irresistible instinct of nature: for that led us to a quite different system, which is acknowledged fallible and even erroneous. And to justify this pretended philosophical system, by a chain of clear and convincing argument, or even any appearance of argument, exceeds the power of all human capacity.

By what argument can it be proved, that the perceptions of the mind must be caused by external objects, entirely different from them, though resembling them (if that be possible) and could not arise either from the energy of the mind itself, or from the suggestion of some invisible and unknown spirit, or from some other cause still more unknown to us? It is acknowledged, that, in fact, many of these perceptions arise not from anything external, as in dreams, madness, and other diseases. And nothing can be more inexplicable than the manner, in which body should so operate upon mind as ever to convey an image of itself to a substance, supposed of so different, and even contrary a nature.

It is a question of fact, whether the perceptions of the senses be produced by external objects, resembling them: how shall this question be determined? By experience surely; as all other questions of a like nature. But here experience is, and must be entirely silent. The mind has never anything present to it but the perceptions, and cannot possibly reach any experience of their connexion with objects. The supposition of such a connexion is, therefore, without any foundation in reasoning.

To have recourse to the veracity of the Supreme Being, in order to prove the veracity of our senses, is surely making a very unexpected circuit. If his veracity were at all concerned in this matter, our senses would be entirely infallible; because it is not possible that he can ever deceive. Not to mention, that, if the external world be once called in question, we shall be at a loss to find arguments, by which we may prove the existence of that Being or any of his attributes.

This is a topic, therefore, in which the profounder and more philosophical scep-tics will always triumph, when they endeavour to introduce an universal doubt into all subjects of human knowledge and enquiry. Do you follow the instincts and propensi-ties of nature, may they say, in assenting to the veracity of sense? But these lead you to believe that the very perception or sensible image is the external object. Do you dis-claim this principle, in order to embrace a more rational opinion, that the perceptions are only representations of something external? You here depart from your natural propensities and more obvious sentiments; and yet are not able to satisfy your reason, which can never find any convincing argument from experience to prove, that the per-ceptions are connected with any external objects.

There is another sceptical topic of a like nature, derived from the most profound philosophy, which might merit our attention, were it requisite to dive so deep, in order to discover arguments and reasonings, which can so little serve to any serious purpose. It is universally allowed by modern enquirers, that all the sensible qualities of objects, such as hard, soft, hot, cold, white, black, etc. are merely secondary, and exist not in the objects themselves, but are perceptions of the mind, without any external archetype or model, which they represent. If this be allowed, with regard to secondary qualities, it must also follow, with regard to the supposed primary qualities of extension and solidity; nor can the latter be any more entitled to that denomination than the former. The idea of extension is entirely acquired from the senses of sight and feeling; and if all the qualities, perceived by the senses, be in the mind, not in the object, the same conclusion must reach the idea of extension, which is wholly dependent on the sensible ideas or the ideas of secondary qual-ities. Nothing can save us from this conclusion, but the asserting, that the ideas of those primary qualities are attained by *Abstraction,* an opinion, which, if we examine it accu-rately, we shall find to be unintelligible, and even absurd. An extension, that is neither tangible nor visible, cannot possibly be conceived: and a tangible or visible extension, which is neither hard nor soft, black or white, is equally beyond the reach of human con-ception. Let any man try to conceive a triangle in general, which is neither *Isosceles* nor *Scalenum,* nor has any particular length or proportion of sides; and he will soon perceive the absurdity of all the scholastic notions with regard to abstraction and general ideas.*

Thus the first philosophical objection to the evidence of sense or to the opinion of external existence consists in this, that such an opinion, if rested on natural instinct, is contrary to reason, and if referred to reason, is contrary to natural instinct, and at the same time carries no rational evidence with it, to convince an impartial enquirer. The second objection goes farther, and represents this opinion as contrary to reason: at least, if it be a principle of reason, that all sensible qualities are in the mind, not in the object. Bereave matter of all its intelligible qualities, both primary and secondary, you in a manner annihilate it, and leave only a certain unknown, inexplicable *something*, as the cause of our perceptions; a notion so imperfect, that no sceptic will think it worth while to contend against it.

---

*This argument is drawn from Dr. Berkeley; and indeed most of the writings of that very ingenious author form the best lessons of scepticism, which are to be found either among the ancient or modern philosophers. Bayle not excepted. He professes, however, in his title-page (and undoubtedly with great truth) to have composed his book against the sceptics as well as against the atheists and freethinkers. But that all his arguments, though otherwise intended, are, in reality, merely sceptical, appears from this, that *they admit of no answer and produce no conviction.* Their only effect is to cause that momentary amazement and irreso-lution and confusion, which is the result of scepticism.

PART II

It may seem a very extravagant attempt of the sceptics to *destroy* reason by argument and ratiocination; yet is this the grand scope of all their enquiries and disputes. They endeavour to find objections, both to our abstract reasonings, and to those which regard matter of fact and existence.

The chief objection against all *abstract* reasonings is derived from the ideas of space and time; ideas, which, in common life and to a careless view, are very clear and intelligible, but when they pass through the scrutiny of the profound sciences (and they are the chief object of these sciences) afford principles, which seem full of absurdity and contradiction. No priestly *dogmas,* invented on purpose to tame and subdue the rebellious reason of mankind, ever shocked common sense more than the doctrine of the infinite divisibility of extension, with its consequences; as they are pompously displayed by all geometricians and metaphysicians, with a kind of triumph and exultation. A real quantity, infinitely less than any finite quantity, containing quantities infinitely less than itself, and so on *in infinitum*; this is an edifice so bold and prodigious, that it is too weighty for any pretended demonstration to support, because it shocks the clearest and most natural principles of human reason.* But what renders the matter more extraordinary, is, that these seemingly absurd opinions are supported by a chain of reasoning, the clearest and most natural; nor is it possible for us to allow the premises without admitting the consequences. Nothing can be more convincing and satisfactory than all the conclusions concerning the properties of circles and triangles; and yet, when these are once received, how can we deny, that the angle of contact between a circle and its tangent is infinitely less than any rectilineal angle, that as you may increase the diameter of the circle *in infinitum,* this angle of contact becomes still less, even *in infinitum,* and that the angle of contact between other curves and their tangents may be infinitely less than those between any circle and its tangent, and so on, *in infinitum?* The demonstration of these principles seems as unexceptionable as that which proves the three angles of a triangle to be equal to two right ones, though the latter opinion be natural and easy, and the former big with contradiction and absurdity. Reason here seems to be thrown into a kind of amazement and suspense, which, without the suggestions of any sceptic, gives her a diffidence of herself, and of the ground on which she treads. She sees a full light, which illuminates certain places; but that light borders upon the most profound darkness. And between these she is so dazzled and confounded, that she scarcely can pronounce with certainty and assurance concerning any one object.

The absurdity of these bold determinations of the abstract sciences seems to become, if possible, still more palpable with regard to time than extension. An infinite number of real parts of time, passing in succession, and exhausted one after another, appears so evident a contradiction, that no man, one should think, whose judgment is not corrupted, instead of being improved, by the sciences, would ever be able to admit of it.

Yet still reason must remain restless, and unquiet, even with regard to that scepticism, to which she is driven by these seeming absurdities and contradictions. How any clear, distinct idea can contain circumstances, contradictory to itself, or to any other clear, distinct idea, is absolutely incomprehensible; and is, perhaps, as absurd as

---

*Whatever disputes there may be about mathematical points, we must allow that there are physical points; that is, parts of extension which cannot be divided or lessened, either by the eye or imagination. These images, then, which are present to the fancy or senses, are absolutely indivisible, and consequently must be allowed by mathematicians to be infinitely less than any real part of extension; and yet nothing appears more certain to reason, than that an infinite number of them composes an infinite extension. How much more an infinite number of those infinitely small parts of extension, which are still supposed infinitely divisible.

any proposition, which can be formed. So that nothing can be more sceptical, or more full of doubt and hesitation, than this scepticism itself, which arises from some of the paradoxical conclusions of geometry or the science of quantity.*

The sceptical objections to *moral* evidence, or to the reasonings concerning matter of fact, are either *popular* or *philosophical*. The popular objections are derived from the natural weakness of human understanding; the contradictory opinions, which have been entertained in different ages and nations; the variations of our judgement in sickness and health, youth and old age, prosperity and adversity; the perpetual contradiction of each particular man's opinions and sentiments; with many other topics of that kind. It is needless to insist farther on this head. These objections are but weak. For as, in common life, we reason every moment concerning fact and existence, and cannot possibly subsist, without continually employing this species of argument, any popular objections, derived from thence, must be insufficient to destroy that evidence. The great subverter of *Pyrrhonism* or the excessive principles of scepticism is action, and employment, and the occupations of common life. These principles may flourish and triumph in the schools; where it is, indeed, difficult, if not impossible, to refute them. But as soon as they leave the shade, and by the presence of the real objects, which actuate our passions and sentiments, are put in opposition to the more powerful principles of our nature, they vanish like smoke, and leave the most determined sceptic in the same condition as other mortals.

The sceptic, therefore, had better keep within his proper sphere, and display those *philosophical* objections, which arise from more profound researches. Here he seems to have ample matter of triumph; while he justly insists, that all our evidence for any matter of fact, which lies beyond the testimony of sense or memory, is derived entirely from the relation of cause and effect; that we have no other idea of this relation than that of two objects, which have been frequently *conjoined* together; that we have no argument to convince us, that objects, which have, in our experience, been frequently conjoined, will likewise, in other instances, be conjoined in the same manner; and that nothing leads us to this inference but custom or a certain instinct of our nature; which it is indeed difficult to resist, but which, like other instincts, may be fallacious and deceitful. While the sceptic insists upon these topics, he shows his force, or rather, indeed, his own and our weakness; and seems, for the time at least, to destroy all assurance and conviction. These arguments might be displayed at greater length, if any durable good or benefit to society could ever be expected to result from them.

For here is the chief and most confounding objection to *excessive* scepticism, that no durable good can ever result from it; while it remains in its full force and vigour. We need only ask a sceptic, *What his meaning is? And what he proposes by all these curious researches?* He is immediately at a loss, and knows not what to answer. A Copernican or Ptolemaic, who supports each his different system of astronomy, may hope to produce a conviction, which will remain constant and durable, with his audi-

---

*It seems to me not impossible to avoid these absurdities and contradictions, if it be admitted, that there is no such thing as abstract or general ideas, properly speaking; but that all general ideas are, in reality, particular ones, attached to a general term, which recalls, upon occasion, other particular ones that resemble, in certain circumstances, the idea, present to the mind. Thus when the term Horse is pronounced, we immediately figure to ourselves the idea of a black or a white animal, of a particular size or figure: But as that term is also usually applied to animals of other colours, figures and sizes these ideas, though not actually present to the imagination, are easily recalled, and our reasoning and conclusion proceed in the same way, as if they were actually present. If this be admitted (as seems reasonable) it follows that all the ideas of quantity, upon which mathematicians reason, are nothing but particular, and such as are suggested by the senses and imagination, and consequently, cannot be infinitely divisible. It is sufficient to have dropped this hint at present, without prosecuting it any farther. It certainly concerns all lovers of science not to expose themselves to the ridicule and contempt of the ignorant by their conclusions; and this seems the readiest solution of these difficulties.

ence. A Stoic or Epicurean displays principles, which may not be durable, but which have an effect on conduct and behaviour. But a Pyrrhonian cannot expect, that his philosophy will have any constant influence on the mind: or if it had, that its influence would be beneficial to society. On the contrary, he must acknowledge, if he will acknowledge anything, that all human life must perish, were his principles universally and steadily to prevail. All discourse, all action would immediately cease; and men remain in a total lethargy, till the necessities of nature, unsatisfied, put an end to their miserable existence. It is true; so fatal an event is very little to be dreaded. Nature is always too strong for principle. And though a Pyrrhonian may throw himself or others into a momentary amazement and confusion by his profound reasonings; the first and most trivial event in life will put to flight all his doubts and scruples, and leave him the same, in every point of action and speculation, with the philosophers of every other sect, or with those who never concerned themselves in any philosophical researches. When he awakes from his dream, he will be the first to join in the laugh against himself, and to confess, that all his objections are mere amusement, and can have no other tendency than to show the whimsical condition of mankind, who must act and reason and believe; though they are not able, by their most diligent enquiry, to satisfy themselves concerning the foundation of these operations, or to remove the objections, which may be raised against them.

PART III

There is, indeed, a more *mitigated* scepticism or *academical* philosophy, which may be both durable and useful, and which may, in part, be the result of this Pyrrhonism, or excessive scepticism, when its undistinguished doubts are, in some measure, corrected by common sense and reflection. The greater part of mankind are naturally apt to be affirmative and dogmatical in their opinions; and while they see objects only on one side, and have no idea of any counterpoising argument, they throw themselves precipitately into the principles, to which they are inclined; nor have they any indulgence for those who entertain opposite sentiments. To hesitate or balance perplexes their understanding, checks their passion, and suspends their action. They are, therefore, impatient till they escape from a state, which to them is so uneasy: and they think, that they could never remove themselves far enough from it, by the violence of their affirmations and obstinacy of their belief. But could such dogmatical reasoners become sensible of the strange infirmities of human understanding, even in its most perfect state, and when most accurate and cautious in its determination; such a reflection would naturally inspire them with more modesty and reserve, and diminish their fond opinion of themselves, and their prejudice against antagonists. The illiterate may reflect on the disposition of the learned, who, amidst all the advantages of study and reflection, are commonly still diffident in their determinations: and if any of the learned be inclined, from their natural temper, to haughtiness and obstinacy, a small tincture of Pyrrhonism might abate their pride, by showing them, that the few advantages, which they may have attained over their fellows, are but inconsiderable, if compared with the universal perplexity and confusion, which is inherent in human nature. In general, there is a degree of doubt, and caution, and modesty, which, in all kinds of scrutiny and decision, ought for ever to accompany a just reasoner.

Another species of *mitigated* scepticism which may be of advantage to man-kind, and which may be the natural result of the Pyrrhonian doubts and scruples, is the limitation of our enquiries to such subjects as are best adapted to the narrow capacity of human understanding. The *imagination* of man is naturally sublime, delighted with whatever is remote and extraordinary, and running, without control, into the most distant parts of space and time in order to avoid the objects, which custom has rendered too familiar to it. A correct *judgement* observes a contrary method, and avoiding all distant and high enquiries, confines itself to common life, and to such subjects as fall under daily practice and experience; leaving the more sublime topics to the embellishment of poets and orators, or to the arts of priests and politicians. To bring us to so salutary a determination, nothing can be more serviceable, than to be once thoroughly convinced of the force of the Pyrrhonian doubt, and of the impossibility, that anything, but the strong power of natural instinct, could free us from it. Those who have a propensity to philosophy, will still continue their researches; because they reflect, that, besides the immediate pleasure, attending such an occupation, philosophical decisions are nothing but the reflections of common life, methodized and corrected. But they will never be tempted to go beyond common life, so long as they consider the imperfection of those faculties which they employ, their narrow reach, and their inaccurate operations. While we cannot give a satisfactory reason, why we believe, after a thousand experiments, that a stone will fall, or fire burn; can we ever satisfy ourselves concerning any determination, which we may form, with regard to the origin of worlds, and the situation of nature, from, and to eternity?

This narrow limitation, indeed, of our enquiries, is, in every respect, so reasonable, that it suffices to make the slightest examination into the natural powers of the human mind and to compare them with their objects, in order to recommend it to us. We shall then find what are the proper subjects of science and enquiry.

It seems to me, that the only objects of the abstract science or of demonstration are quantity and number, and that all attempts to extend this more perfect species of knowledge beyond these bounds are mere sophistry and illusion. As the component parts of quantity and number are entirely similar, their relations become intricate and involved; and nothing can be more curious, as well as useful, than to trace, by a variety of mediums their equality or inequality, through their different appearances. But as all other ideas are clearly distinct and different from each other, we can never advance farther, by our utmost scrutiny, than to observe this diversity, and, by an obvious reflection, pronounce one thing not to be another. Or if there be any difficulty in these decisions, it proceeds entirely from the undeterminate meaning of words, which is corrected by juster definitions. That *the square of the hypothenuse is equal to the square of the other two sides*, cannot be known, let the terms be ever so exactly defined, without a train of reasoning and enquiry. But to convince us of this proposition, *that where there is no property, there can be no injustice*, it is only necessary to define the terms, and explain injustice to be a violation of property. This proposition is, indeed, nothing but a more imperfect definition. It is the same case with all those pretended syllogistical reasonings, which may be found in every other branch of learning, except the sciences of quantity and number and these may safely, I think, be pronounced the only proper objects of knowledge and demonstration.

All other enquiries of men regard only matter of fact and existence; and these are evidently incapable of demonstration. Whatever *is* may *not be*. No negation of a fact can involve a contradiction. The non-existence of any being, without exception, is as clear and distinct an idea as its existence. The proposition, which affirms it not to be, however false, is no less conceivable and intelligible, than that which affirms it to be. The case is different with the sciences, properly so called. Every proposition, which is not true, is there confused and unintelligible. That the cube root of 64 is equal to the half of 10, is a false proposition, and can never be distinctly conceived. But that Caesar, or the angel Gabriel, or any being never existed, may be a false proposition, but still is perfectly conceivable, and implies no contradiction.

The existence, therefore, of any being can only be proved by arguments from its cause or its effect; and these arguments are founded entirely on experience. If we reason *a priori,* anything may appear able to produce anything. The falling of a pebble may, for aught we know, extinguish the sun; or the wish of a man control the planets in their orbits. It is only experience, which teaches us the nature and bounds of cause and effect, and enables us to infer the existence of one object from that of another.* Such is the foundation of moral reasoning, which forms the greater part of human knowledge, and is the source of all human action and behaviour.

Moral reasonings are either concerning particular or general facts. All deliberations in life regard the former; as also all disquisitions in history, chronology, geography, and astronomy.

The sciences, which treat of general facts, are politics, natural philosophy, physic, chemistry, etc. where the qualities, causes and effects of a whole species of objects are enquired into.

Divinity or Theology, as it proves the existence of a Deity, and the immortality of souls, is composed partly of reasonings concerning particular, partly concerning general facts. It has a foundation in *reason,* so far as it is supported by experience. But its best and most solid foundation is *faith* and divine revelation.

Morals and criticism are not so properly objects of the understanding as of taste and sentiment. Beauty, whether moral or natural, is felt, more properly than perceived. Or if we reason concerning it, and endeavour to fix its standard, we regard a new fact, to wit, the general tastes of mankind, or some such fact, which may be the object of reasoning and enquiry.

When we run over libraries, persuaded of these principles, what havoc must we make? If we take in our hand any volume; of divinity or school metaphysics, for instance; let us ask, *Does it contain any abstract reasoning concerning quantity or number?* No. *Does it contain any experimental reasoning concerning matter of fact and existence?* No. Commit it then to the flames: for it can contain nothing but sophistry and illusion.

DIALOGUES CONCERNING NATURAL RELIGION

PAMPHILUS TO HERMIPPUS

It has been remarked, my Hermippus, that, though the ancient philosophers conveyed most of their instruction in the form of dialogue, this method of composition has been little practised in later ages, and has seldom succeeded in the hands of those who have attempted it. Accurate and regular argument, indeed, such as is now expected of philosophical enquirers, naturally throws a man into the methodical and didactic manner; where he can immediately, without preparation, explain the point at which he aims;

---

*That impious maxim of the ancient philosophy, *Ex nihilo, nihil fit* [From nothing, nothing issues], by which the creation of matter was excluded, ceases to be a maxim according to this philosophy. Not only the will of the Supreme Being may create matter; but, for aught we know *a priori,* the will of any other being might create it, or any other cause, that the most whimsical imagination can assign.

and thence proceed, without interruption, to deduce the proofs, on which it is established. To deliver a System in conversation scarcely appears natural; and while the dialogue-writer desires, by departing from the direct style of composition, to give a freer air to his performance, and avoid the appearance of *author* and *reader,* he is apt to run into a worse inconvenience, and convey the image of *pedagogue* and *pupil.* Or if he carries on the dispute in the natural spirit of good company, by throwing in a variety of topics, and preserving a proper balance among the speakers; he often loses so much time in preparations and transitions, that the reader will scarcely think himself compensated, by all the graces of dialogue, for the order, brevity, and precision, which are sacrificed to them.

There are some subjects, however, to which dialogue-writing is peculiarly adapted, and where it is still preferable to the direct and simple method of composition.

Any point of doctrine, which is so *obvious,* that it scarcely admits of dispute, but at the same time so *important,* that it cannot be too often inculcated, seems to require some such method of handling it; where the novelty of the manner may compensate the triteness of the subject, where the vivacity of conversation may enforce the precept, and where the variety of lights, presented by various personages and characters, may appear neither tedious nor redundant.

Any question of philosophy, on the other hand, which is so *obscure* and *uncertain,* that human reason can reach no fixed determination with regard to it; if it should be treated at all; seems to lead us naturally into the style of dialogue and conversation. Reasonable men may be allowed to differ, where no one can reasonably be positive: Opposite sentiments, even without any decision, afford an agreeable amusement: And if the subject be curious and interesting, the book carries us, in a manner, into company; and unites the two greatest and purest pleasures of human life, study and society.

Happily, these circumstances are all to be found in the subject of natural religion. What truth so obvious, so certain, as the *being* of a God, which the most ignorant ages have acknowledged, for which the most refined geniuses have ambitiously striven to produce new proofs and arguments? What truth so important as this, which is the ground of all our hopes, the surest foundation of morality, the firmest support of society, and the only principle which ought never to be a moment absent from our thoughts and meditations? But in treating of this obvious and important truth; what obscure questions occur, concerning the *nature* of that divine Being; his attributes, his decrees, his plan of providence? These have been always subjected to the disputations of men: Concerning these, human reason has not reached any certain determination: But these are topics so interesting, that we cannot restrain our restless enquiry with regard to them; though nothing but doubt, uncertainty, and contradiction, have, as yet, been the result of our most accurate researches.

This I had lately occasion to observe, while I passed, as usual, part of the summer season with Cleanthes, and was present at those conversations of his with Philo and Demea, of which I gave you lately some imperfect account. Your curiosity, you then told me, was so excited, that I must of necessity enter into a more exact detail of their reasonings, and display those various systems which they advanced with regard to so delicate a subject as that of natural religion. The remarkable contrast in their characters still farther raised your expectations; while you opposed the accurate philosophical turn of Cleanthes to the careless scepticism of Philo, or compared either of their dispositions with the rigid inflexible orthodoxy of Demea. My youth rendered me a mere auditor of their disputes; and that curiosity, natural to the early season of life, has so deeply imprinted in my memory the whole chain and connection of their arguments, that, I hope, I shall not omit or confound any considerable part of them in the recital.

PART I

After I joined the company, whom I found sitting in Cleanthes's library, Demea paid Cleanthes some compliments, on the great care which he took of my education, and on his unwearied perseverance and constancy in all his friendships. The father of Pamphilus, said he, was your intimate friend: The son is your pupil, and may indeed be regarded as your adopted son; were we to judge by the pains which you bestow in conveying to him every useful branch of literature and science. You are no more wanting, I am persuaded, in prudence than in industry. I shall, therefore, communicate to you a maxim, which I have observed with regard to my own children, that I may learn how far it agrees with your practice. The method I follow in their education is founded on the saying of an ancient, "That students of philosophy ought first to learn logics, then ethics, next physics, last of all, of the nature of the Gods." This science of natural theology, according to him, being the most profound and abstruse of any, required the maturest judgment in its students; and none but a mind, enriched with all the other sciences, can safely be entrusted with it.

Are you so late, says Philo, in teaching your children the principles of religion? Is there no danger of their neglecting or rejecting altogether, those opinions, of which they have heard so little during the whole course of their education? It is only as a science, replied Demea, subjected to human reasoning and disputation, that I postpone the study of natural theology. To season their minds with early piety is my chief care; and by continual precept and instruction, and I hope too, by example, I imprint deeply on their tender minds an habitual reverence for all the principles of religion. While they pass through every other science, I still remark the uncertainty of each part, the eternal disputations of men, the obscurity of all philosophy, and the strange, ridiculous conclusions, which some of the greatest geniuses have derived from the principles of mere human reason. Having thus tamed their mind to a proper submission and self-diffidence, I have no longer any scruple of opening to them the greatest mysteries of religion, nor apprehend any danger from that assuming arrogance of philosophy, which may lead them to reject the most established doctrines and opinions.

Your precaution, says Philo, of seasoning your children's minds with early piety, is certainly very reasonable; and no more than is requisite, in this profane and irreligious age. But what I chiefly admire in your plan of education, is your method of drawing advantage from the very principles of philosophy and learning, which, by inspiring pride and self-sufficiency, have commonly, in all ages, been found so destructive to the principles of religion. The vulgar, indeed, we may remark, who are unacquainted with science and profound enquiry, observing the endless disputes of the learned, have commonly a thorough contempt for philosophy; and rivet themselves the faster, by that means, in the great points of theology, which have been taught them. Those who enter a little into study and enquiry, finding many appearances of evidence in doctrines the newest and most extraordinary, think nothing too difficult for human reason; and presumptuously breaking through all fences, profane the inmost sanctuaries of the temple. But Cleanthes will, I hope, agree with me, that, after we have abandoned ignorance, the surest remedy, there is still one expedient left to prevent this profane liberty. Let Demea's principles be improved and cultivated: Let us become thoroughly sensible of the weakness, blindness, and narrow limits of human reason: Let us duly consider its uncertainty and needless contrarieties, even in subjects of common life and practice: Let the errors and deceits of our very senses be set before us; the insuperable difficulties, which attend first principles in all systems; the contradictions, which adhere to the very ideas of matter, cause and effect, extension, space, time, motion; and in a word, quantity of all kinds, the object of the only science, that can fairly pretend to any certainty or evidence. When these topics are displayed in their full light, as they are by some philosophers and almost all divines; who can retain such confidence in this frail faculty of reason as to pay any regard to its determinations in points so sublime, so abstruse, so remote from common life and experience? When the coherence of the parts of a stone, or even that composition of parts, which renders it extended; when these familiar objects, I say, are so inexplicable, and contain circumstances so repugnant and contradictory; with what assurance can we decide concerning the origin of worlds, or trace their history from eternity to eternity?

While Philo pronounced these words, I could observe a smile in the countenances both of Demea and Cleanthes. That of Demea seemed to imply an unreserved satisfaction in the doctrines delivered: But in Cleanthes's features, I could distinguish an air of finesse; as if he perceived some raillery or artificial malice in the reasonings of Philo.

You propose then, Philo, said Cleanthes, to erect religious faith on philosophical scepticism; and you think that if certainty or evidence be expelled from every other subject of enquiry, it will all retire to these theological doctrines, and there acquire a superior force and authority. Whether your scepticism be as absolute and sincere as you pretend, we shall learn bye and bye, when the company breaks up: We shall then see, whether you go out at the door or the window; and whether you really doubt, if your body has gravity, or can be injured by its fall; according to popular opinion, derived from our fallacious senses and more fallacious experience. And this consideration, Demea, may, I think, fairly serve to abate our ill-will to this humourous sect of the sceptics. If they be thoroughly in earnest, they will not long trouble the world with their doubts, cavils, and disputes: If they be only in jest, they are, perhaps, bad railliers, but can never be very dangerous, either to the state, to philosophy, or to religion.

In reality, Philo, continued he, it seems certain, that though a man, in a flush of humour, after intense reflection on the many contradictions and imperfections of human reason, may entirely renounce all belief and opinion; it is impossible for him to persevere in this total scepticism, or make it appear in his conduct for a few hours. External objects press in upon him: Passions solicit him: His philosophical melancholy dissipates; and even the utmost violence upon his own temper will not be able, during any time, to preserve the poor appearance of scepticism. And for what reason impose on himself such a violence? This is a point in which it will be impossible for him ever to satisfy himself, consistently with his sceptical principles: So that upon the whole nothing could be more ridiculous than the principles of the ancient Pyrrhonians; if in reality they endeavoured, as is pretended, to extend throughout, the same scepticism, which they had learned from the declamations of their school, and which they ought to have confined to them.

In this view, there appears a great resemblance between the sects of the Stoics and Pyrrhonians, though perpetual antagonists: And both of them seem founded on this erroneous maxim, that what a man can perform sometimes, and in some dispositions, he can perform always, and in every disposition. When the mind, by Stoical reflections, is elevated into a sublime enthusiasm of virtue, and strongly smit with any *species* of honour or public good, the utmost bodily pain and sufferance will not prevail over such a high sense of duty; and it is possible, perhaps, by its means, even to smile and exult in the midst of tortures. If this sometimes may be the case in fact and reality, much more may a philosopher, in his school, or even in his closet, work himself up to such an enthusiasm, and support in imagination the acutest pain or most calamitous event which he can possibly conceive. But how shall he support this enthusiasm itself? The bent of his mind relaxes, and cannot be recalled at pleasure: Avocations lead him astray: Misfortunes attack him unawares: And the *philosopher* sinks by degrees into the *plebeian*.

I allow of your comparison between the Stoics and Sceptics, replied Philo. But you may observe, at the same time, that though the mind cannot, in Stoicism, support the highest flights of philosophy, yet even when it sinks lower, it still retains somewhat of its former disposition; and the effects of the Stoic's reasoning will appear in his conduct in common life, and through the whole tenor of his actions. The ancient schools, particularly that of Zeno, produced examples of virtue and constancy which seem astonishing to present times.

> Vain Wisdom all and false Philosophy.
> Yet with a pleasing sorcery could charm
> Pain, for a while, or anguish, and excite
> Fallacious Hope, or arm the obdurate breast
> With stubborn Patience, as with triple steel.

In like manner, if a man has accustomed himself to sceptical considerations on the uncertainty and narrow limits of reason, he will not entirely forget them when he turns his reflections on other subjects; but in all his philosophical principles and reasoning, I dare not say, in his common conduct, he will be found different from those, who either never formed any opinions in the case, or have entertained sentiments more favourable to human reason.

To whatever length any one may push his speculative principles of scepticism, he must act, I own, and live, and converse like other men; and for this conduct he is not obliged to give any other reason than the absolute necessity he lies under of so doing. If he ever carries his speculations farther than this necessity constrains him, and philosophises, either on natural or moral subjects, he is allured by a certain pleasure and satisfaction, which he finds in employing himself after that manner. He considers besides, that every one, even in common life, is constrained to have more or less of this philosophy; that from our earliest infancy we make continual advances in forming more general principles of conduct and reasoning; that the larger experience we acquire, and the stronger reason we are endowed with, we always render our principles the more general and comprehensive; and that what we call *philosophy* is nothing but a more regular and methodical operation of the same kind. To philosophise on such subjects is nothing essentially different from reasoning on common life; and we may only expect greater stability, if not greater truth, from our philosophy, on account of its exacter and more scrupulous method of proceeding.

But when we look beyond human affairs and the properties of the surrounding bodies: When we carry our speculations into the two eternities, before and after the present state of things; into the creation and formation of the universe; the existence and properties of spirits; the powers and operations of one universal spirit, existing without beginning and without end; omnipotent, omniscient, immutable, infinite, and incomprehensible: We must be far removed from the smallest tendency to scepticism not to be apprehensive, that we have here got quite beyond the reach of our faculties. So long as we confine our speculations to trade, or morals, or politics, or criticism, we make appeals, every moment, to common sense and experience, which strengthen our philosophical conclusions, and remove (at least, in part) the suspicion, which we so justly entertain with regard to every reasoning that is very subtle and refined. But in theological reasonings, we have not this advantage; while at the same time we are employed upon objects, which, we must be sensible, are too large for our grasp, and of all others, require most to be familiarised to our apprehension. We are like foreigners in a strange country, to whom everything must seem suspicious, and who are in danger every moment of transgressing against the laws and customs of the people with whom they live and converse. We know not how far we ought to trust our vulgar methods of reasoning in such a subject; since, even in common life and in that province which is peculiarly appropriated to them, we cannot account for them, and are entirely guided by a kind of instinct or necessity in employing them.

All sceptics pretend, that, if reason be considered in an abstract view, it furnishes invincible arguments against itself, and that we could never retain any conviction or assurance, on any subject, were not the sceptical reasonings so refined and subtile, that they are not able to counterpoise the more solid and more natural arguments, derived from the senses and experience. But it is evident, whenever our arguments lose this advantage, and run wide of common life, that the most refined scepticism comes to be upon a footing with them, and is able to oppose and counterbalance them. The one has no more weight than the other. The mind must remain in suspense between them; and it is that very suspense or balance, which is the triumph of scepticism.

But I observe, says Cleanthes, with regard to you, Philo, and all speculative sceptics, that your doctrine and practice are as much at variance in the most abstruse points of theory as in the conduct of common life. Wherever evidence discovers itself, you adhere to it, notwithstanding your pretended scepticism; and I can observe, too, some of your sect to be as decisive as those who make greater professions of certainty and assurance. In reality, would not a man be ridiculous, who pretended to reject Newton's explication of the wonderful phenomenon of the rainbow, because that explication gives a minute anatomy of the rays of light; a subject, forsooth, too refined for human comprehension? And what would you say to one, who having nothing particular to object to the arguments of Copernicus and Galilæo for the motion of the earth, should withhold his assent, on that general principle, that these subjects were too magnificent and remote to be explained by the narrow and fallacious reason of mankind?

There is indeed a kind of brutish and ignorant scepticism, as you well observed, which gives the vulgar a general prejudice against what they do not easily understand, and makes them reject every principle which requires elaborate reasoning to prove and establish it. This species of scepticism is fatal to knowledge, not to religion; since we find, that those who make greatest profession of it, give often their assent, not only to the great truths of theism, and natural theology, but even to the most absurd tenets, which a traditional superstition has recommended to them. They firmly believe in witches; though they will not believe nor attend to the most simple proposition of Euclid. But the refined and philosophical sceptics fall into an inconsistence of an opposite nature. They push their researches into the most abstruse corners of science; and their assent attends them in every step, proportioned to the evidence which they meet with. They are even obliged to acknowledge, that the most abstruse and remote objects are those which are best explained by philosophy. Light is in reality anatomized: The true system of the heavenly bodies is discovered and ascertained. But the nourishment of bodies by food is still an inexplicable mystery: The cohesion of the parts of matter is still incomprehensible. These sceptics, therefore, are obliged, in every question, to consider each particular evidence apart, and proportion their assent to the precise degree of evidence which occurs. This is their practice in all natural, mathematical, moral, and political science. And why not the same, I ask, in the theological and religious? Why must conclusions of this nature be alone rejected on the general presumption of the insufficiency of human reason, without any particular discussion of the evidence? Is not such an unequal conduct a plain proof of prejudice and passion?

Ninewells, the Hume family estate, near Berwick in southern Scotland. David Hume lived here until age twelve when he went to the University of Edinburgh. (*Culver Pictures, Inc.*)

Our senses, you say, are fallacious, our understanding erroneous, our ideas even of the most familiar objects, extension, duration, motion, full of absurdities and contradictions. You defy me to solve the difficulties, or reconcile the repugnancies, which you discover in them. I have not capacity for so great an undertaking: I have not leisure for it: I perceive it to be superfluous. Your own conduct, in every circumstance, refutes your principles; and shows the firmest reliance on all the received maxims of science, morals, prudence, and behaviour.

I shall never assent to so harsh an opinion as that of a celebrated writer, who says that the sceptics are not a sect of philosophers: They are only a sect of liars. I may, however, affirm (I hope without offence), that they are a sect of jesters or railliers. But for my part, whenever I find myself disposed to mirth and amusement, I shall certainly choose my entertainment of a less perplexing and abstruse nature. A comedy, a novel, or at most a history, seems a more natural recreation than such metaphysical subtilties and abstractions.

In vain would the sceptic make a distinction between science and common life, or between one science and another. The arguments employed in all, if just, are of a similar nature, and contain the same force and evidence. Or if there be any difference among them, the advantage lies entirely on the side of theology and natural religion. Many principles of mechanics are founded on very abstruse reasoning; yet no man, who has any pretensions to science, even no speculative sceptic, pretends to entertain the least doubt with regard to them. The Copernican system contains the most surprising paradox, and the most contrary to our natural conceptions, to appearances, and to our very senses: Yet even monks and inquisitors are now constrained to withdraw their opposition to it. And shall Philo, a man of so liberal a genius, and extensive knowledge, entertain any general undistinguished scruples with regard to the religious hypothesis, which is founded on the simplest and most obvious arguments, and, unless it meet with artificial obstacles, has such easy access and admission into the mind of man?

And here we may observe, continued he, turning himself towards Demea, a pretty curious circumstance in the history of the sciences. After the union of philosophy with the popular religion, upon the first establishment of Christianity, nothing was more usual, among all religious teachers, than declamations against reason, against the senses, against every principle, derived merely from human research and enquiry. All the topics of the ancient Academics were adopted by the Fathers; and thence propagated for several ages in every school and pulpit throughout Christendom. The Reformers embraced the same principles of reasoning, or rather declamation; and all panegyrics on the excellency of faith were sure to be interlarded with some severe strokes of satire against natural reason. A celebrated prelate too, of the Romish communion, a man of the most extensive learning, who wrote a demonstration of Christianity, has also composed a treatise, which contains all the cavils of the boldest and most determined Pyrrhonism. Locke seems to have been the first Christian, who ventured openly to assert, that *faith* was nothing but a species of *reason*, that religion was only a branch of philosophy, and that a chain of arguments, similar to that which established any truth in morals, politics, or physics, was always employed in discovering all the principles of theology, natural and revealed. The ill use, which Bayle and other libertines made of the philosophical scepticism of the Fathers and first Reformers, still farther propagated the judicious sentiment of Mr. Locke: And it is now, in a manner, avowed, by all pretenders to reasoning and philosophy, that atheist and sceptic are almost synonymous. And as it is certain, that no man is in earnest, when he professes the latter principle; I would fain hope that there are as few, who seriously maintain the former.

Don't you remember, said Philo, the excellent saying of Lord Bacon on the head? That a little philosophy, replied Cleanthes, makes a man an atheist: A great deal converts him to religion. That is a very judicious remark too, said Philo. But what I have in my eye is another passage, where, having mentioned David's fool, who said in his heart there is no God, this great philosopher observes, that the atheists now a days have a double share of folly: For they are not contented to say in their hearts there is no God, but they also utter that impiety with their lips, and are thereby guilty of multiplied indiscretion and imprudence. Such people, though they were ever so much in earnest, cannot, methinks, be very formidable.

But though you should rank me in this class of fools, I cannot forbear communicating a remark that occurs to me from the history of the religious and irreligious scepticism with which you have entertained us. It appears to me, that there are strong symptoms of priestcraft in the whole progress of this affair. During ignorant ages, such as those which followed the dissolution of the ancient schools, the priests perceived, that atheism, deism, or heresy of any kind, could only proceed from the presumptuous questioning of received opinions, and from a belief that human reason was equal to everything. Education had then a mighty influence over the minds of men, and was almost equal in force to those suggestions of the senses and common understanding, by which the most determined sceptic must allow himself to be governed. But at present, when the influence of education is much diminished, and men, from a more open commerce of the world, have learned to compare the popular principles of different nations and ages, our sagacious divines have changed their whole system of philosophy, and talk the language of Stoics, Platonists, and Peripatetics, not that of Pyrrhonians and

Academics. If we distrust human reason, we have now no other principle to lead us into religion. Thus, sceptics in one age, dogmatists in another; whichever system best suits the purpose of these reverend gentlemen, in giving them an ascendant over mankind, they are sure to make it their favourite principle, and established tenet.

It is very natural, said Cleanthes, for men to embrace those principles, by which they find they can best defend their doctrines; nor need we have any recourse to priest-craft to account for so reasonable an expedient. And surely, nothing can afford a stronger presumption, that any set of principles are true, and ought to be embraced, than to observe, that they tend to the confirmation of true religion, and serve to confound the cavils of atheists, libertines, and freethinkers of all denominations.

PART II

I must own, Cleanthes, said Demea, that nothing can more surprise me, than the light, in which you have, all along, put this argument. By the whole tenor of your discourse, one would imagine that you were maintaining the being of a God, against the cavils of atheists and infidels; and were necessitated to become a champion for that fundamental principle of all religion. But this, I hope, is not by any means a question among us. No man; no man, at least, of common sense, I am persuaded, ever entertained a serious doubt with regard to a truth so certain and self-evident. The question is not concerning the *being* but the *nature* of *God*. This, I affirm, from the infirmities of human understanding, to be altogether incomprehensible and unknown to us. The essence of that supreme mind, his attributes, the manner of his existence, the very nature of his duration; these and every particular, which regards so divine a Being, are mysterious to men. Finite, weak, and blind creatures, we ought to humble ourselves in his august presence, and, conscious of our frailties, adore in silence his infinite perfections, which eye hath not seen, ear hath not heard, neither hath it entered into the heart of man to conceive them. They are covered in a deep cloud from human curiosity: It is profaneness to attempt penetrating through these sacred obscurities: And next to the impiety of denying his existence, is the temerity of prying into his nature and essence, decrees and attributes.

But lest you should think, that my *piety* has here got the better of my *philosophy*, I shall support my opinion, if it needs any support, by a very great authority. I might cite all the divines almost, from the foundation of Christianity, who have ever treated of this or any other theological subject: But I shall confine myself, at present, to one equally celebrated for piety and philosophy. It is Father Malebranche, who, I remember, thus expresses himself: "One ought not so much (says he) to call God a spirit, in order to express positively what he is, as in order to signify that he is not matter. He is a Being infinitely perfect: Of this we cannot doubt. But in the same manner as we ought not to imagine, even supposing him corporeal, that he is cloathed with a human body, as the anthropomorphites asserted, under colour that that figure was the most perfect of any; so neither ought we to imagine, that the Spirit of God has human ideas, or bears *any* resemblance to our spirit; under colour that we know nothing more perfect than a human mind. We ought rather to believe, that as he comprehends the perfections of matter without being material . . . he comprehends also the perfections of created spirits, without being spirit, in the manner we conceive spirit: That his true name is, *He that is*, or in other words, Being without restriction, All Being, the Being infinite and universal."

After so great an authority, Demea, replied Philo, as that which you have produced, and a thousand more, which you might produce, it would appear ridiculous in me to add my sentiment, or express my approbation of your doctrine. But surely, where reasonable men treat these subjects, the question can never be concerning the being, but only the *nature* of the Deity. The former truth, as you well observe, is unquestionable and self-evident. Nothing exists without a cause; and the original cause of this universe (whatever it be) we call God; and piously ascribe to him every species of perfection. Whoever scruples this fundamental truth deserves every punishment, which can be inflicted among philosophers, to wit, the greatest ridicule, contempt and disapprobation. But as all perfection is entirely relative, we ought never to imagine, that we comprehend the attributes of this divine Being, or to suppose, that his perfections have any analogy or likeness to the perfections of a human creature. Wisdom, thought, design, knowledge; these we justly ascribe to him; because these words are honourable among men, and we have no other language or other conceptions, by which we can express our adoration of him. But let us beware, lest we think, that our ideas any wise correspond to his perfections, or that his attributes have any resemblance to these qualities among men. He is infinitely superior to our limited view and comprehension; and is more the object of worship in the temple, than of disputation in the schools.

In reality, Cleanthes, continued he, there is no need of having recourse to that affected scepticism, so displeasing to you, in order to come at this determination. Our ideas reach no farther than our experience: We have no experience of divine attributes and operations: I need not conclude my syllogism: You can draw the inference yourself. And it is a pleasure to me (and I hope to you too) that just reasoning and sound piety here concur in the same conclusion, and both of them establish the adorably mysterious and incomprehensible nature of the supreme Being.

Not to lose any time in circumlocutions, said Cleanthes, addressing himself to Demea, much less in replying to the pious declamations of Philo; I shall briefly explain how I conceive this matter. Look round the world: Contemplate the whole and every part of it: You will find it to be nothing but one great machine, subdivided into an infinite number of lesser machines, which again admit of subdivisions, to a degree beyond what human senses and faculties can trace and explain. All these various machines, and even their most minute parts, are adjusted to each other with an accuracy, which ravishes into admiration all men, who have ever contemplated them. The curious adapting of means to ends, throughout all nature, resembles exactly, though it much exceeds, the productions of human contrivance; of human design, thought, wisdom, and intelligence. Since therefore the effects resemble each other, we are led to infer, by all the rules of analogy, that the causes also resemble; and that the Author of nature is somewhat similar to the mind of man; though possessed of much larger faculties, proportioned to the grandeur of the work, which he has executed. By this argument *a posteriori*, and by this argument alone, we do prove at once the existence of a Deity, and his similarity to human mind and intelligence.

I shall be so free, Cleanthes, said Demea, as to tell you, that from the beginning, I could not approve of your conclusion concerning the similarity of the Deity to men; still less can I approve of the mediums, by which you endeavour to establish it. What! No demonstration of the being of a God! No abstract arguments! No proofs *a priori!* Are these, which have hitherto been so much insisted on by philosophers, all fallacy, all sophism? Can we reach no farther in this subject than experience and probability? I will not say, that this is betraying the cause of a Deity: But surely, by this affected candour, you give advantage to atheists, which they never could obtain, by the mere dint of argument and reasoning.

What I chiefly scruple in this subject, said Philo, is not so much, that all religious arguments are by Cleanthes reduced to experience, as that they appear not to be even the most certain and irrefragable of that inferior kind. That a stone will fall, that fire will burn, that the earth has solidity, we have observed a thousand and a thousand times; and when any new instance of this nature is presented, we draw without hesitation the accustomed inference. The exact similarity of the cases gives us a perfect assurance of a similar event; and a stronger evidence is never desired nor sought after. But wherever you depart, in the least, from the similarity of the cases, you diminish proportionably the evidence; and may at last bring it to a very weak *analogy*, which is confessedly liable to error and uncertainty. After having experienced the circulation of the blood in human creatures, we make no doubt that it takes place in Titius and Mævius: But from its circulation in frogs and fishes, it is only a presumption, though a strong one, from analogy, that it takes place in men and other animals. The analogical reasoning is much weaker, when we infer the circulation of the sap in vegetables from our experience that the blood circulates in animals; and those, who hastily followed that imperfect analogy, are found, by more accurate experiments, to have been mistaken.

If we see a house, Cleanthes, we conclude, with the greatest certainty, that it had an architect or builder; because this is precisely that species of effect, which we have experienced to proceed from that species of cause. But surely you will not affirm, that the universe bears such a resemblance to a house, that we can with the same certainty infer a similar cause, or that the analogy is here entire and perfect. The dissimilitude is so striking, that the utmost you can here pretend to is a guess, a conjecture, a presumption concerning a similar cause; and how that pretension will be received in the world, I leave you to consider.

It would surely be very ill received, replied Cleanthes; and I should be deservedly blamed and detested, did I allow that the proofs of a Deity amounted to no more than a guess or conjecture. But is the whole adjustment of means to ends in a house and in the universe so slight a resemblance? The œconomy of final causes? The order, proportion, and arrangement of every part? Steps of a stair are plainly contrived, that human legs may use them in mounting; and this inference is certain and infallible. Human legs are also contrived for walking and mounting; and this inference, I allow, is not altogether so certain, because of the dissimilarity which you remark; but does it, therefore, deserve the name only of presumption or conjecture?

Good God! cried Demea, interrupting him, where are we? Zealous defenders of religion allow, that the proofs of a Deity fall short of perfect evidence! And you, Philo, on whose assistance I depended, in proving the adorable mysteriousness of the divine nature, do you assent to all these extravagant opinions of Cleanthes? For what other name can I give them? Or why spare my censure, when such principles are advanced, supported by such an authority, before so young a man as Pamphilus?

You seem not to apprehend, replied Philo, that I argue with Cleanthes in his own way; and by showing him the dangerous consequences of his tenets, hope at last to reduce him to our opinion. But what sticks most with you, I observe, is the representation which Cleanthes has made of the argument *a posteriori;* and finding that that argument is likely to escape your hold and vanish into air, you think it so disguised that you can scarcely believe it to be set in its true light. Now, however much I may dissent, in other respects, from the dangerous principles of Cleanthes, I must allow, that he has fairly represented that argument; and I shall endeavour so to state the matter to you, that you will entertain no farther scruples with regard to it.

Were a man to abstract from every thing which he knows or has seen, he would be altogether incapable, merely from his own ideas, to determine what kind of scene the universe must be, or to give the preference to one state or situation of things above another. For as nothing, which he clearly conceives, could be esteemed impossible or implying a contradiction, every chimera of his fancy would be upon an equal footing; nor could he assign any just reason, why he adheres to one idea or system, and rejects the others, which are equally possible.

Again; after he opens his eyes, and contemplates the world, as it really is, it would be impossible for him, at first, to assign the cause of any one event; much less, of the whole of things or of the universe. He might set his fancy a rambling; and she might bring him in an infinite variety of reports and representations. These would all be possible; but being all equally possible, he would never, of himself, give a satisfactory account for his preferring one of them to the rest. Experience alone can point out to him the true cause of any phenomenon.

Now according to this method of reasoning, Demea, it follows (and is, indeed, tacitly allowed by Cleanthes himself) that order, arrangement, or the adjustment of final causes is not, of itself, any proof of design; but only so far as it has been experienced to proceed from that principle. For aught we can know *a priori*, matter may contain the source or spring of order originally, within itself, as well as mind does; and there is no more difficulty in conceiving, that the several elements, from an internal unknown cause, may fall into the most exquisite arrangement, than to conceive that their ideas, in the great, universal mind, from a like internal, unknown cause, fall into that arrangement. The equal possibility of both these suppositions is allowed. By experience we find (according to Cleanthes), that there is a difference between them. Throw several pieces of steel together, without shape or form; they will never arrange themselves so as to compose a watch: Stone, and mortar, and wood, without an architect, never erect a house. But the ideas in a human mind, we see, by an unknown, inexplicable œconomy, arrange themselves so as to form the plan of a watch or house. Experience, therefore, proves, that there is an original principle of order in mind, not in matter. From similar effects we infer similar causes. The adjustment of means to ends is alike in the universe, as in a machine of human contrivance. The causes, therefore, must be resembling.

I was from the beginning scandalised, I must own, with this resemblance, which is asserted, between the Deity and human creatures; and must conceive it to imply such a degradation of the supreme Being as no sound theist could endure. With your assistance, therefore, Demea, I shall endeavour to defend what you justly call the adorable mysteriousness of the divine nature, and shall refute this reasoning of Cleanthes; provided he allows, that I have made a fair representation of it.

When Cleanthes had assented, Philo, after a short pause, proceeded in the following manner.

That all inferences, Cleanthes, concerning fact, are rounded on experience, and that all experimental reasonings are founded on the supposition, that similar causes prove similar effects, and similar effects similar causes; I shall not, at present, much dispute with you. But observe, I entreat you, with what extreme caution all just reasoners proceed in the transferring of experiments to similar cases. Unless the cases be exactly similar, they repose no perfect confidence in applying their past observation to any particular phenomenon. Every alteration of circumstances occasions a doubt concerning the event; and it requires new experiments to prove certainly, that the new circumstances are of no moment or importance. A change in bulk, situation, arrangement, age, disposition of the air, or surrounding bodies; any of these particulars may be attended with the most unexpected consequences: And unless the objects be quite familiar to us, it is the highest temerity to expect with assurance, after any of these changes, an event similar to that which before fell under our observation. The slow and deliberate steps of philosophers, here, if any where, are distinguished from the precipitate march of the vulgar, who, hurried on by the smallest similitude, are incapable of all discernment or consideration.

But can you think, Cleanthes, that your usual phlegm and philosophy have been preserved in so wide a step as you have taken, when you compared to the universe houses, ships, furniture, machines; and from their similarity in some circumstances inferred a similarity in their causes? Thought, design, intelligence, such as we discover in men and other animals, is no more than one of the springs and principles of the universe, as well as heat or cold, attraction or repulsion, and a hundred others, which fall under daily observation. It is an active cause, by which some particular parts of nature, we find, produce alterations on other parts. But can a conclusion, with any propriety, be transferred from parts to the whole? Does not the great disproportion bar all comparison and inference? From observing the growth of a hair, can we learn any thing concerning the generation of a man? Would the manner of a leaf's blowing, even though perfectly known, afford us any instruction concerning the vegetation of a tree?

But allowing that we were to take the *operations* of one part of nature upon another for the foundation of our judgment concerning the *origin* of the whole (which never can be admitted) yet why select so minute, so weak, so bounded a principle as the reason and design of animals is found to be upon this planet? What peculiar privilege has this little agitation of the rain which we call thought, that we must thus make it the model of the whole universe? Our partiality in our own favour does indeed present it on all occasions: But sound philosophy ought carefully to guard against so natural an illusion.

So far from admitting, continued Philo, that the operations of a part can afford us any just conclusion concerning the origin of the whole, I will not allow any one part to form a rule for another part, if the latter be very remote from the former. Is there any reasonable ground to conclude, that the inhabitants of other planets possess thought, intelligence, reason, or any thing similar to these faculties in men? When nature has so extremely diversified her manner of operation in this small globe; can we imagine, that she incessantly copies herself throughout so immense a universe? And if thought, as we may well suppose, be confined merely to this narrow corner, and has even there so limited a sphere of action; with what propriety can we assign it for the original cause of all things? The narrow views of a peasant, who makes his domestic œconomy the rule for the government of kingdoms, is in comparison a pardonable sophism.

But were we ever so much assured, that a thought and reason, resembling the human, were to be found throughout the whole universe, and were its activity elsewhere vastly greater and more commanding than it appears in this globe: Yet I cannot see, why the operations of a world, constituted, arranged, adjusted, can with any propriety be extended to a world, which is in its embryo-state, and is advancing towards that constitution and arrangement. By observation, we know somewhat of the œconomy, action, and nourishment of a finished animal; but we must transfer with great caution that observation to the growth of a fetus in the womb, and still more, to the formation of an animalcule in the loins of its male parent. Nature, we find, even from our limited experience, possesses an infinite number of springs and principles, which incessantly discover themselves on every change of her position and situation. And what new and unknown principles would actuate her in so new and unknown a situation as that of the formation of a universe, we cannot, without the utmost temerity, pretend to determine.

(A very small part of this great system, during a very short time, is very imperfectly discovered to us: And do we thence pronounce decisively concerning the origin of the whole?)

Admirable conclusion! Stone, wood, brick, iron, brass have not, at this time, in this minute globe of earth, an order or arrangement without human art and contrivance: Therefore the universe could not originally attain its order and arrangement, without something similar to human art. But is a part of nature a rule for another part very wide of the former? Is it a rule for the whole? Is a very small part a rule for the universe? Is nature in one situation, a certain rule for nature in another situation, vastly different from the former?

And can you blame me, Cleanthes, if I here imitate the prudent reserve of Simonides, who, according to the noted story, being asked by Hiero, *What God was?* desired a day to think of it, and then two days more; and after that manner continually prolonged the term, without ever bringing in his definition or description? Could you even blame me, if I had answered at first, *that I did not know,* and was sensible that this subject lay vastly beyond the reach of my faculties? You might cry out sceptic and raillier as much as you pleased: But having found, in so many other subjects, much more familiar, the imperfections and even contradictions of human reason, I never should expect any success from its feeble conjectures, in a subject, so sublime, and so remote from the sphere of our observation. When two *species* of objects have always been observed to be conjoined together, I can *infer,* by custom, the existence of one wherever I see the existence of the other: And this I call an argument from experience. But how this argument can have place, where the objects, as in the present case, are single, individual, without parallel, or specific resemblance, may be difficult to explain. And will any man tell me with a serious countenance, that an orderly universe must arise from some thought and art, like the human; because we have experience of it? To ascertain this reasoning, it were requisite, that we had experience of the origin of worlds; and it is not sufficient surely, that we have seen ships and cities arise from human art and contrivance. . . .

Philo was proceeding in this vehement manner, somewhat between jest and earnest, as it appeared to me; when he observed some signs of impatience in Cleanthes, and then immediately stopped short. What I had to suggest, said Cleanthes, is only that you would not abuse terms, or make use of popular expressions to subvert philosophical reasonings. You know, that the vulgar often distinguish reason from experience, even where the question relates only to matter of fact and existence; though it is found, where that *reason* is properly analysed, that it is nothing but a species of experience. To prove by experience the origin of the universe from mind is not more contrary to common speech than to prove the motion of the earth from the same principle. And a caviller might raise all the same objections to the Copernican system, which you have urged against my reasonings. Have you other earths, might he say, which you have seen to move? Have . . .

Yes! cried Philo, interrupting him, we have other earths. Is not the moon another earth, which we see to turn round its centre? Is not Venus another earth, where we observe the same phenomenon? Are not the revolutions of the sun also a confirmation, from analogy, of the same theory? All the planets, are they not earths, which revolve about the sun? Are not the satellites moons, which move round Jupiter and Saturn, and along with these primary planets, round the sun? These analogies and resemblances, with others, which I have not mentioned, are the sole proofs of the Copernican system: And to you it belongs to consider, whether you have any analogies of the same kind to support your theory.

In reality, Cleanthes, continued he, the modern system of astronomy is now so much received by all enquirers, and has become so essential a part even of our earliest education, that we are not commonly very scrupulous in examining the reasons upon which it is founded. It is now become a matter of mere curiosity to study the first writers on that subject, who had the full force of prejudice to encounter, and were obliged to turn their arguments on every side, in order to render them popular and convincing. But if we peruse Galilæo's famous Dialogues concerning the system of the world, we shall find, that that great genius, one of the sublimest that ever existed, first bent all his endeavours to prove, that there was no foundation for the distinction commonly made between elementary and celestial substances. The schools, proceeding from the illusions of sense, had carried this distinction very far; and had established the latter substances to be ingenerable, incorruptible, unalterable, impassible; and had assigned all the opposite qualities to the former. But Galilæo, beginning with the moon, proved its similarity in every particular to the earth; its convex figure, its natural darkness when not illuminated, its density, its distinction into solid and liquid, the variations of its phases, the mutual illuminations of the earth and moon, their mutual eclipses, the inequalities of the lunar surface, etc. After many instances of this kind, with regard to all the planets, men plainly saw, that these bodies became proper objects of experience; and that the similarity of their nature enabled us to extend the same arguments and phenomena from one to the other.

In this cautious proceeding of the astronomers, you may read your own condemnation, Cleanthes; or rather may see, that the subject in which you are engaged exceeds all human reason and enquiry. Can you pretend to show any such similarity between the fabric of a house, and the generation of a universe? Have you ever seen nature in any such situation as resembles the first arrangement of the elements? Have worlds ever been formed under your eye? and have you had leisure to observe the whole progress of the phenomenon, from the first appearance of order to its final consummation? If you have, then cite your experience, and deliver your theory.

PART III

Now the most absurd argument, replied Cleanthes, in the hands of a man of ingenuity and invention, may acquire an air of probability! Are you not aware, Philo, that it became necessary for Copernicus and his first disciples to prove the similarity of the terrestrial and celestial matter; because several philosophers, blinded by old systems, and supported by some sensible appearances, had denied this similarity? But that it is by no means necessary, that theists should prove the similarity of the works of nature to those of art; because this similarity is self-evident and undeniable? The same matter, a like form: What more is requisite to show an analogy between their causes, and to ascertain the origin of all things from a divine purpose and intention? Your objections, I must freely tell you, are no better than the abstruse cavils of those philosophers, who denied motion; and ought to be refuted in the same manner, by illustrations, examples, and instances, rather than by serious argument and philosophy.

Suppose, therefore, that an articulate voice were heard in the clouds, much louder and more melodious than any which human art could ever reach: Suppose, that this voice were extended in the same instant over all nations, and spoke to each nation in its own language and dialect: Suppose, that the words delivered not only contain a just sense and meaning, but convey some instruction altogether worthy of a benevolent Being, superior to mankind: Could you possibly hesitate a moment concerning the cause of this voice? And must you not instantly ascribe it to some design or purpose? Yet I cannot see but all the same objections (if they merit that appellation) which lie against the system of theism, may also be produced against this inference.

Might you not say, that all conclusions concerning fact were founded on experience: That when we hear an articulate voice in the dark, and thence infer a man, it is only the resemblance of the effects, which leads us to conclude that there is a like resemblance in the cause: But that this extraordinary voice, by its loudness, extent, and flexibility to all languages, bears so little analogy to any human voice, that we have no reason to suppose any analogy in their causes: And consequently, that a rational, wise, coherent speech proceeded, you knew not whence, from some accidental whistling of the winds, not from any divine reason or intelligence? You see clearly your own objections in these cavils; and I hope too, you see clearly, that they cannot possibly have more force in the one case than in the other.

But to bring the case still nearer the present one of the universe, I shall make two suppositions, which imply not any absurdity or impossibility. Suppose, that there is a natural, universal, invariable language, common to every individual of human race; and that books are natural productions, which perpetuate themselves in the same manner with animals and vegetables, by descent and propagation. Several expressions of our passions contain a universal language: All brute animals have a natural speech, which, however limited, is very intelligible to their own species. And as there are infinitely fewer parts and less contrivance in the finest composition of eloquence, than in the coarsest organized body, the propagation of an *Iliad* or *Æneid* is an easier supposition than that of any plant or animal.

Suppose, therefore, that you enter into your library, thus peopled by natural volumes, containing the most refined reason and most exquisite beauty: Could you possibly open one of them, and doubt, that its original cause bore the strongest analogy to mind and intelligence? When it reasons and discourses; when it expostulates, argues, and enforces its views and topics; when it applies sometimes to the pure intellect, sometimes to the affections; when it collects, disposes, and adorns every consideration suited to the subject: could you persist in asserting, that all this, at the bottom, had really no meaning, and that the first formation of this volume in the loins of its original parent proceeded not from thought and design? Your obstinacy, I know, reaches not that degree of firmness: Even your sceptical play and wantonness would be abashed at so glaring an absurdity.

But if there be any difference, Philo, between this supposed case and the real one of the universe, it is all to the advantage of the latter. The anatomy of an animal affords many stronger instances of design than the perusal of Livy or Tacitus: And any objection which you start in the former case, by carrying me back to so unusual and extraordinary a scene as the first formation of worlds, the same objection has place on the supposition of our vegetating library. Choose, then, your party, Philo, without ambiguity or evasion: Assert either that a rational volume is no proof of a rational cause, or admit of a similar cause to all the works of nature.

Let me here observe too, continued Cleanthes, that this religious argument, instead of being weakened by that scepticism, so much affected by you, rather acquires force from it, and becomes more firm and undisputed. To exclude all argument or reasoning of every kind is either affectation or madness. The declared profession of every reasonable sceptic is only to reject abstruse, remote and refined arguments; to adhere to common sense and the plain instincts of nature; and to assent, wherever any reasons strike him with so full a force, that he cannot, without the greatest violence, prevent it. Now the arguments for natural religion are plainly of this kind; and nothing but the most perverse, obstinate metaphysics can reject them. Consider, anatomize the eye: Survey its structure and contrivance; and tell me, from your own feeling, if the idea of a contriver does not immediately flow in upon you with a force like that of sensation.

The most obvious conclusion surely is in favour of design; and it requires time, reflection and study, to summon up those frivolous, though abstruse, objections, which can support infidelity. Who can behold the male and female of each species, the correspondence of their parts and instincts, their passions and whole course of life before and after generation, but must be sensible, that the propagation of the species is intended by nature? Millions and millions of such instances present themselves through every part of the universe; and no language can convey a more intelligible, irresistible meaning, than the curious adjustment of final causes. To what degree, therefore, of blind dogmatism must one have attained, to reject such natural and such convincing arguments?

(Some beauties in writing we may meet with, which seem contrary to rules, and which gain the affections, and animate the imagination, in opposition to all the precepts of criticism, and to the authority of the established masters of art. And if the argument for theism be, as you pretend, contradictory to the principles of logic: its universal, its irresistible influence proves clearly, that there may be arguments of a like irregular nature. Whatever cavils may be urged; an orderly world, as well as a coherent, articulate speech, will still be received as an incontestable proof of design and intention.)

It sometimes happens, I own, that the religious arguments have not their due influence on an ignorant savage and barbarian; not because they are obscure and difficult, but because he never asks himself any question with regard to them. Whence arises the curious structure of an animal? From the copulation of its parents. And these whence? From *their* parents. A few removes set the objects at such a distance, that to him they are lost in darkness and confusion; nor is he actuated by any curiosity to trace them farther. But this is neither dogmatism nor scepticism, but stupidity; a state of mind very different from your sifting, inquisitive disposition, my ingenious friend. You can trace causes from effects: You can compare the most distant and remote objects: And your greatest errors proceed not from barrenness of thought and invention, but from too luxuriant a fertility, which suppresses your natural good sense, by a profusion of unnecessary scruples and objections.

Here I could observe, Hermippus, that Philo was a little embarrassed and confounded: But while he hesitated in delivering an answer, luckily for him, Demea broke in upon the discourse, and saved his countenance.

Your instance, Cleanthes, said he, drawn from books and language, being familiar, has, I confess, so much more force on that account; but is there not some danger too in this very circumstance, and may it not render us presumptuous, by making us imagine we comprehend the Deity, and have some adequate idea of his nature and attributes? When I read a volume, I enter into the mind and intention of the author: I become him, in a manner, for the instant; and have an immediate feeling and conception of those ideas, which revolved in his imagination, while employed in that composition. But so near an approach we never surely can make to the Deity. His ways are not our ways. His attributes are perfect, but incomprehensible. And this volume of nature contains a great and inexplicable riddle, more than any intelligible discourse or reasoning.

The ancient Platonists, you know, were the most religious and devout of all the pagan philosophers: Yet many of them, particularly Plotinus, expressly declare, that intellect or understanding is not to be ascribed to the Deity, and that our most perfect worship of him consists, not in acts of veneration, reverence, gratitude or love; but in a certain mysterious self-annihilation or total extinction of all our faculties. These ideas are, perhaps, too far stretched; but still it must be acknowledged, that, by representing the Deity as so intelligible, and comprehensible, and so similar to a human mind, we are guilty of the grossest and most narrow partiality, and make our selves the model of the whole universe.

All the *sentiments* of the human mind, gratitude, resentment, love, friendship, approbation, blame, pity, emulation, envy, have a plain reference to the state and situation of man, and are calculated for preserving the existence, and promoting the activity of such a being in such circumstances. It seems therefore unreasonable to transfer such sentiments to a supreme existence, or to suppose him actuated by them; and the phenomena, besides, of the universe will not support us in such a theory. All our *ideas*, derived from the senses, are confessedly false and illusive; and cannot, therefore, be supposed to have place in a supreme intelligence: And as the ideas of internal sentiment, added to those of the external senses, compose the whole furniture of human understanding, we may conclude, that none of the *materials* of thought are in any respect similar in the human and in the divine intelligence. Now, as to the *manner* of thinking; how can we make any comparison between them, or suppose them any wise resembling? Our thought is fluctuating, uncertain, fleeting, successive, and compounded; and were we to remove these circumstances, we absolutely annihilate its essence, and it would, in such a case, be an abuse of terms to apply to it the name of thought or reason. At least, if it appear more pious and respectful (as it really is) still to retain these terms, when we mention the supreme Being, we ought to acknowledge, that their meaning, in that case, is totally incomprehensible; and that the infirmities of our nature do not permit us to reach any ideas, which in the least correspond to the ineffable sublimity of the divine attributes.

PART IV

It seems strange to me, said Cleanthes, that you, Demea, who are so sincere in the cause of religion, should still maintain the mysterious, incomprehensible nature of the Deity, and should insist so strenuously, that he has no manner of likeness or resemblance to human creatures. The Deity, I can readily allow, possesses many powers and attributes, of which we can have no comprehension: But if our ideas, so far as they go, be not just and adequate, and correspondent to his real nature, I know not what there is in this subject worth insisting on. Is the name, without any meaning, of such mighty importance? Or how do you mystics, who maintain the absolute incomprehensibility of the Deity, differ from sceptics or atheists, who assert, that the first cause of All is unknown and unintelligible? Their temerity must be very great, if, after rejecting the production by a mind; I mean, a mind resembling the human (for I know of no other), they pretend to assign, with certainty, any other specific, intelligible cause: And their conscience must be very scrupulous indeed, if they refuse to call the universal, unknown cause a God or Deity; and to bestow on him as many sublime eulogies and unmeaning epithets, as you shall please to require of them.

Who could imagine, replied Demea, that Cleanthes, the calm, philosophical Cleanthes, would attempt to refute his antagonists, by affixing a nick-name to them; and like the common bigots and inquisitors of the age, have recourse to invective and declamation, instead of reasoning? Or does he not perceive, that these topics are easily retorted, and that *anthropomorphite* is an appellation as invidious, and implies as dangerous consequences, as the epithet of *mystic*, with which he has honoured us? In reality, Cleanthes, consider what it is you assert, when you represent the Deity as similar to a human mind and understanding. What is the soul of man? A composition of various faculties, passions, sentiments, ideas; united, indeed, into one self or person, but still distinct from each other. When it reasons, the ideas, which are the parts of its discourse, arrange themselves in a certain form or order; which is not preserved entire for a moment, but immediately gives place to another arrangement. New opinions, new passions, new affections, new feelings arise, which continually diversify the mental scene, and produce in it the greatest variety, and most rapid succession imaginable. How is this compatible with that perfect immutability and simplicity, which all true theists ascribe to the Deity? By the same act, say they, he sees past, present, and future: His love and his hatred, his mercy and his justice are one individual operation: He is entire in every point of space; and complete in every instant of duration. No succession, no change, no acquisition, no diminution. What he is implies not in it any shadow of distinction or diversity. And what he is, this moment, he ever has been, and ever will be, without any new judgment, sentiment, or operation. He stands fixed in one simple, perfect state; nor can you ever say, with any propriety, that this act of his is different from that other, or that this judgment or idea has been lately formed, and will give place, by succession, to any different judgment or idea.

I can readily allow, said Cleanthes, that those who maintain the perfect simplicity of the supreme Being, to the extent in which you have explained it, are complete *mystics*, and chargeable with all the consequences which I have drawn from their opinion. They are, in a word, atheists, without knowing it. For though it be allowed, that the Deity possesses attributes, of which we have no comprehension; yet ought we never to ascribe to him any attributes, which are absolutely incompatible with that intelligent nature, essential to him. A mind, whose acts and sentiments and ideas are not distinct and successive; one, that is wholly simple, and totally immutable; is a mind which has no thought, no reason, no will, no sentiment, no love, no hatred; or in a word, is no mind at all. It is an abuse of terms to give it that appellation; and we may as well speak of limited extension without figure, or of number without composition.

Pray consider, said Philo, whom you are at present inveighing against. You are honouring with the appellation of atheist all the sound, orthodox divines almost, who have treated of this subject; and you will, at last, be, yourself, found, according to your reckoning, the only sound theist in the world. But if idolaters be atheists, as, I think may justly be asserted, and Christian theologians the same; what becomes of the argument, so much celebrated, derived from the universal consent of mankind?

But because I know you are not much swayed by names and authorities, I shall endeavour to show you, a little more distinctly, the inconveniences of that anthropomorphism, which you have embraced; and shall prove, that there is no ground to suppose a plan of the world to be formed in the divine mind, consisting of distinct ideas, differently arranged; in the same manner as an architect forms in his head the plan of a house which he intends to execute.

It is not easy, I own, to see, what is gained by this supposition, whether we judge of the matter by *reason* or by *experience*. We are still obliged to mount higher, in order to find the cause of this cause, which you had assigned as satisfactory and conclusive.

If reason (I mean abstract reason, derived from enquiries *a priori*) be not alike mute with regard to all questions concerning cause and effect; this sentence at least it will venture to pronounce, That a mental world or universe of ideas requires a cause as much as does a material world or universe of objects; and if similar in its arrangement must require a similar cause. For what is there in this subject, which should occasion a different conclusion or inference? In an abstract view, they are entirely alike; and no difficulty attends the one supposition, which is not common to both of them.

Again, when we will needs force *experience* to pronounce some sentence, even on these subjects, which lie beyond her sphere; neither can she perceive any material difference in this particular, between these two kinds of worlds, but finds them to be governed by similar principles, and to depend upon an equal variety of causes in their operations. We have specimens in miniature of both of them. Our own mind resembles the one: A vegetable or animal body the other. Let experience, therefore, judge from these samples. Nothing seems more delicate with regard to its causes than thought; and as these causes never operate in two persons after the same manner, so we never find two persons, who think exactly alike. Nor indeed does the same person think exactly alike at any two different periods of time. A difference of age, of the disposition of his body, of weather, of food, of company, of books, of passions; any of these particulars or others more minute, are sufficient to alter the curious machinery of thought, and communicate to it very different movements and operations. As far as we can judge, vegetables and animal bodies are not more delicate in their motions, nor depend upon a greater variety or more curious adjustment of springs and principles.

How therefore shall we satisfy ourselves concerning the cause of that Being, whom you suppose the Author of nature, or, according to your system of anthropomorphism, the ideal world, into which you trace the material? Have we not the same reason to trace that ideal world into another ideal world, or new intelligent principle? But if we stop, and go no farther; why go so far? Why not stop at the material world? How can we satisfy ourselves without going on *in infinitum?* And after all, what satisfaction is there in that infinite progression? Let us remember the story of the Indian philosopher and his elephant. It was never more applicable than to the present subject. If the material world rests upon a similar ideal world, this ideal world must rest upon some other; and so on, without end. It were better, therefore, never to look beyond the present material world. By supposing it to contain the principle of its order within itself, we really assert it to be God; and the sooner we arrive at that divine Being so much the better. When you go one step beyond the mundane system you only excite an inquisitive humour, which it is impossible ever to satisfy.

To say, that the different ideas, which compose the reason of the supreme Being, fall into order, of themselves, and by their own nature, is really to talk without any precise meaning. If it has a meaning, I would fain know, why it is not as good sense to say, that the parts of the material world fall into order, of themselves, and by their own nature? Can the one opinion be intelligible, while the other is not so?

We have, indeed, experience of ideas, which fall into order, of themselves, and without any *known* cause: But, I am sure, we have a much larger experience of matter, which does the same; as in all instances of generation and vegetation, where the accurate analysis of the cause exceeds all human comprehension. We have also experience of particular systems of thought and of matter, which have no order; of the first, in madness, of the second, in corruption. Why then should we think, that order is more essential to one than the other? And if it requires a cause in both, what do we gain by your system, in tracing the universe of objects into a similar universe of ideas? The first step, which we make, leads us on for ever. It were, therefore, wise in us, to limit all our enquiries to the present world, without looking farther. No satisfaction can ever be attained by these speculations, which so far exceed the narrow bounds of human understanding.

It was usual with the Peripatetics, you know, Cleanthes, when the cause of any phenomenon was demanded, to have recourse to their *faculties* or *occult qualities,* and to say, for instance, that bread nourished by its nutritive faculty, and senna purged by its purgative: But it has been discovered, that this subterfuge was nothing but the disguise of ignorance; and that these philosophers, though less ingenuous, really said the same thing with the sceptics or the vulgar, who fairly confessed, that they knew not the cause of these phenomena. In like manner, when it is asked, what cause produces order in the ideas of the supreme Being, can any other reason be assigned by you, anthropomorphites, than that it is a *rational* faculty, and that such is the nature of the Deity? But why a similar answer will not be equally satisfactory in accounting for the order of the world, without having recourse to any such intelligent Creator as you insist on, may be difficult to determine. It is only to say, that *such* is the nature of material objects, and that they are all originally possessed of a *faculty* of order and proportion. These are only more learned and elaborate ways of confessing our ignorance; nor has the one hypothesis any real advantage above the other, except in its greater conformity to vulgar prejudices.

You have displayed this argument with great emphasis, replied Cleanthes: You seem not sensible, how easy it is to answer it. Even in common life, if I assign a cause for any event; is it any objection, Philo, that I cannot assign the cause of that cause, and answer every new question, which may incessantly be started? And what philosophers could possibly submit to so rigid a rule? philosophers, who confess ultimate causes to be totally unknown, and are sensible, that the most refined principles, into which they trace the phenomena, are still to them as inexplicable as these phenomena themselves are to the vulgar. The order and arrangement of nature, the curious adjustment of final causes, the plain use and intention of every part and organ; all these bespeak in the clearest language an intelligent cause or Author. The heavens and the earth join in the same testimony: The whole chorus of nature raises one hymn to the praises of its Creator: You alone, or almost alone, disturb this general harmony. You start abstruse doubts, cavils, and objections: You ask me, what is the cause of this cause? I know not; I care not; that concerns not me. I have found a Deity; and here I stop my enquiry. Let those go farther, who are wiser or more enterprising.

(I pretend to be neither, replied Philo: And for that very reason, I should never perhaps have attempted to go so far; especially when I am sensible, that I must at last be contented to sit down with the same answer, which, without farther trouble, might have satisfied me from the beginning. If I am still to remain in utter ignorance of causes, and can absolutely give an explication of nothing, I shall never esteem it any advantage to shove off for a moment a difficulty, which, you acknowledge, must immediately, in its full force, recur upon me. Naturalists indeed very justly explain particular effects by more general causes; though these general causes themselves should remain in the end totally inexplicable: But they never surely thought it satisfactory to explain a particular effect by a particular cause, which was no more to be accounted for than the effect itself.) An ideal system, arranged of itself, without a precedent design, it not a whit more explicable than a material one, which attains its order in a like manner; nor is there any more difficulty in the latter supposition than in the former.

PART V

But to show you still more inconveniences, continued Philo, in your anthropomorphism; please to take a new survey of your principles. *Like effects prove like causes.* This is the experimental argument; and this, you say too, is the sole theological argument. Now it is certain, that the liker the effects are, which are seen, and the liker the causes, which are inferred, the stronger is the argument. Every departure on either side diminishes the probability, and renders the experiment less conclusive. You cannot doubt of this principle: Neither ought you to reject its consequences.

All the new discoveries in astronomy, which prove the immense grandeur and magnificence of the works of nature, are so many additional arguments for a Deity, according to the true system of theism: But according to your hypothesis of experimental theism, they become so many objections, by removing the effect still farther from all resemblance to the effects of human art and contrivance. For if Lucretius, even following the old system of the world, could exclaim,

Quis regere immensi summam, quis habere profundi Indu manu validas potis est moderanter habenas? Quis pariter cœlos omnes convertere? et omnes Ignibus ætheriis tetras suffire feraces? Omnibus inve locis esse omni tempore præsto?*

If Tully esteemed this reasoning so natural, as to put it into the mouth of his Epicurean:

Quibus enim oculis animi intueri potuit vester Plato fabricam illam tanti operis, qua construi a Deo atque ædificari mundum facit? quæ molitio? quæ ferramenta? qui vectes? quæ machinæ? qui ministri tanti muneris fuerunt? quemadmodum autem obedire et arere voluntati architecti aer, ignis, aqua, tetra potuerunt?**

If this argument, I say, had any force in former ages; how much greater must it have at present; when the bounds of nature are so infinitely enlarged, and such a magnificent scene is opened to us? It is still more unreasonable to form our idea of so unlimited a cause from our experience of the narrow productions of human design and invention.

The discoveries by microscopes, as they open a new universe in miniature, are still objections, according to you; arguments, according to me. The farther we push our researches of this kind, we are still led to infer the universal cause of All to be vastly different from mankind, or from any object of human experience and observation.

And what say you to the discoveries in anatomy, chemistry, botany? . . . These surely are no objections, replied Cleanthes: They only discover new instances of art and contrivance. It is still the image of mind reflected on us from unnumerable objects. Add, a mind *like the human,* said Philo. I know of no other, replied Cleanthes. And the liker the better, insisted Philo. To be sure, said Cleanthes.

Now, Cleanthes, said Philo, with an air of alacrity and triumph, mark the consequences. *First,* By this method of reasoning, you renounce all claim to infinity in any of the attributes of the Deity. For as the cause ought only to be proportioned to the effect, and the effect, so far as it falls under our cognisance, is not infinite; what pretensions have we, upon your suppositions, to ascribe that attribute to the divine Being? You will still insist, that, by removing him so much from all similarity to human creatures, we give into the most arbitrary hypothesis, and at the same time weaken all proofs of his existence.

Secondly, You have no reason, on your theory, for ascribing perfection to the Deity, even in his finite capacity; or for supposing him free from every error, mistake, or incoherence in his undertakings. There are many inexplicable difficulties in the works of nature, which, if we allow a perfect Author to be proved *a priori,* are easily solved, and become only seeming difficulties, from the narrow capacity of man, who cannot trace infinite relations. But according to your method of reasoning, these difficulties become all real; and perhaps will be insisted on, as new instances of likeness to human art and contrivance. At least, you must acknowledge, that it is impossible for us to tell, from our limited views, whether this system contains any great faults, or deserves any considerable praise, if compared to other possible, and even real systems. Could a peasant, if the *Æneid* were read to him, pronounce that poem to be absolutely

---

*"Who can rule the sun, who hold in his hand with controlling force the strong reins, of the immeasurable deep? Who can at least make all the different heavens to roll and warm with ethereal fires all the fruitful earths, or be present in all places at all times?" *De Rerum Natura,* Bk. XI, Chap. 2.

**"For with what eyes of the mind could your Plato see the construction of so vast a work which, according to him, God was putting together and building? What materials, what tools, what bars, what machines, what servants were employed in such gigantic work? How could the air, fire, water, and earth pay obedience and submit to the will of the architect?" *De Natura Deorum,* Bk. I, Chap. 8.

faultless, or even assign to it its proper rank among the productions of human wit; he, who had never seen any other production?

But were this world ever so perfect a production, it must still remain uncertain, whether all the excellencies of the work can justly be ascribed to the workman. If we survey a ship, what an exalted idea must we form of the ingenuity of the carpenter, who framed so complicated, useful, and beautiful a machine? And what surprise must we entertain, when we find him a stupid mechanic, who imitated others, and copied an art, which, through a long succession of ages, after multiplied trials, mistakes, corrections, deliberations, and controversies, had been gradually improving? Many worlds might have been botched and bungled, throughout an eternity, ere this system was struck out: Much labour lost: Many fruitless trials made: And a slow, but continued improvement carried on during infinite ages in the art of world-making. In such subjects, who can determine, where the truth; nay, who can conjecture where the probability, lies; amidst a great number of hypotheses which may be proposed, and a still greater number which may be imagined?

And what shadow of an argument, continued Philo, can you produce, from your hypothesis, to prove the unity of the Deity? A great number of men join in building a house or ship, in rearing a city, in framing a commonwealth: Why may not several Deities combine in contriving and framing a world? This is only so much greater similarity to human affairs. By sharing the work among several, we may so much farther limit the attributes of each, and get rid of that extensive power and knowledge, which must be supposed in one Deity, and which, according to you, can only serve to weaken the proof of his existence. And if such foolish, such vicious creatures as man can yet often unite in framing and executing one plan; how much more those Deities or Dæmons, whom we may suppose several degrees more perfect?

To multiply causes, without necessity, is indeed contrary to true philosophy: But this principle applies not to the present case. Were one Deity antecedently proved by your theory, who were possessed of every attribute requisite to the production of the universe; it would be needless, I own (though not absurd) to suppose any other Deity existent. But while it is still a question, whether all these attributes are united in one subject, or dispersed among several independent Beings: By what phenomena in nature can we pretend to decide the controversy? Where we see a body raised in a scale, we are sure that there is in the opposite scale, however concealed from sight, some counterpoising weight equal to it: But it is still allowed to doubt, whether that weight be an aggregate of several distinct bodies, or one uniform united mass. And if the weight requisite very much exceeds any thing which we have ever seen conjoined in any single body, the former supposition becomes still more probable and natural. An intelligent Being of such vast power and capacity, as is necessary to produce the universe, or, to speak in the language of ancient philosophy, so prodigious an animal, exceeds all analogy, and even comprehension.

But farther, Cleanthes; men are mortal, and renew their species by generation; and this is common to all living creatures. The two great sexes of male and female, says Milton, animate the world. Why must this circumstance, so universal, so essential, be excluded from those numerous and limited Deities? Behold then the theogony of ancient times brought back upon us.

And why not become a perfect anthropomorphite? Why not assert the Deity or Deities to be corporeal, and to have eyes, a nose, mouth, ears, etc.? Epicurus maintained, that no man had ever seen reason but in a human figure; therefore the gods must have a human figure. And this argument, which is deservedly so much ridiculed by Cicero, becomes, according to you, solid and philosophical.

In a word, Cleanthes, a man, who follows your hypothesis, is able, perhaps, to assert, or conjecture, that the universe, sometime, arose from something like design: But beyond that position he cannot ascertain one single circumstance, and is left afterwards to fix every point of his theology, by the utmost licence of fancy and hypothesis. This world, for aught he knows, is very faulty and imperfect, compared to a superior standard; and was only the first rude essay of some infant Deity, who afterwards abandoned it, ashamed of his lame performance; it is the work only of some dependent, inferior Deity; and is the object of derision to his superiors: it is the production of old age and dotage in some superannuated Deity; and ever since his death, has run on at adventures, from the first impulse and active force, which it received from him. . . . You justly give signs of horror, Demea, at these strange suppositions: But these, and a thousand more of the same kind, are Cleanthes's suppositions, not mine. From the moment the attributes of the Deity are supposed finite, all these have place. And I cannot, for my part, think, that so wild and unsettled a system of theology is, in any respect, preferable to none at all.

These suppositions I absolutely disown, cried Cleanthes: They strike me, however, with no horror; especially, when proposed in that rambling way in which they drop from you. On the contrary, they give me pleasure, when I see, that, by the utmost indulgence of your imagination, you never get rid of the hypothesis of design in the universe; but are obliged, at every turn, to have recourse to it. To this concession I adhere steadily; and this I regard as a sufficient foundation for religion.

PART VI

It must be a slight fabric, indeed, said Demea, which can be erected on so tottering a foundation. While we are uncertain, whether there is one Deity or many; whether the Deity or Deities, to whom we owe our existence, be perfect or imperfect, subordinate or supreme, dead or alive; what trust or confidence can we repose in them? What devotion or worship address to them? What veneration or obedience pay them? To all the purposes of life, the theory of religion becomes altogether useless: And even with regard to speculative consequences, its uncertainty, according to you, must render it totally precarious and unsatisfactory.

To render it still more unsatisfactory, said Philo, there occurs to me another hypothesis, which must acquire an air of probability from the method of reasoning so much insisted on by Cleanthes. That like effects arise from like causes: This principle he supposes the foundation of all religion. But there is another principle of the same kind, no less certain, and derived from the same source of experience; that where several known circumstances are *observed* to be similar, the unknown will also be *found* similar. Thus, if we see the limbs of a human body, we conclude, that it is also attended with a human head, though hid from us. Thus, if we see, through a chink in a wall, a small part of the sun, we conclude, that, were the wall removed, we should see the whole body. In short, this method of reasoning is so obvious and familiar, that no scruple can ever be made with regard to its solidity.

Now if we survey the universe, so far as it falls under our knowledge, it bears a great resemblance to an animal or organized body, and seems actuated with a like principle of life and motion. A continual circulation of matter in it produces no disorder: A continual waste in every part is incessantly repaired: The closest sympathy is perceived throughout the entire system: And each part or member, in performing its proper offices, operates both to its own preservation and to that of the whole. The world, therefore, I infer, is an animal, and the Deity is the soul of the world, actuating it, and actuated by it.

You have too much learning, Cleanthes, to be at all surprised at this opinion, which, you know, was maintained by almost all the theists of antiquity, and chiefly prevails in their discourses and reasonings. For though sometimes the ancient philosophers reason from final causes, as if they thought the world the workmanship of God; yet it appears rather their favourite notion to consider it as his body, whose organization renders it subservient to him. And it must be confessed, that as the universe resembles more a human body than it does the works of human art and contrivance; if our limited analogy could ever, with any propriety, be extended to the whole of nature, the inference seems juster in favour of the ancient than the modern theory.

There are many other advantages too, in the former theory, which recommended it to the ancient theologians. Nothing more repugnant to all their notions, because nothing more repugnant to common experience, than mind without body; a mere spiritual substance, which fell not under their senses nor comprehension, and of which they had not observed one single instance throughout all nature. Mind and body they knew, because they felt both: An order, arrangement, organization, or internal machinery in both they likewise knew, after the same manner: And it could not but seem reasonable to transfer this experience to the universe, and to suppose the divine mind and body to be also coevala, and to have, both of them, order and arrangement naturally inherent in them, and inseparable from them.

Here therefore is a new species of anthropomorphism, Cleanthes, on which you may deliberate; and a theory which seems not liable to any considerable difficulties. You are too much superior surely to *systematical prejudices,* to find any more difficulty in supposing an animal body to be, originally, of itself, or from unknown causes, possessed of order and organization, than in supposing a similar order to belong to mind. But the *vulgar prejudice,* that body and mind ought always to accompany each other, ought not, one should think, to be entirely neglected; since it is founded on *vulgar experience,* the only guide which you profess to follow in all these theological inquiries. And if you assert, that our limited experience is an unequal standard, by which to judge of the unlimited extent of nature; you entirely abandon your own hypothesis, and must thenceforward adopt our mysticism, as you call it, and admit of the absolute incomprehensibility of the divine nature.

This theory, I own, replied Cleanthes, has never before occurred to me, though a pretty natural one; and I cannot readily, upon so short an examination and reflection, deliver any opinion with regard to it. You are very scrupulous, indeed, said Philo; were I to examine any system of yours, I should not have acted with half that caution and reserve, in starting objections and difficulties to it. However, if any thing occur to you, you will oblige us by proposing it.

Why then, replied Cleanthes, it seems to me that, though the world does, in many circumstances, resemble an animal body; yet is the analogy also effective in many circumstances, the most material: No organs of sense; no seat of thought or reason; no one precise origin of motion and action. In short, it seems to bear a stronger resemblance to a vegetable than to an animal; and your inference would be so far inconclusive in favour of the soul of the world.

But in the next place, your theory seems to imply the eternity of the world; and that is a principle which, I think, can be refuted by the strongest reasons and probabilities. I shall suggest an argument to this purpose, which, I believe, has not been insisted on by any writer. Those, who reason from the late origin of arts and sciences, though their inference wants not force, may perhaps be refuted by considerations derived from the nature of human society, which is in continual revolution between ignorance and knowledge, liberty and slavery, riches and poverty; so that it is impossible for us, from our limited experience, to foretell with assurance what events may or may not be expected. Ancient learning and history seem to have been in great danger of entirely perishing after the inundation of the barbarous nations; and had these convulsions continued a little longer, or been a little more violent, we should not probably have now known what passed in the world a few centuries before us. Nay, were it not for the superstition of the Popes, who preserved a little jargon of Latin, in order to support the appearance of an ancient and universal church, that tongue must have been utterly lost: In which case, the Western world, being totally barbarous, would not have been in a fit disposition for receiving the Greek language and learning, which was conveyed to them after the sacking of Constantinople. When learning and books had been extinguished, even the mechanical arts would have fallen considerably to decay; and it is easily imagined, that fable or tradition might ascribe to them a much later origin than the true one. This vulgar argument, therefore, against the eternity of the world, seems a little precarious.

But here appears to be the foundation of a better argument. Lucullus was the first that brought cherry-trees from Asia to Europe; though that tree thrives so well in many European climates, that it grows in the woods without any culture. Is it possible, that, throughout a whole eternity, no European had ever passed into Asia, and thought of transplanting so delicious a fruit into his own country? Or if the tree was once transplanted and propagated, how could it ever afterwards perish? Empires may rise and fall; liberty and slavery succeed alternately; ignorance and knowledge give place to each other; but the cherry-tree will still remain in the woods of Greece, Spain and Italy, and will never be affected by the revolutions of human society.

It is not two thousand years since vines were transplanted into France; though there is no climate in the world more favourable to them. It is not three centuries since horses, cows, sheep, swine, dogs, corn, were known in America. Is it possible, that, during the revolutions of a whole eternity, there never arose a Columbus, who might open the communication between Europe and that continent? We may as well imagine, that all men would wear stockings for ten thousand years, and never have the sense to think of garters to tie them. All these seem convincing proofs of the youth, or rather infancy, of the world; as being founded on the operation of principles more constant and steady than those by which human society is governed and directed. Nothing less than a total convulsion of the elements will ever destroy all the European animals and vegetables, which are now to be found in the Western world.

And what argument have you against such convulsions? replied Philo. Strong and almost incontestable proofs may be traced over the whole earth, that every part of this globe has continued for many ages entirely covered with water. And though order were supposed inseparable from matter, and inherent in it; yet may matter be susceptible of many and great revolutions, through the endless periods of eternal duration. The incessant changes, to which every part of it is subject, seem to intimate some such general transformations; though at the same time, it is observable, that all the changes and corruptions, of which we have ever had experience, are but passages from one state of order to another; nor can matter ever rest in total deformity and confusion. What we see in the parts, we may infer in the whole; at least, that is the method of reasoning on which you rest your whole theory. And were I obliged to defend any particular system of this nature (which I never willingly should do), I esteem none more plausible than that which ascribes an eternal, inherent principle of order to the world; though attended with great and continual revolutions and alterations. This at once solves all difficulties;

and if the solution, by being so general, is not entirely complete and satisfactory, it is, at least, a theory, that we must, sooner or later, have recourse to, whatever system we embrace. How could things have been as they are, were there not an original, inherent principle of order somewhere, in thought or in matter? And it is very indifferent to which of these we give the preference. Chance has no place, on any hypothesis, sceptical or religious. Every thing is surely governed by steady, inviolable laws. And were the inmost essence of things laid open to us, we should then discover a scene, of which, at present, we can have no idea. Instead of admiring the order of natural beings, we should clearly see, that it was absolutely impossible for them, in the smallest article, ever to admit of any other disposition.

Were any one inclined to revive the ancient Pagan Theology, which maintained, as we learn from Hesiod, that this globe was governed by 30,000 Deities, who arose from the unknown powers of nature: You would naturally object, Cleanthes, that nothing is gained by this hypothesis, and that it is as easy to suppose all men and animals, beings more numerous, but less perfect, to have sprung immediately from a like origin. Push the same inference a step farther; and you will find a numerous society of Deities as explicable as one universal Deity, who possesses, within himself, the powers and perfections of the whole society. All these systems, then, of scepticism, polytheism, and theism, you must allow, on your principles, to be on a like footing, and that no one of them has any advantages over the others. You may thence learn the fallacy of your principles.

PART VII

But here, continued Philo, in examining the ancient system of the soul of the world, there strikes me, all on a sudden, a new idea, which, if just, must go near to subvert all your reasoning, and destroy even your first inferences, on which you repose such confidence. If the universe bears a greater likeness to animal bodies and to vegetables, than to the works of human art, it is more probable that its cause resembles the cause of the former than that of the latter, and its origin ought rather to be ascribed to generation or vegetation than to reason or design. Your conclusion, even according to your own principles, is therefore lame and defective.

Pray open up this argument a little farther, said Demea. For I do not rightly apprehend it, in that concise manner in which you have expressed it.

Our friend, Cleanthes, replied Philo, as you have heard, asserts, that since no question of fact can be proved otherwise than by experience, the existence of a Deity admits not of proof from any other medium. The world, says he, resembles the works of human contrivance: Therefore its cause must also resemble that of the other. Here we may remark, that the operation of one very small part of nature, to wit man, upon another very small part, to wit that inanimate matter lying within his reach, is the rule by which Cleanthes judges of the origin of the whole; and he measures objects, so widely disproportioned, by the same individual standard. But to waive all objections drawn from this topic; I affirm, that there are other parts of the universe (besides the machines of human invention) which bear still a greater resemblance to the fabric of the world, and which therefore afford a better conjecture concerning the universal origin of this system. These parts are animals and vegetables. The world plainly resembles more an animal or a vegetable, than it does a watch or a knitting-loom. Its cause, therefore, it is more probable, resembles the cause of the former. The cause of the former is generation or vegetation. The cause, therefore, of the world, we may infer to be some thing similar or analogous to generation or vegetation.

A Philosopher Giving a Lecture at the Orrery, ca. 1763–1765, by Joseph Wright of Derby (1734–1797). Using a lamp to represent the sun, this model represents the universe as a gigantic clocklike mechanism—an analogy that Hume questioned. (*Derby Art Gallery Collection*)

But how is it conceivable, said Demea, that the world can arise from any thing similar to vegetation or generation?

Very easily, replied Philo. In like manner as a tree sheds its seed into the neighbouring fields, and produces other trees; so the great vegetable, the world, or this planetary system, produces within itself certain seeds, which, being scattered into the surrounding chaos, vegetate into new worlds. A comet, for instance, is the seed of a world; and after it has been fully ripened, by passing from sun to sun, and star to star, it is at last tossed into the unformed elements, which everywhere surround this universe, and immediately sprouts up into a new system.

Or if, for the sake of variety (for I see no other advantage), we should suppose this world to be an animal; a comet is the egg of this animal; and in like manner as an ostrich lays its egg in the sand, which, without any farther care, hatches the egg, and produces a new animal; so . . .

I understand you, says Demea: But what wild, arbitrary suppositions are these? What *data* have you for such extraordinary conclusions? And is the slight, imaginary resemblance of the world to a vegetable or an animal sufficient to establish the same inference with regard to both? Objects, which are in general so widely different; ought they to be a standard for each other?

Right, cries Philo: This is the topic on which I have all along insisted. I have still asserted, that we have no *data* to establish any system of cosmogony. Our experience, so imperfect in itself, and so limited both in extent and duration, can afford us no probable conjecture concerning the whole of things. But if we must needs fix on some hypothesis; by what rule, pray, ought we to determine our choice? Is there any other rule than the greater similarity of the objects compared? And does not a plant or an animal, which springs from vegetation or generation, bear a stronger resemblance to the world, than does any artificial machine, which arises from reason and design?

But what is this vegetation and generation of which you talk? said Demea. Can you explain their operations, and anatomize that fine internal structure, on which they depend?

As much, at least, replied Philo, as Cleanthes can explain the operations of reason, or anatomize that internal structure, on which *it* depends. But without any such elaborate disquisitions, when I see an animal, I infer, that it sprang from generation; and that with as great certainty as you conclude a house to have been reared by design. These words, *generation, reason*, mark only certain powers and energies in nature, whose effects are known, but whose essence is incomprehensible; and one of these principles, more than the other, has no privilege for made being a standard to the whole of nature.

In reality, Demea, it may reasonably be expected, that the larger the views are which we take of things, the better will they conduct us in our conclusions concerning such extraordinary and such magnificent subjects. In this little corner of the world alone, there are four principles, *reason, instinct, generation, vegetation*, which are similar to each other, and are the causes of similar effects. What a number of other principles may we naturally suppose in the immense extent and variety of the universe, could we travel from planet to planet and from system to system, in order to examine each part of this mighty fabric? Any one of these four principles above mentioned (and a hundred others which lie open to our conjecture) may afford us a theory, by which to judge of the origin of the world; and it is a palpable and egregious partiality, to confine our view entirely to that principle, by which our own minds operate. Were this principle more intelligible on that account, such a partiality might be somewhat excusable: But reason, in its internal fabric and structure, is really as little known to us as instinct or vegetation; and perhaps even that vague, undeterminate word, nature, to which the vulgar refer every thing, is not at the bottom more inexplicable. The effects of these principles are all known to us from experience: But the principles themselves, and their manner of operation, are totally unknown: Nor is it less intelligible, or less conformable to experience to say, that the world arose by vegetation from a seed shed by another world, than to say that it arose from a divine reason or contrivance, according to the sense in which Cleanthes understands it.

But methinks, said Demea, if the world had a vegetative quality, and could sow the seeds of new worlds into the infinite chaos, this power would be still an additional argument for design in its Author. For whence could arise so wonderful a faculty but from design? Or how can order spring from any thing, which perceives not that order which it bestows?

You need only look around you, replied Philo, satisfy yourself with regard to this question. A tree bestows order and organization on that tree which springs from it, without knowing the order: an animal, in the same manner, on its offspring: a bird, on its nest: And instances of this kind are even more frequent in the world, than those of order, which arise from reason and contrivance. To say that all this order in animals and vegetables proceeds ultimately from design is begging the question; nor can that great point be ascertained otherwise than by proving *a priori*, both that order is, from its nature, inseparably attached to thought, and that it can never, of itself, or from original unknown principles, belong to matter.

But farther, Demea; this objection, which you urge, can never be made use of by Cleanthes, without renouncing a defence which he has already made against one of my objections. When I enquired concerning the cause of that supreme reason and intelligence, into which he resolves every thing; he told me, that the impossibility of satisfying such enquiries could never be admitted as an objection in any species of philosophy. *We must stop somewhere, says he; nor is it ever within the reach of human capacity to explain ultimate causes, or show the last connections of any objects. It is sufficient, if the steps, so far as we go, are supported by experience and observation.* Now that vegetation and generation, as well as reason, are experienced to be principles of order in nature, is undeniable. If I rest my system of cosmogony on the former, preferably to the latter, it is at my choice. The matter seems entirely arbitrary. And when Cleanthes asks me what is the cause of my great vegetative or generative faculty, I am equally entitled to ask him the cause of his great reasoning principle. These questions we have agreed to forbear on both sides; and it is chiefly his interest on the present occasion to stick to this agreement. Judging by our limited and imperfect experience, generation has some privileges above reason: For we see every day the latter arise from the former, never the former from the latter.

Compare, I beseech you, the consequences on both sides. The world, say I, resembles an animal, therefore it is an animal, therefore it arose from generation. The steps, I confess, are wide; yet there is some small appearance of analogy in each step. The world, says Cleanthes, resembles a machine, therefore it is a machine, therefore it arose from design. The steps are here equally wide, and the analogy less striking. And if he pretends to carry on *my* hypothesis a step farther, and to infer design or reason from the great principle of generation, on which I insist; I may, with better authority, use the same freedom to push farther *his* hypothesis, and infer a divine generation or theogony from his principle of reason. I have at least some faint shadow of experience, which is the utmost that can ever be attained in the present subject. Reason, in innumerable instances, is observed to arise from the principle of generation, and never to arise from any other principle.

Hesiod, and all the ancient mythologists, were so struck with this analogy, that they universally explained the origin of nature from an animal birth, and copulation. Plato too, so far as he is intelligible, seems to have adopted some such notion in his Timeus.

The Brahmins assert, that the world arose from an infinite spider, who spun this whole complicated mass from his bowels, and annihilates afterwards the whole or any part of it, by absorbing it again, and resolving it into his own essence. Here is a species of cosmogony, which appears to us ridiculous; because a spider is a little contemptible animal, whose operations we are never likely to take for a model of the whole universe. But still here is a new species of analogy, even in our globe. And were there a planet wholly inhabited by spiders (which is very possible), this inference would there appear as natural and irrefragable as that which in our planet ascribes the origin of all things to design and intelligence, as explained by Cleanthes. Why an orderly system may not be spun from the belly as well as from the brain, it will be difficult for him to give a satisfactory reason.

I must confess, Philo, replied Cleanthes, that of all men living, the task which you have undertaken, of raising doubts and objections, suits you best, and seems, in a manner, natural and unavoidable to you. So great is your fertility of invention, that I am not ashamed to acknowledge myself unable, in a sudden, to solve regularly such out-of-the-way difficulties as you incessantly start upon me: Though I clearly see, in general, their fallacy and error. And I question not, but you are yourself, at present, in the same case, and have not the solution so ready as the objection; while you must be sensible, that common sense and reason is entirely against you, and that such whimsies, as you have delivered, may puzzle, but never can convince us.

PART VIII

What you ascribe to the fertility of my invention, replied Philo, is entirely owing to the nature of the subject. In subjects, adapted to the narrow compass of human reason, there is commonly but one determination, which carries probability or conviction with it; and to a man of sound judgment, all other suppositions, but that one, appear entirely absurd and chimerical. But in such questions as the present, a hundred contradictory views may preserve a kind of imperfect analogy; and invention has here full scope to exert itself. Without any great effort of thought, I believe that I could, in an instant, propose other systems of cosmogony, which would have some faint appearance of truth; though it is a thousand, a million to one, if either yours or any one of mine be the true system.

For instance; what if I should revive the old Epicurean hypothesis? This is commonly, and I believe, justly, esteemed the most absurd system, that has yet been proposed; yet, I know not, whether, with a few alterations, it might not be brought to bear a faint appearance of probability. Instead of supposing matter infinite, as Epicurus did; let us suppose it finite. A finite number of particles is only susceptible of finite transpositions: And it must happen, in an eternal duration, that every possible order or position must be tried an infinite number of times. This world, therefore, with all its events, even the most minute, has before been produced and destroyed, and will again be produced and destroyed, without any bounds and limitations. No one, who has a conception of the powers of infinite, in comparison of finite, will ever scruple this determination.

But this supposes, said Demea, that matter can acquire motion, without any voluntary agent or first mover.

And where is the difficulty, replied Philo, of that supposition? Every event, before experience, is equally difficult and incomprehensible; and every event, after experience, is equally easy and intelligible. Motion, in many instances, from gravity, from elasticity, from electricity, begins in matter, without any known voluntary agent; and to suppose always, in these cases, an unknown voluntary agent, is mere hypothesis; and hypothesis attended with no advantages. The beginning of motion in matter itself is as conceivable *a priori* as its communication from mind and intelligence.

Besides, why may not motion have been propagated by impulse through all eternity, and the same stock of it, or nearly the same, be still upheld in the universe? As much as is lost by the composition of motion, as much is gained by its resolution. And whatever the causes are, the fact is certain, that matter is, and always has been in continual agitation, as far as human experience or tradition reaches. There is not probably, at present, in the whole universe, one particle of matter at absolute rest.

And this very consideration too, continued Philo, which we have stumbled on in the course of the argument, suggests a new hypothesis of cosmogony, that is not absolutely absurd and improbable. Is there a system, an order, an œconomy of things, by which matter can preserve that perpetual agitation, which seems essential to it, and yet maintain a constancy in the forms, which it produces? There certainly is such an œconomy: For this is actually the case with the present world. The continual motion of matter, therefore, in less than infinite transpositions, must produce this œconomy or order; and by its very nature, that order, when once established, supports itself, for many ages, if not to eternity. But wherever matter is so poised, arranged, and adjusted as to continue in perpetual motion, and yet preserve a constancy in the forms, its situation must, of necessity, have all the same appearance of art and contrivance which we observe at present. All the parts of each form must have a relation to each other, and to the whole: And the whole itself must have a relation to the other parts of the universe; to the element, in which the form subsists; to the materials, with which it repairs its waste and decay; and to every other form, which is hostile or friendly. A defect in any of these particulars destroys the form; and the matter, of which it is composed, is again set loose, and is thrown into irregular motions and fermentations, till it unite itself to some other regular form. If no such form be prepared to receive it, and if there be a great quantity of this corrupted matter in the universe, the universe itself is entirely disordered; whether it be the feeble embryo of a world in its first beginnings, that is thus destroyed, or the rotten carcass of one, languishing in old age and infirmity. In either case, a chaos ensures; till finite, though innumerable revolutions produce at last some forms, whose parts and organs are so adjusted as to support the forms amidst a continued succession of matter.

Suppose (for we shall endeavour to vary the expression), that matter were thrown into any position, by a blind, unguided force; it is evident that this first position must in all probability be the most confused and most disorderly imaginable, without any resemblance to those works of human contrivance, which, along with a symmetry of parts, discover an adjustment of means to ends and a tendency to self-preservation. If the actuating force cease after this operation, matter must remain for ever in disorder, and continue an immense chaos, without any proportion or activity. But suppose, that the actuating force, whatever it be, still continues in matter, this first position will immediately give place to a second, which will likewise in all probability be as disorderly as the first, and so on, through many successions of changes and revolutions. No particular order or position ever continues a moment unaltered. The original force, still remaining in activity, gives a perpetual restlessness to matter. Every possible situation is produced, and instantly destroyed. If a glimpse or dawn of order appears for a moment, it is instantly hurried away, and confounded, by that never-ceasing force, which actuates every part of matter.

Thus the universe goes on for many ages in a continued succession of chaos and disorder. But is it not possible that it may settle at last, so as not to lose its motion and active force (for that we have supposed inherent in it), yet so as to preserve an uniformity of appearance, amidst the continual motion and fluctuation of its parts? This we find to be the case with the universe at present. Every individual is perpetually changing, and every part of every individual, and yet the whole remains, in appearance, the same. May we not hope for such a position, or rather be assured of it, from the eternal revolutions of unguided matter, and may not this account for all the appearing wisdom and contrivance which is in the universe? Let us contemplate the subject a little, and we shall find, that this adjustment, if attained by matter, of a seeming stability in the forms, with a real and perpetual revolution or motion of parts, affords a plausible, if not a true solution of the difficulty.

It is in vain, therefore, to insist upon the uses of the parts in animals or vegetables, and their curious adjustment to each other. I would fain know how an animal could subsist, unless its parts were so adjusted? Do we not find, that it immediately perishes whenever this adjustment ceases, and that its matter corrupting tries some new form? It happens, indeed, that the parts of the world are so well adjusted, that some regular form immediately lays claim to this corrupted matter: And if it were not so, could the world subsist? Must it not dissolve as well as the animal, and pass through new positions and situations; till in a great, but finite succession, it fall at last into the present or some such order?

It is well, replied Cleanthes, you told us, that this hypothesis was suggested on a sudden, in the course of the argument. Had you had leisure to examine it, you would soon have perceived the insuperable objections, to which it is exposed. No form, you say, can subsist, unless it possess those powers and organs, requisite for its subsistence: Some new order or œconomy must be tried, and so on, without intermission; till at last some order, which can support and maintain itself, is fallen upon. But according to this hypothesis, whence arise the many conveniences and advantages which men and all animals possess? Two eyes, two ears, are not absolutely necessary for the subsistence of the species. Human race might have been propagated and preserved, without horses, dogs, cows, sheep, and those innumerable fruits and products which serve to our satisfaction and enjoyment. If no camels had been created for the use of man in the sandy deserts of Africa and Arabia, would the world have been dissolved? If no loadstone had been framed to give that wonderful and useful direction to the needle, would human society and the human kind have been immediately extinguished? Though the maxims of nature be in general very frugal, yet instances of this kind are far from being rare; and any one of them is a sufficient proof of design, and of a benevolent design, which gave rise to the order and arrangement of the universe.

At least, you may safely infer, said Philo, that the foregoing hypothesis is so far incomplete and imperfect; which I shall not scruple to allow. But can we ever reasonably expect greater success in any attempts of this nature? Or can we ever hope to erect a system of cosmogony, that will be liable to no exceptions, and will contain no circumstance repugnant to our limited and imperfect experience of the analogy of nature? Your theory itself cannot surely pretend to any such advantage; even though you have run into *anthropomorphism,* the better to preserve a conformity to common experience. Let us once more put it to trial. In all instances which we have ever seen, ideas are copied from real objects, and are ectypal, not archetypal, to express myself in learned terms: You reverse this order, and give thought the precedence. In all instances which we have ever seen, thought has no influence upon matter, except where that matter is so conjoined with it, as to have an equal reciprocal influence upon it. No animal can move immediately any thing but the members of its own body; and indeed, the equality of action and reaction seems to be an universal law of nature: But your theory implies a contradiction to this experience. These instances, with many more, which it were easy to collect (particularly the supposition of a mind or system of thought that is eternal, or in other words, an animal ingenerable and immortal), these instances, I say, may teach, all of us, sobriety in condemning each other, and let us see, that as no system of this kind ought ever to be received from a slight analogy, so neither ought any to be rejected on account of a small incongruity. For that is an inconvenience from which we can justly pronounce no one to be exempted.

All religious systems, it is confessed, are subject to great and insuperable difficulties. Each disputant triumphs in his turn; while he carries on an offensive war, and exposes the absurdities, barbarities, and pernicious tenets of his antagonist. But all of them, on the whole, prepare a complete triumph for the *sceptic*; who tells them, that no system ought ever to be embraced with regard to such subjects: For this plain reason, that no absurdity ought ever to be assented to with regard to any subject. A total suspense of judgment is here our only reasonable resource. And if every attack, as is commonly observed, and no defence, among theologians, is successful; how complete must be his victory, who remains always, with all mankind, on the offensive, and has himself no fixed station or abiding city, which he is ever, on any occasion, obliged to defend?

PART IX

But if so many difficulties attend the argument *a posteriori*, said Demea; had we not better adhere to that simple and sublime argument *a priori*, which, by offering to us infallible demonstration, cuts off at once all doubt and difficulty? By this argument, too, we may prove the infinity of the divine attributes, which, I am afraid, can never be ascertained with certainty from any other topic. For how can an effect, which either is finite, or, for aught we know, may be so; how can such an effect, I say, prove an infinite cause? The unity too of the divine nature, it is very difficult, if not absolutely impossible, to deduce merely from contemplating the works of nature; nor will the uniformity alone of the plan, even were it allowed, give us any assurance of that attribute. Whereas the argument *a priori* . . .

You seem to reason, Demea, interposed Cleanthes, as if those advantages and conveniences in the abstract argument were full proofs of its solidity. But it is first proper, in my opinion, to determine what argument of this nature you choose to insist on; and we shall afterwards, from itself, better than from its *useful* consequences, endeavour to determine what value we ought to put upon it.

The argument, replied Demea, which I would insist on is the common one. Whatever exists must have a cause or reason of its existence; it being absolutely impossible for any thing to produce itself, or be the cause of its own existence. In mounting up, therefore, from effects to causes, we must either go on in tracing an infinite succession, without any ultimate cause at all, or must at last have recourse to some ultimate cause, that is *necessarily* existent: Now that the first supposition is absurd may be thus proved. In the infinite chain or succession of causes and effects, each single effect is determined to exist by the power and efficacy of that cause which immediately preceded; but the whole eternal chain or succession, taken together, is not determined or caused by any thing: And yet it is evident that it requires a cause or reason, as much as any particular object, which begins to exist in time. The question is still reasonable, why this particular succession of causes existed from eternity, and not any other succession, or no succession at all. If there be no necessarily existent Being, any supposition, which can be formed, is equally possible; nor is there any more absurdity in nothing's having existed from eternity, than there is in that succession of causes, which constitutes the universe. What was it, then, which determined something to exist rather than nothing, and bestowed being on a particular possibility, exclusive of the rest? *External* causes, there are supposed to be none. *Chance* is a word without a meaning. Was it *nothing*? But that can never produce any thing. We must, therefore, have recourse to a necessarily existent Being, who carries the reason of his existence in himself; and who cannot be supposed not to exist without an express contradiction. There is consequently such a Being, that is, there is a Deity.

I shall not leave it to Philo, said Cleanthes (though I know that the starting objections is his chief delight), to point out the weakness of this metaphysical reasoning. It seems to me so obviously ill-grounded, and at the same time of so little consequence to the cause of true piety and religion, that I shall myself venture to show the fallacy of it.

I shall begin with observing, that there is an evident absurdity in pretending to demonstrate a matter of fact, or to prove it by any arguments *a priori*. Nothing is demonstrable, unless the contrary implies a contradiction. Nothing, that is distinctly conceivable, implies a contradiction. Whatever we conceive as existent, we can also conceive as non-existent. There is no Being, therefore, whose non-existence implies a contradiction. Consequently there is no Being, whose existence is demonstrable. I propose this argument as entirely decisive, and am willing to rest the whole controversy upon it.

It is pretended that the Deity is a necessarily existent Being; and this necessity of his existence is attempted to be explained by asserting, that, if we knew his whole essence or nature, we should perceive it to be as impossible for him not to exist as for twice two not to be four. But it is evident, that this can never happen, while our faculties remain the same as at present. It will still be possible for us, at any time, to conceive the non-existence of what we formerly conceived to exist; nor can the mind ever lie under a necessity of supposing any object to remain always in being; in the same manner as we lie under a necessity of always conceiving twice two to be four. The words, therefore, *necessary existence*, have no meaning; or, which is the same thing, none that is consistent.

But farther; why may not the material universe be the necessarily existent Being, according to this pretended explication of necessity? We dare not affirm that we know all the qualities of matter; and for aught we can determine, it may contain some qualities, which, were they known, would make its non-existence appear as great a contradiction as that twice two is five. I find only one argument employed to prove, that the material world is not the necessarily existent Being; and this argument is derived from the contingency both of the matter and the form of the world. "Any particle of matter," it is said, "may be *conceived* to be annihilated; and any form may be *conceived* to be altered. Such an annihilation or alteration, therefore, is not impossible." But it seems a great partiality not to perceive, that the same argument extends equally to the Deity, so far as we have any conception of him; and that the mind can at least imagine him to be nonexistent, or his attributes to be altered. It must be some unknown, inconceivable qualities, which can make his non-existence appear impossible, or his attributes unalterable: And no reason can be assigned, why these qualities may not belong to matter. As they are altogether unknown and inconceivable, they can never be proved incompatible with it.

Add to this, that in tracing an eternal succession of objects, it seems absurd to inquire for a general cause or first Author. How can any thing, that exists from eternity, have a cause, since that relation implies a priority in time and a beginning of existence?

In such a chain too, or succession of objects, each part is caused by that which preceded it, and causes that which succeeds it. Where then is the difficulty? But the whole, you say, wants a cause. I answer, that the uniting of these parts into a whole, like the uniting of several distinct counties into one kingdom, or several distinct members into one body, is performed merely by an arbitrary act of the mind, and has no influence on the nature of things. Did I show you the particular causes of each individual in a collection of twenty particles of matter, I should think it very unreasonable, should you afterwards ask me, what was the cause of the whole twenty. This is sufficiently explained in explaining the cause of the parts.

Though the reasonings, which you have urged, Cleanthes, may well excuse me, said Philo, from starting any farther difficulties; yet I cannot forbear insisting still upon another topic. It is observed by arithmeticians, that the products of 9 compose always either 9 or some lesser product of 9; if you add together all the characters, of which any of the former products is composed. Thus, of 18, 27, 36, which are products of 9, you make 9 by adding 1 to 8, 2 to 7, 3 to 6. Thus 369 is a product also of 9; and if you add 3, 6, and 9, you make 18, a lesser product of 9. To a superficial observer, so wonderful a regularity may be admired as the effect either of chance or design; but a skillful algebraist immediately concludes it to be the work of necessity, and demonstrates, that it must for ever result from the nature of these numbers. Is it not probable, I ask, that the whole œconomy of the universe is conducted by a like necessity, though no human algebra can furnish a key which solves the difficulty? And instead of admiring the order of natural beings, may it not happen, that, could we penetrate into the intimate nature of bodies, we should clearly see why it was absolutely impossible, they could ever admit of any other disposition? So dangerous is it to introduce this idea of necessity into the present question! And so naturally does it afford an inference directly opposite to the religious hypothesis!

But dropping all these abstractions, continued Philo; and confining ourselves to more familiar topics; I shall venture to add an observation, that the argument *a priori* has seldom been found very convincing, except to people of a metaphysical head, who have accustomed themselves to abstract reasoning, and who finding from mathematics, that the understanding frequently leads to truth, through obscurity, and contrary to first appearances, have transferred the same habit of thinking to subjects where it ought not to have place. Other people, even of good sense and the best inclined to religion, feel always some deficiency in such arguments, though they are not perhaps able to explain distinctly where it lies. A certain proof, that men ever did, and ever will, derive their religion from other sources than from this species of reasoning.

PART X

It is my opinion, I own, replied Demea, that each man feels, in a manner, the truth of religion within his own breast; and from a consciousness of his imbecility and misery, rather than from any reasoning, is led to seek protection from that Being, on whom he and all nature is dependent. So anxious or so tedious are even the best scenes of life, that futurity is still the object of all our hopes and fears. We incessantly look forward, and endeavour, by prayers, adoration, and sacrifice, to appease those unknown powers, whom we find, by experience, so able to afflict and oppress us. Wretched creatures that we are! What resource for us amidst the innumerable ills of life, did not religion suggest some methods of atonement, and appease those terrors, with which we are incessantly agitated and tormented?

I am indeed persuaded, said Philo, that the best and indeed the only method of bringing every one to a due sense of religion is by just representations of the misery and wickedness of men. And for that purpose a talent of eloquence and strong imagery is more requisite than that of reasoning and argument. For is it necessary to prove, what every one feels within himself? It is only necessary to make us feel it, if possible, more intimately and sensibly.

The people, indeed, replied Demea, are sufficiently convinced of this great and melancholy truth. The miseries of life, the unhappiness of man, the general corruptions of our nature, the unsatisfactory enjoyment of pleasures, riches, honours; these phrases have become almost proverbial in all languages. And who can doubt of what all men declare from their own immediate feeling and experience?

In this point, said Philo, the learned are perfectly agreed with the vulgar; and in all letters, *sacred* and *profane*, the topic of human misery has been insisted on with the most pathetic eloquence that sorrow and melancholy could inspire. The poets, who speak from sentiment, without a system, and whose testimony has therefore the more authority, abound in images of this nature. From Homer down to Dr. Young, the whole inspired tribe have ever been sensible, that no other representation of things would suit the feeling and observation of each individual.

As to authorities, replied Demea, you need not seek them. Look round this library of Cleanthes. I shall venture to affirm, that, except authors of particular sciences, such as chemistry or botany, who have no occasion to treat of human life, there scarce is one of those innumerable writers, from whom the sense of human misery has not, in some passage or other, extorted a complaint and confession of it. At least, the chance is entirely on that side; and no one author has ever, so far as I can recollect, been so extravagant as to deny it.

There you must excuse me, said Philo: Leibnitz has denied it; and is perhaps the first, who ventured upon so bold and paradoxical an opinion; at least, the first, who made it essential to his philosophical system.

And by being the first, replied Demea, might he not have been sensible of his error? For is this a subject in which philosophers can propose to make discoveries, especially in so late an age? And can any man hope by a simple denial (for the subject scarcely admits of reasoning) to bear down the united testimony of mankind, founded on sense and consciousness?

And why should man, added he, pretend to an exemption from the lot of all other animals? The whole earth, believe me, Philo, is cursed and polluted. A perpetual war is kindled amongst all living creatures. Necessity, hunger, want, stimulate the strong and courageous: Fear, anxiety, terror, agitate the weak and infirm. The first entrance into life gives anguish to the new-born infant and to its wretched parent: Weakness, impotence, distress, attend each stage of that life: And it is at last finished in agony and horror.

Observe too, says Philo, the curious artifices of nature, in order to embitter the life of every living being. The stronger prey upon the weaker, and keep them in perpetual terror and anxiety. The weaker too, in their turn, often prey upon the stronger, and vex and molest them without relaxation. Consider that innumerable race of insects, which either are bred on the body of each animal, or flying about infix their stings in him. These insects have others still less than themselves, which torment them. And thus on each hand, before and behind, above and below, every animal is surrounded with enemies, which incessantly seek his misery and destruction.

Man alone, said Demea, seems to be, in part, an exception to this rule. For by combination in society, he can easily master lions, tigers, and bears, whose greater strength and agility naturally enable them to prey upon him.

On the contrary, it is here chiefly, cried Philo, that the uniform and equal maxims of nature are most apparent. Man, it is true, can, by combination, surmount all his real enemies, and become master of the whole animal creation: But does he not immediately raise up to himself *imaginary* enemies, the dæmons of his fancy, who haunt him with superstitious terrors, and blast every enjoyment of life? His pleasure, as he imagines, becomes, in their eyes, a crime: His food and repose give them umbrage and offence: His very sleep and dreams furnish new materials to anxious fear: And even death, his refuge from every other ill, presents only the dread of endless and innumerable woes. Nor does the wolf molest more the timid flock, than superstition does the anxious breast of wretched mortals.

Besides, consider, Demea; this very society, by which we surmount those wild beasts, our natural enemies; what new enemies does it not raise to us? What woe and misery does it not occasion? Man is the greatest enemy of man. Oppression, injustice, contempt, contumely, violence, sedition, war, calumny, treachery, fraud; by these they mutually torment each other: And they would soon dissolve that society which they had formed, were it not for the dread of still greater ills, which must attend their separation.

But though these external insults, said Demea, from animals, from men, from all the elements, which assault us, form a frightful catalogue of woes, they are nothing in comparison of those, which arise within ourselves, from the distempered condition of our mind and body. How many lie under the lingering torment of diseases? Hear the pathetic enumeration of the great poet.

> Intestine stone and ulcer, colic-pangs,
> Daemoniac frenzy, moping melancholy,
> And moon-struck madness, pining atrophy,
> Marasmus and wide-wasting pestilence.
> Dire was the tossing, deep the groans: Despair
> Tended the sick, busiest from couch to couch.
> And over them triumphant Death his dart
> Shook, but delay'd to strike, tho' oft invok'd
> With vows, as their chief good and final hope.

The disorders of the mind, continued Demea, though more secret, are not perhaps less dismal and vexatious. Remorse, shame, anguish, rage, disappointment, anxiety, fear, dejection, despair; who has ever passed through life without cruel inroads from these tormentors? How many have scarcely ever felt any better sensations? Labour and poverty, so abhorred by every one, are the certain lot of the far greater number: And those few privileged persons, who enjoy ease and opulence, never reach contentment or true felicity. All the goods of life united would not make a very happy man: But all the ills united would make a wretch indeed; and any one of them almost (and who can be free from every one), nay often the absence of one good (and who can possess all) is sufficient to render life ineligible.

Were a stranger to drop, in a sudden, into this world, I would show him, as a specimen of its ills, an hospital full of diseases, a prison crowded with malefactors and debtors, a field of battle strowed with carcasses, a fleet floundering in the ocean, a nation languishing under tyranny, famine, or pestilence. To turn the gay side of life to him, and give him a notion of its pleasures; whither should I conduct him? to a ball, to an opera, to court? He might justly think, that I was only showing him a diversity of distress and sorrow.

There is no evading such striking instances, said Philo, but by apologies, which still farther aggravate the charge. Why have all men, I ask, in all ages, complained incessantly of the miseries of life? . . . They have no just reason, says one: These complaints proceed only from their discontented, repining, anxious disposition . . . And can there possibly, I reply, be a more certain foundation of misery, than such a wretched temper?

But if they were really as unhappy as they pretend, says my antagonist, why do they remain in life? . . .

Not satisfied with life, afraid of death.

This is the secret chain, say I, that holds us. We are terrified, not bribed to the continuance of or existence.

It is only a false delicacy, he may insist, which a few spirits indulge, and which has spread these complaints among the whole race of mankind. . . . And what is this delicacy, I ask, which you blame? Is it any thing but a greater sensibility to all the pleasures and pains of life? and if the man of a delicate, refined temper, by being so much more alive than the rest of the world, is only so much more unhappy; what judgment must we form in general of human life?

Let men remain at rest, says our adversary; and they will be easy. They are willing artificers of their own misery. . . . No! reply I; an anxious languor follows their repose: Disappointment, vexation, trouble, their activity and ambition.

I can observe something like what you mention in some others, replied Cleanthes: But I confess, I feel little or nothing of it in myself; and hope that it is not so common as you represent it.

If you feel not human misery yourself, cried Demea, I congratulate you on so happy a singularity. Others, seemingly the most prosperous, have not been ashamed to vent their complaints in the most melancholy strains. Let us attend to the great, the fortunate Emperor, Charles V, when, tired with human grandeur, he resigned all his extensive dominions into the hands of his son. In the last harangue, which he made on that memorable occasion, he publicly avowed, *that the greatest prosperities which he had ever enjoyed, had been mixed with so many adversities, that he might truly say he had never enjoyed any satisfaction or contentment.* But did the retired life, in which he sought for shelter, afford him any greater happiness? If we may credit his son's account, his repentance commenced the very day of his resignation.

Cicero's fortune, from small beginnings, rose to the greatest lustre and renown; yet what pathetic complaints of the ills of life do his familiar letters, as well as philosophical discourses, contain? And suitably to his own experience, he introduces Cato, the great, the fortunate Cato, protesting in his old age, that, had he a new life in his offer, he would reject the present.

Ask yourself, ask any of your acquaintance, whether they would live over again the last ten or twenty years of their life. No! but the next twenty, they say, will be better:

> And from the dregs of life, hope to receive
> What the first sprightly running could not give.

Thus at last they find (such is the greatness of human misery; it reconciles even contradictions) that they complain, at once, of the shortness of life, and of its vanity and sorrow.

And it is possible, Cleanthes, said Philo, that after all these reflections, and infinitely more, which might be suggested, you can still persevere in your anthropomorphism, and assert the moral attributes of the Deity, his justice, benevolence, mercy, and rectitude, to be of the same nature with these virtues in human creatures? His power we allow infinite: Whatever he wills is executed: But neither man nor any other animal are happy: Therefore he does not will their happiness. His wisdom is infinite: He is never mistaken in choosing the means to any end: But the course of nature tends not to human or animal felicity: Therefore it is not established for that purpose. Through the whole compass of human knowledge, there are no inferences more certain and infallible than these. In what respect, then, do his benevolence and mercy resemble the benevolence and mercy of men?

Epicurus's old questions are yet unanswered. Is he willing to prevent evil, but not able? then is he impotent. Is he able, but not willing? then is he malevolent. Is he both able and willing? whence then is evil?

You ascribe, Cleanthes (and I believe justly) a purpose and intention to nature. But what, I beseech you, is the object of that curious artifice and machinery, which she has displayed in all animals? The preservation alone of individuals and propagation of the species. It seems enough for her purpose, if such a rank be barely upheld in the universe, without any care or concern for the happiness of the members that compose it. No resource for this purpose: No machinery, in order merely to give pleasure or ease: No fund of pure joy and contentment: No indulgence without some want or necessity accompanying it. At least, the few phenomena of this nature are overbalanced by opposite phenomena of still greater importance.

Our sense of music, harmony, and indeed beauty of all kinds, gives satisfaction, without being absolutely necessary to the preservation and propagation of the species. But what racking pains, on the other hand, arise from gouts, gravels, megrims, toothaches, rheumatisms; where the injury to the animal-machinery is either small or incurable? Mirth, laughter, play, frolic, seem gratuitous satisfactions, which have no farther tendency: Spleen, melancholy, discontent, superstition, are pains of the same nature. How then does the divine benevolence display itself, in the sense of you anthropomorphites? None but we mystics, as you were pleased to call us, can account for this strange mixture of phenomena, by deriving it from attributes, infinitely perfect, but incomprehensible.

And have you at last, said Cleanthes smiling, betrayed your intentions, Philo? Your long agreement with Demea did indeed a little surprise me; but I find you were all the while erecting a concealed battery against me. And I must confess, that you have now fallen upon a subject worthy of your noble spirit of opposition and controversy. If you can make out the present point, and prove mankind to be unhappy or corrupted, there is an end at once of all religion. For to what purpose establish the natural attributes of the Deity, while the moral are still doubtful and uncertain?

You take umbrage very easily, replied Demea, at opinions the most innocent, and the most generally received even amongst the religious and devout themselves: And nothing can be more surprising than to find a topic like this, concerning the wickedness and misery of man, charged with no less than atheism and profaneness. Have not all pious divines and preachers, who have indulged their rhetoric on so fertile a subject; have they not easily, I say, given a solution of any difficulties which may attend it? This world is but a point in comparison of the universe: This life but a moment in comparison of eternity. The present evil phenomena, therefore, are rectified in other regions, and in some future period of existence. And the eyes of men, being then opened to larger views of things, see the whole connection of general laws, and trace, with adoration, the benevolence and rectitude of the Deity, through all the mazes and intricacies of his providence.

No! replied Cleanthes, No! These arbitrary suppositions can never be admitted, contrary to matter of fact, visible and uncontroverted. Whence can any cause be known but from its known effects? Whence can any hypothesis be proved but from the apparent phenomena? To establish one hypothesis upon another is building entirely in the air; and the utmost we ever attain, by these conjectures and fictions, is to ascertain the bare possibility of our opinion; but never can we, upon such terms, establish its reality.

The only method of supporting divine benevolence (and it is what I willingly embrace) is to deny absolutely the misery and wickedness of man. Your representations are exaggerated: Your melancholy views mostly fictitious: Your inferences contrary to fact and experience. Health is more common than sickness: Pleasure than pain: Happiness than misery. And for one vexation which we meet with, we attain, upon computation, a hundred enjoyments.

Admitting your position, replied Philo, which yet is extremely doubtful, you must, at the same time, allow, that, if pain be less frequent than pleasure, it is infinitely more violent and durable. One hour of it is often able to outweigh a day, a week, a month of our common insipid enjoyments: And how many days, weeks, and months are passed by several in the most acute torments? Pleasure, scarcely in one instance, is ever able to reach ecstasy and rapture: And in no one instance can it continue for any time at its highest pitch and altitude. The spirits evaporate; the nerves relax; the fabric is disordered; and the enjoyment quickly degenerates into fatigue and uneasiness. But pain often, Good God, how often! rises to torture and agony; and the longer it continues, it becomes still more genuine agony and torture. Patience is exhausted; courage languishes; melancholy seizes us; and nothing terminates our misery but the removal of its cause, or another event, which is the sole cure of all evil, but which, from our natural folly, we regard with still greater horror and consternation.

But not to insist upon these topics, continued Philo, though most obvious, certain, and important; I must use the freedom to admonish you, Cleanthes, that you have put this controversy upon a most dangerous issue, and are unawares introducing a total scepticism into the most essential articles of natural and revealed theology. What! no method of fixing a just foundation for religion, unless we allow the happiness of human life, and maintain a continued existence even in this world, with all our present pains, infirmities, vexations, and follies, to be eligible and desirable! But this is contrary to every one's feeling and experience: It is contrary to an authority so established as nothing can subvert: No decisive proofs can ever be produced against this authority; nor is it possible for you to compute, estimate, and compare all the pains and all the pleasures in the lives of all men and of all animals: And thus by your resting the whole system of religion on a point, which, from its very nature, must for ever be uncertain, you tacitly confess, that that system is equally uncertain.

But allowing you, what never will be believed; at least, what you never possibly can prove, that animal, or at least, human happiness, in this life, exceeds its misery; you have yet done nothing: For this is not, by any means, what we expect from infinite power, infinite wisdom, and infinite goodness. Why is there any misery at all in the world? Not by chance surely. From some cause then. Is it from the intention of the Deity? But he is perfectly benevolent. Is it contrary to his intention? But he is almighty. Nothing can shake the solidity of this reasoning, so short, so clear, so decisive; except we assert, that these subjects exceed all human capacity, and that our common measures of truth and falsehood are not applicable to them; a topic, which I have all along insisted on, but which you have, from the beginning, rejected with scorn and indignation.

But I will be contented to retire still from this intrenchment: For I deny that you can ever force me in it: I will allow, that pain or misery in man is *compatible* with infinite power and goodness in the Deity, even in your sense of these attributes: What are you advanced by all these concessions? A mere possible compatibility is not sufficient. You must *prove* these pure, unmixed, and uncontrollable attributes from the present mixed and confused phenomena, and from these alone. A hopeful undertaking! Were the phenomena ever so pure and unmixed, yet being finite, they would be insufficient for that purpose. How much more, were they are also so jarring and discordant?

Here, Cleanthes, I find myself at ease in my argument. Here I triumph. Formerly, when we argued concerning the natural attributes of intelligence and design, I needed all my sceptical and metaphysical subtilty to elude your grasp. In many views of the universe, and of its parts, particularly the latter, the beauty and fitness of final causes strike us with such irresistible force, that all objections appear (what I believe they really are) mere cavils and sophisms; nor can we then imagine how it was ever possible for us to repose any weight on them. But there is no view of human life, or of the condition of mankind, from which, without the greatest violence, we can infer the moral attributes, or learn that infinite benevolence, conjoined with infinite power and infinite wisdom, which we must discover by the eyes of faith alone. It is your turn now to tug the labouring oar, and to support your philosophical subtilties against the dictates of plain reason and experience.

Part XI

I scruple not to allow, said Cleanthes, that I have been apt to suspect the frequent repetition of the word, *infinite*, which we meet with in all theological writers, to savour more of panegyric than of philosophy, and that any purposes of reasoning, and even of religion, would be better served, were we to rest contented with more accurate and more moderate expressions. The terms, *admirable, excellent, superlatively great, wise,* and *holy*; these sufficiently fill the imaginations of men; and any thing beyond, besides that it leads into absurdities, has no influence on the affections or sentiments. Thus, in the present subject, if we abandon all human analogy, as seems your intention, Demea, I am afraid we abandon all religion, and retain no conception of the great object of our adoration. If we preserve human analogy, we must for ever find it impossible to reconcile any mixture of evil in the universe with infinite attributes; much less, can we ever prove the latter from the former. But supposing the Author of nature to be finitely perfect, though far exceeding mankind; a satisfactory account may then be given of natural and moral evil, and every untoward phenomenon be explained and adjusted. A less evil may then be chosen, in order to avoid a greater: Inconveniences be submitted to, in order to reach a desirable end: And in a word, benevolence, regulated by wisdom, and limited by necessity, may produce just such a world as the present. You, Philo, who are so prompt at starting views, and reflections, and analogies; I would gladly hear, at length, without interruption, your opinion of this new theory; and if it deserve our attention, we may afterwards, at more leisure, reduce it into form.

My sentiments, replied Philo, are not worth being made a mystery of; and therefore, without any ceremony, I shall deliver what occurs to me with regard to the present subject. It must, I think, be allowed, that, if a very limited intelligence, whom we shall suppose utterly unacquainted with the universe, were assured, that it were the production of a very good, wise, and powerful Being, however finite, he would, from his conjectures, form *beforehand* a different notion of it from what we find it to be by experience; nor would he ever imagine, merely from these attributes of the cause, of which he is informed, that the effect could be so full of vice and misery and disorder, as it appears in this life. Supposing now, that this person were brought into the world, still assured, that it was the workmanship of such a sublime and benevolent Being; he might, perhaps, be surprised at the disappointment; but would never retract his former belief, if founded on any very solid argument; since such a limited intelligence must be sensible of his own blindness and ignorance, and must allow, that there may be many solutions of those phenomena, which will for ever escape his comprehension. But supposing, which is the real case with regard to man, that this creature is not antecedently convinced of a supreme intelligence, benevolent, and powerful, but is left to gather such a belief from the appearances of things; this entirely alters the case, nor will he ever find any reason for such a conclusion. He may be fully convinced of the narrow limits of his understanding; but this will not help him in forming an inference concerning the goodness of superior powers, since he must form that inference from what he knows, not from what he is ignorant of. The more you exaggerate his weakness and ignorance, the more diffident you render him, and give him the greater suspicion, that such subjects are beyond the reach of his faculties. You are obliged, therefore, to reason with him merely from the known phenomena, and to drop every arbitrary supposition or conjecture.

Did I show you a house or palace, where there was not one apartment convenient or agreeable; where the windows, doors, fires, passages, stairs, and the whole œconomy of the building were the source of noise, confusion, fatigue, darkness, and the extremes of heat and cold; you would certainly blame the contrivance, without any farther examination. The architect would in vain display his subtilty, and prove to you, that if this door or that window were altered, greater ills would ensue. What he says, may be strictly true: The alteration of one particular, while the other parts of the building remain, may only augment the inconveniences. But still you would assert in general, that, if the architect had had skill and good intentions, he might have formed such a plan of the whole, and might have adjusted the parts in such a manner, as would have remedied all or most of these inconveniences. His ignorance, or even your own ignorance of such a plan, will never convince you of the impossibility of it. If you find many inconveniences and deformities in the building, you will always, without entering into any detail, condemn the architect.

In short, I repeat the question: Is the world considered in general, and as it appears to us in this life, different from what a man or such a limited being would, *be-*

forehand, expect from a very powerful, wise, and benevolent Deity? It must be strange prejudice to assert the contrary. And from thence I conclude, that, however consistent the world may be, allowing certain suppositions and conjectures, with the idea of such a Deity, it can never afford us an inference concerning his existence. The consistence is not absolutely denied, only the inference. Conjectures, especially where infinity is excluded from the divine attributes, may, perhaps, be sufficient to prove a consistence; but can never be foundations for any inference.

There seem to be *four* circumstances, on which depend all, or the greatest part of the ills, that molest sensible creatures; and it is not impossible but all these circumstances may be necessary and unavoidable. We know so little beyond common life, or even of common life, that, with regard to the œconomy of a universe, there is no conjecture, however wild, which may not be just; nor any one, however plausible, which may not be erroneous. All that belongs to human understanding, in this deep ignorance and obscurity, is to be sceptical, or at least cautious; and not to admit of any hypothesis, whatever; much less, of any which is supported by no appearance of probability. Now this I assert to be the case with regard to all the causes of evil, and the circumstances on which it depends. None of them appear to human reason, in the least degree, necessary or unavoidable; nor can we suppose them such, without the utmost licence of imagination.

The *first* circumstance which introduces evil, is that contrivance or œconomy of the animal creation, by which pains, as well as pleasures, are employed to excite all creatures to action, and make them vigilant in the great work of self-preservation. Now pleasure alone, in its various degrees, seems to human understanding sufficient for this purpose. All animals might be constantly in a state of enjoyment; but when urged by any of the necessities of nature, such as thirst, hunger, weariness; instead of pain, they might feel a diminution of pleasure, by which they might be prompted to seek that object, which is necessary to their subsistence. Men pursue pleasure as eagerly as they avoid pain; at least, might have been so constituted. It seems, therefore, plainly possible to carry on the business of life without any pain. Why then is any animal ever rendered susceptible of such a sensation? If animals can be free from it an hour, they might enjoy a perpetual exemption from it; and it required as particular a contrivance of their organs to produce that feeling, as to endow them with sight, hearing, or any of the senses. Shall we conjecture, that such a contrivance was necessary, without any appearance of reason? And shall we build on that conjecture as on the most certain truth?

But a capacity of pain would not alone produce pain, were it not for the *second* circumstance, viz. the conducting of the world by general laws; and this seems nowise necessary to a very perfect Being. It is true; if every thing were conducted by particular volitions, the course of nature would be perpetually broken, and no man could employ his reason in the conduct of life. But might not other particular volitions remedy this inconvenience? In short, might not the Deity exterminate all ill, wherever it were to be found; and produce all good, without any preparation or long progress of causes and effects?

Besides, we must consider, that, according to the present œconomy of the world, the course of nature, though supposed exactly regular, yet to us appears not so, and many events are uncertain, and many disappoint our expectations. Health and sickness, calm and tempest, with an infinite number of other accidents, whose causes are unknown and variable, have a great influence both on the fortunes of particular persons and on the prosperity of public societies: And indeed all human life, in a manner, depends on such accidents. A Being, therefore, who knows the secret springs of the universe, might easily, by particular volitions, turn all these accidents to the good of mankind, and render the whole world happy, without discovering himself in any operation. A fleet, whose purposes were salutary to society, might always meet with a fair

wind: Good princes enjoy sound health and long life: Persons born to power and authority, be framed with good tempers and virtuous dispositions. A few such events as these,
regularly and wisely conducted, would change the face of the world; and yet would no
more seem to disturb the course of nature or confound human conduct, than the present
œconomy of things, where the causes are secret, and variable, and compounded. Some
small touches, given to Caligula's brain in his infancy, might have converted him into a
Trajan: One wave, a little higher than the rest, by burying Cæsar and his fortune in the
bottom of the ocean, might have restored liberty to a considerable part of mankind.
There may, for aught we know, be good reasons, why providence interposes not in this
manner; but they are unknown to us: And though the mere supposition, that such reasons exist, may be sufficient to *save* the conclusion concerning the divine attributes, yet
surely it can never be sufficient to *establish* that conclusion.

If every thing in the universe be conducted by general laws, and if animals be
rendered susceptible of pain, it scarcely seems possible but some ill must arise in the
various shocks of matter, and the various concurrence and opposition of general laws:
But this ill would be very rare, were it not for the *third* circumstances, which I proposed to mention, viz. the great frugality with which all powers and faculties are distributed to every particular being. So well adjusted are the organs and capacities of all
animals, and so well fitted to their preservation, that, as far as history or tradition
reaches, there appears not to be any single species which has yet been extinguished in
the universe. Every animal has the requisite endowments; but these endowments are
bestowed with so scrupulous an œconomy, that any considerable diminution must entirely destroy the creature. Wherever one power is increased, there is a proportional
abatement in the others. Animals, which excel in swiftness, are commonly defective in
force. Those, which possess both, are either imperfect in some of their senses, or are
oppressed with the most craving wants. The human species, whose chief excellency is
reason and sagacity, is of all others the most necessitous, and the most deficient in bodily advantages; without clothes, without arms, without food, without lodging, without
any convenience of life, except what they owe to their own skill and industry. In short,
nature seems to have formed an exact calculation of the necessities of her creatures;
and like a *rigid master,* has afforded them little more powers or endowments, than
what are strictly sufficient to supply those necessities. An *indulgent parent* would have
bestowed a large stock, in order to guard against accidents, and secure the happiness
and welfare of the creature, in the most unfortunate concurrence of circumstances.
Every course of life would not have been so surrounded with precipices, that the least
departure from the true path, by mistake or necessity, must involve us in misery and
ruin. Some reserve, some fund would have been provided to ensure happiness; nor
would the powers and the necessities have been adjusted with so rigid an œconomy.
The Author of nature is inconceivably powerful: His force is supposed great, if not altogether inexhaustible: Nor is there any reason, as far as we can judge, to make him
observe this strict frugality in his dealings with his creatures. It would have been better, were his power extremely limited, to have created fewer animals, and to have endowed these with more faculties for their happiness and preservation. A builder is
never esteemed prudent, who undertakes a plan, beyond what his stock will enable him
to finish.

In order to cure most of the ills of human life, I require not that man should have
the wings of the eagle, the swiftness of the stag, the force of the ox, the arms of the
lion, the scales of the crocodile or rhinoceros; much less do I demand the sagacity of
an angel or cherubim. I am contented to take an increase in one single power of faculty
of his soul. Let him be endowed with a greater propensity to industry and labour; a

more vigorous spring and activity of mind; a more constant bent to business and application. Let the whole species possess naturally an equal diligence with that which many individuals are able to attain by habit and reflection; and the most beneficial consequences, without any allay of ill, is the immediate and necessary result of this endowment. Almost all the moral, as well as natural evils of human life arise from idleness; and were our species, by the original constitution of their frame, exempt from this vice or infirmity, the perfect cultivation of land, the improvement of arts and manufactures, the exact execution of every office and duty, immediately follow; and men at once may fully reach that state of society, which is so imperfectly attained by the best-regulated government. But as industry is a power, and the most valuable of any, nature seems determined, suitably to her usual maxims, to bestow it on men with a very sparing hand; and rather to punish him severely for his deficiency in it, than to reward him for his attainments. She has so contrived his frame, that nothing but the most violent necessity can oblige him to labour; and she employs all his other wants to overcome, at least in part, the want of diligence, and to endow him with some share of a faculty, of which she has thought fit naturally to bereave him. Here our demands may be allowed very humble, and therefore the more reasonable. If we required the endowments of superior penetration and judgment, of a more delicate taste of beauty, of a nicer sensibility to benevolence and friendship; we might be told, that we impiously pretend to break the order of nature, that we want to exalt ourselves into a higher rank of being, that the presents which we require, not being suitable to our state and condition, would only be pernicious to us. But it is hard; I dare to repeat it, it is hard, that being placed in a world so full of wants and necessities; where almost every being and element is either our foe or refuses us their assistance; we should also have our own temper to struggle with, and should be deprived of that faculty which can alone fence against these multiplied evils.

The *fourth* circumstance, whence arises the misery and ill of the universe, is the inaccurate workmanship of all the springs and principles of the great machine of nature. It must be acknowledged, that there are few parts of the universe, which seem not to serve some purpose, and whose removal would not produce a visible defect and disorder in the whole. The parts hang all together; nor can one be touched without affecting the rest, in a greater or less degree. But at the same time, it must be observed, that none of these parts or principles, however useful, are so accurately adjusted, as to keep precisely within those bounds in which their utility consists; but they are, all of them, apt, on every occasion, to run into the one extreme or the other. One would imagine, that this grand production has not received the last hand of the maker; so little finished is every part, and so coarse are the strokes, with which it is executed. Thus, the winds are requisite to convey the vapours along the surface of the globe, and to assist men in navigation: But how oft, rising up to tempests and hurricanes, do they become pernicious? Rains are necessary to nourish all the plants and animals of the earth: But how often are they defective? how often excessive? Heat is requisite to all life and vegetation; but is not always found in the due proportion. On the mixture and secretion of the humours and juices of the body depend the health and prosperity of the animal: But the parts perform not regularly their proper function. What more useful than all the passions of the mind, ambition, vanity, love, anger? But how oft do they break their bounds, and cause the greatest convulsions in society? There is nothing so advantageous in the universe, but what frequently becomes pernicious, by its excess or defect; nor has nature guarded, with the requisite accuracy, against all disorder or confusion. The irregularity is never, perhaps, so great as to destroy any species; but is often sufficient to involve the individuals in ruin and misery.

On the concurrence, then, of these *four* circumstances does all or the greatest part of natural evil depend. Were all living creatures incapable of pain, or were the world administered by particular volitions, evil never could have found access into the universe: And were animals endowed with a large stock of powers and faculties, beyond what strict necessity requires; or were the several springs and principles of the universe so accurately framed as to preserve always the just temperament and medium; there must have been very little ill in comparison of what we feel at present. What then shall we pronounce on this occasion? Shall we say, that these circumstances are not necessary, and that they might easily have been altered in the contrivance of the universe? This decision seems too presumptuous for creatures so blind and ignorant. Let us be more modest in our conclusions. Let us allow, that, if the goodness of the Deity (I mean a goodness like the human) could be established on any tolerable reasons *a priori*, these phenomena, however untoward, would not be sufficient to subvert that principle; but might easily, in some unknown manner, be reconcilable to it. But let us still assert, that as this goodness is not antecedently established, but must be inferred from the phenomena, there can be no grounds for such an inference, while there are so many ills in the universe, and while these ills might so easily have been remedied, as far as human understanding can be allowed to judge on such a subject. I am sceptic enough to allow, that the bad appearances, notwithstanding all my reasonings, may be compatible with such attributes as you suppose: But surely they can never prove these attributes. Such a conclusion cannot result from scepticism; but must arise from the phenomena, and from our confidence in the reasonings which we deduce from these phenomena.

Look round this universe. What an immense profusion of beings, animated and organized, sensible and active! You admire this prodigious variety and fecundity. But inspect a little more narrowly these living existences, the only beings worth regarding. How hostile and destructive to each other! How insufficient all of them for their own happiness! How contemptible or odious to the spectator! The whole presents nothing but the idea of a blind nature, impregnated by a great vivifying principle, and pouring forth from her lap, without discernment or parental care, her maimed and abortive children.

Here the Manichæan system occurs as a proper hypothesis to solve the difficulty: And no doubt, in some respects, it is very specious, and has more probability than the common hypothesis, by giving a plausible account of the strange mixture of good and ill which appears in life. But if we consider, on the other hand, the perfect uniformity and agreement of the parts of the universe, we shall not discover in it any marks of the combat of a malevolent with a benevolent Being. There is indeed an opposition of pains and pleasures in the feelings of sensible creatures: But are not all the operations of nature carried on by an opposition of principles, of hot and cold, moist and dry, light and heavy? The true conclusion is, that the original source of all things is entirely indifferent to all these principles, and has no more regard to good above ill than to heat above cold, or to drought above moisture, or to light above heavy.

There may *four* hypotheses be framed concerning the first causes of the universe: *that* they are endowed with perfect goodness, *that* they have perfect malice, *that* they are opposite and have both goodness and malice, *that* they have neither goodness nor malice. Mixed phenomena can never prove the two former unmixed principles. And the uniformity and steadiness of general laws seem to oppose the third. The fourth, therefore, seems by far the most probable.

What I have said concerning natural evil will apply to moral, with little or no variation; and we have no more reason to infer, that the rectitude of the supreme Being resembles human rectitude than that his benevolence resembles the human. Nay, it will be thought, that we have still greater cause to exclude from him moral sentiments, such as we feel them; since moral evil, in the opinion of many, is much more predominant above moral good than natural evil above natural good.

But even though this should not be allowed, and though the virtue, which is in mankind, should be acknowledged much superior to the vice; yet so long as there is any vice at all in the universe, it will very much puzzle you anthropomorphites, how to account for it. You must assign a cause for it, without having recourse to the first cause. But as every effect must have a cause, and that cause another; you must either carry on the progression *in infinitum*, or rest on that original principle, who is the ultimate cause of all things . . .

Hold! Hold! cried Demea: Whither does your imagination hurry you? I joined in alliance with you, in order to prove the incomprehensible nature of the divine Being, and refute the principles of Cleanthes, who would measure every thing by a human rule and standard. But I now find you running into all the topics of the greatest libertines and infidels; and betraying that holy cause, which you seemingly espoused. Are you secretly, then, a more dangerous enemy than Cleanthes himself?

And are you so late in perceiving it? replied Cleanthes. Believe me, Demea; your friend Philo, from the beginning, has been amusing himself at both our expence; and it must be confessed, that the injudicious reasoning of our vulgar theology has given him but too just a handle of ridicule. The total infirmity of human reason, the absolute incomprehensibility of the divine nature, the great and universal misery and still greater wickedness of men; these are strange topics surely to be so fondly cherished by orthodox divines and doctors. In ages of stupidity and ignorance, indeed, these principles may safely be espoused; and perhaps, no views of things are more proper to promote superstition, than such as encourage the blind amazement, the diffidence, and melancholy of mankind. But at present . . .

Blame not so much, interposed Philo, the ignorance of these reverend gentlemen. They know how to change their style with the times. Formerly it was a most popular theological topic to maintain, that human life was vanity and misery, and to exaggerate all the ills and pains which are incident to men. But of late years, divines, we find, begin to retract this position, and maintain, though still with some hesitation, that there are more goods than evils, more pleasures than pains, even in this life. When religion stood entirely upon temper and education, it was thought proper to encourage melancholy; as indeed, mankind never have recourse to superior powers so readily as in that disposition. But as men have now learned to form principles, and to draw consequences, it is necessary to change the batteries, and to make use of such arguments as will endure, at least some scrutiny and examination. This variation is the same (and from the same causes) with that which I formerly remarked with regard to scepticism.

Thus Philo continued to the last his spirit of opposition, and his censure of established opinions. But I could observe, that Demea did not at all relish the latter part of the discourse; and he took occasion soon after, on some pretence or other, to leave the company.

PART XII

After Demea's departure, Cleanthes and Philo continued the conversation in the following manner. Our friend, I am afraid, said Cleanthes, will have little inclination to revive this topic of discourse, while you are in company; and to tell truth, Philo, I should rather wish to reason with either of you apart on a subject so sublime and interesting. Your spirit of controversy, joined to your abhorrence of vulgar superstition, carries you strange lengths, when engaged in an argument; and there is nothing so sacred and venerable, even in your own eyes, which you spare on that occasion.

I must confess, replied Philo, that I am less cautious on the subject of natural religion than on any other; both because I know that I can never, on that head, corrupt the principles of any man of common sense, and because no one, I am confident, in whose eyes I appear a man of common sense, will ever mistake my intentions. You, in particular, Cleanthes, with whom I live in unreserved intimacy; you are sensible, that, notwithstanding the freedom of my conversation, and my love of singular arguments, no one has a deeper sense of religion impressed on his mind, or pays more profound adoration to the divine Being, as he discovers himself to reason, in the inexplicable contrivance and artifice of nature. A purpose, an intention, or design strikes everywhere the most careless, the most stupid thinker; and no man can be so hardened in absurd systems, as at all times to reject it. *That nature does nothing in vain,* is a maxim established in all the schools, merely from the contemplation of the works of nature, without any religious purpose; and, from a firm conviction of its truth, an anatomist, who had observed a new organ or canal, would never be satisfied till he had also discovered its use and intention. One great foundation of the Copernican system is the maxim, *that nature acts by the simplest methods, and chooses the most proper means to any end;* and astronomers often, without thinking of it, lay this strong foundation of piety and religion. The same thing is observable in other parts of philosophy: And thus all the sciences almost lead us insensibly to acknowledge a first intelligent Author; and their authority is often so much the greater, as they do not directly profess that intention.

It is with pleasure I hear Galen reason concerning the structure of the human body. The anatomy of a man, says he, discovers above 600 different muscles; and whoever duly considers these, will find, that in each of them nature must have adjusted at least ten different circumstances, in order to attain the end which she proposed; proper figure, just magnitude, right disposition of the several ends, upper and lower position of the whole, the due insertion of the several nerves, veins, and arteries: So that, in the muscles alone, above 6,000 several views and intentions must have been formed and executed. The bones he calculates to be 284: The distinct purposes, aimed at in the structure of each, above forty. What a prodigious display of artifice, even in these simple and homogeneous parts? But if we consider the skin, ligaments, vessels, glandules, humours, the several limbs and members of the body; how must our astonishment rise upon us, in proportion to the number and intricacy of the parts so artificially adjusted? The farther we advance in these researches, we discover new scenes of art and wisdom: But descry still, at a distance, farther scenes beyond our reach; in the fine internal structure of the parts, in the œconomy of the brain, in the fabric of the seminal vessels. All these artifices are repeated in every different species of animal, with wonderful variety, and with exact propriety, suited to the different intentions of nature, in framing each species. And if the infidelity of Galen, even when these natural sciences were still imperfect, could not withstand such striking appearances; to what pitch of pertinacious obstinacy must a philosopher in this age have attained, who can now doubt of a supreme intelligence?

Could I meet with one of this species (who, I thank God, are very rare) I would ask him: Supposing there were a God, who did not discover himself immediately to our senses; were it possible for him to give stronger proofs of his existence, than what appear on the whole face of nature? What indeed could such a divine Being do, but copy the present œconomy of things; render many of his artifices so plain, that no stupidity could mistake them; afford glimpses of still greater artifices, which demonstrate his prodigious superiority above our narrow apprehensions; and conceal altogether a great many from such imperfect creatures? Now according to all rules of just reasoning, every fact must pass for undisputed, when it is supported by all the arguments which its nature admits of, even though these arguments be not, in themselves, very numerous or forcible: How much more, in the present case, where no human imagination can compute their number, and no understanding estimate their cogency?

I shall farther add, said Cleanthes, to what you have so well urged, that one great advantage of the principle of theism, is, that it is the only system of cosmogony which can be rendered intelligible and complete, and yet can throughout preserve a strong analogy to what we every day see and experience in the world. The comparison of the universe to a machine of human contrivance is so obvious and natural, and is justified by so many instances of order and design in nature, that it must immediately strike all unprejudiced apprehensions, and procure universal approbation. Whoever attempts to weaken this theory, cannot pretend to succeed by establishing in its place any other that is precise and determinate: It is sufficient for him, if he start doubts and difficulties; and by remote and abstract views of things, reach that suspence of judgment, which is here the utmost boundary of his wishes. But besides that this state of mind is in itself unsatisfactory, it can never be steadily maintained against such striking appearances as continually engage us into the religious hypothesis. A false, absurd system, human nature, from the force of prejudice, is capable of adhering to with obstinacy and perseverance: But no system at all, in opposition to a theory, supported by strong and obvious reason, by natural propensity, and by early education, I think it absolutely impossible to maintain or defend.

So little, replied Philo, do I esteem this suspense of judgment in the present case to be possible, that I am apt to suspect there enters somewhat of a dispute of words into this controversy, more than is usually imagined. That the works of nature bear a great analogy to the productions of art is evident; and according to all the rules of good reasoning, we ought to infer, if we argue at all concerning them, that their causes have a proportional analogy. But as there are also considerable differences, we have reason to suppose a proportional difference in the causes; and in particular ought to attribute a much higher degree of power and energy to the supreme cause than any we have ever observed in mankind. Here then the existence of a Deity is plainly ascertained by reason; and if we make it a question, whether, on account of these analogies, we can properly call him a *mind* or *intelligence*, notwithstanding the vast difference, which may reasonably be supposed between him and human minds; what is this but a mere verbal controversy? No man can deny the analogies between the effects: To restrain ourselves from enquiring concerning the causes is scarcely possible: From this enquiry, the legitimate conclusion is, that the causes have also an analogy: And if we are not contented with calling the first and supreme cause a God or Deity, but desire to vary the expression; what can we call him but mind or thought, to which he is justly supposed to bear a considerable resemblance?

All men of sound reason are disgusted with verbal disputes, which abound so much in philosophical and theological enquiries; and it is found, that the only remedy for this abuse must arise from clear definitions, from the precision of those ideas which enter into any argument, and from the strict and uniform use of those terms which are employed. But there is a species of controversy, which, from the very nature of language and of human ideas, is involved in perpetual ambiguity, and can never, by any precaution or any definitions, be able to reach a reasonable certainty or precision. These are the controversies concerning the degrees of any quality or circumstance. Men may argue to all eternity, whether Hannibal be a great, or a very great, or a superlatively great man, what degree of beauty Cleopatra possessed, what epithet of praise Livy or Thucydides is entitled to, without bringing the controversy to any determination. The disputants may here agree in their sense and differ in the terms, or *vice versa;* yet never be able to define their terms, so as to enter into each other's meaning: Because the degrees of these qualities are not, like quantity or number, susceptible of any exact mensuration, which may be the standard in the controversy. That the dispute concerning theism is of this nature, and consequently is merely verbal, or perhaps, if possible, still more incurably ambiguous, will appear upon the slightest enquiry. I ask the theist, if he does not allow, that there is a great and immeasurable, because incomprehensible, difference between the *human* and the *divine mind:* The more pious he is, the more readily will he assent to the affirmative, and the more will he be disposed to magnify the difference: He will even assert, that the difference is of a nature which cannot be too much magnified. I next turn to the atheist, who, I assert, is only nominally so, and can never possibly be in earnest; and I ask him, whether, from the coherence and apparent sympathy in all the parts of this world, there be not a certain degree of analogy among all the operations of nature, in every situation and in every age; whether the rotting of a turnip, the generation of an animal, and the structure of human thought be not energies that probably bear some remote analogy to each other: It is impossible he can deny it: He will readily acknowledge it. Having obtained this concession, I push him still farther in his retreat; and I ask him, if it be not probable, that the principle which first arranged, and still maintains, order in this universe, bears not also some remote inconceivable analogy to the other operations of nature, and among the rest to the œconomy of human mind and thought. However reluctant, he must give his assent. Where then, cry I to both these antagonists, is the subject of your dispute? The theist allows, that the original intelligence is very different from human reason: The atheist allows, that the original principle of order bears some remote analogy to it. Will you quarrel, Gentlemen, about the degrees, and enter into a controversy, which admits not of any precise meaning, nor consequently of any determination? If you should be so obstinate, I should not be surprised to find you insensibly change sides; while the theist on the one hand exaggerates the dissimilarity between the supreme Being, and frail, imperfect, variable, fleeting, and mortal creatures; and the atheist on the other magnifies the analogy among all the operations of nature, in every period, every situation, and every position. Consider then, where the real point of controversy lies, and if you cannot lay aside your disputes, endeavour, at least, to cure yourselves of your animosity.

And here I must also acknowledge, Cleanthes, that, as the works of nature have a much greater analogy to the effects of *our* art and contrivance, than to those of *our* benevolence and justice; we have reason to infer that the natural attributes of the Deity have a greater resemblance to those of man, than his moral have to human virtues. But what is the consequence? Nothing but this, that the moral qualities of man are more defective in their kind than his natural abilities. For, as the supreme Being is allowed to be absolutely and entirely perfect, whatever differs most from him departs the farthest from the supreme standard of rectitude and perfection.

These, Cleanthes, are my unfeigned sentiments on this subject; and these sentiments, you know, I have ever cherished and maintained. But in proportion to my veneration for true religion, is my abhorrence of vulgar superstitions; and I indulge a peculiar pleasure, I confess, in pushing such principles, sometimes into absurdity, sometimes into impiety. And you are sensible, that all bigots, notwithstanding their great aversion to the latter above the former, are commonly equally guilty of both.

My inclination, replied Cleanthes, lies, I own, a contrary way. Religion, however corrupted, is still better than no religion at all. The doctrine of a future state is so strong and necessary a security to morals, that we never ought to abandon or neglect it. For if finite and temporary rewards and punishments have so great an effect, as we daily find: How much greater must be expected from such as are infinite and eternal?

How happens it then, said Philo, if vulgar superstition be so salutary to society, that all history abounds so much with accounts of its pernicious consequences on public affairs? Factions, civil wars, persecutions, subversions of government, oppression, slavery; these are the dismal consequences which always attend its prevalency over the minds of men. If the religious spirit be ever mentioned in any historical narration, we are sure to meet afterwards with a detail of the miseries which attend it. And no period of time can be happier or more prosperous, than those in which it is never regarded, or heard of.

The reason of this observation, replied Cleanthes, is obvious. The proper office of religion is to regulate the heart of men, humanize their conduct, infuse the spirit of temperance, order, and obedience; and as its operation is silent, and only enforces the motives of mortality and justice, it is in danger of being overlooked, and confounded with these other motives. When it distinguishes itself, and acts as a separate principle over men, it has departed from its proper sphere, and has become only a cover to faction and ambition.

And so will all religion, said Philo, except the philosophical and rational kind. Your reasonings are more easily eluded than my facts. The inference is not just, because finite and temporary rewards and punishments have so great influence, that therefore such as are infinite and eternal must have so much greater. Consider, I beseech you, the attachment, which we have to present things, and the little concern which we discover for objects so remote and uncertain. When divines are declaiming against the common behaviour and conduct of the world, they always represent this principle as the strongest imaginable (which indeed it is) and describe almost all human kind as lying under the influence of it, and sunk into the deepest lethargy and unconcern about their religious interests. Yet these same divines, when they refute their speculative antagonists, suppose the motives of religion to be so powerful, that, without them, it were impossible for civil society to subsist; nor are they ashamed of so palpable a contradiction. It is certain, from experience, that the smallest grain of natural honesty and benevolence has more effect on men's conduct, than the most pompous views suggested by theological theories and systems. A man's natural inclination works incessantly upon him; it is for ever present to the mind; and mingles itself with every view and consideration: Whereas religious motives, where they act at all, operate only by starts and bounds; and it is scarcely possible for them to become altogether habitual to the mind. The force of the greatest gravity, say the philosophers, is infinitely small, in comparison of that of the least impulse; yet it is certain that the smallest gravity will, in the end, prevail above a great impulse; because no strokes or blows can be repeated with such constancy as attraction and gravitation.

Another advantage of inclination: It engages on its side all the wit and ingenuity of the mind; and when set in opposition to religious principles, seeks every method and art of eluding them: In which it is almost always successful. Who can explain the heart of man, or account for those strange salvos and excuses, with which people satisfy themselves, when they follow their inclinations, in opposition to their religious duty? This is well understood in the world; and none but fools ever repose less trust in a man, because they hear, that, from study and philosophy, he has entertained some speculative doubts with regard to theological subjects. And when we have to do with a man, who makes a great profession of religion and devotion; has this any other effect upon several, who pass for prudent, than to put them on their guard, lest they be cheated and deceived by him?

We must farther consider, that philosophers, who cultivate reason and reflection, stand less in need of such motives to keep them under the restraint of morals: And that the vulgar, who alone may need them, are utterly incapable of so pure a religion as represents the Deity to be pleased with nothing but virtue in human behaviour. The recommendations to the Divinity are generally supposed to be either frivolous observances, or rapturous ecstasies, or a bigoted credulity. We need not run back into antiquity, or wander into remote regions, to find instances of this degeneracy. Amongst ourselves, some have been guilty of that atrociousness, unknown to the Egyptian and Grecian superstitions, of declaiming, in express terms, against morality, and representing it as a sure forfeiture of the divine favour, if the least trust or reliance be laid upon it.

But even though superstition or enthusiasm should not put itself in direct opposition to morality; the very diverting of the attention, the raising up a new and frivolous species of merit, the preposterous distribution which it makes of praise and blame, must have the most pernicious consequences, and weaken extremely men's attachment to the natural motives of justice and humanity.

Such a principle of action likewise, not being any of the familiar motives of human conduct, acts only by intervals on the temper, and must be roused by continual efforts, in order to render the pious zealot satisfied with his own conduct, and make him fulfil his devotional task. Many religious exercises are entered into with seeming fervour, where the heart, at the time, feels cold and languid: A habit of dissimulation is by degrees contracted: And fraud and falsehood become the predominant principle. Hence the reason of that vulgar observation, that the highest zeal in religion and the deepest hypocrisy, so far from being inconsistent, are often or commonly united in the same individual character.

The bad effects of such habits, even in common life, are easily imagined: But where the interests of religion are concerned, no morality can be forcible enough to bind the enthusiastic zealot. The sacredness of the cause sanctifies every measure which can be made use of to promote it.

The steady attention alone to so important an interest as that of eternal salvation is apt to extinguish the benevolent affections, and beget a narrow, contracted selfishness. And when such a temper is encouraged, it easily eludes all the general precepts of charity and benevolence.

Thus the motives of vulgar superstition have no great influence on general conduct; nor is their operation very favourable to morality, in the instances where they predominate.

Is there any maxim in politics more certain and infallible, than that both the number and authority of priests should be confined within very narrow limits, and that the civil magistrate ought, for ever, to keep his *fasces* and *axes* from such dangerous hands? But if the spirit of popular religion were so salutary to society, a contrary maxim ought to prevail. The greater number of priests, and their greater authority and riches, will always augment the religious spirit. And though the priests have the guidance of this spirit, why may we not expect a superior sanctity of life, and greater benevolence and moderation, from persons who are set apart for religion, who are continually inculcating it upon others, and who must themselves imbibe a greater share of it? Whence comes it then, that, in fact, the utmost a wise magistrate can propose with regard to popular religions, is, as far as possible, to make a saving game of it, and to prevent their pernicious consequences with regard to society? Every expedient which he tries for so humble a purpose is surrounded with inconveniences. If he admits only one religion among his subjects, he must sacrifice, to an uncertain prospect of tranquillity, every consideration of public liberty, science, reason, industry, and even his own independency. If he gives indulgence to several sects, which is the wiser maxim, he must preserve a very philosophical indifference to all of them, and carefully restrain the pretensions of the prevailing sect; otherwise he can expect nothing but endless disputes, quarrels, factions, persecutions, and civil commotions.

True religion, I allow, has no such pernicious consequences: But we must treat of religion, as it has commonly been found in the world; nor have I any thing to do with that speculative tenet of theism, which, as it is a species of philosophy, must partake of the beneficial influence of that principle, and at the same time must lie under a like inconvenience, of being always confined to very few persons.

Oaths are requisite in all courts of judicature; but it is a question whether their authority arises from any popular religion. It is the solemnity and importance of the occasion, the regard to reputation, and the reflecting on the general interests of society, which are the chief restraints upon mankind. Custom-house oaths and political oaths are but little regarded even by some who pretend to principles of honesty and religion: And a Quaker's asseveration is with us justly put upon the same footing with the oath of any other person. I know, that Polybius ascribes the infamy of Greek faith to the prevalency of the Epicurean philosophy; but I know also, that Punic faith had as bad a reputation in ancient times, as Irish evidence has in modern; though we cannot account for these vulgar observations by the same reason. Not to mention, that Greek faith was infamous before the rise of the Epicurean philosophy; and Euripides, in a passage which I shall point out to you, has glanced a remarkable stroke of satire against his nation, with regard to this circumstance.

Take care, Philo, replied Cleanthes, take care: Push not matters too far: Allow not your zeal against false religion to undermine your veneration for the true. Forfeit not this principle, the chief, the only great comfort in life; and our principle support amidst all the attacks of adverse fortune. The most agreeable reflection, which it is possible for human imagination to suggest, is that of genuine theism, which represents us as the workmanship of a Being perfectly good, wise, and powerful; who created us for happiness, and who, having implanted in us immeasurable desires of good, will prolong our existence to all eternity, and will transfer us into an infinite variety of scenes, in order to satisfy those desires, and render our felicity complete and durable. Next to such a Being himself (if the comparison be allowed) the happiest lot which we can imagine, is that of being under his guardianship and protection.

These appearances, said Philo, are most engaging and alluring; and with regard to the true philosopher, they are more than appearances. But it happens here, as in the former case, that, with regard to the greater part of mankind, the appearances are deceitful, and that the terrors of religion commonly prevail above its comforts.

It is allowed, that men never have recourse to devotion so readily as when dejected with grief or depressed with sickness. Is not this a proof, that the religious spirit is not so nearly allied to joy as to sorrow?

But men, when afflicted, find consolation in religion, replied Cleanthes. Sometimes, said Philo: But it is natural to imagine, that they will form a notion of those unknown Beings, suitably to the present gloom and melancholy of their temper, when they betake themselves to the contemplation of them. Accordingly, we find the tremendous images to predominate in all religions; and we ourselves, after having employed the most exalted expression in our descriptions of the Deity, fall into the flattest contradiction, in affirming, that the damned are infinitely superior in number to the elect.

I shall venture to affirm, that there never was a popular religion, which represented the state of departed souls in such a light, as would render it eligible for human kind, that there should be such a state. These fine models of religion are the mere product of philosophy. For as death lies between the eye and the prospect of futurity, that event is so shocking to nature, that it must throw a gloom on all the regions which lie beyond it; and suggest to the generality of mankind the idea of Cerberus and Furies; devils, and torrents of fire and brimstone.

It is true; both fear and hope enter into religion; because both these passions, at different times, agitate the human mind, and each of them forms a species of divinity, suitable to itself. But when a man is in a cheerful disposition, he is fit for business or company or entertainment of any kind; and he naturally applies himself to these, and thinks not of religion. When melancholy, and dejected, he has nothing to do but brood upon the terrors of the invisible world, and to plunge himself still deeper in affliction. It may, indeed, happen, that after he has, in this manner, engraved the religious opinions deep into his thought and imagination, there may arrive a change of health or circumstances, which may restore his good humour, and raising cheerful prospects of futurity, make him run into the other extreme of joy and triumph. But still it must be acknowledged, that, as terror is the primary principle of religion, it is the passion which always predominates in it, and admits but of short intervals of pleasure.

Not to mention, that these fits of excessive, enthusiastic joy, by exhausting the spirits, always prepare the way for equal fits of superstitious terror and dejection; nor is there any state of mind so happy as the calm and equable. But this state it is impossible to support, where a man thinks, that he lies, in such profound darkness and uncertainty, between an eternity of happiness and an eternity of misery. No wonder, that such an opinion disjoints the ordinary frame of the mind, and throws it into the utmost confusion. And though that opinion is seldom so steady in its operation as to influence all the actions; yet it is apt to make a considerable breach in the temper, and to produce that gloom and melancholy, so remarkable in all devout people.

It is contrary to common sense to entertain apprehensions or terrors, upon account of any opinion whatsoever, or to imagine that we run any risk hereafter, by the freest use of our reason. Such a sentiment implies both an *absurdity* and an *inconsistency*. It is an absurdity to believe that the Deity has human passions, and one of the lowest of human passions, a restless appetite for applause. It is an inconsistency to believe, that, since the Deity has this human passion, he has not others also; and, in particular, a disregard to the opinions of creatures so much inferior.

To know God, says Seneca, *is to worship him*. All other worship is indeed absurd, superstitious, and even impious. It degrades him to the low condition of mankind, who are delighted with entreaty, solicitation, presents, and flattery. Yet is this impiety the smallest of which superstition is guilty. Commonly, it depresses the Deity far below the condition of mankind; and represents him as a capricious Dæmon, who exercises his power without reason and without humanity! And were that divine Being disposed to be offended at the vices and follies of silly mortals, who are his own workmanship; ill would it surely fare with the votaries of most popular superstitions. Nor would any of human race merit his *favour,* but a very few, the philosophical theists, who entertain, or rather indeed endeavour to entertain, suitable notions of his divine perfections: As the only persons entitled to his *compassion* and *indulgence* would be the philosophical sceptics, a sect almost equally rare, who, from a natural diffidence of their own capacity, suspend, or endeavour to suspend all judgment with regard to such sublime and such extraordinary subjects.

If the whole of natural theology, as some people seem to maintain, resolves itself into one simple, though somewhat ambiguous, at least undefined proposition, *that the cause or causes of order in the universe probably bear some remote analogy to human intelligence:* If this proposition be not capable of extension, variation, or more particular explication: If it afford no inference that affects human life, or can be the source of any action or forbearance: And if the analogy, imperfect as it is, can be carried no farther than to the human intelligence; and cannot be transferred, with any appearance of probability, to the other qualities of the mind: If this really be the case, what can the most inquisitive, contemplative, and religious man do more than give a plain, philosophical assent to the proposition, as often as it occurs; and believe that the arguments, on which it is established, exceed the objections which lie against it? Some astonishment indeed will naturally arise from the greatness of the object: Some melancholy from its obscurity: Some contempt of human reason, that it can give no solution more satisfactory with regard to so extraordinary and magnificent a question. But believe me, Cleanthes, the most natural sentiment, which a well-disposed mind will feel on this occasion, is a longing desire and expectation, that Heaven would be pleased to dissipate, at least alleviate, this profound ignorance, by affording some more particular revelation to mankind, and making discoveries of the nature, attributes, and operations of the divine object of our Faith. A person, seasoned with a just sense of the imperfections of natural reason, will fly to revealed truth with the greatest avidity: While the haughty dogmatist, persuaded that he can erect a complete system of theology by the mere help of philosophy, disdains any farther aid, and rejects this adventitious instructor. To be a philosophical sceptic is, in a man of letters, the first and most essential step towards being a sound, believing Christian; a proposition which I would willingly recommend to the attention of Pamphilus: And I hope Cleanthes will forgive me for interposing so far in the education and instruction of his pupil.

Cleanthes and Philo pursued not this conversation much farther; and as nothing ever made greater impression on me than all the reasonings of that day; so I confess, that, upon a serious review of the whole, I cannot but think, that Philo's principles are more probable than Demea's; but that those of Cleanthes approach still nearer to the truth.

THOMAS REID
1710–1796

Thomas Reid was born in the Scottish village of Strachan, Kincardineshire, on April 25, 1710—exactly one year to the day before the birth of his fellow Scottish philosopher and primary philosophical target, David Hume. Following a pleasant childhood, Reid entered Marishcal College, Aberdeen, at age twelve. At the college, Reid came under the influence of George Turnbull, a follower of Berkeley. In developing Berkeley's idealism, Turnbull held that common sense resolved intellectual and moral disputes—a position Reid championed the rest of his life.

Following graduation from the college in 1726, Reid studied theology for several years. Starting in 1733, he served as librarian at his alma mater for three years. Reid then left Scotland for the only time in his life, touring the English cities of London, Oxford, and Cambridge. Upon his return to Scotland, he become a pastor in the parish of New Machar, Aberdeenshire, married, and had nine children.

Reid's seventeen years as pastor were externally uneventful. But near the beginning of his pastorate, he discovered Hume, and Reid's life was never the same. Just as Immanuel Kant would later say that Hume had awakened him from his "dogmatic slumbers," so also Reid found his own thinking transformed by the Edinburgh philosopher. Reid studied Hume's *Treatise of Human Nature* intently and developed his own response to the challenge he found there.

In 1751, Reid left the pastorate and became a regent and lecturer in philosophy at King's College, Aberdeen University. Here he helped found the Aberdeen Philosophical Society and began a correspondence with Hume. In 1764, Reid published his first book, *Inquiry into the Human Mind on the Principles of Common Sense*. The same year, he accepted the Chair of Moral Philosophy at

Old College, Glasgow University. Reid's version of what he called "Common Sense Philosophy" grew in influence while he was at Glasgow, and several of his students, including Dugald Stewart, received important positions in Scottish universities. This was the period when Scottish philosophy was at its peak in creativity and influence. Reid's ideas found their way to America and influenced generations of thinkers—especially in philosophical theology at schools such as Princeton.

Following his retirement in 1780, Reid assembled his lecture notes and writings and published the most complete statements of his ideas in *Essays on the Intellectual Powers of Man* (1785) and *Essays on the Active Powers* (1788). Reid remained intellectually active until his death in 1796, having outlived his wife and all his nine children save one daughter.

***

In the writings of David Hume, Reid found a "system of skepticism, which leaves no ground to believe any one thing rather than its contrary."* As he examined Hume's philosophy, Reid came to the conclusion that Hume's skepticism was the natural conclusion to a belief accepted by almost every philosopher since Descartes. If one accepted what Reid called the "theory of ideas," a theory held by Descartes, Locke, Berkeley, and many others, one is bound to become a skeptic. Interposing "ideas" between the mind and known objects cuts one off from the actual world. According to Reid, one can then claim to know only one's mental states and not what those mental states are *of*. Moreover, this theory of ideas cuts one off from the mind itself. Berkeley had claimed that there is in fact nothing in nature except minds and ideas. But, as Reid explained, Hume had followed the logic of ideas to the conclusion that "there is nothing in nature but ideas only; for what we call a mind is nothing but a train of ideas connected by certain relations between themselves."

In the reading given here, from Chapters 14 and 15 of the *Essays on the Intellectual Powers of Man*, Reid presents four problems with the theory of ideas. In the first place, such a theory is "directly contrary to the universal sense of men who have not been instructed in philosophy." When we observe an object that appears far away, we all assume that what we are observing is far away—not that what we are observing is actually ideas in our minds. Second, Reid examines a series of arguments that had been advanced in favor of the existence of "ideas" and finds each argument wanting. As he puts it, "If no better arguments can be found, I cannot help thinking that the whole history of philosophy has never furnished an instance of an opinion so unanimously entertained by philosophers upon so slight grounds." Third, that every philosopher who held the theory of ideas seems to have had a different opinion about the nature of ideas and the way in which they are known undermines the value of the theory held. Finally, Reid asks how this theory of ideas help us understand the operations of the mind. Despite the theory's almost universal appeal to philosophers, Reid concluded that it must be dropped.

In place of a theory of ideas, Reid proposed a philosophy of common sense. By appealing to the "original and natural judgements"** we make about objects,

---

*Inquiry into the Human Mind on the Principles of Common Sense, dedication.
**Essays, Chapter 6 (not included in this reading).

we can avoid the skepticism of Hume. As our reading concludes, such a commonsense philosophy "puts the philosopher and the peasant upon a level, and neither of them can give any other reason for believing his senses than that he finds it impossible for him to do otherwise."

The nature and scope of the common sense's "original and natural judgements" have been a matter of debate (see the suggested readings that follow); and the value of common-sense philosophy as a whole has been questioned. By the time of his death, Reid's thought had been overwhelmed by Kant's influential writings. Still, Scottish common-sense philosophy has remained interesting and in recent years it has experienced a renaissance of sorts. In the early twentieth century, G.E. Moore championed the cause of "common sense," and in the second half of the twentieth century, Roderick Chisholm, Richard Taylor, William Alston, Alvin Plantinga, and Nicholas Wolterstorff have saluted Reid's thought.

*   *   *

The best single source for study of Reid's philosophy is Keith Lehrer, *Thomas Reid* (London: Routledge, 1989). Louise Marcil-Lacoste, *Claude Buffier and Thomas Reid: Two Common-Sense Philosophers* (Kingston, Ont.: McGill-Queen's University Press, 1982), and Roger D. Gallie, *Thomas Reid and "The Way of Ideas"* (Dordrecht, The Netherlands: Kluwer Academic, 1989) are also useful. The classic studies of Reid's common-sense philosophy are A. Seth Pringle-Pattison, *Scottish Philosophy: A Comparison of the Scottish and German Answers to Hume*, 4th edition (Edinburgh: W. Blackwood and Sons, 1907), and S.A. Grave, *The Scottish Philosophy of Common Sense* (Oxford: Clarendon Press, 1960). Recent comparative studies which discuss Reid include John W. Yolton, *Perceptual Acquaintance from Descartes to Reid* (Minneapolis: University of Minnesota Press, 1984); Stephen K. Land, *The Philosophy of Language in Britain: Major Theories from Hobbes to Thomas Reid* (New York: AMS Press, 1986); M. Jamie Ferreira, *Skepticism and Reasonable Doubt: The British Naturalist Tradition in Wilkins, Hume, Reid, and Newman* (Oxford: Oxford University Press, 1986); Peter Gilmour, ed., *Philosophers of the Enlightenment* (Edinburgh: Edinburgh University Press, 1989); John Skorupski, *English-Language Philosophy 1750–1945* (Oxford: Oxford University Press, 1993); and James W.F. Somerville, *The Enigmatic Parting Shot* (Aldershot, England: Avebury, 1995). For studies in specific areas of Reid's thought, see Norman Daniels, *Thomas Reid's Inquiry: The Geometry of Visibles and the Case for Realism* (New York: Burt Franklin, 1974), and William L. Rowe, *Thomas Reid on Freedom and Morality* (Ithaca, NY: Cornell University Press, 1991). Finally, for collections of essays that include Reid, see Stephen F. Barker and Tom L. Beauchamp, eds., *Thomas Reid: Critical Interpretations* (Philadelphia: University City Science Center, 1976); Melvin Dalgarno and Eric Matthews, eds., *The Philosophy of Thomas Reid* (Dordrecht, The Netherlands: Kluwer Academic, 1989); and Peter Jones, ed., *The "Science of Man" in the Scottish Enlightenment: Hume, Reid, and Their Contemporaries* (Edinburgh: Edinburgh University Press, 1989).

ESSAYS ON THE INTELLECTUAL POWERS OF MAN (in part)

Chapter 14: Reflections on the Common Theory of Ideas

After so long a detail of the sentiments of philosophers, ancient and modern, concerning ideas, it may seem presumptuous to call in question their existence. But no philosophical opinion, however ancient, however generally received, ought to rest upon authority. There is no presumption in requiring evidence for it, or in regulating our belief by the evidence we can find.

To prevent mistakes, the reader must again be reminded that if by ideas are meant only the acts or operations of our minds in perceiving, remembering, or imagining objects, I am far from calling in question the existence of those acts; we are conscious of them every day and every hour of life; and I believe no man of a sound mind ever doubted of the real existence of the operations of mind, of which he is conscious. Nor is it to be doubted that, by the faculties which God has given us, we can conceive things that are absent as well as perceive those that are within the reach of our senses; and that such conceptions may be more or less distinct, and more or less lively and strong. We have reason to ascribe to the all-knowing and all-perfect Being distinct conceptions of all things existent and possible, and of all their relations; and if these conceptions are called his eternal ideas, there ought to be no dispute among philosophers about a word. The ideas, of whose existence I require the proof, are not the operations of any mind, but supposed objects of those operations. They are not perception, remembrance, or conception, but things that are said to be perceived, or remembered, or imagined.

Nor do I dispute the existence of what the vulgar call the objects of perception. These, by all who acknowledge their existence, are called real things, not ideas. But philosophers maintain that, besides these, there are immediate objects of perception in the mind itself: that, for instance, we do not see the sun immediately, but an idea; or, as Mr. Hume calls it, an impression in our own minds. This idea is said to be the image, the resemblance, the representative of the sun, if there be a sun. It is from the existence of the idea that we must infer the existence of the sun. But the idea, being immediately perceived, there can be no doubt, as philosophers think, of its existence.

In like manner, when I remember, or when I imagine anything, all men acknowledge that there must be something that is remembered or that is imagined; that is, some object of those operations. The object remembered must be something that did exist in time past: the object imagined may be something that never existed. But, say the philosophers, besides these objects which all men acknowledge, there is a more immediate object which really exists in the mind at the same time we remember or imagine. This object is an idea or image of the thing remembered or imagined.

The *first* reflection I would make on this philosophical opinion is, that it is directly contrary to the universal sense of men who have not been instructed in philosophy. When we see the sun or moon, we have no doubt that the very objects which we immediately see are very far distant from us, and from one another. We have not the least doubt that this is the sun and moon which God created some thousands of years ago, and which have continued to perform their revolutions in the heavens ever since. But how are we astonished when the philosopher informs us that we are mistaken in all this; that the sun and moon which we see are not, as we imagine, many miles distant from us, and from each other, but they are in our own mind; that they had no existence before we saw them, and will have none when we cease to perceive and to think of them; because the objects we perceive are only ideas in our own mind, which can have no existence a moment longer than we think of them!

If a plain man, uninstructed in philosophy, has faith to receive these mysteries, how great must be his astonishment! He is brought into a new world where everything he sees, tastes, or touches, is an idea—a fleeting kind of being which he can conjure into existence, or can annihilate in the twinkling of an eye.

After his mind is somewhat composed, it will be natural for him to ask his philosophical instructor, Pray, sir, are there then no substantial and permanent beings called the sun and moon, which continue to exist whether we think of them or not?

Here the philosophers differ. Mr. Locke, and those that were before him, will answer to this question that it is very true there are substantial and permanent beings called the sun and moon; but they never appear to us in their own person, but by their representatives, the ideas in our own minds, and we know nothing of them but what we can gather from those ideas.

Bishop Berkeley and Mr. Hume would give a different answer to the question proposed. They would assure the querist that it is a vulgar error, a mere prejudice of the ignorant and unlearned, to think that there are any permanent and substantial beings called the sun and moon; that the heavenly bodies, our own bodies, and all bodies whatsoever, are nothing but ideas in our minds; and that there can be nothing like the ideas of one mind, but the ideas of another mind. There is nothing in nature but minds and ideas, says the Bishop;—nay, says Mr. Hume, there is nothing in nature but ideas only; for what we call a mind is nothing but a train of ideas connected by certain relations between themselves.

In this representation of the theory of ideas there is nothing exaggerated or misrepresented, as far as I am able to judge; and surely nothing further is necessary to show that, to the uninstructed in philosophy, it must appear extravagant and visionary, and most contrary to the dictates of common understanding.

There is the less need of any further proof of this, that it is very amply acknowledged by Mr. Hume in his *Essay on the Academical or Sceptical Philosophy**

It is therefore acknowledged by this philosopher to be a natural instinct or prepossession, a universal and primary opinion of all men, a primary instinct of nature, that the objects which we immediately perceive by our senses are not images in our minds, but external objects, and that their existence is independent of us and our perception.

In this acknowledgment Mr. Hume indeed seems to me more generous, and even more ingenuous, than Bishop Berkeley, who would persuade us that his opinion does not oppose the vulgar opinion, but only that of the philosophers; and that the external existence of a material world is a philosophical hypothesis, and not the natural dictate of our perceptive powers.

A *second* reflection upon this subject is—that the authors who have treated of ideas have generally taken their existence for granted, as a thing that could not be called in question; and such arguments as they have mentioned incidentally, in order to prove it, seem too weak to support the conclusion.

Mr. Locke, in the Introduction to his Essay, tells us that he uses the word idea to signify whatever is the immediate object of thought; and then adds, "I presume it will

---

Enquiry Concerning Human Understanding, 12, I [pages 413–416 in this volume].

be easily granted me that there are such *ideas* in men's minds; everyone is conscious of them in himself; and men's words and actions will satisfy him that they are in others."* I am indeed conscious of perceiving, remembering, imagining; but that the objects of these operations are images in my mind, I am not conscious. I am satisfied, by men's words and actions, that they often perceive the same objects which I perceive, which could not be if those objects were ideas in their own minds.

Mr. Norris is the only author I have met with who professedly puts the question whether material things can be perceived by us immediately. He has offered four arguments to show that they cannot. *First*, "Material objects are without the mind, and therefore there can be no union between the object and the percipient." Answer, This argument is lame, until it is shown to be necessary that in perception there should be a union between the object and the percipient. *Second*, "Material objects are disproportioned to the mind, and removed from it by the whole diameter of Being." This argument I cannot answer, because I do not understand it. *Third*, "Because, if material objects were immediate objects of perception, there could be no physical science—things necessary and immutable being the only object of science." Answer, Although things necessary and immutable be not the immediate objects of perception, they may be immediate objects of other powers of the mind. *Fourth*, "If material things were perceived by themselves, they would be a true light to our minds, as being the intelligible form of our understandings, and consequently perfective of them, and indeed superior to them."** If I comprehend anything of this mysterious argument, it follows from it that the Deity perceives nothing at all, because nothing can be superior to his understanding or perfective of it.

There is an argument which is hinted at by Malebranche, and by several other authors, which deserves to be more seriously considered. As I find it most clearly expressed and most fully urged by Dr. Samuel Clarke, I shall give it in his words, in his second reply to Leibniz, §4: "The soul, without being present to the images of the things perceived, could not possibly perceive them. A living substance can only there perceive, where it is present, either to the things themselves (as the omnipresent God is to the whole universe) or to the images of things, as the soul is in its proper *sensorium*."

Sir Isaac Newton expresses the same sentiment, but with his usual reserve, in a query only.***

The ingenious Dr. Porterfield, in his *Essay concerning the Motions of our Eyes*, adopts this opinion with more confidence. His words are: "How body acts upon mind, or mind upon body, I know not; but this I am very certain of, that nothing can act, or be acted upon, where it is not; and therefore our mind can never perceive anything but its own proper modifications, and the various states of the sensorium, to which it is present: so that it is not the external sun and moon which are in the heavens, which our mind perceives, but only their image or representation impressed upon the sensorium. How the soul of a seeing man sees these images, or how it receives those ideas, from such agitations in the sensorium, I know not; but I am sure it can never perceive the external bodies themselves, to which it is not present."†

These, indeed, are great authorities: but in matters of philosophy we must not be guided by authority, but by reason. Dr. Clarke, in the place cited, mentions slightly, as the reason of his opinion, that "nothing can any more act, or be acted upon when it is not present, that it can be where it is not." And again, in his third reply to Leibniz, §11:

---

*An Essay Concerning Human Understanding, I, 1, 8 [p. 173 in this volume].
**Essay Towards the Theory of the Ideal or Intelligible World, Pt. II, Ch. 6.
***Optics, Qu. 28.
†Cf. his Treatise on the Eye, III, 2, 7.

"We are sure the soul cannot perceive what it is not present to, because nothing can act, or be acted upon, where it is not." The same reason we see is urged by Dr. Porterfield.

That nothing can act immediately where it is not, I think must be admitted: for I agree with Sir Isaac Newton, that power without substance is inconceivable.* It is a consequence of this, that nothing can be acted upon immediately where the agent is not present: let this, therefore, be granted. To make the reasoning conclusive, it is further necessary that, when we perceive objects, either they act upon us or we act upon them. This does not appear self-evident, nor have I ever met with any proof of it. I shall briefly offer the reasons why I think it ought not to be admitted.

When we say that one being acts upon another, we mean that some power or force is exerted by the agent which produces, or has a tendency to produce, a change in the thing acted upon. If this be the meaning of the phrase, as I conceive it is, there appears no reason for asserting that, in perception, either the object acts upon the mind or the mind upon the object.

An object, in being perceived, does not act at all. I perceive the walls of the room where I sit; but they are perfectly inactive, and therefore act not upon the mind. To be perceived is what logicians call an external denomination which implies neither action nor quality in the object perceived. Nor could men ever have gone into this notion that perception is owing to some action of the object upon the mind, were it not that we are so prone to form our notions of the mind from some similitude we conceive between it and body. Thought in the mind is conceived to have some analogy to motion in a body: and as a body is put in motion by being acted upon by some other body, so we are apt to think the mind is made to perceive by some impulse it receives from the object. But reasonings drawn from such analogies ought never to be trusted. They are, indeed, the cause of most of our errors with regard to the mind. And we might as well conclude that minds may be measured by feet and inches, or weighed by ounces and drams; because bodies have those properties.

I see as little reason, in the second place, to believe that in perception the mind acts upon the object. To perceive an object is one thing, to act upon it is another; nor is the last at all included in the first. To say that I act upon the wall by looking at it is an abuse of language, and has no meaning. Logicians distinguish two kinds of operations of mind: the first kind produces no effect without the mind; the last does. The first they call *immanent acts*, the second *transitive*. All intellectual operations belong to the first class; they produce no effect upon any external object. But, without having recourse to logical distinctions, every man of common sense knows that to think of an object, and to act upon it, are very different things.

As we have, therefore, no evidence that in perception the mind acts upon the object, or the object upon the mind, but strong reasons to the contrary, Dr. Clarke's argument against our perceiving external objects immediately falls to the ground.

This notion that, in perception, the object must be contiguous to the percipient seems, with many other prejudices, to be borrowed from analogy. In all the external senses there must, as has been before observed, be some impression made upon the organ of sense by the object, or by something coming from the object. An impression supposes contiguity. Hence we are led by analogy to conceive something similar in the operations of the mind.

When we lay aside those analogies and reflect attentively upon our perception of the object of sense, we must acknowledge that, though we are conscious of perceiving objects, we are altogether ignorant how it is brought about, and know as little how we perceive objects as how we were made. And, if we should admit an image in the mind,

Principia, Bk. 3.

or contiguous to it, we know as little how perception may be produced by this image as by the most distant object. Why, therefore, should we be led, by a theory which is neither grounded on evidence nor, if admitted, can explain any one phenomenon of perception, to reject the natural and immediate dictates of those perceptive powers to which, in the conduct of life, we find a necessity of yielding implicit submission?

There remains only one other argument that I have been able to find urged against our perceiving external objects immediately. It is proposed by Mr. Hume, who, in the essay already quoted, after acknowledging that it is a universal and primary opinion of all men that we perceive external objects immediately, subjoins what follows:

> But this universal and primary opinion of all men is soon destroyed by the slightest philosophy, which teaches us that nothing can ever be present to the mind but an image or perception; and that the senses are only the inlets through which these images are received, without being ever able to produce any immediate intercourse between the mind and the object. The table, which we see, seems to diminish as we remove further from it: but the real table, which exists independent of us, suffers no alteration. It was, therefore, nothing but its image which was present to the mind. These are the obvious dictates of reason; and no man who reflects ever doubted that the existences which we consider, when we say *this house* and *that tree*, are nothing but perceptions in the mind, and fleeting copies and representations of other existences, which remain uniform and independent. So far, then, we are necessitated, by reasoning, to depart from the primary instincts of nature, and to embrace a new system with regard to the evidence of our senses.*

We have here a remarkable conflict between two contradictory opinions, wherein all mankind are engaged. On the one side stand all the vulgar, who are unpractised in philosophical researches, and guided by the uncorrupted primary instincts of nature. On the other side stand all the philosophers, ancient and modern; every man, without exception, who reflects. In this division, to my great humiliation, I find myself classed with the vulgar.

The passage now quoted is all I have found in Mr. Hume's writings upon this point: and, indeed, there is more reasoning in it than I have found in any other author. I shall, therefore, examine it minutely.

First, He tells us that "this universal and primary opinion of all men is soon destroyed by the slightest philosophy, which teaches us that nothing can ever be present to the mind but an image or perception."

The phrase of being present to the mind has some obscurity, but I conceive he means being an immediate object of thought; an immediate object, for instance, of perception, of memory, or of imagination. If this be the meaning (and it is the only pertinent one I can think of), there is no more in this passage but an assertion of the proposition to be proved, and an assertion that philosophy teaches it. If this be so, I beg leave to dissent from philosophy till she gives me reason for what she teaches. For, though common sense and my external senses demand my assent to their dictates upon their own authority, yet philosophy is not entitled to this privilege. But, that I may not dissent from so grave a personage without giving a reason, I give this as the reason of my dissent: I see the sun when he shines; I remember the battle of Culloden; and neither of these objects is an image or perception.

He tells us, in the next place, "That the senses are only the inlets, through which these images are received."

I know that Aristotle and the schoolmen taught that images or species flow from objects, and are let in by the senses, and strike upon the mind; but this has been so effec-

Ibid., 12; I [page 415 in this volume].

tually refuted by Descartes, by Malebranche, and many others, that nobody now pretends to defend it. Reasonable men consider it as one of the most unintelligible and unmeaning parts of the ancient system. To what cause is it owing that modern philosophers are so prone to fall back into this hypothesis, as if they really believed it? For of this proneness I could give many instances besides this of Mr. Hume; and I take the cause to be that images in the mind, and images let in by the senses, are so nearly allied, and so strictly connected, that they must stand or fall together. The old system consistently maintained both: but the new system has rejected the doctrine of images let in by the senses, holding, nevertheless, that there are images in the mind; and, having made this unnatural divorce of two doctrines which ought not to be put asunder, that which they have retained often leads them back involuntarily to that which they have rejected.

Mr. Hume surely did not seriously believe that an image of sound is let in by the ear, an image of smell by the nose, an image of hardness and softness, of solidity and resistance, by the touch. For besides the absurdity of the thing, which has often been shown, Mr. Hume and all modern philosophers maintain that the images which are the immediate objects of perception have no existence when they are not perceived; whereas if they were let in by the senses, they must be, before they are perceived, and have a separate existence.

He tells us, further, that philosophy teaches that the senses are unable to produce any immediate intercourse between the mind and the object. Here I still require the reasons that philosophy gives for this; for, to my apprehension, I immediately perceive external objects, and this I conceive is the immediate intercourse here meant.

Hitherto I see nothing that can be called an argument. Perhaps it was intended only for illustration. The argument, the only argument, follows:

The table which we see, seems to diminish as we remove farther from it; but the real table, which exists independent of us, suffers no alteration. It was, therefore, nothing but its image which was presented to the mind. These are the obvious dictates of reason.

Let us suppose, for a moment, that it is the real table we see: Must not this real table seem to diminish as we remove farther from it? It is demonstrable that it must. How then can this apparent diminution be an argument that it is not the real table? When that which must happen to the real table, as we remove farther from it, does actually happen to the table we see, it is absurd to conclude from this, that it is not the real table we see. It is evident, therefore, that this ingenious author has imposed upon himself by confounding real magnitude with apparent magnitude, and that his argument is a mere sophism.

I observed that Mr. Hume's argument not only has no strength to support his conclusion, but that it leads to the contrary conclusion—to wit, that it is the real table we see; for this plain reason, that the table we see has precisely that apparent magnitude which it is demonstrable the real table must have when placed at that distance.

This argument is made much stronger by considering that the real table may be placed successively at a thousand different distances, and, in every distance, in a thousand different positions; and it can be determined demonstratively, by the rules of geometry and perspective, what must be its apparent magnitude and apparent figure in each of those distances and positions. Let the table be placed successively in as many of those different distances and different positions as you will, or in them all; open your eyes and you shall see a table precisely of that apparent magnitude, and that apparent figure, which the real table must have in that distance and in that position. Is not this a strong argument that it is the real table you see?

In a word, the appearance of a visible object is infinitely diversified according to its distance and position. The visible appearances are innumerable when we confine ourselves to one object, and they are multiplied according to the variety of objects. Those appearances have been matter of speculation to ingenious men at least since the time of Euclid. They have accounted for all this variety, on the supposition that the objects we see are external and not in the mind itself. The rules they have demonstrated about the various projections of the sphere, about the appearances of the planets in their progressions, stations, and retrogradations, and all the rules of perspective, are built on the supposition that the objects of sight are external. They can each of them be tried in thousands of instances. In many arts and professions innumerable trials are daily made; nor were they ever found to fail in a single instance. Shall we say that a false supposition, invented by the rude vulgar, has been so lucky in solving an infinite number of phenomena of nature? This, surely, would be a greater prodigy than philosophy ever exhibited: add to this, that, upon the contrary hypothesis—to wit, that the objects of sight are internal—no account can be given of any one of those appearances, nor any physical cause assigned why a visible object should, in any one case, have one apparent figure and magnitude rather than another.

Thus, I have considered every argument I have found advanced to prove the existence of ideas, or images of external things, in the mind; and, if no better arguments can be found, I cannot help thinking that the whole history of philosophy has never furnished an instance of an opinion so unanimously entertained by philosophers upon so slight grounds.

A *third* reflection I would make upon this subject is, that philosophers, notwithstanding their unanimity as to the existence of ideas, hardly agree in any one thing else concerning them. If ideas be not a mere fiction, they must be, of all objects of human knowledge, the things we have best access to know, and to be acquainted with; yet there is nothing about which men differ so much.

Some have held them to be self-existent, others to be in the Divine mind, others in our own minds, and others in the brain or *sensorium*. I considered the hypothesis of images in the brain, in the fourth chapter of this essay. As to images in the mind, if anything more is meant by the image of an object in the mind than the thought of that object, I know not what it means. The distinct conception of an object may, in a metaphorical or analogical sense, be called an *image* of it in the mind. But this image is only the conception of the object, and not the object conceived. It is an act of the mind, and not the object of that act.

Some philosophers will have our ideas, or a part of them, to be innate; others will have them all to be adventitious: some derive them from the senses alone; others from sensation and reflection: some think they are fabricated by the mind itself; others that they are produced by external objects; others that they are the immediate operation of the Deity; others say that impressions are the causes of ideas, and that the causes of impressions are unknown: some think that we have ideas only of material objects, but none of minds, of their operations, or of the relations of things; others will have the immediate object of every thought to be an idea: some think we have abstract ideas, and that by this chiefly we are distinguished from the brutes; others maintain an abstract idea to be an absurdity, and that there can be no such thing: with some they are the immediate objects of thought, with others the only objects.

A *fourth* reflection is, that ideas do not make any of the operations of the mind to be better understood, although it was probably with that view that they have been first invented, and afterwards so generally received.

We are at a loss to know how we perceive distant objects; how we remember things past; how we imagine things that have no existence. Ideas in the mind seem to account for all these operations: they are all by the means of ideas reduced to one operation—to a kind of feeling, or immediate perception of things present and in contact with the percipient; and feeling is an operation so familiar that we think it needs no explication, but may serve to explain other operations.

But this feeling, or immediate perception, is as difficult to be comprehended as the things which we pretend to explain by it. Two things may be in contact without any feeling or perception; there must therefore be in the percipient a power to feel or to perceive. How this power is produced, and how it operates, is quite beyond the reach of our knowledge. As little can we know whether this power must be limited to things present, and in contact with us. Nor can any man pretend to prove that the Being who gave us the power to perceive things present may not give us the power to perceive things that are distant, to remember things past, and to conceive things that never existed.

Some philosophers have endeavoured to make all our senses to be only different modifications of touch; a theory which serves only to confound things that are different, and to perplex and darken things that are clear. The theory of ideas resembles this, by reducing all the operations of the human understanding to the perception of ideas in our own minds. This power of perceiving ideas is as inexplicable as any of the powers explained by it; and the contiguity of the object contributes nothing at all to make it better understood; because there appears no connection between contiguity and perception, but what is grounded on prejudices drawn from some imagined similitude between mind and body, and from the supposition that, in perception, the object acts upon the mind, or the mind upon the object. We have seen how this theory has led philosophers to confound those operations of mind which experience teaches all men to be different, and teaches them to distinguish in common language; and that it has led them to invent a language inconsistent with the principles upon which all language is grounded.

CHAPTER 15: AN ACCOUNT OF THE SYSTEM OF LEIBNIZ

*   *   *

After this long account of the theories advanced by philosophers, to account for our perception of external objects, I hope it will appear that neither Aristotle's theory of sensible species, nor Malebranche's of our seeing things in God, nor the common theory of our perceiving ideas in our own minds, nor Leibniz's theory of monads and a preestablished harmony, give any satisfying account of this power of the mind, or make it more intelligible than it is without their aid. They are conjectures, and, if they were true, would solve no difficulty but raise many new ones. It is, therefore, more agreeable to good sense and to sound philosophy, to rest satisfied with what our consciousness and attentive reflection discover to us of the nature of perception, than, by inventing hypotheses, to attempt to explain things which are above the reach of human understanding. I believe no man is able to explain how we perceive external objects any more than how we are conscious of those that are internal. Perception, consciousness, memory, and imagination, are all original and simple powers of the mind and parts of its constitution. For this reason, though I have endeavoured to show that the theories of philosophers on this subject are ill grounded and insufficient, I do not attempt to substitute any other theory in their place.

Every man feels that perception gives him an invincible belief of the existence of that which he perceives; and that this belief is not the effect of reasoning, but the immediate consequence of perception. When philosophers have wearied themselves and their readers with their speculations upon this subject, they can neither strengthen this belief nor weaken it; nor can they show how it is produced. It puts the philosopher and the peasant upon a level, and neither of them can give any other reason for believing his senses than that he finds it impossible for him to do otherwise.

IMMANUEL KANT
1724–1804

Whereas most modern philosophers (such as Descartes, Berkeley, and Hume) arrived at their basic philosophical positions early in life, Immanuel Kant did not work out his views until well into middle age. Whereas the earlier thinkers wrote major works when still young, Kant's important pieces were written between the ages of fifty-seven and sixty-seven. Whereas the others' works were written for a broad general audience and are relatively accessible to educated readers, Kant wrote in an academic style that is notoriously difficult to follow. Whereas most of the earlier philosophers traveled widely, Kant never left the provincial city in which he was born. Unlike his predecessors, who held many different positions and practiced philosophy on the side, Kant earned his living as a professor of philosophy. Yet Kant is the most important and influential of all modern philosophers.

Kant was born, raised, lived, and died in the town of Königsberg in East Prussia. His parents were lower middle-class, hard-working, simple folk. They belonged to the Lutheran Pietist movement, which cultivated high moral standards and personal devotion to God in Christ. Like Hume, who had a similar religious upbringing (Calvinist Presbyterian), Kant was later critical of his background. But unlike Hume, he remained a deeply religious man.

Through the intervention of his mother's favorite preacher, who was also a professor at the University of Königsberg, young Immanuel gained admittance to a local high school. There he received a solid Pietist education and a firm grounding in the classics. At sixteen, Kant was admitted to the university, where he planned to study the classics. But under the influence of a strong teacher, Martin Knutzen, Kant moved into philosophy and was attracted to the comprehensive scholasticism of Christian Wolff (1679–1754), who had developed Leibniz's philosophy into a rationalistic system.

Following his university studies, Kant worked as a private tutor to wealthy families. By 1755, he was back in the university, where he was employed as an unsalaried lecturer for the next fifteen years. (Given the difficulty of his writing, it is worth noting that his lectures were very popular.) His early lectures focused on the external world, dealing with issues in physics and physical geography. He published an important early work, *Universal History of Nature and Theory of the Heavens* (1755), which explained the structure of the universe in terms of Newtonian physics, without reference to God. During this period, Kant's focus began to shift to the inner world of the mind and the nature of morality. At this time, he also encountered the writings of Hume, which challenged the rationalism he had imbibed from Wolff. He later said that Hume "interrupted my dogmatic slumber, and gave my investigations in the field of speculative philosophy quite a new direction."

In 1770, Kant was given what he had long desired—the chair of logic and metaphysics at the University of Königsberg. In his inaugural address, *Dissertation on the Form and Principles of Sensible and Intelligible Worlds,* Kant declared his intention to reconstruct philosophy. Over the next ten years, he carefully and quietly thought through all his ideas. Finally he wrote his major work, *Critique of Pure Reason.* He wrote it, as he later told a friend, "within four or five months, with the utmost attention to the contents, but with less concern for the presentation or for making things easy for the reader." Unfortunately, when the book appeared, his indifference to readers left most people lost. In 1783, he restated his main points in a work "for the benefit of teachers," the *Prolegomena to Any Future Metaphysics,* and in 1787 he rewrote the *Critique* itself.

Kant's first major work on ethics, *Foundation for the Metaphysics of Morals,* was published in 1785. A further development of his moral views, *Critique of Practical Reason,* appeared in 1788. In 1790, Kant published his third and last critique, the *Critique of Judgment,* which deals with aesthetic judgments and the question of purpose in nature. Kant's other important works include *Metaphysical Foundations of Natural Science* (1786), *Religion Within the Limits of Reason Alone* (1793), *Toward Eternal Peace* (1795), and *Metaphysics of Morals* (1797).

Whereas Kant's writings revolutionized the philosophical world, his personal life was quiet, almost boring. With one minor exception late in life, he was never involved in any scandals or controversies. He never traveled more than a few miles outside Königsberg. A lifelong bachelor, he is said to have awakened and gone to bed at exactly the same time each day. His daily walks were reportedly so regular that people could set their clocks by his approach. A rather frail man, he so carefully guarded his health that he lived a long, productive life. Yet he was also a delightful conversationalist and host, and he had many friends and admirers. At his death in 1804, he was the best-known philosopher in Germany, read, if not understood, throughout Europe.

*   *   *

Responding to the skeptical empiricism of Hume, Kant argued that the mind is not simply a repository of impressions and ideas but it is actively involved in knowing the objects it experiences. Prior to Kant, most thinkers believed that the mind, in knowing, conformed to objects: that the ideas of the mind took on the "shape" of the world outside the mind. Kant argued instead that objects conform to the mind: that how one experiences the world is a result of the way the mind operates. Knowledge is a result of human understanding applied to sense experience.

Space and time are two ways the mind operates. They are not "objects" in the world, derived from sense experience; rather, they are the precondition for our having sense-experience at all: They are the *a priori* (meaning "known independently of sense perceptions," "indubitable") foundations of sensibility. Space and time must be presupposed in order to have experience at all.

Kant goes on to consider the *a priori* foundations of human understanding. He argues that there must be categories of the mind, such as causality and substance, that unify our perceptions. These categories are not found in sense experience; they are innate structures of the mind and the necessary conditions for having any knowledge at all. Without these categories, the world of experience would be utterly chaotic and unknowable.

Of course this knowledge is only a knowledge of things as we experience them in the "phenomenal world." The way things really are, apart from our experience of them, the "noumenal world" of the "things-in-themselves," is not available to us by pure reason. This, according to Kant, means that we cannot have knowledge of God, the world, or even the substantial self. But rather than letting this end in Humean skepticism, Kant suggests that these three "ideas of reason" (God, world, self) stimulate and unify knowledge. They point beyond themselves to possibilities in the noumenal world that pure reason cannot reach. As long as we do not think that we have real knowledge of their objects, these three ideas of reason serve a useful purpose.

Turning to moral theory, Kant develops a "deontological," or "duty-based," theory of morality. An action is good not because it produces consequences such as pleasure or happiness, but because it is done out of duty by a good will. To establish what a person's duty is, Kant develops the "categorical imperative." In the *Foundation for the Metaphysics of Morals*, Kant discusses several versions of this imperative, the most important of which is this: "Act only on that maxim whereby you can at the same time will that it should become a universal law."

Although Kant is best known for his work in epistemology and ethics, he wrote on many topics. His earlier essay "Idea for a Universal History with Cosmopolitan Intent" (1784) is an example of Kant at his nontechnical best. Here the Königsberg recluse shows himself as a brilliant citizen of the world when he introduces the idea of a League of Nations:

> By means of wars and the high tension of never relaxed armaments for these wars, and by means of the distress which every nation must thus suffer, even during times of peace, [Nature] drives man at first to imperfect attempts, but finally, after many devastations and disturbances and even exhaustion of all powers, she drives toward a situation which reason might have anticipated without so many sad experiences: Men leave the lawless state of savages and enter a League of Nations. Thus every state, including the smallest, can find a guarantee for its security and its rights, not in its own power or in its own views of what is just, but in this great League of Nations. . . .

The selection from Kant's *Critique of Pure Reason* presented here goes through the "Transcendental Deduction" section (with Professor Kaufmann's editing) and gives a sense of this monumental work. I have used Norman Kemp Smith's translation of the second edition. Kant's condensation of the *Critique*, the

Prolegomena to Any Future Metaphysics, and his *Foundation for the Metaphysics of Morals* are both given here (complete) in the Lewis White Beck translations.

*　*　*

Among the many available books on Kant, Stephen Körner, *Kant* (Baltimore, MD: Penguin Books, 1955) is almost universally accepted as the best introduction. John Kemp, *The Philosophy of Kant* (Oxford: Oxford University Press, 1968); Ralph C.S. Walker, *Kant: The Arguments of the Philosophers* (London: Routledge & Kegan Paul, 1978); C.D. Broad, *Kant: An Introduction* (Cambridge: Cambridge University Press, 1978); Ernst Cassirer, *Kant's Life and Thought*, translated by James Haden (New Haven, CT: Yale University Press, 1982); Ermanno Bencivenga, *Kant's Copernican Revolution* (Oxford: Oxford University Press, 1987); and Otfried Höffe, *Immanuel Kant*, translated by Marshall Farrier (Albany, NY: SUNY Press, 1994) are also helpful. A.C. Ewing, *A Short Commentary on Kant's Critique of Pure Reason* (London: Methuen, 1950) provides an accessible commentary to this difficult work, while Norman Kemp Smith, *A Commentary to Kant's Critique of Pure Reason* (London: Macmillan, 1930) is standard. H.J. Paton, *Kant's Metaphysic of Experience*, two volumes (New York: Humanities Press, 1936) is an alternative interpretation to the N.K. Smith study. T.D. Weldon, *Kant's Critique of Pure Reason* (Oxford: Oxford University Press, 1945, 2nd edition, 1958); Henry E. Allison, *Kant's Transcendental Idealism: An Interpretation and Defense* (New Haven, CT: Yale University Press, 1983); and Lorne Falkenstein, *Kant's Intuitionism: A Commentary on the Transcendental Aesthetic* (Toronto: University of Toronto Press, 1995) are also useful. For works on Kant's moral theory, see W.D. Ross, *Kant's Ethical Theory: A Commentary on the Grundlegung zur Metaphysik der Sitten [Foundation for the Metaphysic of Morals]* (Oxford: Clarendon Press, 1954); Lewis White Beck, *A Commentary on Kant's Critique of Practical Reason* (Chicago: University of Chicago Press, 1960); H.J. Paton, *The Categorical Imperative* (London: 1947; reprinted, New York: Harper & Row, 1967); Roger Sullivan, *An Introduction to Kant's Ethics* (Cambridge: Cambridge University Press, 1994); and Paul Guyer, ed., *Kant's Groundwork of the Metaphysics of Morals* (Lanham, MD: Rowan & Littlefield, 1997). Howard Caygill, *A Kant Dictionary* (Oxford: Basil Blackwell, 1995) provides a useful reference work. For collections of essays, see Lewis White Beck, ed., *Studies in the Philosophy of Kant* (Indianapolis, IN: Bobbs-Merrill, 1965); R.P. Wolff, *Kant* (Garden City, NY: Doubleday, 1967); Ralph C.S. Walker, ed., *Kant on Pure Reason* (Oxford: Oxford University Press, 1982); Beryl Logan, ed., *Immanuel Kant's Prolegomena to Any Future Metaphysics in Focus* (Oxford: Routledge, 1996); and Robin May Schott, ed., *Feminist Interpretations of Kant* (College Park, PA: Pennsylvania State University Press, 1997).

CRITIQUE OF PURE REASON (in part)

CONTENTS

Immanuel Kant's Critique of Pure Reason, translated by Norman Kemp Smith (London: Macmillan; New York: St. Martin's Press, 1963).

    *[The first edition had a fifteen-line table of contents; the second had none at all; the third featured the first-edition table as an appendix. In the fourth edition (1794), and in most editions ever since, the table of contents continued for pages and pages and comprised well over one hundred items. The table offered here was constructed especially for this volume, to help clarify the structure of Kant's work. In both this table of contents and in the text, the page numbers in brackets are those of the second edition. (In scholarly citations they are preceded by a *B,* to distinguish them from references to the first edition, which are preceded by an *A.*) The numbers following the brackets in this table of contents indicate the page numbers in this volume for those sections that are excerpted here.]

PREFACE TO THE SECOND EDITION

Whether the treatment of such knowledge as lies within the province of reason does or does not follow the secure path of a science, is easily to be determined from the outcome. For if after elaborate preparations, frequently renewed, it is brought to a stop immediately it nears its goal; if often it is compelled to retrace its steps and strike into some new line of approach; or again, if the various participants are unable to agree in any common plan of procedure, then we may rest assured that it is very far from having entered upon the secure path of a science, and is indeed a merely random groping. In these circumstances, we shall be rendering a service to reason should we succeed in discovering the path upon which it can securely travel, even if, as a result of so doing, much that is comprised in our original aims, adopted without reflection, may have to be abandoned as fruitless.

That logic has already, from the earliest times, proceeded upon this sure path is evidenced by the fact that since Aristotle it has not required to retrace a single step, unless, indeed, we care to count as improvements the removal of certain needless subtleties or the clearer exposition of its recognised teaching, features which concern the elegance rather than the certainty of the science. It is remarkable also that to the present day this logic has not been able to advance a single step, and is thus to all appearance a closed and completed body of doctrine. If some of the moderns have thought to enlarge it by introducing *psychological* chapters on the different faculties of knowledge (imagination, wit, etc.), *metaphysical* chapters on the origin of knowledge or on the different kinds of certainty according to difference in the objects (idealism, scepticism, etc.), or *anthropological* chapters on prejudices, their causes and remedies, this could only arise from their ignorance of the peculiar nature of logical science. We do not enlarge but disfigure sciences, if we allow them to trespass upon one another's ter-

ritory. The sphere of logic is quite precisely delimited; its sole concern is to give an exhaustive exposition and a strict proof of the formal rules of all thought, whether it be *a priori* or empirical, whatever be its origin or its object, and whatever hindrances, accidental or natural, it may encounter in our minds.

That logic should have been thus successful is an advantage which it owes entirely to its limitations, whereby it is justified in abstracting—indeed, it is under obligation to do so—from all objects of knowledge and their differences, leaving the understanding nothing to deal with save itself and its form. But for reason to enter on the sure path of science is, of course, much more difficult, since it has to deal not with itself alone but also with objects. Logic, therefore, as a propaedeutic, forms, as it were, only the vestibule of the sciences; and when we are concerned with specific modes of knowledge, while logic is indeed presupposed in any critical estimate of them, yet for the actual acquiring of them we have to look to the sciences properly and objectively so called.

Now if reason is to be a factor in these sciences, something in them must be known *a priori*, and this knowledge may be related to its object in one or other of two ways, either as merely *determining* it and its concept (which must be supplied from

elsewhere) or as also *making it actual.* The former is *theoretical,* the latter *practical* knowledge of reason. In both, that part in which reason determines its object completely *a priori,* namely, the *pure* part—however much or little this part may contain— must be first and separately dealt with, in case it be confounded with what comes from other sources. For it is bad management if we blindly pay out what comes in, and are not able, when the income falls into arrears, to distinguish which part of it can justify expenditure, and in which line we must make reductions.

Mathematics and physics, the two sciences in which reason yields theoretical knowledge, have to determine their objects *a priori,* the former doing so quite purely, the latter having to reckon, at least partially, with sources of knowledge other than reason.

In the earliest times to which the history of human reason extends, *mathematics,* among that wonderful people, the Greeks, had already entered upon the sure path of science. But it must not be supposed that it was as easy for mathematics as it was for logic—in which reason has to deal with itself alone—to light upon, or rather to construct for itself, that royal road. On the contrary, I believe that it long remained, especially among the Egyptians, in the groping stage, and that the transformation must have been due to a *revolution* brought about by the happy thought of a single man, the experiment which he devised marking out the path upon which the science must enter, and by following which, secure progress throughout all time and in endless expansion is infallibly secured. The history of this intellectual revolution—far more important than the discovery of the passage round the celebrated Cape of Good Hope—and of its fortunate author, has not been preserved. But the fact that Diogenes Laertius, in handing down an account of these matters, names the reputed author of even the least important among the geometrical demonstrations, even of those which, for ordinary consciousness, stand in need of no such proof, does at least show that the memory of the revolution, brought about by the first glimpse of this new path, must have seemed to mathematicians of such outstanding importance as to cause it to survive the tide of oblivion. A new light flashed upon the mind of the first man (be he Thales or some other) who demonstrated the properties of the isosceles triangle. The true method, so he found, was not to inspect what he discerned either in the figure, or in the bare concept of it, and from this, as it were, to read off its properties; but to bring out what was necessarily implied in the concepts that he had himself formed *a priori,* and had put into the figure in the construction by which he presented it to himself. If he is to know anything with *a priori* certainty he must not ascribe to the figure anything save what necessarily follows from what he has himself set into it in accordance with his concept.

Natural science was very much longer in entering upon the highway of science. It is, indeed, only about a century and a half since Bacon, by his ingenious proposals, partly initiated this discovery, partly inspired fresh vigour in those who were already on the way to it. In this case also the discovery can be explained as being the sudden outcome of an intellectual revolution. In my present remarks I am referring to natural science only in so far as it is founded on *empirical* principles.

When Galileo caused balls, the weights of which he had himself previously determined, to roll down an inclined plane; when Torricelli made the air carry a weight which he had calculated beforehand to be equal to that of a definite volume of water; or in more recent times, when Stahl changed metals into oxides, and oxides back into metal, by withdrawing something and then restoring it,* a light broke upon all students of nature. They learned that reason has insight only into that which it produces after a plan of its own, and that it must not allow itself to be kept, as it were, in nature's leading-strings, but must itself show the way with principles of judgment based upon fixed laws, constraining nature to give answer to questions of reason's own determining. Accidental observations, made in obedience to no previously thought-out plan, can never be made to yield a necessary law, which alone reason is concerned to discover. Reason, holding in one hand its principles, according to which alone concordant appearances can be admitted as equivalent to laws, and in the other hand the experiment which it has

xi

xii

xiii

---

*I am not, in my choice of examples, tracing the exact course of the history of the experimental method; we have indeed no very precise knowledge of its first beginnings.

devised in conformity with these principles, must approach nature in order to be taught by it. It must not, however, do so in the character of a pupil who listens to everything that the teacher chooses to say, but of an appointed judge who compels the witnesses to answer questions which he has himself formulated. Even physics, therefore, owes the beneficent revolution in its point of view entirely to the happy thought, that while reason must seek in nature, not fictitiously ascribe to it, whatever as not being knowable through reason's own resources has to be learnt, if learnt at all, only from nature, it must adopt as its guide, in so seeking, that which it has itself put into nature. It is thus that the study of nature has entered on the secure path of a science, after having for so many centuries been nothing but a process of merely random groping.

xiv

Metaphysics is a completely isolated speculative science of reason, which soars far above the teachings of experience, and in which reason is indeed meant to be its own pupil. Metaphysics rests on concepts alone—not, like mathematics, on their application to intuition. But though it is older than all other sciences, and would survive even if all the rest were swallowed up in the abyss of an all-destroying barbarism, it has not yet had the good fortune to enter upon the secure path of a science. For in it reason is perpetually being brought to a stand, even when the laws into which it is seeking to have, as it professes, an *a priori* insight are those that are confirmed by our most common experiences. Ever and again we have to retrace our steps, as not leading us in the direction in which we desire to go. So far, too, are the students of metaphysics from exhibiting any kind of unanimity in their contentions, that metaphysics has rather to be regarded as a battle-ground quite peculiarly suited for those who desire to exercise themselves in mock combats, and in which no participant has ever yet succeeded in gaining even so much as an inch of territory, not at least in such manner as to secure him in its permanent possession. This shows, beyond all questioning, that the procedure of metaphysics has hitherto been a merely random groping, and, what is worst of all, a groping among mere concepts.

xv

What, then, is the reason why, in this field, the sure road to science has not hitherto been found? Is it, perhaps, impossible of discovery? Why, in that case, should nature have visited our reason with the restless endeavour whereby it is ever searching for such a path, as if this were one of its most important concerns? Nay, more, how little cause have we to place trust in our reason, if, in one of the most important domains of which we would fain have knowledge, it does not merely fail us, but lures us on by deceitful promises, and in the end betrays us! Or if it be only that we have thus far failed to find the true path, are there any indications to justify the hope that by renewed efforts we may have better fortune than has fallen to our predecessors?

The examples of mathematics and natural science, which by a single and sudden revolution have become what they now are, seem to me sufficiently remarkable to suggest our considering what may have been the essential features in the changed point of view by which they have so greatly benefited. Their success should incline us, at least by way of experiment, to imitate their procedure, so far as the analogy which, as species of rational knowledge, they bear to metaphysics may permit. Hitherto it has been assumed that all our knowledge must conform to objects. But all attempts to extend our knowledge of objects by establishing something in regard to them *a priori*, by means of concepts, have, on this assumption, ended in failure. We must therefore make trial whether we may not have more success in the tasks of metaphysics, if we suppose that objects must conform to our knowledge. This would agree better with what is desired, namely, that it should be possible to have knowledge of objects *a priori*, determining something in regard to them prior to their being given. We should then be proceeding precisely on the lines of Copernicus' primary hypothesis. Failing of satisfactory progress in explaining the movements of the heavenly bodies on the supposition

xvi

that they all revolved round the spectator, he tried whether he might not have better success if he made the spectator to revolve and the stars to remain at rest. A similar experiment can be tried in metaphysics, as regards the *intuition* of objects. If intuition must conform to the constitution of the objects, I do not see how we could know anything of the latter *a priori;* but if the object (as object of the senses) must conform to the constitution of our faculty of intuition, I have no difficulty in conceiving such a possibility. Since I cannot rest in these intuitions if they are to become known, but must relate them as representations to something as their object, and determine this latter through them, either I must assume that the *concepts,* by means of which I obtain this determination, conform to the object, or else I assume that the objects, or what is the same thing, that the *experience* in which alone, as given objects, they can be known, conform to the concepts. In the former case, I am again in the same perplexity as to how I can know anything *a priori* in regard to the objects. In the latter case the outlook is more hopeful. For experience is itself a species of knowledge which involves understanding; and understanding has rules which I must presuppose as being in me prior to objects being given to me, and therefore as being *a priori.* They find expression in *a priori* concepts to which all objects of experience necessarily conform, and with which they must agree. As regards objects which are thought solely through reason, and indeed as necessary, but which can never—at least not in the manner in which reason thinks them—be given in experience, the attempts at thinking them (for they must admit of being thought) will furnish an excellent touchstone of what we are adopting as our new method of thought, namely, that we can know *a priori* of things only what we ourselves put into them.*

This experiment succeeds as well as could be desired, and promises to metaphysics, in its first part—the part that is occupied with those concepts *a priori* to which the corresponding objects, commensurate with them, can be given in experience—the secure path of a science. For the new point of: view enables us to explain how there can be knowledge *a priori;* and, in addition, to furnish satisfactory proofs of the laws which form the *a priori* basis of nature, regarded as the sum of the objects of experience—neither achievement being possible on the procedure hitherto followed. But this deduction of our power of knowing *a priori,* in the first part of metaphysics, has a consequence which is startling, and which has the appearance of being highly prejudicial to the whole purpose of metaphysics, as dealt with in the second part. For we are brought to the conclusion that we can never transcend the limits of possible experience, though that is precisely what this science is concerned, above all else, to achieve. This situation yields, however, just the very experiment by which, indirectly, we are enabled to prove the truth of this first estimate of our *a priori* knowledge of reason, namely, that such knowledge has to do only with appearances, and must leave the thing in itself as indeed real *per se,* but as not known by us. For what necessarily forces us to transcend the limits of experience and of all appearances is the *unconditioned,* which reason, by necessity and by right, demands in things in themselves, as required to complete the series of condi-

---

*This method, modelled on that of the student of nature, consists in looking for the elements of pure reason in *what admits of confirmation or refutation by experiment.* Now the propositions of pure reason, especially if they venture out beyond all limits of possible experience, cannot be brought to the test through any experiment with their *objects,* as in natural science. In dealing with those *concepts* and *principles* which we adopt *a priori;* all that we can do is to contrive that they be used for viewing objects from two different points of view—on the one hand, in connection with experience, as objects of the senses and of the understanding, and on the other hand, for the isolated reason that strives to transcend all limits of experience, as objects which are thought merely. If, when things are viewed from this twofold standpoint, we find that there is agreement with the principle of pure reason, but that when we regard them only from a single point of view reason is involved in unavoidable self-conflict, the experiment decides in favour of the correctness of this distinction.

tions. If, then, on the supposition that our empirical knowledge conforms to objects as things in themselves, we find that the unconditioned *cannot be thought without contradiction,* and that when, on the other hand, we suppose that our representation of things, as they are given to us, does not conform to these things as they are in themselves, but that these objects, as appearances, conform to our mode of representation, *the contradiction vanishes;* and if, therefore, we thus find that the unconditioned is not to be met with in things, so far as we know them, that is, so far as they are given to us, but only so far as we do not know them, that is, so far as they are things in themselves, we are justified in concluding that what we at first assumed for the purposes of experiment is now definitely confirmed. But when all progress in the field of the supersensible has thus been denied to speculative reason, it is still open to us to enquire whether, in the practical knowledge of reason, data may not be found sufficient to determine reason's transcendent concept of the unconditioned, and so to enable us, in accordance with the wish of metaphysics, and by means of knowledge that is possible *a priori,* though only from a practical point of view, to pass beyond the limits of all possible experience. Speculative reason has thus at least made room for such an extension; and if it must at the same time leave it empty, yet none the less we are at liberty, indeed we are summoned, to take occupation of it, if we can, by practical data of reason. . . .*

    But, it will be asked, what sort of a treasure is this that we propose to bequeath to posterity? What is the value of the metaphysics that is alleged to be thus purified by criticism and established once for all? On a cursory view of the present work it may seem that its results are merely *negative,* warning us that we must never venture with speculative reason beyond the limits of experience. Such is in fact its primary use. But such teaching at once acquires a *positive* value when we recognise that the principles with which speculative reason ventures out beyond its proper limits do not in effect *extend* the employment of reason, but, as we find on closer scrutiny, inevitably *narrow* it. These principles properly belong [not to reason but] to sensibility, and when thus employed they threaten to make the bounds of sensibility coextensive with the real, and so to supplant reason in its pure (practical) employment. So far, therefore, as our Critique limits speculative reason, it is indeed *negative;* but since it thereby removes an obstacle which stands in the way of the employment of practical reason, nay threatens to destroy it, it has in reality a *positive* and very important use. At least this is so, immediately we are convinced that there is an absolutely necessary *practical* employment of pure reason—the *moral*—in which it inevitably goes beyond the limits of sensibility. Though [practical] reason, in thus proceeding, requires no assistance from speculative reason, it must yet be assured against its opposition, that reason may not be brought into conflict with itself. To deny that the service which the Critique renders is *positive* in character, would thus be like saying that the police are of no positive benefit, inasmuch as their main business is merely to prevent the violence of which citizens stand in mutual fear, in order that each may pursue his vocation in peace and security. That space and time are only forms of sensible intuition, and so only conditions of the existence of things as appearances; that, moreover, we have no concepts of understanding,

xxi

xxii

xxv

---

*Similarly, the fundamental laws of the motions of the heavenly bodies gave established certainty to what Copernicus had at first assumed only as an hypothesis, and at the same time yielded proof of the invisible force (the Newtonian attraction) which holds the universe together. The latter would have remained for ever undiscovered if Copernicus had not dared, in a manner contradictory of the senses, but yet true, to seek the observed movements, not in the heavenly bodies, but in the spectator. The change in point of view, analogous to this hypothesis, which is expounded in the *Critique,* I put forward in this preface as an hypothesis only, in order to draw attention to the character of these first attempts at such a change, which are always hypothetical. But in the *Critique* itself it will be proved, apodeictically not hypothetically, from the nature of our representations of space and time and from the elementary concepts of the understanding.

and consequently no elements for the knowledge of things, save in so far as intuition   xxvi
can be given corresponding to these concepts; and that we can therefore have no
knowledge of any object as thing in itself, but only in so far as it is an object of sensible intuition, that is, an appearance—all this is proved in the analytical part of the Critique. Thus it does indeed follow that all possible speculative knowledge of reason is
limited to mere objects of *experience*. But our further contention must also be duly
borne in mind, namely, that though we cannot *know* these objects as things in themselves, we must yet be in position at least to *think* them as things in themselves;* otherwise we should be landed in the absurd conclusion that there can be appearance with-   xxvii
out anything that appears. Now let us suppose that the distinction, which our Critique
has shown to be necessary, between things as objects of experience and those same
things as things in themselves, had not been made. In that case all things in general, as
far as they are efficient causes, would be determined by the principle of causality, and
consequently by the mechanism of nature. I could not, therefore, without palpable contradiction, say of one and the same being, for instance the human soul, that its will is
free and yet is subject to natural necessity, that is, is not free. For I have taken the soul
in both propositions *in one and the same sense,* namely as a thing in general, that is, as
a thing in itself; and save by means of a preceding critique, could not have done otherwise. But if our Critique is not in error in teaching that the object is to be taken *in a
twofold sense,* namely as appearance and as thing in itself; if the deduction of the concepts of understanding is valid, and the principle of causality therefore applies only to
things taken in the former sense, namely, in so far as they are objects of experience—
these same objects, taken in the other sense, not being subject to the principle—then
there is no contradiction in supposing that one and the same will is, in the appearance,   xxviii
that is, in its visible acts, necessarily subject to the law of nature, and so far *not free,*
while yet, as belonging to a thing in itself, it is not subject to that law, and is therefore
free. My soul, viewed from the latter standpoint, cannot indeed be known by means of
speculative reason (and still less through empirical observation); and freedom as a
property of a being to which I attribute effects in the sensible world, is therefore also
not knowable in any such fashion. For I should then have to know such a being as determined in its existence, and yet as not determined in time—which is impossible,
since I cannot support my concept by any intuition. But though I cannot *know,* I can
yet *think* freedom; that is to say, the representation of it is at least not self-contradictory, provided due account be taken of our critical distinction between the two modes
of representation, the sensible and the intellectual, and of the resulting limitation of the
pure concepts of understanding and of the principles which flow from them.

If we grant that morality necessarily presupposes freedom (in the strictest sense)
as a property of our will; if, that is to say, we grant that it yields practical principles—
original principles, proper to our reason—as *a priori* data of reason, and that this
would be absolutely impossible save on the assumption of freedom; and if at the same   xxix
time we grant that speculative reason has proved that such freedom does not allow of
being thought, then the former supposition—that made on behalf of morality—would
have to give way to this other contention, the opposite of which involves a palpable
contradiction. For since it is only on the assumption of freedom that the negation of

---

*To *know* an object I must be able to prove its possibility, either from its actuality as attested by experience, or *a priori* by means of reason. But I can *think* whatever I please, provided only that I do not contradict myself, that is, provided my concept is a possible thought. This suffices for the possibility of the concept, even though I may not be able to answer for there being, in the sum of all possibilities, an object
corresponding to it. But something more is required before I can ascribe to such a concept objective validity,
that is, real possibility; the former possibility is merely logical. This something, more need not, however, be
sought in the theoretical sources of knowledge; it may lie in those that are practical.

morality contains any contradiction, freedom, and with it morality, would have to yield to the mechanism of nature.

Morality does not, indeed, require that freedom should be understood, but only that it should not contradict itself, and so should at least allow of being thought, and that as thus thought it should place no obstacle in the way of a free act (viewed in another relation) likewise conforming to the mechanism of nature. The doctrine of morality and the doctrine of nature may each, therefore, make good its position. This, however, is only possible in so far as criticism has previously established our unavoidable ignorance of things in themselves, and has limited all that we can theoretically know to mere appearances.

xxx

This discussion as to the positive advantage of critical principles of pure reason can be similarly developed in regard to the concept of *God* and of the *simple nature* of our *soul;* but for the sake of brevity such further discussion may be omitted. [From what has already been said, it is evident that] even the *assumption*—as made on behalf of the necessary practical employment of my reason—of *God, freedom,* and *immortality* is not permissible unless at the same time speculative reason be deprived of its pretensions to transcendent insight. For in order to arrive at such insight it must make use of principles which, in fact, extend only to objects of possible experience, and which, if also applied to what cannot be an object of experience, always really change this into an appearance, thus rendering all *practical extension* of pure reason impossible. I have therefore found it necessary to deny *knowledge,* in order to make room for *faith. . . .*

xxxi

All objections to morality and religion will be for ever silenced, and this in Socratic fashion, namely, by the clearest proof of the ignorance of the objectors. There has always existed in the world, and there will always continue to exist, some kind of metaphysics, and with it the dialectic that is natural to pure reason. It is therefore the first and most important task of philosophy to deprive metaphysics, once and for all, of its injurious influence, by attacking its errors at their very source.

xxxii

Notwithstanding this important change in the field of the sciences, and the *loss* of its fancied possessions which speculative reason must suffer, general human interests remain in the same privileged position as hitherto, and the advantages which the world has hitherto derived from the teachings of pure reason are in no way diminished. The loss affects only the *monopoly of the schools,* in no respect the *interests of humanity.* I appeal to the most rigid dogmatist, whether the proof of the continued existence of our soul after death, derived from the simplicity of substance, or of the freedom of the will as opposed to a universal mechanism, arrived at through the subtle but ineffectual distinctions between subjective and objective practical necessity, or of the existence of God as deduced from the concept of an *ens realissimum* (of the contingency of the changeable and of the necessity of a prime mover), have ever, upon passing out from the schools, succeeded in reaching the public mind or in exercising the slightest influence on its convictions? That has never been found to occur, and in view of the unfitness of the common human understanding for such subtle speculation, ought never to have been expected. Such widely held convictions, so far as they rest on rational grounds, are due to quite other considerations. The hope of a *future life* has its source in that notable characteristic of our nature, never to be capable of being satisfied by what is temporal (as insufficient for the capacities of its whole destination); the con-

xxxiii

sciousness of *freedom* rests exclusively on the clear exhibition of duties, in opposition to all claims of the inclinations; the belief in a wise and great *Author of the world* is generated solely by the glorious order, beauty, and providential care everywhere displayed in nature. When the Schools have been brought to recognise that they can lay no claim to higher and fuller insight in a matter of universal human concern than that which is equally within the reach of the great mass of men (ever to be held by us in the highest esteem), and that, as Schools of philosophy, they should limit themselves to the study of those universally comprehensible, and, for moral purposes, sufficient grounds of proof, then not only do these latter possessions remain undisturbed, but through this very fact they acquire yet greater authority. . . .

This critique is not opposed to the *dogmatic procedure* of reason in its pure knowledge, as science, for that must always be dogmatic, that is, yield strict proof from sure principles *a priori.* It is opposed only to *dogmatism,* that is, to the presumption that it is possible to make progress with pure knowledge, according to principles, from concepts alone (those that are philosophical), as reason has long been in the habit of doing; and that it is possible to do this without having first investigated in what way and by what right reason has come into possession of these concepts. Dogmatism is thus the dogmatic procedure of pure reason, *without previous criticism of its own powers.* In withstanding dogmatism we must not allow ourselves to give free rein to that loquacious shallowness, which assumes for itself the name of popularity, nor yet to scepticism, which makes short work with all metaphysics. On the contrary, such criticism is the necessary preparation for a thoroughly grounded metaphysics, which, as science, must necessarily be developed dogmatically, according to the strictest demands of system, in such manner as to satisfy not the general public but the requirements of the Schools. For that is a demand to which it stands pledged, and which it may not neglect, namely, that it carry out its work entirely *a priori,* to the complete satisfaction of speculative reason. In the execution of the plan prescribed by the critique, that is, in the future system of metaphysics, we have therefore to follow the strict method of the celebrated Wolff, the greatest of all the dogmatic philosophers. He was the first to show by example (and by his example he awakened that spirit of thoroughness which is not extinct in Germany) how the secure progress of a science is to be attained only through orderly establishment of principles, clear determination of concepts, insistence upon strictness of proof, and avoidance of venturesome, non-consecutive steps in our inferences. He was thus peculiarly well fitted to raise metaphysics to the dignity of a science, if only it had occurred to him to prepare the ground beforehand by a critique of the organ, that is, of pure reason itself. The blame for his having failed to do so lies not so much with himself as with the dogmatic way of thinking prevalent in his day, and with which the philosophers of his time, and of all previous times, have no right to reproach one another. Those who reject both the method of Wolff and the procedure of a critique of pure reason can have no other aim than to shake off the fetters of *science* altogether, and thus to change work into play, certainty into opinion, philosophy into philodoxy. . . .

xxxvi

xxxvii

KÖNIGSBERG, *April* 1787

INTRODUCTION

1

I. THE DISTINCTION BETWEEN PURE AND EMPIRICAL KNOWLEDGE

There can be no doubt that all our knowledge begins with experience. For how should our faculty of knowledge be awakened into action did not objects affecting our senses partly of themselves produce representations, partly arouse the activity of our understanding to compare these representations, and, by combining or separating them, work up the raw material of the sensible impressions into that knowledge of objects which is entitled experience? In the order of time, therefore, we have no knowledge antecedent to experience, and with experience all our knowledge begins.

But though all our knowledge begins with experience, it does not follow that it all arises out of experience. For it may well be that even our empirical knowledge is made up of what we receive through impressions and of what our own faculty of knowledge (sensible impressions serving merely as the occasion) supplies from itself. If our faculty of knowledge makes any such addition, it may be that we are not in a position to distinguish it from the raw material, until with long practice of attention we have become skilled in separating it.

This, then, is a question which at least calls for closer examination, and does not allow of any off-hand answer:—whether there is any knowledge that is thus independent of experience and even of all impressions of the senses. Such knowledge is entitled *a priori,* and distinguished from the empirical, which has its sources *a posteriori,* that is, in experience.

The expression *"a priori"* does not, however, indicate with sufficient precision the full meaning of our question. For it has been customary to say, even of much knowledge that is derived from empirical sources, that we have it or are capable of having it *a priori,* meaning thereby that we do not derive it immediately from experience, but from a universal rule—a rule which is itself, however, borrowed by us from experience. Thus we would say of a man who undermined the foundations of his house, that he might have known *a priori* that it would fall, that is, that he need not have waited for the experience of its actual falling. But still he could not know this completely *a priori.* For he had first to learn through experience that bodies are heavy, and therefore fall when their supports are withdrawn.

In what follows, therefore, we shall understand by *a priori* knowledge, not knowledge independent of this or that experience, but knowledge absolutely independent of all experience. Opposed to it is empirical knowledge, which is knowledge possible only *a posteriori,* that is, through experience. *A priori* modes of knowledge are entitled pure when there is no admixture of anything empirical. Thus, for instance, the proposition, "every alteration has its cause," while an *a priori* proposition, is not a pure proposition, because alteration is a concept which can be derived only from experience.

II. WE ARE IN POSSESSION OF CERTAIN MODES OF *A PRIORI* KNOWLEDGE, AND EVEN THE COMMON UNDERSTANDING IS NEVER WITHOUT THEM

What we here require is a criterion by which to distinguish with certainty between pure and empirical knowledge. Experience teaches us that a thing is so and so, but not that it cannot be otherwise. First, then, if we have a proposition which in being thought is thought as *necessary,* it is an *a priori* judgment; and if, besides, it is not derived from any proposition except one which also has the validity of a necessary judgment, it is an absolutely *a priori* judgment. Secondly, experience never confers on its judgments true or strict, but only assumed and comparative *universality,* through induction. We can properly only say, therefore, that, so far as we have hitherto observed, there is no exception to this or that rule. If, then, a judgment is thought with strict universality, that is, in such manner that no exception is allowed as possible, it is not derived from experience, but is valid absolutely *a priori.* Empirical universality is only an arbitrary extension of a validity holding in most cases to one which holds in all, for instance, in the proposition, "all bodies are heavy." When, on the other hand, strict universality is essential to a judgment, this indicates a special source of knowledge, namely, a faculty of *a priori* knowledge. Necessity and strict universality are thus sure criteria of *a priori* knowledge, and are inseparable from one another. But since in the employment of these criteria the contingency of judgments is sometimes more easily shown than their empirical limitation, or, as sometimes also happens, their unlimited universality can be more convincingly proved than their necessity, it is advisable to use the two criteria separately, each by itself being infallible.

Now it is easy to show that there actually are in human knowledge judgments which are necessary and in the strictest sense universal, and which are therefore pure *a priori* judgments. If an example from the sciences be desired, we have only to look to any of the propositions of mathematics; if we seek an example from the understanding in its quite ordinary employment, the proposition, "every alteration must have a cause," will serve our purpose. In the latter case, indeed, the very concept of a cause so manifestly contains the concept of a necessity of connection with an effect and of the strict universality of the rule, that the concept would be altogether lost if we attempted to derive it, as Hume has done, from a repeated association of that which happens with that which precedes, and from a custom of connecting representations, a custom originating in this repeated association, and constituting therefore a merely subjective necessity. Even without appealing to such examples, it is possible to show that pure *a priori* principles are indispensable for the possibility of experience, and so to prove their existence *a priori*. For whence could experience derive its certainty, if all the rules, according to which it proceeds, were always themselves empirical, and therefore contingent? Such rules could hardly be regarded as first principles. At present, however, we may be content to have established the fact that our faculty of knowledge does have a pure employment, and to have shown what are the criteria of such an employment. 5

Such *a priori* origin is manifest in certain concepts, no less than in judgments. If we remove from our empirical concept of a body, one by one, every feature in it which is [merely] empirical, the colour, the hardness or softness, the weight, even the impenetrability, there still remains the space which the body (now entirely vanished) occupied, and this cannot be removed. Again, if we remove from our empirical concept of any object, corporeal or incorporeal, all properties which experience has taught us, we yet cannot take away that property through which the object is thought as substance or as inhering in a substance (although this concept of substance is more determinate than that of an object in general). Owing, therefore, to the necessity with which this concept of substance forces itself upon us, we have no option save to admit that it has its seat in our faculty of *a priori* knowledge. 6

III. PHILOSOPHY STANDS IN NEED OF A SCIENCE WHICH SHALL
DETERMINE THE POSSIBILITY, THE PRINCIPLES, AND THE EXTENT
OF ALL *A PRIORI* KNOWLEDGE

But what is still more extraordinary than all the preceding is this, that certain modes of knowledge leave the field of all possible experiences and have the appearance of extending the scope of our judgments beyond all limits of experience, and this by means of concepts to which no corresponding object can ever be given in experience.

It is precisely by means of the latter modes of knowledge, in a realm beyond the world of the senses, where experience can yield neither guidance nor correction, that our reason carries on those enquiries which owing to their importance we consider to be far more excellent, and in their purpose far more lofty, than all that the understanding can learn in the field of appearances. Indeed we prefer to run every risk of error rather than desist from such urgent enquiries, on the ground of their dubious character, 7 or from disdain and indifference. [These unavoidable problems set by pure reason it-self are *God, freedom,* and *immortality*. The science which, with all its preparations, is in its final intention directed solely to their solution is metaphysics; and its procedure is at first dogmatic, that is, it confidently sets itself to this task without any previous ex-amination of the capacity or incapacity of reason for so great an undertaking.]

Now it does indeed seem natural that, as soon as we have left the ground of ex-perience, we should, through careful enquiries, assure ourselves as to the foundations of any building that we propose to erect, not making use of any knowledge that we possess without first determining whence it has come, and not trusting to principles without knowing their origin. It is natural, that is to say, that the question should first be considered, how the understanding can arrive at all this knowledge *a priori,* and what extent, validity, and worth it may have. Nothing, indeed, could be more natural, if by the term "natural" we signify what fittingly and reasonably ought to happen. But if we mean by "natural" what ordinarily happens, then on the contrary nothing is more natural and more intelligible than the fact that this enquiry has been so long neglected. For one part of this knowledge, the mathematical, has long been of established reliabil-ity, and so gives rise to a favourable presumption as regards the other part, which may yet be of quite different nature. Besides, once we are outside the circle of experience, we can be sure of not being *contradicted* by experience. The charm of extending our knowledge is so great that nothing short of encountering a direct contradiction can suf-fice to arrest us in our course; and this can be avoided, if we are careful in our fabrica-tions—which none the less will still remain fabrications. Mathematics gives us a shin-ing example of how far, independently of experience, we can progress in *a priori* knowledge. It does, indeed, occupy itself with objects and with knowledge solely in so far as they allow of being exhibited in intuition. But this circumstance is easily over-looked, since this intuition can itself be given *a priori,* and is therefore hardly to be dis-tinguished from a bare and pure concept. Misled by such a proof of the power of rea-son, the demand for the extension of knowledge recognises no limits. The light dove, cleaving the air in her free flight, and feeling its resistance, might imagine that its flight would be still easier in empty space. It was thus that Plato left the world of the senses, as setting too narrow limits to the understanding, and ventured out beyond it on the wings of the ideas, in the empty space of the pure understanding. He did not observe that with all his efforts he made no advance—meeting no resistance that might, as it were, serve as a support upon which he could take a stand, to which he could apply his powers, and so set his understanding in motion. It is, indeed, the common fate of human reason to complete its speculative structures as speedily as may be, and only af-terwards to enquire whether the foundations are reliable. All sorts of excuses will then be appealed to, in order to reassure us of their solidity, or rather indeed to enable us to dispense altogether with so late and so dangerous an enquiry. But what keeps us, dur-ing the actual building, free from all apprehension and suspicion, and flatters us with a seeming thoroughness, is this other circumstance, namely, that a great, perhaps the greatest, part of the business of our reason consists in analysis of the concepts which we already have of objects. This analysis supplies us with a considerable body of knowledge, which, while nothing but explanation or elucidation of what has already been thought in our concepts, though in a confused manner, is yet prized as being, at least as regards its form, new insight. But so far as the matter or content is concerned, there has been no extension of our previously possessed concepts, but only an analysis of them. Since this procedure yields real knowledge *a priori,* which progresses in an assured and useful fashion, reason is so far misled as surreptitiously to introduce, with-out itself being aware of so doing, assertions of an entirely different order, in which it

8

9

10

attaches to given concepts others completely foreign to them, and moreover attaches *a priori*. And yet it is not known how reason can be in position to do this. Such a question is never so much as thought of. I shall therefore at once proceed to deal with the difference between these two kinds of knowledge.

IV. THE DISTINCTION BETWEEN ANALYTIC AND SYNTHETIC JUDGMENTS

In all judgments in which the relation of a subject to the predicate is thought (I take into consideration affirmative judgments only, the subsequent application to negative judgments being easily made), this relation is possible in two different ways. Either the predicate B belongs to the subject A, as something which is (covertly) contained in this concept A; or B lies outside the concept A, although it does indeed stand in connection with it. In the one case I entitle the judgment analytic, in the other synthetic. Analytic judgments (affirmative) are therefore those in which the connection of the predicate with the subject is thought through identity; those in which this connection is thought without identity should be entitled synthetic. The former, as adding   11 nothing through the predicate to the concept of the subject, but merely breaking it up into those constituent concepts that have all along been thought in it, although confusedly, can also be entitled explicative. The latter, on the other hand, add to the concept of the subject a predicate which has not been in any wise thought in it, and which no analysis could possibly extract from it; and they may therefore be entitled ampliative. If I say, for instance, "All bodies are extended," this is an analytic judgment. For I do not require to go beyond the concept which I connect with "body" in order to find extension as bound up with it. To meet with this predicate, I have merely to analyse the concept, that is, to become conscious to myself of the manifold which I always think in that concept. The judgment is therefore analytic. But when I say, "All bodies are heavy," the predicate is something quite different from anything that I think in the mere concept of body in general; and the addition of such a predicate therefore yields a synthetic judgment.

Judgments of experience, as such, are one and all synthetic. For it would be absurd to found an analytic judgment on experience. Since, in framing the judgment, I must not go outside my concept, there is no need to appeal to the testimony of experience in its support. That a body is extended is a proposition that holds *a priori* and is not   12 empirical. For, before appealing to experience, I have already in the concept of body all the conditions required for my judgment. I have only to extract from it, in accordance with the principle of contradiction, the required predicate, and in so doing can at the same time become conscious of the necessity of the judgment—and that is what experience could never have taught me. On the other hand, though I do not include in the concept of a body in general the predicate "weight," none the less this concept indicates an object of experience through one of its parts, and I can add to that part other parts of this same experience, as in this way belonging together with the concept. From the start I can apprehend the concept of body analytically through the characters of extension, impenetrability, figure, etc., all of which are thought in the concept. Now, however, looking back on the experience from which I have derived this concept of body, and finding weight to be invariably connected with the above characters, I attach it as a predicate to the concept; and in doing so I attach it synthetically, and am therefore extending my knowledge. The possibility of the synthesis of the predicate "weight" with the concept of "body" thus rests upon experience. While the one concept is not contained in the other, they yet belong to one another, though only contingently, as parts of a whole, namely, of an experience which is itself a synthetic combination of intuitions.

13   But in *a priori* synthetic judgments this help is entirely lacking. [I do not here have the advantage of looking around in the field of experience.] Upon what, then, am I to rely, when I seek to go beyond the concept A, and to know that another concept B is connected with it? Through what is the synthesis made possible? Let us take the proposition, "Everything which happens has its cause." In the concept of "something which happens," I do indeed think an existence which is preceded by a time, etc., and from this concept analytic judgments may be obtained. But the concept of a "cause" lies entirely outside the other concept, and signifies something different from "that which happens," and is not therefore in any way contained in this latter representation. How come I then to predicate of that which happens something quite different, and to apprehend that the concept of cause, though not contained in it, yet belongs, and indeed necessarily belongs, to it? What is here the unknown = X which gives support to the understanding when it believes that it can discover outside the concept A a predicate B foreign to this concept, which it yet at the same time considers to be connected with it? It cannot be experience, because the suggested principle has connected the second representation with the first, not only with greater universality, but also with the character of necessity, and therefore completely *a priori* and on the basis of mere concepts. Upon such synthetic, that is, ampliative principles, all our *a priori* speculative knowledge must ultimately

14   rest; analytic judgments are very important, and indeed necessary, but only for obtaining that clearness in the concepts which is requisite for such a sure and wide synthesis as will lead to a genuinely new addition to all previous knowledge.

V. IN ALL THEORETICAL SCIENCES OF REASON SYNTHETIC *A PRIORI* JUDGMENTS ARE CONTAINED AS PRINCIPLES

1. *All mathematical judgments, without exception, are synthetic.* This fact, though incontestably certain and in its consequences very important, has hitherto escaped the notice of those who are engaged in the analysis of human reason, and is, indeed, directly opposed to all their conjectures. For as it was found that all mathematical inferences proceed in accordance with the principle of contradiction (which the nature of all apodeictic certainty requires), it was supposed that the fundamental propositions of the science can themselves be known to be true through that principle. This is an erroneous view. For though a synthetic proposition can indeed be discerned in accordance with the principle of contradiction, this can only be if another synthetic proposition is presupposed, and if it can then be apprehended as following from this other proposition; it can never be so discerned in and by itself.

First of all, it has to be noted that mathematical propositions, strictly so called, are always judgments *a priori,* not empirical; because they carry with them necessity, which cannot be derived from experience. If this be demurred to, I am willing to limit

15   my statement to pure mathematics, the very concept of which implies that it does not contain empirical, but only pure *a priori* knowledge.

We might, indeed, at first suppose that the proposition $7 + 5 = 12$ is a merely analytic proposition, and follows by the principle of contradiction from the concept of a sum of 7 and 5. But if we look more closely we find that the concept of the sum of 7 and 5 contains nothing save the union of the two numbers into one, and in this no thought is being taken as to what that single number may be which combines both. The concept of 12 is by no means already thought in merely thinking this union of 7 and 5;

and I may analyse my concept of such a possible sum as long as I please, still I shall never find the 12 in it. We have to go outside these concepts, and call in the aid of the intuition which corresponds to one of them, our five fingers, for instance, or, as Segner does in his *Arithmetic*, five points, adding to the concept of 7, unit by unit, the five given in intuition. For starting with the number 7, and for the concept of 5 calling in the aid of the fingers of my hand as intuition, I now add one by one to the number 7 the units which I previously took together to form the number 5, and with the aid of that figure 2 [the hand] see the number 12 come into being. That 5 should be added to 7, I have indeed already thought in the concept of a sum = 7 + 5, but not that this sum is equivalent to the number 12. Arithmetical propositions are therefore always synthetic. This is still more evident if we take larger numbers. For it is then obvious that, however we might turn and twist our concepts, we could never, by the mere analysis of them, and without the aid of intuition, discover what [the number is that] is the sum. 16

Just as little is any fundamental proposition of pure geometry analytic. That the straight line between two points is the shortest, is a synthetic proposition. For my concept of *straight* contains nothing of quantity, but only of quality. The concept of the shortest is wholly an addition, and cannot be derived, through any process of analysis, from the concept of the straight line. Intuition, therefore, must here be called in; only by its aid is the synthesis possible. What here causes us commonly to believe that the predicate of such apodeictic judgments is already contained in our concept, and that the judgment is therefore analytic, is merely the ambiguous character of the terms used. We are required to join in thought a certain predicate to a given concept, and this necessity is inherent in the concepts themselves. But the question is not what we *ought* to join in thought to the given concept, but what we *actually* think in it, even if only obscurely; and it is then manifest that, while the predicate is indeed attached necessarily to the concept, it is so in virtue of an intuition which must be added to the concept, not as thought in the concept itself. 17

Some few fundamental propositions, presupposed by the geometrician, are, indeed, really analytic, and rest on the principle of contradiction. But, as identical propositions, they serve only as links in the chain of method and not as principles; for instance, *a = a;* the whole is equal to itself; or *(a + b) > a,* that is, the whole is greater than its part. And even these propositions, though they are valid according to pure concepts, are only admitted in mathematics because they can be exhibited in intuition.

2. *Natural science (physics) contains* a priori *synthetic judgments as principles.* I need cite only two such judgments: that in all changes of the material world the quantity of matter remains unchanged; and that in all communication of motion, action and reaction must always be equal. Both propositions, it is evident, are not only necessary, and therefore in their origin *a priori,* but also synthetic. For in the concept of matter I do not think its permanence, but only its presence in the space which it occupies. I go outside and beyond the concept of matter, joining to it *a priori* in thought something which I have not thought *in* it. The proposition is not, therefore, analytic, but synthetic, and yet is thought *a priori;* and so likewise are the other propositions of the pure part of natural science. 18

3. *Metaphysics,* even if we look upon it as having hitherto failed in all its endeavours, is yet, owing to the nature of human reason, a quite indispensable science, and *ought to contain* a priori *synthetic knowledge.* For its business is not merely to analyse concepts which we make for ourselves *a priori* of things, and thereby to clarify them analytically, but to extend our *a priori* knowledge. And for this purpose we must employ principles which add to the given concept something that was not contained in it, and through *a priori* synthetic judgments venture out so far that experience is quite unable to follow us, as, for instance, in the proposition, that the world must have a first

beginning, and such like. Thus metaphysics consists, at least *in intention,* entirely of *a priori* synthetic propositions.

19   VI. THE GENERAL PROBLEM OF PURE REASON

Much is already gained if we can bring a number of investigations under the formula of a single problem. For we not only lighten our own task, by defining it accurately, but make it easier for others, who would test our results, to judge whether or not we have succeeded in what we set out to do. Now the proper problem of pure reason is contained in the question: How are *a priori* synthetic judgments possible?

That metaphysics has hitherto remained in so vacillating a state of uncertainty and contradiction, is entirely due to the fact that this problem, and perhaps even the distinction between analytic and synthetic judgments, has never previously been considered. Upon the solution of this problem, or upon·a sufficient proof that the possibility which it desires to have explained does in fact not exist at all, depends the success or failure of metaphysics. Among philosophers, David Hume came nearest to envisaging this problem, but still was very far from conceiving it with sufficient definiteness and universality. He occupied himself exclusively with the synthetic proposition regarding the connection of an effect with its cause (*principium causali-*
20   *tatis*), and he believed himself to have shown that such an *a priori* proposition is entirely impossible. If we accept his conclusions, then all that we call metaphysics is a mere delusion whereby we fancy ourselves to have rational insight into what, in actual fact, is borrowed solely from experience, and under the influence of custom has taken the illusory semblance of necessity. If he had envisaged our problem in all its universality, he would never have been guilty of this statement, so destructive of all pure philosophy. For he would then have recognised that, according to his own argument, pure mathematics, as certainly containing *a priori* synthetic propositions, would also not be possible; and from such an assertion his good sense would have saved him.

In the solution of the above problem, we are at the same time deciding as to the possibility of the employment of pure reason in establishing and developing all those sciences which contain a theoretical *a priori* knowledge of objects, and have therefore to answer the questions:

How is pure mathematics possible?
How is pure science of nature possible?

Since these sciences actually exist, it is quite proper to ask *how* they are possible; for
21   that they must be possible is proved by the fact that they exist.* But the poor progress which has hitherto been made in metaphysics, and the fact that no system yet propounded can, in view of the essential purpose of metaphysics, be said really to exist, leaves everyone sufficient ground for doubting as to its possibility.

---

*Many may still have doubts as regards pure natural science. We have only, however, to consider the various propositions that are to be found at the beginning of (empirical) physics, properly so called, those, for instance, relating to the permanence in the quantity of matter, to inertia, to the equality of action and re-action, etc., in order to be soon convinced that they constitute a *physica pura,* or *rationalis,* which well deserves, as an independent science, to be separately dealt with in its whole extent, be that narrow or wide.

Yet, in a certain sense, this *kind of knowledge* is to be looked upon as given; that is to say, metaphysics actually exists, if not as a science, yet still as natural disposition (*metaphysica naturalis*). For human reason, without being moved merely by the idle desire for extent and variety of knowledge, proceeds impetuously, driven on by an inward need, to questions such as cannot be answered by any empirical employment of reason, or by principles thence derived. Thus in all men, as soon as their reason has become ripe for speculation, there has always existed and will always continue to exist some kind of metaphysics. And so we have the question:

How is metaphysics, as natural disposition, possible?   22

that is, how from the nature of universal human reason do those questions arise which pure reason propounds to itself, and which it is impelled by its own need to answer as best it can?

But since all attempts which have hitherto been made to answer these natural questions—for instance, whether the world has a beginning or is from eternity—have always met with unavoidable contradictions, we cannot rest satisfied with the mere natural disposition to metaphysics, that is, with the pure faculty of reason itself, from which, indeed, some sort of metaphysics (be it what it may) always arises. It must be possible for reason to attain to certainty whether we know or do not know the objects of metaphysics, that is, to come to a decision either in regard to the objects of its enquiries or in regard to the capacity or incapacity of reason to pass any judgment upon them, so that we may either with confidence extend our pure reason or set to it sure and determinate limits. This last question, which arises out of the previous general problem, may, rightly stated, take the form:

How is metaphysics, as science, possible?

Thus the critique of reason, in the end, necessarily leads to scientific knowledge; while its dogmatic employment, on the other hand, lands us in dogmatic assertions to which other assertions, equally specious, can always be opposed—that is, in *scepticism.*   23

This science cannot be of any very formidable prolixity, since it has to deal not with the objects of reason, the variety of which is inexhaustible, but only with itself and the problems which arise entirely from within itself, and which are imposed upon it by its own nature, not by the nature of things which are distinct from it. When once reason has learnt completely to understand its own power in respect of objects which can be presented to it in experience, it should easily be able to determine, with completeness and certainty, the extent and the limits of its attempted employment beyond the bounds of all experience.

We may, then, and indeed we must, regard as abortive all attempts, hitherto made, to establish a metaphysic *dogmatically.* For the analytic part in any such attempted system, namely, the mere analysis of the concepts that inhere in our reason *a priori,* is by no means the aim of, but only a preparation for, metaphysics proper, that is, the extension of its *a priori* synthetic knowledge. For such a purpose, the analysis of concepts is useless, since it merely shows what is contained in these concepts, not how we arrive at them *a priori.* A solution of this latter problem is required, that we may be able to determine the valid employment of such concepts in regard to the ob-   24
jects of all knowledge in general. Nor is much self-denial needed to give up these claims, seeing that the undeniable, and in the dogmatic procedure of reason also un-

avoidable, contradictions of reason with itself have long since undermined the authority of every metaphysical system yet propounded. Greater firmness will be required if we are not to be deterred by inward difficulties and outward opposition from endeavouring, through application of a method entirely different from any hitherto employed, at last to bring to a prosperous and fruitful growth a science indispensable to human reason—a science whose every branch may be cut away but whose root cannot be destroyed.

VII. THE IDEA AND DIVISION OF A SPECIAL SCIENCE, UNDER THE TITLE "CRITIQUE OF PURE REASON"

In view of all these considerations, we arrive at the idea of a special science which can be entitled the Critique of Pure Reason. For reason is the faculty which supplies the principles of *a priori* knowledge. Pure reason is, therefore, that which contains the principles whereby we know anything absolutely *a priori.* . . . I entitle *transcendental* all knowledge which is occupied not so much with objects as with the mode of our knowledge of objects in so far as this mode of knowledge is to be possible *a priori.* A system of such concepts might be entitled transcendental philosophy. But that is still, at this stage, too large an undertaking. For since such a science must contain, with completeness, both kinds of *a priori* knowledge, the analytic no less than the synthetic, it is, so far as our present purpose is concerned, much too comprehensive. We have to carry the analysis so far only as is indispensably necessary in order to comprehend, in their whole

26   extent, the principles of *a priori* synthesis, with which alone we are called upon to deal. It is upon this enquiry, which should be entitled not a doctrine, but only a transcendental critique, that we are now engaged. Its purpose is not to extend knowledge, but only to correct it, and to supply a touchstone of the value, or lack of value, of all *a priori* knowledge. . . .

What has chiefly to be kept in view in the division of such a science, is that no concepts be allowed to enter which contain in themselves anything empirical, or, in other words, that it consist in knowledge wholly *a priori.* Accordingly, although the highest principles and fundamental concepts of morality are *a priori* knowledge, they have no place in transcendental philosophy, because, although they do not lay at the

29   foundation of their precepts the concepts of pleasure and pain, of the desires and inclinations, etc., all of which are of empirical origin, yet in the construction of a system of pure morality these empirical concepts must necessarily be brought into the concept of duty, as representing either a hindrance, which we have to overcome, or an allurement, which must not be made into a motive. Transcendental philosophy is therefore a philosophy of pure and merely speculative reason. All that is practical, so far as it contains motives, relates to feelings, and these belong to the empirical sources of knowledge.

. . . By way of introduction or anticipation we need only say that there are two stems of human knowledge, namely, *sensibility* and *understanding,* which perhaps spring from a common, but to us unknown, root. Through the former, objects are given

30   to us; through the latter, they are thought. Now in so far as sensibility may be found to contain *a priori* representations constituting the condition under which objects are given to us, it will belong to transcendental philosophy. And since the conditions under which alone the objects of human knowledge are given must precede those under which they are thought, the transcendental doctrine of sensibility will constitute the first part of the science of the elements.

TRANSCENDENTAL DOCTRINE OF ELEMENTS

FIRST PART

TRANSCENDENTAL AESTHETIC

§1

In whatever manner and by whatever means a mode of knowledge may relate to objects, *intuition* is that through which it is in immediate relation to them, and to which all thought as a means is directed. But intuition takes place only in so far as the object is given to us. This again is only possible, to man at least, in so far as the mind is affected in a certain way. The capacity (receptivity) for receiving representations through the mode in which we are affected by objects, is entitled *sensibility*. Objects are *given* to us by means of sensibility, and it alone yields us *intuitions;* they are *thought* through the understanding, and from the understanding arise *concepts.* But all thought must, directly or indirectly, by way of certain characters, relate ultimately to intuitions, and therefore, with us, to sensibility, because in no other way can an object be given to us.

The effect of an object upon the faculty of representation, so far as we are affected by it, is *sensation.* That intuition which is in relation to the object through sensation, is entitled *empirical.* The undetermined object of an empirical intuition is entitled *appearance.*

That in the appearance which corresponds to sensation I term its *matter;* but that   34
which so determines the manifold of appearance that it allows of being ordered in certain relations, I term the *form* of appearance. That in which alone the sensations can be posited and ordered in a certain form, cannot itself be sensation; and therefore, while the matter of all appearance is given to us *a posteriori* only, its form must lie ready for the sensations *a priori* in the mind, and so must allow of being considered apart from all sensation.

I term all representations *pure* (in the transcendental sense) in which there is nothing that belongs to sensation. The pure form of sensible intuitions in general, in which all the manifold of intuition is intuited in certain relations, must be found in the mind *a priori.* This pure form of sensibility may also itself be called *pure intuition.*   35
Thus, if I take away from the representation of a body that which the understanding thinks in regard to it, substance, force, divisibility, etc., and likewise what belongs to sensation, impenetrability, hardness, colour, etc., something still remains over from this empirical intuition, namely, extension and figure. These belong to pure intuition, which, even without any actual object of the senses or of sensation, exists in the mind *a priori* as a mere form of sensibility.

The science of all principles of *a priori* sensibility I call *transcendental aesthetic.* There must be such a science, forming the first part of the transcendental doc-   36
trine of elements, in distinction from that part which deals with the principles of pure thought, and which is called transcendental logic.

In the transcendental aesthetic we shall, therefore, first *isolate* sensibility, by taking away from it everything which the understanding thinks through its concepts, so that nothing may be left save empirical intuition. Secondly, we shall also separate off from it everything which belongs to sensation, so that nothing may remain save pure intuition and the mere form of appearances, which is all that sensibility can supply *a priori.* In the course of this investigation it will be found that there are two pure forms of sensible intuition, serving as principles of *a priori* knowledge, namely, space and time. To the consideration of these we shall now proceed.

37   THE TRANSCENDENTAL AESTHETIC

SECTION I

SPACE

§2

Metaphysical Exposition of this Concept

By means of outer sense, a property of our mind, we represent to ourselves objects as outside us, and all without exception in space. In space their shape, magnitude, and relation to one another are determined or determinable. Inner sense, by means of which the mind intuits itself or its inner state, yields indeed no intuition of the soul itself as an object; but there is nevertheless a determinate form [namely, time] in which alone the intuition of inner states is possible, and everything which belongs to inner determinations is therefore represented in relations of time. Time cannot be outwardly intuited, any more than space can be intuited as something in us. What, then, are space and time? Are they real existences? Are they only determinations or relations of things, yet such as would belong to things even if they were not intuited? Or are space and time such that they belong only to the form of intuition, and therefore to the subjective constitution of our mind, apart from which they could not be ascribed to anything whatsoever? In order to obtain light upon these questions, let us first give an exposition of the concept of space. By *exposition* (expositio) I mean the clear, though not necessarily exhaustive, representation of that which belongs to a concept: the exposition is *metaphysical* when it contains that which exhibits the concept *as given a priori*.

1. Space is not an empirical concept which has been derived from outer experiences. For in order that certain sensations be referred to something outside me (that is, to something in another region of space from that in which I find myself), and similarly in order that I may be able to represent them as outside and alongside one another, and accordingly as not only different but as in different places, the representation of space must be presupposed. The representation of space cannot, therefore, be empirically obtained from the relations of outer appearance. On the contrary, this outer experience is itself possible at all only through that representation.

2. Space is a necessary *a priori* representation, which underlies all outer intuitions. We can never represent to ourselves the absence of space, though we can quite well think it as empty of objects. It must therefore be regarded as the condition of the possibility of appearances, and not as a determination dependent upon them. It is an *a priori* representation, which necessarily underlies outer appearances.

3. Space is not a discursive or, as we say, general concept of relations of things in general, but a pure intuition. For, in the first place, we can represent to ourselves only one space; and if we speak of diverse spaces, we mean thereby only parts of one and the same unique space. Secondly, these parts cannot precede the one all-embracing space, as being, as it were, constituents out of which it can be composed; on the contrary, they can be thought only as *in* it. Space is essentially one; the manifold in it, and therefore the general concept of spaces, depends solely on [the introduction of] limitations. Hence it follows that an *a priori,* and not an empirical, intuition underlies all concepts of space. For kindred reasons, geometrical propositions, that, for instance, in a triangle two sides together are greater than the third, can never be derived from the general concepts of line and triangle, but only from intuition, and this indeed *a priori*, with apodeictic certainty.

38

39

4. Space is represented as an infinite *given* magnitude. Now every concept must 40 be thought as a representation which is contained in an infinite number of different possible representations (as their common character), and which therefore contains these *under* itself; but no concept, as such, can be thought as containing an infinite number of representations *which* itself. It is in this latter way, however, that space is thought; for all the parts of space coexist *ad infinitum*. Consequently, the original representation of space is an *a priori* intuition, not a concept.

§3

The Transcendental Exposition
of the Concept of Space

I understand by a transcendental exposition the explanation of a concept, as a principle from which the possibility of other *a priori* synthetic knowledge can be understood. For this purpose it is required (1) that such knowledge does really flow from the given concept, (2) that this knowledge is possible only on the assumption of a given mode of explaining the concept.

Geometry is a science which determines the properties of space synthetically, and yet *a priori*. What, then, must be our representation of space, in order that such knowledge of it may be possible? It must in its origin be intuition; for from a mere 41 concept no propositions can be obtained which go beyond the concept—as happens in geometry (Introduction, V). Further, this intuition must be *a priori*, that is, it must be found in us prior to any perception of an object, and must therefore be pure, not empirical, intuition. For geometrical propositions are one and all apodeictic, that is, are bound up with the consciousness of their necessity; for instance, that space has only three dimensions. Such propositions cannot be empirical or, in other words, judgments of experience, nor can they be derived from any such judgments (Introduction, II).

How, then, can there exist in the mind an outer intuition which precedes the objects themselves, and in which the concept of these objects can be determined *a priori?* Manifestly, not otherwise than in so far as the intuition has its seat in the subject only, as the formal character of the subject, in virtue of which, in being affected by objects, it obtains *immediate representation,* that is, intuition, of them; and only in so far, therefore, as it is merely the form of outer *sense* in general.

Our explanation is thus the only explanation that makes intelligible the *possibility* of geometry, as a body of *a priori* synthetic knowledge. Any mode of explanation which fails to do this, although it may otherwise seem to be somewhat similar, can by this criterion be distinguished from it with the greatest certainty.

Conclusions from the above Concepts 42

(*a*) Space does not represent any property of things in themselves, nor does it represent them in their relation to one another. That is to say, space does not represent any determination that attaches to the objects themselves, and which remains even when abstraction has been made of all the subjective conditions of intuition. For no determinations, whether absolute or relative, can be intuited prior to the existence of the things to which they belong, and none, therefore, can be intuited *a priori*.

(*b*) Space is nothing but the form of all appearances of outer sense. It is the subjective condition of sensibility, under which alone outer intuition is possible for us. Since, then, the receptivity of the subject, its capacity to be affected by objects, must necessarily precede all intuitions of these objects, it can readily be understood how the form of all appearances can be given prior to all actual perceptions, and so exist in the mind *a priori,* and how, as a pure intuition, in which all objects must be determined, it can contain, prior to all experience, principles which determine the relations of these objects.

It is, therefore, solely from the human standpoint that we can speak of space, of extended things, etc. If we depart from the subjective condition under which alone we can

43   have outer intuition, namely, liability to be affected by objects, the representation of space stands for nothing whatsoever. This predicate can be ascribed to things only in so far as they appear to us, that is, only to objects of sensibility. The constant form of this receptivity, which we term sensibility, is a necessary condition of all the relations in which objects can be intuited as outside us; and if we abstract from these objects, it is a pure intuition, and bears the name of space. Since we cannot treat the special conditions of sensibility as conditions of the possibility of things, but only of their appearances, we can indeed say that space comprehends all things that appear to us as external, but not all things in themselves, by whatever subject they are intuited, or whether they be intuited or not. For we cannot judge in regard to the intuitions of other thinking beings, whether they are bound by the same conditions as those which limit our intuition and which for us are universally valid. If we add to the concept of the subject of a judgment the limitation under which the judgment is made, the judgment is then unconditionally valid. The proposition, that all things are side by side in space, is valid under the limitation that these things are viewed as objects of our sensible intuition. If, now, I add the condition to the concept, and say that all things, as outer appearances, are side by side in space, the rule is valid universally and

44   without limitation. Our exposition therefore establishes the *reality,* that is, the objective validity, of space in respect of whatever can be presented to us outwardly as object, but also at the same time the *ideality* of space in respect of things when they are considered in themselves through reason, that is, without regard to the constitution of our sensibility. We assert, then, the *empirical reality* of space, as regards all possible outer experience; and yet at the same time we assert its *transcendental ideality*—in other words, that it is nothing at all, immediately we withdraw the above condition, namely, its limitation to possible experience, and so look upon it as something that underlies things in themselves. . . .

46   ## TRANSCENDENTAL AESTHETIC

SECTION II

TIME

§4

Metaphysical Exposition of the Concept of Time

1. Time is not an empirical concept that has been derived from any experience. For neither coexistence nor succession would ever come within our perception, if the representation of time were not presupposed as underlying them *a priori.* Only on the presupposition of time can we represent to ourselves a number of things as existing at one and the same time (simultaneously) or at different times (successively).

2. Time is a necessary representation that underlies all intuitions. We cannot, in respect of appearances in general, remove time itself, though we can quite well think time as void of appearances. Time is, therefore, given *a priori.* In it alone is actuality

of appearances possible at all. Appearances may, one and all, vanish; but time (as the universal condition of their possibility) cannot itself be removed.

3. The possibility of apodeictic principles concerning the relations of time, or of 47 axioms of time in general, is also grounded upon this *a priori* necessity. Time has only one dimension; different times are not simultaneous but successive (just as different spaces are not successive but simultaneous). These principles cannot be derived from experience, for experience would give neither strict universality nor apodeictic certainty. We should only be able to say that common experience teaches us that it is so; not that it must be so. These principles are valid as rules under which alone experiences are possible; and they instruct us in regard to the experiences, not by means of them.

4. Time is not a discursive, or what is called a general concept, but a pure form of sensible intuition. Different times are but parts of one and the same time; and the representation which can be given only through a single object is intuition. Moreover, the proposition that different times cannot be simultaneous is not to be derived from a general concept. The proposition is synthetic, and cannot have its origin in concepts alone. It is immediately contained in the intuition and representation of time.

5. The infinitude of time signifies nothing more than that every determinate mag- 48 nitude of time is possible only through limitations of one single time that underlies it. The original representation, *time,* must therefore be given as unlimited. But when an object is so given that its parts, and every quantity of it, can be determinately represented only through limitation, the whole representation cannot be given through concepts, since they contain only partial representations; on the contrary, such concepts must themselves rest on immediate intuition.

§5

*The Transcendental Exposition
of the Concept of Time*

I may here refer to No. 3 [i.e., §4, No. 3, just above], where, for the sake of brevity, I have placed under the title of metaphysical exposition what is properly transcendental. Here I may add that the concept of alteration, and with it the concept of motion, as alteration of place, is possible only through and in the representation of time; and that if this representation were not an *a priori* (inner) intuition, no concept, no matter what it might be, could render comprehensible the possibility of an alteration, that is, of a combination of contradictorily opposed predicates in one and the same object, for instance, the being and not-being of one and the same thing in one and the same place. Only in time can two contradictorily opposed predicates meet in one 49 and the same object, namely, *one after the other.* Thus our concept of time explains the possibility of that body of *a priori* synthetic knowledge which is exhibited in the general doctrine of motion, and which is by no means unfruitful.

§6

Conclusions from these Concepts

(*a*) Time is not something which exists of itself, or which inheres in things as an objective determination, and it does not, therefore, remain when abstraction is made of all subjective conditions of its intuition. Were it self-subsistent, it would be something which would be actual and yet not an actual object. Were it a determination or order inhering in things themselves, it could not precede the objects as their condition, and be known and intuited *a priori* by means of synthetic propositions. But this last is quite possible if time is nothing but the subjective condition under which alone intuition can take place in us. For that being so, this form of inner intuition can be represented prior to the objects, and therefore *a priori*.

(*b*) Time is nothing but the form of inner sense, that is, of the intuition of ourselves and of our inner state. It cannot be a determination of outer appearances; it has to do neither with shape nor position, but with the relation of representations in our inner state. And just because this inner intuition yields no shape, we endeavour to make up for this want by analogies. We represent the time-sequence by a line progressing to infinity, in which the manifold constitutes a series of one dimension only; and we reason from the properties of this line to all the properties of time, with this one exception, that while the parts of the line are simultaneous the parts of time are always successive. From this fact also, that all the relations of time allow of being expressed in an outer intuition, it is evident that the representation is itself an intuition.

(*c*) Time is the formal *a priori* condition of all appearances whatsoever. Space, as the pure form of all outer intuition, is so far limited; it serves as the *a priori* condition only of outer appearances. But since all representations, whether they have for their objects outer things or not, belong, in themselves, as determinations of the mind, to our inner state; and since this inner state stands under the formal condition of inner intuition, and so belongs to time, time is an *a priori* condition of all appearance whatsoever. It is the immediate condition of inner appearances (of our souls), and thereby the mediate condition of outer appearances. Just as I can say *a priori* that all outer appearances are in space, and are determined *a priori* in conformity with the relations of space, I can also say, from the principle of inner sense, that all appearances whatsoever, that is, all objects of the senses, are in time, and necessarily stand in time-relations.

If we abstract from *our* mode of inwardly intuiting ourselves—the mode of intuition in terms of which we likewise take up into our faculty of representation all outer intuitions—and so take objects as they may be in themselves, then time is nothing. It has objective validity only in respect of appearances, these being things which we take *as objects of our senses*. It is no longer objective, if we abstract from the sensibility of our intuition, that is, from that mode of representation which is peculiar to us, and speak of *things in general*. Time is therefore a purely subjective condition of our (human) intuition (which is always sensible, that is, so far as we are affected by objects), and in itself, apart from the subject, is nothing. Nevertheless, in respect of all appearances, and therefore of all the things which can enter into our experience, it is necessarily objective. We cannot say that all things are in time, because in this concept of things in general we are abstracting from every mode of their intuition and therefore from that condition under which alone objects can be represented as being in time. If, however, the condition be added to the concept, and we say that all things as appearances, that is, as objects of sensible intuition, are in time, then the proposition has legitimate objective validity and universality *a priori*.

What we are maintaining is, therefore, the *empirical reality* of time, that is, its objective validity in respect of all objects which allow of ever being given to our senses. And since our intuition is always sensible, no object can ever be given to us in experience which does not conform to the condition of time. On the other hand, we deny to time all claim to absolute reality; that is to say, we deny that it belongs to things absolutely, as their condition or property, independently of any reference to the form of our sensible intuition; properties that belong to things in themselves can never be given to us through the senses. This, then, is what constitutes the *transcendental ideality* of time. What we mean by this phrase is that if we abstract from the subjective conditions of sensible intuition, time is nothing, and cannot be ascribed to the objects in themselves (apart from their relation to our intuition) in the way either of subsistence or of inherence. . . .

§7

Elucidation

Against this theory, which admits the empirical reality of time, but denies its ab-   53
solute and transcendental reality, I have heard men of intelligence so unanimously voicing an objection, that I must suppose it to occur spontaneously to every reader to whom this way of thinking is unfamiliar. The objection is this. Alterations are real, this being proved by change of our own representations—even if all outer appearances, together with their alterations, be denied. Now alterations are possible only in time, and time is therefore something real. There is no difficulty in meeting this objection. I grant the whole argument. Certainly time is something real, namely, the real form of inner intuition. It has therefore subjective reality in respect of inner experience; that is, I really have the representation of time and of my determinations in it. Time is there-   54
fore to be regarded as real, not indeed as object but as the mode of representation of myself as object. If without this condition of sensibility I could intuit myself, or be intuited by another being, the very same determinations which we now represent to ourselves as alterations would yield knowledge into which the representation of time, and therefore also of alteration, would in no way enter. Thus empirical reality has to be allowed to time, as the condition of all our experiences; on our theory, it is only its absolute reality that has to be denied. It is nothing but the form of our inner intuition.* If we take away from our inner intuition the peculiar condition of our sensibility, the concept of time likewise vanishes; it does not inhere in the objects, but merely in the subject which intuits them.

But the reason why this objection is so unanimously urged, and that too by those   55
who have nothing very convincing to say against the doctrine of the ideality of space, is this. They have no expectation of being able to prove apodeictically the absolute reality of space; for they are confronted by idealism, which teaches that the reality of outer objects does not allow of strict proof. On the other hand, the reality of the object of our inner sense (the reality of myself and my state) is, [they argue,] immediately evident through consciousness. The former may be merely an illusion; the latter is, on their view, undeniably something real. What they have failed, however, to recognise is that both are in the same position; in neither case can their reality as representations be questioned, and in both cases they belong only to appearance, which always has two sides, the one by which the object is viewed in and by itself (without regard to the mode of intuiting it—its nature therefore remaining always problematic), the other by which the form of the intuition of this object is taken into account. This form is not to be looked for in the object in itself, but in the subject to which the object appears; nevertheless, it belongs really and necessarily to the appearance of this object.

. . . Those . . . who maintain the absolute reality of space and time, whether as subsistent or only as inherent, must come into conflict with the principles of experience

---

*I can indeed say that my representations follow one another; but this is only to say that we are conscious of them as in a time sequence, that is, in conformity with the form of inner sense. Time is not, therefore, something in itself, nor is it an objective determination inherent in things.

itself. For if they decide for the former alternative (which is generally the view taken by mathematical students of nature), they have to admit two eternal and infinite self-subsistent non-entities (space and time), which are there (yet without there being anything real) only in order to contain in themselves all that is real. If they adopt the latter alternative (as advocated by certain metaphysical students of nature), and regard space and time as relations of appearances, alongside or in succession to one another—relations abstracted from experience, and in this isolation confusedly represented—they are obliged to deny that *a priori* mathematical doctrines have any validity in respect of real things (for instance, in space), or at least to deny their apodeictic certainty. For such certainty is not to be found in the *a posteriori*. On this view, indeed, the *a priori* concepts of space and time are merely creatures of the imagination, whose source must really be sought in experience, the imagination framing out of the relations abstracted from experience something that does indeed contain what is general in these relations, but which cannot exist without the restrictions which nature has attached to them. The former thinkers obtain at least this advantage, that they keep the field of appearances open for mathematical propositions. On the other hand, they have greatly embarrassed themselves by those very conditions [space and time, eternal, infinite, and self-subsistent], when with the understanding they endeavour to go out beyond this field. The latter have indeed an advantage, in that the representations of space and time do not stand in their way if they seek to judge of objects, not as appearances but merely in their relation to the understanding. But since they are unable to appeal to a true and objectively valid *a priori* intuition, they can neither account for the possibility of *a priori* mathematical knowledge, nor bring the propositions of experience into necessary agreement with it. On our theory of the true character of these two original forms of sensibility, both difficulties are removed.

*   *   *

74   TRANSCENDENTAL DOCTRINE OF ELEMENTS

SECOND PART

TRANSCENDENTAL LOGIC

INTRODUCTION

IDEA OF A TRANSCENDENTAL LOGIC

I

LOGIC IN GENERAL

Our knowledge springs from two fundamental sources of the mind; the first is the capacity of receiving representations (receptivity for impressions), the second is the power of knowing an object through these representations (spontaneity [in the production] of concepts). Through the first an object is *given* to us, through the second the object is *thought* in relation to that [given] representation (which is a mere determination of the mind). Intuition and concepts constitute, therefore, the elements of all our knowledge, so that neither concepts without an intuition in some way corresponding to them, nor intuition without concepts, can yield knowledge. Both may be either pure or empirical. When they contain sensation (which presupposes the actual presence of the object), they are empirical. When there is no mingling of sensation with the representation, they are pure. Sensation may be entitled the material of sensible knowledge. Pure intuition, therefore, contains only the form under which something is intuited; the pure concept only the form of the thought of an object in general. Pure intuitions or pure concepts alone are possible *a priori,* empirical intuitions and empirical concepts only *a posteriori.* 75

If the *receptivity* of our mind, its power of receiving representations in so far as it is in any wise affected, is to be entitled sensibility, then the mind's power of producing representations from itself, the *spontaneity* of knowledge, should be called the understanding. Our nature is so constituted that our *intuition* can never be other than sensible; that is, it contains only the mode in which we are affected by objects. The faculty, on the other hand, which enables us to *think* the object of sensible intuition is the understanding. To neither of these powers may a preference be given over the other. Without sensibility no object would be given to us, without understanding no object would be thought. Thoughts without content are empty, intuitions without concepts are blind. It is, therefore, just as necessary to make our concepts sensible, that is, to add the object to them in intuition, as to make our intuitions intelligible, that is, to bring them under concepts. These two powers or capacities cannot exchange their functions. The understanding can intuit nothing, the senses can think nothing. Only through their union can knowledge arise. But that is no reason for confounding the contribution of 76 either with that of the other; rather is it a strong reason for carefully separating and distinguishing the one from the other. We therefore distinguish the science of the rules of sensibility in general, that is, aesthetic, from the science of the rules of the understanding in general, that is, logic.

* * *

IV. The Division of Transcendental Logic into Transcendental Analytic and Dialectic 87

In a transcendental logic we isolate the understanding—as above, in the Transcendental Aesthetic, the sensibility—separating out from our knowledge that part of thought which has its origin solely in the understanding. The employment of this pure knowledge depends upon the condition that objects to which it can be applied be given to us in intuition. In the absence of intuition all our knowledge is without objects, and therefore remains entirely empty. That part of transcendental logic which deals with the elements of the pure knowledge yielded by understanding, and the principles without which no object can be thought, is transcendental analytic. It is a logic of truth. For no knowledge can contradict it without at once losing all content, that is, all relation to any object, and therefore all truth. But since it is very tempting to use these pure modes of knowledge of the understanding and these principles by themselves, and even beyond the limits of experience, which alone can yield the matter (objects) to which 88 those pure concepts of understanding can be applied, the understanding is led to incur

View of Königsberg Castle, Kant's house in foreground. (*British Museum*)

the risk of making, with a mere show of rationality, a material use of its pure and merely formal principles, and of passing judgments upon objects without distinction—upon objects which are not given to us, nay, perhaps cannot in any way be given. Since, properly, this transcendental analytic should be used only as a canon for passing judgment upon the empirical employment of the understanding, it is misapplied if appealed to as an organon of its general and unlimited application, and if consequently we venture, with the pure understanding alone, to judge synthetically, to affirm, and to decide regarding objects in general. The employment of the pure understanding then becomes dialectical. The second part of transcendental logic must therefore form a critique of this dialectical illusion, and is called transcendental dialectic. . . .

89 TRANSCENDENTAL LOGIC

FIRST DIVISION

TRANSCENDENTAL ANALYTIC

Transcendental analytic consists in the dissection of all our *a priori* knowledge into the elements that pure understanding by itself yields. In so doing, the following are the points of chief concern: (1) that the concepts be pure and not empirical; (2) that they belong, not to intuition and sensibility, but to thought and understanding; (3) that they be fundamental and be carefully distinguished from those which are derivative or composite; (4) that our table of concepts be complete, covering the whole field of the pure understanding. When a science is an aggregate brought into existence in a merely experimental manner, such completeness can never be guaranteed by any kind of mere estimate. It is possible only by means of *an idea of the totality* of the *a priori* knowledge yielded by the understanding; such an idea can furnish an exact classification of

90 the concepts which compose that totality, exhibiting their *interconnection in a system*. Pure understanding distinguishes itself not merely from all that is empirical but com-

pletely also from all sensibility. It is a unity self-subsistent, self-sufficient, and not to be increased by any additions from without. The sum of its knowledge thus constitutes a system, comprehended and determined by one idea. The completeness and articulation of this system can at the same time yield a criterion of the correctness and genuineness of all its components. This part of transcendental logic requires, however, for its complete exposition, two books, the one containing the *concepts,* the other the *principles* of pure understanding

* * *

TRANSCENDENTAL ANALYTIC

BOOK I

ANALYTIC OF CONCEPTS

CHAPTER 1

THE CLUE TO THE DISCOVERY OF ALL PURE CONCEPTS OF THE UNDERSTANDING

... Transcendental philosophy, in seeking for its concepts, has the advantage and also   92
the duty of proceeding according to a single principle. For these concepts spring, pure and unmixed, out of the understanding which is an absolute unity; and must therefore be connected with each other according to one concept or idea. Such a connection supplies us with a rule, by which we are enabled to assign its proper place to each pure concept of the understanding, and by which we can determine in an *a priori* manner their systematic completeness. Otherwise we should be dependent in these matters on our own discretionary judgment or merely on chance.

THE TRANSCENDENTAL CLUE TO THE DISCOVERY OF ALL PURE CONCEPTS OF THE UNDERSTANDING

SECTION I

THE LOGICAL EMPLOYMENT OF THE UNDERSTANDING

The understanding has thus far been explained merely negatively, as a non-sensible faculty of knowledge. Now since without sensibility we cannot have any intuition, understanding cannot be a faculty of intuition. But besides intuition there is no other mode of knowledge except by means of concepts. The knowledge yielded by under-   93 standing, or at least by the human understanding, must therefore be by means of concepts, and so is not intuitive, but discursive. Whereas all intuitions, as sensible, rest on affections, concepts rest on functions. By "function" I mean the unity of the act of bringing various representations under one common representation. Concepts are based on the spontaneity of thought, sensible intuitions on the receptivity of impressions. Now the only use which the understanding can make of these concepts is to judge by means of them. Since no representation, save when it is an intuition, is in immediate relation to an object, no concept is ever related to an object immediately, but to some other representation of it, be that other representation an intuition, or itself a concept. Judgment is therefore the mediate knowledge of an object, that is, the representation of a representation of it. In every judgment there is a concept which holds of many representations, and among them of a given representation that is immediately related to an object. Thus in the judgment, "all bodies are divisible" the concept of the divisible applies to various other concepts, but is here applied in particular to the concept of body, and this concept again to certain appearances that present themselves to us. These objects, therefore, are mediately represented through the concept of divisibil-

94   ity. Accordingly, all judgments are functions of unity among our representations; instead of an immediate representation, a *higher* representation, which comprises the immediate representation and various others, is used in knowing the object, and thereby much possible knowledge is collected into one. Now we can reduce all acts of the understanding to judgments, and the *understanding* may therefore be represented as a *faculty of judgment.* For, as stated above, the understanding is a faculty of thought. Thought is knowledge by means of concepts. But concepts, as predicates of possible judgments, relate to some representation of a not yet determined object. Thus the concept of body means something, for instance, metal, which can be known by means of that concept. It is therefore a concept solely in virtue of its comprehending other representations, by means of which it can relate to objects. It is therefore the predicate of a possible judgment, for instance, "every metal is a body." The functions of the understanding can, therefore, be discovered if we can give an exhaustive statement of the functions of unity in judgments. That this can quite easily be done will be shown in the next section.

95

THE CLUE TO THE DISCOVERY OF ALL PURE CONCEPTS OF THE UNDERSTANDING

SECTION 2

§9

THE LOGICAL FUNCTION OF THE UNDERSTANDING IN JUDGMENTS

If we abstract from all content of a judgment, and consider only the mere form of understanding, we find that the function of thought in judgment can be brought under four heads, each of which contains three moments. They may be conveniently represented in the following table:

I
Quantity of Judgments
Universal
Particular
Singular

II
Quality
Affirmative
Negative
Infinite

III
Relation
Categorical
Hypothetical
Disjunctive

IV
Modality
Problematic
Assertoric
Apodeictic

*   *   *

THE CLUE TO THE DISCOVERY OF ALL PURE CONCEPTS OF THE UNDERSTANDING

SECTION 3

§10

THE PURE CONCEPTS OF THE UNDERSTANDING, OR CATEGORIES

General logic, as has been repeatedly said, abstracts from all content of knowledge, and looks to some other source, whatever that may be, for the representations which it is to transform into concepts by process of analysis. Transcendental logic, on the other hand, has lying before it a manifold of *a priori* sensibility, presented by transcendental aesthetic, as material for the concepts of pure understanding. In the absence of this material those concepts would be without any content, therefore entirely empty. Space and time contain a manifold of pure *a priori* intuition, but at the same time are conditions of the receptivity of our mind—conditions under which alone it can receive representations of objects, and which therefore must also always affect the concept of these objects. But if this manifold is to be known, the spontaneity of our thought requires that it be gone through in a certain way, taken up, and connected. This act I name *synthesis*. . . .

Synthesis in general, as we shall hereafter see, is the mere result of the power of imagination, a blind but indispensable function of the soul, without which we should have no knowledge whatsoever, but of which we are scarcely ever conscious. To bring this synthesis *to concepts* is a function which belongs to the understanding, and it is through this function of the understanding that we first obtain knowledge properly so called. . . . The same understanding, through the same operations by which in concepts, by means of analytical unity, it produced the logical form of a judgment, also introduces a transcendental content into its representations, by means of the synthetic unity of the manifold in intuition in general. On this account we are entitled to call these rep-

102

resentations pure concepts of the understanding, and to regard them as applying *a priori* to objects—a conclusion which general logic is not in a position to establish.

In this manner there arise precisely the same number of pure concepts of the understanding which apply *a priori* to objects of intuition in general, as, in the preceding table, there have been found to be logical functions in all possible judgments. For these functions specify the understanding completely, and yield an exhaustive inventory of its powers. These concepts we shall, with Aristotle, call *categories,* for our primary purpose is the same as his, although widely diverging from it in manner of execution.

106
TABLE OF CATEGORIES

I
Of Quantity
Unity
Plurality
Totality

II
Of Quality
Reality
Negation
Limitation

III
Of Relation
Of Inherence and Subsistence
(*substantia et accidens*)
Of Causality and Dependence
(*cause and effect*)
Of Community (reciprocity
between agent and patient)

IV
Of Modality
Possibility—Impossibility
Existence—Nonexistence
Necessity—Contingency

This then is the list of all original pure concepts of synthesis that the understanding contains within itself *a priori.* Indeed, it is because it contains these concepts that it is called pure understanding; for by them alone can it *understand* anything in the manifold of intuition, that is, think an object of intuition. This division is developed systematically from a common principle, namely, the faculty of judgment (which is the same as the faculty of thought). It has not arisen rhapsodically, as the result of a haphazard search after pure concepts, the complete enumeration of which, as based on induction

107 only, could never be guaranteed. Nor could we, if this were our procedure, discover why just these concepts, and no others, have their seat in the pure understanding. It was an enterprise worthy of an acute thinker like Aristotle to make search for these fundamental concepts. But as he did so on no principle, he merely picked them up as they came his way, and at first procured ten of them, which he called *categories* (predicaments). Afterwards he believed that he had discovered five others, which he added under the name of post-predicaments. But his table still remained defective. Besides, there are to be found in it some modes of pure sensibility (*quando, ubi, situs,* also *prius, simul*), and an empirical concept (*motus*), none of which have any place in a table of the concepts that trace their origin to the understanding. Aristotle's list also enumerates among the original concepts some derivative concepts (*actio, passio*); and of the original concepts some are entirely lacking.

*   *   *

DEDUCTION OF THE PURE CONCEPTS
OF THE UNDERSTANDING

[As restated in the second edition]

SECTION 2

TRANSCENDENTAL DEDUCTION OF THE PURE CONCEPTS   129
OF THE UNDERSTANDING

§15

*The Possibility of Combination
in General*

The manifold of representations can be given in an intuition which is purely sensible, that is, nothing but receptivity; and the form of this intuition can lie *a priori* in our faculty of representation, without being anything more than the mode in which the subject is affected. But the combination (*conjunctio*) of a manifold in general can never come to us through the senses, and cannot, therefore, be already contained in the pure form of sensible intuition. For it is an act of spontaneity of the   130 faculty of representation; and since this faculty, to distinguish it from sensibility, must be entitled understanding, all combination—be we conscious of it or not, be it a combination of the manifold of intuition, empirical or non-empirical, or of various concepts—is an act of the understanding. To this act the general title "synthesis" may be assigned, as indicating that we cannot represent to ourselves anything as combined in the object which we have not ourselves previously combined, and that of all representations *combination* is the only one which cannot be given through objects. Being an act of the self activity of the subject, it cannot be executed save by the subject itself. It will easily be observed that this action is originally one and is equipollent for all combination, and that its dissolution, namely, *analysis,* which appears to be its opposite, yet always presupposes it. For where the understanding has not previously combined, it cannot dissolve, since only as having been combined *by the understanding* can anything that allows of analysis be given to the faculty of representation.

But the concept of combination includes, besides the concept of the manifold and of its synthesis, also the concept of the unity of the manifold. Combination is representation of the *synthetic* unity of the manifold. The representation of this   131 unity cannot, therefore, arise out of the combination. On the contrary, it is what, by adding itself to the representation of the manifold, first makes possible the concept of the combination. This unity, which precedes *a priori* all concepts of combination, is not the category of unity (§10); for all categories are grounded in logical functions of judgment, and in these functions combination, and therefore unity of given concepts, is already thought. Thus the category already presupposes combination. We must therefore look yet higher for this unity (as qualitative, §12), namely in that which itself contains the ground of the unity of diverse concepts in judgment, and therefore of the possibility of the understanding, even as regards its logical employment.

§16

*The Original Synthetic Unity
of Apperception*

132   It must be possible for the "I think" to accompany all my representations; for otherwise something would be represented in me which could not be thought at all, and that is equivalent to saying that the representation would be impossible, or at least would be nothing to me. That representation which can be given prior to all thought is entitled intuition. All the manifold of intuition has, therefore, a necessary relation to the "I think" in the same subject in which this manifold is found. But this representation is an act of *spontaneity,* that is, it cannot be regarded as belonging to sensibility. I call it *pure apperception,* to distinguish it from empirical apperception, or, again, *original apperception,* because it is that self-consciousness which, while generating the representation *"I think"* (a representation which must be capable of accompanying all other representations, and which in all consciousness is one and the same), cannot itself be accompanied by any further representation. The unity of this apperception I likewise entitle the *transcendental* unity of self-consciousness, in order to indicate the possibility of *a priori* knowledge arising from it. For the manifold representations, which are given in an intuition, would not be one and all *my* representations, if they did not all belong to one self-consciousness. As *my* representations (even if I am not conscious of them as such) they must conform to the condition under which alone they *can* stand together in
133   one universal self-consciousness, because otherwise they would not all without exception belong to me. From this original combination many consequences follow.

This thoroughgoing identity of the apperception of a manifold which is given in intuition contains a synthesis of representations, and is possible only through the consciousness of this synthesis. For the empirical consciousness, which accompanies different representations, is in itself diverse and without relation to the identity of the subject. That relation comes about, not simply through my accompanying each representation with consciousness, but only in so far as I *conjoin* one representation with another, and am conscious of the synthesis of them. Only in so far, therefore, as I can unite a manifold of given representations in *one consciousness,* is it possible for me to represent to myself the *identity of the consciousness in [i.e. throughout] these representations.* In other words, the analytic unity of apperception is possible only under the presupposition of a certain *synthetic* unity.

134   The thought that the representations given in intuition one and all belong to me, is therefore equivalent to the thought that I unite them in one self-consciousness, or can at least so unite them; and although this thought is not itself the consciousness of the *synthesis* of the representations, it presupposes the possibility of that synthesis. In other words, only in so far as I can grasp the manifold of the representations in one consciousness, do I call them one and all *mine.* For otherwise I should have as many-coloured and diverse a self as I have representations of which I am conscious to myself. Synthetic unity of the manifold of intuitions, as generated *a priori,* is thus the ground of the identity of apperception itself, which precedes *a priori* all *my* determinate thought. Combination does not, however, lie in the objects, and cannot be borrowed from them, and so, through perception, first taken up into the understanding. On the contrary, it is an affair of the understanding alone, which itself is nothing but the
135   faculty of combining *a priori,* and of bringing the manifold of given representations under the unity of apperception. The principle of apperception is the highest principle in the whole sphere of human knowledge.

This principle of the necessary unity of apperception is itself, indeed, an identical, and therefore analytic, proposition; nevertheless it reveals the necessity of a synthesis of the manifold given in intuition, without which the thoroughgoing identity of self-consciousness cannot be thought. For through the "I," as simple representation, nothing manifold is given; only in intuition, which is distinct from the "I," can a manifold be given; and only through *combination* in one consciousness can it be thought. An understanding in which through self-consciousness all the manifold would *eo ipso* be given, would be *intuitive;* our understanding can only *think,* and for intuition must look to the senses. I am conscious of the self as identical in respect of the manifold of representations that are given to me in an intuition, because I call them one and all *my* representations, and so apprehend them as constituting *one* intuition. This amounts to saying, that I am conscious to myself *a priori* of a necessary synthesis of representations—to be entitled the original synthetic unity of apperception—under which all representations that are given to me must stand, but under which they have also first to be brought by means of a synthesis.

136

§17

The Principle of the Synthetic Unity is the
Supreme Principle of all Employment of
the Understanding

The supreme principle of the possibility of all intuition in relation to sensibility is, according to the Transcendental Aesthetic, that all the manifold of intuition should be subject to the formal conditions of space and time. The supreme principle of the same possibility, in its relation to understanding, is that all the manifold of intuition should be subject to conditions of the original synthetic unity of apperception.* In so far as the manifold representations of intuition are given to us, they are subject to the former of these two principles; in so far as they must allow of being *combined* in one consciousness, they are subject to the latter. For without such combination nothing can be thought or known, since the given representations would not have in common the act of the apperception "I think," and so could not be apprehended together in one self-consciousness.

137

Understanding is, to use general terms, *the faculty of knowledge.* This knowledge consists in the determinate relation of given representations to an object; and an *object* is that in the concept of which the manifold of a given intuition is *united.* Now all unification of representations demands unity of consciousness in the synthesis of them. Consequently it is the unity of consciousness that alone constitutes the relation of representations to an object, and therefore their objective validity and the fact that they are modes of knowledge; and upon it therefore rests the very possibility of the understanding.

The first pure knowledge of understanding, then, upon which all the rest of its employment is based, and which also at the same time is completely independent of all

*Space and time, and all their parts, are *intuitions,* and are, therefore, with the manifold which they contain, singular representations (see the Transcendental Aesthetic). Consequently they are not mere concepts through which one and the same consciousness is found to be contained in a number of representations. On the contrary, through them many representations are found to be contained in one representation, and in the consciousness of that representation; and they are thus composite. The unity of that consciousness is therefore synthetic and yet is also original. The *singularity* of such intuitions is found to have important consequences.

conditions of sensible intuition, is the principle of the original synthetic unity of apperception. Thus the mere form of outer sensible intuition, space, is not yet [by itself] knowledge; it supplies only the manifold of *a priori* intuition for a possible knowledge. To know anything in space (for instance, a line), I must *draw* it, and thus synthetically bring into being a determinate combination of the given manifold, so that the unity of this act is at the same time the unity of consciousness (as in the concept of a line); and it is through this unity of consciousness that an object (a determinate space) is first known. The synthetic unity of consciousness is, therefore, an objective condition of all knowledge. It is not merely a condition that I myself require in knowing an object, but is a condition under which every intuition must stand in order *to become an object for me.* For otherwise, in the absence of this synthesis, the manifold would *not* be united in one consciousness. . . .

138

* * *

§18

The Objective Unity of Self-Consciousness

The transcendental unity of apperception is that unity through which all the manifold given in an intuition is united in a concept of the object. It is therefore entitled *objective,* and must be distinguished from the *subjective* unity of consciousness, which is a *determination* of *inner sense*—through which the manifold of intuition for such [objective] combination is empirically given. Whether I can become *empirically* conscious of the manifold as simultaneous or as successive depends on circumstances or empirical conditions. Therefore the empirical unity of consciousness, through association of representations, itself concerns an appearance, and is wholly contingent. But the pure form of intuition in time, merely as intuition in general, which contains a given manifold, is subject to the original unity of consciousness, simply through the necessary relation of the manifold of the intuition to the one *"I think,"* and so through the pure synthesis of understanding which is the *a priori* underlying ground of the empirical synthesis. Only the original unity is objectively valid; the empirical unity of apperception, upon which we are not here dwelling, and which besides is merely derived from the former under given conditions *in concreto,* has only subjective validity. To one man, for instance, a certain word suggests one thing, to another some other thing; the unity of consciousness in that which is empirical is not, as regards what is given, necessarily and universally valid.

140

§19

The Logical Form of all Judgments consists in the Objective Unity of the Apperception of the Concepts which they contain

I have never been able to accept the interpretation which logicians give of judgment in general. It is, they declare, the representation of a relation between two concepts. I do not here dispute with them as to what is defective in this interpretation— that in any case it applies only to *categorical,* not to hypothetical and disjunctive judgments (the two latter containing a relation not of concepts but of judgments), an

141

oversight from which many troublesome consequences have followed. I need only point out that the definition does not determine in what the asserted *relation* consists.

But if I investigate more precisely the relation of the given modes of knowledge in any judgment, and distinguish it, as belonging to the understanding, from the relation according to laws of the reproductive imagination, which has only subjective validity, I find that a judgment is nothing but the manner in which given modes of knowledge are brought to the objective unity of apperception. This is what is intended by the copula "is." It is employed to distinguish the objective unity of given representations   142 from the subjective. It indicates their relation to original apperception, and its *necessary unity*. It holds good even if the judgment is itself empirical, and therefore contingent, as, for example, in the judgment, "Bodies are heavy." I do not here assert that these representations *necessarily* belong *to one another* in the empirical intuition, but that they belong to one another *in virtue of the necessary unity* of apperception in the synthesis of intuitions, that is, according to principles of the objective determination of all representations, in so far as knowledge can be acquired by means of these representations—principles which are all derived from the fundamental principle of the transcendental unity of apperception. Only in this way does there arise from this relation a *judgment,* that is, a relation which is *objectively valid,* and so can be adequately distinguished from a relation of the same representations that would have only subjective validity—as when they are connected according to laws of association. In the latter case, all that I could say would be, "If I support a body, I feel an impression of weight"; I could not say, "It, the body, is heavy." Thus to say "The body is heavy" is not merely to state that the two representations have always been conjoined in my perception, however often that perception be repeated; what we are asserting is that they are combined *in the object,* no matter what the state of the subject may be.

§20   143

*All Sensible Intuitions are subject
to the Categories, as Conditions
under which alone their Manifold can
come together in one Consciousness*

The manifold given in a sensible intuition is necessarily subject to the original synthetic *unity* of apperception, because in no other way is the unity of intuition possible (§17). But that act of understanding by which the manifold of given representations (be they intuitions or concepts) is brought under one apperception, is the logical function of judgment (cf. §19). All the manifold, therefore, so far as it is given in a single empirical intuition, is *determined* in respect of one of the logical functions of judgment, and is thereby brought into one consciousness. Now the *categories* are just these functions of judgment, in so far as they are employed in determination of the manifold of a given intuition (cf. §13). Consequently, the manifold in a given intuition is necessarily subject to the categories.

§21   144

Observation

. . . In the above proof there is one feature from which I could not abstract, the feature, namely, that the manifold to be intuited must be given prior to the synthesis of understanding, and independently of it. How this takes place, remains here undetermined. For were I to think an understanding which is itself intuitive (as, for example, a divine understanding which should not represent to itself given objects, but through whose representation the objects should themselves be given or produced), the categories would have no meaning whatsoever in respect of such a mode of knowledge. They are merely rules for an understanding whose whole power consists in thought, consists, that is, in the act whereby it brings the synthesis of a manifold, given to it from elsewhere in intuition, to the unity of apperception—a faculty, therefore, which by itself knows nothing whatsoever, but merely combines and arranges the material of knowledge, that is, the intuition, which must be given to it by the object. This peculiarity of our understanding, that it can produce *a priori* unity of apperception solely by means of the categories, and only by such and so many, is as little capable of further explanation as why we have just these and no other functions of judgment, or why space and time are the only forms of our possible intuition.

§22

The Category has no other Application
in Knowledge than to Objects
of Experience

To *think* an object and to *know* an object are thus by no means the same thing Knowledge involves two factors: first, the concept, through which an object in general is thought (the category); and secondly, the intuition, through which it is given. For if no intuition could be given corresponding to the concept, the concept would still indeed be a thought, so far as its form is concerned, but would be without any object, and no knowledge of anything would be possible by means of it. So far as I could know, there would be nothing, and could be nothing, to which my thought could be applied. Now, as the Aesthetic has shown, the only intuition possible to us is sensible; consequently, the thought of an object in general, by means of a pure concept of understanding, can become knowledge for us only in so far as the concept is related to objects of the senses . . . In other words, they serve only for the possibility of *empirical knowledge;* and such knowledge is what we entitle experience. Our conclusion is therefore this: the categories, as yielding knowledge of *things,* have no kind of application, save only in regard to things which may be objects of possible experience.

§23

The above proposition is of the greatest importance; for it determines the limits of the employment of the pure concepts of understanding in regard to objects, just as the Transcendental Aesthetic determined the limits of the employment of the pure form of our sensible intuition. Space and time, as conditions under which alone objects can possibly be given to us, are valid no further than for objects of the senses, and therefore only for experience Beyond these limits they represent nothing; for they are only in the senses, and beyond them have no reality. The pure concepts of understanding are free from this limitation, and extend to objects of intuition in general, be the intuition like or unlike ours, if only it be sensible and not intellectual. But this extension of concepts beyond *our* sensible intuition is of no advantage to us. For as concepts of objects they are then empty, and do not even enable us to judge of their objects whether or not they are possible. . . .

§24

The Application of the Categories   150
to Objects of the Senses in General

. . . This is a suitable place for explaining the paradox which must have been obvious to everyone in our exposition of the form of inner sense (§6): namely, that this sense represents to consciousness even our own selves only as we appear to ourselves,   153 not as we are in ourselves. For we intuit ourselves only as we are inwardly *affected,* and this would seem to be contradictory, since we should then have to be in a passive relation [of active affection] to ourselves. It is to avoid this contradiction that in systems of psychology *inner sense,* which we have carefully distinguished from the faculty of *apperception,* is commonly regarded as being identical with it. . . .

How the "I" that thinks can be distinct from the "I" that intuits itself (for I can represent still other modes of intuition as at least possible), and yet, as being the same subject, can be identical with the latter; and how, therefore, I can say: "I, as intelligence and *thinking* subject, know myself as an object that is *thought,* in so far as I am given to myself [as something other or] beyond that [I] which is [given to myself] in intuition, and yet know myself, like other phenomena, only as I appear to myself, not as I am to the understanding"—these are questions that raise no greater nor less difficulty than how I can be an object to myself at all, and, more particularly, an object of intuition and of inner perceptions. Indeed, that this is how it must be, is easily shown—   156 if we admit that space is merely a pure form of the appearances of outer sense—by the fact that we cannot obtain for ourselves a representation of time, which is not an object of outer intuition, except under the image of a line, which we draw, and that by this mode of depicting it alone could we know the singleness of its dimension; and similarly by the fact that for all inner perceptions we must derive the determination of lengths of time or of points of time from the changes which are exhibited to us in outer things, and that the determinations of inner sense have therefore to be arranged as appearances in time in precisely the same manner in which we arrange those of outer sense in space. If, then, as regards the latter, we admit that we know objects only in so far as we are externally affected, we must also recognise, as regards inner sense, that by means of it we intuit ourselves only as we are inwardly affected *by ourselves;* in other words, that, so far as inner intuition is concerned, we know our own subject only as appearance, not as it is in itself.*

§25   157

On the other hand, in the transcendental synthesis of the manifold of representations in general, and therefore in the synthetic original unity of apperception, I am conscious of myself, not as I appear to myself, nor as I am in myself, but only that I am. This *representation* is a *thought,* not an *intuition.* Now in order to *know* ourselves, there is required in addition to the act of thought, which brings the manifold of every possible intuition to the unity of apperception, a determinate mode of intuition, whereby this manifold is given; it therefore follows that although my existence is not

*I do not see why so much difficulty should be found in admitting that our inner sense is affected by ourselves. Such affection finds exemplification in each and every act of *attention.* In every act of attention the understanding determines inner sense, in accordance with the combination which it thinks, to that inner intuition which corresponds to the manifold in the synthesis of the understanding. How much the mind is usually thereby affected, everyone will be able to perceive in himself.

indeed appearance (still less mere illusion), the determination of my existence* can
take place only in conformity with the form of inner sense, according to the special
mode in which the manifold, which I combine, is given in inner intuition. Accordingly
I have no *knowledge* of myself as I am but merely as I appear to myself. The consciousness of self is thus very far from being a knowledge of the self, notwithstanding
all the categories which [are being employed to] constitute the thought of an *object in
general,* through combination of the manifold in one apperception. Just as for knowledge of an object distinct from me I require, besides the thought of an object in general
(in the category), an intuition by which I determine that general concept, so for knowledge of myself I require, besides the consciousness, that is, besides the thought of myself, an intuition of the manifold in me, by which I determine this thought. I exist as an
intelligence which is conscious solely of its power of combination; but in respect of the
manifold which it has to combine I am subjected to a limiting condition (entitled inner
sense), namely, that this combination can be made intuitable only according to relations of time, which lie entirely outside the concepts of understanding, strictly regarded. Such an intelligence, therefore, can know itself only as it appears to itself in respect of an intuition which is not intellectual and cannot be given by the understanding
itself, not as it would know itself if its *intuition* were intellectual.

158

159

§26

*Transcendental Deduction of the Universally
Possible Employment in Experience of the
Pure Concepts of the Understanding*

. . . Categories are concepts which prescribe laws *a priori* to appearances, and
therefore to nature, the sum of all appearances (*natura materialiter spectata*). The
question therefore arises, how it can be conceivable that nature should have to proceed
in accordance with categories which yet are not derived from it, and do not model
themselves upon its pattern; that is, how they can determine *a priori* the combination
of the manifold of nature, while yet they are not derived from it. The solution of this
seeming enigma is as follows.

164   That the *laws* of appearances in nature must agree with the understanding and its
a priori form, that is, with its faculty of *combining* the manifold in general, is no more
surprising than that the appearances themselves must agree with the form of *a priori*
sensible intuition. For just as appearances do not exist in themselves but only relatively
to the subject in which, so far as it has senses, they inhere, so the laws do not exist in
the appearances but only relatively to this same being, so far as it has understanding.
Things in themselves would necessarily, apart from any understanding that knows
them, conform to laws of their own. But appearances are only representations of things
which are unknown as regards what they may be in themselves. As mere representations, they are subject to no law of connection save that which the connecting faculty

---

*The "I think" expresses the act of determining my existence. Existence is already given thereby, but
the mode in which I am to determine this existence, that is, the manifold belonging to it, is not thereby given.
In order that it be given, self-intuition is required; and such intuition is conditioned by a given *a priori* form,
namely, time, which is sensible and belongs to the receptivity of the determinable [in me]. Now since I do
not have another selfintuition which gives the *determining* in me (I am conscious only of the spontaneity of
it) prior to the act of *determination,* as time does in the case of the determinable, I cannot determine my existence as that of a self-active being; all that I can do is to represent to myself the spontaneity of my thought,
that is, of the determination; and my existence is still only determinable sensibly, that is, as the existence of
an appearance. But it is owing to this spontaneity that I entitle myself an *intelligence.*

prescribes. Now it is imagination that connects the manifold of sensible intuition; and imagination is dependent for the unity of its intellectual synthesis upon the understanding, and for the manifoldness of its apprehension upon sensibility. All possible perception is thus dependent upon synthesis of apprehension, and this empirical synthesis in turn upon transcendental synthesis, and therefore upon the categories. Consequently, all possible perceptions, and therefore everything that can come to empirical consciousness, that is, all appearances of nature, must, so far as their connection is concerned, be subject to the categories. Nature, considered merely as nature in general, is dependent upon these categories as the original ground of its necessary conformity to law (*natura formaliter spectata*). Pure understanding is not, however, in a position, through mere categories, to prescribe to appearances any *a priori* laws other than those which are involved in a *nature in general,* that is, in the conformity to law of all appearances in space and time. Special laws, as concerning those appearances which are empirically determined, cannot in their specific character be *derived* from the categories, although they are one and all subject to them. To obtain any knowledge whatsoever of these special laws, we must resort to experience; but it is the *a priori* laws that alone can instruct us in regard to experience in general, and as to what it is that can be known as an object of experience.

165

§27

*Outcome of this Deduction of the
Concepts of Understanding*

We cannot think an object save through categories; we cannot *know* an object so thought save through intuitions corresponding to these concepts. Now all our intuitions are sensible; and this knowledge, in so far as its object is given, is empirical. But empirical knowledge is experience. *Consequently, there can be no* a priori *knowledge, except of objects of possible experience.**

166

But although this knowledge is limited to objects of experience, it is not therefore all derived from experience. The pure intuitions [of receptivity] and the pure concepts of understanding are elements in knowledge, and both are found in us *a priori.* There are only two ways in which we can account for a *necessary* agreement of experience with the concepts of its objects: either experience makes these concepts possible or these concepts make experience possible. The former supposition does not hold in respect of the categories (nor of pure sensible intuition); for since they are *a priori* concepts, and therefore independent of experience, the ascription to them of an empirical origin would be a sort of *generatio aequivoca* [spontaneous generation]. There remains, therefore, only the second supposition—a system, as it were, of the *epigenesis* of pure reason—namely, that the categories contain, on the side of the understanding, the grounds of the possibility of all experience in general. How they make experience possible, and what are the principles of the possibility of experience that they supply in their application to appearances, will be shown more fully in the following chapter on the transcendental employment of the faculty of judgment.

167

*Lest my readers should stumble at the alarming evil consequences which may over-hastily be inferred from this statement, I may remind them that *for thought* the categories are not limited by the conditions of our sensible intuition, but have an unlimited field. It is only the *knowledge* of that which we think, the determining of the object, that requires intuition. In the absence of intuition, the thought of the object may still have its true and useful consequences, as regards the subject's *employment of reason.* The use of reason is not always directed to the determination of the object, that is, to knowledge, but also to the determination of the subject and of its volition—a use which cannot therefore be here dealt with.

A middle course may be proposed between the two above mentioned, namely, that the categories are neither *self-thought* first principles *a priori* of our knowledge nor derived from experience, but subjective dispositions of thought, implanted in us from the first moment of our existence, and so ordered by our Creator that their employment is in complete harmony with the laws of nature in accordance with which experience proceeds—a kind of *preformation-system* of pure reason. Apart, however, from the objection that on such an hypothesis we can set no limit to the assumption of predetermined dispositions to future judgments, there is this decisive objection against the suggested middle course, that the *necessity* of the categories, which belongs to their very conception, would then have to be sacrificed. The concept of cause, for instance, which expresses the necessity of an event under a presupposed condition, would be false if it rested only on an arbitrary subjective necessity, implanted in us, of connecting certain empirical representations according to the rule of causal relation. I would not then be able to say that the effect is connected with the cause in the object, that is to say, necessarily, but only that I am so constituted that I cannot think this representation otherwise than as thus connected. This is exactly what the sceptic most desires. For if this be the situation, all our insight, resting on the supposed objective validity of our judgments, is nothing but sheer illusion; nor would there be wanting people who would refuse to admit this subjective necessity, a necessity which can only be felt. Certainly a man cannot dispute with anyone regarding that which depends merely on the mode in which he is himself organised.

Brief Outline of this Deduction

The deduction is the exposition of the pure concepts of the understanding, and therewith of all theoretical *a priori* knowledge, as principles of the possibility of experience—the principles being here taken as the *determination* of appearances in space and time *in general,* and this determination, in turn, as ultimately following from the *original* synthetic unity of apperception, as the form of the understanding in its relation to space and time, the original forms of sensibility.

PROLEGOMENA TO ANY FUTURE METAPHYSICS

INTRODUCTION

These *Prolegomena* are for the use, not of mere learners, but of future teachers, and even the latter should not expect that they will be serviceable for the systematic exposition of a ready-made science, but merely for the discovery of the science itself.

There are scholarly men to whom the history of philosophy (both ancient and modern) is philosophy itself; for these the present *Prolegomena* are not written. They must wait till those who endeavor to draw from the fountain of reason itself have com-

Immanuel Kant, *Prolegomena to Any Future Metaphysics,* a revision of the Paul Carus translation with an introduction by Lewis White Beck (New York: Macmillan/Library of the Liberal Arts, 1950).

pleted their work; it will then be the turn of these scholars to inform the world of what has been done. Unfortunately, nothing can be said which, in their opinion, has not been said before, and truly the same prophecy applies to all future time; for since the human reason has for many centuries speculated upon innumerable objects in various ways, it is hardly to be expected that we should not be able to discover analogies for every new idea among the old sayings of past ages.

My purpose is to persuade all those who think metaphysics worth studying that it is absolutely necessary to pause a moment and, regarding all that has been done as though undone, to propose first the preliminary question, "Whether such a thing as metaphysics be even possible at all?"

If it be science, how is it that it cannot, like other sciences, obtain universal and lasting recognition? If not, how can it maintain its pretensions and keep the human mind in suspense with hopes never ceasing, yet never fulfilled? Whether then we demonstrate our knowledge or our ignorance in this field, we must come once for all to a definite conclusion respecting the nature of this so-called science, which cannot possibly remain on its present footing. It seems almost ridiculous, while every other science is continually advancing, that in this, which pretends to be wisdom incarnate, for whose oracle everyone inquires, we should constantly move round the same spot, without gaining a single step. And so its votaries having melted away, we do not find men confident of their ability to shine in other sciences venturing their reputation here, where everybody, however ignorant in other matters, presumes to deliver a final verdict, because in this domain there is actually as yet no standard weight and measure to distinguish sound knowledge from shallow talk.

After all it is nothing extraordinary in the elaboration of a science that, when men begin to wonder how far it has advanced, the question should at last occur whether and how such a science is possible at all. Human reason so delights building that it has several times built up a tower and then razed it to see how the foundation was laid. It is never too late to become reasonable and wise; but if the knowledge comes late, there is always more difficulty in starting a reform.

The question whether a science be possible presupposes a doubt as to its actuality. But such a doubt offends the men whose whole fortune consists of this supposed jewel; hence he who raises the doubt must expect opposition from all sides. Some, in the proud consciousness of their possessions, which are ancient and therefore considered legitimate, will take their metaphysical compendia in their hands and look down on him with contempt; others, who never see anything except it be identical with what they have elsewhere seen before, will not understand him, and everything will remain for a time as if nothing had happened to excite the concern or the hope for an impending change.

Nevertheless, I venture to predict that the independent reader of these *Prolegomena* will not only doubt his previous science, but ultimately be fully persuaded that it cannot exist unless the demands here stated on which its possibility depends be satisfied; and, as this has never been done, that there is, as yet, no such thing as metaphysics. But as it can never cease to be in demand*—since the interest of common sense are so intimately interwoven with it—he must confess that a radical reform, or

*Says Horace:
Rusticus expectat, dum defluat amnis, at ille
Labitur et labetur in omne volubilis aevum.

["A rustic fellow waiteth on the shore
For the river to flow away,
But the river flows, and flows on as before,
And it flows forever and aye."]

Epistle I, 2, 42f.

rather a new birth of the science, after a new plan, is unavoidable, however men may struggle against it for a while.

Since the *Essays* of Locke and Leibniz, or rather since the origin of metaphysics so far as we know its history, nothing has ever happened which could have been more decisive to its fate than the attack made upon it by David Hume. He threw no light on this species of knowledge, but he certainly struck a spark by which light might have been kindled had it caught some inflammable substance and had its smouldering fire been carefully nursed and developed.

Hume started chiefly from a single but important concept in metaphysics, namely, that of the connection of cause and effect (including its derivatives force and action, and so on). He challenged reason, which pretends to have given birth to this concept of herself, to answer him by what right she thinks anything could be so consti-tuted that if that thing be posited, something else also must necessarily be posited; for this is the meaning of the concept of cause. He demonstrated irrefutably that it was perfectly impossible for reason to think *a priori* and by means of concepts such a com-bination, for it implies necessity. We cannot at all see why, in consequence of the exis-tence of one thing, another must necessarily exist or how the concept of such a combi-nation can arise *a priori.* Hence he inferred that reason was altogether deluded with reference to this concept, which she erroneously considered as one of her own chil-dren, whereas in reality it was nothing but a bastard of imagination, impregnated by experience, which subsumed certain representations under the law of association and mistook a subjective necessity (habit) for an objective necessity arising from insight. Hence he inferred that reason had no power to think such combinations, even in gen-eral, because her concepts would then be purely fictitious and all her pretended *a priori* cognitions nothing but common experiences marked with a false stamp. In plain lan-guage, this means that there is not and cannot be any such thing as metaphysics at all.*

However hasty and mistaken Hume's inference may appear, it was at least founded upon investigation, and this investigation deserved the concentrated attention of the brighter spirits of his day as well as determined efforts on their part to discover, if possible, a happier solution of the problem in the sense proposed by him, all of which would have speedily resulted in a complete reform of the science.

But Hume suffered the usual misfortune of metaphysicians, of not being under-stood. It is positively painful to see how utterly his opponents, Reid, Oswald, Beattie, and lastly Priestley, missed the point of the problem; for while they were ever taking for granted that which he doubted, and demonstrating with zeal and often with impu-dence that which he never thought of doubting, they so misconstrued his valuable sug-gestion that everything remained in its old condition, as if nothing had happened. The question was not whether the concept of cause was right, useful, and even indispens-able for our knowledge of nature, for this Hume had never doubted; but whether that concept could be thought by reason *a priori,* and consequently whether it possessed an inner truth, independent of all experience, implying a perhaps more extended use not restricted merely to objects of experience. This was Hume's problem. It was solely a question concerning the *origin,* not concerning the *indispensable* need of using the

---

*Nevertheless Hume called this destructive science metaphysics and attached to it great value. "Metaphysics and morals," he declares, "are the most considerable branches of science. Mathematics and natural philosophy are not half so valuable" ["Of the Rise and Progress of the Arts and Sciences," *Essays Moral, Political, and Literary,* XIV (edited by Green and Grose, I, 187)]. But the acute man merely regarded the negative use arising from the moderation of extravagant claims of speculative reason, and the complete settlement of the many endless and troublesome controversies that mislead mankind. He overlooked the pos-itive injury which results if reason be deprived of its most important prospects, which can alone supply to the will the highest aim for all its endeavors.

concept. Were the former decided, the conditions of the use and the sphere of its valid application would have been determined as a matter of course.

But to satisfy the conditions of the problem, the opponents of the great thinker should have penetrated very deeply into the nature of reason, so far as it is concerned with pure thinking—a task which did not suit them. They found a more convenient method of being defiant without any insight, namely, the appeal to *common sense*. It is indeed a great gift of God to possess right or (as they now call it) plain common sense. But this common sense must be shown in action by well-considered and reasonable thoughts and words, not by appealing to it as an oracle when no rational justification for one's position can be advanced. To appeal to common sense when insight and science fail, and no sooner—this is one of the subtle discoveries of modern times, by means of which the most superficial ranter can safely enter the lists with the most thorough thinker and hold his own. But as long as a particle of insight remains, no one would think of having recourse to this subterfuge. Seen clearly, it is but an appeal to the opinion of the multitude, of whose applause the philosopher is ashamed, while the popular charlatan glories and boasts in it. I should think that Hume might fairly have laid as much claim to common sense as Beattie and, in addition, to a critical reason (such as the latter did not possess), which keeps common sense in check and prevents it from speculating, or, if speculations are under discussion, restrains the desire to decide because it cannot satisfy itself concerning its own premises. By this means alone can common sense remain sound. Chisels and hammers may suffice to work a piece of wood, but for etching we require an etcher's needle. Thus common sense and speculative understanding are each serviceable, but each in its own way: the former in judgments which apply immediately to experience; the latter when we judge universally from mere concepts, as in metaphysics, where that which calls itself, in spite of the inappropriateness of the name, sound common sense, has no right to judge at all.

I openly confess my recollection* of David Hume was the very thing which many years ago first interrupted my dogmatic slumber and gave my investigations in the field of speculative philosophy a quite new direction. I was far from following him in the conclusions at which he arrived by regarding, not the whole of his problem, but a part, which by itself can give us no information. If we start from a well-founded, but undeveloped, thought which another has bequeathed to us, we may well hope by continued reflection to advance farther than the acute man to whom we owe the first spark of light.

I therefore first tried whether Hume's objection could not be put into a general form, and soon found that the concept of the connection of cause and effect was by no means the only concept by which the understanding thinks the connection of things *a priori,* but rather that metaphysics consists altogether of such concepts. I sought to ascertain their number; and when I had satisfactorily succeeded in this by starting from a single principle, I proceeded to the deduction of these concepts, which I was now certain were not derived from experience, as Hume had attempted to derive them, but sprang from the pure understanding. This deduction (which seemed impossible to my acute predecessor, which had never even occurred to anyone else, though no one had hesitated to use the concepts without investigating the basis of their objective validity) was the most difficult task which ever could have been undertaken in the service of metaphysics; and the worst was that metaphysics, such as it is, could not assist me in the least because this deduction alone can render metaphysics possible. But as soon as I had succeeded in solving Hume's problem, not merely in a particular case, but with respect to the whole faculty of pure reason, I could proceed safely, though slowly, to

---

*[*Erinnerung.* Kant had probably read Hume before 1760, but only much later (1772?) did he begin to follow "a new direction" under Hume's influence—L.W.B.]

determine the whole sphere of pure reason completely and from universal principles, in its boundaries as well as in its contents. This was required for metaphysics in order to construct its system according to a safe plan.

But I fear that the execution of Hume's problem in its widest extent (namely, my *Critique of Pure Reason*) will fare as the problem itself fared when first proposed. It will be misjudged because it is misunderstood, and misunderstood because men choose to skim through the book and not to think through it—a disagreeable task, because the work is dry, obscure, opposed to all ordinary notions, and moreover long-winded. I confess, however, I did not expect to hear from philosophers complaints of want of popularity, entertainment, and facility when the existence of highly prized and indispensable knowledge is at stake, which cannot be established otherwise than by the strictest rules of a scholastic precision. Popularity may follow, but is inadmissible at the beginning. Yet as regards a certain obscurity, arising partly from the diffuseness of the plan, owing to which the principal points of the investigation are easily lost sight of, the complaint is just, and I intend to remove it by the present *Prolegomena.*

The first-mentioned work, which discusses the pure faculty of reason in its whole compass and bounds, will remain the foundation, to which the *Prolegomena,* as a preliminary exercise, refer; for critique as a science must first be established as complete and perfect before we can think of letting metaphysics appear on the scene or even have the most distant hope of attaining it.

We have been long accustomed to seeing antiquated knowledge produced as new by taking it out of its former context and fitting it into a systematic garment of any fancy pattern with new titles. Most readers will set out by expecting nothing else from the *Critique;* but these *Prolegomena* may persuade him that it is a perfectly new science, of which no one has ever even thought, the very idea of which was unknown, and for which nothing hitherto accomplished can be of the smallest use, except it be the suggestion of Hume's doubts. Yet even he did not suspect such a formal science, but ran his ship ashore, for safety's sake, landing on scepticism, there to let it lie and rot; whereas my object is rather to give it a pilot, who, by means of safe principles of navigation drawn from a knowledge of the globe, and provided with a complete chart and compass, may steer the ship safely whither he listeth.

If in a new science which is wholly isolated and unique in its kind, we started with the prejudice that we can judge of things by means of alleged knowledge previously acquired—though this is precisely what has first to be called in question—we should only fancy we saw everywhere what we had already known, because the expressions have a similar sound. But everything would appear utterly metamorphosed, senseless, and unintelligible, because we should have as a foundation our own thoughts, made by long habit a second nature, instead of the author's. But the long-windedness of the work, so far as it depends on the subject and not on the exposition, its consequent unavoidable dryness and its scholastic precision, are qualities which can only benefit the science, though they may discredit the book.

Few writers are gifted with the subtlety and, at the same time, with the grace of David Hume, or with the depth, as well as the elegance, of Moses Mendelssohn. Yet I flatter myself I might have made my own exposition popular had my object been merely to sketch out a plan and leave its completion to others, instead of having my heart in the welfare of the science to which I had devoted myself so long; in truth, it required no little constancy, and even self-denial, to postpone the sweets of an immediate success to the prospect of a slower, but more lasting, reputation.

Making plans is often the occupation of an opulent and boastful mind, which thus obtains the reputation of a creative genius by demanding what it cannot itself supply, by censuring what it cannot improve, and by proposing what it knows not where to find. And yet something more should belong to a sound plan of a general critique of pure reason than mere conjectures if this plan is to be other than the usual declamations of pious aspirations. But pure reason is a sphere so separate and self-contained that we cannot touch a part without affecting all the rest. We can do nothing without first determining the position of each part and its relation to the rest; for, as our judgment within this sphere cannot be corrected by anything without, the validity and use of every part depends upon the relation in which it stands to all the rest within the domain of reason. As in the structure of an organized body, the end of each member can only be deduced from the full conception of the whole. It may, then, be said of such a critique that it is never trustworthy except it be perfectly complete, down to the most minute elements of pure reason. In the sphere of this faculty you can determine and define either everything or nothing.

But although a mere sketch preceding the *Critique of Pure Reason* would be unintelligible, unreliable, and useless, it is all the more useful as a sequel. It enables us to grasp the whole, to examine in detail the chief points of importance in the science, and to improve in many respects our exposition, as compared with the first execution of the work.

With that work complete, I offer here a sketch based on an *analytical* method, while the *Critique* itself had to be executed in the *synthetical* style, in order that the science may present all its articulations, as the structure of a peculiar cognitive faculty, in their natural combination. But should any reader find this sketch, which I publish as the *Prolegomena to Any Future Metaphysics,* still obscure, let him consider that not everyone is bound to study metaphysics; that many minds will succeed very well in the exact and even in deep sciences more closely allied to the empirical, while they cannot succeed in investigations dealing exclusively with abstract concepts. In such cases men should apply their talents to other subjects. But he who undertakes to judge or, still more, to construct a system of metaphysics must satisfy the demands here made, either by adopting my solution or by thoroughly refuting it and substituting another. To evade it is impossible.

In conclusion, let it be remembered that this much abused obscurity (frequently serving as a mere pretext under which people hide their own indolence or dullness) has its uses, since all who in other sciences observe a judicious silence speak authoritatively in metaphysics and make bold decisions, because their ignorance is not here contrasted with the knowledge of others. Yet it does contrast with sound critical principles, which we may therefore commend in the words of Virgil:

*Ignavum, fucos, pecus a praesepibus arcent.**

PROLEGOMENA

PREAMBLE ON THE PECULIARITIES OF ALL METAPHYSICAL KNOWLEDGE

§ I. Of the Sources of Metaphysics

If it becomes desirable to organize any knowledge as science, it will be necessary first to determine accurately those peculiar features which no other science has in common with it, constituting its peculiarity; otherwise the boundaries of all sciences become confused, and none of them can be treated thoroughly according to its nature.

*["They defend the hives against drones, those indolent creatures"—Georgics IV 168.]

The peculiar characteristic of a science may consist of a simple difference of object, or of the sources of knowledge, or of the kind of knowledge, or perhaps of all three conjointly. On these, therefore, depends the idea of a possible science and its territory.

First, as concerns the sources of metaphysical knowledge, its very concept implies that they cannot be empirical. Its principles (including not only its maxims but its basic notions) must never be derived from experience. It must not be physical but metaphysical knowledge, namely, knowledge lying beyond experience. It can therefore have for its basis neither external experience, which is the source of physics proper, nor internal, which is the basis of empirical psychology. It is therefore *a priori* knowledge, coming from pure understanding and pure reason.

But so far metaphysics would not be distinguishable from pure mathematics; it must therefore be called *pure philosophical* knowledge; and for the meaning of this term I refer to the *Critique of the Pure Reason,** where the distinction between these two employments of reason is sufficiently explained. So far concerning the sources of metaphysical knowledge.

§ 2. Concerning the Kind of Knowledge Which Can Alone Be Called Metaphysical

a. On the Distinction between Analytical and Synthetical Judgments in General.— The peculiarity of its sources demands that metaphysical knowledge must consist of nothing but *a priori* judgments. But whatever be their origin or their logical form, there is a distinction in judgments, as to their content, according to which they are either merely *explicative,* adding nothing to the content of knowledge, or *expansive,* increasing the given knowledge. The former may be called *analytical,* the latter *synthetical,* judgments.

Analytical judgments express nothing in the predicate but what has been already actually thought in the concept of the subject, though not so distinctly or with the same (full) consciousness. When I say: "All bodies are extended," I have not amplified in the least my concept of body, but have only analyzed it, as extension was really thought to belong to that concept before the judgment was made, though it was not expressed. This judgment is therefore analytical. On the contrary, this judgment, "All bodies have weight," contains in its predicate something not actually thought in the universal concept of body; it amplifies my knowledge by adding something to my concept, and must therefore be called synthetical.

b. The Common Principle of All Analytical Judgments Is the Law of Contradiction.—All analytical judgments depend wholly on the law of contradiction, and are in their nature *a priori* cognitions, whether the concepts that supply them with matter be empirical or not. For the predicate of an affirmative analytical judgment is already contained in the concept of the subject, of which it cannot be denied without contradiction. In the same way its opposite is necessarily denied of the subject in an analytical, but negative, judgment, by the same law of contradiction. Such is the nature of the judgments: "All bodies are extended," and "No bodies are unextended (that is, simple)."

For this very reason all analytical judgments are *a priori* even when the concepts are empirical, as, for example, "Gold is a yellow metal"; for to know this I require no experience beyond my concept of gold as a yellow metal. It is, in fact, the very concept, and I need only analyze it without looking beyond it.

**Critique of Pure Reason,* "Methodology," Ch. I, Sec. 2.

c. Synthetical Judgments Require a Different Principle from the Law of Contra-diction.—There are synthetical *a posteriori* judgments of empirical origin; but there are also others which are certain *a priori,* and which spring from pure understanding and reason. Yet they both agree in this, that they cannot possibly spring from the principle of analysis, namely, the law of contradiction, alone. They require a quite different principle from which they may be deduced, subject, of course, always to the law of contradiction, which must never be violated, even though everything cannot be deduced from it. I shall first classify synthetical judgments.

1. *Judgments of Experience* are always synthetical. For it would be absurd to base an analytical judgment on experience, as our concept suffices for the purpose without requiring any testimony from experience. That body is extended is a judgment established *a priori,* and not an empirical judgment. For before appealing to experience, we already have all the conditions of the judgment in the concept, from which we have but to elicit the predicate according to the law of contradiction, and thereby to become conscious of the necessity of the judgment, which experience could not in the least teach us.

2. *Mathematical Judgments* are all synthetical. This fact seems hitherto to have altogether escaped the observation of those who have analyzed human reason: it even seems directly opposed to all their conjectures, though it is incontestably certain and most important in its consequences. For as it was found that the conclusions of mathematicians all proceed according to the law of contradiction (as is demanded by all apodictic certainty), men persuaded themselves that the fundamental principles were known from the same law. This was a great mistake, for a synthetical proposition can indeed be established by the law of contradiction, but only by presupposing another synthetical proposition from which it follows, but never by that law alone.

First of all, we must observe that all strictly mathematical judgments are *a priori,* and not empirical, because they carry with them necessity, which cannot be obtained from experience. But if this be not conceded to me, very good; I shall confine my assertion to *pure mathematics,* the very notion of which implies that it contains pure *a priori* and not empirical knowledge.

It must at first be thought that the proposition 7 + 5 = 12 is a mere analytical judgment, following from the concept of the sum of seven and five, according to the law of contradiction. But on closer examination it appears that the concept of the sum of 7 + 5 contains merely their union in a single number, without its being at all thought what the particular number is that unites them. The concept of twelve is by no means thought by merely thinking of the combination of seven and five; and, analyze this possible sum as we may, we shall not discover twelve in the concept. We must go beyond these concepts, by calling to our aid some intuition which corresponds to one of the concepts—that is, either our five fingers or five points (as Segner has it in his *Arithmetic*)—and we must add successively the units of the five given in the intuition to the concept of seven. Hence our concept is really amplified by the proposition 7 + 5 = 12, and we add to the first concept a second concept not thought in it. Arithmetical judgments are therefore synthetical, and the more plainly according as we take larger numbers; for in such cases it is clear that, however closely we analyze our concepts without calling intuition to our aid, we can never find the sum by such mere dissection.

Just as little is any principle of geometry analytical. That a straight line is the shortest path between two points is a synthetical proposition. For my concept of straight contains nothing of quantity, but only a quality. The concept "shortest" is therefore altogether additional and cannot be obtained by any analysis of the concept "straight line." Here, too, intuition must come to aid us. It alone makes the synthesis possible. What usually makes us believe that the predicate of such apodictic judgments is already contained in our concept, and that the judgment is therefore analytical, is the duplicity of the expression. We must think a certain predicate as attached to a given concept, and necessity indeed belongs to the concepts. But the question is not what we must join in thought *to* the given concept, but what we actually think together with and in it, though obscurely; and so it appears that the predicate belongs to this concept necessarily indeed, yet not directly but indirectly by means of an intuition which must be present.

Some other principles, assumed by geometers, are indeed actually analytical, and depend on the law of contradiction; but they only serve, as identical propositions, as a method of concatenation, and not as principles—for example $a = a$, the whole is equal to itself, or $a + b > a$, the whole is greater than its part. And yet even these, though they are recognized as valid from mere concepts, are admitted in mathematics only because they can be represented in some intuition.

The essential and distinguishing feature of pure mathematical knowledge among all other *a priori* knowledge is that it cannot at all proceed from concepts, but only by means of the construction of concepts.* As therefore in its propositions it must proceed beyond the concept to that which its corresponding intuition contains, these propositions neither can, nor ought to, arise analytically, by dissection of the concept, but are all synthetical.

I cannot refrain from pointing out the disadvantage resulting to philosophy from the neglect of this easy and apparently insignificant observation. Hume being prompted to cast his eye over the whole field of *a priori* cognitions in which human understanding claims such mighty possessions (a calling he felt worthy of a philosopher) heedlessly severed from it a whole, and indeed its most valuable, province, namely, pure mathematics; for he imagined its nature or, so to speak, the state constitution of this empire depended on totally different principles, namely, on the law of contradiction alone; and although he did not divide judgments in this manner formally and universally as I have done here, what he said was equivalent to this: that mathematics contains only analytical, but metaphysics synthetical, *a priori* propositions. In this, however, he was greatly mistaken, and the mistake had a decidedly injurious effect upon his whole conception. But for this, he would have extended his question concerning the origin of our synthetical judgments far beyond the metaphysical concept of causality and included in it the possibility of mathematics *a priori* also, for this latter he must have assumed to be equally synthetical. And then he could not have based his metaphysical propositions on mere experience without subjecting the axioms of mathematics equally to experience, a thing which he was far too acute to do. The good company into which metaphysics would thus have been brought would have saved it from the danger of a contemptuous ill-treatment, for the thrust intended for it must have reached mathematics, which was not and could not have been Hume's intention. Thus that acute man would have been led into considerations which must needs be similar to those that now occupy us, but which would have gained inestimably by his inimitably elegant style.

[3.] *Metaphysical Judgments,* properly so called, are all synthetical. We must distinguish judgments pertaining to metaphysics from metaphysical judgments properly so called. Many of the former are analytical, but they only afford the means for metaphysical judgments, which are the whole end of the science and which are always synthetical. For if there be concepts pertaining to metaphysics (as, for example, that of substance), the judgments springing from simple analysis of them also pertain to metaphysics, as, for example, substance is that which only exists as subject, etc.; and by

Critique of Pure Reason, "Methodology," Ch. I, Sec. 1.

means of several such analytical judgments we seek to approach the definition of the concepts. But as the analysis of a pure concept of the understanding (the kind of concept pertaining to metaphysics) does not proceed in any different manner from the dissection of any other, even empirical, concepts, not belonging to metaphysics (such as, air is an elastic fluid, the elasticity of which is not destroyed by any known degree of cold), it follows that the concept indeed, but not the analytical judgment, is properly metaphysical. This science has something peculiar in the production of its *a priori* cognitions, which must therefore be distinguished from the features it has in common with other rational knowledge. Thus the judgment that all the substance in things is permanent is a synthetical and properly metaphysical judgment.

If the *a priori* concepts which constitute the materials and tools of metaphysics have first been collected according to fixed principles, then their analysis will be of great value; it might be taught as a particular part (as a *philosophia definitiva*), containing nothing but analytical judgments pertaining to metaphysics, and could be treated separately from the synthetical which constitute metaphysics proper. For indeed these analyses are not of much value except in metaphysics, that is, as regards the synthetical judgments which are to be generated by these previously analyzed concepts.

The conclusion drawn in this section then is that metaphysics is properly concerned with synthetical propositions *a priori,* and these alone constitute its end, for which it indeed requires various dissections of its concepts, namely, analytical judgments, but wherein the procedure is not different from that in every other kind of knowledge, in which we merely seek to render our concepts distinct by analysis. But the generation of *a priori* knowledge by intuition as well as by concepts, in fine, of synthetical propositions *a priori,* especially in philosophical knowledge, constitutes the essential subject of metaphysics.

§ 3. A Remark on the General Division of Judgment into Analytical and Synthetical

This division is indispensable, as concerns the critique of human understanding, and therefore deserves to be called classical in such critical investigation, though otherwise it is of little use. But this is the reason why dogmatic philosophers, who always seek the sources of metaphysical judgments in metaphysics itself, and not apart from it in the pure laws of reason generally, altogether neglected this apparently obvious distinction. Thus the celebrated Wolff and his acute follower Baumgarten came to seek the proof of the principle of sufficient reason, which is clearly synthetical, in the principle of contradiction. In Locke's *Essay,* however, I find an indication of my division. For in the fourth book (Chapter III, § 9, seq.), having discussed the various connections of representations in judgments, and their sources, one of which he makes "identity or contradiction" (analytical judgments) and another the coexistence of ideas in a subject (synthetical judgments), he confesses (§ 10) that our (*a priori*) knowledge of the latter is very narrow and almost nothing. But in his remarks on this species of knowledge, there is so little of what is definite and reduced to rules that we cannot wonder if no one, not even Hume, was led to make investigations concerning this sort of proposition. For such general and yet definite principles are not easily learned from other men, who have had them only obscurely in their minds. One must hit on them first by one's own reflection; then one finds them elsewhere, where one could not possibly have found them at first because the authors themselves did not know that such an idea lay at the basis of their observations. Men who never think independently have nevertheless the acuteness to discover everything, after it has been once shown them, in what was said long since, though no one was ever able to see it there before.

§ 4. The General Question of the Prolegomena:
Is Metaphysics at All Possible?

Were a metaphysics which could maintain its place as a science really in existence, could we say: "Here is metaphysics; learn it and it will convince you irresistibly and irrevocably of its truth"? This question would then be useless, and there would only remain that other question (which would rather be a test of our acuteness than a proof of the existence of the thing itself): "How is the science possible, and how does reason come to attain it?" But human reason has not been so fortunate in this case. There is no single book to which you can point as you do to Euclid, and say: "This is metaphysics; here you may find the noblest objects of this science, the knowledge of a highest being and of a future existence, proved from principles of pure reason." We can be shown indeed many propositions, demonstrably certain and never questioned; but these are all analytical, and rather concern the materials and the scaffolding for metaphysics than the extension of knowledge, which is our proper object in studying it (§ 2). Even supposing you produce synthetical judgments (such as the law of sufficient reason, which you have never proved, as you ought to, from pure reason *a priori,* though we gladly concede its truth), you lapse, when you try to employ them for your principal purpose, into such doubtful assertions that in all ages one metaphysics has contradicted another, either in its assertions or their proofs, and thus has itself destroyed its own claim to lasting assent. Nay, the very attempts to set up such a science are the main cause of the early appearance of skepticism, a mental attitude in which reason treats itself with such violence that it could never have arisen save from complete despair of ever satisfying its most important aspirations. For long before men began to inquire into nature methodically, they consulted abstract reason, which had to some extent been exercised by means of ordinary experience; for reason is ever present, while laws of nature must usually be discovered with labor. So metaphysics floated to the surface, like foam, which dissolved the moment it was scooped off. But immediately there appeared a new supply on the surface, to be ever eagerly gathered up by some; while others, instead of seeking in the depths the cause of the phenomenon, thought they showed their wisdom by ridiculing the idle labor of their neighbors.

Weary therefore of dogmatism, which teaches us nothing, and of skepticism, which does not even promise us anything—even the quiet state of a contented ignorance—disquieted by the importance of knowledge so much needed, and rendered suspicious by long experience of all knowledge which we believe we possess or which offers itself in the name of pure reason, there remains but one critical question on the answer to which our future procedure depends, namely, "Is metaphysics at all possible?" But this question must be answered, not by sceptical objections to the asseverations of some actual system of metaphysics (for we do not as yet admit such a thing to exist), but from the conception, as yet only problematical, of a science of this sort.

In the *Critique of Pure Reason* I have treated this question synthetically, by making inquiries into pure reason itself and endeavoring in this source to determine the elements as well as the laws of its pure use according to principles. The task is difficult and requires a resolute reader to penetrate by degrees into a system based on no data except reason itself, and which therefore seeks, without resting upon any fact, to unfold knowledge from its original germs. The *Prolegomena,* however, are designed for preparatory exercises; they are intended to point out what we have to do in order to make a science actual if it is possible, rather than to propound it. The *Prolegomena* must therefore rest upon something already known as trustworthy, from which we can set out with confidence and ascend to sources as yet unknown, the discovery of which will not only explain to us what we knew but exhibit a sphere of many cognitions which all spring from the same sources. The method of prolegomena, especially of those designed as a preparation for future metaphysics, is consequently analytical.

But it happens, fortunately, that though we cannot assume metaphysics to be an actual science, we can say with confidence that there is actually given certain pure *a priori* synthetical cognitions, pure mathematics and pure physics; for both contain propositions which are unanimously recognized, partly apodictically certain by mere reason, partly by general consent arising from experience and yet as independent of experience. We have therefore at least some uncontested synthetical knowledge *a priori* and need not ask *whether* it be possible, for it is actual, but *how* it is possible, in order that we may deduce from the principle which makes the given knowledge possible the possibility of all the rest.

§ 5. The General Problem: How Is Knowledge from Pure Reason Possible?

We have already learned the significant distinction between analytical and synthetical judgments. The possibility of analytical propositions was easily comprehended, being entirely founded on the law of contradiction. The possibility of synthetical *a posteriori* judgments, of those which are gathered from experience, also requires no particular explanations, for experience is nothing but a continued synthesis of perceptions. There remain therefore only synthetical propositions *a priori,* of which the possibility must be sought or investigated, because they must depend upon other principles than the law of contradiction.

But here we need not first establish the possibility of such propositions so as to ask whether they are possible. For there are enough of them which indeed are of undoubted certainty; and, as our present method is analytical, we shall start from the fact that such synthetical but purely rational knowledge actually exists; but we must now inquire into the ground of this possibility and ask *how* such knowledge is possible, in order that we may, from the principles of its possibility, be enabled to determine the conditions of its use, its sphere and its limits. The real problem upon which all depends, when expressed with scholastic precision, is therefore: "How are synthetic propositions *a priori* possible?"

For the sake of popular understanding I have above expressed this problem somewhat differently, as an inquiry into purely rational knowledge, which I could do for once without detriment to the desired insight, because, as we have only to do here with metaphysics and its sources, the reader will, I hope, after the foregoing reminders, keep in mind that when we speak of knowing by pure reason we do not mean analytical but synthetical knowledge.*

Metaphysics stands or falls with the solution of this problem; its very existence depends upon it. Let anyone make metaphysical assertions with ever so much plausibility, let him overwhelm us with conclusions; but if he has not previously proved able to answer this question satisfactorily, I have a right to say: This is all vain, baseless

---

*It is unavoidable that, as knowledge advances, certain expressions which have become classical after having been used since the infancy of science will be found inadequate and unsuitable, and a newer and more appropriate application of the terms will give rise to confusion. [This is the case with the term "analytical."] The analytical method, so far as it is opposed to the synthetical, is very different from one that consists of analytical propositions; it signifies only that we start from what is sought, as if it were given, and ascend to the only conditions under which it is possible. In this method we often use nothing but synthetical propositions, as in mathematical analysis, and it were better to term it the *regressive* method, in contradistinction to the *synthetic* or *progressive.* A principal part of logic too is distinguished by the name of analytic, which here signifies the logic of truth in contrast to dialectic, without considering whether the cognitions belonging to it are analytical or synthetical.

philosophy and false wisdom. You speak through pure reason and claim, as it were, to create cognitions *a priori* not only by dissecting given concepts, but also by asserting connections which do not rest upon the law of contradiction, and which you claim to conceive quite independently of all experience; how do you arrive at this, and how will you justify such pretensions? An appeal to the consent of the common sense of mankind cannot be allowed, for that is a witness whose authority depends merely upon rumor. Says Horace:

*Quodcunque ostendis mihi sic, incredulus odi.**

The answer to this question is as indispensable as it is difficult; and although the principal reason that it was not sought long ago is that the possibility of the question never occurred to anybody, there is yet another reason, namely, that a satisfactory answer to this one question requires a much more persistent, profound, and painstaking reflection than the most diffuse work on metaphysics, which on its first appearance promised immortal fame to its author. And every intelligent reader, when he carefully reflects what this problem requires, must at first be struck with its difficulty, and would regard it as insoluble and even impossible did there not actually exist pure synthetical cognitions *a priori*. This actually happened to David Hume, though he did not conceive the question in its entire universality as is done here and as must be done if the answer is to be decisive for all metaphysics. For how is it possible, says that acute man, that when a concept is given me I can go beyond it and connect with it another which is not contained in it, in such a manner as if the latter *necessarily* belonged to the former? Nothing but experience can furnish us with such connections (thus he concluded from the difficulty which he took to be impossibility), and all that vaunted necessity or, what is the same thing, knowledge assumed to be *a priori* is nothing but a long habit of accepting something as true, and hence of mistaking subjective necessity for objective.

Should my reader complain of the difficulty and the trouble which I shall occasion him in the solution of this problem, he is at liberty to solve it himself in an easier way. Perhaps he will then feel under obligation to the person who has undertaken for him a labor of so profound research and will rather feel some surprise at the facility with which, considering the nature of the subject, the solution has been attained. Yet it has cost years of work to solve the problem in its whole universality (using the term in the mathematical sense, namely, for that which is sufficient for all cases), and finally to exhibit it in the analytical form, as the reader will find it here.

All metaphysicians are therefore solemnly and legally suspended from their occupations till they shall have adequately answered the question, "How are synthetic cognitions *a priori* possible?" For the answer contains the only credentials which they must show when they have anything to offer us in the name of pure reason. But if they do not possess these credentials, they can expect nothing else of reasonable people, who have been deceived so often, than to be dismissed without further inquiry.

If they, on the other hand, desire to carry on their business, not as a science, but as an art of wholesome persuasion suitable to the common sense of man, this calling cannot in justice be denied them. They will then speak the modest language of a rational belief; they will grant that they are not allowed even to conjecture, far less to know, anything which lies beyond the bounds of all possible experience, but only to assume

*["To all that which thou provest me thus, I refuse to give credence, and hate"—*Epistle* II, 3, 188.]

(not for speculative use, which they must abandon, but for practical use only) the existence of something possible and even indispensable for the guidance of the understanding and of the will in life. In this manner alone can they be called useful and wise men, and the more so as they renounce the title of metaphysicians. For the latter profess to be speculative philosophers; and since, when judgments *a priori* are under discussion, poor probabilities cannot be admitted (for what is declared to be known *a priori* is thereby announced as necessary), such men cannot be permitted to play with conjectures, but their assertion must be either science or nothing at all.

It may be said that the entire transcendental philosophy, which necessarily precedes all metaphysics, is nothing but the complete solution of the problem here propounded, in systematic order and completeness, and hence we have hitherto never had any transcendental philosophy. For what goes by its name is properly a part of metaphysics, whereas the former science is intended only to constitute the possibility of the latter and must therefore precede all metaphysics. And it is not surprising that when a whole science, deprived of all help from other sciences and consequently in itself quite new, is required to answer a single question satisfactorily, we should find the answer troublesome and difficult, nay, even shrouded in obscurity.

As we now proceed to this solution according to the analytical method, in which we assume that such cognitions from pure reason actually exist, we can only appeal to two sciences of theoretical knowledge (which alone is under consideration here), namely, pure mathematics and pure natural science. For these alone can exhibit to us objects in intuition, and consequently (if there should occur in them a cognition *a priori*) can show the truth or conformity of the cognition to the object *in concreto,* that is, its actuality, from which we could proceed to the ground of its possibility by the analytical method. This facilitates our work greatly for here universal considerations are not only applied to facts, but even start from them, while in a synthetic procedure they must strictly be derived *in abstracto* from concepts.

But in order to rise from these actual and, at the same time, well-grounded pure cognitions *a priori* to a possible knowledge of the kind as we are seeking, namely, to metaphysics as a science, we must comprehend that which occasions it—I mean the mere natural, though in spite of its truth still suspect, cognition *a priori* which lies at the basis of that science, the elaboration of which without any critical investigation of its possibility is commonly called metaphysics. In a word, we must comprehend the natural conditions of such a science as a part of our inquiry, and thus the transcendental problem will be gradually answered by a division into four questions:

1. How is pure mathematics possible?
2. How is pure natural science possible?
3. How is metaphysics in general possible?
4. How is metaphysics as a science possible?

It may be seen that the solution of these problems, though chiefly designed to exhibit the essential matter of the *Critique,* has yet something peculiar, which for itself alone deserves attention. This is the search for the sources of given sciences in reason itself, so that its faculty of knowing something *a priori* may by its own deeds be investigated and measured. By this procedure these sciences gain, if not with regard to their contents, yet as to their proper use; and while they throw light on the higher question concerning their common origin, they give, at the same time, an occasion better to explain their own nature.

FIRST PART OF THE MAIN TRANSCENDENTAL PROBLEM

How Is Pure Mathematics Possible?

§ 6. Here is a great and established branch of knowledge, encompassing even now a wonderfully large domain and promising an unlimited extension in the future, yet carrying with it thoroughly apodictic certainty, that is, absolute necessity, and therefore resting upon no empirical grounds. Consequently it is a pure product of reason; and, moreover, it is thoroughly synthetical. [Hence the question arises:] "How then is it possible for human reason to produce such knowledge entirely *a priori?*"

Does not this faculty [which produces mathematics], as it neither is nor can be based upon experience, presuppose some ground of knowledge *a priori,* which lies deeply hidden but which might reveal itself by these its effects if their first beginnings were but diligently ferreted out?

§ 7. But we find that all mathematical cognition has this peculiarity: it must first exhibit its concept in intuition and indeed *a priori;* therefore in an intuition which is not empirical but pure. Without this mathematics cannot take a single step; hence its judgments are always *intuitive;* whereas philosophy must be satisfied with *discursive* judgments from mere concepts, and though it may illustrate its doctrines through an intuition, can never derive them from it. This observation on the nature of mathematics gives us a clue to the first and highest condition of its possibility, which is that some pure intuition must form its basis, in which all its concepts can be exhibited or constructed, *in concreto* and yet *a priori.* If we can uncover this pure intuition and its possibility, we may thence easily explain how synthetical propositions *a priori* are possible in pure mathematics, and consequently how this science itself is possible. For just as empirical intuition [namely, sense-perception] enables us without difficulty to enlarge the concept which we frame of an object of intuition by new predicates which intuition itself presents synthetically in experience, so also pure intuition does likewise, only with this difference, that in the latter case the synthetical judgment is *a priori* certain and apodictic, in the former only *a posteriori* and empirically certain; because this latter contains only that which occurs in contingent empirical intuition, but the former that which must necessarily be discovered in pure intuition. Here intuition, being an intuition *a priori,* is inseparably joined with the concept *prior to all experience* or particular perception.

§ 8. But with this step our perplexity seems rather to increase than to lessen. For the question now is, "How is it possible to intuit anything *a priori?*" An intuition is such a representation as would immediately depend upon the presence of the object. Hence it seems impossible to intuit spontaneously *a priori,* because intuition would in that event have to take place without either a former or a present object to refer to, and in consequence could not be intuition. Concepts indeed are such that we can easily form some of them *a priori,* namely, such as contain nothing but the thought of an object in general; and we need not find ourselves in an immediate relation to the object. Take, for instance, the concepts of quantity, of cause, etc. But even these require, in order to be meaningful and significant, a certain concrete use—that is, an application to some intuition by which an object of them is given us. But how can the intuition of the object precede the object itself?

§ 9. If our intuition were of such a nature as to represent things as they are in themselves, there would not be any intuition *a priori,* but intuition would be always empirical. For I can only know what is contained in the object in itself if it is present and given to me. It is indeed even then incomprehensible how the intuition of a present thing should make me know this thing as it is in itself, as its properties cannot migrate into my faculty of representation. But even granting this possibility, an intuition of that sort would not take place *a priori,* that is, before the object were presented to me; for without this latter fact no ground of a relation between my representation and the object can be imagined, unless it depend upon a direct implantation.

Therefore in one way only can my intuition anticipate the actuality of the object, and be a cognition *a priori,* namely: *if my intuition contains nothing but the form of sensibility, antedating in my mind all the actual impressions through which I am affected by objects.*

For that objects of sense can only be intuited according to this form of sensibility I can know *a priori.* Hence it follows that propositions which concern this form of sensuous intuition only are possible and valid for objects of the senses; as also, conversely, that intuitions which are possible *a priori* can never concern any other things than objects of our senses.

§ 10. Accordingly, it is only the form of sensuous intuition by which we can intuit things *a priori,* but by which we can know objects only as they *appear* to us (to our senses), not as they are in themselves; and this assumption is absolutely necessary if synthetical propositions *a priori* be granted as possible or if, in case they actually occur, their possibility is to be comprehended and determined beforehand.

Now, the intuitions which pure mathematics lays at the foundation of all its cognitions and judgments which appear at once apodictic and necessary are space and time. For mathematics must first present all its concepts in intuition, and pure mathematics in pure intuition; that is, it must construct them. If it proceeded in any other way, it would be impossible to take a single step; for mathematics proceeds, not analytically by dissection of concepts, but synthetically, and if pure intuition be wanting there is nothing in which the matter for synthetical judgments *a priori* can be given. Geometry is based upon the pure intuition of space. Arithmetic achieves its concept of number by the successive addition of units in time, and pure mechanics cannot attain its concepts of motion without employing the representation of time. Both representations, however, are only intuitions; for if we omit from the empirical intuitions of bodies and their alterations (motion) everything empirical, that is, belonging to sensation, space and time still remain, which are therefore pure intuitions that lie *a priori* at the basis of the empirical. Hence they can never be omitted; but at the same time, by their being pure intuitions *a priori,* they prove that they are mere forms of our sensibility, which must precede all empirical intuition, that is, perception of actual objects, and conformably to which objects can be known *a priori,* but only as they appear to us.

§ 11. The problem of the present section is therefore solved. Pure mathematics, as synthetical cognition *a priori,* is possible only by referring to no other objects than those of the senses. At the basis of their empirical intuition lies a pure intuition (of space and of time) which is *a priori,* because the latter intuition is nothing but the mere form of sensibility, which precedes the actual appearance of the objects, since in fact it makes them possible. Yet this faculty of intuiting *a priori* affects not the matter of the phenomenon (that is, the sensation in it, for this constitutes that which is empirical), but its form, namely, space and time. Should any man venture to doubt that these are determinations adhering not to things in themselves, but to their relation to our sensibility, I should be glad to know how he can find it possible to know *a priori* how their intuition will be characterized before we have any acquaintance with them and before they are presented to us. Such, however, is the case with space and time. But this is quite comprehensible as soon as both count for nothing more than formal conditions of our sensibility, while the objects count merely as phenomena; for then the form of the phenomenon, that is, pure intuition, can by all means be represented as proceeding from ourselves, that is, *a priori.*

§ 12. In order to add something by way of illustration and confirmation, we need only watch the ordinary and unavoidable procedure of geometers. All proofs of the complete congruence of two given figures (where the one can in every respect be substituted for the other) come ultimately to this, that they may be made to coincide, which is evidently nothing else than a synthetical proposition resting upon immediate intuition; and this intuition must be pure or given *a priori,* otherwise the proposition could not rank as apodictically certain, but would have empirical certainty only. In that case, it could only be said that it is always found to be so and holds good only as far as our perception reaches. That everywhere space (which [in its entirety] is itself no longer the boundary of another space) has three dimensions and that space cannot in any way have more is based on the proposition that not more than three lines can intersect at right angles in one point; but this proposition cannot by any means be shown from concepts, but rests immediately on intuition, and indeed on pure and *a priori* intuition because it is apodictically certain. That we can require a line to be drawn to infinity (*in indefinitum*) or that a series of changes (for example, spaces traversed by motion) shall be infinitely continued presupposes a representation of space and time, which can only attach to intuition—namely, so far as it in itself is bounded by nothing— for from concepts it could never be inferred. Consequently, the basis of mathematics actually is pure intuitions, which make its synthetical and apodictically valid propositions possible. Hence our transcendental deduction of the notions of space and of time explains at the same time the possibility of pure mathematics. Without such a deduction and the assumption "that everything which can be given to our senses (to the external senses in space, to the internal one in time) is intuited by us as it appears to us, not as it is in itself," the truth of pure mathematics may be granted, but its existence could by no means be understood.

§ 13. Those who cannot yet rid themselves of the notion that space and time are actual qualities inherent in things in themselves may exercise their acumen on the following paradox. When they have in vain attempted its solution and are free from prejudices at least for a few moments, they will suspect that the degradation of space and time to mere forms of our sensuous intuition may perhaps be well founded.

If two things are quite equal in all respects as much as can be ascertained by all means possible, quantitatively and qualitatively, it must follow that the one can in all cases and under all circumstances replace the other, and this substitution would not occasion the least perceptible difference. This in fact is true of plane figures in geometry; but some spherical figures exhibit, notwithstanding a complete internal agreement, such a difference in their external relation that the one figure cannot possibly be put in the place of the other. For instance, two spherical triangles on opposite hemispheres, which have an arc of the equator as their common base, may be quite equal, both as regards sides and angles, so that nothing is to be found in either, if it be described for itself alone and completed, that would not equally be applicable to both; and yet the one cannot be put in the place of the other (that is, upon the opposite hemisphere). Here, then, is an internal difference between the two triangles, which difference our understanding cannot describe as internal and which only manifests itself by external relations in space. But I shall adduce examples, taken from common life, that are more obvious still.

What can be more similar in every respect and in every part more alike to my hand and to my ear than their images in a mirror? And yet I cannot put such a hand as is seen in the glass in the place of its original; for if this is a right hand, that in the glass is a left one, and the image or reflection of the right ear is a left one, which never can take the place of the other. There are in this case no internal differences which our understanding could determine by thinking alone. Yet the differences are internal as the senses teach, for, notwithstanding their complete equality and similarity, the left hand cannot be enclosed in the same bounds as the right one (they are not congruent); the glove of one hand cannot be used for the other. What is the solution? These objects are not representations of things as they are in themselves and as some mere* understanding would know them, but sensuous intuitions, that is, appearances whose possibility rests upon the relation of certain things unknown in themselves to something else, namely, to our sensibility. Space is the form of the external intuition of this sensibility, and the internal determination of every space is possible only by the determination of its external relation to the whole of space, of which it is a part (in other words, by its relation to the outer sense). That is to say, the part is possible only through the whole, which is never the case with things in themselves, as objects of the mere understanding, but which may well be the case with mere appearances. Hence the difference between similar and equal things which are not congruent (for instance, two symmetric helices) cannot be made intelligible by any concept, but only by the relation to the right and the left hands which immediately refers to intuition.

Remark I

Pure mathematics, and especially pure geometry, can have objective reality only on condition that they refer merely to objects of sense. But in regard to the latter the principle holds good that our sense representation is not a representation of things in themselves, but of the way in which they appear to us. Hence it follows that the propositions of geometry are not the results of a mere creation of our poetic imagination, and that therefore they cannot be referred with assurance to actual objects; but rather that they are necessarily valid of space, and consequently of all that may be found in space, because space is nothing else than the form of all external appearances, and it is this form alone in which objects of sense can be given to us. Sensibility, the form of which is the basis of geometry, is that upon which the possibility of external appearance depends. Therefore these appearances can never contain anything but what geometry prescribes to them.

It would be quite otherwise if the senses were so constituted as to represent objects as they are in themselves. For then it would not by any means follow from the representation of space, which, with all its properties, serves to the geometer as an *a priori* foundation, that this foundation and everything which is thence inferred must be so in nature. The space of the geometer would be considered a mere fiction, and it would not be credited with objective validity because we cannot see how things must of necessity agree with an image of them which we make spontaneously and previous to our acquaintance with them. But if this image, or rather this formal intuition, is the essential property of our sensibility by means of which alone objects are given to us, and if this sensibility represents not things in themselves but their appearances, then we shall easily comprehend, and at the same time indisputably prove, that all external objects of our world of sense must necessarily coincide in the most rigorous way with the propositions of geometry; because sensibility, by means of its form of external intuition, namely, by space, with which the geometer is occupied, makes those objects possible as mere appearances.

*[In German, *pure*. The clause is meant ironically.—L.W.B.]

It will always remain a remarkable phenomenon in the history of philosophy that there was a time when even mathematicians who at the same time were philosophers began to doubt, not of the accuracy of their geometrical propositions so far as they concerned space, but of their objective validity and the applicability of this concept itself, and of all its corollaries, to nature. They showed much concern whether a line in nature might not consist of physical points, and consequently that true space in the object might consist of simple parts, while the space which the geometer has in his mind cannot be such. They did not recognize that this thought space renders possible the physical space, that is, the extension of matter itself; that this pure space is not at all a quality of things in themselves, but a form of our sensuous faculty of representation; and that all objects in space are mere appearances, that is, not things in themselves but representations of our sensuous intuition. But such is the case, for the space of the geometer is exactly the form of sensuous intuition which we find *a priori* in us, and contains the ground of the possibility of all external appearances (according to their form); and the latter must necessarily and most rigorously agree with the propositions of the geometer, which he draws, not from any fictitious concept, but from the subjective basis of all external appearances which is sensibility itself. In this and no other way can geometry be made secure as to the undoubted objective reality of its propositions against all the intrigues of a shallow metaphysics, which is surprised at them [the geometrical propositions] because it has not traced them to the sources of their concepts.

Remark II

Whatever is given us as object must be given us in intuition. All our intuition, however, takes place by means of the senses only; the understanding intuits nothing but only reflects. And as we have just shown that the senses never and in no manner enable us to know things in themselves, but only their appearances, which are mere representations of the sensibility, we conclude that "all bodies, together with the space in which they are, must be considered nothing but mere representations in us, and exist nowhere but in our thoughts." Is not this manifest idealism?

Idealism consists in the assertion that there are none but thinking beings, all other things which we think are perceived in intuition, being nothing but representations in the thinking beings, to which no object external to them in fact corresponds. I, on the contrary, say that things as objects of our senses existing outside us are given, but we know nothing of what they may be in themselves, knowing only their appearances, that is, the representations which they cause in us by affecting our senses. Consequently I grant by all means that there are bodies without us, that is, things which, though quite unknown to us as to what they are in themselves, we yet know by the representations which their influence on our sensibility procures us. These representations we call "bodies," a term signifying merely the appearance of the thing which is unknown to us, but not therefore less actual. Can this be termed idealism? It is the very contrary.

Long before Locke's time, but assuredly since him, it has been generally assumed and granted without detriment to the actual existence of external things that many of their predicates may be said to belong, not to the things in themselves, but to their appearances, and to have no proper existence outside our representation. Heat, color, and taste, for instance, are of this kind. Now, if I go farther and, for weighty reasons, rank as mere appearances the remaining qualities of bodies also, which are called primary—such as extension, place, and, in general, space, with all that which belongs to it (impenetrability or materiality, shape, etc.)—no one in the least can adduce the reason of its being inadmissible. As little as the man who admits colors not to be properties of the object in itself, but only as modifications of the sense of sight, should on that account be called an idealist, so little can my thesis be named idealistic merely because I find that more, nay, *all the properties which constitute the intuition of a body belong merely to its appearance.*

The existence of the thing that appears is thereby not destroyed, as in genuine idealism, but it is only shown that we cannot possibly know it by the senses as it is in itself.

I should be glad to know what my assertions must be in order to avoid all idealism. Undoubtedly, I should say that the representation of space is not only perfectly conformable to the relation which our sensibility has to objects—that I have said—but that it is quite similar to the object—an assertion in which I can find as little meaning as if I said that the sensation of red has a similarity to the property of cinnabar which excites this sensation in me.

Remark III

Hence we may at once dismiss an easily foreseen but futile objection, "that by admitting the ideality of space and of time the whole sensible world would be turned into mere sham." After all philosophical insight into the nature of sensuous cognition was spoiled by making the sensibility merely a confused mode of representation, according to which we still know things as they are, but without being able to reduce everything in this our representation to a clear consciousness, I proved that sensibility consists, not in this logical distinction of clearness and obscurity, but in the genetic one of the origin of knowledge itself. For sensuous perception represents things not at all as they are, but only the mode in which they affect our senses; and consequently by sensuous perception appearances only, and not things themselves, are given to the understanding for reflection. After this necessary correction an objection rises from an unpardonable and almost intentional misconception, as if my doctrine turned all the things of the world of sense into mere illusion.

When an appearance is given us, we are still quite free as to how we should judge the matter. The appearance depends upon the senses, but the judgment upon the understanding; and the only question is whether in the determination of the object there is truth or not. But the difference between truth and dreaming is not ascertained by the nature of the representations which are referred to objects (for they are the same in both cases), but by their connection according to those rules which determine the coherence of the representations in the concept of an object, and by ascertaining whether they can subsist together in experience or not. And it is not the fault of the appearances if our cognition takes illusion for truth, that is, if the intuition, by which an object is given us, is considered a concept of the thing or even of its existence which the understanding can only think. The senses represent to us the course of the planets as now progressive, now retrogressive; and herein is neither falsehood nor truth, because as long as we hold this to be nothing but appearance we do not judge of the objective character of their motion. But as a false judgment may easily arise when the understanding is not on its guard against this subjective mode of representation being considered objective, we say they appear to move backward; it is not the senses however which must be charged with the illusion, but the understanding, whose province alone it is to make an objective judgment from appearances.

Thus, even if we did not at all reflect on the origin of our representations, whenever we connect our intuitions of sense (whatever they may contain) in space and in time, according to the rules of the coherence of all knowledge in experience, illusion or truth will arise according as we are negligent or careful. It is merely a question of the use of sensuous representations in the understanding, and not of their origin. In the same way, if I consider all the representations of the senses, together with their form, space and time, to be nothing but appearances, and space and time to be a mere form of the sensibility, which is not to be met with in objects out of it, and if I make use of these representations in reference to possible experience only, there is nothing in my regarding them as appearances that can lead astray or cause illusion. For all that they can correctly cohere according to rules of truth in experience. Thus all the propositions of geometry hold good of space as well as of all the objects of the senses, consequently, of all possible experience, whether I consider space as a mere form of the sensibility or as something cleaving to the things themselves. In the former case, however, I comprehend how I can know *a priori* these propositions concerning all the objects of external intuition. Otherwise, everything else as regards all possible experience remains just as if I had not departed from the common view.

But if I venture to go beyond all possible experience with my concepts of space and time, which I cannot refrain from doing if I proclaim them characters inherent in things in themselves (for what should prevent me from letting them hold good of the same things, even though my senses might be different, and unsuited to them?), then a grave error may arise owing to an illusion, in which I proclaim to be universally valid what is merely a subjective condition of the intuition of things and certain only for all objects of senses—namely, for all possible experience; I would refer this condition to things in themselves, and not limit it to conditions of experience.

My doctrine of the ideality of space and of time, therefore, far from reducing the whole sensible world to mere illusion, is the only means of securing the application of one of the most important kinds of knowledge (that which mathematics propounds *a priori*) to actual objects and of preventing its being regarded as mere illusion. For without this observation it would be quite impossible to make out whether the intuitions of space and time, which we borrow from no experience and which yet lie in our representation *a priori,* are not mere phantasms of our brain to which objects do not correspond, at least not adequately; and, consequently, whether we have been able to show its unquestionable validity with regard to all the objects of the sensible world just because they are mere appearances.

Secondly, though these my principles make appearances of the representations of the senses, they are so far from turning the truth of experience into mere illusion that they are rather the only means of preventing the transcendental illusion, by which metaphysics has hitherto been deceived and led to the childish endeavor of catching at bubbles, because appearances, which are mere representations, were taken for things in themselves. Here originated the remarkable occurrence of the antinomy of reason which I shall mention later and which is solved by the single observation that appearance, as long as it is employed in experience, produces truth; but the moment it transgresses the bounds of experience, and consequently becomes transcendent, produces nothing but illusion.

Inasmuch, therefore, as I leave to things as we obtain them by the senses their actuality and only limit our sensuous intuition of these things to this: that it represents in no respect, not even in the pure intuitions of space and of time, anything more than mere appearance of those things, but never their constitution in themselves, this is not a sweeping illusion invented for nature by me. My protestation, too, against all charges of idealism is so valid and clear as even to seem superfluous, were there not incompetent judges who, while they would have an old name for every deviation from their perverse though common opinion and never judge of the spirit of philosophic nomenclature, but cling to the letter only, are ready to put their own conceits in the place of well-defined notions, and thereby deform and distort them. I have myself given this my theory the name of transcendental idealism, but that cannot authorize anyone to confound it either with the empirical idealism of Descartes (indeed, his was only an insoluble problem, owing to which he thought everyone at liberty to deny the existence of the corporeal world because it could never be proved satisfactorily), or with the mystical and visionary idealism of Berkeley, against which and other similar phantasms our *Critique* contains the proper antidote. My idealism concerns not the existence of things (the doubting of which, however, constitutes idealism in the ordinary sense), since it never came into my head to doubt it, but it concerns the sensuous representation of things to which space and time especially belong. Of these [namely, space and time], consequently of all appearances in general, I have only shown that they are neither things (but mere modes of representation) nor determinations belonging to things in themselves. But the word "transcendental," which with me never means a reference of our knowledge to things, but only to the cognitive faculty, was meant to obviate this misconception. Yet rather than give further occasion to it by this word, I now retract it and desire this idealism of mine to be called "critical." But if it be really an objectionable idealism to convert actual things (not appearances) into mere representations, by what name shall we call him who conversely changes mere representations to things? It may, I think, be called "dreaming idealism," in contradistinction to the former, which may be called "visionary," both of which are to be refuted by my transcendental or, better, *critical* idealism.

SECOND PART OF THE MAIN TRANSCENDENTAL PROBLEM

How Is Pure Science of Nature Possible?

§ 14. Nature is the existence of things, so far as it is determined according to universal laws. Should nature signify the existence of things in themselves, we could never know it either *a priori* or *a posteriori*. Not *a priori*, for how can we know what belongs to things in themselves, since this never can be done by the dissection of our concepts (in analytical propositions)? For I do not want to know what is contained in my concept of a thing (for that belongs to its logical essence), but what in the actuality of the thing is superadded to my concept and by which the thing itself is determined in its existence apart from the concept. My understanding and the conditions on which alone it can connect the determination of things in their existence do not prescribe any rule to things [in] themselves; these do not conform to my understanding, but it would have to conform itself to them; they would therefore have to be first given me in order to gather these determinations from them, wherefore they would not be known *a priori*.

But knowledge of the nature of things in themselves *a posteriori* would be equally impossible. For, if experience is to teach us laws to which the existence of things is subject, these laws, if they have reference to things in themselves, would have to hold them of necessity even outside our experience. But experience teaches us what exists and how it exists, but never that it must necessarily exist so and not otherwise. Experience therefore can never teach us the nature of things in themselves.

§ 15. We nevertheless actually possess a pure science of nature in which are propounded, *a priori* and with all the necessity requisite to apodictical propositions, laws to which nature is subject. I need only call to witness that propaedeutic of natural science which, under the title of the universal science of nature, precedes all physics (which is founded upon empirical principles). In it we have mathematics applied to appearances, and also merely discursive principles (or those derived from concepts), which constitute the philosophical part of the pure knowledge of nature. But there are several things in it which are not quite pure and independent of empirical sources, such as the concept of *motion,* that of *impenetrability* (upon which the empirical concept of matter rests), that of *inertia,* and many others, which prevent its being called a perfectly pure science of nature. Besides, it only refers to objects of the outer sense, and therefore does not give an example of a universal science of nature, in the strict sense, for such a science must bring nature in general, whether it regards the object of the outer or that of the inner sense (the object of physics as well as psychology), under universal laws. But among the principles of this universal physics there are a few which actually have the required universality; for instance, the propositions that "substance is permanent," that "every event is determined by a cause according to constant laws," etc. These are actually universal laws of nature, which hold completely *a priori.* There is then in fact a pure science of nature, and the question arises, *How is it possible?*

§ 16. The word *nature* assumes yet another meaning which defines the object, whereas in the former sense it only denotes the conformity to law of the determinations of the existence of things generally. If we consider it *materialiter,* "nature is the complex of all the objects of experience." And with this only are we now concerned, for anyhow things which can never be objects of experience, if they had to be known as to their nature, would oblige us to have recourse to concepts whose meaning could never be given *in concreto* (by any example of possible experience). Consequently we would have to form for ourselves a list of concepts of their nature, the reality whereof could never be determined. That is, we could never learn whether they actually referred to objects or were mere creations of thought. The knowledge of what cannot be an object of experience would be hyperphysical, and with things hyperphysical we are here not concerned, but only with the knowledge of nature, the actuality of which can be confirmed by experience, though this knowledge is possible *a priori* and precedes all experience.

§ 17. The formal aspect of nature in this narrower sense is therefore the conformity to law of all the objects of experience and, so far as it is known *a priori,* their *necessary* conformity. But it has just been shown that the laws of nature can never be known *a priori* in objects so far as they are considered, not in reference to possible experience, but as things in themselves. And our inquiry here extends, not to things in themselves (the properties of which we pass by), but to things as objects of possible experience, and the complex of these is what we here properly designate as nature. And now I ask, when the possibility of knowledge of nature *a priori* is in question, whether it is better to arrange the problem thus: "How can we know *a priori* that things as objects of experience necessarily conform to law?" or thus: "How is it possible to know *a priori* the necessary conformity to law of experience itself as regards all its objects generally?"

Closely considered, the solution of the problem represented in either way amounts, with regard to the pure knowledge of nature (which is the point of the question at issue), entirely to the same thing. For the subjective laws, under which alone an empirical knowledge of things is possible, hold good of these things as objects of possible experience (not as things in themselves, which are not considered here). It is all the same whether I say: "A judgment of perception can never rank as experience without the law that, whenever an event is observed, it is always referred to some antecedent, which it follows according to a universal rule," or: "Everything of which experience teaches that it happens must have a cause."

It is, however, more suitable to choose the first formula. For we can *a priori* and prior to all given objects have a knowledge of those conditions on which alone experience of them is possible, but never of the laws to which things may in themselves be subject, without reference to possible experience. We cannot, therefore, study the nature of things *a priori* otherwise than by investigating the conditions and the universal (though subjective) laws, under which alone such a cognition as experience (as to mere form) is possible, and we determine accordingly the possibility of things as objects of experience. For if I should choose the second formula and seek the *a priori* conditions under which nature as an object of experience is possible, I might easily fall into error and fancy that I was speaking of nature as a thing in itself, and then move round in endless circles, in a vain search for laws concerning things of which nothing is given me.

Accordingly, we shall here be concerned with experience only and the universal conditions of its possibility, which are given *a priori*. Thence we shall define nature as the whole object of all possible experience. I think it will be understood that I here do not mean the rules of the observation of a nature that is already given, for these already presuppose experience. Thus I do not mean how (through experience) we can study the laws of nature, for these would not then be laws *a priori* and would yield us no pure science of nature; but [I mean to ask] how the conditions *a priori* of the possibility of experience are at the same time the sources from which all universal laws of nature must be derived.

§ 18. In the first place we must state that, while all judgments of experience are empirical (that is, have their ground in immediate sense-perception), all empirical judgments are not judgments of experience; but, besides the empirical, and in general besides what is given to the sensuous intuition, special concepts must yet be superadded—concepts which have their origin wholly *a priori* in the pure understanding, and under which every perception must be first of all subsumed and then by their means changed into experience.

Empirical judgments, so far as they have objective validity, are *judgments of experience,* but those which are only subjectively valid I name mere *judgments of perception.* The latter require no pure concept of the understanding, but only the logical connection of perception in a thinking subject. But the former always require, besides the representation of the sensuous intuition, special *concepts originally begotten in the understanding,* which make possible the objective validity of the judgment of experience.

All our judgments are at first merely judgments of perception; they hold good only for us (that is, for our subject), and we do not till afterward give them a new reference (to an object) and desire that they shall always hold good for us and in the same way for everybody else; for when a judgment agrees with an object, all judgments concerning the same object must likewise agree among themselves, and thus the objective validity of the judgment of experience signifies nothing else than its necessary universal validity. And conversely when we have ground for considering a judgment as necessarily having universal validity (which never depends upon perception, but upon the pure concept of the understanding under which the perception is subsumed), we must consider that it is objective also—that is, that it expresses not merely a reference of our perception to a subject, but a characteristic of the object. For there would be no reason for the judgments of other men necessarily agreeing with mine if it were not the unity of the object to which they all refer and with which they accord; hence they must all agree with one another.

§ 19. Therefore objective validity and necessary universality (for everybody) are equivalent terms, and though we do not know the object in itself, yet when we consider a judgment as universal, and hence necessary, we thereby understand it to have objective validity. By this judgment we know the object (though it remains unknown as it is in itself) by the universal and necessary connection of the given perceptions. As this is the case with all objects of sense, judgments of experience take their objective validity, not from the immediate knowledge of the object (which is impossible), but from the condition of universal validity of empirical judgments, which, as already said, never rests upon empirical or, in short, sensuous conditions, but upon a pure concept of the understanding. The object in itself always remains unknown; but when by the concept of the understanding the connection of the representations of the object, which it gives to our sensibility, is determined as universally valid, the object is determined by this relation, and the judgment is objective.

To illustrate the matter: when we say, "The room is warm, sugar sweet, and wormwood bitter,"* we have only subjectively valid judgments. I do not at all expect that I or any other person shall always find it as I now do; each of these sentences only expresses a relation of two sensations to the same subject, that is, myself, and that only in my present state of perception; consequently they are not valid of the object. Such are judgments of perception. Judgments of experience are of quite a different nature. What experience teaches me under certain circumstances, it must always teach me and everybody; and its validity is not limited to the subject nor to its state at a particular time. Hence I pronounce all such judgments objectively valid. For instance, when I say the air is elastic, this judgment is as yet a judgment of perception only; I do nothing but refer two of my sensations to each other. But if I would have it called a judgment of experience, I require this connection to stand under a condition which makes it universally valid. I desire therefore that I and everybody else should always connect necessarily the same perceptions under the same circumstances.

§ 20. We must consequently analyze experience in general in order to see what is contained in this product of the senses and of the understanding, and how the judgment of experience itself is possible. The foundation is the intuition of which I become conscious, that is, perception (*perceptio*), which pertains merely to the senses. But in the next place, there is judging (which belongs only to the understanding). But this judging may be twofold: first, I may merely compare perceptions and connect them in a consciousness of my particular state; or, secondly, I may connect them in consciousness in general. The former judgment is merely a judgment of perception, and hence is of subjective validity only; it is merely a connection of perceptions in my mental state, without reference to the object. Hence it does not, as is commonly imagined, suffice for experience that perceptions are compared and connected in consciousness through judgment; thence arises no universal validity and necessity by virtue of which alone consciousness can be objectively valid, that is, can be called experience.

Quite another judgment therefore is required before perception can become experience. The given intuition must be subsumed under a concept which determines the form of judging in general relatively to the intuition, connects empirical consciousness of intuition in consciousness in general, and thereby procures universal validity for empirical judgments. A concept of this nature is a pure *a priori* concept of the understanding, which does nothing but determine for an intuition the general way in which it can be used for judgments. Let the concept be that of cause; then it determines the intuition which is subsumed under it, for example, that of air, relative to judging in general—

---

*I freely grant that these examples do not represent such judgments of perception as ever could become judgments of experience, even though a concept of the understanding were superadded, because they refer merely to feeling, which everybody knows to be merely subjective and which of course can never be attributed to the object, and consequently never become objective. I only wished to give here an example of a judgment that is merely subjectively valid, containing no ground for necessary universal validity and thereby for a relation to the object. An example of the judgments of perception which become judgments of experience by superadded concepts of the understanding will be given in the next note.

namely, the concept of air in respect to its expansion serves in the relation of antecedent to consequent in a hypothetical judgment. The concept of cause accordingly is a pure concept of the understanding, which is totally disparate from all possible perception and only serves to determine the representation subsumed under it, with respect to judging in general, and so to make a universally valid judgment possible.

Before, therefore, a judgment of perception can become a judgment of experience, it is requisite that the perception should be subsumed under some such concept of the understanding; for instance, air belongs under the concept of cause, which determines our judgment about it in respect to its expansion as hypothetical.* Thereby the expansion of the air is represented, not as merely belonging to the perception of the air in my present state or in several states of mine, or in the perceptual state of others, but as belonging to it necessarily. The judgment, "Air is elastic," becomes universally valid and a judgment of experience only because certain judgments precede it which subsume the intuition of air under the concept of cause and effect; and they thereby determine the perceptions, not merely with respect to one another in me, but with respect to the form of judging in general (which is here hypothetical), and in this way they render the empirical judgment universally valid.

If all our synthetical judgments are analyzed so far as they are objectively valid, it will be found that they never consist of mere intuitions connected only (as is commonly believed) by comparison into a judgment; but that they would be impossible were not a pure concept of the understanding superadded to the concepts abstracted from intuition, under which concept these latter are subsumed and in this manner only combined into an objectively valid judgment. Even the judgments of pure mathematics in their simplest axioms are not exempt from this condition. The principle, "A straight line is the shortest distance between two points," presupposes that the line is subsumed under the concept of magnitude, which certainly is no mere intuition, but has its seat in the understanding alone and serves to determine the intuition (of the line) with regard to the judgments which may be made about it, in respect to their quantity, that is, to plurality (as *judicia plurativa*).** For under them it is understood that in a given intuition there is contained a plurality of homogeneous parts.

§ 21. To prove, then, the possibility of experience so far as it rests upon pure concepts of the understanding a priori, we must first represent what belongs to judging in general and the various functions of the understanding in a complete table. For the pure concepts of the understanding must run parallel to these functions, as such concepts are nothing more than concepts of intuitions in general, so far as these are determined by one or other of these functions of judging, in themselves, that is, necessarily and universally. Hereby also the *a priori* principles of the possibility of all experience, as objectively valid empirical knowledge, will be precisely determined. For they are nothing but propositions which subsume all perception (under certain universal conditions of intuition) under those pure concepts of the understanding.

---

*As an easier example, we may take the following: "When the sun shines on the stone, it grows warm." This judgment, however often I and others may have perceived it, is a mere judgment of perception and contains no necessity; perceptions are only usually conjoined in this manner. But if I say, "The sun warms the stone," I add to the perception a concept of the understanding, namely, that of cause, which necessarily connects with the concept of sunshine that of heat, and the synthetical judgment becomes of necessity universally valid, namely, objective, and is converted from a perception into experience.

**This name seems preferable to the term *particularia*, which is used for these judgments in logic. For the latter implies the idea that they are not universal. But when I start from unity (in singular judgments) and so proceed to totality, I must not [even indirectly and negatively] imply any reference to totality. I think plurality merely without totality, and not the exception from totality. This is necessary if logical distinctions are to form the basis of the pure concepts of the understanding. However, logical usage need not be changed.

LOGICAL TABLE OF JUDGMENTS

1	2
As to Quantity	*As to Quality*
Universal	Affirmative
Particular	Negative
Singular	Infinite

3	4
As to Relation	*As to Modality*
Categorical	Problematic
Hypothetical	Assertoric
Disjunctive	Apodeictic

TRANSCENDENTAL TABLE OF THE CONCEPTS OF THE UNDERSTANDING

1	2
As to Quantity	*As to Quality*
Unity (Measure)	Reality
Plurality (Magnitude)	Negation
Totality (Whole)	Limitation

3	4
As to Relation	*As to Modality*
Substance	Possibility
Cause	Existence
Community	Necessity

PURE PHYSICAL TABLE OF THE UNIVERSAL PRINCIPLES OF THE SCIENCE OF NATURE

1	2
Axioms of Intuition	Anticipations of Perception

3	4
Analogies of Experience	Postulates of Empirical Thinking Generally

§ 21a. In order to comprise the whole matter in one idea, it is first necessary to remind the reader that we are discussing, not the origin of experience, but that which lies in experience. The former pertains to empirical psychology and would even then never be adequately explained without the latter, which belongs to the critique of knowledge, and particularly of the understanding.

Experience consists of intuitions, which belong to the sensibility, and of judgments, which are entirely a work of the understanding. But the judgments which the understanding forms solely from sensuous intuitions are far from being judgments of experience. For in the one case the judgment connects only the perceptions as they are given in sensuous intuition, while in the other the judgments must express what experience in general and not what the mere perception (which possesses only subjective validity) contains. The judgment of experience must therefore add to the sensuous intuition and its logical connection in a judgment (after it has been rendered universal by comparison) something that determines the synthetical judgment as necessary and therefore as universally valid. This can be nothing else than that concept which represents the intuition as determined in itself with regard to one form of judgment rather than another, namely, a concept of that synthetical unity of intuitions which can only be represented by a given logical function of judgments.

§ 22. The sum of the matter is this: the business of the senses is to intuit, that of the understanding is to think. But thinking is uniting representations in one consciousness. This union originates either merely relative to the subject and is accidental and subjective, or takes place absolutely and is necessary or objective. The union of representations in one consciousness is judgment. Thinking, therefore, is the same as judging or referring representations to judgments in general. Hence judgments are either merely subjective, when representations are referred to a consciousness in one subject only and united in it, or objective, when they are united in consciousness in general, that is, necessarily. The logical functions of all judgments are but various modes of uniting representations in consciousness. But if they serve for concepts, they are concepts of the necessary union of representations in [any] consciousness, and so are principles of objectively valid judgments. This union in consciousness is either analytical, by identity, or synthetical, by the combination and addition of various representations one to another. Experience consists in the synthetical connection of phenomena (perceptions) in consciousness, so far as this connection is necessary. Hence the pure concepts of the understanding are those under which all perceptions must be subsumed ere they can serve for judgments of experience, in which the synthetical unity of the perceptions is represented as necessary and universally valid.*

§ 23. Judgments, when considered merely as the condition of the union of given representations in a consciousness, are rules. These rules, so far as they represent the union as necessary, are rules *a priori,* and, insofar as they cannot be deduced from higher rules, are principles. But in regard to the possibility of all experience, merely in relation to the form of thinking in it, no conditions of judgments of experience are higher than those which bring the appearances, according to the various form of their intuition, under pure concepts of the understanding, which render the empirical judgment objectively valid. These are therefore the *a priori* principles of possible experience.

The principles of possible experience are then at the same time universal laws of nature, which can be known *a priori.* And thus the problem of our second question, "How is the pure science of nature possible?" is solved. For the system which is required for the form of a science is to be met with in perfection here, because, beyond the above-mentioned formal conditions of all judgments in general (and hence of all rules in general) offered in logic, no others are possible, and these constitute a logical system. The concepts grounded thereupon, which contain the *a priori* conditions of all synthetical and necessary judgments, accordingly constitute a transcendental system. Finally the principles, by means of which all phenomena are subsumed under these

---

*But how does the proposition that judgments of experience contain necessity in the synthesis of perceptions agree with my statement so often before inculcated that experience as cognition *a posteriori* can afford contingent judgments only? When I say that experience teaches me something, I mean only the perception that lies in experience—for example, that heat always follows the shining of the sun on a stone; consequently the proposition of experience is always so far accidental. That this heat necessarily follows the shining of the sun is contained indeed in the judgment of experience (by means of the concept of cause), yet is a fact not learned by experience; for conversely, experience is first of all generated by this addition of the concept of the understanding (of cause) to perception. How perception attains this addition may be seen by referring in the *Critique* itself to the [first] section of the "Transcendental Faculty of Judgment."

concepts, constitute a physical system, that is, a system of nature, which precedes all empirical knowledge of nature, and makes it possible. It may in strictness be denominated the universal and pure science of nature.

§ 24. The first of the physical principles subsumes all phenomena, as intuitions in space and time, under the concept of quantity, and is thus a principle of the application of mathematics to experience. The second one subsumes the strictly empirical element, namely, sensation, which denotes the real in intuitions, not indeed directly under the concept of quantity, because sensation is not an intuition that *contains* either space or time, though it places the respective object corresponding to it in both. But still there is between reality (sense-representation) and the zero, or total void of intuition in time, a difference which has a quantity. For between every given degree of light and of darkness, between every degree of heat and of absolute cold, between every degree of weight and of absolute lightness, between every degree of occupancy space and of totally void space, diminishing degrees can be conceived, in the same manner as between consciousness and total unconsciousness (psychological darkness) ever-diminishing degrees obtain. Hence there is no perception that can prove an absolute absence; for instance, no psychological darkness that cannot be considered as consciousness which is only outbalanced by a stronger consciousness. This occurs in all cases of sensation, and so the understanding can anticipate even sensations, which constitute the peculiar quality of empirical representations (appearances), by means of the principle that they all have degree (and consequently that what is real in all appearance has degree). Here is the second application of mathematics (*mathesis intensorum*) to the science of nature.

§ 25. Anent the relation of appearances merely with a view to their existence, the determination of the relation is not mathematical but dynamical, and can never be objectively valid, consequently never fit for experience, if it does not come under *a priori* principles by which the empirical knowledge relative to appearances first becomes possible. Hence appearances must be subsumed under the concept of substance, which as a concept of a thing is the foundation of all determination of existence; or, secondly—so far as a succession is found among appearances, that is, an event—under the concept of an effect with reference to cause; or lastly—so far as coexistence is to be known objectively, that is, by a judgment of experience—under the concept of community (action and reaction). Thus *a priori* principles form the basis of objectively valid, though empirical, judgments—that is, of the possibility of experience so far as it must connect objects as existing in nature. These principles are the real laws of nature, which may be termed "dynamical."

Finally knowledge of the agreement and connection, not only of appearances among themselves in experience, but of their relation to experience in general, belongs to the judgments of experience. This relation contains either their agreement with the formal conditions, which the understanding recognizes, or their coherence with the materials of the senses and of perception, or combines both into one concept. Consequently, their relation to experience in general entails possibility, actuality, and necessity, according to universal laws of nature. This would constitute the physical doctrine of method for distinguishing truth from hypotheses and for determining the limits of certainty of the latter.

§ 26. The third table of principles drawn by the critical method from the nature of the understanding itself shows an inherent perfection, which raises it far above every other table which has hitherto, though in vain, been tried or may yet be tried by analyzing the objects themselves dogmatically. It exhibits all synthetical *a priori* principles completely and according to one principle, namely, the faculty of judging in general, constituting the essence of experience as regards the understanding; so that we can be certain that there are no more such principles. This affords a satisfaction which can never be attained by the dogmatic method. Yet this is not all; there is a still greater merit in it.

We must carefully bear in mind the premise which shows the possibility of this cognition *a priori* and, at the same time, limits all such principles to a condition which must never be lost sight of if we desire it not to be misunderstood and extended in use beyond the original sense which the understanding attaches to it. This limit is that they contain nothing but the conditions of possible experience in general so far as it is subjected to laws *a priori*. Consequently, I do not say that things *in themselves* possess a magnitude; that their reality possesses a degree, their existence a connection of accidents in a substance, etc. This nobody can prove, because such a synthetical connection from mere concepts, without any reference to sensuous intuition on the one side or connection of it in a possible experience on the other, is absolutely impossible. The essential limitation of the concepts in these principles then is that all things *as objects of experience only* stand necessarily *a priori* under the aforementioned conditions.

Hence there follows, secondly, a specifically peculiar mode of proof of these principles; they are not directly referred to appearances and to their relation, but to the possibility of experience, of which appearances constitute the matter only, not the form. Thus they are referred to objectively and universally valid synthetical propositions, in which we distinguish judgments of experience from those of perception. This takes place because appearances, as mere intuitions *occupying a part of space and time,* come under the concept of quantity, which synthetically unites their multiplicity *a priori* according to rules. Again, insofar as the perception contains, besides intuition, sensation, and between the latter and nothing (that is, the total disappearance of sensation), there is an ever-decreasing transition, it is apparent that the real within appearances must have a degree, so far as it (namely, the sensation) *does not itself occupy any part of space or of time.** Still the transition to this real from empty time or empty space is possible only in time. Consequently, although sensation, as the quality of empirical intuition specifically differentiating it from other sensations, can never be known *a priori,* yet it can, in a possible experience in general, as quantity of perception be intensively distinguished from every other similar perception. Hence the application of mathematics to nature, as regards the sensuous intuition by which nature is given to us, thus becomes possible and definite.

Above all, the reader must pay attention to the mode of proof of the principles which occur under the title of "analogies of experience." For these do not refer to the genesis of intuitions, as do the principles of applying mathematics to natural science in general, but to the connection of their existence in an experience; and this can be nothing but the determination of their existence in time according to necessary laws, under which alone the connection is objectively valid and thus becomes experience. The proof, therefore, does not turn on the synthetical unity in the connection of things in themselves, but merely of perceptions; and of these, not in regard to their matter, but to the determination of time and of the relation of their existence in it according to uni-

---

*Heat and light are in a small space just as large, as to degree, as in a large one; in like manner the internal representations, pain, consciousness generally, whether they last a short or a long time, need not vary as to the degree. Hence the quantity is here in a point and in a moment just as great as in any space or time, however great. Degrees are quantities not in intuition, but in mere sensation (or the quantity of the content [*Grundes*] of an intuition). Hence they can only be estimated quantitatively by the relation of 1 to 0, namely, by their capability of decreasing by infinite intermediate degrees to disappearance, or of increasing from naught through infinite gradations to a determinate sensation in a certain time. *Quantitas qualitatis est gradus.* "The quantity of quality is degree."

versal laws. If the empirical determination in relative time is indeed to be objectively valid (that is, to be experience), these universal laws must contain the necessary determination of existence in time generally (namely, according to a rule of the understanding *a priori*).

As these are prolegomena I cannot here further descant on the subject, but my reader (who has probably been long accustomed to consider experience a mere empirical synthesis of perceptions, and hence has not considered that it goes much beyond them since it imparts to empirical judgments universal validity, and for that purpose requires a pure and *a priori* unity of the understanding) is recommended to pay special attention to this distinction of experience from a mere aggregate of perceptions and to judge the mode of proof from this point of view.

§ 27. Now we are prepared to remove Hume's doubt. He justly maintains that we cannot comprehend by reason the possibility of causality, that is, of the reference of the existence of one thing to the existence of another which is necessitated by the former. I add that we comprehend just as little the concept of subsistence, that is, the necessity that at the foundation of the existence of things there lies a subject which cannot itself be a predicate of any other thing; nay, we cannot even form a notion of the possibility of such a thing (though we can point out examples of its use in experience). The very same incomprehensibility affects the community of things, as we cannot comprehend how from the state of one thing an inference to the state of quite another thing beyond it, and *vice versa,* can be drawn, and how substances which have each their own separate existence should depend upon one another necessarily. But I am very far from holding these concepts to be derived merely from experience, and the necessity represented in them to be imaginary and a mere illusion produced in us by long habit. On the contrary, I have amply shown that they and the principles derived from them are firmly established *a priori* before all experience and have their undoubted objective value, though only with regard to experience.

§ 28. Although I have no notion of such a connection of things in themselves, how they can either exist as substances, or act as causes, or stand in community with others (as parts of a real whole), and I can just as little conceive such properties in appearances as such (because those concepts contain nothing that lies in the appearances, but only what the understanding alone must think), we have yet a concept of such a connection of representations in our understanding and in judgments generally. This concept is: that representations appear, in one sort of judgments, as subject in relation to predicates; in another, as ground in relation to consequent; and, in a third, as parts which constitute together a total possible cognition. Furthermore, we know *a priori* that without considering the representation of an object as determined in one or the other of these respects, we can have no valid knowledge of the object; and, if we should occupy ourselves about the object in itself, there is not a single possible attribute by which I could know that it is determined under any of these aspects, that is, under the concept either of substance, or of cause, or (in relation to other substances) of community, for I have no concept of the possibility of such a connection of existence. But the question is not how things in themselves but how the empirical knowledge of things is determined, as regards the above aspects of judgments in general; that is, how things, as objects of experience, can and must be subsumed under these concepts of the understanding. And then it is clear that I completely comprehend, not only the possibility, but also the necessity, of subsuming all appearances under these concepts—that is, of using them for principles of the possibility of experience.

§ 29. In order to test Hume's problematical concept (his *crux metaphysicorum*), the concept of cause, we are first given *a priori*, by means of logic, the form of a conditional judgment in general; that is, we have one cognition given as antecedent and another as consequent. But it is possible that in perception we may meet with a rule of relation which runs thus: that a certain appearance is constantly followed by another (though not conversely); and this is a case for me to use the hypothetical judgment and, for instance, to say if the sun shines long enough upon a body it grows warm. Here there is indeed as yet no necessity of connection or concept of cause. But I proceed and say that, if this proposition, which is merely a subjective connection of perceptions, is to be a proposition of experience, it must be seen as necessary and universally valid. Such a proposition would be that the sun is by its light the cause of heat. The empirical rule is now considered as a law, and as valid, not merely of appearances but valid of them for the purposes of a possible experience which requires universal and therefore necessarily valid rules. I therefore easily comprehend the concept of cause, as a concept necessarily belonging to the mere form of experience, and its possibility as a synthetical union of perceptions in consciousness in general; but I do not at all comprehend the possibility of a thing in general as a cause, because the concept of cause denotes a condition not at all belonging to things, but to experience. For experience can be nothing but objectively valid knowledge of appearances and of their succession, only so far as the earlier can be conjoined with the later according to the rule of hypothetical judgments.

§ 30. Hence if even the pure concepts of the understanding are thought to go beyond objects of experience to things in themselves (*noumena*), they have no meaning whatever. They serve, as it were, only to decipher appearances, that we may be able to read them as experience. The principles which arise from their reference to the sensible world only serve our understanding for empirical use. Beyond this they are arbitrary combinations without objective reality, and we can neither know their possibility *a priori* nor verify—or even render intelligible by any example—their reference to objects; because examples can only be borrowed from some possible experience, and consequently the objects of these concepts can be found nowhere but in a possible experience.

This complete (though to its originator unexpected) solution of Hume's problem rescues for the pure concepts of the understanding their *a priori* origin and for the universal laws of nature their validity as laws of the understanding, yet in such a way as to limit their use to experience, because their possibility depends solely on the reference of the understanding to experience, but with a completely reversed mode of connection which never occurred to Hume—they do not derive from experience, but experience derives from them.

This is, therefore, the result of all our foregoing inquiries: "All synthetical principles *a priori* are nothing more than principles of possible experience" and can never be referred to things in themselves, but to appearances as objects of experience. And hence pure mathematics as well as a pure science of nature can never be referred to anything more than mere appearances, and can only represent either that which makes experience in general possible, or else that which, as it is derived from these principles, must always be capable of being represented in some possible experience.

§ 31. And thus we have at last something definite upon which to depend in all metaphysical enterprises, which have hitherto, boldly enough but always blindly, attempted everything without discrimination. That the aim of their exertions should be so near struck neither the dogmatic thinkers nor those who, confident in their supposed sound common sense, started with concepts and principles of pure reason (which were legitimate and natural, but destined for mere empirical use) in quest of insights to which they neither knew nor could know any definite bounds, because they had never reflected nor were able to reflect on the nature or even on the possibility of such a pure understanding.

Many a naturalist of pure reason (by which I mean the man who believes he can decide in matters of metaphysics without any science) may pretend that he, long ago, by the prophetic spirit of his sound sense, not only suspected but knew and comprehended what is here propounded with so much ado, or, if he likes, with prolix and pedantic pomp: "that with all our reason we can never reach beyond the field of experience." But when he is questioned about his rational principles individually, he must grant that there are many of them which he has not taken from experience and which are therefore independent of it and valid *a priori.* How then and on what grounds will he restrain both himself and the dogmatist, who makes use of these concepts and principles beyond all possible experience because they are recognized to be independent of it? And even he, this adept in sound sense, in spite of all his assumed and cheaply acquired wisdom, is not exempt from wandering inadvertently beyond objects of experience into the field of chimeras. He is often deeply enough involved in them; though, in announcing everything as mere probability, rational conjecture, or analogy, he gives by his popular language a color to his groundless pretensions.

§ 32. Since the oldest days of philosophy, inquirers into pure reason have conceived, besides the things of sense, or appearances (*phenomena*), which make up the sensible world, certain beings of the understanding (*noumena*), which should constitute an intelligible world. And as appearance and illusion were by those men identified (a thing which we may well excuse in an undeveloped epoch), actuality was only conceded to the beings of the understanding.

And we indeed, rightly considering objects of sense as mere appearances, confess thereby that they are based upon a thing in itself, though we know not this thing as it is in itself but only know its appearances, namely, the way in which our senses are affected by this unknown something. The understanding, therefore, by assuming appearances, grants the existence of things in themselves also; and to this extent we may say that the representation of such things as are the basis of appearances, consequently of mere beings of the understanding, is not only admissible but unavoidable.

Our critical deduction by no means excludes things of that sort (*noumena*), but rather limits the principles of the Aesthetic* to this, that they shall not extend to all things—as everything would then be turned into mere appearance—but that they shall hold good only of objects of possible experience. Hereby, then, beings of the understanding are granted, but with the inculcation of this rule which admits of no exception: that we neither know nor can know anything at all definite of these pure beings of the understanding, because our pure concepts of the understanding as well as our pure intuitions extend to nothing but objects of possible experience, consequently to mere things of sense; and as soon as we leave this sphere, these concepts retain no meaning whatever.

§ 33. There is indeed something seductive in our pure concepts of the understanding which tempts us to a transcendent use—a use which transcends all possible experience. Not only are our concepts of substance, of power, of action, of reality, and others, quite independent of experience, containing nothing of sense appearance, and so apparently applicable to things in themselves (*noumena*), but, what strengthens this conjecture, they contain a necessity of determination in themselves, which experience never attains. The concept of cause implies a rule according to which one state follows another necessarily; but experience can only show us that one state of things often or, at most, commonly follows another, and therefore affords neither strict universality nor necessity.

*[That is, the first part of the *Critique of Pure Reason,* establishing space and time as pure intuitions.—L.W.B.]

Hence the concepts of the understanding seem to have a deeper meaning and import than can be exhausted by their merely empirical use, and so the understanding inadvertently adds for itself to the house of experience a much more extensive wing, which it fills with nothing but beings of thought, without ever observing that it has transgressed with its otherwise legitimate concepts the bounds of their use.

§ 34. Two important and even indispensable, though very dry, investigations therefore became indispensable in the *Critique of Pure Reason* [namely, the chapters "The Schematism of the Pure Concepts of the Understanding" and "On the Ground of the Distinction of All Objects as Phenomena and Noumena."] In the former it is shown that the senses furnish, not the pure concepts of the understanding *in concreto,* but only the schema for their use, and that the object conformable to it occurs only in experience (as the product of the understanding from materials of the sensibility). In the latter it is shown that, although our pure concepts of the understanding and our principles are independent of experience, and despite the apparently greater sphere of their use, still nothing whatever can be thought by them beyond the field of experience, because they can do nothing but merely determine the logical form of the judgment relatively to given intuitions. But as there is no intuition at all beyond the field of the sensibility, these pure concepts, as they cannot possibly be exhibited *in concreto,* are void of all meaning; consequently all these *noumena,* together with their complex, the intelligible world,* are nothing but representation of a problem, of which the object in itself is possible but the solution, from the nature of our understanding, totally impossible. For our understanding is not a faculty of intuition, but of the connection of given intuitions in one experience. Experience must therefore contain all the objects for our concepts; but beyond it no concepts have any significance, as there is no intuition that might offer them a foundation.

§ 35. The imagination may perhaps be forgiven for occasional vagaries and for not keeping carefully within the limits of experience, since it gains life and vigor by such flights and since it is always easier to moderate its boldness than to stimulate its languor. But the understanding which ought to *think* can never be forgiven for indulging in vagaries; for we depend upon it alone for assistance to set bounds, when necessary, to the vagaries of the imagination.

But the understanding begins its aberrations very innocently and modestly. It first brings to light the elementary cognitions which inhere in it prior to all experience, but which yet must always have their application in experience. It gradually drops these limits—and what is there to prevent it, as it has quite freely derived its principles from itself? It then proceeds first to newly imagined powers in nature, then to beings outside nature—in short, to a world for whose construction the materials cannot be wanting, because fertile fiction furnishes them abundantly, and though not confirmed it is never refuted by experience. This is the reason that young thinkers are so partial to metaphysics constructed in a truly dogmatic manner, and often sacrifice to it their time and their talents, which might be otherwise better employed.

But there is no use in trying to moderate these fruitless endeavors of pure reason by all manner of cautions as to the difficulties of solving questions so occult, by complaints of the limits of our reason, and by degrading our assertions into mere conjec-

---

*We speak of the "intelligible world," not (as the usual expression is) "intellectual world." For cognitions are intellectual through the understanding and refer to our world of sense also; but objects, in so far as they can be represented merely by the understanding, and to which none of our sensible intuitions can refer, are termed "intelligible." But as some possible intuition must correspond to every object, we would have to assume an understanding that intuits things immediately; but of such we have not the least notion, nor have we any notion of the *beings of the understanding* to which it should be applied.

tures. For if their impossibility is not distinctly shown, and reason's knowledge of itself does not become a true science, in which the field of its right use is distinguished, so to say, with geometrical certainty from that of its worthless and idle use, these fruitless efforts will never be wholly abandoned.

§ 36. How is nature itself possible? This question—the highest point that transcendental philosophy can ever reach, and to which, as its boundary and completion, it must proceed—really contains two questions.

First: How is nature in the material sense, that is, as to intuition, or considered as the totality of appearances, possible; how are space, time, and that which fills both—the object of sensation—possible generally? The answer is: By means of the constitution of our sensibility, according to which it is in its own way affected by objects which are in themselves unknown to it and totally distinct from those appearances. This answer is given in the *Critique* itself in the "Transcendental Aesthetic," and in these *Prolegomena* by the solution of the first general problem.

Secondly: How is nature possible in the formal sense, as the totality of the rules under which all appearances must come in order to be thought as connected in experience? The answer must be this: It is only possible by means of the constitution of our understanding, according to which all the above representations of the sensibility are necessarily referred to a consciousness, and by which the peculiar way in which we think (namely, by rules) and hence experience also are possible, but must be clearly distinguished from an insight into the objects in themselves. This answer is given in the *Critique* itself in the "Transcendental Logic" and in these *Prolegomena,* in the course of the solution of the second main problem.

But how this peculiar property of our sensibility itself is possible, or that of our understanding and of the apperception which is necessarily its basis and that of all thinking, cannot be further analyzed or answered, because it is of them that we are in need for all our answers and for all our thinking about objects.

There are many laws of nature which we can know only by means of experience; but conformity to law in the connection of appearances, that is, in nature in general, we cannot discover by any experience, because experience itself requires laws which are *a priori* at the basis of its possibility.

The possibility of experience in general is therefore at the same time the universal law of nature, and the principles of experience are the very laws of nature. For we know nature only as the totality of appearances, that is, of representations in us; and hence we can only derive the laws of their connection from the principles of their connection in us, that is, from the conditions of their necessary union in one consciousness which constitutes the possibility of experience.

Even the main proposition expounded throughout this section—that universal laws of nature can be known *a priori*—leads naturally to the proposition that the highest legislation of nature must lie in ourselves, that is, in our understanding; and that we must not seek the universal laws of nature in nature by means of experience, but conversely must seek nature, as to its universal conformity to law, in the conditions of the possibility of experience which lie in our sensibility and in our understanding. For how were it otherwise possible to know *a priori* these laws, as they are not rules of analytical knowledge but truly synthetical extensions of it?

Such a necessary agreement of the principles of possible experience with the laws of the possibility of nature can only proceed from one of two causes: either these laws are drawn from nature by means of experience, or conversely nature is derived from the laws of the possibility of experience in general and is quite the same as the mere universal conformity to law of the latter. The former is self-contradictory, for the universal laws of nature can and must be known *a priori* (that is, independently of all experience) and be the foundation of all empirical use of the understanding; the latter alternative therefore alone remains.*

But we must distinguish the empirical laws of nature, which always presuppose particular perceptions, from the pure or universal laws of nature, which, without being based on particular perceptions, contain merely the conditions of their necessary union in experience. In relation to the latter, nature and possible experience are quite the same; and as the conformity to law in the latter depends upon the necessary connection of appearances in experience (without which we cannot know any object whatever in the sensible world), consequently upon the original laws of the understanding, it seems at first strange, but is not the less certain, to say: *The understanding does not derive its laws* (a priori) *from, but prescribes them to, nature.*

§ 37. We shall illustrate this seemingly bold proposition by an example, which will show that laws which we discover in objects of sensuous intuition (especially when these laws are known as necessary) are commonly held by us to be such as have been placed there by the understanding, in spite of their being similar in all points to the laws of nature which we ascribe to experience.

§ 38. If we consider the properties of the circle, by which this figure combines in itself so many arbitrary determinations of space in a universal rule, we cannot avoid attributing a constitution to this geometrical thing. Two straight lines, for example, which intersect each other and the circle, howsoever they may be drawn, are always divided so that the rectangle constructed with the segments of the one is equal to that constructed with the segments of the other. The question now is: Does this law lie in the circle or in the understanding? That is, does this figure, independently of the understanding, contain in itself the ground of the law; or does the understanding, having constructed according to its concepts (of the equality of the radii) the figure itself, introduce into it this law of the chords intersecting in geometrical proportion? When we follow the proofs of this law, we soon perceive that it can only be derived from the condition on which the understanding founds the construction of this figure, namely, the concept of the equality of the radii. But if we enlarge this concept to pursue further the unity of various properties of geometrical figures under common laws and consider the circle as a conic section, which of course is subject to the same fundamental conditions of construction as other conic sections, we shall find that all the chords which intersect within the ellipse, parabola, and hyperbola always intersect so that the rectangles of their segments are not indeed equal but always bear a constant ratio to one another. If we proceed still farther to the fundamental teachings of physical astronomy, we find a physical law of reciprocal attraction applicable to all material nature, the rule of which is that it decreases inversely as the square of the distance from each attracting point, that is, as the spherical surfaces increase over which this force spreads, which law seems to be necessarily inherent in the very nature of things, and hence is usually propounded as knowable *a priori*. Simple as the sources of this law are, merely resting upon the relation of spherical surfaces of different radii, its consequences are so valuable with regard to the variety and simplicity of their agreement that not only are all possible orbits of the celestial bodies conic sections, but such a relation of these orbits to one another results that no other law of attraction than that of the inverse square of the distance can be imagined as fit for a cosmical system.

---

*Crusius alone thought of a compromise: that a spirit, who can neither err nor deceive, implanted these laws in us originally. But since false principles often intrude themselves, as indeed the very system of this man shows in not a few instances, we are involved in difficulties as to the use of such a principle in the absence of sure criteria to distinguish the genuine origin from the spurious, since we never can know certainly what the spirit of truth or the father of lies may have instilled into us.

A drawing from Andreas Cellarius's *Harmonia Macrocosmica* (1661) with some of the greatest names of astronomy and cosmology, including (from left to right): Tycho Brahe (1546–1601), Ptolemy (fl. A.D. 130), St. Augustine (A.D. 354–430), Nicholas Copernicus (1473–1543), Galileo Galilei (with pointer) (1564–1642), and Andreas Cellarius (seated at right). (*Library of Congress*)

Here accordingly is nature, which rests upon laws that the understanding knows *a priori,* and chiefly from the universal principles of the determination of space. Now I ask: Do the laws of nature lie in space, and does the understanding learn them by merely endeavoring to find out the enormous wealth of meaning that lies in space; or do they inhere in the understanding and in the way in which it determines space according to the conditions of the synthetical unity in which its concepts are all centered?

Space is something so uniform and as to all particular properties so indeterminate that we should certainly not seek a store of laws of nature in it. Whereas that which determines space to assume the form of a circle, or the figures of a cone and a sphere, is the understanding, so far as it contains the ground of the unity of their constructions.

The mere universal form of intuition, called space, must therefore be the substratum of all intuitions determinable to particular objects; and in it, of course, the condition of the possibility and of the variety of these intuitions lies. But the unity of the objects is entirely determined by the understanding and on conditions which lie in its own nature; and thus the understanding is the origin of the universal order of nature, in that it comprehends all appearances under its own laws and thereby produces, in an *a priori* manner, experience (as to its form), by means of which whatever is to be known only by experience is necessarily subjected to its laws. For we are not concerned with the nature of things in themselves, which is independent of the conditions both of our sensibility and our understanding, but with nature as an object of possible experience; and in this case the understanding, since it makes experience possible, thereby insists that the sensuous world is either not an object of experience at all or that it is nature [namely, the existence of things determined according to universal laws].

Appendix to the Pure Science of Nature

§ 39. *Of the System of the Categories.* There can be nothing more desirable to a philosopher than to be able to derive the scattered multiplicity of the concepts or principles which had occurred to him in concrete use from a principle *a priori,* and to unite everything in this way in one cognition. He formerly only believed that those things which remained after a certain abstraction, and seemed by comparison among one another to constitute a particular kind of cognitions, were completely collected; but this was only an *aggregate.* Now he knows that just so many, neither more nor less, can constitute the kind of cognition, and perceives the necessity of his division. This constitutes comprehension; and only then has he attained a *system.*

To search in our common knowledge for the concepts which do not rest upon particular experience and yet occur in all knowledge from experience, of which they as it were constitute the mere form of connection, presupposes neither greater reflection nor deeper insight than to detect in a language the rules of the actual use of words generally and thus to collect elements for a grammar (in fact both researches are very nearly related), even though we are not able to give a reason why each language has just this and no other formal constitution, and still less why any precise number of such formal determinations in general, neither more nor less, can be found in it.

Aristotle collected ten pure elementary concepts under the name of *categories.** To these, which are also called "predicaments," he found himself obliged afterward to add five post-predicaments,** some of which however (*prius, simul,* and *motus*) are contained in the former; but this rhapsody must be considered (and commended) as a mere hint for future inquirers, not as an idea developed according to rule; and hence it has, in the present more advanced state of philosophy, been rejected as quite useless.

After long reflection on the pure elements of human knowledge (those which contain nothing empirical), I at last succeeded in distinguishing with certainty and in separating the pure elementary notions of the sensibility (space and time) from those of the understanding. Thus the seventh, eighth, and ninth categories had to be excluded from the old list. And the others were of no service to me because there was no principle on which the understanding could be exhaustively investigated, and all the functions, whence its pure concepts arise, determined exhaustively and precisely.

But in order to discover such a principle, I looked about for an act of the understanding which comprises all the rest and is distinguished only by various modifications or phases, in reducing the multiplicity of representation to the unity of thinking in general. I found this act of the understanding to consist in judging. Here, then, the labors of the logicians were ready at hand, though not yet quite free from defects; and with this help I was enabled to exhibit a complete table of the pure functions of the understanding, which are however undetermined with respect to any object. I finally referred these functions of judging to objects in general, or rather to the condition of de-

---

*1. *Substantia.* 2. *Qualitas.* 3. *Quantitas.* 4. *Relatio.* 5. *Actio.* 6. *Passio.* 7. *Quando.* 8. *Ubi.* 9. *Situs.* 10. *Habitus.*

**Oppositum. Prius. Simul. Motus. Habere.*

termining judgments as objectively valid; and so there arose the pure concepts of the understanding, concerning which I could make certain that these, and this exact number only, constitute our whole knowledge of things by pure understanding. I was justified in calling them by their old name "categories," while I reserved for myself the liberty of adding, under the title of "predicables," a complete list of all the concepts deducible from them by combinations, whether among themselves, or with the pure form of the appearance, that is, space or time, or with its matter, so far as it is not yet empirically determined (namely, the object of sensation in general), as soon as a system of transcendental philosophy should be completed, with the construction of which I was engaged in the *Critique of Pure Reason* itself.

Now the essential point in this system of categories, which distinguishes it from the old rhapsody which proceeded without any principle and for which alone it deserves to be considered as philosophy, consists in this: that, by means of it, the true significance of the pure concepts of the understanding and the condition of their use could be precisely determined. For here it became obvious that they are themselves nothing but logical functions, and as such do not produce the least concept of an object, but require sensuous intuition as a basis. These concepts, therefore, only serve to determine empirical judgments (which are otherwise undetermined and indifferent as regards all functions of judging) with respect to the functions of judging, thereby procuring them universal validity and, by means of them, making judgments of experience in general possible.

Such an insight into the nature of the categories, which limits them at the same time to use merely in experience, never occurred either to their first author or to any of his successors; but without this insight (which immediately depends upon their derivation or deduction), they are quite useless and only a miserable list of names, without explanation or rule for their use. Had the ancients ever conceived such a notion, doubtless the whole study of pure rational knowledge, which under the name of metaphysics has for centuries spoiled many a sound mind, would have reached us in quite another shape and would have enlightened the human understanding, instead of actually exhausting it in obscure and vain speculations and rendering it unfit for true science.

This system of categories makes all treatment of every object of pure reason itself systematic, and affords a direction or clue how and through what points of inquiry every metaphysical consideration must proceed in order to be complete; for it exhausts all the possible functions of the understanding, among which every concept must be classed. In like manner the table of principles has been formulated, the completeness of which we can only vouch for by the system of the categories. Even in the division of the concepts,* which must go beyond the physical application of the understanding, it is always the very same clue, which, as it must always be determined *a priori* by the same fixed points of the human understanding, always forms a closed circle. There is no doubt that the object of a pure concept, either of the understanding or of reason, so far as it is to be estimated philosophically and on *a priori* principles, can in this way be completely known. I could not therefore omit to make use of this clue with regard to one of the most abstract ontological divisions, namely, the various distinctions of the concepts of something and of nothing, and to construct accordingly** a systematic and necessary table of their divisions.***

---

*Cf. the tables in the *Critique of Pure Reason* in the chapters on "The Paralogisms of Pure Reason" and the "System of Cosmological Ideas."

**In the chapter on "The Amphiboly of the Concepts of Reflection," in the *Critique of Pure Reason.*

***On the table of the categories many neat observations may be made, for instance: (1) that the third arises from the first and the second, joined in one concept; (2) that in those of quantity and of quality

And this system, like every other true one founded on a universal principle, shows its inestimable value in that it excludes all foreign concepts which might otherwise intrude among the pure concepts of the understanding, and determines the place of every cognition. Those concepts, which under the name of "concepts of reflection" have been likewise arranged in a table according to the clue of the categories, intrude into ontology without any privilege or just claim to be among the pure concepts of the understanding. The latter are concepts of connection, and thereby of the objects themselves, whereas the former are only concepts of mere comparison of concepts already given, and hence are of quite another nature and use. By my systematic division* they are saved from this confusion. But the value of the special table of the categories will be still more obvious when we separate—as we are about to do—the table of the transcendental concepts of reason from the concepts of the understanding. As the transcendental concepts of reason are of an entirely different nature and origin, the table of them must have quite another form than the table of categories. This so necessary separation has never yet been made in any system of metaphysics, where, as a rule, these Ideas of reason are all mixed up with the concepts of the understanding, as if they were children of the same family—a confusion which was unavoidable in the absence of a definite system of categories.

THIRD PART OF THE MAIN TRANSCENDENTAL PROBLEM

How Is Metaphysics in General Possible?

§ 40. Pure mathematics and pure science of nature had, for their own safety and certainty, no need for such a deduction as we have made of both. For the former rests upon its own evidence, and the latter (though sprung from pure sources of the understanding) upon experience and its thorough confirmation. The pure science of nature cannot altogether refuse and dispense with the testimony of experience; because with all its certainty it can never, as philosophy, rival mathematics. Both sciences, therefore, stood in need of this inquiry, not for themselves, but for the sake of another science: metaphysics.

Metaphysics has to do not only with concepts of nature, which always find their application in experience, but also with pure rational concepts, which never can be given in any possible experience whatever. Consequently it deals with concepts whose objective reality (namely, that they are not mere chimeras) and with assertions whose

---

there is merely a progress from unity to totality or from something to nothing (for this purpose the categories of quality must stand thus: reality, limitation, total negation), without *correlata* or *opposita,* whereas those of relation and of modality have them; (3) that, as in logic categorical judgments are the basis of all others, so the category of substance is the basis of all concepts of actual things; (4) that, as modality in the judgment is not a particular predicate, so by the modal concepts a determination is not superadded to things, etc. Such observations are of great use. If we enumerate all the predicables, which we can find pretty completely in any good ontology (for example, Baumgarten's), and arrange them in classes under the categories, in which operation we must not neglect to add as complete a dissection of all these concepts as possible, there will then arise a merely analytical part of metaphysics which does not contain a single synthetical proposition, which might precede the second (the synthetical) and would, by its precision and completeness, be not only useful but, in virtue of its system, be even to some extent elegant.

*See *Critique of Pure Reason,* "The Amphiboly of the Concepts of Reflection."

truth or falsity cannot be discovered or confirmed by any experience. This part of metaphysics, however, is precisely what constitutes its essential end, to which the rest is only a means, and thus this science is in need of such a deduction for its own sake. The third question now proposed relates therefore as it were to the root and peculiarity of metaphysics, that is, the occupation of reason merely with itself and the supposed knowledge of objects arising immediately from this brooding over its own concepts, without requiring, or indeed being able to reach that knowledge through, experience.*

Without solving this problem, reason can never satisfy itself. The empirical use to which reason limits the pure understanding does not fully satisfy the proper calling of reason. Every single experience is only a part of the whole sphere of its domain, but the absolute totality of all possible experience is itself not experience. Yet it is a necessary problem for reason, the mere representation of which requires concepts quite different from the pure concepts of the understanding, whose use is only *immanent,* or refers to experience, so far as it can be given. Whereas the concepts of reason aim at the completeness, that is, the collective unity of all possible experience, and thereby transcend every given experience. Thus they become *transcendent.*

As the understanding stands in need of categories for experience, reason contains in itself the source of Ideas, by which I mean necessary concepts whose object *cannot* be given in any experience. The latter are inherent in the nature of reason, as the former are in that of the understanding. While the former carry with them an illusion likely to mislead, the illusion of the latter is inevitable, though it certainly can be kept from misleading us.

Since all illusion consists in holding the subjective ground of our judgments to be objective, a self-knowledge of pure reason in its transcendent (presumptuous) use is the sole preservative from the aberrations into which reason falls when it mistakes its calling and transcendently refers to the object that which concerns only its own subject and its guidance in all immanent use.

§ 41. The distinction of Ideas—that is, of pure concepts of reason—from categories, or pure concepts of the understanding, as cognitions of a quite distinct species, origin, and use, is so important a point in founding a science which is to contain the system of all these *a priori* cognitions that, without this distinction, metaphysics is absolutely impossible or is at best a random, bungling attempt to build a castle in the air without a knowledge of the materials or of their fitness for this or any purpose. Had the *Critique of Pure Reason* done nothing but first point out this distinction, it would thereby have contributed more to clear up our conception of, and to guide our inquiry in, the field of metaphysics than all the vain efforts which had hitherto been made to satisfy the transcendent problems of pure reason, but which had never surmised that we were in quite another field than that of the understanding, and hence classed concepts of the understanding and those of reason together as if they were of the same kind.

§ 42. All pure cognitions of the understanding have this feature that their concepts present themselves in experience, and their principles can be confirmed by it; whereas the transcendent cognitions of reason cannot either, as Ideas, appear in experience or, as propositions, ever be confirmed or refuted by it. Hence whatever errors may slip in unawares can only be discovered by pure reason itself—a discovery of much difficulty, because this very reason naturally becomes dialectical by means of its Ideas; and this unavoidable illusion cannot be limited by any objective and dogmatic researches into things, but only by a subjective investigation of reason itself as a source of ideas.

*If we can say that a science is actual, at least in the idea of all men, as soon as it appears that the problems which lead to it are proposed to everybody by the nature of human reason, and that therefore many (though faulty) endeavors are unavoidably made in its behalf, then we are bound to say that metaphysics is subjectively (and indeed necessarily) actual, and therefore, we justly ask, how is it (objectively) possible.

§ 43. In the *Critique of Pure Reason* it was always my greatest care to endeavor, not only carefully to distinguish the several species of knowledge, but to derive concepts belonging to each one of them from their common source. I did this in order that, by knowing whence they originated, I might determine their use with safety and also have the unanticipated but invaluable advantage of knowing, according to principles, the completeness of my enumeration, classification, and specification of concepts *a priori*. Without this, metaphysics is mere rhapsody, in which no one knows whether he has enough or whether and where something is still wanting. We can indeed have this advantage only in pure philosophy, but of this philosophy it constitutes the very essence.

As I had found the origin of the categories in the four logical forms of all the judgments of the understanding, it was quite natural to seek the origin of the Ideas in the three forms of syllogisms. For as soon as these pure concepts of reason (the transcendental Ideas) are given, they could hardly, except they be held innate, be found anywhere else than in the same activity of reason, which, so far as it regards mere form, constitutes the logical element of syllogisms; but, so far as it represents judgments of the understanding as determined *a priori* with respect to one or another form, constitutes transcendental concepts of pure reason.

The formal distinction of syllogisms renders necessary their division into categorical, hypothetical, and disjunctive. The concepts of reason founded on them contain therefore, first, the Idea of the complete subject (the substantial); secondly, the Idea of the complete series of conditions; thirdly, the determination of all concepts in the Idea of a complete complex of that which is possible.* The first idea is psychological, the second cosmological, the third theological; and, as all three give occasion to dialectic, yet each in its own way, the division of the whole dialectic of pure reason into its paralogism, its antinomy, and its Ideal was arranged accordingly. Through this deduction we may feel assured that all the claims of pure reason are completely represented and that none can be wanting, because the faculty of reason itself, whence they all take their origin, is thereby completely surveyed.

§ 44. In these general considerations it is also remarkable that the Ideas of reason, unlike the categories, are of no service to the use of our understanding in experience, but quite dispensable, and become even an impediment to the maxims of a rational knowledge of nature. Yet in another aspect still to be determined they are necessary. Whether the soul is or is not a simple substance is of no consequence to us in the explanation of its phenomena. For we cannot render the concept of a simple being sensuous and thus concretely intelligible by any possible experience. The concept is therefore quite void as regards all hoped-for insight into the cause of appearances and cannot at all serve as a principle of the explanation of that which inner or outer experience supplies. Similarly, the cosmological Ideas of the beginning of the world or of its eternity (*a parte ante*) cannot be of any service to us for the explanation of any event in the world itself. And finally we must, according to a right maxim of the philosophy of nature, refrain from explaining the design of nature as drawn from the will of a Supreme Being, because this would not be natural philosophy but a confession that we have come to the end of it. The use of these Ideas, therefore, is quite dif-

---

*In disjunctive judgments, we consider all possibility as divided in respect to a particular concept. By the ontological principle of the universal determination of a thing in general, I understand the principle that either the one or the other of all possible contradictory predicates must be assigned to any object. This is, at the same time, the principle of all disjunctive judgments, constituting the foundation of a complete whole of possibility, and in it the possibility of every object in general is considered as determined. This may serve as a slight explanation of the above propositions: that the activity of reason in disjunctive syllogisms is formally the same as that by which it fashions the idea of a complete whole of all reality, containing in itself that which is positive in all pairs of contradictory predicates.

ferent from that of those categories by which (and by the principles built upon which) experience itself first becomes possible. But our laborious Analytic of the understanding would be superfluous if we had nothing else in view than the mere knowledge of nature as it can be given in experience; for reason does its work, both in mathematics and in the science of nature, quite safely and well without any of this subtle deduction. Therefore our critical examination of the understanding combines with the Ideas of pure reason for a purpose which lies beyond the empirical use of the understanding; but such an extended use of the understanding we have above declared to be totally inadmissible and without any object or meaning. Yet there must be a harmony between the nature of reason and that of the understanding, and the former must contribute to the perfection of the latter and cannot possibly upset it.

The solution of this question is as follows: Pure reason does not in its Ideas point to particular objects which lie beyond the field of experience, but only requires completeness of the use of the understanding in the system of experience. But this completeness can be a completeness of principles only, not of intuitions and of objects. In order, however, to represent the Ideas definitely, reason conceives them after the fashion of the knowledge of an object. This knowledge is, as far as these rules are concerned, completely determined; but the object is only an Idea [invented for the purpose of] bringing the knowledge of the understanding as near as possible to the completeness indicated by that Idea.

PREFATORY REMARK TO THE DIALECTIC OF PURE REASON

§ 45. We have shown in §§ 33 and 34 that the purity of the categories from all admixture of sensuous restrictions may mislead reason into extending their use beyond all experience to things in themselves; for though these categories themselves find no intuition which can give them meaning or sense *in concreto,* they, as mere logical functions, can represent a thing in general, but not give by themselves alone a determinate concept of anything. Such hyperbolical objects are distinguished by the appellation of *noumena,* or pure beings of the understanding (or better, beings of thought)—such as, for example, "substance"—but conceived without permanence in time, or "cause," but not acting in time, etc. Here predicates that only serve to make the conformity-to-law of experience possible are applied to these concepts, and yet they are deprived of all the conditions of intuition on which alone experience is possible, and so these concepts lose all significance.

There is no danger, however, of the understanding spontaneously making an excursion so very wantonly beyond its own bounds into the field of the mere beings of thought unless it is impelled by foreign laws. But when reason, which cannot be fully satisfied with any empirical use of the rules of the understanding, as being always conditioned, requires a completion of this chain of conditions, then the understanding is forced out of its sphere. And then it partly represents objects of experience in a series so extended that no experience can grasp it; partly even (with a view to complete the series) it seeks entirely beyond it *noumena,* to which it can attach that chain; and so, having at last escaped from the conditions of experience, it makes its stand as it were final. These are then the transcendental Ideas, which, in accord with the true but hidden ends of the natural destiny of our reason, aim, not at extravagant concepts, but at an unbounded extension of their empirical use, yet seduce the understanding by an unavoidable illusion to a transcendent use, which, though deceitful, cannot be restrained within the bounds of experience by any resolution, but only by scientific instruction and with much difficulty.

I. The Psychological Ideas*

§ 46. People have long since observed that in all substances the subject proper, that which remains after all the accidents (as predicates) are abstracted, consequently the *substantial,* remains unknown, and various complaints have been made concerning these limits to our knowledge. But it will be well to consider that the human understanding is not to be blamed for its inability to know the substance of things—that is, to determine it by itself—but rather for demanding definitely to know substance, which is a mere Idea, as though it were a given object. Pure reason requires us to seek for every predicate of a thing its own subject, and for this subject, which is itself necessarily nothing but a predicate, its subject, and so on indefinitely (or as far as we can reach). But hence it follows that we must not hold anything at which we can arrive to be an ultimate subject, and that substance itself never can be thought by our understanding, however deep we may penetrate, even if all nature were unveiled to us. For the specific nature of our understanding consists in thinking everything discursively, that is, by concepts, and so by mere predicates, to which, therefore, the absolute subject must always be wanting. Hence all the real properties by which we know bodies are mere accidents—not excepting even impenetrability, which we can only represent to ourselves as the effect of a power of which the subject is unknown to us.

Now we appear to have this substance in the consciousness of ourselves (in the thinking subject), and indeed in an immediate intuition; for all the predicates of an internal sense refer to the *ego,* as a subject, and I cannot conceive myself as the predicate of any other subject. Hence completeness in the reference of the given concepts as predicates to a subject—not merely an Idea, but an object—that is, the absolute subject itself, seems to be given in experience. But this expectation is disappointed. For the ego is not a concept,** but only the indication of the object of the inner sense, so far as we know it by no further predicate. Consequently it cannot indeed be itself a predicate of any other thing; but just as little can it be a definite concept of an absolute subject, but is, as in all other cases, only the reference of the inner phenomena to their unknown subject. Yet this idea (which serves very well as a regulative principle totally to destroy all materialistic explanations of the internal phenomena of the soul) occasions by a very natural misunderstanding a very specious argument, which infers its nature from this supposed knowledge of the substance of our thinking being. This is specious so far as the knowledge of it falls quite without the complex of experience.

§ 47. But though we may call this thinking self (the soul) "substance," as being the ultimate subject of thinking which cannot be further represented as the predicate of another thing, it remains quite empty and without significance if permanence—the quality which renders the concept of substances in experience fruitful—cannot be proved of it.

But permanence can never be proved of the concept of a substance as a thing in itself, but for the purposes of experience only. This is sufficiently shown by the first Analogy of Experience,*** and whoever will not yield to this proof may try for himself whether he can succeed in proving, from the concept of a subject which does not exist itself as the predicate of another thing, that its existence is absolutely permanent and that it cannot either in itself or by any natural cause originate or be annihilated.

---

*See *Critique of Pure Reason,* "The Paralogisms of Pure Reason."

**Were the representation of the apperception (the Ego) a concept, by which anything whatever could be thought, it could be used as a predicate of other things or contain predicates in itself. But it is nothing more than the feeling of an existence without the least concept and is only the representation of that to which all thinking stands in relation (*relatione accidentis*).

***In the *Critique of Pure Reason.*

These synthetical *a priori* propositions can never be proved in themselves, but only in reference to things as objects of possible experience.

§ 48. If, therefore, from the concept of the soul as a substance we would infer its permanence, this can hold good as regards possible experience only, not of the soul as a thing in itself and beyond all possible experience. Life is the subjective condition of all our possible experience; consequently we can only infer the permanence of the soul in life, for the death of a man is the end of all experience which concerns the soul as an object of experience, except the contrary be proved—which is the very question in hand. The permanence of the soul can therefore only be proved (and no one cares to do that) during the life of man, but not, as we desire to do, after death. The reason for this is that the concept of substance, so far as it is to be considered necessarily combined with the concept of permanence, can be so combined only according to the principles of possible experience, and therefore for the purposes of experience only.*

§ 49. That there is something real outside us which not only corresponds but must correspond to our outer perceptions can likewise be proved to be, not a connection of things in themselves, but for the sake of experience. This means that there is something empirical, that is, some appearance in space without us, that admits of a satisfactory proof; for we have nothing to do with other objects than those which belong to possible experience, because objects which cannot be given us in any experience are nothing for us. Empirically outside me is that which is intuited in space; and space, together with all the appearances it contains, belongs to the representations whose connection, according to laws of experience, proves their objective truth, just as the connection of the appearances of the inner sense proves the actuality of my soul (as an object of the inner sense). By means of outer experience I am conscious of the actuality of bodies as external appearances in space, in the same manner as by means of the inner experience I am conscious of the existence of my soul in time; but this soul is known only as an object of the inner sense by appearances that constitute an inner state and of which the being in itself, which forms the basis of these appearances, is unknown. Cartesian idealism therefore does nothing but distinguish outer experience from a dream and the conformity to law (as a criterion of its truth) of the former from the irregularity and false illusion of the latter. In both it presupposes space and time as conditions of the existence of objects, and it only inquires whether the objects of the outer senses which we, when awake, put in space, are as actually to be found in it as the object of the internal sense, the soul, is in time; that is, whether experience carries with it sure criteria to distinguish it from imagination. This doubt, however, may easily be disposed of, and we always do so in common life by investigating the connection of

---

*It is indeed very remarkable how carelessly metaphysicians have always passed over the principle of the permanence of substances without ever attempting a proof of it; doubtless because they found themselves abandoned by all proofs as soon as they began to deal with the concept of substance. Common sense, which felt distinctly that without this presupposition no union of perceptions in experience is possible, supplied the want by a postulate. From experience itself it never could derive such a principle, partly because material things (substances) cannot be so traced in all their alterations and dissolutions that the matter can always be found undiminished, partly because the principle contains *necessity*, which is always the sign of an *a priori* principle. People then boldly applied this postulate to the concept of soul as a *substance*, and concluded a necessary continuance of the soul after the death of man (especially as the simplicity of this substance, which is inferred from the indivisibility of consciousness, secured it from destruction by dissolution). Had they found the genuine source of this principle—a discovery which requires deeper researches than they were ever inclined to make—they would have seen that the law of the permanence of substances arises for the purposes of experience only, and hence can hold good of things so far as they are to be known and conjoined with others in experience, but never independently of all possible experience, and consequently cannot hold good of the soul after death.

appearances in both space and time according to universal laws of experience, and we cannot doubt, when the representation of external things throughout agrees therewith that they constitute truthful experience. Material idealism, in which appearances are considered as such only according to their connection in experience may accordingly be very easily refuted; and it is just as sure an experience that bodies exist outside us (in space) as that I myself exist according to the representation of the inner sense (in time), for the concept "outside us" only signifies existence in space. However, as the Ego in the proposition "I am" means not only the object of inner intuition (in time) but the subject of consciousness, just as body means not only outer intuition (in space) but the thing in itself which is the basis of this appearance, then the question whether bodies (as appearances of the outer sense) exist as bodies in nature apart from my thoughts may without any hesitation be denied. But the question whether I myself as an appearance of the inner sense (the soul according to empirical psychology) exist apart from my faculty of representation in time is an exactly similar one and must likewise be answered in the negative. And in this manner everything, when it is reduced to its true meaning, is decided and certain. The formal (which I have also called "transcendental") actually abolishes the material, or Cartesian, idealism. For if space be nothing but a form of my sensibility, it is as a representation in me just as actual as I myself am, and nothing but the empirical truth of the appearances in it remains for consideration. But if this is not the case, if space and the appearances in it are something existing outside us, then all the criteria of experience besides our perception can never prove the actuality of these objects outside us.

II. The Cosmological Ideas*

§ 50. This product of pure reason in its transcendent use is its most remarkable phenomenon. It serves as a very powerful agent to rouse philosophy from its dogmatic slumber and to stimulate it to the arduous task of undertaking a critical examination of reason itself.

I term this Idea cosmological because it always takes its object only in the sensible world and does not need any other world than one whose object is given to sense; consequently it remains in this respect in its native home, does not become transcendent, and is therefore so far not an Idea; whereas to conceive the soul as a simple substance, on the contrary, means to conceive such an object (the simple) as cannot be presented to the senses. Yet, in spite of this, the cosmological idea extends the connection of the conditioned with its condition (whether this is mathematical or dynamical) so far that experience never can keep up with it. It is therefore with regard to this point always an Idea, whose object never can be adequately given in any experience.

§ 51. In the first place, the use of a system of categories becomes here so obvious and unmistakable that, even if there were not several other proofs of it, this alone would sufficiently prove it indispensable in the system of pure reason. There are only four such transcendent Ideas, as many as there are classes of categories; in each of which, however, they refer only to the absolute completeness of the series of the conditions for a given conditioned. In accordance with these cosmological Ideas, there are only four kinds of dialectical assertions of pure reason, which, being dialectical, prove that to each of them, on equally specious principles of pure reason, a contradictory assertion stands opposed. As all the metaphysical art of the most subtle distinction cannot prevent this opposition, it compels the philosopher to recur to the first sources of

---

*Cf. *Critique of Pure Reason,* "The Antinomy of Pure Reason."

pure reason itself. This antinomy, not arbitrarily invented but founded in the nature of human reason, and hence unavoidable and never ceasing, contains the following four theses together with their antitheses:

1
Thesis
The world has, as to time and space, a beginning (limit).

Antithesis
The world is, as to time and space, infinite.

2
Thesis
Everything in the world consists of [elements that are] simple.

Antithesis
There is nothing simple, but everything is composite.

3
Thesis
There are in the world causes through freedom.

Antithesis
There is no freedom, but all is nature.

4
Thesis
In the series of the world-causes there is some necessary being.

Antithesis
There is nothing necessary in the world, but in this series all is contingent.

§ 52*a*. Here is the most singular phenomenon of human reason, no other instance of which can be shown in any other use of reason. If we, as is commonly done, represent to ourselves the appearances of the sensible world as things in themselves, if we assume the principles of their combination as principles universally valid of things in themselves and not merely of experience, as is usually, nay, without our *Critique* unavoidably, done, there arises an unexpected conflict which never can be removed in the common dogmatic way; because the thesis, as well as the antithesis, can be shown by equally clear, evident, and irresistible proofs—for I pledge myself as to the correctness of all these proofs—and reason therefore perceives that it is divided against itself, a state at which the skeptic rejoices, but which must make the critical philosopher pause and feel ill at ease.

§ 52*b*. We may blunder in various ways in metaphysics without any fear of being detected in falsehood. If we but avoid self-contradiction, which in synthetical though purely fictitious propositions is quite possible, then whenever the concepts which we connect are mere Ideas that cannot be given (with respect to their whole content) in experience, we cannot be refuted by experience. For how can we make out by experience whether the world is from eternity or had a beginning, whether matter is infinitely divisible or consists of simple parts? Such concepts cannot be given in any experience, however extensive, and consequently the falsehood either of the affirmative or the negative proposition cannot be discovered by this touchstone.

The only possible way in which reason could have revealed unintentionally its secret dialectic, falsely announced as its dogmatics, would be when it were made to ground an assertion upon a universally admitted principle and to deduce the exact contrary with the greatest accuracy of inference from another which is equally granted. This is actually here the case with regard to four natural Ideas of reason, whence four assertions on the one side and as many counterassertions on the other arise, each consistently following from universally acknowledged principles. Thus they reveal, by the use of these principles, the dialectical illusion of pure reason, which would otherwise forever remain concealed.

This is therefore a decisive experiment, which must necessarily expose any error lying hidden in the assumptions of reason.* Contradictory propositions cannot both be false, except the concept on which each is founded is self-contradictory; for example, the propositions, "A square circle is round," and "A square circle is not round," are both false. For, as to the former, it is false that the circle is round because it is quadrangular; and it is likewise false that it is not round, that is, angular, because it is a circle. For the logical criterion of the impossibility of a concept consists in this that, if we presuppose it, two contradictory propositions both become false; consequently, as no middle between them is conceivable, nothing at all is thought by that concept.

§ 52c. The first two antinomies, which I call mathematical because they are concerned with the addition or division of the homogeneous, are founded on such a contradictory concept; and hence I explain how it happens that both the thesis and antithesis of the two are false.

When I speak of objects in time and in space, it is not of things in themselves, of which I know nothing, but of things in appearance, that is, of experience, as the particular way of knowing objects which is afforded to man. I must not say of what I think in time or in space, that in itself, and independent of these my thoughts, it exists in space and in time, for in that case I should contradict myself; because space and time, together with the appearances in them, are nothing existing in themselves and outside of my representations, but are themselves only modes of representation, and it is palpably contradictory to say that a mere mode of representation exists without our representation. Objects of the senses therefore exist only in experience, whereas to give them a self-subsisting existence apart from experience or before it is merely to represent to ourselves that experience actually exists apart from experience or before it.

Now if I inquire into the magnitude of the world, as to space and time, it is equally impossible, as regards all my concepts, to declare it infinite or to declare it finite. For neither assertion can be contained in experience, because experience either of an infinite space or of an infinite elapsed time, or again, of the boundary of the world by a void space or by an antecedent void time, is impossible; these are mere Ideas. The magnitude of the world, decided either way, would therefore have to exist in the world itself apart from all experience. But this contradicts the concept of a world of sense, which is merely a complex of the appearances whose existence and connection occur only in our representations, that is, in experience; since this latter is not an object in itself but a mere mode of representation. Hence it follows that, as the concept of an ab-

---

*I therefore would be pleased to have the critical reader to devote to this antinomy of pure reason his chief attention, because nature itself seems to have established it with a view to stagger reason in its daring pretensions and to force it to self-examination. For every proof which I have given of both thesis and antithesis I undertake to be responsible, and thereby to show the certainty of the inevitable antinomy of reason. When the reader is brought by this curious phenomenon to fall back upon the proof of the presumption upon which it rests, he will feel himself obliged to investigate the ultimate foundation of all knowledge by pure reason with me more thoroughly.

solutely existing world of sense is self-contradictory, the solution of the problem concerning its magnitude, whether attempted affirmatively or negatively, is always false.

The same holds of the second antinomy, which relates to the division of appearances. For these are mere representations; and the parts exist merely in their representation, consequently in the division—that is, in a possible experience in which they are given—and the division reaches only as far as the possible experience reaches. To assume that an appearance, for example, that of body, contains in itself before all experience all the parts which any possible experience can ever reach is to impute to a mere appearance, which can exist only in experience, an existence previous to experience. In other words, it would mean that mere representations exist before they can be found in our faculty of representation. Such an assertion is self-contradictory, as also every solution of our misunderstood problem, whether we maintain that bodies in themselves consist of an infinite number of parts or of a finite number of simple parts.

§ 53. In the first (the mathematical) class of antinomies the falsehood of the presupposition consists in representing in one concept something self-contradictory as if it were compatible (that is, an appearance as a thing in itself). But, as to the second (the dynamical) class of antinomies, the falsehood of the presupposition consists in representing as contradictory what is compatible; so that while in the former case the opposed assertions were both false, in this case, on the other hand, where they are opposed to one another by mere misunderstanding, they may both be true.

Any mathematical connection necessarily presupposes homogeneity of what is connected (in the concept of magnitude), while the dynamical one by no means requires this. When we have to deal with extended magnitudes all the parts must be homogeneous with one another and with the whole, whereas in the connection of cause and effect homogeneity may indeed likewise be found but is not necessary; for the concept of causality (by means of which something is posited through something else quite different from it) does not in the least require it.

If the objects of the world of sense are taken for things in themselves and the above laws of nature for laws of things in themselves, the contradiction would be unavoidable. So also, if the subject of freedom were, like other objects, represented as mere appearance, the contradiction would be just as unavoidable; for the same predicate would at once be affirmed and denied of the same kind of object in the same sense. But if natural necessity is referred merely to appearances and freedom merely to things in themselves, no contradiction arises if we at the same time assume or admit both kinds of causality, however difficult or impossible it may be to make the latter kind conceivable.

In appearance every effect is an event, or something that happens in time; it must, according to the universal law of nature, be preceded by a determination of the causal act of its cause—this determination being a state of the cause—which it follows according to a constant law. But this determination of the cause to a causal act must likewise be something that takes place or happens; the cause must have begun to act, otherwise no succession between it and the effect could be conceived. Otherwise the effect, as well as the causal act of the cause, would have always existed. Therefore the determination of the cause to act must also have originated among appearances and must consequently, like its effect, be an event, which must again have its cause, and so on; hence natural necessity must be the condition on which efficient causes are determined. Whereas if freedom is to be a property of certain causes of appearances, it must, as regards these, which are events, be a faculty of starting them spontaneously. That is, it would not require that the causal act of the cause should itself begin [in time], and hence it would not require any other ground to determine its start. But then the cause, as to its causal act, could not rank under time-determinations of its state; that is, it could not be an appearance, but would have to be considered a thing in itself, while only its effects would be appearances.* If without contradiction we can think of the beings of understanding as exercising such an influence on appearances, then natural necessity will attach to all connections of cause and effect in the sensuous world; though, on the other hand, freedom can be granted to the cause which is itself not an appearance (but the foundation of appearance). Nature and freedom therefore can without contradiction be attributed to the very same thing, but in different relations—on one side as an appearance, on the other as a thing in itself.

We have in us a faculty which not only stands in connection with its subjective determining grounds [motives] which are the natural causes of its actions and is so far the faculty of a being that itself belongs to appearances, but is also related to objective grounds which are only Ideas so far as they can determine this faculty. This connection is expressed by the word *ought.* This faculty is called "reason," and, so far as we consider a being (man) entirely according to this objectively determinable reason, he cannot be considered as a being of sense; this property is a property of a thing in itself, a property whose possibility we cannot comprehend. I mean we cannot comprehend how the *ought* should determine (even if it never has actually determined) its activity and could become the cause of actions whose effect is an appearance in the sensible world. Yet the causality of reason would be freedom with regard to the effects in the sensuous world, so far as we can consider *objective grounds,* which are themselves Ideas, as their determinants. For its action in that case would not depend upon subjective conditions, consequently not upon those of time, and of course not upon the law of nature which serves to determine them, because grounds of reason give the rule universally to actions, according to principles, without influence of the circumstances of either time or place.

What I adduce here is merely meant as an example to make the thing intelligible and does not necessarily belong to our problem, which must be decided from mere concepts independently of the properties which we meet in the actual world.

Now I may say without contradiction that all the actions of rational beings, so far as they are appearances (met with in any experience), are subject to the necessity of nature, but the very same actions, as regards merely the rational subject and its faculty of acting according to mere reason, are free. For what is required for the necessity of nature? Nothing more than the determinability of every event in the world of sense according to constant laws, that is, a reference to cause in the [world of] appearance; in this process the thing in itself at its foundation and its causality remain unknown. But, I say, the law of nature remains, whether the rational being is the cause of the effects in the sensuous world from reason—that is, through freedom—or whether it does not determine them on grounds of reason. For if the former is the case, the action is performed according to maxims, the effect of which as appearance is always conformable to constant laws; if the latter is the case, and the action not performed on principles of reason, it is subjected to the empirical laws of the sensibility, and in both cases the effects are connected according to constant laws; more than this we do not require or know concerning natural necessity. But in the former case reason is the cause of these

---

*The Idea of freedom occurs only in the relation of the intellectual, as cause, to the appearance, as effect. Hence we cannot attribute freedom to matter in regard to the incessant action by which it fills its space, though this action takes place from an internal principle. We can likewise find no notion of freedom suitable to purely rational beings, for instance, to God, so far as his action is immanent. For his action, though independent of external determining causes, is determined in his eternal reason, that is, in the divine *nature.* It is only if *something is to start* by an action, and so the effect occurs in the sequence of time, or in the world of sense (for example, the beginning of the world), that we can put the question whether the causal act of the cause must in its turn have been started or whether the cause can originate an effect without its causal act itself beginning. In the former case, the concept of this activity is a concept of natural necessity; in the latter, that of freedom. From this the reader will see that as I explained freedom to be the faculty of starting an event spontaneously, I have exactly hit the concept which is the problem of metaphysics.

laws of nature, and therefore free; in the latter, the effects follow according to mere natural laws of sensibility, because reason does not influence it. But reason itself is not determined on that account by the sensibility (which is impossible) and is therefore free in this case too. Freedom is therefore no hindrance to natural law in appearances; neither does this law abrogate the freedom of the practical use of reason, which is connected with things in themselves, as determining grounds.

Thus practical freedom, namely, the freedom in which reason possesses causality according to objectively determining grounds, is rescued; and yet natural necessity is not in the least curtailed with regard to the very same effects, as appearances. The same remarks will serve to explain what we had to say concerning transcendental freedom and its compatibility with natural necessity in the same subject, but not taken in the same context. For, as to this, every beginning of the action of a being from objective causes regarded as determining grounds is always a *first beginning,* though the same action is in the series of appearances only a *subordinate beginning,* which must be preceded by a state of the cause which determines it and is itself determined in the same manner by another immediately preceding. Thus we are able, in rational beings, or in beings generally so far as their causality is determined in them as things in themselves, to think of a faculty of beginning from themselves a series of states without falling into contradiction with the laws of nature. For the relation of the action to objective grounds of reason is not a time relation; in this case that which determines the causality does not precede in time the action, because such determining grounds represent, not a reference to objects of sense, for example, to causes in the appearances, but to determining causes as things in themselves, which do not fall under conditions of time. And in this way the action, with regard to the causality of reason, can be considered as a first beginning, while in respect to the series of appearances as merely a subordinate beginning. We may therefore without contradiction consider it in the former aspect as free, but in the latter (as it is merely appearance) as subject to natural necessity.

As to the fourth antinomy, it is solved in the same way as the conflict of reason with itself in the third. For, provided the cause *in* the appearance is distinguished from the cause *of* the appearances (so far as it can be thought as a thing in itself), both propositions are perfectly reconcilable: the one, that there is nowhere in the sensuous world a cause (according to similar laws of causality) whose existence is absolutely necessary; the other, that this world is nevertheless connected with a necessary being as its cause (but of another kind and according to another law). The incompatibility of these propositions rests entirely upon the mistake of extending what is valid merely of appearances to things in themselves and in confusing both in one concept.

§ 54. This, then, is the exposition, and this the solution of the whole antinomy in which reason finds itself involved in the application of its principles to the sensible world. The former alone (the mere exposition) would be a considerable service in the cause of our knowledge of human reason, even though the solution might fail fully to satisfy the reader, who has here to combat a natural illusion which has been but recently exposed to him and which he had hitherto always regarded as genuine. For one result at least is unavoidable. As it is quite impossible to prevent this conflict of reason with itself—so long as the objects of the sensible world are taken for things in themselves and not for mere appearances, which they are in fact—the reader is thereby compelled to examine over again the deduction of all our *a priori* knowledge and the proof which I have given of my deduction in order to come to a decision on the question. This is all I require at present; for when in this occupation he shall have thought himself deep enough into the nature of pure reason, those concepts by which alone the solution of the conflict of reason is possible will become sufficiently familiar to him. Without this preparation, I cannot expect an unreserved assent even from the most attentive reader.

III. The Theological Idea*

§ 55. The third transcendental Idea, which affords matter for the most important but (if pursued only speculatively) transcendent and thereby dialectical use of reason, is the Ideal of pure reason. Reason in this case does not, as with the psychological and the cosmological Ideas, begin from experience and err by exaggerating its grounds in striving to attain, if possible, the absolute completeness of their series. Rather, it totally breaks with experience and from mere concepts of what constitutes the absolute completeness of a thing in general; and thus, by means of the Idea of a most perfect primal Being, it proceeds to determine the possibility and therefore the actuality of all other things. And so the mere presupposition of a Being conceived, not in the series of experience yet for the purposes of experience, for the sake of comprehending its connection, order, and unity—in a word, the Idea—is more easily distinguished from the concept of the understanding here than in the former cases. Hence we can easily expose the dialectical illusion which arises from our making the subjective conditions of our thinking objective conditions of objects themselves, and from making an hypothesis necessary for the satisfaction of our reason into a dogma. As the observations of the *Critique* on the pretensions of transcendental theology are intelligible, clear, and decisive, I have nothing more to add on the subject.

General Remark on the Transcendental Ideas

§ 56. The objects which are given us by experience are in many respects incomprehensible, and many questions to which the law of nature leads us when carried beyond a certain point (though still quite conformably to the laws of nature) admit of no answer. An example is the question: Why do material things attract one another? But if we entirely quit nature or, in pursuing its combinations, exceed all possible experience, and so enter the realm of mere Ideas, we cannot then say that the object is incomprehensible and that the nature of things proposes to us insoluble problems. For we are not then concerned with nature or even with given objects, but with mere concepts which have their origin solely in our reason, and with mere beings of thought; and all the problems that arise from our concepts of them must be solved, because of course reason can and must give a full account of its own procedure.** As the psychological, cosmological, and theological Ideas are nothing but pure concepts of reason which cannot be given in any experience, the questions which reason asks us about them are put to us, not by the objects, but by mere maxims of our reason for the sake of its own satisfaction. They must all be capable of satisfactory answers, which are given by showing that they are principles which bring our use of the understanding into thorough agreement, completeness, and synthetical unity, and that they thus hold good of experience only, but of experience as a whole.

Although an absolute whole of experience is impossible, the Idea of a whole of knowledge according to principles must impart to our knowledge a peculiar kind of

---

*Cf. *Critique of Pure Reason,* "The Transcendental Ideal."

**Herr Platner, in his *Aphorismen,* acutely says (§§ 728, 729), "If reason be a criterion, no concept which is incomprehensible to human reason can be possible. Incomprehensibility has place in what is actual only. Here incomprehensibility arises from the insufficiency of the acquired ideas." It sounds paradoxical, but is otherwise not strange to say that in nature there is much that is incomprehensible (for example, the faculty of reproduction); but if we mount still higher and go even beyond nature, everything again becomes comprehensible. For we then quit entirely the objects which can be given us and occupy ourselves merely about Ideas, in which occupation we can easily comprehend the law that reason prescribes by them to the understanding for its use in experience, because the law is the reason's own production.

unity, that of a system, without which it is nothing but piecework and cannot be used for proving the existence of a highest purpose (which can only be the general system of all purposes). I do not here refer only to the practical, but also to the highest purpose of the speculative use of reason.

The transcendental Ideas therefore express the peculiar vocation of reason as a principle of systematic unity in the use of the understanding. Yet if we assume this unity of the mode of knowledge to pertain to the object of knowledge, if we regard that which is merely *regulative* to be *constitutive,* and if we persuade ourselves that we can by means of these Ideas widen our knowledge transcendently or far beyond all possible experience, while it only serves to render experience within itself as nearly complete as possible, that is, to limit its progress by nothing that cannot belong to experience—if we do this, I say—we suffer from a mere misunderstanding in our estimate of the proper role of our reason and of its principles, and a dialectic arises which both confuses the empirical use of reason and sets reason at variance with itself.

CONCLUSION

On the Determination of the Bounds of Pure Reason

§ 57. Having adduced the clearest arguments, it would be absurd for us to hope that we can know more of any object than belongs to the possible experience of it or lay claim to the least knowledge of anything not assumed to be an object of possible experience which would determine it according to the constitution it has in itself. For how could we determine anything in this way, since time, space, and all the concepts of the understanding, and still more all the concepts formed by empirical intuition (perception) in the sensible world, have and can have no other use than to make experience possible? And if this condition is omitted from the pure concepts of the understanding, they do not determine any object and have no meaning whatever.

But it would be, on the other hand, a still greater absurdity if we conceded no things in themselves or set up our experience as the only possible mode of knowing things, our intuition of them in space and in time for the only possible intuition and our discursive understanding for the archetype of every possible understanding; for this would be to wish to have the principles of the possibility of experience considered universal conditions of things in themselves.

Our principles, which limit the use of reason to possible experience, might in this way become transcendent and the limits of our reason be set up as limits of the possibility of things in themselves (as Hume's *Dialogues* may illustrate) if a careful critique did not guard the bounds of our reason with respect to its empirical use and set a limit to its pretensions. Skepticism originally arose from metaphysics and its anarchic dialectic. At first it might, merely to favor the empirical use of reason, announce everything that transcends this use as worthless and deceitful; but by and by, when it was perceived that the very same principles that are used in experience insensibly and apparently with the same right led still further than experience extends, then men began to doubt even the principles of experience. But here there is no danger, for common sense will doubtless always assert its rights. A certain confusion, however, arose in science, which cannot determine how far reason is to be trusted, and why only so far and no farther; and this confusion can only be cleared up and all future relapses obviated by a formal determination, on principle, of the boundary of the use of our reason.

We cannot indeed, beyond all possible experience, form a definite concept of what things in themselves may be. Yet we are not at liberty to abstain entirely from inquiring into them; for experience never satisfies reason fully but, in answering questions, refers us further and further back and leaves us dissatisfied with regard to their complete solution. This anyone may gather from the dialectic of pure reason, which therefore has its good subjective grounds. Having acquired, as regards the nature of our soul, a clear conception of the subject, and having come to the conviction that its manifestations cannot be explained materialistically, who can refrain from asking what the soul really is and, if no concept of experience suffices for the purpose, from accounting for it by a concept of reason (that of a simple immaterial being), though we cannot by any means prove its objective reality? Who can satisfy himself with mere empirical knowledge in all the cosmological questions of the duration and of the magnitude of the world, of freedom or of natural necessity, since every answer given on principles of experience begets a fresh question, which likewise requires its answer and thereby clearly shows the insufficiency of all physical modes of explanation to satisfy reason? Finally, who does not see in the thoroughgoing contingency and dependence of all his thoughts and assumptions on mere principles of experience the impossibility of stopping there? And who does not feel himself compelled, notwithstanding all interdictions against losing himself in transcendent Ideas, to seek rest and contentment, beyond all the concepts which he can vindicate by experience, in the concept of a Being the possibility of the Idea of which cannot be conceived but at the same time cannot be refuted, because it relates to a mere being of the understanding and without it reason must needs remain forever dissatisfied?

Bounds (in extended beings) always presuppose a space existing outside a certain definite place and inclosing it; limits do not require this, but are mere negations which affect a quantity so far as it is not absolutely complete. But our reason, as it were, sees in its surroundings a space for knowledge of things in themselves, though we can never have definite concepts of them and are limited to appearances only.

As long as the knowledge of reason is homogeneous, definite bounds to it are inconceivable. In mathematics and in natural philosophy, human reason admits of limits but not of bounds, namely, it admits that something indeed lies without it, at which it can never arrive, but not that it will at any point find completion in its internal progress. The enlarging of our views in mathematics and the possibility of new discoveries are infinite; and the same is the case with the discovery of new properties of nature, of new powers and laws, by continued experience and its rational combination. But limits cannot be mistaken here, for mathematics refers to appearances only, and what cannot be an object of sensuous intuition, such as the concepts of metaphysics and of morals, lies entirely without its sphere; it can never lead to them, but neither does it require them. There is, therefore, not a continual progress and approximation towards these sciences, and there is not, as it were, any point or line of contact. Natural science will never reveal to us the internal constitution of things, which, though not appearance, yet can serve as the ultimate ground for explaining appearances. Nor does that science require this for its physical explanations. Nay, even if such grounds should be offered from other sources (for instance, the influence of immaterial beings), they must be rejected and not used in the progress of its explanations. For these explanations must only be grounded upon that which as an object of sense can belong to experience, and be brought into connection with our actual perceptions and empirical laws.

But metaphysics leads us towards bounds in the dialectical attempts of pure reason (not undertaken arbitrarily or wantonly, but stimulated thereto by the nature of reason itself). And the transcendental Ideas, as they do not admit of evasion but are never capable of realization, serve to point out to us actually not only the bounds of the pure use of reason, but also the way to determine them. Such is the end and the use of this natural predisposition of our reason, which has brought forth metaphysics as its favorite child, whose generation, like every other in the world, is not to be ascribed to blind chance but to an original germ, wisely organized for great ends. For metaphysics, in its fundamental features, perhaps more than any other science, is placed in us by nature itself and cannot be considered the production of an arbitrary choice or a casual enlargement in the progress of experience from which it is quite disparate.

Reason through all its concepts and laws of the understanding which are sufficient to it for empirical use, that is, within the sensible world, finds in it no satisfaction, because ever-recurring questions deprive us of all hope of their complete solution. The transcendental Ideas which have that completion in view are such problems of reason. But it sees clearly that the sensuous world cannot contain this completion; neither, consequently, can all the concepts which serve merely for understanding the world of sense, for example, space and time, and what we have adduced under the name of pure concepts of the understanding. The sensuous world is nothing but a chain of appearances connected according to universal laws; it has therefore no subsistence by itself; it is not the thing in itself, and consequently must point to that which contains the basis of this appearance, to beings which cannot be known merely as appearances, but as things in themselves. In the knowledge of them alone can reason hope to satisfy its desire for completeness in proceeding from the conditioned to its conditions.

We have above (§§ 33 and 34) indicated the limits of reason with regard to all knowledge of mere beings of thought. Now, since the transcendental Ideas have made it necessary to approach them and thus have led us, as it were, to the spot where the occupied space (namely, experience) touches the void (that of which we can know nothing, namely, *noumena*), we can determine the bounds of pure reason. For in all bounds there is something positive (for example, a surface is the boundary of corporeal space, and is therefore itself a space; a line is a space, which is the boundary of the surface, a point the boundary of the line, but yet always a place in space), but limits contain mere negations. The limits pointed out in those paragraphs are not enough after we have discovered that beyond them there still lies something (though we can never know what it is in itself). For the question now is, What is the attitude of our reason in this connection of what we know with what we do not, and never shall, know? This is an actual connection of a known thing with one quite unknown (and which will always remain so), and though what is unknown should not become in the least more known—which we cannot even hope—yet the concept of this connection must be definite and capable of being rendered distinct.

We must therefore think an immaterial being, a world of understanding, and a Supreme Being (all mere *noumena*), because in them only, as things in themselves, reason finds that completion and satisfaction which it can never hope for in the derivation of appearances from their homogeneous grounds, and because these actually have reference to something distinct from them (and totally heterogeneous), as appearances always presuppose an object in itself and therefore suggest its existence whether we can know more of it or not.

But as we can never know these beings of understanding as they are in themselves, that is, as definite, yet must assume them as regards the sensible world and connect them with it by reason, we are at least able to think this connection by means of such concepts as express their relation to the world of sense. If we represent to ourselves a being of the understanding by nothing but pure concepts of the understanding, we then indeed represent nothing definite to ourselves, and consequently our concept has no significance; but if we think of it by properties borrowed from the sensuous world, it is no longer a being of understanding, but is conceived phenomenally and belongs to the sensible world. Let us take an instance from the notion of the Supreme Being.

The deistic conception is a quite pure concept of reason, but represents only a thing containing all reality, without being able to determine any one reality [in it]; because for that purpose an example must be taken from the world of sense, in which case I should have an object of sense only, not something quite heterogeneous which can never be an object of sense. Suppose I attribute to the Supreme Being understanding, for instance; I have no concept of an understanding other than my own, one that must receive its intuitions by the senses and which is occupied in bringing them under rules of the unity of consciousness. Then the elements of my concept would always lie in the appearance; I should, however, by the insufficiency of the appearance have to go beyond them to the concept of a being which neither depends upon appearances nor is bound up with them as conditions of its determination. But if I separate understanding from sensibility to obtain a pure understanding, then nothing remains but the mere form of thinking without intuition, by which form alone I can know nothing definite and consequently no object. For that purpose I should finally have to conceive another understanding, such as would intuit its objects but of which I have not the least concept, because the human understanding is discursive and can know only by means of general concepts. And the very same difficulties arise if we attribute a will to the Supreme Being, for I have this concept only by drawing it from my inner experience, and therefore from my dependence for satisfaction upon objects whose existence I require; and so the concept rests upon sensibility, which is absolutely incompatible with the pure concept of the Supreme Being.

Hume's objections to deism are weak, and affect only the proofs and not the deistic assertion itself. But as regards theism, which depends on a stricter determination of the concept of the Supreme Being, which in deism is merely transcendent, they are very strong and, as this concept is formed, in certain (in fact in all common) cases irrefutable. Hume always insists that by the mere concept of an original being to which we apply only ontological predicates (eternity, omnipresence, omnipotence) we think nothing definite, and that properties which could yield a concept *in concreto* would have to be superadded. He further insists that it is not enough to say it is cause, but we must explain the nature of its causality, for example, that it is that of an understanding and of a will. He then begins his attacks on the essential point itself, that is, theism, as he had previously directed his battery only against the proofs of deism, an attack which is not very dangerous to it in its consequences. All his dangerous arguments refer to anthropomorphism, which he holds to be inseparable from theism and to make it contradictory in itself; but if the former be abandoned, the latter must vanish with it and nothing remain but deism, of which nothing can come, which is of no value and which cannot serve as any foundation to religion or morals. If this anthropomorphism were really unavoidable, no proofs whatever of the existence of a Supreme Being, even were they all granted, could determine for us the concept of this Being without involving us in contradictions.

If we connect with the command to avoid all transcendent judgments of pure reason the command (which apparently conflicts with it) to proceed to concepts that lie beyond the field of its immanent (empirical) use, we discover that both can subsist together, but only at the boundary of all permitted use of reason. For this boundary belongs to the field of experience as well as to that of the beings of thought, and we are thereby taught how these so remarkable Ideas serve merely for marking the bounds of human reason. On the one hand, they give warning not boundlessly to extend knowledge of experience, as if nothing but world remained for us to know, and yet, on the other hand, not to transgress the bounds of experience and to think of judging about things beyond them as things in themselves.

But we stop at this boundary if we limit our judgment merely to the relation which the world may have to a Being whose very concept lies beyond all the knowledge which we can attain within the world. For we then do not attribute to the Supreme Being any of the properties in themselves by which we represent objects of experience, and thereby avoid *dogmatic* anthropomorphism; but we attribute them to the relation of this Being to the world and allow ourselves a *symbolical* anthropomorphism, which in fact concerns language only and not the object itself.

If I say that we are compelled to consider the world *as if* it were the work of a Supreme Understanding and Will, I really say nothing more than that a watch, a ship, a regiment, bears the same relation to the watchmaker, the shipbuilder, the commanding officer as the world of sense (or whatever constitutes the substratum of this complex of appearances) does to the unknown, which I do not hereby know as it is in itself but as it is for me, that is, in relation to the world of which I am a part.

§ 58. Such a cognition is one of analogy and does not signify (as is commonly understood) an imperfect similarity of two things, but a perfect similarity of relations between two quite dissimilar things.* By means of this analogy, however, there remains a concept of the Supreme Being sufficiently determined *for us,* though we have left out everything that could determine it absolutely or *in itself;* for we determine it as regards the world and hence as regards ourselves, and more do we not require. The attacks which Hume makes upon those who would determine this concept absolutely, by taking the materials for so doing from themselves and the world, do not affect us; and he cannot object to us that we have nothing left if we give up the objective anthropomorphism of the concept of the Supreme Being.

For let us assume at the outset (as Hume in his *Dialogues* makes Philo grant Cleanthes), as a necessary hypothesis, the deistic concept of the First Being, in which this Being is thought by the mere ontological predicates of substance, of cause, and so on. This must be done because reason, actuated in the sensible world by mere conditions which are themselves always conditional, cannot otherwise have any satisfaction; and it therefore can be done without falling into anthropomorphism (which transfers predicates from the world of sense to a Being quite distinct from the world) because those predicates are mere categories which, though they do not give a determinate concept of that Being, yet give a concept not limited to any conditions of sensibility. Thus nothing can prevent our predicating of this Being a causality through reason with regard to the world, and thus passing to theism, without being obliged to attribute to this Being itself this kind of reason, as a property inherent in it. For as to the former, the only possible way of prosecuting the use of reason (as regards all possible experience in complete harmony with itself) in the world of sense to the highest point is to assume a supreme reason as a cause of all the connections in the world. Such a principle must

---

*There is, for example, an analogy between the juridical relation of human actions and the mechanical relation of moving forces. I never can do anything to another man without giving him a right to do the same to me on the same conditions; just as no mass can act with its moving forces on another mass without thereby occasioning the other to react equally against it. Here right and moving force are quite dissimilar things, but in their relation there is complete similarity. By means of such an analogy, I can obtain a notion of the relation of things which absolutely are unknown to me. For instance, as the promotion of the welfare of children (= a) is to the love of parents (= b), so the welfare of the human species (= c) is to that unknown character in God (= x), which we call love; not as if it had the least similarity to any human inclination, but because we can suppose its relation to the world to be similar to that which things of the world bear one another. But the concept of relation in this case is a mere category, namely, the concept of cause, which has nothing to do with sensibility.

be quite advantageous to reason and can hurt it nowhere in its application to nature. As to the latter, reason is thereby not transferred as a property to the First Being in itself, but only to its relation to the world of sense, and so anthropomorphism is entirely avoided. For nothing is considered here but the cause of the form of reason which is perceived everywhere in the world, and reason is indeed attributed to the Supreme Being so far as it contains the ground of this form of reason in the world, but according to analogy only—that is, so far as this expression shows merely the relation which the Supreme Cause, unknown to us, has to the world in order to determine everything in it conformably to reason in the highest degree. We are thereby kept from using reason as an attribute for the purpose of conceiving God, but not from conceiving the world in such a manner as is necessary to have the greatest possible use of reason within it according to principle. We thereby acknowledge that the Supreme Being is quite inscrutable and even unthinkable in any definite way as to what it is in itself. We are thereby kept, on the one hand, from making a transcendent use of the concepts which we have of reason as an efficient cause (by means of the will), in order to determine the Divine Nature by properties which are only borrowed from human nature, and from losing ourselves in gross and extravagant notions; and, on the other hand, from deluging the contemplation of the world with hyperphysical modes of explanation according to our notions of human reason which we transfer to God, and so from losing for this contemplation its proper rôle, according to which it should be a rational study of mere nature and not a presumptuous derivation of its appearances from a Supreme Reason. The expression suited to our feeble notions is: we conceive the world *as if* it came, in its existence and internal plan, from a Supreme Reason. By this, on the one hand, we know the constitution which belongs to the world itself without pretending to determine the nature of its cause in itself; and, on the other hand, we transfer the ground of this constitution (of the form of reason in the world) upon the *relation* of the Supreme Cause to the world, without finding the world sufficient by itself for that purpose.*

Thus the difficulties which seem to oppose theism disappear by combining with Hume's principle, "not to carry the use of reason dogmatically beyond the field of all possible experience," this other principle, which he quite overlooked, "not to consider the field of experience as one which bounds itself in the eyes of our reason." The *Critique of Pure Reason* here points out the true mean between dogmatism, which Hume combats, and skepticism, which he would substitute for it—a mean which is not like others that we find advisable to determine for ourselves, as it were mechanically (by adopting something from one side and something from the other), and by which nobody is taught a better way, but such a one as can be precisely determined on principles.

§ 59. At the beginning of this note I made use of the metaphor of a boundary, in order to establish the limits of reason in regard to its suitable use. The world of sense contains merely appearances, which are not things in themselves; but the understanding, because it recognizes that the objects of experience are mere appearances, must assume that there are things in themselves, namely, *noumena*. In our reason both are comprehended, and the question is, How does reason proceed to set boundaries to the understanding as regards both these fields? Experience, which contains all that belongs to the sensible world, does not bound itself; it only proceeds in every case from the

---

*I may say that the causality of the Supreme Cause holds the same place with regard to the world that human reason does with regard to its works of art. Here the nature of the Supreme Cause itself remains unknown to me; I only compare its effects (the order of the world), which I know, and their conformity to reason to the effects of human reason, which I also know; and hence I term the former "reason," without attributing to it on that account what I understand in man by this term, or attaching to it anything else known to me as its property.

conditioned to some other equally conditioned object. That which bounds it must lie quite without it, and this is the field of the pure beings of the understanding. But this field, so far as the *determination* of the nature of these beings is concerned, is an empty space for us; and apart from dogmatically defined concepts, we cannot pass beyond the field of possible experience. But as a boundary itself is something positive, which belongs to that which lies within as well as to the space that lies without the given content, it is still an actual positive cognition which reason only acquires by enlarging itself to this boundary, yet without attempting to pass it because it there finds itself in the presence of an empty space in which it can conceive forms of things, but not things themselves. But the setting of a boundary to the field of the understanding by something which is otherwise unknown to it is still a cognition which belongs to reason even at this point, and by which it is neither confined within the sensible nor strays beyond it, but only limits itself, as befits the knowledge of a boundary, to the relation between that which lies beyond it and that which is contained within it.

Natural theology is such a concept at the boundary of human reason, being constrained to look beyond this boundary to the Idea of a Supreme Being (and, for practical purposes, to that of an intelligible world also), not in order to determine anything relatively to this pure being of the understanding, and thus to determine something that lies beyond the world of sense, but in order to guide the use of reason within it according to principles of the greatest possible (theoretical as well as practical) unity. For this purpose, it makes use of the reference of the world of sense to an independent reason as the cause of all its connections. Thereby it does not just *invent* a being, but, as beyond the sensible world there must be something that can be thought only by the pure understanding, it determines that something in this particular way, though only of course by analogy.

And thus there remains our original proposition, which is the *résumé* of the whole *Critique:* "Reason by all its *a priori* principles never teaches us anything more than objects of possible experience, and even of these nothing more than can be known in experience." But this limitation does not prevent reason from leading us to the objective boundary of experience, namely, to the relation to something which is not itself an object of experience but is the ground of all experience. Reason does not, however, teach us anything concerning the thing in itself; it only instructs us as regards its own complete and highest use in the field of possible experience. But this is all that can be reasonably desired in the present case, and with it we have cause to be satisfied.

§ 60. Thus we have fully exhibited metaphysics, in its subjective possibility, as it is actually given in the natural predisposition of human reason and in that which constitutes the essential end of its pursuit. Though we have found that this merely natural use of such a predisposition of our reason, if no discipline arising only from a scientific critique bridles and sets limits to it, involves it in transcendent and specious inferences and really conflicting dialectical inferences, and this fallacious metaphysics is not only unnecessary as regards the promotion of our knowledge of nature but even disadvantageous to it, there yet remains a problem worthy of investigation, which is to find out the natural ends intended by this disposition to transcendent concepts in our nature, because everything that lies in nature must be originally intended for some useful purpose.

Such an inquiry is of a doubtful nature, and I acknowledge that what I can say about it is conjecture only, like every speculation about the ultimate ends of nature. Such conjecture may be allowed me here, for the question does not concern the objective validity of metaphysical judgments but our natural predisposition to them, and therefore does not belong to the system of metaphysics but to anthropology.

When I compare all the transcendental Ideas, the totality of which constitutes the proper problem of natural pure reason, compelling it to quit the mere contemplation of nature, to transcend all possible experience, and in this endeavor to produce the thing (be it knowledge or fiction) called metaphysics, I think I perceive that the aim of this natural tendency is to free our concepts from the fetters of experience and from the limits of the mere contemplation of nature so far as at least to open to us a field containing mere objects for the pure understanding which no sensibility can reach, not indeed for the purpose of speculatively occupying ourselves with them (for there we can find no ground to stand on), but in order that practical principles [may be assumed as at least possible]; for practical principles, unless they find scope for their necessary expectation and hope, could not expand to the universality which reason unavoidably requires from a moral point of view.

So I find that the psychological Idea (however little it may reveal to me the nature of the human soul, which is elevated above all concepts of experience), shows the insufficiency of these concepts plainly enough and thereby deters me from materialism, a psychological concept which is unfit for any explanation of nature and which moreover confines reason in practical respects. The cosmological Ideas, by the obvious insufficiency of all possible knowledge of nature to satisfy reason in its legitimate inquiry, serve in the same manner to keep us from naturalism, which asserts nature to be sufficient for itself. Finally, all natural necessity in the sensible world is conditional, as it always presupposes the dependence of things upon others, and unconditional necessity must be sought only in the unity of a cause different from the world of sense. But as the causality of this cause, in its turn, were it merely nature, could never render the existence of the contingent (as its consequent) comprehensible, reason frees itself by means of the theological Idea from fatalism (both as a blind natural necessity in the coherence of nature itself, without a first principle, and as a blind causality of this principle itself) and leads to the concept of a cause possessing freedom or of a Supreme Intelligence. Thus the transcendental Ideas serve, if not to instruct us positively, at least to destroy the narrowing assertions of materialism, of naturalism, and of fatalism, and thus to afford scope for the moral Ideas beyond the field of speculation. These considerations, I should think, explain in some measure the natural predisposition of which I spoke.

The practical value, which a merely speculative science may have, lies without the bounds of this science, and can therefore be considered as a scholium merely, and like all scholia does not form part of the science itself. This application, however, surely lies within the bounds of philosophy, especially of philosophy drawn from the pure sources of reason, where its speculative use in metaphysics must necessarily be at one with its practical use in morals. Hence the unavoidable dialectic of pure reason, considered in metaphysics as a natural tendency, deserves to be explained not as a mere illusion, which is to be removed, but also, if possible, as a natural provision as regards its end, though this task, a work of supererogation, cannot justly be assigned to metaphysics proper.

The solutions of these questions which are treated in the *Critique** should be considered a second scholium, which, however, has a greater affinity with the subject of metaphysics. For there certain rational principles are expounded which determine *a priori* the order of nature or rather of the understanding, which seeks nature's laws through experience. They seem to be constitutive and legislative with regard to experience, though they spring from pure reason, which cannot be considered, like the understanding, as a principle of possible experience. Now whether or not this harmony rests

---

Critique of Pure Reason, "Regulative Use of the Ideas of Pure Reason."

upon the fact that, just as nature does not inhere in appearances or in their source (the sensibility) itself, but only in the relation of the latter to the understanding, a thorough unity in applying the understanding to bring about an entirety of all possible experience (in a system) can only belong to the understanding when in relation to reason, with the consequence that experience is in this way mediately subordinate to the legislation of reason—this question may be discussed by those who desire to trace the nature of reason even beyond its use in metaphysics, into the general principles, which will make a history of nature in general systematic. I have presented this task as important, but not attempted its solution in the book itself.*

And thus I conclude the analytical solution of the main question which I had proposed: "How is metaphysics in general possible?" by ascending from the data of its actual use, as shown in its consequences, to the grounds of its possibility.

SOLUTION OF THE GENERAL QUESTION OF THE *PROLEGOMENA*

How Is Metaphysics Possible as Science?

Metaphysics, as a natural disposition of reason, is actual; but if considered by itself alone (as the analytical solution of the third principal question showed), dialectical and illusory. If we think of taking principles from it, and in using them follow the natural, but on that account not less false, illusion, we can never produce science, but only a vain dialectical art, in which one school may outdo another but none can ever acquire a just and lasting approbation.

In order that as a science metaphysics may be entitled to claim, not mere fallacious plausibility, but insight and conviction, a critique of reason itself must exhibit the whole stock of *a priori* concepts, their division according to their various sources (sensibility, understanding, and reason), together with a complete table of them, the analysis of all these concepts, with all their consequences, and especially the possibility of synthetical knowledge *a priori* by means of a deduction of these concepts, the principles and the bounds of their application, all in a complete system. Critique, therefore, and critique alone contains in itself the whole well-proved and well-tested plan, and even all the means, required to establish metaphysics as a science; by other ways and means it is impossible. The question here, therefore, is not so much how this performance is possible as how to set it going and to induce men of clear heads to quit their hitherto perverted and fruitless cultivation for one that will not deceive, and how such a union for the common end may best be directed.

This much is certain, that whoever has once tasted critique will be ever after disgusted with all dogmatic twaddle which he formerly had to put up with because his reason had to have something and could find nothing better for its support.

Critique stands in the same relation to the common metaphysics of the schools as chemistry does to alchemy, or as astronomy to the astrology of the fortune teller. I pledge myself that nobody who has thought through and grasped the principles of critique, even in these *Prolegomena* only, will ever return to that old and sophistical

---

*Throughout in the *Critique* I never lost sight of the plan not to neglect anything, were it ever so recondite, that could render the inquiry into the nature of pure reason complete. Everybody may afterward carry his research as far as he pleases, when he has been merely shown what yet remains to be done. This can reasonably be expected of him who has made it his business to survey the whole field, in order to consign it to others for future cultivation and allotment. And to this branch both the scholia belong, which will hardly recommend themselves because of their dryness to amateurs, and hence are added here for connoisseurs only.

pseudo-science; but will rather with a certain delight look forward to metaphysics, which is now indeed in his power, requiring no more preparatory discoveries and affording permanent satisfaction to reason at last. For here is an advantage upon which, of all possible sciences, metaphysics alone can with certainty reckon: that it can be brought to such completion and fixity as to be in need of no further change or be subject to any augmentation by new discoveries; because here reason has the sources of its knowledge in itself, not in objects and their observation, by which its stock of knowledge could be further increased. When, therefore, it has exhibited the fundamental laws of its faculty completely and so definitely as to avoid all misunderstanding, there remains nothing further which pure reason could know *a priori;* nay, there is no ground even to raise further questions. The sure prospect of knowledge so definite and so compact has a peculiar charm, even though we should set aside all its advantages, of which I shall hereafter speak.

All false art, all vain wisdom, lasts its time but finally destroys itself, and its highest culture is also the epoch of its decay. That this time is come for metaphysics appears from the state into which it has fallen among all learned nations, despite all the zeal with which other sciences of every kind are prosecuted. The old arrangement of our university studies still preserves its shadow. Now and then an academy of science tempts men by offering prizes to write some essay on it, but it is no longer numbered among the rigorous sciences; and let anyone judge for himself how a sophisticated man, if he were called a great metaphysician, would receive the compliment, which may be well meant but is scarcely envied by anybody.

Yet, though the period of the downfall of all dogmatic metaphysics has undoubtedly arrived, we are yet far from being able to say that the period of its regeneration is come by means of a thorough and complete critique of reason. All transitions from a tendency to its contrary pass through the stage of indifference, and this moment is the most dangerous for an author but, in my opinion, the most favorable for the science. For when party spirit has died out by a total dissolution of former connections, minds are in the best state to listen to several proposals for an organization according to a new plan.

When I say that I hope these *Prolegomena* will excite investigation in the field of critique and afford a new and promising object to sustain the general spirit of philosophy, which seems on its speculative side to want sustenance, I can imagine beforehand that everyone whom the thorny paths of my *Critique* have tired and put out of humor will ask me upon what I found this hope. My answer is: upon the irresistible law of necessity.

That the human mind will ever give up metaphysical researches is as little to be expected as that we, to avoid inhaling impure air, should prefer to give up breathing altogether. There will, therefore, always be metaphysics in the world; nay, everyone, especially every reflective man, will have it and, for want of a recognized standard, will shape it for himself after his own pattern. What has hitherto been called metaphysics cannot satisfy any critical mind, but to forego it entirely is impossible; therefore a *Critique of Pure Reason* itself must now be attempted or, if one exists, investigated and brought to the full test, because there is no other means of supplying this pressing want which is something more than mere thirst for knowledge.

Ever since I have come to know critique, whenever I finish reading a book of metaphysical contents which, by the preciseness of its notions, by variety, order, and an easy style, was not only entertaining but also helpful, I cannot help asking, "Has this author indeed advanced metaphysics a single step?" The learned men whose works have been useful to me in other respects and always contributed to the culture of my mental powers will, I hope, forgive me for saying that I have never been able to find either their essays or my own less important ones (though self-love may recommend them to me) to have advanced the science of metaphysics in the least.

There is a very obvious reason for this: metaphysics did not then exist as a science, nor can it be gathered piecemeal; but its germ must be fully preformed in critique. But, in order to prevent all misconception, we must remember what has been already said—that, by the analytical treatment of our concepts, the understanding gains indeed a great deal; but the science of metaphysics is thereby not in the least advanced, because these dissections of concepts are nothing but the materials from which the intention is to carpenter our science. Let the concepts of substance and of accident be ever so well dissected and determined; all this is very well as a preparation for some future use. But if we cannot prove that in all which exists the substance endures and only the accidents vary, our science is not the least advanced by all our analyses.

Metaphysics has hitherto never been able to prove *a priori* either this proposition or that of sufficient reason, still less any more complex theorem such as belongs to psychology or cosmology, or indeed any synthetical proposition. By all its analyzing, therefore, nothing is affected, nothing obtained or forwarded; and the science, after all this bustle and noise, still remains as it was in the days of Aristotle, though there were far better preparations for it than of old if only the clue to synthetical cognitions had been discovered.

If anyone thinks himself offended, he is at liberty to refute my charge by producing a single synthetical proposition belonging to metaphysics which he would prove dogmatically *a priori;* for until he has actually performed this feat I shall not grant that he has truly advanced the science, even if this proposition should be sufficiently confirmed by common experience. No demand can be more moderate or more equitable and, in the (inevitably certain) event of its nonperformance, no assertion more just than that hitherto metaphysics has never existed as a science.

But there are two things which, in case the challenge be accepted, I must deprecate: first, trifling about probability and conjecture, which are suited as little to metaphysics as to geometry; and secondly, a decision by means of the magic wand of so-called common sense, which does not convince everyone but accommodates itself to personal peculiarities.

For as to the former, nothing can be more absurd than in metaphysics, a philosophy from pure reason, to think of grounding our judgments upon probability and conjecture. Everything that is to be known *a priori* is thereby announced as apodictically certain, and must therefore be proved in this way. We might as well think of grounding geometry or arithmetic upon conjectures. As to the calculus of probabilities in the latter, it does not contain probable but perfectly certain judgments concerning the degree of the possibility of certain cases under given uniform conditions, which, in the sum of all possible cases, must infallibly happen according to the rule, though the rule is not sufficiently definite with respect to every single instance. Conjectures (by means of induction and of analogy) can be suffered in an empirical science of nature only, yet even there at least the possibility of what we assume must be quite certain.

The appeal to common sense is even more absurd—if anything more absurd can be imagined—when it is a question of concept and principles claimed as valid, not in so far as they hold with regard to experience, but beyond the conditions of experience. For what is common sense? It is normal good sense, so far it judges right. But what is normal good sense? It is the faculty of the knowledge and use of rules *in concreto,* as distinguished from the speculative understanding, which is a faculty of knowing rules *in abstracto.* Common sense can hardly understand the rule that every event is determined by means of its cause and can never comprehend it in its generality. It therefore demands an example from experience; and when it hears that this rule means nothing but what it always thought when a pane was broken or a kitchen utensil missing, it then understands the principle and grants it. Common sense, therefore, is only of use so far as it can see its rules (though they actually are *a priori*) confirmed by experience; consequently to comprehend them *a priori,* or independently of experience, belongs to the speculative understanding and lies quite beyond the horizon of common sense. But the province of metaphysics is entirely confined to the latter kind of knowledge, and it is certainly a bad sign of common sense to appeal to it as a witness, for it cannot here form any opinion whatever, and men look down upon it with contempt until they are in straits and can find in their speculation neither advice nor help.

It is a common subterfuge of those false friends of common sense (who occasionally prize it highly, but usually despise it) to say that there must surely be at all events some propositions which are immediately certain and of which there is no occasion to give any proof, or even any account at all, because we otherwise could never stop inquiring into the grounds of our judgments. But if we except the principle of contradiction, which is not sufficient to show the truth of synthetical judgments, they can never adduce, in proof of this privilege, anything else indubitable which they can immediately ascribe to common sense, except mathematical propositions, such as twice two make four, between two points there is but one straight line, etc. But these judgments are radically different from those of metaphysics. For in mathematics I can by thinking itself construct whatever I represent to myself as possible by a concept: I add to the first two the other two, one by one, and myself make the number four, or I draw in thought from one point to another all manner of lines, equal as well as unequal; yet I can draw one only which is like itself in all its parts. But I cannot, by all my power of thinking, extract from the concept of a thing the concept of something else whose existence is necessarily connected with the former; for this I must call in experience. And though my understanding furnishes me *a priori* (yet only in reference to possible experience) with the concept of such a connection (that is causation), I cannot exhibit it, like the concepts of mathematics, by intuiting it *a priori,* and so show its possibility *a priori.* This concept, together with the principles of its application, always requires, if it shall hold *a priori*—as is requisite in metaphysics—a justification and deduction of its possibility, because we cannot otherwise know how far it holds good and whether it can be used in experience only or beyond it also.

Therefore in metaphysics, as a speculative science of pure reason, we can never appeal to common sense, but may do so only when we are forced to surrender it and to renounce all pure speculative knowledge which must always be theoretical cognition, and thereby under some circumstances to forego metaphysics itself and its instruction for the sake of adopting a rational faith which alone may be possible for us, sufficient to our wants, and perhaps even more salutary than knowledge itself. For in this case the state of affairs is quite altered. Metaphysics must be science, not only as a whole, but in all its parts; otherwise it is nothing at all; because, as speculation of pure reason, it finds a hold only on common convictions. Beyond its field, however, probability and common sense may be used justly and with advantage, but on quite special principles, the importance of which always depends on their reference to practical life.

This is what I hold myself justified in requiring for the possibility of metaphysics as a science.

APPENDIX

ON WHAT CAN BE DONE TO MAKE METAPHYSICS AS A SCIENCE ACTUAL

Since all the ways heretofore taken have failed to attain the goal, and since without a preceding critique of pure reason it is not likely ever to be attained, the present attempt has a right to an accurate and careful examination, unless it be thought more advisable to give up all pretensions to metaphysics, to which, if men but would consistently adhere to their purpose, no objection can be made.

If we take the course of things as it is, not as it ought to be, there are two sorts of judgments: (1) one a judgment which precedes investigation (in our case one in which the reader from his own metaphysics pronounces judgment on the *Critique of Pure Reason,* which was intended to discuss the very possibility of metaphysics); (2) the other a judgment subsequent to investigation. In the latter, the reader is enabled to ignore for a while the consequences of the critical researches that may be repugnant to his formerly adopted metaphysics, and first examines the grounds whence those consequences are derived. If what common metaphysics propounds were demonstrably certain, as is the case with the theorems of geometry, the former way of judging would hold good. For if the consequences of certain principles are repugnant to established truths, these principles are false and without further inquiry to be repudiated. But if metaphysics does not possess a stock of indisputably certain (synthetical) propositions, and should it even be the case that there are a number of them, which, though among the most plausible, are by their consequences in mutual conflict, and if no sure criterion of the truth of peculiarly metaphysical (synthetical) propositions is to be met with in it, then the former way of judging is not admissible, but the investigation of the principles of the *Critique* must precede all judgments as to its value.

A SPECIMEN OF A JUDGMENT OF THE CRITIQUE PRIOR TO ITS EXAMINATION

Such a judgment is to be found in the *Göttingische gelehrte Anzeigen,* in the supplement to the third part, of January 19, 1782, pages 40 *et seq.*

When an author who is familiar with the subject of his work and endeavors to present his independent reflections in its elaboration falls into the hands of a reviewer who, in his turn, is keen enough to discern the points on which the worth or worthlessness of the book rests, who does not cling to words but goes to the heart of the subject, sifting and testing the principles which the author takes as his point of departure, the severity of the judgment may indeed displease the author, but the public does not care, as it gains thereby. And the author himself may be contented, as an opportunity of correcting or explaining his positions is afforded to him at an early date by the examination of a competent judge, in such a manner that if he believes himself fundamentally right, he can remove in time any stumbling block that might hurt the success of his work.

I find myself, with my reviewer, in quite another position. He seems not to see at all the real matter of the investigation with which (successfully or unsuccessfully) I have been occupied. It is either impatience at thinking out a lengthy work, or vexation at a threatened reform of a science in which he believed he had brought everything to perfection long ago, or, what I am reluctant to suspect, real narrow-mindedness that prevents him from ever carrying his thoughts beyond his school metaphysics. In short, he passes impatiently in review a long series of propositions, of which, without knowing their premises, one can understand nothing, intersperses here and there his censure, the reason of which the reader understands just as little as the propositions against which it is directed; and hence [his report] can neither serve the public nor damage me in the judgment of experts. I should, for these reasons, have passed over this judgment altogether, were it not that it may afford me occasion for some explanations which may in some cases save the readers of these *Prolegomena* from a misconception.

In order to take a position from which my reviewer could most easily set the whole work in a most unfavorable light, without venturing to trouble himself with any special investigation, he begins and ends by saying: "This work is a system of transcendental (or, as he translates it, of higher*) idealism."

A glance at this line soon showed me the sort of criticism that I had to expect, much as though the reviewer were one who had never seen or heard of geometry, having found a Euclid and coming upon various figures in turning over its leaves, were to say, on being asked his opinion of it: "The work is a textbook of drawing; the author introduces a peculiar terminology, in order to give dark, incomprehensible directions, which in the end teach nothing more than what everyone can effect by a fair natural accuracy of eye, etc."

Let us see, in the meantime, what sort of an idealism it is that goes through my whole work, although it does not by a long way constitute the soul of the system.

The dictum of all genuine idealists, from the Eleatic school to Bishop Berkeley, is contained in this formula: "All knowledge through the senses and experience is nothing but sheer illusion, and only in the ideas of the pure understanding and reason is there truth."

The principle that throughout dominates and determines my idealism, is on the contrary: "All knowledge of things merely from pure understanding or pure reason is nothing but sheer illusion, and only in experience is there truth."

But this is directly contrary to idealism proper. How came I then to use this expression for quite an opposite purpose, and how came my reviewer to see it everywhere?

The solution of this difficulty rests on something that could have been very easily understood from the general bearing of the work if the reader had only desired to understand it. Space and time, together with all that they contain, are not things in themselves or their qualities, but belong merely to the appearances of the things in themselves. Up to this point I am one in confession with the above idealists. But these, and among them more particularly Berkeley, regarded space as a mere empirical representation that, like the appearances it contains, is, together with its determinations, known to us only by means of experience or perception. I, on the contrary, prove in the first place that space (and also time, which Berkeley did not consider) and all its

---

*By no means "higher." High towers and metaphysically great men resembling them, round both of which there is commonly much wind, are not for me. My place is the fruitful bathos of experience; and the word "transcendental," the meaning of which is so often explained by me but not once grasped by my reviewer (so carelessly has he regarded everything), does not signify something passing beyond all experience but something that indeed precedes it *a priori,* but that is intended simply to make knowledge of experience possible. If these conceptions overstep experience, their employment is termed "transcendent," which must be distinguished from the immanent use, that is, use restricted to experience. All misunderstandings of this kind have been sufficiently guarded against in the work itself, but my reviewer found his advantage in misunderstanding me.

a priori determinations can be known by us, because, no less than time, it inheres in us as a pure form of our sensibility before all perception or experience and makes all intuition of the form, and therefore all appearances, possible. It follows from this that, as truth rests on universal and necessary laws as its criteria, experience, according to Berkeley, can have no criteria of truth because its phenomena* (according to him) have nothing *a priori* at their foundation, whence it follows that experience is nothing but sheer illusion; whereas with us, space and time (in conjunction with the pure concept of the understanding) prescribe their law to all possible experience *a priori* and, at the same time, afford the certain criterion for distinguishing truth from illusion therein.

My so-called (properly critical) idealism is of quite a special character, in that it subverts the ordinary idealism and in that only through it all *a priori* knowledge, even that of geometry, receives objective reality, which, without my demonstrated ideality of space and time, could not be maintained by the most zealous realists. This being the state of the case, I could wish, in order to avoid all misunderstanding, to have named this conception of mine otherwise, but to alter it altogether is probably impossible. It may be permitted me however, in future, as has been above intimated, to term it "formal" or, better still, "critical" idealism, to distinguish it from the dogmatic idealism of Berkeley and from the skeptical idealism of Descartes.

Beyond this, I find nothing remarkable in the judgment of my book. The reviewer makes sweeping criticisms, a mode prudently chosen, since it does not betray one's own knowledge or ignorance; a single thorough criticism in detail, had it touched the main question, as is only fair, would have exposed either my error or my reviewer's measure of insight into this species of research. It was, moreover, not a badly conceived plan, in order at once to take from readers (who are accustomed to form their conceptions of books from newspaper reports) the desire to read the book itself, to pour out in one breath a number of passages in succession which, torn from their connection with their premises and explanations, must necessarily sound senseless, especially considering how antipathetic they are to all school-metaphysics; to exhaust the reader's patience *ad nauseam,* and then, having made me acquainted with the lucid proposition that persistent illusion is truth, to conclude with the crude paternal moralization: to what end, then, the quarrel with accepted language; to what end, and whence, the idealistic distinction? A judgment which seeks all that is characteristic of my book, first supposed to be metaphysically heterodox, in a mere innovation of the nomenclature proves clearly that my would-be judge has understood nothing of the subject and, in addition, has not understood himself.**

My reviewer speaks like a man who is conscious of important and superior insight which he keeps hidden, for I am aware of nothing recent with respect to meta-

---

*Idealism proper always has a mystical tendency, and can have no other, but mine is solely designed for the purpose of comprehending the possibility of our *a priori* knowledge of objects of experience, which is a problem never hitherto solved or even suggested. In this way all mystical idealism falls to the ground, for (as may be seen in Plato) it inferred from our cognitions *a priori* (even from those of geometry) another intuition different from that of the senses (namely, an intellectual intuition), because it never occurred to anyone that the senses themselves might intuit *a priori.*

**The reviewer often fights with his own shadow. When I oppose the truth of experience to dream, he never thinks that I am here speaking simply of the well-known *somnio objective sumto* of the Wolffian philosophy, which is merely formal, and with which the distinction between sleeping and waking is in no way concerned—a distinction which can indeed have no place in a transcendental philosophy. For the rest, he calls my deduction of the categories and table of the principles of the understanding "common well-known axioms of logic and ontology, expressed in an idealistic manner." The reader need only consult these *Prolegomena* upon this point to convince himself that a more miserable and historically incorrect judgment could hardly be made.

physics that could justify his tone. But he should not withhold his discoveries from the world, for there are doubtless many who, like myself, have not been able to find in all the fine things that have for long past been written in this department anything that has advanced the science by so much as a finger's breadth; we find indeed the giving a new point to definitions, the supplying of lame proofs with new crutches, the adding to the crazy-quilt of metaphysics fresh patches or changing its pattern. But all this is not what the world requires. The world is tired of metaphysical assertions; it wants [to know] the possibility of this science, the sources from which certainty therein can be derived, and certain criteria by which it may distinguish the dialectical illusion of pure reason from truth. To this the critic seems to possess a key, otherwise he would never have spoken out in such a high tone.

But I am inclined to suspect that no such requirement of the science has ever entered his thoughts, for in that case he would have directed his judgment to this point, and even a mistaken attempt in such an important matter would have won his respect. If that be the case, we are once more good friends. He may penetrate as deeply as he likes into his metaphysics, without any one hindering him; only as concerns that which lies outside metaphysics, its sources, which are to be found in reason, he cannot form a judgment. That my suspicion is not without foundation is proved by the fact that he does not mention a word about the possibility of synthetic knowledge *a priori,* the special problem upon the solution of which the fate of metaphysics wholly rests and upon which my *Critique* (as well as the present *Prolegomena*) entirely hinges. The idealism he encountered and which he hung upon was only taken up in the doctrine as the sole means of solving the above problem (although it received its confirmation on other grounds), and hence he must have shown either that the above problem does not possess the importance I attribute to it (even in these *Prolegomena*) or that, by my conception of appearances, it is either not solved at all or can be better solved in another way; but I do not find a word of this in the criticism. The reviewer, then, understands nothing of my work and possibly also nothing of the spirit and essential nature of metaphysics itself; and it is not, what I would rather assume, the hurry of a reviewer to finish his review, incensed at the labor of plodding through so many obstacles, that threw an unfavorable shadow over the work lying before him and made its fundamental features unrecognizable.

There is a good deal to be done before a learned journal, it matters not with what care its writers may be selected, can maintain its otherwise well-merited reputation in the field of metaphysics as elsewhere. Other sciences and branches of knowledge have their standard. Mathematics has it in itself, history and theology in profane or sacred books, natural science and the art of medicine in mathematics and experience, jurisprudence in law books, and even matters of taste in the examples of the ancients. But for the judgment of the thing called metaphysics, the standard has yet to be found. I have made an attempt to determine it, as well as its use. What is to be done, then, until it be found when works of this kind have to be judged of? If they are of a dogmatic character, one may do what one likes; no one will play the master over others here for long before someone else appears to deal with him in the same manner. If, however, they are critical in character, not indeed with reference to other works but to reason itself, so that the standard of judgment cannot be assumed but has first of all to be sought for, then, though objection and blame may indeed be permitted, yet a certain degree of leniency is indispensable, since the need is common to us all and the lack of the necessary insight makes the high-handed attitude of judge unwarranted.

In order, however, to connect my defense with the interest of the philosophical commonwealth, I propose a test, which must be decisive as to the mode whereby all metaphysical investigations may be directed to their common purpose. This is nothing more than what mathematicians have done in establishing the advantage of their methods by competition. I challenge my critic to demonstrate, as is only just, on *a priori* grounds, in his own way, any single really metaphysical proposition asserted by him. Being metaphysical, it must be synthetical and known *a priori* from concepts, but it may also be any one of the most indispensable propositions, as, for instance, the principle of the persistence of substance or of the necessary determination of events in the world by their causes. If he cannot do this (silence however is confession), he must admit that, since metaphysics without apodictic certainty of propositions of this kind is nothing at all, its possibility or impossibility must before all things be established in a critique of pure reason. Thus he is bound either to confess that my principles in the *Critique* are correct, or he must prove their invalidity. But as I can already foresee that, confidently as he has hitherto relied on the certainty of his principles, when it comes to a strict test he will not find a single one in the whole range of metaphysics he can boldly bring forward, I will concede to him an advantageous condition, which can only be expected in such a competition, and will relieve him of the *onus probandi* by laying it on myself.

He finds in these *Prolegomena* and in my *Critique** eight propositions, of which one in each pair contradicts the other, but each of which necessarily belongs to metaphysics, by which it must either be accepted or rejected (although there is not one that has not in its time been assumed by some philosopher). Now he has the liberty of selecting any one of these eight propositions at his pleasure and accepting it without any proof, of which I shall make him a present, but only one (for waste of time will be just as little serviceable to him as to me), and then of attacking my proof of the opposite proposition. If I can save this one and at the same time show that, according to principles which every dogmatic metaphysics must necessarily recognize, the opposite of the proposition adopted by him can be just as clearly proved, it is thereby established that metaphysics has an hereditary failing not to be explained, much less set aside, until we ascend to its birthplace, pure reason itself. And thus my *Critique* must either be accepted or a better one take its place; at least it must be studied, which is the only thing I now require. If, on the other hand, I cannot save my demonstration, then a synthetic proposition *a priori* from dogmatic principles is to be reckoned to the score of my opponent, and I shall deem my impeachment of ordinary metaphysics unjust and pledge myself to recognize his stricture on my *Critique* as justified (although this would not be the consequence by a long way). To this end it would be necessary, it seems to me, that he should step out of his incognito. Otherwise I do not see how it could be avoided that, instead of dealing with one, I should be honored or besieged by several challenges coming from anonymous and unqualified opponents.

Proposals as to an Investigation of the "Critique" Upon Which a Judgment May Follow

I feel obliged to the learned public even for the silence with which it for a long time honored my *Critique,* for this proves at least a postponement of judgment and some supposition that, in a work leaving all beaten tracks and striking out on a new path, in which one cannot at once perhaps so easily find one's way, something may perchance

---

*[The reference is to the theses and antitheses of the antinomies.—L.W.B.]

lie from which an important but at present dead branch of human knowledge may derive new life and productiveness. Hence may have originated a solicitude for the as yet tender shoot, lest it be destroyed by a hasty judgment. A specimen of a judgment, delayed for the above reasons, is now before my eye in the *Gothaische gelehrte Zeitung,* the thoroughness of which—disregarding my praise, which might be suspicious—every reader will himself perceive from the clear and unperverted presentation of a fragment of one of the first principles of my work.

Since an extensive structure cannot be judged of as a whole from a hurried glance, I suggest that it be tested piece by piece from the ground up, and in this, the present *Prolegomena* may fitly be used as a general outline with which the work itself may occasionally be compared. This notion, if it were founded on nothing more than my conceit of importance, such as vanity commonly attributes to all of one's own productions, would be immodest and would deserve to be repudiated with indignation. But now the interests of speculative philosophy have arrived at the point of total extinction, while human reason hangs upon them with inextinguishable affection; and only after having been ceaselessly deceived, does it vainly attempt to change this into indifference.

In our thinking age, it is not to be supposed but that many deserving men would use any good opportunity of working for the common interest of the more and more enlightened reason, if there were only some hope of attaining the goal. Mathematics, natural science, laws, arts, even morality, etc., do not completely fill the soul; there is always a space left over reserved for pure and speculative reason, the emptiness of which prompts us to seek in vagaries, buffooneries, and mysticism for what seems to be employment and entertainment, but what actually is mere pastime undertaken in order to deaden the troublesome voice of reason, which, in accordance with its nature, requires something that can satisfy it and does not merely subserve other ends or the interests of our inclinations. A consideration, therefore, which is concerned only with reason as it exists for it itself has, as I may reasonably suppose, a great fascination for everyone who has attempted thus to extend his conceptions, and I may even say a greater fascination than any other theoretical branch of knowledge, for which he would not willingly exchange it because here all other branches of knowledge and even purposes must meet and unite themselves in a whole.

I offer, therefore, these *Prolegomena* as a sketch and textbook for this investigation, and not the work itself. Although I am even now perfectly satisfied with the latter as far as contents, order, and mode of presentation, and the care that I have expended in weighing and testing every sentence before writing it down are concerned (for it has taken me years to satisfy myself fully, not only as regards the whole, but in some cases even as to the sources of one particular proposition); yet I am not quite satisfied with my exposition in some sections of the Doctrine of Elements,* as for instance in the deduction of the concepts of the understanding or in the chapter on the paralogisms of pure reason, because a certain diffuseness takes away from their clearness, and in place of them what is here said in the *Prolegomena* respecting these sections may be made the basis of the test.**

It is the boast of the Germans that, where steady and continuous industry are requisite, they can carry things farther than other nations. If this opinion be well founded,

---

*[The first part of the *Critique of Pure Reason,* the other being the Methodology.—L.W.B.]

**[These sections were almost completely rewritten in the second edition of the *Critique* (1787), though the new deduction of the categories does not follow the argument of the *Prolegomena.*—L.W.B.]

an opportunity, a task, presents itself the successful issue of which we can scarcely doubt and in which all thinking men can equally take part, though they have hitherto been unsuccessful in accomplishing it and in thus confirming the above good opinion. This is chiefly because the science in question is of so peculiar a kind that it can all at once be brought to completion and to that enduring state beyond which it can never be developed, in the least degree enlarged by later discoveries, or changed if we leave out of account adornment by greater clearness in some places or additional uses. This is an advantage no other science has or can have, because there is none so fully isolated and independent of others and so exclusively concerned with the faculty of cognition pure and simple. And the present moment seems not to be unfavorable to my expectation, for just now, in Germany, no one seems to know wherewith to occupy himself, apart from the so-called useful sciences, so as to pursue not mere play but a business possessing an enduring purpose.

To discover how the endeavors of the learned may be united in such a purpose I must leave to others. In the meantime, it is not my intention to persuade anyone merely to follow my propositions or even to flatter me with the hope that he will do so; but attacks, repetitions, limitations, or confirmation, completion, and extension, as the case may be, should be appended. If the matter be but investigated from its foundation, it cannot fail that a system, albeit not my own, shall be erected that shall be a possession for future generations for which they may have reason to be grateful.

It would lead us too far here to show what kind of metaphysics may be expected when the principles of criticism have been perfected and how, though the old false feathers have been pulled out, it need by no means appear poor and reduced to an insignificant figure but may be in other respects richly and respectably adorned. But other and great uses which would result from such a reform strike one immediately. The ordinary metaphysics had its uses, in that it sought out the elementary concepts of the pure understanding in order to make them clear through analysis and definite through definitions. In this way it was a training for reason, in whatever direction it might be turned. But this was all the good it did. The service was subsequently effaced when it favored conceit by venturesome assertions, sophistry by subtle distinctions and adornment, and shallowness by the ease with which it decided the most difficult problems by means of a little school wisdom, which is only the more seductive the more it has the choice, on the one hand, of taking something from the language of science and, on the other, from that of popular discourse—thus being everything to everybody but in reality nothing at all. By criticism, however, a standard is given to our judgment whereby knowledge may be with certainty distinguished from pseudo-science and firmly founded, being brought into full operation in metaphysics—a mode of thought extending by degrees its beneficial influence over every other use of reason, at once infusing into it the true philosophical spirit. But the service that metaphysics performs also for theology, by making it independent of the judgment of dogmatic speculation and thereby assuring it completely against the attacks of all such opponents, is certainly not to be valued lightly. For ordinary metaphysics, although it promised theology much advantage, could not keep this promise, and by summoning speculative dogmatics to its assistance did nothing but arm enemies against itself. Mysticism, which can prosper in a rationalistic age only when it hides itself behind a system of school metaphysics, under the protection of which it may venture to rave with a semblance of rationality, is driven from theology, its last hiding place, by critical philosophy. Last, but not least, it cannot be otherwise than important to a teacher of metaphysics to be able to say with universal assent that what he expounds is *science,* and that by it genuine services will be rendered to the commonweal.

FOUNDATION FOR THE METAPHYSICS OF MORALS

PREFACE

Ancient Greek philosophy was divided into three sciences: physics, ethics, and logic. This division conforms perfectly to the nature of the subject, and one need improve on it perhaps only by supplying its principle in order both to insure its exhaustiveness and to define correctly the necessary subdivisions.

All rational knowledge is either material, and concerns some object, or formal, and is occupied only with the form of understanding and reason itself and with the universal rules of thinking, without regard to distinctions among objects. Formal philosophy is called logic. Material philosophy, however, which has to do with definite objects and the laws to which they are subject, is divided into two parts. This is because these laws are either laws of nature or laws of freedom. The science of the former is called physics, and that of the latter ethics. The former is also called theory of nature and the latter theory of morals.

Logic can have no empirical part—a part in which universal and necessary laws of thinking would rest upon grounds taken from experience. For in that case it would not be logic (i.e., a canon for understanding or reason which is valid for all thinking and which must be demonstrated). Natural and moral philosophy, on the other hand, can each have its empirical part. The former must do so, for it must determine the laws of nature as an object of experience, and the latter must do so because it must determine the human will so far as it is affected by nature. The laws of the former are laws according to which everything happens; those of the latter are laws according to which everything ought to happen, but allow for conditions under which what ought to happen often does not.

All philosophy, so far as it is based on experience, may be called empirical; but, so far as it presents its doctrines solely on the basis of *a priori* principles, it may be called pure philosophy. Pure philosophy, when formal only, is logic; when limited to definite objects of the understanding, it is metaphysics.

In this way there arises the idea of a two-fold metaphysics—a metaphysics of nature and a metaphysics of morals. Physics, therefore, will have an empirical part and also a rational part, and ethics likewise. In ethics, however, the empirical part may be called more specifically practical anthropology; the rational part, morals proper.

All crafts, handiworks, and arts have gained by the division of labor, for when one person does not do everything but each limits himself to a particular job which is distinguished from all the others by the treatment it requires, he can do it with greater perfection and more facility. Where work is not thus differentiated and divided, where everyone is a jack-of-all-trades, the crafts remain at a primitive level. It might be worth considering whether pure philosophy in each of its parts does not require a man particularly devoted to it, and whether it would not be better for the learned profession as a whole to warn those who are in the habit of catering to the taste of the public by mixing up the empirical with the rational in all sorts of proportions which they themselves

Immanuel Kant, *Foundation for the Metaphysics of Morals,* 2nd edition, translated by Lewis White Beck (New York: Macmillan/Library of the Liberal Arts, 1990).

do not know—a warning to those who call themselves independent thinkers and who give the name of speculator to those who apply themselves exclusively to the rational part of philosophy. This warning would be that they should not, at one and the same time, carry on two employments which differ widely in the treatment they require, and for each of which perhaps a special talent is required, since the combination of these talents in one person produces only bunglers. I only ask whether the nature of the science does not require that a careful separation of the empirical from the rational part be made, with a metaphysics of nature put before real (empirical) physics and a metaphysics of morals before practical anthropology. Each branch of metaphysics must be carefully purified of everything empirical so that we can know how much pure reason can accomplish in each case and from what sources it creates its *a priori* teaching, whether the latter inquiry be conducted by all moralists (whose name is legion) or only by some who feel a calling to it.

Since my purpose here is directed to moral philosophy, I narrow my proposed question to this: Is it not of the utmost necessity to construct a pure moral philosophy which is completely freed from everything which may be only empirical and thus belong to anthropology? That there must be such a philosophy is self-evident from the common idea of duty and moral laws. Everyone must admit that a law, if it is to hold morally (i.e., as a ground of obligation), must imply absolute necessity; he must admit that the command: Thou shalt not lie, does not apply to men only as if other rational beings had no need to observe it. The same is true for all other moral laws properly so called. He must concede that the ground of obligation here must not be sought in the nature of man or in the circumstances in which he is placed but *a priori* solely in the concepts of pure reason, and that every precept which rests on principles of mere experience, even a precept which is in certain respects universal, so far as it leans in the least on empirical grounds (perhaps only in regard to the motive involved) may be called a practical rule but never a moral law.

Thus not only are moral laws together with their principles essentially different from all practical knowledge in which there is anything empirical, but all moral philosophy rests solely on its pure part. Applied to man, it borrows nothing from knowledge of him (anthropology) but gives man, as a rational being, *a priori* laws. No doubt these laws require a power of judgment sharpened by experience partly in order to decide in which cases they apply and partly to procure for them access to man's will and to provide an impetus to their practice. For man is affected by so many inclinations that, though he is capable of the Idea of a practical pure reason, he is not so easily able to make it concretely effective in the conduct of his life.

A metaphysics of morals is therefore indispensable, not merely because of motives to speculation on the source of the *a priori* practical principles which lie in our reason, but also because morals themselves remain subject to all kinds of corruption so long as the guide and supreme norm for their correct estimation is lacking. For it is not sufficient to that which should be morally good that it conform to the law; it must be done for the sake of the law. Otherwise its conformity is merely contingent and spurious because, though the unmoral ground may indeed now and then produce lawful actions, more often it brings forth unlawful ones. But the moral law can be found in its purity and genuineness (which is the central concern in the practical) nowhere else than in a pure philosophy; therefore metaphysics must lead the way, and without it there can be no moral philosophy. Philosophy which mixes pure principles with empirical ones does not deserve the name, for what distinguishes philosophy from common sense knowledge is its treatment in separate sciences of what is confusedly apprehended in such knowledge. Much less does it deserve the name of moral philosophy, since by this confusion it spoils the purity of morals themselves, and works contrary to its own end.

It should not be thought that what is here required is already present in the celebrated Wolff's propaedeutic to his moral philosophy (i.e., in what he calls *Universal Practical Philosophy*) and that it is not an entirely new field which is to be opened. Precisely because his work was to be universal practical philosophy, it contained no will of any particular kind, such as one determined without any empirical motives by *a priori* principles; in a word, it had nothing which could be called a pure will, since it considered only volition in general with all the actions and conditions which pertain to it in this general sense. Thus his propaedeutic differs from a metaphysic of morals in the same way that general logic is distinguished from transcendental philosophy, the former expounding the actions and rules of thinking in general, and the latter presenting the actions and rules of pure thinking (thinking by which objects are known completely *a priori*). For the metaphysics of morals is meant to investigate the Idea and principles of a possible pure will and not the actions and conditions of human volition as such, which for the most part are drawn from psychology.

That universal practical philosophy discussed (though improperly) laws and duty is no objection to my assertion. For the authors of this science remain even here true to their idea of it. They do not distinguish the motives which are presented completely *a priori* by reason alone and which are thus moral in the proper sense of the world, from empirical motives which the understanding raises to universal concepts by comparing experiences. Rather, they consider motives without regard to the difference in their source but only with reference to their larger or smaller number (as they are considered to be all of the same kind); they thus formulate their concept of obligation, which is anything but moral, but which is all that can be desired in a philosophy which does not decide whether the origin of all possible practical concepts is *a priori* or *a posteriori*.

As a preliminary to a *Metaphysics of Morals* which I intend to publish someday, I issue these *Foundations*. There is, to be sure, no other foundation for such a metaphysics than a critical examination of pure practical reason, just as there is no other foundation for metaphysics than the already published critical examination of pure speculative reason. But, in the first place, a critical examination of pure practical reason is not of such extreme importance as that of the speculative reason, because human reason, even in the commonest mind, can easily be brought to a high degree of correctness and completeness in moral matters while, on the other hand, in its theoretical but pure use it is wholly dialectical. In the second place, I require of a critical examination of pure practical reason, if it is to be complete, that its unity with the speculative be subject to presentation under a common principle, because in the final analysis there can be but one and the same reason which must be different only in application. But I could not bring this to such a completeness without bringing in observations of an altogether different kind and without thereby confusing the reader. For these reasons I have employed the title, *Foundations of the Metaphysics of Morals,* instead of *Critique of Pure Practical Reason.*

Because, in the third place, a *Metaphysics of Morals,* in spite of its forbidding title, is capable of a high degree of popular adaptation to common understanding, I find it useful to separate this preliminary work of laying the foundation, in order not to have to introduce unavoidable subtleties into the latter, more comprehensible work.

The present foundations, however, are nothing more than the search for and establishment of the supreme principle of morality. This constitutes a task altogether complete in design and one which should be kept separate from all other moral inquiry. My conclusions concerning this important question, which has not yet been discussed nearly enough, would, of course, be clarified by application of the principle to the whole system of morality, and it would receive much confirmation by the adequacy which it would everywhere show. But I must forego this advantage which would be, in the final analysis, more personally gratifying than commonly useful, because ease of use and apparent adequacy of a principle are not any sure proof of correctness, but rather awaken a certain partiality which prevents a rigorous investigation and evaluation of it for itself without regard to consequences.

I have adopted in this writing the method which is, I think, most suitable if one wishes to proceed analytically from common knowledge to the determination of its supreme principle, and then synthetically from the examination of this principle and its sources back to common knowledge where it finds its application. The division is therefore as follows:

1. First Section. Transition from Common Sense Knowledge of Morals to the Philosophical
2. Second Section. Transition from Popular Moral Philosophy to the Metaphysics of Morals
3. Third Section. Final Step from the Metaphysics of Morals to the Critical Examination of Pure Practical Reason

FIRST SECTION

TRANSITION FROM COMMON SENSE* KNOWLEDGE OF MORALS TO THE PHILOSOPHICAL

Nothing in the world—indeed nothing even beyond the world—can possibly be conceived which could be called good without qualification except a GOOD WILL. Intelligence, wit, judgment, and other talents of the mind however they may be named, or courage, resoluteness, and perseverance as qualities of temperament, are doubtless in many respects good and desirable; but they can become extremely bad and harmful if the will, which is to make use of these gifts of nature and which in its special constitution is called character, is not good. It is the same with gifts of fortune. Power, riches, honor, even health, general well-being and the contentment with one's condition which is called happiness make for pride and even arrogance if there is not a good will to correct their influence on the mind and on its principle of action, so as to make it generally fitting to its entire end. It need hardly be mentioned that the sight of a being adorned with no feature of a pure and good will yet enjoying lasting good fortune can never give pleasure to an impartial rational observer. Thus the good will seems to constitute the indispensable condition even of worthiness to be happy.

---

*[*gemeine Vernunfterkenntnis* ("common rational knowledge") is one of several expressions Kant uses which may sometimes best be translated as "common sense." Kant is very strict in his censure of those who appeal to common sense as an arbiter in philosophical disputes, yet he accepts it as a starting point, especially in ethics, where he says that the man of common sense has at least as much chance to be right as the philosopher. In this title "common sense" is not being used as a technical term; it just means "what everyone knows" about morality.]

Some qualities seem to be conducive to this good will and can facilitate its action, but in spite of that they have no intrinsic unconditional worth. They rather presuppose a good will, which limits the high esteem which one otherwise rightly has for them and prevents their being held to be absolutely good. Moderation in emotions and passions, self-control, and calm deliberation not only are good in many respects but seem even to constitute part of the inner worth of the person. But however unconditionally they were esteemed by the ancients, they are far from being good without qualification, for without the principles of a good will they can become extremely bad, and the coolness of a villain makes him not only far more dangerous but also more directly abominable in our eyes than he would have seemed without it.

The good will is not good because of what it effects or accomplishes or because of its competence to achieve some intended end; it is good only because of its willing (i.e., it is good in itself). And, regarded for itself, it is to be esteemed as incomparably higher than anything which could be brought about by it in favor of any inclination or even of the sum total of all inclinations. Even if it should happen that, by a particularly unfortunate fate or by the niggardly provision of a step-motherly nature, this will should be wholly lacking in power to accomplish its purpose, and if even the greatest effort should not avail it to achieve anything of its end, and if there remained only the good will—not as a mere wish, but as the summoning of all the means in our power—it would sparkle like a jewel all by itself, as something that had its full worth in itself. Usefulness or fruitlessness can neither diminish nor augment this worth. Its usefulness would be only its setting, as it were, so as to enable us to handle it more conveniently in commerce or to attract the attention of those who are not yet connoisseurs, but not to recommend it to those who are experts or to determine its worth.

But there is something so strange in this idea of the absolute worth of the will alone, in which no account is taken of any use, that, notwithstanding the agreement even of common sense, the suspicion must arise that perhaps only high-flown fancy is its hidden basis, and that we may have misunderstood the purpose of nature in appointing reason as the ruler of our will. We shall therefore examine this idea from this point of view.

In the natural constitution of an organized being (i.e., one suitably adapted to life), we assume as an axiom that no organ will be found for any purpose which is not the fittest and best adapted to that purpose. Now if its preservation, its welfare, in a word its happiness, were the real end of nature in a being having reason and will, then nature would have hit upon a very poor arrangement in appointing the reason of the creature to be the executor of this purpose. For all the actions which the creature has to perform with this intention of nature, and the entire rule of his conduct, would be dictated much more exactly by instinct, and the end would be far more certainly attained by instinct than it ever could be by reason. And if, over and above this, reason should have been granted to the favored creature, it would have served only to let him contemplate the happy constitution of his nature, to admire it, to rejoice in it, and to be grateful for it to its beneficent cause. But reason would not have been given in order that the being should subject his faculty of desire to that weak and delusive guidance and to meddle with the purpose of nature. In a word, nature would have taken care that reason did not break forth into practical use nor have the presumption, with its weak insight, to think out for itself the plan of happiness and the means of attaining it. Nature would have taken over the choice not only of ends but also of the means, and with wise foresight she would have entrusted both to instinct alone.

And, in fact, we find that the more a cultivated reason deliberately devotes itself to the enjoyment of life and happiness, the more the man falls short of true contentment. From this fact there arises in many persons, if only they are candid enough to admit it, a certain degree of misology, hatred of reason. This is particularly the case with those who are most experienced in its use. After counting all the advantages which they draw—I will not say from the invention of the arts of common luxury— from the sciences (which in the end seem to them to be also a luxury of the understanding), they nevertheless find that they have actually brought more trouble on their shoulders instead of gaining in happiness; they finally envy, rather than despise, the common run of men who are better guided by merely natural instinct and who do not permit their reason much influence on their conduct. And we must at least admit that a morose attitude or ingratitude to the goodness with which the world is governed is by no means found always among those who temper or refute the boasting eulogies which are given of the advantages of happiness and contentment with which reason is supposed to supply us. Rather, their judgment is based on the Idea of another and far more worthy purpose of their existence for which, instead of happiness, their reason is properly intended; this purpose, therefore, being the supreme condition to which the private purposes of men must, for the most part, defer.

Since reason is not competent to guide the will safely with regard to its objects and the satisfaction of all our needs (which it in part multiplies), to this end an innate instinct would have led with far more certainty. But reason is given to us as a practical faculty (i.e., one which is meant to have an influence on the will). As nature has elsewhere distributed capacities suitable to the functions they are to perform, reason's proper function must be to produce a will good in itself and not one good merely as a means, since for the former, reason is absolutely essential. This will need not be the sole and complete good, yet it must be the condition of all others, even of the desire for happiness. In this case it is entirely compatible with the wisdom of nature that the cultivation of reason, which is required for the former unconditional purpose, at least in this life restricts in many ways—indeed, can reduce to nothing—the achievement of the latter unconditional purpose, happiness. For one perceives that nature here does not proceed unsuitably to its purpose, because reason, which recognizes its highest practical vocation in the establishment of a good will, is capable of a contentment of its own kind (i.e., one that springs from the attainment of a purpose determined by reason), even though this injures the ends of inclination.

We have, then, to develop the concept of a will which is to be esteemed as good in itself without regard to anything else. It dwells already in the natural and sound understanding and does not need so much to be taught as only to be brought to light. In the estimation of the total worth of our actions it always takes first place and is the condition of everything else. In order to show this, we shall take the concept of duty. It contains the concept of a good will, though with certain subjective restrictions and hindrances, but these are far from concealing it and making it unrecognizable, for they rather bring it out by contrast and make it shine forth all the more brightly.

I here omit all actions which are recognized as opposed to duty, even though they may be useful in one respect or another, for with these the question does not arise as to whether they may be done from duty, since they conflict with it. I also pass over actions which are really in accord with duty and to which one has no direct inclination, rather doing them because impelled to do so by another inclination. For it is easily decided whether an action in accord with duty is done from duty or for some selfish purpose. It is far more difficult to note this difference when the action is in accord with duty and, in addition, the subject has a direct inclination to do it. For example, it is in accord with duty that a dealer should not overcharge an inexperienced customer, and wherever there is much trade the prudent merchant does not do so, but has a fixed price for everyone so that a child may buy from him as cheaply as any other. Thus the customer is honestly served, but this is far from sufficient to warrant the belief that the merchant has behaved in this way from duty and principles of honesty. His own advantage required this behavior, but it cannot be assumed that over and above that he had a direct inclination to his customers and that, out of love, as it were, he gave none an advantage in price over another. The action was done neither from duty nor from direct inclination but only for a selfish purpose.

On the other hand, it is a duty to preserve one's life, and moreover everyone has a direct inclination to do so. But for that reason, the often anxious care which most men take of it has no intrinsic worth, and the maxim of doing so has no moral import. They preserve their lives according to duty, but not from duty. But if adversities and hopeless sorrow completely take away the relish for life; if an unfortunate man, strong in soul, is indignant rather than despondent or dejected over his fate and wishes for death, and yet preserves his life without loving it and from neither inclination nor fear but from duty—then his maxim has moral merit.

To be kind where one can is a duty, and there are, moreover, many persons so sympathetically constituted that without any motive of vanity or selfishness they find an inner satisfaction in spreading joy and rejoice in the contentment of others which they have made possible. But I say that, however dutiful and however amiable it may be, that kind of action has no true moral worth. It is on a level with [actions done from] other inclinations, such as the inclination to honor, which, if fortunately directed to what in fact accords with duty and is generally useful and thus honorable, deserve praise and encouragement, but no esteem. For the maxim lacks the moral import of an action done not from inclination but from duty. But assume that the mind of that friend to mankind was clouded by a sorrow of his own which extinguished all sympathy with the lot of others, and though he still had the power to benefit others in distress their need left him untouched because he was preoccupied with his own. Now suppose him to tear himself, unsolicited by inclination, out of his dead insensibility and to do this action only from duty and without any inclination—then for the first time his action has genuine moral worth. Furthermore, if nature has put little sympathy into the heart of a man, and if he, though an honest man, is by temperament cold and indifferent to the sufferings of others perhaps because he is provided with special gifts of patience and fortitude and expects and even requires that others should have them too—and such a man would certainly not be the meanest product of nature—would not he find in himself a source from which to give himself a far higher worth than he could have got by having a good-natured temperament? This is unquestionably true even though nature did not make him philanthropic, for it is just here that the worth of character is brought out, which is morally the incomparably highest of all: he is beneficent not from inclination, but from duty.

To secure one's own happiness is at least indirectly a duty, for discontent with one's condition under pressure from many cares and amid unsatisfied wants could easily become a great temptation to transgress against duties. But, without any view to duty, all men have the strongest and deepest inclination to happiness, because in this Idea all inclinations are summed up. But the precept of happiness is often so formulated that it definitely thwarts some inclinations, and men can make no definite and certain concept of the sum of satisfaction of all inclinations, which goes under the name of happiness. It is not to be wondered at, therefore, that a single inclination, definite as to what it promises and as to the time at which it can be satisfied, can outweigh a fluctuating idea and that, for example, a man with the gout can choose to enjoy what he likes and to suffer what he may, because according to his calculations at least on this occasion he has not sacrificed the enjoyment of the present moment to a perhaps groundless expectation of a happiness supposed to lie in health. But even in this case if the universal inclination to happiness did not determine his will, and if health were not at least for him a necessary factor in these calculations, there would still remain, as in all other cases, a law that he ought to promote his happiness not from inclination but from duty. Only from this law could his conduct have true moral worth.

It is in this way, undoubtedly, that we should understand those passages of Scripture which command us to love our neighbor and even our enemy, for love as an inclination cannot be commanded. But beneficence from duty, even when no inclination impels it and even when it is opposed by a natural and unconquerable aversion, is practical love, not pathological* love; it resides in the will and not in the propensities of feeling, in principles of action and not in tender sympathy; and it alone can be commanded.

[Thus the first proposition of morality is that to have genuine moral worth, an action must be done from duty.] The second proposition is: An action done from duty does not have its moral worth in the purpose which is to be achieved through it but in the maxim whereby it is determined. Its moral value, therefore, does not depend upon the realization of the object of the action but merely on the principle of the volition by which the action is done irrespective of the objects of the faculty of desire. From the preceding discussion it is clear that the purposes we may have for our actions and their effects as ends and incentives of the will cannot give the actions any unconditional and moral worth. Wherein, then, can this worth lie, if it is not in the will in its relation to its hoped-for effect? It can lie nowhere else than in the principle of the will irrespective of the ends which can be realized by such action. For the will stands, as it were, at the crossroads halfway between its *a priori* principle which is formal and its posteriori incentive which is material. Since it must be determined by something, if it is done from duty it must be determined by the formal principle of volition as such, since every material principle has been withdrawn from it.

The third principle, as a consequence of the two preceding, I would express as follows: Duty is the necessity to do an action from respect for law. I can certainly have an inclination to an object as an effect of the proposed action, but I can never have respect for it precisely because it is a mere effect and not an activity of a will. Similarly, I can have no respect for any inclination whatsoever, whether my own or that of another; in the former case I can at most approve of it and in the latter I can even love it (i.e., see it as favorable to my own advantage). But that which is connected with my will merely as ground and not as consequence, that which does not serve my inclination but overpowers it or at least excludes it from being considered in making a choice—in a word, law itself—can be an object of respect and thus a command. Now as an act from duty wholly excludes the influence of inclination and therewith every object of the will, nothing remains which can determine the will objectively except law and subjectively except pure respect for this practical law. This subjective element is the maxim** that I should follow such a law even if it thwarts all my inclinations.

---

*[Here as elsewhere Kant uses the word pathological to describe motives and actions arising from feeling or bodily impulses, with no suggestion of abnormality or disease.]

**A maxim is the subjective principle of volition. The objective principle (i.e., that which would serve all rational beings also subjectively as a practical principle if reason had full power over the faculty of desire) is the practical law.

Thus the moral worth of an action does not lie in the effect which is expected from it or in any principle of action which has to borrow its motive from this expected effect. For all these effects (agreeableness of my own condition, indeed even the promotion of the happiness of others) could be brought about through other causes and would not require the will of a rational being, while the highest and unconditional good can be found only in such a will. Therefore the preeminent good can consist only in the conception of law in itself (which can be present only in a rational being) so far as this conception and not the hoped-for effect is the determining ground of the will. This preeminent good, which we call moral, is already present in the person who acts according to this conception, and we do not have to look for it first in the result.*

But what kind of law can that be, the conception of which must determine the will without reference to the expected result? Under this condition alone can the will be called absolutely good without qualification. Since I have robbed the will of all impulses which could come to it from obedience to any law, nothing remains to serve as a principle of the will except universal conformity to law as such. That is, I ought never to act in such a way that I could not also will that my maxim should be a universal law. Strict conformity to law as such (without assuming any particular law applicable to certain actions) serves as the principle of the will, and it must serve as such a principle if duty is not to be a vain delusion and chimerical concept. The common sense of mankind (*gemeine Menschenvernunft*) in its practical judgments is in perfect agreement with this and has this principle constantly in view.

Let the question, for example, be: May I, when in distress, make a promise with the intention not to keep it? I easily distinguish the two meanings which the question can have, viz., whether it is prudent to make a false promise, or whether it conforms to duty. The former can undoubtedly be often the case, though I do see clearly that it is not sufficient merely to escape from the present difficulty by this expedient, but that I must consider whether inconveniences much greater than the present one may not later spring from this lie. Even with all my supposed cunning, the consequences cannot be so easily foreseen. Loss of credit might be far more disadvantageous than the misfortune I am now seeking to avoid, and it is hard to tell whether it might not be more prudent to act according to a universal maxim and to make it a habit not to promise anything without intending to fulfill it. But it is soon clear to me that such a maxim is based only on an apprehensive concern with consequences.

To be truthful from duty, however, is an entirely different thing from being truthful out of fear of untoward consequences, for in the former case the concept of the

---

*It might be objected that I seek to take refuge in an obscure feeling behind the word "respect," instead of clearly resolving the question with a concept of reason. But though respect is a feeling, it is not one received through any [outer] influence but is self-wrought by a rational concept; thus it differs specifically from all feelings of the former kind which may be referred to inclination or fear. What I recognize directly as a law for myself I recognize with respect, which means merely the consciousness of the submission of my will to a law without the intervention of other influences on my mind. The direct determination of the will by law and the consciousness of this determination is respect; thus respect can be regarded as the effect of the law on the subject and not as the cause of the law. Respect is properly the conception of a worth which thwarts my self-love. Thus it is regarded as an object neither of inclination nor of fear, though it has something analogous to both. The only object of respect is law, and indeed only the law which we impose on ourselves and yet recognize as necessary in itself. As a law we are subject to it without consulting self-love; as imposed on us by ourselves, it is a consequence of our will. In the former respect it is analogous to fear and in the latter to inclination. All respect for a person is only respect for the law (of righteousness, etc.) of which the person provides an example. Because we see the improvement of our talents as a duty, we think of a person of talent as the example of a law, as it were (the law that we should by practice become like him in his talents), and that constitutes our respect. All so-called moral interest consists solely in respect for the law.

action itself contains a law for me, while in the latter I must first look about to see what results for me may be connected with it. To deviate from the principle of duty is certainly bad, but to be unfaithful to my maxim of prudence can sometimes be very advantageous to me, though it is certainly safer to abide by it. The shortest but most infallible way to find the answer to the question as to whether a deceitful promise is consistent with duty is to ask myself: Would I be content that my maxim of extricating myself from difficulty by a false promise should hold as a universal law for myself as well as for others? And could I say to myself that everyone may make a false promise when he is in a difficulty from which he otherwise cannot escape? Immediately I see that I could will the lie but not a universal law to lie. For with such a law there would be no promises at all, inasmuch as it would be futile to make a pretense of my intention in regard to future actions to those who would not believe this pretense or—if they overhastily did so—would pay me back in my own coin. Thus my maxim would necessarily destroy itself as soon as it was made a universal law.

I do not, therefore, need any penetrating acuteness to discern what I have to do in order that my volition may be morally good. Inexperienced in the course of the world, incapable of being prepared for all its contingencies, I only ask myself: Can I will that my maxim become a universal law? If not, it must be rejected, not because of any disadvantage accruing to myself or even to others, but because it cannot enter as a principle into a possible enactment of universal law, and reason extorts from me an immediate respect for such legislation. I do not as yet discern on what it is grounded (this is a question the philosopher may investigate), but I at least understand that it is an estimation of a worth which far outweighs all the worth of whatever is recommended by the inclinations, and that the necessity that I act from pure respect for the practical law constitutes my duty. To duty every other motive must give place, because duty is the condition of a will good in itself, whose worth transcends everything.

Thus within the moral knowledge of ordinary human reason (*gemeine Menschenvernunft*) we have attained its principle. To be sure, ordinary human reason does not think this principle abstractly in such a universal form, but it always has the principle in view and uses it as the standard for its judgments. It would be easy to show how ordinary human reason, with this compass, knows well how to distinguish what is good, what is bad, and what is consistent or inconsistent with duty. Without in the least teaching common reason anything new, we need only to draw its attention to its own principle (in the manner of Socrates), thus showing that neither science nor philosophy is needed in order to know what one has to do in order to be honest and good, and even wise and virtuous. We might have conjectured beforehand that the knowledge of what everyone is obliged to do and thus also to know would be within the reach of everyone, even of the most ordinary man. Here we cannot but admire the great advantages which the practical faculty of judgment has over the theoretical in ordinary human understanding. In the theoretical, if ordinary reason ventures to go beyond the laws of experience and perceptions of the senses, it falls into sheer inconceivabilities and self-contradictions, or at least into a chaos of uncertainty, obscurity, and instability. In the practical, on the other hand, the power of judgment first shows itself to advantage when common understanding excludes all sensuous incentives from practical laws. It then even becomes subtle, quibbling with its own conscience or with other claims to what should be called right, or wishing to determine accurately, for its own instruction, the worth of certain actions. But the most remarkable thing about ordinary human understanding in its practical concern is that it may have as much hope as any philosopher of hitting the mark. In fact, it is almost more certain to do so that the philosopher, for while he has no principle which common understanding lacks, his judgment is easily confused by a mass of irrelevant considerations so that it easily turns aside from the correct way. Would it not, therefore, be wiser in moral matters to acquiesce in ordinary reasonable judgment and at most to call in philosophy in order to make the system of morals more complete and comprehensible and its rules more convenient for use (especially in disputation), than to steer the ordinary understanding from its happy simplicity in practical matters and to lead it through philosophy into a new path of inquiry and instruction?

Innocence is indeed a glorious thing, but it is very sad that it cannot well maintain itself, being easily led astray. For this reason, even wisdom—which consists more in acting than in knowing—needs science, not so as to learn from it but to secure admission and permanence to its precepts. Man feels in himself a powerful counterpoise against all commands of duty which reason presents to him as so deserving of respect. This counterpoise is his needs and inclinations, the complete satisfaction of which he sums up under the name of happiness. Now reason issues inexorable commands without promising anything to the inclinations. It disregards, as it were, and holds in contempt those claims which are so impetuous and yet so plausible, and which refuse to be suppressed by any command. From this a natural dialectic arises, i.e., a propensity to argue against the stern laws of duty and their validity, or at least to place their purity and strictness in doubt and, where possible, to make them more accordant with our wishes and inclinations. This is equivalent to corrupting them in their very foundations and destroying their dignity—a thing which even ordinary practical reason cannot finally call good.

In this way ordinary human reason is impelled to go outside its sphere and to take a step into the field of practical philosophy. But it is forced to do so not by any speculative need, which never occurs to it so long as it is satisfied to remain merely healthy reason; rather, it is impelled on practical grounds to obtain information and clear instruction respecting the source of its principle and the correct definition of this principle in its opposition to the maxims based on need and inclination. It seeks this information in order to escape from the perplexity of opposing claims and to avoid the danger of losing all genuine moral principles through the equivocation in which it is easily involved. Thus when ordinary practical reason cultivates itself, a dialectic surreptitiously ensues which forces it to seek aid in philosophy, just as the same thing happens in the theoretical use of reason. Ordinary practical reason, like theoretical reason, will find rest only in a complete critical examination of our reason.

SECOND SECTION

TRANSITION FROM POPULAR MORAL PHILOSOPHY TO THE METAPHYSICS OF MORALS

Although we have derived our earlier concept of duty from the ordinary use of our practical reason, it is by no means to be inferred that we have treated it as an empirical concept. On the contrary, if we attend to our experience of the way men act, we meet frequent and, as we must confess, justified complaints that we cannot cite a single sure example of the disposition to act from pure duty. There are also justified complaints that, though much may be done that accords with what duty commands, it is nevertheless always doubtful whether it is done from duty and thus whether it has moral worth.

There have always been philosophers who for this reason have absolutely denied the reality of this disposition in human actions, attributing everything to more or less refined self-love. They have done so without questioning the correctness of the concept of morality. Rather they spoke with sincere regret of the frailty and corruption of human nature, which is noble enough to take as its precept an Idea so worthy of respect but which at the same time is too weak to follow it, employing reason, which should give laws for human nature, only to provide for the interest of the inclinations either singly or, at best, in their greatest possible harmony with one another.

It is, in fact, absolutely impossible by experience to discern with complete certainty a single case in which the maxim of an action, however much it might conform to duty, rested solely on moral grounds and on the conception of one's duty. It sometimes happens that in the most searching self-examination we can find nothing except the moral ground of duty which could have been powerful enough to move us to this or that good action and to such great sacrifice. But from this we cannot by any means conclude with certainty that a secret impulse of self-love, falsely appearing as the Idea of duty, was not actually the true determining cause of the will. For we like to flatter ourselves with a pretended nobler motive, while in fact even the strictest examination can never lead us entirely behind the secret incentives, for when moral worth is in question it is not a matter of actions which one sees but of their inner principles which one does not see.

Moreover, one cannot better serve the wishes of those who ridicule all morality as a mere phantom of human imagination overreaching itself through self-conceit than by conceding that the concepts of duty must be derived only from experience (for they are ready, from indolence, to believe that this is true of all other concepts too). For, by this concession, a sure triumph is prepared for them. Out of love for humanity I am willing to admit that most of our actions are in accord with duty; but if we look more closely at our thoughts and aspirations, we come everywhere upon the dear self, which is always turning up, and it is this instead of the stern command of duty (which would often require self-denial) which supports our plans. One need not be an enemy of virtue, but only a cool observer who does not confuse even the liveliest aspiration for the good with its actuality, to be sometimes doubtful whether true virtue can really be found anywhere in the world. This is especially true as one's years increase and the power of judgment is made wiser by experience and more acute in observation. This being so, nothing can secure us against the complete abandonment of our ideas of duty and preserve in us a well-founded respect for its law except the conviction that, even if there never were actions springing from such pure sources, our concern is not whether this or that was done, but that reason of itself and independently of all appearances commanded what ought to be done. Our concern is with actions of which perhaps the world has never had an example, with actions whose feasibility might be seriously doubted by those who base everything on experience, and yet with actions inexorably commanded by reason. For example, pure sincerity in friendship can be demanded of every man, and this demand is not in the least diminished if a sincere friend has never existed, because this duty, as duty in general, prior to all experience lies in the Idea of reason which determines the will on *a priori* grounds.

No experience, it is clear, can give occasion for inferring the possibility of such apodictic laws. This is especially clear when we add that, unless we wish to deny all truth to the concept of morality and renounce its application to any possible object, we cannot refuse to admit that the law is of such broad significance that it holds not merely for men but for all rational beings as such; we must grant that it must be valid with absolute necessity, and not merely under contingent conditions and with exceptions. For

Immanuel Kant and Luncheon Guests, 1893, by E. Doestling. While Kant led a simple,
routine-filled life, he was known as a delightful conversationalist and host who had many
friends and admirers. (*The Bettmann Archive*)

with what right could we bring into unlimited respect something that might be valid
only under contingent human conditions? And how could laws of the determination of
our will be held to be laws of the determination of the will of any rational being whatever and of ourselves in so far as we are rational beings, if they were merely empirical
and did not have their origin completely *a priori* in pure, but practical, reason?

Nor could one given poorer counsel to morality than to attempt to derive it from
examples. For each example of morality which is exhibited must itself have been previously judged according to principles of morality to see whether it was worthy to
serve as an original example or model. By no means could it authoritatively furnish the
concept of morality. Even the Holy One of the Gospel must be compared with our
ideal of moral perfection before He is recognized as such; even He says of Himself,
"Why call ye Me (Whom you see) good? None is good (the archetype of the good) except God only (Whom you do not see)." But whence do we have the concept of God as
the highest good? Solely from the Idea of moral perfection which reason formulates *a*

priori and which it inseparably connects with the concept of a free will. Imitation has no place in moral matters, and examples serve only for encouragement. That is, they put beyond question the possibility of performing what the law commands, and they make visible that which the practical rule expresses more generally. But they can never justify our guiding ourselves by examples and our setting aside their true original, which lies in reason.

If there is thus no genuine supreme principle of morality which does not rest on pure reason alone independent of all possible experience, I do not believe it is necessary even to ask whether it is well to exhibit these concepts generally (in abstracto), which, together with the principles belonging to them, are established *a priori*. At any rate, the question need not be asked if knowledge of them is to be distinguished from ordinary knowledge and called philosophical. But in our times this question may be necessary. For if we collected votes as to whether pure rational knowledge separated from all experience (i.e., a metaphysics of morals) or popular practical philosophy is to be preferred, it is easily guessed on which side the majority would stand.

This condescension to popular notions is certainly very commendable once the ascent to the principles of pure reason has been satisfactorily accomplished. That would mean the prior establishment of the doctrine of morals on metaphysics and then, when it is established, procuring a hearing for it through popularization. But it is extremely absurd to want to achieve popular appeal in the first investigation, where everything depends on the correctness of the fundamental principles. Not only can this procedure never make claim to that rarest merit of true philosophical popularity, since there is really no art in being generally comprehensible if one thereby renounces all basic insight; but it produces a disgusting jumble of patched-up observations and half-reasoned principles. Shallow pates enjoy this, for it is very useful in everyday chitchat, while the more sensible feel confused and dissatisfied and avert their eyes without being able to help themselves. But philosophers, who see through this delusion, get little hearing when they call people away from this would-be popularity so that they may have genuine popular appeal once they have gained a definite understanding.

One need only look at the essays on morality favored by popular taste. One will sometimes meet with the particular vocation of human nature (but occasionally with the Idea of a rational nature in general), sometimes perfection and sometimes happiness, here moral feeling, there fear of God, a little of this and a little of that in a marvelous mixture. It never occurs to the authors, however, to ask whether the principles of morality are, after all, to be sought anywhere in knowledge of human nature (which we can derive only from experience). And if this is not the case, if the principles are *a priori*, free from everything empirical, and found exclusively in pure rational concepts and not at all in any other place, they never ask whether they should undertake this investigation as a separate inquiry (i.e., as pure practical philosophy) or (if one may use a name so decried) a metaphysics* of morals. They never think of dealing with it alone and bringing it by itself to completeness and of requiring the public, which desires popularization, to await the outcome of this undertaking.

But a completely isolated metaphysics of morals, mixed with no anthropology, no theology, no physics or hyperphysics, and even less with occult qualities (which

---

*If one wishes, the pure philosophy (metaphysics) of morals can be distinguished from the applied (i.e., applied to human nature), just as pure mathematics and pure logic are distinguished from applied mathematics and applied logic. By this designation one is immediately reminded that moral principles are not founded on the peculiarities of human nature but must stand of themselves *a priori*, and that from such principles practical rules for every rational nature, and accordingly for man, must be derivable.

might be called hypophysical), is not only an indispensable substrate of all theoretically sound and definite knowledge of duties; it is also a desideratum of the highest importance to the actual fulfillment of its precepts. For the thought of duty and of the moral law generally, with no admixture of empirical inducements, has an influence on the human heart so much more powerful than all other incentives* which may be derived from the empirical field that reason, in the consciousness of its dignity, despises them and gradually becomes master over them. It has this influence only through reason alone, which thereby first realizes that it can of itself be practical. A mixed theory of morals which is put together from incentives of feelings and inclinations and from rational concepts must, on the other hand, make the mind vacillate between motives which cannot be brought together under any principle and which can lead only accidentally to the good, and frequently lead to the bad.

From what has been said it is clear that all moral concepts have their seat and origin entirely *a priori* in reason. This is just as much the case in the most ordinary reason as in the reason which is speculative to the highest degree. It is obvious that they can be abstracted from no empirical and hence merely contingent cognitions. In the purity of origin lies their worthiness to serve us as supreme practical principles, and to the extent that something empirical is added to them, just this much is subtracted from their genuine influence and from the unqualified worth of actions. Furthermore, it is evident that it is not only of the greatest necessity from a theoretical point of view when it is a question of speculation but also of the utmost practical importance to derive the concepts and laws of morals from pure reason and to present them pure and unmixed, and to determine the scope of this entire practical but pure rational knowledge (the entire faculty of pure practical reason) without making the principles depend upon the particular nature of human reason, as speculative philosophy may permit and even find necessary. But since moral laws should hold for every rational being as such, the principles must be derived from the universal concept of a rational being in general. In this manner all morals, which need anthropology for their application to men, must be completely developed first as pure philosophy (i.e., metaphysics), independently of anthropology (a thing feasibly done in such distinct fields of knowledge). For we know well that if we are not in possession of such a metaphysics, it is not merely futile [to try to] define accurately for the purposes of speculative judgment the moral element of duty in all actions which accord with duty, but impossible to base morals on legitimate principles for even ordinary practical use, especially in moral instruction; and it is only in this manner that pure moral dispositions can be produced and engrafted on men's minds for the purpose of the highest good in the world.

In this study we do not advance merely from the common moral judgment (which here is very worthy of respect) to the philosophical, as this has already been done; but we advance by natural stages from popular philosophy (which goes no farther than it can grope by means of examples) to metaphysics (which is not held back

---

*I have a letter from the late excellent Sulzer in which he asks me why the theories of virtue accomplish so little even though they contain so much that is convincing to reason. My answer was delayed in order that I might make it complete. The answer is only that the teachers themselves have not completely clarified their concepts, and when they wish to make up for this by hunting in every quarter for motives to the morally good so as to make their physic right strong, they spoil it. For the commonest observation shows that if we imagine an act of honesty performed with a steadfast soul and sundered from all view to any advantage in this or another world and even under the greatest temptations of need or allurement, it far surpasses and eclipses any similar action which was affected in the least by any foreign incentive; it elevates the soul and arouses the wish to be able to act in this way. Even moderately young children feel this impression, and one should never represent duties to them in any other way.

by anything empirical and which, as it must measure out the entire scope of rational knowledge of this kind, reaches even Ideas, where examples fail us). In order to make this advance, we must follow and clearly present the practical faculty of reason from its universal rules of determination to the point where the concept of duty arises from it.

Everything in nature works according to laws. Only a rational being has the capacity of acting according to the *conception* of laws (i.e., according to principles). This capacity is the will. Since reason is required for the derivation of actions from laws, will is nothing less than practical reason. If reason infallibly determines the will, the actions which such a being recognizes as objectively necessary are also subjectively necessary. That is, the will is a faculty of choosing only that which reason, independently of inclination, recognizes as practically necessary (i.e., as good). But if reason of itself does not sufficiently determine the will, and if the will is subjugated to subjective conditions (certain incentives) which do not always agree with the objective conditions—in a word, if the will is not of itself in complete accord with reason (which is the actual case with men), then the actions which are recognized as objectively necessary are subjectively contingent, and the determination of such a will according to objective laws is a constraint. That is, the relation of objective laws to a will which is not completely good is conceived as the determination of the will of a rational being by principles of reason to which this will is not by its nature necessarily obedient.

The conception of an objective principle, so far as it constrains a will, is a command (of reason), and the formula of this command is called an *imperative*.

All imperatives are expressed by an "ought" and thereby indicate the relation of an objective law of reason to a will which is not in its subjective constitution necessarily determined by this law. This relation is that of constraint. Imperatives say that it would be good to do or to refrain from doing something, but they say it to a will which does not always do something simply because the thing is presented to it as good to do. Practical good is what determines the will by means of the conception of reason and hence not by subjective causes but objectively, on grounds which are valid for every rational being as such. It is distinguished from the pleasant, as that which has an influence on the will only by means of a sensation from purely subjective causes, which hold for the senses only of this or that person and not as a principle of reason which holds for everyone.*

A perfectly good will, therefore, would be equally subject to objective laws of the good, but it could not be conceived as constrained by them to accord with them, because it can be determined to act by its own subjective constitution only through the conception of the good. Thus no imperatives hold for the divine will or, more generally, for a holy will. The "ought" here is out of place, for the volition of itself is neces-

---

*The dependence of the faculty of desire on sensations is called inclination, and inclination always indicates a need. The dependence of a contingently determinable will on principles of reason, however, is called interest. An interest is present only in a dependent will which is not of itself always in accord with reason; in the divine will we cannot conceive of an interest. But even the human will can take an interest in something without thereby acting from interest. The former means the practical interest in the action; the latter, the pathological interest in the object of the action. The former indicates only the dependence of the will on principles of reason in themselves, while the latter indicates dependence on the principles of reason for the purpose of inclination, since reason gives only the practical rule by which the needs of inclination are to be aided. In the former case the action interests me, and in the latter the object of the action (so far as it is pleasant for me) interests me. In the First Section we have seen that, in the case of an action done from duty, no regard must be given to the interest in the object, but merely to the action itself and its principle in reason (i.e., the law).

sarily in unison with the law. Therefore imperatives are only formulas expressing the relation of objective laws of volition in general to the subjective imperfection of the will of this or that rational being, for example, the human will.

All imperatives command either *hypothetically* or *categorically*. The former present the practical necessity of a possible action as a means to achieving something else which one desires (or which one may possibly desire). The categorical imperative would be one which presented an action as of itself objectively necessary, without regard to any other end.

Since every practical law presents a possible action as good and thus as necessary for a subject practically determinable by reason, all imperatives are formulas of the determination of action which is necessary by the principle of a will which is in any way good. If the action is good only as a means to something else, the imperative is hypothetical; but if it is thought of as good in itself, and hence as necessary in a will which of itself conforms to reason as the principle of this will, the imperative is categorical.

The imperative thus says what action possible for me would be good, and it presents the practical rule in relation to a will which does not forthwith perform an action simply because it is good, in part because the subject does not always know that the action is good, and in part (when he does know it) because his maxims can still be opposed to the objective principles of a practical reason.

The hypothetical imperative, therefore, says only that the action is good to some purpose, possible or actual. In the former case, it is a problematical, in the latter an assertorical, practical principle. The categorical imperative, which declares the action to be of itself objectively necessary without making any reference to any end in view (i.e., without having any other purpose), holds as an apodictical practical principle.

We can think of what is possible only through the powers of some rational being as a possible end in view of any will. As a consequence, the principles of action thought of as necessary to attain a possible end in view which can be achieved by them, are in reality infinitely numerous. All sciences have some practical part consisting of problems which presuppose some purpose as well as imperatives directing how it can be reached. These imperatives can therefore be called, generally, imperatives of skill. Whether the purpose is reasonable and good is not in question at all, for the questions concerns only what must be done in order to attain it. The precepts to be followed by a physician in order to cure his patient and by a poisoner to bring about certain death are of equal value in so far as each does that which will perfectly accomplish his purpose. Since in early youth we do not know what purposes we may have in the course of our life, parents seek to let their children learn a great many things and provide for skill in the use of means to all sorts of ends which they might choose, among which they cannot determine whether any one of them will become their child's actual purpose, though it may be that someday he may have it as his actual purpose. And this anxiety is so great that they commonly neglect to form and correct their children's judgment on the worth of the things which they may make their ends.

There is one end, however, which we may presuppose as actual in all rational beings so far as imperatives apply to them, that is, so far as they are dependent beings. There is one purpose which they not only can have but which we can presuppose that they all *do* have by a necessity of nature. This purpose is happiness. The hypothetical imperative which represents the practical necessity of an action as means to the promotion of happiness is an assertorical imperative. We may not expound it as necessary to a merely uncertain and merely possible purpose, but as necessary to a purpose which we can *a priori* and with assurance assume for everyone because it belongs to his essence. Skill in the choice of means to one's own highest well-being can be called prudence* in the narrowest sense. Thus the imperative which refers to the choice of means to one's own happiness (i.e., the precept of prudence) is still only hypothetical, and the action is not commanded absolutely but commanded only as a means to another end in view.

Finally, there is one imperative which directly commands certain conduct without making its condition some purpose to be reached by it. This imperative is categorical. It concerns not the material of the action and its intended result, but the form and principle from which it originates. What is essentially good in it consists in the mental disposition, the result being what it may. This imperative may be called the imperative of morality.

Volition according to these three principles is plainly distinguished by the dissimilarity in the constraints by which they subject the will. In order to clarify this dissimilarity, I believe that they are most suitably named if one says that they are either rules of skill, counsels of prudence, or commands (laws) of morality, respectively. For law alone implies the concept of an unconditional and objective and hence universally valid necessity, and commands are laws which must be obeyed even against inclination. Counsels do indeed involve necessity, but a necessity that can hold only under a subjectively contingent condition (i.e., whether this or that man counts this or that as part of his happiness). The categorical imperative, on the other hand, is restricted by no condition. As absolutely, though practically, necessary it can be called a command in the strict sense. We could also call the first imperatives technical (belonging to art), the second *pragmatic** (belonging to well-being), and the third moral (belonging to free conduct as such, i.e., to morals).

The question now arises: How are all these imperatives possible? This question does not require an answer as to how the action which the imperative commands can be performed, but only an answer as to how the constraint of the will, which the imperative expresses in setting the problem, can be conceived. How an imperative of skill is possible requires no particular discussion. Whoever wills the end, so far as reason has decisive influence on his action, wills also the indispensably necessary steps to it that he can take. This proposition, in what concerns the will, is analytical; for, in the willing of an object as an effect, my causality, as an acting cause of this effect shown in my use of the means to it, is already thought, and the imperative derives the concept of actions necessary to this purpose from the concept of willing this purpose. Synthetical propositions undoubtedly are necessary for determining the means to a proposed end, but they do not concern the ground, the act of the will, but only the way to achieve the object. Mathematics teaches, by synthetical propositions only, that in order to bisect a line according to an infallible principle, I must make two intersecting arcs from each of its extremities; but if I know the proposed result can be obtained only by such an ac-

---

*The word "prudence" may be taken in two senses, and it may bear the names of prudence with reference to things of the world and private prudence. The former sense means the skill of a man in having an influence on others so as to use them for his own purposes. The latter is the ability to unite all these purposes to his own lasting advantage. The worth of the first is finally reduced to the latter, and of one who is prudent in the former sense but not in the latter we might better say that he is clever and cunning yet, on the whole, imprudent.

**It seems to me that the proper meaning of the word "pragmatic" could be most accurately defined in this way. For sanctions which properly flow not from the law of states as necessary statutes but from provision for the general welfare are called pragmatic. A history is pragmatically composed when it teaches prudence (i.e., instructs the world how it could provide for its interest better than, or at least as well as, has been done in the past).

tion, then it is an analytical proposition that, if I fully will the effect, I must also will the action necessary to produce it. For it is one and the same thing to conceive of something as an effect which is in a certain way possible through me, and to conceive of myself as acting in this way.

If it were only easy to give a definite concept of happiness, the imperatives of prudence would perfectly correspond to those of skill and would likewise be analytical. For it could then be said in this case as well as in the former that whoever wills the end wills also (necessarily according to reason) the only means to it which are in his power. But it is a misfortune that the concept of happiness is so indefinite that, although each person wishes to attain it, he can never definitely and self-consistently state what it is that he really wishes and wills. The reason for this is that all elements which belong to the concept of happiness are empirical (i.e., they must be taken from experience), while for the Idea of happiness an absolute whole, a maximum, of well-being is needed in my present and in every future condition. Now it is impossible for even a most clear-sighted and most capable but finite being to form here a definite concept of that which he really wills. If he wills riches, how much anxiety, envy, and intrigues might he not thereby draw upon his shoulders! If he wills much knowledge and vision, perhaps it might become only an eye that much sharper to show him as more dreadful the evils which are now hidden from him and which are yet unavoidable; or it might be to burden his desires—which already sufficiently engage him—with even more needs! If he wills long life, who guarantees that it will not be long misery! If he wills at least health, how often has not the discomfort of his body restrained him from excesses into which perfect health would have led him? In short, he is not capable, on any principle and with complete certainty, of ascertaining what would make him truly happy; omniscience would be needed for this. He cannot, therefore, act according to definite principles so as to be happy, but only according to empirical counsels (e.g., those of diet, economy, courtesy, restraint, etc.) which are shown by experience best to promote well-being on the average. Hence the imperatives of prudence cannot, in the strict sense, command (i.e., present actions objectively as practically necessary); thus they are to be taken as counsels (*consilia*) rather than as commands (*praecepta*) of reason, and the task of determining infallibly and universally what action will promote the happiness of a rational being is completely unsolvable. There can be no imperative which would, in the strict sense, command us to do what makes for happiness, because happiness is an ideal not of reason but of imagination, depending only on empirical grounds which one would expect in vain to determine an action through which the totality of consequences—which in fact is infinite—could be achieved. Assuming that the means to happiness could be infallibly stated, this imperative of prudence would be an analytically practical proposition for it differs from the imperative of skill only in that its purpose is given, while in the imperative of skill it is merely a possible purpose. Since both, however, command the means to that which one presupposes as a willed purpose, the imperative which commands the willing of the means to him who wills the end is in both cases analytical. There is, consequently, no difficulty in seeing the possibility of such an imperative.

To see how the imperative of morality is possible, then, is without doubt the only question needing an answer. It is not hypothetical, and thus the objectively conceived necessity cannot be supported by any presupposed purpose, as was the case with the hypothetical imperatives. But it must not be overlooked that it cannot be shown by any example (i.e., it cannot be empirically shown) that there is such an imperative. Rather, it is to be suspected that all imperatives which appear to be categorical are tacitly hypothetical. For instance, when it is said, "Thou shalt not make a false promise," we assume that the necessity of this prohibition is not a mere counsel for the sake of escaping some other evil, so that it would read: "Thou shalt not make a false promise, lest, if it comes to light, thou ruinest thy credit." [In so doing] we assume that an action of this kind must be regarded as in itself bad and that the imperative prohibiting it is categorical, but we cannot show with certainty by any example that the will is here determined by the law alone without any other incentives, although it appears to be so. For it is always possible that secretly fear of disgrace, and perhaps also obscure apprehension of other dangers, may have had an influence on the will. Who can prove by experience the nonexistence of a cause when experience shows us only that we do not perceive the cause? In such a case the so-called moral imperative, which as such appears to be categorical and unconditional, would be actually only a pragmatic precept which makes us attentive to our own advantage and teaches us to consider it.

Thus we shall have to investigate purely *a priori* the possibility of a categorical imperative, for we do not have the advantage that experience would show us the reality of this imperative so that the [demonstration of its] possibility would be necessary only for its explanation, and not for its establishment. In the meantime, this much at least may be seen: the categorical imperative alone can be taken as a practical law, while all other imperatives may be called principles of the will but not laws. This is because what is necessary merely for the attainment of some chosen end can be regarded as itself contingent and we get rid of the precept once we give up the end in view, whereas the unconditional command leaves the will no freedom to choose the opposite. Thus it alone implies the necessity which we require of a law.

Secondly, in the case of the categorical imperative or law of morality, the cause of the difficulty in discerning its possibility is very weighty. This imperative is an *a priori* synthetical practical proposition* and since to discern the possibility of propositions of this sort is so difficult in theoretical knowledge it may well be gathered that it will be no less difficult in practical knowledge.

In attacking this problem, we will first inquire whether the mere concept of a categorical imperative does not also furnish the formula containing the proposition which alone can be a categorical imperative. For even when we know the formula of the imperative, to learn how such an absolute command is possible will require difficult and special labors which we shall postpone to the last Section.

If I think of a hypothetical imperative as such, I do not know what it will contain until the condition is stated [under which it is an imperative]. But if I think of a categorical imperative, I know immediately what it will contain. For since the imperative contains, besides the law, only the necessity of the maxim** of acting in accordance with the law, while the law contains no condition to which it is restricted, nothing remains except the universality of law as such to which the maxim of the action should conform; and this conformity alone is what is represented as necessary by the imperative.

---

*I connect *a priori*, and hence necessarily, the action with the will without supposing as a condition that there is any inclination [to the action] (though I do so only objectively, i.e., under the Idea of a reason which would have complete power over all subjective motives). This is, therefore, a practical proposition which does not analytically derive the willing of an action from some other volition already presupposed (for we do not have such a perfect will); it rather connects it directly with the concept of the will of a rational being as something which is not contained within it.

**A maxim is the subjective principle of acting and must be distinguished from the objective principle (i.e., the practical law). The former contains the practical rule which reason determines according to the conditions of the subject (often his ignorance or inclinations) and is thus the principle according to which the subject acts. The law, on the other hand, is the objective principle valid for every rational being, and the principle by which it ought to act, i.e., an imperative.

There is, therefore, only one categorical imperative. It is: Act only according to that maxim by which you can at the same time will that it should become a universal law.

Now if all imperatives of duty can be derived from this one imperative as a principle, we can at least show what we understand by the concept of duty and what it means, even though it remain undecided whether that which is called duty is an empty concept or not.

The universality of law according to which effects are produced constitutes what is properly called nature in the most general sense (as to form) (i.e., the existence of things so far as it is determined by universal laws). [By analogy], then, the universal imperative of duty can be expressed as follows: Act as though the maxim of your action were by your will to become a universal law of nature.

We shall now enumerate some duties, adopting the usual division of them into duties to ourselves and to others and into perfect and imperfect duties.*

1. A man who is reduced to despair by a series of evils feels a weariness with life but is still in possession of his reason sufficiently to ask whether it would not be contrary to his duty to himself to take his own life. Now he asks whether the maxim of his action could become a universal law of nature. His maxim, however is: For love of myself, I make it my principle to shorten my life when by a longer duration it threatens more evil than satisfaction. But it is questionable whether this principle of self-love could become a universal law of nature. One immediately sees a contradiction in a system of nature whose law would be to destroy life by the feeling whose special office is to impel the improvement of life. In this case it would not exist as nature; hence that maxim cannot obtain as a law of nature, and thus it wholly contradicts the supreme principle of all duty.

2. Another man finds himself forced by need to borrow money. He well knows that he will not be able to repay it, but he also sees that nothing will be lent him if he does not firmly promise to repay it at a certain time. He desires to make such a promise, but he has enough conscience to ask himself whether it is not improper and opposed to duty to relieve his distress in such a way. Now, assuming he does decide to do so, the maxim of his action would be as follows: When I believe myself to be in need of money, I will borrow money and promise to repay it, although I know I shall never be able to do so. Now this principle of self-love or of his own benefit may very well be compatible with his whole future welfare, but the question is whether it is right. He changes the pretension of self-love into a universal law and then puts the question: How would it be if my maxim became a universal law? He immediately sees that it could never hold as a universal law of nature and be consistent with itself; rather it must necessarily contradict itself. For the universality of a law which says that anyone who believes himself to be in need could promise what he pleased with the intention of not fulfilling it would make the promise itself and the end to be accomplished by it impossible; no one would believe what was promised to him but would only laugh at any such assertion as vain pretense.

3. A third finds in himself a talent which could, by means of some cultivation, make him in many respects a useful man. But he finds himself in comfortable circum-

---

*It must be noted here that I reserve the division of duties for a future *Metaphysics of Morals* and that the division here stands as only an arbitrary one (chosen in order to arrange my examples). For the rest, by a perfect duty I here understand a duty which permits no exception in the interest of inclination; thus I have not merely outer but also inner perfect duties. This runs contrary to the usage adopted in the schools, but I am not disposed to defend it here because it is all one to my purpose whether this is conceded or not.

stances and prefers indulgence in pleasure to troubling himself with broadening and improving his fortunate natural gifts. Now, however, let him ask whether his maxim of neglecting his gifts, besides agreeing with his propensity to idle amusement, agrees also with what is called duty. He sees that a system of nature could indeed exist in accordance with such a law, even though man (like the inhabitants of the South Sea Islands) should let his talents rust and resolve to devote his life merely to idleness, indulgence, and propagation—in a word, to pleasure. But he cannot possibly will that this should become a universal law of nature or that it should be implanted in us by a natural instinct. For, as a rational being, he necessarily wills that all his faculties should be developed, inasmuch as they are given him and serve him for all sorts of purposes.

4. A fourth man, for whom things are going well, sees that others (whom he could help) have to struggle with great hardships, and he asks, "What concern of mine is it? Let each one be as happy as heaven wills, or as he can make himself; I will not take anything from him or even envy him; but to his welfare or to his assistance in time of need I have no desire to contribute." If such a way of thinking were a universal law of nature, certainly the human race could exist, and without doubt even better than in a state where everyone talks of sympathy and good will or even exerts himself occasionally to practice them while, on the other hand, he cheats when he can and betrays or otherwise violates the right of man. Now although it is possible that a universal law of nature according to that maxim could exist, it is nevertheless impossible to will that such a principle should hold everywhere as a law of nature. For a will which resolved this would conflict with itself, since instances can often arise in which he would need the love and sympathy of others, and in which he would have robbed himself, by such a law of nature springing from his own will, of all hope of the aid he desires.

The foregoing are a few of the many actual duties, or at least of duties we hold to be actual, whose derivation from the one stated principle is clear. We must be able to will that a maxim of our action become a universal law; this is the canon of the moral estimation of our action generally. Some actions are of such a nature that their maxim cannot even be *thought* as a universal law of nature without contradiction, far from it being possible that one could will that it should be such. In others this internal impossibility is not found, though it is still impossible to *will* that that maxim should be raised to the universality of a law of nature, because such a will would contradict itself. We easily see that a maxim of the first kind conflicts with stricter or narrower (imprescriptable) duty, that of the latter with broader (meritorious) duty. Thus all duties, so far as the kind of obligation (not the object of their action) is concerned, have been completely exhibited by these examples in their dependence upon the same principle.

When we observe ourselves in any transgression of a duty, we find that we do not actually will that our maxim should become a universal law. That is impossible for us; rather, the contrary of this maxim should remain as a law generally, and we only take the liberty of making an exception to it for ourselves or for the sake of our inclination, and for this one occasion. Consequently, if we weighed everything from one and the same standpoint, namely, reason, we would come upon a contradiction in our own will, viz., that a certain principle is objectively necessary as a universal law and yet subjectively does not hold universally but rather admits exceptions. However, since we regard our action at one time from the point of view of a will wholly conformable to reason and then from that of a will affected by inclinations, there is actually no contradiction, but rather an opposition of inclination to the precept of reason (*antagonismus*). In this the universality of the principle (*universalitas*) is changed into mere generality (*generalitas*), whereby the practical principle of reason meets the maxim halfway. Although this cannot be justified in our own impartial judgment, it does show that we actually acknowledge the validity of the categorical imperative and allow ourselves (with all respect to it) only a few exceptions which seem to us to be unimportant and forced upon us.

We have thus at least established that if duty is a concept which is to have significance and actual law-giving authority for our actions, it can be expressed only in categorical imperatives and not at all in hypothetical ones. For every application of it we have also clearly exhibited the content of the categorical imperative which must contain the principle of all duty (if there is such). This is itself very much. But we are not yet advanced far enough to prove *a priori* that that kind of imperative really exists, that there is a practical law which of itself commands absolutely and without any incentives, and that obedience to this law is duty.

With a view to attaining this, it is extremely important to remember that we must not let ourselves think that the reality of this principle can be derived from the particular constitution of human nature. For duty is practical unconditional necessity of action; it must, therefore, hold for all rational beings (to which alone an imperative can apply), and only for that reason can it be a law for all human wills. Whatever is derived from the particular natural situation of man as such, or from certain feelings and propensities, or even from a particular tendency of the human reason which might not hold necessarily for the will of every rational being (if such a tendency is possible), can give a maxim valid for us but not a law; that is, it can give a subjective principle by which we might act if only we have the propensity and inclination, but not an objective principle by which we would be directed to act even if all our propensity, inclination, and natural tendency were opposed to it. This is so far the case that the sublimity and intrinsic worth of the command is the better shown in a duty the fewer subjective causes there are for it and the more they are against it; the latter do not weaken the constraint of the law or diminish its validity.

Here we see philosophy brought to what is, in fact, a precarious position, which should be made fast even though it is supported by nothing in either heaven or earth. Here philosophy must show its purity, as the absolute sustainer of its laws, and not as the herald of laws which an implanted sense or who knows what tutelary nature whispers to it. Those may be better than nothing at all, but they can never afford fundamental principles, which reason alone dictates. These fundamental principles must originate entirely *a priori* and thereby obtain their commanding authority; they can expect nothing from the inclination of men but everything from the supremacy of the law and due respect for it. Otherwise they condemn man to self-contempt and inner abhorrence.

Thus everything empirical is not only wholly unworthy to be an ingredient in the principle of morality but is even highly prejudicial to the purity of moral practices themselves. For, in morals, the proper and inestimable worth of an absolutely good will consists precisely in the freedom of the principle of action from all influences from contingent grounds which only experience can furnish. We cannot too much or too often warn against the lax or even base manner of thought which seeks its principles among empirical motives and laws, for human reason in its weariness is glad to rest on this pillow. In a dream of sweet illusions (in which it embraces not Juno but a cloud), it substitutes for morality a bastard patched up from limbs of very different parentage, which looks like anything one wishes to see in it, but not like virtue to anyone who has ever beheld her in her true form.*

---

*To behold virtue in her proper form is nothing else than to exhibit morality stripped of all admixture of sensuous things and of every spurious adornment of reward or self-love. How much she then eclipses everything which appears charming to the senses can easily be seen by everyone with the least effort of his reason, if it be not spoiled for all abstraction.

The question then is: Is it a necessary law for all rational beings that they should always judge their actions by such maxims as they themselves could will to serve as universal laws? If there is such a law, it must be connected wholly *a priori* with the concept of the will of a rational being as such. But in order to discover this connection, we must, however reluctantly, take a step into metaphysics, although in a region of it different from speculative philosophy, namely into the metaphysics of morals. In a practical philosophy it is not a question of assuming grounds for what happens but of assuming laws of what ought to happen even though it may never happen (that is to say, we assume objective practical laws). Hence in practical philosophy we need not inquire into the reasons why something pleases or displeases, how the pleasure of mere feeling differs from taste, and whether this is distinct from a general satisfaction of reason. Nor need we ask on what the feeling of pleasure or displeasure rests, how desires and inclinations arise, and how, finally, maxims arise from desires and inclination under the co-operation of reason. For all these matters belong to empirical psychology, which would be the second part of physics if we consider it as philosophy of nature so far as it rests on empirical laws. But here it is a question of objectively practical laws and thus of the relation of a will to itself so far as it determines itself only by reason, for everything which has a relation to the empirical automatically falls away, because if reason of itself alone determines conduct, it must necessarily do so *a priori*. The possibility of reason's thus determining conduct must now be investigated.

The will is thought of as a faculty of determining itself to action in accordance with the conception of certain laws. Such a faculty can be found only in rational beings. That which serves the will as the objective ground of its self-determination is a purpose, and if it is given by reason alone it must hold alike for all rational beings. On the other hand, that which contains the ground of the possibility of the action, whose result is an end, is called the means. The subjective ground of desire is the incentive (Triebfeder) while the objective ground of volition is the motive (Bewegungsgrund). Thus arises the distinction between subjective purposes, which rest on incentives, and objective purposes, which depend on motives valid for every rational being. Practical principles are formal when they disregard all subjective purposes; they are material when they have subjective purposes and thus certain incentives as their basis. The purposes that a rational being holds before himself by choice as consequences of his action are material purposes and are without exception only relative, for only their relation to a particularly constituted faculty of desire in the subject gives them their worth. And this worth cannot afford any universal principles for all rational beings or any principles valid and necessary for every volition. That is, they cannot give rise to any practical laws. All these relative purposes, therefore, are grounds for hypothetical imperatives only.

But suppose that there were something the existence of which in itself had absolute worth, something which, as an end in itself, could be a ground of definite laws. In it and only in it could lie the ground of a possible categorical imperative (i.e., of a practical law).

Now, I say, man and, in general, every rational being exists as an end in himself and not merely as a means to be arbitrarily used by this or that will. In all his actions, whether they are directed toward himself or toward other rational beings, he must always be regarded at the same time as an end. All objects of inclination have only conditional worth, for if the inclinations and needs founded on them did not exist, their object would be worthless. The inclinations themselves as the sources of needs, however, are so lacking in absolute worth that the universal wish of every rational being must be indeed to free himself completely from them. Therefore, the worth of any objects to be obtained by our actions is at times conditional. Beings whose existence does not depend on our will but on nature, if they are not rational beings, have only relative worth as means, and are therefore called "things"; rational beings, on the other hand, are designated "persons" because their nature indicates that they are ends in themselves (i.e., things which may not be used merely as means). Such a being is thus an object of respect, and as such restricts all [arbitrary] choice. Such beings are not merely subjective ends whose existence as a result of our action has a worth for us, but are objective ends (i.e., beings whose existence is an end in itself). Such an end is one in the place of which no other end, to which these beings should serve merely as means, can be put. Without them, nothing of absolute worth could be found, and if all worth is conditional and thus contingent, no supreme practical principle for reason could be found anywhere.

Thus if there is to be a supreme practical principle and a categorical imperative for the human will, it must be one that forms an objective principle of the will from the conception of that which is necessarily an end for everyone because it is an end in itself. Hence this objective principle can serve as a universal law. The ground of this principle is: rational nature exists as an end in itself. Man necessarily thinks of his own existence in this way, and thus far it is a subjective principle of human actions. Also every other rational being thinks of his existence on the same rational ground which holds also for myself;* thus it is at the same time an objective principle from which, as a supreme practical ground, it must be possible to derive all laws of the will. The practical imperative, therefore, is the following: Act so that you treat humanity, whether in your own person or in that of another, always as an end and never as a means only. Let us now see whether this can be achieved. To return to our previous examples:

First, according to the concept of necessary duty to oneself, he who contemplates suicide will ask himself whether his action can be consistent with the idea of humanity as an end in itself. If in order to escape from burdensome circumstances he destroys himself, he uses a person merely as a means to maintain a tolerable condition up to the end of life. Man, however, is not a thing, and thus not something to be used merely as a means; he must always be regarded in all his actions as an end in himself. Therefore I cannot dispose of man in my own person so as to mutilate, corrupt, or kill him. (It belongs to ethics proper to define more accurately this basic principle so as to avoid all misunderstanding, e.g., as to amputating limbs in order to preserve myself, or to exposing my life to danger in order to save it; I must therefore omit them here.)

Second, as concerns necessary or obligatory duties to others, he who intends a deceitful promise to others sees immediately that he intends to use another man merely as a means, without the latter at the same time containing the end in himself. For he whom I want to use for my own purposes by means of such a promise cannot possibly assent to my mode of acting against him and thus share in the purpose of this action. This conflict with the principle of other men is even clearer if we cite examples of attacks on their freedom and property, for then it is clear that he who violates the rights of men intends to make use of the person of others merely as means, without considering that, as rational beings, they must always be esteemed at the same time as ends (i.e., only as beings who must be able to embody in themselves the purpose of the very same action).**

*Here I present this proposition as a postulate, but in the last Section grounds for it will be found.

**Let it not be thought that the banal "what you do not wish to be done to you . . ." could here serve as guide or principle, for it is only derived from the principle and is restricted by various limitations. It cannot be a universal law, because it contains the ground neither of duties to one's self nor of the benevolent duties to others (for many a man would gladly consent that others should not benefit him, provided only that he might be excused from showing benevolence to them). Nor does it contain the ground of obligatory duties to another, for the criminal would argue on this ground against the judge who sentences him. And so on.

Third, with regard to contingent (meritorious) duty to oneself, it is not sufficient that the action not conflict with humanity in our person as an end in itself; it must also harmonize with it. In humanity there are capacities for greater perfection which belong to the purpose of nature with respect to humanity in our own person, and to neglect these might perhaps be consistent with the preservation of humanity as an end in itself, but not with the furtherance of that end.

Fourth, with regard to meritorious duty to others, the natural purpose that all men have is their own happiness. Humanity might indeed exist if no one contributed to the happiness of others, provided he did not intentionally detract from it, but this harmony with humanity as an end in itself is only negative, not positive, if everyone does not also endeavor, as far as he can, to further the purposes of others. For the ends of any person, who is an end in himself, must as far as possible be also my ends, if that conception of an end in itself is to have its full effect on me.

This principle of humanity, and in general of every rational creature an end in itself, is the supreme limiting condition on the freedom of action of each man. It is not borrowed from experience, first, because of its universality, since it applies to all rational beings generally, and experience does not suffice to determine anything about them; and secondly, because in experience humanity is not thought of (subjectively) as the purpose of men (i.e., as an object which we of ourselves really make our purpose). Rather it is thought of as the objective end which ought to constitute the supreme limiting condition of all subjective ends whatever they may be. Thus this principle must arise from pure reason. Objectively the ground of all practical legislation lies (according to the first principle) in the rule and form of universality, which makes it capable of being a law (at least a natural law); subjectively it lies in the end. But the subject of all ends is every rational being as an end in itself (by the second principle); from this there follows the third practical principle of the will as the supreme condition of its harmony with universal practical reason, viz, the Idea of the will of every rational being as making universal law.

By this principle all maxims are rejected which are not consistent with the will's giving universal law. The will is not only subject to the law, but subject in such a way that it must be conceived also as itself prescribing the law, of which reason can hold itself to be the author; it is on this ground alone that the will is regarded as subject to the law.

By the very fact that the imperatives are thought of as categorical, either way of conceiving them—as imperatives demanding the lawfulness of actions, resembling the lawfulness of the natural order; or as imperatives of the universal prerogative of the purposes of rational beings as such—excludes from their sovereign authority all admixture of any interest as an incentive to obedience. But we have been assuming the imperatives to be categorical, for that was necessary if we wished to explain the concept of duty; that there are practical propositions which command categorically could not of itself be proved independently, just as little as it can be proved anywhere in this section. One thing, however could have been done: to indicate in the imperative itself, by some determination inherent in it, that in willing from duty the renunciation of all interest is the specific mark of the categorical imperative, distinguishing it from the hypothetical. And this is now done in the third formulation of the principle, viz., in the Idea of the will of every rational being as a will giving universal law. A will which is subject to laws can be bound to them by an interest, but a will giving the supreme law cannot possibly depend upon any interest, for such a dependent will would itself need still another law which would restrict the interest of its self-love to the condition that its [maxim] should be valid as a universal law.

Thus the principle of every human will as a will giving universal law in all its maxims* is very well adapted to being a categorical imperative, provided it is otherwise correct. Because of the Idea of giving universal law, it is based on no interest; and thus of all possible imperatives, it alone can be unconditional. Or, better, converting the proposition: if there is a categorical imperative (a law for the will of every rational being), it can command only that everything be done from the maxim of its will as one which could have as its object only itself considered as giving universal law. For only in this case are the practical principle and the imperative which the will obeys unconditional, because the will can have no interest as its foundation.

If now we look back upon all previous attempts which have ever been undertaken to discover the principle of morality, it is not to be wondered at that they all had to fail. Man was seen to be bound to laws by his duty, but it was not seen that he is subject to his own, but still universal, legislation, and that he is bound to act only in accordance with his own will, which is, however, designed by nature to be a will giving universal law. For if one thought of him as only subject to a law (whatever it may be), this necessarily implied some interest as a stimulus or compulsion to obedience because the law did not arise from his will. Rather, his will had to be constrained by something else to act in a certain way. By this strictly necessary consequence, however, all the labor of finding a supreme ground for duty was irrevocably lost, and one never arrived at duty but only at the necessity of acting from a certain interest. This might be his own interest or that of another, but in either case the imperative always had to be conditional, and could not at all serve as a moral command. The moral principle I will call the principle of *autonomy* of the will in contrast to all other principles which I accordingly count under *heteronomy*.

The concept of any rational being as a being that must regard itself as giving universal law through all the maxims of its will, so that it may judge itself and its actions from this standpoint, leads to a very fruitful concept, namely that of a *realm of ends*.

By *realm* I understand the systematic union of different rational beings through common laws. Because laws determine which ends have universal validity, if we abstract from personal differences of rational beings, and thus from all content of their private purposes, we can think of a whole of all ends in systematic connection, a whole of rational beings as ends in themselves as well as a whole of particular purposes which each may set for himself. This is a realm of ends, which is possible on the principles stated above. For all rational beings stand under the law that each of them should treat himself and all others never merely as means, but in every case at the same time as an end in himself. Thus there arises a systematic union of rational beings through common objective laws. This is a realm which may be called a realm of ends (certainly only an ideal) because what these laws have in view is just the relation of these beings to each other as ends and means.

A rational being belongs to the realm of ends as a member when he gives universal laws in it while also himself subject to these laws. He belongs to it as sovereign when, as legislating, he is subject to the will of no other. The rational being must regard himself always as legislative in a realm of ends possible through the freedom of the will whether he belongs to it as member or as sovereign. He cannot maintain his position as sovereign merely through the maxims of his will, but only when he is a completely independent being without need and with unlimited power adequate to his will.

---

*I may be excused from citing examples to elucidate this principle, for those that have already illustrated the categorical imperative and its formula can here serve the same purpose.

Morality, therefore, consists in the relation of every action to the legislation through which alone a realm of ends is possible. This legislation must be found in every rational being. It must be able to arise from his will, whose principle then is to do no action according to any maxim which would be inconsistent with its being a universal law, and thus to act only so that the will through its maxims could regard itself at the same time as giving universal law. If the maxims do not by their nature already necessarily conform to this objective principle of rational beings as giving universal law, the necessity of acting according to that principle is called practical constraint, which is to say: duty. Duty pertains not to the sovereign of the realm of ends, but rather to each member and to each in the same degree.

The practical necessity of acting according to this principle (duty) does not rest at all on feelings, impulses, and inclinations; it rests solely on the relation of rational beings to one another, in which the will of a rational being must always be regarded as legislative, for otherwise it could not be thought of as an end in itself. Reason, therefore, relates every maxim of the will as giving universal laws to every other will and also to every action towards itself; it does not do so for the sake of any other practical motive or future advantage but rather from the Idea of the dignity of a rational being who obeys no law except one which he himself also gives.

In the realm of ends everything has either a *price* or a *dignity*. Whatever has a price can be replaced by something else as its equivalent; on the other hand, whatever is above all price and therefore admits of no equivalent, has dignity.

That which is related to general human inclinations and needs has a *market price*. That which, without presupposing any need, accords with a certain taste (i.e., with pleasure in the purposeless play of our faculties) has a *fancy price*. But that which constitutes the condition under which alone something can be an end in itself does not have mere relative worth (price) but an intrinsic worth (*dignity*).

Morality is the condition under which alone a rational being can be an end in himself, because only through it is it possible to be a lawgiving member in the realm of ends. Thus morality, and humanity so far as it is capable of morality, alone have dignity. Skill and diligence in work have a market value; wit, lively imagination, and humor have a fancy price; but fidelity in promises and benevolence on principle (not benevolence from instinct) have intrinsic worth. Nature and likewise art contain nothing which could make up for their lack, for their worth consists not in the effects which flow from them nor in any advantage and utility which they procure; it consists only in mental dispositions, maxims of the will, which are ready to reveal themselves in this manner through actions even though success does not favor them. These actions need no recommendation from my subjective disposition or taste in order that they may be looked upon with immediate favor and satisfaction, nor do they have need of any direct propensity or feeling directed to them. They exhibit the will which performs them as the object of an immediate respect, since nothing but reason is required in order to impose them upon the will. The will is not to be cajoled into them, for this, in the case of duties, would be a contradiction. This esteem lets the worth of such a turn of mind be recognized as dignity and puts it infinitely beyond any price; with things of price it cannot in the least be brought into any competition or comparison without, as it were, violating its holiness.

And what is it that justifies the morally good disposition or virtue in making such lofty claims? It is nothing less that the participation it affords the rational being in giving universal laws. He is thus fitted to be a member in a possible realm of ends, to which his own nature already destined him. For, as an end in himself, he is destined to be a lawgiver in the realm of ends, free from all laws of nature and obedient only to those laws which he himself gives. Accordingly, his maxims can belong to a universal legislation to which he is at the same time subject. A thing has no worth other than that determined for it by the law. The lawgiving which determines all worth must therefore have a dignity (i.e., an unconditional and incomparable worth). For the esteem which a rational being must have for it, only the word "respect" is suitable. Autonomy is thus the basis of the dignity of both human nature and every rational nature.

The three aforementioned ways of presenting the principle of morality are fundamentally only so many formulas of the very same law, and each of them unites the others in itself. There is, nevertheless, a difference between them, but the difference is more subjectively than objectively practical, for the difference is intended to bring an Idea of reason closer to intuition (by means of a certain analogy) and thus nearer to feeling. All maxims have:

1. A form, which consists in universality, and in this respect the formula of the moral imperative requires that maxims be chosen as though they should hold as universal laws of nature.
2. A material (i.e., an end), and in this respect the formula says that the rational being, as by its nature an end and thus as an end in itself, must serve in every maxim as the condition restricting all merely relative and arbitrary ends.
3. A complete determination of all maxims by the formula that all maxims which stem from autonomous legislation ought to harmonize with a possible realm of ends as with a realm of nature.*

There is a progression here like that through the categories of the unity of the form of the will (its universality), the plurality of material (the objects, ends), to the all-comprehensiveness or totality of the system of ends. But it is better in moral valuation to follow the rigorous method and to make the universal formula of the categorical imperative the basis: Act according to the maxim which can at the same time make itself a universal law. But if one wishes to gain a hearing for the moral law, it is very useful to bring one and the same action under the three stated principles and thus, so far as possible, bring it nearer to intuition.

We can now end where we started, with the concept of an unconditionally good will. That will is absolutely good which cannot be bad, and thus it is a will whose maxim, when made universal law, can never conflict with itself. Thus this principle is also its supreme law: Always act according to that maxim whose universality as law you can at the same time will. This is the only condition under which a will can never come into conflict with itself, and such an imperative is categorical. Because the validity of the will as a universal law for possible actions has an analogy with the universal connection of the existence of things under universal laws, which is the formal element of nature in general, the categorical imperative can be expressed also as follows: Act on those maxims which can at the same time have themselves as universal laws of nature as their object. Such, then, is the formula of an absolutely good will.

Rational nature is distinguished from others in that it proposes an end to itself. This end would be the material of every good will. Since, however, in the Idea of an absolutely good will without the limiting condition that this or that end be achieved, we must abstract from every end to be actually effected (as any particular end would

---

*Teleology considers nature as a realm of ends; morals regards a possible realm of ends as a realm of nature. In the former the realm of ends is a theoretical Idea for the explanation of what actually is. In the latter it is a practical Idea for bringing about that which does not exist but which can become actual through our conduct and for making it conform with this Idea.

make each will only relatively good), we must conceive the end here not as one to be brought about, but as a self-existent end, and thus merely negatively, as that which must never be acted against and which consequently must never be valued merely as a means but in every volition also as an end. Now this end can never be other than the subject of all possible ends themselves, because this is at the same time the subject of a possible will which is absolutely good, for the latter cannot without contradiction be made secondary to any other object. The principle: Act with reference to every rational being (whether yourself or another) so that in your maxim it is an end in itself, is thus basically identical with the principle: Act by a maxim which involves its own universal validity for every rational being.

That in the use of means to any end I should restrict my maxim to the condition of its universal validity as a law for every subject is tantamount to saying that the subject of ends (i.e., the rational being itself) must be made the basis of all maxims of actions and thus be treated never as a mere means but as the supreme limiting condition in the use of all means (i.e., as at the same time an end).

It follows incontestably that every rational being must be able to regard himself as an end in himself with reference to all laws to which he may be subject whatever they may be, and thus see himself as giving universal laws. For it is just the fitness of his maxims to universal legislation that indicates that he is an end in himself. It also follows that his dignity (his prerogative) over all merely natural beings entails that he must take his maxims from the point of view that regards himself, and hence also every other rational being, as legislative. Rational beings are, on this account, called persons. In this way, a world of rational beings (*mundus intelligibilis*) is possible as a realm of ends, because of the legislation belonging to all persons as members. Consequently every rational being must act as if by his maxims he were at all times a legislative member of the universal realm of ends. The formal principle of these maxims is: So act as if your maxims should serve at the same time as universal law (for all rational beings).

A realm of ends is thus possible only by analogy with a realm of nature. The former is possible only by maxims (i.e., self-imposed rules), while the latter is possible by laws of efficient causes of things externally necessitated. Regardless of this difference, by analogy we call the natural whole a realm of nature so far as it is related to rational beings as its end; we do so even though the natural whole is looked upon as a machine. Such a realm of ends would actually be realized through maxims whose rule is prescribed to all rational beings by the categorical imperative, if they were universally obeyed. But a rational being, though he scrupulously follow this maxim, cannot for that reason expect every other rational being to be true to it, nor can he expect the realm of nature and its orderly design to harmonize with him as a fitting member of a realm of ends which is possible through himself. That is, he cannot count on its favoring his expectation of happiness. Still the law: Act according to the maxim of a member of a merely potential realm of ends who gives universal law, remains in full force because it commands categorically. And just in this lies the paradox that simply the dignity of humanity as rational nature without any end or advantage to be gained by it, and thus respect for a mere Idea, should serve as the inflexible precept of the will. [There is the further paradox that] the sublimity of the maxims and the worthiness of every rational subject to be a law-giving member in the realm of ends consist precisely in the independence of his maxims from all such incentives. Otherwise he would have to be viewed as subject to only the natural law of his needs. Although the realm of nature as well as that of ends would be thought of as united under a sovereign, so that the latter would no longer remain a mere Idea but would receive true reality, the realm of ends would undoubtedly gain a strong urge in its favor though its intrinsic worth would not be augmented. Regardless of this, even the one and only absolute legislator would still have to be conceived as judging the worth of rational beings only by the disinterested conduct which they prescribe to themselves merely from the Idea. The essence of things is not changed by their external relations, and without reference to these relations a man must be judged only by what constitutes his absolute worth, and this is true whoever his judge may be, even if it be the Supreme Being. Morality is thus the relation of actions to the autonomy of the will (i.e., to the possible giving of universal law by the maxims of the will). The action which can be compatible with the autonomy of the will is permitted; that which does not agree with it is prohibited. The will whose maxims are necessarily in harmony with the laws of autonomy is a holy will or an absolutely good will. The dependence of a will not absolutely good on the principle of autonomy (moral constraint) is *obligation*. Hence obligation cannot be predicated of a holy will. The objective necessity of an action from obligation is called *duty*.

From what has just been said, it can easily be explained how it happens that, although in the concept of duty we think of subjection to law, we do nevertheless at the same time ascribe a certain sublimity and dignity to the person who fulfills all his duties. For though there is no sublimity in him in so far as he is subject to the moral law, yet he is sublime in so far as he is the giver of the law and subject to it for this reason only. We have also shown above how neither fear of nor inclination to the law is the incentive which can give moral worth to action; only respect for it can do so. Our own will, so far as it would act only under the condition of a universal legislation rendered possible by its maxims—this will ideally possible for us—is the proper object of respect, and the dignity of humanity consists just in its capacity to give universal laws under the condition that it is itself subject to this same legislation.

The Autonomy of the Will as the Supreme Principle of Morality

Autonomy of the will is that property of it by which it is a law to itself independent of any property of the objects of its volition. Hence the principle of autonomy is: Never choose except in such a way that the maxims of the choice are comprehended as universal law in the same volition. That this practical rule is an imperative, that is, that the will of every rational being is necessarily bound to it as a condition, cannot be proved by a mere analysis of the concepts occurring in it, because it is a synthetical proposition. To prove it, we would have to go beyond the knowledge of objects to a critical examination of the subject (i.e., to a critique of pure practical reason), for this synthetical proposition which commands apodictically must be susceptible of being known *a priori*. This matter, however, does not belong in the present section. But that the principle of autonomy, which is now in question, is the sole principle of morals can be readily shown by mere analysis of the concepts of morality; for by this analysis we find that its principle must be a categorical imperative and that the imperative commands neither more nor less than this very autonomy.

The Heteronomy of the Will as the Source of All Spurious Principles of Morality

If the will seeks the law which is to determine it elsewhere than in the fitness of its maxims to be given as universal law, and if thus it goes outside and seeks the law in the property of any of its objects, heteronomy always results. For then the will does not give itself the law, but the object through its relation to the will gives the law to it. This relation, whether it rests on inclination or on conceptions of reason, admits of only hypothetical imperatives: I should do something for the reason that I will something else. The moral (categorical) imperative, on the other hand, says that I should act in this or that way even though I have not willed anything else. For example, the former says that I should not lie if I wish to keep my good name. The latter says that I should not lie even though it would not cause me the least injury. The latter, therefore, must disregard every object to such an extent that it has absolutely no influence on the will; it must so disregard it that practical reason (will) may not just minister to any interest not its own but rather show its commanding authority as the supreme legislation. Thus, for instance, I should seek to further the happiness of others, not as though its realization were of consequence to me (because of a direct inclination or some satisfaction related to it indirectly through reason); I should do so solely because the maxim which excludes it from my duty cannot be comprehended as a universal law in one and the same volition.

Classification of All Possible Principles of Morality Following from the Assumed Principle of Heteronomy

Here as everywhere in the pure use of reason so long as a critical examination of it is lacking, human reason tries all possible wrong ways before it succeeds in finding the one true way.

All principles which can be taken from this point of view are either empirical or rational. The former, drawn from the principles of happiness, are based on physical or moral feeling; the latter, drawn from the principle of perfection, are based either on the rational concept of perfection as a possible result or on the concept of an independent perfection (the will of God) as the determining ground of the will.

Empirical principles are not at all suited to serve as the basis of moral laws. For if the basis of the universality by which they should be valid for all rational beings without distinction (the unconditional practical necessity which is thereby imposed upon them) is derived from a particular tendency of human nature or the accidental circumstance in which it is found, that universality is lost. But the principle of one's own happiness is the most objectionable of the empirical principles. This is not merely because it is false and because experience contradicts the supposition that well-being is always proportional to good conduct, nor yet because this principle contributes nothing to the establishment of morality inasmuch as it is a very different thing to make a man happy from making him good, and to make him prudent and farsighted for his own advantage is far from making him virtuous. Rather, it is because this principle supports morality with incentives which undermine it and destroy all its sublimity, for it puts the motives to virtue and those to vice in the same class, teaching us only to make a better calculation while obliterating the specific difference between them. On the other hand, there is the alleged special sense,* the moral feeling. The appeal to it is superficial, since those who cannot think expect help from feeling, even with respect to that which concerns universal laws; they do so even though feelings naturally differ so infinitely

---

*I count the principle of moral feeling under that of happiness, because every empirical interest promises to contribute to our well-being by the agreeableness that a thing affords, either directly and without a view to future advantage or with a view to it. We must likewise, with Hutcheson, count the principle of sympathy with the happiness of others under the moral sense which he assumed.

in degree that they are incapable of furnishing a uniform standard of the good and bad, and also in spite of the fact that one cannot validly judge for others by means of one's own feeling. Nevertheless, the moral feeling is nearer to morality and its dignity, inasmuch as it pays virtue the honor of ascribing the satisfaction and esteem for her directly to morality, and does not, as it were, say to her face that it is not her beauty but only our advantage which attaches us to her.

Among the rational principles of morality, there is the ontological concept of perfection. It is empty, indefinite, and consequently useless for finding in the immeasurable field of possible reality the greatest possible sum which is suitable to us; and, in specifically distinguishing the reality which is here in question from all other reality, it inevitably tends to move in a circle and cannot avoid tacitly presupposing the morality which it ought to explain. Nevertheless, it is better than the theological concept, which derives morality from a most perfect divine will. It is better not merely because we cannot intuit the perfection of the divine will, having rather to derive it only from our own concepts of which morality itself is foremost, but also because if we do not so derive it (and to do so would involve a most flagrant circle in explanation), the only remaining concept of the divine will is made up of the attributes of desire for glory and dominion combined with the awful conceptions of might and vengeance, and any system of ethics based on them would be directly opposed to morality.

But if I had to choose between the concept of the moral sense and that of perfection in general (neither of which at any rate weakens morality, though neither is capable of serving as its foundation), I would decide for the latter, because it preserves the indefinite Idea of a will good in itself free from corruption until it can be more narrowly defined. It at least withdraws the decision on the question from the realm of sensibility and brings it to the court of pure reason, although it does not even there decide the question.

For the rest, I think I may be excused from a lengthy refutation of all these doctrines. It is so easy, and presumably so well understood even by those whose office requires them to decide for one of these theories (since their students would not tolerate suspension of judgment), that such a refutation would be superfluous. What interests us more, however, is to know that all these principles set up nothing other than heteronomy of the will as the first ground of morality, and thus they necessarily miss their goal.

In every case in which the object of the will must be assumed as prescribing the rule which is to determine the will, the rule is nothing else than heteronomy. The imperative in this case is conditional, stating that if or because one wills such and such an object, one ought to act thus or so. Therefore the imperative can never coinmand morally, that is, categorically. The object may determine the will by means of inclination, as in the principle of one's own happiness, or by means of reason directed to objects of our possible volition in general, as in the principle of perfection; but the will in these cases never determines itself directly by the conception of the action itself but only by the incentive which the foreseen result of the action incites in the will—that is: I ought to do something because I will something else. And here still another law must be assumed in me as the basis for this imperative; it would be a law by which I would necessarily will that other thing; but this law would in its turn require an imperative to restrict this maxim. Since the conception of a result to be obtained by one's own powers incites in the will an impulse which depends upon the natural characteristic of the subject, either of his sensibility (inclination and taste) or understanding and reason; and since these faculties according to the particular constitution of their nature find satisfaction in exercising themselves on the result of the voluntary action, it follows that it would really be nature which would give the law [to the action]. This law, as a law of nature, would have to be known and proved by experience, and as in itself contingent it would be unfit to be an apodictical practical rule such as the moral rule must be. Such a law always represents heteronomy of the will: the will does not give itself the law, but an external impulse gives the law to the will according to nature of the subject which is susceptible to receive it.

The absolutely good will, the principle of which must be a categorical imperative, is thus undetermined with reference to any object. It contains only the form of volition in general, and this form is autonomy. That is, the capability of the maxims of every good will to make themselves universal laws is itself the sole law which the will of every rational being imposes on himself, and it does not need to support this by any incentive or interest.

How such a synthetical practical *a priori* proposition is possible and why it is necessary is a problem whose solution does not lie within the boundaries of the metaphysics of morals. Moreover, we have not here affirmed its truth, and even less professed to command a proof of it. We showed only through the development of the generally received concept of morals that autonomy of the will is unavoidably connected with it, or rather that it is its foundation. Whoever, therefore, holds morality to be something real and not a chimerical idea without truth must also concede its principle which has been derived here. Consequently, this section, like the first, was merely analytical. To prove that morality is not a mere phantom of the mind—and if the categorical imperative, and with it the autonomy of the will, is true and absolutely necessary as an *a priori* proposition, it follows that it is no phantom—requires that a synthetical use of pure practical reason be possible. But we must not venture on this use without first making a critical examination of this faculty of reason. In the last section we shall give the principal features of such an examination that will be sufficient for our purpose.

THIRD SECTION

TRANSITION FROM THE METAPHYSICS OF MORALS TO THE CRITICAL EXAMINATION OF PURE PRACTICAL REASON

*The Concept of Freedom Is the Key
to the Explanation of the Autonomy
of the Will*

As will is a kind of causality of living beings so far as they are rational, freedom would be that property of this causality by which it can be effective independent of foreign causes determining it, just as natural necessity is the property of the causality of all irrational beings by which they are determined to activity by the influence of foreign causes.

The preceding definition of freedom is negative and therefore affords no insight into its essence. But a positive concept of freedom flows from it which is so much the richer and more fruitful. Since the concept of a causality entails that of laws according to which something (i.e., the effect) must be established through something else which we call cause, it follows that freedom is by no means lawless even though it is not a property of the will according to laws of nature. Rather, it must be a causality of a peculiar kind according to immutable laws. Otherwise a free will would be an absurdity. Natural necessity is, as we have seen, a heteronomy of efficient causes, for every effect is possible only according to the law that something else determines the efficient cause to its causality. What else, then, can the freedom of the will be but autonomy (i.e., the property of the will to be law to itself)? The proposition that the will is a law to itself in all its actions, however, only expresses the principle that we should act according to no other maxim than that which can also have itself as a universal law for its object. And this is just the formula of the categorical imperative and the principle of morality. Therefore a free will and a will under moral laws are identical.

Thus if freedom of the will is presupposed, morality together with its principle follows from it by the mere analysis of its concepts. But the principle: An absolutely good will is one whose maxim can always include itself as a universal law, is nevertheless a synthetical proposition. It is synthetical because by analysis of the concept of an absolutely good will that property of the maxim cannot be found in it. Such synthetical propositions, however, are made possible only by the fact that the two cognitions are connected with each other through their union with a third in which both are to be found. The positive concept of freedom furnishes this third cognition, which cannot be, as in the case of physical causes, the sensible world of nature, in the concept of which we find conjoined the concepts of something as cause in relation to something else as effect. We cannot yet show directly what this third cognition is to which freedom directs us and of which we have an *a priori* Idea, nor can we yet explain the deduction of the concept of freedom from pure practical reason, and therewith the possibility of a categorical imperative. For this, some further preparation is needed.

Freedom Must be Presupposed as the Property of the Will of All Rational Beings

It is not enough to ascribe freedom to our will, on whatever grounds, if we do not also have sufficient grounds for attributing it to all rational beings. For since morality serves as a law for us only as rational beings, it must hold for all rational beings, and since it must be derived exclusively from the property of freedom, freedom as a property of the will of all rational beings must be demonstrated. And it does not suffice to prove it from certain alleged experiences of human nature (which is indeed impossible, as it can be proved only *a priori*), but we must prove it as belonging universally to the activity of rational beings endowed with a will. Now I say that every being which cannot act otherwise than under the Idea of freedom is thereby really free in a practical respect. That is to say, all laws which are inseparably bound with freedom hold for it just as if its wills were proved free in itself by theoretical philosophy.* Now I affirm that we must necessarily grant that every rational being who has a will also has the Idea of freedom and that it acts only under this Idea. For in such a being we think of a reason which is practical (i.e., a reason which has causality with respect to its object). Now we cannot conceive of a reason which, in making its judgments, consciously responds to a bidding from the outside, for then the subject would attribute the determination of its

---

*I propose this argument as sufficient to our purpose: Freedom as an Idea is posited by all rational beings as the basis for their actions. I do so in order to avoid having to prove freedom also in its theoretical aspect. For even if the latter is left unproved, the laws which would obligate a being who was really free would hold for a being who cannot act except under the Idea of his own freedom. Thus we escape the onus which has been pressed on theory.

power of judgment not to reason but to an impulse. Reason must regard itself as the author of its principles, independently of alien influences; consequently as practical reason or as the will of a rational being it must regard itself as free. That is to say, the will of a rational being can be a will of its own only under the Idea of freedom, and therefore from a practical point of view such a will must be ascribed to all rational beings.

Of the Interest Attaching to the Ideas of Morality

We have finally reduced the definite concept of morality to the Idea of freedom, but we could not prove freedom to be actual in ourselves and in human nature. We saw only that we must presuppose it if we would think of a being as rational and conscious of its causality with respect to actions, that is, as endowed with a will; and so we find that on the very same grounds we must ascribe to each being endowed with reason and will the property of determining itself to action under the Idea of its freedom.

From presupposing this Idea [of freedom] there followed also the consciousness of a law of action: that the subjective principles of actions (i.e., maxims) must in every instance be so chosen that they can hold also as objective (i.e., universal) principles, and can thus serve as principles for our giving universal laws. But why should I, as a rational being, and why should all other beings endowed with reason, subject ourselves to this law? I will admit that no interest impels me to do so, for that would then give no categorical imperative. But I must nevertheless take an interest in it and see how it comes about, for this *ought* is properly a *would* that is valid for every rational being provided reason were practical for it without hindrance [i.e., exclusively determined its action]. For beings who, like ourselves, are affected by the senses as incentives different from reason, and who do not always do that which reason by itself alone would have done, that necessity of action is expressed as only an *ought*. The subjective necessity is thus distinguished from the objective.

It therefore seems that we have only presupposed the moral law, the principle of the autonomy of the will in the Idea of freedom, as if we could not prove its reality and objective necessity by itself. Even if that were so, we would still have gained something because we would at least have defined the genuine principle more accurately than had been done before; but with regard to its validity and the practical necessity of subjection to it, we would not have advanced a single step, for we could give no satisfactory answer to anyone who asked us why the universal validity of our maxim as a law had to be the restricting condition of our action. We could not tell on what is based the worth which we ascribe to actions of this kind—a worth so great that there can be no higher interest—nor could we tell how it happens that man believes that it is only through this that he feels his own personal worth, in contrast to which the worth of a pleasant or unpleasant state is to be regarded as nothing.

We do find sometimes that we can take an interest in a personal quality which involves no [personal] interest in any [external] condition, provided only that the [possession of] this quality makes us fit to participate in the [desired] condition in case reason were to effect the allotment of this condition. That is, being worthy of happiness, even without the motive of partaking in happiness, can interest of itself. But this judgment is in fact only the effect of the importance already ascribed to moral laws (if by the Idea of freedom we detach ourselves from every empirical interest). But that we ought so to detach ourselves from every empirical interest, to regard ourselves as free in acting and yet as subject to certain laws, in order to find a worth wholly in our person which would compensate for the loss of everything which could make our situation desirable—how this is possible and hence on what grounds the moral law obligates us still cannot be seen in this way.

We must openly confess that there is a kind of circle here from which it seems that there is no escape. We assume that we are free in the order of efficient causes so that we can conceive of ourselves as subject to moral laws in the order of ends. And then we think of ourselves subject to these laws because we have ascribed freedom of the will to ourselves. This is circular because freedom and self-legislation of the will are both autonomy and thus are reciprocal concepts, and for that reason one of them cannot be used to explain the other and to furnish a ground for it. At most they can be used for the logical purpose of bringing apparently different conceptions of the same object under a single concept (as we reduce different fractions of the same value to the lowest common terms).

One recourse, however, remains open to us, namely, to inquire whether we do not assume a different standpoint when we think of ourselves as causes *a priori* efficient through freedom from that which we occupy when we conceive of ourselves in the light of our actions as effects which we see before our eyes.

The following remark requires no subtle reflection, and we may suppose that even the commonest understanding can make it, though it does so, after its fashion, by an obscure discernment of judgment which it calls feeling: all conceptions, like those of the senses, which come to us without our choice enable us to know objects only as they affect us, while what they are in themselves remains unknown to us; therefore, as regards this kind of conception, even with the closest attention and clearness which understanding may ever bring to them we can attain only a knowledge of appearances and never a knowledge of things as they are in themselves. When this distinction is once made (perhaps merely because of a difference noticed between conceptions which are given to us from somewhere else and to which we are passive, and those which we produce from ourselves only and in which we show our own activity), it follows of itself that we must admit and assume behind the appearances something else which is not appearance, i.e., things as they are in themselves, although we must admit that we cannot approach them more closely and can never know what they are in themselves, since they can never be known by us except as they affect us. This must furnish a distinction, though a crude one, between a world of sense and a world of understanding. The former, by differences in our sensible faculties, can be very different to various observers, while the latter, which is its foundation, remains always the same. A man may not presume to know even himself as he really is by knowing himself through inner sensation. For since he does not, as it were, produce himself or derive his concept of himself *a priori* but only empirically, it is natural that he obtain his knowledge of himself through inner sense and consequently only through the appearance of his nature and the way in which his consciousness is affected. But beyond the characteristic of his own subject which is compounded of these mere appearances, he necessarily assumes something else as its basis, namely, his ego as it is in itself. Thus in respect to mere perception and receptivity to sensations he must count himself as belonging to the world of sense; but in respect to that which may be pure activity in himself (i.e., in respect to that which reaches consciousness directly and not by affecting the senses) he must reckon himself as belonging to the intellectual world. But he has no further knowledge of that world.

To such a conclusion the thinking man must come with respect to all things which may present themselves to him. Presumably it is to be met with in the commonest understanding which, as is well known, is very much inclined to expect behind the objects of the senses something else invisible and acting of itself. But common understanding soon spoils it by trying to make the invisible again sensible (i.e., to make it an object of intuition). Thus the common understanding becomes not in the least wiser.

Now man really finds in himself a faculty by which he distinguishes himself from all other things, even from himself so far as he is affected by objects. This faculty is reason. As a pure, spontaneous activity it is elevated even above understanding. For though the latter is also a spontaneous activity and does not, like sense, which is passive, merely contain representations which arise only when one is affected by things, it cannot produce by its activity any other concepts than those which serve to bring the sensible representations under rules and thereby to unite them in one consciousness. Without this use of sensibility it would think nothing at all; on the other hand, reason shows such a pure spontaneity in the case of Ideas that it far transcends anything that sensibility can give to consciousness, and shows its chief occupation in distinguishing the world of sense from the world of understanding, thereby prescribing limits to the understanding itself.

For this reason a rational being must regard itself qua intelligence (and not from the side of his lower faculties) as belonging to the world of understanding and not to that of the senses. Thus it has two standpoints from which it can consider itself and recognize the laws [governing] the employment of its powers and all its actions: first, as belonging to the world of sense, under the laws of nature (heteronomy), and, second, as belonging to the intelligible world under laws which, independent of nature, are not empirical but founded on reason alone.

As a rational being and thus as belonging to the intelligible world, man cannot think of the causality of his own will except under the Idea of freedom, for independence from the determining causes of the world of sense (an independence which reason must always ascribe to itself) is freedom. The concept of autonomy is inseparably connected with the Idea of freedom, and with the former there is inseparably bound the universal principle of morality, which is the ground in Idea of all actions of rational beings, just as natural law is the ground of all appearances.

We have now removed the suspicion which we raised that there might be a hidden circle in our reasoning from freedom to autonomy and from the latter to the moral law. This suspicion was that we laid down the Idea of freedom for the sake of the moral law in order later to derive the law from freedom, and that we were thus unable to give any basis for the law, presenting it only as a *petitio principii* [begging the question] which well-disposed minds might gladly allow us, but which we could never advance as a demonstrable proposition. But we now see that, if we think of ourselves as free, we transport ourselves into the intelligible world as members of it and know the autonomy of the will together with its consequence, morality; whereas if we think of ourselves as obligated, we consider ourselves as belonging both to the world of sense and at the same time to the intelligible world.

How Is a Categorical Imperative Possible?

The rational being counts himself, *qua* intelligence, as belonging to the intelligible world, and only as an efficient cause belonging to it does he call his causality will. On the other side, however, he is conscious of himself as a part of the world of sense in which his actions are found as mere appearances of that causality. But we do not discern how they are possible on the basis of that causality which we do not know; rather, those actions must be regarded as determined by other appearances, namely, desires and inclinations belonging to the world of sense. As a member of the intelligible world only, all my actions would completely accord with the principle of the autonomy of the pure will, and as a part only of the world of sense would they have to be assumed to conform wholly to the natural law of desires and inclinations and thus to the heteronomy of nature. (The former actions would rest on the supreme principle of morality, and the latter on that of happiness.) But since the intelligible world contains the ground of the world of sense and hence of its laws, the intelligible world is (and must be conceived as) directly legislative for my will, which belongs wholly to the intelligible world. Therefore I recognize myself *qua* intelligence as subject to the law of the world of understanding and to the autonomy of the will. That is, I recognize myself as subject to the law of reason which contains in the Idea of freedom the law of the intelligible world, while at the same time I must acknowledge that I am a being which belongs to the world of sense. Therefore I must regard the laws of the intelligible world as imperatives for me, and actions in accord with this principle as duties.

Thus categorical imperatives are possible because the Idea of freedom makes me a member of an intelligible world. Consequently, if I were a member of that world only, all my actions *would* always be in accordance with the autonomy of the will. But since I intuit myself at the same time as a member of the world of sense, my actions *ought* to conform to it, and this categorical "ought" presents a synthetic *a priori* proposition, since besides my will affected by my sensuous desires there is added the Idea of exactly the same will as pure, practical of itself, and belonging to the intelligible world, which according to reason contains the supreme condition of the sensuously affected will. It is similar to the manner in which concepts of the understanding, which of themselves mean nothing but lawful form in general, are added to the intuitions of the sensible world, thus rendering possible *a priori* synthetic propositions on which all knowledge of a system of nature rests.

The practical use of ordinary human reason confirms the correctness of this deduction. When we present examples of honesty of purpose, of steadfastness in following good maxims, and of sympathy and general benevolence even with great sacrifices of advantage and comfort, there is no man, not even the most malicious villain (provided he is otherwise accustomed to using his reason), who does not wish that he also might have these qualities, but because of his inclinations and impulses cannot bring this about, yet at the same time wishes to be free from such inclinations which are burdensome even to him. He thus proves that with a will free from all impulses of sensibility, he in thought transfers himself into an order of things altogether different from that of his desires in the field of sensibility. He cannot expect to obtain by that wish any gratification of desires or any state which would satisfy his actual or even imagined inclinations, for the Idea itself, which elicits this wish from him, would lose its preeminence if he had any such expectation. He imagines himself to be this better person when he transfers himself to the standpoint of a member of the intelligible world to which he is involuntarily impelled by the Idea of freedom (i.e., of independence from the determining causes in the world of sense); and from this standpoint he is conscious of a good will, which on his own confession constitutes the law for his bad will as a member of the world of sense. He acknowledges the authority of the law even while he transgresses it. The moral "ought" is therefore his own volition as a member of the intelligible world, and it is conceived by him as an "ought" only insofar as he regards himself at the same time as a member of the world of sense.

On the Extreme Boundary of All Practical Philosophy

In respect to their will, all men think of themselves as free. Hence arise all judgments of acts as being such as ought to have been done, although they were not done.

But this freedom is not an empirical concept and cannot be such, for it continues to hold even though experience shows the contrary of the demands which are necessarily conceived to be consequences of the supposition of freedom. On the other hand it is equally necessary that everything that happens should be inexorably determined by natural laws, and this natural necessity is likewise no empirical concept because it implies the concept of necessity and thus of *a priori* knowledge. But this concept of a system of nature is confirmed by experience, and it is inevitably presupposed if experience, which is knowledge of the objects of the sense interconnected by universal laws, is to be possible. Therefore freedom is only an Idea of reason whose objective reality in itself is doubtful, while nature is a concept of the understanding which shows and must necessarily show its reality by examples of experience.

There now arises a dialectic of reason, since the freedom ascribed to the will seems to stand in contradiction to natural necessity. At this parting of the ways reason in its speculative aspect finds the path of natural necessity more well-beaten and usable than that of freedom, but in its practical aspect the path of freedom is the only one on which it is possible to make use of reason in our conduct. Hence it is as impossible for the subtlest philosophy as for the commonest reasoning to argue freedom away. Philosophy must therefore assume that no true contradiction will be found between freedom and natural necessity in the same human actions, for it cannot give up the concept of nature any more than that of freedom.

Hence if we should never be able to conceive how freedom is possible, at least this apparent contradiction must be convincingly eradicated. For if even the thought of freedom contradicted itself or nature, it would have to be surrendered in competition with natural necessity.

But it would be impossible to escape this contradiction if the subject, who seems to himself to be free, thought of himself in the same sense or in the same relationship when he calls himself free as when he assumes that in the same action he is subject to natural law. Therefore it is an inescapable task of speculative philosophy to show at least that its illusion of contradiction rests on the fact that we [do not] think of man in a different sense and relationship when we call him free from that in which we consider him as part of nature and subject to its laws. It must show not only that they can very well coexist but also that they must be thought of as necessarily united in one and the same subject; for otherwise no ground could be given as to why we should burden reason with an Idea which, though it may without contradiction be united with another that is sufficiently established, nevertheless involves us in a perplexity which sorely embarrasses reason in its theoretical use. This duty is imposed only on theoretical philosophy, so that it may clear the way for practical philosophy. Thus the philosopher has no choice as to whether he will remove the apparent contradiction or leave it untouched, for in the latter case the theory of it would be unoccupied land, into the possession of which the fatalist could rightly enter and drive all morality from its alleged property as occupying it without title.

Yet we cannot say here that we have reached the boundary of practical philosophy. For the settlement of the controversy does not belong to practical philosophy, as the latter only demands from theoretical reason that it put an end to the discord in which it entangles itself in theoretical questions, so that practical reason may have rest and security from outward attacks which could dispute it the ground on which it desires to erect its edifice.

The title to freedom of the will claimed by ordinary reason is based on the consciousness and the conceded presupposition of the independence of reason from merely subjectively determining causes which together constitute what belongs only to sensation and is included under the general name of sensibility. Man, who in this way regards himself as intelligence, puts himself in a different order of things and in a relationship to determining grounds of an altogether different kind when he thinks of himself as intelligence with a will and thus as endowed with causality, compared with that other order of things and that other set of determining grounds which become relevant when he perceives himself as a phenomenon in the world of sense (as he really is also) and submits his causality to external determination according to natural laws. Now he soon realizes that both can subsist together—indeed, that they must. For there is not the least contradiction between a thing in appearance (as belonging to the world of sense) being subject to certain laws from which, as a thing or being regarded as it is in itself, it is independent. That he must think of himself in this twofold manner rests, with regard to the first, on the consciousness of himself as an object affected through the senses, and, with regard to what is required by the second, on the consciousness of himself as intelligence (i.e., as independent of sensible impressions in the use of reason), and thus as belonging to the intelligible world.

This is why man claims to possess a will which does not make him accountable for what belongs only to his desires and inclinations, but thinks of actions which can be done only by disregarding all his desires and sensuous attractions as possible and indeed as necessary for him. The causality of these actions lies in him as an intelligence and in effects and actions in accordance with principles of an intelligible world, of which he knows only that reason alone, and indeed pure reason independent of sensibility, gives the law in it. Moreover, since it is only as intelligence that he is his proper self (as man he is only appearance of himself), he knows that those laws apply to him directly and categorically, so that that to which inclinations and impulses and hence the entire nature of the world of sense incite him cannot in the least impair the laws of his volition as an intelligence. He does not even hold himself responsible for these inclinations and impulses or attribute them to his proper self (i.e., his will), though he does impute to his will the indulgence which he may grant to them when he permits them to influence his maxims to the detriment of the rational laws of his will.

When practical reason thinks itself into an intelligible world, it does in no way transcend its boundaries. It would do so, however, if it tried to intuit or feel itself into it. The intelligible world is only a negative thought with respect to the world of sense, which does not give reason any laws for determining the will. It is positive only in the single point that freedom as negative determination is at the same time connected with a positive power and even a causality of reason. This causality we call a will to act so that the principle of actions will accord with the essential characteristic of a rational cause (i.e., with the condition of universal validity of a maxim as law). But if it were to borrow an object of the will (i.e., a motive) from the intelligible world, it would overstep its boundaries and pretend to be acquainted with something of which it knows nothing. The concept of a world of understanding is therefore only a standpoint from which reason sees itself forced to take outside appearances, in order to think of itself as practical. If the influences of sensibility were determining for man, this would not be possible; but it is necessary unless he is to be denied the consciousness of himself as an intelligence, and thus as a rational and rationally active cause (i.e., a cause acting in freedom). This thought certainly implies the Idea of an order and legislation different from that of natural mechanism, which applies to the world of sense; and it makes necessary the concept of an intelligible world, the whole of rational beings as things regarded as they are in themselves. But it does not give us the least occasion to think of it otherwise than according to its formal condition only (i.e., the universality of the maxim of the will as law and thus the autonomy of the will), which alone is consistent with freedom. All laws, on the other hand, which are directed to an object make for heteronomy, which belongs only to natural laws and which can apply only to the world of sense.

But reason would overstep its bounds if it undertook to explain how pure reason can be practical, which is the same problem as explaining how freedom is possible.

We can explain nothing but what we can reduce to laws whose object can be given in some possible experience. But freedom is only an Idea, the objective reality which can in no way be shown to accord with natural laws or to be in any possible experience. Since no example in accordance with any analogy can support it, it can never be comprehended or even imagined. It holds only as the necessary presupposition of reason in a being who believes himself conscious of a will (i.e., of a faculty different from the mere faculty of desire, or a faculty of determining himself to act as an intelligence and thus according to laws of reason independently of natural instincts. But where determination according to natural laws comes to an end, there too all explanation ceases, and nothing remains but defense (i.e., refutation of the objections from those who pretend to have seen more deeply into the essence of things and who boldly declare freedom to be impossible). We can show them only that the supposed contradiction they have discovered lies nowhere else than in their necessarily regarding man [only] as appearance in order to make natural law valid with respect to human actions, and now when we require them to think of man *qua* intelligence as a thing regarded as it is in itself, they still persist in considering him as appearance [only]. Obviously, then, the detachment of his causality (his will) from all natural laws of the world of sense in one and the same subject is a contradiction, but this disappears when they reconsider and confess, as is reasonable, that behind the appearances things regarded as they are in themselves must stand as their hidden ground, and that we cannot expect the laws of the activity of these grounds to be the same as those under which their appearances stand.

The subjective impossibility of explaining the freedom of the will is the same as the impossibility of discovering and explaining an interest* which man can take in moral laws. Nevertheless, he does actually take an interest in them, and the foundation of this interest in us we will call the moral feeling. This moral feeling has been erroneously construed by some as the standard for our moral judgment, whereas it must be regarded rather as the subjective effect which the law has upon the will to which reason alone gives objective grounds.

In order to will an action which reason alone prescribes to the sensuously affected rational being as the action which he ought to will, there is certainly required a power of will to instill a feeling of pleasure of satisfaction in the fulfilment of duty, and hence there must be a causality of reason to determine sensibility in accordance with its own principles. But it is wholly impossible to discern, i.e., to make *a priori* conceivable, how a mere thought containing nothing sensuous is able to produce a sensation of pleasure or displeasure. For that is a particular kind of causality of which, as of

---

*Interest is that by which reason becomes practical (i.e., a cause determining the will). We therefore say only of a rational being that he takes an interest in something; irrational creatures feel only sensuous impulses. A direct interest in the action is taken by reason only if the universal validity of its maxim is a sufficient determining ground of the will. Only such an interest is pure. But if reason can determine the will only by means of another object of desire or under the presupposition of a particular feeling of the subject, reason takes merely an indirect interest in the action, and since reason for itself alone without experience can discover neither objects of the will nor a particular feeling which lies at its root, that indirect interest would be only empirical and not a pure interest of reason. The logical interest of reason in advancing its insights is never direct but rather presupposes purposes for which they are to be used.